2003
POET'S
1,800+ PLACES TO
PUBLISH YOUR POETRY
MARKET®

EDITOR
NANCY BREEN

ASSISTANT EDITOR
VANESSA LYMAN

WRITER'S DIGEST BOOKS
CINCINNATI, OH

Important Market Listing Information

• Listings are based on questionnaires completed by editors and on subsequent verified copy. Listings are not advertisements *nor* are markets necessarily endorsed by the editors of this book.

• Information in the listings comes directly from the publishers and is as accurate as possible. However, publications and editors come and go, and poetry needs fluctuate between the publication date of this directory and the date of purchase.

• If you are a poetry publisher and would like to be considered for a listing in the next edition, send a SASE (or SAE and IRC) with your request for a questionnaire to *Poet's Market*—QR, 4700 East Galbraith Road, Cincinnati OH 45236. Questionnaires received after February 15, 2003, will be held for the 2005 edition.

• *Poet's Market* reserves the right to exclude any listing that does not meet its requirements.

Complaint Procedure

If you feel you have not been treated fairly by a market listed in *Poet's Market*, we advise you to take the following steps:

• First, try to contact the market. Sometimes one phone call or letter can quickly clear up the matter. Document all your communications with the market.

• When you contact us with a complaint, provide the details of your submission, the date of your first contact with the market, and the nature of your subsequent communication.

• We will file a record of your complaint and further investigate the market.

• The number and severity of complaints will be considered when deciding whether or not to delete a market from the next edition of *Poet's Market*.

Editorial Director, Annuals Department: Barbara Kuroff
Supervisory Editor, Annuals Department: Alice Pope

Writer's Market website: www.writersmarket.com
Writer's Digest Books website: www.writersdigest.com

International Standard Serial Number 0883-5470
International Standard Book Number 1-58297-124-2

Front Cover Image: © Pedro Lobo/Photonica

Attention Booksellers: This is an annual directory of F&W Publications. Return deadline for this edition is December 31, 2003.

Contents

THE MARKETS

RESOURCES

INDEXES

From the Editor

As poets and as individuals, we all had different reactions to the tragedies of September 11, 2001. Beyond my own overwhelming sense of horror and mourning, artistically I shrank into myself. How in the world could I ever write my little poems again in the aftermath of so much death, suffering, and loss?

Yet it was poetry that helped many cope with the earth-shattering circumstances of September 11. Poems were e-mailed between friends, posted in the streets and at memorials, and published in very nonpoetic newspapers and magazines. They were read over the airwaves, shared at special readings and services, circulated electronically with the "pass it along" frequency of chain letters, and submitted to numerous websites inviting literary responses to the tragedy.

Many poets, including some of our leading artists, found it difficult to address the terrorist attacks in their work. Others, however, poured out their anger, despair, and confusion as they struggled to make sense of what had happened. Despite my initial feeling that I'd never be able to attempt my "irrelevant" poetry again, I wound up writing several poems about the disaster. Whether or not they were "good" poems didn't matter; I desperately needed to examine and record my impressions through the unique medium of poetry. Perhaps you felt the same way.

As we've all discovered since September 11, we don't need "permission" to write our poetry, no matter how insignificant we feel it may be at times. Rather, we have an obligation to live and write, whether we're celebrating, ranting, meditating, grieving, or simply capturing a certain place and time.

During a period of shock and sadness, it helped to be reminded that poetry matters. As you explore the articles, listings, and resources in this book, I hope you find just what you need to create and share *your* poetry.

Nancy Breen
poetsmarket@fwpubs.com

What's New for 2003?

There are a few changes in the 2003 edition of *Poet's Market*, plus some important new items we wanted to bring to your attention:

New Address. Yes, *Poet's Market* has a new home. We can now be reached at 4700 East Galbraith Road, Cincinnati OH 45236. Please make a note of this new address for inquiries, listing changes, and questionnaire requests.

New Website for *Writer's Digest*. The folks at *Writer's Digest* have redesigned their website—with a web page especially for poetry! Check out www.writersdigest.com for a wealth of features, information, and "goodies" regarding *all* areas of writing. (Content will be changing regularly, so check back often!)

Change in Listing Icons. We've made some changes in the way we define and use icons to better reflect each listing's preferences. See the "Keys to Symbols" printed on the inside covers of this book for updated explanations of each icon.

Note, too, that we've deleted three icons. We've eliminated the ☑ indicating changes in a listing's contact information. The reason? With the number of websites and e-mail addresses being added each year, plus the continual changes in existing addresses, a majority of listings would have required this icon, decreasing its usefulness.

To help ease visual clutter we've also deleted the ▣ icon for online/electronic markets and the ◘ icon for poetry written by children. However, never fear—you can still locate these special markets easily by turning to the Subject Index. Check under the headings for "Online Markets," "Poetry by Children," and a new designation, "Poetry for Children."

We've also tightened our use of the ◎ icon to reflect markets with a true specialization that sets them apart (or markets with a single focus, such as science fiction). However, we've categorized many general markets with areas of special interest (those that accept translations, for example) under appropriate headings in the Subject Index. Check these categorized lists to further help you choose the right magazines and publishers for your work.

Page Numbers in Indexes. We now list page numbers in all indexes (including the Geographical and Subject Indexes) to make it easier to find the markets you're looking for.

Publications Accepting E-mail Submissions. Today there are so many markets welcoming electronic submissions that this reference has become superfluous; check individual listings for their openness to receiving e-mail submissions and their preferred formats.

Glossary of Listing Terms. We've moved this reference to the Publishers of Poetry section to make it more visible and accessible.

Glossary of Poetry Terms. This reference is back, updated and expanded.

Poets in Education. We've provided a contact list for those interested in Poets in the Schools and similar programs.

New currency symbol. Are you familiar with the € symbol? It appears in some of our foreign listings and is the sign of the euro, the new single currency for the 11 member countries of the European Union. The abbreviation EUR when appearing with a monetary amount also refers to the euro. Be aware that some publishers still list monetary amounts in their former local currency. Also, nonmember countries, such as Great Britain, continue to use their traditional currency.

We're always looking for ways to improve *Poet's Market* for our readers. Let us know your comments and suggestions for the 2004 edition.

Getting Started (and Using This Book)

Delving into the pages of *Poet's Market* indicates a commitment—you've decided to take that big step and begin submitting your poems for publication. Three cheers for you! How do you *really* begin, though? To smooth the way, here are eight quick tips to help make sense of the marketing/submission process. Follow these suggestions, study the markets in this book carefully, and give proper attention to the preparation of your manuscript. Before you know it you'll be well under way in pursuit of your dream—seeing your poems in print.

1. **Read. And read. Then read some more.** There's a tendency among poets, young and old, not to read poetry. Kind of a puzzle, isn't it? It's also a big mistake. You'll never develop your skills if you don't immerse yourself in poetry of all kinds. It's essential to study the masters; but from a marketing standpoint, it's equally vital to read what your contemporaries are writing and publishing. Read journals and magazines, chapbooks and collections, anthologies for a variety of voices; scope out the many poetry sites on the Internet. Develop an eye for quality, then use that eye to assess your own work. Don't rush to publish until you know you're writing the best poetry you're capable of producing.

2. **Know what you like to write—and what you write best.** Ideally you should be experimenting with all kinds of poetic forms, from free verse to villanelles. However, there's sure to be a certain style with which you feel most comfortable, that conveys your true "voice." Whether you're into more formal, traditional verse or avant-garde poetry that breaks all the rules, you should identify which markets publish work similar to yours. Those are the magazines and presses you should target to give your submissions the best chance of being read favorably—and accepted! (See the Subject Index beginning on page 546 to get an idea of how some magazines and presses specify their needs.)

3. **Learn the "biz."** Poetry may not be a high-paying writing market, but there's still a right way to go about the "business" of submitting and publishing poems. Learn all you can by reading writing-related books and magazines. Read the articles and interviews in this book for plenty of helpful advice. Surf the Net for a wealth of sites filled with writing advice, market news, and informative links. (See Websites of Interest on page 520 for some leads.)

4. **Research those markets.** Start by studying the listings in *Poet's Market*. Each gathers the names, addresses, figures, editorial preferences, and other pertinent information all in one place. (The Publishers of Poetry section begins on page 27, with the Contests & Awards section following on page 427. Also, the indexes at the back of this book provide insights to what a publication or publisher might be looking for.)

   You're already reading a variety of published poetry (or at least you should be). That's the best way to gauge the kinds of poetry a market publishes. However, you need to go a step further. It's best to study several issues of a magazine/journal or several of a press's books to get a feel for the style and content of each. If the market has a Web address (when available, websites are included in the contact information for each listing in this book), log on and take a look. Check out the site for poetry samples, reviews and other content, and especially guidelines! If a market isn't online, send for guidelines and sample copies. Guidelines give you the lowdown on what an editor expects of submissions, the kind of "insider information" that's too valuable to ignore.

5. **Start slowly.** As tempting as it may be to send your work straight to *The New Yorker*, try to adopt a more modest approach if you're just starting out. Most listings in this book show symbols that reflect the level of writing a magazine or publisher would prefer to receive. The (☐) symbol indicates a market that welcomes submissions from beginning or unpublished poets. As you gain confidence and experience (and increased skill in your writing), move on to markets coded with the (◨) symbol. Later, when you've built a publication history, submit to the more prestigious magazines and presses (the ◖ markets). Although it may tax your patience, slow and steady progress is a proven route to success.

6. **Be professional.** Professionalism, on the other hand, is not something you should "work up to." Make it show in your very first submission, from the way you prepare your manuscript to the attitude you project in your communications with editors.

   Follow guidelines. Submit a polished manuscript. (See Frequently Asked Questions on page 7 for details on manuscript formatting and preparation.) Choose poems carefully with the editor's needs in mind. *Always* include a SASE (self-addressed stamped envelope) with any submission or inquiry. Not only do such practices show respect for the editor, the publication, and the process; they reflect *your* self-respect and the fact that you take your work seriously. Editors love that; and even if your work is rejected, you've made a good first impression that could help your chances with your next submission.

7. **Keep track of your submissions.** First, do *not* send out the only copies of your work. There are no guarantees that your submission won't get lost in the mail, misplaced in a busy editorial office, or vanish into a black hole if the market winds up closing shop. Create a special file folder for poems you are submitting. Even if you use a word processing program and store your manuscripts on disk, keep a hard copy file as well.

   Second, establish a tracking system so you always know which poems are where. This can be extremely simple: index cards, a chart made up on the computer, or even a simple notebook used as a log. (You can photocopy an enlarged version of the Submission Tracker on page 6 or use it as a model to design your own.) Note the titles of the poems submitted (or the title of the manuscript, if submitting a collection); the name of the publication, press, or contest; date sent; and date returned *or* date accepted. Additional information you may want to log includes the name of the editor/contact, date the accepted piece is published, the pay received, rights acquired by the publication or press, and any pertinent comments.

   Without a tracking system you risk forgetting where and when pieces were submitted. This is even more problematic if you simultaneously send the same poems to different magazines. And if you learn of an acceptance at one magazine, you must notify the others that the poem you sent them is no longer available. You have a bigger chance of overlooking someone without an organized approach. This causes hard feelings among editors you may have inconvenienced, hurting your chances with these markets in the future.

   Besides, a tracking system gives you a sense of accomplishment, even if your acceptances are infrequent at first. After all, look at all those poems you've sent out! You're really working at it, and that's something to be proud of.

8. **Learn from rejection.** No one enjoys rejection, but every writer faces it. The best way to turn a negative into a positive is to learn as much as you can from your rejections. Don't let them get you down. A rejection slip isn't a permission slip to doubt yourself, condemn your poetry, or give up. Look over the rejection. Did the editor provide any comments about your work or reasons why your poems were rejected? Probably he or she didn't. Editors are extremely busy and don't necessarily have time to comment on rejections. If that's the case, move on to the next magazine or publisher you've targeted and send your work out again.

   If, however, the editor *has* commented on your work, pay attention. It counts for something that the editor took the time and trouble to say anything, however brief, good, or bad. And consider any remark or suggestion with an open mind. You don't have to agree, but you shouldn't automatically disregard it, either. Tell your ego to sit down and be quiet, then use the editor's comments to review your work from a new perspective. You might be surprised how much you'll learn from a single scribbled word in the margin; or how encouraged you'll feel from a simple "Try again!" written on the rejection slip.

Keep these eight tips in mind as you prepare your poetry manuscript, and keep *Poet's Market* close at hand to help you along. Believe in yourself and don't give up! As the 1,800+ listings in this book show, there are many opportunities for beginning poets to become published poets. Why shouldn't you be one of them?

GUIDE TO LISTING FEATURES

Below is an example of the market listings you'll find in the Publishers of Poetry section. Note the callouts that identify various format features of the listing. The front and back covers of this book contain a key to the symbols used at the beginning of all listings.

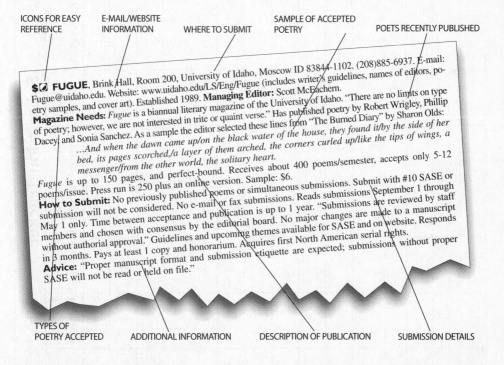

ICONS FOR EASY REFERENCE — E-MAIL/WEBSITE INFORMATION — WHERE TO SUBMIT — SAMPLE OF ACCEPTED POETRY — POETS RECENTLY PUBLISHED

$☑ FUGUE, Brink Hall, Room 200, University of Idaho, Moscow ID 83844-1102. (208)885-6937. E-mail: Fugue@uidaho.edu. Website: www.uidaho.edu/LS/Eng/Fugue (includes writer's guidelines, names of editors, poetry samples, and cover art). Established 1989. **Managing Editor:** Scott McEachern.
Magazine Needs: *Fugue* is a biannual literary magazine of the University of Idaho. "There are no limits on type of poetry; however, we are not interested in trite or quaint verse." Has published poetry by Robert Wrigley, Phillip Dacey, and Sonia Sanchez. As a sample the editor selected these lines from "The Burned Diary" by Sharon Olds:
...And when the dawn came up/on the black water of the house, they found it/by the side of her bed, its pages scorched,/a layer of them arched, the corners curled up/like the tips of wings, a messenger/from the other world, the solitary heart.
Fugue is up to 150 pages, and perfect-bound. Receives about 400 poems/semester, accepts only 5-12 poems/issue. Press run is 250 plus an online version. Sample: $6.
How to Submit: No previously published poems or simultaneous submissions. Submit with #10 SASE or submission will not be considered. No e-mail or fax submissions. Reads submissions September 1 through May 1 only. Time between acceptance and publication is up to 1 year. "Submissions are reviewed by staff members and chosen with consensus by the editorial board. No major changes are made to a manuscript without authorial approval." Guidelines and upcoming themes available for SASE and on website. Responds in 3 months. Pays at least 1 copy and honorarium. Acquires first North American serial rights.
Advice: "Proper manuscript format and submission etiquette are expected; submissions without proper SASE will not be read or held on file."

TYPES OF POETRY ACCEPTED — ADDITIONAL INFORMATION — DESCRIPTION OF PUBLICATION — SUBMISSION DETAILS

For More Information

If you're interested in writing for greeting card companies, *Writer's Market* (Writer's Digest Books, www.writersmarket.com) includes a section devoted to the greeting card/giftware industry. If you write song lyrics as well as poetry, *Songwriter's Market* (Writer's Digest Books) is an ideal resource for this field. Both books are available through your local library or bookstore, or can be ordered directly through the publisher at (800)448-0915 or www.writersdigest.com.

Submission Tracker

Poem Title	Publication/ Contest	Editor/Contact	Date Sent	Date Returned	Date Accepted	Date Published	Pay Received	Comments

Frequently Asked Questions

"What is a chapbook?"
"How many poems per page should I include in a manuscript?"
"What do I say in a cover letter?"

These are the kinds of questions we hear regularly at *Poet's Market*, so it made sense to provide our readers with a handy FAQ section ("frequently asked questions"). The answers it contains provide the expert knowledge it takes to submit your poetry like a pro.

Important Note: Most basic questions such as "How many poems should I send?", "How long should I wait for a reply?", and "Are simultaneous submissions okay?" can be answered by simply reading the listings in the Publishers of Poetry section. See the introduction to that section for an explanation of the information contained in the listings. Also, see the Glossary of Listing Terms on page 29.

Is it okay to submit handwritten poems?

Usually no. Now and then a publisher or editor makes an exception and accepts handwritten manuscripts. However, check the preferences stated in each listing. If no mention is made of handwritten submissions, assume your poetry should be typed or computer-printed.

How should I format my poems for submission to magazines and journals?

If you're submitting poems by regular mail (also referred to as *land mail*, *postal mail*, or *snail mail*), follow this format:

Poems should be typed or computer-printed on white 8½ × 11 paper of at least 20 lb. weight. Left, right, and bottom margins should be at least one inch. Starting ½ inch from the top of the page, type your name, address, telephone number, and e-mail address (if you have one), and number of lines in the poem in the *upper right* corner, individual lines, single spaced. Space down about six lines and type the poem title, either centered or flush left. The title may appear in all caps or in upper and lower case. Space down another two lines (at least) and begin to type your poem. Poems are usually single spaced, although some magazines may request double-spaced submissions. (Be alert to each market's preferences.) Double space between stanzas. Type one poem to a page. For poems longer than one page, type your name in the *upper left* corner; on the next line type a key word from the title of your poem, the page number, and indicate whether the stanza begins or is continued on the new page (i.e., BROKEN SHOELACE, Page 2, continue stanza *or* begin new stanza).

If you're submitting poems by e-mail:

First, make sure the publication accepts e-mail submissions. This information, when available, is included in all *Poet's Market* listings. In most cases include poems within the body of your e-mail, *not* as attachments. This is the preference of many editors accepting e-mail submissions because of the danger of viruses, the possibility of software incompatibility, and other concerns. Editors who consider e-mail attachments taboo may even delete the message without ever opening the attachment.

Of course, other editors do accept, and even prefer e-mail submissions as attachments. This information should be clearly stated in the market listing. If it's not, you're probably safer submitting your poems in the body of the e-mail. (All the more reason to pay close attention to details given in the listings.)

Note, too, the number of poems the editor recommends including in the e-mail submission. If no quantity is given specifically for e-mails, go with the number of poems an editor recommends submitting in general. Identify your submission with a notation in the subject line. Some editors simply want the words "Poetry Submission" while others want poem titles. Check the market listing for preferences. If you're uncertain about any aspect of e-mail submission formats, double-check the website (if available) for information or contact the publication for directions.

If you're submitting poems by disk:

Submit poems by disk *only* when the publication indicates this is acceptable. Even then, if no formatting preferences are given, contact the publisher for specifics before sending the disk. Always include a hardcopy (i.e., printed copy) of your submission with the disk.

What is a chapbook? How is it different from a regular poetry book?

A chapbook is a booklet averaging 24-50 pages in length (some may be shorter), usually digest sized (5½×8½, although chapbooks can come in all sizes, even published within the pages of a magazine). Typically a chapbook is saddle-stapled with a soft cover (card or special paper); however, chapbooks can also be produced with a plain paper cover the same weight as the pages, especially if the booklet is photocopied.

A chapbook is a much smaller collection of poetry than a full-length book (which runs anywhere from 50 pages to well over 100 pages, longer for "best of" collections and retrospectives). There are probably more poetry chapbooks being published than full-length books, and that's an important point to consider. Don't think of the chapbook as a poor relation to the full-length collection. While it's true a chapbook won't attract big reviews, qualify for major prizes, or find national distribution through large bookstores, it's a terrific way for a poet to build an audience (and reputation) in increments, while developing the kind of publishing history that may eventually attract the attention of a book publisher.

Although some presses consider chapbook-length submissions, many choose manuscripts through competitions. Check each publisher's listing for requirements, send for guidelines or visit the website (absolutely vital if a competition is involved), and check out some sample chapbooks the press has already produced (these are usually available from the publisher). Keep in mind that chapbook publishers are usually just as choosy as book publishers about the quality of work they accept. Submit your best work in a professional manner. (See the Chapbook Publishers Index on page 525 for markets that consider chapbook manuscripts.)

How do I format a collection of poems to submit to a book/chapbook publisher?

Before you send a manuscript to a book/chapbook publisher, request guidelines (or consult the publisher's website, if one is available). Requirements vary regarding formatting, query letters and samples, length, and other considerations. Usually you will be using 8½×11 20 lb. paper; left, right, and bottom margins of at least one inch; your name and title of your collection in the top left corner of every page; one poem to a page (although poems certainly may run longer than one page); and pages numbered consecutively. Individual publisher requirements may include a title page, table of contents, credits page (indicating where previously published poems originally appeared), and biographical note.

If you're submitting your poetry book or chapbook manuscript to a competition, you *must* read and follow the guidelines. Failure to do so could disqualify your manuscript. Often guidelines for a competition call for a special title page, a minimum and maximum number of pages, the absence of the poet's name anywhere in the manuscript, and even a special entry form to accompany the submission.

What is a cover letter? Do I have to send one? What should it say?

A cover letter is your introduction to the editor, telling him a little about yourself and your work. Most editors have indicated their preferences regarding cover letters in their listings in the Publishers of Poetry section. If an editor states that a cover letter is "required," absolutely send one! It's also better to send one if a cover letter is "preferred." Experts disagree on the necessity and appropriateness of cover letters, so use your own judgment when preferences aren't clear in the listing.

A cover letter should be professional but also allow you to present your work in a personal manner. (See the fictional cover letter on page 10 as an example.) Keep your letter brief, no more than one page. Address your letter to the correct contact person. (Use "Poetry Editor" if no contact name appears in the listing.) Include your name, address, phone number, and e-mail address (if available). If a biographical note is requested, include 2-3 lines about your job, interests, why you write poetry, etc. Avoid praising yourself or your poems in your letter (your submission should speak for itself). Include titles (or first lines) of the poems you're submitting. List a few of your most recent publishing credits, but no more than five. (If you haven't published any poems yet, you may skip this. However, be aware that some editors are interested in and make an effort to publish new writers.) Show your familiarity with the magazine to which you're submitting—comment on a poem you saw printed there, tell the editor why you chose to submit to her magazine, mention poets the magazine has published. Use a business-style format for a professional appearance, and proofread carefully; typos, misspellings, and other errors make a poor first impression. Remember that editors are people, too. Respect, professionalism, and kindness go a long way in poet/editor relationships.

What is a SASE? An IRC (with SAE)?

A SASE is a self-addressed stamped envelope. Don't let your submission leave home without it! You should also include a SASE if you send an inquiry to an editor. If your submission is too large for an envelope (for instance a bulky book-length collection of poems), use a box and include a self-addressed mailing label with adequate return postage (paper clip the return postage to the return mailing label).

An IRC is an International Reply Coupon, enclosed in place of a SASE with manuscripts submitted to foreign markets. Each coupon is equivalent in value to the minimum postage rate for an unregistered airmail letter. IRCs may be exchanged for postage stamps at post offices in all foreign countries that are members of the Universal Postal Union (UPU). When you provide the adequate number of IRCs and a self-addressed envelope (SAE), you give a foreign editor financial means to return your submission (U.S. postage stamps cannot be used to send mail *to* the United States from outside the country). Purchase price is $1.75 per coupon. Call your local post office to check for availability (sometimes only larger post offices sell them).

To save trouble and money, poets sometimes send disposable manuscripts to foreign markets and inform the editor to discard the manuscript after it's been read. Some enclose an IRC and SAE for reply only; others establish a deadline after which they will withdraw the manuscript from consideration and market it elsewhere.

How much postage does my submission need?

As much as it takes; you do *not* want your manuscript to arrive postage due! Purchase a postage scale or take your manuscript to the post office for weighing. Remember you'll need postage on two envelopes: the one containing your submission and SASE, and the return envelope itself. Submissions without SASEs usually will not be returned (and possibly may not even be read).

At press time the U.S. Postal Service was proposing a First-Class Mail rate increase from 34 cents for the first ounce to 37 cents; each additional ounce would cost 23 cents per ounce up to 13 ounces. So, at these new rates, if your submission weighs in at five ounces, you'll need to apply $1.29 in postage. Note that three pages of poetry, a cover letter, and a SASE can be mailed for one first-class stamp using a #10 (business-size) envelope; the SASE should be either a #10 envelope folded in thirds or a #9 envelope. Larger envelopes may require different rates, so check with your post office.

First Class mail over 13 ounces is classified Priority; at press time, for $3.95 you can mail

Perry Lineskanner
1954 Eastern Blvd.
Pentameter, OH 45007
(852)555-5555
soneteer@trochee.vv.cy

April 24, 2003

Spack Saddlestaple, Editor
The Squiggler's Digest
Double-Toe Press
P.O. Box 54X
Submission Junction, AZ 85009

Dear Mr. Saddlestaple:

Enclosed are three poems for your consideration for *The Squiggler's Digest*:
"His Tired Feet," "Boogie Lunches," and "Circling Piccadilly."

Although I'm a long-time reader of *The Squiggler's Digest*, this is my first
submission to your publication. However, my poetry has appeared in other
magazines, including *The Bone-Whittle Review*, *Bumper Car Reverie*, and *Stock
Still*. I've won several awards through the annual *Buckeye Versefest!* contests
and my chapbook manuscript was a finalist in the competition sponsored
by Hollow Banana Press. While I devote a great deal of time to poetry
(both reading and writing), I'm employed as a coffeehouse manager—which
inspires more poetry than you might imagine!

Thank you for the opportunity to submit my work. Your time and attention
are much appreciated, and I look forward to hearing from you.

Sincerely,

Perry Lineskanner

An example of what to include in a cover letter. Note: The names used in this letter are intended to be
fictional; any resemblance to real people, publications, or presses is purely coincidental.

a package of up to two pounds with two-day service offered to most domestic destinations. You can simply mark your envelope "Priority Mail" or use labels, envelopes, or boxes provided free by the Postal Service. Matter sent in a flat-rate envelope provided by the Postal Service may be mailed for the newly proposed rate of $3.85 (actually a 10 cent decrease), regardless of weight or destination.

For complete U.S. Postal Service information, including rates and increases, a postage calculator, and the option to buy stamps online with a credit card, see their website at www.usps.gov. Canadian Postal Service information is available at www.canadapost.ca.

What does it mean when an editor says "no previously published" poems? Does this include poems that have appeared in anthologies?

If your poem appears *anywhere* in print for a public audience, it's considered "previously" published. That includes magazines, anthologies, websites and online magazines, and even programs (say for a church service, wedding, etc.). See the following explanation of rights, especially *second serial (reprint) rights* and *all rights* for additional concerns about previously published material.

What rights should I offer for my poems? What do these different rights mean?

Usually editors indicate in their listings what rights they acquire. Most journals and magazines license *first rights* (a.k.a. *first serial rights*), which means the poet offers the right to publish the poem for the first time in any periodical. All other rights to the material remain with the poet. (Note that some editors state that rights to poems "revert to authors upon publication" when first rights are acquired.) When poems are excerpted from a book prior to publication and printed in a magazine/journal, this is also called *first serial rights*. The addition of *North American* indicates the editor is the first to publish a poem in a U.S. or Canadian periodical. The poem can still be submitted to editors outside of North America or to those who acquire reprint rights.

When a magazine/journal licenses *one-time rights* to a poem (also known as *simultaneous rights*), the editor has *nonexclusive* rights to publish the poem once. The poet can submit that same poem to other publications at the same time (usually markets that don't have overlapping audiences).

Editors/publishers open to submissions of work already published elsewhere seek *second serial (reprint) rights*. The poet is obliged to inform them where and when the poem previously appeared so they can give proper credit to the original publication. In essence, chapbook or book collections license reprint rights, listing the magazines in which poems previously appeared somewhere in the book (usually on the copyright page or separate credits page).

If a publisher or editor requires you to relinquish *all rights*, be aware that you are giving up ownership of that poem or group of poems. You cannot resubmit the work elsewhere, nor can you include it in a poetry collection without permission or negotiating for reprint rights to be returned to you. Before you agree to this type of arrangement, ask the editor first if she is willing to acquire first rights instead of all rights. If she refuses, simply write a letter withdrawing your work from consideration. Some editors will reassign rights to a writer after a given amount of time, such as one year.

With the growth in Internet publishing opportunities, *electronic rights* have become very important. These cover a broad range of electronic media, including online magazines, CD recordings of poetry readings, and CD-ROM editions of magazines. When submitting to an electronic market of any kind, find out what rights the market acquires upfront (many online magazines also stipulate the right to archive poetry they've published so it's continually available on their websites).

What is a copyright? Should I have my poems copyrighted before I submit them for publication?

Copyright is a proprietary right that gives you the power to control your work's reproduction, distribution, and public display or performance, as well as its adaptation to other forms. In other words, you have legal right to the exclusive publication, sale, or distribution of your poetry. What's more, your "original works of authorship" are protected as soon as they are "fixed in a tangible form of expression," or written down. Since March 1989, copyright notices are no longer required to secure protection, so it's not necessary to include them on your poetry manuscript. Also, in many editors' minds copyright notices signal the work of amateurs distrustful and paranoid about having work stolen.

If you still want to indicate copyright, use the (c) symbol or the word *copyright*, your name, and the year. Furthermore, if you wish you can register your copyright with the Copyright Office for a $30 fee. (Since paying $30 per poem is costly and impractical, you may prefer to copyright a group of poems for that single fee.) Further information is available from the U.S. Copyright Office, Library of Congress, Washington DC 20559-6000. You can also call the Copyright Public Information Office at (202)707-3000 between 8:30 a.m. and 5:00 p.m. weekdays (EST). Copyright forms can be ordered from (202)707-9100 or downloaded from www.loc.gov/copyright (this Library of Congress website includes advice on filling out forms, general copyright information, and links to copyright-related websites).

Special note regarding the Copyright Office: Because of last year's anthrax scare in Washington, mail delivery to the Copyright Office was halted on October 17, 2001. Delivery resumed on March 4, 2002, but catch-up on the backlog of undelivered mail was expected to take several months. This also impacted the "effective date of registration" for copyright applications (usually the day the Copyright Office actually receives all elements of the application—application form, fee, and copies of work being registered). *For delayed mail only*, the Copyright Office has established certain guidelines to determine receipt dates based on the postmark dates on envelopes or packages. These standards differ depending on the type of delivery method used by the applicant, so check the website at www.loc.gov/copyright/mail.html for a complete breakdown of the standards the Copyright Office is using, plus additional information and on-going updates. You may also call (202)707-3000 for a recorded message or to speak with an Information Specialist regarding this situation *only*.

Editors' Roundtable: Four Top Magazines and What They Like

BY WILL ALLISON

The magazines represented in this interview range considerably in size. The press runs of *Barrow Street* (1,000 copies) and *Crab Orchard Review* (1,600 copies) are modest compared to that of *Poetry* (12,000 copies), which in turn is modest compared to *The Atlantic Monthly*'s circulation of half a million. Despite these differences in size, these magazines have in common a reputation for first-rate verse, and recent editions of *Best American Poetry* have featured work from all four.

The editors who participated in this roundtable include Patricia Carlin, Peter Covino, Lois Hirshkowitz, and Melissa Hotchkiss of *Barrow Street*; Allison Joseph, poetry editor of *Crab Orchard Review*; Joseph Parisi, editor of *Poetry*; and Peter Davison, poetry editor of *The Atlantic Monthly*.

(For more information on the magazines featured in this interview, see the individual listings in the Publishers of Poetry section, page 27.)

How would you characterize the poetry in your magazine?

Barrow Street editors: We would characterize our magazine as exceptionally eclectic. We strive to represent the diversity of poems being written today, as well as the varying tastes of the editors (we are all poets). I don't think anyone would read *Barrow Street* and say, "Oh, it's this type of poetry or that type of poetry." Bottom line: We look for strong work, in any form. We would never want our journal to become predictable; and if it does, we hope we notice or someone will tell us! We want to surprise readers because that is what good writing does. We want each issue to be a little different; we want readers to see the book and think, "What's in there this time?" We don't want readers to skim the back of the journal, see the names, and say, "I've seen this before."

*Peter Davison, **The Atlantic Monthly**:* Since *The Atlantic Monthly* is a general magazine of literature, politics, science, and human affairs, the poetry we publish is chosen with that context in mind. I'm interested in poems of all sorts, by poets of all ages and degrees of eminence, from all parts of the United States, dealing with all walks of life, cast in a wide variety of poetic forms. We receive upwards of 60,000 poetry submissions a year, but we have space for no more than three dozen poems a year, not many of them long. I tend to avoid poems that are specifically about poetry, and we cannot afford to publish more than a very few translations.

*Allison Joseph, **Crab Orchard Review**:* At *Crab Orchard Review*, we seek literate, engaging poetry for a wide audience, an audience beyond just poets and writers themselves. We like poems that take on a wide variety of topics; once a year, we even give poets a topic with our thematic issues. We like poems that writers and readers of all backgrounds can appreciate, poems that embody common ground for today's divergent cultures. We strive to publish poems that

---

WILL ALLISON *is former executive editor of* Story. *His short stories have appeared in* Shenandoah, American Short Fiction, *and other magazines.*

poets will admire and readers will enjoy. We publish both free verse and formal poetry, with more free verse than formal verse because we see more free verse, though I have noted an increase in certain forms being submitted, such as the villanelle and sestina.

Joseph Parisi, **Poetry:** We sort of take the poems as they come in, one at a time, and do the best we can trying to judge them on their own merits rather than on some preconceived notion about what a poem is supposed to be. Even though it's rarer and rarer nowadays, we have a number of unpublished poets who come in over the transom, and they strike it on the first go. We're also one of the very few places that still publish longer poems or sequences. We're not particularly looking for them, to tell you the truth. Most people have a hard enough time writing twelve lines, let alone twelve pages. In any case, long poems do seem to be in vogue at the moment. The writing programs seem to be telling these kids, "Oh, you should write long poems and sequences." That's the last thing they should probably be doing.

When you're reading submissions, what are the most important qualities you look for?

Barrow Street *editors:* A strong, original voice; powerful language; a new way of looking at things (a perspective that is original and singular); and integrity.

Peter Davison, **The Atlantic Monthly:** When I read poems, it's the sound that I listen for first: what does this poem make me hear, what sort of freshness of experience has invigorated its sound, what emotions or music ruffle its surface, what passions have made it sing? Our magazine contains substance of many kinds, but our poetry must ring with the truth of genuine emotion, whether it be mirth or anger, melancholy or lassitude, indignation or love. In the long history of our magazine since its founding in 1857, the two most frequently published *Atlantic* poets have been Henry Wadsworth Longfellow and W. S. Merwin; but I would always prefer accepting a poet not yet known.

Allison Joseph, **Crab Orchard Review:** I look for poems that embody contradictions: poems that are both lucid and mysterious, accessible yet challenging. As a poet myself, I look for poems that make me jealous; poems that make me say, "I wish I wrote that one!"; poems that make me turn to my managing editor (also a poet) to say, "Look at this; you've just got to read this poem." I want poems that stay with me, ones I remember after hours of reading poems and logging in submissions, work so good that I stop the routine of my day to immerse myself in it. On a more formal level, I look for poems where all the elements are working in concert, where the line breaks, images, figurative language, rhythms, and word choices all work together to make that poem undeniably what it is. As a reader, I admire both elegance and daring.

Joseph Parisi, **Poetry:** Here's a simple criterion: Would you want to read this poem twice? You can tell very quickly, usually. It's not something that's necessarily just intellectual. It's not a question of content; certainly not that. There is a certain confidence you have right off the bat, when you read a poem and you know you're in good hands, even if you don't know what's going to happen. It's a question of music, of voice, of tone, of rhythm—all these things just seem to be very right. And there's usually also an element of strangeness.

Are there any types of poems that turn up again and again in your submission pile? And are these poems, by virtue of their familiarity, at a disadvantage?

Barrow Street *editors:* We never mind hearing or seeing something again if it is written in a new way with fresh, challenging language. I don't think any particular poem is at a disadvantage, if someone has sent his or her best work.

Peter Davison, **The Atlantic Monthly:** The poems most frequently submitted to *The Atlantic* are those that grieve for a loss or for the death of a relative; those that express sexual yearning (but seldom fulfillment); those that attempt to describe familiar landscape; those that dilate upon marital or sexual discontent; those that wish to illuminate the poetic process. Even more common than these categories of subject matter is the form in which the submissions are cast: something like 60% are written in the present indicative, which has somehow in recent years become the fashionable form in which every aspirant poet thinks he or she is obliged to write. Why, I don't know.

Allison Joseph, **Crab Orchard Review:** We see many poems about personal losses: death within families, divorce and/or ill-fated romance, loss of a loved one—a spouse or a partner—to disease or injury. The work we see these days seems more elegiac and less sociopolitical. These poems aren't necessarily at a disadvantage because of the subject matter. I don't say "Oh no, not another cancer poem!" but I do expect the writing in such poems to be just as accomplished as the writing in poems on other subjects. I want to be moved by the language and imagery, not just by the situation, as tragic as it may be. When we do thematic issues, certain topics spring up again and again. We did an issue titled "The City: Past, Present, and Future," and we got a lot of poems on homeless people. We did an issue on music, and we received quite a few poems on the tyranny of childhood music lessons.

Joseph Parisi, **Poetry:** There are certain fashions. In the seventies and eighties, there was a lot of confessional dreck ("My mother hates me, I despise my father."). And then there are the perennial favorites: the grandfather/grandmother poems, the photograph poems, the ekphrastic poems—"I just went to the Vermeer exhibit, and now I'm going to tell you what that painting is all about" poem—we get tons of those. Then there are the favored diseases of the current year, besides cancer, which is the perennial. Alzheimer's poems—lots of those coming in nowadays.

  Even if they're very, very well done—and not many of them are—there's only so many of those I can do, so I may have to send back a fairly decent one about Aunt Hilda's Alzheimer's, just because I can't stand to read another one, and my readers wouldn't stand for it. This is a paraliterary criterion, I'm afraid.

What are the most common weaknesses you see in the poems you receive?

Barrow Street *editors:* Dead/empty language; cliched or self-conscious diction; and an overall sense that we have read a clone of the poem many times before.

Peter Davison, **The Atlantic Monthly:** The most common weakness (aside from clinging feebly to the present tense) is the incapacity of most poets to find verbs that awaken their utterance. Younger poets are especially prone to multiplying adjectives, when the verb could have enlivened their poems from the inside, had the verb only been found. Some people blame contemporary poetry for being "formless." That's often true among those aspiring to write it, but it's not a matter of importance to me whether a poem rhymes or does not rhyme. It's extremely important whether it takes to the waves, rides on its own melting, as Robert Frost put it, breathes with its own breath.

Allison Joseph, **Crab Orchard Review:** There are different levels of weaknesses. There's the beginner level where rhymes are expected, cliched phrases appear with regularity, and the topics are obvious (love with a capital L, for example). There's a level beyond that in which the poet is progressing, but the subjects in the poems are still a bit broadly familiar, the writing not as sharp as it could be. Then there's the level where the poet is more accomplished, often well published, but the poems in that particular submission are not up to previous levels. We do see poems that feel hurried, rushed, as if gaining a publication credit were more important to the poet than the poem itself.

*Joseph Parisi, **Poetry:*** Verbosity. Just blah, blah—too much filler and repetition. The poem would be twice as good if it were half as long. Perhaps it's a function of the fact that people are using computers more, and so they can keep on adding stuff so easily. And they do. So you have these things going on and on. I do get irritated after a while, and I think the reader would be, too, saying, "Why are you telling me all this? Get to the point." One of the reasons you're reading poetry supposedly is to have a distilled, intense experience, not more of the blabbing that you can hear around the coffeepot. I think people are much too easily pleased, perhaps—particularly pleased with the sounds of their own voices.

What is your single best piece of advice for poets hoping to publish work in your magazine?

Barrow Street editors: Send us your best work.

*Peter Davison, **The Atlantic Monthly:*** My single piece of advice is to read more than you write, to be sincere in your writing without attempting to sound like anyone else, to certify to what you write after you have written it, and to believe what you have set down before you ship it off to an editor. Poetry is not a career, it is the servant to your life; it will never make you famous (certainly not in your lifetime), but it can satisfy you so long as you have fully expressed and passed along what your life has taught you. Perhaps, if you turn out to have talent, people will discover that what you have told them is true. But publication means very little except helping you speak to the people you most care about reaching.

*Allison Joseph, **Crab Orchard Review:*** Since we do one thematic issue each year, it's good for poets to keep up with what we're doing so they don't send inappropriate work at the wrong time. If we're working on a thematic issue, we want to see only work for that issue (we work on thematic issues from April to October). Poets can keep up with our plans for *Crab Orchard Review* by checking our website (www.siu.edu/~crborchd), by writing us for submission guidelines (we'll gladly send them if you send us a self-addressed, stamped envelope), or by subscribing (calls for submissions are printed with the journal itself). Knowing one's market always helps.

*Joseph Parisi, **Poetry:*** One word: revise.

A Look at Alternatives in Publishing

BY MELANIE RIGNEY

If you're reading this book, you want to see your poems published. Yet, as you're probably all too aware, getting poetry published today is tough. Many of the hundreds of markets here are looking for poetry of a certain style. If your work doesn't fit their requirements, they won't publish it. If it fits the requirements, you're often competing against dozens or hundreds of others to get published. Mainstream magazines are publishing less poetry, and traditional book publishers aren't likely to take a chance on a volume of work by an unknown author. What's a poet to do?

More and more poets today are exploring the worlds of self-publishing and print-on-demand (POD). In addition to traditional custom printing and subsidy arrangements, publishing your book electronically is also an option today. In general, these alternative publishers will publish any work—short of pornography or hate speech—as long as the poet can pay the bill.

Poets are embracing these new technologies. The *Writer's Digest* 2001 National Self-Published Book Awards drew 125 poetry entrants vs. 74 the previous year, an increase of nearly 70 percent. But how do you know which option is right for you?

CUSTOM PRINTING

Working with a custom printer on your book or chapbook of poetry is similar to working with your local printer on posters or fliers. Custom printers typically produce a minimum of 200 books per press run for as low as $4.50 per book; the unit cost goes down with the volume ordered and goes up when color, illustrations, and photos are added.

Advantages: On a per-unit basis, probably the best value for poets who plan to use the book in a class setting or who are prepared to participate in a large number of public readings to sell chapbooks. You retain all rights, since all that is involved is a printing agreement. That means you can republish poems from the collection elsewhere. It also means you keep all the money from sales rather than receiving a monthly or quarterly royalty.

Disadvantages: You're the cook and chief bottle washer. If you want a proofreader or copyeditor, you'll have to look elsewhere and incur additional costs. While you'll see galleys, finding errors is totally your responsibility. In general, if you want to copyright the work, get an International Standard Book Number (most bookstores won't sell a book that doesn't carry one), and get a bar code, you'll have to do that yourself. Your entire press run will be delivered to your house, and you will be responsible for storing the books and processing and fulfilling orders. You also will be responsible for all marketing.

PRINT-ON-DEMAND (POD)

With this digital technology, copies literally are printed one at a time. Some experts expect all books to use digital printing within the next ten years—you'd go to your local bookstore, take a copy of the cover to the front, and have a cup of coffee while you wait ten minutes for the book to be printed and bound. We're not quite convinced that that's what the future holds, but it's a viable option for some poets. You'll typically pay somewhere between $200 and $600

MELANIE RIGNEY *is editorial director of* Writer's Digest Books *and editor of* Writer's Digest. *She speaks on publishing technology at several writer's conferences each year.*

in setup fees. Some POD companies provide ISBNs and bar codes as part of the basic service; others charge extra. Editorial services sometimes are available, but generally, there is an additional fee. Similarly, many POD companies will promote your book at their site and submit information to third-party sellers. Many offer additional marketing services for additional fees.

Advantages: This is about the lowest up-front monetary investment a poet can expect to find for a full-length book. Once you've signed off on corrections, you can typically expect books within a few weeks. There are no books to warehouse—whenever an order comes in, the POD company prints the book and ships it out. This is an excellent option for poets who expect to sell or give away fewer than 100 books. It's also a good way to test the salability of your book with minimal risk.

Disadvantages: POD is an expensive option for the poet who realistically expects to sell more than 100 books. The *à la carte* menu concept (a fee for editing, a fee for marketing, a fee for getting your ISBN) can get more expensive than you expected very quickly. Typically, the name of the POD company, not your business, is listed as the book's publisher on the spine and jacket. Read the rights section of your publishing agreement carefully. Some PODs take the exclusive right to publish the work in English for the life of the agreement and claim subrights (film, book club, and so on) they would be unlikely ever to exercise.

E-BOOKS

The impact of electronic books on the market so far has been underwhelming, to say the least, with the exception of Stephen King's experiments. Your poems are saved in a proprietary format or as an Adobe PDF file and are then readable only via a special reader. Proponents say e-readers' portability and ability to hold text for several books at once ensure the technology's ultimate success; others don't see electrons replacing paper in a serious way any time soon. Several e-book pioneers now also offer print-on-demand paperback or hardback options.

Advantages: Your investment is even more minimal than in POD and sometimes is nonexistent. The e-publisher typically handles creating the file downloads and processing orders.

Disadvantages: So far, acceptance of e-books by consumers has been minimal.

SUBSIDY PUBLISHING

In subsidy publishing, you'll find it difficult to publish your book of poetry for an investment of less than $5,000. Reputable companies will tell you that few writers make back that initial investment despite royalty rates in the 40 to 60 percent range. The initial press run will be between 450 and 1,000 and will be set by the company, as will the book's price. Who controls the rights varies; some companies hold rights until the contract with you expires (typically three years) while others take no rights.

Advantages: Some sort of marketing plan for your book and some editing services typically are included in the base price. Do make sure you understand what you'll get before signing the agreement. Also, subsidy publishers generally handle fulfillment—that is, they warehouse your book and process orders. This option is for poets who have some money and want some TLC while their book is being produced and who don't want to stuff books into envelopes and take them to the post office.

Disadvantages: You have to invest what for many poets is a good chunk of money up front (some subsidy companies do provide payment plans) with little likelihood of recouping that investment. Depending on the contract, you may give up all rights to your poems for the life of the contract, meaning you can't submit them to contests, magazines, and elsewhere during that time. The process typically takes six months to a year. Finally, rightly or wrongly, there still is a sense that subsidy published books aren't as "good" as those published by traditional publishing houses.

LET THE POET BEWARE

Before you embrace one of these alternative publishing modes, we urge you to consider what's important to you. No two poets are alike. For one, simply having five volumes of her poetry to give the family for Christmas may be a cherished dream; retaining various rights and including illustrations may not be important. For another, the goal may be to sell 5,000 copies in the first year in hopes of interesting a traditional publisher. For another, controlling all rights and keeping all the money from selling books at poetry readings may be paramount. Set your goals, then find the option that's best for you.

Additional Resources

Groups

American Self-Publisher Association, P.O. Box 232233, Sacramento CA 95823. (800)929-7889. Website: www.members.aol.com/ASPublish). Helps authors learn how to self-publish and market their books on a limited budget.

National Association of Independent Publishers, P.O. Box 430, Highland City FL 33846-0430. (863)648-4420. Website: www.publishersreport.com. An informal organization of publishers, authors, and vendors that shares publishing information via an e-mail newsletter.

Small Publishers Association of North America, P.O. Box 1306, 425 Cedar St., Buena Vista, CO 81211. (719)395-4790. Website: www.spannet.org. A nonprofit organization for independent publishers.

Books

The Complete Guide to Self-Publishing by Tom and Marilyn Ross (Writer's Digest Books)
The Self-Publishing Manual by Dan Poynter (ParaPublishing)

The Niche Market of Poetry Translation

BY VANESSA LYMAN

Translations are like women, the old proverb goes. If they're faithful, they're not beautiful; if they're beautiful, they're not faithful. The originator of the proverb undoubtedly had a fit of inspiration after pouring over a bad interpretation of *The Iliad*, but is there any truth to the saying?

Just enough truth to make a translator smile; but under scrutiny the black and white categories of "faithful" and "beautiful" melt into gray. Faithfulness, one might ask, on what level?

David Lee Garrison, translator, poet, and professor of modern languages at Wright State University, uses one of his own experiences to illustrate the difference between faithfulness to the language and faithfulness to the spirit of the poem. Both he and John Frederick Nimms translated the same poem by 17th century Spanish poet Lope de Vega. "I stuck mainly to what Lope said but [Nimms] took these enormous liberties with it, and yet his poem is a riot. It's exactly what Lope intended. I've got to hand it to Nimms. I think my own translation is truer to the Spanish, but in terms of effect created, his is phenomenal. The translation's a *tour de force*."

There is also faithfulness regarding form. Annie Finch, considered a leading New Formalist poet, says, "If I have a choice between form and meaning, I will go for the form, since I feel my particular skill is in accurately conveying the music of form—a music I believe has its own meaning and truth just as important, or even more so than the denotative meaning of words." Her forthcoming book, *The Poetry of Louise Labé* (University of Chicago Press), is a translation of the French Renaissance poet's complete body of work, and the only translation to keep the original Petrarchan sonnet rather than substituting, for example, the Shakespearean form.

Finch describes three stages she experienced in translating Labé's poetry. "I started by being completely faithful to all the Renaissance conventions, every ah and oh, every odd comma and oft-repeated word." Then she muted the archaic diction just enough to keep it from being distracting. Finally, Finch set aside the originals and approached the translations as if they were her own work, "feeling free to loosen the syntax and word-for-word correspondence up a bit wherever beauty or creative life were lacking. I didn't do much tinkering at this stage, but it was a crucial stage."

Crucial, indeed. "One problem translators make is becoming too tied to the text," says Garrison. "If you don't make it a poem in English, if it can't stand on its own, it's 'translationese.' And, boy, there's translationese out there."

"I don't think the best translations are word-for-word translations," agrees George Looney, translation editor for *Mid-American Review*, "but instead [the translator] thinks about the way language is being used in the original, especially in terms of figurative language. [The translator] tries to find the appropriate or equivalent context in English for whatever the Italian is doing in the Italian, for example. Since we're not going to publish any poems just so we can have poems in another language, the translation has to be work we would publish as an English language poem."

VANESSA LYMAN *is assistant editor of both* Poet's Market *and* Novel & Short Story Writer's Market, *as well as editor of writersdigest.com's fiction web page. She knows a smattering of dirty limericks in different languages but declined to translate them for this article.*

Looney confesses *Mid-American Review* doesn't receive as many translations as he would like. Often he seeks out a translator whose work he has read elsewhere. In the case of *Mid-American Review*'s Translation Chapbook Series (a slice of each volume of *Mid-American Review* devoted to one translator, with originals on the facing page), Looney frequently contacts a translator who had submitted only a few poems and asks for a wider selection. On occasion, *Mid-American Review* will place a call for submissions in the American Literary Translators Association's (ALTA) regular newsletter.

Quality translations of good poetry are a rare commodity in the literary world. Many journals closed to unsolicited submissions are more than willing, even *eager* to see translations of poetry. "Certainly it is easier to publish translations. I had publishers snapping up the Labé, while my own poetry books still take years to persuade someone to publish," says Finch. When the University of Chicago Press accepted her Labé manuscript for their Early Modern Women Writers series, Finch agreed for more than one reason. "I knew if Chicago published it, it would become the definitive, authoritative translation of Labé and would remain in print forever. And Chicago will attract the academic audience, and that may bring some new readers to my own poems." In hope of doing the reverse—attracting readers to Labé—Finch included three of the translations in her current manuscript, *Brutal Flowers*.

Expanding the audience for a certain poet or poetry of another region is probably the most cited reason, by writers and publishers alike, for why they translate or publish translations.

Looney describes it as a service. "It helps our readers (and many of our readers are writers) to see what is being done elsewhere in the world. The only way most of our readers can be exposed to writing from other places is through translation. There's a lot of work not necessarily in English that deserves to be read."

Or deserves to be read the way it was originally constructed. "I did feel a duty to translate [Labé] properly—she is such a wonderfully passionate, exciting poet," says Finch. Labé's work had been translated before, though never into her own sonnet form. "Nowadays, so few people are able to write sonnets well that it seemed unlikely that anyone else would do it if I didn't. And I wanted an excuse to start a poem with the words, 'Kiss me again!' "

There is another, very strong attraction to translating poetry. "It's a chance to get inside the soul of another poet, especially the soul of a great poet—in the soul, in the mind, to see how they work," says Garrison. "That's essentially what you're doing when you try to recreate a poem in English that exists in another language. I find it increases my own creativity, it gives me new ideas, new ways of looking at and thinking about things, and new ways of doing poetry."

For poets, this is one of the most rewarding aspects of translation: developing stronger skills to use in their own poetry. "One of the poems I translated was a sonnet about the act of writing a sonnet," says Garrison. "If you were to translate that and not make it rhyme, it wouldn't have any meaning. The whole point is 'How do you come up with 14 lines that rhyme *abba*?' " After struggling to make rhymed Spanish poetry rhyme in its English counterpart, Garrison became interested in trying rhyme in his own poetry, with some success.

Finch also credits her translation work with teaching her a great deal about rhyme and the sonnet form. "I call it an apprenticeship, since the process involves learning technical skills by hearing the other poet at work in a very literal way. Certainly, if the poet is well-chosen to complement one's own weaknesses, it enriches one's work."

"Trying to figure out what a poet is doing in another language and come up with an equivalent in English is going to help your skills as a poet in English," Looney says. "The same way reading critically—not only what the poet has done but how they're doing it, which you *have* to do when you're translating—that's going to help you when you approach the page. You have a more varied ammunition to attack the page with."

This benefit isn't limited to translators, however. Just as a translator specializes in one region's dialect, a particular form, or even one poet in order to learn the nuances of style and expression, so too can a poet benefit from reading the entire works of a single English-language poet.

"Trying to figure out over the span of a career what their work has done, how it has changed, how it's doing the same thing but doing it differently—those kinds of things will help a writer learn many different approaches," says Looney. "The more you know about craft and the more you know what has been done, then the more you bring to what you can do."

A technique Garrison uses in his poetry workshops involves translating from English to English. "I give them a poem in Spanish by [Juan Ramón] Jiménez and then I give them the [Robert] Bly translation and also a very literal translation. I tell them to try to do something with it, either translating with different words or doing a takeoff and making their own poem out of it. I find that can be very creative."

So a poet can gain skills and exposure by translating poetry. What about money?

"You don't make much money," Garrison is quick to point out. Publishing a translation in a journal is not all that different from publishing original poetry. "Nobody's in it for the money. Occasionally, I'll get ten or twenty dollars and the protocol is that you always split it with the original poet 50/50. So if I get a check for fifty dollars, I send twenty-five to the poet." The same courtesy extends to contributor's copies.

When submitting to a journal or publisher, a translator's chances of being published increase by being as professional as possible. "With your cover letter, include information about the poet you're translating so you give the editor some context for looking at the poems," says Looney. Your own credits are important, but the original poet's credits are more so. In other words, tell the editor why he or she should be interested in these poems. Adds Looney, "If the translator includes the written documentation of permission with the initial submission, a) it's going to look more professional, b) it's going to give the submission some authority, and c) it will save time later."

Mid-American Review will not publish translated poetry without written permission from either the author or, if the poet is no longer alive, the poet's estate. Required primarily to prevent legal complications, the permissions do, however, serve one other, very important purpose.

In Looney's case, the permissions provide a security measure. Because he speaks only a little German and therefore can't catch every mistake in every language, Looney depends on the permissions to mean that either the original writer or the writer's publisher has read and is satisfied with the work. Not many editors can live up to the standards of an ideal translations editor ("Someone who knows or has some facility with several languages and is well versed in terms of contemporary poetics," as Looney describes it), so permissions give a translator's work a reassuring authority.

Obtaining permission can be difficult or easy, depending on the fame of the selected poet. Garrison says of a translation he did of a Gabriela Mistral poem, "That took months to get permission because she had won the Nobel Prize and she had an agent, and they were very sticky about everything. Usually, if the poet is not known, it's easy because everybody wants to be translated."

If you're interested in submitting translations for publication, what's the simplest way to get permission? Write to the original poet or the poet's most recent publisher; request written permission to translate and publish a specific poem or group of poems in the literary magazine of your choice. When submitting translations for publication, send a copy of the written permission along with your work, the source document (if requested), a SASE, and your cover letter (which clearly indicates you have permission). The more professional the package, the more at ease the editor, which is exactly what you want.

The best way, however, to ease an editor is to send him or her beautiful poetry. As Finch discovered with Labé's poetry, you may find "the unfaithfulness necessary to make the poems work was not adultery but mild flirtation, a flicker of freedom across the beautifully faithful bones."

Editor's Note: *See "Breaking into Print" on ALTA's website at www.utdallas.edu/research/ cts/alta.htm.*

Promote Yourself and Your Work: Five Quick Tips

Whether you're a poet, editor of a magazine, or publisher with a book to sell, you want the public to know about you and what you have to offer. Here are some tips for promoting your work and increasing your audience:

1. Get involved in readings. If you're a poet, contact bookstore and coffeehouse managers to let them know you're available for readings. Find out when and where open mic readings are being held; go, sign up, and read some of your poems. If you're the editor of a magazine, organize a reading of local poets appearing in your latest issue. Be sure to provide plenty of copies for sale at the reading (and perhaps at the bookstore or coffeehouse on a permanent basis). If you're a publisher, talk to the author of your latest poetry book about scheduling a "circuit" of publicity readings within a convenient radius of his/her hometown. Arrange for a book signing to follow the readings.

2. Make connections. Explore networking, and not just locally. Groups and associations in your own area are important (and easy to reach). However, don't overlook such opportunities as state poetry societies, publishing- or poetry-oriented organizations with national affiliations, and writer's newsletters (whether their readership is county-wide or country-wide). Tap into the Internet for an overwhelming array of networking possibilities, from online forums and bulletin boards to poetry websites of every description.

3. Contact the media. Send out press releases, especially to community newspapers—often they're very open to printing newsy tidbits (such as a poet's latest award or print appearance), and they may be on the lookout for feature story possibilities (such as a small local press or literary journal). Also, the calendar sections of newspapers are ideal to promote readings and book signings. Be sure to provide all the necessary details, including your contact information.

Don't overlook TV and radio stations, which may broadcast arts and entertainment calendars at various times during the day. There may also be locally produced TV or radio programs willing to feature a poet, editor, or publisher with area connections. Contact the appropriate producer (be polite, not pushy).

Again, turn to the Internet—many electronic newsletters for writers carry all kinds of announcements about poets and poetry publishers. Check and follow their submission guidelines.

4. Get a business card. Business cards are easy to design on the computer; you can even buy special stock for printing them out yourself, or you can take your design to your local quick-print center (costs are usually quite reasonable for a generous quantity of cards). Be sure to include all pertinent information and try to make the card eye-catching but professional. And don't be shy about passing cards out everywhere to everyone.

5. Create a website. Even a basic website can be extremely valuable, whether you're a poet who wants to post some samples of your work or a press with several chapbooks to promote. A website can be as complicated or as simple as you wish. There are plenty of books and software programs available to help, even if you're a first-timer with few computer skills. There's also a lot of free information on the Web, from tutorials to HTML guides. Enter the words "basic web development" or "beginner web development" (include quotation marks) or similar phrases in your favorite search engine to call up all the resources you'll need.

Are You Being Taken?

There are many publishing opportunities for poets, from traditional magazines and journals to contests, websites, and anthologies. Along with that good news comes this warning: There are also many opportunities for poets to be taken. How do you know whether an opportunity is legitimate? Listed below are some of the most common situations that cost poets disappointment, frustration—and cash. Watch out for them when you're submitting your work, and *don't* let your vanity be your guide.

Anthologies

You know the drill. There's an ad in a perfectly respectable publication announcing a poetry contest with big cash prizes. You enter and receive a glowing letter congratulating you on your exceptional poem, which the contest sponsor wants to include in his deluxe hardbound anthology of the best poetry submitted to the contest. The anthology costs only $45 (or whatever, could be more). You don't have to buy it to have your poem published, of course, but wouldn't you be proud to own one? And wouldn't it be nice to buy additional copies to give to family and friends? And for an extra charge you can include a biographical note. And so on . . .

Of course, when the anthology arrives you may be disappointed. The quality of the poetry isn't what you were expecting, with several poems crammed unattractively onto a page. It turns out everyone who entered the contest was invited to be published, and you basically paid cash to see your poem appear in a phone book-like volume with no literary merit at all.

Are you being taken? Depends on how you look at it. If you bought into the flattery heaped on you and believed you were being published in an exclusive, high quality publication, no doubt you feel duped. On the other hand, if all you were after was seeing your poem in print, even knowing you'd have to pay for the privilege, then you got what you wanted. (Unless you've deceived yourself into believing you've truly won an honor and now have a worthy publishing credit; you don't).

You'll really feel taken if you fall for any other spiels, like having your poem printed on coffee mugs and t-shirts (you can do this much cheaper yourself through quick-print centers) or spending large sums on awards banquets and conferences. Also, find out what rights the contest sponsor acquires before you submit a single line of poetry. You may be relinquishing all rights to your poem simply by mailing it in or submitting it through a website. The poem may no longer belong to you and the publisher can do whatever he wishes with it. Don't let your vanity propel you into a situation you'll always regret.

Reading and contest fees

You notice a promising market for your poetry, but the editor requires a set fee simply to consider your work. You see a contest that interests you, but the sponsors want money from you just to enter. Are you being taken?

In the case of reading fees, keep these points in mind: Is the market so exceptional that you feel it's worth risking the cost of the reading fee to have your work considered? What makes it so much better than markets that do *not* charge fees? Has the market been around awhile, with an established publishing schedule? What are you paid if your work is accepted? Are reasonably priced samples available so you can judge the production values and quality of the writing?

Reading fees don't necessarily signal a suspicious market. In fact, they're becoming increasingly popular as editors struggle with the costs of publishing books and magazines, including the man-hours required to read loads of (often bad) submissions. However, fees represent an additional financial burden on poets, who often don't receive any monetary reward for their poems to begin with. It's really up to individual poets to decide whether paying a fee is beneficial to their publishing efforts. Think long and hard about fee-charging markets that are new and untried, don't pay poets for their work (at the very least a print publication should offer a contributor's copy), charge high prices for sample copies, or set fees that seem unreasonable ($1/poem is an average fee).

Entry fees for contests are less worrisome. Usually these funds are used to establish prizes, pay judges, cover the expenses of running and promoting the contest (including publishing a "prize" issue of a magazine). Other kinds of contests charge entry fees, from Irish dancing competitions to bake-offs at a county fair. Why not poetry contests?

That's not to say you shouldn't be cautious. Watch out for contests that charge fees that are higher than average, especially if the fees are out of proportion to the amount of prize money being given. (Look through the Contests & Awards section beginning on page 427 to get a sense of what most competitions charge; you'll also find contests in listings throughout the Publishers of Poetry section, page 27.) Try to find out how long the contest has been around and whether prizes have been awarded each year. In the case of book and chapbook contests, send for a sample copy to confirm that the publisher puts out a quality product. Beware any contest that tells you you've won something, then demands payment for an anthology, trophy, or other item. (It's okay if a group offers an anthology for a modest price without providing winners with free copies. Most state poetry societies have to do this, but they also present cash awards in each category of the contest and charge low entry fees.)

Subsidy Publishers

Poetry books are a hard sell. Few of the big publishers handle them, and those that do feature the "name" poets, major prize winners and contemporary masters with breathtaking reputations. Even the small presses publish only so many books per year—far less than the number of poets writing.

No wonder poets feel desperate enough to turn to subsidy publishers (also called "vanity publishers"). These operations charge a sum to print a given number of copies of a poetry book. They promise promotion and distribution, and the poet receives a certain percentage of the print run along with a promise of royalties after the printing costs are met.

Are you being taken? Sounds okay, except the whole picture is painted rosier than it really is. Often the sum the publisher charges is inflated and the finished books may be of dubious quality. Bookstores won't stock subsidy-published books (especially poetry), and promotion efforts often consist of sending review copies far and wide, even though such volumes are rarely reviewed. In some particularly tricky situations the poet may not even own rights to his or her own work any more. Regardless, the poet is left with a stack of unsold books, perhaps with an offer from the publisher to sell the balance of the print run to the poet for a certain price. What seemed to be a dream realized turns out to be a dead end.

Before shelling out huge sums of money to a subsidy publisher for more books than you'll ever need, consider self-publishing. Literary history is starred with great poets who published their own works (Walt Whitman is one of the most well known). Talk to some local printers about the kind of book you have in mind, see what's involved, and get some price quotes. If the cost is too high for your budget, consider doing a more modest publication through a quick-print center. Chapbooks (about 24 pages) are an ideal length and can be produced attractively, softbound and saddle-stapled, for a reasonable cost. (You can even lay out and typeset the whole chapbook on your computer.) You'll have something beautiful to share with family and friends, to sign and sell at readings, and you might be able to persuade a supportive local bookstore to put a few copies on its shelves. Best of all, you'll still own and control your work; and if you turn a profit, every cent goes to you. (For another discussion of alternatives to traditional publishing, see Melanie Rigney's article on page 17.)

Obviously, poets who don't stay on their toes may find themselves preyed upon. And a questionable publishing opportunity doesn't have to be an out-and-out rip-off for you to feel cheated. In every situation, you have a choice *not* to participate. Exercise that choice, or at least develop a healthy sense of skepticism before you fling yourself and your poetry at the first smooth talker who compliments your work. Poets get burned because they're much too impatient to see their work in print. Calm your ego, slow down, and devote that time, energy, and money toward reading other poets and improving your own writing. You'll find that getting published will eventually take care of itself.

Important Market Listing Information

• Listings are based on questionnaires completed by editors and on subsequent verified copy. Listings are not advertisements *nor* are markets necessarily endorsed by the editors of this book.

• Information in the listings comes directly from the publishers and is as accurate as possible. However, publications and editors come and go, and poetry needs fluctuate between the publication date of this directory and the date of purchase.

• If you are a poetry publisher and would like to be considered for a listing in the next edition, send a SASE (or SAE and IRC) with your request for a questionnaire to *Poet's Market*—QR, 4700 East Galbraith Road, Cincinnati OH 45236. Questionnaires received after February 15, 2003, will be held for the 2005 edition.

• *Poet's Market* reserves the right to exclude any listing that does not meet its requirements.

Complaint Procedure

If you feel you have not been treated fairly by a market listed in *Poet's Market*, we advise you to take the following steps:

• First, try to contact the market. Sometimes one phone call or letter can quickly clear up the matter. Document all your communications with the market.

• When you contact us with a complaint, provide the details of your submission, the date of your first contact with the market, and the nature of your subsequent communication.

• We will file a record of your complaint and further investigate the market.

• The number and severity of complaints will be considered when deciding whether or not to delete a market from the next edition of *Poet's Market*.

The Markets

Publishers of Poetry

These days, poetry is being published in a variety of venues: in magazines; in literary and academic journals; in books and chapbooks produced by both large and small presses; in anthologies assembled by poetry societies and other groups; on CDs and tapes that feature poets reading their own work; and on the Internet in sites ranging from individual web pages to sophisticated digital publications. There are probably others as well, not to mention new cutting-edge opportunities not yet widely known.

In this edition of *Poet's Market* we've striven to gather as much information about these markets as possible. Each listing in the Publishers of Poetry section gives an overview of the various activities for a single operation as described by the editors/publishers we queried. These include magazines/journals, books/chapbooks, contests, workshops, readings, organizations, and whatever else the editor/publisher thinks will be of interest to you. For those few publishers with projects at different addresses, or who requested their activities to be broken out into the appropriate sections of the book, we've cross-referenced the listings so the overview will be complete.

HOW LISTINGS ARE FORMATTED

To organize all this information within each listing, we follow a basic format:

Symbols. Each listing begins with symbols that reflect various aspects of that operation: (N) a market new to this edition; ( ) a Canadian or ( ) international market; ( ) an award-winning market (including publications with work appearing in *The Best American Poetry*); ($) a cash-paying market (as opposed to one that pays in copies); ( ) this market welcomes submissions from beginning poets; ( ) this market prefers submissions from skilled, experienced poets but will consider work from beginning poets; ( ) this market prefers submissions from poets with a high degree of skill and experience; ( ) this market has a specialized focus (listed in parentheses after title); and ( ) this market is currently closed to *all* submissions. (Keys to these symbols are listed on the inside front and back covers of this book; they also appear in blurbs at the bottom of pages scattered throughout each section.)

Contact Information. Next you'll find all the information you need to contact the market, as provided by each editor/publisher: names (in bold) of all operations associated with the market (with areas of specialization noted in parentheses where appropriate); regular mail address; telephone number; fax number; e-mail address; website address; year the market was established; the name of the person to contact (with that person's title in bold); and membership in small press/publishing organizations (when provided).

Magazine Needs: This is an important section to study as you research potential markets. Here you'll find the editor's or publisher's overview of the operation and stated preferences (often in his or her own words), plus a list of recently published poets; poetry sample; production information about the market (size of publication, printing/binding methods, art/graphics); statistics regarding the number of submissions the market receives vs. the number accepted; and distribution and price information.

How to Submit: Another important section. This one gets down to specifics—how many poems to send; minimum/maximum number of lines; preferences regarding previously published poems and simultaneous submissions, as well as electronic submissions; payment, rights, and response times; and a lot more.

Book/Chapbook Needs and How to Submit: Same as the information for magazines with added information tailored to book/chapbook publishers.

Also Offers: The section to check for contests, conferences/workshops, readings, or organizations sponsored by or affiliated with the market.

Advice: Want to hear what an editor or publisher has to say? In this section you'll find direct quotes about everything from pet peeves to tips on writing to views on the state of poetry today.

WHERE TO START?

If you don't have a publisher in mind, just begin reading through the listings, possibly making notes as you go (don't hesitate to write in the margins, underline, use highlighters; it also helps to flag markets that interest you with Post-it Notes). Browsing the listings is an effective way to familiarize yourself with the information presented and the publishing opportunities available.

If you have a specific market in mind, however, begin with the General Index. This is where *all* listings are alphabetized (i.e., all the markets included within a single listing). For instance, what if you want to check out Pickle Gas Press? If you turn to the "P" listings in the Publishers of Poetry section, you won't find this publisher. The information appears as part of *The Aardvark Adventurer* listing (along with *The Armchair Aesthete*). In the General Index, though, Pickle Gas Press is listed individually along with the page number for *The Aardvark Adventurer* so you can go straight to the source for the information you need. (Sound confusing? Try it, it works.)

The General Index also lists those markets in the 2002 edition that do not appear in this book, along with a two-letter code explaining the absence (see the introduction to the General Index on page 554 for an explanation of these codes). In addition, markets that have changed names since the 2002 edition are listed in the General Index, cross-referenced to the new titles.

REFINE YOUR SEARCH

In addition to the General Index, we provide several more specific indexes to help you refine your marketing plan for your poems. Note that the editors/publishers themselves indicate how and where they want their listings indexed, and not every listing appears in an index. Therefore, use indexes only to supplement your other research efforts:

Chapbook Publishers Index provides a breakdown of markets that publish chapbooks.

Book Publishers Index indicates markets looking for book-length collections of poetry.

Openness to Submissions Index breaks out markets according to the symbols (⬭ ⬰ ⬯ ◎) that appear at the beginning of each listing, signposts indicating the level of writing a market prefers to see. (For an explanation of these symbols, see the previous page or the inside front and back covers of this book.)

Geographical Index sorts markets by state. Some markets are more open to poets from their region, so use this index when you're pinpointing local opportunities.

Subject Index groups markets into categories according to areas of interest. These include all specialized markets (appearing with the ◎ symbol) as well as broader categories such as online markets, poetry for children, markets that consider translations, and others. Save time when looking for a specific type of market by checking this index first.

THE NEXT STEP

Once you know how to interpret the listings in this section to identify markets for your work, the next step is to start submitting your poems. See Getting Started (and Using This Book) on page 3 and Frequently Asked Questions on page 7 for advice, guidelines about preparing your manuscript, and proper submission procedures.

ADDITIONAL INFORMATION

The Publishers of Poetry section includes six Insider Reports: Informative interviews with editors **Larry Smith** (Bottom Dog Press) and **C.J. Houghtaling** (*miller's pond*/H&H Press); discussions of craft with poets **Mark Doty** and **Wanda Coleman**; an overview of the Christian poetry market with comments from poets **Luci Shaw, Jill Peláez Baumgaertner,** and **Jeanne Murray Walker**; and a timely essay from poet **Fred Marchant** about trauma and poetry. These pieces provide special insights and advice from some of the top names in contemporary poetry.

This section also features the covers of eleven literary magazines reflecting the range of print publications being produced today. Such images tell a lot about a publication's style and content, as do the accompanying comments by editors regarding why the cover images were selected. (When evaluating a potential market for your work, consider everything that makes up the product—poets published, style and quality of content, guidelines, editorial comments, cover art, and even ads.)

And remember, the opportunities in the Publishers of Poetry section are only part of the picture. Be sure to look at the sections that follow (Contests & Awards, Conferences & Workshops, Organizations, and Publications of Interest) for additional market leads, competitions, and educational and informational sources of special interest to poets.

Glossary of Listing Terms

A3, A4, A5. Metric equivalents of 11¾ × 16½, 8¼ × 11¾ and 5⅞ × 8¼ respectively.

Anthology. A collection of selected writings by various authors.

Attachment. A computer file electronically "attached" to an e-mail message.

b&w. Black & white (photo or illustration).

Bio. A short biographical statement often requested with a submission.

Camera-ready. Poems ready for copy camera platemaking; camera-ready poems usually appear in print exactly as submitted.

Chapbook. A small book of about 24-50 pages.

Circulation. The number of subscribers to a magazine/journal.

Contributor's copy. Copy of book or magazine containing a poet's work, sometimes given as payment.

Cover letter. Brief introductory letter accompanying a poetry submission.

Cover stock. Heavier paper used as the cover for a publication.

Digest-sized. About 5½ × 8½, the size of a folded sheet of conventional printer paper.

Download. To "copy" a file, such as a registration form, from a website.

Electronic magazine. See Online magazine.

E-mail. Mail sent electronically using computer and modem or similar means.

Euro. Currency unit for the 11 member countries of the European Union; designated by EUR or the € symbol.

FAQ. Frequently Asked Questions.

Font. The style/design of type used in a publication; typeface.

Galleys. First typeset version of a poem, magazine, or book/chapbook.

Honorarium. A token payment for published work.

Internet. A worldwide network of computers offering access to a variety of electronic resources.

IRC. International Reply Coupon; a publisher can exchange IRCs for postage to return a manuscript to another country.

Magazine-sized. About $8\frac{1}{2} \times 11$, the size of an unfolded sheet of conventional printer paper.

ms. Manuscript; **mss**. Manuscripts.

Multi-book review. Several books by the same author or by several authors reviewed in one piece.

Offset-printed. Printing method in which ink is transferred from an image-bearing plate to a "blanket" and then from blanket to paper.

Online magazine. Publication circulated through the Internet or e-mail.

p&h. Postage & handling.

p&p. Postage and packing.

"Pays in copies." See "contributor's copy."

Perfect-bound. Publication with glued, flat spine; also called "flat-spined."

POD. See print-on-demand.

Press run. The total number of copies of a publication printed at one time.

Previously published. Work that has appeared before in print, in any form, for public consumption.

Print-on-demand. Publishing method that allows copies of books to be published as they're requested, rather than all at once in a single press run.

Publishing credits. A poet's magazine publications and book/chapbook titles.

Query letter. Letter written to an editor to raise interest in a proposed project.

Reading fee. A monetary amount charged by an editor or publisher to consider a poetry submission without any obligation to accept the work.

Rights. A poet's legal property interest in his/her literary work; an editor or publisher may acquire certain rights from the poet to reproduce that work.

ROW. "Rest of world."

Royalties. A percentage of the retail price paid to the author for each copy of a book sold.

Saddle-stapled. A publication folded, then stapled along that fold; also called "saddle-stitched."

SAE. Self-addressed envelope.

SASE. Self-addressed, stamped envelope.

Simultaneous submission. Submission of the same manuscript to more than one publisher at the same time.

Subsidy press. Publisher who requires the poet to pay all costs, including typesetting, production, and printing; sometimes called a "vanity publisher."

Tabloid-sized. 11×15 or larger, the size of an ordinary newspaper folded and turned sideways.

Text file. A file containing only textual characters (i.e., no graphics or special formats).

Unsolicited manuscript. A manuscript an editor did not ask specifically to receive.

Website. A specific address on the Internet that provides access to a set of documents (or "pages").

⬤ ◎ **THE AARDVARK ADVENTURER; THE ARMCHAIR AESTHETE; PICKLE GAS PRESS (Specialized: humor)**, 31 Rolling Meadows Way, Penfield NY 14526. (585)388-6968. E-mail: bypaul@netacc.net. Established 1996. **Editor:** Paul Agosto.

Magazine Needs: *The Aardvark Adventurer* is "a quarterly family-fun newsletter-style zine of humor, thought, and verse. Very short stories (less than 500 words) are sometimes included." Prefers "light, humorous verse; any style; any 'family acceptable' subject matter; length limit 32 lines. Nothing obscene, overly forboding, no graphic gore or violence." Has published poetry by Paul Humphrey, Ray Gallucci, Max Gutmann, and Theone DiRocco. As a sample the editor selected his untitled poem:

> When once you err take ample care/to demonstrate good form,/remember, it's best always eating/crow
> when it's still warm.

The Aardvark Adventurer is 6-12 pages, 8½×14, photocopied, corner-stapled, with many playful b&w graphics. Receives about 500 poems/year, accepts about 40%. Press run is 150 for 100 subscribers. Single copy: $2; subscription: $5. Sample: $2. Make checks payable to Paul Agosto. "Subscription not required but subscribers given preference."

Magazine Needs: Also publishes *The Armchair Aesthete*, a quarterly digest-sized zine of "fiction and poetry of thoughtful, well-crafted concise works. Interested in more fiction submissions than poetry though." Line length for poetry is 30 maximum. *The Armchair Aesthete* is 40-60 pages, 5½×8½, quality desktop-published, photocopied, card cover, includes ads for other publications and writers' available chapbooks. Each issue usually contains 10-15 poems and 9-14 stories. Receives about 300 poems/year, accepts about 25-30%. Subscription: $10/year. Sample postpaid: $3. Make checks payable to Paul Agosto.

How to Submit: For both publications, accepts previously published poems and simultaneous submissions, if indicated. Accepts e-mail submissions, include in body of message. Cover letter preferred. Time between acceptance and publication is up to 9 months. Seldom comments on rejected poems. *The Aardvark Adventurer* occasionally publishes theme issues, but *The Armchair Aesthete* does not. Guidelines available by SASE for both publications. Responds in 2 months. Pays 1 contributor's copy. Acquire one-time rights. The staff of *The Aardvark Adventurer* reviews books and chapbooks of poetry in 100 words. The staff of *The Armchair Aesthete* occasionally reviews chapbooks. Send books for review consideration.

Advice: "*The Aardvark Adventurer* is a perfect opportunity for the aspiring poet, a newsletter-style publication with a very playful format."

⬤ **ABBEY; ABBEY CHEAPOCHAPBOOKS**, 5360 Fallriver Row Court, Columbia MD 21044. E-mail: greisman@aol.com. Established 1970. **Editor:** David Greisman.

Magazine Needs & How to Submit: *Abbey*, a quarterly, aims "to be a journal but to do it so informally that one wonders about my intent." Wants "poetry that does for the mind what that first sip of Molson Ale does for the palate. No pornography or politics." Has published poetry and artwork by Richard Peabody, Vera Bergstrom, D.E. Steward, Carol Hamilton, Harry Calhoun, Wayne Hogan, and Cheryl Townsend. *Abbey* is 20-26 pages, magazine-sized, photocopied. Publishes about 150 of 1,000 poems received/year. Press run is 200. Subscription: $2. Sample: 50¢. Guidelines are available for SASE. Responds in 1 month. Pays 1-2 copies.

Book/Chapbook Needs & How to Submit: *Abbey Cheapochapbooks* come out 1-2 times/year averaging 10-15 pages. For chapbook consideration query with 4-6 samples, bio, and list of publications. Responds in 2 months. Pays 25-50 copies.

Advice: The editor says he is "definitely seeing poetry from two schools—the nit'n'grit school and the textured/reflective school. I much prefer the latter."

⬤ ◎ **ABLE MUSE (Specialized: form/style); ERATOSPHERE**, 467 Saratoga Ave., #602, San Jose CA 95129-1326. Phone/fax: (801)729-3509. E-mail: submission@ablemuse.com. Website: www.ablemuse.com. Established 1999. **Editor:** Alex Pepple.

Magazine Needs: *Able Muse: a review of metrical poetry* "spotlights formal poetry via a quarterly online presentation, in the supportive environment of art and photography, essays, interviews, book reviews, fiction, and a literary forum. Also includes electronic books of poetry. *Able Muse* exclusively publishes formal poetry. We are looking for well-crafted poems of any length or subject that employ skillful and imaginative use of meter, or meter and rhyme, executed in contemporary idiom, that reads as naturally as your free-verse poems. Do not send us free-verse, greeting card verse, or poetry campaigning for the revival of archaic language." Has published poetry by Mark Jarman, Andrea Hollander Budy, Rhina P. Espaillat, Len Krisak, John William Watkins, and Patrick Daly. As a sample the editor selected these lines from "Heart Attack" by Beth Houston:

> Even now, her last day blessed with a flood/Of roses, only one closed flower will do,/One last bud
> clinging to color like blood/Flowing from its thorn, her old heart's issue,/Love held so deep, so cold,
> that stillborn bud/In ice, that wound's child clutching one fist, two.

Receives about 800 poems/year, accepts about 10%. Publish 20 poems/issue.

How to Submit: Submit 1-5 poems at a time. No previously published poems or simultaneous submissions. Accepts e-mail and disk submissions. "E-mail is the preferred medium of submission, but we also welcome snail mail, or submit directly from the website with the automated online submission form." Cover letter preferred. Time between acceptance and publication is 4-10 weeks. Often comments on rejected poems. Occasionally publishes theme issues. Guidelines and a list of upcoming themes available by e-mail or on website. Responds in 1 month. Sometimes sends prepublication galleys. Acquires first rights. Reviews books of poetry. Poets may send books for review consideration.

Also Offers: "*Eratosphere* is provided online for the posting and critique of poetry and other literary work. It is a 'virtual' workshop! Literary online chats also provided featuring the scheduled appearance of guest celebrity poets."

Advice: "Despite the rush to publish everything online, most of web-published poetry has been free verse. This is surprising given formal poetry's recent rise in popularity and number of print journals that exclusively publish formal poetry. *Able Muse* attempts to fill this void bringing the best contemporary formalists online. Remember, content is just as important as form."

⊘ ☺ ◉ **ABRAXAS MAGAZINE; GHOST PONY PRESS (Specialized: lyric poetry)**, P.O. Box 260113, Madison WI 53726-0113. (608)238-0175. E-mail: abraxaspress@hotmail.com or ghostponypress@hotmail.com. Website: www.geocities.com/Paris/4614 (include guidelines and submission dates; book prices; and links to the editor). *Abraxas* established in 1968 by James Bertolino and Warren Woessner; Ghost Pony Press in 1980 by editor/publisher Ingrid Swanberg. **Contact:** Ingrid Swanberg (for both presses).

Magazine Needs & How to Submit: *Abraxas* **no longer considers unsolicited material**, except as announced as projects arise. Interested in poetry that is "contemporary lyric, experimental, and poetry in translation." Does not want to see "political posing; academic regurgitations. Please include original with submissions of translation." Has published poetry by William Stafford, Ivan Argüelles, Denise Levertov, César Vallejo, and Andrea Moorhead. As a sample the editor selected these lines from "the silence of lascaux" by próspero saíz:

> in the silence of lascaux a wavering light is fading/outside the cave the bones of slaughter linger still/
> traces of mass killings beneath the cliffs of stone/yet far from the equine ossuary stubby ponies tumble/
> in the vanishing lines of the sacred terror of the horse . . .

Abraxas is up to 80 pages (160 pages, double issues), 6×9, flat-spined (saddle-stapled with smaller issues), litho-offset, original art on matte card cover, with "unusual graphics in text, original art and collages, concrete poetry, exchange ads only, letters from contributors, essays." Appears "irregularly, 9- to 12-month intervals or much longer." Press run is 600 for 500 subscribers of which 150 are libraries. Subscription: $16/4 issues, $20/4 issues Canada, Mexico, and overseas. Sample: $4 ($8 double issues). *Abraxas* will announce submission guidelines as projects arise. Pays 1 copy plus 40% discount on additional copies.

Book/Chapbook Needs & How to Submit: To submit to Ghost Pony Press, inquire with SASE plus 5-10 poems and cover letter. Accepts previously published material for book publication by Ghost Pony Press. Editor sometimes comments briefly on rejected poems. Submissions by post only; no e-mail submissions. Responds to queries in 1-3 months, to mss in 3 months or longer. "We currently have a considerable backlog of mss." Payment varies per project. Send SASE for catalog to buy samples. Has published three books of poetry by próspero saíz including *the bird of nothing & other poems*; 168 pages, 7×10, sewn and wrapped binding, paperback available for $20 (signed and numbered edition is $35), as well as *Zen Concrete + Etc.*, by d.a. levy; 268 pages, 8½×11, perfect-bound, illustrated, paperback for $27.50.

Advice: "Ghost Pony Press is a small press publisher of poetry books; *Abraxas* is a literary journal publishing contemporary poetry, criticism, and translations. Do not confuse these separate presses!"

N $ ⊘ **ABUNDANCE—A HARVEST OF LIFE, LITERATURE AND ART; ABUNDANCE PRESS**, 265 SW Port Saint Lucie Blvd., PMB #175, Port Saint Lucie FL 34984. (561)336-3793. Fax: (561)336-4176. E-mail: editor@abundancepress.com. Website: www.abundancepress.com. Established 1995. Online Editor: Suzanne Robinson. **Contact:** Anthony Watkins, editor.

Magazine Needs: *Abundance* is "a bimonthly literary magazine published and distributed throughout South Florida's Treasure Coast dedicated to promoting the arts in our community which now includes the world. We publish 1 poem by 6-10 poets per issue. Poems should be 20-30 lines unless haiku, do not send religious, rhyming or humorous poetry. Write honestly, use words that you might actually speak on occasion. We want a piece of your life, not a fantasy of a world you know not of." Also accepts poetry written by children. As a sample the editors selected these lines from "The Sound of Grapes" by Stephanie J. Arnal:

> She watches the stain of his words form tattoos on her arm,/and you could see in her stiffness visions
> of iron kettles being thrown as his head.//But instead she continues cleaning grapes./Seething moans
> under her lips./And her hands move more vigorously as she imagines the purple skin she's tearing is
> his./While each little seed she rips from the center magically takes the shape of his heart.

Abundance is about 30 pages, published in tabloid and online formats. Receives about 100 submissions per issue and prints about 8 poems. Press run is 6,000. See website for archives.

How to Submit: Submit 3-4 typed poems at a time. Line length for poetry is 30 maximum. Accepts previously published poems and simultaneous submissions. E-mail submissions preferred, include in body of message. "Make sure your name and address are on each page if you submit by snail-mail, work is passed around to all editors and title page can get separated from poems. If you are submitting work to multiple publications, we reserve the right to publish if you do not withdraw your submission in writing within 30 days of notice of intent to publish." Cover letter preferred ("more about you, less about publishing credits"). Time between acceptance and publication is usually 3 months. Often comments on rejected poems via phone or e-mail. "Sometimes editor will call you with suggestions, so be prepared, Anthony likes to talk to 'his' poets." Guidelines available for e-mail and online. Tries to respond within 1 month. Pays 10 copies and/or cash. $5 per poem; 5¢ per word in fiction, up to $75. Acquires one-time rights plus reprint rights for "Best of" Collections. Reviews books and chapbooks of poetry. Poets may send books for review consideration.

Advice: "We do not print poetry or fiction by the same author more than once per year. We do, however, consider both poetry and fiction by the same author. So if we publish your poetry, you might consider submitting fiction."

$ ACM (ANOTHER CHICAGO MAGAZINE); LEFT FIELD PRESS; CHICAGO LITERARY PRIZE, 3709 N. Kenmore, Chicago IL 60613. Website: www.anotherchicagomag.com (includes guidelines, contest guidelines, subscription info, and current issues info). Established 1977. **Poetry Editor:** Barry Silesky.

- Work published in *ACM* has been frequently included in *The Best American Poetry* and *Pushcart Prize* anthologies.

Magazine Needs: *ACM* is a literary biannual, with emphasis on quality, experimental, politically aware prose, fiction, poetry, reviews, cross-genre work, and essays. No religious verse. Has published prose and poetry by Albert Goldbarth, Michael McClure, Jerome Sala, Nadja Tesich, Wanda Coleman, Charles Simic, and Diane Wakoski. *ACM* is 220 pages, digest-sized, offset-printed, with b&w art and ads. Appreciates traditional to experimental verse with an emphasis on message, especially poems with strong voices articulating social or political concerns. Press run is 2,000 for 500 subscribers of which 100 are libraries.

How to Submit: Submit 3-4 typed poems at a time. Accepts simultaneous submissions; no previously published poems. Reads submissions from February 1 through August 31. Responds in 3 months, has 3- to 6-month backlog. Sends prepublication galleys. Pays "if funds permit," and/or 1 contributor's copy and 1 year subscription. Acquires first serial rights. Reviews books of poetry in 250-800 words. Poets may send books for review consideration.

Also Offers: Sponsors Chicago Literary Prize. Deadline: December.

Advice: "Buy a copy—subscribe and support your own work."

$ ACORN: A JOURNAL OF CONTEMPORARY HAIKU (Specialized: forms, haiku); REDFOX PRESS, P. O. Box 186, Philadelphia PA 19105. E-mail: missias@earthlink.net. Website: http://home.earthlink.net/~missias/Acorn.html (includes contact info, links, samples from journal, guidelines, info on special issues, subscription info). Established 1998. **Editor:** A. C. Missias.

Magazine Needs: *Acorn: a journal of contemporary haiku* appears biannually and is dedicated to publishing "the best of contemporary English language haiku, and in particular to showcasing individual poems that reveal the extraordinary moments found in everyday life." No restrictions on form or absolute subject matter, "but the approach should generally be that of 'traditional' haiku: images taken from reality, juxtaposed in a way that elicits (indirectly) an emotional response, insight, or deeper resonance." Does not want "epigrams, musings, and overt emotion poured into 17 syllables; surreal, sci-fi, or political commentary 'ku'; strong puns or raunchy humor. Syllable counting generally discouraged." Accepts poetry written by children; poetry judged on same standards as adult poetry. Recently published poetry by Yu Chang, Michael McClintock, Matter Merden, and John Stevenson. As a sample the editor selected this haiku by W.F. Owen:
> *Summer evening/the screen porch/fills the darkness.*

Acorn is 60 pages plus flyleaf, 4¼×7, offset-printed/photocopied, saddle-stapled, cardstock cover with set graphic. Receives about 2,000 poems/year, accepts about 12%. Publishes about 115 poems/issue. Press run is 350 for 180 subscribers of which 6 are libraries, 30 shelf sales; 20 are distributed free to potential subscribers. Single copy: $6; subscription: $11.50/year, $27/2 years and supplement volume. Sample: $5. Make checks payable to redfox press.

How to Submit: Submit 5-25 poems at a time. Line length for poetry is 1 minimum, 5 maximum. No previously published poems or simultaneous submissions. Accepts e-mail submissions; no fax or disk submissions. "Snail mail should include SASE; e-mail submissions in e-mail text only (no attachments); several poems/page preferred." Reads submissions year round. Deadlines: February 28(9) and August 31 for spring and fall issues. Time between acceptance and publication is 1-6 months. "Decisions made by editor on a rolling basis. Poems judged purely on their own merits, not dependent on other work taken. Sometimes acceptance conditional on minor edits. Attempt to respond to submissions within 2 weeks." Often comments on rejected poems. Occasionally publishes theme issues, supplemental volumes only (released with every 3rd issue; solicited content only). Theme for 2003 spring issue: linked forms in the haiku/haikai tradition. Upcoming themes available in magazine. Guidelines are available in magazine, for SASE, by e-mail, and on website. Responds in 3 weeks. Pays $2/accepted snail mail submission with SASE, $1/accepted e-mail submission. Acquires first rights and one-time rights. Poets may send books for review consideration to A. C. Missias, c/o redfox press (reviews posted online or for Haiku Society of America, not in journal).

Book/Chapbook Needs & How to Submit: redfox press publishes "occasional book projects, mostly solicited. Focus on haiku, with some interest in poets whose work spans haiku and other poetry."

Also Offers: Periodic supplement issues released with *Acorn* on particular topics chosen by the editor. Descriptions and ordering information available on website.

Advice: "Write focused poems that capture a real moment and make the reader immediately discover what made it jump out—less thinking, more showing!"

THE ACORN; EL DORADO WRITERS' GUILD (Specialized: regional, Western Sierra), P.O. Box 1266, El Dorado CA 95623-1266. (530)621-1833. Fax: (530)621-3939. E-mail: theacorn@visto.com. Established 1993. **Editors:** Kirk Colvin, Harlon Stafford, Frank Seveson, Joy Burris.

Magazine Needs: *the ACORN* is a quarterly journal of the Western Sierra, published by the El Dorado Writers' Guild, a nonprofit literary organization. It includes "fiction and nonfiction, history and reminiscence, story and legend, and poetry." Wants poetry "up to 30 lines long, though we prefer shorter. Focus should be on western slope Sierra Nevada. No erotica, pornography, or religious poetry." Has published poetry by Nancy Cherry, Jeanne Wagner, Joyce Odam, and Edward C. Lynskey. As a sample the poetry consultant selected these lines from "Talking Water" by Blaine Hammond:

> It has been the hawk/after it was a rat/eaten by the hawk. Listen!/It was your lover/after she breathed moist oxygen/once exhaled by the pine,/which gave its limbs a perch/to the hawk, breathed/carbon dioxide expiration.//It has passed through so many cells,/been alive so many times/without dying, by now/it has become aware./You should taste/its memory.

the ACORN is 44 pages, 5½×8½, offset-printed, saddle-stapled, light card cover. Receives about 400 poems/year, accepts about 15%. Press run is 200 for 110 subscribers. Subscription: $12. Sample: $3.

How to Submit: Submit 3-5 poems, neatly typed or printed, at a time. Accepts previously published poems (indicate where published), but no simultaneous submissions. E-mail submissions encouraged; "prefer attachment in MSWord format. However, in body of message is acceptable." Cover letter with short (75-word) bio and publication credits preferred. "Our issues favor topical items suitable for the season." Deadlines are February 1, May 1, August 1. "January is our contest issue." Time between acceptance and publication is 1 month. "Five editors score the poems for content, form, and suitability. Graphics editor selects to fit space available." Often comments on rejected poems. Responds within 1 month after deadline. Pays 2 copies.

Also Offers: Sponsors annual contest. 1st Prize: $100, 2nd Prize: $50, 3rd Prize: $20, 2 $10 honorable mentions. Entry fee: $10/3 poems, 40 lines maximum/poem. Deadline: December 31. All winning entries are published in the contest edition of *the ACORN* in January. Send SASE for complete rules.

Advice: "If your poetry is about nature, be accurate with the species' names, colors, etc. If you describe a landscape, be sure it fits our region. Metered rhyming verse had better be precise. (We have an editor with an internal metronome!) Slant rhyme and free verse are welcome. Avoid trite phrases."

ACUMEN MAGAZINE; EMBER PRESS; THE LONG POEM GROUP NEWSLETTER, 6 The Mount, Higher Furzeham, Brixham, South Devon TQ5 8QY England. Phone: (01803)851098. Press established 1971. *Acumen* established 1984. **Poetry Editor:** Patricia Oxley.

Magazine Needs: *Acumen* appears 3 times/year (in January, May, and September) and is a "small press publisher of a general literary magazine with emphasis on good poetry." Wants "well-crafted, high quality, imaginative poems showing a sense of form. No experimental verse of an obscene type." Has published poetry by Elizabeth Jennings, William Oxley, Gavin Ewart, D.J. Enright, Peter Porter, Kathleen Raine, and R.S. Thomas. As a sample the editor selected these lines from "Learning A Language" by Danielle Hope:

> . . . And I walk to the sea/to look for messages in dunes/and sea-grass/but I find a tangle of red flowers
> I cannot identify./The sea shuffles/illegible scatters of sand.

Acumen is 100 pages, A5, perfect-bound. "We aim to publish 120 poems out of 12,000 received." Press run is 650 for 400 subscribers of which 20 are libraries. Subscription: $45 surface/$50 air. Sample copy: $15.

How to Submit: Submit 5-6 poems at a time. Accepts simultaneous submissions, if not submitted to UK magazines; no previously published poems. Responds in 1 month. Pays "by negotiation" and 1 copy. Staff reviews books of poetry up to 300 words, single format or 600 words, multi-book. Send books for review consideration to Glyn Pursglove, 25 St. Albans Rd., Brynmill, Swansea, West Glamorgan SA2 0BP Wales.

Also Offers: Publishes *The Long Poem Group Newsletter,* established in 1995, which features short articles about long poems and reviews long poems. Free for large SASE (or SAE with IRC).

Advice: "Read *Acumen* carefully to see what kind of poetry we publish. Also read widely in many poetry magazines, and don't forget the poets of the past—they can still teach us a great deal."

◑ADASTRA PRESS, 16 Reservation Rd., Easthampton MA 01027-2536. Established 1980. **Publisher:** Gary Metras.
Book/Chapbook Needs: "Adastra is primarily a chapbook publisher using antique equipment and methods, i.e., hand-set type, letterpress printed, hand-sewn bindings. Any titles longer than chapbook length are by special arrangement and are from poets who have previously published a successful chapbook or two with Adastra. Editions are generally released with a flat-spine paper wrapper, and some titles have been bound in cloth. Editions are limited, ranging from 200-400 copy print runs. Some of the longer titles have gone into reprint and these are photo-offset and perfect-bound. Letterpress chapbooks by themselves are not reprinted as single titles. Once they go out of print, they are gone. Instead, I have released *The Adastra Reader, Collected Chapbooks, 1979-1986* (1987), and am assembling *The Adastra Reader II, Collected Chapbooks, 1987-1992*. These anthologies collect the first twelve chapbooks and the second twelve, respectively, and I am now planning the third series. I am biased against poems that rhyme and/or are religious in theme. Sequences and longish poems are always nice to present in a chapbook format. There are no guidelines other than these. Competition is keen. Less than .5% of submissions are accepted."
Poets published include W.D. Ehrhart (*Beautiful Wreckage, New & Selected Poems*), Linda Lee Harper (*Blue Flute*), Martha Carlson-Bradley (*A Nest Full of Cries*), Ed Ochester (*Cooking in Key West*). As a sample the editor selected these lines from the title poem from *Breaking the Voodoo* by M.L. Lieber:
> *I break the voodoo/On all older women who forgot/To take their calcium when they were young./ Straighten up!/Straighten up!/You're FREE./Well, as free as Republicans/Allow.*
Publishes 2-4 chapbooks/year. Sample hand-crafted chapbook: $6 postpaid.
How to Submit: Send a complete chapbook ms of 12-18 pages, double-spaced preferred, during the month of February. Notification of acceptance/rejection by April. "I choose 1 or 2 mss to publish the following year." Query with a sample of 5 poems from a chapbook ms in the Fall. "If I like what I see, I'll ask you to submit the chapbook ms in February. Always include an SASE." Time between acceptance and publication is up to 2 years. Payment is 10% of the print run in copies with a discount on additional copies.

◑ADEPT PRESS; SMALL BRUSHES, P.O. Box 391, Long Valley NJ 07853-0391. Established 1999. **Editor:** Jan Epps Turner.
Magazine Needs: Published quarterly, *Small Brushes* wants "to be another showcase for good poetry from many voices. We prefer poems of 36 lines or fewer, and we are unlikely to use any poem over 42 lines. We want poetry of all forms springing from important human emotions, ethics, and realizations. We value unity, coherence, emphasis, and accessibility. We will not use material containing vulgarity, explicit sexual references, or words or descriptions that might reasonably offend anyone. We avoid issues of a narrow religious, social, or political nature." Has published poetry by Paul D. McGlynn, Gerald Zipper, Paul Truttman, Giovanni Malito, Robert Cooperman, and Kelley Jean White. As a sample the editor selected these lines from "Perception Pond" by Claudia Showers Drezga:
> *But who struck this fire/of imploding sun,/whose mindful death/winks creative tongue/into my patterned, watery span,/reflecting a wider purpose plan.*
Small Brushes is 32 pages, digest-sized, desktop-published, photocopied and saddle-stapled, with parchment cover, color graphics. Receives about 740 poems/year, accepts about 20%. Publishes 37-39 poems/issue. Press run is 100 for contributors, subscriptions, and shelf sales. Single copy: $3; subscription: $10/year (4 issues). Sample: $2. Make checks payable to Adept Press.
How to Submit: Submit 3-4 poems at a time. No previously published poems or simultaneous submissions. Cover letter requested. "Please include a brief bio in your cover letter, place your name and address at the top of each manuscript page and type or print clearly. Please send SASE for our comments or contact." Reads submissions all year. Submit seasonal poems 2 months in advance. Time between acceptance and publication is up to 18 months. Seldom comments on rejected poems. Guidelines available for SASE. Responds in up to 3 months. Sometimes sends prepublication galleys. Pays 1 copy/published poem. Rights remain with authors and artists.
Advice: "Read poetry, including the masters. Ignore the trends. Write from your own experiences and deep feelings."

▧ ◑ ◎ THE ADIRONDACK REVIEW (Specialized: French, German poetry, both original and translations), 1206 Superior St., Suite F-24, Watertown NY 13601-1142. E-mail: AdkReview@aol.com. Website: www.adirondackreview.homestead.com. Established 2000. **Editor:** Colleen Ryor.
Magazine Needs: *The Adirondack Review* is a quarterly online literary journal dedicated to quality free verse poetry and short fiction as well as art, photography, and interviews. "We are open to both new and established writers. Our only requirement is excellence. We would like to publish more French and German poetry translations as well as original poems in these languages. We publish an eclectic mix of voices and styles, but all poems should show attention to craft. We are open to beginners who demonstrate talent, as

well as established voices. The work should speak for itself." Wants well-crafted, thoughtful writing full of imagery. Does not want religious, overly sentimental, horror/gothic, rhyming, greeting card, pet-related, humor, or science fiction poetry. Recently published poetry by Walt McDonald, Natasha Sajé, D.C. Berry, Allan Peterson, Robert Klein Engler, and Frank Matagrano. As a sample the editor selected these lines from "Nuclear Sites May Always Be Unsafe" by Ace Boggess:

> . . . when conscience sings. If we could,/we would forgive you, but your hands/have distracted us with monuments that/last almost forever, to such a time when we/and you are not memories, not even/ideas the many despise, not anymore.

The Adirondack Review is published online. Accepts about 3-5% of poems submitted. Publishes about 30 poems/issue.

How to Submit: Submit 2-7 poems at a time. Accepts previously published poems and simultaneous submissions. Accepts e-mail submissions; no fax or disk submissions. "All submissions should be pasted into the body of an e-mail (no attached files, please)." Cover letter is preferred. Reads submissions year round. Submit seasonal poems 3 months in advance. Time between acceptance and publication is 1-3 months. Seldom comments on rejected poems. Guidelines available on website. Responds in 1 month. Acquires first or one-time rights. Reviews books of poetry. Poets may send books/chapbooks for review consideration "but query by e-mail first."

Advice: "Get your hands on all the good writing you can, including international, past, contemporary, web-based, and print. Read much, write well, and send us what you love."

○ ADVOCATE, PKA's PUBLICATION, 301A Rolling Hills Park, Prattsville NY 12468. (518)299-3103. Established 1987.

Magazine Needs: *Advocate* is a bimonthly advertiser-supported tabloid, 12,000 copies distributed free, using "original, previously unpublished works, such as feature stories, essays, 'think' pieces, letters to the editor, profiles, humor, fiction, poetry, puzzles, cartoons, or line drawings." Wants "nearly any kind of poetry, any length, but not religious or pornographic. Poetry ought to speak to people and not be so oblique as to have meaning only to the poet. If I had to be there to understand the poem, don't send it. Now looking for horse-related poems, stories, drawings, and photos." Accepts about 25% of poems received. Sample: $4.

How to Submit: No previously published poems or simultaneous submissions. Time between acceptance and publication is an average of 6 months. "Occasionally" comments on rejected poems. Responds in 2 months. Pays 2 copies. Acquires first rights only.

Advice: "All submissions and correspondence must be accompanied by a self-addressed, stamped envelope with sufficient postage."

◑ ⊚ AETHLON: THE JOURNAL OF SPORT LITERATURE (Specialized: sports/recreation), Dept. PM, English Dept., East Tennessee State University, Box 70270, Johnson City TN 37614-0270. Established 1983. **General Editor:** Don Johnson, Dean, Arts & Sciences, ETSU. **Poetry Editor:** Robert W. Hamblin, Professor of English, Southeast Missouri State University, Cape Girardeau MO 63701.

Magazine Needs: *Aethlon* publishes a variety of sport-related literature, including scholarly articles, fiction, poetry, and reviews; two issues annually in fall and spring. Subject matter must be sports-related; no restrictions regarding form, length, style, or purpose. Does not want "doggerel, cliché-ridden, or oversentimental" poems. Poets published include Joseph Bathanti, David Allen Evans, John Grey, John B. Lee, Barbara Smith, and Matthew J. Spireng. *Aethlon* is 200 pages, digest-sized, offset-printed, flat-spined, with illustrations and some ads. Publishes 12-15 poems/issue. Circulation is 1,000 for 750 subscribers of which 250 are libraries. Subscription included with membership ($40) in the Sport Literature Association. Sample: $15.

How to Submit: "Only typed mss with SASE considered." No simultaneous submissions. Responds in up to 2 months. Backlog is up to 1 year. Pays 5 offprints and a copy of the issue in which poem appears.

◑ ⊚ AFRICAN VOICES (Specialized: ethnic, people of color), 270 W. 96th St., New York NY 10025. (212)865-2982. Fax: (212)316-3335. E-mail: annebutts@aol.com. Website: www.africanvoices. com (includes history of magazine, submission guidelines, subscription information, spotlighted artists, a calendar of events, flash animation, etc.). Established 1992. **Poetry Editor:** Layding Kalida.

Magazine Needs: *African Voices* is a quarterly "art and literary magazine that highlights the work of people of color. We publish ethnic literature and poetry on any subject. We also consider all themes and styles: avant-garde, free verse, haiku, light verse, and traditional. We do not wish to limit the reader or author." Accepts poetry written by children. Has published poetry by Reg E. Gaines, Maya Angelou, Jessica Care Moore, Asha Bandele, Tony Medina, and Louis Reyes Rivera. *African Voices* is about 48 pages, 8½×11, professionally printed, saddle-stapled, paper cover, with b&w photos and illustrations. Receives about 100 submissions/year, accepts about 30%. Press run is 20,000 for 5,000 subscribers of which 30 are libraries, 40% shelf sales. Single copy: $3; subscription: $12. Sample: $5.

How to Submit: Submit no more than 5 poems at any one time. Accepts previously published poems and simultaneous submissions. Accepts e-mail submissions in body of message. Cover letter and SASE required. Seldom comments on rejected poems. Guidelines and upcoming themes available for SASE or on website. Responds in 3 months. Pays 5 copies. Acquires first or one-time rights. Reviews books of poetry in 500-1,000 words. Poets may send books for review consideration, attn. Layding Kaliba.

Also Offers: Sponsors periodic poetry contests and readings. Send SASE for details.

Advice: "We strongly encourage new writers/poets to send in their work and not give up if their work is not accepted the first time. Accepted contributors are encouraged to subscribe."

THE AGUILAR EXPRESSION (Specialized: social issues), 1329 Gilmore Ave., Donora PA 15033. (724)379-8019. Established 1986. **Editor/Publisher:** Xavier F. Aguilar.

Magazine Needs: *Aguilar Expression* appears annually in October. "In publishing poetry, I try to exhibit the unique reality that we too often take for granted and acquaint as mediocre. We encourage poetics that deal with *now*, which our readers can relate to. We are particularly interested in poetry dealing with social issues: corrupt politics, racism, police misconduct, discrimination, etc." Has published poetry by Martin Kich and Gail Ghai. As a sample the editor selected these lines from "The Water Truck" by Donna Taylor Burgess:

> *But pockets are as empty/As the taps/In a government day/And water has never been free.*

Aguilar Expression is 4-20 pages, photocopied on 8½×11 sheets, corner-stapled. Receives about 20-30 poems/ month, accepts about 5-10. Circulation is 300. Sample: $6. Make checks payable to *Aguilar Expression*.

How to Submit: "We insist that all writers send a SASE for writer's guidelines before submitting." Submit up to 3 poems at a time in a clear, camera-ready copy, 30-line limit, any topic/style. Cover letter, including writing background, and SASE for contact purposes, required with submissions. Reads mss. in January, February, March. Manuscripts received in any other months will be discarded unopened. "Send copies; mss will not be returned." Responds in 2 months. Pays 2 copies.

AHSAHTA PRESS; SAWTOOTH POETRY PRIZE, MFA Program in Creative Writing, Boise State University, Boise ID 83725. (208)426-2195. Fax: (208)426-4373. E-mail: ahsahta@boisestate. edu. Website: http://ahsahtapress.boisestate.edu (includes guidelines, contact information, bios, contest information, and catalog). Director: Janet Holmes. **Contact:** Editor.

Book/Chapbook Needs: Ahsahta Press has been publishing contemporary poetry of the American West since 1976. "It has since expanded its scope to publish poets nationwide, seeking out and publishing the best new poetry from a wide range of aesthetics—poetry that is technically accomplished, distinctive in style, and thematically fresh." Has published *Corpus Socius*, by Lance Phillips; *Esse*, by David Mutschlecner; *Fictional Teeth*, by Linda Dyer; *The Widow's Coat*, by Miriam Sagan as well as work by Craig Cotler, Sandra Alcosser, and Cynthia Hogue. As a sample here are lines from Wyn Cooper's "Fun," in the collection *The Country of Here Below* (set to music, it is Sheryl Crow's Grammy-winning "All I Wanna Do"):

> *"All I want is to have a little fun/Before I die," says the man next to me/Out of nowhere, apropos of nothing. He says/His name is William but I'm sure he's Bill/Or Billy, Mac or Buddy: he's plain ugly to me,/And I wonder if he's ever had fun in his life.*

How to Submit: Submit only during their January 1 through March 31 reading period. Send complete ms and SASE for reply. Accepts multiple and simultaneous submissions. Responds in up to 3 months. Forthcoming, new, and backlist titles available from website. Most backlist titles: $9.95; current titles: $12.95.

Also Offers: Sawtooth Poetry Prize publishes a book-length collection of poetry judged by a nationally recognized poet (2001 judge was Brenda Hillman). Publishes a letterpress broadside series drawn from Ahsahta Press authors. Beginning in 2002, will publish 1 letterpress chapbook/year. Query first.

Advice: "Ahsahta seeks distinctive, non-imitative, unpredictible, and innovatively crafted work. Please check out our website for examples of what we publish."

AIM MAGAZINE (Specialized: social issues, ethnic, political), P.O. Box 1174, Maywood IL 60153. (773)874-6184. Fax: (206)543-2746. E-mail: mapilado@aol.com. Website: www.aimmaga zine.org (includes advertising, subscription information). Established 1974. **Poetry Editor:** Ruth Apilado.

Magazine Needs: *Aim* appears quarterly, "dedicated to racial harmony and peace." Uses 3-4 poems ("poetry with social significance mainly"—average 32 lines) in each issue. Accepts poetry written by high school students. Has published poetry by J. Douglas Studer, Wayne Dowdy, Ned Pendergast, and Maria

DeGuzman. *Aim* is magazine-sized with glossy cover. Receives about 30 submissions/year, accepts about half. Circulation is 10,000 for 3,000 subscribers of which 15 are libraries. Single copy: $3; subscription: $12. Sample: $4.

How to Submit: Accepts simultaneous submissions. A list of upcoming themes is available for SASE. Responds in 6 weeks. Pays $3/poem and 1 copy. Does not send an acceptance notice: "We simply send payment and magazine copy."

Advice: "Read the work of published poets."

ALASKA QUARTERLY REVIEW, University of Alaska Anchorage, 3211 Providence Dr., Anchorage AK 99508. Phone/fax: (907)786-6916. E-mail: ayaqr@uaa.alaska.edu. Website: www.uaa.alask a.edu/aqr. Established 1981. **Executive Editor:** Ronald Spatz.

• Poetry published in *Alaska Quarterly Review* has been selected for inclusion in *The Best American Poetry*, *Pushcart Prize,* and *Beacon's Best* anthologies.

Magazine Needs: *Alaska Quarterly Review* "is a journal devoted to contemporary literary art. We publish both traditional and experimental fiction, poetry, literary nonfiction, and short plays." Has published poetry by Kim Addonizio, Tom Lux, Pattiann Rogers, John Balaban, Albert Goldbarth, Jane Hirshfeld, Billy Collins, and Dorianne Laux. Wants all styles and forms of poetry with the most emphasis perhaps on voice and content that displays "risk," or intriguing ideas or situations. Publishes two double-issues/year, each using between 25-50 pages of poetry. *Alaska Quarterly Review* is 262 pages, 6×9, professionally printed, perfect-bound, card cover with b&w photo. Receives up to 3,000 submissions/year, accepts about 40-60. Circulation is 2,200 for 500 subscribers of which 32 are libraries. Subscription: $10. Sample: $6.

How to Submit: Does not accept fax or e-mail submissions. Manuscripts are *not* read from May 15 through August 15. Responds in up to 4 months, sometimes longer during peak periods in late winter. Pay depends on funding. Acquires first North American serial rights. Guest poetry editors have included Stuart Dybek, Jane Hirshfield, Stuart Dischell, Maxine Kumin, Pattiann Rogers, Dorianne Laux, and Billy Collins.

ALBATROSS; THE ANABIOSIS PRESS (Specialized: nature), 2 South New St., Bradford MA 01835. (978)469-7085. E-mail: rsmyth@mva.net. Website: http://members.mva.net/rsmyth/anabiosis (includes guidelines, contact info, contest info, and current and back issues in PDF format). **Editor:** Richard Smyth.

Magazine Needs: *Albatross* appears "as soon as we have accepted enough quality poems to publish an issue. We consider the albatross to be a metaphor for an environment that must survive. This is not to say that we publish only environmental or nature poetry, but that we are biased toward such subject matters. We publish mostly free verse, 200 lines/poem maximum, and we prefer a narrative style, but again, this is not necessary. We do not want trite rhyming poetry which doesn't convey a deeply felt experience in a mature expression with words." Also publishes interviews with established writers. Has published poetry by William Doreski, James Grinwis, Teresa Starr, E.G. Burrows, and Susan Johnson. As a sample the editors selected these lines by Richard Alan Bunch:

> Beneath theologies/blue shadows interlace the journey—/behold: this lingering fruit/the lovers almost.

Albatross is 28 pages, 5½×8½, laser-typeset, linen cover, with some b&w drawings. Subscription: $5/2 issues. Sample: $3.

How to Submit: Submit 3-5 poems at a time. "Poems should be typed single-spaced, with name, address, and phone number in upper left corner." No simultaneous submissions. Accepts e-mail submissions if included in body of message. Name and address must accompany e-mail submissions. Cover letter not required; "We do, however, need bio notes and SASE for return or response." Guidelines available for SASE and on website. Responds in up to 1 month, has 3-month backlog. Pays 1 copy. Acquires all rights. Returns rights provided that "previous publication in *Albatross* is mentioned in all subsequent reprintings."

Also Offers: Holds a chapbook contest. Submit 20 pages of poetry, any theme, any style. Deadline is June 30 of each year. Include name, address, and phone number on the title page. Charges $7 reading fee (check payable to Anabiosis Press). Winner receives $100 and at least 50 copies of his/her published chapbook. All entering receive a free copy of the winning chapbook. Also publishes the Anabiosis Press Pocket Book series. These are 5×3½, laser typeset with linen cover. Initial print run of 100. Send 350 lines of poetry, preferably from a single long poem. Guidelines on website or for SASE.

Advice: "We expect a poet to read as much contemporary poetry as possible. We seek deeply felt experiences expressed maturely in a unique style of writing. We want to be moved. When you read our poetry, we hope that it moves you in the same way that it moves us. We try to publish the kind of poetry that you would want to read again and again."

$ ⊘ ◎ **ALIVE NOW (Specialized: spirituality, themes); POCKETS (Specialized: religious, children, themes); DEVO'ZINE (Specialized: religious, youth, themes); WEAVINGS; THE UPPER ROOM**, 1908 Grand Ave., P.O. Box 340004, Nashville TN 37203-0004. E-mail: alivenow@upper room.org. Website: www.alivenow.org or www.upperroom.org (include guidelines, subscription information, daily devotionals, news, bookstore, etc.). This publishing company brings out about 30 books/year and 5 magazines: *The Upper Room, Alive Now, Pockets, Devo'Zine*, and *Weavings*. Of these, three use unsolicited poetry.

Magazine Needs & How to Submit: *Pockets, Devotional Magazine for Children*, which comes out 11 times/year, circulation 90,000, is for children 6-12. "Offers stories, activities, prayers, poems—all geared to giving children a better understanding of themselves as children of God. Some of the material is not overtly religious but deals with situations, special seasons and holidays, and ecological concerns from a Christian perspective." Uses 3-4 pages of poetry/issue. Sample free with 7½×10½ SAE and 4 first-class stamps. Accepts e-mail submissions; include text in body of message. Ordinarily 24-line limit on poetry. Upcoming themes and guidelines available for SASE and on website. Pays $25-50.

Magazine Needs & How to Submit: *Alive Now* is a bimonthly, circulation 70,000, for a general Christian audience interested in reflection and meditation. Buys 20 poems/year, avant-garde and free verse. Submit 5 poems, 10-45 lines. Guidelines and upcoming themes available for SASE and on website. Pays $25 and up.

Magazine Needs & How to Submit: *Devo'Zine: Just for Teens* is a bimonthly devotional magazine for youth ages 13-18. Offers meditations, scripture, prayers, poems, stories, songs, and feature articles to "aid youth in their prayer life, introduce them to spiritual disciplines, help them shape their concept of God, and encourage them in the life of discipleship." Ordinarily 20-line limit on poetry. Guidelines and upcoming themes available for SASE and on website. Pays $25.

Also Offers: *The Upper Room* magazine does not accept poetry.

N ⊘ **AMARYLLIS**, P.O. Box 6330, Montgomery AL 36106-0330. Fax: (334)244-3740. E-mail: anders on@strudel.aum.edu. Established 1985. **Editors:** Nancy Anderson, Lynn Jinks, Donald Nobles.

Magazine Needs: *Amaryllis* appears annually in December, "more often depending on submissions." A national magazine publishing high quality poetry, fiction, essays, and reviews, *Amaryllis* is open to all forms and styles, including experimental forms, with no restriction on subject. Does not want trite verse or inspirational work. *Amaryllis* is 75-150 pages, digest-sized, professionally offset-printed, perfect-bound, heavy matte cardstock cover with line illustration. Accepts about 5% of poems submitted. Press run is 500. Single copy: $5. Sample: $3. Make checks payable to *Amaryllis*.

How to Submit: Submit 7 poems at a time. Any length poetry will be considered. No previously published poems or simultaneous submissions. No fax, e-mail, or disk submissions. Cover letter is required. "Please submit in triplicate and include SASE for response." Reads submissions year round. Time between acceptance and publication varies. Poems are circulated to an editorial board. "All submissions are discussed by three editors; works are reviewed in a roundtable discussion." Seldom comments on rejected poems. Guidelines available in magazine, for SASE, or by fax or e-mail. Responds in 2 months. Sometimes sends prepublication galleys. Pays 5 contributor's copies. Acquires one-time rights. Reviews books of poetry in 1,000 words, single and multi-book format.

N ⊕ ⊘ **AMBIT**, 17 Priory Gardens, Highgate, London N6 5QY England. Phone: 0181-340-3566. Website: www.ambit.co.uk. **Editor:** Martin Bax. **Poetry Editors:** Martin Bax, Carol Ann Duffy and Henry Graham. Prose Editors: J.G. Ballard and Geoff Nicholson. Art Editor: Mike Foreman.

Magazine Needs: *Ambit* is a 96-page quarterly of avant-garde, contemporary and experimental work. Subscription: £24 individuals, £35 institutions (UK); £26 ($52) individuals, £37 ($74) institutions (overseas). Sample: £6.

How to Submit: Submit up to 6 poems at a time, typed double-spaced. No previously published poems or simultaneous submissions. Pay is "variable plus 2 free copies. SAE vital for reply." Staff reviews books of poetry. Send books for review consideration, attn. review editor.

Also Offers: Website includes names of editors and poetry and prose selected from the magazine's latest number.
Advice: "Read a copy of the magazine before submitting!"

◐ AMERICA; FOLEY POETRY CONTEST, 106 W. 56th St., New York NY 10019. (212)581-4640. Fax: (212)399-3596. Website: www.americapress.org. Established 1909. **Poetry Editor:** Paul Mariani
Magazine Needs: *America* is a weekly journal of opinion published by the Jesuits of North America. Primarily publishes articles on religious, social, political, and cultural themes. *America* is 36 pages, magazine-sized, professionally printed on thin stock, thin paper cover. Circulation is 39,000. Subscription: $42. Sample: $2.25.
How to Submit: "Because of a large backlog, we are only accepting poems submitted for the Foley Poetry Contest." The annual Foley Poetry Contest offers a prize of $1,000, usually in June. Send SASE for rules. "Poems for the Foley Contest should be submitted between January and April. Poems submitted for the Foley Contest between July and December will be returned unread."
Advice: "*America* is committed to publishing quality poetry as it has done for the past 89 years. We encourage more established poets to submit their poems to us."

◨ ◎ THE AMERICAN DISSIDENT(Specialized: political, social issues), 1837 Main St., Concord MA 01742. E-mail: enmarge@aol.com. Website: www.geocities.com/enmarge (includes guidelines, sample poems and essays, names of editors, and contact information). Established 1998. **Editor:** G. Tod Slone.
Magazine Needs: *The American Dissident* appears 2-3 times/year to "provide an outlet for critics of America." Wants "well-written dissident work (poetry and short 250-950 word essays) in English, French, or Spanish. Submissions should be iconoclastic and anti-obfuscatory in nature and should criticize some aspect of the American scene." As a sample the editor selected these lines from "Shadow Group Think" by Mary Gribble:

> *The September eleventh of murderous theocrats/torments us, yet does not retard/our holy duty to ask/ why preexisting secret agendas/due to horror, now find to ask/why preexisting secret agendas/due to horror, now find a safe cave./The Star Wars fantasy tiptoes through . . .*

The American Dissident is 56 pages, digest-sized, offset-printed, perfect-bound, card cover, with political cartoons. Press run is 200. Single copy: $7. Subscription: $14.
How to Submit: Submit 3 poems at a time. Accepts simultaneous submissions; no previously published poems. No e-mail submissions. "Include SASE and cover letter containing short bio (Manifest humility! Don't list credits and prizes), including de-programing and personal dissident information and specific events that may have pushed you to shed the various national skins of indoctrination and stand apart from your friends and/or colleagues to howl against corruption." Time between acceptance and publication up to 6 months. Almost always comments on rejected poems. Guidelines available for SASE. Responds in 1 month. Pays 1 copy. Acquires first North American serial rights. Reviews books and chapbooks of poetry and other magazines in 250 words, single book format. Poets may send books for review consideration.
Advice: "Do not submit work apt to be accepted by the multitudinous valentine and academic journals and presses that clog up the piping of the nation's bowels. *The American Dissident* is concerned about the overly successful indoctrination of the citizenry and resultant pervasive happy-face fascism. It is concerned that too many citizens have become clonified team players, networkers, and blind institutional patriots for whom loyalty *(semper fi)* has overwhelming priority over the truth. *The American Dissident* is interested in unique insights and ways of looking at the national infrastructure of hypocrisy, fraud, and corruption, the glue that seems to be holding America together."

Ⓝ ◎ AMERICAN INDIAN STUDIES CENTER; AMERICAN INDIAN CULTURE AND RESEARCH JOURNAL (Specialized: ethnic/nationality, Native American), 3220 Campbell Hall, Box 951548, UCLA, Los Angeles CA 90095-1548. (310)825-7315. Fax: (310)206-7060. E-mail: aiscpubs @ucla.edu. Website: www.sscnet.UCLA.edu/esp/aisc/index.html. Established 1975.
Magazine Needs: The *American Indian Culture and Research Journal* is a quarterly which publishes new research and literature about American Indians. All work must have Native American content. The journal is 300 pages, 6×9, perfect-bound. Receives about 50-70 poems/year, accepts approximately 30. Press run is 1,200 for 1,000 subscribers of which 400 are libraries, 10 shelf sales. Subscription: $25 individual, $60 institution. Sample: $12. Make checks payable to Regents of the University of California.
How to Submit: Submit 5-6 poems at a time. No previously published poems or simultaneous submissions. No fax or e-mail submissions. Cover letter preferred. Time between acceptance and publication is 6 months. Poems are circulated to an editorial board. Often comments on rejected poems. Publishes theme issues. Responds in 2 months. Always sends prepublication galleys. Pays 1 copy.

Book/Chapbook Needs & How to Submit: The American Indian Studies Center also publishes 1-2 paperback books of poetry in their Native American Literature Series. Has published *The Light on the Tent Wall: A Bridging* by Mary TallMountain and *Old Shirts & New Skins* by Sherman Alexie. Pays author's copies and offers 40% discount on additional copies. Send SASE for a complete list of the center's publications.

AMERICAN LITERARY REVIEW, University of North Texas, P.O. Box 311307, Denton TX 76203-1307. (940)565-2755. E-mail: americanliteraryreview@yahoo.com. Website: www.engl.unt.edu/alr (includes guidelines, contact information, archives, contest information, subscription information, and editorial policy). **Editors:** Corey Marks and Barbara Rodman. **Poetry Editors:** Bruce Bond and Corey Marks.
Magazine Needs: *American Literary Review* is a biannual publishing all forms and modes of poetry and fiction. "We are especially interested in originality, substance, imaginative power, and lyric intensity." Has published poetry by Matthew Rohrer, Dara Wier, Pattiann Rogers, Donald Revell, Laura Kasischke, and David Biespiell. *American Literary Review* is about 120 pages, 6×9, attractively printed, perfect-bound, color card cover with photo. Subscription: $10/year, $18/2 years. Sample: $6 (US), $7 (elsewhere).
How to Submit: Submit up to 5 typewritten poems at a time. No fax or e-mail submissions. Cover letter with author's name, address, phone number, and poem titles required. Guidelines available for SASE and on website. Responds in 2 months. Pays 2 contributor's copies.
Also Offers: Sponsors poetry and fiction contest in alternating years. Next poetry contest will be in 2002. Send SASE for details.

AMERICAN RESEARCH PRESS (Specialized: paradoxism); "FLORENTIN SMARAN-DACHE" AWARD FOR PARADOXIST POETRY, P.O. Box 141, Rehoboth NM 87322. E-mail: M_L_Perez@yahoo.com. Website: www.gallup.unm.edu/~smarandache/lit.htm (includes features of paradoxism). Established 1990. **Publisher:** Minh Perez.
Book/Chapbook Needs: American Research Press publishes 2-3 poetry paperbacks per year. Wants experimental poetry dealing with paradoxism. No classical poetry. See website for poetry samples. Has published poetry by Al. Florin Tene, Anatol Ciocanu, Nina Josu, and Al Bantos.
How to Submit: Submit 3-4 poems at a time. No previously published poems or simultaneous submissions. Cover letter preferred. Submit seasonal poems 1 month in advance. Time between acceptance and publication is 1 year. Seldom comments on rejected poems. Responds to queries in 1 month. Pays 100 author's copies. Order sample books by sending SASE.
Also Offers: Sponsors the "Florentin Smarandache" Award for Paradoxist Poetry.

N **$** **THE AMERICAN SCHOLAR**, 1785 Massachusetts Ave., NW, 4th Floor, Washington DC 20036. (202)265-3808. Established 1932. Website: www.pbk.org/americanscholar.htm. **Poetry Editor:** Robert Farnsworth. **Associate Editor:** Sandra Costich.
 • Poetry published here has also been included in the 2002 *Pushcart Prize* anthology.
Magazine Needs: *American Scholar* is an academic quarterly which uses about 5 poems/issue. "The usual length of our poems is 34 lines." The magazine has published poetry by John Updike, Philip Levine, and Rita Dove. What little poetry is used in this high-prestige magazine is accomplished, intelligent, and open (in terms of style and form). Study before submitting. Sample: $6.95; subscription: $25/year, $48/2 years, $69/3 years.
How to Submit: Submit up to 4 poems at a time; "no more for a careful reading. Poems should be typed, on one side of the paper, and each sheet should bear the name and address of the author and the name of the poem." Guidelines available for SASE. Responds in 4 months. Always sends prepublication galleys. Pays $50/poem and 3 contributor's copies. Acquires first rights only.

AMERICAN TANKA (Specialized: form/style, tanka), P.O. Box 120-024, Staten Island NY 10312. E-mail: editor@americantanka.com. Website: www.americantanka.com (includes news, guidelines, sample poems from issues, editorial policy, subscription information, information about the tanka form, a tanka bibliography, and a submission form). Established 1996. **Contact:** Editor.
Magazine Needs: *American Tanka* appears twice/year (May and November) and is devoted to single English-language tanka. Wants "concise and vivid language, good crafting, and echo of the original Japanese form." Does not want anything that is not tanka. Has published poetry by Sanford Goldstein, ai li, Jane Reichhold, and George Swede. As a sample the editor selected this tanka by Marianne Bluger:

> *Headed back/from good-byes at the airport/I keep checking/in rear-view the sky/where your contrail lingers.*

American Tanka is 95-120 pages, 8½×5½, perfect-bound, glossy cover, with b&w original drawings. Single copy: $10; subscription: $20.

How to Submit: Submit up to 5 poems at a time; "submit only once per reading period." No previously published poems or simultaneous submissions. Accepts submissions in e-mail text box and through online submission form. Reads manuscripts from November 1 to February 15; May 1 to August 15. Guidelines available for SASE or on website. Responds in up to 2 months. Pays 1 copy. Acquires first North American serial rights.

Advice: "Become familiar with the tanka form by reading both translations and English-language tanka. In your own tanka, be natural and concrete and vivid. Avoid clichés, overcrowded imagery, or attempting to imitate Japanese poems."

AMERICAN TOLKIEN SOCIETY; MINAS TIRITH EVENING-STAR; W.W. PUBLICATIONS (Specialized: science fiction/fantasy, Tolkien), P.O. Box 7871, Flint MI 48507-0871. Phone/fax: (727)585-0985. Established 1967. **Editor:** Philip W. Helms.

Magazine Needs & How to Submit: Journals and chapbooks use poetry of fantasy about Middle-Earth and Tolkien. Accepts poetry written by children. Has published poetry by Thomas M. Egan, Anne Etkin, Nancy Pope, and Martha Benedict. *Minas Tirith Evening-Star* is digest-sized, offset from typescript, with cartoon-like b&w graphics. Press run is 400 for 350 subscribers of which 10% are libraries. Single copy: $3.50; subscription: $10. Sample: $1.50. Make checks payable to American Tolkien Society. No simultaneous submissions; previously published poems "maybe." Cover letter preferred. "We do not return phone calls unless collect." Editor sometimes comments on rejected poems. Occasionally publishes theme issues. Guidelines available for SASE. Responds in 2 weeks. Sometimes sends prepublication galleys. Pays contributor's copies. Reviews related books of poetry; length depends on the volume, "a sentence to several pages." Poets may send books to Paul Ritz, Reviews, P.O. Box 901, Clearwater FL 33757 for review consideration.

Book/Chapbook Needs & How to Submit: Under the imprint of W.W. Publications, publishes collections of poetry 50-100 pages. For book or chapbook consideration, submit sample poems. Publishes 2 chapbooks/year.

Also Offers: Membership in the American Tolkien Society is open to all, regardless of country of residence, and entitles one to receive the quarterly journal. Dues are $10 per annum to addresses in US, $12.50 in Canada, and $15 elsewhere. Sometimes sponsors contests.

AMERICAN WRITING: A MAGAZINE; NIERIKA EDITIONS (Specialized: form/style), 4343 Manayunk Ave., Philadelphia PA 19128. Established 1990. **Editor:** Alexandra Grilikhes.

• Since *American Writing* began, 60 of their authors have won national awards after appearing in the magazine.

Magazine Needs: *American Writing* appears twice/year using poetry that is "experimental and the voice of the loner, writing that takes risks with form, point of view, language, and ways of perceiving. Interested in the powers of intuition and states of being, the artist as shaman. No cerebral, academic poetry. Poets often try to make an experience 'literary' through language, instead of going back to the original experience and finding the original images. What we are interested in: the voice that speaks those images." Has published poetry by Ryan Van Cleave, Millie Mae Wieklund, Virgil Suarez, Cristina Biaggi, Saikat Mazumdar, and Jerry Harp. *American Writing* is 96 pages, digest-sized, professionally printed, flat-spined, matte card cover. Press run is 1,800 for 1,000 subscribers. Subscription: $10/year, $18/2 years. Sample: $6.

How to Submit: Submit 8 poems at a time. Accepts simultaneous submissions; no previously published poems. Guidelines available for SASE. Responds anywhere from 6 weeks to 6 months. Pays 2 copies/accepted submission group.

Advice: "Many magazines print the work of the same authors (the big names) who often publish 'lesser' works that way. *American Writing* is interested in the work itself, its particular strength, energy, and voice, not necessarily in the 'status' of the authors. We like to know *something* about the authors, however. We recommend reading a sample issue before just blindly submitting work."

$ ANCIENT PATHS (Specialized: religious, Christian). E-mail: skylar.burris@gte.net. Website: http://ancientpaths.LiteratureClassics.com (includes submission guidelines, online seasonal issues, sample literature, advice and resources for writers, contact and subscription information, links, and Bible trivia). Established 1998. **Editor:** Skylar H. Burris.

• *Ancient Paths* underwent an address change after this edition went to press. Check website for updated contact information.

Magazine Needs: *Ancient Paths* is published semiannually in Spring and Fall "to provide a forum for quality Christian literature. It contains poetry, short stories, and art." Wants "traditional rhymed/metrical forms or free verse; Christian images, issues, events or themes. I seek poetry that makes the reader both think and feel. No 'preachy' poetry or obtrusive rhyme; no stream of conscious or avant-garde work; no esoteric academic poetry." Has published poetry by Giovanni Malito, Diane Glancy, Walt McDonald, and Donna Farley. As a sample the editor selected these lines from "A Sudden Death in the House" by Jene Erick Beardsley:

> *How thoughtless of you to get up on that morning—unsteady/In bathrobe and slippers, with toothbrush*
> *and washcloth ready,/Breakfast frying in the kitchen, soon leaving for work—merely/To die, the day*
> *in your absence resuming so queerly.*

Ancient Paths is 40 pages, digest-sized, photocopied, side-stapled, cardstock cover, with b&w art. Receives about 350 poems/year, accepts about 15%. Press run is 150 for about 40 paid subscribers, 30 individual copy sales; 50 distributed free to churches, libraries, and authors. Subscription: $12/2 years. Sample: $3. Make checks payable to Skylar Burris.

How to Submit: Submit up to 5 poems at a time, single-spaced. Line length for poetry is 60 maximum. Accepts previously published poems and simultaneous submissions. Accepts e-mail submissions, but regular mail submissions preferred. "E-mail submissions should be pasted directly into the message, single spaced, one poem per message, using a small or normal font size, with name and address at the top of each submission. Specify that it is a submission to the *Ancient Paths* printed journal." Cover letter not required. "Name, address, and line count on first page. Note if the poem is previously published and what rights (if any) were purchased." Time between acceptance and publication is up to a year. Often comments on rejected poems. Guidelines available for SASE. Responds in "2-3 weeks if rejected, longer if being seriously considered." Pays $1/poem and 1 copy. Acquires one-time or reprint rights. Reviews other magazines and chapbooks in 100 words. The online journal contains original content not found in the print edition. "Easter and Christmas poems needed for online seasonal issues. Authors published online will receive one free copy of the printed publication (no cash payment for online publication)." Contact Skylar H. Burris.

Advice: "Read the great religious poets: John Donne, George Herbert, T.S. Eliot, Lord Tennyson. Remember not to preach. This is a literary magazine, not a pulpit. This does not mean you do not communicate morals or celebrate God. It means you are not overbearing or simplistic when you do so."

◐ ANHINGA PRESS; ANHINGA PRIZE, P.O. Box 10595, Tallahassee FL 32302-0595. (850)521-9920. Fax: (850)442-6323. E-mail: info@anhinga.org. Website: www.anhinga.org (includes guidelines, contact information, bios, archives, contest information, catalog, links, and editorial policy). Established 1972. **Poetry Editors:** Rick Campbell.

Book/Chapbook Needs: The press publishes "books and anthologies of poetry. We want to see contemporary poetry which respects language. We're inclined toward poetry that is not obscure, that can be understood by any literate audience." Has published *The Secret History of Water* by Silvia Curbelo as well as works by Naomi Shibab Nye, Robert Dana, Lola Haskins, and Ruth L. Schwartz (the 2000 Anhinga Prize winner).

How to Submit: Considers simultaneous submissions. Include SASE with all submissions.

Also Offers: The annual Anhinga Prize awards $2,000 and publication to a book-length poetry ms. Send SASE for rules. Submissions accepted January 1 to March 31 only. Entry fee: $20. The contest has been judged by such distinguished poets as William Stafford, Louis Simpson, Henry Taylor, Hayden Carruth, Marvin Bell, Donald Hall, and Joy Harjo. "Everything we do is on our website."

Advice: "Write good poetry. Read contemporary poetry. Not necessarily in that order."

◐ ◎ ANNA'S JOURNAL (Specialized: childlessness issues), P.O. Box 341, Ellijay GA 30540. Phone/fax: (706)276-2309. E-mail: annas@ellijay.com. Website: www.annasjournal.com (includes guidelines, contact info, archives, subscription information, and editorial policy). Established 1995. **Editor:** Catherine Ward-Long.

Magazine Needs: *Anna's Journal* is an online publication offering "spiritual support for childless couples who for the most part have decided to stay that way." Wants any type of poetry as long as it relates to childless issues. Receives about 10 poems/year, accepts approximately 50%.

How to Submit: Submit 3 poems at a time (maximum). Accepts previously published poems; no simultaneous submissions. Accepts e-mail submissions; include text in body of message. Cover letter preferred. Guidelines available on website. Publishes theme issues occasionally. Submit seasonal poems 3 months in advance. Acquires first rights and reprint rights. Reviews books of poetry, single book format. Poets may send books for review consideration.

Advice: "Looking for innovative ways to improve the child-free lifestyle and self-esteem."

N ⊘ **ANTHOLOGY; ANTHOLOGY, INC.**, P.O. Box 4411, Mesa AZ 85211-4411. Website: www.a nthologymagazine.com (includes submission guidelines, sample poems and prose, contact information, issue availability, events, interesting links, and contest information). Executive Editor: Sharon Skinner. Publisher: Bob Nelson. **Contact:** Poetry Editor.

Magazine Needs: *Anthology* appears every 2 months and intends to be "the best poetry, prose and art magazine." Wants "poetry with clear conceit. Evocative as opposed to provocative. We do not dictate form or style but creative uses are always enjoyed. Graphic horror and pornography are not encouraged." Accepts poetry written by children. Has published poetry by Buddy Wakefield, Gregory Ekey, Tom Hendrix, and Virgil Suarez. As a sample the editor selected these lines from "Bloodworthy" by Katie McKy:

> I was born with blood./It oiled the way to my first, raw suck/of air./And now I am borne by blood./It is the pulse of me.

Anthology is 28-32 pages, 8½ × 11, saddle-stapled, b&w drawings and clip art inside. Press run is 1,000 for 150 subscribers of which 10 are libraries, with 50-75 distributed free to local coffeehouses, beauty parlors, doctors' offices, etc. Single copy: $3.95; subscription: $20 (6 issues). Make checks payable to *Anthology*.

How to Submit: Submit up to 5 poems at a time with SASE. Accepts simultaneous submissions. "Do not send handwritten work or unusual fonts." Include name and address on each page of submission. Time between acceptance and publication is up to 8 months. Guidelines available for SASE and on website. Responds in 3 months. Pays 1 copy. Acquires one-time rights.

Also Offers: Sponsors annual contest with cash and other prizes for both poetry and short stories. Entry fee: $1/poem required. Send SASE for guidelines.

Advice: "Send what you write, not what you think an editor wants to hear. And always remember that a rejection is seldom personal, it is just one step closer to a yes."

⊘ ◎ **THE ANTHOLOGY OF NEW ENGLAND WRITERS; ROBERT PENN WARREN POETRY AWARDS (Specialized: form, free verse); NEW ENGLAND WRITERS CONFERENCE; VERMONT POETS ASSOCIATION; NEWSCRIPT**, P.O. Box 483, Windsor VT 05089. (802)674-2315. Fax: (802)674-5503. E-mail: newvtpoet@aol.com. Website: www.hometown.aol.com/new vtpoet/myhomepage/profile.html (includes names of the panelists, workshop leaders, judges of fiction and poetry contests, and conference date and location). Established 1986. **Editor:** Frank Anthony. **Associate Editor:** Susan Anthony.

Magazine Needs: *The Anthology of New England Writers* appears annually in November. All poems published in this annual are winners of their contest. Wants "unpublished, original, free verse poetry only; 10-30 line limit." Open to *all* poets, not just New England. Also accepts poetry written by teenagers. Has published poetry by Richard Eberhart, Rosanna Warren, David Kirby, and Vivian Shipley. *Anthology* is 44 pages, 5½ × 8½, professionally printed, perfect-bound, colored card cover, with b&w illustrations. Press run is 400. Single copy: $4.95. Sample: $4. Make checks payable to New England Writers.

How to Submit: Submit 3-9 poems at a time with contest reading fee (3 poems: $6; 6 poems: $10; 9 poems: $15). Include 3 × 5 card with name, address, and titles of poems. No previously published poems or simultaneous submissions. Reads submissions September through June 15 (post mark) only. Guidelines available for SASE or by e-mail. Responds 6 weeks after June 15 deadline. Sends prepublication galleys. Pays 1 copy. All rights revert to author upon publication.

Also Offers: Sponsors an annual free verse contest with The Robert Penn Warren Poetry Awards. Awards $300 for first, $200 for second, and $100 for third. Also awards 10 Honorable Mentions ($20 each), 10 Commendables, and 10 Editor's Choice. Entry fee: $6/3 poems. Winners announced at the New England Writers Conference in July. All submissions are automatically entered in contest. The Vermont Poets Association was established in 1986 "to encourage precision and ingenuity in the practice of writing and speaking, whatever the form and style." Currently has 500 members. Writing information is included in the biannual newsletter, *NewScript*. Meetings are held several times/year. Membership dues: $10, $7 senior citizens and students. Send SASE or e-mail for additional information. Also sponsors the annual New England Writers Conference with nationally known writers and editors involved with workshops, open mike readings, and a writer's panel. 2001 date: July 21. Conference lasts one day and is "affordable," and open to the public.

M $ **ANTIETAM REVIEW**, Washington County Arts Council, 41 S. Potomac St., Hagerstown MD 21740-5512. (301)791-3132. Fax: (240)420-1754. E-mail: winnie@washingtoncountyarts.com. Website: http://washingtoncountyarts.com (includes guidelines, contact information, contest info, subscription info). Established 1980. **Managing Editor:** Winnie Wagaman. **Poetry Editor:** Paul Grant.

• Public Radio's series *The Poet and the Poem* recognized *The Antietam Review* as an "outstanding contributor to American Letters."

Vicki Kelch, West Virginia freelance artist, photographer, and writer, shot this rainy morning image in Old Havana. The editors of *Antietam Review* felt the photo captured the essence of Cuba: "The beauty of the photograph is the illumination of the rain. The historical car, which has become an icon of Cuba, takes on a powerful symbolism, with the man looking out from the darkness into the light."

Magazine Needs: *The Antietam Review* appears annually in June and looks for "well-crafted literary quality poems." Needs 25 poems/issue, up to 30 lines each. Has published poetry by Ace Boggess, Joshua Poteat, and Susan Printz Robb. As a sample the editor selected these lines from "Circuit Breaker" by Llewellyn McKernan:

> In Twin Towers dorm, she's electric, she's/wired, her eyebrows sizzle, her rollers/smoke and pop, her brain a lightning rod where/neurons leap and spark as her fingertips/whiz across a mini-rechargeable/ espresso-toaster & Christmas-/lights-attached laptop.

Antietam Review is 72 pages, 8½×11, saddle-stapled, glossy paper with glossy card cover and b&w photos throughout. Press run is 1,000. Sample: $5.25 back issue, $6.30 current.

How to Submit: Submit 3 typed poems at a time. "We prefer a cover letter stating other publications, although we encourage new and emerging writers. We do not accept previously published poems and reluctantly take simultaneous submissions." No fax or e-mail submissions; "we share offices with the Washington County Arts Council, and this creates a problem for other staff." Do not submit mss from February through August. "We read from September 1 through February 1 annually." Guidelines available for SASE and on website. Pays $25/ poem, plus 2 copies. Acquires first North American serial rights.

Also Offers: Sponsors a Summer Literary Contest. Send SASE for details.

$ **THE ANTIOCH REVIEW**, P.O. Box 148, Yellow Springs OH 45387. (937)769-1365. Website: www.antioch.edu/review (includes guidelines, subscription info, and 2 excerpted poems). Established 1941. **Poetry Editor:** Judith Hall.

• Work published in this review has been frequently included in *The Best American Poetry* and *Pushcart Prize* anthologies.

Magazine Needs: *The Antioch Review* "is an independent quarterly of critical and creative thought . . . For well over 50 years, creative authors, poets and thinkers have found a friendly reception . . . regardless of formal reputation. We get far more poetry than we can possibly accept, and the competition is keen. Here, where form and content are so inseparable and reaction is so personal, it is difficult to state requirements or limitations. Studying recent issues of *The Review* should be helpful. No 'light' or inspirational verse." Has published poetry by Harryette Mullen, Jorie Graham, Jacqueline Osherow, and Mark Strand. Receives about 3,000 submissions/year, publishes 16 pages of poetry in each issue, and has about a 6-month backlog. Circulation is 5,000, with 70% distributed through bookstores and newsstands. Large percentage of subscribers are libraries. Subscription: $35. Sample: $6.

How to Submit: Submit 3-6 poems at a time. No previously published poems. Reads submissions September 1 through May 1 only. Guidelines available for SASE or on website. Responds in 2 months. Pays $10/ published page plus 2 copies. Reviews books of poetry in 300 words, single format.

$ **ANTIPODES (Specialized: regional, Australia)**, 8 Big Island, Warwick NY 10990. E-mail: kane@vassar.edu. Established 1987. **Poetry Editor:** Paul Kane.

Magazine Needs: *Antipodes* is a biannual of Australian poetry, fiction, criticism, and reviews of Australian writing. Wants work from Australian poets only. No restrictions as to form, length, subject matter, or style. Has published poetry by A.D. Hope, Judith Wright, and Les Murray. *Antipodes* is 180 pages, 8½×11, perfect-bound, with graphics, ads, and photos. Receives about 500 submissions/year, accepts about 10%. Press run is 500 for 200 subscribers. Subscription: $20. Sample: $17.

How to Submit: Submit 3-5 poems at a time. No previously published poems or simultaneous submissions. Cover letter with bio note required. Prefers submission of photocopies which do not have to be returned. Seldom comments on rejected poems. Responds in 2 months. Pays $50/poem plus 1 copy. Acquires first North American serial rights. Staff reviews books of poetry in 500-1,500 words. Send books for review consideration.

APPALACHIA; THE APPALACHIA POETRY PRIZE (Specialized: animals, nature), 5 Joy St., Boston MA 02108. Website: www.outdoors.org. Established 1949. **Editor:** Lucille Daniel. **Poetry Editor:** Parkman Howe.

Magazine Needs: *Appalachia* is a "semiannual journal of mountaineering and conservation which describes activities outdoors and asks questions of an ecological nature." Open to all forms of poetry relating to the outdoors and nature—specifically weather, mountains, rivers, lakes, woods, and animals. "No conquerors' odes." Recently published poetry by Mary Oliver, Jean Hollander, Francis Blessington, and Thomas Reiter. As a sample the editor selected these lines from "Early October" by Carolyn Miller:

> So many bronze torches to lead us down/into darkness, dark lamb's blood/of dogwood, low flames of
> sumac/and sassafras, and here and there, a few bright coins/for the hooded boatman on the shore

Appalachia is 160 pages, digest-sized, professionally-printed, perfect-bound, color cover using photos, with art/graphics and a few ads. Receives about 200 poems/year, accepts about 5%. Press run is 15,000. Subscription: $10/year. Sample: $5. Make checks payable to *Appalachia*.

How to Submit: Submit 5 poems at a time. "We favor shorter poems—maximum of 36 lines usually." No previously published poems or simultaneous submissions. Cover letter preferred. SASE required. Time between acceptance and publication is 6 months. Seldom comments on rejected poems. Occasionally publishes theme issues. Guidelines available for SASE. Responds in 3 months. Pays 1 contributor's copy. Acquires first rights. Staff reviews books of poetry in 500 words, multi-book format. Poets may send book for review consideration to Parkman Howe, poetry editor.

Also Offers: An annual award, The Appalachia Poetry Prize, given since 1975 to poets published in the journal. Write for details.

Advice: "Our readership is very well versed in the outdoors—mountains, rivers, lakes, animals. We look for poetry that helps readers see the natural world in fresh ways. No generalized accounts of the great outdoors."

APPLES & ORANGES POETRY MAGAZINE; LA GRANDE POMME AWARD. E-mail: editor@aopoetry.com. Website: www.aopoetry.com. Established 1997. **Editor:** Tom Fallon.

Magazine Needs: *Apples & Oranges Poetry Magazine* appears online. "All poetry forms accepted from international, U.S., Maine, and student poets. See Submission Guide at www.aopoetry.com/pmsubmit.html ." Wants "any poetry form: free verse, prose poems, traditional poetry, experimental forms. Satire, the erotic, humorous, serious religious poetry okay." Does not want greeting card, pornographic, or discriminatory poetry. Recently published poetry by Brendan O'Neill, Kucinta Setia, Ruth Daigon, Nancy Henry, Miguel de Asen, and George Van Deventer. As a sample the editor selected these lines from "Absence" by Robert Phelps:

> Absence doesn't do a thing for me/Doesn't make my heart grow anything but/weeds, and those weeds
> grow down into my soul soil/where the worms follow. Like some terrible dow jones/the life in my heart
> rides bulls and bears,/and the falls and surges blow ulcer holes in who I am.

Receives about 2,000 poems/year, accepts about 10%. Publishes about 50 poems/issue.

How to Submit: Poets should submit 3-5 poems at a time. No simultaneous submissions or previously published poems. Cover letter is preferred. "E-mail submissions only: poems in the body of the message. No attachments. See Submission Guide." Reads submissions September 1 through May 1. Time between acceptance and publication is 3 months. "The three-month selection period allows multiple readings of each submission." Never comments on rejected poems. Guidelines available on website. Responds in 3 months. Acquires one-time rights.

Also Offers: La Grande Pomme Award of $300 granted to poetry published in *Apples & Oranges* by an international or US poet during the year.

Advice: "Beginning poets should read *Poet's Market* and the *Apple's & Oranges* submission guide before e-mailing poems to the magazine. And *Apples & Oranges* unequivocally supports a poet's freedom to explore poetic form in any direction."

APROPOS (Specialized: subscribers), Ashley Manor, 450 Buttermilk Rd., Easton PA 18042. Established 1989. **Editor:** Ashley C. Anders.

Magazine Needs: *Apropos* publishes all poetry submitted by subscribers except that judged by the editor to be pornographic or in poor taste. As a sample the editor selected her own poem "With Pen in Hand":

> *With pen in hand I can confess/my innermost unhappiness,/or wonder in the things I see—/a newborn bird; a lovely tree.//This gift that God has given me/Allows my feelings to be free./With pen in hand I always say/whatever's on my mind each day.*

Apropos is 90 pages, desktop-published, digest-sized, plastic ring bound, with heavy stock cover. $25 for 6 issues. Sample: $3.

How to Submit: Submit 1 poem at a time. Line length for poetry is 40 maximum—50 characters/line. Editor prefers to receive sample of poetry prior to acceptance of subscription. Samples will not be returned. Accepts previously published poems; no simultaneous submissions. Guidelines available for SASE. All poems are judged by subscribers. Prizes for regular issues are $50, $25, $10, and $5.

N ⊕ ◢ AQUARIUS, Flat 4, Room B, 116 Sutherland Ave., Maida-Vale, London W9 2QP England. **Poetry Editor:** Eddie Linden.

Magazine Needs & How to Submit: *Aquarius* is a literary biannual publishing poetry, fictional prose, essays, interviews, and reviews. "Please note the magazine will not accept work unless writers have bought the magazine and studied the style/form of the work published." Single copy: $10; subscription: $50 (US). Payment is by arrangement.

N ◯ ◎ ARACHNE, INC. (Specialized: rural), 2363 Page Rd., Kennedy NY 14747-9717. Established 1980. **Senior Editor:** Susan L. Leach.

Book/Chapbook Needs: *Arachne* focuses on the work of "America's finest rural poets" and publishes 2 chapbooks/year (500 press run). Wants "any style, as long as its theme is rural in nature. No purient subjects." Chapbooks are usually 30 pages, staple-bound, #10 cover, no graphics.

How to Submit: Submit 7 poems at a time. No previously published poems or simultaneous submissions. Cover letter preferred. "Please include a SASE for return and correspondence." Reads submissions January and June only. Time between acceptance and publication is 6 months. Poems are circulated to an editorial board. "Poems selected initially by membership, presented to board for final decision." Seldom comments on rejected poems. Responds to queries and mss within 3 months.

Advice: "We will not consider any material of a sexually questionable nature. We remain a conservative press."

N ✉ ▼ $◢ ARC: CANADA'S NATIONAL POETRY MAGAZINE; THE CONFEDERATION POETS PRIZE; POEM OF THE YEAR CONTEST, P.O. Box 7368, Ottawa, Ontario K1L 8E4 Canada. E-mail: arc.poetry@cyberus.ca. Website: www.cyberus.ca/~arc.poetry (includes guidelines, contact and subscription info, upcoming themes, bios, editorial policy, and contest info). Established 1978. **Co-Editors:** Rita Donovan and John Barton.

• *Arc* received both gold and silver National Magazine Awards in 2001.

Magazine Needs: *Arc* is a biannual of poetry, poetry-related articles, interviews and book reviews. "Our tastes are eclectic. Our focus is Canadian, but we also publish writers from elsewhere." Has published poetry by Evelyn Lau, Michael Crummey, Erin Mouré, Patricia Young, and Joelene Heathcote. *Arc* is 112 pages, perfect-bound, with laminated 2-color cover, artwork and ads. Receives about 500 submissions/year, accepts approximately 40-50 poems. Press run is 1,500 for 1,000 subscribers. Single copy: $11.50 Canadian/Canada, $16 Canadian/US, $18 Canadian/overseas; subscription (4 issues): $36 Canadian/Canada, $48 Canadian/US, $62 Canadian/overseas. Cost of sample varies.

How to Submit: Submit 5-8 poems, single spaced, with name and address on each page. No previously published poems or simultaneous submissions. Cover letter required. Guidelines available for SAE and IRC and on website; upcoming themes on website and in publication. Responds in 3-6 months. Pays $30 Canadian/page plus 2 copies. Acquires first North American serial rights.

Also Offers: The Confederation Poets Prize is an annual award of $100 for the best poem published in *Arc* that year. *Arc* also sponsors a "Poem of the Year Contest." Awards first prize of $1,000, second prize of $750 and third prize of $500. Deadline in June.

N ⊕ $◙ ARC PUBLICATIONS, Nanholme Mill, Shaw Wood Rd., Todmorden, Lancashire OL14 6DA United Kingdom. Phone (01706)812338. Established 1969. **Partners:** Tony Ward, Angela Jarman, and Rosemary Jones.

Book/Chapbook Needs: ARC publishes 8 paperback books of poetry/year. Wants "literary, literate, contemporary poetry. No religious or children's verse. We specialize not only in contemporary poetry of the U.K. but also in poetry written in English from across the world." Has published books of poetry by Michael Haslam (UK), Emma-Jane Arkady (UK), and Louis Armand (Australia). Their books are 64-100 pages, 5½×8½, offset litho and perfect-bound with card covers in 2-3 colors.

How to Submit: Query first with 10 sample poems and a cover letter with brief bio and publication credits. "No submissions replied to if there is no IRC." Accepts previously published poems and simultaneous submissions. Mss are read by at least 2 editors before possible acceptance. Seldom comments on rejected poems. Responds to queries in up to 4 months. Pays 7-10% royalties and 5 author's copies (out of a press run of 600). Send SASE (or SAE and IRCs) for current list to order samples.

Advice: "Poets should have a body of work already published in magazines and journals, and should be acquainted with our list of books, before submitting."

⊘ ARCTOS PRESS; HOBEAR PUBLICATIONS, P.O. Box 401, Sausalito CA 94966-0401. (415)331-2503. E-mail: runes@aol.com. Website: www.members.aol.com/RUNES (includes guidelines, contact info, contest info, subscription info, upcoming themes). Established 1997. **Editor:** CB Follett.

Book/Chapbook Needs: Arctos Press, under the imprint HoBear Publications, publishes 1-2 paperbacks each year. "We publish quality books and anthologies of poetry, usually theme-oriented, in runs of 1,000, paper cover, perfect-bound." Has published *GRRRRR, A Collection of Poems About Bears* (anthology), *Eye of the Holocaust*, by Susan Terris; *Beside the Sleeping Maiden*, by the poets of Marin County (anthology); and *The Mouth of Home*, by Janell Moon. As a sample the editor selected these lines from "Every Day" by Ellery Akers:

> It is not impersonal, the world./Or strict. If she is awake to every stalk./If she can watch the hyacinths
> hammer their green beaks/through the ground.

How to Submit: "We do not accept unsolicited mss unless a current call has been posted in *Poets & Writers* and/or elsewhere, at which time up to 5 poems related to the theme should be sent." Accepts previously published poems (if author holds the rights) and simultaneous submissions ("if we are kept informed"). Accepts submissions by post only. Guidelines and upcoming themes available on website and for SASE. Pays 1 copy; discounts available on additional copies.

Also Offers: *Runes, A Review of Poetry* (see separate listing in this section).

Ⓝ ⊘ ARIES: A JOURNAL OF CREATIVE EXPRESSION, Dept. of English, 1201 Wesleyan St., Fort Worth TX 76105-1536. (817)531-4444. Fax: (817)531-6503. E-mail: aries_journal@hotmail.com. Website: http://web.txwes.edu/languagesliterature/aries.html (includes guidelines, editors, occasional excerpts). Established 1973. **General Editor:** Thom D. Chesney.

Magazine Needs: *Aries* appears annually in June publishing quality poetry, b&w art, fiction, essays, and one-act plays. Wants any form up to 50 lines. "Special needs: Spanish language poetry and translation thereof (send *both* versions)." Does not want erotica. Recently published poetry by Virgil Suarez, Richard Robbins, Susan Smith Nash, and Lynn Veach Sadler. As a sample the editor selected these lines from "Iron Gallery" by Mario Milosevic:

> The rail yards of Chicago/are home to midnight prowlers/rattling spray cans in hand/dodging bosses
> wielding clubs/risking bruises cuts and worse/for the joy of painting pictures . . .

Aries is 60 pages, digest-sized, offset-printed, perfect-bound, heavy cardstock cover, with b&w art (1500 dpi scans). Receives about 400 poems/year, accepts about 10%. Publishes about 40 poems/issue. Press run is 300 for 100 subscribers of which 3 are libraries, 125 shelf sales; 50 distributed free to contributors. Single copy: $6; subscription: $6. Sample: $6. Make checks payable to *Aries* general editor.

How to Submit: Submit 1-5 poems at a time. Line length for poetry is 3 minimum, 50 maximum. Accepts simultaneous submissions; no previously published poems. No fax, e-mail, or disk submissions. Cover letter is required. "Blind submissions only: cover letter with titles; no identifying marks on submissions." Reads submissions September 1-January 31 only. Time between acceptance and publication is 3-5 months. "Three editors read every submission blindly. Personal response to *every* submission accompanied by a SASE or functioning e-mail address." Always comments on rejected poems. Guidelines available in magazine, by e-mail, or on website. Responds in up to 6 months. Pays 1 contributor's copy. Acquires first rights.

Advice: "Write in the voice that's most comfortable for you. Our editors tend to choose works where 'there's something at stake.' "

⊘ Ⓒ ARJUNA LIBRARY PRESS; JOURNAL OF REGIONAL CRITICISM (Specialized: surrealism, science fiction/fantasy, spirituality, symbols), 1025 Garner St. D, Space 18, Colorado Springs CO 80905-1774. Library established 1963; press established 1979. **Editor-in-Chief:** Count Prof. Joseph A. Uphoff, Jr.

Magazine Needs: "The Arjuna Library Press is avant-garde, designed to endure the transient quarters and marginal funding of the literary phenomenon (as a tradition) while presenting a context for the development of current mathematical ideas in regard to theories of art, literature, and performance; photocopy printing allows for very limited editions and irregular format. Quality is maintained as an artistic materialist practice." Publishes "surrealist prose poetry, visual poetry, dreamlike, short and long works; no obscene, profane (will criticize but not publish), unpolished work." Has published work by Niran Bahjat-Abbas, Kurt Beiswenger, Woodrow G. Moore, II, Timothy Savage, Matt Counte, and Larry R. Brooks. As a sample the editor selected these lines from "LET FREE" by Ryan Jason Jackson:

> NOT TO MAKE THE PROBLEMS WORSE/RESPONSIBLE FOR FIGHTING/THAT ONLY NOW/
> PUNISHMENT BECOMES THE PROBLEM/THAT ONLY WED BECOME FREE OF ANYWAY/
> FINALLY UNTIL THAT DAY WHEN/WE ARE LET FREE OF OURSELVES

Journal of Regional Criticism is published on loose photocopied pages of collage, writing, and criticism, appearing frequently in a varied format. Press run is 1 copy each. Reviews books of poetry "occasionally." Poets may send books for review consideration. "Upon request will treat material as submitted for reprint, one-time rights."

Book/Chapbook Needs & How to Submit: Arjuna Library Press publishes 6-12 chapbooks/year, averaging 50 pages. Sample: $2.50. Currently accepting one or two short poems, with a cover letter and SASE, to be considered for publication. Accepts submissions by post only. Guidelines available by SASE.

Advice: "The Arjuna Library Press and Associated Poets will examine a series of concepts that modify the word surrealism to come up with special theories for such as Surrealist Naturalism, Surrealist Materialism, and Cultural Surrealism. Poetry that refers to Pataphysical Subjects, that investigates existential theorems, or that describes the Process of Contradiction should narrate philosophy in the context of fiction by expressive language and metaphor."

ARKANSAS REVIEW: A JOURNAL OF DELTA STUDIES (Specialized: regional), P.O. Box 1890, State University AR 72467-1890. (870)972-3043. Fax: (870)972-3045. E-mail: delta@toltec.astate. edu. Website: www.clt.astate/arkreview (includes past table of contents, guidelines for contributors, list of editors). Established 1968 (as *Kansas Quarterly*). **General Editor:** William M. Clements. **Creative Materials Editor:** Norman E. Stafford.

Magazine Needs: Appearing 3 times/year, the *Arkansas Review* is "a regional studies journal devoted to the seven-state Mississippi River Delta. Interdisciplinary in scope, we publish academic articles, relevant creative material, interviews, and reviews. Material must respond to or evoke the experiences and landscapes of the seven-state Mississippi River Delta (St. Louis to New Orleans)." Has published poetry by Walt McDonald, Gordon Osing, Lora Dunetz, and Mark DeFoe. As a sample the editors selected this untitled poem:

> On her good old stove, her hardy skillet/waits, iron sentinel guarding those grim days/when her food
> stuck to the field hand's ribs./Her stove is as yellow now as an old/wedding gown. It stands, perfuming
> the air/with the just aroma of Mr. Clean.

Arkansas Review is 92 pages, magazine-sized, photo offset-printed, saddle-stapled, 4-color cover, with photos, drawings, and paintings. Receives about 500 poems/year, accepts about 5%. Press run is 600 for 400 subscribers of which 300 are libraries, 20 shelf sales; 50 distributed free to contributors. Subscription: $20. Sample: $7.50. Make checks payable to ASU Foundation.

How to Submit: No limit on number of poems submitted at a time. No previously published poems or simultaneous submissions. Accepts e-mail and disk submissions. Cover letter with SASE preferred. Time between acceptance and publication is about 6 months. Poems are circulated to an editorial board. "The Creative Materials Editor makes the final decision based—in part—on recommendations from other readers." Often comments on rejections. Occasionally publishes theme issues. Guidelines available by e-mail or for SASE. Responds in 4 months. Pays 5 copies. Acquires first rights. Staff reviews books and chapbooks of poetry in 500 words, single and multi-book format. Send books for review consideration to William M. Clements. ("Inquire in advance.")

ARSENIC LOBSTER, P.O. Box 484, Pocatello ID 83204. Established 2000. **Editors:** Martin Vest and Jen Hawkins.

Magazine Needs: *Arsenic Lobster* appears biannually, "prints succulent poems for toxic people. Honed lyricisms or stripped narratives." Wants "surgical steel punk, disasters that die laughing, riddles solved with a gunshot, poetry written down on its knees. Be charlie-horse hearted and heavily quirked." Does not want "marmalade, hyacinths, or the art of gardening. No cicadas, wheelbarrows, or fond reflections on the old county fair. Nothing about Tai Chi. Nothing written with a cat on your lap." Has published poetry by John Bradley, Antler, and J.C. Watson. As a sample the editors selected these lines from "Labyrinth" by C.J. Sage:

> I am a space/between two teeth./A wedding hides/inside me./My walls/have fallen/on the doorstep.

Arsenic Lobster is 35 pages, digest-sized, saddle-stapled, illustrated card stock cover. Publishes about 30-40 poems/issue. Press run is 300. Single copy $4; subscription: $8/year. Make checks payable to Jen Hawkins.

How to Submit: Submit 4-7 poems at a time. Accepts previously published poems and simultaneous submissions. ("Please inform us.") No fax, e-mail, or disk submissions. Cover letter preferred. "Free verse and biographical cover letters (not credit lists) preferred; SASE a must." Reads submissions all year. Time between acceptance and publication is 6 months. Responds immediately. Pays 1 contributor's copy. Acquires first/one-time rights. Reviews chapbooks and other magazines/journals. Poets may send books for review consideration Attn: Jen Hawkins.

ART TIMES: COMMENTARY AND RESOURCE FOR THE FINE & PERFORMING ARTS, P.O. Box 730, Mount Marion NY 12456-0730. Phone/fax: (845)246-6944. E-mail: poetry@arttimesjournal. com. Website: www.arttimesjournal.com. **Poetry Editor:** Raymond J. Steiner.
Magazine Needs: *Art Times* is a monthly tabloid newspaper devoted to the arts. Focuses on cultural and creative articles and essays, but also publishes some poetry and fiction. Wants "poetry that strives to express genuine observation in unique language; poems no longer than 20 lines each." As a sample the editor selected these lines from "Satin" by Paul Camacho:

> *an encounter with a noticed article,/the satin of a bias smile,/which causes the novice to speak/of no experience save his own:/what is beauty, but articulate bone?*

Art Times is 20-26 pages, newsprint, with reproductions of artwork, some photos, advertisement-supported. Receives 300-500 poems/month, accepts about 40-50/year. Circulation is 24,000, of which 5,000 are subscriptions; most distribution is free through galleries, theatres, etc. Subscription: $15/year. Sample: $1 with 9 × 12 SAE and 3 first-class stamps.
How to Submit: Submit 4-5 typed poems at a time, up to 20 lines each. "All topics; all forms." Include SASE with all submissions. No e-mail submissions. Has an 18-month backlog. Guidelines available for SASE. Responds in 6 months. Pays 6 copies plus 1-year subscription.

$ ARTFUL DODGE, Dept. of English, College of Wooster, Wooster OH 44691. Established 1979. **Poetry Editor:** Daniel Bourne.
Magazine Needs: *Artful Dodge* is an annual literary magazine that "takes a strong interest in poets who are continually testing what they can get away with successfully in regard to subject, perspective, language, etc., but who also show mastery of current American poetic techniques—its varied textures and its achievement in the illumination of the particular. What all this boils down to is that we require high craftsmanship as well as a vision that goes beyond one's own storm windows, grandmothers, or sexual fantasies—to paraphrase Hayden Carruth. Poems can be on any subject, of any length, from any perspective, in any voice, but we don't want anything that does not connect with both the human and the aesthetic. Thus, we don't want cute, rococo surrealism, someone's warmed-up, left-over notion of an avant-garde that existed 10-100 years ago, or any last bastions of rhymed verse in the civilized world. On the other hand, we are interested in poems that utilize stylistic persuasions both old and new to good effect. We are not afraid of poems which try to deal with large social, political, historical, and even philosophical questions—especially if the poem emerges from one's own life experience and is not the result of armchair pontificating. We often offer encouragement to writers whose work we find promising, but *Artful Dodge* is more a journal for the already emerging writer than for the beginner looking for an easy place to publish. We also have a sustained commitment to translation, especially from Polish and other East European literatures, and we feel the interchange between the American and foreign works on our pages is of great interest to our readers. We also feature interviews with outstanding literary figures." Has published poetry by Gregory Orr, Julia Kasdorf, Denise Duhamel, Gary Gildner, and John Haines. As a sample the editor selected these lines from "How It Was" by Jeff Gundy:

> *. . . It was the last year of the old world, the last spring/of the old time, you don't believe me but watch it/or next thing you know you'll be carving sticks/by the scant fire and waiting for somebody to ask you,/hey grandpa, about all that, and nobody will.*

Artful Dodge is digest-sized, perfect-bound, professionally printed, glossy cover, with art, ads. There are about 60-80 pages of poetry in each issue. Receives at least 2,000 poems/year, accepts about 60. Press run is 1,000 for 100 subscribers of which 30 are libraries. Sample: $7 for current issue, $3 for others.
How to Submit: "No simultaneous submissions. Please limit submissions to 6 poems. Long poems may be of any length, but send only one at a time. We encourage translations, but we ask as well for original text and statement from translator that he/she has copyright clearance and permission of author." Responds in up to 1 year. Pays 2 copies, plus, currently, $5/page honorarium because of grants from Ohio Arts Council. Poets may send books for review consideration; however, "there is no guarantee we can review them!"

N ⊘ SHERMAN ASHER PUBLISHING, P.O. Box 2853, Santa Fe NM 87504. (505)984-2686. Fax: (505)820-2744. E-mail: SApublish@alt.net. Website: www.shermanasher.com (includes guidelines, contact information, poetry, interviews with authors, and catalog). Established 1994. **Contact:** Nancy Fay.
 • *The Rain at Midnight*, by Joseph Hutchinson was a finalist for the Colorado Book Award.
Book Needs: "We are dedicated to changing the world one book at a time, committed to the power of truth and the craft of language expressed by publishing fine poetry. We specialize in anthologies. We do

not publish chapbooks." Publishes 3-5 paperbacks/year. "Please see our current books as an example of what we look for in poetry. We enjoy well-crafted form. No rhymed doggerel, cowboy poetry or stiff academic work." Has published poetry by Joseph Hutchinson, Marjorie Agosín, and Judyth Hill.

How to Submit: Closed to poetry submissions until 2004.

Advice: "Take an unflinching look at our list. Does your work fit?"

 **ASHEVILLE POETRY REVIEW**, P.O. Box 7086, Asheville NC 28802. (828)649-0217. Established 1994. **Founder/Managing Editor:** Keith Flynn.

Magazine Needs: *Asheville Poetry Review* appears biannually. "We publish the best regional, national, and international poems we can find. We publish translations, interviews, essays, historical perspectives, and book reviews as well." Wants "quality work with well-crafted ideas married to a dynamic style. Any subject matter is fit to be considered so long as the language is vivid with a clear sense of rhythm." Has published poetry by Robert Bly, Yevgeny Yevtushenko, Eavan Boland, and Fred Chappell. *Asheville Poetry Review* is 160-180 pages, 6×9, perfect-bound, laminated, full-color cover, b&w art inside. Receives about 1,200 poems/year, accepts about 10-15%. Press run is 600-750. Subscription: $22.50/1 year, $43.50/2 years. Sample: $13. "We prefer poets purchase a sample copy prior to submitting."

How to Submit: Submit 3-5 poems at a time. Accepts simultaneous submissions; no previously published poems. Cover letter required. Include comprehensive bio, recent publishing credits, and SASE. Submission deadlines: January 15 and July 15. Time between acceptance and publication is up to 5 months. Poems are circulated to an editorial board. Seldom comments on rejected poems. Publishes theme issues occasionally. Guidelines and upcoming themes available for SASE. Responds in up to 5 months. Pays 1 copy. Rights revert back to author upon publication. Reviews books and chapbooks of poetry. Poets may send books for review consideration.

ASIAN PACIFIC AMERICAN JOURNAL; ASIAN AMERICAN WRITERS' WORKSHOP (Specialized: ethnic/nationality, anthology), 16 W. 32nd St., Suite 10A, New York NY 10001. (212)494-0061. Fax: (212)494-0062. E-mail: desk@aaww.org. Website: www.aaww.org (includes information about AAWW publications, creative writing workshops, programs and events, guidelines, and a comprehensive seasonal calendar). Established 1992. **Contact:** Poetry Editor.

Magazine Needs: The *APA Journal* is a semiannual published by the AAWW, a not-for-profit organization. It is "dedicated to the best of contemporary Asian-American writing." Has published poetry by Arthur Sze, Meera Alexander, Luis Cabalquinto, and Sesshu Foster. *APA Journal* is 200 pages, digest-sized, typeset, perfect-bound, 2-color cover, with ads. Receives about 150 poems/year, accepts about 30%. Press run is 1,500 for 400 subscribers of which 50 are libraries, 800 shelf sales. Single copy: $10; subscription/membership: $45; institutional membership: $55. Sample: $12.

How to Submit: Submit 4 copies of up to 10 pages of poetry, maximum of one poem/page. No previously published poems. No fax or e-mail submission. Cover letter with phone and fax numbers and 1- to 4-sentence biographical statement required. Deadlines are usually August 15 for the issue appearing December 1 and March 15 for the issue appearing June 1. "We will work with authors who are promising." Guidelines available for SASE or on website. Responds in up to 4 months. Pays 2 copies. Acquires one-time rights. In 1999, *The Nuyorasian Anthology: Asian American Writings about NYC* was published followed by *Take Out: Queer Writing from Asian America* in 2001.

Also Offers: The AAWW offers creative writing workshops, a newsletter, a bookselling service, readings, and fellowships to young Asian-American writers. Write for details.

ATLANTA REVIEW; POETRY 2003, P.O. Box 8248, Atlanta GA 31106. E-mail: dan@atlanta review.com. Website: www.atlantareview.com (includes submission and contest guidelines, names of editors, poetry samples from several issues, and a free issue offer). Established 1994. **Editor:** Dan Veach.

• Work published in this review has been included in the *Pushcart Prize* anthologies.

Magazine Needs: *Atlanta Review* is a semiannual primarily devoted to poetry, but also featuring fiction, interviews, essays, and fine art. Wants "quality poetry of genuine human appeal." Has published poetry by Seamus Heaney, Derek Walcott, Maxine Kumin, Rachel Hadas, Charles Simic, Louis Simpson, and Naomi Shihab Nye. As a sample the editor selected these lines from "It Rains on Gaza" by David Moolten:

> Today, it rains on Gaza, that blessed strip/Of desert by the sea. It rains on the fig trees,/And on the
> one-room homes in cramped rows/Like the ramps of praying men, every inch occupied . . .

Atlanta Review is 128 pages, 6×9, professionally printed on acid-free paper, flat-spined, glossy color cover, with b&w artwork. Receives about 10,000 poems/year, accepts about 1%. Press run is 3,500 for 1,000 subscribers of which 50 are libraries, 2,000 shelf sales. Single copy: $6; subscription: $10. Sample: $5.

How to Submit: No previously published poems. No e-mail submissions. Issue deadlines are June 1 and December 1. Time between acceptance and publication is 3 months. Seldom comments on rejected poems. Each spring issue has an International Feature Section. Guidelines available for SASE. Responds in 2 weeks. Pays 2 copies plus author's discounts. Acquires first North American serial rights.

Also Offers: *Atlanta Review* also sponsors POETRY 2003, an annual international poetry competition. Prizes are $2,003, $500, and $250, plus 50 International Merit Awards. Winners are announced in leading literary publications. All entries are considered for publication in *Atlanta Review*. Entry fee is $5 for the first poem, $2 for each additional. No entry form or guidelines necessary. Send to POETRY 2003 at the above address. Postmark deadline: May 2, 2003.

Advice: "We are giving today's poets the international audience they truly deserve."

$ THE ATLANTIC MONTHLY, Dept. PM, 77 North Washington St., Boston MA 02114. (617)854-7700. Website: www.theatlantic.com. Established 1857. **Poetry Editor:** Peter Davison. **Assistant Poetry Editor:** David Barber.

● Poetry published here has been included in every volume of *The Best American Poetry*.

Magazine Needs: *The Atlantic Monthly* publishes some of the most distinguished poetry in American literature, including work by William Matthews, Andrew Hudgins, Stanley Kunitz, Rodney Jones, May Swenson, Galway Kinnell, Philip Levine, Richard Wilbur, Jane Kenyon, Donald Hall, and W.S. Merwin. Has a circulation of 500,000, of which 5,800 are libraries. Receives some 50,000 poems/year, accepts about 30-35, has an "accepted" backlog of 6-12 months. Sample: $3.

How to Submit: Submit 3-5 poems with SASE. No simultaneous submissions. No fax or e-mail submissions. Publishes theme issues. Responds in 3 weeks. Always sends prepublication galleys. Pays about $4/ line. Acquires first North American serial rights only.

Advice: Wants "to see poetry of the highest order; we do *not* want to see workshop rejects. Watch out for workshop uniformity. Beware of the present tense. Be yourself."

AURA LITERARY ARTS REVIEW, HUC 135, University of Alabama at Birmingham, 1530 Third Ave. S., Birmingham AL 35294-1150. (205)934-3216. E-mail: aura@popmail.com. Website: http://students .uab.edu (includes guidelines, bios, archives, contact information, contest information, links, editorial policy). Established 1974. **Editor:** Chris Giganti. **Poetry Editor:** Daniel Robbins.

Magazine Needs: *Aura* appears biannually in September and January and publishes poetry, prose, and visual art. The editors "prefer quality, experienced work." *Aura* has published poetry by Phillip Levine, Robert Collins, William Stafford, Danny Gamble, R.T. Smith, and Jim Mersmann. The 6×9 magazine is 120-145 pages, perfect-bound, printed on white matte with b&w artwork and the front and back cover in color. Circulation is 5,000, of which 40-50 are subscriptions; other sales are to students and Birmingham residents. Subscription: $6. Sample postpaid: $3.

How to Submit: Submit up to 10 previously unpublished, typed, double-spaced pages of poetry. No simultaneous submissions; "poets who retract work will be shunned for life." Include SASE or receive no response. "Poetry editor is a hard-ass." Guidelines available for SASE, by e-mail, on website, and in publication. Responds in 3 months. Pays 2 copies.

THE AUROREAN: A POETIC QUARTERLY; THE UNROREAN; ENCIRCLE PUBLICA-TIONS, P.O. Box 219, Sagamore Beach MA 02562. Phone/fax: (508)833-0805 (no fax submissions). E-mail: cafpoet37@aol.com (no e-mail submissions). Press established 1992. Magazine established 1995. **Editor:** Cynthia Brackett-Vincent.

Magazine Needs: *The Aurorean*, which appears in March, June, September, and December, seeks to publish "poetry that is inspirational (but not religious), meditational, or reflective of the Northeast. Strongly encouraged (but not limited to) topics: positiveness, recovery, and nature. Maximum length: 38 lines. No hateful, overly religious or poetry that uses four-letter words for four-letter words' sake. Use mostly free-verse; occasional rhyme; I am biased toward haiku and well-written humor. I'm *always* in need of short (2-6 lines), seasonal poems. For seasonal poems, please note specific deadlines in our guidelines." Welcomes submissions from both beginning and experienced poets. Accepts poetry written by children. Has published poetry by Henry Berne, Lyn Lifshin, Dennis Rhodes, and Lainie Senechal. As a sample the editor selected these lines from "No John Milton" by Joanna Nealon:

> *Soft chant of changing light on water,/Swift colloquies of clouds,/And those low secrets/Uttered only by eyes.*

The Aurorean is 36 pages of poetry, 5 pages of contributor's bios, 5½ × 8½, professionally printed, perfect-bound with papers and colors varying from season to season. Open to exchange ads. Press run is 550. Single copy: $6 US, $7 international. Subscription: $21 US, $25 international. Make checks payable to Encircle Publications or *The Aurorean*.

How to Submit: Submit 3-5 poems at a time. No previously published poems or simultaneous submissions. No e-mail or fax submissions. "Make it clear what you're submitting. Please do not fold poems individually. Type if possible; if not, write as clearly as possible." Cover letter strongly preferred with first submission. Sometimes comments on rejected poems. Guidelines available for SASE. Authors notified when ms received if SASE or e-mail address included. Responds on acceptance in up to 3 months. Always sends prepublication galleys. Pays 3 copies/poem with an-up-to 50-word bio in the "Who's Who" section. Also features a "Poet-of-the-Quarter" each issue with publication of up to 3 poems and an extended bio (100 words). The "Poet-of-the-Quarter" receives 10 copies and a 1-year subscription.

Also Offers: "New contests for *The Aurorean:* each issue an independent judge picks Best-Poems-of-Last-Issue; winner receives $20. Send entries for Poetic-Quote-of-the-Season (cannot be acknowledged or returned); 4 lines maximum, quote by not-too-obscure poet." Source must be cited. Winner receives 2 free issues. "New broadsheet, *The Unrorean*, will appear 2/year . . . experimental, risque, and for poems that might not fit *The Aurorean*. Still, nothing hateful. SASE for return/reply. No proofs, acknowledgements, deadlines, or bio listings. 11 × 17; laser-printed. $2 each postpaid." Pays one copy/poem published. Unless otherwise requested, work sent to *The Aurorean* will also be considered for the broadsheet.

Advice: "Study *Poet's Market*. Be familiar with any journal before submitting."

N $⊘ **AUSABLE PRESS**, 46 East Hill Rd., Keene NY 12942-9719. E-mail: editor@ausablepress. com. Website: www.ausablepress.com (includes books available and forthcoming, submissions guidelines). Established 1999. **Editor:** Chase Twichell. Member: CLMP.

Book/Chapbook Needs & How to Submit: Ausable Press wants poetry "that investigates and expresses human consciousness in language that goes where prose cannot." Does not want children's poetry or poetry for children, light verse, inspirational poetry, illustrated poetry, or journal entries. Recently published poetry by C.K. Williams, Steve Orlen, Julianne Buchsbaum, and James Richardson. As a sample the editor selected these lines from "Gossip of the Inner Life" by Steve Orlen from *This Particular Eternity*:

> *My good friend who these days despises the newspapers/complains they aren't news but gossip, a talking down,/in brief sidebars, in the mathematics of the intellect,/from the highest to the lowest common denominator . . .*

Publishes 4-6 paperback or hardback titles/year. Number of pages varies, offset-printed, paper and cloth editions. "Please send SASE for submission guidelines or visit our website (www.ausablepress.com)." Accepts unsolicited mss in June and July only. **Charges reading fee of $20.** Responds to queries in 1 week; to mss in up to 4 months. Pays royalties of 5-8%, advance of $1,000 and 20 author's copies (out of a press run of 2,000).

Advice: "This is not a contest. Ausable Press is under no obligation to publish any of the manuscripts submitted. Response time can be as long as 3-4 months, so please be patient."

⊘ **AUSTRALIAN GOTHICA**, P.O. Box 6492, Destin FL 32550. Established 1993. **Editor:** Rebecca Lu Kiernan.

Magazine Needs: Currently accepting mss by invitation only. *Australian Gothica* appears biannually. "We publish tightly crafted, impressive works of art, poetry, short stories, the exotic and erotic, and science fiction of the highest literary value." As a sample, the editor selected these lines from "Pre-emptive" by Rebecca Lu Kiernan:

> *I will have a rib removed/and mail it to you/in a sanitary jar/saving you the/trouble/of robbing me/in my sleep.//Incision is easier sewn/than the slow jagged/tearing/of stealing back/a bone.*

Australian Gothica is 38-50 pages, 6 × 9, professionally printed, flat spined. Press run is 1,000 for 600 subscribers.

Advice: "We have a sense of horror and humor. Tell us something we will never forget!"

◎ **AVOCET, A JOURNAL OF NATURE POEMS (Specialized: nature, spirituality)**, P.O. Box 8041, Calabasas CA 91372-8041. E-mail: patricia.j.swenson@csun.edu. Website: www.csun.edu/~pjs44 945/avocet.html (includes writer's guidelines, editor's e-mail address, deadlines, and sample poems). First issue published fall 1997. **Editor:** Patricia Swenson.

Magazine Needs: *Avocet* is a quarterly poetry journal "devoted to poets seeking to understand the beauty of nature and its interconnectedness with humanity." Wants "poetry that shows man's interconnectedness with nature; discovering the Divine in nature." Does not want "poems that have rhyme or metrical schemes, cliché, abstraction, and sexual overtones." Has recently published poetry by Donna J. Waidtlow, Fred Boltz, Joan Goodwin, Paul B. Roth, Sharron Kollmeyer, and Judy Snow. *Avocet* is 30 pages, 4¼×5½, professionally printed, saddle-stapled, card cover, with some illustrations. Single copy: $5; subscription: $20. Make checks payable to Pat Swenson.

How to Submit: Submit up to 5 poems at a time. Accepts previously published poems if acknowledged; no simultaneous submissions. Accepts e-mail submissions with name, city, state, and e-mail address; include submission in body of message, no attachments. Cover letter required including SASE. Time between acceptance and publication is up to 6 months. Responds in 8 weeks. Pays 1 contributor's copy.

AXE FACTORY REVIEW; CYNIC PRESS, P.O. Box 40691, Philadelphia PA 19107. E-mail: cynicpress@yahoo.com. *Axe Factory* established 1986. Cynic Press established 1996. **Editor/Publisher:** Joseph Farley.

Magazine Needs: *Axe Factory* is published 1-4 times/year and its purpose is to "spread the disease known as literature. The content is mostly poetry and essays. We now use short stories too." Wants "eclectic work. Will look at anything but suggest potential contributors purchase a copy of magazine first to see what we're like. No greeting card verse." Accepts poetry written by children. "Parents should read magazine to see if they want their children in it as much material is adult in nature." Has published *River Architecture: poems from here & there* by Louis McKee and poetry by Taylor Graham, A.D. Winans, Normal, and John Sweet. As a sample the editor selected these lines from "Starting Over" by Louis McKee:

> I kept the doll I found/in the yard, a Barbie with matted/blond hair and not a stitch/of clothing. A new
> wife,/I thought, and I proposed to her

Axe Factory is 20-40 pages, 8½×11, saddle-stapled, neatly printed with light card cover. Press run is 100. Current issue: $9; sample: $8; subscription: $24 for 4 issues. Make checks payable to Cynic Press or Joseph Farley.

How to Submit: Submit up to 10 poems. Accepts previously published poems "sometimes, but let me know up front" and simultaneous submissions. Cover letter preferred "but not a form letter, tell me about yourself." Often comments on rejected poems. Pays 1-2 copies. " 'Featured poet' receives more." Reserves right to anthologize poems under Cynic Press; all other rights returned. Several anthologies planned; upcoming themes available for SASE, by e-mail, and in publication. Reviews books of poetry in 10-1,000 words. Poets may send books for review consideration.

Book/Chapbook Needs & How to Submit: Cynic Press occasionally publishes chapbooks. Published *Yellow Flower Girl* by Xu Juan, *Under the Dogwoods* by Joseph Banford, *Ceiling of Mirrors* by Shane Allison, and *13 Ways of Looking at Godzilla* by Michael Hafer. Send $10 reading fee with ms. No guarantee of publication. All checks to Cynic Press. Contest information available by e-mail.

Advice: "Writing is a form of mental illness, spread by books, teachers, and the desire to communicate."

BABYSUE®, P.O. Box 33369, Decatur GA 30033. Established 1985. Website: www.babysue.com. **Editor/Publisher:** Don W. Seven.

Magazine Needs: *babysue* appears twice/year publishing obtuse humor for the extremely open-minded. "We are open to all styles, but prefer short poems." No restrictions. Has published poetry by Edward Mycue, Susan Andrews, and Barry Bishop. *babysue* is 32 pages, offset-printed. "We print prose, poems, and cartoons. We usually accept about 5% of what we receive." Subscription: $16 for 4 issues. Sample: $4.

How to Submit: Accepts previously published poems and simultaneous submissions. Deadlines are March 30 and September 30 of each year. Seldom comments on rejected poems. Responds "immediately, if we are interested." Pays 1 copy. "We do occasionally review other magazines."

Advice: "We have received no awards, but we are very popular on the underground press circuit and sell our magazine all over the world."

THE BALTIMORE REVIEW; BALTIMORE WRITER'S ALLIANCE, P.O. Box 410, Riderwood MD 21139. (410)377-5265. Fax: (410)377-4325. E-mail: hdiehl@bcpl.net. Website: ww.baltimorewriters. org (includes writer's guidelines and distributor information). *Baltimore Review* established 1996, Baltimore Writers' Alliance established 1980. **Editor:** Barbara Diehl.

Magazine Needs: *The Baltimore Review* appears 2 times/year (winter and summer) and showcases the "best short stories and poems of writers from the Baltimore area and beyond." No restrictions on poetry except they do not want to see "sentimental-mushy, loud, or very abstract work; corny humor; poorly crafted or preachy poetry." *Baltimore Review* is 128 pages, 6×9, offset lithography, perfect-bound with 10 pt. CS1 cover, back cover photo only. Publish 20-30 poems/issue. Single copy: $7.95; subscription: $14/year (2 issues). Sample: $8. Make checks payable to Baltimore Writers' Alliance.

How to Submit: Submit up to 5 poems at a time. Accepts simultaneous submissions; no previously published poems. No e-mail or fax submissions. Cover letter preferred. Time between acceptance and publication is up to 6 months. "Poems and short stories are circulated to at least 2 reviewers." Sometimes comments on rejected poems. Responds in up to 4 months. Pays 2 copies, reduced rate for additional copies.

Also Offers: The Baltimore Writers' Alliance is "a vital organization created to foster the professional growth of writers in the metro Baltimore area." The Alliance meets monthly and sponsors workshops, an annual conference, and an annual contest. It also publishes *WordHouse*, a monthly newsletter for members. Write for details.

⬜ **BARBARIC YAWP; BONEWORLD PUBLISHING**, 3700 County Route 24, Russell NY 13684. (315)347-2609. Established 1996. **Editors:** John and Nancy Berbrich.

Magazine Needs: *Barbaric Yawp* appears quarterly, "publishing the best fiction, poetry, and essays available"; encourages beginning writers. "We are not preachers of any particular poetic or literary school. We publish any type of quality material appropriate for our intelligent and wide-awake audience; all types considered, blank, free, found, concrete, traditional rhymed and metered forms. We do not want any pornography, gratuitous violence, or any whining, pissing, or moaning." Has published poetry by Errol Miller, Mark Spitzer, and Gary Jurechka. As a sample the editors selected these lines from "A Good Day" by Virginia Burnett:

> He will step outside/with certainty in his boots./He will listen to his buckets,/and judge the breeze with
> his face./He will turn to us/with a smile/and he will tell me why/this is a good day for sugarin'.

Barbaric Yawp is a 60-page booklet, stapled with 67 lb. cover, line drawings. Receives 1,000 poems/year, accepts about 5%. Press run is 120 for 40 subscribers of which 3 are libraries. Single copy: $4; subscription: $15/year for 4 issues. Sample: $3. Make checks payable to John Berbrich.

How to Submit: Submit up to 5 poems at a time, no more than 50 lines each, and include SASE. All types considered. Accepts previously published poems and simultaneous submissions. Accepts submissions by postal mail only. One-page cover letter preferred, include a short publication history (if available) and a brief bio. No deadlines; reads year round. Time between acceptance and publication is up to 6 months. Often comments on rejected poems. Guidelines available for SASE. Responds in up to 2 months. Pays 1 copy. Acquires one-time rights.

Advice: "We are primarily concerned with work that means something to the author but which is able to transcend the personal into the larger more universal realm. Send whatever is important to you. We will use yin and yang. We really like humor."

Ⓝ ⬤ **BARDSONG PRESS; CELTIC VOICE ANNUAL CONTESTS (Specialized: Celtic-themed)**, P.O. Box 775396, Steamboat Springs CO 80477-5396. Fax: (970)879-2657. E-mail: celts@bards ongpress.com. Website: www.bardsongpress.com (includes book catalog, guidelines and info promoting subjects of interest). Established 1997. **Editor:** Ann Gilpin. Member: SPAN, PMA, CIPA.

Book/Chapbook Needs: At Bardsong Press "our quest is to encourage and celebrate Celtic heritage and culture through poetry, short stories, essays, creative nonfiction, and historical novels. We are looking for poetry that reflects the ageless culture, history, symbolism, mythology, and spirituality that belongs to Celtic heritage. Any style or format is welcome. If it is not Celtic-themed, don't submit it." As a sample we selected these lines from "Dance the Circle on Midwinter Night" by Kathleen Cunningham Guler from *Offerings for the Green Man*:

> And you see their eyes/Brilliant and intense and intoxicating/As your arms and theirs twine across
> each other's shoulders//You turn together face to face/And become one dancer . . .

Bardsong Press publishes 1 paperback/year. Book is usually offset-printed, perfect-bound.

How to Submit: Query first, with a few sample poems and cover letter with brief bio and publication credits. Book mss may not include previously published poems. Responds to queries in 1 month; to mss in 3 months. Pays 25 author's copies (out of a press run of 500). Order sample books by sending $11.95 to Bardsong Press.

Also Offers: "We also sponsor an annual 'Celtic Voice' writing contest which usually includes a poetry category. Entry fee is $10. Small cash award and copies of anthology in which poem is published." Guidelines available for SASE, by e-mail, or on website. Deadline is September 30.

Advice: "Please follow the publisher's guidelines; neatness counts, too."

💲⬤ **BARNWOOD PRESS; BARNWOOD**, P.O. Box 146, Selma IN 47383. (765)288-0149. Fax: (765)285-3765. E-mail: tkoontz@gw.bsu.edu. Website: www.barnwoodpress.org (includes sample poems, guidelines, contact information, bios, catalog, subscription information, links, and editorial policy). Established 1975. **Editor:** Tom Koontz.

Magazine Needs: *Barnwood* appears 3 times/year "to serve poets and readers by publishing excellent poems." Does not want "expressions of prejudice such as racism, sexism." Has published poetry by Bly, Goedicke, and Stafford. As a sample the editor selected these lines from "Prophecy" by Alice Friman:

> I've already told you what I want:/that sloshing sea of you turned in this direction,/my arms reaching into you like jetties./The tides taking care of the rest.

Barnwood is 12 pages, magazine-sized, photocopied and saddle-stapled with paper cover. Receives about 500 poems/year, accepts about 4%. Press run is 200 for 150 subscribers of which 30 are libraries. Single copy: $5; subscription: $15/3 issues. Sample: $5.

How to Submit: Submit 1-3 poems at a time. Accepts simultaneous submissions; no previously published poems. Accepts submissions by postal mail only. "SASE or no response." Reads submissions September 1 through May 31 only. Time between acceptance and publication is 6 months. Poems are circulated to an editorial board. "Submissions screened by assistant editors. Editor makes final decisions." Seldom comments on rejected poems. Responds in 1 month. Pays $25/poem and 2 copies. Acquires one-time rights.

Book/Chapbook Needs & How to Submit: Barnwood Press publishes 1 paperback and 1 chapbook of poetry/year. Has recently published *The White Poems* by Barbara Crooker and *Whatever You Carry* by Stephen Herz. Chapbooks are usually 12-32 pages, size varies, offset printed and saddle-stapled with paper cover and cover art. Query first with a few sample poems and cover letter with brief bio and publication credits. Responds to queries and mss in 1 month. Payment varies. Order sample books or chapbooks by sending price of book plus $2.50.

Advice: "Emphasize imagination, passion, engagement, artistry."

BARROW STREET, P.O. Box 2017, Old Chelsea Station, New York NY 10113-2017. E-mail: info@barrowstreet.org. Website: www.barrowstreet.org (includes guidelines, contact information, archives, contest information, subscription information, links, and editorial policy). Established 1998. **Editors:** Patricia Carlin, Peter Covino, Lois Hirshkowitz, Melissa Hotchkiss.

- Poetry published in *Barrow Street* has been selected for inclusion in *The Best American Poetry 2000, 2001* and *2002*.

Magazine Needs: "*Barrow Street*, a poetry journal appearing twice yearly, is dedicated to publishing new and established poets." Wants "poetry of the highest quality; open to all styles and forms." Has published poetry by Kim Addonizio, Elaine Equi, Brian Henry, Jane Hirshfield, Phillis Levin, and Molly Peacock. *Barrow Street* is 96-120 pages, 6×9, professionally printed and perfect-bound with glossy cardstock cover with color and photography. Receives about 3,000 poems/year, accepts about 3%. Press run is 1,000. Subscription: $15/1 year, $28/2 years, $42/3 years. Sample: $8.

How to Submit: Submit up to 5 poems at a time. Accepts simultaneous submissions (when notified); no previously published poems. Cover letter with brief bio preferred. Reads submissions year round. Poems are circulated to an editorial board. Seldom comments on rejected poems. Publishes theme issues occasionally. Guidelines available for SASE or on website. Responds in approximately 6 months. Always sends prepublication galleys. Pays 2 copies. Acquires first rights.

Book/Chapbook Needs & How to Submit: Barrow Street Press was established in 2002. Submit ms to Barrow Street Press Book Contest. Publication of ms in book form and $1,000 awarded to "best previously unpublished manuscript of poetry in English." Manuscript should be single-spaced and on white 8½×11 paper. Photocopies acceptable. Include 2 title pages and acknowledgement page listing where any poem has appeared in a publication. Author's name, address, and daytime phone should appear on first title page only. Include SASE for notification and $25 entry fee. Make checks payable to Barrow Street. Deadline in 2002 was May 1, judge was Robert Pinsky.

Advice: "Submit your strongest work."

BATHTUB GIN; PATHWISE PRESS; THE BENT, P.O. Box 2392, Bloomington IN 47402. E-mail: charter@bluemarble.net. Website: www.bluemarble.net/~charter/btgin.htm (includes guidelines, contact info, catalog, archives, subscription and patronage info, outlets, links to small presses, and resources). Established 1997. **Editor:** Christopher Harter.

Magazine Needs: *Bathtub Gin*, a biannual appearing in April and October, is "an eclectic aesthetic . . . we want to keep you guessing what is on the next page." Wants poetry that "takes a chance with language or paints a vivid picture with its imagery . . . has the kick of bathtub gin, which can be experimental or a sonnet. No trite rhymes . . . Bukowski wannabes (let the man rest) . . . confessional (nobody cares about your family but you)." Has published poetry by Kell Robertson, Mark Terrill, Carmen Garmain, and Susan Terris. As a sample the editor selected these lines from "The Water Horses" by John Gohmann:

> Whiskey had slit poetry's throat in a barfight/So painting was the only exorcism I could muster/And as I set out my oils and brushes,/Cubism seemed the logical tool/To pulverise two separate nightmares/Into a communal pile of rubble

Bathtub Gin is approximately 60 pages, digest-sized, laser-printed, saddle stapled, 80 lb. cover stock cover, includes "eclectic" art. "We feature a 'News' section where people can list their books, presses, events, etc." Receives about 1,200 poems/year, accepts about 5%. Press run is 250 for 50 subscribers, 60 shelf sales; 10 distributed free to reviewers, other editors, and libraries. Subscription: $8. Sample: $5; foreign orders add $2; back issues: $3.50. Make checks payable to Christopher Harter.

How to Submit: Submit 4-6 poems at a time. Include SASE. Accepts previously published poems and simultaneous submissions. Accepts submissions by postal mail and by e-mail (include ms in text box). "Three to five line bio required if you are accepted for publication . . . if none [given], we make one up." Cover letter preferred. Reads submissions July 1 through September 15 and January 1 through March 15 only. Time between acceptance and publication is up to 4 months. Often comments on rejected poems. Guidelines available for SASE, by e-mail, on website, and in publication. Responds in 2 months. Pays 1 contributor's copy. "We also sell extra copies to contributors at a discount, which they can give away or sell at full price." Reviews books and chapbooks of poetry and spoken word recordings. Poets may send books for review consideration.

Book/Chapbook Needs & How to Submit: Pathwise Press's goal is to publish chapbooks, broadsides, and "whatever else tickles us." Has published *Bone White/Raven Black* by John Gohmann and *You Write Your Life Like Fiction* by Gordon Annand. For co-operative publishing guidelines, send SASE or visit website.

Also Offers: "We also publish a newsletter, *The Bent*, which features reviews. Price is $1."

Advice: "Submission etiquette goes a long way. Always include a cover letter—I receive too many submissions with no cover letter to explain what the poems are for (*Bathtub Gin* or a chapbook or what?). Make sure the poems are neat and without typos; if you don't care about your submission, why should I?"

⬤ BAY AREA POETS COALITION (BAPC); POETALK, P.O. Box 11435, Berkeley CA 94712-2435. E-mail: poetalk@aol.com. Established 1974. Direct submissions to Editorial Committee. Coalition sends quarterly poetry journal, *Poetalk*, to over 300 people. Also publishes an annual anthology (24th edition: 150 pages, out in Spring 2003), giving one page to each member of BAPC (minimum 6 months) who has had work published in *Poetalk* during the previous year.

Magazine Needs: *Poetalk* publishes approximately 70 poets each issue. BAPC has 150 members, 70 subscribers, but *Poetalk* is open to all. No particular genre. Short poems (under 35 lines) are preferred. "Longer poems of outstanding quality accepted. Rhyme must be well done." Membership: $15/year of *Poetalk*, copy of anthology and other privileges; extra outside US. Also offers a $50 patronage, which includes a subscription and anthology for another individual of your choice, and a $25 beneficiary/memorial, which includes membership plus subscription for friend. Subscriptions: $6/year. As a sample the editors selected these lines from "La Poésie Contre Le Pouvoir" by Phyllis Henry-Jordan:

> *Too late to believe in/Merovingian crowns, the wingéd helmet of/the heldentenor, the soprano's corncob/*
> *braids. No place left for satin rivers/of song, for Mozart's graceful lunacy,/his redemptive foolishness*

Poetalk is 36 pages, 5½ × 8½, photocopied, saddle-stapled with heavy card cover. Send SASE with 80¢ postage for a free complimentary copy.

How to Submit: Submit up to 4 poems, typed and single-spaced, with SASE, no more than twice a year. "Manuscripts should be clearly typewritten and include author's name and mailing address on every page. Include e-mail address if you have one." Accepts simultaneous and previously published work, but must be noted. Response time is up to 4 months. Pays 1 copy. All rights revert to authors upon publication.

Also Offers: BAPC holds monthly readings (in Berkeley, CA) and a yearly contest, etc. Send SASE in early September for contest guidelines, or request via e-mail.

Advice: "If you don't want suggested revisions you need to say so clearly in your cover letter or indicate on each poem submitted."

⬤ ◎ BAY WINDOWS (Specialized: gay/lesbian), 631 Tremont St., Boston MA 02118. E-mail: rKikel@baywindows.com. Website: http://BayWindows.com. Established 1983. **Poetry Editor:** Rudy Kikel.

Magazine Needs: *Bay Windows* is a weekly gay and lesbian newspaper published for the New England community, regularly using "short poems of interest to lesbians and gay men. Poetry that is 'experiential' seems to have a good chance with us, but we don't want poetry that just 'tells it like it is.' Our readership doesn't read poetry all the time. A primary consideration is giving pleasure. We'll overlook the poem's (and the poet's) tendency not to be informed by the latest poetic theory, if it does this: pleases. Pleases, in particular, by articulating common gay or lesbian experience, and by doing that with some attention to form. I've found that a lot of our choices were made because of a strong image strand. Humor is always welcome—and hard to provide with craft. Obliquity, obscurity? Probably not for us. We won't presume on our audience." Has published poetry by Robert Cataldo, Bob McCranie, Ron Mohring, Sheryl L. Nelms, Dennis Rhodes, and Stacey Waite. As a sample the editor selected these lines from "A Note to Narcissus" by Eric Norris:

> *Narcissus, I'm your well:/Look deeply into me./And try to love your Self—/Not the thing you see.*

"We try to run four poems each month." Receives about 300 submissions/year, accepts about 1 in 10, has a 3-month backlog. Press run is 13,000 for 700 subscribers of which 15 are libraries. Single copy: 50¢; subscription: $40. Sample: $3.

How to Submit: Submit 3-5 poems at a time, "up to 30 lines are ideal; include short biographical blurb and SASE. No submissions via e-mail, but poets may request info via e-mail." Responds in 3 months. Pays 1 copy "unless you ask for more." Acquires first rights. Editor "often" comments on rejected poems. Reviews books of poetry in about 750 words—"Both single and omnibus reviews (the latter are longer)."

$ ◎ THE BEAR DELUXE (Specialized: nature/ecology), P.O. Box 10342, Portland OR 97296-0342. (503)242-1047. Fax: (503)243-2645. E-mail: bear@teleport.com. Website: www.orlo.org. Established 1993. **Editor:** Tom Webb. **Contact:** poetry editor.

● Note: *The Bear Deluxe* is published by Orlo, a nonprofit organization exploring environmental issues through the creative arts.

Magazine Needs: *The Bear Deluxe*, formerly *Bear Essential*, is a quarterly that "provides a fresh voice amid often strident and polarized environmental discourse. Street-level, non-dogmatic, and solution-oriented, *The Bear Deluxe* presents lively creative discussion to a diverse readership." Wants poetry with "innovative environmental perspectives, not much longer than 50 lines. No rants." Has published poetry by Judith Barrington, Robert Michael Pyle, Mary Winters, Stephen Babcock, Carl Hanni, and Derek Sheffield. As a sample the editor selected these lines from "Smoking" by Leanne Grabel:

> I wonder what I/think's going to/happen if I/breathe only/air.

Bear Deluxe is 60 pages, 11 × 14, newsprint with brown Kraft paper cover, saddle-stapled, with lots of original graphics and b&w photos. Receives about 1200 poems/year, accepts about 20-30. Press run is 19,000 for 750 subscribers of which 20 are libraries, 18,000 distributed free on the streets of the Western US and beyond. Subscription: $16. Sample: $3. Make checks payable to Orlo.

How to Submit: Submit 3-5 poems at a time up to 50 lines each. Accepts previously published poems and simultaneous submissions, "so long as noted." Accepts e-mail submissions, "in body of message. We can't respond to e-mail submissions but do look at them." Poems are reviewed by a committee of 7-9 people. Publishes 1 theme issue/year. Guidelines and a list of upcoming themes available for SASE. Responds in 6 months. Pays $10/poem, 5 copies (more if willing to distribute), and subscription. Acquires first or one-time rights.

$ ◑ ◎ BEAR STAR PRESS; DOROTHY BRUNSMAN POETRY PRIZE (Specialized: regional), 185 Hollow Oak Dr., Cohasset CA 95973. (530)891-0360. Website: www.bearstarpress.com (includes sample poems from books published, guidelines, contest information, bios, and a link to a secure-server for credit card transcations). Established 1996. **Publisher/Editor:** Beth Spencer.

Book/Chapbook Needs: Bear Star Press accepts work by poets from Western and Pacific states ("Those in Mountain or Pacific time zones"). "Bear Star is committed to publishing the best poetry it can attract. Each year it sponsors a contest open to poets from Western and Pacific states, although other eligibility requirements change depending on the composition of our list up to that point. From time to time we add to our list other poets from our target area whose work we admire." Wants "well-crafted poems. No restrictions as to form, subject matter, style or purpose." Has published *Poems in Which* by Joseph Di Prisco, *The Archival Birds* by Melissa Kwaswy, *The Bandsaw Riots* by Arlitia Jones, *Closet Drama* by Kandie St. Germain, and *The Orphan Conducts the Dovehouse Orchestra* by Deborah Woodard. As a sample the publisher selected these lines from "Beeman" by Deborah Woodard:

> Bitten near the mouth, he keeps/completely still under his burred coat./The bees have flung a leopard skin/over the shoulders of a strong man./And then intractable as ivy,/they dedicate themselves to hanging on,

Publishes 1-2 paperbacks and occasionally chapbooks. Books are usually 35-75 pages, size varies, professionally printed, and perfect-bound. Chapbooks are usually $7; full-length collections, $12.

How to Submit: "Poets should enter our annual book competition. Other books are occasionally solicited by publisher, sometimes from among contestants who didn't win." Accepts previously published poems and simultaneous submissions. "Prefer single-spaced manuscripts in plain font such as Times New Roman. SASE required for results. Manuscripts not returned but are recycled." Generally reads submissions September through November. Guidelines available for SASE or on website. Contest entry fee: $16. Time between acceptance and publication is up to 9 months. Poems are circulated to an editorial board. "I occasionally hire a judge. More recently I have taken on the judging with help from poets whose taste I trust." Seldom comments on rejected poems. Responds to queries regarding competitions in 1-2 weeks. Contest winner notified February 1 or before. Contest pays $1,000 and 25 author's copies (out of a press run of up to 750).

Advice: "Send your best work, consider its arrangement. A 'Wow' poem early on keeps me reading."

◐ BELLINGHAM REVIEW; 49TH PARALLEL POETRY AWARD, M.S. 9053, Western Washington University, Bellingham WA 98225. E-mail: bhreview@cc.wwu.edu. Website: www.wwu.edu/~bhreview/ (includes submissions and contest guidelines, names of editors and staff, and selections from recent issue). Established 1975. **Editor:** Brenda Miller. **Contact:** Poetry Editor.

Magazine Needs: *Bellingham Review* appears twice/year. "We want well-crafted poetry but are open to all styles," no specifications as to form. Accepts poetry written by children. Has published poetry by David Shields, Tess Gallagher, Gary Soto, Jane Hirshfield, Albert Goldbarth, R.T. Smith, and Rebecca McClanahan. As a sample the editor selected these lines from "Sitting at Dusk in the Back Yard After the Mondrian Retrospective" by Charles Wright:

> Form imposes, structure allows—/the slow destruction of form/So as to bring it back resheveled, reorganized,/Is the hard heart of the enterprise./Under its camouflage,/The light, relentless shill and cross-dresser, pools and deals./Inside its short skin, the darkness burns.

Bellingham Review is 6×9, perfect-bound, with art and glossy cover. Each issue has about 60 pages of poetry. Circulation is 1,500 with 500 subscriptions. Subscription: $14/year, $27/2 years. Sample: $5. Make checks payable to The Western Foundation/*Bellingham Review*.

How to Submit: Submit 3-5 poems at a time with SASE. Accepts simultaneous submissions with notification. No fax or e-mail submissions. Reads submissions October 1 through February 1 only. Guidelines available for SASE or on website. Responds in 2 months. Pays 1 copy, a year's subscription plus monetary payment (if funding allows). Acquires first North American serial rights.

Also Offers: The 49th Parallel Poetry Award, established in 1983, awards a $1,000 first prize, $300 second prize and $200 third prize, plus a year's subscription to the *Bellingham Review*. Submissions must be unpublished and may be entered in other contests. Guidelines available for SASE or website. Most recent award winner was Don Judson (2001). Judge was Davin Lee. Winners will be announced in summer.

◐ BELLOWING ARK; BELLOWING ARK PRESS, P.O. Box 55564, Shoreline WA 98155. (206)440-0791. Established 1984. **Editor:** Robert R. Ward.

Magazine Needs: *Bellowing Ark* is a bimonthly literary tabloid that "publishes only poetry which demonstrates in some way the proposition that existence has meaning or, to put it another way, that life is worth living. We have no strictures as to length, form or style; only that the work we publish is to our judgment life-affirming." Does not want "academic poetry, in any of its manifold forms." Has published poetry by Irene Culver, Muriel Karr, Esther Cameron, Ute Carbone, and Jacqueline Hill. *Bellowing Ark* is 32 pages, tabloid-sized, printed on electrobright stock with b&w photos and line drawings. Circulation is 1,000, of which 275 are subscriptions and 500 are sold on newsstands. Subscription: $15/year. Sample: $3.

How to Submit: Submit 3-6 poems at a time. "Absolutely *no* simultaneous submissions." No fax or e-mail submissions. Responds to submissions in up to 12 weeks and publishes within the next 1 or 2 issues. Occasionally will criticize a ms if it seems to "display potential to become the kind of work we want." Sometimes sends prepublication galleys. Pays 2 copies. Reviews books of poetry. Send books for review consideration.

Book/Chapbook Needs & How to Submit: Bellowing Ark Press publishes collections of poetry by *invitation only*.

◐ ◎ BELL'S LETTERS POET (Specialized: subscribers), P.O. Box 2187, Gulfport MS 39505-2187. E-mail: jimbelpoet@aol.com. Established 1956. **Publisher/Editor:** Jim Bell.

Magazine Needs: *Bell's Letters Poet* is a quarterly which you must buy ($5.50/issue, $22 subscription) to be included. "Many say they stop everything the day it arrives," and judging by the many letters from readers, that seems to be the case. Though there is no payment for poetry accepted, many patrons send cash awards to the poets whose work they especially like. Poems are "four to 20 lines in good taste." Accepts poetry written by subscribers' children, ages 8-12. Has published poetry by Eve J. Blohm, Kalman Gayler, Patrick Flavin, and Raymond J. Flory. As a sample the editor selected these lines from "The Poet" by C. David Hay:

> Although an artist I'll never be/I accept the fate of those like me,/Painting visions in black and white—/ God gives to us the will to write.

Bell's Letters Poet is about 60 pages, digest-sized, photocopied on plain bond paper (including cover) and saddle-stapled. Sample (including guidelines): $5. "Send a poem (20 lines or under, in good taste) with your sample order and we will publish in our next issue."

How to Submit: Submit 4 poems at a time. No simultaneous submissions. Accepts previously published poems "if cleared by author with prior publisher." Accepts submissions by regular mail only. Accepted poems by subscribers go immediately into the next issue. Guidelines available for SASE and in publication. Deadline for poetry submissions is 2 months prior to publication. Reviews books of poetry by subscribers in "one abbreviated

paragraph." "The Ratings" is a competition in each issue. Readers are asked to vote on their favorite poems, and the "Top 40" are announced in the next issue, along with awards sent to the poets by patrons. *Bell's Letters Poet* also features a telephone and e-mail exchange among poets, a birth-date listing, and a profile of its poets.
Advice: "Tired of seeing no bylines this year? Subscription guarantees a byline in each issue."

THE BELOIT POETRY JOURNAL; CHAD WALSH POETRY PRIZE, 24 Berry Cove Rd., Lamoine ME 04605-4617. (207)667-5598. E-mail: sharkey@maine.edu (for information only). Website: www.bpj.org (includes contact information, biographical notes, contest and subscription information, links, editorial policy, guidelines, magazine history, sample poems, a 52-year index, and table of contents of recent issues). Established 1950. **Editor:** Marion K. Stocking.
● Poetry published in *The Beloit Poetry Journal* has also been included in *The Best American Poetry* (1994, 1996, and 2000) and *Pushcart Prize* anthologies.
Magazine Needs: *The Beloit Poetry Journal* is a well-known, long-standing quarterly of quality poetry and reviews. "We publish the best poems we receive, without bias as to length, school, subject, or form. It is our hope to discover the growing tip of poetry and to introduce new poets alongside established writers. We publish occasional chapbooks to diversify our offerings. These are almost never the work of one poet." Wants "fresh, imaginative poetry, with a distinctive voice. We tend to prefer poems that make the reader share an experience rather than just read about it, and these we keep for up to four months, circulating them among our readers, and continuing to winnow for the best. At the quarterly meetings of the Editorial Board we read aloud all the surviving poems and put together an issue of the best we have." Has published poetry by Bei Dao, A.E. Stallings, Glori Simmons, and Janet Holmes. As a sample the editor selected the poem "Song Beside a Sippy Cup" by Jenny Factor:
> In the never truly ever/truly dark dark night, ever/blinds-zipped, slat-cut,/dark-parked light,/you (late) touch my toes./with your broad flat own/horny-nailed cold toes./clock-tock, wake-shock.
The Beloit Poetry Journal averages 48 pages, 6×9, saddle-stapled, and attractively printed with tasteful art on the card cover. Circulation is 1,100 for 724 subscribers of which 227 are libraries. Subscription: individuals $18/year, institutions $23/year. Sample (including guidelines): $5. Guidelines without sample available for SASE.
How to Submit: Submit any time, without query, any legible form. "No previously published poems or simultaneous submissions. Any length of ms, but most poets send what will go in a business envelope for one stamp. Don't send your life's work." No e-mail submissions. Pays 3 copies. Acquires first serial rights. Editor reviews books by and about poets in an average of 500 words, usually single format. Send books for review consideration.
Also Offers: The journal awards the Chad Walsh Poetry Prize ($3,000 in 2001) to a poem or group of poems published in the calendar year. "Every poem published in 2003 will be considered for the 2003 prize."
Advice: "We are always watching for new poets, fresh insights, live forms and language."

$ BIBLE ADVOCATE (Specialized: religious), P.O. Box 33677, Denver CO 80233. E-mail: bibleadvocate@cog7.org. Website: www.cog7.org/BA (includes writer's guidelines). Established 1863. **Associate Editor:** Sherri Langton.
Magazine Needs: *Bible Advocate*, published 10 times/year, features "Christian content—to advocate the Bible and represent the church." Wants "free verse, some traditional; 5-20 lines, with Christian/Bible themes." Does not want "avant garde poetry." *Bible Advocate* is 24 pages, 8¾×11⅞ with most poetry set up with 4-color art. Receives about 30-50 poems/year, accepts about 10-20. Press run varies for 13,500 subscribers with all distributed free.
How to Submit: Submit no more than 5 poems at a time, 5-20 lines each. Accepts previously published poems (with notification) and simultaneous submissions. Accepts e-mail submissions with text included in body of message; no attachments. "No fax or handwritten submissions, please." Cover letter preferred. Time between acceptance and publication is up to 12 months. "I read them first and reject those that won't work for us. I send good ones to editor for approval." Seldom comments on rejected poems. Publishes theme issues. Guidelines and upcoming themes available for SASE and on website. Responds in 2 months. Pays $20 and 2 contributor's copies. Acquires first, reprint, electronic, and one-time rights.
Advice: "Avoid trite, or forced rhyming. Be aware of the magazine's doctrinal views (send for doctrinal beliefs booklet)."

BIBLIOPHILOS (Specialized: bilingual/foreign language, ethnic/nationality, political, social issues, writing), 200 Security Building, Fairmont WV 26554. (304)366-8107. Established 1981. **Editor:** Gerald J. Bobango.
Magazine Needs: "*Bibliophilos* is a quarterly academic journal, for the literati, illuminati, amantes artium, and those who love animals; scholastically oriented, for the liberal arts. Topics include fiction and nonfiction; literature and criticism, history, art, music, theology, philosophy, natural history, educational

theory, contemporary issues and politics, sociology, and economics. Published in English, French, German, Romanian." Wants "traditional forms, formalism, structure, rhyme; also blank verse. Aim for concrete visual imagery, either in words or on the page. No inspirational verse, or anything that Ann Landers or Erma Bombeck would publish." Accepts poetry written by children, ages 10 and up. Has published poetry by Belle Randall, Jack Lloyd Packard, and Edward Locke. As a sample the editor selected these lines from "Twists of Truth" by Edward Locke:

> *And so he stood upon his windowsill/In that calm afternoon of Mobius May,/And with two earnest and*
> *flighty winds,/Both bird and man as brothers flew away—*

Bibliophilos is 68 pages, 5½×8, laser photography printed and saddle-stapled with light card, includes clip art, ads. Receives about 100 poems/year, accepts about 33%. Press run is 200 for 150 subscribers. Subscription: $18/year, $35/2 years. Sample: $5.25. Make checks payable to *The Bibliophile*. West Virginia residents please add 6% sales tax.

How to Submit: Closed to unsolicited submissions. Query first with SASE and $5.25 for sample and guidelines. Then, if invited, submit 3-5 poems at a time. Accepts previously published poems and simultaneous submissions. Cover letter with brief bio preferred. No submissions read during 2002. Time between acceptance and publication is up to 6 months. Often comments on rejected poems. Guidelines available for SASE. Responds in 2 weeks. Pays 2 copies "and money, in some cases." Acquires first North American serial rights. Staff reviews books and chapbooks of poetry in 750-1,000 words, single book format. Send books for review consideration.

Also Offers: Sponsors poetry contest. Send SASE for rules. 1st Prize $25 plus publication.

Advice: "Query, get a sample issue of our poetry number(s) and read it, and read our listing and our interests first. Do not send unsolicited material. Once we've accepted something for publication from you, do not pester us with letters asking when it will appear. Once it appears, do not assume you have an open forum to send material at once, without asking."

BILINGUAL REVIEW PRESS; BILINGUAL REVIEW/REVISTA BILINGÜE (Specialized: ethnic/Hispanic, bilingual/Spanish), Hispanic Research Center, Arizona State University, Box 872702, Tempe AZ 85287-2702. (480)965-3867. Journal established 1974, press in 1976. **Managing Editor:** Karen Van Hooft.

Magazine Needs: "We are a small press publisher of U.S. Hispanic creative literature and of a journal containing poetry and short fiction in addition to scholarship." *Bilingual Review/Revista Billingüe,* published 3 times/year, contains some poetry in most issues. "We publish poetry by and/or about U.S. Hispanics and U.S. Hispanic themes. We do not publish translations in our journal or literature about the experiences of Anglo-Americans in Latin America. We have published a couple of poetry volumes in bilingual format (Spanish/English) of important Mexican poets." Has published poetry by Alberto Ríos, Martín Espada, Judith Ortiz Cofer, and Marjorie Agosín. The journal is 96 pages, 7×10, offset-printed and flat-spined, with 2-color cover. Accepts less than 10% of hundreds of submissions received each year. Press run is 1,000 for 700 subscribers. Subscriptions: $23 for individuals, $38 for institutions. Sample: $7 individuals/$12 institutions.

How to Submit: Submit "two copies, including ribbon original if possible, with loose stamps for return postage." Cover letter required. Pays 2 copies. Acquires all rights. Reviews books of US Hispanic literature only. Send books, Attn: Editor, for review consideration.

$ ☑ ◎ BIRCH BROOK PRESS (Specialized: nature, sports/recreation), P.O. Box 81, Delhi NY 13753. (212)353-3326 (messages only). Website: www.birchbrookpress.com ("tells how we produce our books, lists media coverage, and our latest titles"). Established 1982. **Contact:** Tom Tolnay. Member: American Academy of Poets, Small Press Center, American Typefounders Fellowship.

Book/Chapbook Needs: Birch Brook "is a letterpress book printer/typesetter/designer that uses monies from these activities to publish several titles of its own each year with cultural and literary interest." Specializes in literary work, flyfishing, baseball. Has published *Uncertain Relations* by Joel Chace; *Waiting On Pentecost* by Tom Smith; *Walking the Perimeters of the Plate Glass Window Factory* by Jared Smith; *Repercussions* by Marcus Rome; and *Risking the Wind* by Warren Carrier. Publishes 4-6 paperbacks and/or hardbacks per year. The press specializes "mostly in anthologies with specific subject matter. Birch Brook Press occasionally publishes one or two books annually by individuals with high-quality literary work on a co-op basis." Books are "handset letterpress editions printed in our own shop."

How to Submit: Query first with sample poems or send entire ms. "Must include SASE with submissions." Occasionally comments on rejected poems. Authors may obtain sample books by sending SASE for catalog. Pays from $5-20 for publication in anthology.

Advice: "Send your best work, and see other Birch Brook Press books."

THE BITTER OLEANDER; FRANCES LOCKE MEMORIAL AWARD, 4983 Tall Oaks Dr., Fayetteville NY 13066-9776. (315)637-3047. Fax: (315)637-5056. E-mail: bones44@ix.netcom.com. Website: www.bitteroleander.com (includes guidelines, contact info, links, editorial policy, and subscription and contest info). Established 1974. **Editor/Publisher:** Paul B. Roth.

● Poetry published in *The Bitter Oleander* has been included in *The Best American Poetry 1999*.

Magazine Needs: *The Bitter Oleander* appears biannually in April and October, publishing "imaginative poetry; poetry in translation; serious language." Wants "highly imaginative poetry whose language is serious. We prefer short poems of no more than 25 lines. We are not interested in very long poems and prefer not to receive poems about the common values and protests of society." Accepts translations. Has published poetry by Robert Bly, Alan Britt, Duane Locke, Silvia Scheibli, Anthony Seidman, and Charles Wright. *The Bitter Oleander* is 128 pages, digest-sized, offset-printed, perfect-bound with glossy 4-color cover, cover art, ads. Receives about 6,000 poems/year, accepts about 2%. Press run is 1,500; 1,000 shelf sales. Single copy: $8; subscription: $15. Make checks payable to Bitter Oleander Press.

How to Submit: Submit up to 8 poems at a time with name and address on each page. No previously published poems or simultaneous submissions. No e-mail submissions. Cover letter preferred. Does not read mss during July. Time between acceptance and publication is 6 months. Guidelines available for SASE and on website. "All poems are read by the editor only and all decisions are made by this editor." Often comments on rejected poems. Responds within a month. Pays 1 copy.

Also Offers: Sponsors the Frances Locke Memorial Award, awarding $1,000 and publication. Submit any number of poems. Entry fee: $10/5 poems, $2 each additional poem. Open to submissions March 15 through June 15 only.

Advice: "We simply want poetry that is imaginative and serious in its performance of language. So much flat-line poetry is written today that anyone reading one magazine or another cannot tell the difference."

BLACK BEAR PUBLICATIONS; BLACK BEAR REVIEW (Specialized: social issues), 1916 Lincoln St., Croydon PA 19021-8026. E-mail: BBReview@earthlink.net. Website: http://BlackBearR eview.com (includes recent issues, a list of upcoming themes, complete guidelines, links, and current needs). Established 1984. **Poetry and Art Editor:** Ave Jeanne. **Business Manager:** Ron Zettlemoyer.

Magazine Needs: *Black Bear Review* is a semiannual international literary and fine arts magazine in print and online. "We like well-crafted poetry that mirrors real life—void of camouflage. We seek energetic poetry, avant-garde, free verse and haiku which relate to the world today. We seldom publish the beginner. No traditional poetry is used. The underlying theme of *Black Bear Publications* is social and political, but the review is interested also in environmental, war/peace, ecological, human rights, poverty, discrimination, apathy, and minorities themes. We would like to receive more ideas on mental health, life styles, and current political topics." Has recently published poetry by Phillip Hyams, Peter Connors, John Grey, Alan Catlin, and Carlos Martinez. As a sample the editor selected these lines from "Among the Poor" by Juan Sequeira:

> I was born among the poor/who carry hope in melancholic eyes/dreams in furrowed shoulders/They
> rise to the alarm of dawn/leave the nests of the families/for the chilled streets, wounded fields/assembly
> lines suffocating air . . .

Black Bear Review is 64 pages, digest-sized, perfect-bound, offset from typed copy on white stock, with line drawings, collages, and woodcuts. Circulation is 500 for 300 subscribers of which 15 are libraries. Subscription: $12, $18 overseas. Sample: $6; back copies when available are $5 (overseas add $3/copy). Make checks payable to Ron Zettlemoyer.

How to Submit: Submit 5 poems at a time by e-mail only. "E-mail submissions are answered within a week, use Arial font. Include snail mail address. No attached files please." Simultaneous submissions are not considered. Time between acceptance and publication is 6 months. Guidelines available for SASE or on website. Pays 1 copy. Acquires first North American serial rights and electronic rights, "as work may appear on our website."

Book/Chapbook Needs & How to Submit: Publishes 2 chapbooks/year. "Publication is now on a subsidy basis." Chapbook series requires a **reading fee of $5**, complete ms, and cover letter sent via snail mail. Guidelines available for SASE. For book publication, they require that "*Black Bear Publications* has published the poet and is familiar with his/her work." Author receives one-half print run. Recently published *Tracers* by Gerald Wheeler.

Also Offers: "Our yearly poetry competition offers cash awards to poets." Deadline: November 30. Guidelines available for SASE. "Our website is designed and maintained by Ave Jeanne and is updated regularly to meet the diverse needs of our readers. *Bear Facts* is our online newsletter, which readers can subscribe to for free. Details can be found on website. Mark Zettlemoyer, *Bear Facts* Editor MarkZett@earthlink.net."

Advice: "We appreciate a friendly, brief cover letter. All submissions are handled with objectivity and timeliness. Keep e-mail submissions professional. We are always interested in aiding those who support small press. We frequently suggest poets keep up with the current edition of *Poet's Market*. We make an effort to keep our readers informed and on top of the small press scene. Camera-ready ads are printed free of charge as a support to small press publishers. We also run an ad page on the Internet, 'InterActions,' for all interested poets and writers to advertise. We do suggest poets and artists read issues before submitting to absorb the flavor and spirit of our publication. Send your best!" "Visit our applauded website. *Black Bear* will continue to print in our paperback format as well as art and poems online. We are financially supported by our poets, artists, readers, and editors."

N Ø BLACK HAT PRESS, P.O. Box 12, Goodhue MN 55027. (651)923-4590. Established 1982. **Poetry Editor/Publisher:** Beverly Voldseth.

● Black Hat Press is no longer publishing *Rag Mag*.

Book/Chapbook Needs & How to Submit: Black Hat Press is *not* considering chapbooks or book-length mss of any kind until further notice. Has published *Boom Town* by Diane Glancy and *Crawling Out the Window* (a book of prose poems) by Tom Hennen.

N $ Ø © THE BLACK LILY (Specialized: high fantasy, Medieval; Russian and Swedish language submissions), 8444 Cypress Circle, Sarasota FL 34243-2006. E-mail: pohhtheromantic@yaho o.com or ellie149@hotmail.com. Website: www.blacklily.org (includes excerpts, guidelines, staff guides, print version of new and past issue available to subscribers). Established 1996. **Chief Editor:** Vincent Kuklewski.

Magazine Needs: *The Black Lily* appears quarterly publishing "high fantasy with dragons, elves, goblins, magic. Medieval and Renaissance with crusaders, longships, castles, tourneys. Both free form and historical forms ranging from Anglo-Saxon to sonnets to haiku. Absolutely no work, fantasy or Medieval, with post-1600 A.D. subjects or elements." Recently published poetry by Susan Spilecki, Nancy Bennett, Barbara Johnson-Haddad, Elizabeth Enaid, and Ralph Robinson. As a sample the editor selected these lines from "King Stephen's Prayer" by Susan Spilecki:

> *May God and my sister Maude forgive me/All my sins: this seige, this long carnage/Burning across England, the green glade singed/To brown, the wheat unharvested,/The boys in buckskin and muddy wool flinging/Themselves onto swords for their King's sake.*

The Black Lily is 64 pages, magazine-sized, saddle-stapled, b&w cardstock cover, with "quite a lot" of art and graphics, some ads. (The print edition also appears online.) Receives about 180-200 poems/year, accepts about 55%. Publishes about 16-20 poems/issue. Press run is 225 for 45 subscribers, 110 shelf sales. Single copy: $5; subscription: $16. Sample: $5. Make checks payable to Vincent Kuklewski.

How to Submit: Submit 8 poems at a time maximum. Line length for poetry is 200 maximum. Accepts previously published poems; no simultaneous submissions. "Previously published work cannot have been published within the past 3 years and must be identified as previously published and in which publications." Accepts e-mail submissions. Cover letter is required. Include SASE. Reads submissions January 1 to November 20 **only**. Time between acceptance and publication is 1-4 months. "Chief editor is responsible for reading and accepting poetry." Often comments on rejected poems. Regularly publishes theme issues. A list of upcoming themes and guidelines available for SASE or by e-mail. Responds in up to 2 months. Pays $1-10 and 1 contributor's copy. Acquires all rights; rights are returned "upon publication unless otherwise agreed upon for reprint option."

Also Offers: "Twice per year we publish special theme issues in addition to regular issue. Twice a year we have a poetry contest with $20 prize."

Advice: "Never, ever send us poetry with post-1600 A.D. themes, subjects, elements. The chief editor loves forests, castles, elves, swords, ships, dragons, dryads, and nymphs. He is a student of Medieval studies of Old English and Old Icelandic. Be nice to him in this regard. *The Black Lily* is sent to five countries. Will accept submissions in Russian and Swedish."

N Ø BLACK SPARROW PRESS, 24 10th St., Santa Rosa CA 95401. E-mail: books@blacksparrowp ress.com. Website: www.blacksparrowpress.com/ (includes catalog, authors' bios, and ordering info). Established 1966.

● Black Sparrow Press is the distinguished publisher of American avant-garde and experimental poetry, prose, and literary criticism. Black Sparrow poets include Charles Bukowski, Diane Wakoski, Andrei Codrescu, Lyn Lifshin, Wanda Coleman, and Laura Chester.

Ø BLACK SPRING PRESS, 63-89 Saunders, 6G, Rego Park NY 11374. E-mail: stjulian66@juno.com. Established 1997. **Editor/Publisher:** John Gallo.

Book/Chapbook Needs: Black Spring Press wants "strong, emotional writing that isn't afraid to take risks." Publishes broadside series called Mezzotints for individual poets. Has published *Bloody and Living* by Ed Galing, *Naked Brunch* by Laura Joy Lustig, *Scrape That Violin More Darkly Then Hover Like Smoke in the Air* by John Gallo, and *Suck Out the Marrow of Life* by Linda La Porte. Chapbooks are usually 20-40 pages, 5½×8½, photocopied, and saddle-stapled with card stock cover. Sample: $5. Responds to mss in up to 1 month. Pays 30 author's copies (out of a press run of 100).

How to Submit: Submit up to 6 poems, "do not send the entire manuscript." Accepts submissions by e-mail (include in text box or attach) and by postal mail. Guidelines and upcoming themes available for SASE and by e-mail.

Also Offers: "Co-op publishing is offered. Write for details." Black Spring Press may also publish a yearly anthology to replace its now defunct journal, *Black Spring Review*. Contact for more information.

Advice: "Write from deep within you. Find your own voice. Bukowski already did Bukowski and Ginsberg already did Ginsberg. Black Spring Press respects the Beat tradition but is not interested in resurrecting a by-gone era. It's the 21st century now. Time to move forward. Also, take whatever you may have learned in college literature courses or writing workshops and ignore it. Good writing does not necessarily come out of the universities. Keep your ego in check. There are an awful lot of people writing out there, and a small press will not make you rich and famous beyond your wildest dreams. However small presses have been a nice stepping stone to bigger and better things. Just don't think I am going to get you the Pulitzer prize. Remember what small in 'small press' means. We feel it should be a network of independent writers and artists to share ideas and their work since none of the large houses would ever look our way unless there's a million dollars to be made."

BLACK TIE PRESS, P.O. Box 440004, Houston TX 77244-0004. Fax: (713)789-5119. Established 1986. **Publisher and Editor:** Peter Gravis.

Book/Chapbook Needs: "Black Tie Press is committed to publishing innovative, distinctive, and engaging writing. We publish books; we are not a magazine or literary journal. We are not like the major Eastern presses, university presses, or other small presses in poetic disposition. To get a feel for our publishing attitude, we urge you to buy one or more of our publications before submitting. Prefer the exotic, the surreal, the sensual—work that provokes, shocks . . . work that continues to resonate long after being read. Surprise us." Does not want "rhyme or fixed forms, unless remarkably well done. No nature, animal, religious, or pet themes." Has published poetry by Steve Wilson, Guy Beining, Laura Ryder, Donald Rawley, Harry Burrus, and Jenny Kelly. As a sample the editor selected these lines from "Late November, Los Angeles" in *Steaming* by Donald Rawley:

> In this rubbed dusk,/the false fall sky/silvers itself/into a pale, nude witch,/a sun of mother's cologne,/
> and a neck of distanced chill

Sample: $8.

How to Submit: "We have work we want to publish, hence, unsolicited material is not encouraged. However, we will read and consider material from committed, serious writers as time permits. Query with four sample poems. Write, do not call about material. No reply without SASE." Cover letter with bio preferred. Responds in 6 weeks. Always sends prepublication galleys. Author receives percent of press run.

Advice: "Too many writers are only interested in getting published and not interested in reading or supporting good writing. Black Tie hesitates to endorse a writer who does not, in turn, promote and patronize (by actual purchases) small press publications. Once Black Tie publishes a writer, we intend to remain with that artist."

$ BLACK WARRIOR REVIEW; WARRIOR WEB, P.O. Box 862936, Tuscaloosa AL 35486-0027. (205)348-4518. E-mail: bwr@ua.edu. Website: http://webdelsol.com/bwr (includes guidelines, bios, editorial policy, links, poems, a comprehensive index, contact and subscription information). Established 1974. **Poetry Editor:** Don Gilliland. **Editor:** Ander Monson.

• Poetry published in *Black Warrior Review* has been included in the 1997, 1999, and 2000 volumes of *The Best American Poetry* and *Pushcart Prize* anthologies.

Magazine Needs: *Black Warrior Review* is a biannual review appearing in March and October. Has published poetry by W.S. Merwin, Anne Carson, Mark Doty, Jane Miller, Medbh McGuckian, Jane Houlihan, and C.D. Wright. As a sample the editor selected these lines from "Some Kind of Osiris" by Reginald Shepherd:

> fail to reply, my fingers filled/with leaves, mouth with remains/of leaves. The day skilled in italics/
> declines my nouns of wait and sleep

Black Warrior Review is 200 pages, 6×9. Press run is 2,000. Subscription: $14/year, $25/2 years, $30/3 years. Sample: $8. Make checks payable to the University of Alabama.

How to Submit: Submit 3-6 poems at a time. Accepts simultaneous submissions if noted. No electronic submissions. Responds in 4 months. Pays $25-50 and year subscription. Acquires first rights. Reviews books of poetry in single or multi-book format. Poets may send books for review consideration.

Also Offers: Awards one $500 prize annually to a poet whose work appeared in either the fall or spring issue. Also offers *Warrior Web*, the online publishing arm of Black Warrior Review. Features web-exclusive poetry, fiction, reviews, artwork, and chapbooks. For more information, contact the editor at bwr@us.edu.

Advice: "We solicit a nationally-known poet for a chapbook section. The remainder of the issue is chosen from unsolicited submissions. Many of our poets have substantial publication credits, but our decision is based simply on the quality of the work submitted."

N: ◙ BLEEDING HEARTS MAGAZINE; BLEEDING HEARTS ANTHOLOGY, P.O. Box 882, Delhi CA 95315. E-mail: spector-intelligence@aaemail.com. Established 1996. **Poetry Editor:** Spector 6.
Magazine Needs: *Bleeding Hearts Magazine* appears quarterly and is "a free-for-all blitz of the surreal and the all too real; a mesh of art, insanity, fiction, and poetry. Each issue also features interviews, contests, and giveaways. All submissions considered. No rants or juvenile angst." Recently published poetry by Ben Pleasants, M. Schepler, Angelique X, Jonathyn Sinistre, Promethius Twig, and Charlotte Shai. As a sample the editor selected these lines from "Visions in The Mist" by Promethius Twig:

> *He gives her love with a twist of the hip and touches the Gods under/The crack of her whip. She trusts*
> *no one and no words spoken,/And even less when the day's light is upon them. She feeds from/Darkness*
> *and lets it fill her like he does tonight gently on top of her./All three are made of ice and scars, held*
> *together carefully by their lies/And the aligning stars.*

Bleeding Hearts Magazine is 64 pages, magazine-sized, digital output, saddle-stapled, full color cover, with heavy, graphically intense content, with ads. Receives about 200 poems/year, accepts about 25%. Publishes about 20 poems/issue. Press run is 500 for 150 subscribers of which 20 are libraries, 200 shelf sales; 50 distributed free to various sources. Single copy: $5 plus s&h; subscription: $20 plus s&h. Sample: $4 plus s&h. Make checks payable to C.D. Wofford.
How to Submit: Submit 5 poems at a time maximum. Line length for poetry is 100 maximum. Accepts previously published poems and simultaneous submissions. Accepts e-mail and disk submissions; no fax submissions. Cover letter is preferred. "Include SASE if you wish your submissions returned." Reads submissions year round. Submit seasonal poems 4 months in advance. Time between acceptance and publication is usually months. "All poems are read by the poetry editor. Those under consideration are then reviewed by the poetry staff and a final decision is made." Never comments on rejected poems. "Should poet request criticism, a $5 charge/piece is applicable." Guidelines available in magazine, for SASE, or by e-mail. Responds in up to 6 weeks. Pays 1 contributor's copy. Acquires one-time rights. Reviews books and chapbooks of poetry in 360-400 words. Poets may send books/chapbooks for review consideration to *Bleeding Hearts*, Attn: Spector 6.
Book/Chapbook Needs & How to Submit: Bleeding Hearts Publications/B.H.E. publishes 1 anthology/ year, oversize chapbook format. Anthologies are usually 24 pages, digital output, saddle-stapled, 4-color cover, with heavy art/graphics. "Our anthologies are only created with material that we have previously published in *Bleeding Hearts Magazine*—material which stands over the top." Pays 1 contributor's copy (out of a press run of 100). Order sample anthologies by sending $25 to C.D. Wofford.
Advice: "This journal is designed to be a platform for art; as such, the editorial role at Bleeding Heart is solely to place deserving works, regardless of style or content, where they will hopefully be seen and appreciated. And we like cheese that is smooth and creamy."

◎ BLIND BEGGAR PRESS; LAMPLIGHT EDITIONS; NEW RAIN (Specialized: ethnic, anthology, children), P.O. Box 437, Williamsbridge Station, Bronx NY 10467. Phone/fax: (914)683-6792. Established 1976. **Literary Editor:** Gary Johnston. **Business Manager:** C.D. Grant.
Book/Chapbook Needs: Publishes work "relevant to Black and Third World people, especially women." *New Rain* is an annual anthology of such work. Wants to see "quality work that shows a concern for the human condition and the condition of the world—art for people's sake." Has published work by Judy D. Simmons, A.H. Reynolds, Mariah Britton, Kurt Lampkin, Rashidah Ismaili, Jose L. Garza, and Carletta Wilson. *New Rain* is a 60- to 200-page book, digest-sized, finely printed, saddle-stapled or perfect-bound, with simple art, card covers. Sample: $5. Also publishes about 3 collections of poetry by individuals each year, 60-100 pages, flat-spined paperback, glossy, color cover, good printing on good paper. Sample: $5.95.
How to Submit: For either the anthology or book publication, first send sample of 5-10 poems with cover letter including biographical background, philosophy, and poetic principles. Considers simultaneous submissions. Reads submissions January 15 through September 1 only. Responds to queries in 4 weeks, to submissions in 3 months. Pays copies (the number depending on the print run). Acquires all rights. Returns them "unconditionally." Willing to work out individual terms for subsidy publication. Catalog available for SASE.
Also Offers: Lamplight Editions is a subsidiary that publishes "educational materials such as children's books, manuals, greeting cards with educational material in them, etc."

OPENNESS TO SUBMISSIONS: ❏ beginners; ◢ beginners and experienced;
◖ mostly experienced, few beginners; ◎ specialized; ◿ closed to all submissions.

◐ **THE BLIND MAN'S RAINBOW**, P.O. Box 1557, Erie PA 16507-0557. E-mail: editor@bmrpoetry. com. Website: www.bmrpoetry.com (includes writer's guidelines, subscription information, poets, and covers from latest issues). Established 1993. **Editor:** Melody Sherosky.

Magazine Needs: *Blind Man's Rainbow* is a quarterly publication "whose focus is to create a diverse collection of quality poetry and art." Wants "all forms of poetry (Beat, rhyme, free verse, haiku, etc.), though excessively long poems are less likely to be accepted. All subject matter accepted." Does not want "anything excessively sexual or violent." Accepts poetry written by children though they are held to the same standards as adults. As a sample the editor selected these lines from "Some Kids Are Bowling Balls" by Kathy Kieth:

> Show them an alley and they'll head straight/down it: straight-arrow for the pins: no time//wasted on
> curveballs or sidetracks, no sir: all/business, then wash your hands, resin up move

The Blind Man's Rainbow is 20-24 pages, 8½×11, photocopied and side-stapled, paper cover with art, line drawings inside. Receives about 500 submissions a month. Subscription: $10 US, $14 foreign. Sample: $3 US, $4 foreign. Make checks payable to Melody Sherosky.

How to Submit: Submit 2-10 poems at a time with name and address on each poem. Include SASE. Accepts previously published poems and simultaneous submissions, "but it is nice to let us know." Accepts submissions on disk and by post only; no e-mail. Cover letter preferred. "Submissions only returned if requested and with adequate postage." Time between acceptance and publication is up to 6 months. Often comments on rejected poems. Guidelines available for SASE, by e-mail or on website. Responds in 3 months. Pays 1 copy. Acquires one-time rights.

◐ ◎ **BLUE COLLAR REVIEW; PARTISAN PRESS; WORKING PEOPLE'S POETRY COMPETITION (Specialized: political, social issues, women/feminism, working class)**, P.O. Box 11417, Norfolk VA 23517. E-mail: redart@infi.net. Website: www.angelfire.com/va/bcr (includes mission statement, sample poetry, rate of publication, subscription information, and a list of available chapbook collections). *Blue Collar Review* established 1997. Partisan Press established 1993. **Editor:** A. Markowitz. **Co-Editor:** Mary Franke.

Magazine Needs: *Blue Collar Review* (*Journal of Progressive Working Class Literature*) is published quarterly and contains poetry, short stories, and illustrations "reflecting the working class experience, a broad range from the personal to the societal. Our purpose is to promote and expand working class literature and an awareness of the connections between workers of all occupations and the social context in which we live. Also to inspire the creativity and latent talent in 'common' working people." Wants "writing of high quality which reflects the working class experience from delicate internal awareness to the militant. We accept a broad range of style and focus—but are generally progressive, political/social. Nothing racist, sexist-misogynist, right wing, or overly religious. No 'bubba' poetry, nothing overly introspective or confessional, no academic/abstract or 'Vogon' poetry. No simple beginners rhyme or verse." Has published poetry by Jeff Vande Zande, Joya Lonsdale, Antler, Jim Daniels, Kathryn Kirkpatrick, Alan Catlin, and Rob Whitbeck. As a sample we selected these lines from "Talking Late with Old Friends" by Robert Edwards:

> One part of me, the part that has lived/a hundred years in a sip of water,/that has paid double for food
> that never arrived,/makes me want to throw my arms open/to this creditscape of portfolios/and toxic
> conversation and ask: who's to blame/if our compasses and dictionaries don't agree?

Blue Collar Review is 56 pages, 8½×5½, offset-printed and saddle-stapled with colored card cover, includes b&w illustrations and literary ads. Receives hundreds of poems/year, accepts about 30%. Press run is 350 for 200 subscribers of which 8 are libraries, 50 shelf sales. Subscription: $15/year. Sample: $5. Make checks payable to Partisan Press.

How to Submit: Submit up to 4 poems at a time; "no complete manuscripts please." Accepts previously published poems and simultaneous submissions. Accepts submissions by e-mail (include in text box) and by post. Cover letter preferred. "Poems should be typed as they are to appear upon publication. Author's name and address should appear on every page. Overly long lines reduce chances of acceptance as line may have to be broken to fit the page size and format of the journal." Time between acceptance and publication is 3 months to 1 year. Poems are reviewed by editor and co-editor. Seldom comments on rejected poems. SASE for response. Responds in 3 months. Sends prepublication galleys only upon request. Pays 1-3 copies. Reviews of chapbooks and journals accepted.

Book/Chapbook Needs & How to Submit: Partisan Press looks for "poetry of power that reflects a working class consciousness and which moves us forward as a society. Must be good writing reflecting social/political issues, militancy desired but not didactic screed." Publishes about 3 chapbooks/year and are not presently open to unsolicited submissions. "Submissions are requested from among the poets published in the *Blue Collar Review*." Has published *Dictation* by Anne Babson and *Dreambuilders* by Armando Zuniga. Chapbooks are usually 20-60 pages, 5½×8½, offset-printed and saddle-stapled with card or glossy cover. Sample chapbooks are $5 and listed on website.

Also Offers: Sponsors the Working People's Poetry Competition. Entry fee: $15 per entry. Prize: $100 and 1-year subscription to *Blue Collar Review*. Deadline: May 1. Winner of the 2001 Working People's Poetry Competition was Luis Cuauhtemoc Berriozabal. "Include cover letter with entry and make check payable to Partisan Press."

Advice: "Don't be afraid to try. Read a variety of poetry and find your own voice. Write about reality, your own experience, and what moves you."

BLUE LIGHT PRESS; THE BLUE LIGHT POETRY PRIZE AND CHAPBOOK CONTEST,

P.O. Box 642, Fairfield IA 52556. (641)472-7882. E-mail: bluelightpress@aol.com. Established 1988. **Chief Editor:** Diane Frank.

Book/Chapbook Needs: Publishes 2 paperbacks, 3 chapbooks/year. "We like poems that are imagistic, emotionally honest, and uplifting, where the writer pushes through the imagery to a deeper level of insight and understanding. No rhymed poetry." Has published poetry by Kate Gray, Viktor Tichy, Tom Centolella, Christopher Buckley, and Diane Averill. As a sample the editor selected these lines from *Against the Blue* by Christopher Buckley:

> *until I stand in the consuming sun with images/Of a world re-made/Whirling through my hands again, and the day-mists lifting/All this space/In its weightlessness—in its high, white, primrose bloom . . .*

Against the Blue is 32 pages, digest-sized, professionally printed and flat-spined with elegant matte card cover. Cost is $8 plus $1.50 p&h. Also published 3 anthologies of visionary poets.

How to Submit: Does not accept e-mail submissions. Send SASE for submission deadlines. Guidelines available for SASE or by e-mail. Has an editorial board. "We work in person with local poets, have an ongoing poetry workshop, give classes, and will edit/critique poems by mail—$30 for 4-5 poems."

Also Offers: Sponsors the Blue Light Poetry Prize and Chapbook Contest. "The winner will be published by Blue Light Press, receive a $100 honorarium and 50 copies of his or her book, which can be sold for $8 each, for a total of $500." Submit ms of 10-24 pages, typed or printed with a laser or inkjet printer, between March 1, 2002 and May 1, 2002. Entry fee: $10. Make checks payable to Blue Light Press. Include SASE. No ms will be returned without a SASE. Winner will be announced on or before September 1, 2002, and the book will be published in April, 2003. Send SASE for more information.

Advice: "Read some of the books we publish, especially one of the anthologies. We like to publish poets with a unique and expanded vision and gorgeous or unusual language. Stay in the poem longer and see what emerges in your vision and language."

BLUE MESA REVIEW, Dept. of English, Humanities Bldg. #217, University of New Mexico,

Albuquerque NM 87131-1106. (505)277-6155. Fax: (505)277-5573. E-mail: bluemesa@unm.edu. Website: www.unm.edu/~bluemesa (includes current news about recent issues, sample cover art and writing, and guidelines). Established 1989 by Rudolfo Anaya. **Editor:** Julie Shigekuni. **Fiction Editor:** Dan Mueller. **Poetry Editor:** Amy Beeder.

Magazine Needs: *Blue Mesa Review* is an annual review of poetry, short fiction, creative essays, and book reviews. Wants "all kinds of free, organic verse; poems of place encouraged. Limits: four poems or six pages of poetry; one story; one essay. We accept theoretical essays as well as fiction, poetry, and nonfiction." Has published poetry by Virgil Suarez, David Axelrod, Paula Gunn Allen, and Brian Swann. *Blue Mesa Review* is about 250 pages, 6×9, professionally printed and flat-spined with glossy cover, photos, and graphics. This hefty publication includes a number of long poems—several spanning 3 pages. Receives about 1,000 poems/year, accepts about 10% or less. Press run is 1,000 for 600 shelf sales. Sample: $12.

How to Submit: "Please submit two copies of everything with your name, address and telephone number on each page. Fax numbers and e-mail addresses are also appreciated." No previously published poems or simultaneous submissions. No electronic submissions. Cover letter required. Accepts mss from July 1 through October 1 only. Poems are then passed among readers and voted on. Guidelines available on website. Reports on mss by mid-December to mid-January. Pays 2 copies.

BLUE UNICORN, A TRIQUARTERLY OF POETRY; BLUE UNICORN POETRY CONTEST,

22 Avon Rd., Kensington CA 94707. (510)526-8439. Established 1977. **Poetry Editors:** Ruth G. Iodice, John Hart, and Fred Ostrander.

Magazine Needs: *Blue Unicorn* wants "well-crafted poetry of all kinds, in form or free verse, as well as expert translations on any subject matter. We shun the trite or inane, the soft-centered, the contrived poem. Shorter poems have more chance with us because of limited space." Has published poetry by James Applewhite, Kim Cushman, Patrick Worth Gray, Joan LaBombard, James Schevill, and Gail White. As a sample the editors selected these lines from "An Evening Chat in John Burrough's Field" by Austin MacRae:

We sat and talked, John's grave nearby,/about the way a poem grows, the art/of smoothing out a twist of words, a pinched/old line. And then his voice, like an oar,/turned us to tales of backwoods streams,/ the ripple of a hermit's song . . .

Blue Unicorn is "distinguished by its fastidious editing, both with regard to contents and format." It is 56 pages, narrow digest-sized, finely-printed, saddle-stapled, with some art. Features 40-50 poems in each issue, all styles, with the focus on excellence and accessibility. Receives over 35,000 submissions/year, accepts about 200, has a year's backlog. Single copy: $6, foreign add $2; subscription: $14/3 issues, foreign add $6.

How to Submit: Submit 3-5 typed poems on 8½×11 paper. No simultaneous submissions or previously published poems. "Cover letter OK, but will not affect our selection." Guidelines available for SASE. Responds in 3 months (generally within 6 weeks), sometimes with personal comment. Pays 1 copy.

Also Offers: Sponsors an annual contest with small entry fee, with prizes of $150, $75, $50, and sometimes special awards; distinguished poets as judges, publication of 3 top poems and 6 honorable mentions in the magazine. Entry fee: $6 for first poem, $3 for others to a maximum of 5. Write for current guidelines. Criticism occasionally offered.

Advice: "We would advise beginning poets to read and study poetry—both poets of the past and of the present; concentrate on technique; and discipline yourself by learning forms before trying to do without them. When your poem is crafted and ready for publication, study your markets and then send whatever of your work seems to be compatible with the magazine you are submitting to."

BLUELINE (Specialized: regional), Dept. PM, English Dept., Potsdam College, Potsdam NY 13676. Fax: (315)267-2043. E-mail: blueline@potsdam.edu. Established 1979. **Editor-in-Chief:** Rick Henry and an editorial board. Member: CLMP.

Magazine Needs: Appearing in May, *Blueline* "is an annual literary magazine dedicated to prose and poetry about the Adirondacks and other regions similar in geography and spirit." Wants "clear, concrete poetry pertinent to the countryside and its people. It must go beyond mere description, however. We prefer a realistic to a romantic view. We do not want to see sentimental or extremely experimental poetry." Usually uses poems of 75 lines or fewer, though "occasionally we publish longer poems" on "nature in general, Adirondack Mountains in particular. Form may vary, can be traditional or contemporary." Has published poetry by L.M. Rosenberg, John Unterecker, Lloyd Van Brunt, Laurence Josephs, Maurice Kenny, and Nancy L. Nielsen. *Blueline* is 200 pages, 6×9, with 90 pages of poetry in each issue. Press run is 600. Sample copies: $4 for back issues.

How to Submit: Submit 3 poems at a time. Include short bio. No simultaneous submissions. Submit September 1 through November 30 only. Occasionally comments on rejected poems. Guidelines available for SASE or by e-mail. Responds in 10 weeks. Pays 1 copy. Acquires first North American serial rights. Reviews books of poetry in 500-750 words, single or multi-book format.

Advice: "We are interested in both beginning and established poets whose poems evoke universal themes in nature and show human interaction with the natural world. We look for thoughtful craftsmanship rather than stylistic trickery."

BOA EDITIONS, LTD., 260 East Ave., Rochester NY 14604. (716)546-3410. E-mail: boaedit@front iernet.net. Website: www.info-boaeditions.org. Established 1976. **Poetry Editor:** Thom Ward. Has published some of the major American poets, such as W.D. Snodgrass, John Logan, Isabella Gardner, Richard Wilbur, and Lucille Clifton. Also publishes introductions by major poets of those less well-known. For example, Gerald Stern wrote the foreword for Li-Young Lee's *Rose*. Guidelines available for SASE. Pays 10 copies.

BOGG PUBLICATIONS; BOGG, (Specialized: form/style, experimental, humor), 422 N. Cleveland St., Arlington VA 22201-1424. Established 1968. **Poetry Editors:** John Elsberg (USA), George Cairncross (UK: 31 Belle Vue St., Filey, N. Yorkshire YO 14 9HU England), Wilga Rose (Australia: 13 Urara Rd., Avalon Beach, NSW 2107 Australia), and Sheila Martindale (Canada: P.O. Box 23148, 380 Wellington St., London, Ontario NGA 5N9 Canada).

Magazine Needs: Appearing at least twice/year, *Bogg* is "a journal of contemporary writing with an Anglo-American slant. Its contents combines innovative American work with a range of writing from England and the Commonwealth. It includes poetry (to include haiku, prose poems, and experimental/ visual poems), very short experimental or satirical fiction, interviews, essays on the small press scenes both in America and in England /the Commonwealth, reviews, review essays, and line art. We also publish occasional free-for-postage pamphlets." The magazine uses a great deal of poetry in each issue (with several featured poets)—"poetry in all styles, with a healthy leavening of shorts (under ten lines). Prefer original voices." Accepts all styles, all subject matter. "Some have even found the magazine's sense of play offensive. Overt religious and political poems have to have strong poetical merits—statement alone is not sufficient." *Bogg* started in England and in 1975 began including a supplement of American work; it now is published in the US and mixes US, Canadian, Australian, and UK work with reviews of small press publications from all of those areas. Has published work by Martin Galvin, John M. Bennett, Marcia Arrieta, Harriet Zinnes, and Steve Sneyd. As a sample the editors selected these lines from the prose poem "The Word" by Harriet Zinnes:

> It is time to be open. To be free of metaphor. To let desire walk/naked. In the word. The word, stripped,
> bare, not even in swaddling/clothes. The word that is not an object. Not a frame of meaning. Like/a
> stone, the word.

Bogg is 72 pages, typeset, saddle-stapled, in a 6×9 format that leaves enough white space to let each poem stand and breathe alone. There are about 50 pages of poetry/issue. Receives over 10,000 American poems/year, accepts about 100-150. Press run is 850 for 400 subscribers of which 20 are libraries. Single copy: $5.50; subscription: $15 for 3 issues. Sample: $3.50.

How to Submit: Submit 6 poems at a time. No simultaneous submissions. Cover letters preferred. "They can help us get a 'feel' for the writer's intentions/slant." SASE required or material discarded ("no exceptions.") Prefer typewritten manuscripts, with author's name and address on each sheet. "We will reprint previously published material, but with a credit line to a previous publisher." Guidelines available for SASE. Responds in 1 week. Pays 2 copies. Acquires one-time rights. Reviews books and chapbooks of poetry in 250 words, single book format. Poets may send books to relevant editor (by region) for review consideration.

Book/Chapbook Needs & How to Submit: Their occasional pamphlets and chapbooks are by *invitation only*, the author receiving 25% of the print run, and you can get chapbook samples free for 6×9 SASE. "At least 2 ounces worth of postage."

Advice: "Become familiar with a magazine before submitting to it. Long lists of previous credits irritate me. Short notes about how the writer has heard about *Bogg* or what he or she finds interesting or annoying in the magazine I read with some interest."

BOMBAY GIN, Naropa University, 2130 Arapahoe Ave., Boulder CO 80302. (303)546-3540. Fax: (303)546-5297. E-mail: bgin@naropa.edu. Website: www.naropa.edu/gin.html (includes writer's guidelines, sample poems from most recent issue, and current cover art). Established 1974. **Contact:** Judith Huntera.

Magazine Needs: "*Bombay Gin*, appearing in June, is the annual literary magazine of the Jack Kerouac School of Disembodied Poetics at Naropa University. Produced and edited by MFA students, *Bombay Gin* publishes established writers alongside those who have been previously unpublished. It has a special interest in works that push conventional literary boundaries. Submission of poetry, prose, visual art, and works involving hybrid forms and cross-genre exploration are encouraged." Recent issues have included works by Lisa Jarnot, Anne Waldman, Wang Ping, Thalia Field, Anselm Hollo, and Alice Notley. As a sample the editor selected these lines from "Permanent Home 2" by Mei-mei Brussenburge:

> a drawing of the house takes on qualities of a home, then exceeds it in these qualities./Space in front
> of the house is panoramic, as if all my last homes could be accommodated at the same time/
> Accommodation is a perception, not abstract, like a space painted white./The sublime divides itself
> from what's great—nature, my wonderful home, space, etc., and casts these as prose.

Bombay Gin is 124 pages, 6×9, professionally printed, perfect-bound with color card cover, includes art and photos. Receives about 300 poems/year, accepts about 5%. Press run is 500, 400 shelf sales; 100 distributed free to contributors. Single copy: $10. Sample: $5.

How to Submit: "Submit up to 3 pages of poetry or up to 8 pages of prose/fiction (12 pt. Times New Roman). Art may be submitted as slides, negatives, or prints." No previously published poems or simultaneous submissions. Accepts disk submissions (PC format). Cover letter preferred. Reply with SASE only. Deadline: December 1. Submissions read December 15 through March 15. Guidelines available for SASE or on website. Notification of acceptance/rejection: April 15. Pays 2 copies. Acquires one-time rights.

BONE & FLESH PUBLICATION, P.O. Box 349, Concord NH 03302-0349. Phone/fax: (603)225-0521. Website: www.essentialbooks.com. Established 1988. **Publisher/Editor-in-Chief:** Lester Hirsh. **Assistant Editor:** Roy Morrison.

Book/Chapbook Needs: Accepting mss for annual contest. Publishes 1-2 chapbooks a year through competition. Wants "well seasoned, professional poetry. Looking for good material, sometimes cutting-edge." Does not want banality or erotica. Has published poetry by Thomas Raine Crowe, Keith Flynn, Lyn Lifshin, Joel Openheimer, and Mary Winters. Chapbooks are 50-60 pages, 8½×11, perfect-bound, "aesthetically nice." Welcomes "tasteful artwork that is black and white or can be reproduced in black and white." Press run is about 300. Single copy: $10 (includes postage); subscription: $20 for award-winning issue and another chapbook.

How to Submit: Submit mss of up to 55 pages with a **$15 reading fee**. Reads submissions July through September only. "Given time and money, other submissions will be considered for a supplemental anthology." Guidelines available for SASE.

$ ⬭ ◎ BORDIGHERA, INC.; VOICES IN ITALIAN AMERICANA; VIA FOLIOS; THE BORDIGHERA POETRY PRIZE; ANIELLO LAURI AWARD (Specialized: ethnic/nationality, Italian-American), P.O. Box 1374, Lafayette IN 47902-1374. Phone/fax: (765)474-6330. E-mail: atamburri@fau.edu. Established 1990. **Editors:** Anthony Julian Tamburri, Paolo Giordano, and Fred Gardaphé.

Magazine Needs: *Voices in Italian Americana* (*VIA*) is "a semiannual literary and cultural review devoted to the dissemination of information concerning the contributions of and about Italian Americans to the cultural and art worlds of North America." Open to all kinds of poetry. Has published poetry by Daniela Gioseffi, David Citino, Felix Stefanile, and Dana Gioia. As a sample the editor selected these lines from "Coming To Know Empedokles" by Diane diPrima:

> *A couple of millennia seems like a moment:/This song cd be planting rite of black Sicilians/in autumn fields behind a small house/the sounds / the colors as if/intervening greys & anglo stillness/had never entered.*

VIA is about 250 pages, 8½×5½, docutech printed, perfect-bound with glossy paper cover, includes art and ads. Receives about 150 poems/year, accepts about 25%. Press run is 500 for 300 subscribers of which 50 are libraries, 50 shelf sales; 50 distributed free to contributors. Subscription: $20 individual; $15 student/senior citizen; $25 institutional; $30 foreign. Sample: $10. Make checks payable to Bordighera, Inc.

How to Submit: No previously published poems or simultaneous submissions. Accepts e-mail and disk submissions. Cover letter required. Reads submissions October 1 through May 31 only. Time between acceptance and publication is 3 months. Poems are circulated to an editorial board. Often comments on rejected poems. Publishes theme issues occasionally. Guidelines and upcoming themes available for SASE. Responds in 6 weeks. Always sends prepublication galleys. Acquires all rights. Rights returned upon publication. "But in subsequent publications, poet must acknowledge first printing in *VIA*." Reviews books and chapbooks of poetry in 500-1,000 words, single book format. Poets may send books for review consideration to Fred Gardaphé, Center for Italian Studies, State University of New York, Stony Brook NY 11794-3358.

Book/Chapbook Needs & How to Submit: Bordighera, under the imprint *VIA Folios*, has published *The Silver Lake of Love Poems* by Emmanuel di Pasquale, *Going On* by Daniela Gioseffi, *Sardinia/Sardegna* by Robert Lima, and *The Book of Madness and Love* by Arthur L. Clements. Publishes 5 titles/year with the print run for each paperback being 550. Books are usually 50-75 pages, 8½×5½, docutech printed and perfect-bound with glossy paper cover and art. Query first, with a variety of sample poems and a cover letter with brief bio and publication credits. Responds to queries in 2 weeks; to mss in 6 weeks. Pays 10% royalties. Offers subsidy arrangements. Poets are required to subsidize 50% of publishing costs. "Author regains subsidy through sales with 50% royalties up to subvention paid, 10% thereafter."

Also Offers: Sponsors the Bordighera Poetry Prize, which awards book publication and $2,000, and the Aniello Lauri Award, which awards $150 plus publication in *Voices in Italian Americana*. Contest rules available for SASE.

▨ ⬭ ◎ BOREALIS PRESS; TECUMSEH PRESS LTD.; JOURNAL OF CANADIAN POETRY (Specialized: regional, Canadian), 8 Mohawk Crescent, Ottawa, Ontario K2H 7G6 Canada. (613)829-0150. Fax: (613)829-3783. E-mail: borealis@istar.ca. Website: www.borealispress.com. Established 1972. Editor: Glenn Clever. **Contact:** Poetry Editor.

Book/Chapbook Needs & How to Submit: "We publish most genres but specialize in Canadian authored or oriented material. We are in the market only for material that seriously involves the human situation, in mature, skillful manner and interesting, well-written style." Has recently published *Deeper Than Mind* by Fred Cogswell, *The Altering Eye* by Susan McCaskill, *Irregular People* by Janet Fehr, *Unlearning Ice* by Liliane Welsh, *Woman Is Goddess* by Brenda Fleet, and *Lifting the Veil* by Judith Avinsen. "We do not offer an editing service and consider only manuscripts already edited for composition, grammar, spelling, punctuation, etc., to professional standards. For acceptance for publication we require a copy on diskette as well as a copy on 8½×11 pages, one side only, numbered, in loose sheets." Query first; no unsolicited or simultaneous submissions. Include samples with adequately sized return envelope and sufficient return postage/IRCs. "Material arriving without such prepaid return is normally scrapped." Accepts submissions by post only. Guidelines available for SASE or by e-mail. Responds in 4 months. Pays 10% royalty on net price. Time between acceptance and publication is up to 2 years. Catalog available for $3.

Also Offers: The *Journal of Candian Poetry* is an annual that publishes articles, reviews, and criticism, not poetry. Sample: $15.95.

N 🌑 **BORN MAGAZINE**, P.O. Box 1313, Portland OR 97207-1313. E-mail: editor@bornmagazine. org. Website: www.bornmagazine.org. Established 1996. **Editor:** Anmarie Trimble. **Contributing Editors:** Jennifer Grotz, Bruce Smith.

Magazine Needs: *Born Magazine* appears quarterly as "an experimental online revue that marries literary arts and interactive media. We publish six to eight multimedia 'interpretations' of poetry and prose each issue, created by interactive artists in collaboration with poets and writers." Wants poems suited to "interpretation into a visual or interactive form. Due to the unusual, collaborative nature of our publication, we represent a variety of styles and forms of poetry." Recently published poetry by Paisley Rekdal, Bruce Smith, Cate Marvin, Tenaya Darlington, Michele Glazer, and Philip Jenks. Publishes about 6-8 poems/ online issue.

How to Submit: Submit 2-5 poems at a time. Accepts previously published poems; no simultaneous submissions. Accepts e-mail submissions; no fax submissions. "Prefer electronic submissions as Word documents or .txt files. Also accept hard copies; electronic format on disk or via e-mail will be required upon acceptance." Reads submissions year round. Submit seasonal poems 4 months in advance. Time between acceptance and publication is 1-3 months. "Poems must be accepted by the editor and one contributing editor. Selected works are forwarded to our art department, which chooses an artist partner to work with the writer. Artist and writer collaborate on a concept, to be realized by the artist." Never comments on rejected poems. Guidelines available on website. Responds in 3 weeks to e-mail queries. Always sends prepublication galleys. No pay. "We can offer only the experience of participating in a collaborative community, as well as a broad audience. (We receive approximately 20,000-30,000 unique visitors to our site per month.)" Acquires one-time rights.

Advice: "We accept new and previously published work. *Born*'s mission is to nurture creativity and collaboration between different artistic genres to further the development of new literary art forms on the Web."

N 🎯 **BOTTOM DOG PRESS, INC. (Specialized: working class literature)**, % Firelands College, Huron OH 44839. Website: http://members.aol.com/lsmithdog/bottomdog/ (includes guidelines, newsletter, and catalog). **Editors:** Larry Smith, David Shevin, Laura Smith.

Book/Chapbook Needs & How to Submit: Bottom Dog Press, Inc. "is a nonprofit literary and educational organization dedicated to publishing the best writing and art from the Midwest." Bottom Dog poets include Jeff Gundy, Ray McNiece, Maj Ragain, David Kherdian, and Sue Doro. See website for guidelines.

Ⓥ $ 🌑 **BOULEVARD**, 4579 Laclede Ave., Suite 332, St. Louis MO 63108-2103. Website: www.boul evardmagazine.com. Established 1985. **Editor:** Richard Burgin.

   • Poetry published in *Boulevard* has been frequently included inclined in *The Best American Poetry* and *Pushcart Prize* anthologies.

Magazine Needs: *Boulevard* appears 3 times/year. "*Boulevard* strives to publish only the finest in fiction, poetry, and nonfiction (essays and interviews; we do not accept book reviews). While we frequently publish writers with previous credits, we are very interested in publishing less experienced or unpublished writers with exceptional promise. We've published everything from John Ashbery to Donald Hall to a wide variety of styles from new or lesser known poets. We're eclectic. Do not want to see poetry that is uninspired, formulaic, self-conscious, unoriginal, insipid." Has published poetry by Amy Clampitt, Molly Peacock, Jorie Graham, and Mark Strand. *Boulevard* is 200 pages, digest-sized, professionally printed, flat-spined, with glossy card cover. Their press run is 3,500 with 1,200 subscribers of which 200 are libraries. Subscription: $12/3 issues, $20/6 issues, $25/9 issues. Sample: $7 plus 5 first-class stamps and SASE. Make checks payable to Opojaz, Inc.

How to Submit: Submit up to 5 poems at a time. Line length for poetry is 200 maximum. No previously published poems. "*Boulevard* does allow, even encourages, simultaneous submissions, but we want to be notified of this fact." Does not accept fax or e-mail submissions. All submissions must include an SASE. Author's name and address must appear on each submission, with author's first and last name on each page. Cover letters encouraged but not required. Reads submissions October 1 through April 30 only. Editor sometimes comments on rejected poems. Responds in about 2 months. Pays $25-300/poem, depending on length, plus 1 copy. Acquires first-time publication and anthology rights.

Advice: "Write from your heart as well as your head."

N $ 🌑 **BOVINE FREE WYOMING**. E-mail: submissions@bovinefreewyoming.com. Website: www. bovinefreewyoming.com (includes entire publication online). Established 2000. **Co-Editor:** Vickie L. Knestaut.

insider report

Working class voices, Midwestern values

Bottom Dog Press, based in Huron, Ohio, and edited by Larry Smith, has gained a distinctive profile since its founding in 1985. The press's name comes from Edward Dahlberg's 1933 novel, *Bottom Dog*. "It's the story of his struggle with poverty in Cleveland and then Kansas City," Smith says. "It's the underdog theme, and it fits us. But that bottom dog has to be feisty to survive, and that fits us, too." That name gives the flavor of Bottom Dog's thematic focus: Midwestern and working-class literature, chiefly poetry and fiction, with occasional nonfiction added. The press publishes a variety of anthologies, single poet and chapbook collections, and collections of short fiction.

Larry Smith

Among the prominent contemporary authors published by Bottom Dog Press are Ohio poet Jeff Gundy; Pennsylvania poet and fiction writer Jim Daniels; New York poet Naton Leslie; Ohio poet and essayist Richard Hague; and poet Chris Llewellyn, whose first collection, *Fragments from the Fire*, won the prestigious Walt Whitman Award from the Academy of American Poets. Bottom Dog has also published the works of some major writers, such as the collected love poems of Kenneth Patchen and his biography (in conjunction with several other small presses).

Smith, a widely published poet himself, founded the press to expand an interest he had taken in publishing. "It really started because, well, I knew I could do it. I'd had a couple books of poems published already by Northwood Press and Cleveland State Poetry Center, and I felt I could do better myself," Smith says. "I had also been researching the San Francisco Poetry Renaissance in Berkeley and San Francisco, and my going through those original magazines and chapbooks taught me how to go about it. I knew a lot of deserving writers and writings, and so decided to start locally, in Ohio and the Midwest."

Bottom Dog quickly grew into focusing beyond Ohio writers. "I was pretty strongly into 'sense of place' writings, which said to be where you are," says Smith. "Also, I sensed that our press had to find an identity, not try to publish just anything, and find out what mattered to us, then do that. It's what Gary Snyder calls 'the real work,' what you do that confirms yourself and your world."

Though "working class" and "Midwestern" are difficult to define, Smith has a definite sense of what the terms mean to him and how they influence Bottom Dog's editorial decisions. "I would define 'working class' as a culture and not merely a socio-economic status. It's about people and values, and the writing must reflect and speak to those same people. The worker must have a place of respect in the writing; his/her values and voice must be heard." Smith says "Midwest" is "an open and experiential concept. It is felt or sensed, but geographically its broadest definition is the 12 states between the Rockies and Pennsylvania, above the Mason-Dixon Line. It can also include parts of Canada. At Bottom Dog Press we don't restrict the definition; we read the work and sense whether it is located or not in the place and values of the Midwest."

Smith's advice to writers seeking to place books with publishers is simple: Understand the publisher's needs. He says Bottom Dog gets many books that are simply inappropriate in terms of subject or style. "A book begins with an idea that might get shaped into an anthology, or most often it begins with a manuscript we receive or maybe a couple manuscripts we can pair together. We look for good writing first, but it needs to fit our Midwest and working-class vision," Smith says. "We receive a lot of manuscripts about almost anything from folks from California, Florida, New York, Maine, and usually I just return it with a note: 'Thanks, but no thanks. We are a Midwest publisher.' We know who we are even if eager writers don't take the time to notice."

Like many small presses, Bottom Dog is incorporated as a non-profit organization, which makes it eligible for grant support from foundations and state agencies; the press receives some of its support from the Ohio Arts Council. But that doesn't mean the press is immune to the concerns that affect for-profit businesses as well. "Like everything else, small presses are a business facing the changes into a corporate economy. Fortunately, we have survived by not changing too much, not trying to grow too fast. We work at supporting our writers and developing an audience. You can't go wrong doing that," Smith says.

Bottom Dog, however, steers away from a practice that an increasing number of small publishers use to finance their books. "Bottom Dog Press has never done a contest with a 'reading fee,'" Smith states, "though I know that's becoming an economic necessity for many presses. There are a lot of ways to build a house. We do get supporting grants from the Ohio Arts Council, but with Ohio's budget cuts, those have gotten smaller. So our main income is from sales, as it should be. What good is a press that doesn't work to sell its books? We stay in the black each year and put any small profit into next year's books. To survive in the small press world is an accomplishment."

Smith plans to continue the press in the future (this year Bottom Dog reaches a milestone by publishing its 70th book), although he doesn't have plans for unbridled growth. There is such a thing as growing too fast and losing the focus of one's original business. "An early book on publishing by Michael Cain suggested that one should watch carefully what the big presses are doing, and then not do any of it," Smith explains, "because one can't afford the waste and failures they create. I've followed that by publishing writing that has a home and by building slowly and staying small."

The Internet has transformed publishing, with the emergence of online retailers such as Amazon.com, the development of e-books, and online opportunities for writers to get published. Bottom Dog has responded by establishing its own website at http://members.aol.com/lsmithdog/bottomdog/. Still, Smith says, the basic work of publishing remains the same—find work suitable for your audience, produce it in an attractive edition, and market the work.

"Many people are turning from the independent bookstores to corporate ones and from bookstores to Internet booksellers. We haven't been blind to this shift, and you can find our books on Amazon.com as well as our own distributor's Small Press Books Distribution Internet ordering page at http://spdbooks.org. And we have our own homepages," he points out. "We advertise in state, regional, and national market areas. We work to get our books reviewed. That's the same as it always has been. And, trust me, the book is not vanishing. The Internet and e-books are just another way to get the word out. They haven't hurt our market."

Because Smith views publishing as a type of "real," or essential work, just like writing, it's not surprising that his own concerns as a writer mirror his focus as a publisher. The author of several books of poetry, fiction, and nonfiction, his work takes an unsparing look at life in the industrial Ohio Valley of northeast Ohio, where he grew up. Perhaps his finest book is *Steel Valley: Letters and Postcards* (Pig Iron Press, 1992), a collection of poems in letter form spoken by individuals from that region over several decades. Like his new *Milldust and Roses: Memoirs* (Detroit: Ridgeway Press, 2002), the writing captures the region's difficulty and hope of life in spare, elegant lyrics.

"As I said, most small press publishers are writers who got into the business because they felt they could do a good job of it, do some 'real work.' I had three books of poetry and two literary biographies published before I got into it as a publisher," Smith says. "My writing is deeply located in a place sense; usually that harsh and beautiful Ohio Valley of my past or in the natural beauty and family depth of life along Lake Erie. I've done some spiritual growth in Eastern thought, Taoism and Buddhism, and so that becomes a part of my own real work as well. My work seems to always come home to that Ohio Valley."
—*Kevin Walzer*

Magazine Needs: *Bovine Free Wyoming* is a quarterly electronic publication of literature. "We want to see quality poetry that appeals to a general reading audience. We do not want to see poetry that alienates the average reader." Recently published poetry by Michael A. Arnzen, Matt Mason, Deborah Bacharach, geoff davis, Frank Matagrano, and Roger Pfingston. *Bovine Free Wyoming* is published in html format. Receives about 400 poems/year, accepts about 10%. Publishes about 10 poems/issue.
How to Submit: Submit 4 poems at a time. Line length for poetry is open. Accepts previously published poems and simultaneous submissions. Accepts e-mail submissions; no fax or disk submissions. Cover letter is required. "Please review submission guidelines before making a submission." Reads submissions year round. Submit seasonal poems 3 months in advance. Time between acceptance and publication is 3 months. Poems are circulated to an editorial board. "Staff reads and rates poems. Poems that score a certain rating or more are accepted for publication." Seldom comments on rejected poems. Guidelines available on website. Responds in 1 month. Always sends prepublication galleys. Pays $10. Acquires one-time electronic rights.
Advice: "It may be old hat, but it still needs to be said: Proof your work and know your market. If a poet doesn't care enough to send clean copies that adhere to the guidelines, then why should an editor care enough to publish it?"

BRANCHES; UCCELLI PRESS; BEST OF BRANCHES, P.O. Box 85394, Seattle WA 98145-1394. E-mail: editor@branchesquarterly.com. Website: www.branchesquarterly.com (includes guidelines, excerpts, contributor bios, current/past issues, links of interest). Established 2001. **Editor:** Toni La Ree Bennett.
Magazine Needs: *Branches* is a quarterly online journal "dedicated to publishing the best of known and unknown artists and authors, presenting, when possible, verbal and visual art together in a way that expands their individual meaning." Wants poetry that is "educated but not pretentious. Seeking an eclectic, sophisticated mix of poetry, short prose, art, photos, fiction, essays, translations. Would like to see more 'light' or 'comic' submissions. No rhyming unless specific form. No greeting card verse, no openly sectarian religious verse (spirituality okay)." Recently published poetry by John Amen, Janet Buck, A.E. Stallings, Richard Jordan, Britt East, and Adam Sorkin. As a sample the editor selected these lines from "The Cat Escapes" by Richard Jordan:
> Then you see a hole in the screen,/about the height and width of a cat./Someplace far away, you know/
> There is a ponderous hole/Made to your own specifications./Nearby, a baby is crying.

Branches is published online, equivalent to about 30 pages in print. *Best of Branches* is an annual print version. Receives about 500 poems/year, accepts about 20%. Publishes about 25 poems/issue.
How to Submit: Submit 3-5 poems at a time. Accepts simultaneous submissions; no previously published poems "unless by invitation." Accepts fax and e-mail submissions; no disk submissions. Cover letter is preferred. "Preferred method of submission is to e-mail work in body of message to submit@branchesquarterly.com. Send art/photos as jpeg attachments. Submitters must be willing to have their work appear with other verbal or visual art of editor's choosing." Reads submissions continually; see website for issue deadlines. Submit seasonal poems

3 months in advance. Time between acceptance and publication is 1-3 months. Seldom comments on rejected poems. Guidelines available on website. Responds in 6 weeks. Always sends prepublication galleys (online only). Pays 1 contributor's copy of *Best of Branches* annual print version. Acquires first rights and retains right to archive online.

Also Offers: $25 cash contest each issue for Best Visual (art, photo, etc.) Response to a Verbal Piece and Best Verbal Response to a Visual Piece. See website for details.

Advice: "*Branches* is a place where 'the undefined and exact combine' (Verlaine). Artists live in a privileged, neglected place in our society. We are expected to make concrete the fluid, to tell the future, to work without recompense, and walk around naked. I'm looking for solid craftsmanship and an honest attempt to articulate the undefined."

N ⚡ ◎ THE BREAD OF LIFE MAGAZINE (Specialized: religious), 209 MacNab St. N., P.O. Box 395, Hamilton, Ontario L8N 3H8 Canada. (905)529-4496. Fax: (905)529-5373. Website: www.thebreadoflife.com. Established 1977. **Editor:** Fr. Peter Coughlin.

Magazine Needs: *The Bread of Life* is "a Catholic charismatic magazine, published bimonthly and designed to encourage spiritual growth in areas of renewal in the Catholic Church today." It includes articles, poetry and artwork. As a sample the editor selected these lines from "To Know His Love" by Margaret Larrivee:

> *In times when all is going well/on His great love we seldom dwell./It's only when we are laid low/His*
> *abundant love we start to know.//It comes in cards with loving words/get well wishes, written, heard./*
> *Calls and visits cheerfully bring/joy to my soul, my heart to sing.*

The Bread of Life is 34 pages, 8½ × 11, professionally printed and saddle-stapled with glossy paper cover, includes original artwork and photos. Receives about 50-60 poems/year, accepts approximately 25%. Press run is 3,600 for subscribers only. "It's good if contributors are members of *The Bread of Life*."

How to Submit: Accepts previously published poems and simultaneous submissions. Cover letter preferred. Publishes theme issues. Send SAE with IRCs for upcoming themes.

◐ ◎ BREAKAWAY BOOKS (Specialized: sports), P.O. Box 24, Halcottsville NY 12438-0024. (212)898-0408. E-mail: Garth@breakawaybooks.com. Website: www.breakawaybooks.com. Established 1994. **Publisher:** Garth Battista.

Book/Chapbook Needs & How to Submit: Breakaway Books publishes "sports literature—fiction, essays, and poetry on the athletic experience." Wants "Poetry on sports only—for intelligent, literate athletes; book-length collections or book-length poems only." Accepts previously published poems and simultaneous submissions. Accepts e-mail submissions; no disk submissions. Query first, with a few sample poems and a cover letter with brief bio and publication credits. Responds to queries in 2 weeks; to mss in 2 months. Seldom comments on rejections. Pays royalties of 7-12%.

⚡ ◐ THE BRIAR CLIFF REVIEW, Briar Cliff College, 3303 Rebecca St., Sioux City IA 51104-2340. E-mail: emmons@briarcliff.edu. Website: www.briarcliff.edu/administrative/publications/bccrevie/bcreview.htm (includes writer's guidelines, annual contest guidelines, and sample contest winners). Established 1989. **Managing Editor:** Tricia Currans-Sheehan. **Poetry Editor:** Jeanne Emmons.

● *The Briar Cliff Review* received the 1999 Columbia Scholastic Association Gold Crown and the 2000 Associated Collegiate Press Peacemaker Award.

Magazine Needs: *The Briar Cliff Review*, appearing in April, is an attractive annual "eclectic literary and cultural magazine focusing on (but not limited to) Siouxland writers and subjects." Wants "quality poetry with strong imagery; especially interested in regional, Midwestern content with tight, direct, well-wrought language. No allegorical emotional landscapes." Has published poetry by Sandra Adelmund, Vivian Shipley, and Michael Carey. As a sample the editor selected these lines from "An Early Fall" by Margaret J. Hoehn:

> *I have walked back against the/curve of time to find you, into/the shadows of the houses where/we*
> *slept . . .*

The Briar Cliff Review is 64 pages, 8½ × 11, professionally printed on 80 lb. dull text paper, perfect-bound, four-color cover on dull stock, b&w and color photos inside. Receives about 600 poems/year, accepts about 15. Press run is 1,000, all shelf sales. Sample: $10.

How to Submit: Submissions should be typewritten or letter quality, with author's name and address on the first page, with name on following pages. Accepts simultaneous submissions; no previously published poems. No fax or e-mail submissions. "We will assume that submissions are not simultaneous unless notified." Cover letter with short bio required. "No manuscripts returned without SASE." Reads submissions August 1 through November 1 only. Time between acceptance and publication is up to 6 months. Seldom comments on rejected poems. Responds in 6 months. Pays 2 copies. Acquires first serial rights.

⬤ ◎ **BRICKHOUSE BOOKS, INC.; NEW POETS SERIES, INC./CHESTNUT HILLS PRESS; STONEWALL SERIES** (Specialized, Stonewall only: gay/lesbian/bisexual), 541 Piccadilly Rd., Baltimore MD 21204. (410)830-2869 or 828-0724. Fax: (410)830-3999. E-mail: charriss@towson.edu. Website: www.towson.edu/harriss/ (includes writer's guidelines, names of editors, list of in-print publications, plus sample poetry from individual books). Established 1970. **Editor/Director:** Clarinda Harriss. NPS, along with Chestnut Hills Press, Stonewall is now a division of BrickHouse Books.

Book/Chapbook Needs: BrickHouse and The New Poets Series, Inc. brings out first books by promising new poets. Poets who have previously had book-length mss published are not eligible. Prior publication in journals and anthologies is strongly encouraged. Wants "excellent, fresh, nontrendy, literate, intelligent poems. Any form (including traditional), any style." BrickHouse Books and New Poets Series pay 20 author's copies (out of a press run of 1,000), the sales proceeds going back into the corporation to finance the next volume. "BrickHouse has been successful in its effort to provide writers with a national distribution; in fact, The New Poets Series was named an Outstanding Small Press by the prestigious Pushcart Awards Committee, which judges some 5,000 small press publications annually." Chestnut Hills Press publishes author-subsidized books—"High quality work only, however. Chestnut Hills Press has achieved a reputation for prestigious books, printing only the top 10% of mss Chestnut Hills Press and New Poets Series receive." Chestnut Hills Press authors receive proceeds from sale of their books. The Stonewall series publishes work with a gay, lesbian, or bisexual perspective. New Poets Series/Chestnut Hills Press has published books by Chester Wickwire, Ted McCrorie, Sharon White, Mariquita McManus, and Jeff Mann. As a sample the editor selected these lines from *To Move Into the House* from "Just After Dawn" by Richard Fein:

> *I woke to the murmur of my words./Leaning against the headboard/I yielded to the words that took*
> *me back/to my mother's slow death, how I finally stopped wishing/I had a sister to take her off my*
> *hands,/how we worked through that long illness to embrace/and she called me* Ruvn. Ruvn.

Brickhouse publishes 64-112 page works. Chapbooks: $8. Full-length books: $10.

How to Submit: Send a 50- to 55-page ms, $10 reading fee and cover letter giving publication credits and bio. Indicate if ms is to be considered for BrickHouse, New Poets Series, Chestnut Hills Press or Stonewall. Accepts simultaneous submissions. No e-mail submissions. Cover letters should be very brief, businesslike and include an accurate list of published work. Editor sometimes comments briefly on rejected poems. Responds in up to 1 year. Mss "are circulated to an editorial board of professional, publishing poets. BrickHouse is backlogged, but the best 10% of the mss it receives are automatically eligible for Chestnut Hills Press consideration," a subsidy arrangement. Send $5 and a 7×10 SASE for a sample volume.

Also Offers: Stonewall Series offers a chapbook contest whose winner is published by New Poets Series. Send 20-30 poems with $20 entry fee, postmarked no later than August 15. Rane Arroyo's *The Naked Thief* is a recent Stonewall winner.

$ ◎ **BRIDGES: A JOURNAL FOR JEWISH FEMINISTS AND OUR FRIENDS** (Specialized: ethnic, women/feminism, social issues), P.O. Box 24839, Eugene OR 97402. Phone/fax: (541)343-7617. E-mail: clare@bridgesjournal.org. Website: www.bridgesjournal.org. Established 1990. **Managing Editor:** Clare Kinberg.

Magazine Needs: The biannual *Bridges* is "a showcase for Jewish women's creativity and involvement in social justice activism." Wants "anything original by Jewish women, not purely religious." Has published poetry by Emily Warn, Willa Schneberg, and Ellen Bass. As a sample the managing editor selected these lines from "I'll Tell You What My People Know of the Land" by Judith Arcana:

> *Later, much later, who can say how it came to be, there were market stalls in Kiev, Bobroisk, the*
> *Ukraine, changing names and shifting borders with the decades. Every war made new rules to learn,*
> *new names, but still they came in the night to burn and tear at us. So we climbed on the wagon, hid*
> *our boxes under the straw, and rode out across the meadows by moonlight. The leather straps creaked*
> *all night, they made me think of something, something before.*

Bridges is 128 pages, 7×10, professionally printed on 50% recycled paper, perfect-bound, with 2-color cover, b&w photos inside. Receives about 200 poems/year, accepts about 20. Press run is 3,000 for 1,500 subscribers of which 70 are libraries, 300 shelf sales; 200 distributed free to exchanges, board members, funders. Subscription: $15/year. Sample: $7.50.

How to Submit: Submit 6-10 poems at a time. No previously published poems or simultaneous submissions. Cover letter preferred with 40 word bio. Time between acceptance and publication is 6 months. Poems are circulated to an editorial board. "Two poetry readers and sometimes others decide on poems." Often comments on rejected poems. Publishes theme issues. Guidelines available for SASE. Responds in 9 months. Sometimes sends prepublication galleys. Pays $50 per selection plus 3 copies. Sometimes reviews books of poetry. Poets may send books for review consideration.

⬤ ⊚ **BRILLIANT CORNERS: A JOURNAL OF JAZZ & LITERATURE (Specialized: jazz-related literature)**, Lycoming College, Williamsport PA 17701. (570)321-4279. Fax: (570)321-4090. E-mail: bc@lycoming.edu. Website: www.lycoming.edu/BrilliantCorners. Established 1996. **Editor:** Sascha Feinstein.

Magazine Needs: *Brilliant Corners*, a biannual, publishes jazz-related poetry, fiction, and nonfiction. "We are open to length and form, but want work that is both passionate and well crafted—work worthy of our recent contributors. No sloppy hipster jargon or improvisatory nonsense." Has published poetry by Amiri Baraka, Jayne Cortez, Philip Levine, Colleen McElroy, and Al Young. As a sample the editor selected these lines from "Rhythm Method" by Yusef Komunyakaa:

> *If you can see blues/in the ocean, light & dark,/can feel worms ease through/a subterranean path/*
> *beneath each footstep,/Baby, you got rhythm.*

Brilliant Corners is 100 pages, 6×9, commercially printed and perfect-bound with color card cover with original artwork, ads. Accepts about 5% of work received. Press run is 1,800 for 200 subscribers. Subscription: $12. Sample: $7.

How to Submit: Submit 3-5 poems at a time. Previously published poems "very rarely, and only by well established poets"; no simultaneous submissions. No e-mail or fax submissions. Cover letter preferred. Reads submissions September 1 through May 15 only. Seldom comments on rejected poems. Responds in 2 months. Pays 2 copies. Acquires first North American serial rights. Staff reviews books of poetry. Poets may send books for review consideration.

🌐 ⬤ **THE BROBDINGNAGIAN TIMES**, 96 Albert Rd., Cork, Ireland. Phone: 353-21-4311227. Established 1996. **Editor:** Giovanni Malito.

Magazine Needs: *The Brobdingnagian Times* appears quarterly. "Its purpose and contents are international and eclectic. We wish to present a small sample of what is happening out there in the 'world' of poetry." Open to all kinds of poetry of 40 lines or less. "Translations are very welcome. Not very partial to rhyming forms." Has published poetry by Miroslav Holub, Leonard Cirino, Ion Codescru, John Martone, and John Millet. *The Brobdingnagian Times* is 8 pages, A3 sheet folded twice, photocopied from laser original. Receives about 300 poems/year, accepts about 10%. Press run is 250 for 65 subscribers, variable shelf sales; 12 distributed free to writers' groups. Subscription: $5 or equivalent in loose stamps. Sample: $1 or postage. Make checks payable to Giovanni Malito.

How to Submit: Submit 4-8 poems at a time. Line length for poetry is 1 minimum, 40 maximum. Accepts previously published poems and simultaneous submissions. Cover letter preferred. "SASE is required. If IRCs are not convenient then loose stamps for trade with Irish stamps are fine." Time between acceptance and publication is up to 6 months. Often comments on rejected poems. Publishes occasional theme issues as supplements. Guidelines and upcoming themes available for SASE. Responds in 1 month. Pays 1 copy. Acquires one-time rights. Staff reviews books and chapbooks of poetry in 300-500 words, single book format. Send books for review consideration.

Book/Chapbook Needs & How to Submit: The Brobdingnagian Times Press is open to any type of prose and/or poetry and publishes 2-4 chapbooks/year. Chapbooks are usually "palmtop" in size, photocopied from laser original and side-stapled with slightly heavier stock colored paper, cover art only. "The palmtops are quite small. They may be one long poem (8 pages) or several (8-16) short poems (less than 6 lines) or something in between. Collections (unless haiku/senryu) must be more or less themed." Responds to queries in 1 week; to mss in up to 3 weeks. Pays 50 author's copies (out of a press run of 100). "Poets outside of Ireland are asked to cover the postage." Order sample chapbooks by sending 2 IRCs.

Advice: "Nerve and verve and the willingness to edit: these are three qualities a poet must possess."

⬤ ⊚ **BROKEN BOULDER PRESS; GESTALTEN; NEOTROPE (Specialized: form/style)**, P.O. Box 6305, Santa Barbara CA 93160. E-mail: apowell10@hotmail.com or paulsilvia@hotmail.com. Website: www.brokenboulder.com (includes editor's information, submission guidelines, catalog, archives, subscription information, links, editorial policy). Established 1996. **Co-Editors:** Adam Powell and Paul Silvia.

Magazine Needs & How to Submit: *gestalten* appears 2 times/year and publishes experimental poetry from new and established writers. "We want experimental, abstract, collage, visual, language, asemic, found, system, proto, non, and simply strange forms of poetry. Coherence and words are optional. No vampire poetry; religious/inspirational poetry; Bukowski rip offs; no poems containing the word 'poetry'." Has published poetry by John Lowther, Spencer Selby, Peter Ganick, John M. Bennett, Michael Lenhart, and the Atlanta Poet's Group. As a sample the editors selected this poem, "24/7" by Sheila E. Murphy:

> *Allow forth format, gem/The interimshot letterfest/Play to altercations/Summative in form of plenty/*
> *folded latitude*

gestalten is a 100 page perfect-bound journal with full-color cover, includes "tons" of art/graphics and a few small-press ads. Receives about 750 poems/year, accepts about 10%. Publish 70 poems/issue. Press run is 250 for 50 subscribers. Subscription: $7/2 issues. Sample: $4. Make checks payable to Broken Boulder Press. Submit 5-20 poems at a time. No previously published poems or simultaneous submissions. No fax or e-mail submissions. Cover letter preferred. "SASE required. No e-mail submissions, please. We like casual and quirky cover letters." Time between acceptance and publication is up to 8 months. Always comments on rejected poems. Guidelines available for SASE and on website. Responds in 3 weeks. Sometimes sends prepublication galleys. Pays 2 copies. Acquires one-time rights.

Magazine Needs & How to Submit: Published annually in January, *neotrope* "focuses primarily on experimental fiction and drama, with some visual poetry and abstract art. We publish primarily fiction and want to see visual poetry, collages, and abstract art only (Visual/text hybrids OK.) No traditional or text poetry. If you send text poems we will send them back unread." Has published poetry by Jim Leftwich, John M. Bennett, Michael Basinski, and Dave Chirot. *neotrope* is 200 pages, digest-sized, professionally printed and perfect-bound with full-color glossy cover, includes 10-20 pages of art per issue, some ads included on an exchange basis. Receives about 30 poems/year, accepts about 20%. Publish 5-8 poems/issue. Press run is 1,500 for 250 subscribers of which 50 are libraries, 1,000 shelf sales; 30 distributed free to review publications. Subscription: $11/2 issues. Sample: $6. Make checks payable to Broken Boulder Press. Submit up to 10 poems at a time. Accepts simultaneous submissions; no previously published poems. Accepts e-mail submissions. Cover letter with brief bio preferred. "Electronic submissions should be sent in Quark or Pagemaker format, if possible. E-mail us to make other arrangements." Time between acceptance and publication is about 6 months. Always comments on rejected poems. Guidelines available for SASE and on website. Responds in 1 month. Sometimes sends prepublication galleys. Pays 2 copies. Acquires one-time rights.

Book/Chapbook Needs & How to Submit: Broken Boulder Press publishes 2 chapbooks per year. "We want to promote experimental writing; we're biased toward work by underappreciated and beginning poets." Chapbooks are usually 24-32 pages, 5½×8½, photocopied, and saddle-stapled with cardstock cover, includes lots of art. In the future, Broken Boulder Press will focus on e-chapbooks published in PDF format and featured on the website. "Normally we like to see the whole manuscript, but if it's a long one you can send 5-10 sample poems. Publishing in our journals is certainly not required but nearly all of our chapbook authors have done so." Responds to queries and mss in 1 month. Pays 12 author's copies (out of a press run of 50). Order sample chapbooks by sending $1.50 per title.

Advice: "You can't do anything new until you know what's already been done. For every hour you spend writing, spend five hours reading other writers."

N **⊘** **BROODING HERON PRESS**, 101 Bookmonger Rd., Waldron Island WA 98297. Established 1984. **Co-Publishers:** Sam and Sally Green.

Book/Chapbook Needs: Brooding Heron Press publishes up to 3 chapbooks/year. "No restrictions other than excellence." Does not want "prose masquerading as poetry or poems written for form's sake." Has published books by Denise Levertov, James Laughlin, John Haines, David Lee, Donald Hall, and Gary Snyder.

How to Submit: "We're too backlogged to look at anything new until 2006." Accepts previously published poems; no simultaneous submissions. Cover letter required. Time between acceptance and publication varies. Never comments on rejected poems. Responds within 6 weeks. "We print 300 books per title, bound in paper and cloth. Payment is 10% of the press run. Author retains copyright." This press has received many awards for fine printing. Write for catalog to order samples.

N **⊘** **BRYANT LITERARY REVIEW**, Faculty Suite F, Bryant College, Smithfield RI 02917. Website: http://web.bryant.edu/~blr. Established 2000. **Editor:** Tom Chandler. Member: The Council of Literary Magazines and Presses (CLMP).

Magazine Needs: *Bryant Literary Review* appears annually in May and publishes poetry, fiction, photography, and art. "Our only standard is quality." Recently published poetry by Michael S. Harper, Mary Crow, Cathleen Calbert, and Allison Joseph. *Bryant Literary Review* is 125 pages, digest-sized, offset-printed, perfect-bound, 4-color cover, with art or photo. Receives about 2,500 poems/year, accepts about 1%. Publishes about 25 poems/issue. Press run is 2,500. Single copy: $8; subscription: $8.

How to Submit: Submit 3-5 poems at a time. Cover letter is required. "Include SASE; please submit only *once* each reading period." Reads submissions September 1-December 31. Time between acceptance and publication is 5 months. Seldom comments on rejected poems. Guidelines available on website and in publication. Responds in 3 months. Pays 2 contributors copies. Acquires one-time rights.

Advice: "No abstract expressionist or l-a-n-g-u-a-g-e poems, please. We prefer accessible work of depth and quality."

$ **⊘** **◎** **BUGLE: JOURNAL OF ELK COUNTRY AND THE HUNT (Specialized: animals, nature/rural/ecology, elk conservation)**, Rocky Mountain Elk Foundation, P.O. Box 8249, Missoula

MT 59807-8249. (406)523-4570. Fax: (406)543-7710. E-mail: bugle@rmef.org. Website: www.elkfoundati on.org (includes guidelines, contact information, and archives). Established 1984. **Assistant Editor:** Lee Cromrich.

Magazine Needs: *Bugle* is the bimonthly publication of the nonprofit Rocky Mountain Elk Foundation, whose mission is to ensure the future of elk, other wildlife, and their habitat. "The goal of *Bugle* is to advance this mission by presenting original, critical thinking about wildlife conservation, elk ecology, and hunting." Wants "high quality poems that explore the realm of elk, the 'why' of hunting, or celebrate the hunting experience as a whole. Prefer one page. Free verse preferred. No 'Hallmark' poetry." Has published poetry by Mike Fritch, John Whinery, and Ted Horea. *Bugle* is 130 pages, 8½×11, professionally printed on coated stock and saddle-stapled with full-color glossy cover containing photos, illustrations, ads. Receives about 50 poems/year, accepts about 10%. Press run is 130,000. Subscription: $30 membership fee. Sample: $5.95. Make checks payable to Rocky Mountain Elk Foundation.

How to Submit: "Poets may submit as many poems as they'd like at a time." Accepts simultaneous submissions. Accepts e-mail (prefer attached file in Word), fax, and disk submissions. Cover letter preferred. Time between acceptance and publication varies. "Poems are screened by assistant editor first, those accepted then passed to editorial staff for review and comment, final decision based on their comments. We will evaluate your poem based on content, quality, and our needs for the coming year." Rarely comments on rejected poems. Publishes special sections. Guidelines available for SASE, by fax, by e-mail, and on website. Responds in 3 months. "The Rocky Mountain Elk Foundation is a nonprofit conservation organization committed to putting membership dollars into protecting elk habitat. So we appreciate, and still receive, donated work. However, if you would like to be paid for your work, our rate is $100 a poem, paid on acceptance. Should your poem appear in *Bugle*, you will receive three complimentary copies of the issue." Acquires first North American serial rights. Staff reviews other magazines.

Advice: "Although poetry has appeared periodically in *Bugle* over the years, it has never been a high priority for us, nor have we solicited it. A lack of high-quality work and poetry appropriate for the focus of the magazine has kept us from making it a regular feature. However, we've decided to attempt to give verse a permanent home in the magazine. . . . Reading a few issues of *Bugle* prior to submitting will give you a better sense of the style and content of the magazine."

◐ BULK HEAD; BRIDGE BURNER'S PUBLISHING, P.O. Box 5255, Mankato MN 56002-5255. E-mail: editor@bulkhead.org. Website: www.bulkhead.org. Established 2000. **Editor:** Curtis Meyer.

Magazine Needs: *Bulk Head* appears online quarterly, publishing quality poetry, fiction, and nonfiction. "We like angst. We like anything experimental. Shorter poems. No religious stuff (unless angry). Nothing rhyming. No song lyrics." Recently published poetry by Paul Dilsaver, Janet Buck, Greg Kosmicki, Leslie Bentley, Matt Mason, and Duane Locke. As a sample the editor selected these lines from "Date with Pete" by Cassandra Labairon:

> We stop at McDonalds/for soda. His brother/is there, giggling/with a group/of high school/girls, Pete
> winks/and whispers,/"Ladies man./It's in the genes."

Bulk Head is published online only with b&w photos. Receives about 120 poems/year, accepts about 30%. Publishes about 10-20 poems/issue. Single copy: free online; subscription: free online.

How to Submit: Submit 3 poems at a time. Line length for poetry is 2-4 minimum, 50 maximum. No previously published or simultaneous submissions. Accepts e-mail submissions only. Cover letter is required. "Include a short bio." Reads submissions up to the date of publication. Time between acceptance and publication is up to 3 months. "For now, this is a one-man operation." Seldom comments on rejected poems. Guidelines are available in magazine and on website. Responds in up to 3 months. Acquires first rights, one-time rights. Reviews books and chapbooks of poetry and other magazines/journals. Poets may send books for review consideration.

Book/Chapbook Needs & How to Submit: Bridge Burner's Publishing presents work of "genius, anger, unpublished greatness." Publishes 1-2 paperback, 1-2 chapbooks/year. Books/chapbooks are usually 16-80 pages. Query first, with a few sample poems and a cover letter with brief bio and publication credits. "We will consider polished collections for chapbooks." Responds to queries in 2 weeks; to mss in 2 months. Order sample books/chapbooks by sending $15 to Bridge Burner's.

Also Offers: Annual Bulk Head Poetry Contest. Entry fee: $1. Check website for details. "We've decided to publish a print edition of *Bulk Head* starting later this year. Details will be on the website."

USE THE GENERAL INDEX in the back of this book to find the page number of a specific market. Also, markets listed in the 2002 edition but not included in this edition appear in the General Index with a code explaining their absence from the listings.

Advice: "We are open to anything, but we prefer writing stripped of all romance and glamour. We especially like constructive angst. Don't shoot up your office or school! Write a poem instead."

☾ BURNING BUSH PUBLICATIONS; IN OUR OWN WORDS; THE PART-TIMER POST; PEOPLE BEFORE PROFITS POETRY PRIZE, P.O. Box 9636, Oakland CA 94613. (510)482-9996. E-mail: editor@bbbooks.com. Website: www.bbbooks.com (includes "the inspiration behind Burning Bush Publications", lists our mail order titles, writer's guidelines, contest guidelines, and features literary e-zines). Established 1996. **Contact:** Acquisitions Editor.

Book/Chapbook Needs: Burning Bush serves "voices that are underserved by mainstream presses." Wants "uplifting writing that believes in a more harmonious and equitable world with an emphasis on social justice and conscience." Does not want "any work that is degrading to humans or other lifeforms." Has published poetry by Morton Marcus, Lyn Lifshin, Patti Sirens, Opal Palmer Adisa, Abby Lynn Bogomolny, and Grace Paley. As a sample the editor selected these lines from "Grito de vieques" by Aya de Leon:

> Tender shoots of grass push up toward the sky./A lizard sneaks back to sun itself on a chunk of shrapnel./ A butterfly alights on a rusted out jet./Fish slowly make their way back toward my shores,/no longer reverberating with shockwaves of violation.

Books are usually 144 pages, 5½ × 8½, offset, perfect-bound with medium card cover and photographs.

How to Submit: Press is not accepting mss until further notice.

Magazine Needs & How to Submit: "Writers may submit poetry, fiction, or essays for our online e-zines, *In Our Own Words* and *The Part-Timer Post* or send entries to our People Before Profits Poetry Prize." Seldom comments on rejected work. Guidelines available for SASE or on website. Responds in 2 months. "Authors are paid in publication and by individual contract."

Also Offers: People Before Profits Poetry Prize awards a $200 first prize and two Honorable Mentions. Submit up to 3 poems in any style or form. Include name, title of poems, address, entry fee, phone and e-mail address on separate sheet. Entry fee: $10. Guidelines available for SASE and on website. Winners published in e-zine. Books are distributed to the trade by Bookpeople, Baker & Taylor, and Small Press Distribution.

⊘ BUTTON MAGAZINE, 3 Oak Ave., Lunenburg MA 01462. E-mail: buttonx26@aol.com. Website: http://moonsigns.net (includes contact and subscription information). Established 1993. **Editor:** Sally Cragin. **Contact:** Maude Piper.

Magazine Needs: *Button* "is New England's tiniest magazine of fiction, poetry, and gracious living." Wants "poetry about the quiet surprises in life, not sentimental, and true moments carefully preserved. Brevity counts." Has published poetry by William Corbett, Amanda Powell, Brendan Galvin, Jean Monahan, Diana Der-Hovanessian, Kevin McGrath, and Sappho ("Hey, we have a fabulous translator in Julia Dubnoff!"). As a sample the editor selected these lines from "Cereal Haiku" by Richard Boursy:

> Bumpy and crunchy/the Golden flakes of Total/bursting with goodness

Button appears twice/year and is 30 pages, 4¼ × 5½, saddle-stapled, card stock 4-color cover with illustrations that incorporate one or more buttons. Press run is 1,200 for more than 500 subscribers; 750 shelf sales. Subscription: $5/2 years, $25/lifetime. Sample: $2 and a first class stamp.

How to Submit: Submit no more than 2 poems at a time. No previously published poems. Cover letter required. Time between acceptance and publication is up to 6 months. Poems are circulated to an editorial board. Often comments on rejected poems. Guidelines available by e-mail. Responds in 4 months. Pays honorarium, subscription, and at least 5 copies. Acquires first North American serial rights.

Advice: "Read good work by giants in the field. Eradicate 'I'. Revise. Wait. Revise some more. Wait some more. Keep submissions at least 6 months apart so you can revise. Wait. Revise."

$ ⊘ ◎ BYLINE MAGAZINE; BYLINE LITERARY AWARDS (Specialized: writing), P.O. Box 5240, Edmond OK 73083-0001. (405)348-5591. E-mail: MPreston@bylinemag.com. Website: www.byline mag.com (features guidelines, contest listings, subscription info, and sample column or article from magazine). Established 1981. **Poetry Editor:** Sandra Soli. **Editor:** Marcia Preston.

Magazine Needs: *ByLine* is a magazine for the encouragement of writers and poets, using 8-10 poems/issue about writers or writing. Has published poetry by Judith Tate O'Brien, Katheryn Howd Machan, and Henry B. Stobbs. *ByLine* is magazine-sized, professionally printed, with illustrations, cartoons, and ads. Has more than 3,000 subscriptions and receives about 2,500 poetry submissions/year, of which about 100 are used. Subscription: $22. Sample: $4.

How to Submit: Submit up to 3 poems at a time, no reprints. No e-mail or fax submissions, please. Guidelines available for SASE or on website. Responds within 6 weeks. Pays $10/poem. Acquires first North American serial rights.

Also Offers: Sponsors up to 20 poetry contests, including a chapbook competition open to anyone. Send #10 SASE for details. Also sponsors the *ByLine* Short Fiction and Poetry Awards. Prize: $250. Send SASE for guidelines.

Advice: "We are happy to work with new writers, but please read a few samples to get an idea of our style. We would like to see more serious poetry about the creative experience (as it concerns writing)."

N ✉ ◎ BYTES OF POETRY; LOVESTORIES.COM; BACKUP COMPUTER RESOURCES (Specialized: anthologies), 905 S. 30th St., Broken Arrow OK 74014. Phone/fax: (918)251-4652. E-mail: webmaster@lovestories.com. Website: www.lovestories.com. Website established September 1997. **Founder/Editor:** Alanna Webb.

Book/Chapbook Needs: Under *Bytes of Poetry*, Backup Computer Resources publishes 2-4 poetry anthologies per year. "We are looking for heartfelt poetry. Our emphasis is poetry written by everyday people. We review poetry written by all ages, on a wide range of topics, and in a wide range of styles. We do not accept poetry that contains profanity, or very explicit subject matter. We do accept sensual poetry though." Has published poetry by C.J. Heck, Paula Duquette, Susan Fridkin, Randall Longshore, Max the Poet, and Chuck Pool. As a sample the editor selected this poem, "Live on (Peter's Poem)" by Julia Warfel:

> Love could not hold you,/Nor could our tears./You suffered in silence,/Enslaved by your fears./Now
> mortal boundaries,/Keep us apart,/But live in my memory./Live on in my heart.

Books are usually 150-170 pages, 5½×8½, offset printed and perfect-bound with full-color paper cover, custom designed

How to Submit: "We only print poetry anthologies of poetry posted by people on our website. Poets can post 5 poems/24 hours onto our website. To post, poets must sign up for our free Poet Account." Accepts previously published poems and simultaneous submissions. Submit seasonal poems 4 months in advance. Time between acceptance and publication is 3 months. "Poetry for our books are selected by our internal staff with the help of nominations by fellow poets on the website." Seldom comments on rejected poems. Responds in 1 month. Pays 1 author's copy/published poem (out of a press run of 5,000). Order sample books by calling Book Clearing House at (800)431-1579 or ordering online at www.bytesofpoetry.com.

Also Offers: Sponsors weekly and monthly poetry contests, voted by visitors and staff. Winners are reviewed for possible inclusion in books. Also, visit their website to vote for the weekly Top 10 Poems. "Our staff and sponsors select the Poem of the Month winners from all poems posted on a monthly topic. Our website (Lovestories.com) has one of the largest poetry sections on the Internet, as part of our love and romance community. BytesofPoetry.com is our special domain that contains details on the books we publish, including sample poems, forms to contact the poets, Our News Releases, and reviews and order information." Also posts e-mail interviews with poets and publishers.

Advice: "We believe that there is a lot of untapped talent in everyday people who haven't studied poetry formally. Our goal is to promote poetry written at the grassroots level and to promote poetry to everyone. We encourage people to make poetry reading part of their everyday life. The Internet can be a wonderful way to learn about poetry, get feedback and recognition for your poetry, and interact with other poets. Just be wary of contest scams and check out the sites you frequent and post at."

◗ CALIFORNIA QUARTERLY; CALIFORNIA STATE POETRY SOCIETY, P.O. Box 7126, Orange CA 92863-7126. (949)854-8024. E-mail: jipalley@aol.com. Website: www.chapman.edu/comm/english/CSPS (includes guidelines, contact information, contest information, subscription information). Established 1972. **Editors:** Julian Palley and Kate Ozbirn.

Magazine Needs: *California Quarterly* is the official publication of the California State Poetry Society (an affiliate of the National Federation of State Poetry Societies) and is designed "to encourage the writing and dissemination of poetry." Wants poetry on any subject, 60 lines maximum. "No geographical limitations. Quality is all that matters." Has published poetry by Michael L. Johnson, Lyn Lifshin, and Robert Cooperman. *California Quarterly* is 64 pages, 5½×8½, offset-printed, perfect-bound, heavy paper cover with art. Receives 3,000-4,000 poems/year, accepts about 5%. Press run is 500 for 300 subscribers of which 24 are libraries, 20-30 shelf sales. Membership in CSPS is $20/year and includes a subscription to *California Quarterly.* Sample (including guidelines): $5. Guidelines available for SASE.

How to Submit: Submit up to 6 "relatively brief" poems at a time; name and address on each sheet. Include SASE. Prefer no previously published poems. Accepts submissions by post only; no e-mail submissions. Seldom comments on rejected poems. Responds in up to 8 months. Pays 1 copy. Acquires first rights. Rights revert to poet after publication.

Also Offers: CSPS also sponsors an annual poetry contest. Awards vary. All entries considered for *California Quarterly.*

Advice: "Since our editor changes with each issue, we encourage poets to resubmit."

🔟 🗖 🗐 **CALLALOO (Specialized: ethnic)**, Dept. of English, Texas A&M University, 4227 TAMU, College Station TX 77843-4227. (979)458-3108. Fax: (979)458-3275. E-mail: callaloo@tamu.edu. Website: http://callaloo.tamu.edu. Established 1976. **Editor:** Charles H. Rowell.

● Poetry published in *Callaloo* has been frequently included in volumes of *The Best American Poetry.*

Magazine Needs: *Callaloo: A Journal of African Diaspora Arts & Letters* is devoted to poetry dealing with the African Diaspora, including North America, Europe, Africa, Latin and Central America, South America, and the Caribbean. Has published poetry by Nathaniel Mackey, Lucille Clifton, Harryette Mullen, Audre Lorde, Will Alexander, and Cave Canem poets. This thick quarterly journal features about 15-20 poems (all forms and styles) in each issue along with short fiction, interviews, literary criticism, and concise and scholarly book reviews. Circulation is 1,600 subscribers of which half are libraries. Subscription: $36, $92 for institutions.

How to Submit: Submit complete ms in triplicate. Include cover letter with name, mailing address, e-mail address if available, and SASE. No fax or e-mail submissions. Responds in 6 months. Pays copies.

🗖 🗐 **CALYX, A JOURNAL OF ART & LITERATURE BY WOMEN (Specialized: women, lesbian, multicultural); CALYX BOOKS**, P.O. Box B, Corvallis OR 97339-0539. (541)753-9384. Fax: (541)753-0515. E-mail: calyx@proaxis.com. Established 1976. **Senior Editor:** Beverly McFarland. **Managing Editor:** Micki Reaman.

Magazine Needs: *Calyx* is a journal edited by a collective editorial board. Publishes poetry, prose, art, book reviews, and interviews by and about women. Wants "excellently crafted poetry that also has excellent content." Has published poetry by Maurya Simon, Diane Averill, Carole Boston Weatherford, and Eleanor Wilner. As a sample the editor selected these lines from "Transparent Woman" by Donna Henderson:

> in the basement of the science museum,/half-lit, naked, and marvelous with her perfect/posture, lucite
> arms straight and slightly apart,/palms turned toward us like the Blessed Virgin's,/helplessly
> welcoming.

Calyx appears 3 times every 18 months and is 6×8, handsomely printed on heavy paper, flat-spined, glossy color cover, 128-144 pages, of which 50-60 are poetry. Poems tend to be lyric free verse that makes strong use of image and symbol melding unobtrusively with voice and theme. Single copy: $9.50. Sample: $11.50.

How to Submit: Send up to 6 poems with SASE and short bio. "We accept copies in good condition and clearly readable. We focus on new writing, but occasionally publish a previously published piece." Accepts simultaneous submissions, "if kept up-to-date on publication." No fax or e-mail submissions. *Calyx* is open to submissions October 1 through December 31 only. Mss received when not open to reading will be returned unread. Guidelines available for SASE or e-mail. Responds in 9 months. Pays 1 copy/poem and subscription. Poets may send books for review consideration.

Book/Chapbook Needs & How to Submit: Calyx Books publishes 1 book of poetry/year. All work published is by women. Recently published: *Black Candle* by Chitra Divakaruni. However, Calyx Books is closed for ms submissions until further notice.

Advice: "Read the publication and be familiar with what we have published."

🔟 🗐 **CANADIAN WOMAN STUDIES (Specialized: women)**, 212 Founders College, York University, 4700 Keele St., North York, Ontario M3J 1P3 Canada. (416)736-5356. Fax: (416)736-5765. E-mail: cwscf@yorku.ca. Website: www.yorku.ca/cwscf (includes tables of contents, policies, order information, guidelines for submissions, and calls for papers). Established 1978. **Literary Editor:** Marlene Kadar.

Magazine Needs: *Canadian Woman Studies* appears quarterly and focuses on "women's studies; experiential and academic articles, poetry, book reviews, and artwork." Wants poetry "exploring women's lives/ perspectives. No long poems (i.e., more than 50 lines)." Has published poetry by Libby Scheier, Patience Wheatley, and Lyn Lifshin. *Canadian Woman Studies* is about 152 pages, magazine-sized, offset-printed and perfect-bound with full color cover, includes art and ads. Receives 400 poems/year, accepts about 15%. Press run is 4,000 for 1,500 subscribers of which 500 are libraries, 1,000 shelf sales; 250 distributed free to women's groups. Single copy: $10; subscription: $36 plus $2.52 gst/year plus $15 for US orders. Sample: $13.

How to Submit: Submit 5 poems at a time. No previously published poems or simultaneous submissions. Accepts e-mail submissions. Cover letter required. "SASE (or SAE and IRC) appreciated, bio note must accompany submission." Time between acceptance and publication is 5 months. Publishes theme issues. Responds in 5 months. Pays 1 copy. "Poets maintain copyright of their work at all times." Reviews books and chapbooks of poetry in 750 words, single and multi-book format. Poets may send books for review consideration to Fran Beer, book review editor.

$ 🗓 📷 **CANADIAN WRITER'S JOURNAL (Specialized: writing)**, White Mountain Publications, Box 5180, New Liskeard, Ontario P0J 1P0 Canada. (705)647-5424. Fax: (705)647-8366. E-mail: cwj@cwj.ca. Website: www.cwj.ca (includes writer's guidelines and information on subscription, contests, and contacting). **Editor:** Deborah Ranchuk.

Magazine Needs: *Canadian Writer's Journal* is a digest-sized bimonthly, publishing mainly short "how-to" articles of interest to writers at all levels. Use a few "short poems or portions thereof as part of 'how-to' articles relating to the writing of poetry and occasional short poems with tie-in to the writing theme. We try for 90% Canadian content but prefer good material over country of origin, or how well you're known." Subscription: $35/year, $67.50/2 years, add 7% gst in Canada. Sample: $8.

How to Submit: Submit up to 5 poems ("poems should be titled"). Include SASE ("U.S. postage accepted; do not affix to envelope"). No previously published poems. Accepts e-mail and fax submissions. "Include in body of message, not as attachment. Write 'Submission' in the subject line." Hard copy and SASE (or SAE and IRC) required if accepted." Responds in 3 months. Token payment. Pays $2-7.50 and 1 copy/poem.

$ 🗓 **THE CAPILANO REVIEW**, 2055 Purcell Way, North Vancouver, British Columbia V7J 3H5 Canada. (604)984-1712. E-mail: tcr@capcollege.bc.ca. Website: www.capcollege.bc.ca/dept/TCR/ (includes guidelines, excerpts, subscription info, contest info, etc.). Established 1972. **Editor:** Sharon Thesen.

Magazine Needs: *The Capilano Review* is a literary and visual arts review appearing 3 times/year. Wants "avant-garde, experimental, previously unpublished work, poetry of sustained intelligence and imagination. We are interested in poetry that is new in concept and in execution." Has published poetry by bill bissett, Phyllis Webb, and Michael Ondaatje. *The Capilano Review* comes in a handsome digest-sized format, 115 pages, flat-spined, finely printed, semi-glossy stock with a glossy full-color card cover. Circulation is 1,000. Sample: $9 prepaid.

How to Submit: Submit 5-6 poems, minimum, with cover letter and SAE and IRC (no US postage). No simultaneous submissions. No e-mail or disk submissions. Responds in up to 5 months. Pays $50-200, subscription, plus 2 copies. Acquires first North American serial rights.

Advice: "*The Capilano Review* receives several manuscripts each week; unfortunately the majority of them are simply inappropriate for the magazine. The best advice we can offer is to read the magazine before you submit."

$ ◯ 🗓 📷 **CAPPER'S; BRAVE HEARTS (Specialized: inspirational, humor, themes)**, 1503 SW 42nd St., Topeka KS 66609-1265. (785)274-4300. Fax: (785)274-4305. Website: www.cappers.com (includes guidelines and summary of current issue). Established 1879. **Editor:** Ann Crahan.

Magazine Needs & How to Submit: *Capper's* is a biweekly tabloid (newsprint) going to 240,000 mail subscribers, mostly small-town and rural families. Wants short poems (4-16 lines preferred, lines of one-column width) "relating to everyday situations, nature, inspirational, humorous. Most poems used in *Capper's* are upbeat in tone and offer the reader a bit of humor, joy, enthusiasm, or encouragement." Accepts poetry written by children, ages 12 and under and 13-19. Has published poetry by Elizabeth Searle Lamb, Robert Brimm, Margaret Wiedyke, Helena K. Stefanski, Sheryl L. Nelms, and Claire Puneky. Send $1.95 for sample. Uses 6-8 poems in each issue. Not available on newsstand. Submit 5-6 poems at a time, 14-16 lines. No simultaneous submissions. No e-mail or fax submissions. Returns mss with SASE. Publishes seasonal theme issues. Upcoming themes available for SASE. Responds in 3 months. Pays $10-15/poem. Additional payment of $5 if poem is used on website. Acquires one-time rights.

Magazine Needs & How to Submit: *Brave Hearts* is an inspirational magazine appearing quarterly in February, May, August, and November. Features themes and humorous poems. "Poems should be short (16 lines or less)." Sample: $4.95. Does not accept poetry by children. Guidelines and themes available for SASE. Accepts submissions by postal mail only. Pays on acceptance and 1 copy.

Advice: "Poems chosen are upbeat, sometimes humorous, always easily understood. Short poems of this type fit our format best."

🏴 ◯ 📷 **THE CARIBBEAN WRITER (Specialized: regional, Caribbean); THE DAILY NEWS PRIZE; THE CANUTE A. BRODHURT PRIZE; THE CHARLOTTE AND ISIDOR PAIEWONSKY PRIZE; DAVID HOUGH LITERARY PRIZE; THE MARGUERITE COBB MCKAY PRIZE**, University of the Virgin Islands, RR 02, P.O. Box 10,000, Kingshill, St. Croix, USVI

00850. (340)692-4152. Fax: (340)692-4026. E-mail: qmars@uvi.edu. Website: www.TheCaribbeanWriter. com (includes guidelines, bios, themes, links, as well as information on how to contact, subscribe, and enter contest). Established 1987. **Editor:** Dr. Erika Waters. **Contact:** Ms. Quilin Mars.

• Poetry published in *The Caribbean Writer* has been included in the 2002 *Pushcart Prize* anthology.

Magazine Needs: *The Caribbean Writer* is a literary anthology, appearing in July, with a Caribbean focus. The Caribbean must be central to the literary work or the work must reflect a Caribbean heritage, experience or perspective. Has published poetry by Virgil Suarez, Thomas Reiter, Kamau Brathwaite, and Opal Palmer Adisa. *The Caribbean Writer* magazine is over 300 pages, 6×9, handsomely printed on heavy stock, perfect-bound, with glossy card cover, using advertising and b&w art by Caribbean artists. Press run is 1,200. Single copy: $12 plus $4 postage; subscription: $20. Sample: $7 plus $4 postage. Guidelines are available for SASE. (Note: postage to and from the Virgin Islands is the same as within the US.)

How to Submit: Submit up to 5 poems. Accepts simultaneous submissions; no previously published poems. Accepts submissions by e-mail (attached file), on disk, and by post; no fax submissions. Blind submissions only: name, address, phone number, and title of ms should appear in cover letter along with brief bio. Title only on ms. Deadline is September 30 of each year. Publishes theme issues. Guidelines available for SASE, by e-mail, on website, and in publication. Pays 2 copies. Acquires first North American serial rights. Reviews books of poetry and fiction in 1,000 words. Poets may send books for review consideration.

Also Offers: The magazine annually awards the Daily News Prize ($300) for the best poem or poems, The Marguerite Cobb McKay Prize to a Virgin Island author ($100), the David Hough Literary Prize to a Caribbean author ($500), the Canute A. Brodhurst Prize for Fiction ($400), and the Charlotte and Isidor Paiewonsky Prize ($200) for first-time publication.

CATAMOUNT PRESS; COTYLEDON (Specialized: short poems, haiku, tanka), 2519 Roland Rd. SW, Huntsville AL 35805-4147. Established 1992. **Editor:** Georgette Perry.

Magazine Needs: *Cotyledon*, established in 1997 and published 4 times/year, is a miniature magazine. Wants poems up to 8 lines. Nature and the environment are favorite subjects, but a variety of subject matter is needed. Poets recently published include Gerrye Payne, John Cantey Knight, and Ross Figgins. As a sample the editor has selected these lines by Tommy Curran:

> *midsummer pond/small dark fishes motionless/in all directions*

Cotyledon is 16 pages, 3½×4¼, photocopied, saddle-stapled, with bond cover and b&w art. Sample: $1 or 3 unattached first class stamps.

How to Submit: Submit 3-6 poems at a time with cover letter and SASE. Accepts previously published poems if identified as such. Send three unattached first-class stamps for a sample *Cotyledon*, guidelines, and news of press offerings and plans. Responds in 2 months. Pays at least 2 copies.

Book/Chapbook Needs & How to Submit: "Catamount Press publishes very few chapbooks, so please do not submit a ms. Get acquainted with us first by submitting to *Cotyledon*, or querying."

CAVEAT LECTOR, 400 Hyde St., Apt. 606, San Francisco CA 94109-7445. Phone/fax: (415)928-7431. Website: http://caveat-lector.org (includes archives, links, editorial policy, and information on subscription and how to contact). Established 1989. **Editors:** Christopher Bernard, Ho Lin, James Bybee, and Andrew Towne.

Magazine Needs: Appearing 2 times/year, "*Caveat Lector* is devoted to the arts and to cultural and philosophical commentary. We publish visual art and music as well as literary and theoretical texts. We are looking for accomplished poems, something that resonates in the mind long after the reader has laid the poem aside. We want work that has authenticity of emotion and high craft; whether raw or polished, that rings true—if humorous, actually funny, or at least witty. Classical to experimental. 500-line limit." Has published poetry by Deanne Bayer, Simon Perchik, Alfred Robinson, and E.S. Hilbert. As a sample the editor selected these lines from "To A Friend Who Has Not Written," by Christopher Hewitt:

> *You must have some news./I do. The asters bloomed. There's/still no rain./Oh and I go often to/A place*
> *I found/Where leaves are letters falling/All of which I've written.//How I exhaust myself/Catching*
> *them!*

Caveat Lector is 36-64 pages, 11×4¼, photocopied and saddle-stapled with b&w card cover. Receives 600-800 poems/year, accepts about 2%. Press run is 300 for 30 subscribers, 200 shelf sales. Single copy: $3.50; subscription: $15/4 issues. Sample: $3.

How to Submit: Submit up to 6 short poems (up to 50 lines each), 3 medium length poems (51-100 lines), or 1 long poem (up to 500 lines) at a time "on any subject, in any style, as long as the work is authentic in feeling and appropriately crafted." Place name, address, and (optional) telephone number on each page. Include SASE, cover letter, and brief bio (30 words or less). Accepts simultaneous submissions, "but please inform us." Guidelines available for SASE. Time between acceptance and publication is 1 year. Reads submissions from January to June. Sometimes comments on rejected poems. Responds in 1 month. Pays 2 copies. Acquires first publication rights.

Advice: "The two rules of writing are: 1. Rewrite it again. 2. Rewrite it again. The writing level of most of our submissions is pleasingly high. A rejection by us is not always a criticism of the work, and we try to provide comments to our more promising submitters."

$⬤ CC. MARIMBO, P.O. Box 933, Berkeley CA 94701-0933. Established 1996. **Editor:** Peggy Golden.

Book/Chapbook Needs: CC. Marimbo "promotes the work of underpublished poets/artists by providing a well-crafted, cheap (people's prices) and therefore affordable/accessible, collection." Publishes 2-3 poetry titles per year. "Books are issued as 'minichaps' to introduce underpublished poets/artists to the public. Runs done by alphabet, lettered A-Z, AA-ZZ, etc. Short poems for the small format, styles, and content welcome in whatever variation. We do not want to see already published work, unless poems previously in print in magazines (attributed), i.e., poems OK, reprintable books not OK." Has published poetry by David Stone, Mark States, and Marie Kazala. As a sample the editor selected this poem, "These Kids," from *My Back Yardstick* by Tom Plante:
> Singing, these kids/kicking that eternal ball

Chapbooks are usually 40 pages, 4¼ × 5¼ or 5½ × 4¼, offset-printed and photocopied, mainly handsewn binding with matt cover, includes art/graphics according to project.

How to Submit: Query first, with a few sample poems and cover letter with brief bio and publication credits, include SASE. Line length for poetry is 25 maximum. Responds in 2 months to queries; 3 months to mss. Pays 5 author's copies (out of a press run of 26), additional copies paid for larger press runs. "Author gets 10% of cover price on all copies sold, except for copies sold to author." Order sample chapbooks by sending $5 (5¢ for p&h).

Advice: "We must keep seeking."

Ⓝ $◎ CC MOTORCYCLE NEWS MAGAZINE (Specialized: sports/recreation), P.O. Box 808, Nyack NY 10960-0808. (914)353-MOTO. Fax: (914)353-5240. E-mail: info@motorcyclenews.cc. Website: www.motorcyclenews.cc. Established 1990.

Magazine Needs: *CCMNM* is a monthly containing regional motorcycle news and features. Wants motorcycle-related poetry. *CCMNM* is tabloid-sized and printed on newsprint. Circulation of 60,000; available in 1,000 motorcycle shops from Washington, DC to Rhode Island to Chicago. Sample: $4. Offers subscriptions. Make checks payable to Motomag Corp.

How to Submit: Submit up to 5 poems at a time. Accepts previously published poems and simultaneous submissions. Cover letter required including SASE. Time between acceptance and publication is 1-4 months. Often comments on rejected poems. Publishes theme issues. Send SASE for guidelines and upcoming themes. Responds in 1 month. Pays $10-25. Buys one-time regional rights and Internet rights.

◯ CHAFF, P.O. Box 632, McHenry IL 60051-0632. E-mail: jordan5450@aol.com. Established 1996. First issue 1997. **Editor/Co-publisher:** Jordan Taylor Young.

Magazine Needs: *Chaff* is a semiannual publication "dedicated to the Lord, for the express purpose of reaching out to a lost and dying world, as well as uniting Christian poets through the publication of their work." Wants "free verse poetry—rhyme and meter only if exceptional quality—romance, nature, aging, friendship, family life, animals, senior citizens, social issues, children, and humor. Nothing satanic, obscene, violent, sensual, erotic, or homosexual." As a sample the editor selected this poem, "This Miracle Mile" by Jordan Taylor Young:
> Who gives music to the songbird, feathered limbs for flight, what determines when the stars should
> shine, and bid the morning night. I often ask on bended knee by what possessed this smile, for I am
> but a feeble guest upon this miracle mile.

Chaff is 20-30 pages, 5½ × 8, laser-printed and stapled. Press run is 50-100. Single copy: $12. Poetry may be complemented by appropriate photographs, illustrations, or scripture. In addition, *Chaff* includes a "Featured Poet" segment, consisting of a short bio and photograph.

How to Submit: Submit no more than 6 poems; there is a reading fee of $5 for two poems. Make checks payable to Jordan Taylor Young, editor. Accepts previously published poems and simultaneous submissions. Accepts e-mail submissions; no fax submissions. Cover letter and SASE required. Responds in 1 month. Guidelines available for SASE and in publication. Pays 2 copies, 3 copies to Featured Poet.

Advice: "Often poets are not recognized for their artistry, separated like chaff from wheat. The name *Chaff* stems from the editors' deep conviction that we are like chaff, and separated from God we can do nothing! 'All flesh is grass and its loveliness is like the flower of the fields. The grass withers, the flower fades, because the breath of the Lord blows upon us . . . But the word of our God stands forever.' (Isaiah 40:6-8). We intend to provide a stronger link to self, helping new and aspiring poets to find their own voices through the publication of their work. 'For where your treasure is, there will your heart be also.' (Matthew 6:21)."

⬤ CHAFFIN JOURNAL, Dept. of English, Case Annex 467, Eastern Kentucky University, Richmond KY 40475-3102. (859)622-3080. Established 1998. **Editor:** Robert W. Witt.

Magazine Needs: *The Chaffin Journal* appears annually. Publishes quality short fiction and poetry by new and established writers/poets. Wants any form, subject matter, or style. Does not want "poor quality." Recently published poetry by Pat Boran, James Doyle, Corey Mesler, Simon Perchik, Philip St. Clair, and Virgil Suarez. As a sample the editor selected these lines from "The Home Place" by Philip St. Clair:

> *It's Saturday morning, and a fiftyish woman sits in a booth/in a family-style restaurant, staring/out of the window as she smokes mentholated cigarettes/one after another. The walls/are hung with sepia photos and antique tools, conjuring/bygone days, country virtues . . .*

The Chaffin Journal is 120 pages, digest-sized, offset-printed, perfect-bound, plain cover with title only. Receives about 200 poems/year, accepts about 25%. Publishes about 40-50 poems/issue. Press run is 300 for 65 subscribers of which 3 are libraries, 180 shelf sales; 40-50 are distributed free to contributors. Single copy: $5; subscription: $5 annually. Make checks payable to *The Chaffin Journal*.

How to Submit: Submit 5 poems at a time. Accepts simultaneous submission; no previousy published poems. No fax, e-mail, or disk submissions. Cover letter is preferred. "Submit typed, double-spaced pages with only one poem per page. Enclose SASE." Reads submissions June 1 through November 1. Time between acceptance and publication is 6 months. Poems are reviewed by the general editor and 2 poetry editors. Never comments on rejected poems. Guidelines available in magazine. Responds in 3 months. Pays 1 contributor's copy. Acquires one-time rights.

🍁 ◯ ◎ CHALLENGER INTERNATIONAL; MCNAUGHTON EDITIONS (Specialized: teen/young adult). (250)991-5567. E-mail: lukivdan@hotmail.com. Website: http://challengerinternation al.20m.com/index.html. Established 1978. **Editor:** Dan Lukiv.

Magazine Needs: *Challenger international*, a literary quarterly, contains poetry, short fiction, novel excerpts, and black pen drawings. Open to "any type of work, especially by teenagers (*Ci*'s mandate: to encourage young writers, and to publish their work alongside established writers), providing it is not pornographic, profane, or overly abstract." *Ci* has published poetry from Canada, the US, Switzerland, Russia, Ireland, Korea, and Columbia. As a sample the editor selected a haiku from *Thirteen Goslings* by Dan Lukiv:

> *Rain/Fills the forest/With sound.*

Ci is about 20 pages, 8½×11, photocopied and side-stapled. Press run is 50. *Ci* is distributed free to McNaughton Center-secondary alternate-students.

How to Submit: Accepts previously published poems and simultaneous submissions. Cover letter required with list of credits, if any. Accepts only e-mail submissions. "Sometimes we edit to save the poet rejection." Responds in 4 months. Pays 1 copy.

Book/Chapbook Needs & How to Submit: McNaughton Editions publishes chapbooks of work by authors featured in *Ci*. Pays 3 copies. Copyright remains with author. Distribution of free copies through McNaughton Center.

Advice: "Concrete imagery and clear themes get our attention."

🌐 ◗ ◎ CHAPMAN (Specialized: ethnic); CHAPMAN PUBLISHING, 4 Broughton Place, Edinburgh EH1 3RX Scotland. Phone: (0131)557-2207. Fax: (0131)556-9565. E-mail: editor@chapman-pub.co.uk. Website: www.chapman-pub.co.uk (includes sample of current issue, guidelines, back list of issues, and publications). Established 1970. **Editor:** Joy Hendry.

Magazine Needs: "*Chapman* magazine is controversial, influential, outspoken, and intelligent. Established in 1970, it has become a dynamic force in Scottish culture covering theatre, politics, language, and the arts. Our highly-respected forum for poetry, fiction, criticism, review, and debate makes it essential reading for anyone interested in contemporary Scotland. *Chapman* publishes the best in Scottish writing—new work by well-known Scottish writers in the context of lucid critical discussion. It also, increasingly, publishes international writing. With our strong commitment to the future, we energetically promote new writers, new ideas and new approaches." Has published poetry and fiction by Alasdair Gray, Liz Lochhead, Sorley MacLean, T.S. Law, Edwin Morgan, Willa Muir, Tom Scott, and Una Flett. As a sample the editor selected these lines from Judy Steel's poem "For Nicole Boulanger" who, Steel says, "was born in the same year as my daughter and died in the Lockerbie air disaster of 1988":

You died amongst these rolling Border hills:/The same our daughters played and rode and walked in -/
They make a nursery fit to shape and mould/A spirit swift as water, free as air.//But you, west-winging
through the Christmas dark/Found them no playground but a mortuary -/Your young life poised for
flight to woman's years/Destroyed as wantonly as moorland game.

Chapman appears 3 times/year in a 6×9, perfect-bound format, 144 pages, professionally printed in small type on matte stock with glossy card cover, art in 2 colors. Press run is 2,000 for 900 subscribers of which 200 are libraries. Receives "thousands" of poetry submissions/year, accepts about 200, has a 4- to 6-month backlog. Single copy: £6; subscription: £18. Sample: £4 (overseas).

How to Submit: "We welcome submissions which must be accompanied by a SASE/IRC. Please send sufficient postage to cover the return of your manuscript. Do not send foreign stamps." Submit 4-10 poems at a time, one poem/page. "We do not usually publish single poems." No simultaneous submissions. Cover letter required. Responds "as soon as possible." Always sends prepublication galleys. Pays copies. Staff reviews books of poetry. Send books for review consideration.

Book/Chapbook Needs: Chapman Publishing is currently not accepting submissions.

Advice: "Poets should not try to court approval by writing poems especially to suit what they perceive as the nature of the magazine. They usually get it wrong and write badly." Also, they are interested in receiving poetry dealing with women's issues and feminism.

N **C** **CHAPULTEPEC PRESS**, 111 E. University #3, Cincinnati OH 45219. (513)281-9248. E-mail: chapultepecpress@hotmail.com. Established 2001. **Contact:** David Garza.

Book/Chapbook Needs & How to Submit: Chapultepec Press publishes books of poetry/literature, essays, social/political issues, art, music, film, library/archive issues, history, popular science, and bilingual. Wants "poetry/literature that works as a unit, that is caustic, fun, open-ended, worldly, mature, relevant, stirring, evocative. Bilingual. No poetry/literature collections without a purpose, that are mere collections." Publishes 5-7 books/year. Books are usually 5-50 pages, with art/graphics. Query first, with a few sample poems and cover letter with brief bio and publication credits. Responds to queries and mss in 1 month. Pays advance of $10-15 and 3-5 author's copies. Order sample books by sending $4 to David Garza.

Also Offers: Currently seeking bawdy limericks for anthology.

Advice: "Write as if your life depends on it . . . because it does."

$ **C** **THE CHARITON REVIEW**, Truman State University, Kirksville MO 63501. (816)785-4499. Established 1975. **Editor:** Jim Barnes.

Magazine Needs: *The Chariton Review* began in 1975 as a twice yearly literary magazine and in 1978 added the activities of the press (now defunct). The poetry published in the magazine is, according to the editor, "open and closed forms—traditional, experimental, mainstream. We do not consider verse, only poetry in its highest sense, whatever that may be. The sentimental and the inspirational are not poetry for us. Also, no more 'relativism': short stories and poetry centered around relatives." Has published poetry by Michael Spence, Kim Bridgford, Sam Maio, Andrea Budy, Charles Edward Eaton, Wayne Dodd, and J'laine Robnolt. There are 40-50 pages of poetry in each issue of the *The Chariton Review*, a 6×9, flat-spined magazine of over 100 pages, professionally printed, glossy cover with photographs. Receives 8,000-10,000 submissions/year, accepts about 35-50, with never more than a 6-month backlog. Press run is about 600 for 400 subscribers of which 100 are libraries. Subscription: $9/1 year, $15/2 years. Sample: $5.

How to Submit: Submit 5-7 poems at a time, typescript single-spaced. No simultaneous submissions. Do *not* write for guidelines. Responds quickly; accepted poems often appear within a few issues of notification. Always sends prepublication galleys. Pays $5/printed page. Acquires first North American serial rights. Contributors are expected to subscribe or buy copies. Poets may send books for review consideration.

N **©** **CHARM CITY REVIEW (Specialized: middle and high school students)**, Ben Franklin Junior High School, 1201 Cambria St., Baltimore MD 21225. (410)396-1373. Fax: (410)396-8434. E-mail: benwildcats@yahoo.com. Established 1999. **Advising Editor:** Kim LaVigueur.

Magazine Needs: *Charm City Review* appears annually in April. Publishes poetry, fiction, and b&w art by middle school and high school students from across the nation. Produced by junior high school students. Wants "all forms, all subject matters, all styles or purposes. Nothing risqué." Accepts poetry written by children. Recently published poetry by Matthew Gonzalez, Michael Townes, and Tamara Foulke. *Charm City Review* is 64 pages, digest-sized, commercially printed, perfect-bound, matte cover, with b&w photos and art, ad swaps for other publications. Receives about 180 poems/year, accepts about 65%. Publishes about 45 poems/issue. Press run is 1,000 for 320 subscribers; all distributed free to Baltimore City Public School Students, contributors and by request. Single copy: free; subscription: $2.95 for shipping. Sample: $2.95. Make checks payable to Benjamin Franklin Junior High School.

How to Submit: Submit 3-5 poems at a time. Accepts previously published poems and simultaneous submissions. Accepts fax, e-mail and disk submissions. Cover letter is required. "If submitted on disk, please no Mac-based. Submit .doc or .txt." Reads submissions September 1 through March 15. Time between acceptance and publication is up to 7 months. Poems are circulated to an editorial board who meets and votes on selections. Never comments on rejected poems. Responds in up to 7 months. Pays 2 contributors copies. Acquires one-time rights.

Also Offers: $25 Prize (one each per publication) to a poet, fiction writer, artist/photographer.

Advice: "Write about what you know/experience."

⬤ CHASE PARK, P.O. Box 9136, Oakland CA 94613-0136. E-mail: twentymule@yahoo.com. Established 2000. **Editor:** David Horton.

Magazine Needs: *Chase Park*, published biannually, is a journal of poetry and poetics. "We attempt to publish a wide range of voices in the contemporary national and international schools and scenes as well as new and independent voices. Open to style and form. Open to experimental, language, concrete, visual, and more traditional approaches." Recently published poetry by Richard Kostelanetz, Elizabeth Robinson, Spencer Selby, Ryan G. Van Cleave, and Rosmarie Waldrop. *Chase Park* is 60-80 pages, digest-sized, perfect-bound, card stock cover with art/graphics on cover only. Receives about 1,000 poems/year, accepts about 5-10%. Publishes about 40-60 poems, 50-70 pages/issue. Press run is 500 for 10 subscribers of which 10 are libraries, 300 shelf sales. Single copy: $7; subscription: $12. Sample: $5. Make checks payable to *Chase Park*.

How to Submit: "Submit up to 7 poems/15 pages. Name and address should appear on all pages." Accepts simultaneous submissions if notified of acceptance elsewhere immediately. No previously published poems. SASE required. No e-mail or disk submissions. "If submitting visual poetry, you may be asked for disk upon acceptance." Reads submissions year-round, "but responses may be slower in summer." Submit seasonal poems 4 months in advance. Time between acceptance and publication is up to 6 months. "Poems are read by editorial assistants who make recommendations to editor. Editor makes final decisions." Seldom comments on rejected poems. Guidelines available for SASE or by e-mail. Responds in 4 months. Sometimes sends prepublication galleys. Pays contributor's copies. Acquires first North American serial rights. Reviews chapbooks and books of poetry and other magazines/journals in 250-500 words, single and multi-book format. Send books for review consideration to the review editor.

$⬤ THE CHATTAHOOCHEE REVIEW, Georgia Perimeter College, 2101 Womack Rd., Dunwoody GA 30338. (770)551-3019. Website: www.chattahoochee-review.org. Established 1980. **Editor-in-Chief:** Lawrence Hetrick. **Poetry Editor:** John Warwick.

Magazine Needs: *The Chattahoochee Review* is a quarterly of poetry, short fiction, essays, reviews, and interviews, published by Georgia Perimeter College. "We publish a number of Southern writers, but *Chattahoochee Review* is not by design a regional magazine. All themes, forms, and styles are considered as long as they impact the whole person: heart, mind, intuition, and imagination." Has published poetry by A.E. Stalling, Carolyne Wright, Coleman Barks, Ron Rash, and Fred Chappell. *Chattahoochee Review* is 140 pages, 6×9, professionally printed on cream stock with reproductions of artwork, flat-spined, with one-color card cover. Recent issues feature a wide range of forms and styles augmenting prose selections. Press run is 1,250, of which 300 are complimentary copies sent to editors and "miscellaneous VIPs." Subscription: $16/year. Sample: $6.

How to Submit: Writers should send 1 copy of each poem and a cover letter with bio material. No simultaneous submissions. Time between acceptance and publication is up to 4 months. Publishes theme issues. Guidelines and a list of upcoming themes available for SASE. Queries will be answered in 1-2 weeks. Responds in 3 months. Pays $50/poem and 2 copies. Acquires first rights. Staff reviews books of poetry and short fiction in 1,500 words, single or multi-book format. Send books for review consideration.

▼ $⬤ CHELSEA; CHELSEA AWARD COMPETITION, P.O. Box 773, Cooper Station, New York NY 10276-0773. E-mail: chelseareview@yahoo.com. Established 1958. **Editor:** Alfredo de Palchi. **Associate Editor:** Andrea Lockett.

 • Work published in *Chelsea* has been included in the 1995, 1997, and 1998 volumes of *The Best American Poetry* and the 1999 and 2000 *Beacon's Best* anthologies.

Magazine Needs: *Chelsea* is a long-established, high quality literary biannual, appearing in June and December, that aims to promote intercultural communication. "We look for intelligence and sophisticated technique in both experimental and traditional forms. We are also interested in translations of contemporary poets. Although our tastes are eclectic, we lean toward the cosmopolitan avant-garde. We would like to see more poetry by writers of color. Do not want to see 'inspirational' verse, pornography or poems that rhyme merely for the sake of rhyme." Has published poetry by D.A. Powell, Joy Katz, Robin Benn, Mark Wunderlich, Diane Ackerman, and Bob Hicok. As an example of "the kind of attention to language and imagery" wanted for *Chelsea*, the editor selected these lines from "The Eye-mote" by Sylvia Plath, which first appeared in *Chelsea* in 1960:

> What I want back is what I was/Before the bed, before the knife,/Before the brooch-pin and the salve/ Fixed me in this parenthesis;/Horses fluent in the wind,/A place, a time gone out of mind.

Chelsea is 192-240 pages, 6×9, perfect-bound, offset-printed, full-color cover art on card cover, occasional photos, ads. Press run is 2,100 for 900 subscribers of which 200 are libraries. Subscription: $13 domestic, $16 foreign. Sample: $7.

How to Submit: *Chelsea* will again be accepting submissions after October 1, 2001. Submissions of 5-7 pages of poetry are ideal; long poems should not exceed 10 pages; must be typed; include brief bio. No previously published poems or simultaneous submissions. E-mail for queries only, not for submissions. "We try to comment favorably on above-average mss; otherwise, we do not have time to provide critiques." Responds within 3 months. Always sends prepublication galleys. Guidelines available for SASE. Pays $20/page and 2 copies. Acquires first North American serial rights and one-time nonexclusive reprint rights.

Also Offers: Sponsors the annual Chelsea Award Competition (deadline December 15), $1,000 for poetry. Guidelines available for SASE.

Advice: "Beginners should realize editors of little magazines are always overworked and that it is necessary haste and not a lack of concern or compassion that makes rejections seem coldly impersonal."

N 🌐 🔲 ◎ **CHERRYBITE PUBLICATIONS; HELICON (Specialized: subscription)**, Linden Cottage, 45 Burton Rd., Little Neston, South Wirral CH64 4AE England. E-mail: helicon@globalnet.co.uk. Website: www.cherrybite.co.uk. Established 1993. **Editor:** Shelagh Nugent.

Magazine Needs: *Helicon* has combined with *Reach* to become a monthly publication. Poems may be any style or length. Poets are strongly advised to study the magazine before submitting. Accepts poetry written by children. Has published poetry by Albert Russo, M. Munro Gibson, RL Cook, and Fiona Curnow. *Helicon* is 40 pages, A5, saddle-stitched with card cover, occasionally includes line drawings, ads. Receives about 2,000 poems/year, accepts approximately 2%. Press run is 400. Single copy: 9 IRCs; subscription: 31 IRCs; sample: 3 IRCs. "Must buy at least one copy before submitting. The standard is high."

How to Submit: Submit 6 poems at a time. All mss must be accompanied by a "submissions form" which can be found inside each current issue. Accepts previously published poems; no simultaneous submissions. "No e-mail submissions accepted"; postal mail only. Cover letter required. Time between acceptance and publication is 6 months. Often comments on rejected poems. Guidelines available on website. Responds in 2 weeks. Copyright remains with the author. Every month, readers vote to award £50.

Also Offers: Sponsors regular competitions and "several booklets of use to poets and writers." Publishes the *Competitions Bulletin*, a bimonthly magazine containing details of UK writing competitions. Send IRC for details.

Advice: "Never send submissions without studying a magazine first. Always send a cover letter."

🔲 **CHILDREN, CHURCHES AND DADDIES; DOWN IN THE DIRT; SCARS PUBLICA-TIONS**, 824 Brian Court, Gurnee IL 60031. E-mail: ccandd96@aol.com. Website: http://scars.tv (includes writer's guidelines, past issues, archives, past books archives, writers' work, art, awards, interactive poetry, names of editors, poetry, interviews). Established 1993. **Editor/Publisher:** Janet Kuypers.

Magazine Needs: *Children, Churches and Daddies (the unreligious, non-family oriented literary magazine)* is published "monthly or bimonthly depending on year and contains news, humor, poetry, prose, and essays. We specialize in electronic issues and collection books. We accept poetry of almost any genre, but we're not keen on rhyme for rhyme's sake, and we're not keen on religious poems (look at our current issue for a better idea of what we're like). We like gay/lesbian/bisexual, nature/rural/ecology, political, social issues, women/feminism. We do accept longer works, but within two pages for an individual poem is appreciated. We don't go for racist, sexist (therefore we're not into pornography either), or homophobic stuff." Has published poetry by Rochelle Holt, Virginia Love Long, Pete McKinley, and Janine Canan. As a sample we selected these lines from the publisher's own poem "Scars 1997":

> I wear my scars like badges./These deep marks show through from under my skin/like war paint on an Apache chief./Decorated with feathers, the skins of his prey.

The print version of *Children, Churches and Daddies* is about 100 pages, 8×11, photocopied and saddle-stapled, cover, with art and ads. Receives hundreds of poems/year, accepts about 40%. Press run "depends." Sample: $5.50. Make checks payable to Janet Kuypers.

How to Submit: Prefers electronic submissions. Submit via e-mail in body of message, explaining in preceding paragraph that it is a submission. Or mail floppy disk with ASCII text or Macintosh disk. Accepts previously published poems and simultaneous submissions. Seldom comments on rejected poems. Guidelines available for SASE, e-mail, or on website. Responds in 2 weeks.

Magazine Needs & How to Submit: *Down in the Dirt* appears "as often as work is submitted to us to guarantee a good-length issue." Does not want smut, rhyming poetry, or poetry already accepted for *Children, Churches and Daddies*. Has published work by I.B. Rad, Jennifer Rowan, Cheryl A. Townsend, Tom Racine, David-Matthew Barnes, and Michael Estabrook. *Down in the Dirt* is published electronically, either on the web or in e-book form (PDF files). Prefers e-mail submissions. Accepts disk submissions formatted for Macintosh. Guidelines and sample issues available on website. Accepts previously published material.

Also Offers: Scars Publications sometimes sponsors a book contest. Write or e-mail for information. "The website is a more comprehensive view of what *Children, Churches and Daddies* does. All the information is there." Also able to publish chapbooks. Write for more information.

◉ CHIRON REVIEW; CHIRON BOOKS; KINDRED SPIRIT PRESS, 702 N. Prairie, St. John KS 67576-1516. (620)786-4955. E-mail: chironreview@hotmail.com. Website: www.geocities.com/SoHo/ Nook/1748/ (includes guidelines, sample poems, news and notes, and Personal Publishing Program information). Established 1982 as *The Kindred Spirit*. **Editor:** Michael Hathaway.

Magazine Needs: *Chiron Review* is a quarterly tabloid using photographs of featured writers. No taboos. Accepts poetry written by children. Has published poetry by Felice Picano, Robert Cooperman, Ruth Moon Kempher, Ed Ochester, Peter Morris, and Susan Terris. As a sample the editor selected this poem "To the Student Who Said Nothing Rhymes with 'Orange' " by Jay Dougherty:

> Dear child, Something utterly horrifying/rhymes with "orange."/We just haven't found it yet./But oh, don't worry:/It will find us.

Each issue "contains dozens of poems." Press run is about 1,000. Subscription: $14 US, $28 overseas. Sample: $5 US, $10 overseas or institutions.

How to Submit: Submit 3-6 poems at a time, "typed or printed legibly." No simultaneous submissions or previously published poems. No e-mail submissions; accepts postal mail only. Very seldom publishes theme issues. Guidelines and upcoming themes available for SASE or on website. Responds in 2 months. Pays 1 copy with a discount on additional copies. Acquires first-time rights. Reviews books of poetry in 500-700 words. Poets may send books for review consideration.

Book/Chapbook Needs & How to Submit: For book publication, query. Publishes 1-3 chapbooks/year, flat-spined, professionally printed, paying 25% of press run of 100-200 copies.

Also Offers: Personal Publishing Program is offered under the Kindred Spirit Press imprint. "Through special arrangements with a highly specialized printer, we can offer extremely short run publishing at unbelievably low prices." Information available for SASE.

Ⓝ $⦿ ◎ THE CHRISTIAN CENTURY (Specialized: religious, social issues), Dept. PM, 104 S. Michigan Ave., Suite 700, Chicago IL 60603. (312)263-7510. Fax: (312)263-7540. Website: www. ChristianCentury.com. Established 1884. Named *The Christian Century* 1900, estab. again 1908, joined by *New Christian* 1970. **Poetry Editor:** Jill Peláez Baumgaertner.

Magazine Needs: This "ecumenical weekly" is a liberal, sophisticated journal of news, articles of opinion and reviews from a generally Christian point-of-view, using approximately 1 poem/issue, not necessarily on religious themes but in keeping with the literate tone of the magazine. Wants "poems that are not statements but experiences, that do not talk about the world, but show it. We want to publish poems that are grounded in images and that reveal an awareness of the sounds of language and the forms of poetry even when the poems are written in free verse." Does not want "pietistic or sentimental doggerel." Has published poetry by Jeanne Murray Walker, Ida Fasel, Kathleen Norris, Luci Shaw, J. Barrie Shepherd, and Wendell Berry. As a sample the editor selected this poem, "Rapture" by Ashley Mace Havird:

> In a straight-backed pew/on the balcony's front row,/I keep my distance./Still, the sunburst/of red-hot gladiolus,/fireball mums,/spikes me blind. . . .

Christian Century is magazine-sized, printed on quality newsprint, using b&w art, cartoons and ads, about 30 pages, saddle-stapled. Sample: $3.

How to Submit: Submit poems of up to 20 lines, typed and double-spaced, 1 poem/page. Include your name, address and phone number on the first page of each poem. "Prefer shorter poems." No simultaneous submissions. Submissions without SASE or SAE and IRCs will not be returned. Pays usually $20/poem plus 1 copy and discount on additional copies. Acquires all rights. Inquire about reprint permission. Reviews books of poetry in 300-400 words, single format; 400-500 words, multi-book format.

Ⓝ ◉ CHRISTIANITY AND LITERATURE, Dept. of English, University of Delaware, Newark DE 19716-2537. **Poetry Editor:** Prof. Jeanne Murray Walker.

Magazine Needs: *Christianity and Literature* is a quarterly scholarly journal publishing about 6-8 poems/ issue. Press run is 1,350 for 1,125 subscribers of which 525 are libraries, 600 individuals. Single copy: $7; subscription: $25/1 year, $45/2 years. Make checks payable to CCL.

How to Submit: Submit 1-6 poems at a time. No previously published poems or simultaneous submissions. Accepts submissions by surface mail only. Cover letter is required. Submissions must be accompanied by SASE. Time between acceptance and publication is 6-9 months. "Poems are chosen by our poetry editor." Responds within 1 month. Pays 2 contributor's copies "and a dozen offprints to poets whose work we publish." Rights revert to poets upon written request. Reviews poetry collections in each issue (no chapbooks).

N **$** **CHRYSALIS READER (Specialized: spirituality, themes)**, Rt. 1 Box 184, Dillwyn VA 23936-9616. Fax: (434)983-1074. E-mail: chrysalis@hovac.com. Established 1985. **Poetry Editor:** Robert F. Lawson. **Editor:** Carol S. Lawson.

Magazine Needs: *Chrysalis Reader* is published by the Swedenborg Foundation as a "contribution to the search for spiritual wisdom." Appearing annually, it is a "book series that draws upon diverse traditions to engage thought on questions that challenge inquiring minds using literate and scholarly fiction, essays and poetry." Wants poetry that is "spiritually related and focused on the particular issue's theme. Nothing overly religious or sophomoric." Has published work by Jan Frazier, William Kloefkorn, Linda Pastan, Wesley McNair, Julia Randall, Robert Bly, Peter Bethanis, Pat Schneider and Tom O'Grady. As a sample the editor selected these lines from "The Only Love That Lasts" by Kate Gleason:

> *I want to grow alike/in the grand tradition of great marriages,/want our faces to wrinkle like wax paper/that's been used and smoothed and used again.*

Chrysalis Reader is 208 pages, 7 × 10, professionally printed on archival paper and perfect-bound with coated cover stock, illustrations and photos. Receives about 1,000 poems/year, accepts approximately 2-5%. Press run is 3,500. Sample: $10.

How to Submit: Submit no more than 5 poems at one time. No previously published poems; accepts simultaneous submissions. Time between acceptance and publication is typically 18 months. Send SASE for themes and guidelines. Upcoming themes include "Spiritual Well-Being" and "Letting Go." Responds in 3 months. Always sends prepublication galleys. Pays $25 and 3 copies. Acquires first-time rights. "We expect to be credited for reprints after permission is given."

Advice: "When time permits, editorial suggestions are offered in the spirit of all good literature."

CIDER PRESS REVIEW, P.O. Box 881914, San Diego CA 92168. Established 1997. **Co-Editors:** Caron Andregg and Robert Wynne.

Magazine Needs: *Cider Press Review* appears twice/year and features "the best new work from contemporary poets." Wants "thoughtful, well-crafted poems with vivid language and strong images. We prefer poems that have something to say. We would like to see more well-written humor. No didactic, inspirational, greeting-card verse; therapy or religious doggerel." Has published poetry by Jackson Wheeler, Janet Holmes, W.D. Snodgrass, Thomas Lux, Linda Pastan, and Gary Young. As a sample the editors selected these lines from "The Lesser Days" by Cecilia Woloch:

> *And I mean to make the most of what has/fallen in my path. The brown-haired man; the smiling clerk; the/branch I've broken from the branch. I mean you can. Give in or not./Take something like the juice of too few stars, anoint yourself.*

Cider Press Review is 120 pages, digest-sized, offset printed and perfect-bound with 2-color coated card cover. Receives about 1,500 poems/year, accepts about 5%. Press run is 750. Subscription: $22/2 issues. Sample: $10.

How to Submit: Submit up to 5 poems at a time. Accepts simultaneous submissions; no previously published poems. Cover letter with short bio preferred. "Please include a SASE. Poets whose work is accepted will be expected to provide a copy of the poem on disk. Do not send unsolicited disk submissions." Editors read from April to August, but will accept submissions any time. Time between acceptance and publication is up to 10 months. Poems are circulated to an editorial board. Seldom comments on rejected poems. Responds in up to 6 months. Pays 1 copy. Acquires first North American serial rights.

$ **CIMARRON REVIEW**, 205 Morrill Hall, Oklahoma State University, Stillwater OK 74078-0135. Website: http://cimarronreview.okstate.edu (includes guidelines and information on subscriptions and how to contact). Established 1967. **Editor:** E.P. Walkiewicz. **Poetry Editor:** Lisa Lewis, Ai.

THE SUBJECT INDEX in the back of this book helps you identify potential markets for your work.

insider report

Poetry and a Christian worldview

Trace Western poetry through the ages and you'll find lines laced with Christian thought, theme, and image. Such literary giants as Shakespeare, Milton, and Eliot wrote from a Judaeo-Christian worldview. Mention Christian poetry today, however, and many people think hymns and greeting cards. Is literary Christian poetry dead?

Not according to these three highly respected poet/editors:

● Jill Peláez Baumgaertner, Dean of Humanities and Theological Studies and Professor of English at Wheaton College, is poetry editor of the *Christian Century*. She has authored three books of poetry, *Finding Cuba*, *Leaving Eden*, and *Namings*, as well as the text-book, *Poetry*.

● Luci Shaw, Writer in Residence at Regent College in Vancouver and poetry editor of *Radix*, has authored nine books of poetry, including *Angles of Light* and *The Green Earth: Poems of Creation*. She has also edited three poetry anthologies.

● Jeanne Murray Walker, Professor of English at the University of Delaware, is the poetry editor of *Christianity and Literature* and author of five books of poetry, including *Gaining Time* and *Stranger than Fiction*. She also writes for the theater.

Though the hymn and greeting card variety of Christian poetry may be more diffusive, these poet/editors agree that literary Christian poets are making their mark. The most obvious showplaces are Christian or religious journals. *Christianity and Literature*, *Christian Century*, *Radix*, *Image*, *The Cresset*, *Weavings*, *America*, *U.S. Catholic*, *Spirituality and Health*, and *First Things* feature some of the best and brightest Christian poets.

But religious journals aren't the only avenue for Christian poetry today. Says Shaw, "Even magazines like *The New Yorker*, *The Atlantic Monthly*, and *Harper's Magazine* will publish poems with religious content, and it doesn't seem to be a taboo subject anymore. I'm really grateful that their editors are open to using poetry that has a deeply spiritual commitment behind it—a Christian worldview, perhaps. It's not always overt, but it's there." Walker, too, has noticed a shift in secular publishing. "Particularly in the last two or three years, I think, there is a kind of longing or hunger for some way of coming to grips with various really serious life issues."

Baumgaertner says, "I've been able to find more poems in the secular journals that speak

Photo by John Flak

Jill Peláez Baumgaertner

Luci Shaw

Jeanne Murray Walker

to me as a Christian." She especially noticed in the three months after the September 11, 2001 terrorist attacks that "even poems in *The New Yorker*, for the first time in years, were filled with references to God."

A fourth editor, Mary Kenagy of *Image*, also senses acceptance by secular publications of poems with a religious viewpoint. "So many of our contributors are poets at work in the mainstream of the contemporary poetry world—people like Scott Cairns, Mark Jarman, Mary Oliver, and Julia Dasdorf, who teach at major universities, get published and anthologized all over the place, and their work is profoundly religious."

Religious content is one thing, but what about specifically Christian content? And what are the characteristics of Christian poetry being published today?

Walker warns against "didactic" poetry. "There aren't many editors who are willing to publish that, even in religious publications. It's necessary to try to write what's in your heart, but an overlay of some didactic message is probably not a good idea."

Baumgaertner, who guest-edited the all-poetry 50th anniversary issue of *Christianity and Literature*, says, "I'm not looking for a particular religious orthodoxy; I am looking for the deep human questions. Whatever their faith, the best poets always ask these questions: Who am I? What does it mean to be human? Who is God? Where can he be found in our daily life? Why is he sometimes silent? I don't want pat, easy answers. I want poems that make connections beyond themselves."

"To a Friend"

Yes, Time is my adversary, too—

but for you
he is an armed guard
patrolling the far end of a one-way road
Various with sunlight, weeds, rare stones—
way too short;

while for me
he is a hefty wrestler
pounding me on the ropes
of one after another squared-off ring—
match too incessant.

And you believe
that someday—loaf and ramble how you will—
you must reach that black-barred roadblock,
and Time, awaiting no password,
gun you down—

while I believe
that someday—shove, wrench, throw me how he will—
Time must hear the last bell rung on him,
and I, loosed from his hold,
roll free.

(by Nancy Esther James, published in *Christianity and Literature*; reprinted with permission of the author)

Shaw says, "I think the key is poetry of a high literary quality. If it's good poetry, it's going to have a better chance of acceptance." She says the quality is more important "than certain 'buzz' words. You can use 'God' words. You can use Christian symbolism from the Old or the New Testament, and it's generally recognized as such, but it's in the context of a poem that opens up different layers of meaning and metaphor."

Creative use of Biblical references and symbolism is not to be equated with King James language. This doesn't work, Baumgaertner explains, "because it's not contemporary language; it's not the language we use every day. It becomes a distraction for the reader, and a distancer."

Delineating her selection criteria, Walker says, "I look for the same thing as somebody else would look for who is just reading for a regular journal. I look for poems to be clear. I look for them to be surprising. I look for them to create images that are memorable and new. I look for them to have a point of view which seems authentic and which seems to come from some specific person as opposed to being the kind of general poet-in-the-sky. I look for them to have a voice."

A demand for high quality is understandable; but one may wonder what, in terms of poetry, sets apart Christian from secular journals.

Walker admits, "It's something that's pretty subtle. Part of the way that comes about is we have a self-selected group of people who send work. They tend to be people who are thinking about the great themes of Christianity. It's hard to characterize that it's absolutely Christian. I am really one of those people who believe that the great works of literature are almost all deeply religious; that, in fact, the great religious questions are the great human questions. Sure, there is absolutely a relationship between Christianity and the content of these poems [in *Christianity and Literature*], and I would never publish anything, even if it were good, if it was destructive of Christianity. But our poems don't always have an overt link with Christianity."

What advice, then, for poets who want to create high-quality poetry with that overt Christian link?

Baumgaertner points out, "What they're setting out to do is one of the hardest things to do with writing. The common language, which they have heard used for years both in Scripture and in their churches, is language that needs to be revitalized. They can't use clichés. These writers need to ground their experience in concrete image. What they're going to want to do is leap immediately into abstractions. I need to remind them of what the Incarnation is. It is the Spirit becoming flesh, and that's what they must work at doing in their poetry, bringing the Spirit into flesh."

Shaw believes the work is worth the effort. "To me the art of poetry is more recognition of a connection or a theme that comes to mind, where you begin to see what you've never seen before in something quite ordinary. You can write a poem about anything in the world, but you have to be able to see it from a fresh, surprising angle. It's an amazing experience for people to realize that they can begin to do that, that they can think and write in a way that opens their own minds as well as the minds of their readers."

—Holly Davis

Magazine Needs: *Cimarron* is a quarterly literary journal. "We take pride in our eclecticism. We like evocative poetry (lyric or narrative) controlled by a strong voice. No sing-song verse. No quaint prairie verse. No restrictions as to subject matter. We look for poems whose surfaces and structures risk uncertainty and which display energy, texture, intelligence, and intense investment." Among poets they have published are Tess Gallagher, Nin Andrews, W.D. Ehrhart, Mark Halliday, Jerome Rothenberg, and Paul Hoover. *Cimarron Review*, 100-150 pages, 6×9, perfect-bound, boasts a handsome design, including a color cover and attractive printing. Poems lean toward free verse, lyric, and narrative, although all forms and styles seem welcome. There are 15-25 pages of poetry in each issue. Circulation is 500 of which most are libraries. Single copy: $7; subscription: $24/year ($28 Canada), $65/3 years ($72 Canada).

How to Submit: Submit 3-5 poems, name and address on each, typed single- or double-spaced. No simultaneous submissions. No response without SASE. Guidelines available on website. Responds in 3 months. Pays $15 for each poem published, 1 copy, and a subscription. Acquires first North American serial rights only. Reviews books of poetry in 500-900 words, single book format, occasionally multi-book. All reviews are assigned.

⬛ ◐ ◎ THE CLAREMONT REVIEW (Specialized: teens/young adults), 4980 Wesley Rd., Victoria, British Columbia V8Y 1Y9 Canada. (250)658-5221. Fax: (250)658-5387. E-mail: editor@theClaremontReview.com. Website: www.theClaremontReview.com (includes guidelines, samples, editorial policy, and subscription and monthly contest information). Established 1991. **Contact:** Susan Field.

Magazine Needs: *The Claremont Review* is a biannual review which publishes poetry and fiction written by those ages 13 to 19. Each fall issue also includes an interview with a prominent Canadian writer. Wants "vital, modern poetry with a strong voice and living language. We prefer works that reveal something of the human condition. No clichéd language nor copies of 18th and 19th century work." Has published poetry by Jen Wright, Erin Egan, and Max Rosenblum. As a sample the editors selected these lines from "The Last Room" by Jen Wright:

> These men study death./They say it is congestive heart failure,/brain hemorrhage, invasive tumor./But
> that's not what you showed me/one child's day/after we found a robin, frozen, on the porch.

The Claremont Review is 110 pages, 6×9, professionally printed and perfect-bound with an attractive color cover. Receives 600-800 poems/year, accepts about 120. Press run is 700 for 200 subscribers of which 50 are libraries, 250 shelf sales. Subscription: $12/year, $20/2 years. Sample: $6.

How to Submit: Submit poems typed one to a page with author's name at the top of each. Accepts simultaneous submissions; no previously published poems. Cover letter with brief bio required. Reads submissions September through June only. Always comments on rejected poems. Guidelines available for SASE (or SAE and IRC), on website, and in publication. Publishes theme issues; upcoming themes available on website and in publication. Responds in up to 6 weeks (excluding July and August). Pays 1 copy and funds when grants allow it. Acquires first North American serial rights.

Advice: "We strongly urge potential contributors to read back issues of *The Claremont Review*. That is the best way for you to learn what we are looking for."

◐ ◎ CLARK STREET REVIEW (Specialized: form/style, narrative and prose poetry), P.O. Box 1377, Berthoud CO 80513. E-mail: clarkreview@earthlink.net. Established 1998. **Editor:** Ray Foreman.

Magazine Needs: Appearing 8 times/year, *Clark Street Review* publishes narrative poetry and short shorts—"to give writers and poets cause to keep writing by publishing their best work." Wants "narrative poetry under 100 lines that reach readers who are mostly published poets and writers. Subjects are open. No obscure and formalist work." Has published poetry by Steven Levi, Errol Miller, Ray Dickson, Michael Ketchek, and Al Negemova. As a sample the editor selected these lines from "Night Run to Norfolk" by Thomas Feeny:

> The express to Norfolk/slips down the highway. Tight/behind the dreaming driver/sits black Maisie,
> shedding/petals of Love's Sweet Song/onto the heavy air.

Clark Street Review is 20 pages, digest-sized, photocopied, and saddle-stapled with paper cover. Receives about 500 poems/year, accepts about 10%. Press run is 200 for 90 subscribers. Subscription: $10 for 10 issues postpaid. Single copy: $2. Make checks payable to R. Foreman.

How to Submit: Submit 1-10 poems at a time. Line length for poetry is 30 minimum, 100 maximum. Accepts previously published poems and simultaneous submissions. "Disposable copies only—sharp copies. Maximum width—65 characters. SASE or e-mail address for reply. No cover letter." Time between acceptance and publication is 3 months. "Editor reads everything with a critical eye of 30 years of experience in writing and publishing small press work." Often comments on rejected poems. Publishes theme issues occasionally. Guidelines available for SASE and by e-mail. "If one writes narrative poetry, they don't need guidelines. They feel it." Responds in 3 weeks. Acquires one-time rights.

Advice: "*Clark Street Review* is geared to the more experienced poet and writer. There are tips throughout each issue writers appreciate. As always, the work we print speaks for the writer and the magazine. We encourage communication between our poets by listing their e-mail and home addresses. Publishing excellence and giving writers a cause to write is our only aim."

◎ THE CLASSICAL OUTLOOK (Specialized: themes, translations, classics, Latin), Classics Dept., Park Hall, University of Georgia, Athens GA 30602-6203. (706)542-9257. Fax: (706)542-8503.

E-mail: mricks@arches.uga.edu. Website: www.classics.uga.edu/classout.html. Established 1924. **Editor:** Prof. Richard LaFleur. **Poetry Editors:** Prof. David Middleton (original English verse) and David Slavitt (translations and original Latin verse).

Magazine Needs: *The Classical Outlook* "is an internationally circulated quarterly journal (4,200 subscriptions, of which 250 are libraries) for high school and college Latin and Classics teachers, published by the American Classical League." They invite submissions of "original poems in English on classical themes, verse translations from Greek and Roman authors, and original Latin poems. Submissions should, as a rule, be written in traditional poetic forms and should demonstrate skill in the use of meter, diction, and rhyme if rhyme is employed. Original poems should be more than mere exercise pieces or the poetry of nostalgia. Translations should be accompanied by a photocopy of the original Greek or Latin text. Latin originals should be accompanied by a literal English rendering of the text. Submissions should not exceed 50 lines." Has published work by Burt Porter and Susan McLean. As a sample the editors selected these lines from "Icarus" by Francis Fike:

> *Icarus, in his rising pride,/Goes for a catastrophic ride/On wings of feather and wax./Not happy with a mere escape/To nearby safety of a cape,/He, unlike Father, overreacts/And soars toward Helios-heat,/Which will all waxen wings defeat.*

There are 2-3 magazine-sized pages of poetry in each issue. Receives about 300 submissions/year, uses 12%. Has a 12-month backlog, 4-month lead time. Single copy: $10.

How to Submit: Submit 2 anonymous copies, double-spaced, no more than 5 poems at a time. No previously published or simultaneous submissions. Poetry is refereed by poetry editors. Guidelines available for SASE, by e-mail, or by fax. Responds in up to 3-6 months. Pays 2 copies. Sample copies are available from the American Classical League, Miami University, Oxford OH 45056 for $10. Reviews books of poetry "if the poetry is sufficiently classical in nature."

Advice: "Since our policy is to have poetry evaluated anonymously, names and addresses on poems, etc., just make work at this end. Cover letters are not forwarded to the poetry editors. Also, we never knowingly publish any works which have been or will be published elsewhere."

CLAY PALM REVIEW: ART AND LITERARY MAGAZINE, 8 Huntington St., Suite 307, Shelton CT 06484-5228. E-mail: claypalm@cs.com. Website: www.claypalmreview.com (includes guidelines, statement of purpose, archives, contact information, bios, purchasing information, etc.). Established 1999 (premier issue, spring/summer 2000). **Founder/Editor:** Lisa Cisero.

Magazine Needs: Clay Palm Review will be on hiatus until late 2003 and will not be accepting submissions. Has published poetry by Naomi Shihab Nye, Marge Piercy, Duane Locke, Virgil Suarez, and John Smelcer. *Clay Palm Review* is about 120 pages, "a bit larger than digest-sized," offset-printed and perfect-bound with glossy cover, includes colored artwork, b&w photography, short fiction, essays, interviews, collage, sculpture, and ads. Samples available for the discounted price of $7.95 (includes s&h). Both full issues, when purchased together, cost $14.95.

$ ▢ ◎ CLEANING BUSINESS MAGAZINE; CLEANING CONSULTANT SERVICES, INC. (Specialized: cleaning, self-employment), P.O. Box 1273, Seattle WA 98111. (206)622-4241. Fax: (206)622-6876. E-mail: wgriffin@cleaningconsultant.com. Website: www.cleaningconsultants.com (includes subscription information and catalog). Established 1976. **Poetry Editor:** William R. Griffin.

Magazine Needs: *Cleaning Business Magazine* is "a monthly magazine for cleaning and maintenance professionals" and uses some poetry relating to their interests. "To be considered for publication in *Cleaning Business*, submit poetry that relates to our specific audience—cleaning and self-employment." Has published poetry by Don Wilson, Phoebe Bosche, Trudie Mercer, and Joe Keppler. *Cleaning Business Magazine* is 100 pages, 8½×11, offset litho printed, using ads, art, and graphics. Receives about 50 poems/year, accepts about 10. Press run is 5,000 for 3,000 subscribers of which 100 are libraries, 500 shelf sales. Single copy: $5; subscription: $20. Sample: $3.

How to Submit: Accepts simultaneous submissions; no previously published poems. Accepts submissions by e-mail (attachment or in text box), by fax, or by regular mail. Guidelines available for SASE, by fax, and by e-mail. Pays $5-10 plus 1 copy.

Advice: "Poets identify a specific market and work to build a readership that can be tapped again and again over a period of years with new books. Also write to a specific audience that has a mutual interest. We buy poetry about cleaning, but seldom receive anything our subscribers would want to read."

◢ ◎ CLEVELAND STATE UNIVERSITY POETRY CENTER; CSU POETRY SERIES; CLEVELAND POETS SERIES (Specialized: regional); CSU POETRY CENTER PRIZES, 1983 E. 24 St., Cleveland OH 44115-2440. (216)687-3986 or toll-free: (888)278-6473. Fax: (216)687-6943.

E-mail: poetrycenter@csuohio.edu. Website: www.csuohio.edu/poetrycenter (including contest guidelines and catalog of publications). The Poetry Center was established in 1962, first publications in 1971. **Coordinator:** Rita Grabowski. **Director:** Ted Lardner.

Book Needs: The Poetry Center publishes the CSU Poetry Series for poets in general and the Cleveland Poets Series for Ohio poets. "Open to many kinds of form, length, subject matter, style, and purpose. Should be well-crafted, clearly of professional quality, ultimately serious (even when humorous). No light verse, devotional verse or verse in which rhyme and meter seem to be of major importance." Recent CSU Poetry Series publications include *Short History of Pets* by Carol Potter, *The Largest Possible Life* by Alison Luterman, and *Before the Blue Hour* by Deirdre O'Connor. Publications in the Cleveland Poets Series include *Attendant Ghosts* by George Looney and *Willow from the Willow* by Margaret H. Young. As a sample the editors selected this excerpt from the title poem of *Before the Blue Hour* by Deirdre O'Connor:

> *Obviously there was something I craved/in all of that, the unacknowledged violence of your mind,//*
> *the heights you fell from into me—with permission—/terrified child who had been happy, or happy*
> *enough,//buoyed by longing to be disciplined, thus muscular, thus loved/with the kind of urgency that*
> *sins. Blessed with fear,//I left the brink of me to you. Now you're gone, and lilacs soften/the edges of*
> *my walk. Finally I dive into you like a ghost.*

Books are chosen for publication from the entries to the two categories of the CSU Poetry Center Prize Contests: First Book and Open Competition. (Write and send $2 for catalog of Poetry Center books.) Postmark deadline: February 1. Entry fee: $20. Winners receive $1,000, 50 copies, and publication. May publish other entrants in the Poetry Series, providing 50 copies (out of a press run of 1,000) and $300 lump sum. The Cleveland Poets Series (for Ohio poets) offers 80 copies of a press run of 800.

How to Submit: To submit for all series, send ms between November 1 and February 1 only. Responds to all submissions for the year by the end of July. No e-mail submissions. Manuscripts should be "clearly typed, contain a minimum of 40 pages of poetry and a table of contents, pages numbered." Manuscript should include two cover sheets—the first including ms title, poet's name, address, phone number, and e-mail; the second including ms title only. Poet's name should appear on first cover sheet and nowhere else on ms. Do not send acknowledgements, cover letters, or bio. Accepts previously published and simultaneous submissions (if notified of acceptance elsewhere). Guidelines available for SASE, by e-mail, by fax, or on website.

◨ ◎ **THE CLIMBING ART (Specialized: nature/ecology, sports/recreation, mountaineering)**, 6390 E. Floyd Dr., Denver CO 80222. Phone/fax: (303)757-0541. E-mail: rmorrow@dnvr.uswest.net. Established 1986. **Editor:** Ron Morrow.

Magazine Needs: *The Climbing Art* is an annual journal appearing in June "read mainly by mountain enthusiasts who appreciate good writing about mountains and mountaineering. We are open to all forms and lengths. The only requirement is that the work be fresh, well-written, and in some way of interest to those who love the mountains." Accepts poetry written by children. Has published poetry by Terry Gifford, Allison Hunter, Paul Willis, Denise K. Simon, and Barry Govenor. *The Climbing Art* is 160 pages, digest-sized, professionally printed on heavy stock with glossy card cover. Accepts 12-20 poems/issue, receives 50 submissions/month. Press run is 1,500 for 700 subscribers of which 10 are libraries, 500 shelf sales. Subscription: $18. Sample: $4.

How to Submit: Accepts simultaneous submissions and previously published poems. Accepts submissions on disk, by fax, by e-mail (attachment), and by regular mail. Responds in 6 months. Sometimes sends prepublication galleys. Pays 2 copies and subscription. Acquires one-time rights. Reviews books of poetry only if they concern mountains.

▦ ◎ **CLÓ IAR-CHONNACHTA (Specialized: bilingual/foreign language, Irish)**, Indreabhán, Co. Galway, Ireland. Phone: +353-91-593307. Fax: +353-91-593362. E-mail: cic@iol.ie. Website: www.cic.ie. Established 1985. **Contact:** Róisin Ní Mhianáin, editor.

Book/Chapbook Needs: Publishes paperback books of Irish language poetry, one of which is selected through a competition. Has published collections of poetry by Cathal Ó Searcaigh, Nuala Ni Dhomhnaill, Gabriel Rosenstock, Michael Davitt, and Liam Ó Muirthile.

How to Submit: Query by postal mail with 20 sample poems and a cover letter with brief bio and publication credits. Mss are read by an editorial panel. No payment information provided.

$◪ **CLOUD RIDGE PRESS**, 815 13th St., Boulder CO 80302. Established 1985. **Editor:** Elaine Kohler.

Book/Chapbook Needs: Cloud Ridge Press is a "literary small press for unique works in poetry and prose." Publishes letterpress and offset books in both paperback and hardcover editions. In poetry, publishes "strong images of the numinous qualities in authentic experience grounded in a landscape and its people."

The first book, published in 1985, was *Ondina: A Narrative Poem* by John Roberts. The book is 6 × 9¼, handsomely printed on buff stock, cloth bound in black with silver decoration and spine lettering, 131 pages 800 copies were bound in Curtis Flannel and 200 copies bound in cloth over boards, numbered, and signed by the poet and artist. This letterpress edition, priced at $18/cloth and $12/paper, is not available in bookstores but only by mail from the press. The trade edition was photo-offset from the original, in both cloth and paper bindings, and is sold in bookstores. The press plans to publish 1-2 books/year.
How to Submit: Since the press is not accepting unsolicited mss, writers should query first. Queries will be answered in 2 weeks and mss reported on in 1 month. Simultaneous submissions are acceptable. Royalties are 10% plus a negotiable number of author's copies. A brochure is free on request; send #10 SASE.

N $ 🔲 🖉 CLUBHOUSE; YOUR STORY HOUR (Specialized: children, teens), P.O. Box 15, Berrien Springs MI 49103. (616)471-3701. Website: www.yourstoryhour.com (includes general information about *Your Story Hour*, current newsletter and the current issue of *Clubhouse*). Established 1949. **Poetry Editor:** Elaine Trumbo.
Magazine Needs: The publication is printed in conjunction with the Your Story Hour radio program, which is designed to teach the Bible and moral life to children. The magazine, *Clubhouse*, started with that title in 1982, but as *Good Deeder*, its original name, it began publication in 1951. "We do like humor or mood pieces. Don't like mushy-sweet 'Christian' poetry. We don't have space for long poems. Best— 16 lines or under." Has published poetry by Lillian M. Fisher, Audrey Osofsky, Sharon K. Motzko, Bruce Bash, and Craig Peters. *Clubhouse*, published monthly, is 20 pages. The magazine has a circulation of 500, all for subscribers of which maybe 5 are libraries. Subscription: $5/year. Sample cost: 3 oz. postage.
How to Submit: Closed to submissions until 2003. Accepts simultaneous submissions. The "evaluation sheet" for returned mss gives reasons for acceptance or rejection. Guidelines available for SASE. Pays about $12 for poems under 24 lines plus 2 copies. Negotiates rights.

🔲 $ 🔲 🖉 CLUBHOUSE JR. (Specialized: children, religious), 8605 Explorer Dr., Colorado Springs CO 80920. Fax: (719)531-3499. Website: www.clubhousemagazine.org/club_jr/. Established 1988. **Assistant Editor:** Suzanne Hadley. **Editor:** Annette Bourland.
• *Clubhouse Jr.* won the Evangelical Press Association Award for Youth Publication.
Magazine Needs: *Clubhouse Jr.* is a monthly magazine published by Focus on the Family for 4-8 year olds. Wants short poems—less than 100 words. "Poetry should have a strong message that supports traditional values. No cute, but pointless work." As a sample the editors selected this poem, "My Friend," by Mary Ryer:

> If I'm feeling very sad/And don't know what to do./If I'm feeling all alone/Or angry through and
> through./I really shouldn't worry/Or sit alone and cry./I always have a friend to help./Jesus is nearby.

Clubhouse Jr. is 16-20 pages, magazine-sized, web-printed on glossy paper and saddle-stapled with 4-color paper cover, includes 4-color art. The magazine has 96,000 subscribers. Single copy: $1.50; subscription: $15/year. Sample: $1.25 with 8 × 10 SASE. Make checks payable to Focus on the Family.
How to Submit: Submit up to 5 poems at a time. Accepts simultaneous submissions; no previously published poems. Cover letter preferred. Accepts fax submissions; no e-mail submissions. Time between acceptance and publication is in up to 1 year. Seldom comments on rejected poems. Occasionally publishes theme issues. Guidelines available for SASE. Responds in up to 2 months. Pays $50-100. Acquires first rights.

🔲 COAL CITY REVIEW, English Dept., University of Kansas, Lawrence KS 66045. Established 1989. **Editor:** Brian Daldorph.
Magazine Needs: Published in the fall, *Coal City Review* is an annual publication of poetry, short stories, reviews, and interviews—"the best material I can find." As for poetry, the editor quotes Pound: " 'Make it new.' " Does not want to see "experimental poetry, doggerel, five-finger exercises, or beginner's verse." Has published poetry by Michael Gregg Michaud, Phil Miller, Walt McDonald, and Denise Low. As a sample the editor selected these lines from "Restless Man" by Thomas Zvi Wilson:

> He was a journeyman everything:/running a job press in Alma,/carrying hod in Tuscaloosa's heat,/
> usher at the Folly in Booneville,/bouncer at Steer Here Bistro in Austin, Texas . . .

Coal City Review is 100 pages, 5½ × 8½, professionally printed on recycled paper and perfect-bound with light, colored card cover. Accepts about 5% of the material received. Press run is 200 for 50 subscribers of which 5 are libraries. Subscription: $10. Sample: $6.
How to Submit: Submit 6 poems at a time with name and address on each page. Accepts previously published poems occasionally; prefers not to receive simultaneous submissions. "Please do not send list of prior publications." Seldom comments on rejected poems. Guidelines available for SASE. Responds in up to 3 months. Pays 1 copy. Reviews books of poetry in 300-1,000 words, mostly single format. Poets may send books for review consideration.

Book/Chapbook Needs & How to Submit: *Coal City Review* also publishes occasional chapbooks and books as issues of the magazine but does not accept unsolicited chapbook submissions. Their most recent book is *Under the Fool Moon* by Gary Lechliter.
Advice: "Care more (much more) about writing than publication. If you're good enough, you'll publish."

$ ☑ **C/OASIS** (formerly *Cyber Oasis*). Fax: (603)971-5013. E-mail: poetmuse@swbell.net. Website: www.sunoasis.com/oasis.html. Established 1996. Editor: David Eide. **Contact:** Vicki Goldsberry Colker.
Magazine Needs: *C/Oasis* is a monthly online journal containing poems, stories, personal essays, articles for writers, and commentary. "The purpose is two-fold. Number one is to publish excellent writing and number two is to explore the web for all the best writing and literary venues. Not only does *C/Oasis* publish original material but it investigates the web each month to deliver the very best material it can find." Wants "poetry that has an active consciousness and has artistic intention. Open on form, length, subject matter, style, purpose, etc. It must deliver the active consciousness and artistic intention. No sing song stuff, fluff stuff, those who write poems without real artistic intent because they haven't given the idea a thought." Has published poetry by Richard Fein, Anne Babson, John Sweet, Rebecca Lu Kiernan, and Jeffrey Altier. "I'm trying to find the right style for the Web. I was inspired by the literary magazine phenomena but find the Web to be a new medium. One that is terrific for poetry." Receives "hundreds" of poems/year, accepts about 15%.
How to Submit: Submit 5 poems at a time. Accepts previously published poems; no simultaneous submissions. Accepts fax and e-mail submissions; "try to include submission in ASCII plain-text in body of e-mail message." Time between acceptance and publication is about 3 months. "If I know I don't want it I'll turn it back that day. If there is something there that warrants further reading I'll put it into a review folder. As the day of publication approaches I'll get the review folder out and start to eliminate stuff. If I eliminate something that I like, I'll put it into next month's folder. Then I come down to a chosen few. One or two I pick for publication, the others I schedule for another month. I then notify the writer of acceptance, I notify the others that I want to publish their poems later and give them updates on that." Often, but not always, comments on rejected poems. Guidelines available for e-mail or website. Responds in 1 month. Pays $10/poem. Acquires first, first North American serial, one time, and reprint rights.
Advice: "Seek to improve the writing; take poetry seriously, treat it as an art and it will treat you well."

▢ ◎ **COCHRAN'S CORNER (Specialized: subscribers)**, 1003 Tyler Court, Waldorf MD 20602-2964. Established 1985. **Executive Editor:** Jeanie Saunders. **Poetry Editor:** Billye Keene.
Magazine Needs: *Cochran's Corner* is a "family type" quarterly open to beginners, preferring poems of 20 lines or less. Must be a subscriber to submit. "Any subject or style (except porn)." Accepts poetry written by children. Has published poetry by Jean B. York, Brian Duthins, C.J. Villiano, and Annette Shaw. As a sample the editor selected this poem, "Journey," (poet unidentified):
> You take me to places/Within myself/Where I have never been—/foreign places/Timidly I follow you
> through/Subterranian chambers/And/Undiscovered essences/to the/mainstream/that/is/I
Cochran's Corner is 58 pages, desktop-published, saddle-stapled, with matte card cover. Press run is 500. Subscription: $20. Sample: $5 plus SASE.
How to Submit: Submit 5 poems at a time. Accepts simultaneous submissions and previously published poems. Guidelines available for SASE. Responds in 3 months. Pays 2 copies. Acquires first or one-time rights. Reviews books of poetry. Send books for review consideration.
Also Offers: Sponsors contests in March and July; $5 entry fee for unlimited poems "if sent in the same envelope. We provide criticism if requested at the rate of $1 per page."
Advice: "Write from the heart, but don't forget your readers. You must work to find the exact words that mirror your feelings, so the reader can share your feelings."

▼ ◖ **COFFEE HOUSE PRESS**, 27 N. Fourth St., Suite 400, Minneapolis MN 55401. (612)338-0125. Established 1984. **Managing Editor:** Christopher Fischbach.
- Coffee House Press books have won numerous honors and awards. As an example, *The Book of Medicines* by Linda Hogan won the Colorado Book Award for Poetry and the Lannan Foundation Literary Fellowship.

Book Needs: Publishes 12 books/year, 4-5 of which are poetry. Wants poetry that is "challenging and lively; influenced by the Beats, the NY School, LANGUAGE and post-LANGUAGE, or Black Mountain." Has published poetry collections by Victor Hernandez Cruz, Anne Waldman, Eleni Siskelianos, and Paul Metcalf.

How to Submit: Submit 8-12 poems at a time. Accepts previously published poems. Cover letter and vita required. "Please include a SASE for our reply and/or the return of your ms." Seldom comments on rejected poems. Responds to queries in 1 month; to mss in up to 8 months. Always sends prepublication galleys. Send SASE for catalog. No phone, fax, or e-mail queries.

$ COLORADO REVIEW; COLORADO PRIZE FOR POETRY, Dept. of English, Colorado State University, Ft. Collins CO 80523. (970)491-5449. E-mail: creview@colostate.edu. Website: www.coloradoreview.com (includes writer's guidelines, list of editorial staff, subscription guidelines, and Colorado Prize for Poetry guidelines). Established 1955 as *Colorado State Review*, resurrected 1967 under "New Series" rubric, renamed *Colorado Review* 1985. **Editor:** David Milofsky. **Poetry Editors:** Jorie Graham and Donald Revell.

• Poetry published in *Colorado Review* has been frequently included in volumes of *The Best American Poetry*.

Magazine Needs: *Colorado Review* is a journal of contemporary literature which appears 3 times/year combining short fiction, poetry, and personal essays. Has published poetry by John Ashbery, Joseph Lease, Tessa Rumsey, Cole Swensen, and Liz Waldner. *Colorado Review* is about 224 pages, 6×9, professionally printed and perfect-bound with glossy card cover. Press run is 1,500 for 1,000 subscribers of which 100 are libraries. Receives about 10,000 submissions/year, accepts about 2%. Subscription: $24/year. Sample: $10.

How to Submit: Submit about 5 poems at a time. No previously published poems or simultaneous submissions. No e-mail submissions. Submissions must include SASE for response. Reads submissions September 1 through May 1 only. Responds in 2 months. Pays $5/printed page for poetry. Acquires first North American serial rights. Reviews books of poetry and fiction, both single and multi-book format. Poets may send books for review consideration.

Also Offers: Also sponsors the annual Colorado Prize for Poetry, established in 1995, offering an honorarium of $2,000. Book as a whole must be unpublished though individual poems may have been published elsewhere. Submit a book-length ms on any subject in any form. Guidelines available for SASE. Entry fee: $25. Deadline: January 8. Most recent award winner was Geoffrey Nutter (2001). Judge was Jorie Graham. Winner announced in May.

COMFUSION REVIEW, 304 S. Third St., San Jose CA 95112. E-mail: wright@comfusionreview. com. Website: www.comfusionreview.com (includes poetry, interviews, reviews, fiction, academic essays, rant/friction, photography, and artwork in varied mediums). Established 1995. **Editors:** Jaime Wright, James Brown, and Stephen Wiley.

Magazine Needs: *Comfusion* appears quarterly; www.comfusion.ws is updated bimonthly. "Our purpose is to showcase new and established talent skillfully manifested within the medium of poetry. We want well-crafted material that is original and edgy. We encourage innovative formal and free verse poetry." Also accepts essays, fiction, and photography. "We do not want to see sappy-sentimental love or devotional poetry. And please, absolutely no inspirational." Recently published poetry by Vadim Litvak, Samuel Maio, Genny Lim, David Holler, Ginger Pielage, and Marc David Pinate. As a sample the editors selected these lines from "Photographer" by Ginger Pielage:

> he penetrates the silver solution/grasps the skin of film/casts me/a dripping rag/drying out in his hands

Comfusion is 60-80 pages, magazine-sized, saddle-stapled, glossy cover, with art/graphics and ads. "Many poems that go unprinted in our yearly publication are featured on our website." Receives about 120 poems/year, accepts about 10%. Publishes 5-10 poems/issue. Press run is 5,000 for 500 subscribers; 4,500 distributed free to independent book stores and cafes. Single copy: free; subscription: $10 for 2 years. Sample: $5. Make checks payable to Lotus Foundation.

How to Submit: Submit 3 poems at a time. Accepts previously published poems; no simultaneous submissions. Accepts e-mail submissions and disk submissions. Cover letter is preferred. "Cover letter should include bio information. Please include SASE with submission. E-mail poems to wright@comfusionreview.com. Each submission needs name, address, phone, and e-mail." Submit seasonal poems 5 months in advance. Time between acceptance and publication is up to 1 year. Poems are circulated to an editorial board. Seldom comments on rejections. "We encourage poets and other artists to check out our website, comfusionreview.com, or purchase one of our back issues before submission." Guidelines available for SASE, by e-mail, or on website. Responds in up to 5 months. Pays 2 contributor's copies. Acquires one-time rights. Reviews books and chapbooks of poetry and other magazines. Poets may send books for review consideration to *comfusion*.

Advice: "Poets should take into account a broad spectrum of poetic tradition as refracted through the spectrum of their own personal irreverence and respect. Please don't insult your collective readers' intelligence by attempting to speak in the voice of the 'common man.' But feel free to make sure we know what you're talking about (James Brown)."

N: $⃝ COMMON GROUND REVIEW; COMMON GROUND POETRY CONTEST, 43 Witch Path #3, West Springfield MA 01089. E-mail: cgreview@home.com. Website: http://members.cox. net/cgreview/ (includes guidelines, FAQs, sample poems, Meet the Editors, list of contributors). Established 1999. **Editor:** Larry O'Brien.

Magazine Needs: *Common Ground Review* appears biannually publishing poetry and original artwork. Wants poetry with strong imagery; well-written free or traditional forms. No greeting card verse, overly sentimental, or political poetry. Recently published poetry by James Doyle, Martin Galvin, Lyn Lifshin, Virgil Suarez, and Rennie McQuilken. As a sample the editor selected these lines from "Sinks and Rises" by Theodore Deppe:

> *Since chemo, Sarah's hair's grown back a startling silver,/color of moonlight on river grass, a boy's*
> *crewcut//that keeps inching out, too lustrous to be gray—/she wants to see what silver looks like*
> *dangling past her chest,//wants silver to cascade to her waist, mermaid's hair, color of/moonlight,*
> *color of river grass, magnificent, and merciless*

Common Ground Review is 40-58 pages, digest-sized, high quality photocopied, saddle-stapled, original artwork/ card cover, with 4-6 pages original artwork. Receives about 1,000 poems/year, accepts less than 10%. Publishes about 35 poems/issue. Press run is 125-150. Single copy: $6.30. Sample: $6.30. Make checks payable to *Common Ground Review.*

How to Submit: Submit 1-5 poems at a time. Line length for poetry is 40 maximum. No previously published poems or simultaneous submissions. Accepts e-mail submissions; no fax or disk submissions. Cover letter is required. "Poems single-spaced, include name, address, phone, e-mail address, brief biography, SASE (submissions without SASE will be discarded)." Reads submissions all year. Submit seasonal poems 6 months in advance. Time between acceptance and publication is 4-6 months. Poems are circulated to an editorial board. "Editor reads and culls submissions. Final decisions made by editorial board." Seldom comments on rejected poems. Guidelines available in magazine, for SASE, by e-mail, or on website. Responds in 2 months. Pays 1 contributor's copy. Acquires one-time rights.

Also Offers: Annual contest. Awards 1st Prize: $100, 2nd Prize: $50, and 3rd Prize: $25. **Reading fee:** $10 for 1-3 unpublished poems. **Deadline:** February 28.

Advice: "Read journal before submitting. Beginning poets need to read what's out there, get into workshops, and work on revising. Attend writers' conferences. Listen and learn."

◎ COMMON THREADS; OHIO HIGH SCHOOL POETRY CONTESTS; OHIO POETRY ASSOCIATION (Specialized: membership, students), 3520 State Route 56, Mechanicsburg OH 43044. (937)834-2666. Website: www.crosswinds.net/~opa (includes the history of the OPA, most recent newsletter, membership applications, poets' library, and links). Established 1928. **Editor:** Amy Jo Zook. Ohio Poetry Association (Michael Lepp, treasurer, 1798 Sawgrass Dr., Reynoldsburg OH 43068), is a state poetry society open to members from outside the state, an affiliate of the National Federation of State Poetry Societies.

Magazine Needs: *Common Threads* is the Ohio Poetry Association's biannual poetry magazine, appearing in April and October. Only members of OPA may submit poems. Does not want to see poetry which is highly sentimental, overly morbid, religiously coercive, or pornographic—and nothing over 40 lines. "We use beginners' poetry, but would like it to be good, tight, revised. In short, not first drafts. Too much is sentimental or prosy when it could be passionate or lyric. We'd like poems to make us think as well as feel something." Accepts poetry written by children "if members or high school contest winners." Has published poetry by Yvonne Hardenbrook, Betsy Kennedy, Rose Ann Spaith, and Dalene Workman Stull. As a sample the editor selected these lines from "Talking to Flowers," by Cathryn Essinger:

> *And then we spoke about silence/and the fragile gestures made by flowers/and the single word spoken/*
> *by each blossom, mouth to mouth.*

Common Threads is 52 pages, digest-sized, computer-typeset, with matte card cover. "Ours is a forum for our members, and we do use reprints, so new members can get a look at what is going well in more general magazines." Annual dues including 2 issues *Common Threads*: $15. Senior (over 65): $12. Single copies: $2.

How to Submit: Accepts previously published poems, if "author is upfront about them. All rights revert to poet after publication." Accepts submissions by regular mail only. Frequently publishes seasonal poems. Guidelines available on website.

Also Offers: Ohio Poetry Association sponsors an annual contest for unpublished poems written by high school students in Ohio with categories of traditional, modern, and several other categories. March deadline, with 3 money awards in each category. For contest information write Ohio Poetry Association, % Elouise Postle, 4761 Willow Lane, Lebanon OH 45036. "We publish student winners in a book of winning poems before reprinting their work in *Common Threads*. Also, we have a quarterly contest open to all poets, entry fee, two money awards and publication. Write to Janeen Lepp, 1798 Sawgrass Dr., Reynoldsburg OH 43068 (#10 SASE) or e-mail janeenlepp@juno.com for dates and themes." (Also see separate listing for Ohio Poetry Association in the Organizations section.)

N ☐ ◎ A COMPANION IN ZEOR (Specialized: science fiction/fantasy), 1622 Swallow Crest Dr., Edgewood MD 21040-1751. Fax: (410)676-0164. E-mail: klitman323@aol.com or karenlitman@juno. com. Website: www.simegen.com/sgfandom/rimonslibrary/cz/ (includes guidelines, contact information, bios, archives, contest information, links, and editorial policy). Established 1978. **Editor:** Karen MacLeod.

Magazine Needs: *A Companion in Zeor* is a science fiction/fantasy fanzine appearing irregularly on the Internet. "Material used is now limited to creations based solely on works (universes) of Jacqueline Lichtenberg. No other submission types considered. Prefer nothing obscene. Homosexuality not acceptable unless very relevant to the piece. Prefer a 'clean' publication image." Accepts poetry written by young writers over 13.

How to Submit: Accepts submissions on disk, by fax, by e-mail (in text box), or by regular mail. Cover letter preferred with submissions; note whether to return or dispose of rejected mss. Guidelines available for SASE, by fax, by e-mail, and on website. Sometimes sends prepublication galleys. Acquires first rights. "Always willing to work with authors or poets to help in improving their work." Reviews books of poetry. Poets may send books for review consideration.

◐ THE COMSTOCK REVIEW; COMSTOCK WRITERS' GROUP INC.; MURIEL CRAFT BAILEY MEMORIAL PRIZE, 4956 St. John Dr., Syracuse NY 13215. (315)488-8077. E-mail: poetry@c omstockreview.org. Website: www.comstockreview.org (includes guidelines, contact and subscription information, bios, archives, contest information, Poet's Handbook—Resource Guide for Poets, and reviews). Established 1987 as *Poetpourri*, published by the Comstock Writers' Group, Inc. **Contact:** Peggy Sperber Flanders, managing editor.

Magazine Needs: *The Comstock Review* appears biannually; Volume I in summer, Volume II in winter. Uses "well-written free and traditional verse. Metaphor and fresh, vivid imagery encouraged. Poems over 40 lines discouraged. No obscene, obscure, patently religious, or greeting card verse. Few Haiku." Has published poetry by E.G. Burrows, Barbara Crooker, Walt McDonald, Vivian Shipley, Virgil Suarez, and Susan Terris. As a sample they selected these lines from "Naming the Heart" by Bill Van Buskirk:

> . . . I call you harlequin/how easily you give yourself away./I call you bought-and-sold, gypsy and
> dancing bear./I call you Aria. I call you flame./An editor once told me/to lock you out of every poem—/
> that nothing original can be said about you anymore./I call you exile. I call you darkening wood.

The Comstock Review is about 100 pages, digest-sized, professionally printed, perfect-bound. Press run is 600. Subscription: $15/year; $8/issue. Sample from past years: $6.

How to Submit: Submit 3-6 poems at a time; name, e-mail/phone, and address on each page; unpublished poems only. No e-mail submissions. No simultaneous submissions. Cover letter with short bio preferred. Poems are read January 1 through February 28 and July 1 through August 31 only. Poems are held until next reading period for consideration. Guidelines available for SASE, on website, and in publication. Editors sometimes comment on returned submissions. Pays 1 copy. Acquires first North American serial rights.

Also Offers: Offers the Muriel Craft Bailey Memorial Prize yearly with $1,000 1st Prize, $200 2nd Prize, $100 3rd Prize, honorable mentions, publication of all finalists. Entry fee: $3/poem. 40-line limit. No simultaneous submissions or previously published material (includes both print and electronic publications). Deadline: postmark by July 1. Judge for 2001: Mary Oliver; judge for 2002: Kelly Cherry.

◐ CONCHO RIVER REVIEW; FORT CONCHO MUSEUM PRESS, P.O. Box 10894, Angelo State University, San Angelo TX 76909. (915)942-2273. Fax: (915)942-2155. E-mail: bradleyjw@hal.lama r.edu. Website: www.angelo.edu (includes writer's guidelines and names of editors). Established 1984. **Editor:** James A. Moore. **Poetry Editor:** Jerry Bradley.

Magazine Needs: *Concho River Review* is a literary journal published twice/year. "Prefer shorter poems, few long poems accepted; particularly looking for poems with distinctive imagery and imaginative forms and rhythms. The first test of a poem will be its imagery." Short reviews of new volumes of poetry are also published. Has published poetry by Walt McDonald, Robert Cooperman, Mary Winters, William Wenthe, and William Jolliff. *Concho River Review* is 120-138 pages, digest-sized, professionally printed and flat-spined, with matte card cover. Accepts 35-40 of 600-800 poems received/year. Press run is 300 for about 200 subscribers of which 10 are libraries. Subscription: $14. Sample: $5.

How to Submit: "Please submit 3-5 poems at a time. Use regular legal-sized envelopes—no big brown envelopes; no replies without SASE. Type must be letter-perfect, sharp enough to be computer scanned." Accepts submissions by e-mail (attachment). Responds in 2 months. Pays 1 copy. Acquires first rights.

Advice: "We're always looking for good, strong work—from both well-known poets and those who have never been published before."

◐ CONCRETE WOLF, P. O. Box 10250, Bedford NH 03110-0250. E-mail: editors@concretewolf. com. Website: www.concretewolf.com (includes guidelines, excerpts, audio poems, subscription information, archives, contact information, catalog, editorial policy, and contest info). Established 2001. **Editors:** Brent Allard and Lana Ayers. Member: CLMP.

Magazine Needs: *Concrete Wolf* appears quarterly. "We like to see fresh perspectives on common human experiences, with careful attention to words. No specifications as to form, subject matter, or style. Poems that give the impression the poet is in the room." Does not want "poetry that is all head or preaches rather than speaks." Recently published poetry by Martha Miller, Brian Moreau, Nancy Glover, Wunjo, Brian Moreau, Gertrude F. Bantle, and Nancy Brady Cunningham. As a sample the editors selected these lines from "Above the River" by Jim Bell:

> & honor my/shoulder with your small gift//of a hand because you just/can't not all the sins of all//the
> people who never touched me/right seem forgiven

Concrete Wolf is 85 pages, magazine-sized, duplex-printed, perfect-bound, matte card stock cover, with b&w art. Receives about 1,200 poems/year, accepts about 25%. Publishes about 70 poems/issue. Press run is 1,000 for 75 subscribers of which 5 are libraries, 30% shelf sales; 10% are distributed free to writing organizations. Single copy: $7; subscription: $24. Sample: $5. Make checks payable to *Concrete Wolf*.

How to Submit: Submit up to 5 poems at a time. Line length for poetry is 300 maximum. Accepts previously published poems and simultaneous submissions. Accepts e-mail and disk submissions; no fax submissions. "For e-mail submissions, type in body or attach Word file." Reads submissions year round. Time between acceptance and publication is up to 9 months. "Poetry is individually reviewed by two editors and then discussed. Poems agreed upon by both editors are accepted." Often comments on rejected poems. Guidelines available for SASE, by e-mail, in publication, and on website. Responds in up to 4 months. Pays 2 contributor's copies. Acquires one-time rights.

Also Offers: Holds annual chapbook contest; write for details. Website will occasionally post writing exercises. Future plans include a supplementary CD of poets reading their work.

Advice: "Poetry exists for everyone, not just the academic. Remember that poetry is work that requires crafting."

ℕ ◐ CONFLUENCE; OHIO VALLEY LITERARY GROUP, P.O. Box 336, Belpre OH 45714. (304)295-6599. E-mail: wilmaacree@charter.net. Established 1983 as *Gambit*, 1989 as *Confluence*. **Poetry Editors:** Wilma Acree, Barbara McCullough. **Fiction Editor:** Ben Hague, Sandra Tritt.

Magazine Needs: Appearing in June, *Confluence* is an annual "credible platform for established/emerging authors and outstanding student work. This literary magazine is published at Marietta College, Marietta, Ohio, and was named to represent the merging of the Ohio and Muskingum Rivers as well as the collaboration of the Ohio Valley Literary Group with Marietta College." Has published poetry by Virgil Suarez, Mary Winters, Barbara Crooker, and Gerald Zipper. As a sample, the editor selected these lines from "The Mesmeric Quality of Crimson" by Virgil Suarez:

> hairy, prickly, seeds painted like spirochetes/of sperm zeroed in on the ovum, a certain//calling home
> to a meaty center, pulp dreams,/gift-wrapped in onion skin-thin layers, one cut//will take your life, one
> kiss will bring you back,/what's hidden under a green leaf is (like) love . . .

Confluence is 80-100 pages, digest-sized, professionally printed and perfect-bound with full color, coated card cover and b&w graphics. Receives 2,500-5,000 submissions/year, accepts approximately 2%. Press run is 1,000 for 300 subscribers of which 10 are libraries, about 150 shelf sales. Single copy: $5. Sample: $3 backcopy and $1.50 postage.

How to Submit: Submit 5-7 poems with SASE. No previously published poems or simultaneous submissions. Accepts e-mail submissions either in text box or an MS Word or DOS format. Cover letter with brief bio required. Reads submissions September 1 through February 1 only. Time between acceptance and publication is 6 months. Seldom comments on rejected poems. Guidelines available for SASE, by e-mail, and in publication. Responds in up to 6 months. Pays 3 copies. Returns rights upon publication.

Advice: "Strive for precise word choice and effective images. Avoid clichés, passive verbs, and rhyme for rhyme's sake."

$ ◐ ◎ CONFRONTATION MAGAZINE, English Dept., C.W. Post Campus of Long Island University, Brookville NY 11548-1300. (516)299-2720. Fax: (516)299-2735. E-mail: mtucker@liu.edu. Established 1968. **Editor-in-Chief:** Martin Tucker. **Poetry Editor:** Michael Hartnett.

Magazine Needs: *Confrontation Magazine* is "a semiannual literary journal with interest in all forms. Our only criterion is high literary merit. We think of our audience as an educated, lay group of intelligent

THE GEOGRAPHICAL INDEX in the back of this book helps you locate markets in your region.

readers. We prefer lyric poems. Length generally should be kept to two pages. No sentimental verse." Has published poetry by Karl Shapiro, T. Alan Broughton, David Ignatow, Philip Appleman, Jane Mayhall, and Joseph Brodsky. *Confrontation* is about 300 pages, digest-sized, professionally printed, flat-spined, with a press run of 2,000. Receives about 1,200 submissions/year, accepts about 150, has a 6- to 12-month backlog. Subscription: $10/year. Sample: $3.

How to Submit: Submit no more than 10 pages, clear copy. No previously published poems. Accepts submissions by e-mail (include in text box). Do not submit mss June through August. "Prefer single submissions." Publishes theme issues. A list of upcoming themes available for SASE. Responds in 2 months. Sometimes sends prepublication galleys. Pays $5-50 and 1 copy with discount available on additional copies. Staff reviews books of poetry. Send books for review consideration.

Also Offers: Basically a magazine, they do on occasion publish "book" issues or "anthologies." Their most recent "occasional book" is *Clown at Wall*, stories and drawings by Ken Bernard.

Advice: "We want serious poetry, which may be humorous and light-hearted on the surface."

$ ☑ THE CONNECTICUT POETRY REVIEW, P.O. Box 818, Stonington CT 06378. Established 1981. **Poetry Editors:** J. Claire White and Harley More.

Magazine Needs: *The Connecticut Poetry Review* is a "small press annual magazine. We look for poetry of quality which is both genuine and original in content. No specifications except length: 10-40 lines." Has published such poets as John Updike, Robert Peters, Diane Wakoski, and Marge Piercy. Each issue seems to feature a poet. As a sample the editors selected these lines from "Sea" by Miguel Torga (translated by Alexis Levitin):

> *"Sea!/And when will all the suffering reach an end!/And when will we at last no longer bow/To your enchantments, oh, false friend!"*

The flat-spined, large digest-sized journal is "printed letterpress by hand on a Hacker Hand Press from Monotype Bembo." Most of the 45-60 pages are poetry, but they also have reviews. Receives over 2,500 submissions/year, accepts about 20, has a 3-month backlog. Press run is 400 for 80 subscribers of which 35 are libraries. Sample: $3.50.

How to Submit: Reads submissions April through June and September through December only. Responds in 3 months. Pays $5/poem plus 1 copy.

Advice: "Study traditional and modern styles. Study poets of the past. Attend poetry readings and write. Practice on your own."

☑ ☑ CONNECTICUT REVIEW, Southern Community State University, 501 Crescent St., New Haven CT 06473. (203)392-6737. Fax: (203)248-5007. Established 1968. **Editor:** Dr. Vivian Shipley.

- Poetry published in this review has been included in *The Best American Poetry* and *The Pushcart Prize* anthologies, has received special recognition for Literary Excellence from Public Radio's series *The Poet and the Poetry*, and has won the Phoenix Award for Significant Editorial Achievement from the Council of Editors of Learned Journals (CELJ).

Magazine Needs: *Connecticut Review*, published biannually, contains essays, poetry, articles, fiction, b&w photographs, and color artwork. Has published poetry by Robert Phillips, Sherod Santos, Colette Inez, Maxine Kumin, Pattiann Rogers, Alberto Ríos, Dana Gioia, and Marilyn Nelson. As a sample the editor selected these lines from "Flying" by Maxine Kumin:

> *That night in a room not her own/under eaves heavy with rain/and the rue of a disbelieving daughter/ my mother described her grandfather to me:/a passionate man who carried his soul/wedged deep in his pants' watch-pocket*

Connecticut Review is 176 pages, digest-sized, offset-printed, perfect-bound, with glossy 4-color cover and 8-color interior art. Receives about 2,500 poems/year, accepts about 5%. Press run is 3,000 of which 400 are libraries, with 1,000 distributed free to Connecticut State libraries and high schools. Sample: $6. Make checks payable to Connecticut State University.

How to Submit: Submit 3-5 typed poems at a time with name, address, and phone in the upper left corner on 8½ × 11 paper with SASE for return only. Publishes theme issues. Guidelines available for SASE. Pays 2 copies. Acquires first or one-time rights.

☑ CONNECTICUT RIVER REVIEW; ANNUAL CONNECTICUT RIVER REVIEW POETRY CONTEST; BRODINSKY-BRODINE CONTEST; WINCHELL CONTEST; LYNN DECARO HIGH SCHOOL COMPETITION; CONNECTICUT POETRY SOCIETY, P.O. Box 4053, Waterbury CT 06704-0053. E-mail: editorcrr@yahoo.com (queries only). Website: http://pages.prodigy.net/mmwalker/cpsindex.html. Established 1978. **Editor:** Peggy Sapphire.

Magazine Needs: Published by the Connecticut Poetry Society, *Connecticut River Review* appears biannually. Looking for "original, honest, diverse, vital, well-crafted poetry; any form, any subject. Translations and long poems accepted." Has published poetry by Marilyn Nelson (CT Poet Laureate), David Budbill, Charles Rafferty, and JQ Zheng. As a sample the editor selected these lines from "Drought Ending" by Brian Brown:

> *you try not to watch/the arthritis of heat lightning/spinning its ancient curse/on the religion of farmers./*
> *but each mute vein/is a primordial ocean/lapping your dusty brow/drowning you in disbelief.*

Connecticut River Review is attractively printed, digest-sized and contains about 40 pages of poetry, has a press run of about 500 with 175 subscriptions of which 5% are libraries. Receives about 2,000 submissions/year, accepts about 80. Single copy: $7; subscription: $14. CPS membership (including subscription): $25.

How to Submit: Submit up to 3 poems at a time. "Complete contact information typed in upper right corner, SASE required." No previously published poems. Accepts simultaneous submissions if notified of acceptance elsewhere." Cover letter with current bio appreciated. Guidelines available with SASE, by e-mail, and in publication. Responds in up to 6 weeks. Pays 1 copy. "Poet retains copyright."

Also Offers: Annual *Connecticut River Review* Poetry Contest has a $10 entry fee and 3 poem limit. Deadline: April 30. The Brodinsky-Brodine Contest has a $2 entry fee/poem and awards publication in the *Connecticut River Review*. Entries must be postmarked between May 1 and July 31. The Winchell Contest has a $2 entry fee/ poem and awards publication in the *Connecticut River Review*. Entries must be postmarked between October 1 and December 31. The Lynn DeCaro Competition (for Connecticut high school students only) has no entry fee and awards publication in the *Connecticut River Review*. Entries must be postmarked between September 1 and February 27. Affiliated with the National Federation of State Poetry Societies, the Connecticut Poetry Society currently has 150 members. Sponsors conferences, workshops. Publishes *Newsletter*, a bimonthly publication, also available to nonmembers for SASE. Members or nationally known writers give readings that are open to the public. Sponsors open-mike readings. Membership dues are $25/year. Members meet monthly. Send SASE for additional information.

COPIOUS MAGAZINE, #276, 2416 Main St., Vancouver, British Columbia V5T 3E2 Canada. E-mail: editor@copiousmagazine.com. Website: www.copiousmagazine.com (includes guidelines, contact info, archives, links, subscription info). Established 2000. **Editor:** Andrea Grant.

Magazine Needs: *Copious Magazine* appears bimonthly, featuring poetry, artwork, b&w photographs, pulp fiction novel covers, interviews, music, and a new comic series called *Minx*. "I want poems that have that aching knife twist in them. Themes of nocturne, superheroes, mythology, and fairy tales. Larger than life, poems about people. *Copious* features 'the doyenne,' the vixen of *film noir* and hardboiled pulp novels. She defies social expectations as seduction melds with her tragic side - a strong female force! Love poems are always nice, Native Indian themes also." Does not want rhyming, overly sentimental poetry. Accepts poetry written by children. Has published poetry by Ace Boggess, T. Paul Ste. Marie, Joy Reid, B.M. Bradley, Andrea MacPherson, and Laurel Ann Bogen. As a sample the editor selected these lines from a poem by T. Paul Ste. Marie:

> *You've been my junkyard cradle/sanctuary priestess ladelling me over and over/from your bathwater*
> *font cleansing dismal decay/away with daily baptismal rituals/humming lullabyes/bluesy swaddling*
> *spirituals/to a body taunted by excesses stress/real or imagined that aimed bullets at my head.*

Copious Magazine is 46 pages, digest-sized, professionally-printed, glossy cover, with contributed artwork and photos, pulp fiction pictures, and ads for related industries or of reader interest. Publishes about 20 poems/issue. Press run is 1,000 and growing. Single copy: $5; subscription: $10 US/$20 Canada. Sample: $4. Make checks payable to *Copious Magazine*.

How to Submit: Submit 3-5 poems at a time. Accepts previously published poems and simultaneous submissions. Accepts e-mail submissions (in text box). Cover letter is required. "Please provide a short bio, send SASE." Reads submissions year round. Submit seasonal poems 6 months in advance. Time between acceptance and publication is up to 6 months. "Whatever I like, I will publish." Often comments on rejected poems. Occasionally publishes theme issues. Guidelines and upcoming themes available in magazine, for SASE, by e-mail, or on website. Responds in up to 4 months. Pays 1 copy. Acquires one-time rights; reserves right to republish in future anthologies. Poets may send books for review consideration to Andrea Grant.

Advice: "The best poetry comes from the heart and has that haunting little twist. Don't be afraid to take risks."

COPPER CANYON PRESS; HAYDEN CARRUTH AWARD, P.O. Box 271, Port Townsend WA 98368. (877)501-1393. Fax: (360)385-4985. E-mail: poetry@coppercanyonpress.org. Website: www. coppercanyonpress.org. Established 1972. **Editor:** Sam Hamill.

Book/Chapbook Needs: Copper Canyon publishes books of poetry. Has published books of poetry by Lucille Clifton, Hayden Carruth, Carolyn Kizer, Olga Broumas, and Jim Harrison. As a sample, the editor selected these lines from "Comice" in *Below Cold Moutain* by Joseph Stroud:

> *I think of Issa often these days, his poems about the loneliness/of fleas, watermelons becoming frogs*
> *to escape from thieves./Moon in solstice, snowfall under the earth, I dream of a pure life./Issa said of*
> *his child, She smooths the wrinkles from my heart./Yes, it's a dewdrop world. Inside the pear there's*
> *a paradise/we will never know, our only hint the sweetness of its taste.*

How to Submit: Currently accepts no unsolicited poetry. E-mail queries and submissions will go unanswered.
Also Offers: Copper Canyon Press publishes 1 volume of poetry each year by a new or emerging poet through its Hayden Carruth Award. "For the purpose of this award an emerging poet is defined as a poet who has published not more than two books." Winner receives $1,000 advance, book publication with Copper Canyon Press, and a 1-month residency at the Vermont Studio Center. Each unbound ms submitted should be a minimum of 46 typed pages on white paper, paginated consecutively with a table of contents. Author's name or address must not appear anywhere on ms (this includes both title and acknowledgements pages). Please do not staple or paper-clip ms. Include $20 handling fee (check payable to Copper Canyon Press), submission form (available on website), and SASE for notification (mss will be recycled, not returned). Deadline: postmarked between November 1 and November 30, 2002. No entries by e-mail or fax. Winner announced February 21, 2003. Winners include Sascha Feinstein's *Misterioso*, Rebecca Wee's *Uncertain Grace*, and Jenny Factor's *Unraveling at the Name*. Past judges include Hayden Carruth (1999), Jane Miller (2000), Marilyn Hacker (2001). Further guidelines available for SASE and on website.

N **CORONA**, Dept. of History and Philosophy, Montana State University, P.O. Box 172320, Bozeman MT 59717-2320. (406)994-5200. Established 1979. **Poetry Editors:** Lynda and Michael Sexson.
Magazine Needs: *Corona* "is an interdisciplinary occasional journal bringing together reflections from those who stand on the edges of their disciplines; those who sense that insight is located not in things but in relationships; those who have deep sense of playfulness; and those who believe that the imagination is involved in what we know." In regard to poetry they want "no sentimental greeting cards; no slap-dash." Has published poetry by Wendy Battin, William Irwin Thompson, Frederick Turner, and James Dickey. *Corona* is 125-140 pages, perfect-bound, professionally printed. Uses about 20-25 pages of poetry/issue. Press run is 2,000. Sample: $7.
How to Submit: Submit any number of pages. No simultaneous submissions. Responds in up to 9 months. Payment is "nominal" plus 2 copies.
Advice: "Today's poet survives only by the generous spirits of small press publishers. Read and support the publishers of contemporary artists by subscribing to the journals and magazines you admire."

 CORRECTION(S): A LITERARY JOURNAL (Specialized: poetry from prisoners only); CORRECTION(S) CHAPBOOK CONTEST, P.O. Box 1234, New York NY 10276. Established 2001. **Editor:** K. Adams.
Magazine Needs: "*Correction(s)* is a biannual journal dedicated to the poetics and vision of prisoners." Wants "good writing with a sense of one's own poetics." Does not want blantant pornography. Recently published poetry by David Bowman, Torrance Mimms, Christopher Presfield, and Dwight Jordan. *Correction(s)* is 90 pages, digest-sized, perfect-bound, glossy and card stock cover, sometimes with art/graphics. Publishes 25-30 poems/issue. Single copy price: $3 (inmates), $8 (everyone else). Make checks payable to *Correction(s)*.
How to Submit: Submit 3-8 poems at a time. Accepts simultaneous submissions, no previously published poems. Accepts disk submissions; no fax or e-mail submissions. Cover letter is preferred. "Include SASE and brief bio. Handwritten submissions are accepted. Please print as neatly as possible." Reads submissions "all year/all the time." Time between acceptance and publication is about 6 months. Often comments on rejected poems. Will occasionally publish theme issues. Upcoming themes and guidelines are available for SASE. Responds in 2 months. Pays 2 contributor's copies. Acquires first rights. Reviews books and chapbooks of poetry and other magazines/journals. Poets may send books for review consideration to *Correction(s)*.
Book/Chapbook Needs & How to Submit: Correction(s) Press "seeks to publish quality literature written by prisoners." Publishes one paperback, one chapbook/year. Selects chapbook through competition (see **Also Offers** below). Chapbooks are usually 30-45 pages, perfect-bound, varied covers, sometimes with art/graphics. Responds to queries in 6 weeks; to mss in up to 1 year. Pays 30 author's copies. Guidelines available for SASE.
Also Offers: The *Correction(s)* Chapbook Contest accepts submissions in poetry and short fiction. Handwritten mss accepted. Manuscript must not exceed 60 handwritten (45 typed) pages for poetry; 50 handwritten (35 typed) pages for short fiction. **Contest open to prisoners only.** Prize is 30 copies and publication in *Correction(s)*. Entry fee: $1. Deadline: December 1, 2002. Winners will be notified by January 30, 2003.

 COTTONWOOD; COTTONWOOD PRESS, 400 Kansas Union-Box J, University of Kansas, Lawrence KS 66045. (913)864-3777. E-mail: cottonwd@falcon.cc.ukans.edu. Website: www.falcon.cc.ukans.edu/~cottonwd (includes guidelines, names of editors and staff, information on publications, and subscription order form). Established 1965. **Poetry Editor:** Philip Wedge.

Magazine Needs: *Cottonwood* is published biannually. Wants "strong narrative or sensory impact, non-derivative, not 'literary,' not 'academic.' Emphasis on Midwest, but publishes the best poetry received regardless of region. Poems should be 60 lines or fewer, on daily experience, *perception.*" Has published poetry by Rita Dove, Virgil Suarez, Walt McDonad, and Luci Tapahonso. As a sample the editors selected these lines from "The World Remade" by Lyn Plath:

> *Sunlight becomes a room in the city,/an angle of windows, a bar of gold on the floor./In a white vase on a table in the corner/flowers open, pulling the day into themselves,/into the rush and flutter of yellow petals/the way one body draws another body into itself.*

Cottonwood is 112 pages, 6×9, flat-spined, printed from computer offset, with photos, using 10-15 pages of poetry in each issue. Receives about 4,000 submissions/year, accepts about 30, have a maximum of 1-year backlog. Press run of 500-600, with 150 subscribers of which 75 are libraries. Single copy: $8.50. Sample: $5.

How to Submit: Submit up to 5 pages of poetry at a time. No simultaneous submissions. Sometimes provides criticism on rejected mss. Responds in up to 5 months. Pays 1 copy.

Book/Chapbook Needs & How to Submit: The press "is auxiliary to *Cottonwood Magazine* and publishes material by authors in the region. Material is usually solicited." The press published *Violence and Grace* by Michael L. Johnson and *Midwestern Buildings* by Victor Contoski.

Advice: "Read the little magazines and send to ones you like."

$ ◎ COUNTRY WOMAN; REIMAN PUBLICATIONS (Specialized: women, humor), 5925 Country Lane, Greendale WI 53129. Established 1970. **Executive Editor:** Kathy Pohl. **Managing Editor:** Kathleen Anderson.

Magazine Needs: *Country Woman* "is a bimonthly magazine dedicated to the lives and interests of country women. Those who are both involved in farming and ranching and those who love country life. In some ways, it is very similar to many women's general interest magazines, and yet its subject matter is closely tied in with rural living and the very unique lives of country women. We like short (4-5 stanzas, 16-20 lines) traditional rhyming poems that reflect on a season. No experimental poetry or free verse. Poetry will not be considered unless it rhymes. Always looking for poems that focus on the seasons. We don't want rural putdowns, poems that stereotype country women, etc. All poetry must be positive and upbeat. Our poems are fairly simple, yet elegant. They often accompany a high-quality photograph." Has published poetry by Hilda Sanderson, Edith E. Cutting, and Ericka Northrop. *Country Woman* is 68 pages, magazine-sized, printed on glossy paper with much color photography. Receives about 1,200 submissions of poetry/year, accepts about 40-50. Backlog is 3 months. Subscription: $17.98/year. Sample: $2.

How to Submit: Submit up to 6 poems at a time. Photocopy OK if stated not a simultaneous submission. Responds in 3 months. Pays $10-25/poem plus 1 copy. Acquires first rights (generally) or reprint rights (sometimes).

Also Offers: Holds various contests for subscribers only.

Advice: "We're always welcoming submissions, but any poem that does not have traditional rhythm and rhyme is automatically passed over."

◖ CRAB CREEK REVIEW, P.O. Box 840, Vashon Island WA 98070. E-mail: editor@crabcreekreview. org. Website: www.crabcreekreview.org (includes back issue samples, subscriber information, guidelines, and information on readings and appearances). Established 1983. **Editorial Collective:** Eleanor Lee, Harris Levinson, Laura Sinai, and Terri Stone.

Magazine Needs: Published biannually, *Crab Creek Review* publishes "an eclectic mix of energetic poems, free or formal, and more interested in powerful imagery than obscure literary allusion. Wit? Yes. Punch? Sure. Toast dry? No thank you. Translations are welcome—please submit with a copy of the poem in its original language, if possible." Has published poetry by Pauls Toutonghi, Molly Tenenbaum, Judith Skillman, Derek Sheffield, David Lee, and Kevin Miller. *Crab Creek Review* is an 80 to 120-page, perfect-bound paperback. Subscription: $10 (2 issues). Sample: $5.

How to Submit: Submit up to 5 poems at a time. No fax or e-mail submissions. Include SASE ("without one we will not consider the work"). Responds in up to 4 months. Pays 2 copies. Guidelines available for SASE or on website.

▣ $◖ CRAB ORCHARD REVIEW; CRAB ORCHARD AWARD SERIES IN POETRY, English Dept., Faner Hall, Southern Illinois University at Carbondale, Carbondale IL 62901-4503. Website: www.siu.edu/~crborchd (includes guidelines, contact and subscription info, upcoming themes, links, biographical notes, contest requirements and results, archives). Established 1995. **Poetry Editor:** Allison Joseph. **Managing Editor:** Jon C. Tribble.

• *Crab Orchard Review* received a 2001 Literary Award and a 2001 Operating Grant from the Illinois Arts Council. Poetry from *Crab Orchard Review* has also appeared in *The Best American Poetry 1999, 2000,* and *2001* and *Beacon Best of 1999* and 2000.

Magazine Needs: *Crab Orchard Review* appears biannually in June and January. "We are a general interest literary journal publishing poetry, fiction, creative nonfiction, interviews, book reviews, and novel excerpts." Wants all styles and forms from traditional to experimental. No greeting card verse; literary poetry only. Has published poetry by Karen Kovacik, Jeffrey Levine, Brendan Galvin, Ruth Ellen Kocher, and Cornelius Eady. In response to our request for sample lines of poetry the editors say, "We'd prefer not to, since no one excerpt can convey the breadth of poetry we'd like to receive." *Crab Orchard Review* is 250 pages, 5½×8½, professionally printed and perfect-bound with photos, usually glossy card cover containing color photos. Receives about 8,000 poems/year, accepts about 1%. Each issue usually includes 35-40 poems. Press run is 1,600 for 1,100 subscribers of which 60 are libraries, 390 shelf sales; 50 distributed free to exchange with other journals. Subscription: $10. Sample: $6.

How to Submit: Submit up to 5 poems at a time. Accepts simultaneous submissions with notification; no previously published poems. No fax or e-mail submissions. Cover letter preferred. "Indicate stanza breaks on poems of more than one page." Reads submissions April to November for our Spring/Summer special issue, December to April for regular, non-thematic Fall/Winter issue. Time between acceptance and publication is 6-12 months. Poems are circulated to an editorial board. "Poems that are under serious consideration are discussed and decided on by the managing editor, and poetry editor." Seldom comments on rejected poems. Publishes theme issues. Theme for Spring/Summer 2002 issue is "Taste the World: Writers Explore Food." Deadline: December 1, 2002. Guidelines and upcoming themes available for SASE or on website. Responds in up to 8 months. Pays $10/page, $50 minimum plus 2 copies and 1 year's subscription. Acquires first North American serial rights. Staff reviews books of poetry in 500-700 words, single book format. Send books for review consideration to managing editor Jon C. Tribble.

Also Offers: Sponsors the Crab Orchard Award Series in Poetry. The publisher of the books will be Southern Illinois University Press. The competition is open from October 1 to November 16 for US citizens and permanent residents. "The Crab Orchard Award Series in Poetry, launched in 1997, is committed to publishing two book-length manuscripts each year. We also run an annual fiction/nonfiction contest." Books are usually 50-70 pages, 9×6, perfect-bound with color paper covers. Entry fee: $20/submission (each entrant receives a subscription to *Crab Orchard Review*). 1st and 2nd Prize winners each receive a publication contract with Southern Illinois University Press. In addition, the 1st Prize winner will be awarded a $2,000 prize and $1,000 as an honorarium for a reading at Southern Illinois University at Carbondale; also, the 2nd Prize winner will receive $1,000 as an honorarium for a reading at Southern Illinois University at Carbondale. Both readings will follow the publication of the poets' collections by Southern Illinois University Press. 2001 winner was Joy Katz from *Fabulae,* second place winner was Susan Aizenberg for *Muse.* 2001 First Book winner was Joelle Biele Siegwarth for *White Summer.* Also, first book competition for the publication of a poet's first book. Reads for this prize from May 15, 2002 to June 15, 2002 (first book). All questions regarding the Award Series in Poetry should go to Jon C. Tribble, series editor, Crab Orchard Award Series in Poetry. Details available for SASE.

Advice: "Please include SASE with all submissions—let us know whether or not you want poems recycled or returned. Don't send SASEs that are smaller than number 10 envelopes."

CRANIAL TEMPEST; CANNEDPHLEGM PRESS, 410 El Dorado St., Vallejo CA 94590. E-mail: cranialtempest@hotmail.com. Established 1991 (press); 2000 (publication). **Editor:** Jeff Fleming.

Magazine Needs: *Cranial Tempest* appears bimonthly "to publish the best in poetry and short fiction." Wants poetry of all kinds, "we are wide open." Recently published poetry by John Grey, Michael Brownstein, Ed Galing, Tim Scannell, normal, and John Sweet. As a sample the editor selected these lines from "In Traffic" by John Grey:

> you're on the streets,/on a bed of rubber/and rusty springs,/steering life out/of the faraway,/the misty-eyed

Cranial Tempest is 26 pages, digest-sized, photocopied, saddle-stapled, card stock cover. Receives about 600 poems/year, accepts about 40%. Publishes about 25 poems/issue. Press run is 150 for 75 subscribers.

Book/Chapbook Needs & How to Submit: CannedPhlegm Press publishes 3-5 chapbooks/year. Chapbooks are usually 15-30 pages, photocopied, saddle-stapled, card stock cover. Query first, with 3-5 sample poems and a cover letter with brief bio and publication credits. Responds to queries in 2 weeks; to mss in 1 month. Pays 2 author's copies. Order sample chapbooks by sending $3 to Jeff Fleming.

N ◯ CRAZYHORSE; CRAZYHORSE FICTION AND POETRY AWARDS, Dept. of English, College of Charleston, 66 George St., Charleston SC 29424. (843)953-7740. E-mail: crazyhorse@cofc.edu. Established 1960. **Poetry Editors:** Paul Allen and Carol Ann Davis.

Magazine Needs: *Crazyhorse* appears biannually and publishes fine fiction, poetry, and essays. "Send your best words our way. We like to print a mix of writing regardless of its form, genre, school, or politics. We're especially on the lookout for writing that doesn't fit the categories." Does not want "writing with nothing at stake. Before sending, ask 'What's reckoned with that's important for other people to read?'" Recently published poetry by David Wojahn, Mary Ruefle, Nance Van Winkle, Andrew Hudgins, James Grinwis, and Lola Haskins. *Crazyhorse* is 150-200 pages, 9×8, perfect-bound, 4-color glossy cover. Receives about 8,000 poems/year. Publishes about 80 poems/issue. Press run is 1,500. Single copy: $8.50; subscription: $15 for 1 year/2 issues, $25 for 2 years, $40 for 3 years. Sample: $5. Make checks payable to *Crazyhorse*.

How to Submit: Submit 3-5 poems at a time. Accepts simultaneous submissions; no previously published poems. No fax, e-mail, or disk submissions. Cover letter is preferred. Reads submissions year round. "We read slower in summer." Time between acceptance and publication is 6 months. Seldom comments on rejected poems. Guidelines available in magazine, for SASE, or by e-mail. Responds in 3 months. Sometimes sends prepublication galleys. Pays 2 contributor's copies plus a year's subscription (2 issues). Acquires first rights.

Also Offers: The Crazyhorse Fiction and Poetry Awards: $50 and publication in *Crazyhorse*. Send SASE for details.

Advice: "Feel strongly; then write."

N ◯ THE CREAM CITY REVIEW, P.O. Box 413, Dept. of English, University of Wisconsin at Milwaukee, Milwaukee WI 53201. (414)229-4708. E-mail: creamcity@uwm.edu. Website: www.uwm.edu/Dept/English/CCR. **Editors:** Karen Anvinen. **Poetry Editor:** Fran Abbate.

• Poetry published in this review has been included in the 1996 and 1997 volumes of *The Best American Poetry*.

Magazine Needs: *The Cream City Review* is a nationally distributed literary magazine published twice/year by the university's Creative Writing Program. "We seek to publish all forms of writing, from traditional to experimental. We strive to produce issues which are challenging, diverse and of lasting quality. We are not interested in sexist, homophobic, racist or formulaic writings." Has published poetry by William Harrold, Maxine Chernoff, Kate Braverman, Billy Collins, Bob Hicok, and Allison Joseph. They do not include sample lines of poetry; "Best to buy a copy—we publish the best from new and established writers. We like an energetic mix." *The Cream City Rewview* is averaging 200 pages, 5½×8½, perfect-bound, with full-color cover on 70 lb. paper. Press run is 1,000 for 450 subscribers of which 40 are libraries. Single copy: $8; subscription: $15/1 year, $28/2 years. Sample: $5.

How to Submit: "Include SASE when submitting and please submit no more than five poems at a time." Accepts simultaneous submissions when notified. "Please include a few lines about your publication history and other information you think of interest." Reads submissions September 1 through April 1 only. Editors sometimes comment on rejected poems. Accepts submissions by regular mail only. Guidelines available for SASE. Responds in up to 6 months. Payment includes 1-year subscription. Acquires first rights. Reviews books of poetry in 1-2 pages. Poets may send books to the poetry editors for review consideration.

Also Offers: Sponsors an annual contest for poems under 100 lines. Submit 3 poems/entry. Entry fee: $10. Awards $100 plus publication; all entries considered for publication.

◯ CREATIVE JUICES; FORESTLAND PUBLICATIONS, 423 N. Burnham Highway, Canterbury CT 06331. E-mail: forestland1@juno.com. Website: www.geocities.com/geraldinepowell/index.html (includes guidelines, submission info, and subscription forms). Established 1989 (Forestland Publications). **Editor:** Geraldine Hempstead Powell.

Magazine Needs: *Creative Juices*, published bimonthly, features poetry, arts, photos, "something to inspire everyone's creative juices." Wants "any style or subject, 50 lines or less." Does not want pornography. Accepts poetry written by children aged 10 or older. Has published poetry by John Grey, John Allen Jaynes, and David Spiering. As a sample the editor selected this lines from "Love Thus Lost" by John Allen Jaynes:

> O, the mocking laughter of Reality/and the chains clanking upon the ghosts/as I huddle in the corner
> before fate/and watch my princess walk away.

Press run is 100 for 65 subscribers, 30 shelf sales. Receives about 1,000 poems/year, accepts about 350. Single copy: $3; subscription: $20/year; $35/2 years. Sample: $2 and SASE. Make checks payable to Geraldine Powell.

How to Submit: Submit 3-5 poems at a time. Accepts simultaneous submissions. Accepts e-mail submissions; prefers attached file. Cover letter preferred. Time between acceptance and publication is up to 3 months. Submissions reviewed by editor. Often comments on rejected poems. Guidelines available for SASE, on website, by fax, in publication, or by e-mail. Responds in 1 month. Sometimes sends prepublication galleys. Pays 1 or more copies. Acquires first North American serial or one-time rights. Always returns rights. Reviews books of poetry. Poets may send books for review consideration.

Book/Chapbook Needs & How to Submit: Forestland Publications publishes 4-6 chapbooks/year. Has published Nancy Manning's *Amythst Garden* and Reneeta Renganathan's *Sleeping Alone*. Chapbooks are usually 5×7, 20 pages. Send up to 20 poems, **$10 reading fee**, and cover letter with brief bio and publication credits. Responds to mss in 1 month. Obtain sample chapbooks by sending SASE with 2 stamps and $3. "Beginning in 1999, non-subscribers [to *Creative Juices*] should remit a $10 reading fee for chapbook submissions."

Advice: "Please learn to type. Put name and address on *every* page."

CREATIVE WITH WORDS PUBLICATIONS (C.W.W.); SPOOFING (Specialized: themes); WE ARE WRITERS, TOO (Specialized: children); THE ECLECTICS (Specialized: adults), P.O. Box 223226, Carmel CA 93922. Fax: (831)655-8627. E-mail: geltrich@usa.net or cwwpub@usa.net. Website: http://members.tripod.com/CreativeWithWords (includes guidelines, themes, editing information, contest for children and winners). Established 1975. **Poetry Editor:** Brigitta Geltrich.

Magazine Needs: Creative with Words Publications focuses "on furthering folkloristic tall tales and such; creative writing abilities in children (poetry, prose, language art); creative writing in adults (poetry and prose)." Publishes on a wide range of themes relating to human studies and the environment that influence human behaviors. **Reading fee:** $5/poem (includes critique). The publications are anthologies of children's poetry, prose, and language art; anthologies of 'special-interest groups' poetry and prose; *Spoofing: An Anthology of Folkloristic Yarns and Such*; and anthologies with announced themes (nature, animals, love, travel, etc.). "Do not want to see: too mushy; too religious; too didactic; expressing dislike for fellow men; political; pornographic; death and murder poetry and prose." Guidelines and upcoming themes available for SASE or on website. Has published poetry by Daniel Mohler, Hannah Shefsky, Elizabeth Kapp, Nick Emanuele, and Alex Beck. As a sample the editor selected these lines by Ruth Margarete Boehnke:

> Love does not guarantee everthing,/Love is fighting a battle in deepest understanding

Spoofing! and *We are Writers, Too!* are low-budget publications, photocopied from typescript, saddle-stapled, card covers with cartoon-like computer art. Samples: $6 plus p&h. Single copy: $9-12, depending on length; subscription: 12 issues for $60; 6 issues for $36; 3 issues for $21. Libraries and schools receive 10% discount. Make checks payable to Brigitta Ludgate.

How to Submit: Submit poems of 20 lines or less, 46 character maximum line length, poems geared to specific audience and subject matter. No simultaneous submissions or previously published poems. No fax submissions. "Query with sample poems (one poem/page, name and address on each), short personal biography, other publications, poetic goals, where you read about us, for what publication and/or event you are submitting. SASE is a must." Accepts queries by fax. Has "no conditions for publication, but **C.W.W. is dependent on author/poet support by purchase of a copy or copies of publication.**" Offers a 20% reduction on any copy purchased.

Also Offers: Sponsors "Best of the Month" contest, awards publication certificate and 1 copy.

Advice: "Trend is proficiency. Poets should research topic; know audience for whom they write; check topic for appeal to specific audience; should not write for the sake of rhyme, rather for the sake of imagery and being creative with the language. Feeling should be expressed (but no mushiness). Topic and words should be chosen carefully; brevity should be employed; and author should proofread for spelling and grammar. We would like to receive more positive and clean, family-type poetry."

CREATIVITY UNLIMITED PRESS®; ANNUAL CREATIVITY UNLIMITED PRESS® POETRY COMPETITION, 30819 Casilina, Rancho Palos Verdes CA 90275. E-mail: sstockwell@earthlink.net. Established 1978. **Editor:** Shelley Stockwell.

Book/Chapbook Needs: Creativity Unlimited® uses poetry submitted to their contest in published text. $5 fee for 1-5 poems; prizes of $50, $35, and $25 and possible publication. Deadline: December 31. "Clever, quippy, humor, and delightful language encouraged. No inaccessible, verbose, esoteric, obscure poetry. Limit three pages per poem, double-spaced, one side of page."

How to Submit: "Poems previously published will be accepted provided writer has maintained copyright and notifies us." Accepts e-mail submissions. Often uses poems as chapter introductions in self-help books. Always comments on rejected poems. Publishes theme issues. Upcoming themes available for SASE. Sometimes sends prepublication galleys. Pays 2 copies.

Advice: "We are interested in receiving more humorous poetry."

CREOSOTE, Department of English, Mohave Community College, 1977 W. Acoma Blvd., Lake Havasu City AZ 86403. Established 2000. **Editor:** Ken Raines.

Magazine Needs: *Creosote* is an annual publication of poetry, fiction, and literary nonfiction appearing in May. Has "a bias favoring more traditional forms, but interested in any and all quality poems." Has "a bias against confessional and beat-influenced poetry, but will consider everything." Recently published poetry by William Wilborn, Ruth Moose, and Star Coolbrooke. As a sample the editor selected these lines from "Chinook" by William Wilborn:

> Then wind like starlight or, maybe, the Grace/Of God, drops silent, freshening the face/Of mountain
> ranges, sweeps the valleys, swirls/Around you sleeping, turning all the world/To tender sucking sweetly
> breathing mood/Of spring, of our brief aching dream of earth.

Creosote is 48 pages, digest-sized, saddle stapled, card cover. Receives about 150-200 poems/year, accepts about 10%. Publishes about 15 poems/issue. Press run is 500 for 30 subscribers of which 5 are libraries, 200 shelf sales; 100+ are distributed free to contributors and others. Single copy: $4. Sample: $2. Make checks payable to Mohave Community College.

How to Submit: Submit up to 5 poems at a time. Line length for poetry is open. Accepts simultaneous submissions "but please notify us ASAP if accepted elsewhere"; no previously published poems. Accepts disk submissions; no fax or e-mail submissions. Cover letter is preferred. "Disk submissions must be accompanied by a hard copy." Reads submissions September 1-February 28. Time between acceptance and publication is 2-3 months. Poems are circulated to an editorial board. "All work which passes initial screening is considered by at least 2 (usually more) readers." Seldom comments on rejected poems. Guidelines are available for SASE. Responds in 6 months "at most, usually sooner." Pays 2 contributor's copies. Acquires one-time rights. Occasionally reviews books of poetry in 250-500 words. Poets may send books for review consideration to Ken Raines, editor.

Advice: "Love words. Resist the urge to pontificate. Beware a self-congratulatory tone. Shun sloppy expression."

CROSS-CULTURAL COMMUNICATIONS; CROSS-CULTURAL REVIEW OF WORLD LITERATURE AND ART IN SOUND, PRINT, AND MOTION; CROSS-CULTURAL MONTHLY; CROSS-CULTURAL REVIEW CHAPBOOK ANTHOLOGY; INTERNATIONAL WRITERS SERIES (Specialized: translations, bilingual), 239 Wynsum Ave., Merrick NY 11566-4725. (516)868-5635. Fax: (516)379-1901. E-mail: cccmia@juno.com or cccpoetry@aol.com. Established 1971. **Contact:** Stanley H. and Bebe Barkan.

Magazine Needs & How to Submit: *Cross-Cultural Monthly* focuses on bilingual poetry and prose. Subscription (12 issues/editions): $50. Sample postpaid: $7.50. Pays 1 copy.

Book/Chapbook Needs & How to Submit: *Cross-Cultural Review* began as a series of chapbooks (6-12/year) of collections of poetry translated from various languages and continues as the Holocaust, Women Writers, Latin American Writers, African Heritage, Asian Heritage, Italian Heritage, International Artists, Art & Poetry, Jewish, Israeli, Yiddish, Hebrew, Arabic, American, Bengali, Cajun, Chicano, Chinese, Czech, Dutch, Finnish, Gypsy (Roma), Indian, Polish, Russian, Serbian, Sicilian, Swedish, Scandinavian, Turkish, and Long Island and Brooklyn Writers Chapbook Series (with a number of other permutations in the offing)—issued simultaneously in palm-sized and regular paperback and cloth-binding editions and boxed and canned editions, as well as audiocassette and videocassette. Cross-Cultural International Writers Series, focusing on leading poets from various countries, includes titles by Leo Vroman (Holland) and Pablo Neruda (Chile). The Holocaust series is for survivors. In addition to publications in these series, Cross-Cultural Communications has published anthologies, translations, and collections by dozens of poets from many countries. As a sample the editor selected the beginning of a poem by Rainer Maria Rilke, as translated by Stephen Mitchell:

> She was no longer that woman with blue eyes/who once had echoed through the poet's songs,/no
> longer the wide couch's scent and island,/and that man's property no longer.//She was already loosened
> like long hair,/poured out like fallen rain,/shared like a limitless supply.

That's from the bilingual limited poetry and art edition, *Orpheus. Eurydice. Hermes: Notations on a Landscape* (1996) which is 35 pages, 10½×13½, smythe-sewn cloth. Sample chapbook: $10 postpaid. All submissions should be preceded by a query letter with SASE. Guidelines available for SASE. Pays 10% of print run.

Also Offers: Cross-Cultural Communications continues to produce the International Festival of Poetry, Writing and Translation with the International Poets and Writers Literary Arts Week in New York. Cross-Cultural Communications won the Poor Richards Award "for a quarter century of high-quality publishing," presented by The Small Press Center in New York.

CROSSOVER PRESS, P.O. Box 101362, Pittsburgh PA 15237. (412)364-9009. Fax: (412)364-3273. Established 1996. **Editor:** Don H. Laird. **Poetry Editor:** Halley White.

• *"The Threshold* has ceased publication. Crossover Press will continue as a book publisher."

Book/Chapbook Needs & How to Submit: Accepts simultaneous submissions; no previously published poems. No fax submissions. "Poets should provide a brief biography." Time between acceptance and publication is 6 months. Occasionally publishes theme issues. Guidelines available for SASE. Responds in up to 8 months. Pays 1 contributor's copy. Acquires one-time rights.
Advice: "Good writers are a dime a dozen. Good story tellers are priceless!"

CRUCIBLE; SAM RAGAN PRIZE, Barton College, College Station, Wilson NC 27893. (252)399-6456. E-mail: tgrimes@barton.edu. Established 1964. **Editor:** Terrence L. Grimes.
Magazine Needs: *Crucible* is an annual published in November using "poetry that demonstrates originality and integrity of craftsmanship as well as thought. Traditional metrical and rhyming poems are difficult to bring off in modern poetry. The best poetry is written out of deeply felt experience which has been crafted into pleasing form. No very long narratives." Has published poetry by Robert Grey, R.T. Smith, and Anthony S. Abbott. *Crucible* is 100 pages, 6×9, professionally printed on high-quality paper with matte card cover. Press run is 500 for 300 subscribers of which 100 are libraries, 200 shelf sales. Sample: $7.
How to Submit: Submit 5 poems at a time between Christmas and mid-April only. No previously published poems or simultaneous submissions. Responds in up to 4 months. "We require three unsigned copies of the manuscript and a short biography including a list of publications, in case we decide to publish the work." Pays contributor's copies.
Also Offers: Send SASE for guidelines for contests (prizes of $150 and $100), and the Sam Ragan Prize ($150) in honor of the former Poet Laureate of North Carolina.
Advice: Editor leans toward free verse with attention paid particularly to image, line, stanza, and voice. However, he does not want to see poetry that is "forced."

CUMBERLAND POETRY REVIEW; THE ROBERT PENN WARREN POETRY PRIZE, Dept. PM, P.O. Box 120128, Acklen Station, Nashville TN 37212. Established 1981. **Contact:** Eva Touster, editor.
Magazine Needs: *Cumberland Poetry Review* is a biannual journal presenting poetry, poetry criticism, and poets of diverse origins to a widespread audience. "We place no restrictions on form, subject, or style. Our aim is to support the poet's effort to keep up the language. We accept a special responsibility for reminding our readers that excellent poems in English are written by citizens of many counties around the world. We have published such poets as Dan Stryk, Ovid (in translation), James Sutherland-Smith, and C.K. Stead." *Cumberland Poetry Review* is 75-100 pages, 6×9, flat-spined. Circulation is 500. Sample: $9.
How to Submit: Send poetry, translations, or poetry criticism with SASE or SAE with IRC. Submit up to 6 poems at a time. No previously published poems. "We accept, but do not like to receive simultaneous submissions." Cover letter with brief bio required. Responds in 6 months. Pays 2 copies. Acquires first rights. Returns rights "on request of author providing he acknowledges original publication in our magazine."
Also Offers: Awards the Robert Penn Warren Poetry Prize annually. Winners receive $500, $300, and $200 and publication in the review. Entry fee: $18. For contest guidelines, send SASE.

CURBSIDE REVIEW, P.O. Box 667189, Houston TX 77266-7189. (713)529-0198. E-mail: rcastl2335@aol.com. Established 2000. **Co-Editors/Publishers:** Carolyn Adams and R.T. Castleberry.
Magazine Needs: *Curbside Review* appears monthly. "Our motto on the masthead is from W.B. Yeats: 'Our words must seem to be inevitable.' " Wants mature, crafted work in all styles and forms, "though we prefer modern free verse and prose poetry. We like intensity, dark humor, and wit." Recently published poetry by Larry D. Thomas, Robert Phillips, Lorenzo Thomas, Virgil Suarez, and Lyn Lifshin. As a sample the editors selected these lines from "Transformations (Stele for Luigi Nono)" by John Shreffler:

> The falling dialectic of the birds/Pelting the fleeing sun with off-rhythms/Or spaces, the leaf about to embark/Mindless upon the torrent

Curbside Review is 4 pages, magazine-sized, copier-printed, folded. Receives about 1,200 poems/year, accepts about 20%. Publishes about 10 poems/issue. Press run is 400; all distributed free to local poetry groups and events, local independent bookstores. Single copy: free with #10 SASE.
How to Submit: Submit 5 poems at a time. Line length for poetry is 50 maximum. Accepts simultaneous submissions; no previously published poems. No fax, e-mail, or disk submissions. Cover letter is preferred. "We have a strict 'don't ask, don't tell' policy on previously published/simultaneous submissions. We read continuously throughout the year." Submit seasonal poems 4 months in advance. Time between acceptance and publication varies. Poems are circulated to an editorial board. "We often take more than one poem from writers, so publication

is ongoing. Rather than reject, we often ask for revisions on promising poems." Never comments on rejected poems. Guidelines available in magazine, for SASE, or by e-mail. Responds in 3 months. Pays 2 contributor's copies. Acquires one-time rights.

Advice: "We publish *poetry* only. Since a sample copy is free, please take advantage of that to read it for a sense of our style."

N ⊕ ⊘ CURRENT ACCOUNTS; BANK STREET WRITERS; BANK STREET WRITERS COMPETITION, 16-18 Mill Lane, Horwich, Bolton, Lancashire BL6 6AT England. Phone/fax: (01204)669858. E-mail: rodriesco@cs.com. Website: http://ourworld.compuserve.co.uk/bswscribe/myhom epage/writing.html (includes guidelines, contact and subscription information, links, editorial policy). Established 1994. **Editor:** Rod Riesco.

Magazine Needs: *Current Accounts* is a biannual publishing poetry, fiction, and nonfiction by members of Bank Street Writers and other contributors. Open to all types of poetry; maximum 100 lines. Accepts poetry written by children. Has published poetry by Pat Winslow, M.R. Peacocke, and Gerald England. As a sample the editor selected these lines from "Spinal Tap" by Geoff Stevens:

> *All bronzes, and stone sculptures, are bald.//And yet backbone is a long plait/bronzed or marbled to the flesh.//It is the necessary fibre/the rhino whip lashing together head and hip.//A blind man that has never seen the Andes/can recognize the chain of the human frame.//It bumps under his fingers//from nape to coccyx.*

Current Accounts is 24-48 pages, A5, photocopied, saddle-stapled, card cover with b&w or color photo or artwork. Receives about 300 poems/year, accepts about 5%. Press run is 50 for 3 subscribers, 30 shelf sales; 8 distributed free to competition winners. Subscription: UK £4. Sample: UK £2. Make checks payable to Bank Street Writers (sterling checks only). "No requirements, although some space is reserved for members."

How to Submit: Submit up to 6 poems at a time. Unpublished poems preferred; no simultaneous submissions. Accepts e-mail and fax submissions. Cover letter required and SAE or IRC essential for postal submissions. Guidelines available for SASE, by fax, by e-mail, and on website. Time between acceptance and publication is 6 months. Seldom comments on rejected poems. Responds in 1 month. Pays 1 contributor's copy. Acquires first rights.

Also Offers: Sponsors the annual Bank Street Writers Poetry and Short Story Competition. Submit poems up to 40 lines, any subject or style. Deadline: October 31. Entry fee: £2/poem. Entry form available for SAE and IRC. Also, the Bank Street Writers meets once a month and offers workshops, guest speakers and other activities. Write for details.

Advice: "We like originality of ideas, images, and use of language. No inspirational or religious verse unless it's also good in poetic terms."

N ◯ ◎ CURRICULUM VITAE LITERARY SUPPLEMENT; SIMPSON PUBLICATIONS (Specialized: themes, Nature/Rural/Ecology, Political, Women/Feminism), Grove City Factory Store, P.O. Box 1309, Grove City PA 16127. E-mail: simpub@hotmail.com. Established 1995. **Managing Editor:** Amy Dittman.

Magazine Needs: *Curriculum Vitae Literary Supplement* appears biannually in January and July and is "a thematic zine, but quality work is always welcome whether or not it applies to our current theme. We'd like to see more metrical work, especially more translations, and well-crafted narrative free verse is always welcome. However, we do not want to see rambling Bukowski-esque free verse or poetry that overly relies on sentimentality. We are a relatively new publication and focus on unknown poets." As a sample the editor selected these lines from "Faye's Loose Hair" by Andy Krackow:

> *Grandma called you Susan,/But Mom I named you Faye/To my ninth grade classmates/Because it was romantic and I wanted you/To be a movie star with a murderous man.*

Curriculum Vitae Literary Supplement is 40 pages, digest-sized, photocopied, saddle-stapled, with a 2-color card stock cover. Receives about 500 poems/year, accepts about 75. Press run is 1,000 for 300 subscribers of which 7 are libraries, 200 shelf sales. Subscription: $6 (4 issues). Sample: $4.

How to Submit: Submit 3 poems at a time. "Submissions without a SASE cannot be acknowledged due to postage costs." Accepts previously published poems and simultaneous submissions. Accepts e-mail submissions (as attachment). Cover letter "to give us an idea of who you are" preferred. Time between acceptance and publication is 8 months. Poetry is circulated among 3 board members. Often comments on rejected poems. Publishes theme issues. Guidelines and upcoming themes available for SASE or by e-mail. Responds within 1 month. Pays 2 contributor's copies plus 1-year subscription.

Book/Chapbook Needs & How to Submit: Simpson Publications also publishes about 5 chapbooks/year. Interested poets should query.

Also Offers: "We are currently looking for poets who would like to be part of our Poetry Postcard series." Interested writers should query to The *CVLS* Poetry Postcard Project at the above address for more information.

⊕ ⊘ CYBER LITERATURE, c/o Dr. Chhote Lal Khatri, Saketpuri, Road No-I, Hanuman Nagar, Fatna, 800020 Bihar, India. Phone: 0612-363326. Fax: 0612-669188. Established 1997. **Contact:** Dr. Chhote Lal Khatri.

Magazine Needs: *Cyber Literature* appears biannually to "nurture creativity and serve humanity by spreading the voice of muse and foster world peace and fellow-feeling." "Open to all sorts of poems within 25 lines that have authenticity of experience and vitality of expression, well knit, compact and crisp, preference to structural verse. No sermons, prosaic, experimental work without any purpose." Has published poetry by Ruth Wildes Schuler, R.K. Singh, and I.H. Rizvi. *Cyber Literature* is 70-80 pages, offset-printed and saddle-stapled with paper back cover, includes ads. Receives about 200 poems/year, accepts about 30-40%. Press run is 500 for 300 subscribers of which 20 are libraries, 100 shelf sales; 40-60 distributed free to editors, celebrities. Single copy: $5; subscription: $10. Sample: $5. Make checks payable to Dr. Chhote Lal Khatri.

How to Submit: Submit 3-6 poems at a time. Line length for poetry is 25 maximum. Accepts previously published poems and simultaneous submissions. Cover letter preferred. Include SASE or IRC and a bio. Reads submissions March 1-April 30 and September 1-October 30 only. Time between acceptance and publication is 6 months. "Poems are circulated among associate editors. They are returned to the editor for final decision." Seldom comments on rejections. Membership or purchase of copy required for consideration. Responds in 1 month. Pays 1 contributor's copy. Acquires one-time rights. Reviews books and chapbooks of poetry and other magazines in 500 words, single book format. Poets may send books for review consideration.

Also Offers: Publishes an anthology of poets from both India and abroad.

Ⓝ ⊘ ⊚ CYCLE PRESS; INTERIM BOOKS; CAYO MAGAZINE (Specialized: regional), 715 Baker's Lane, Key West FL 33040. Established 1968. **Contact:** Kirby Congdon.

Magazine Needs & How to Submit: *Cayo* is a quarterly regional literary magazine focusing on the Florida Keys. *Cayo* is 40 pages, magazine-sized, offset printed and saddle-stapled with self-cover, includes photography. Receives about 100 poems/year, accepts approximately 20%. Press run is 1,000 for 100 subscribers, 400 shelf sales; 500 distributed free to sponsors/contributors. Single copy: $3; subscription: $16. Sample: $4. Submit 3 poems at a time. Accepts previously published poems and simultaneous submissions. Cover letter preferred. SASE required. Reads submissions July through August and October through April only. Time between acceptance and publication is 3-6 months. Poems are circulated to an editorial board. "The poetry editor finalizes his choices with the publisher and editor-in-chief." Often comments on rejected poems. Responds in 3 months. Pays 2 copies. Acquires one-time rights.

Book/Chapbook Needs: Cycle Press and Interim Books publish poems that are "contemporary in experience and thought. We concentrate on single poems, rather than more elaborate projects, for the author to distribute as he sees fit—usually in numbered copies of 50 to 300 copies." Wants "provocative, uncertain queries; seeking resolutions rather than asserting solutions. No nineteenth century platitudes." As a sample Mr. Congdon selected these lines from his poem "Discus Thrower":

> His figure, cut in silhouette/with no excess expended/nor stint in measure,/takes its careful aim.

Books are usually 6-12 pages, 5×8, computer-generated with hand-sewn binding, paper jackets, some photos. **How to Submit:** Submit 3 poems at a time. Accepts simultaneous submissions. Cover letter preferred. "If spelling, punctuation and grammer are secondary concerns to the author. I feel the ideas and experience have to be secondary too." Time between acceptance and publication is 1 year. Often comments on rejected poems. "No requirements except a feeling of rapport with the author's stance."

⊠ ⊘ DALHOUSIE REVIEW, Dalhousie University, Halifax, Nova Scotia B3H 1X1 Canada. (902)494-2541. Fax: (902)494-3561. E-mail: dalhousie.review@dal.ca. Website: www.dal.ca/~dalrev. Established 1921. **Editor:** Dr. Ronald Huebert.

Magazine Needs: *Dalhousie Review* appears 3 times/year. Recently published poetry by Martin Bennett, Ogaga Ifowodo, Kanina Dawson, Jacqueline Karp, and David Rachel. *Dalhousie Review* is 144 pages, 6×9. Accepts about 10% of poems received. Press run is 600 for 400 subscribers. Single copy: $10 (Canadian); subscription: $22 (Canadian); 28 (US). Sample: $10 (Canadian). Make checks payable to *Dalhousie Review.*

How to Submit: No previously published poems. Accepts e-mail and disk submissions. "Contributions should be typed on plain white paper, double-spaced throughout. Spelling preferences are those of *The Canadian Oxford Dictionary*: catalogue, colour, program, travelling, theatre, and so on. Beyond this, writers of fiction and poetry are encouraged to follow whatever canons of usage might govern the particular story or poem in question, and to be inventive with language, ideas and form. Poems should in general not exceed 40 lines, but there will of course be valid exceptions to these rules. Initial submissions are by means of hard copy only." Reads submissions year-round. Seldom comments on rejected poems. Occasionally publishes theme issues. Upcoming themes and guidelines available for SAE and IRC. Pays 2 contributor's copies and 10 off-prints.

$ ⬡ DANA LITERARY SOCIETY ONLINE JOURNAL, P.O. Box 3362, Dana Point CA 92629-8362. Website: www.danaliterary.org (includes poetry, fiction, and nonfiction, also editorial commentary, writer's guidelines, and recommended resources; edited by Ronald D. Hardcastle). Established 2000. **Director:** Robert L. Ward.

Magazine Needs: *Dana Literary Society Online Journal* appears monthly. Contains poetry, fiction, and nonfiction. "All styles are welcome—rhyming/metrical, free verse, and classic—but they must be well-crafted and throught-provoking. We want no pornography. Neither do we want works that consist of pointless flows of words with no apparent significance." Recently published poetry by Earl J. Perel, Heidi Schwartz, Laurence W. Thomas, and Elinor Phillips Cubbage. As a sample the editor selected these lines from "Unrequited" by A.B. Jacobs:

> And as I knelt in rapture there,/The orchid writhed in grim despair./As if to show my love denied,/
> Forlornly in my arms it died.

Dana Literary Society Online Journal is equivalent to approximately 40 printed pages. Receives about 600 poems/year, accepts about 10%. Publishes about 5 poems/issue.

How to Submit: Submit up to 3 poems at a time. Line length for poetry is 120 maximum. Accepts previously published poems and simultaneous submissions. Accepts submissions by regular mail only. Time between acceptance and publication is 3 months. Poems are selected by Society director and *Online Journal* editor. Often comments on rejected poems. Guidelines are available on website. Responds in 2 weeks. Pays $25 for each poem accepted. Acquires right to display in *Online Journal* for one month.

Advice: "We desire works that are well-crafted and thought-provoking. Neither pornography nor meaningless flows of words are welcome."

⊕ ◯ ◎ DANDELION ARTS MAGAZINE; FERN PUBLICATIONS (Specialized: membership/subscription), 24 Frosty Hollow, East Hunsbury, Northants NN4 OSY England. Fax: 01604-701730. Established 1978. **Editor/Publisher:** Mrs. Jacqueline Gonzalez-Marina M.A.

• Fern Publications subsidizes costs for their books, paying no royalties.

Magazine Needs: *Dandelion Arts Magazine*, published biannually, is "a platform for new and established poets and prose writers to be read throughout the world." Wants poetry "not longer than 35-40 lines. Modern but not wild." Does not want "bad language poetry, religious or political, nor offensive to any group of people in the world." Has published poetry by Andrew Duncan, Donald Ward, Andrew Pye, John Brander, and Gerald Denley. As a sample the editor selected these lines from her own poem:

> . . . The human spirit without a planned path/to follow, is a sad landscape,/only grass and weeds, and
> nothing more/to expect.

Dandelion is about 25 pages, A4, thermal binding with b&w and color illustrations, original cover design, some ads. Receives about 200-300 poems/year, accepts about 40%. Press run is up to 1,000 for 100 subscribers of which 10% are universities and libraries, some distributed free to chosen organizations. Subscription: £12 (UK), £18 (Europe). Sample: half price of subscription. Make checks payable to J. Gonzalez-Marina.

How to Submit: Poets must become member-subscribers of *Dandelion Arts Magazine* and poetry club in order to be published. Submit 4-6 poems at a time. Accepts simultaneous submissions; no previously published poems. Cover letter required. "Poems must be typed out clearly and ready for publication, if possible, accompanied by a SAE or postal order to cover the cost of postage for the reply. Reads submissions any time of the year. Time between acceptance and publication is 2-6 months. "The poems are read by the editor when they arrive and a decision is taken straight away." Some constructive comments on rejected poems. Guidelines available for SASE (or SAE and IRC). Responds within 3 weeks. Reviews books of poetry. Poets may send books for review consideration.

Also Offers: *Dandelion* includes information on poetry competitions and art events.

Book/Chapbook Needs & How to Submit: Fern Publications is a subsidy press of artistic, poetic, and historical books and publishes 2 paperbacks/year. Books are usually 50-80 pages, A5 or A4, "thermal bound" or hand finished. Query first with 6-10 poems. Requires authors to subscribe to *Dandelion Arts Magazine*. Responds to queries and mss in 3 weeks. "All publications are published at a minimum cost agreed beforehand and paid in advance."

Advice: "Consider a theme from all angles and to explore all the possibilities, never forgetting grammar! Stay away from religious or political or offensive issues."

$ ⬡ JOHN DANIEL AND COMPANY, PUBLISHER; FITHIAN PRESS, a division of Daniel & Daniel, Publishers, Inc., P.O. Box 21922, Santa Barbara CA 93121-1922. (805)962-1780. Fax: (805)962-

8835. E-mail: dandd@danielpublishing.com. Website: www.danielpublishing.com (includes writer's guide-lines, author profiles, description of books, and "opinionated advice for writers"). Established 1980. Re-established 1985.

Book/Chapbook Needs: John Daniel, a general small press publisher, specializes in literature, both prose, and poetry. "Book-length mss of any form or subject matter will be considered, but we do not want to see pornographic, libelous, illegal, or sloppily written poetry." Has published *Between the Totems of Labor and Love* by Burton D. Wasserman, *Skins* by Joyce Thomas, and *Hang Time* by W.R. Wilkins. As a sample John Daniel selected "At Sea" from the book *Between the Totems of Labor and Love*, by Burton D. Wasserman:

> The thinking man/who dives deep/for ultimate answers/comes up naked,/races for/the fading shore.

Publishes about 4 flat-spined poetry paperbacks, averaging 80 pages, each year. Press runs average between 500-1,000. For free catalog of either imprint, send #10 SASE.

How to Submit: Send 12 sample poems and bio. Responds to queries in 2 weeks, to mss in 2 months. Accepts simultaneous submissions. No fax or e-mail submissions. Always sends prepublication galleys. Pays 10% royalties of net receipts. Acquires English-language book rights. Returns rights upon termination of contract.

Also Offers: Fithian Press books (50% of his publishing) are subsidized, the author paying production costs and receiving royalties of 60% of net receipts. Books and rights are the property of the author, but publisher agrees to warehouse and distribute for one year if desired.

Advice: "We receive over five thousand unsolicited manuscripts and query letters a year. We publish only a few books a year, of which fewer than half were received unsolicited. Obviously the odds are not with you. For this reason we encourage you to send out multiple submissions and we do not expect you to tie up your chances while waiting for our response. Also, poetry does not make money, alas. It is a labor of love for both publisher and writer. But if the love is there, the rewards are great."

DEAD FUN (Specialized: gothic/horror), P.O. Box 752, Royal Oak MI 48068-0752. E-mail: terror@deadfun.com. Website: www.deadfun.com (includes submission guidelines, previews of issues, and other information). **Editoress:** Kelli.

Magazine Needs: *Dead Fun* appears sporadically. "I have to refrain from accepting poetry submissions this time around. I've gotten absolutely swamped with submissions and my 'hold' file is overflowing. I'll still read and respond to those who send submissions but all I can offer at this time is for their work to be placed in our files for possible future use." Prefers "gothic and horror-related, religious/sacrilegious ma-terial." Does not want poetry that is "political, flowery." Has published poetry by Jessica Ocasio, Ben Wilensky, and Chris Albanese. As a sample the editor selected these lines from "After the Feast" by John Grey:

> What a meal,/no . . . a banquet:/eyes like grapes,/spaghetti veins,/flesh tender/on the bone./I lick her lips,/knowing she would/if she could.

Dead Fun is about 50 pages, digest-sized, photocopied and stapled with cardstock cover, includes pen and ink drawings, charcoal art, photography, as well as ads for zines, bands, and "anything relative." Accept approxi-mately 30% of poetry submitted. Sample: $3 plus $1.03 postage (inside US) or IRC. Make money orders payable to Kelli or send well-concealed cash.

How to Submit: Submit up to 3 poems at a time. Accepts previously published poems and simultaneous submissions. Accepts e-mail submissions (in text box). Cover letter strongly preferred. Time between acceptance and publication up to 6 months "unless otherwise agreed." Guidelines available for SASE, on website, or by e-mail. Responds in 6 weeks or a few days for e-mail requests. Pays 1 contributor's copy. Staff reviews books of poetry in approximately 40 words. Send books for review consideration.

DEAD METAPHOR PRESS, P.O. Box 2076, Boulder CO 80306-2076. Established 1992. **Contact:** Richard Wilmarth.

Book/Chapbook Needs: Publishes 1-2 chapbooks of poetry and prose/year through an annual chapbook contest. "No restrictions in regard to subject matter and style." Has published poetry by John McKernan, Tracy Davis, Aimée Grunberger, Mark DuCharme, Thomas R. Peters, Jr., and Randy Roark. As a sample we selected these lines from "Epileptic" by Maureen Foley:

> On the verge of a/seizure at every moment. All her synapses misfiring/at once.

Chapbooks are usually 20-80 pages, sizes differ, printed, photocopied, saddle-stapled or perfect-bound, some with illustrations.

How to Submit: Submit 24 pages of poetry or prose with a bio, acknowledgments. Manuscripts are not returned. "Entries must be typed or clearly reproduced and bound only by a clip. Do not send only copy of manuscript." Accepts previously published poems and simultaneous submissions. Does not accept fax or e-mail submissions. SASE for notification. Guidelines and booklist available for SASE. **Reading fee: $12.** Deadline: October 31. Winner receives 10% of press run plus discounted copies. For sample chapbooks, send $6.

DEBUT REVIEW, P.O. Box 412184, Kansas City MO 64141-2184. Established 1999. **Editor:** Michael Lorenzo.
Magazine Needs & How to Submit: *Debut Review* appears annually to "showcase the work of a select few talented poets." *Debut Review* is "somewhere between 25-30 pages, printed in a somewhat informal manner, but highly professsional. I prefer one-page poems; nothing trite, unpolished or vulgar."

$ DENVER QUARTERLY; LYNDA HULL POETRY AWARD, Dept. of English, University of Denver, Denver CO 80208. (303)871-2892. Fax: (303)871-2853. Established 1965. **Editor:** Bin Ramke.
   • Poetry published here has also been included in the 1997, 1998, and 1999 volumes of *The Best American Poetry.*
Magazine Needs: *Denver Quarterly* is a quarterly literary journal that publishes fiction, poems, book reviews and essays. There are no restrictions on the type of poetry wanted. Poems here focus on language and lean toward the avant-garde. Length is open, with some long poems and sequences also featured. Translations are also published. Has published poetry by John Ashbery, Jorie Graham, Arthur Sze, and Paul Hoover. *Denver Quarterly* is about 130 pages, 6×9, handsomely printed on buff stock and perfect-bound with 2-color matte card cover. Press run is 1,900 for 900 subscribers of which 300 are libraries, about 700 shelf sales. Subscription: $20/year to individuals and $24 to institutions. Sample: $6.
How to Submit: Submit 3-5 poems at a time. Include SASE. Accepts simultaneous submissions. Do not submit between May 15 and September 15 each year. Publishes theme issues. Responds in 3 months. "Will request diskette upon acceptance." Pays 2 copies and $5/page. Reviews books of poetry.
Also Offers: The Lynda Hull Poetry Award of $500 is awarded annually for the best poem published in a volume year. All poems published in the *Denver Quarterly* are automatically entered.

$ DESCANT (Specialized: themes), Box 314, Station P, Toronto, Ontario M5S 2S8 Canada. (416)593-2557. E-mail: descant@web.net. Website: www.descant.on.ca (includes writer's guidelines, editors, themes, subscription info, and excerpts). Established 1970. **Editor-in-Chief:** Karen Mulhallen.
Magazine Needs: *Descant* is "a quarterly journal of the arts committed to being the finest in Canada. While our focus is primarily on Canadian writing we have published writers from around the world." Has published are Lorna Crozier, Eric Ormsby, and Jan Zwicky. *Descant* is 140 pages, over-sized digest format, elegantly printed and illustrated on heavy paper, flat-spined with colored, glossy cover. Receives 1,200 unsolicited submissions/year, accepts less than 100, has a 2-year backlog. Press run is 1,200. Sample: $8.50 plus postage.
How to Submit: Submit typed ms of no more than 6 poems, name and address on first page and last name on each subsequent page. Include SASE with Canadian stamps or SAE and IRCs. "Please include an extra stamp, or an e-mail address, or fax number, so that we may acknowledge receipt of your submission." No previously published poems or simultaneous submissions. Guidelines and upcoming themes available for SASE (or SAE and IRC). Responds within 4 months. Pays "approximately $100." Acquires first rights.
Advice: "The best advice is to know the magazine you are submitting to. Please read the magazine before submitting."

DESCANT: FORT WORTH'S JOURNAL OF POETRY AND FICTION, English Dept., Box 297270, Texas Christian University, Fort Worth TX 76129. Fax: (817)257-6239. E-mail: descant@tcu.edu. Website: www.eng.tcu.edu./usefulsites/descant.htm. Established 1956. **Editor:** Dave Kuhne.
Magazine Needs: *descant* appears annually during the summer months. Wants "well-crafted poems of interest. No restrictions as to subject matter or forms. We usually accept poems 60 lines or fewer but sometimes longer poems." *descant* is more than 100 pages, 6×9, professionally printed and bound with matte card cover. "We publish 30-40 pages of poetry per year. We receive probably 3,000 poems annually." Press run is 500 for 350 subscribers. Single issue: $12, $18 outside US. Sample: $6.
How to Submit: No simultaneous submissions. No fax or e-mail submissions. Reads submissions September through April only. Responds in 6 weeks. Pays 2 copies.

THE OPENNESS TO SUBMISSIONS INDEX in the back of this book lists markets according to the level of writing they prefer to see.

Also Offers: The Betsy Colquitt Award for poetry, $500 prize awarded annually to the best poem or series of poems by a single author in an issue. Complete contest rules and guidelines available for SASE or by e-mail.

DEVIL BLOSSOMS, P.O. Box 5122, Seabrook NJ 08302-3511. Established 1997. E-mail: theeditor @asteriuspress.com. Website: www.asteriuspress.com (includes guidelines, publication information, contest updates, etc). **Editor:** John C. Erianne.

Magazine Needs: *Devil Blossoms* appears irregularly, 1-2 times/year, "to publish poetry in which the words show the scars of real life. Sensual poetry that's occasionally ugly. I'd rather read a poem that makes me sick than a poem without meaning." Wants poetry that is "darkly comical, ironic, visceral, horrific; or any tidbit of human experience that moves me." Does not want religious greetings, 'I'm-so-happy-to-be-alive' tree poetry. Has published poetry by John Sweet, T. Kilgore Splake, Dennis Saleh, and Alan Catlin. As a sample the editor selected these lines from "The Big News" by Karl Wachter:

> A serpent is waiting/beneath the sewer drain/winged angels are asked/for change and the darkness/in
> a god's eyes is mistaken/for dirt.

Devil Blossoms is 24 pages, 7×10, saddle-stapled, with a matte-card cover and ink drawings (cover only). Receives about 10,000 poems/year, accepts about 1%. Press run is 750, 200 shelf sales. Single copy: $5; subscription: $14. Make checks payable to John C. Erianne.

How to Submit: Submit 2-5 poems at a time. Accepts simultaneous submissions. Accepts e-mail submissions; include in body of message. Cover letter preferred. Time between acceptance and publication is up to 6 months. "I promptly read submissions, divide them into a 'no' and a 'maybe' pile. Then I read the 'maybes' again." Seldom comments on rejected poems. Guidelines available for SASE. Responds in up to 5 weeks. Pays 1 contributor's copy. Acquires first rights.

Advice: "Write from love; don't expect love in return, don't take rejection personally and don't let anyone stop you."

DIALOGOS: HELLENIC STUDIES REVIEW (Specialized: Greek culture), Dept. of Byzantine and Modern Greek Studies, King's College, Strand Campus, London WC2R 2LS England. Fax: 0044-020-7848-2830. E-mail: david.ricks@kcl.ac.uk. Website: www.frankcass.com (includes current table of contents). Established 1994. **Co-Editors:** David Ricks and Michael Trapp.

Magazine Needs: *Dialogos* is an annual of "Greek language and literature, history and archaeology, culture and thought, present and past." Wants "poems with reference to Greek or the Greek world, any period (ancient, medieval, modern), translations of Greek poetry." Does not want "holiday pictures or watery mythological musings." Has published poetry by Homer (translated by Oliver Taplin) and Nikos Engonopoulos (translated by Martin McKinsey). As a sample the editors selected these lines by C. Haim Gouri, translated by Avi Sharon:

> "Error always returns" said Odysseus to his weary heart/and came to the crossroads of the next town/
> to find that the way home was not water.

Dialogos is 150 pages, professionally printed and bound. Receives about 50 poems/year, accepts about 2%. Press run is 500 for 150 subscribers of which 100 are libraries. Sample: $45. Make checks payable to Frank Cass & Co. Ltd.

How to Submit: Submit 6 poems at a time. No previously published poems or simultaneous submissions. No e-mail or fax submissions. Time between acceptance and publication is 1 year. Poems are circulated to an editorial board of 2 editors. Seldom comments on rejected poems. Responds within 2 months. Always sends prepublication galleys. Pays 1 copy and 25 offprints. Acquires all rights. Returns rights. Reviews books of direct Greek interest, in multi-book review. Poets may send books for review consideration.

JAMES DICKEY NEWSLETTER (Specialized: membership/subscription, nature/ rural/ecology), 1753 Dyson Dr., Atlanta GA 30307. Fax: (404)373-2989. E-mail: joycepair@mindspring. com. Website: www.jamesdickey.org (includes biography of Dickey, bylaws of society, contacts, study help, subscription info, etc.). Established 1984. **Editor:** Joyce M. Pair.

Magazine Needs: *James Dickey Newsletter* is a biannual newsletter published in the spring and fall devoted to critical articles/studies of James Dickey's works/biography and bibliography. "Publishes a few poems of high quality. No poems lacking form or meter or grammatical correctness." Has published poetry by Linda Roth, Paula Goff, John Van, and Peenen. *James Dickey Newsletter* is 30 pages of ordinary paper, neatly offset (back and front), with a card back-cover, stapled top left corner. Subscription to individuals: $12/year (includes membership in the James Dickey Society), $14 to institutions in the US; outside the US send $14/year individuals, $15.50 institutions. Sample available for $3.50 postage.

How to Submit: Contributors should follow MLA style and standard ms form, sending 1 copy, double-spaced. Cover letter required. Accepts e-mail submissions (in text box) and fax submissions. "However, if a poet wants written comments/suggestions line by line, then mail ms with SASE." Pays 3 copies. Acquires first rights. Reviews "only works on Dickey or that include Dickey."

Advice: "We accept only grammatically correct, full sentences (except rarely a telling fragment). No first person narratives."

THE DIDACTIC, 11702 Webercrest, Houston TX 77048. Established 1993. **Editor:** Charlie Mainze.

Magazine Needs: *The Didactic* is a monthly publishing "only, only didactic poetry. That is the only specification. Some satire might be acceptable as long as it is didactic."

How to Submit: Accepts previously published poems and simultaneous submissions. Time between acceptance and publication is about a year. "Once it is determined that the piece is of self-evident quality and is also didactic, it is grouped with similar or contrasting pieces. This may cause a lag time for publication." Responds "as quickly as possible." Pay is "nominal." Acquires one-time rights. Considering a general review section, only using staff-written reviews. Poets may send books for review consideration.

DINER; POETRY OASIS, P.O. Box 60676, Greendale Station Worcester MA 01606-2378. Website: www.spokenword.to/diner (includes guidelines, editors, feature information). Established 2000. **Editors:** Eve Rifkah and Abby Millager.

Magazine Needs: *Diner* appears biannually in June and November with the intent of continuing the Worcester poetry tradition—Bishop, Knight, Kunitz, O'Hara. Features 1-2 native poets per issue. Encourages general submissions from all regions and will also include short reviews. "Open to all types of poetry. Like to see imaginative work, with attention to diction, sound, imagery." Recently published poetry by Joseph Langland, Bill Tremblay, Marin Sorescu (translated by Adam Sorkin and Lidea Vianu), and Fran Quinn. *Diner* is 100 pages, digest-sized, perfect-bound, glossy card cover with photo. Publishes about 50 poems/issue. Press run is 500. Single copy: $10; subscription: $18. Sample: $8. Make checks payable to Poetry Oasis.

How to Submit: Submit no more than 5 poems. Accepts simultaneous submissions; no previously published poems. Accepts e-mail submissions from abroad only. Cover letter is required. "SASE a must. Cover letter should include your name and poems submitted." Reads submissions year round. Time between acceptance and publication up to 6 months. Often comments on rejected poems. Guidelines are available for SASE or on website. Responds in up to 6 months. Pays 1 copy. Acquires first rights. Reviews books and chapbooks of poetry in single book format. Poets may send books for review consideration if poet "is from central New England."

Also Offers: The *Diner* Annual Poetry Contest. Send entries to the contest % Wayne-Daniel Berard, 51 Park St., Mansfield MA 02048. First place, $500; second place, $100; third place, $50. All winning poems published in Fall/Winter edition of *Diner*. "Do not list your name on submitted poems. Send a cover letter with name, address, e-mail, and titles of poems." No previously published poems. More information available on website.

Advice: "Find a group, share your work, get feedback. Read not only classics but also work currently being published. Don't worry about rejections—buy lots of stamps."

THE DISTILLERY, Motlow State Community College, P.O. Box 88100, Lynchburg TN 37352-8500. (931)393-1700. Fax: (931)393-1761. Established 1994. **Editor:** Dawn Copeland.

Magazine Needs: *The Distillery* appears twice/year and publishes "the highest quality poetry, fiction, and criticism. We are looking for poetry that pays careful attention to line, voice, and image. We like poems that take emotional risks without giving in to easy sentimentality or staged cynicism." Has published poetry by Walter McDonald, Thomas Rabbitt, Virgil Suarez, and John Sisson. As a sample the editor selected these lines from "Toward a Theology of Headgear" by G.C. Waldrep:

> In the town of my youth one mansion's cupola/beckoned with its shadow, burned a darker//shade of night and hid the moon so perfectly/it seemed a part of space itself, wheeling,//in collusion with the small mean stars.

Distillery is 88 pages, digest-sized, professionally printed on matte paper, perfect-bound, color cover, b&w photography. Receives about 800 poems/year, accepts approximately 2%. Press run is 750. Subscription: $15/year (2 issues). Sample: $7.50.

How to Submit: Submit 4-6 poems at a time with SASE. Accepts simultaneous submissions "if poet informs us immediately of acceptance elsewhere"; no previously published poems. Cover letter preferred. Reads submissions August 15 through May 15 only. Time between acceptance and publication is 6-12 months. Poems are circulated to an editorial board. "Poems are read by three preliminary readers then passed to the poetry editor." Seldom comments on rejected poems. Send SASE for guidelines. Responds in 3 months. Pays 2 copies. Acquires first North American serial rights.

Advice: "We continue to publish the best poetry sent to us, regardless of name or reputation. We like poets who look as if they would write poems even if there were no magazines in which to publish them."

DMQ REVIEW; THE MUSES AWARD, (formerly Disquieting Muses). E-mail: editors@disquietin gmuses.com. Website: www.disquietingmuses.com (includes full text of magazine). **Editor-in-Chief:** J.P. Dancing Bear. **Managing Editor:** C.J. Sage. **Editor:** D.E. Shephard.

Magazine Needs: *DMQ Review* appears quarterly as "a quality online magazine of poetry presented with visual art." Wants "intriguing themes; unique, strong imagery; metaphor; and fresh, concise language over a base of smarts and discovery. The best poems enter the reader like songs and make the body rock. We are interested in finely crafted poetry of any style." Does not want "Form without compelling content, narratives without interesting imagery or underlying musicality." Recently published poetry by Jane Hirshfield, William Logan, John Kennedy, Sidney Wade, Robley Wilson, and John Brehm. As a sample the editor selected these lines from "Psalm" by Gary Short:

> Then the boy breathes harder into the goose,/cradles it and listens,//until there is music, a swell of air/ returned over the bird's vocal chords, a purr,/a dirge, a lost-soul quaver./A blue cone of sound, humanmade,/or made human.

DMQ Review is published online; art/photography appears with the poetry. Receives about 3,000-5,000 poems/ year, accepts about 1%. Publishes about 20-25 poems/issue.

How to Submit: Submit 3-5 poems at a time. Accepts simultaneous submissions (with notifications only); no previously published poems. E-mail submissions only. "Paste poems in the body of an e-mail only; no attachments will be read. Please read and follow complete submissions guidelines on our website." Reads submissions year round. Time between acceptance and publication is 1-3 months. Poems circulated to an editorial board. "The editor-in-chief, managing editor, and a third editor read and vote on all submissions. Seldom comments on rejected poems. Responds in up to 6 weeks. Acquires first rights.

Also Offers: The Muses Award, an annual prize of $100 for the best poem to first appear in *DMQ Review* during the year. No entry fee or special entry process. "Our editors will select a winner from all poems first published in the magazine. To be eligible, contributors must simply adhere to all regular submission guidelines as outlined in our Guidelines page and, if using a pen name, include their legal name with the submission. Previously published poems are ineligible for the award." Also nominates 6 poems/year for the Pushcart Prize. "We also consider submissions of visual art, which we publish with the poems in the magazine with links to artists' sites."

Advice: "Send your best work. To delight is great; to instruct is fine. To surprise and dazzle with innovation, with craft, with your depth and courage to stand out in a crowd? Fantastic."

$ DOVETAIL: A JOURNAL BY AND FOR JEWISH/CHRISTIAN FAMILIES (Specialized: interfaith marriage), 775 Simon Greenwell Lane, Boston KY 40107. (502)549-5499. Fax: (502)549-3543. E-mail: DI-IFR@Bardstown.com. Website: www.dovetailinstitute.org (includes guidelines, contact and subscription information, catalog, upcoming themes, and conference info). Established 1991. **Editor:** Mary Rosenbaum.

Magazine Needs: *Dovetail*, published bimonthly, provides "strategies and resources for interfaith couples, their families and friends." Wants poetry related to Jewish/Christian marriage issues, no general religious themes. Has published work by Janet Landman and Eric Wolk Fried. As a sample the editor selected these lines from "Composed on a Braided Base" by Janet Landman:

> No, she tells her friends, No,/she doesn't miss a Christmas tree./It's no disaster./She hugs to herself/ those eight waxing nights/along with our odd worldling rite./She stands composed/on a braided base.

Dovetail is 12-16 pages, magazine-sized, stapled, includes 1-5 ads. Receives about 10 poems/year, accepts about 1%. Press run is 1,000 for 700 subscribers. Single copy: $5; subscription: $29.95. Make checks payable to DI-IFR.

How to Submit: Submit 1 poem at a time. Accepts previously published poems and simultaneous submissions. Accepts e-mail (in text box). Time between acceptance and publication is up to 1 year. Poems are circulated to an editorial board. "Clergy and other interfaith professionals review draft issues." Seldom comments on rejected poems. Publishes theme issues. Guidelines and upcoming themes available for SASE and on website. Responds in 1 month. Pays $10-20 plus copies. Acquires first North American serial rights. Reviews other magazines in 500 words, single and multi-book format.

Advice: "Do not send general 'inspirational' or denomination-oriented proselytizing material."

[N] [⊕] [O] DRAGON HEART PRESS; LIVING POETS ONLINE POETRY JOURNAL; DRAG-ONHEART PRESS POETRY COMPETITION, 11 Menin Rd., Allestree, Derby, Derbyshire DE22 2NL England. E-mail: dragonheartpress@seanwoodward.com. Website: http://welcome.to/livingpoets. Established 1985. **Executive Editor:** Mr. S. Woodward.

Magazine Needs: *Living Poets* is an online showcase for poetry. Wants "crafted poetry with strong imagery. No constrained rhyming structures." As a sample the editor selected these lines from his poem "Shades of 1870":

> *The elegant lead lines in sweeping jesture/Frame the head/of one seen only in a vision.//This is the dread sovereign/Blake has seen/whose temple afire/Drain all colour from the world*

Receives about 400 poems/year, accepts about 20%. Sample (printed): $10. Make checks payable to S. Woodward.

How to Submit: Submit 3 poems at a time. Accepts previously published poems and simultaneous submissions. Cover letter with bio and publication credits preferred. Time between acceptance and publication is 1-2 months. Often comments on rejected poems. Publishes theme issues. Guidelines available for SASE, by e-mail, or on website. Responds in 1 month. Pays 1 copy. Reviews books and chapbooks of poetry or other magazines in single book format. Poets may send books for review consideration to Review Editor, Dragon Heart Press.

Also Offers: Sponsors Dragonheart Press Poetry Competition. Send SAE (or SAE and IRC) for details.

[◐] [◎] DREAM INTERNATIONAL QUARTERLY (Specialized: dreams/fantasy/horror), 809 W. Maple St., Champaign IL 61820-2810. Established 1981. **Editor-in-Chief/Publisher:** Charles I. (Chuck) Jones. **Senior Poetry Editor:** Carmen M. Pursifull.

Magazine Needs: "Poetry must be dream-inspired and/or dream-related. This can be interpreted loosely, even to the extent of dealing with the transitory as a theme. Nothing written expressly or primarily to advance a political or religious ideology. We have published everything from neo-Romantic sonnets to stream-of-consciousness, a la 'Beat Generation.' " Has published poetry by Carmen M. Pursifull, Ursula Le Guin, Errol Miller, and Dr. Dimitri Mihalas. As a sample the senior poetry editor selected these lines from Heather Winters' poem "Ripening":

> *she opens purple eyes/yawning shaking wiping/away Past's sleep sand/to a young man with/a sunrise beard &/a red wine twinkle/in his eyebound eye/*

Dream International Quarterly is 120-150 pages, 8½ × 11, with vellum cover and drawings. Receives 300 poems/year, accepts about 30. Press run is 300 for 20 subscribers. Subscription: $56/year, $112/2 years. Sample: $14. All orders should be addressed to Chuck Jones, Editor-in-Chief/Publisher, *Dream International Quarterly*, 411 14th St., #H-, Ramona CA 92605-2769. All checks/money orders should be in US Funds and made payable to Charles I. Jones.

How to Submit: Submit up to 3 typed poems at a time. Accepts previously published poems and simultaneous submissions. No fax or e-mail submissions. Cover letter including publication history, if any. "As poetry submissions go through the hands of two readers, poets should enclose 2 loose stamps, along with the standard SASE." Do not submit mss in September or October. Time between acceptance and publication is up to 2 years. Comments on rejected poems if requested. Guidelines available for large SASE with 2 first-class stamps plus $2. Responds in 2 weeks. Sometimes sends prepublication galleys. Occasionally pays 1 copy, "less postage. Postage/handling for contributor's copy costs $4." Also, from time to time, "exceptionally fine work has been deemed to merit a complimentary subscription." Acquires first North American serial or nonexclusive reprint rights.

Advice: "A) no profanity. B) use a dictionary for spelling. C) we prefer free verse. D) if poem rhymes, it should not be sing-song; rhyme should be unique not clichéd."

[N] [◐] DREXEL ONLINE JOURNAL, Dept. of English & Philosophy, MacAlister Hall, Drexel University, Philadelphia PA 19104. (215)895-6469. Fax: (215)895-1071. E-mail: doj@drexel.edu. Website: www.drexel.edu/doj (includes guidelines, online journal). Established 2001. **Contact:** Poetry Editor.

Magazine Needs: *Drexel Online Journal* is "a general interest, somewhat literary bimonthly. No limitations as to form; but if it rhymes, it should be unobtrusive (unless it is deliberately obtrusive rhyme). Recently published poetry by Barbara Daniels, Lynn Levin, Valerie Fox, Besnik Mustafaj, Jenn McCreary, and Michael McGoolaghan. As a sample the editor selected these lines from "Periwinkle" by Barbara Daniels:

> *A clipped moon through/uncurtained windows./My big book of cancer/lists 68 words for pain./I light two candles./Eat saltines to settle my stomach.*

Drexel Online Journal is published online. Accepts about 5% of poems received. Publishes about 5 poems/issue. Sample available free online at www.drexel.edu/doj.

How to Submit: Submit 1-6 poems at a time. Cover letter is preferred. "SASE should be included. Electronic submissions are not taken." Reads submissions year round. Submit seasonal poems 3 months in advance. Time between acceptance and publication is 2 months. Poems are circulated to an editorial board. "We currently have two readers who go by consensus." Often comments on rejected poems. Guidelines available on website. Responds in 6 weeks. Pay varies. Acquires first rights. Reviews books of poetry. Poets may send books for review consideration to Bood Editor, Drexel Online Journal, Dept. of English and Philosophy, MacAlister Hall, Drexel University, Philadelphia PA 19104.

Advice: "We like original work. Read widely."

◐ ◎ THE DRIFTWOOD REVIEW (Specialized: regional, Michigan), P.O. Box 2042, Bay City MI 48707. Established 1996. **Poetry Editor:** Jeff Vande Zande.

Magazine Needs: "An annual publication, *The Driftwood Review* strives to publish the best poetry and fiction being written by Michigan writers—known and unknown. We consider any style, but are particularly fond of poetry that conveys meaning through image. Rhyming poetry stands a poor chance." Has published poetry by Daniel James Sundahl, Danny Rendleman, Anca Vlasopolos, Terry Blackhawk, and Linda Nemec Foster. *The Driftwood Review* is 100-125 pages, digest-sized, professionally-printed, perfect-bound with glossy card cover containing b&w artwork. Receives about 500 poems/year, accepts about 5-7%. Press run is 200 for 75 subscribers. Subscription: $6.

How to Submit: Submit 3-5 poems at a time. No previously published poems or simultaneous submissions. Cover letter preferred. "Cover letter should include a brief bio suitable for contributors notes. No SASE? No reply." Reads submissions January 1 through September 15 only. Time between acceptance and publication is 9 months. Seldom comments on rejected poems. "Will comment on work that's almost there." Responds in 3 months. Pays 1 copy and includes the opportunity to advertize a book. Acquires first North American serial rights. Staff reviews chapbooks of poetry by Michigan writers only in 500 words, single book format. Send chapbooks for review consideration.

Also Offers: Sponsors a Reader's Choice Award.

Advice: "Strive to express what you have to say with image."

Ⓝ ◐ ◎ DRY BONES PRESS; THE COMPLEAT NURSE (Specialized: nursing), P.O. Box 1437, Roseville CA 95678-0597. Voice mail/fax: (415)707-2129. E-mail: jrankin@drybones.com. Website: www.drybones.com (includes guidelines, contact info, bios, links, editorial policy, etc.). Established 1992 (Dry Bones Press). **Editor/Publisher:** Jim Rankin, RN, MSN.

Magazine Needs: *the Compleat Nurse*, a monthly newsletter, "is a voice of independent nursing featuring matters of interest to nurses—a very broad range, indeed." Has published poetry by James Snydal, Richard Bunch, Cae Cordell, Cherise Wynehen, and J. Rankin. *the Compleat Nurse* is 4 pages, 8½×11, desktop-published, folded with clip art; occasionally published as an anthology. Receives about 10-20 poems/year, "accepts most, if in our range." Press run is 500-1,000 with all distributed free. Sample for SASE.

How to Submit: Submit 2-3 poems at a time. Accepts previously published poems and simultaneous submissions. Accepts e-mail submissions (in text box or as attachment). Cover letter preferred. Time between acceptance and publication "varies greatly; 1 month to 2 years." Poems are selected by editor with consideration of space availability. Always comments on rejected poems. Responds "within 30 days." Sometimes sends prepublication galleys. Pays 4 copies. Acquires "one-time rights, plus right to include in anthology." Reviews books or chapbooks of poetry. Poets may send books for review consideration.

Book/Chapbook Needs & How to Submit: Dry Bones Press seeks "to encourage nurses, or just do things we like, or want to take a flyer on." Publishes 1-3 paperbacks and 2-3 chapbooks/year as well as occasional anthologies. Books are usually 5½×8½, offset, stapled or "fine wire-O" bound with glossy, b&w cover. Responds to queries and mss in 1 month. Pays 10 author's copies, on traditional publishing efforts; or special offer on print-on-demand newsletter—4 copies.

◐ ◎ DWAN (Specialized: gay/lesbian/bisexual, translations, bilingual/foreign language), Box 411, Swarthmore PA 19081-0411. E-mail: dwanzine@hotmail.com. Website: www.geocities.com/dwanzine/. Established 1993. **Editor:** Donny Smith.

Magazine Needs: Published every 2 to 3 months, *Dwan* is a "queer poetry zine; some prose; some issues devoted to a single poet or a single theme ('Jesus' or 'Mom and Dad,' for instance)." Wants "poetry exploring gender, sexuality, sex roles, identity, queer politics, etc. Heterosexuals usually welcome." Has published poetry by Melanie Hemphill, Susana Cattaneo, and Fabián Iriarte. As a sample the editor selected these lines from "The Russian Twins" by Lola Arias:

> To kill the father./The twin kisses her sister on the mouth./Shameless, snow falls on the impossible kiss./That country, that father.

Dwan is 20 pages, 5½×8½, photocopied on plain white paper, and stapled. Receives 400-500 pages of poetry/year, accepts less than 10%. Press run is 100. Sample available for $2 (free to prisoners). Make checks payable to Donny Smith.

How to Submit: Submit 5-15 poems typed. Accepts previously published poems and simultaneous submissions. Accepts e-mail submissions, "no attachments." Cover letter required. Time between acceptance and publication is 6-18 months. Often comments on rejected poems. Guidelines available on website. Responds in 3 months. Pays copies. The editor reviews books, chapbooks, and magazines usually in 25-150 words. Send books for review consideration.

Advice: "Be honest in your writing. Work hard. Read a lot."

◯ EAGLE'S FLIGHT; EAGLE'S FLIGHT BOOKS, 1505 N. Fifth St., Sayre OK 73662. (580)928-2298. Established 1989. **Editor/Publisher:** Shyamkant Kulkarni.

Magazine Needs: *Eagle's Flight* is a quarterly "platform for poets and short story writers—new and struggling to come forward." Wants "well-crafted literary quality poetry, any subject, any form, including translations. Translations should have permission of original poets." Has published poetry by Maria Keplinger, Cynthia Ruth Flynn, Jane Stuart, Rekha Kulkarni, and Daniel Green. As a sample the editor selected these lines from "Sudden Creatures" by Jane Stuart:

> Times rises out of fire and from flood/That steeped this world inside/a whirling shower/Of wrathful
> waters that another/power turned into serene lakes/of hope and good.

Eagle's Flight is 8-12 pages, 7 × 8½, printed on colored paper and saddle-stapled, including simple art, few ads. Receives about 200 poems/year, accepts about 10%. Press run is 200 for 100 subscribers. Subscription: $5. Sample: $1.50.

How to Submit: Submit up to 5 poems at a time, no more than 21 lines each. No previously published poems or simultaneous submissions. Cover letter required; include short bio, up to 4 lines. Reads submissions January 1 through June 30 only. Time between acceptance and publication is up to 3 years. Seldom comments on rejected poems. "All material accepted for publication is subject to editing according to our editorial needs." Guidelines available for SASE. Responds in 6 months. Pays 1 copy. Acquires first publication rights. Reviews books of poetry in 250-750 words, single format.

Advice: "We expect poets to be familiar with our publication and our expectations and our limitations. To be a subscriber is one way of doing this. Everybody wants to write poems and, in his heart, is a poet. Success lies in getting ahead of commonplace poetry. To do this one has to read, to be honest, unashamed and cherish decent values of life in his heart. Then success is just on the corner of the next block."

⚃ $◯ ◎ ÉCRITS DES FORGES; ESTUAIRE; ARCADE (Specialized: women only); EXIT (All Specialized: foreign language, French), 1497 Laviolette, Trois-Rivières, Québec G9A 5G4 Canada. (819)379-9813. Fax: (819)376-0774. E-mail: ecrits.desforges@tr.cgocable.ca. Established 1971. **Président:** Gaston Bellemare. **Directrice Générale:** Maryse Baribeau.

Magazine Needs: Écrits des Forges publishes 3 poetry journals each year: *Estuaire* appears 5 times/year and wants poetry from well-known poets; *Exit* appears 4 times/year and wants poetry from beginning poets; and *Arcade* appears 3 times/year and wants poetry from women only. All three publications only accept work in French. Wants poetry that is "authentic and original as a signature." "We have published poetry from more than a thousand poets coming from most of the francophone's countries: André Romus (Belgium), Amadou Lamine Sall (Sénégal), Nicole Brossard, Claudine Bertrand, Denise Brassard, Tony Tremblay, and Jean-Paul Daoust (Québec)." As a sample the editor selected these lines from "La peau fragile du ciel" by Bernard Pozier:

> l'infini défait ses gris hérités de la pluie/dans la brume laiteuse du soir/et l'on tente de distinguer la
> plage le ciel et l'océan/en flottant dans ce néant/et c'est comme essayer enfin de savoir/s'il est plus
> facile de faire parler le poème/ou bien faire taire la mer

The 3 journals are 88-108 pages, 5½ × 8, perfect-bound with art on cover, includes ads from poetry publishers. Receives more than 1,000 poems/year, accepts less than 5%. Press run for *Estuaire* is 750 for 450 subscribers of which 250 are libraries. Press run for *Arcade* is 650 for 375 subscribers of which 260 are libraries. Press run for *Exit* is 500 for 110 subscribers of which 235 are libraries. Subscription for *Estuaire* is $45 plus p&h; for *Arcade* is $27 plus p&h; for *Exit* is $36 plus p&h. Samples: $10 each. For *Exit* make checks payable to Éditions Gaz Moutarde. For *Estuaire* and *Arcade*, make checks payable to the respective publication.

How to Submit: Submit 10 poems at a time. No previously published poems or simultaneous submissions. "We make decisions on submissions in February, May, September, and December." Time between acceptance and publication is 3-12 months. Poems are circulated to an editorial board. "Nine persons read the submissions and send their recommendations to the editorial board." *Arcade* publishes theme issues. Upcoming themes are listed in the journal. Guidelines available by e-mail. Responds in 5 months. Pays "10% of the market price based on number of copies sold." Acquires all rights for 1 year. Retains rights to reprint in anthology for 10 years. Staff reviews books and chapbooks of poetry and other magazines on 1 page, double-spaced, single book format. Send books for review consideration.

Book/Chapbook Needs & How to Submit: Écrits des Forges inc. publishes poetry only—40-50 paperbacks/year. Books are usually 80-88 pages, 5½ × 8, perfect-bound with 2-color cover with art. Query first with a few sample poems and cover letter with brief bio and publication credits. Responds to queries in 3-6 months. Pays royalties of 10-20%, advance of 50% maximum, and 25 author's copies. Order sample books by writing or faxing.

Also Offers: Sponsors the International Poetry Festival/Festival international de la poésie. "250 poets from 30 countries based on the 5 continents read their poems over 10-day period in 70 different cafés, bars, restaurants, etc. 30,000 persons attend. All in French." For more information, see website: www.fiptr.com.

ECW PRESS, 2120 Queen St. E., Suite 200, Toronto, Ontario M4E 1E2 Canada. (416)694-3348. Fax: (416)698-9906. E-mail: ecw@sympatico.ca. Website: www.ecwpress.com Established 1979. **Literary Editor:** Michael Holmes.

Book/Chapbook Needs: ECW Press typically publishes 4 Canadian-authored paperback titles/year. Wants interesting—structurally challenging poetry. No greeting card doggerel. Has published poetry by Robert Priest, Sky Gilbert, David McGimpsey, Mark Sinnett, and Libby Scheier. Books are usually 96-150 pages, 5×8, perfect-bound with full color covers.

How to Submit: Not accepting unsolicited manuscripts.

THE EDGE CITY REVIEW (Specialized: form/style, traditional; social issues), 10912 Harpers Square Court, Reston VA 20191. E-mail: tponick@earthlink.net. Website: www.edge-city. com (includes guidelines, contact and subscription info, archives, links, and editorial policy). Established 1991. **Editor:** F.S. Ponick.

Magazine Needs: *The Edge City Review* appears 3 times/year and "publishes poetry, fiction, criticism, and book reviews for a combined lay and academic audience—iconoclastic, conservative, and not hospitable to left-wing crusaders." Wants poetry in traditional forms (sonnets, ballads, rhyme), narrative, satire; quality verse. No free verse; no greeting card verse. Has published poetry by Dana Gioia, R.S. Gwynn, Jared Carter, Thomas Carper, and X.J. Kennedy. As a sample the editor selected these lines from "Bachelorhood" by Leslie Monsour:

> No family pictures on the wall, no books,/A drafting desk, one travel magazine;/No children, one
> divorce, a satellite dish,/A cold efficient exercise machine,/And in the corner with the firewood,/A stack
> of videos.

Edge City Review is 48-52 pages, 8½×11, neatly printed and saddle-stapled with 80 lb. colored stock cover, only occasionally includes ads. Receives about 250 poems/year, accepts approximately 15%. Press run is 535 for 305 subscribers of which 25 are libraries, 75 shelf sales; 130 distributed free for promotional purposes. Subscription: $17/year (3 issues). Sample: $6.

How to Submit: Accepts simultaneous submissions "if so indicated"; no previously published poems. Accepts e-mail and disk submissions. "Disk submissions can be Mac or PC, Word or WordPerfect preferred. For e-mail, send poems in the body of the message. Only send attachment if crucial to format." Cover letter preferred. Do not submit mss in December. Time between acceptance and publication is 6 months. Poems are circulated to an editorial board. "Poetry editor makes first cut, final selections based on consensus." Seldom comments on rejected poems. Responds in 4 months. Pays 2 copies. Acquires first North American serial rights. Staff reviews books of poetry and other magazines in 800-1,000 words, single book format. Send books for review consideration.

Advice: "Write in meter and rhyme."

EDGEWISE PRESS, INC., 24 Fifth Ave., #224, New York NY 10011. Website: www.edgewise.com. Has published Alan Jones, Cid Corman, and Nanni Cagnone. Order sample books by sending $10, plus $2 p&h. Currently accepts no unsolicited poetry.

EDGZ, Edge Publications, P.O. Box 799, Ocean Park WA 98640. Established 2000. **Publisher/Editor:** Blaine R. Hammond.

Magazine Needs: *Edgz* appears semiannually in March and September and publishes "poetry of all sorts of styles and schools. Our purpose is to present poetry with transpersonal intentions or applications and to put poets on a page next to other poets they are not used to appearing next to." Wants "a broad variety of styles with a transpersonal intent. *Edgz* has two main reasons for existence: My weariness with the attitude that whatever kind of poetry someone likes is the only legitimate poetry; and my desire to present poetry addressing large issues of life: meaning; oppression; exaltation; and whatever else you can think of. Must be engaged; intensity helps." Does not want "anything with a solely personal purpose; dense language poetry, which I'm not good at; poetry that does not take care with the basics of language, or displays an ignorance of modern poetry. No clichés, gushing, sentimentalism, or lists of emotions. Nothing vague or abstract. No light verse, but humor is fine" Accepts poetry by children; "I do not have a children's section, but do not discriminate by age." Has published poetry by David Small Bird, Taylor Graham,

Thomas Lowe Taylor, David Campiche, Patricia Wellingham-Jones, and Ron Offen. *Edgz* is digest-sized, laser-printed, saddle-stapled or perfect-bound (depends on number of pages), 94 lb. card stock cover with art/graphics (not comix). Printed on paper "made of no virgin wood fibers." 2003 prices are single copy: $7; subscription: $13 (2 issues). Sample: $3.50 when available. Make checks payable to Edge Publications.
How to Submit: Submit 3-5 poems at a time; "a longer poem may be submitted by itself." No limits on line length. Accepts simultaneous submissions; no previously published poems. No e-mail submissions. "I don't mind more than one poem to a page or well-traveled submissions; these are ecologically sound practices. I like recycled paper. Submissions without SASE will be gratefully used as note paper. Handwritten OK if poor or incarcerated." Reads submissions all year. Deadlines: February 1 and August 1 for winter and summer issues. Time between acceptance and publication is 1-6 months. Often comments on rejections "as I feel like it. I don't provide criticism services." Guidelines available for SASE. Responds in up to 6 months. Pays 1 copy with discounts on additional copies. Acquires first rights plus anthology rights ("just in case").
Advice: "It is one thing to require subscriptions in order to be published. It is something else to charge reading fees. In a world that considers poetry valueless, reading fees say it is less than valueless—editors should be compensated for being exposed to it. I beg such editors to cease the practice. I advise everyone else not to submit to them, or the practice will spread."

⊠ ◎ EIDOS: SEXUAL FREEDOM & EROTIC ENTERTAINMENT FOR CONSENTING ADULTS (Specialized: erotica), P.O. Box 990095, Boston MA 02199-0095. E-mail: eidos@eidos.org. Website: www.eidos.org. Established 1982. **Poetry Editor:** Brenda Loew.
Magazine Needs: "Our website publishes erotic literature, poetry, photography, and artwork. Our purpose is to provide an alternative to women's images and male images and sexuality depicted in mainstream publications like *Playboy*, *Penthouse*, *Playgirl*, etc. We provide a forum for the discussion and examination of two highly personalized dimensions of human sexuality: desire and satisfaction. We do not want to see angry poetry or poetry that is demeaning to either men or women. We like experimental, avant-garde material that makes a personal, political, cultural statement about mutually respectful sensu-sexuality." Has published poetry by Nancy Young, Miriam Carroll, Linwood M. Ross, Ann Tweedy, and Mona J. Perkins. *Eidos* is now publishing online only. Receives hundreds of poems/year, accepts approximately 10-20.
How to Submit: Only accepts sexually-explicit erotic material. Length for poetry is 1-page maximum, format flexible. Must be 18 or over; age statement required. Accepts simultaneous submissions; no previously published poems. "Poets must submit their work e-mail." Publishes bio information as space permits. Comment or criticism provided as often as possible. Acquires first North American serial rights.
Advice: "There is so much poetry submitted for consideration that a rejection can sometimes mean a poet's timing was poor. We let poets know if the submission was appropriate for our publication and suggest they resubmit at a later date. Keep writing, keep submitting, keep a positive attitude."

$ ◐ THE EIGHTH MOUNTAIN PRESS, 624 SE 29th Ave., Portland OR 97214. Established 1985. **Editor:** Ruth Gundle.
Book/Chapbook Needs: Eighth Mountain is a "small press publisher of literary works by women." Has published poetry by Lucinda Roy, Maureen Seaton, Irena Klepfisz, Almitra David, Judith Barrington, and Elizabeth Woody. Publishes 1 book of poetry averaging 128 pages every few years. "Our books are handsomely designed and printed on acid-free paper in both quality trade paperbacks and library editions." Initial press run for poetry is 2,500.
How to Submit: "We expect to receive a query letter along with a few poems. A résumé of published work, if any, should be included. Work should be typed, double-spaced, and with your name on each page. If you want to know if your work has been received, enclose a separate, stamped postcard." Responds within 6 weeks. SASE (#10 envelope) must be included for response. "Full postage must be included if return of the work submitted is desired." Pays 7-8% royalties. Acquires all rights. Returns rights if book goes out of print.

◐ 88: A JOURNAL OF CONTEMPORARY AMERICAN POETRY, % Hollyridge Press, P. O. Box 2872, Venice CA 90294. (310)712-1238. Fax: (310)828-4860. E-mail: T88AJournal@aol.com. Established 1999. **Managing Editor:** Ian Wilson. Member: PMA.
Magazine Needs: *88: A Journal of Contemporary American Poetry* appears annually, includes essays on poetry and poetics, also reviews. Wants mainstream, lyric, lyric narrative, prose poems, experimental.

"Will consider work that incorporates elements of humor, elements of surrealism. No light verse, limericks, children's poetry, concrete poetry." *88* is 176 pages, 6×9, printed on-demand, perfect-bound, 4-color soft cover, with very limited art/graphics, ads. Publishes about 80 poems/issue. Single copy: $13.95.

How to Submit: Submit 5 poems at a time. No previously published poems or simultaneous submissions. No fax, e-mail, or disk submissions. Cover letter is required. Poems should be typed, single spaced on one side, indicate stanza breaks if poem is longer than one page. Name and address should appear on every page. "Unsolicited submissions accompanied by a proof-of-purchase coupon clipped from the back of the journal are read year round. Without proof-of-purchase, unsolicited submissions are considered March 1 through May 31 only. Unsolicited submissions received outside these guidelines will be returned unread. Submissions sent without SASE will be discarded." Time between acceptance and publication is up to 9 months. "Managing editor has the final decision of inclusion, but every poem is considered by an editorial board consisting of contributing editors whose suggestions weigh heavily in the process." Guidelines available in magazine and for SASE. Responds in 3 months. Sometimes sends prepublication galleys. Pays 1 copy. Acquires one-time rights. Reviews books of poetry in 500-1,000 words, single book and multi-book format. Poets may send books for review consideration to Ian Wilson, managing editor.

Advice: "We believe it's important for poets to support the journals to which they submit. Because of print-on-demand, *88* is always available. We recommend becoming familiar with the journal before submitting."

EKPHRASIS (Specialized: ekphrastic verse); FRITH PRESS; OPEN POETRY CHAP-BOOK COMPETITION, P.O. Box 161236, Sacramento CA 95816-1236. Website: www.hometown.aol.com/ekphrasis1 (includes journal and competition guidelines as well as a list of publications). *Ekphrasis* established Summer 1997, Frith Press 1995. **Editors:** Laverne Frith and Carol Frith.
- William Reichard's "To Be Quietly Spoken" was winner of the 2001 Open Poetry Chapbook Competition.

Magazine Needs: *Ekphrasis*, appearing in March and September, is a biannual "outlet for the growing body of poetry focusing on individual works from any artistic genre." Wants "poetry whose main content is based on individual works from any artistic genre. Poetry should transcend mere description. Form open. No poetry without ekphrastic focus. No poorly crafted work. No archaic language." Nominates for Pushcart Prize. Has published poetry by Jeffrey Levine, Linda Nemec Foster, David Hamilton, Simon Perchik, Joseph Stanton, and Virgil Suarez. *Ekphrasis* is 40-50 pages, digest-sized, photocopied and saddle-stapled. Subscription: $12/year. Sample: $6. Make checks payable, in US funds, to Laverne Frith.

How to Submit: Submit 3-7 poems at a time with SASE. Accepts previously published poems "occasionally, must be credited"; no simultaneous submissions. Cover letter required including short bio with representative credits and phone number. Time between acceptance and publication is up to 1 year. Seldom comments on rejected poems. Guidelines available for SASE. Responds in 4 months. Pays 1 copy. Acquires first North American serial or one-time rights.

Book/Chapbook Needs & How to Submit: Frith Press publishes well-crafted poems—all subjects and forms considered—through their annual Open Poetry Chapbook Competition. Submit 16-24 pages of poetry with **$10 reading fee** (US funds). Include cover sheet with poet's name, address, phone number, and e-mail. Previously published poems must be credited. "No poems pending publication elsewhere." Deadline: October 31. Winner receives $100, publication, and 50 copies of their chapbook.

Advice: "With the focus on ekphrastic verse, we are bringing attention to the interconnections between various artistic genres and dramatizing the importance and universality of language. Study in the humanities is essential background preparation for the understanding of these interrelations."

ELEMENTS MAGAZINE, 2820 Houston St., Alexandria LA 71301. (318)445-5055. Established 1979. **Editor/Publisher:** Bernard Washington.

Magazine Needs: *Elements* appears bimonthly and is "designed to be a communications tool to be used to demonstrate positive contributions from all sorts of writers. All poetry is accepted. None is excluded." Accepts poetry written by children. Recently published poetry by Tim Scannell, Amy Littlefield, C. David Hay, Laura Stamps, Taalia Whitehead, and B.Z. Niditch. As a sample the editor selected these lines from "Antal the Gypsy Violinist to His Audience" by Joanne Lowery:

> you come to watch and listen/I wear my best black hat/for a coin or two/let my violin become yours/
> my love tremble like yours though there is no resemblance/And it's/true I know your truth/Life is one
> bitter nettle stew

Element is 50 pages, magazine-sized, commercial inkjet-printed, stapled, soft cover, with b&w, cut and paste art/graphics and business and personal ads. Receives about 15 poems/year, accepts about 100%. Publishes about 15

Salt Lake City photographer Kyle McCoun used color slide film and an underwater camera (while standing poolside) to capture this arresting image. The bright turquoise coloring of the original and the visual impact suited *Ellipsis'* bold mix of fiction and poetry, say the editors; and "we liked the way the woman's fingertips point to the name of the journal."

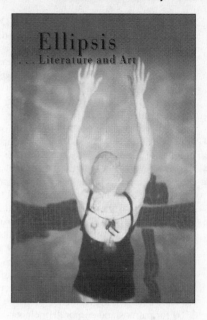

poems/issue. Press run is 500 subscribers of which 2 are libraries, 10 shelf sales; 3 are distributed free to individuals. Single copy: $7/US, $9/foreign. Subscription: $30/year, $50/2 years, $65/3 years. Make checks payable to Bernard Washington.

How to Submit: Line length for poetry is open. Accepts previously published poems and simultaneous submissions. No fax, e-mail, or disk submissions. Cover letter is required. "All submissions must be put on both sides of paper. Always include a SASE, biographical info in cover letter, very short stories." Reads submissions January 1-December 24. Submit seasonal poems 1 month in advance. Time between acceptance and publication is weeks. "Poems are read for clarity and content and accepted on the basis of their merit." Never comments on rejected poems. Occasionally publishes theme issues. Upcoming themes and guidelines available for SASE. Responds in 3 weeks. Sometimes sends prepublication galleys. Pays 1 copy. Acquires one-time rights. Reviews books and chapbooks of poetry and other magazines/journals in 1,200 words, single book format. Poets may send books for review consideration to *Elements Magazine*.

Advice: "Young poets should remember a poem is about teaching. A poet explains himself or herself over and over and further and further. The poet must write to please self and ultimately please others. Always seek knowledge, not just pieces of information."

$⏣ **ELLIPSIS MAGAZINE**, Westminster College of Salt Lake City, 1840 S. 1300 East, Salt Lake City UT 84105. (801)832-2321. E-mail: Ellipsis@westminstercollege.edu. Website: www.westminstercollege.edu/ellipsis (includes guidelines, contact information, bios, archives, contest info, editorial policy, subscription info). Established 1967. **Faculty Advisor:** Natasha Sajé. **Contact:** Poetry Editor (rotating editors).

Magazine Needs: *Ellipsis* is an annual appearing in April. Needs "good literary poetry, fiction essays, plays, and visual art." Has published work by Allison Joseph, Molly McQuade, Virgil Suarez, Maurice Kilwein-Guevara, Richard Cecil, and Ron Carlson. *Ellipsis* is 120 pages, digest-sized, perfect-bound, with color cover. Press run is 2,000 with most copies distributed free through college. Sample: $7.50.

How to Submit: Submit 3-5 poems or prose to 3,000 words. No previously published submissions. No fax or e-mail submissions. Accepts simultaneous submissions if notified of acceptance elsewhere. Include SASE and brief bio. Reads submissions August 1 to November 1. Responds in up to 5 months. Pays $10/poem, plus 1 copy.

Also Offers: "All accepted poems are eligible for the *Ellipsis* Award which includes a $100 prize. Past judges have included Jorie Graham, Sandra Cisneros, Phillip Levine, and Stanley Plumly." Also, Westminster College hosts Writers@Work, an annual literary conference, which sponsors fellowship competition and features distinguished faculty. (See separate listing for Writers@Work in the Conferences & Workshops section).

⏣ ◎ **EMERALD COAST REVIEW; THE LEGEND** (Specialized: Membership); **WEST FLORIDA LITERARY FEDERATION; DR. FRANCIS P. CASSIDY LITERARY CENTER;**

W.I.S.E. (WRITERS IN SERVICE TO EDUCATION); W.I.S.T.S. (WRITERS IN SERVICE TO SENIORS) PROGRAMS (Specialized: regional), 400 S. Jefferson St., Suite 212, Pensacola FL 32501. (850)435-0942. E-mail: WFLitFed@aol.com. Website: www.WestFloridaLiteraryFed.com. The WFLF was established in 1987 and began the Dr. Francis P. Cassidy Literary Center, a regional writers' resource and special collections library. *Emerald Coast Review* **Contact:** Submissions Committee. *Legend* **Editor:** Robin Travis-Murphree.

Magazine Needs & How to Submit: The *Emerald Coast Review* is published every odd year and is usually limited to Coast regional writers and members of the West Florida Literary Federation. Sample: $11. Guidelines available for SASE or on website. Submit with required form (included in guidelines) January 1 through May 15 only. Pays copies.

Magazine Needs & How to Submit: "*The Legend*, the WFLF monthly newsletter, publishes literary art news, events and contests, members' poetry, essays, and articles. Members may submit poetry short essays and articles in the body of an e-mail at WFLitFed@aol.com (no more than three poems or one article/essay per month), or by snail mail to the WFLF office attn: Robin Travis-Murphree, *Legend* Editor. Deadline is the 15th of each month for the next month's newsletter."

Also Offers: The WFLF offers many programs for writers. One program, W.I.S.E. (Writers In Service to Education), allows area writers to volunteer their time and talents to local students. Sponsors a Student Writers Network for students in grades 9-12 and also sponsors a PenWISE poetry contest for grades 1-12. Back Door Poets, one of their subgroups, conducts open microphone poetry readings the third Saturday of each month. WFLF also hosts a writing workshop the first Saturday of every month. W.I.S.T.S. (Writers In Service to Seniors) provides volunteer area writers to nursing homes and assisted living facilities to read and entertain the residents. Membership dues range from $10/year for students and senior citizens to $100 for patrons and corporate memberships.

EMPLOI PLUS; DGR PUBLICATION, 1256 Principale N. St. #203, L'Annonciation, Quebec J0T 1T0 Canada. Phone/fax: (819)275-3293. Established 1988 (DGR Publication), 1990 (*Emploi Plus*). **Publisher:** Daniel G. Reid.

Magazine Needs: *Emploi Plus*, published irregularly, features poems and articles in French or English. Has published poetry by Robert Ott. Recently published *Alexiville, Planet Earth* by D.G. Reid. *Emploi Plus* is 12 pages, $7 \times 8\frac{1}{2}$, photocopied, stapled, with b&w drawings, and pictures, no ads. Press run is 500 distributed free. Sample: free.

How to Submit: *Does not accept unsolicited submissions.*

EMRYS JOURNAL, P.O. Box 8813, Greenville SC 29604. Website: www.emrys.org. Established 1982. **Editor:** Jeanine Halva-Neubauer. **Contact:** poetry editor.

Magazine Needs: *Emrys Journal* is an annual appearing in April. Publishes "the accessible poem over the fashionably sophisticated, the touching dramatic or narrative poem over the elaborately meditative, the humorous poem over the ponderously significant, the modest poem over the showily learned." Has published poetry by Ken Autrey, Virgil Suarez, Michael S. Smith, and Rosanne Singer. As a sample the editor selected these lines from "Florida Straight" by Virgil Suarez:

> Out here on the high seas, the ocean ispossessed/of a thousand hues between lapis lazuli and emerald,/
> and on this makeshift raft headed north, another/family prays to Santa Barbara, Holy Mother

Emrys Journal is up to 120 pages, 6×9, handsomely printed, flat-spined. Press run is 400 for 250 subscribers of which 10 are libraries. "About 10 poems are selected for inclusion." Single copy: $12.

How to Submit: Not accepting submissions in 2003.

ENGLISH JOURNAL, Dept. of English, Youngstown State University, Youngstown OH 44555. (330)742-1781. Fax: (330)742-1782. E-mail: mangelotti@ou.edu. **Poetry Editor:** Michael Angelotti.

Magazine Needs: The *English Journal* is looking for the best poems under 40 lines, and if its subject matter is teaching or learning, so much the better. "We are an education journal open to all topics but erotica, etc. that are not appropriate for teacher/student audiences."

How to Submit: Submit 1 copy of no more than 5 typed poems with cover letter and SASE between September and May. No previously published poems or simultaneous submissions. No e-mail or fax submissions. Publishes theme issues. Guidelines available in publication. Pays 2 copies.

ENGLISH STUDIES FORUM, Dept. of English, Ball State University, Muncie IN 47306. (765)285-8580. Fax: (765)285-3765. E-mail: tkoontz@gw.bsu.edu. Website: www.bsu.edu/english/cwp/forum (includes contact information, bios, archives, links, editorial policy). Established 2000. **Editors-in-Chief:** Tom Koontz and Patti White.

Magazine Needs: *English Studies Forum* is an online publication created with the "purpose of distributing art and ideas. It contains creative writing, scholarship and commentary." Has no specifications for poetry submissions. However, they do not want to see weak artistry or prejudiced thought.

How to Submit: Submit 1-3 poems at a time. No previously published poems or simultaneous submissions. Accepts fax submissions. Cover letter preferred with SASE, brief bio and other pertinent info. Reads submissions September 1 through April 30 only. Poems are circulated to an editorial board. "Poems reviewed by editorial board of faculty and students. Editors-in-chief make final decisions." Seldom comments on rejected poems. Upcoming theme issues include "Image, Story, Conversation"; "The Post Modern Imagination"; "Postcolonial Writing and Theory." Guidelines and upcoming themes available on website. Responds in 1 month. Acquires first rights.

Advice: "Emphasize imagination, passion, engagement, artistry."

ENITHARMON PRESS, 26B Caversham Rd., London NW5 2DU United Kingdom. Phone: (20)7482 5967. Fax: (20)7284 1787. E-mail: books@enitharmon.co.uk. Established 1967. **Poetry Editor:** Stephen Stuart-Smith.

Book/Chapbook Needs: Enitharmon is a publisher of fine editions of poetry and literary criticism in paperback and some hardback editions, about 15 volumes/year averaging 100 pages. Has published books of poetry by John Heath-Stubbs, Ted Hughes, David Gascoyne, Thom Gunn, Ruth Pitter, and Anthony Thwaite.

How to Submit: "Substantial backlog of titles to produce, so no submissions possible before 2004."

EPICENTER, P.O. Box 367, Riverside CA 92502. E-mail: poetry@epicentermagazine.org. Website: www.epicentermagazine.org (includes guidelines, contact information, archives, links, and latest issue). Established 1994.

Magazine Needs: *Epicenter* is a biannual poetry and short story forum open to all styles. "*Epicenter* is looking for ground-breaking poetry, essays, and short stories from new and established writers. No angst-ridden, sentimental, or earthquake poetry. We are not adverse to graphic images if the work is well presented and contains literary merit." Has published poetry by Michael Vaughn, Virgil Suarez, Lon Risley, Max Berkovitz, Stan Nemeth, and Vicki Solheid. As a sample the editor selected these lines from "Missing Person" by B.Z. Niditch:

> you are declared/a non person/by the newly stateless/without a passport/carrying only a poem for the
> underground.

Epicenter is 44 pages, digest-sized, and saddle-stapled with semi-glossy paper cover and b&w graphics. Receives about 1,000 submissions/year, accepts about 5%. Press run is 400 for 250 shelf sales. Single copy: $4.50. Sample: $4.50. Make checks payable to Rowena Silver.

How to Submit: Submit up to 5 poems. Include SASE with sufficient postage for return of materials. Accepts previously published poems and simultaneous submissions. Accepts e-mail submissions (as attachment or in e-mail). Seldom comments on rejected poems. Guidelines available for SASE, by e-mail, on website, in publication. Pays 1 copy. Acquires one-time and electronic rights.

$ EPOCH, 251 Goldwin Smith, Cornell University, Ithaca NY 14853. (607)255-3385. Established 1947. **Poetry Editor:** Nancy Vieira Couto.

Magazine Needs: *Epoch* has a distinguished and long record of publishing exceptionally fine poetry and fiction. Has published work by such poets as Ashbery, Ammons, Eshleman, Wanda Coleman, Molly Peacock, Robert Vander Molen, and Alvin Aubert. *Epoch* appears 3 times/year in a 6×9, professionally printed, flat-spined format with glossy color cover, 128 pages, which goes to 1,000 subscribers. Accepts less than 1% of the many submissions received each year, have a 2- to 12-month backlog. Sample: $5. Subscription: $11/year domestic, $15/year foreign.

How to Submit: "We don't read unsolicited mss between April 15 and September 15." Responds in 2 months. Occasionally provides criticism on mss. Pays $5-10/page. "We pay more when we have more!" Acquires first serial rights.

Advice: "It's extremely important for poets to read other poets. It's also very important for poets to read the magazines that they want to publish in. Directories are not enough."

EUROPEAN JUDAISM (Specialized: religious, ethnic), Kent House, Rutland Gardens, London SW7 1BX England. Established 1966. **Poetry Editor:** Ruth Fainlight.

Magazine Needs: *European Judaism* is a "twice-yearly magazine with emphasis on European Jewish theology/philosophy/literature/history, with some poetry in every issue. It should preferably be short and have some relevance to matters of Jewish interest." Has published poetry by Linda Pastan, Elaine Feinstein, Daniel Weissbort, and Dannie Abse. As a sample the editor selected these lines from a poem by Michael Heller:

> *I took silence into time, marking the absence/of our late vocabularies in their conspirings,/these new mythologies, as they fell from on high//through our skies and through our roofs/scouring the mind as cosmic rays leave/traceries in the cool white lime of tunnels.*

European Judaism is a glossy, elegant, 6×9, flat-spined magazine, rarely art or graphics, 110 pages Has a press run of 950, about 50% of which goes to subscribers (few libraries). Subscription: $27.

How to Submit: Submit 3-4 poems at a time. No material dealt with or returned if not accompanied by SASE (or SAE with IRCs). "We cannot use American stamps. Also, I prefer unpublished poems, but poems from published books are acceptable." Cover letter required. Pays 1 copy.

N $ ⬛ ◎ EVANGEL; LIGHT AND LIFE COMMUNICATIONS (Specialized: religious, Christian), P.O. Box 535002, Indianapolis IN 46253-5002. Established 1897. **Editor:** J. Innes.

Magazine Needs: *Evangel* is a weekly adult Sunday school paper. "Devotional in nature, it lifts up Christ as the source of salvation and hope. The mission of *Evangel* is to increase the reader's understanding of the nature and character of God and the nature of a life lived for Christ. Material that fits this mission that isn't more than one page will be considered." No rhyming work. *Evangel* is 8 pages, 5½×8½ (2 8½×11 sheets folded), printed in 4 color and unbound with photos and graphics used. Accepts approximately 5% of poetry received. Press run is approximately 20,000 for 19,000 subscribers. Subscription: $1.99/quarter (13 weeks).

How to Submit: Submit no more than 5 poems at a time. Accepts simultaneous submissions. Cover letter preferred. Seldom comments on rejected poems. "Poetry must be typed on 8½×11 inch white paper. In the upper left-hand corner of each page, include your name, address, phone number, and social security number. In the upper right-hand corner of cover page, specify what rights you are offering. One-eighth of the way down the page, give the title. All subsequent material must be double-spaced, one-inch margins." Submit seasonal material one year in advance. Guidelines and sample available for #10 SASE; "write 'guidelines request' on your envelope so we can sort it from the submissions." Responds in up to 2 months. Pays $10 plus 2 copies on publication. Acquires one-time rights.

Advice: "Poetry is used primarily as filler. Send for sample and guidelines to better understand what and who the audience is."

N ▼ ⬤ THE EVANSVILLE REVIEW, 1800 Lincoln Ave., Evansville IN 47722. Phone/fax: (812)488-1042. Established 1989. **Editor:** Leeandra Nolting. **Contact:** Elisabeth Meyer.

● Poetry published in *The Evansville Review* has been included in *Best American Poetry* (2001) and the *Pushcart Prize* anthology (2002).

Magazine Needs: *The Evansville Review* appears annually and publishes "prose, poems and drama of literary merit." Wants "anything of quality." No experimental work or erotica. Has published poetry by John Updike, Willis Barnstone, Carol Muske, Vivian Shipley, David Ignatow, and Tess Galagher. As a sample the editor selected these lines from "Beckett Had Only One Student" by James Ragan:

> *As a tutor, Beckett taught only one/thought to a farmer who had pushed/a stone up pasture with a leg,/ how to add/a syllable to the name of <u>God</u>/and reverse direction in the space of letters/from the dauphin <u>to</u> to the expanse of <u>ot</u>,/and to skip the space that followed/as a symbol of regret.*

The Evansville Review is 200 pages, digest-sized, perfect-bound, includes art on cover only. Receives about 1,000 poems/year, accepts approximately 2%. Publish 45 poems/issue. Press run is 3,000; all distributed free to students and attendees at conferences. Sample: $5.

How to Submit: Submit 5 poems at a time. Accepts previously published poems and simultaneous submissions. Cover letter required. Include SASE for reply for return and brief bio. Reads submissions September 1 through December 10 only. Time between acceptance and publication is 3 months. Poems are circulated to an editorial board. Seldom comments on rejected poems. Guidelines available for SASE. Responds in 5 months. Pays 2 copies. Rights remain with poet. "We are not copywritten."

◎ EXIT 13 (Specialized: geography/travel), % Tom Plante, P.O. Box 423, Fanwood NJ 07023-1162. (908)889-5298. Established 1987. **Editor:** Tom Plante.

Magazine Needs: *Exit 13* is a "contemporary poetry annual" using poetry that is "short, to the point, with a sense of geography." Has published poetry by Ruth Moon Kempher, John McDermott, Carol Gordon, Hadara Bar-Nadav, Ray Skjelbred, and Walter Griffin. As a sample the editor selected these lines by from "Tsunami" by Carole Felix:

In travel brochures I see jagged fault lines/beneath a placid ocean./Suddenly, azure waves are in kitchens/and bedrooms, a cook is swept away, a maid/clings to a bed where a couple with sandy bodies/tried to produce a pearl.

Exit 13, #10, was 72 pages. Press run is 300. Sample: $7.

How to Submit: Accepts simultaneous submissions and previously published poems. Guidelines available for SASE and in publication. Responds in 4 months. Pays 1 copy. Acquires one-time and possible anthology rights. Staff reviews books of poetry and magazines in a "Publications Received" column, using 25-30 words/listing. Send books for review consideration.

Advice: "Write about what you know. Study geography. *Exit 13* looks for adventure. Every state, region, and ecosystem is welcome. Send a snapshot of an 'Exit 13' road sign and receive a free copy of the issue in which it appears."

EXPEDITION PRESS, 411 Stanwood St., Apt. D, Kalamazoo MI 49006-4543. (616)349-6413. Established 1978. **Publisher:** Bruce W. White.

Book/Chapbook Needs: Expedition Press publishes chapbooks that are "offbeat and bohemian with egalitarian appeal." Open to any style. This press is "not for snobs." He has published poetry by J. Kline Hobbs, Robin Reish, Todd Zimmerman, Margaret Tyler, Martin Cohen and C. VanAllsburg. As a sample the publisher selected his own couplet:

The moon is always full/The sun is always high.

Sample chapbooks: $5. Make checks payable to Bruce White.

How to Submit: Submit typed ms of 20-30 pages and cover letter with brief bio. Accepts submissions on cassette. **Reading fee: $5.** Please send SASE. Responds in 1 month. Sometimes sends prepublication galleys. Pays 100 contributor's copies. Bruce White provides "much" criticism on rejected mss.

EXPERIMENTAL FOREST PRESS (Specialized: bilingual/foreign language, political, social issues), 223 A Bosler Ave., Lemoyne PA 17043. (717)730-2143. E-mail: xxforest@yahoo.com. Website: http://maxpages.com/xxforest. Established 1999. **Co-Editors:** Jeanette Trout and Kevyn Knox.

Magazine Needs: *Experimental Forest* is published bimonthly "to show the world that there is more out there than meets the eye. Please, no sappy love poetry!" Has published poetry by Richard Kostelanetz, John M. Bennett, Taylor Graham, T. Kilgore Splake, Marty Esworthy, and Snow. As a sample the editor selected these lines by Kerry Shawn Keys:

E-mail is humming in pythagorean space/Chopin composes the flesh of a nocturne/Pink white apple blossoms/inner-tubes bearing naiads drift down the Delaware.

Experimental Forest is 60 pages, 5½ × 8½, stapled, b&w artwork on cover stock, also inside art. Receives about 1,000 poems/year, accepts about 20%. Publishes 30 poems/issue. Press run is 250 for 25 subscribers of which 5 are libraries, 75 shelf sales; 25 distributed free to fellow editors. Single copy: $5; subscription: $21.50/year. Sample: $5. Make checks payable to Jeanette Trout and/or Kevyn Knox.

How to Submit: Submit up to 5 poems at a time. Accepts e-mail submissions; no fax submissions. Cover letter preferred. "We prefer to have a short bio for our contributors page. We also require a SASE." Time between acceptance and publication is 6 months. Often comments on rejected poems. Publishes theme issues occasionally. A list of upcoming themes available for SASE. Responds in 2 months. Pays 1 copy. Acquires one-time rights.

Also Offers: Sponsors a poetry contest every fall with a $100 1st Prize and a short story contest each spring with a $100 1st Prize. Guidelines available for SASE or by e-mail.

Advice: "We accept poetry of any style or subject. We look for poetic voices that have something fresh and new to say. Remember, we are called '*Experimental*' Forest."

EXPLORATIONS; EXPLORATIONS AWARD FOR LITERATURE, UAS, 11120 Glacier Highway, Juneau AK 99801-8761. E-mail: art.petersen@uas.alaska.edu. Website: www.geocities.com/artp etersen. Established 1981. **Editor:** Professor Art Petersen.

Magazine Needs: *Explorations* is the literary magazine of the University of Alaska Southeast and appears annually in July. "Submissions are welcome from all poets and writers. The editors respond favorably to language really spoken by men and women. Standard form and innovation are encouraged as well as appropriate and fresh aspects of imagery (allusion, metaphor, simile, symbol . . .)." *Explorations* is digest-sized, nicely printed and saddle-stapled, with front and back cover illustration in one color. The editors tend to go for smaller-length poems (with small line breaks for tension) and often print two on a page—mostly lyric free verse with a focus on voice. Sample: $5.

MARKETS LISTED in the 2002 edition of *Poet's Market* that do not appear this year are identified in the General Index with a code explaining their absence from the listings.

How to Submit: An entry/reading fee is required: $6 for 1 or 2 poems (60 lines/poem maximum), add $3/poem for more than 2 poems; those paying reader/contest entry fees receive a copy of the publication. Checks should be made payable to "UAS Explorations." Mss must be typed with name, address, and 3- to 4-line biography on the back of each first page. Accepts simultaneous submissions. Submit January through May 15 only. Mss are not returned. Guidelines available for SASE, on website, or by e-mail. Responds in July. Pays 2 copies. Acquires one-time rights.

Also Offers: Sponsors the Explorations Awards for Literature. First place (for a poem or short story): $1,000; second place (for best work in a genre different from first place winner): $500; and third places for poetry and prose: $100. Entry fee: $6 for 1-2 poems, $3/poem for 3-5 poems. Judges are founding editors Art Petersen and Ron Silva.

☉ FAILBETTER.COM, 63 Eighth Ave., #3A, Brooklyn NY 11217. E-mail: submissions@failbetter. com. Website: www.failbetter.com (portal to current issue and archive of past issues). Established 2000. **Editors:** Thom Didato and David McLendon.

Magazine Needs: *failbetter.com* is a quarterly webzine "in the spirit of a traditional literary journal, dedicated to publishing quality fiction, poetry, and artwork. While the Web plays host to hundreds, if not thousands, of genre-related literary sites (i.e., science fiction and horror, many of which have merit), *failbetter.com* is not one of them. We place a high degree of importance on originality, believing that even in this age of trends it is still possible." Recently published poetry by Dick Davis, Cooper Estaban, M. Sarki, Terrence Hayes, and Melissa McCreedy. As a sample the editors selected these lines from "Daniella in the Palace" by M. Sarki:

> Grapa knew I was gulping/the warp of her back/leeward to the blut//And still she willed/herself to lie still . . .

failbetter.com is published exclusively online with art/graphics. Receives about 300 poetry submissions/year, accepts about 9-12. Publishes 3-4 poets/issue.

How to Submit: Submit 4-6 poems at a time. Line length for poetry is open. "We are not concerned with length: One good sentence may find a home here; as the bulk of mediocrity will not." Accepts simultaneous submissions; no previously published poems. Encourages e-mail submissions. "All e-mail submissions should include title in header. All poetry submissions must be included in the body of your e-mail. Please do not send attached files. If for whatever reason you wish to submit a MS Word attachment, please query first." Submissions also accepted by regular mail. "Please note, however, any materials accepted for publication must ultimately be submitted in electronic format in order to appear on our site." Cover letter is preferred. Reads submissions year round. Time between acceptance and publication ranges from up to 4 months. Poems are circulated to an editorial board. Often comments on rejected poems. "There have been several incidences where poets have been asked to re-submit, and their subsequent submissions have been accepted." Guidelines available on website. Responds in 3 weeks to e-mail submissions; up to 3 months for submissions by regular mail. "We will not respond to any e-mail inquiry regarding receipt confirmation or status of any work under consideration." No payment. Acquires exclusive first-time Internet rights; works will also be archived online. All other rights, including opportunity to publish in traditional print form, revert to the artist.

Also Offers: *failbetter presents*, a New York-based reading series featuring both established and emerging poets and fiction writers. Inquiries regarding reading series can be made at failbetterpresents@yahoo.com.

Advice: "We strongly recommend that you not only read the previous issue, but also sign up on our e-mail list (subscribe@failbetter.com) to be notified of future publications. Most importantly, know that what you are saying could only come from you. When you are sure of this, please feel free to submit."

☉ THE FAIRFIELD REVIEW, 544 Silver Spring Rd., Fairfield CT 06430-1947. (203)255-1119. E-mail: fairfieldreview@hpmd.com. Website: www.farifieldreview.org (includes all publications and related info). Established 1997. **Editors:** Janet and Edward Granger-Happ.

Magazine Needs: *The Fairfield Review* appears 3 times/year as an e-zine featuring poetry and short stories from new and established authors. "We prefer free style poems, approachable on first reading, but with the promise of a rich vein of meaning coursing along under the consonants and vowels." Does not want "something better suited for a Hallmark card." Accepts poetry written by children; requires parents' permission/release for children under 18. Recently published poetry by David Meuel, Halsted, Richard Fewell, E. Doyle-Gillespie, and Doug Tanoury. As a sample the editors selected these lines from "Bulb & Seed" by Taylor Graham:

> The old dogs are blooming where we planted/them with daffodils, the lemon-yellow heads/nodding this March afternoon, with ruffs/as bright as egg yolk. I name them/to remember: Lady-Bear and Pepper, Roxy,/Pattycake . . .

Fairfield Review is 20-30 pages published online (HTML). Receives about 350 poems/year, accepts about 8%. Publishes about 10 poems/issue.

How to Submit: Submit 3 poems at a time. Line length for poetry is 75 maximum. Accepts previously published poems with permission; no simultaneous submissions. Accepts fax, e-mail, and disk submissions. Cover letter is preferred. "We strongly prefer submission via e-mail or e-mail attachment. Notifications are sent exclusively via e-mail, unless SASE is sent with submissions." Reads submissions continually. Time between acceptance and publication is up to 6 months. Poems are circulated to an editorial board. Often comments on rejected poems, if requested and submitted via e-mail. Guidelines are available on website. Responds in up to 4 months. Always sends prepublications galleys (online only). Acquires first rights and right to retain publication in online archive issues. Reviews books of poetry. "We consider reviews of books from authors we have published or who are referred to us."

Also Offers: "We select poems from each issue for 'reader's choice' awards based on readership frequency."

Advice: "Read our article on 'Writing Qualities to Keep in Mind.' "

⬤⬤ ◎ FANTASTIC STORIES OF THE IMAGINATION (Specialized: science fiction/fantasy), P.O. Box 329, Brightwaters NY 11718. Established 1992. **Editor:** Edward J. McFadden. (Published by DNA Publications. Send all business-related inquiries and subscriptions to DNA Publications, P.O. Box 2988, Radford VA 24143.)

Magazine Needs: *Fantastic Stories* is a quarterly magazine "filled with fiction, poetry, art, and reviews by top name professionals and tomorrow's rising stars." Wants all forms and styles of poetry "within our genres—fantasy and science fiction. Best chance is 20 lines or less. No crude language or excessive violence. No pornography, horror, western, or romance. Poems should be typed with exact capitalization and punctuation suited to your creative needs." Has published poetry by Nancy Springer, Jane Yolen, and John Grey. *Fantastic Stories* is 72 pages, magazine-sized and saddle-stapled with a full-color cover, and b&w art throughout. Receives about 150 poetry submissions/year, accepts about 15-25 poems. Subscription: $16/4 issues, $27/8 issues. Sample: $4.95.

How to Submit: Accepts simultaneous submissions. Cover letter required; include credits, if applicable. Often comments on rejected poems. Guidelines available for SASE. Responds in 4 months. Pays 1-2 copies and 50¢ a line. Acquires first North American serial rights. Also "reserves the right to print in future volumes of *Fantastic Stories* anthology."

$ ⬤ ◎ FARRAR, STRAUS & GIROUX/BOOKS FOR YOUNG READERS (Specialized: children), 19 Union Square W., New York NY 10003. (212)741-6900. Website: www.fsgbooks.com. Established 1946. **Contact:** Children's Editorial Dept.

Book/Chapbook Needs: Publishes one book of children's poetry "every once in a while," in both hardcover and paperback editions. Open to book-length submissions of children's poetry only. Has published collections of poetry by Valerie Worth and Deborah Chandra.

How to Submit: Query first with sample poems and cover letter with brief bio and publication credits. Accepts previously published in magazines and simultaneous submissions. Seldom comments on rejected poems. Send SASE for reply. Responds to queries in up to 2 months, to mss in up to 4 months. "We pay an advance against royalties; the amount depends on whether or not the poems are illustrated, etc." Also pays 10 copies.

⬤ FAT TUESDAY, 560 Manada Gap Rd., Grantville PA 17028. (717)469-7159. E-mail: lionelstevroid@ yahoo.com. Website: www.egroups.com/group/FatTuesday. Established 1981. **Editor-in-Chief:** F.M. Cotolo. **Editor:** Lionel Stevroid.

Magazine Needs: *Fat Tuesday* publishes irregularly as "a Mardi Gras of literary, visual, and audio treats featuring voices, singing, shouting, sighing, and shining, expressing the relevant to irreverent." Wants "prose poems, poems of irreverence, gems from the gut. Particularly interested in hard-hitting 'autofiction.' " Accepts poetry written by children. Has published poetry by Chuck Taylor, Charles Bukowski, Mark Cramer, and Cotolo Patrick Kelly. *Fat Tuesday* is up to 60 pages, typeset (large type, heavy paper), saddle-stapled, card covers, usually chapbook style (sometimes magazine-sized, unbound) with cartoons, black line art, and ads. Press run is 1,000/year with poetry on 80% of the pages. Receives hundreds of submissions each year, accepts about 3-5%, have a 3- to 5-month backlog "but usually try to respond with personal, not form, letters." All editions are $5, postage paid. "Contact us about our new purchase-and-publish plan."

How to Submit: Submit any number of poems at a time. No previously published poems or simultaneous submissions. Accepts e-mail submissions (in text box). "Cover letters are fine, the more amusing the better." Publishes theme issues. Guidelines and upcoming themes available for SASE and by e-mail. Responds in up to 3 months. Pays 2 copies if audio. Rights revert to author after publication.

Also Offers: "In 1998 *Fat Tuesday* was presented in a different format with the production of a stereo audio cassette edition. *Fat Tuesday's Cool Noise* features readings, music, collage, and songs, all in the spirit of *Fat*'s printed versions. Other *Cool Noise* editions will follow. *Fat Tuesday* solicits artists who wish to have their material produced professionally in audio form. Call the editors about terms and prices on how you can release a stereo audio cassette entirely of your own material. *Fat Tuesday* has released *Seven Squared*, by Frank Cotolo and is looking for other audio projects. In-print magazines will still be produced as planned. You can hear Cotolo music and purchase CDs at our website."
Advice: "Support the magazine that publishes your work!"

FAULTLINE, Dept. of English & Comparative Literature, University of California—Irvine, Irvine CA 92697-2650. (949)824-1573. E-mail: faultline@uci.edu. Website: www.humanities.uci.edu/faultline (includes guidelines, contact and subscription information, contest rules). Established 1991. **Editor:** Elaine Kelly. **Contact:** Poetry Editor.
   • Poetry published by this journal has also been selected for inclusion in a *Pushcart Prize* anthology.
Magazine Needs: On shelves in May, *Faultline* is an annual journal of art and literature occasionally edited by guest editors and published at the University of California, Irvine. Has published poetry by Thomas Lux, Heather McHugh, Amy Genstler, and Yusef Komunyakaa. As a sample the editor selected these lines from "Late for Work" by Ralph Angel:

> Maybe I knelt there/for since they have vanished the lamps/in the shop windows//flicker within.
> Somebody/flinching. A red/umbrella and that part of the town swept from the hip

Faultline is approximately 120 pages, 6×9, professionally printed on 60 lb. paper, perfect-bound with 80 lb. cover stock and featuring b&w art and photos. Receives about 1,500 poems/year, accepts about 5%. Press run is 1,000. Single copy: $12. Sample: $5.
How to Submit: Submit up to 5 poems at a time. Accepts simultaneous submissions. No fax or e-mail submissions. Cover letter preferred. Do not include name and address on ms to assist anonymous judging. Reads submissions September 15 to March 1 only. Poems are selected by a board of up to 6 readers. Seldom comments on rejected poems. Guidelines available for SASE and on website. Responds in 3 months. Pays 2 copies. Acquires first or one-time rights.
Also Offers: "2002 was the first year of the annual Ahio Scott Watt Poetry Contest. Entry fee: $12; prize: $1,000."

$ FAUQUIER POETRY JOURNAL, P.O. Box 68, Bealeton VA 22712-0068. Established 1994. **Managing Editor:** Donna Clement.
Magazine Needs: *Fauquier Poetry Journal* is a quarterly that contains poetry, poetry commentary, editorials, contest announcements, and book reviews. Wants "fresh, creative, well-crafted poetry, any style. Due to format, longer poems over 40 lines are not often used. Do not want overly sentimental or religious themes, overdone subjects, or overly obscure work." Has published poetry by Sean Brendan-Brown, Robert Cooperman, Richard Arnold, Nancy Ryan, and Kenneth Wanamaker. *Fauquier Poetry Journal* is 40-50 pages, digest-sized, laser-printed on plain white paper and saddle-stapled with bright colored paper cover. Press run is more than 300 for 100 subscribers, including libraries. Subscription: $20. Sample: $5.
How to Submit: The editor encourages subscriptions by requiring a **reading fee for nonsubscribers** ($5 for 1-5 poems only per month); no reading fee for subscribers. Submit up to 5 poems with name and address in the upper left corner of each page and include SASE and in publication. Accepts previously published poems and simultaneous submissions. Sometimes comments on rejected poems. Guidelines and upcoming themes available for SASE. Responds within 6 weeks. Editor's Choice Awards of $5-25 granted to the best entries in each issue. Pays 1 copy to remainder of published poets. Acquires one-time rights.
Also Offers: Sponsors quarterly poetry contests, explained in the journal. Entry fee: $5. Prizes range from $15-75, and winners are published in the following issue. In addition to poetry, *Fauquier Poetry Journal* occasionally prints articles by guest columnists. Articles should deal with some aspect of poetry, the writing experience, reactions to particular poems or poets, the mechanics (how to), etc. No reading fee, no guidelines other than word limit (around 1,000 words). "Pretty much anything goes as long as it's interesting and well-written." Pays 2¢/word.
Advice: "Let us see a variety in your submission; what one editor likes, another won't. Send a range of work that illustrates the breadth and depth of your talent; this helps us decide if there's something we like. We encourage submissions from anyone who is writing mature, well-crafted poetry."

FEATHER BOOKS; THE POETRY CHURCH MAGAZINE; CHRISTIAN HYMNS & SONGS, P.O. Box 438, Shrewsbury, SY3 0WN United Kingdom. Phone/fax: (01743)872177. E-mail: john@waddysweb.freeuk.com. Website: www.waddysweb.freeuk.com (includes directors and editors and their specialized areas, a list of publications, and the top twenty most popular selling books). Feather Books established 1982. *Poetry Church Magazine* established 1996. **Contact:** Rev. John Waddington-Feather, editor.

Magazine Needs: *The Poetry Church Magazine* appears quarterly and contains Christian poetry and prayers. Wants "Christian or good religious poetry—usually around 20 lines, but will accept longer." Does not want "unreadable blasphemy." Accepts poetry written by children over ten. Has published poetry by M.A.B. Jones, Joan Smith, Idris Caffrey, Walter Nash, and the Glyn family. *The Poetry Church Magazine* is 40 pages, digest-sized, photocopied, saddle-stapled with laminated cover and b&w cover art. Receives about 1,000 poems/year, accepts about 500. Press run is 1,000 for 400 subscribers of which 10 are libraries. Single copy free; subscription: £7 ($15 US). Sample: $5. Make checks payable in sterling to Feather Books. Payment can also be made through website.

How to Submit: Submit 2 typed poems at a time. Accepts previously published poems and simultaneous submissions. Accepts e-mail submissions in attached file. Cover letter preferred with information about the poet. All work must be submitted by mail with SASE (or SAE and IRC). Time between acceptance and publication is 4 months. "The editor does a preliminary reading; then seeks the advice of colleagues about uncertain poems." Guidelines available for SASE (or SAE and IRC), by e-mail, or by fax. Responds within 1 week. Pays 1 copy. Poets retain copyright.

Book/Chapbook Needs & How to Submit: Feather Books publishes the Feather Books Poetry Series, books of Christian poetry, and prayers. Has recently published poetry collections by the Glyn family, Walter Nash, David Grieve, and Rossi Morgan Barry. "We have now published 158 poetry collections by individual Christian poets." Books are usually photocopied and saddle-stapled with laminated covers. "Poets' works are selected for publication in collections of around 20 poems in our Feather Books Poetry Series. We do not insist, but most poets pay for small run-offs of their work, e.g., around 50-100 copies for which we charge $270 per fifty. If they can't afford it, but are good poets, we stand the cost. We expect poets to read our *Poetry Church Magazine* to get some idea of our standards."

Also Offers: Feather Books also publishes *Christian Hymns & Songs*, a quarterly supplement by Grundy and Feather. And, each fall and summer, selected poems that have been published throughout the year in *Poetry Church Magazine* appear in *The Poetry Church Anthology*, the leading Christian poetry anthology used in churches and schools. Began a new chapbook collection, the "Christianity and Literature Series," which focuses on academic work. "The first, just published, is a paper by Dr. William Ruleman, of Wesley College, Tennessee, entitled *W.H. Auden's Search for Faith*. Other numbers include *Six Contemporary Women Christian Poets*, by Dr. Patricia Batstone; *In a Quiet Place: J.B. Priestley & Religion*, by Michael Nelson; and *'The Dream of the Road,' 'The Wanderer,' 'The Seafarer': Three Old English Early Christian Poems of the 8th Century*, newly translated by Reverend John Waddington-Feather, with an introduction by Professor Walter Nash."

Advice: "We find it better for poets to master rhyme and rhythm before trying free verse. Many poets seem to think that if they write 'down' a page they're writing poetry, when all they're doing is writing prose in a different format."

◯ FEELINGS OF THE HEART, P.O. Box 1022, Gulfport MS 39502-1022. (228)864-0766. E-mail: aharnischfitchie@hotmail.com. Website: www.feelingsoftheheart.net (includes staff bios, featured authors, guidelines, subscription information). Established 1999. **Editor/Publisher/Founder:** Alice M. Harnisch-Fitchie.

Magazine Needs: *Feelings of the Heart* appears biannually as the Winter/Spring issue and the Summer/Fall issue. Wants "*good* poetry from the heart." Recently published poetry by Vernon A. Fitchie, Elijah St. Ives, Frank L. Kunkel, Richard Sponougle, Melvin Sandburg, and Gary Edwards. As a sample the editor selected these lines from "River of Life" by Geneva Jo Anthony:

> The words flow across the page/Like running water in a river/swirling in eddies and bubbling over rocks/splashing and flowing over boulders/Bubbling and still among the reeds/only to settle into some quiet stream/resting beside the ferns/as a young lady whispers to her lover . . .

Feelings of the Heart is 50 pages, magazine-sized, computer-printed, stapled, artist cover, with ads from other publications. Receives about 100 poems/year, accepts about 95%. Publishes 20+ poems/issue. Press run is 100 for 80 subscribers. Single copy: $6; subscription: $18/year, $34/2 years. Sample: $4.50. Make checks payable to Alice M. Harnisch.

How to Submit: Submit 5 poems at a time with "name and address on every poem submitted." Line length for poetry is 20-40. Accepts previously published poems and simultaneous submissions. Accepts e-mail and disk submissions, up to 5 poems per e-mail but only 3 e-mail per day. Cover letter is required. "Please enclose SASE or IRC with all correspondence." Submit seasonal poems 2 months in advance. Time between acceptance and publication is 2 weeks. Poems "are read by me, the editor, and decided by the poetic intent of poetry submitted."

Often comments on rejections. Guidelines available for SASE or on website. Responds in 2 weeks with SASE. Sometimes sends prepublication galleys. Acquires first rights. Reviews books and chapbooks of poetry and other magazines in 200 words or less, single book format. Poets may send books for review consideration to Alice M. Fitchie.

Advice: "Send poetry that you believe in, not something you just scribbled on a napkin."

🅐 🅒 **FEMINIST STUDIES (Specialized: women/feminism)**, 0¦03 Taliaferro Hall, University of Maryland, College Park MD 20742. (301)405-7415. Fax: (301)405-8395. E-mail: femstud@umail.umd. edu. Website: www.feministstudies.org (includes editorial policy as well as contact and subscription information). Established 1969. **Contact:** Creative Writing Editor.

Magazine Needs: *Feminist Studies* appears 3 times/year and "welcomes a variety of work that focuses on women's experience, on gender as a category of analysis, and that furthers feminist theory and consciousness." Has published poetry by Janice Mirikitani, Paula Gunn Allen, Cherrie Moraga, Audre Lorde, Valerie Fox, and Diane Glancy. *Feminist Studies* is 250 pages, elegantly printed, flat-spined paperback. Press run is 8,000 for 7,000 subscribers, of which 1,500 are libraries. There are 4-10 pages of poetry in each issue. Sample: $15.

How to Submit: "All subscribers should send one copy (no SASE) to the above address. Work will not be returned." No simultaneous submissions; will only consider previously published poems under special circumstances. No fax or e-mail submissions. Manuscripts are reviewed twice a year, in May and December. Deadlines are May 1 and December 1. Authors will receive notice of the board's decision by July 10 and February 10. Guidelines are available on website. Always sends prepublication galleys. Pays 2 copies. Commissions reviews of books of poetry. Poets may send books to Claire G. Moses for review consideration.

🅥 $ 🅒 🅒 **FIELD: CONTEMPORARY POETRY AND POETICS; FIELD TRANSLATION SERIES; FIELD POETRY PRIZE; FIELD POETRY SERIES; OBERLIN COLLEGE PRESS**, 10 N. Professor St., Oberlin College, Oberlin OH 44074. (440)775-8408. Fax: (440)775-8124. E-mail: oc.press @oberlin.edu. Website: www.oberlin.edu/~ocpress (includes guidelines, contact and subscription information, catalog, links, and editorial policy). Established 1969. **Poetry Editors:** David Young and Martha Collins.

● Work published in *FIELD* has also been included in the 1992, 1993, 1994, 1995, and 1998 volumes of *The Best American Poetry.*

Magazine Needs: *FIELD* is a literary journal appearing in October and April with "emphasis on poetry, translations, and essays by poets." Wants the "best possible" poetry. Has published poetry by Marianne Boruch, Miroslav Holub, Charles Wright, Billy Collins, Jon Loomis, Charles Simic, and Sandra McPherson. As a sample the editors selected these lines from "Ars Poetica," a poem in *The Pleasure Principle* by Jon Loomis:

> It's not the dog, or even the ghost/of the dog, but the ghost of the dog's/lean shadow, camera obscura
> sketched//on the canvas—the north window's/steeped light not the light in the painting,/the girl in the
> painting not the girl . . .

FIELD is digest-sized, flat-spined, has 100 pages, rag stock with glossy card color cover. Although most poems fall under the lyrical free verse category, you'll find narratives and formal work here on occasion, much of it sensual, visually appealing, and resonant. Press run is 1,500, with 400 library subscriptions. Subscription: $14/ year, $24/2 years. Sample: $7.

How to Submit: Submit up to 5 poems at a time. Include cover letter and SASE. Reads submissions year-round. No previously published or simultaneous submissions. Does not accept fax or e-mail submissions. Seldom comments on rejected poems. Responds in 2 months. Time between acceptance and publication is up to 6 months. Always sends prepublication galleys. Guidelines available for SASE, by e-mail, on website. Pays $15/page plus 2 copies. Staff reviews books of poetry. Poets and publishers may send books for review consideration.

Book/Chapbook Needs & How to Submit: Publishes books of translations in the *FIELD* Translation Series, averaging 150 pages, flat-spined and hardcover editions. Query regarding translations. Pays 7½-10% royalties and author's copies. Also has a *FIELD* Poetry Series. Has published *Ill Lit* by Franz Wright; and *The Pleasure Principle* by Jon Loomis. This series is by invitation only. Write for catalog to buy samples.

Also Offers: Sponsors the *FIELD* Poetry Prize, the winning ms will be published in the *FIELD* poetry series and receive $1,000 award. Submit mss of 50-80 pages with a $22 reading fee in May only. Contest guidelines available for SASE.

🅐 **FINISHING LINE PRESS; MM REVIEW; MUTANT MULE; NEW WOMEN'S VOICES CHAPBOOK SERIES; FINISHING LINE PRESS OPEN CHAPBOOK COMPETITION**, P.O. Box 1016, Cincinnati OH 45201-1016. E-mail: finishingl@aol.com. Established 1998. **Editor:** C.J. Morrison (and occasionally guest editors). **Contact:** Poetry Editor.

Magazine Needs: *MM Review* is a biannual literary arts magazine publishing mostly poetry, but also short stories, short drama, essays and, sometimes, reviews. "We hope to discover new talent." Wants "quality verse. We are open to any style or form, but prefer free verse." Has published poetry by Errol Miller, Dennis Saleh, Denise Brennan Watson, Mark McCloskey, Rane Arroyo, and Alexandra Grilikhes. As a sample the editor selected these lines from "Feeling Fireworks" by Leah Maines:

> *Fireflowers bloom/in the warm summer air/your hand/unaware/brushes my breast*

MM Review is 40 pages, digest-sized, laser-printed and saddle-stapled with glossy cover, includes b&w photos. Receives about 1,000 poems/year, accepts 4%. Press run is 500 for 300 subscribers. Single copy: $6; subscription: $10. Sample: $6. Make checks payable to Finishing Line Press.

How to Submit: Submit up to 3 poems at a time. Include SASE. Accepts simultaneous submissions; no previously published poems. Brief cover letter with 50- to 75-word bio required, include past publication credits. Time between acceptance and publication is 6 months. Poems are circulated to an editorial board. Often comments on rejected poems. Guidelines available for SASE. Responds in 4 months. Sometimes sends prepublication galleys. Pays 1 contributor's copy. Acquires all rights. Returns rights upon publication. Staff reviews books and chapbooks of poetry in 200 words, multi-book format. Send books for review consideration to Finishing Line Press.

Book/Chapbook Needs & How to Submit: Finishing Line Press seeks to "discover new talent" and hopes to publish 20 new chapbooks/year by both men and women poets who have not previously published a book or chapbook of poetry. Has published *Looking to the East with Western Eyes* by Leah Maines; *Like the Air* by Joyce Sidman; *Startling Art* by Dorothy Sutton; *Mama Thoughts* by Gayle Pierce; *Man Overboard* by Steven Barza. Chapbooks are usually 25-30 pages, digest-sized, laser-printed and saddle-stapled with card cover with textured matte wrapper, includes b&w photos. Submit ms of 16-24 pages with cover letter, bio, acknowledgements and **$10 reading fee.** Responds to queries in 3-4 weeks, to mss in 3-4 months. Pay varies; pays in copies. "Sales profits, if any, go to publish the next new poet." Obtain sample chapbooks by sending $6.

Also Offers: Sponsors New Women's Voices chapbook competition. Entry fee: $12. Deadline: December 31. Finishing Line Press Open Chapbook Competition. Open to all poets regardless of past publications. Deadline: June 30.

Advice: "We are very open to new talent. If the poetry is great, we will consider it for a chapbook."

FIRE, Field Cottage, Old Whitehill, Tackley, Kidlington, Oxfordshire OX5 3AB United Kingdom. Website: www.poetical.org (includes guidelines, contact and subscription info as well as poetry from current issue, list of authors appearing in next issue, and a webpage of children's poetry). Established 1994. **Editor:** Jeremy Hilton.

Magazine Needs: *Fire* appears 3 times/year "to publish little-known, unfashionable or new writers alongside better known ones." Wants "experimental, unfashionable, demotic work; longer work encouraged. Use of rhyme schemes and other strict forms *not* favored." Accepts poetry written by children. Has published poetry by Marilyn Hacker, Adrian C. Louis, Tom Pickard, Allen Fisher, Gael Turnbull, and David Hart. *Fire* is 150 pages, A5. Receives about 400 poems/year, accepts about 35%. Press run is 250 for 180 subscribers of which 20 are libraries. Single copy: £4, add £1 postage Europe, £2 postage overseas. Subscription (3 issues): £7, add £2 postage Europe, £4 postage overseas.

How to Submit: Accepts previously published poems; no simultaneous submissions. Cover letter preferred. Time between acceptance and publication "varies enormously." Often comments on rejected poems. Guidelines available for SASE and on website. Responds in 2 months. Sometimes sends prepublication galleys, "but rarely to overseas contributors." Pays 1 copy.

Advice: "Read a copy first. Don't try to tailor your work to any particular style, format, or formula. Free expression, strongly imaginative work preferred."

FIREWEED: A FEMINIST QUARTERLY (Specialized: women), P.O. Box 279, Station B, Toronto, Ontario M5T 2W2 Canada. (416)504-1339. E-mail: fireweed@web.net. Established 1978. **Contact:** editorial collective.

Magazine Needs: *Fireweed*, edited by the Fireweed editorial/collective, is a feminist journal of writing, politics, art, and culture that "especially welcomes contributions by women of color, working-class women, native women, lesbians, and women with disabilities." As a sample they selected the opening lines of "Remembering My Voice" by Treena Kortje:

> *Today the baby discovers sound under water./It is my own voice she recognizes,/how it reached her*
> *once through soft folds of skin,/to the swell in my belly where she began*

Fireweed is 88 pages, 6¾×9¾, professionally printed and perfect-bound with 3- or 4-color glossy cover, includes b&w art. Press run is 1,500. Subscription: $22 individuals, $35 institutions in Canada; $30 individuals, $45 institutions in US. Sample: $5-15 (double issues), Canadian or US funds.

How to Submit: Submit up to 5 poems, single-spaced. Accepts simultaneous submissions. Send cover letter with brief bio and publication credits, if any. Publishes theme issues. Send SASE (or SAE and IRC) for upcoming themes. Responds in up to 1 year. "Please include SAE and IRC for reply." Pays contributors' fee and 2 copies of issue in which work appears.

◑ FIRST CLASS; FOUR-SEP PUBLICATIONS, P.O. Box 12434, Milwaukee WI 53212. E-mail: christopherm@four-sep.com. Website: www.four-sep.com (includes guidelines, contact and subscription information, bios, archives, catalog, and editorial policy). Established 1994. **Editor:** Christopher M.
Magazine Needs: *First Class* appears in May and November and "publishes excellent/odd writing for intelligent/creative readers." Wants "short postmodern poems, also short fiction." No traditional work. Has published poetry by Bennett, Locklin, Roden, Splake, Catlin, and Huffstickler. *First Class* is 56-66 pages, 4½×11, printed, saddle-stapled with colored cover. Receives about 1,500 poems/year, accepts about 30. Press run is 200-400. Sample (including guidelines): $6 or mini version $1. Make checks payable to Christopher M.
How to Submit: Submit 5 poems at a time. Accepts previously published poems and simultaneous submissions. Does not accept fax or e-mail submissions. Cover letter preferred. Time between acceptance and publication is 2-4 months. Often comments on rejected poems. Guidelines available for SASE, on website, and in publication. Responds in 3 weeks. Pays in 1 copy. Acquires one-time rights. Reviews books of poetry. Poets may send books for review consideration.
Also Offers: Chapbook production available.
Advice: "Belt out a good, short, thought-provoking, graphic, uncommon piece."

Ⓝ ⊕ ◎ FIRST OFFENSE (Specialized: form/style), Syringa, Stodmarsh, Canterbury, Kent CT3 4BA England. E-mail: enquiries@firstoffense.co.uk. Website: www.firstoffense.co.uk (includes guidelines, contact info, bios, catalog, subscription info, and editorial policy). Established 1985. Contact: Tim Fletcher.
Magazine Needs: *First Offense* is published 1-2 times/year. "The magazine is for contemporary poetry and is not traditional, but is received by most ground-breaking poets." Wants "contemporary, language, and experimental poetry and articles. No traditional work." *First Offense* is photocopied, "so we need well typed manuscripts, word processed." Press run is 300. Subscription: £2.50 plus 75¢ p&h. Make checks payable to Tim Fletcher.
How to Submit: No previously published poems. "No reply without SASE or SAE and IRC." Reviews books and chapbooks of poetry and other magazines.
Advice: "Always buy a copy before submitting for research so as not to waste everyone's time."

◐ FISH DRUM, P.O. Box 966, Murray Hill Station, New York NY 10156. Website: www.fishdrum.com. Established in 1988 by Robert Winson (1959-1995). **Editor:** Suzi Winson.
Magazine Needs: *Fish Drum* is a literary magazine appearing 2/year. Wants "West Coast poetry, the exuberant, talky, often elliptical and abstract 'continuous nerve movie' that follows the working of the mind and has a relationship to the world and the reader. Philip Whalen's work, for example, and much of *Calafia, The California Poetry*, edited by Ishmael Reed. Also magical-tribal-incantatory poems, exemplified by the future/primitive *Technicians of the Sacred*, ed. Rothenberg. *Fish Drum* has a soft spot for schmoozy, emotional, imagistic stuff. Literate, personal material that sings and surprises, OK?" Has published poetry by Philip Whalen, Arthur Sze, Nathaniel Tarn, Alice Notley, Jessica Hagedorn, and Leo Romero. As a sample the editor selected these lines from "Glossolalia" by Kate Bremer:

> *Everywhere I look I see amino acids on the ground./When I close my eyes, I see molecules and pieces*
> *of Sanskrit:/I hear syllables and alphabets.*

Fish Drum is approximately 80 pages, professionally printed, perfect-bound. Press run is 2,000 for subscribers, libraries, and shelf sales. Subscription: $24/4 issues. Sample: $6.
How to Submit: Publishes theme issues. Sends prepublication galleys. Pays 2 copies. Acquires first serial rights. Reviews books or chapbooks of poetry in long essays and/or capsule reviews. Open to unsolicited reviews. Poets may send books for review consideration.
Advice: "We're looking for prose, fiction, essays, what-have-you, and artwork, scores, cartoons, etc.—just send it along. We are also interested in poetry, prose, and translations concerning the practice of Zen. We publish chapbooks, but solicit these from our authors." She also adds, "It is my intention to complete Robert's work and to honor his memory by continuing to publish *FishDrum*."

◐ 5 AM, P.O. Box 205, Spring Church PA 15686. Established 1987. **Editors:** Ed Ochester and Judith Vollmer.
Magazine Needs: *5 AM* is a poetry publication that appears twice/year. Open in regard to form, length, subject matter, and style. However, they do not want poetry that is "religious or naive rhymers." Has

published poetry by Virgil Suarez, Nin Andrews, Alicia Ostriker, Edward Field, Billy Collins, and Denise Duhamel. *5 AM* is a 24-page, offset tabloid. Receives about 3,000 poems/year, accepts about 2%. Press run is 1,000 for 550 subscribers of which 25 are libraries, about 300 shelf sales. Subscription: $12/4 issues. Sample: $4.

How to Submit: No previously published poems or simultaneous submissions. Seldom comments on rejected poems. Responds within 1 month. Pays 2 copies. Acquires first rights.

580 SPLIT, P.O. Box 9982, Mills College, Oakland CA 94613-0982. (510)430-2217. Fax: (510)430-3398. E-mail: five80split@yahoo.com. Website: www.mills.edu/580Split (includes guidelines, contact information, bios, and table of contents to past issues). Established 1999. **Contact:** Poetry Editor. Member: CLMP.

Magazine Needs: *580 Split* appears annually in May. Publishes "high-quality, innovative poetry and fiction. Open to style and form. Rhyming poetry must be stellar. Open to experimental, visual, language, and concrete poetry." Recently published poetry by Lisa Jarnot, Lyn Hejinian, Clark Coolidge, D.A. Powell, Liz Waldner, Wenceslau Maldonado. *580 Split* is 100 pages, digest-sized, professionally printed, perfect-bound, cardstock cover with b&w photo, b&w art/graphics. Receives about 2,000 poems/year, accepts 1-5%. Publishes about 25 pages/issue. Press run is 625 for 20 subscribers of which 15 are libraries, 500 shelf sales. Single copy: $7.50; subscription: $7.50. Sample: $5. Make checks payable to *580 Split*.

How to Submit: Submit up to 5 poems at a time. No previously published poems or simultaneous submissions. No e-mail or disk submissions. Cover letter is preferred. "Poems not accompanied by SASE are recycled immediately." Reads submissions July 1 through November 1. Time between acceptance and publication is 4 months. Poems circulate to an editorial board and are voted on. Seldom comments on rejected poems. Guidelines available for SASE, in publication, by e-mail, and on website. Responds in up to 5 months. Sometimes sends prepublication galleys. Pays 2 contributor's copies. Acquires first North American serial rights.

Advice: "Familiarize yourself with our magazine and editorial vision to find out if we're the best place for your work."

FLAMING ARROWS, County Sligo VEC, Riverside, Sligo, Ireland. Phone: (+353)7145844. Fax: (+353)7143093. E-mail: leoregan@eircom.net. Established 1989. **Editor:** Leo Regan, A.E.O.

Magazine Needs: *Flaming Arrows*, published annually in January, features poetry and prose. Wants "cogent, lucid, coherent, technically precise poetry. Poems of the spirit, mystical, metaphysical but sensuous, tactile, and immediate to the senses." Has published poetry by Sydney Bernard Smith, Medbh McGuckian, Ben Wilensky, James Liddy, and Ciaran O'Driscoll. As a sample the editor selected these lines from "Alickadoo's Great Debate About Nothing" by S.B. Smith:

> . . . Re-enter Plato, expectation buoyed/by proven fact. Fact is, we're mostly hole;/which-body apart-
> leaves lots of room for-soul!//"That is, if soul were willing to subsist/within the same continuum or
> space/as petty particles, however wist-/ful, winsome, energetic, full of grace

Flaming Arrows is 80-102 pages, A5, offset-printed, perfect-bound or saddle-stapled, with 2-color cover stock. Receives about 500 poems/year, accepts about 6%. Press run is 600 for 150 subscribers of which 30 are libraries, 180 shelf sales; 100 distributed free to writer's groups, contributors, literary events. Issues 2 and 3 are $6; issues 4, 5, and 6 are $3; postage $1.25. Make checks payable to County Sligo VEC.

How to Submit: Submit 5 poems "typed, A4, in 10 or 12 pt. for scanning or discs for Word 7 in Windows 95." Accepts previously published poems and simultaneous submissions. Cover letter required. Time between acceptance and publication is 10 months. Responds in 3 months. Pays 1 copy, additional copies at cost. Include SASE with IRC.

Advice: "Inspection of previous issues, especially 2, 3, 5, or 6 will inform prospective contributors of style and standard required."

$ **FLESH AND BLOOD: QUIET TALES OF DARK FANTASY & HORROR (Specialized: horror, dark fantasy, off-beat, supernatural)**, 121 Joseph St., Bayville NJ 08721. E-mail: HorrorJack@aol.com. Website: http://zombie.horrorseek.com/horror/fleshnblood/ (includes guidelines, updates, news, editors, issue contents, etc.). Established 1997. **Senior Editor:** Jack Fisher.

Magazine Needs: Appearing 3 times/year, *Flesh and Blood* publishes work of dark fantasy and the supernatural. Wants surreal, bizarre, and avant-garde poetry. No "rhyming or love poems, epics, killers, etc." Has published poetry by Charles Jacob, Mark McLaughlin, Kurt Newton, Wendy Rathbone, J.W. Donnelly and Donna Taylor Burgess. *Flesh and Blood* is 50-52 pages, 5½×8½, saddle-stapled with glossy full-color cover, includes art/graphics and ads. Receives about 200 poems/year, accepts about 10%. Publishes 4-6 poems/issue. Press run is 500 for 400 subscribers, 100 shelf sales; 50 distributed free to reviewers. Subscription: $15. Sample: $4.50. Make checks payable to John or Jack Fisher.

How to Submit: Submit up to 5 poems at a time. Line length for poetry is 3 minimum, 30 maximum. Accepts previously published poems; no simultaneous submissions. Accepts e-mail submissions (include text in body of e-mail). Cover letter preferred. "Poems should be on separate pages, each with the author's address. Cover letter should include background credits." Time between acceptance and publication is up to 10 months. Guidelines available for SASE or on website. Responds in 2 months. Pays $5-10/poem and 1 copy.

Advice: "Be patient, professional, tactful, and courteous."

Ⓐ FLINT HILLS REVIEW, Department of English, Box 4019, Emporia State University, Emporia KS 66801. Fax: (620)341-5547. E-mail: heldricp@emporia.edu or webbamy@emporia.edu. Website: www.emporia.edu/fhr/index.htm (includes guidelines, contact and subscription information, editorial policy, contest information, samples, "a comprehensive web presence"). Established 1995. **Contact:** Editors.

Magazine Needs: Published annually in June, *Flint Hills Review* is "a regionally focused journal presenting writers of national distinction alongside burgeoning authors." Open to all forms except "rhyming, sentimental or gratuitous verse." Has published poetry by E. Ethelbert Miller, Elizabeth Dodd, Vivian Shipley, and Gwendolyn Brooks. *Flint Hills Review* is about 100 pages, digest-sized, offset-printed and perfect-bound with glossy card cover with b&w photo, also includes b&w photos. Receives about 2,000 poems/year, accepts about 5%. Single copy: $5.50.

How to Submit: Submit 3-5 poems at a time. Accepts simultaneous submissions; no previously published poems. Accepts submissions by e-mail (in text box), by fax, or postal mail. Cover letter with SASE required. Reads submissions January through March only. Time between acceptance and publication is about 1 year. Seldom comments on rejected poems. Occasionally publishes theme issues. Guidelines and a list of upcoming themes available for SASE or on website. Pays 1 copy. Acquires first rights.

Also Offers: Sponsors the annual Bluestem Press Award. See listing in the Contests & Awards section of this book.

Advice: "Send writing with evidences of a strong sense of place."

Ⓜ Ⓖ FLOATING BRIDGE PRESS (Specialized: regional, Washington State), P.O. Box 18814, Seattle WA 98118. E-mail: ppereira5@aol.com. Website: www.scn.org/arts/floatingbridge (includes guidelines, sample poems, poet bios, ordering information, and links to other sites of interest to poets). Established 1994. **Contact:** editor.

Book/Chapbook Needs: Floating Bridge press is "supported by Seattle Arts Commission, King County Arts Commission, Washington State Arts Commission, and the Allen Foundation for the Arts." The press publishes chapbooks and anthologies by Washington state poets, selected through an annual contest. Recently published *The End of Forgiveness* by Joseph Green, *X: a poem* by Chris Forhan, *Sonnets from the Mare Imbrium* by Bart Baxter, and *Blue Willow* by Molly Tenenbaum. In 1997 the press began publishing *Pontoon*, an annual anthology featuring the work of Washington state poets. *Pontoon* is 96 pages, digest-sized, offset-printed and perfect-bound with matte cardstock cover. For a sample chapbook or anthology, send $7 postpaid.

How to Submit: For consideration, Washington poets (only) should submit a chapbook ms of 20-24 pages of poetry with $10 entry fee and SASE (for results only). The usual reading period is November 1 to February 15. Accepts previously published individual poems and simultaneous submissions. Author's name must not appear on the ms; include a separate page with title, name, address, telephone number, and acknowledgments of any previous publication. Mss are judged anonymously and will not be returned. In addition to publication, the winner receives $500, 50 copies, and a reading in the Seattle area. All entrants receive a copy of the winning chapbook. All entrants will be considered for inclusion in *Pontoon*, a poetry anthology.

Ⓝ Ⓐ THE FLORIDA REVIEW, Dept. of English, University of Central Florida, Orlando FL 32816. (407)823-2038. Website: http://pegasus.cc.ucf.edu/~english/floridareview/home.htm (includes contents of past issues, information about Editors' Awards competition, and submission guidelines). Established 1972. **Contact:** The Editors.

Magazine Needs: *Florida Review* is a "literary biannual with emphasis on short fiction and poetry." Wants "poems filled with real things, real people and emotions, poems that might conceivably advance our knowledge of the human heart." Has published poetry by Knute Skinner, Elton Glaser, Silvia Curbelo, and Walter McDonald. *Florida Review* is 144 pages, professionally printed, flat-spined, with glossy card cover. Press run is 1,000 for 600 subscribers. Subscription: $10. Sample: $6.

How to Submit: Submit no more than 5 poems at a time. No correspondence, including mss, will be read or acknowledged unless accompanied by a SASE. Accepts simultaneous submissions. Editor comments on submissions "occasionally." Guidelines available for SASE or on website. Responds in 3 months. Always sends prepublication galleys. Pays 3 copies, small honorarium occasionally available. Acquires "first publication rights only. After publication, all rights return to author with first publication citation requested." Reviews books of poetry in 1,500 words, single book format; 2,500-3,000 words, multi-book format. Send books for review consideration.

N ⬤ FLUME PRESS, California State University at Chico, 400 W. First St., Chico CA 95929-0830. (530)898-5983. E-mail: flumepress@csuchico.edu. Website: www.csuchico.edu/engl/huff/index.html (includes guidelines and contact and contest information). Established 1984. **Poetry Editor:** Casey Huff.
Book/Chapbook Needs: Flume Press publishes poetry chapbooks. "We have few biases about form, although we appreciate control and crafting, and we tend to favor a concise, understated style, with emphasis on metaphor rather than editorial commentary." Has published chapbooks by Tina Barr, Luis Omar Salinas, Pamela Uschuk, Martha M. Vertreace, Carol Gordon, and David Graham. As a sample the editors selected these lines from "Hopeless Love" by Joanne Allred:

> I sit on a porch wearing nothing/but hot ambition under a cool cotton shift, waiting/for a boy who never shows. He can't get a car,/or off work, or the nerve, or some needed luck/circumstance won't grant in its plot to keep me pure./My virginity aches like a loose milk tooth.

How to Submit: Chapbooks are chosen from an annual competition. $20 entry fee (each entrant receives a copy of the winning chapbook). Submit 24-32 pages, including title, contents, and acknowledgments. Considers simultaneous submissions. Sometimes sends prepublication galleys. Winner receives $500 and 25 copies. Sample: $8. **Postmark deadline:** December 1.

⬤ FLYWAY, A LITERARY REVIEW, 206 Ross Hall, Iowa State University, Ames IA 50011-1201. Fax: (515)294-6814. E-mail: flyway@iastate.edu. Website: www.engl.iastate.edu/publications/flyway/hom epage.html. Established 1961. **Editor:** Stephen Pett.
Magazine Needs: Appearing 3 times/year, *Flyway* "is one of the best literary magazines for the money; it is packed with some of the most readable poems being published today—all styles and forms, lengths and subjects." The editor shuns elite-sounding free verse with obscure meanings and pretty-sounding formal verse with obvious meanings. *Flyway* is 112 pages, 6×9, professionally printed and perfect-bound with matte card cover with color. Press run is 600 for 400 subscribers of which 100 are libraries. Subscription: $20. Sample: $7.
How to Submit: Submit 4-6 poems at a time. Cover letter preferred. "We do not read mss between the end of May and mid-August." May be contacted by fax. Publishes theme issues (Chicano, Latino). Responds in 6 weeks (often sooner). Pays 1 copy. Acquires first rights.
Also Offers: Sponsors an annual award for poetry, fiction, and nonfiction. Details available for SASE.

N ☐ ◎ FOR CRYING OUT LOUD, INC. (Specialized: women survivors of sexual abuse), 46 Pleasant St., Cambridge MA 02139. E-mail: fcol_snlc@hotmail.com. Website: www.forcryingoutloud. org (includes selected prose, poetry, and editorials from quarterly newsletter). Established 1985. **Contact:** Survivors Newsletter Collective.
Magazine Needs: *For Crying Out Loud* appears quarterly "to provide a forum for the voices of women survivors of childhood sexual abuse. Each issue focuses on a theme. Recent themes include Trust; Justice; Memory; and Incest, Politics and Power. We publish poetry by women abuse survivors, often (though not always) on topics related to abuse and healing from abuse, any form or style." Does not want poetry that is anti-survivor or anti-woman. *For Crying Out Loud* is 12 pages, magazine-sized, offset-printed in b&w, side-stapled, paper cover, with occasional line drawings and clip art. Receives about 75 poems/year, accepts about 25%. Publishes 4 poems/issue. Press run is 400 for 200 subscribers of which 10 are libraries, 20 shelf sales; 50 are distributed free to Cambridge, MA Women's Center. Single copy: $3; subscription: $10/ 4 issues, $18/8 issues, $25/12 issues. Sample: $3. Make checks payable to Survivors Newsletter Collective.
How to Submit: Submit 3-6 poems at a time. Accepts previously published poems and simultaneous submissions. No fax, e-mail, or disk submissions. Cover letter is preferred. Reads submissions year round. Submit seasonal poems 3 months in advance. Time between acceptance and publication is 3 months. "The newsletter is edited by an editorial collective which votes on all submissions." Never comments on rejected poems. Regularly publishes theme issues. List of upcoming themes available for SASE. Guidelines available in magazine or for SASE. Responds in 3 months; **does not return submitted work.** Pays 1 contributor's copy plus a year's subscription. Acquires one-time rights. Reviews books and chapbooks of poetry

and other magazines/journals in 500 words, single book format. "We often review books and other resources that we feel will be of interest to our readers." Poets may send materials for review consideration to Survivors Newsletter Collective.

Advice: "Our mission is to break the silence around childhood sexual abuse and to empower survivors of abuse. We are interested in poetry (and prose of up to 500 words) that is related to this mission. We especially like to see work that is related to the theme of a particular issue."

THE FORMALIST; HOWARD NEMEROV SONNET AWARD (Specialized: form, metrical), 320 Hunter Dr., Evansville IN 47711. Website: www2.evansville.edu/theformalist/. Established 1990. **Editor:** William Baer.

Magazine Needs: *The Formalist*, appears twice/year, "dedicated to contemporary *metrical* poetry written in the great tradition of English-language verse. We're looking for well-crafted poetry in a contemporary idiom which uses meter and the full range of traditional poetic conventions in vigorous and interesting ways. We're especially interested in sonnets, couplets, tercets, ballads, the French forms, etc. We're not, however, interested in haiku (or syllabic verse of any kind) or sestinas. Only rarely do we accept a poem over 2 pages, and we have no interest in any type of erotica, blasphemy, vulgarity, or racism. Finally, we suggest that those wishing to submit to *The Formalist* become familiar with the journal beforehand. We are also interested in metrical translations of the poetry of major, formalist, non-English poets—from the ancient Greeks to the present." Has published poetry by Derek Walcott, John Updike, Maxine Kumin, X.J. Kennedy, May Swenson, W.D. Snodgrass, and Louis Simpson. As a sample the editor selected the opening stanza from "The Amateurs of Heaven" by Howard Nemerov:

> Two lovers to a midnight meadow came/High in the hills, to lie there hand in hand/Like effigies and look up at the stars,/The never-setting ones set in the North/To circle the Pole in idiot majesty,/And wonder what was given them to wonder.

The Formalist is 128 pages, digest-sized, offset-printed on bond paper and perfect-bound, with colored card cover. Subscription: $14/year; $26/2 years (add $7/year for foreign subscription). Sample: $7.50.

How to Submit: Submit 3-5 poems at a time. No simultaneous submissions, previously published work, or disk submissions. A brief cover letter is recommended and a SASE is necessary for a reply and return of ms. Responds within 2 months. Guidelines available for SASE. Pays 2 copies. Acquires first North American serial rights.

Also Offers: The Howard Nemerov Sonnet Award offers $1,000 and publication in *The Formalist* for the best unpublished sonnet. The final judge for 2002 was Wyatt Prunty. Entry fee: $3/sonnet. Postmark deadline: June 15. Guidelines available for SASE. Contestants must subscribe to *The Formalist* to enter.

FORPOETRY.COM, E-mail: submissions@forpoetry.com. Website: www.forpoetry.com. Established March 1999. **Editor:** Jackie Marcus.

Magazine Needs: *ForPoetry.Com* is a web magazine with daily updates. "We wish to promote new and emerging poets, with or without MFAs. We will be publishing established poets, but our primary interest is in publishing excellent poetry, prose, essays, reviews, paintings, and photography. We are interested in lyric poetry, vivid imagery, open form, natural landscape, philosophical themes but not at the expense of honesty and passion: model examples: Robert Hass, James Wright, Charles Wright's *The Other Side of the River*, Montale, Neruda, Levertov, and Karen Fish. No city punk, corny sentimental fluff, or academic workshop imitations." Has published poetry by Sherod Santos, John Koethe, Jane Hirshfield, Dana Gioir, Erin Believ, and Kathy Fasaw. As a sample the editor selected these lines from "Of Haloes & Saintly Aspects" by Sherod Santos:

> Out of a ripple in the sea grass,/Two unhoused fiddler crabs/sidestep past the almost-dead/hawksbill turtle turned over/on the beach and left there/staked with a broom—

"We receive lots of submissions and are very selective about acceptances, but we will always try to send a note back on rejections."

How to Submit: Submit no more than 2 poems at a time. Accepts simultaneous submissions; no previously published poems. E-mail submissions only; include text in body of message. Cover letter preferred. Reads submissions September through May only. Time between acceptance and publication is 2-6 weeks. Poems are circulated to an editorial board. "We'll read all submissions and then decide together on the poems we'll publish." Comments on rejected poems "as often as possible." Guidelines and upcoming themes available on website. Responds in 2 weeks. Reviews books and chapbooks of poetry and other magazines in 800 words.

Advice: "As my friend Kevin Hull said, 'Get used to solitude and rejection.' Sit on your poems for several months or more. Time is your best critic."

○ ◎ **4*9*1 NEO-NAIVE IMAGINATION (Specialized: neo-naive)**, P.O. Box 91212, Lakeland FL 33804-1212. E-mail: stompdncr@aol.com or juanbeaumontez@aol.com. Website: www.491.20m.com (includes guidelines, contact information, bios, archives, links, editorial policy, and manifesto). Established 1997. **Editor:** Donald Ryburn. **Assistant Editor:** Juan Beauregard-Montez.

Magazine Needs: *4*9*1 Neo-Naive Imagination* appears continuously as an online publication and publishes poetry, art, photography, essays and interviews. Wants "poetry of neo-naive genre. No academic poetry, limited and fallacious language." Accepts poetry written by children. Has published poetry by Aubrey and Jesus Morales-Montez. As a sample the editor selected these lines from "Alexandra in Sicilia" by Donald Ryburn:

> *I slept beside her in the unforgiving sun,/Dreamed of a perfect world,/without icons, burial shrouds,*
> *burdens,/I awoke to Alexandra's breath/On my breast,/Perfect white sand flowed,/From her thin mouth.*

How to Submit: Submit 3-6 poems at a time. Accepts previously published poems and simultaneous submissions. E-mail, fax, disk, and CD-ROM submissions preferred; include e-mail submissions in body of message. "No attachments accepted or opened." Note "submission" in subject area. "Would like to hear the poets own words not some standard format." Cover letter with picture and SASE preferred. Time between acceptance and publication varies. Response time varies. Payment varies. Acquires first or one-time rights. Reviews books and chapbooks of poetry and other magazines. Poets may send books for review consideration.

Also Offers: Sponsors a series of creative projects. Write for details or visit the website.

▨ ◗ **FOURTEEN HILLS: THE SFSU REVIEW**, Creative Writing Dept., San Francisco State University, 1600 Holloway Ave., San Francisco CA 94132. (415)338-3083. Fax: (415)338-7030. E-mail: hills@ sfsu.edu. Website: www.mercury.sfsu.edu/~hills (includes guidelines, contact info, subscription info, links, and editorial policy). Established 1994. **Contact:** poetry editor.

Magazine Needs: *Fourteen Hills* is semiannual appearing in December and May. "We are seeking high quality, innovative work." Has published poetry by Alice Notley, CD Wright, Sherman Alexie, and Virgil Suarez. As a sample the editor selected these lines from "Rodeo of Outer Mind" by Joshua Corey:

> *A lens in the wind,/a burn in the thighs of the century,/knees crashing down, eyes raised to Vega . . ./*
> *to a glittering condor unfolding/like a knife in the new sky . . .*

Fourteen Hills is 170 pages, 6×9, professionally printed and perfect-bound with glossy card cover. Receives about 600 poems/year, accepts approximately 5-10%. Press run is 600 for 125 subscribers of which 25 are libraries. Single copy: $7; subscription: $12/year, $21/2 years. Sample: $5.

How to Submit: Submit 5 poems at a time. Accepts simultaneous submissions; no previously published poems. Cover letter preferred. Reads submissions August-September for the fall issue; January-February for the spring. "The editorial staff is composed entirely of graduate students from the Creative Writing Program at SFSU." Seldom comments on rejected poems. Guidelines available in publication and on website. Responds in 6 months. Always sends prepublication galleys. Pays 2 copies.

Advice: "Please read an issue of *Fourteen Hills* before submitting."

◗ **FOX CRY REVIEW**, University of Wisconsin-Fox Valley, 1478 Midway Rd., Menasha WI 54952-1297. (920)832-2600. Website: www.uwfoxvalley.uwc.edu. Established 1974. **Editor:** Darren Defrain.

Magazine Needs: *Fox Cry Review* is a literary annual, published in August, using poems of any length or style, include brief bio, deadline February 1. Has published poetry by Doug Flaherty, Paula Sergi, and Ellen Kort, and A.J. Rathburn. As a sample the editor selected these lines from "Let the Words of My Mouth" by Beverly Voldseth, which was nominated for a Pushcart Prize:

> *We take comfort in these lines/that wait on our tongues—/to be rolled out to bank tellers//neighbors*
> *we pass on the street/strangers in the post office./What little boredoms our lives//are made up of, how*
> *they stand/in the mouth like truth.*

Fox Cry Review is 115 pages, digest-sized, professionally printed and perfect-bound with light card cover with b&w illustration, also contains b&w illustrations. Press run is 300. Single copy: $7.50 plus $1 postage.

How to Submit: Submit maximum of 3 poems from September 1 through February 1 only. Include SASE. "Include name, address and phone number on each poem." No previously published poems. No fax or e-mail submissions. Guidelines available in publication. Pays 1 copy.

▨ **$** ◗ **FRANK: AN INTERNATIONAL JOURNAL OF CONTEMPORARY WRITING AND ART**, 32 rue Edouard Vaillant, 93100 Montreuil France. Phone: (33)(1)48596658. Fax: (33)(1)48596668. E-mail: sub@ReadFrank.com. Website: www.ReadFrank.com (includes guidelines, bios, contact and subscription information, archives). Established 1983. **Editor:** David Applefield.

Magazine Needs: *Frank* is a literary semiannual that "encourages work of seriousness and high quality which falls often between existing genres. Looks favorably at true internationalism and stands firm against ethnocentric values. Likes translations. Publishes foreign dossier in each issue. Very eclectic." There are no subject specifications, but the magazine "discourages sentimentalism and easy, false surrealism. Although we're in Paris, most Paris-poems are too thin for us. Length is open." Has published poetry by Billy Collins, C.K. Williams, Michael Anania, Jim Morrison, Raymond Carver, Tomas Tranströmer, James Laughlin, Breytenbach, Michaux, Gennadi Aigi, W.S. Merwin, Edmond Jabes, John Berger, and many lesser known poets. The journal is 256 pages, digest-sized, flat-spined and offset in b&w with color cover flaps and photos, drawings and ads. Circulation is 4,000 of which 2,000 are bookstore sales and subscriptions. Subscription: $38/€40 (individuals), $60/€65 (institutions) for 4 issues. Sample: $10 airmail from Paris.

How to Submit: Accepts submissions on disk, by e-mail (as attachment or in text box), by online submission form, or by regular mail. Guidelines and upcoming themes available on website. Poems must be previously unpublished. The editor often provides some criticism on rejected mss. Responds in 3 months, publication is in 3-6 months. Pay is $5/printed page and 2 copies. Editor organizes readings in US and Europe for *Frank* contributors. "Poets are encouraged to submit news of readings, new publications, and literary events on *Frank*'s calendar online. We are also collecting for publication in an anthology the best, most telling rejection and/or cover letters poets have received."

Advice: "Send only what you feel is fresh, original, and provocative in either theme or form. Work of craft that also has political and social impact is encouraged. We are very open to translations from lesser known countries and languages as well as interviews with engaging poets."

FREE FOCUS (Specialized: women/feminist); OSTENTATIOUS MIND (Specialized: form/style), P.O. Box 7415, JAF Station, New York NY 10116. *Free Focus* established 1985. *Ostentatious Mind* established 1987. **Poetry Editor:** Patricia D. Coscia.

Magazine Needs: *Free Focus* "is a literary magazine only for creative women, who reflect their ideas of love, nature, beauty, and men and also express the pain, sorrow, joy, and enchantment that their lives generate. *Free Focus* needs poems of all types on the subject matters above. Nothing X-rated, please. The poems can be as short as two lines or as long as two pages. The objective of this magazine is to give women poets a chance to be fullfilled in the art of poetry, for freedom of expression for women is seldom described in society." Has published poetry by Jill Bornstein, Joan Mazza, Janet Stuart, Patricia A. Pierkowski, Crystal Beckner, and Carol L. Clark. *Ostentatious Mind* "is a co-ed literary magazine for material of stream of consciousness and experimental poems. The poets deal with the political, social, and psychological." Has published poetry by Edward Janz, J. Fyfe, Tom Baer, Matt Hutchinson, Rod Farmer, and Joe Lackey. Both magazines are printed on 8 × 14 paper, folded in the middle and stapled to make a 10-page (including cover) format, with simple b&w drawings on the cover and inside. The two magazines appear every 6-8 months. Sample of either is $4.

How to Submit: Submit only 3 poems at a time. Poems should be typed neatly and clearly on white typing paper. Accepts simultaneous submissions and previously published poems. Publishes theme issues. Guidelines and upcoming themes available for SASE. Responds "as soon as possible." Sometimes sends prepublication galleys. Pays 1 copy.

Advice: "I think that anyone can write a poem who can freely express intense feelings about their experiences. A dominant thought should be ruled and expressed in writing, not by the spoken word, but the written word."

FREE LUNCH, P.O. Box 7647, Laguna Niguel CA 92607-7647. Website: www.poetsfreelunch.org (includes information about *Free Lunch*, submission guidelines, a poem and the cover art from most recent issue, subscription and contact information, editorial policy). Established 1988. **Editor:** Ron Offen.

Magazine Needs: *Free Lunch* is a "poetry journal interested in publishing the whole spectrum of what is currently being produced by American poets. Features a 'Mentor Series,' in which an established poet introduces a new, unestablished poet. Mentors have included Maxine Kumin, Billy Collins, Lucille Clifton, Donald Hall, Carolyn Forché, Wanda Coleman, Lyn Lifshin, and Stephen Dunn. Especially interested in experimental work and work by unestablished poets. Hope to provide all serious poets living in the US with a free subscription. For details on free subscription send SASE. Regarding the kind of poetry we find worthwhile, we like metaphors, similes, arresting images, and a sensitive and original use of language. We are interested in all genres—experimental poetry, protest poetry, formal poetry, etc. No restriction on form, length, subject matter, style, purpose. No aversion to form, rhyme." Poets published include Thomas Carper, Jared Carter, Billy Collins, David Wagoner, Donald Hall, D. Nurkse, and Cathy Song. As a sample the editor selected "Coastline" by Billy Collins:

> I draw a fingernail over your skin/like the pen-point/of a blind mapmaker/tracing the outline of an island.//Let us go slowly now/in the dark/as the moon rises/into the curtainless window./Let me print the name of every bay and cove.

Free Lunch, published 2 times/year, is 32-40 pages, digest-sized, attractively printed and designed, saddle-stapled, featuring free verse that shows attention to craft with well-knowns and newcomers alongside each other. Press run is 1,200 for 1,000 free subscriptions and 200 paid of which 15 are libraries. Subscription: $12 ($15 foreign). Sample: $5 ($6 foreign).

How to Submit: "Submissions must be limited to three poems and are considered only between September 1 and May 31. Submissions sent at other times will be returned unread. Although a cover letter is not mandatory, I like them. I especially want to know if a poet is previously unpublished, as I like to work with new poets." Accepts simultaneous submissions; no previously published poems. Editor comments on rejected poems and tries to return submissions in 2 months. Guidelines available for SASE. Pays 1 copy plus subscription.

Also Offers: A prize of $200 is awarded to one poem in each issue of *Free Lunch*. The winning poem of the Rosine Offen Memorial Award is selected solely by the Board of Directors of Free Lunch Arts Alliance. Winners announced in next issue.

Advice: "Archibald MacLeish said, 'A poem should not mean/ But be.' I have become increasingly leery of the ego-centered lyric that revels in some past wrong, good-old-boy nostalgia, or unfocused ecstatic experience. Poetry is concerned primarily with language, rhythm, and sound; fashions and trends are transitory and to be eschewed; perfecting one's work is often more important than publishing it."

FREEFALL, Undead Poets Press, 15735 Kerstyn St., Taylor MI 48180. (248)543-6858. E-mail: mauru spoet@yahoo.com. Established 1999. **Editor/Publishers:** Marc Maurus and T. Anders Carson.

Magazine Needs: *freefall* appears biannually, publishing the quality work of beginners as well as established poets. "Free verse or formal poetry is okay, and our acceptance policy is broad. No concrete, shape, or greeting card verse. No gratuitous language or sex. No fuzzy animals or syrupy nature poems." Recently published poetry by T. Anders Carson, Kristin Hatch, Mary Hedger, Ann Holdreith, and Cara Jane Houlberg. As a sample the editor selected these lines from "Winter Wolf" by Nathan Roberts:

> *silent howls deafen/the lonely moonlit sky/and the raven carries/a fletched twig arrow/to build his nest*
> *of souls*

freefall is 40 pages, digest-sized, laser-printed, saddle-stapled, card stock cover. Receives about 200 poems/year, accepts about 50%. Publishes about 30-40 poems/issue. Press run is 250 for 50 subscribers fo which 10 are libraries, 25 shelf sales; 25 are distributed free to small press reviewers. Single copy: $5; subscription: $7.50. Sample: $5. Make checks payable to Marc Maurus.

How to Submit: Submit 5-10 poems at a time. Line length for poetry is 3 minimum, 80 maximum. Accepts previously published poems with notification; no simultaneous submissions. Accepts e-mail submissions; no fax or disk submissions. Cover letter is preferred. "Snail mail preferred, please send SASE. E-mail submissions in body, not attached." Reads submissions all year. Submit seasonal poems 6 months in advance. Time between acceptance and publication is 6 months. Poems are circulated to an editorial board. "If a poem is high quality, I accept it right away, poor work is rejected immediately, and those on the fence are circulated to as many as 3 other guest editors." Often comments on rejected poems. *Poems may be sent for critique only for $2 each plus SASE.* Guidelines are available for SASE. Responds in 2 weeks. Always sends prepublication galleys. Pays 2 contributor's copies. Acquires first rights; rights always revert to author on publication. Reviews chapbooks of poetry and other magazines/journals in 500 words, single book format. Poets may send books for review consideration to Marc Maurus.

Advice: "We prefer to see crafted work, not unedited one-offs. We welcome as much formal verse as we can because we feel there is a place for it."

FREEHAND, 15 Meols Dr., Hoylake, Wirral CH47 4AD United Kingdom. Phone: (44)0151-625-0969. E-mail: josephinewood@compuserve.com. Established 1996. **Editor:** Jo Wood.

Magazine Needs: *Freehand* appears bimonthly "to spread availability and access to those starting out in writing and to offer a platform for promising writers." Does not want "foul language." Accepts poetry written by children. As a sample the editor selected these lines from "For Dad—The Seasons of Life" by Jo Burns:

> *In early spring you rocked me in your arms/The world was far too big for me/And so your rose lay*
> *cradled in her green and leafy gown/But you were there, and frost and snow/Could never penetrate*
> *that blanket love had thrown around her*

Freehand is 36 pages, magazine-sized, stapled with 100g paper cover, includes various ads. Receives about 300 poems/year, accepts approximately 70%. Press run is 250 for 220 subscribers. Single copy: £2; subscription: £18 overseas, £12 UK. Sample: £2 plus postage. "Prefer subscribers."

How to Submit: Submit 5 poems at a time. Accepts previously published poems and simultaneous submissions. Accepts e-mail and disk submissions. Cover letter preferred. "SAE's especially from overseas." Reads submissions all year. Time between acceptance and publication is 2 months. "Sole member of staff reads submissions." Often comments on rejected poems. Publishes theme issues occasionally. Guidelines available by SASE (or SAE and IRC) or by e-mail. Responds in 2 weeks. Acquires first British serial rights. Reviews books of poetry and other magazines in 300 words. Poets may send books for review consideration.
Also Offers: Offers free reviews of subscriber's books and free ads for subscribers.
Advice: "Try a sample copy."

FREEXPRESSION, P.O. Box 4, West Hoxton NSW 2171 Australia. Phone: (02)9607 5559. Fax: (02)9826 6612. E-mail: frexprsn@bigpond.com.au. Established 1993. **Managing Editor:** Peter F. Pike.
Magazine Needs: *FreeXpresSion* is a monthly publication containing "creative writing, how-to articles, short stories, and poetry including cinquain, haiku, etc., and bush verse." Open to all forms. "Christian themes OK. Humorous material welcome. No gratuitous sex; bad language OK. We don't want to see anything degrading." Has published poetry by Ron Stevens, John Ryan, and Ken Dean. As a sample the editor selected these lines from "The Riding of Tearaway" by Ellis Campbell:

> I wasn't scared of any horse—or of the ringer's jeers—/I'd rode the worst to come my way since early childhood years./While droving with my father—since the day my mother died—/I'd often bested older men and showed them how to ride./But years diminish glory and I'm weary of the fray;/I had no inclination for the scalp of Tearaway.

FreeXpresSion is 24 pages, magazine-sized, offset-printed and saddle-stapled with paper cover, includes b&w graphics. Receives about 1,500 poems/year, accepts about 50%. Press run is 500 for 300 subscribers of which 20 are libraries. Single copy: $3.50 AUS; subscription: $35 AUS ($55 overseas airmail). For sample, send large SAE with $1 stamp.
How to Submit: Submit 3-4 poems at a time. Accepts previously published poems and simultaneous submissions. Accepts fax and e-mail submissions (include in body of message). Cover letter preferred. "Very long poems are not desired but would be considered." Time between acceptance and publication is 2 months. Seldom comments on rejected poems. Publishes theme issues. Guidelines and upcoming themes available for fax or SAE and IRC. Responds in 2 months. Sometimes sends prepublication galleys. Pays 1 copy, additional copies available at half price. Acquires first Australian rights only. Reviews books of poetry in 500 words. Poets may send books for review consideration.
Also Offers: Sponsors annual contest with 2 categories for poetry: blank verse (up to 40 lines), traditional verse (up to 80 lines). 1st Prize (in both categories): $200, 2nd Prize: $100. *FreeXpresSion* also publishes books up to 200 pages through subsidy arrangements with authors.
Advice: "Keep it short and simple."

FROGMORE PAPERS; FROGMORE POETRY PRIZE, 18 Nevill Rd., Lewes, East Sussex BN7 1PF England. Website: www.frogmorepress.co.uk (includes list of titles in print, submission guidelines, details of the Frogmore Poetry Prize). Established 1983. **Poetry Editor:** Jeremy Page.
Magazine Needs: *Frogmore Papers* is a biannual literary magazine with emphasis on new poetry and short stories. "Quality is generally the only criterion, although pressure of space means very long work (over 100 lines) is unlikely to be published." Has published "Other Lilies" by Marita Over and "A Plutonian Monologue" by Brian Aldiss and poetry by Carole Satyamurti, John Mole, Linda France, Elizabeth Garrett, John Harvey, and John Latham. As a sample the editor selected these lines by Tobias Hill:

> if I stand just here, just right/and look up, I can see the rain/coming, and light on aeroplanes/high and certain, crossing time zones.

Frogmore Papers is 42 pages, saddle-stapled with matte card cover, photocopied in photoreduced typescript. Accepts 3% of the poetry received. Their press run is 300 for 120 subscribers. Subscription: £7 ($20). Sample: £2 ($5). (US payments should be made in cash, not check.)
How to Submit: Submit 5-6 poems at a time. Considers simultaneous submissions. Editor rarely comments on rejected poems. Responds in 6 months. Pays 1 copy. Staff reviews books of poetry in 2-3 sentences, single book format. Send books for review consideration to Catherine Smith, 24 South Way, Lewes, East Sussex BN7 1LU England.
Also Offers: Sponsors the annual Frogmore Poetry Prize. Write for information.
Advice: "My advice to people starting to write poetry would be: Read as many recognized modern poets as you can and don't be afraid to experiment."

$ FROGPOND: INTERNATIONAL HAIKU JOURNAL; HAIKU SOCIETY OF AMERICA; HAIKU SOCIETY OF AMERICA AWARDS/CONTESTS (Specialized: form/style, haiku and related forms; translation), P.O. Box 2461, Winchester VA 22604-1661. (540)722-2156.

Fax: (708)810-8992. E-mail: redmoon@shentel.net. Website: www.octet.com/~hsa/ (includes general information on haiku and the Haiku Society of America, plus contests, guidelines, publications, subscription and contact information, links, editorial policy, and special features). Established 1978. **Editor:** Jim Kacian.

Magazine Needs: *Frogpond* is the international journal of the Haiku Society of America and is published triannually. Wants "contemporary English-language haiku, ranging from 1-4 lines or in a visual arrangement, focusing on a moment keenly perceived and crisply conveyed, using clear images and non-poetic language." Also accepts "related forms: senryu, sequences, linked poems, and haibun. It welcomes translations of any of these forms." Accepts poetry written by children. As a sample the editor selected these poems by Robert Mainone and Burneu Gippy:

> *All around/Light failing in a field/of fireflies/—Robert Mainone//Commuter trains/abandoned crossword/the early darkness/—Burneu Gippy*

Frogpond is 96 pages, 5½×8½, perfect-bound, and has 60 pages of poetry. Receives about 20,000 submissions/year, accepts about 500. *Frogpond* goes to 800 subscribers, of which 15 are libraries, as well as to over a dozen foreign countries. Sample back issues: $7. Make checks payable to Haiku Society of America.

How to Submit: Submit 5-10 poems, with 5 poems per 8½×11 sheet, with SASE (send submissions to Jim Kacian at address mentioned above). No simultaneous submissions. Accepts submissions by e-mail (as attachment or in text box), on disk, by fax, or by regular mail. Information on the HSA and submission guidelines available for SASE. Responds "usually" in 3 weeks or less. Pays $1/accepted item. Poetry reviews usually 1,000 words or less. "Authors are urged to send their books for review consideration."

Also Offers: *Supplement* publishes longer essays, articles, and reviews from quarterly meetings and other haiku gatherings. *Supplement* is 96 pages, 5½×8½, perfect-bound. *HSA Newsletter*, edited by Charles Trumbull, appears 6 times/year and contains reports of the HSA Quarterly meetings, regional activities, news of upcoming events, results of contests, publications activities, and other information. A "best of issue" prize is awarded for each issue through a gift from the Museum of Haiku Literature, located in Tokyo. The Society also sponsors The Harold G. Henderson Haiku Award Contest, the Gerald Brady Senryu Award Contest, the Bernard Lionel Einbond Memorial Renku Contest, the Nicholas A. Virgilio Memorial Haiku Competition for High School Students and the Merit Book Awards for outstanding books in the haiku field.

Advice: "Submissions to *Frogpond* are accepted from both members and nonmembers, although familiarity with the journal will aid writers in discovering what it publishes."

N⃞ ◎ FRONTIERS: A JOURNAL OF WOMEN STUDIES (Specialized: feminist), % Susan Armitage, Wilson 12, Washington State University, Pullman WA 99164-4007. Established 1975.

Magazine Needs: *Frontiers* is published 3 times/year and uses poetry on feminist themes. Has published work by Audré Lorde, Janice Mirikitani, Carol Wolfe Konek and Opal Palmer Adisa. The journal is 200-208 pages, 6×9, flat-spined. Circulation is 500. Sample: $9.

How to Submit: No simultaneous submissions. Responds in 5 months. Pays 2 copies. "We are not currently publishing reviews of books, poetry, essays or otherwise."

$⃞ ◿ FUGUE, Brink Hall, Room 200, University of Idaho, Moscow ID 83844-1102. (208)885-6937. E-mail: Fugue@uidaho.edu. Website: www.uidaho.edu/LS/Eng/Fugue (includes writer's guidelines, names of editors, poetry samples, and cover art). Established 1989. **Managing Editor:** Scott McEachern.

Magazine Needs: *Fugue* is a biannual literary magazine of the University of Idaho. "There are no limits on type of poetry; however, we are not interested in trite or quaint verse." Has published poetry by Robert Wrigley, Phillip Dacey, and Sonia Sanchez. As a sample the editor selected these lines from "The Burned Diary" by Sharon Olds:

> . . . *And when the dawn came up/on the black water of the house, they found it/by the side of her bed, its pages scorched,/a layer of them arched, the corners curled up/like the tips of wings, a messenger/ from the other world, the solitary heart.*

Fugue is up to 150 pages, and perfect-bound. Receives about 400 poems/semester, accepts only 5-12 poems/issue. Press run is 250 plus an online version. Sample: $6.

How to Submit: No previously published poems or simultaneous submissions. Submit with #10 SASE or submission will not be considered. No e-mail or fax submissions. Reads submissions September 1 through May 1 only. Time between acceptance and publication is up to 1 year. "Submissions are reviewed by staff members and chosen with consensus by the editorial board. No major changes are made to a manuscript without authorial approval." Guidelines and upcoming themes available for SASE and on website. Responds in 3 months. Pays at least 1 copy and honorarium. Acquires first North American serial rights.

Advice: "Proper manuscript format and submission etiquette are expected; submissions without proper SASE will not be read or held on file."

◑ FULLOSIA PRESS; THE ROCKAWAY PARK PHILOSOPHICAL SOCIETY, P.O. Box 280, Ronkonkoma NY 11779. Fax: (631)588-9428. E-mail: deanofRPPS@aol.com. Website: http://RPPS_FUL LOSIA_PRESS.tripod.com (includes contact information, bios, archives, upcoming themes, online magazine, guidelines). Established 1971. **Contact:** J.F. Clennan.

Magazine Needs: *Fullosia Press* appears online monthly, presenting news, information, satire, and right-conservative perspective. Wants any style of poetry. "If you have something to say, say it. We consider many different points of view." Does not want "anti-American, anti-Christian." Accepts poetry by children with parental approval. Recently published poetry by J.D. Collins, Thomas Gross, Peter Vetrano, Nathan Whiting, and Rich Kenney. As a sample the editor selected these lines from "The Never Ending Verse" by Thomas Dean:

> Amd we have few/who steeled true/in all the seasons/of disorder

Fullosia Press is published online only. Receives about 50 poems/year, accepts about 40%. Publishes a varied number of poems/issue. Single copy: $5 and SASE—free online. Sample: $5. Subscription: $20/year; free online. Make checks payable to RPPS-Fullosia Press.

How to Submit: Accepts fax, e-mail (in text box), and disk submissions. Cover letter is required. "Electronic submission by disk to address; e-mail preferred. Final submission by disk or e-mail only." Reads submissions when received. Submit seasonal poems 1 month in advance. Time between acceptance and publication varies. "I review all poems: (1) do they say something; (2) is there some thought behind it; (3) is it more than words strung together?" Always comments on rejected poems. Guidelines and upcoming themes available for SASE, by fax, by e-mail, on website, and in publication. Acquires one-time rights. Reviews books and chapbooks of poetry and other magazines/journals. Poets may send books for review consideration to RPPS-Fullosia Press.

Advice: "Say what you have in mind without tripping over your own symbolism. We like poems which are clear, concise, to the point; American traditional heroes; Arthur is nice; American states. Everybody sings about Texas, has anyone written a poem to New Jersey?"

$◻ THE FUNNY PAPER; F/J WRITERS SERVICE, P.O. Box 22557, Kansas City MO 64113-0557. E-mail: felix22557@aol.com. Website: www.angelfire.com/biz/funnypaper (includes guidelines, jokes, descriptive page, and bulletin boards). Established 1985. **Editor:** Felix Fellhauer.

Magazine Needs: *The Funny Paper* appears 4 times/year "to provide readership, help and the opportunity to write for money to budding authors/poets/humorists of all ages." Accepts poetry written by children, ages 8-15. Wants "light verse; space limited; humor always welcome. No tomes, heavy, dismal, trite work, or pornography." As a sample we selected this poem, "Farewell" by Betty R. Cevoli:

> Roughly grasping at my fingers,/They pull at my tee-shirt/My arms scratched as I/clutch them//Bright, sunny orange with/dark hills and valleys/covering their skin.//Roadmaps—promising tender,/juicy, rich flavor—/The last canteloupes of summer.

The Funny Paper is 10 pages, 8½×11, photocopied on colored paper and unbound, includes clip art and cartoons. Receives about 300 poems/year, accepts about 10%. Single copy: $2. Make checks payable to F/J Writers Service.

How to Submit: Submit 1-2 poems at a time. Line length for poetry is 16 lines maximum. Accepts e-mail submissions (include in body of message). "We encourage beginners; handwritten poems OK. Submissions not returned." Seldom comments on rejected poems. Publishes contest theme issues regularly. Guidelines and upcoming themes available for SASE, in publication, or on website. Pays $5-25/published poem and 1 copy. Acquires one-time rights.

Also Offers: Sponsors contests with $100 prize. Guidelines available for SASE or on website.

Advice: "When trying for $100 prize, take us seriously. The competition is fierce."

Ⓝ ◯ ◎ FURROW—THE UNDERGRADUATE LITERARY AND ART REVIEW (Specialized: undergraduates only); THE ORCHARD PRIZE FOR POETRY, UWM Union Box 194, University of Wisconsin-Milwaukee, P.O. Box 413, Milwaukee WI 53201. (414)229-3405. E-mail: furrow@cs d.uwm.edu. Established 1999. **Poetry Editor:** Emily Hall. **Executive Editor:** Heather Berlowitz.

Magazine Needs: *Furrow—The Undergraduate Literary and Art Review* appears 2 times/year. "We simply want to see poetry that does not take for granted any of the prescribed aesthetic functions of a poem. A poem should have a certain felicity of expression and originality but also be sort of dangerous and fun. We want wild associations, pungent images, and layered meanings. For the most part, we are not interested in poetry that reinforces traditional styles or what is fashionable in poetry." Recently published poetry by Erika Mueller, Sarah Schuetze, Mike Krull, Daniel John Frostman, Russ Bickerstaff, and Donald V. Kingsbury. As a sample the editor selected these lines from "Ode to My Period" by Erika Mueller:

> Like ants scurrying to sand/water-proofed doors,/crayoned leaves clattering/wildly toward sewers,/ horsetails whipping/storm-blown shoulders . . ./It will come

Furrow is 45-70 pages, digest-sized, perfect-bound, card stock cover. Receives about 400 poems/year, accepts about 10%. Publishes about 15 poems/issue. Press run is 400 for 25 subscribers of which 5 are libraries, 300 shelf sales; 1 each distributed free to contributors. Single copy: $3; subscription: $6 (2 issues). Sample: $4. Make checks payable to *Furrow*.

How to Submit: Submit 3-5 poems at a time. Accepts simultaneous submissions; no previously published poems. Accepts e-mail and disk submissions. "Please include SASE and cover letter stating school, year in school, brief bio note (no more than 5 sentences), and contact information (address, phone, e-mail)." Reads submissions year round, "although we only publish a spring and a fall issue." Submit seasonal poems 2 months in advance. Time between acceptance and publication is 1-2 months. "Submissions are read by a single editor, acceptances notified upon approval of undergraduate status." Seldom comments on rejected poems. Guidelines available for SASE. Responds in 2 months. Pays 1 contributors copy/accepted piece. Acquires one-time rights. Reviews books and chapbooks of poetry and other magazines in 3,000 words maximum, single book format. Poets may send books for review consideration to Brett Kell.

Advice: "We would like to think that our poets at least have the decency to want to change poetry and make it their own."

$◻ FUTURES MAGAZINE, 3039 38th Ave. S, Minneapolis MN 55406-2142. (612)724-4023. E-mail: futrpoet@mwsc.edu. Website: www.futuresforstorylovers.com (includes writer's guidelines, names of editors, artwork and illustrations, greeting cards for writers, cover art, contests, etc.). Established 1997.
Editor: Dr. Patricia Donaher.
Magazine Needs: *Futures* is a quarterly magazine containing short stories, poetry, artwork and "inspiration for artists of all kinds." "We want creative people with the fire to fly!" Do not want to receive gratuitous profanity or pornography. Has published poetry by R.C. Hildebrandt, Simon Perchik, Kristin Masterson, John Bennett, Karen Davenport, and Ally Reith. *Futures* is 90 pages, 8½×11, with 4-color semigloss cover, includes art and ads. Receives about 250 poems/year, accepts about 10%. Publishes 5-10 poems/issue. Press run is 2,000. Single copy: $10.95; subscription: $52. Sample (including guidelines): $5.
How to Submit: Submit up to 5 poems at a time. Maximum length per poem is 1½ pages. Accepts previously published poems. Accepts *only* e-mail submissions (in text box). On subject line, write "Poetry submissions." Double space between stanzas. "We are asking for submissions via e-mail because our writers, artists, and staff are all over the world. If you need me to make an exception, write and tell me why you cannot follow our guidelines." Cover letter preferred. Reads submissions January 31 through October 31 only. Submit seasonal poems 6 months in advance. Time between acceptance and publication is up to 6 months. Often comments on rejected poems. "If you want to assure a critique of your work, you may enclose a SASE and $3 with your request." Occasionally publishes theme issues. Guidelines available on website. Responds in 6 weeks. Pays up to $50 "for best of the year."
Also Offers: There are 2 Publisher's Choice Awards per issue (not necessarily for poetry). Winners receive $25 plus an award certificate and "their caricature done by our cartoonist James Oddie."
Advice: "If it is flat on the page, it is not a poem. You have to make an impact in few words. In poetry the line is really all—like a commercial—you have to make an emotional statement in a flash."

⊕ ◎ GAIRM; GAIRM PUBLICATIONS (Specialized: ethnic; foreign language, Scottish Gaelic), 29 Waterloo St., Glasgow G2 6BZ Scotland. Phone/fax: (0141)221-1971. Established 1952.
Editor: Derick Thomson.
Magazine Needs: *Gairm* is a quarterly that uses modern/cosmopolitan and traditional/folk verse in Scottish Gaelic only. Has published the work of all significant Scottish Gaelic poets, and much poetry translated from European languages. An anthology of such translations, *European Poetry in Gaelic*, is available for £7.50 or $15. A recent collection is Derick Thomson's *Meall Garbh/The Rugged Mountain*, £7.50 or $15. *Gairm* is 96 pages, digest-sized, flat-spined with coated card cover. Circulation is 1,000. Sample: $3.50.
How to Submit: Submit 3-4 poems at a time, Gaelic only. Staff reviews books of poetry in 500-700 words, single format; 100 words, multi-book format. Occasionally invites reviews. Send books for review consideration. All of the publications of the press are in Scottish Gaelic. Catalog available.

ℕ ♥ GARGOYLE MAGAZINE; PAYCOCK PRESS, P.O. Box 6216, Arlington VA 22206-0216. (202)234-3287. E-mail: atticus@atticusbooks.com. Website: www.atticusbooks.com. Established 1976.
Co-Editors: Richard Peabody and Lucinda Ebersole.
Magazine Needs: *Gargoyle Magazine* appears annually "to publish the best literary magazine we can. We generally run short one page poems. We like wit, imagery, killer lines. Not big on rhymed verse or language school." Has published poetry by Nicole Blackman, Wayne Koestenbaum and Jeremy Reed. As a sample the editors selected these lines from "Abortion Elegy: What I Know About Her" by Rose Solari:

> *There are times I can see her face as if/she were here, as if she had lived—hair darker/than yours or mine, your cheeks, my mouth./She stands over my bed as she did almost/a full year before we knew of her, or runs/through the living room, both hands spread,/chasing a shadow.*

Gargoyle is 365 pages, 6×9, offset printed and perfect-bound, color cover, includes photos, artwork and ads. Accept approximately 10% of the poems received each year. Press run is 3,000. Subscription: $20 for 2; $25 to institutions. Sample: $10. Make checks payable to Atticus Books. "We have international distribution through Bernhard DeBier, Airlift Book Co. and Perigo Distribution."

How to Submit: Submit 5 poems at a time. Accepts simultaneous submissions. Accepts e-mail and disk submissions in Microsoft Word or WordPerfect format. Reads submissions Memorial Day through Labor Day only. Time between acceptance and publication is 5 months. Poems are circulated to an editorial board. "The two editors make some concessions but generally concur." Often comments on rejected poems. Responds in 2 months. Always sends prepublication galleys. Pays 1 copy and ½ off additional copies. Acquires first rights

Book/Chapbook Needs & How to Submit: Paycock Press has published 9-10 books since 1976 and are not currently seeking mss.

[N] ⊘ GAZELLE PUBLICATIONS, 11650 Red Bud Trail, Berrien Springs MI 49106. Phone: (616)471-4717 or (800)650-5076 (orders only). Website: www.gazellepublications.com (includes contact information, biographical notes, catalog). Established 1976. **Editor:** Ted Wade. Publisher for home schools and compatible markets including books of verse for children. Not currently considering unsolicited manuscripts.

⊘ GECKO, P.O. Box 6492, Destin FL 32550. E-mail: geckogalpoet@hotmail.com. Established 1998. **Editor:** Rebecca Lu Kiernan.

Magazine Needs & How to Submit: "Due to the overwhelming response of *Poet's Market* readers and personal projects of the editor, we are currenly closed to unsolicited manuscripts. We hope to change this in the future when an assistant will assume some of the editor's duties."

◎ ⊘ GENERATOR; GENERATOR PRESS (Specialized: visual poetry), 3503 Virginia Ave., Cleveland OH 44109. (216)351-9406. E-mail: generatorpress@msn.com. Established 1987. **Editor:** John Byrum.

Magazine Needs: *Generator* is an annual magazine "devoted to the presentation of all types of experimental poetry, focusing on language poetry and 'concrete' or visual poetic modes."

Book/Chapbook Needs: Generator Press also publishes the Generator Press chapbook series. Approximately 1 new title/year.

How to Submit: Currently not accepting unsolicited manuscripts for either the magazine or chapbook publication.

⊘ THE GENTLE SURVIVALIST (Specialized: ethnic, nature, inspirational), P.O. Box 4004, St. George UT 84770. E-mail: gentle-survivalist@rocketmail.com. Website: www.infowest.com/gentle/ (includes guidelines as well as contact and subscription information). Established 1991. **Editor/Publisher:** Laura Martin-Bühler.

Magazine Needs: *The Gentle Survivalist* is a quarterly newsletter of "harmony—timeless truths and wisdom balanced with scientific developments for Native Americans and all those who believe in the Great Creator." Wants poetry that is "positive, inspirational, on survival of body and spirit, also man's interconnectedness with God and all His creations. Nothing sexually oriented, occult, negative, or depressing." Accepts poetry written by children. Has published poetry by Keith Moore and C.S. Churchman. The issues we have received discuss environmental illness, Eastern medicine, and list common household toxins to avoid. They also offer money-saving tips and ideas on writing a personal history. "We print four poems average per issue." Press run is 200. Subscription: $22. Sample: $5.

How to Submit: Submit 4 poems at a time. Accepts previously published poems and simultaneous submissions. No e-mail submissions. Cover letter required; "just a note would be fine. I find noteless submissions too impersonal." Time between acceptance and publication is up to 4 months. For written evaluation and editing, send $5. "Written evaluation money is returned if writing is inappropriate or rejected. Evaluation and editing does not guarantee writing will be published." Guidelines are available for SASE and on website; no guidelines mailed without sample request and $5. "Folks need to see what they are getting into and I need to weed out frivolous submitters." Responds within 2 months. Does not return poetry. Pays 1 copy.

Also Offers: Sponsors annual contest. Awards a 1-year subscription to the winner. Winner announced in Spring issue.

Advice: "To succeed, one must not seek supporters, but seek to know whom to support. *The Gentle Survivalist* receives a great deal of poetry that is too general in nature. We seek poems of inspiration about God, Man, and our interconnectedness with all living."

GERONIMO REVIEW; MAOMAO PRESS, Box 88, San Geronimo CA 94963-0088. E-mail: geronimoreview@yahoo.com. Website: http://home.att.net/~geronimoreview (includes poetry, reviews, essays). Established 1998. **Editor:** bassetti. **Factotumus Maximus:** Mark C. Peery. **Factotumus Minimus:** Mark Vronin.

Magazine Needs: At this time *geronimo review* appears randomly as a zine. Wants "only the freshest, most original of any form or subject. Must have sight, sound, sense; or imagery, music, and meaning." Does not want "the boring, the earnest, the lifeless—poetry currently in style (i.e. the dead end non sequitur)." Recently published poetry by Mark C. Peery, dada rambass, Albert de Silver, E.E. Glazer, geronimo bassetti, and Élan B. Yergmoul. As a sample the editor selected these lines from "Oily Mourning" by Élan Batieri Yergmoul:

> OILY MOURNING/INSTILL EMBED//bear giddup/ice head/tomb eyes/elf

How to Submit: Submit 3 poems at a time. Line length for poetry is 100 maximum (or the length demanded by the poem). Accepts simultaneous submissions; no previously published poems. Accepts submissions by e-mail (in text box) or on disk. Reads submissions all year. Time between acceptance and publication is 2 weeks. Poems are "read by Wired Writers Workshop (of San Rafael); final decision made by Geronimo Bassetti and Mark C. Peery." Seldom comments on rejections and does not return submissions. Occasionally publishes theme issues. Upcoming themes and guidelines available on website. Responds in 3 weeks. Pays "eternal fame" and 2 contributor's copies "when printing occurs." Acquires all rights; returns to poet "on request." Reviews books and chapbooks of poetry and other magazines in 250-500 words, single book format. Poets may send books for review consideration to *geronimo review*.

Book/Chapbook Needs & How to Submit: MaoMao Press will publish essays on and reviews of poetry in the future. "Not presently accepting book submissions—watch our website."

Also Offers: "We are currently calling for submissions of essays by poets (only) on Shakespeare's sonnets, 1,000-1,500 words."

Advice: "Don't be Susan Wheeler. Be in the tradition of Yeats, Frost, Carroll, Stevens, and be really original and inspire strong reactions."

GERTRUDE: A JOURNAL OF VOICE & VISION (Specialized: gay/lesbian/bisexual/transgender), P.O. Box 270814, Fort Collins CO 80527-0814. E-mail: editor@gertrudejournal.com. Website: www.gertrudejournal.com (includes excerpts from previous issues, writer/artist guidelines, contact and subscription information, bios, archives, contest information, links, editorial policy). Established 1998. **Founding Editor:** Eric Delehoy. **Art Editor:** Ronda Stone.

● *Gertrude* will be relocating to Portland, OR, in July/August 2002. Check website for updated information.

Magazine Needs: "Published two times/year, *Gertrude* is a literary journal showcasing the voices and visions of the gay, lesbian, bisexual, transgendered and straight-supportive community. Provides a positive, nonpornographic forum. Open to all forms and subjects, we'd like to see positive poetry." Does not want "bitter ex-love poetry, five-minute poetry, or Hallmark verse; steer clear of work that portrays gays as victims." Has published poetry by Deanna Kern Ludwin, Jannell Moon, Richard Tayson, Jennifer Perrine, Noah Tysick, and Francisco Aragón. As a sample the editor selected these lines from "leap the gate" by Stephen Kopel:

> the moon and I/tip-toe your slumber/and I wonder/can you tell me, mother,/tell me if I'm in your satin dream

Gertrude is 64 pages, digest-sized, professionally printed and perfect-bound with glossy cardstock cover, includes b&w art/photography. Receives about 200 poems/year, accepts up to 10%. Press run is 500 for about 100 subscribers, 250 shelf sales; 50 distributed free to gay/lesbian/bisexual/transgender organizations. Single copy: $5; subscription: $10/year. Sample: $5.

How to Submit: Submit 3-5 poems at a time. No previously published poems. Accepts simultaneous submissions with notification. Accepts e-mail submissions (as attachment). Cover letter preferred. Include previous publication credits, short bio, and SASE. Time between acceptance and publication is up to 2 months. Poems are circulated to an editorial board. "Three editors apply initial rating system to determine final selections. Final selections are re-read by all editors." Seldom comments on rejected poems. Guidelines available for SASE, by e-mail, in publication, and on website. Responds in 4 months. Pays 1 copy plus discount on additional copies. All rights revert to authors upon publication.

Also Offers: Sponsors Fall Poetry Contest. Also invites contributors to an annual contributors' reading.

Advice: "Write for yourself, not for publication. In this you find your voice and produce your best."

$ ⃞ THE GETTYSBURG REVIEW, Gettysburg College, Gettysburg PA 17325. (717)337-6770. Fax: (717)337-6775. Website: www.gettysburgreview.com (includes guidelines, contact and subscription information, editorial policy, bios, links, and forms, and most importantly, reprints of works published in recent issues. Works—poems, stories, essays—appear in their entirety). Established 1988. **Editor:** Peter Stitt.

> • Work appearing in *The Gettysburg Review* has been frequently included in *The Best American Poetry* and *Pushcart Prize* anthologies. As for the editor, Peter Stitt won the first PEN/Nora Magid Award for Editorial Excellence.

Magazine Needs: *The Gettysburg Review* is a multidisciplinary literary quarterly considering "well-written poems of all kinds." Has published poetry by Rita Dove, Beckian Fritz Goldberg, Charles Wright, Michelle Boisseau, Pattiann Rogers, Mark Doty, and Charles Simic. As a sample, the editor selected these lines from "The Second Act" by Michael Teis:

> One time I thought the things I love would fit inside a hatbox,/inside a quintet as they rounded a difficult corner,//inside a t-shirt or a sentence./They'd fit inside a station wagon then drive around for hours//just hoping for radio stations, hands like jibes out the windows.

Accepts 1-2% of submissions received. Press run is 4,500 for 2,700 subscriptions. Subscription: $24/year. Sample: $7.

How to Submit: Submit 3-5 poems at a time, with SASE. No previously published poems. Simultaneous submissions OK. Cover letter preferred. Reads submissions September through May only. Occasionally publishes theme issues. Response times can be slow during heavy submission periods, especially in the late fall. Pays 1 copy plus subscription plus $2/line. Essay-reviews are featured in each issue. Poets may send books for review consideration.

⊕ $ ⃝ GINNINDERRA PRESS, P.O. Box 53, Charnwood ACT 2615 Australia. E-mail: smgp@cyb erone.com.au. Website: www.ginninderrapress.com.au (includes press history, guidelines, catalog, bios, links, editorial policy, book extracts, as well as contact and ordering information). Established 1996. **Publisher:** Stephen Matthews.

Book/Chapbook Needs: Ginninderra Press works "to give publishing opportunities to new writers." Has published poetry by Alan Gould and Geoff Page. Books are usually up to 56 pages, A5, laser printed and saddle-stapled with board cover, sometimes includes art/graphics.

How to Submit: Query first, with a few sample poems and cover letter with brief bio and publication credits. Accepts previously published poems; no simultaneous submissions. No fax or e-mail submissions. Time between acceptance and publication is 2 months. Seldom comments on rejected poems. Responds to queries in 1 week; to mss in 2 months. Pays royalties of 12½%.

⃝ GLASS TESSERACT, P. O. Box 702, Agoura Hills CA 91376. E-mail: editor@glasstesseract.com. Website: www.glasstesseract.com (includes rotating selections, guidelines, contact and subscription information, and links). Established 2001. **Editor:** Michael Chester.

Magazine Needs: *Glass Tesseract* appears once or twice a year and publishes poems and short stories. "Our purpose is to help bring works of art into the world. Our interests are eclectic." Wants poetry that is "rich in imagery, emotion, ideas, or the sound of language. We are open to all forms from rhyming sonnets to unrhymed, open-ended anything—so long as we feel that the poem is a work of art. We don't want sentimental, moralizing, devotional, cute, coy, or happy face poems." Recently published poetry by Alan Catlin, Tim Cumming, Carol Frith, and Mario Susko. As a sample the editor selected these lines from "A Sighting of Several Ghosts" by Carl Bramblett:

> the dead like to feel my hot breath on the glass,/and I peer through the blur, stars diffusing./The dead speak with great effort. Their voices/amplify the dull, electric prattle of streetlights,/blue tongues nostalgic, regretful . . .

Glass Tesseract is 48-96 pgs., digest-sized, laser-printed, saddle-stapled, cover with art, some issues with b&w line art illustrations. Publishes about 12-20 poems/issue. Single copy: $5; subscription for 2 consecutive issues: $9. Sample: $4. Special edition (spiral comb-bound, linen paper, frontispiece): $12 per copy. Make checks payable to *Glass Tesseract*.

How to Submit: Submit up to 10 poems at a time. Accepts previously published poems and simultaneous submissions. Accepts e-mail submissions; no fax or disk submissions. Cover letter is optional. Include SASE for hard copy submissions. Reads submissions year round. Time between acceptance and hardcopy publication is up to 1 year. Website publication within 2 weeks (not guaranteed to all). "Poems are always read by the editor and are often reviewed by one or more consulting editors. We are particularly alert to strong poems that differ from our own preferred styles." Always comments on rejected poems. Guidelines are available in magazine, for SASE, by e-mail, or on website. Responds in up to 3 months. Sometimes sends prepublication galleys. Pays 3 copies—2 trade and 1 special edition. Acquires one-time rights which revert to author upon publication.

Advice: "Steep yourself in the best enduring poetry found in anthologies or taught in literature classes—then go your own way. Experiment until you find your voice. Keep reading other poets in the magazines that interest you for your own poems."

DAVID R. GODINE, PUBLISHER, 9 Hamilton Place, Boston MA 02108. Website: www.godine. com (includes titles and ordering information). "Our poetry program is completely filled through 2004, and we do not accept any unsolicited materials."

GOOD FOOT, P.O. Box 681, Murray Hill Stn., New York NY 10156. E-mail: submissions@goo dfootmagazine.com. Website: www.goodfootmagazine.com (includes submission guidelines, subscription info, sample poems from previous issues). Established 2000. **Contact:** Matthew Thorburn, editor (submissions). **Editors:** Amanda Lea Johnson, Katherine Sarkis, Carmine Simmons, Matthew Thorburn.
Magazine Needs: *Good Foot* appears biannually and publishes "an eclectic mix of the finest poetry written by established and emerging poets. We welcome a wide cross-section of work without restriction: both free and formal, experimental and traditional, original and in translation, all styles and schools. Our only standard for selection is the quality of the work." Recently published poetry by Rachel Hadas, Matthea Harvey, David Lehman, David Trinidad, Paul Violi, and Diane Wakoski. *Good Foot* is about 100 pages, 7×8.5, professionally offset-printed, perfect-bound, 2-3 color matte card cover, with b&w photos/artwork and back page ads. Receives about 400 poems/year, accepts about 15%. Publishes about 50 poems/issue. Press run is 500. Single copy: $8; subscription: $14. Sample: $8. Make checks payable to *Good Foot Magazine*.
How to Submit: Submit 3 poems at a time. Accepts simultaneous submissions ("with timely notice of acceptance elsewhere"); no previously published poems. Accepts e-mail and disk submissions; no fax submissions. Cover letter is preferred. "Include brief bio in cover letter. Include SASE. Electric submissions accepted, with poems sent as an e-mail attachment, preferably in .rtf or .pdf format." Reads submissions year round. Submit seasonal poems 6 months in advance. Time between acceptance and publication is 6 months. Poems are circulated to an editorial board ("read by all four editors"). Seldom comments on rejected poems. Guidelines available on website. Responds in up to 2 months. Sometimes sends prepublication galleys. Pays 1 contributor's copy. Acquires first North American serial rights. Reviews books of poetry ("reviews not included in every issue but upcoming issues may include them"). Poets may send books for review consideration to the attention of Matthew Thorburn.

GOOSE LANE EDITIONS (Specialized: regional, Canada), 469 King St., Fredericton, New Brunswick E3B 1E5 Canada. (506)450-4251. Established 1956. **Editorial Director:** L. Boone.
Book/Chapbook Needs: Goose Lane is a small literary press publishing Canadian fiction, poetry, and nonfiction. Writers should be advised that Goose Lane considers mss by Canadian poets only. Receives approximately 400 mss/year, publishes 10-15 books yearly, 3 of these being poetry collections. Has published *Conversations* by Herménégilde Chiasson and *Weathers: Poems New and Selected* by Douglas Lockhead.
How to Submit: Not currently reading unsolicited submissions. "Call to inquire whether we are reading submissions." Guidelines available for SASE. Always sends prepublication galleys. Authors may receive royalty of up to 10% of retail sale price on all copies sold. Copies available to author at 40% discount.
Advice: "Many of the poems in a manuscript accepted for publication will have been previously published in literary journals such as *The Fiddlehead, The Dalhousie Review, The Malahat Review,* and the like."

GOTHIC CHAPBOOK SERIES; GOTHIC PRESS (Specialized: supernatural horror), 1701 Lobdell Ave. No. 32, Baton Rouge LA 70806-8242. E-mail: gothicpt12@aol.com. Website: www.gothicpress.com (includes history of Gothic Press, online catalog). Established 1979. **Publisher:** Gary W. Crawford. Member: Science Fiction Poetry Association, Horror Writers Association.
Book/Chapbook Needs & How to Submit: Gothic Chapbook Series publishes poetry with supernatural horror elements. Wants any style or approach. Recently published poetry by Bruce Boston and Joey Froehlich. As a sample the editor selected these lines from "Future Past: An Exercise in Horror" by Bruce Boston:

> *Assume tomorrow has already come and gone/and you now inhabit no more than a string of/damaged*
> *yesterdays haunted by the ghostly/penumbra of your abridged anticipations,/a shadow corridor where*
> *all perspectives/are reduced to parameters of expiration.*

Gothic Press publishes 1-2 chapbooks/year. Chapbooks are usually offset-printed/photocopied, saddle-stapled, card stock cover, with b&w drawings (not always an open market; query first before submitting anything). Responds to queries in 2 weeks; to mss in 1 week. Pays royalties of 10% maximum and 20 author's copies (out of a press run of 100). Order sample chapbooks by sending $6 to Gary W. Crawford.
Advice: "Know horror poetry well."

N ⊘ GRAFFITI RAG; GRAFFITI RAG POETRY AWARD; HELEN YOUNG/LINDA ASH-EAR PRIZE, 304 Varick St., Jersey City NJ 07302. E-mail: hayan.charara@worldnet.att.net. Established 1995. **Editor:** Hayan Charara. **Co-Editor:** Erik Fahren Kopf. **West Coast Editor:** Bayla Winters.
Magazine Needs: *Graffiti Rag*, published annually, is a "poetry journal that seeks to publish work of well-known and gifted unknown poets on the urban experience." Wants "poetry of the highest quality that brings a unique perspective on the shifting and limitless themes of urban life—economic, ethnic, intellectual, political, sexual." Has published poetry by Khaled Mattawa, Catherine Bowman, Wang Ping, Jim Daniels and Chase Twichell. As a sample the editor selected these lines from "A Last Look Back" by Chase Twichell:

> So strange, to inhabit a space/and then leave it vacant, standing open.//Each change in me is a stone
> step/beneath the blur of snow./In spring the sharp edges cut through.//When I look back, I see my
> former selves,/numerous as the trees.

Graffiti Rag is approximately 96 pages, 6×9, perfect-bound, professionally printed with a colored matte cover. Receives about 900-1,500 poems/year, accepts less than 10%. Press run is 750, 400 shelf sales. Single copy: $9.95; subscription: $9.95 plus $1.50 p&h. Sample issue: $7.95 plus $1.50 p&h.
How to Submit: Submit 3-5 poems at a time. No previously published poems or simultaneous submissions. Cover letter preferred. Time between acceptance and publication varies. Poems are circulated to an editorial board. "Guest editor (usually poets) assist in editorial process. Final decisions are made by main editor, Charara." Often comments on rejected poems. Send SASE for guidelines. Responds in 4 months. Pays 1 copy. Acquires first North American serial or one-time rights.
Also Offers: Sponsors the annual Graffiti Rag Poetry Award. Submit 3-5 unpublished poems from February 1 through June 30. Enclose reading fee of $10 (check or money order) and a SASE. Winning poet is featured in the anthology and receives cash award of $1,000. Also sponsors the Helen Young/Linda Ashear Prize for poets between the ages 14-19. No entry fee. Submit 3-5 poems with SASE. 1st Prize: $250 plus publication; 2nd Prize: $150 plus publication; and 3rd Prize: $100 plus publication.
Advice: "Read literary journals to better gauge their 'likes.' "

♣ ▼ $⊘ GRAIN; SHORT GRAIN CONTEST, P.O. Box 67, Saskatoon, Saskatchewan S7K 3K1 Canada. (306)244-2828. Fax: (306)244-0255. E-mail: grain.mag@sk.sympatico.ca. Website: www.sk writer.com (includes guidelines, sample work, contest information, archives, catalog, links, contact and subscription information/online ordering, and editorial policy). Established 1973. **Editor:** Elizabeth Philips. **Poetry Editor:** Séan Virgo.
● Grain was voted Saskatchewan Magazine of the Year, Western Magazine Awards 2001.
Magazine Needs: "*Grain*, a literary quarterly, strives for artistic excellence and seeks poetry that is well-crafted, imaginatively stimulating, distinctly original." Has published poetry by Ken Howe, Elizabeth Ukrainetz, Hilary Clark, Charles Noble, Barry Dempster, and Karen Solie. *Grain* is 128-144 pages, digest-sized, professionally printed. Press run is 1,300 for 1,100 subscribers of which 100 are libraries. Receives about 1,200 submissions of poetry/year, accepts 80-140 poems. Subscription: $26.95/1 year, $39.95/2 years, for international subscriptions provide $4 postage for 1 year, $8 postage for 2 years in US dollars. Sample: $7.95 plus IRC.
How to Submit: Submit up to 8 poems, typed on 8½×11 paper, single-spaced, one side only. No previously published poems or simultaneous submissions. Cover letter required. Include "the number of poems submitted, address (with postal or zip code), and phone number. Submissions accepted by regular post only. No e-mail submissions." Reads submissions August through May only. Guidelines available for SASE (or SAE and IRC), by e-mail, in publication, or on website. Responds in 3 months. "Response by e-mail if address provided (ms recycled). Then IRCs or SASE not required." Pays over $40/page (up to five pages) or a maximum of $175 plus 2 copies. Acquires first North American serial rights.
Also Offers: Holds an annual Short Grain Contest. Entries are either prose poems (a lyric poem written as a prose paragraph or paragraphs in 500 words or less), dramatic monologues, or postcard stories (also 500 words or less). Also sponsors the Long Grain of Truth contest for nonfiction and creative prose (5,000 words or less). "Twelve prizes of $500; three equal prizes in each category." Entry fee of $22 allows up to two entries in the same category, and includes a 1-year subscription. Additional entries are $5 each. "U.S. and international entrants send fees in U.S. funds ($22 for two entries in one category plus $4 to help cover postage)." Entries are normally accepted between September 1 and January 31.

Advice: "Only work of the highest literary quality is accepted. Read several back issues."

◐ **GRASSLANDS REVIEW**, P.O. Box 626, Berea OH 44017. E-mail: GLReview@aol.com. Website: http://hometown.aol.com/GLReview/prof/index.htm (includes guidelines, sample poems,and contest information). Established 1989. **Editor:** Laura B. Kennelly.

Magazine Needs: *Grasslands Review* is a biannual magazine "to encourage beginning writers and to give adult creative writing students experience in editing fiction and poetry; using any type of poetry; shorter poems stand best chance." Has published poetry by Robert Wynne, Lamar Thomas, Deborah Byrne, Linda Roth, Mae Gibson, Ryan G. Van Cleave, and Charles Grosel. As a sample the editor selected these lines from "Geometry" by Robert Wynne:

> *I could tell Mr. Shuster had never been loved,/by the parallelograms he drew on the board,/Sides*
> *bending in their longing for each other.*

Grasslands Review is 80 pages, digest-sized, professionally printed, photocopied, saddle-stapled with card cover. Accepts 30-50 of 600 submissions received. Press run is 200. Subscription (2 issues): $10 for individuals, $20 institutions. Sample: $5 for older issues, $6 for more recent.

How to Submit: Submit only during October and March, no more than 5 poems at a time. No previously published poems or simultaneous submissions. No e-mail submissions. Short cover letter preferred. Send #10 SASE for response. Editor comments on submissions "sometimes." Responds in 4 months. Sometimes sends prepublication galleys. Pays 1 copy.

Also Offers: Sponsors annual Editors' Prize Contest. Prize: $100 and publication. Deadline: April 30. Entry fee: $12 for 5 poems, $1/poem extra for entries over 5 poems. Entry fee includes 1-year subscription. Send SASE for reply.

$◐ GRAVITY PRESSES; NOW HERE NOWHERE, 27030 Havelock, Dearborn Heights MI 48127-3639. (313)563-3663. E-mail: barney@gravitypresses.com. Website: www.gravitypresses.com (includes contact information, guidelines, and subscription information). Established 1998. **Publisher:** Michael J. Barney. **Editor-in-Chief:** Paul Kingston.

Magazine Needs: *Now Here Nowhere* is a quarterly magazine publishing "the best poetry and short prose (fiction and nonfiction) that we can find. We are primarily a poetry magazine but will publish one to two prose pieces per issue. We have no restrictions or requirements as to form, content, length, etc. We publish what we like and what we think is good. No greeting card verse or song lyrics (unless by Leonard Cohen and Tom Waits)." Has published poetry by Simon Perchik, Taylor Graham, Richard Kostelanetz, and Alan Catlin. As a sample the editor selected these lines from "Communication" by Patti Couture:

> *Sometimes my words seemed carved/with the dull clumsy chisels barely scratching/the granite air/I*
> *long for sharp clean edges/to cut precisely/deep through the silent stone*

Now Here Nowhere is 48-52 pages, 6¾×8½, offset-printed or photocopied, saddle-stapled with glossy card cover, includes b&w illustrations. Receives about 500 poems/year, accepts up to 30%. Press run is 100 for 10 subscribers, 85 shelf sales. Single copy: $5.50; subscription: $20/4 issues. Sample: $6. Make checks payable to Gravity Presses.

How to Submit: Submit 5 poems at a time. Accepts simultaneous submissions; no previously published poems. Accepts disk submissions. "International submissions only will be accepted in ASCII format via e-mail." Cover letter preferred. "SASEs should accompany all submissions." Time between acceptance and publication is up to 12 months. Poems are circulated to an editorial board. "All work is seen by at least two editors (of four) and must be accepted by at least two editors. Controversies are settled by the editor-in-chief with no appeals." Seldom comments on rejected poems. Publishes theme issues occasionally. Guidelines and upcoming themes available for SASE. Responds in 6 months. Sometimes sends prepublication galleys. Pays $3-5/issue plus 1 copy. Acquires first North American serial rights.

Book/Chapbook Needs & How to Submit: Gravity Presses is currently not accepting unsolicited mss.

Advice: "The only advice we have for beginners is to write well and submit fearlessly and unrelentingly."

⧆ ♉ ◎ **GRAYWOLF PRESS**, 2402 University Ave., Suite 203, Saint Paul MN 55114. E-mail: wolves@graywolfpress.org (for book catalog requests only). Website: www.graywolfpress.org. Established 1974. **Contact:** Editorial Department.

• Poetry published by Graywolf Press has been included in the 2002 *Pushcart Prize* anthology.

Book/Chapbook Needs: Graywolf Press does not read unsolicited mss. Considers mss *only* by poets widely published in journals of merit. Has published poetry by Jane Kenyon, David Rivard, Vijay Seshadri, John Haines, Eamon Grennan, Tess Gallagher, Tony Hoagland, William Stafford, Linda Gregg, Carl Phillips, and Dana Gioia. Sometimes sends prepublication galleys. No e-mail submissions or queries.

GREEN BEAN PRESS, P.O. Box 237, Canal Street Station, New York NY 10013. Phone/fax: (718)302-1955. E-mail: gbpress@earthlink.net. Website: www.greenbeanpress.com (includes guidelines, contact information, bios, catalog, links, editorial policy). Established 1993. **Editor:** Ian Griffin.

Book/Chapbook Needs: Green Bean Press publishes 6-8 chapbooks and 2-4 full-length books/year. Chapbooks are usually 20-30 pages, priced $3-5 occasional graphics; cover art sometimes provided by author, other times by publisher." Average press run is 125, pays 10 copies and 10% of list price royalty. Full-length books can range from 78-300 pages, usually 5½×8½, list prices $10-16, catalog available upon request. Average press run is 600. Has published *Long Live the 2 of Spades*, by Daniel Crocker and *North Beach Revisited*, by A.D. Winans.

How to Submit: No unsolicited mss are read for full-length books. For chapbooks query first, with 5-10 sample poems and cover letter with brief bio and publication credits by mail, fax, or e-mail. "Not the entire manuscript, please." E-mail submissions preferred in attached RTF file. Responds to queries and mss in 1 month. Pays 35% author's copies out of a press run of 100-125.

GREEN HILLS LITERARY LANTERN, Truman State University, Division of Language & Literature, Kirksville MO 63501. (660)785-4513. E-mail: jksmith@grm.net or jbeneven@truman.edu. **Co-editors:** Joe Benevento (poetry) and Jack Smith (fiction).

Magazine Needs: *Green Hills Literary Lantern*, an annual journal of Truman State University, is open to short fiction and poetry of "exceptional quality." Wants "the best poetry, in any style, preferably understandable. There are no restrictions on subject matter, though pornography and gratuitous violence will not be accepted. Obscurity for its own sake is also frowned upon. Both free and formal verse forms are fine, though we publish more free verse overall. No haiku, limericks, or anything over two pages." Has published poetry by Jim Thomas, Charles Harper Webb, Francine Tolf, and Margeurite Scott. As a sample the editor selected these lines from "I Take Comfort in Golf" by Julie Lechevsky:

> Men like to move on to the next hole./It's like the Stations of the Cross./One does not dwell forever/on the agony in the garden.

Green Hills Literary Lantern is 200-300 pages, 6×9, professionally printed and perfect-bound with glossy, 4-color cover. Receives work by more than 200 poets/year and publishes about 10% of the poets submitting—less than 10% of all poetry received. Press run is 500. Sample: $7.

How to Submit: Send fiction to Jack Smith, *GHLL*, P.O. Box 375, Trenton MO 64683 and poetry to Joe Benevento, *GHLL*, Truman State University, Division of Language & Literature, Kirksville MO 63501. Submit 3-7 poems at a time, typed, 1 poem/page. Accepts simultaneous submissions but not preferred; no previously published poems. No fax or e-mail submissions. Cover letter with list of publications preferred. Often comments on rejected poems. Guidelines available for SASE or by e-mail. Responds within 4 months. Always sends prepublication galleys. Pays 2 copies. Acquires one-time rights.

Advice: "Read the best poetry and be willing to learn from what you encounter. A genuine attempt is made to publish the best poems available, no matter who the writer. First time poets, well-established poets, and those in-between, all can and have found a place in the *Green Hills Literary Lantern*. We try to supply feedback, particularly to those we seek to encourage."

GREEN MOUNTAINS REVIEW, Johnson State College, Johnson VT 05656. (802)635-1350. Fax: (802)635-1294. E-mail: gmr@badger.jsc.vsc.edu. Established 1975. **Poetry Editor:** Neil Shepard.

• Poetry published in *Green Mountains Review* has been selected for inclusion in *The Best American Poetry* (1997 and 1999) and the 1998 *Pushcart Prize* anthology.

Magazine Needs: *Green Mountains Review* appears twice/year and includes poetry (and other writing) by well-known authors and promising newcomers. Has published poetry by Carol Forest, Sharon Olds, Carl Phillips, David St. John, and David Wojahn. *Green Mountains Review* is digest-sized, flat-spined, 150-200 pages. Of 3,000 submissions they publish 30 authors. Press run is 1,800 for 200 subscribers of which 30 are libraries. Subscription: $14/year. Sample back issue: $5, current issue $8.50.

How to Submit: Submit no more than 5 poems at a time. Accepts simultaneous submissions. Reads submissions September 1 through March 1 only. Editor sometimes comments on rejection slip. Publishes theme issues. Guidelines and upcoming themes are available for SASE. Responds in up to 6 months. Pays 2 copies plus 1-year subscription. Acquires first North American serial rights. Send books for review consideration.

GREENHOUSE REVIEW PRESS, 3965 Bonny Doon Rd., Santa Cruz CA 95060. Established 1975. Publishes a series of poetry chapbooks and broadsides. "Unsolicited mss are not accepted."

GREEN'S MAGAZINE, P.O. Box 3236, Regina, Saskatchewan S4P 3H1 Canada. Established 1972. **Editor:** David Green.

Magazine Needs: *Green's Magazine* is a literary quarterly with a balanced diet of short fiction and poetry. Publishes "free/blank verse examining emotions or situations." Does not want greeting card jingles or pale imitations of the masters. Accepts poetry written by children. Has published poetry by Robert L. Tener, B.Z. Niditch, Nannette Swift Melcher, Nancy-Lou Patterson, Giovanni Malito, and Josh Auerbach. As a sample we selected these lines from "The Fifth Freedom" by Warren Keith Wright:

> *Cleanse and restore the hard heart of my enemy./Show that the table prepared seats many./Reveal that the highway leads in two directions./Unscroll a sky where even the clouds have been set free.*

Green's is 96 pages, digest-sized, typeset on buff stock with line drawings, matte card cover, saddle-stapled. Press run is 300. Subscription: $15. Sample: $5.

How to Submit: Submit 4-6 poems at a time. Prefers typescript, complete originals. No simultaneous submissions. "If © used, poet must give permission to use and state clearly the work is unpublished." Time between acceptance and publication is usually 6 months. Comments are usually provided on rejected mss. Guidelines available for SAE and IRC. Responds in 2 months. Pays 2 copies. Acquires first North American serial rights. Occasionally reviews books of poetry in "up to 150-200 words." Send books for review consideration.

Advice: "Would-be contributors are urged to study the magazine first."

◯ THE GREENSBORO REVIEW; GREENSBORO REVIEW LITERARY AWARDS, English Dept., Room 134, McIver Bldg., University of North Carolina, P.O. Box 26170, Greensboro NC 27402. (336)334-5459. E-mail: jlclark@uncg.edu. Website: www.uncg.edu/eng/mfa (includes guidelines, contact and subscription information, and literary award information). Established 1966. **Editor:** Jim Clark. **Contact:** Poetry Editor.

● Work published in this review has been consistently anthologized or cited in *Best American Short Stories, New Stories from the South, Pushcart Prize*, and *Prize Stories: The O. Henry Award*.

Magazine Needs: *The Greensboro Review* appears twice yearly and showcases well-made verse in all styles and forms, though shorter poems (under 50 lines) seem preferred. Has published poetry by Stephen Dobyns, Thomas Lux, Stanley Plumly, Alan Shapiro, David Rivard, and Bruce Smith. As a sample the poetry editor selected these lines from "Double Life" by Daniel Tobin:

> *To have driven along blue levitating roads/this far into land's end, golden, rumpled,/these humps that could be the goddess's bedclothes,/and the red broach of a bridge pinning the continent/together, it is all ample and errant*

The Greensboro Review is 128 pages, digest-sized, professionally printed and flat-spined with colored matte cover. Uses about 25 pages of poetry in each issue, about 1.5% of the 2,000 submissions received for each issue. Subscription: $10/year, $25/3 years. Single/sample: $5.

How to Submit: "Submissions (no more than five poems) must arrive by September 15 to be considered for the Spring issue (acceptances in December) and February 15 to be considered for the Fall issue (acceptances in May). Manuscripts arriving after those dates will be held for consideration with the next issue." No previously published poems or simultaneous submissions. No fax or e-mail submissions. Cover letter not required but helpful. Include number of poems submitted. Guidelines available for SASE, on website, and in publication. Responds in 4 months. Always sends prepublication galleys. Pays 3 copies. Acquires first North American serial rights.

Also Offers: Sponsors an open competition for *The Greensboro Review* Literary Awards, $250 for both poetry and fiction each year. Deadline: September 15. Guidelines available for SASE, on website, and in publication.

Advice: "We want to see the best being written regardless of theme, subject, or style."

◯ GSU REVIEW; GSU REVIEW ANNUAL WRITING CONTEST, Georgia State University, Campus Box 1894, Atlanta GA 30303. (404)651-4804. Fax: (404)651-1710. E-mail: kchaple@emory.edu. Website: www.gsu.edu/~wwwrev/ (includes guidelines and samples). Established 1980. **Editor:** Katie Chaple. **Poetry Editor:** Josephine Pallos.

Magazine Needs: *GSU Review* is a biannual literary magazine publishing fiction, poetry, and photography. Wants "original voices searching to rise above the ordinary. No subject or form biases." Does not want pornography or Hallmark verse. Has published poetry by Gary Sange, Virgil Suarez, Earl Braggs, Charles Fort, Kenneth Chamlee, and Dana Littlepage Smith. *GSU Review* is 112 pages. Press run is 2,500 for 500 subscribers, 600 shelf sales; 500 distributed free to students. Single copy: $5; subscription: $8.

How to Submit: Submit up to 3 poems, "each *no longer* than two pages in length." Name, address, and phone/e-mail must appear on each page of ms. Include SASE and cover letter with 3- to 4-line bio. Accepts simultaneous submissions; no previously published poems. No submissions by e-mail. Time between acceptance and publication is 3 months. Seldom comments on rejected poems. Guidelines available for SASE and by e-mail. Responds in up to 10 weeks. Pays 1 copy.

Also Offers: Sponsors the *GSU Review* Annual Writing Contest, an annual award of $1,000 for the best poem; copy of issue to all who submit. Submissions must be previously unpublished. Submit up to 3 poems on any subject or in any form. "Specify 'poetry' on outside envelope." Guidelines available for SASE and by e-mail. Accepts inquiries via fax and e-mail. Postmark deadline: January 31. Competition receives 200 entries. Past judges include Sharon Olds, Jane Hirschfield, Anthony Hecht, and Phillip Levine. Winner will be announced in the Spring issue.

Advice: "Avoid cliched and sentimental writing but as all advice is filled with paradox—write from the heart. We look for a smooth union of form and content."

GUERNICA EDITIONS INC.; ESSENTIAL POET SERIES, PROSE SERIES, DRAMA SERIES; INTERNATIONAL WRITERS (Specialized: regional, translations, ethnic/nationality), P.O. Box 117, Toronto, Ontario M5S 2S6 Canada. Fax: (416)657-8885. E-mail: guernicaeditions@cs.com. Website: www.guernicaeditions.com. Established 1978. **Poetry Editor:** Antonio D'Alfonso.

Book/Chapbook Needs: "We wish to bring together the different and often divergent voices that exist in Canada and the U.S. We are interested in translations. We are mostly interested in poetry and essays on pluriculturalism." Has published work by Eugénio de Andrade (Portugal), Eugenio Cirese (Italy), Antonio Porta (Italy), Pasquale Verdicchio (Canada), Robert Flanagan (Canada), and Brian Day (Canada).

How to Submit: Query with 1-2 pages of samples. Send SASE (Canadian stamps only) or SAE and IRCs for catalog.

Advice: "We are interested in promoting a pluricultural view of literature by bridging languages and cultures. Besides our specialization in international translation."

GUIDE MAGAZINE (Specialized: regional, Catskill Mountains); FOR THE NATURAL POET, The Catskill Mountain Foundation Inc., P. O. Box 924, 7967 Main St., Hunter NY 12442. (518)263-4908. Fax: (518)263-4459. E-mail: teenspeakpoetry@aol.com. Website: www.catskillregionguide.com (includes events, Elderhostel program, guidelines). Established 1992, new owner since 1999. **Literary Editor:** Faith Lieberman.

Magazine Needs: *Guide Magazine* appears as a monthly journal of arts and culture, outdoor recreation, and country and farm life for the Catskill Mountains and valleys of the Hudson, Mohawk, Delaware, and Susquehana River regions. "All types of verse are acceptable as long as they are accessible. If you use a particular form, please give a brief description. Not interested in profanity or shock value." Accepts poetry by teens. Recently published poetry by Anne-Marie Macari, Gerald Stern, Jason Shinder, Diane Wakoski, Anna DiBello, and Tony Coiro. As a sample the editor selected these lines from "The World Loved by Moonlight" by Jane Hirshfield:

> You must try,/the voice said, to become colder./I understood at once./It is like the bodies of gods: cast in bronze,/braced in stone. Only something heartless could bear the full weight

Guide Magazine is 96 pages, magazine-sized, sheet fed press-printed, saddle-stapled, 70 lb. coated stock cover with 4-color photography, and ads (commercial, arts, sports). Receives about 500 poems/year, accepts about 5%. Publishes about 2 poems/issue. Press run is 30,000. Distributed free to commercial establishments and tourist info centers for 8 counties.

How to Submit: Submit 3 poems at a time. Line length for poetry is 32 maximum. Accepts simultaneous submissions; no previously published poems unless solicited. Accepts fax, e-mail, and disk submissions. Cover letter is preferred. Include SASE. Reads submissions year round. Submit seasonal poems 3 months in advance. Time between acceptance and publication is 2-3 months. Seldom comments on rejected poems. Occasionally publishes theme issues. A list of upcoming themes is available for SASE or by fax. Responds in 2 months. Pays 1 contributor's copy and admission (2) to poetry series and readings. All rights revert to author on publication. Poets may send books for review consideration to Faith Lieberman at the Catskill Mountain Foundation.

Also Offers: " 'For the Natural Poet' series with four or more dates on Saturdays, including seminars, readings, open mics. Bookstore accepts consignment. Happy to hear new ideas and voices, especially teachers and students."

Advice: "To be heard is to be validated. Make punctuation or the lack of it work for you. The spoken word can improve the written word. Poetry should be ageless and timeless."

GULF COAST: A JOURNAL OF LITERATURE AND FINE ART, Dept. of English, University of Houston, Houston TX 77204-3012. (713)743-3223. Website: www.gulfcoast.uh.edu (includes current magazine, submission and subscription information, events and links, contact information, cover art, etc.). Established 1986. **Poetry Editors:** Jennifer Gotz, Brian Barker, and Nick Beer.

Magazine Needs: *Gulf Coast* is published twice/year in October and April. While the journal features work by a number of established poets, editors are also interested in "providing a forum for new and emerging writers who are producing well-crafted work that takes risks." Each issue includes poetry, fiction, essays, interviews, and color reproductions of work by artists from across the nation. Has published poetry by Heather McHugh, Robert Pinsky, Marilyn Nelson, William Logan, Nick Flynn, D.A. Powell, Nancy Eimers, Franz Wright, and Josh Bell. As a sample the editors selected these lines from "Answer to Crowd" by Ed Skoog:

> *You have to ask, what was your war crime?/This is social work, walking around the crowd,/wanting to tell the woman who left hours ago/that her scarf still lies across the bench,/another coworker at a crossroad like yours./At the end of the world one feels worldlier.*

Gulf Coast is 144 pages, 6×9, offset-printed, perfect-bound. Single copy: $7; subscription: $12/year, $22/2 years.
How to Submit: Submit up to 4 poems at a time. Accepts simultaneous submissions with notification; no previously published poems. Cover letter with previous publications, "if any," and a brief bio required. Does not read submissions June through August. Guidelines available for SASE, in publication, or on website. Responds in 6 months. Pays 2 copies and $50 per poem. Returns all rights (except electronic) upon publication.

GULF STREAM MAGAZINE, English Dept. Florida International University, 3000 NE First St., North Miami Campus, North Miami FL 33181. (305)919-5599. Established 1989. **Editor:** John Dufresne. **Associate Editor:** Terri Carrion.
Magazine Needs: *Gulf Stream* is the biannual literary magazine associated with the creative writing program at FIU. Wants "poetry of any style and subject matter as long as it is of high literary quality." Has published poetry by Gerald Costanzo, Naomi Shihab Nye, Jill Bialosky, and Catherine Bowman. *Gulf Stream* is 96 pages, digest-sized, flat-spined, printed on quality stock, glossy card cover. Accepts less than 10% of poetry received. Press run is 750. Subscription: $9. Sample: $5.
How to Submit: Submit no more than 5 poems and include cover letter. Accepts simultaneous submissions (with notification in cover letter). Reads submissions September 15 through April 30 only. Editor comments on submissions "if we feel we can be helpful." Publishes theme issues. Guidelines available for SASE. Responds in 3 months. Pays 2 copies and 2 subscriptions. Acquires first North American serial rights.

$☐ ◎ HADROSAUR TALES (Specialized: science fiction/fantasy), P.O. Box 8468, Las Cruces NM 88006-8468. (505)527-4163. E-mail: hadrosaur.productions@verizon.net. Website: http://hadrosaur.com (includes writer's guidelines, a staff description and company history, links to authors' websites, contact and subscription information, editorial policy, and an online bookstore through Amazon.com). Established 1995. **Editor:** David L. Summers.
Magazine Needs: *"Hadrosaur Tales* is a literary journal that appears 3 times/year and publishes well written, thought-provoking science fiction and fantasy." Wants science fiction and fantasy themes. "We like to see strong visual imagery; strong emotion from a sense of fun to more melancholy is good. We do not want to see poetry that strays too far from the science fiction/fantasy genre." Has published poetry by G.O. Clark, John Grey, Joyce Frohn, Sharon Fotta Anderson, Gary Every, and Merle Taliaferro. As a sample the editor selected these lines from "Star Shadows" by Louise Webster:

> *Icy plateaus of ancient rock/Shift as the universe exhales./The blind eye of cyclops/Snares star shadows/ And drags them into/Bottomless sockets of gravity.*

Hadrosaur Tales is about 100 pages, digest-sized, printed on 60 lb. white paper, perfect-bound with black drawing on card stock cover, uses cover art only, includes minimal ads. Receives about 100 poems/year, accepts up to 25%. Press run is 200 for 40 subscribers. Single copy: $5.95; subscription: $10/year. Sample: $6.95. Make checks payable to Hadrosaur Productions.
How to Submit: Submit 1-5 poems at a time. Accepts previously published poems and simultaneous submissions. Accepts e-mail submissions either in text box or as attachment (RIF format only). Cover letter preferred. "For electronic mail submissions, please place the word, 'Hadrosaur' in the subject line. Submissions that do not include this are subject to being destroyed unread. Poetry will not be returned unless sufficient postage is provided." Time between acceptance and publication is 1 year. Often comments on rejected poems. Occasionally publishes theme issues. Guidelines available for SASE, by e-mail, and on website. Upcoming themes available for SASE. Responds in 1 month. Sends prepublication galleys on request. Pays $2/poem plus 2 copies. Acquires one-time rights.
Advice: "I select poems that compliment the short stories that appear in a given issue. A rejection does not necessarily mean that I disliked your poem, only that the given poem wasn't right for the issue. Keep writing and submitting your poetry."

THE ◎ SYMBOL indicates a market with a specific or unique focus. This specialized area of interest is listed in parentheses behind the market title.

◑ HAIGHT ASHBURY LITERARY JOURNAL, 558 Joost Ave., San Francisco CA 94127. Established 1979-1980. **Editors:** Indigo Hotchkiss, Alice Rogoff, and Conyus.

Magazine Needs: *Haight Ashbury* is a newsprint tabloid that appears 1-3 times/year. Use "all forms including haiku. Subject matter sometimes political, but open to all subjects. Poems of background—prison, minority experience—often published, as well as poems of protest and of Central America. Few rhymes." Has published poetry by Molly Fisk, Laura del Fuego, Dancing Bear, Lee Herrick, Janice King, and Laura Beausoleil. As a sample the editors selected these lines from "in the lines" by Tia Blassingame:

> color boys and girls/leaves the trees in flower/triggers the metal from which year olds drop/drug addict
> babes born on/crack open their skulls/on the ground/color boys and girls/does not become men and
> women

Haight Ashbury Literary Journal is 16 pages with graphics and ads. Press run 2,500. $35 for a lifetime subscription, which includes 3 back issues. Subscription: $12/4 issues. Sample: $3.

How to Submit: Submit up to 6 poems. "Please type one poem to a page, put name and address on every page and include SASE." No previously published poems. Each issue changes its theme and emphasis. Guidelines and upcoming themes available for SASE. Responds in 4 months. Pays 3 copies, small amount to featured writers. Rights revert to author. An anthology of past issues, *This Far Together*, is available for $15.

Also Offers: Writing contest with cash award. Deadline: May 1, 2001.

◑ ◎ HAIKU HEADLINES: A MONTHLY NEWSLETTER OF HAIKU AND SENRYU (Specialized: form), 1347 W. 71st St., Los Angeles CA 90044-2505. (323)778-5337. Established 1988. **Editor/Publisher:** Rengé/David Priebe.

Magazine Needs: *Haiku Headlines* is "America's oldest monthly publication dedicated to the genres of haiku and senryu only." Prefers the 5/7/5 syllabic discipline, but accepts irregular haiku and senryu which display pivotal imagery and contrast. Has published haiku by Dorothy McLaughlin, Jean Calkins, Günther Klinge, and Mark Arvid White. Here are examples of haiku and senryu by Rengé:

> HAIKU: By the very sound/of the splash in the water/—invisible frog!
> SENRYU: The silent facades/of the tall city buildings/teeming with people.

Haiku Headlines is 8 pages, 8½ × 11, corner-stapled and punched for a three-ring binder. "Each issue has a different color graphic front page. The back page showcases a Featured Haiku Poet with a photo-portrait, biography, philosophy, and six of the poet's own favorite haiku." *Haiku Headlines* publishes 100 haiku/senryu a month, including, on the average, work from 6 newcomers. Has 225 subscribers of which 3 are libraries. Single copy: $2 US, $2.25 Canada, $2.50 overseas; subscription: $24 US, $27 Canada, $30 overseas.

How to Submit: Haiku/senryu may be submitted with 12 maximum/single page. Unpublished submissions from subscribers will be considered first. Nonsubscriber submissions will be accepted only if space permits and SASE is included. Guidelines available for SASE and in publication. Responds in 2 months. Pays subscribers half price rebates for issues containing their work; credits applicable to subscription. Nonsubscribers are encouraged to prepay for issues containing their work.

Also Offers: Monthly Readers' Choice Awards of $25, $15, and $10 are shared by the "Top Three Favorites." The "First Timer" with the most votes receives an Award of Special Recognition ($5).

⊕ ◑ ◎ HANDSHAKE; THE EIGHT HAND GANG (Specialized: science fiction/fantasy, horror), 5 Cross Farm, Station Rd., Padgate, Warrington, Cheshire WA2 OQG United Kingdom. Established 1992. **Contact:** J.F. Haines.

Magazine Needs: *Handshake*, published irregularly, "is a newsletter for science fiction poets. It has evolved into being one side of news and information and one side of poetry." Wants "science fiction/fantasy poetry of all styles. Prefer short poems." Does not want "epics or foul language." Has published poetry by Margaret B. Simon, Fleming A. Calder, and Jacqueline Jones. As a sample the editor selected these lines from "A Home in Space" by Jacqueline Jones:

> Blueish splinters and a lightning beauty/Saw us through the orbits throat on earth

Handshake is 1 sheet of A4 paper, photocopied with ads. Receives about 50 poems/year, accepts up to 50%. Press run is 60 for 30 subscribers of which 5 are libraries. Subscription: SAE with IRC. Sample: SAE with IRC.

How to Submit: Submit 2-3 poems, typed and camera-ready. No previously published poems or simultaneous submissions. Cover letter preferred. Time between acceptance and publication varies. Editor selects "whatever takes my fancy and is of suitable length." Seldom comments on rejected poems. Publishes theme issues. Responds ASAP. Pays 1 copy. Acquires first rights. Staff reviews books or chapbooks of poetry or other magazines of very short length. Send books for review consideration.

Also Offers: *Handshake* is also the newsletter for The Eight Hand Gang, an organization for British science fiction poets, established in 1991. They currently have 60 members. Information about the organization is found in their newsletter.

🌐 ◐ **HANDSHAKE EDITIONS; CASSETTE GAZETTE**, Atelier A2, 83 rue de la Tombe Issoire 75014, Paris, France. Phone: 33.1.43.27.17.67. Fax: 33.1.43.20.41.95. E-mail: jim_haynes@wanadoo.fr. Established 1979. **Publisher:** Jim Haynes.
Magazine Needs & How to Submit: *Cassette Gazette* is an audiocassette issued "from time to time. We are interested in poetry dealing with political/social issues and women/feminism themes." Poets published include Yianna Katsoulos, Judith Malina, Elaine Cohen, Amanda Hoover, Roy Williamson, and Mary Guggenheim. Single copy: $10 plus postage. Pays in copies.
Book/Chapbook Needs & How to Submit: Handshake Editions does not accept unsolicited mss for book publication. New Book: "a bilingual English/Spanish edition by Cuban poet, Pablo Armando Fernandez to be co-published with Mosaic Press, Toronto" in early 2001.
Advice: Jim Haynes, publisher, says, "I prefer to deal face to face."

▼ $◻ ◐ **HANGING LOOSE PRESS; HANGING LOOSE**, 231 Wyckoff St., Brooklyn NY 11217. Website: http://omega.cc.umb.edu/~hangloos/ (includes guidelines, index, new titles, etc.). Established 1966. **Poetry Editors:** Robert Hershon, Dick Lourie, Mark Pawlak, and Ron Schreiber.
   ● Poetry published in *Hanging Loose* has been included in the 1995, 1996, and 1997 volumes of *The Best American Poetry.*
Magazine Needs: *Hanging Loose* appears 3 times/year. The magazine has published poetry by Sherman Alexie, Paul Violi, Donna Brook, Kimiko Hahn, Ron Overton, Jack Anderson, and Ha Jin. *Hanging Loose* is 120 pages, flat-spined, offset on heavy stock with a 4-color glossy card cover. One section contains poems by high-school-age poets. The editor says it "concentrates on the work of new writers." Sample: $9.
How to Submit: Submit 4-6 "excellent, energetic" poems. No simultaneous submissions. "Would-be contributors should read the magazine first." Responds in 3 months. Pays small fee and 2 copies.
Book/Chapbook Needs & How to Submit: *Hanging Loose* Press does not accept unsolicited book mss or artwork.

⬛N 🌐 ◐ **HANGMAN BOOKS**, 11 Boundary Rd., Chatham, Kent ME4 6TS England. Established 1982. **Editor:** Jack Ketch. **Administrator:** Juju Hamper.
Book/Chapbook Needs: Hangman publishes selected books of poetry. Wants "personal" poetry, "underground" writing, "none rhyming, none political." As a sample the editor selected these lines from "dead funny" by Billy Childish from his book, *Big Hart and Balls*:
   and with every poem i rite/my fame grows/another nail in my coffin/people feel embarrassed for me/
   everything i utter becomes a cliche//when oh when the people ask/will billy shut up?
How to Submit: When submitting a ms, send sufficient IRCs for return.

$◐ **HANOVER PRESS, LTD.; THE UNDERWOOD REVIEW**, P.O. Box 596, Newtown CT 06470-0596. Established 1994. **Editor:** Faith Vicinanza.
Magazine Needs: *The Underwood Review* appears annually and publishes poetry, short stories, essays, and b&w artwork including photographs. Wants "cutting-edge fiction, poetry, and art. We are not afraid of hard issues, love humor, prefer personal experience over nature poetry. We want poetry that is strong, gutsy, vivid images, erotica accepted. No religious poems; no 'Hallmark' verse." Accepts poetry written by children. Has published poetry by award winning poets Patricia Smith ("Queen of Performance Poetry"), Marc Smith ("Father of Slam Poetry"), Michael Brown, and Vivian Shipley. As a sample the editor selected these lines from "Mommy's Hubby" by Leo Connellan (Poet Laureate of Connecticut):
   Yes, it's Fisk tellin' you split./Imagine it, Fisk tellin' you leave!/Because now I'm Mommy's Hubby and
   we've got our coffins/picked out/plots and perpetual flowers.
The Underwood Review is 120-144 pages, 6×9, offset-printed and perfect-bound with card cover with computer graphics, photos, etc. Receives about 2,000 poems/year, accepts up to 3%. Press run is 1,000. Subscription: $13. Sample: $13. Make checks payable to Hanover Press, Ltd./Faith Vicinanza.
How to Submit: Submit up to 3 poems at a time. Accepts simultaneous submissions; no previously published poems. Accepts disk submissions. Cover letter with short bio (up to 60 words) preferred. Time between acceptance and publication is up to 8 months. Guidelines available for SASE and in publication. Responds in 5 months. Pays 2 copies. Acquires one-time rights.
Book/Chapbook Needs & How to Submit: Hanover Press, Ltd. seeks "to provide talented writers with the opportunity to get published and readers with the opportunity to experience extraordinary poetry." Has published *Crazy Quilt* by Vivian Shipley; *Short Poems/City Poems* by Leo Connellan; *We Are What We Love* by Jim Scrimgeour; *What Learning Leaves* by Taylor Mali; *Dangerous Men* by David Martin; and *The Space Between* by Sandra Bishop Ebner. Publishes 5 paperbacks/year. Books are usually 6×9, offset-printed and perfect-bound

with various covers, include art/graphics. Query first with a few sample poems and cover letter with brief bio and publication credits. Responds to queries in 2 months; to mss in 6 months. Pays 100 author's copies (out of a press run of 1,000). Order sample books by sending $11.

Advice: "Poets so often just mass submit their work without being familiar with the literary journal and its preferences. Please don't waste an editor's time or your postage."

[N] Ø HARCOURT, INC.; HARCOURT CHILDREN'S BOOKS; GULLIVER BOOKS; SILVER WHISTLE, 525 B St., Suite 1900, San Diego CA 92101. (619)231-6616. Harcourt Children's Books, Gulliver Books and Silver Whistle publish hardback and trade paperback books for children. Does not accept unsolicited material.

Ø ◎ HARD ROW TO HOE; POTATO EYES FOUNDATION (Specialized: nature/rural/ecology), P.O. Box 541-I, Healdsburg CA 95448. (707)433-9786. **Editor:** Joe E. Armstrong.

Magazine Needs: *Hard Row to Hoe,* taken over from Seven Buffaloes Press in 1987, is a "book review newsletter of literature from rural America with a section reserved for short stories (about 2,000 words) and poetry featuring unpublished authors. The subject matter must apply to rural America including nature and environmental subjects. Poems of 30 lines or less given preference, but no arbitrary limit. No style limits. Do not want any subject matter not related to rural subjects." As a sample the editor selected these lines from "Patience" by David Black:

> Everything shines with use. . . . The hook where his left hand used to be. . . . After the hook, he was nearly whole./Nearly. That's farming for you—/it starts with one little piece:/sooner or later it'll get the rest.

Hard Row to Hoe is 12 pages, magazine-sized, side-stapled, appearing 3 times/year, 3 pages reserved for short stories and poetry. Press run is 300. Subscription: $8/year. Sample: $3.

How to Submit: Submit 3-4 poems at a time. No simultaneous submissions. Accepts previously published poems only if published in local or university papers. Guidelines available for SASE. Editor comments on rejected poems "if I think the quality warrants." Pays 2 copies. Acquires one-time rights. Reviews books of poetry in 600-700 words. Poets may send books for review consideration.

Ø HARPERCOLLINS PUBLISHERS, 10 East 53rd St., New York NY 10022. Website: www.HarperCollins.com (includes poets, recorded poetry, books and events, workshop, free electronic newsletter subscription). Top publisher of some of America's premier poets. **"Unfortunately the volume of submissions we receive prevents us from reading unsolicited manuscripts or proposals."**

[N] $ Ø HARPUR PALATE; MILTON KESSLER MEMORIAL PRIZE FOR POETRY, Dept. of English, Binghamton University, P.O. Box 6000, Binghamton NY 13902-6000. E-mail: hppoetry@hotmail.com (submissions only). Website: http://harpurpalate.binghamton.edu (includes excerpts, guidelines, contest information, editorial policy, archives, subscription and contact information). Established 2000. **Poetry Editors:** Catherine Dent and Anne Rashid.

Magazine Needs: *Harpur Palate* appears biannually. "We're dedicated to publishing the most eclectic mix of poetry and prose, regardless of style, form, and genre." Wants experimental, blank verse, free verse, haiku, lyrical, narrative, prose poem, sonnet, tanka, villanelle, speculative poetry, and metapoetry. "No light verse, pretentious attitudes, or violence for violence's sake." Recently published poetry by Virgil Suárez, Ryan G. Van Cleave, Eileen Tabios, Danielle L. Gutter, Kake Huck, Allison Joseph, Christina Pugh, and Joyce K. Luzzi. As a sample the editor selected these lines from "Streetlight Pantoum" by Danielle L. Gutter:

> While she's simply listening for someone to ring,/the ancient lady (across the street) sips her dark tea./ Waiting to start its long descent, on a crane's wing/her dying life never whispers a plea.

Harpur Palate is 100-120 pages, digest-sized, offset-printed, perfect-bound, matte or glossy cover. Receives about 700 poems/year, accepts about 35. Publishes about 10-15 poems/issue. Press run is 400-500 of which 50 are shelf sales; 50-100 distributed free to journals in exchange program, award anthologies, contributors, creative writing programs. Single copy: $7.50; subscription: $14/year, 2 issues. Sample: $7.50. Make checks payable to *Harpur Palate*.

How to Submit: Submit 3-5 poems at a time. "No line restrictions, poems must be 10 pages or less." Accepts simultaneous submissions; no previously published poems. Accepts e-mail submissions; no fax or disk submissions. Cover letter is required. "E-mail submissions should be sent as .rtf file attachments (Rich Text Format) *only.*" Reads submissions August 1-October 15 (winter issue); January 1-March 15 (summer issue). Time between acceptance and publication is 2 months. Poems are circulated to an editorial board. "Poetry board consists of first and second readers. Poems accepted for publication have been approved by a first reader and second reader and are selected by the Final Selection Committee consisting of all poetry readers, poetry editors, and managing

The transformation of experience

In his book, *Heaven's Coast*, Mark Doty says, "Apocalypse is played out now on a personal scale; it is not in the sky above us, but in our bed." The question of personal distance from experience is one every poet confronts when trying to write a poem based on a personal experience. The struggle to know an audience and provide well-chosen and forceful details ultimately decides whether the reader will receive the experience the author intended. For Doty, this question is partially addressed by understanding his distance from the experience and by moving back and forth between writing poetry and nonfiction.

Photo by Margaretta K. Mitchell

Mark Doty

An award-winning author in both genres, Doty's work has been honored with the T.S. Eliot Prize, a Whiting Writers' Award, the National Book Critics Circle Award, a PEN/Martha Allbrand Nonfiction Prize, the Witter Bynner Prize for Poetry, and the Lambda Literary Award. In 2000 he received a three-year Lila Wallace-Reader's Digest Writers' Award, and he has been the recipient of fellowships from the New York Public Library Center for Scholars and Writers, the National Endowment for the Arts, and the Guggenheim, Rockefeller, and Ingram Merrill Foundations. Doty's most recent book of poetry, *Source*, was released in 2001 by HarperCollins.

Your poetry career has been successful since the beginning and continues to land you in brighter, more elite circles. What leads you to branch out into nonfiction?

I began to write nonfiction prose because I felt forced to, literally, when my partner died in 1994. There was a period of months when poetry was not available to me. I think I simply felt too overwhelmed by feeling to try to make a poem. I had too much to say, and no distance, and no ability to focus in the way that poetry seems to demand. But I felt if I didn't write *something* I would—well, disappear.

I discovered that I *could* write sentences, and that one sentence led to another. I began writing an essay just to pay attention to the experience of new grief, and when I'd finished that I wrote another. And another. Soon I realized I wasn't writing essays but chapters; I was beginning a chronicle of grief. And my prose could be inclusive and expansive in a way that, just then, poetry couldn't be for me. I didn't have to make decisions, I could put everything in. Later, of course, I had to take lots out! But prose is always a more inclusive, more open form than poetry is; one has room to spread out, tell a related story, meditate on an idea. When I'd finished writing my first memoir, I'd already returned to writing poetry. But I found that I missed that broader field, and now it seems very important to me to have more than one mode of investigation, another way to think.

How do those different ways of thinking inform one another? Does one necessarily fuel the other or do they function separately in your mind?
It depends on the nature of the project. In *Heaven's Coast*, I found that there were images I wasn't quite ready to let go of, after I'd examined them in prose. There seemed to be something more there, and writing a poem involving that same image proved a way to get at it, to mine the image further.

When I was writing *Firebird*, which is a childhood memoir, that material didn't seem to lend itself to poetry. It seemed to want the larger container of the prose book, with its wider sense of context and of history.

Now I'm going back and forth between essays and poems, and the movement feels like a comfortable one. When one form isn't happening for me, the other may be available. And it does feel to me like one pushes the other along. A piece of prose, I mean, might show me the way into a new poem, and vice versa.

Have you ever considered writing fiction?
I'm certainly attracted to fiction. Who doesn't love getting lost in the long arc of a narrative? I like the dimensionality and texture of historical, literary fiction especially—books like A.S. Byatt's *Possession* or Andrea Barrett's *Servants of the Map* I find entirely transporting. But it seems to be the nature of my imagination that I'm stimulated by trying to describe experience. Thus my poems and my nonfiction are almost entirely based in my own life. If I try to make things up, as the novelist must, my imagination just seems to sit there lumpishly. But ask me to describe something I've seen and I'm off!

Absolutely; we can never escape our own experience in writing. In fact, poetry offers the unique quality of being able to discuss a universal condition by exploring a very specific experience. But it is also a very difficult thing to do well, and many young writers fall into tones of melodrama or self-pity. How do you manage to steer clear of those things?
The crucial thing, I think, is to remember that whatever you're describing in the poem isn't important *because* it happened to you, be it the frost on the leaves in your garden or the death of your grandfather. The crucial thing in a poem is not what is reported, but what you make of it, what architecture of sound, form, and meaning you build from that originating experience.

And here is a paradox: By caring about such things, by paying attention to every formal means at your disposal to create the poem, you get yourself out of the way; you stand back from your own emotional involvement and allow the reader to feel. That's the difference between feeling and sentimentality. Feeling is the experience the reader has when a poem works; sentimentality is when the writer's full of feeling, or claims to be, and the reader doesn't share it.

Are there things you have shied away from writing about for a while, just to get the sort of distance you describe?
Absolutely. For instance, I was living in New York on September 11, and I can't imagine trying to speak about those days in a poem just yet. Maybe I won't ever find the right degree of distance. In a way that's one of the great determiners of whether you can write a certain poem or not—finding the stance or position which will allow you to speak at just enough of a remove as to be able to see your subject.

"Fish-R-Us"

Clear sac
of coppery eyebrows
suspended in amnion,
not one moving—

A Mars,
composed entirely
of single lips,
each of them gleaming—

this bag of fish
(have they actually
traveled here like this?)
bulges while they

acclimate, presumably,
to the new terms
of the big tank
at Fish-R-Us. Soon

they'll swim out
into separate waters,
but for now they're
shoulder to shoulder

in this clear and
burnished orb, each fry
about the size of this line,
too many lines for any

bronzy antique epic,
a million of them,
a billion incipient citizens
of a goldfish Beijing,

a Sao Paolo,
a Mexico City.
They seem to have sense
not to move but hang

fire, suspended, held
at just a bit of distance
(a bit is all there is), all
facing outward, eyes

(they can't even blink)
turned toward the skin

of the sac they're in,
this swollen polyethylene.

And though nothing's
actually rippling but their gills,
it's still like looking up
into falling snow,

if all the flakes
were a dull, breathing gold,
as if they were
streaming toward—

not us, exactly,
but what they'll
be . . . Perhaps
they're small enough

—live sparks, for sale
at a nickel apiece—
that one can actually
see them transpiring:

they want to swim
forward, want to
eat, want to take place . . .
Who's going to know

or number or even see them all?
They pulse in their golden ball.

(from *Source* (HarperCollins, 2001); reprinted with permission of the author)

Do you ever feel as though it's a question of what the audience is prepared to read? And do you consider your audience while writing or revising?
In truth, I think an audience will go absolutely anywhere with you, if they feel they're in good hands. I mean that if an artist creates a sense of caring for the reader's experience—through crafted language, through the careful shaping of material—then we trust that writer, and we're willing to go along into dangerous territory.

And yes, I think about audience all the time. Not so much in the sense of pitching my work towards a particular reader, but rather through trying very hard to create an experience for the reader. This is the necessary distinction between self-expression and art. When you write for yourself, in a journal, say, you might as well say things any old way. But when you begin to transform experience for someone else, then you must stand back from your subject matter at least enough to try to say things well. This is the beginning of esthetic distance, and we need at least that kind of distance from our work in order to move the reader.
—Amy Ratto

editors." Seldom comments on rejected poems. Guidelines available for SASE or on website. Responds in 2 months. Pays $5-10 when funding available, and 2 contributors copies. Acquires first North American serial rights.

Also Offers: The Milton Kessler Memorial Prize for Poetry. Prize: $500 and publication in the winter issue of *Harpur Palate*. "Contest opens on July 1." **Postmark deadline:** October 1. "Poems in any style, form or genre are welcome as long as they are 1) no more than 3 pages and 2) previously unpublished. The entry fee is $10/5 poems. You may send as many poems as you wish, but no more than 5 poems per envelope. Please send checks drawn on a US bank or money orders made out to *Harpur Palate*. IMPORTANT: Checks *must* be made out to *Harpur Palate*, or we will not be able to process your check!" Complete guidelines available for SASE or on website. "We publish a Writing By Degrees supplement featuring fiction and poetry in the winter issue. Writing By Degree is a creative writing conference run by graduate students in Binghamton's Creative Writing Program."

Advice: "Please don't take rejection as a sign that we don't like your work. We receive so many quality submissions that there's no way we can publish them all. We're always open to form poetry, experimental poetry, metapoetry, and speculative poetry."

N. Ø HARTWORKS; D.C. CREATIVE WRITING WORKSHOP, 601 Mississippi Ave. SE, Washington DC 20032-3899. (202)297-1957. E-mail: hartwrites@yahoo.com. Established 2000. **Executive Director:** Nancy Schwalb, D.C. Creative Writing Workshop.

● **Although this journal doesn't accept submissions from the general public, it's included here as an outstanding example of what a literary journal can be (for anyone of any age).**

Magazine Needs: *hArtworks* appears 3 times/year. "We publish the poetry of Hart Middle School students (as far as we know, Hart may be the only public middle school in the U.S. with its own poetry magazine) and the writing of guest writers such as Nikki Giovanni, Alan Cheuse, Arnost Lustig, and Henry Taylor, along with an interview between the kids and the grown-up pro. Also publishes work by our writers-in-residence who teach workshops at Hart, and provide trips to readings, slams, museums, and plays." Wants "vivid, precise, imaginative constructions of language that have to do with the heart as well as the intellect, and psychology as well as civic necessity." Does not want "poetry that has no awareness or respect for itself, its tradition, and the neighborhood into which it is born." Recently published poetry by Nikki Giovanni, Larry Robertson, Andy Fogle, Kerry Danner-McDonald, Jessica Young, and Antonio Ashford. As a sample the editor selected these lines from "Ode II" (from an adaptation of Sophocles' *Antigone*) by Larry Robertson:

> There was no Zeus or raging God whose heart throbbed his temporal arteries in eternal punishment./ They weren't fazed when celestial rebellion swarmed their immortality./'Twas America's rich and money-filth mansions swept in gold tooth smiles,/Be costing more than what lies above Olympus,/while standing amidst that sweet yellow that looms above the echoes of the clouds.

hArtworks is 60 pages, magazine-sized, professionally-printed, saddle-stapled, card cover, with photography. Receives about 800 poems/year, accepts about 20%. Publishes about 60 poems/issue. Press run is 500 for 75 subscribers of which 2 are libraries, 100 shelf sales; 100 distributed free to writers, teachers. Single copy: $1; subscription: $5. Sample: $2. Make checks payable to D.C. Creative Writing Workshop.

"Our covers always picture some of our students, because they are the most interesting aspect of the magazine," says Nancy Schwalb, executive director of the D.C. Creative Writing Workshop. She photographed these three young writers in a subway station as they returned from a field trip to see "Hamlet." All three have poetry in *hArtworks*. Cover layout by Holly Mansfield of Free Hand Press.

How to Submit: "Writers-in-residence solicit most submissions from their classes and then a committee of student editors makes the final selections. Each year, our second issue is devoted to responses to the Holocaust."
Advice: "The 'scene,' like our lives, can be tough and so one smart thing to do is dig down into your own individual voice, and stretch out its roots—follow what is interesting and important—inform your work with honesty and awareness. When it comes down to it, it's simple—read, write, think, and so on."

⬛ **HAWAII PACIFIC REVIEW**, 1060 Bishop St., Honolulu HI 96813. (808)544-1107. Fax: (808)544-0862. E-mail: pwilson@hpu.edu. Website: www.hpu.edu (includes contact information, tables of content from back issues, selected sample poems, contributor bios, and guidelines). Established 1986. **Editor:** Patrice Wilson.
Magazine Needs: *Hawaii Pacific Review* is an annual literary journal appearing in August or September. Wants "quality poetry, short fiction, and personal essays from writers worldwide. Our journal seeks to promote a world view that celebrates a variety of cultural themes, beliefs, values, and viewpoints. We wish to further the growth of artistic vision and talent by encouraging sophisticated and innovative poetic and narrative techniques." Has published poetry by Wendy Bishop, B.Z. Niditch, Rick Bursky, Virgil Suarez, and Linda Bierds. *Hawaii Pacific Review* is 80-120 pages, 6×9, professionally printed on quality paper, perfect-bound, with coated card cover; each issue features original artwork. Receives 800-1,000 poems/ year, accepts up to 30-40. Press run is approximately 1,000 for 200 shelf sales. Single copy: $8.95. Sample: $5.
How to Submit: Submit up to 5 poems, maximum 100 lines each. 1 submission/issue. "No handwritten manuscripts." Accepts simultaneous submissions with notification; no previously published poems. No fax or e-mail submissions. Cover letter with 5-line professional bio including prior publications required. "Our reading period is September 1 through December 31 each year." Seldom comments on rejected poems. Guidelines available for SASE or by e-mail. Responds within 3 months. Pays 2 copies. Acquires first North American serial rights.
Advice: "We'd like to receive more experimental verse. Good poetry is eye-opening; it investigates the unfamiliar or reveals the spectacular in the ordinary. Good poetry does more than simply express the poet's feelings; it provides both insight and unexpected beauty. Send us your best work!"

🔳 $⬛ **HAYDEN'S FERRY REVIEW**, Box 871502, Arizona State University, Tempe AZ 85287-1502. (480)965-1243. Website: www.haydensferryreview.com (includes guidelines, submission information, back issues, and excerpts). Established 1986.
● Poetry published in *Hayden's Ferry Review* has been included in the *Pushcart Prize* anthologies (2001 and 2002).
Magazine Needs: *Hayden's Ferry* is a handsome literary magazine appearing in December and May. Has published poetry by Dennis Schmitz, Raymond Carver, Maura Stanton, Ai, and David St. John. *Hayden's Ferry Review* is 6×9, 120 pages, flat-spined with glossy card cover. Press run is 1,300 for 200 subscribers of which 30 are libraries, 800 shelf sales. Accepts about 3% of 5,000 submissions annually. Subscription: $10. Sample: $6.
How to Submit: "No specifications other than limit in number (six)." No electronic submissions. Submissions circulated to two poetry editors. Editor comments on submissions "often." Guidelines available for SASE. Responds in 3 months of deadlines. Deadlines: February 28 for Spring/Summer issue; September 30 for Fall/Winter. Sends contributor's page proofs. Pays $25/page (maximum $100) and 2 copies.

🔳 ⬛ ◎ **HEART—HUMAN EQUITY THROUGH ART (Specialized: social issues); AN-NUAL HEART POETRY CONTEST**, P.O. Box 81038, Pittsburgh PA 15217-0538. (412)244-0122. Fax: (412)244-0210. E-mail: lesanne@ix.netcom.com. Website: http://trfn.clpgh.org/heart/ (includes contest guidelines, journal excerpts, events, subscription/submission info, links). Established 1997. **Poetry Editor:** Leslie Anne Mcilroy. Member: CLMP.
● Named one of "Others to Watch" in literature by the 1998 *Pittsburgh Magazine* Harry Schwalb Excellence in Arts Awards; received Honorable Mention from 1998 Pushcart Prize for "Elizabeth Tines" by Jane McCafferty.
Magazine Needs: *HEArt* appears 3 times/year. "*HEArt* is the nation's only journal of contemporary art, literature, and review devoted to confronting discrimination and promoting social justice. We encourage the role of artists as human rights activists. All poems should address social justice issues including, but not limited to racial, sexual, gender, and class discrimination. Fresh language, vivid imagery, strong craft, concise word choice, economy of language, and poems that 'show,' not tell. Must be accessible, not 'academic,' though intellectual is fine." Does not want "ethereal, romantic, pastoral, or highly academic and inaccessible poetry. We steer away from preachy or rambling work. Personal poems with no social

significance are inappropriate." Accepts poetry written by young adults. Recently published poetry by Tim Seibles, Sherod Santos, Sapphire, Amiri Baraka, Sonia Sanchez, and Linda McCarriston. As a sample the editor selected these lines from "Really Breathing" by Tim Seibles:

> *Fresh prisons and bottom lines/everywhere: terrible jobs, terrible/choices, terrible. Look at the flies/ dead, so close to freedom—/the window smiling,/the glass sweet as a guillotine.*

HEArt is 80 pages, 5×7½, offset/full-bleed-printed, saddle-stapled, computer art graphic/100 lb. uncoated/cover, with art/graphics (encouraged) and 4-8 pages of retail/art/literary ads. Receives about 150 poems/year, accepts about 20%. Publishes about 12 poems/issue. Press run is 1,000 for 500 subscribers of which 5 are libraries, 100 shelf sales; 250 are distributed free to potential subscribers, writing conferences, shelters, social service agencies. Single copy: $7.50; subscription: $21. Sample: $8.50. Make checks payable to *HEArt*.

How to Submit Submit 3 poems at a time. Accepts simultaneous submissions; no previously published poems. Accepts fax, e-mail, and disk submissions. Cover letter is preferred. "Require final version hard copy to proof as well as electronic version to place, preferably in rich text format." Reads submissions all year. Time between acceptance and publication is 4 months. "Poems are reviewed by poetry editor and accepted or rejected. Poems that raise some question or are printable with minor revisions are given to fiction editor for review/suggestions." Seldom comments on rejected poems. Occasionally publishes theme issues. A list of upcoming themes and guidelines are available in magazine, for SASE, by fax, by e-mail, or on website. Responds in up to 6 months. Pays subscription and 2 contributor's copies. Acquires first North American serial rights. Reviews books of poetry in 1,000-1,500 words, single book format. Poets may send books for review consideration to Leslie Anne Mcilroy.

Also Offers: The annual HEArt (Human Equity Through Art) Poetry & Short Fiction Contest. First prize in both categories is publication in *HEArt* and $500. Entries must be previously unpublished and address social justice issues, including but not limited to racial, sexual, gender, and class discrimination. Submissions must be postmarked by December 31. A $15 entry fee includes a copy of the winning issue. For $21, entrants receive a year's subscription to the journal beginning with the winning issue. Make check payable to HEArt. Additional information and guidelines available for SASE, by fax, e-mail, or on website.

Advice: "*HEArt* believes in the power of poetry to affect readers, and thereby affect social change. We encourage poets to use their voices to recognize injustice in the tradition of Pablo Neruda. This is not easy. Many submissions are preachy and trite, though well-meaning. Show, don't tell and balance message with craft."

THE HEARTLANDS TODAY (Specialized: regional, themes), Firelands College, 1 University Rd., Huron OH 44839. (419)433-5560. Fax: (419)433-9696. E-mail: lsmithdog@aol.com. Website: http://theheartlandstoday.net. Established 1990. **Editors:** Larry Smith and Nancy Dunham. Member: CLMP.

Magazine Needs: *The Heartlands Today* is an annual publication of the Firelands Writing Center at Firelands College. Wants work by Midwestern writers about the Midwest Heartlands, "writing and photography that is set in the Midwest today and deals revealingly and creatively with the issues we face—good writing and art that documents our lives." Each issue has a specific theme. Has published poetry by Alberta Turner, Chris Llewellyn, and Lawrence Ferlinghetti. *The Heartlands Today* is 160 pages, 6×9, perfect-bound with 20 b&w photos. Accepts 10-20% of the poetry received. Press run is 800. Single copy: $8.50. Sample: $5.

How to Submit: Submit up to 5 poems at a time. Accepts simultaneous submissions. No e-mail submissions, only queries. Cover letter with brief bio required. Reads submissions January 1 to June 1 only. Often comments on rejected poems. Guidelines and upcoming themes available for SASE. Responds in 2 months once reading period begins. Pays $10 and 2 copies. Acquires first or second rights.

Advice: "We're looking for good writing and art that is set in the midwest today and deals revealingly and creatively with who we are. We seek good writing and art that documents our lives, bears witness to our shared concerns and humanity."

HEAVEN BONE MAGAZINE; HEAVEN BONE PRESS; HEAVEN BONE PRESS INTERNATIONAL CHAPBOOK COMPETITION (Specialized: spiritual, nature/rural/ecology), P.O. Box 486, Chester NY 10918. E-mail: heavenbone@aol.com. Established 1986. **Poetry Editor:** Steve Hirsch.

Magazine Needs: *Heaven Bone* publishes poetry, fiction, essays, and reviews with "an emphasis on spiritual, metaphysical, surrealist, experimental, esoteric, and ecological concerns." Has published poetry and fiction by Richard Kostelanetz, Charles Bukowski, Marge Piercy, Kirpal Gordon, Diane di Prima, and Michael McClure. As a sample the editor selected these lines from "Message of Hope" by G. Sutton Breiding:

> *The screech owl's call/Is vertical: a tower/Rippling in the mist,/A door of oracles/Hung between night/ And dawn that opens/And shuts softly/In the white places/Of sleep.*

Heaven Bone is approximately 144 pages, magazine-sized, perfect-bound, using b&w art, photos on recycled bond stock with glossy 4-color recycled card cover. Receives up to 1,000 poems/year, accepts up to 30. Press run is 2,000. Sample: $10.

How to Submit: Submit 3-10 poems at a time. "I will not read submissions without SASEs." Accepts simultaneous submissions and previously published poems, "if notified." Accepts e-mail submissions (PDF, Microsoft Word). Time between acceptance and publication is up to 1 year. Occasionally publishes theme issues. A list of upcoming themes available for SASE. Responds in up to 6 months. Sometimes sends prepublication galleys. Pays 2 copies. Acquires first North American serial rights. Reviews books of poetry. Poets may send books for review consideration.

Also Offers: The press sponsors the biannual Heaven Bone Press International Chapbook Competition which awards $500 plus publication to an original, unpublished poetry ms of 30 pages or less. Reading fee $10. Guidelines available for SASE.

Advice: Editor advises, "Please be familiar with the magazine before sending mss. We receive too much religious verse. Break free of common 'poetic' limitations and speak freely with no contrivances. No forced end-line rhyming please. Channel the muse and music without being an obstacle to the poem."

N ⊘ HELIKON PRESS, 120 W. 71st St., New York NY 10023. Established 1972. **Poetry Editors:** Robin Prising and William Leo Coakley. "Try to publish the best contemporary poetry in the tradition of English verse. We read (and listen to) poetry and ask poets to build a collection around particular poems. We print fine editions illustrated by good artists. Unfortunately we cannot encourage submissions."

$ ◎ HERALD PRESS; PURPOSE; STORY FRIENDS; ON THE LINE; WITH; CHRISTIAN LIVING (Specialized: religious, children), 616 Walnut Ave., Scottdale PA 15683-1999. (724)887-8500. Send submissions or queries directly to the editor of the specific magazine at address indicated.

Magazine Needs & How to Submit: *Herald Press*, the official publisher for the Mennonite Church in North America, seeks also to serve a broad Christian audience. Each of the magazines listed has different specifications, and the editor of each should be queried for more exact information. *Purpose*, editor James E. Horsch, a "religious young adult/adult monthly in weekly parts," press run 13,000, its focus: "action oriented, discipleship living." It is $5\frac{3}{8} \times 8\frac{3}{8}$, with two-color printing throughout. Buys appropriate poetry up to 12 lines. *Purpose* uses 3-4 poems/week, receives about 2,000/year of which they use 150, has a 10- to 12-week backlog. Guidelines and a free sample are available for SASE. Mss should be double-spaced, one side of sheet only. Accepts simultaneous submissions. Responds in 2 months. Pays $7.50-20/poem plus 2 copies. *On the Line*, edited by Mary C. Meyer, a monthly religious magazine, for children 9-14, "that reinforces Christian values," press run 6,000. Sample free with SASE. Wants poems 3-24 lines. Submit poems "each on a separate $8\frac{1}{2} \times 11$ sheet." Accepts simultaneous submissions and previously published poems. Responds in 1 month. Pays $10-25/poem plus 2 copies. *Story Friends*, edited by Rose Mary Stutzman, is for children 4-9, a "monthly magazine that reinforces Christian values," press run 6,500, uses poems 3-12 lines. Send SASE for guidelines/sample copy. Pays $10. *With*, Editorial Team, Box 347, Newton KS 67114, (316)283-5100. This magazine is for "senior highs, ages 15-18," focusing on empowering youth to radically commit to a personal relationship with Jesus Christ, and to share God's good news through word and actions." Press run 4,000, uses a limited amount of poetry. Poems should be 4-50 lines. Pays $10-25. *Christian Living*, edited by Sarah Kehrberg, published 8 times/year, is "for family, community, and culture," uses poems up to 30 lines. Has published poetry by Julia Kasdorf. As a sample the editor selected these lines from "Sometimes Hope" by Jean Janzen:

> *But sometimes hope/is a black ghost/in a fantastic twist,/an old dream that flickers/in the wind.*

Christian Living is 28-44 pages, 8×10, 1-3 color with photos and artwork. Receives about 75 poems/year, accepts 15-20. Press run is 4,000 for 4,000 subscribers of which 8-10 are libraries, 10-20 shelf sales; 100-300 distributed free. Single copy: $3; subscription: $23.95. Sample free with 9×12 SASE ($1). Make checks payable to *Christian Living*. Submit 3-5 poems at a time. Accepts previously published poems and simultaneous submissions. Time between acceptance and publication is up to 14 months. Seldom comments on rejected poems. Guidelines available for SASE. Responds within 6 months. Pays $1/line plus 2 copies. Acquires first or one-time rights. Staff reviews books or chapbooks of poetry in 200-800 words. Poets may send books for review consideration.

◻ ◎ THE HERB NETWORK (Specialized: herbs), P.O. Box 35983, Las Vegas NV 89133. (702)870-9259. E-mail: editor@herbnetwork.com. Website: www.herbnetwork.com (includes writer's guidelines, membership information, articles, contact and subscription information, upcoming themes, editorial policy, catalog, bios, archives, links, and an interview with the editor). Established 1995. **Editor:** Kathleen O'Mara.

Magazine Needs: *The Herb Network* is a quarterly newsletter of information for herbal enthusiasts. Wants poetry related to herbs or plants—real or folklore. Short poems to 250 words. Also accepts poetry written by children. Has published poetry by Jack Weber, Jene Erick Beardsley, Robert Crowe, Melinda Hamilton Hunter, Roberta Carvelli, and Debra Anne Chapman. As a sample the editor selected "Dandelions" by Elizabeth Willis DeHuff:

> *Slim little girls with green flounced dresses,/Dandelions stand with yellow shaggy hair./Soon they grow*
> *to gray haired ladies,/Whose locks sail away through the air./Ashamed of their baldness, each of these*
> *dears,/Fringes a cap which she always wears.*

The newsletter is 24 pages, 8½×11, neatly printed on plain white paper with a few b&w graphics. The issue we received included recipes, information about herbs used by midwives, an article focusing on lavender, book reviews, and classified ads. Press run is 7,500 for 7,000 subscribers. Subscription: $39/year; student rate; $32/year; international: $50/year.

How to Submit: Submit up to 3 poems at a time, typed double-spaced, one poem/page, name and address on each. Line length for poems is 25 maximum. Accepts previously published poems and simultaneous submissions. Accepts e-mail submissions; include text in body of message. Cover letter preferred. Publishes theme issues. Guidelines available by e-mail, on website, in publication, or for SASE; upcoming themes available on website or in publication. Responds in up to 3 months. Pays with 1 copy and 2 tearsheets or by barter, offering free advertisements, or copies or $1-5 as budget allows. Acquires first or one-time rights.

Advice: "Write from your experience, from your heart about herbs and gifts you receive from nature."

⬤ ◎ **HERNANDO MEDIC (Specialized: health concerns)**, 7443 Oak Tree Lane, Spring Hill FL 34607-2324. (352)688-8116. Fax: (352)686-9477. E-mail: mariasingh@cs.com. Established 2001. **Editor-in-Chief:** Pariksith Singh, MD.

Magazine Needs: *Hernando Medic* appears quarterly, published by the Hernando County Medical Society. Deals with health, healing, and medical aspects of the human experience. Wants any form, style of poetry dealing with health and healing." Does not want slander, racism, or bigotry. Accepts poetry written by children. *Hernando Medic* is 24-36 pages, magazine-sized, offset-printed, stapled, glossy cover. Publishes about 2-3 poems/issue. Press run is 500 for 70 subscribers of which 10 are libraries; rest are distributed free to physicians and medical personnel. Single copy: $5; subscription: $20. Sample: $6. Make checks payable to Hernando County Medical Society.

How to Submit: Submit up to 5 poems at a time. Line length for poetry is 100 lines maximum. Accepts previously published poems and simultaneous submissions. Accepts submissions on disk or by e-mail (as attachment or in text box). Cover letter is preferred. Submissions should be double-spaced, one side of 8½×11 sheet. Include SASE. Time between acceptance and publication is up to 6 months. "Editorial board is composed of 5-6 members. We meet every quarter to review the material received." Always comments on rejected poems. Occasionally publishes theme issues. Upcoming themes and guidelines available for SASE or by e-mail. Responds in up to 1 month. Pays up to $50/page and 1 contributor's copy. Acquires first North American serial rights. Staff reviews books of poetry in 1,000 words, multi-book format. Poets may send books for review consideration to Pariksith Singh, MD.

Also Offers: "I also publish *Midwest Poetry Review*, a journal of poetry." (See separate listing for *Midwest Poetry Review* in this section.)

⬤ **HEY, LISTEN!; SEAWEED SIDESHOW CIRCUS**, 3820 Miami Rd., Apt. 3, Cincinnati OH 45227. (513)271-2214. E-mail: sscircus@aol.com. Website: http://hometown.aol.com/SSCircus/sscweb.html. Established 1994. **Editor:** Andrew Wright Milam.

Magazine Needs: *Hey, listen!* is an annual "small press magazine created to bring personal response back into publishing." Open to all poetry, except rhyme. Has published poetry by Jim Daniels, Susan Firer, James Liddy, and Sarah Fox. As a sample the editor selected these lines from "he found being in love/more difficult than driving/52 hours home" by Erich Ebert:

> *no one wants to be sad/from saying "in 52 hours I'll be home."/especially since we should be/asking*
> *someone "Do the leaves change/when I touch your skin?"*

Hey, listen! is 30 pages, magazine-sized, photocopied, and saddle-stapled with cardstock cover. Receives about 50-100 poems/year, accepts 20-30%. Press run is 100. Subscription: $5/2 years. Sample: $2. Make checks payable to Seaweed Sideshow Circus.

How to Submit: Submit 3-5 poems at a time. No previously published poems or simultaneous submissions. Accepts e-mail submissions (include in body); no fax submissions. Include SASE and name and address on each page. Cover letter preferred. Time between acceptance and publication is 1-2 months. Often comments on rejected poems. Guidelines available for SASE. Responds in 2 months. Pays 1 contributor's copy. Rights revert to author upon publication.

Book/Chapbook Needs & How to Submit: Seaweed Sideshow Circus is "a place for young or new poets to publish a chapbook." Publishes 1 chapbook/year. Chapbooks are usually 30 pages, 8½×5½, photocopied and saddle-stapled with cardstock cover. Send 5-10 sample poems and cover letter with bio and credits. Responds to queries in 3 weeks; to mss in 3 months. Pays royalties of 10 author's copies (out of a press run of 100). Order sample chapbooks by sending $6.

HIDDEN OAK, P.O. Box 2275, Philadelphia PA 19103. E-mail: hidoak@att.net. Established 1999. **Editor:** Louise Larkins.
Magazine Needs: *Hidden Oak* appears 3 times/year. "Hidden Oak seeks well-crafted poems which make imaginative use of imagery to reach levels deeper than the immediate and personal. Both traditional forms and free verse are accepted. Especially welcome are poems which include time-honored poetic devices and reveal an ear for the music of language." *Hidden Oak* is 60-68 pages, 5½ × 8½, photocopied, stapled, original art/photograph on cover, with several b&w drawings. Receives about 500 poems/year, accepts up to 40%. Publishes about 50-60 poems/issue, usually 1 on a page. Press run is 80-100. Single copy: $4; subscription: $11. Sample: $3. Make checks payable to Louise Larkins.
How to Submit: Submit 3-6 poems at a time. Line length for poetry is 30 maximum. Accepts previously published poems; no simultaneous submissions. Accepts e-mail submissions; no disk submissions. Cover letter is preferred. Include SASE. Also accepts small b&w drawings, whether or not they are poem-related. Submit seasonal poems 2-3 months in advance. Time between acceptance and publication is up to 3 months. Seldom comments on rejected poems. Might publish theme issues in the future. Guidelines available for SASE or by e-mail. Responds in 1 week. Pays 1 copy. Does not review books or chapbooks.

$ **HIGH PLAINS PRESS (Specialized: regional, American West)**, P.O. Box 123, Glendo WY 82213. (307)735-4370. Fax: (307)735-4590. Website: www.highplainspress.com (includes guidelines, contact information, and catalog). Established 1985. **Poetry Editor:** Nancy Curtis.
Book/Chapbook Needs: High Plains Press considers books of poetry "specifically relating to Wyoming and the West, particularly poetry based on historical people/events or nature. We're mainly a publisher of historical nonfiction, but do publish one book of poetry every year." Has published *Close at Hand* by Mary Lou Sanelli and *Bitter Creek Junction* by Linda Hasselstrom. As a sample the editor selected these lines from "Gathering Mint" from the book *Glass-Eyed Paint in the Rain* by Laurie Wagner Buyer:

> He returned at dusk, drunk on solitude, singing/in time with the gelding's rocky trot,/moccasined feet
> wet with mud,/the burlap bag he tossed me/stuffed full of mint/from the beaver slough.

How to Submit: Query first with 3 sample poems (from a 50-poem ms). Accepts fax submissions. Responds in 2 months. Time between acceptance and publication is up to 24 months. Always sends prepublication galleys. Pays 10% of sales. Acquires first rights. Catalog available on request; sample books: $5.
Advice: "Look at our previous titles."

HILLTOP PRESS (Specialized: science fiction), 4 Nowell Place, Almondbury, Huddersfield, West Yorkshire HD5 8PB England. Website (online catalog): www.bbr-online.com/catalogue. Established 1966. **Editor:** Steve Sneyd.
Book/Chapbook Needs: Hilltop publishes "mainly science fiction poetry nowadays." Publications include a series of books on poetry in US and UK SFanzines as well as collections, new and reprint, by individual science fiction poets including, recently, Andrew Darlington, Peter Layton, Gavin Salisbury, J.P.V. Stewart, and Andrei Lubensky. As a sample the editor selected these lines from the book *Euroshima, Mon amour: Poems from the Inner Mind to the Outer Limits*, by Andrew Darlington:

> and this man, frozen involcanic glaze/carbon-dated 50 million years old//to show we've passed this
> way before//he points at Earth, and he smiles that particular smile

Orders from the USA can be placed through the website of BBR Solutions Ltd. (see above).
How to Submit: Does not accept unsolicited mss. Query (with SAE/IRC) with proposals for relevant projects.
Advice: "My advice for beginning poets is (a) persist—don't let any one editor discourage you. 'In poetry's house are many mansions,' what one publication hates another may love; (b) be prepared for long delays between acceptance and appearance of work—the small press is mostly self-financed and part time, so don't expect it to be more efficient than commercial publishers; (c) *always* keep a copy of everything you send out, put your name and address on *everything* you send and *always* include adequately stamped SAE."

N **INDICATES A MARKET** that did not appear in the 2002 edition.

🌐 💲🚫 💾 ◎ **HIPPOPOTAMUS PRESS** (Specialized: form); **OUTPOSTS POETRY QUAR-TERLY; OUTPOSTS ANNUAL POETRY COMPETITION**, 22 Whitewell Rd., Frome, Somerset BA11 4EL England. Phone/fax: 01373-466653. *Outposts* established 1943, Hippopotamus Press established 1974. **Poetry Editor:** Roland John.

Magazine Needs: "*Outposts* is a general poetry magazine that welcomes all work either from the recognized or the unknown poet." Wants "fairly mainstream poetry. No concrete poems or very free verse." Has published poetry by Jared Carter, John Heath-Stubbs, Lotte Kramer, and Peter Russell. As a sample we selected these lines from "The Lotus-Eaters" by Ashleigh John:

> Our lives are one long Sunday, when it rained./There were so many things we might have done—/We watched the television-set instead,/And the day ended as it had begun./We are the quick who may as well be dead:/The nothing-ventured, and the nothing gained.

Outposts is 60-120 pages, A5, litho printed and perfect-bound with laminated card cover, includes occasional art and ads. Receives about 46,000 poems/year, accepts approximately 1%. Press run is 1,600 for 1,200 subscribers of which 400 are libraries, 400 shelf sales. Single copy: $8; subscription: $26. Sample (including guidelines): $6. Make checks payable to Hippopotamus Press. "We prefer credit cards because of bank charges."

How to Submit: Submit 5 poems at a time. "IRCs must accompany U.S. submissions." Accepts simultaneous submissions; no previously published poems. Accepts fax submissions. Cover letter required. Time between acceptance and publications is 9 months. Seldom comments on rejected poems, "only if asked." Occasionally publishes theme issues. Upcoming themes available for SASE (or SAE and IRC). Responds in 2 weeks plus post time. Sometimes sends prepublication galleys. Pays £8/poem plus 1 copy. Copyright remains with author. Staff reviews books of poetry in 200 words for "Books Received" page. Also uses full essays up to 4,000 words. Send books for review consideration, attn. M. Pargitter.

Book/Chapbook Needs & How to Submit: Hippopotamus Press publishes 6 books/year. "The Hippopotamus Press is specialized, with an affinity with Modernism. No Typewriter, Concrete, Surrealism." For book publication query with sample poems. Accepts simultaneous submissions and previously published poems. Responds in 6 weeks. Pays 7½-10% royalties plus author's copies. Send for book catalog to buy samples.

Also Offers: The magazine also holds an annual poetry competition.

⚫ **HIRAM POETRY REVIEW**, P.O. Box 162, Hiram OH 44234. (330)569-7512. Fax: (330)569-5166. E-mail: greenwoodwp@hiram.edu. Established 1967. **Poetry Editor:** Willard Greenwood.

Magazine Needs: *Hiram Poetry Review* is an annual publication appearing in November. "We favor new talent—and except for one issue every three to four years, read only unsolicited mss." Interested in "all kinds of high quality poetry" and have published poetry by Austin Hummell, Mike Fournier, and Gabe Gudding. Circulation is 400 for 300 subscriptions of which 150 are libraries. Receives about 5,000 submissions/year, accepts approximately 20, has up to a 6-month backlog. Although most poems appearing here tend to be lyric and narrative free verse under 50 lines, exceptions occur (a few longer, sequence or formal works can be found in each issue). Single copy: $15; subscription: $15. Sample (of printed back issues): $5.

How to Submit: "Send 2-4 of your best poems. We scan poetry text electronically, directly from the typed manuscripts." No simultaneous submissions. Responds in up to 6 months. Pays 2 copies. Acquires first North American serial rights; returns rights upon publication. Reviews books of poetry in single or multi-book format, no set length. Send books for review consideration.

💲 🚫 💾 ◎ **HODGEPODGE SHORT STORIES & POETRY** (Specialized: subscribers), P.O. Box 6003, Springfield MO 65801. E-mail: fictionpub@aol.com. Established 1994. **Editor:** Vera Jane Goodin. **Contact:** poetry editor.

Magazine Needs: *Hodgepodge* appears quarterly to "provide a showcase for new as well as established poets and authors; to promote writing and offer encouragement." Open to all kinds of poetry. Accepts poetry written by children (but makes no special allowance for them). Has published poetry by Bee Neeley Kuckelman, Gloria Trapold Bradford, and William Sowell. As a sample the editor selected these lines from "Ode to a Lawn Flamingo" by William Sowell:

> A pox on you Don Featherstone./Surely someday you must atone/for thinking up the bird that's known/as the flaming pink lawn flamingo.

Hodgepodge is a 24- to 32-page chapbook, photocopied and saddle-stapled with self cover, includes clip art. Receives about 100 poems/year, accepts up to 50%. Press run is about 100 for about 100 subscribers. Single copy: $3; subscription: $10 US/$15 foreign. Sample: $2. Make checks payable to Goodin Communications. "Potential contributors either need to purchase a copy or be annual subscribers."

How to Submit: Submit up to 4 poems at a time. Accepts previously published poems and simultaneous submissions. Accepts e-mail submissions; include text in body of message, no attachments. SASE required for return of poems. Time between acceptance and publication is 3 months. Seldom comments on rejected poems.

Guidelines available for SASE or by e-mail. Responds in 2 months. Pays $1/poem. Acquires one-time rights. Staff reviews books and chapbooks of poetry and other magazines in 250 words, single and multi-book format. Send books for review consideration to Review Editor.

Also Offers: Sponsors a Best-of-the-Year Contest. Any poem published in *Hodgepodge* is eligible for the contest. 1st Place $30, 2nd Place $15, 3rd Place free subscription. Also awards honorable mentions and certificates. "Judging is done by staff, but readers are asked for input." Sponsors the Sunny Edition contest; deadline: June 30, 2001—poems and short stories that are uplifting, touching or funny. Reading fee of $5 covers up to 3 entries. Awards: work published and 1st Place: $25, 2nd Place: $15, 3rd Place: $10, 4th Place: $5. Published in fall. Details available for SASE.

$ ☑ **THE HOLLINS CRITIC**, P.O. Box 9538, Hollins University, Roanoke VA 24020-1538. (540)362-6275. Website: www.hollins.edu/academics/critic. Established 1964. **Editor:** R.H.W. Dillard. **Poetry Editor:** Cathryn Hankla.

Magazine Needs: *The Hollins Critic*, appears 5 times/year, publishing critical essays, poetry, and book reviews. Uses a few short poems in each issue, interesting in form, content or both. Has published poetry by John Engels, Lyn Lifshin, George Garrett, and Dara Wier. As a sample the editor selected these lines from "Carving the Salmon" by John Engels:

> And then it is recognizable, a fish,/and ready for finishing. It quivers//a little at the skew chisel, flinches/
> at the spoonbit. With the straight gouge/I give it eyes, and with the veiner, gills,//and it leaps a little
> in my hand.

The Hollins Critic is 24 pages, magazine-sized. Press run is 500. Subscription: $6/year ($7.50 outside US). Sample: $1.50.

How to Submit: Submit up to 5 poems, must be typewritten with SASE, to Cathryn Hankla, poetry editor. Reads submissions September through May. Submissions received between June 1 and September 1 will be returned unread. Responds in 6 weeks. Pays $25/poem plus 5 copies.

☑ **HOME PLANET NEWS**, Box 415, Stuyvesant Station, New York NY 10009. Established 1979. **Co-Editor:** Enid Dame. **Co-Editor:** Donald Lev.

Magazine Needs: *Home Planet News* appears 3 times/year. "Our purpose is to publish lively and eclectic poetry, from a wide range of sensibilities, and to provide news of the small press and poetry scenes, thereby fostering a sense of community among contributors and readers." Wants "honest, well-crafted poems, open or closed form, on any subject. Poems under 30 lines stand a better chance. We do not want any work which seems to us to be racist, sexist, agist, anti-Semitic, or imposes limitations on the human spirit." Has published poetry by Layle Silbert, Robert Peters, Lyn Lifshin, and Gerald Locklin. As a sample the editor selected these lines from "Milk" by Barry Wallenstein:

> In my tired hand—milk/in my memory—it glows/a white shadow/smear around my younger mouth/
> around what I used to know

Home Planet News is a 24-page tabloid, web offset-printed, includes b&w drawings, photos, cartoons and ads. Receives about 1,000 poems/year, accepts up to 3%. Press run is 1,000 for 300 subscribers. Subscription: $10/4 issues, $18/8 issues. Sample: $3.

How to Submit: Submit 3-6 poems at a time. No previously published poems or simultaneous submissions. Cover letter preferred. "SASEs are a must." Reads submissions February 1 through May 31 only. Time between acceptance and publication is 1 year. Seldom comments on rejected poems. Occasionally publishes theme issues. "We announce these in issues." Guidelines available for SASE, "however, it is usually best to simply send work." Responds in 4 months. Pays 1-year gift subscription plus 3 copies. Acquires first rights. All rights revert to author on publication. Reviews books and chapbooks of poetry and other magazines in 1,200 words, single and multi-book format. Poets may send books for review consideration to Enid Dame. "Note: we do have guidelines for book reviewers; please write for them. Magazines are reviewed by a staff member."

Advice: "Read many publications, attend readings, feel yourself part of a writing community, learn from others."

☑ **HOMESTEAD REVIEW**, Box A-5, 156 Homestead Ave., Hartnell College, Salinas CA 93901. (831)755-6943. Fax: (831)755-6751. E-mail: mtabor@jafar.hartnell.cc.ca.us. Website: www.hartnell.cc.ca.us/Homestead_Review/SPOL (includes guidelines, contact and subscription information, bios, and archives). Established 1985. **Editor:** Maria Garcia Tabor.

Magazine Needs: *Homestead Review* appears biannually (December and May). Wants to see "avant-garde poetry as well as fixed form styles of remarkable quality and originality. We do not want to see Hallmark-style writing or first drafts." Accepts poetry written by children. Recently published poetry by Ray Gonzalez, Kathryn Kirkpatrick, Dana Garrett, Virgil Suarez, Morton Marcus, and Hilary Mosher Buri. As a sample the editor selected these lines from "Why There Can Be No More Chinese Departure Poems" by Dana Garrett:

> Under the digital blue theater sign outside the mall,/White faces stream out behind us./Here we must
> offer our "Later" and "Yea, Later,"/And trek a thousand feet of parking lot in broken glass.

Receives about 1,000 poems/year, accepts about 15%. Publishes about 65 poems/issue. Press run is 500 for 300 subscribers of which 300 are libraries; 200 are distributed free to poets, writers, bookstores. Single copy: $10, subscription: $20/year. Make checks payable to *Homestead Review*.

How to Submit: Submit 3 poems at a time. No previously published poems or simultaneous submissions. No fax, e-mail, or disk submissions. Cover letter is required. "A brief bio should be included in the cover letter." Reads submissions all year. Submit seasonal poems 3 months in advance. Time between acceptance and publication is 2 months. "Manuscripts are read by the staff and discussed. Poems/fiction accepted by majority consensus." Often comments on rejected poems. Guidelines available for SASE. Responds in 2 months. Pays 1 contributor's copy. Acquires one-time rights.

Also Offers: "We accept short fiction, book reviews, and b&w photography/art, and interviews."

Advice: "Poetry is language distilled; do not send unpolished work. Join a workshop group if at all possible."

$ 🌓 📖 ◎ HOUSE OF ANANSI PRESS (Specialized: regional, Canada), 895 Don Mills Road, 400-2 Park Centre, Toronto, Ontario M3C 1W3 Canada. (416)445-3333. Fax: (416)445-5967. E-mail: info@anansi.ca. Website: www.anansi.ca (includes submission guidelines, front list, back list, contact info). Established 1967. **Publisher:** Martha Sharpe. **Editor:** Adrienne Leahey.

Book/Chapbook Needs: House of Anansi publishes literary fiction and poetry by Canadian writers. "We seek to balance the list between well-known and emerging writers, with an interest in writing by Canadians of all backgrounds. We publish Canadian poetry only, and poets must have a substantial publication record—if not in books, then definitely in journals and magazines of repute. No children's poetry and no poetry by previously unpublished poets." Has published *Power Politics* by Margaret Atwood and *Ruin & Beauty* by Patricia Young. As a sample they selected these lines from "The Ecstasy of Skeptics" in the book *The Ecstasy of Skeptics* by Steven Heighton:

> This tongue/is a moment of moistened dust, it must learn/to turn the grit of old books/into hydrogen,
> and burn/The dust of the muscles must burn/down the blood-fuse of the sinews, . . .

Books are generally 96-144 pages, trade paperback with French sleeves, a matte finish cover and full-color cover art.

How to Submit: Canadian poets should query first with 10 sample poems (typed double-spaced) and a cover letter with brief bio and publication credits. Accepts previously published poems and simultaneous submissions. Poems are circulated to an editorial board. Often comments on rejected poems. Responds to queries within 3 months, to mss (if invited) within 4 months. Pays 8-10% royalties, a $750 advance and 10 author's copies (out of a press run of 1,000).

Advice: To learn more about their titles, check their website or write to the press directly for a catalog. "We strongly advise poets to build up a publishing résumé by submitting poems to reputable magazines and journals. This indicates three important things to us: One, that he or she is becoming a part of the Canadian poetry community; two, that he or she is building up a readership through magazine subscribers; and three, it establishes credibility in his or her work. There is a great deal of competition for only three or four spots on our list each year—which always includes works by poets we have previously published."

🌐 📀 HQ POETRY MAGAZINE (THE HAIKU QUARTERLY); THE DAY DREAM PRESS, 39 Exmouth St., Kingshill, Swindon, Wiltshire SN1 3PU England. Phone: 01793-523927. Website: www.nogs.dial.pipex.com/HQ.htm (includes poetry from past and present issues). Established 1990. **Editor:** Kevin Bailey.

Magazine Needs: *HQ Poetry Magazine* is "a platform from which new and established poets can speak and/or experiment with new forms and ideas." Wants "any poetry of good quality." Accepts poetry written by children. Has published poetry by Peter Redgrove, Alan Brownjohn, James Kirkup, and Cid Corman. *HQ Poetry magazine* is 48-64 pages, A5, perfect-bound with art, ads, and reviews. Accepts about 5% of poetry received. Press run is 500-600 for 500 subscribers of which 30 are libraries. Subscription: £10 UK, £13 foreign. Sample: £2.70.

How to Submit: No previously published poems or simultaneous submissions. Cover letter and SASE (or SAE and IRCs) required. Time between acceptance and publication is 3-6 months. Often comments on rejected poems. Responds "as time allows." Pays 1 copy. Reviews books of poetry in about 1,000 words, single book format. Poets may send books for review consideration.

Also Offers: Sponsors "Piccadilly Poets" in London, and "Live Poet's Society" based in Bath, Somerset England.

🌑 HUBBUB; VI GALE AWARD; ADRIENNE LEE AWARD, 5344 SE 38th Ave., Portland OR 97202. Established 1983. **Editors:** L. Steinman and J. Shugrue.

Magazine Needs: Appearing once/year (usually in August/September), *Hubbub* is designed "to feature a multitude of voices from interesting contemporary American poets. We look for poems that are well-crafted, with something to say. We have no single style, subject, or length requirement and, in particular, will consider long poems. No light verse." Has published poetry by Madeline DeFrees, Cecil Giscombe, Carolyn Kizer, Primus St. John, Shara McCallum, and Alice Fulton. *Hubbub* is 50-70 pages, 5½×8½, offset-printed and perfect-bound, cover art only, usually no ads. Receives about 1,200 submissions/year, accepts up to 2%. Press run is 350 for 100 subscribers of which 12 are libraries, about 150 shelf sales. Subscription: $5/year. Sample: $3.35 (back issues), $5 (current issue).

How to Submit: Submit 3-6 typed poems (no more than 6) with SASE. No previously published poems or simultaneous submissions. Guidelines available for SASE. Responds in 4 months. Pays 2 copies. Acquires first North American serial rights. "We review two to four poetry books/year in short (three-page) reviews; all reviews are solicited. We do, however, list books received/recommended." Send books for consideration.

Also Offers: Outside judges choose poems from each volume for two awards: Vi Gale Award ($100) and Adrienne Lee Award ($50). There are no special submission procedures or entry fees involved.

☑ $☑ THE HUDSON REVIEW, 684 Park Ave., New York NY 10021. Website: www.hudsonrevie w.com (includes guidelines, contact and subscription information, and text from magazine). **Editor:** Paula Deitz. **Contact:** Emily D. Montjoy.

• Work published in this review has been included in the 1997 and 1998 volumes of *The Best American Poetry*.

Magazine Needs: *The Hudson Review* is a high-quality, flat-spined quarterly of 176 pages, considered one of the most prestigious and influential journals in the nation. Editors welcome all styles and forms. However, competition is extraordinarily keen, especially since poems compete with prose. Has published poetry by Marilyn Nelson, Hayden Carruth, Louis Simpson, and Dana Gioia. Subscription: $28 ($32 foreign)/1 year, institutions $34 ($38 foreign)/1 year. Sample: $9.

How to Submit: Do not submit more than 10 poems at a time. No previously published or simultaneous submissions. Nonsubscribers may submit poems between April 1 and June 30 only. "Manuscripts submitted by subscribers who so identify themselves will be read throughout the year." Responds in 3 months. Always sends prepublication galleys. Pays 2 copies and 50¢/line.

Advice: "Read the magazine to ascertain our style/sensibility."

☑ ☺ HUNGER MAGAZINE; HUNGER PRESS (Specialized: form, language-image experimentation), 1305 Old Route 28, Phoenicia NY 12464. (845)688-2332. E-mail: hungermag@aol.com. Website: www.hungermagazine.com (includes guidelines, contact and subscription information, catalog, archives, links, and editorial policy). Established 1997. **Publisher/Editor:** J.J. Blickstein.

Magazine Needs: *Hunger Magazine* is an international zine based in the Hudson Valley and appears 2 times/year. "*Hunger* publishes mostly poetry but will accept some short fiction, essays, translations, cover art, and book reviews. Although there are no school/stylistic limitations, our main focus is on language-image experimentation with an edge. We publish no names for prestige and most of our issues are dedicated to emerging talent. Well known poets do grace our pages to illuminate possibilities. No dead kitty elegies; Beat impersonators; Hallmark cards; 'I'm not sure if I can write poems'. All rhymers better be very, very good. We have published poetry by Amiri Baraka, Paul Celan, Robert Kelly, Anne Waldman, Janine Pommy Vega, Antonin Artaud, and Clayton Eshleman." *Hunger* is 75-100 pages, magazine-sized, saddle-stapled with glossy full-color card cover, uses original artworks and drawings. Accepts about 10% of submissions. Press run is 250-500. Single issue: $7 and $1 p&h ($10 foreign); subscription: $14 ($20 foreign). Back issue: $7. Chapbooks: $5. Make checks payable to Hunger Magazine & Press.

How to Submit: "Send 3-10 pages and SASE." Accepts simultaneous submissions, if notified; no previously published poems. Accepts e-mail submissions and queries; include text in body of message "unless otherwise requested." Brief cover letter with SASE preferred. "Manuscripts without SASEs will be recycled. Please proof your work and clearly indicate stanza breaks." Time between acceptance and publication is up to 1 year. Guidelines available for SASE, by e-mail, on website, or in publication. Responds in up to 6 months, depending on backlog. Sends prepublication galleys upon request. Pays 1-5 copies depending on amount of work published. "If invited to be a featured poet we pay a small honorarium and copies." Acquires first North American serial rights.

Advice: "Read, read, read."

☑ THE HUNTED NEWS; THE SUBOURBON PRESS, P.O. Box 9101, Warwick RI 02889. (401)826-7307. Established 1990. **Editor:** Mike Wood.

Magazine Needs: *The Hunted News* is an annual "designed to find good writers and give them one more outlet to get their voices heard." As for poetry, the editor says, "The poems that need to be written are those that need to be read." Does not want to see "the poetry that does not need to be written or which is written only to get a reaction or congratulate the poet." Accepts poetry written by children. *The Hunted News* is 25-30 pages, 8½×11, photocopied, unstapled. "I receive over 200 poems per month and accept perhaps 10%." Press run is 150-200. Sample free with SASE.

How to Submit: Accepts previously published poems; no simultaneous submissions. Always comments on rejected poems. Publishes theme issues. Guidelines and upcoming themes available for SASE. Responds in 1 month. Pays 3-5 copies, more on request. "I review current chapbooks and other magazines and do other random reviews of books, music, etc. Word count varies."

Advice: "I receive mostly beginner's poetry that attempts to be too philosophical, without much experience to back up statements, or self-impressed 'radical' poems by poets who assume that I will publish them because they are beyond criticism. I would like poets to send work whose point lies in language and economy and in experience, not in trite final lines, or worse, in the arrogant cover letter."

HURRICANE ALICE (Specialized: feminist), Dept. of English, Rhode Island College, Providence RI 02908. (401)456-8377. Fax: (401)456-8379. E-mail: mreddy@ric.edu. Established 1983. **Executive Editor:** Maureen Reddy.

Magazine Needs: *Hurricane Alice* is a quarterly feminist review. Poems should be "infused by a feminist sensibility (whether the poet is female or male)." Has published poetry by Alice Walker, Ellen Bass, Patricia Hampl, Nellie Wong, Edith Kur, and Kristen Williams. As a sample the editor selected these lines from "The Gift" by Marjorie Roemer:

> I would give you my right hand/My mother always said/Too many times/As if she really wanted to/As if she needed to.

Hurricane Alice is a "12-page folio with plenty of graphics." Press run is 1,000, of which 450 are subscriptions, about 50 go to libraries, and about 100 shelf sales. Subscription: $12 (or $10 low-income). Sample: $2.50.

How to Submit: Submit no more than 3 poems at a time. Considers simultaneous submissions. Time between acceptance and publication is up to 6 months. Publishes theme issues. Guidelines and upcoming themes available for SASE. Responds in 1 year. Pays 6 copies. Reviews books of poetry.

IAMBS & TROCHEES (Specialized: forms/metrical verse only); IAMBS & TROCHEES ANNUAL POETRY CONTEST, 6801 19th Ave. 5H, Brooklyn NY 11204. (718)232-9268. E-mail: carwill@prodigy.net. Website: www.iambsandtrochees.com (includes essays, responses, contest, guidelines). Established 2001. **Editor/Publisher:** William F. Carlson.

Magazine Needs: *Iambs & Trochees* appears biannually in spring and fall. Welcomes "poetry written in the great tradition of English and American literature. We will consider rhymed verse, blank verse, and metrically regular verse of any type, along with poems written in the various fixed forms. These include (but are not limited to) the sonnet, the villanelle, the ballade, the triolet, and the ottava rima. We are open to all genres: lyric, elegiac, satiric, narrative, or anything else. We have no restrictions on subject matter, nor do we demand that our writers follow any specific approach or ideology when handling their material. Our concern is strictly with the intrinsic aesthetic merit of a poem." Does not want free verse, syllabic verse. Recently published poetry by Alfred Dorn, Rhina Espaillat, Samuel Maio, Rachel Hadas, Jared Carter, and X.J. Kennedy. As a sample we selected the poem "Souvenir" by Jennifer Reeser:

> So many mornings I awoke in tears/from one more dream of crying at her grave,/but she was always there, secure and strong,//perfumed with talc or Oriental spice,/with perfect words, and comfort cold as ice—/the only love I ever held too long.

Iambs & Trochees is 64 pages, 7×9, digitally-printed, perfect-bound, paper cover. Single copy: $8; subscription: $15/year (2 issues). Sample: $8. Make checks payable to Iambs & Trochees Publishing.

How to Submit: No previously published poems or simultaneous submissions. Accepts e-mail and disk submissions; no fax submissions. Include SASE for return of poems not accepted. Time between acceptance and publication is 2 months. Submission deadline: January 30 (Spring) and August 30 (Fall/Winter). Poems are circulated to an editorial board. "We select poems on how well they are crafted." Seldom comments on rejected poems. Guidelines available in magazine or on website. Responds in 2 months. Pays 1 contributor's copy. Acquires first North American serial rights. Reviews books of poetry *only* in 1,500 words.

Also Offers: Sponsors annual poetry contest for metrical poetry. Offers 3 awards of $300, $150, and $50. No entry fee. Guidelines available for SASE or on website.

Advice: "We feel keeping a beautiful tradition alive is possible by presenting poems in the classic tradition."

IBBETSON ST. PRESS, 25 School St., Somerville MA 02143-1721. (617)628-2313. E-mail: ibbetsonstreet@GO.com or Dianner@iopener.net. Website: http://homepage.mac.com/rconte (includes guidelines, contact and subscription info, bios, and samples). Established 1999. **Editor:** Doug Holder. **Co-Editors:** Dianne Robitaille, Richard Wilhelm, Linda H. Conte, and Marc Widershien.

Magazine Needs: Appearing biannually in May and November, *Ibbetson St. Press* is "a poetry magazine that wants 'down to earth' poetry that is well-written; has clean, crisp images; with a sense of irony and humor. We want mostly free verse, but open to rhyme. No maudlin, trite, overly political, vulgar for vulgar's sake, poetry that tells but doesn't show." Has published poetry by Robert K. Johnson, Don Divecchio, Ed Galing, Brian Morrissey, and Oliver Cutshaw. As a sample the editors selected these lines by Ed Chaberek:

> It's down a curving brick/stair, where the cool beer-stale/air gets thick; it's past/the piss-stains and the cracks/left by some wise guy's skull.

Ibbetson St. Press is 30 pages, 8½×11, desktop-published with plastic binding and cream cover stock cover, includes b&w prints and classified ads. Receives about 300 poems/year, accepts up to 40%. Press run is 100 for 20 subscribers. Single copy: $4; subscription: $7. Sample: $2. Make checks payable to Ibbetson St. Press.

How to Submit: Submit 3-5 poems at a time. Accepts previously published poems and simultaneous submissions. Cover letter required. Time between acceptance and publication is up to 5 months. Poems are circulated to an editorial board. "Three editors comment on submissions." Guidelines available by SASE. Responds in 2 weeks. Pays 1 copy. Acquires one-time rights. Reviews books and chapbooks of poetry and other magazines in 250-500 words. Poets may send books for review consideration.

Book/Chapbook Needs & How to Submit: "We also publish chapbooks by newer, little exposed poets of promise. In some cases we pay for all expenses, in others the poet covers publishing expenses." Has published *The Life of All Worlds* by Marc Widershien and *Inaccessibility of the Creator* by Jack Powers. Chapbooks are usually 20-30 pages, 8½×11, photocopied with plastic binding, white coverstock cover, includes b&w prints. "Send complete manuscript for consideration, at least 20-30 poems with or without artwork." Responds to queries in 1 month. Pays 50 author's copies (out of a press run of 100). Order sample books or chapbooks by sending $5.

Advice: "Please buy a copy of the magazine you submit to—support the small press. In your work, be honest. Don't affect."

$⊘ THE ICONOCLAST, 1675 Amazon Rd., Mohegan Lake NY 10547-1804. Established 1992. **Editor/Publisher:** Phil Wagner.

Magazine Needs: *The Iconoclast* is a general interest literary publication appearing 7 times/year. Wants "poems that have something to say—the more levels the better. Nothing sentimental, obscure, or self-absorbed. Try for originality; if not in thought, then expression. No greeting card verse or noble religious sentiments. Look for the unusual in the usual, parallels in opposites, the capturing of what is unique or often unnoticed in an ordinary, or extraordinary moment. What makes us human—and the resultant glories and agonies. Our poetry is accessible to a thoughtful reading public." Has published poetry by John Garmon, Lyle Glazier, and Gerald Kaminski. As a sample, the editor selected these lines from "While My Soul Was in the Shop Awaiting Fixes" by Harry Olive:

> Remembering why we have to/love someone,/as though it were the coming/of an unknown god.

The Iconoclast is 40-64 pages, journal-sized, photo offset on #45 white wove paper, with b&w art, graphics, photos and ads. Receives about 2,000 poems/year, accepts up to 3%. Press run is 500-2,000 for 335 subscribers. Subscription: $15 for 8 issues. Double issue: $3. Sample: $2.50.

How to Submit: Submit 3-4 poems at a time. Time between acceptance and publication is 4-12 months. Sometimes comments on rejected poems. Responds in 1 month. Pays 1 copy per published page or poem, 40% discount on extras, and $2-5 per poem for first North American rights on acceptance. Reviews books of poetry in 250 words, single format.

⊘ ◎ THE IDIOT (Specialized: humor), P.O. Box 69163, Los Angeles CA 90069. E-mail: slavingins rilanka@hotmail.com. Website: http://magicalmeat.com. Established 1993. **President for Life:** Sam Hayes. **Mussolini to My Hitler:** Brian Campbell.

Magazine Needs: *The Idiot* is a biannual humor magazine. "We mostly use fiction, articles, and cartoons, but will use anything funny, including poetry. Nothing pretentious. We are a magazine of dark comedy. Death, dismemberment, and religion are all subjects of comedy. Nothing is sacred. But it needs to be funny, which brings us to . . . Laughs! I don't want whimsical, I don't want amusing, I don't want some fanciful anecdote about childhood. I mean belly laughs, laughing out loud, fall on the floor funny. If it's cute, give it to your sweetheart or your puppy dog. Length doesn't matter, but most comedy is like soup. It's an appetizer, not a meal. Short is often better. Bizarre, obscure, and/or literary references are often appreciated but not necessary." Has published poetry by Brian Campbell, Joe Deasy, Mike Buckley, and Mark Romyn. As a sample the editor selected these lines from "The Cat in the Hat (Millennium Remix)" by Dr. Sardonicus:

> This cat lived alone,/Resentful and bitter./He slept in his hat/Filled with foul smelling litter.//Given his druthers/He hated most others/He hated them all/Even poor old Coruthers!

The Idiot is 48 pages, 5½ × 8½, professionally printed and staple-bound with glossy cover. Receives about 250 submissions/year, accepts up to 3-4. Press run is 300. Subscription: $10. Sample: $6.
How to Submit: Accepts previously published poems and simultaneous submissions. Prefers e-mail submissions if included in body of message. Seldom comments on rejected poems. Responds in 3 months. Pays 1 copy. Acquires one-time rights.
Advice: "Gather round, my children. Oh, come closer. Closer, don't be shy. Okay, scoot back, that's too close. Now listen closely as there's something uncle Sammy wants to tell you. Billy, get those fingers out of your ears and listen. I'd like to give you a little advice about submissions. You see, kids, most people send me poems that just aren't funny. We're a *comedy* magazine, emphasis on the word 'comedy.' We're looking for things that are funny. Anything less than that demeans us both (but mostly you). So please make sure that whatever you send isn't just amusing or cute, but really, really, really hilarious."

◑ ILLUMINATIONS, AN INTERNATIONAL MAGAZINE OF CONTEMPORARY WRIT-ING, % Dept. of English, College of Charleston, 66 George St., Charleston SC 29424-0001. (843)953-1993. Fax: (843)953-3180. E-mail: lewiss@cofc.edu. Website: www.cofc.edu/Illuminations (includes guidelines, contact and subscription information, links, archives). Established 1982. **Editor:** Simon Lewis.
Magazine Needs: *Illuminations* is published annually "to provide a forum for new writers alongside already established ones." Open as to form and style. Do not want to see anything "bland or formally clunky." Has published poetry by Peter Porter, Michael Hamburger, Geri Doran and Anne Born. As a sample the editor selected these lines from "For Stephen Spender" by Louis Bourne:

> Old romantic, imprisoned in your speech,/Steeled in a world racing to its doom,/We've taken in the
> news from your compass-points./You've given us some signs that still can teach.

Illuminations is 64-88 pages, 8 × 5, offset-printed and perfect-bound with 2-color card cover, includes photos and engravings. Receives about 1,500 poems/year, accepts up to 5%. Press run is 400. Subscription: $15/2 issues. Sample: $10.
How to Submit: Submit up to 6 poems at a time. No previously published poems or simultaneous submissions. Accepts e-mail and fax submissions. Brief cover letter preferred. Time between acceptance and publication "depends on when received. Can be up to a year." Publishes theme issues occasionally; "issue 16 [2000] was a Vietnamese special; issue 17 [2001] focuses on Cuban and Latin American writing." Guidelines available by e-mail. Responds within 2 months. Pays 2 copies plus one subsequent issue. Acquires all rights. Returns rights on request.

◉ ILLYA'S HONEY, % Dallas Poets Community, P.O. Box 700865, Dallas TX 75370. Website: www.dallaspoets.org (includes guidelines, contest and subscription information, links, biographies of members, link to e-mail, and sample poems). Established 1994, acquired by Dallas Poets Community in January 1998. **Managing Editor:** Ann Howells. **Contact:** Editor.
Magazine Needs: *Illya's Honey* is a quarterly journal of poetry and micro fiction. "All subjects and styles are welcome, but we admit a fondness for free verse. Poems may be of any length but should be accessible, thought-provoking, fresh, and should exhibit technical skill. Every poem is read by at least three members of our editorial staff, all of whom are poets. No didactic or overly religious verse, please." Recently published poetry by Lyn Lifshin, Joe Ahern, Seamus Murphy, Robert Eastwood, and Brandon Brown. *Illya's Honey* is 40 pages, digest-sized, and saddle-stapled, glossy card cover with b&w photographs. Receives about 2,000 poems/year, accepts about 5-10%. Press run is 250 for 80 subscribers, 50 shelf sales. Subscription: $18. Current issue: $6. Sample: $4.
How to Submit: Submit 3-5 poems at a time. No previously published poems or simultaneous submissions. Cover letter preferred. Include short biography. Occasionally comments on rejected poems. Guidelines available for SASE. Responds in up to 5 months. Pays 1 contributor's copy.
Also Offers: See listing for Dallas Poets Community under Organizations.

$ ◉ ◎ IMAGE: A JOURNAL OF ARTS & RELIGION (Specialized: religious), 3307 3rd Ave. W., Seattle WA 98119. E-mail: image@imagejournal.org. Website: www.imagejournal.org (includes sample material from all back issues; info on The Glen Workshop, an annual writers workshop sponsored by *Image*; guidelines; *Image* Artist of the Month; as well as information on advertising; back issue and subscription ordering). Established 1989. **Publisher:** Gregory Wolfe.
Magazine Needs: *Image*, published quarterly, "explores and illustrates the relationship between faith and art through world-class fiction, poetry, essays, visual art, and other arts." Wants "poems that grapple with religious faith, usually Judeo-Christian." Has published poetry by Philip Levine, Scott Cairns, Annie Dillard, Mary Oliver, Mark Jarman, and Kathleen Norris. As a sample we selected these lines from "Receptionism" by Marjorie Maddox:

> Does our kneeling/bring him down/again, from the wood,/unhinge his stone,/trumpet for ourselves/our
> catalytic salvation?

Image is 136 pages, 10×7, perfect-bound, acid free paper with glossy 4-color cover, averages 10 pages of 4-color art/issue (including cover), ads. Receives about 800 poems/year, accepts up to 2%. Has 4,700 subscribers of which 100 are libraries. Subscription: $36. Sample: $12.

How to Submit: Submit up to 4 poems at a time. No previously published poems. Cover letter preferred. No e-mail submissions. Time between acceptance and publication is 1 year. Guidelines available on website. Responds in 3 months. Always sends prepublication galleys. Pays 4 copies plus $2/line ($150 maximum). Acquires first North American serial rights. Reviews books of poetry in 1,000-1,300 words, single or multi-book format. Poets may send books for review consideration.

◖ **IMAGES INSCRIPT**, P.O. Box 44894, Columbus OH 43204-4894. E-mail: submit@ImagesInscript. com or comments@ImagesInscript.com. Website: www.ImagesInscript.com (includes guidelines, links, contact information, editorial policy, best poem, best short story, subscription and contest information, latest edition, and archives). Established 1998. **Publisher:** H. Roger Baker II. **Editor:** Carla Radwanski.

Magazine Needs: *Images Inscript* is published monthly online "to provide a showcase of poetry and short stories. *Images Inscript* is a place for writers to submit and comment on poetry and interact with other writers. We want to see creative well-written poetry that showcases the writer's talent. We do not want to see excessive use of 'adult' language." Has published poetry by Ben Jones, Susanne Onskog, James William Hoddinott, Maryann Hazen-Stearns, Daniel Green, and Dorothy Doyle Mienko. As a sample they selected these lines from "Annabelle Lynn and the White Bird" by Susanne Onskag:

> Deep in her heart she felt it/this bird knew who she was./He had seen the whole of her/yet smiled and
> understood.

Receives about 1,300 poems/year, accepts up to 5%.

How to Submit: Submit 1 poem at a time. Line length for poetry is 60 maximum. Accepts previously published poems and simultaneous submissions. Accepts submissions by e-mail (in text box) or by online submission form. "Electronic submissions preferred, subject line should read 'I.I. submission' with name, address and age included in 75 word maximum biography—sent to submit@imagesinscript.com." Time between acceptance and publication is up to 6 weeks. Seldom comments on rejected poems. Guidelines available by e-mail or on website. Responds in up to 4 months. Sometimes sends prepublication galleys. Acquires one time electronic rights.

Also Offers: Sponsors a yearly contest where the best poetry and short story writers are awarded a minimum of $50. Also publishes an anthology, *Images Inscript: Reflections*, in June and December as "a showcase of the works by a specific selected author." Not open to poets under 18.

Advice: "Please review *Images Inscript* submissions guidelines and previous issues before submitting."

N ◖ **IMPROVIJAZZATION NATION**, 5806 B Armour Dr., Lacey WA 98513. (360)438-9299. E-mail: rotcod@reachone.com. Website: www.reachone.com. Established 1991. **Editor:** Dick Metcalf.

Magazine Needs: *Improvijazzation Nation* is a webzine "devoted to networking; prime focus is tape/music reviews, includes quite a bit of poetry." Wants "experimental, visual impact and non-establishment poetry, no more than 15 lines. No hearts and flowers, shallow, epic." Has published poetry by John M. Bennett, Joan Payne Kincaid and Anthony Lucero. Receives 50-100 poems/year, accepts approximately 50%.

How to Submit: Submit 3 poems at a time. Accepts previously published poems and simultaneous submissions. E-mail submissions preferred (as attachment or in text box). Often comments on rejected poems. Responds within a week or two. No payment. Reviews books of poetry. Also accepts short essays/commentary on the use of networking to void commercial music markets, as well as material of interest to musical/artist improvisors.

$ ◖ ◎ **IN THE FAMILY (Specialized: gay/lesbian/bisexual/transgender)**, P.O. Box 5387, Takoma Park MD 20913. (301)270-4771. E-mail: lmarkowitz@aol.com. Website: http://inthefamily.com. Established 1995. **Fiction Editor:** Helena Lipstadt.

Magazine Needs: *In the Family* is a quarterly "therapy magazine exploring clinical issues for queer people and their families." We're open to anything but it must refer to a gay/lesbian/bisexual/transgender theme. No long autobiography. No limericks." Has published poetry by Benjamin Goldberg, Penny Perry, and Katrina Gonzalez. As a sample the editor selected these lines from "The Long to Be" by Greg Pokarney:

> My mother and I/wouldn't talk too much./She thought I had/too small of hands,/even though they were/
> exactly the size of hers./Her eyes would blow through the leaves on the street,/and I would count them
> as they fell away./My mother was never so serious as to/count herself among the leaves.

In the Family is 32 pages, 8½×11, offset-printed and saddle-stapled with 2-color cover, includes art and ads. Receives about 50 poems/year, accepts approximately 10%. Press run is 10,000 for 8,000 subscribers of which 10% are libraries, 5% shelf sales; 10% distributed free to direct mail promos. Subscription: $24. Sample: $6. Make checks payable to ITF.

How to Submit: Submit 5 poems at a time. Accepts simultaneous submissions; no previously published poems. No e-mail submissions. Cover letter required. Time between acceptance and publication is up to 3 months. Poems are circulated to an editorial board. "Fiction editor makes recommendations." Publishes theme issues. Responds in 6 weeks. Always sends prepublication galleys. Pays $35 and 5 copies. Acquires first rights. Reviews books of poetry. Poets may send books for review consideration to attn. Reviews.

⚫ ◎ IN THE GROVE (Specialized: regional, California), P.O. Box 16195, Fresno CA 93755. (559)442-4600, ext. 8469. Fax: (559)265-5756. E-mail: inthegrove@rocketmail.com. Website: http://lherri ck.freeyellow.com/inthegrove.html (includes guidelines, submission deadlines, samples from recent issues). Established 1996. **Publisher:** Lee Herrick. **Editor:** Michael Roberts. **Poetry Editor:** Zay Guffy-Bill.
Magazine Needs: *In the Grove* appears 2 times/year and publishes "short fiction, essays, and poetry by new and established writers born or currently living in the Central Valley and throughout California." Wants "poetry of all forms and subject matter. We seek the originality, distinct voice and craftsmanship of a poem. No greeting card verse or forced rhyme. Be fresh. Take a risk." Has published poetry by Gillian Wegener, Andres Montoya, Loren Palsgaard, Amy Uyematsu, and Renny Christopher. *In The Grove* is 80-100 pages, 5½×8½, photocopied and perfect-bound with heavy card stock cover, 4-5 pages of ads. Receives about 500 poems/year, accepts up to 10%. Press run is 150 for 50 subscribers, 75 shelf sales; 25 distributed free to contributors, colleagues. Subscription: $12. Sample: $6.
How to Submit: Submit 3-5 poems at a time. Accepts previously published poems and simultaneous submissions. Cover letter preferred. Time between acceptance and publication is up to 6 months. "Poetry editor reads all submissions and makes recommendations to editor, who makes final decisions." Seldom comments on rejected poems. Guidelines available for SASE or on website. Responds in 3 months. Pays 2 copies. Acquires first or one-time rights. Rights return to poets upon publication.

Ⓝ ⚪ IN THE SPIRIT OF THE BUFFALO, Opportunity Assistance, 233 N. 48th St., Suite MBE 151, Lincoln NE 68504. (402)464-1994. Fax: (978)285-0331. E-mail: webmaster@opportunityassistance.com. Website: www.inthespiritofthebuffalo.com. Established 1996. **Publisher/Editor:** Keith P. Stiencke.
Magazine Needs: *In the Spirit of the Buffalo* is published 2 or 3 times a month online and as an e-mail newsletter to "provide a forum for poets and authors of all experience levels to be a positive influence for social awareness and change through creative personal expression." Wants "poetry that awakens social consciousness while still being positive in tone. Motivational, inspirational, and spiritual writing is highly acceptable. No poetry that promotes racism; no hate poetry; pornographic content is not acceptable."
How to Submit: Submit up to 3 poems at a time. Accepts previously published poems; no simultaneous submissions. Accepts submissions on disk, by e-mail (in text box), by fax, or by regular mail. E-mail preferred. Cover letter preferred; "we would appreciate being able to publish your contact information, however it is not a requirement for publication." Time between acceptance and publication is 3-6 months. Seldom comments on rejected poems. Responds in up to 4 months. Acquires one-time rights. Poets may send books for review consideration.
Also Offers: "We will be offering occasional contests in which cash and other prizes will be awarded. In addition, we will offer a yearly anthology in both paper and e-book format. Purchases will contribute to a pool from which all writers will receive residual income."
Advice: "Proofread, again and again. Read previous editions to see what we may consider as right for publishing."

Ⓝ ⚫ INDEFINITE SPACE (Specialized: style/experimental), P.O. Box 40101, Pasadena CA 91114. Established 1992. **Editor:** Marcia Arrieta.
Magazine Needs: *Indefinite Space* appears annually. Wants experimental, visual, minimalistic poetry. Does not want rhyming poetry. Recently published poetry by Bruna Mori, Dan Campion, Jeffrey Little, Crag Hill, Ann Erickson, and Giovanni Malito. *Indefinite Space* is 36 pages, digest-sized, with b&w art. Single copy: $6; subscription: $10/2 issues. Sample: $6. Make checks payable to Marcia Arrieta.
How to Submit: Accepts simultaneous submissions; no previously published poems. No fax, e-mail, or disk submissions. Seldom comments on rejected poems. Guidelines available for SASE. Responds in up to 3 months. Copyright retained by poets.

▼ ⚫ ◎ INDIAN HERITAGE PUBLISHING; INDIAN HERITAGE COUNCIL QUAR-TERLY; NATIVE AMERICAN POETRY ANTHOLOGY (Specialized: ethnic/nationality, Native American; spirituality/inspirational); P.O. Box 2302, Morristown TN 37816. (423)581-4448. Established 1986. **CEO:** Louis Hooban.

• Indian Heritage Publishing's Native American Poetry Anthology won first prize in literature from the Green Corn Festival 1999 and received the Best Native Literature Award at the National Pow-Wow.

Magazine Needs: *Indian Heritage Council Quarterly*, appearing quarterly, devotes 1 issue to poetry with a Native American theme. Wants "any type of poetry relating to Native Americans, their beliefs, or Mother Earth." Does not want "doggerel." Has published poetry by Running Buffalo and Angela Evening Star Dempsey. As a sample the editor selected these lines from his poem:

   Canopy of trees—evergreen and birch/holier than any man-made church.

Indian Heritage Council Quarterly is 6 pages, 5½×8½ (8½×11 folded sheet with 5½×8½ insert), photocopied. Receives about 300 poems/year, accepts up to 30%. Press run and number of subscribers vary, 50% shelf sales; 50 distributed free to Indian reservations. Subscription: $10. Sample: "negotiable." Make checks payable to Indian Heritage Council.

How to Submit: Submit up to 3 poems at a time. Accepts previously published poems (author must own rights only) and simultaneous submissions. Cover letter required. Time between acceptance and publication is 3 months to 1 year. Poems are circulated to an editorial board. "Our editorial board decides on all publications." Seldom comments on rejected poems. Charges criticism fees "depending on negotiations." Publishes theme issues. Guidelines and upcoming themes available for SASE and in publication. Responds within 3 weeks. Pay is negotiable. Acquires one-time rights. Staff reviews books or chapbooks of poetry or other magazines. Send books for review consideration.

Book/Chapbook Needs & How to Submit: Indian Heritage Publishing publishes chapbooks of Native American themes and/or Native American poets. Format of chapbooks varies. Query first, with a few sample poems and cover letter with brief bio and publication credits. Responds to queries within 3 weeks, varies for mss. Pays 33-50% royalties. Offers subsidy arrangements that vary by negotiations, number of poems, etc. For sample chapbooks, write to the above address.

Also Offers: Sponsors a contest for their anthology, "if approved by our editorial board. Submissions are on an individual basis—always provide a SASE."

Advice: "Write from the heart and spirit—so readers can relate likewise."

$ INDIANA REVIEW, Ballantine Hall 465, 1020 E. Kirkwood Ave., Bloomington IN 47405-7103. (812)855-3439. E-mail: inreview@indiana.edu. Website: www.indiana.edu/~inreview/ir.html (includes writer's guidelines, current news, sample poetry, and fiction from past and current issues). Established 1982. **Contact:** David J. Daniels.

• Poetry published in *Indiana Review* has been frequently selected for inclusion in *The Best American Poetry* and in the 2002 *Pushcart Prize* anthology.

Magazine Needs: *Indiana Review* is a biannual of prose, poetry, and visual art. "We look for an intelligent sense of form and language, and admire poems of risk, ambition and scope. We'll consider all types of poems—free verse, traditional, experimental. Reading a sample issue is the best way to determine if *Indiana Review* is a potential home for your work. Any subject matter is acceptable if it is written well." Has published poetry by Philip Levine, Sherman Alexie, Campbell McGrath, Charles Simic, Mark Strand, and Alberto Rios. The magazine uses about 40-60 pages of poetry in each issue (6×9, flat-spined, 160 pages, color matte cover, professional printing). Receives about 5,000 submissions/year, accepts up to 60. The magazine has 500 subscriptions. Sample: $8.

How to Submit: Submit 4-6 poems at a time, do not send more than 10 pages of poetry per submission. No electronic submissions. Pays $5/page ($10 minimum/poem), plus 2 copies and remainder of year's subscription. Acquires first North American serial rights only. "We try to respond to manuscripts in 2-3 months. Reading time is often slower during summer and holiday months." Brief book reviews are also featured. Send books for review consideration. Holds yearly contests. Guidelines available for SASE.

$ INKWOOD PRESS, P.O. Box 4306, Mankato MN 56002-4306. E-mail: inkwood@inkwood press.com. Website: www.inkwoodpress.com. Established 2002.

Book/Chapbook Needs & How to Submit: Inkwood Press publishes books and chapbooks of both prose and poetry. Wants contemporary poetry that focuses on music, language, and image. Does not want overly experimental or forced-rhyme poetry, or poetry that "tries" to shock. Inkwood Press publishes 1 book and 2-4 chapbooks/year. Books are 40-80 pages, press-printed, perfect-bound, matte cover with art. Chapbooks are 20-32 pages, press-printed, side-stapled, matte cover with art. **Charges $10 reading fee;** runs contest year round. "Submit 20-32 pages of poetry with reading fee. Provide cover letter, acknowledgments, and table of contents with the submission, but include contact info on cover letter only. Staff members vote on submissions." Check website for updated deadlines and guidelines. Responds to mss in up to 6 months. Pays $100 and 25 author's copies (out of a press run of 250). Order sample books/chapbooks by sending $5 to Inkwood Press.

◻ ◙ **INSECTS ARE PEOPLE TWO; PUFF 'N' STUFF PRODUCTIONS (Specialized: insects)**, P.O. Box 146486, Chicago IL 60614-6400. Established 1989. **Publisher:** H.R. Felgenhauer.
Magazine Needs: *Insects Are People Two* is an infrequent publication focusing solely on "poems about insects doing people things and people doing insect things." Accepts poetry written by children. Has published poetry by Bruce Boston, Steve Sneyd, Paul Wieneman, and Lyn Lifshin. As a sample the editor selected these lines from an untitled poem by Steve Sneyd:
>   Is time/of insect moon—/Dry chittering comes down/to us promising hour soon we/too saved
Insects Are People Two is 8½×11, with card cover, b&w art and graphics. Press run is 1,000. Sample: $6.
How to Submit: Accepts previously published poems and simultaneous submissions. Often comments on rejected poems. Publishes theme issues. Responds "immediately." Pay varies. Send books for review consideration.
Book/Chapbook Needs & How to Submit: Puff 'N' Stuff Productions publishes 1 chapbook/year. Responds to queries and mss in 10 days. Pay is negotiable.
Advice: "Hit me with your best shot. Never give up—editors have tunnel-vision. The *BEST* mags you almost *NEVER* even hear about. Don't believe reviews. Write for yourself. Prepare for failure, not success."

◪ **INTERBANG; BERTYE PRESS, INC.**, P.O. Box 1574, Venice CA 90294. (310)450-6372. E-mail: heather@interbang.net. Website: www.interbang.net. Established 1995. **Editor:** Heather Hoffman.
Magazine Needs: *Interbang*, published quarterly, is "Dedicated to Perfection in the Art of Writing." Wants "enticing poetry of any length on any subject. Although we do not have strict standards regarding substance, texture, or structure, your craft, in tandem with your subject matter, should elicit a strong response in the reader: love, hate, shock, sorrow, revulsion, you name it. Write your name, address, and phone number on each page of your submission." Has published poetry by Rob Lipton, John Thomas, Linda Platt Mintz, David Centorbi, and Jessica Pompei. As a sample we selected these lines from "Malted Moksha in 4C41.17" by John Marvin:
>   Louie Louie please say why/you are so exciting for the FBI/Stephen King and the Kingsmen/bravissimo
>   bravishiva/with the clarity of a despot/geometry of the universe
Interbang is 30 pages, 7½×8½, offset-printed and saddle-stapled with colored card stock cover, includes line art and photos. Receives about 500 poems/year, accepts up to 50%. Press run is 2,000 for 100 subscribers of which 10 are libraries, 20 shelf sales; 40 distributed free to other magazines, the rest distributed free at coffeehouses and bookstores in L.A. Send two stamps for a free sample copy.
How to Submit: Submit 5-15 poems at a time. Accepts previously published poems and simultaneous submissions. Accepts e-mail submissions; include text in body of message. Comments on rejected poems on request. *Interbang Writer's Guide* available by e-mail or on website. Responds in 6 months. Always sends prepublication galleys. Pays 5 copies. Reviews chapbooks of poetry and other magazines in 350-400 words, single book format. Poets may send books for review consideration.

◪ **THE INTERFACE; BUTTERMILK ART WORKS**, % GlassFull Productions, P.O. Box 57129, Philadelphia PA 19111-7129. E-mail: madlove3000@excite.com. Website: www.baworks.com/Interface. Established 1997. **Publisher:** Earl Weeks. **Art Director:** Willie McCoy.
Magazine Needs: *The INTERFACE* is published quarterly on the Internet and covers wrestling, comic books, trading cards, science fiction, and politics. Wants "all kinds of work—romantic, political, social commentary. We want poetry that comes from your heart, that makes tears come to the eye or forces one to want to mobilize the troops. No poems of hate or discrimination." Has published poetry by Mike Emrys, Sheron Regular, Cassandra Norris, and Monique Frederick. As a sample the publisher selected his poem "Love is":
>   Love is forever until death do we part/Love is when we never send arrows through each others hearts/
>   Love is me snuggled warmly against your breasts./Love is when you can sleep peacefully at rest.
Receives about 20 poems/year, accepts up to 35%. Publishes 15 poems/issue.
How to Submit: Submit 7 poems at a time. Accepts previously published poems and simultaneous submissions. Accepts submissions by e-mail, through online submission form, and by regular mail. Cover letter preferred. "We will consider accompanying illustration." Submit seasonal poems 6 months in advance. Time between acceptance and publication is 2 months. Poems are circulated to an editorial board. Occasionally publishes theme issues. Guidelines and upcoming themes available for e-mail or on website. Responds in 3 weeks. Acquires one-time rights. Reviews books and chapbooks of poetry and other magazines. Poets may send books for review consideration.
Also Offers: "We publish poetry, essays, videogame reviews, book reviews, fashion, science fiction, art, and more. We are trying to make *The INTERFACE* a meeting place for idea exchanges. We need your opinions and views, so submit them to us."

◪ **INTERIM**, Dept. of English Box 5011, University of Nevada—Las Vegas, Las Vegas NV 89154. (702)895-3333. Fax: (702)895-4801. E-mail: keelanc@nevada.edu. **Editor:** Claudia Keelan.

● Member CLMP, New York. Indexed in *Index of American Periodical Verse*.

Magazine Needs: *Interim* is an annual magazine, appearing in February or March, that publishes poetry, short fiction, essays, and book reviews. "We seek submissions from writers who are testing the boundaries of genre." Has published poetry by Brenda Hillman, Alice Notley, Doug Powell, and Elizabeth Robinson. As a sample the editor selected this poem, "The Paragraph She Gives Me to Live In" by Martha Ronk:

> *"The paragraph she gives me to live in is I don't know how./Description is a phenomenon of walks as obvious as rain./All the outcroppings in a brownish moss I can't get over/The undulation of columns one after another/Through which the distance is an extension of how we think/How someone walks into the room or sits in a chair./She says again you are where you should have begun./She offers copses and seclusion./Or you don't listen to what I say how could I foresee/"bitterns crying I the lintels" or her inner being/whatever insists is what she says I have to do.*

Interim is 100 pages, 6×9, professionally printed and perfect-bound with coated card cover. Press run is 400. Individual subscription: $12/year, $24/2 years. Single copy: $12.

How to Submit: Submit 3-5 poems at a time, SASE, and brief biographical note. No simultaneous submissions. No fax or e-mail submissions. Reads from September to April so "please do not submit anything during summer months." Responds in 3 months. Pays 2 copies. Acquires first serial rights. Poems may be reprinted elsewhere with a permission line noting publication in *Interim*.

◻ ◎ **INTERNATIONAL BLACK WRITERS; BLACK WRITER MAGAZINE (Specialized: ethnic),** P.O. Box 437134, Chicago IL 60690. (312)458-5745. Established 1970. **President/CEO:** Mable Terrell.

Magazine Needs & How to Submit: *Black Writer* is a "quarterly literary magazine to showcase new writers and poets and provide educational information for writers. Open to all types of poetry." *Black Writer* is 30 pages, magazine-sized, offset-printed, with glossy cover. Press run is 1,000 for 200 subscribers. Subscription: $19/year. Sample: $1.50. Responds in 10 days, has 1 quarter backlog. Pays 10 contributor's copies.

Book/Chapbook Needs & How to Submit: For chapbook publication (40 pages), submit 2 sample poems and cover letter with short bio. Accepts simultaneous submissions. Pays copies. For sample chapbook, send SASE with book rate postage.

Also Offers: Offers awards of $100, $50, and $25 for the best poems published in the magazine and presents them to winners at annual awards banquet. International Black Writers is open to all writers.

◑ ◎ **INTERNATIONAL POETRY REVIEW (Specialized: translations),** Dept. of Romance Languages, UNC-Greensboro, Greensboro NC 27402-6170. (336)334-5655. Fax: (336)334-5358. E-mail: k_mather@uncg.edu or tokyorse@aol.com. Website: www.uncg.edu/rom/ipr.htm. Established 1975. **Editor:** Kathleen Koestler.

Magazine Needs: *International Poetry Review* is a biannual primarily publishing translations of contemporary poetry with corresponding originals (published on facing pages) as well as original poetry in English. Recently published work by Richard Exner, René Char, Alvaro Mutis, and Tony Barnstone. *International Poetry Review* is 100 pages, 5½×8½, professionally printed and perfect-bound with 2-3 color cover. "We accept 5% of original poetry in English and about 30% of translations submitted." Press run is 500 for 200 subscribers. Subscription: $12/$20/$30 (for one, two, and three years respectively) for individuals, $20/$35/$50 for institutions. Sample: $5. Make checks payable to *International Poetry Review*.

How to Submit: Submit no more than 6 pages of poetry. Accepts simultaneous submissions; no previously published poems. Reads submissions between September 1 and April 30. Seldom comments on rejected poems. Guidelines and upcoming themes available for SASE. Responds in up to 6 months. Pays 1 copy. All rights revert to authors and translators. Occasionally reviews books of poetry. Poets may send books for review consideration.

Advice: "We strongly encourage contributors to subscribe. We prefer poetry in English to have an international or cross-cultural theme."

◎ **INTRO (Specialized: students),** AWP, MS 1E3, George Mason University, Fairfax VA 22030. Website: http://awpwriter.org. Established 1970. **Publications Manager:** Supriya Bhatnagar.

● See Associated Writing Programs in the Organizations section of this book.

NEED HELP? To better understand and use the information in these listings, see the introduction to this section.

Magazine Needs & How to Submit: Students in college writing programs belonging to AWP may submit to this consortium of magazines publishing student poetry, fiction, and creative nonfiction. Open as to the type of poetry submitted except they do not want "non-literary, haiku, etc." "In our history, we've introduced Dara Wier, Carolyn Forché, Greg Pope, Norman Dubie, and others." All work must be submitted by the writing program. Programs nominate *Intro* works in the fall. Ask the director of your writing program for more information.

🌐 🅞 **IOTA**, 1 Lodge Farm, Snitterfield, Warwicks CV37 0LR United Kingdom. Phone: 01789 730358. Fax: 01789 730320. E-mail: raggedravenpress@aol.com. Website: www.raggedraven.co.uk. Established 1988. **Editors:** Janet Murch and Bob Mee.

Magazine Needs: *Iota* is a quarterly wanting "any style and subject; no specific limitations as to length, though, obviously, the shorter a poem is, the easier it is to get it in, which means that poems over 40 lines can still get in if they seem good enough. No concrete poetry (no facilities) or self-indulgent logorrhea." Accepts poetry written by children (but they have to take their chance with the rest). Has published poetry by James Brockway, David H.W. Grubb, Harland Ristau, Daphne Schiller, and Peter Stavropoulo. *Iota* is 48 pgs., professionally printed and saddle-stapled with light colored card cover. Publishes about 300 of 6,000 poems received. Their press run is 500 with 250 subscribers of which 6 are libraries. Subscription: $20 (£10). Sample: $2 (£1) "but sometimes sent free."

How to Submit: Submit 4-6 poems at a time. Prefers name and address on each poem, typed, "but provided it's legible, am happy to accept anything." Accepts simultaneous submissions, but previously published poems "only if outstanding." Accepts e-mail submissions (in text box); no fax submissions. First response in 3 weeks (unless production of the next issue takes precedence) but final acceptance/ rejection may take up to a year. Pays 2 copies. Acquires first British serial rights only. Editor usually comments on rejected poems, "but detailed comment only when time allows and the poem warrants it." Reviews books of poetry in about 200 words, single or multi-book format. Poets may send books for review consideration.

Advice: "I am after crafted verse that says something; self-indulgent word-spinning is out. All editors have their blind spots; the only advice I can offer a beginning poet is to find a sympathetic editor (and you will only do that by seeing their magazines) and not to be discouraged by initial lack of success. Keep plugging!"

🅜 **$**🅞 **THE IOWA REVIEW; THE TIM McGINNIS AWARD; THE IOWA AWARD**, 308 EPB, University of Iowa, Iowa City IA 52242. (319)335-0462. E-mail: iowa-review@uiowa.edu. Website: www.iowa.edu/~iareview (includes excerpts, guidelines, table of contents, etc.). Established 1970. **Editor:** David Hamilton. **Contact:** editor.

• Poetry published in *The Iowa Review* has been frequently included in *The Best American Poetry* and the *Pushcart Prize* anthologies.

Magazine Needs: *The Iowa Review* appears 3 times/year and publishes fiction, poetry, essays, reviews, interviews, and autobiographical sketches. "We simply look for poems that at the time we read and choose, we admire. No specifications as to form, length, style, subject matter, or purpose. There are around 40 pages of poetry in each issue and we like to give several pages to a single poet. Though we print work from established writers, we're always delighted when we discover new talent." *The Iowa Review* is 200 pages, professionally printed, flat-spined. Receives about 5,000 submissions/year, accepts up to 100. Press run is 2,900 with 1,000 subscribers of which about half are libraries; 1,500 distributed to stores. Subscription: $18. Sample: $6.

How to Submit: Submit 3-6 poems at a time. No e-mail submissions. Cover letter (with title of work and genre) and SASE required. Reads submissions "from Labor Day to April Fool's Day or until we fill our next volume year's issues." Time between acceptance and publication is "around a year. Sometimes people hit at the right time and come out in a few months." Occasionally comments on rejected poems or offers suggestions on accepted poems. Responds in up to 4 months. Pays $20/page, 2 copies, and a year subscription. Acquires first North American serial rights, non-exclusive anthology rights, and non-exclusive electronic rights.

Also Offers: Sponsors the Tim McGinnis Award. "The award, in the amount of $500, is given irregularly to authors of work with a light or humorous touch. We have no separate category of submissions to be considered alone for this award. Instead, any essay, story, or poem we publish which is charged with a distinctly comic vision will automatically come under consideration for the McGinnis Award." Also offers Iowa Award for the single work judged best of the year. Outside judge, any genre.

N ⃠ ◎ **IRIS: A JOURNAL ABOUT WOMEN (Specialized: women/feminism)**, P.O. Box 800588, University of Virginia, Charlottesville VA 22908. (434)924-4500. Fax: (804)982-2801. E-mail: Iris@virginia.edu. Website: http://womenscenter.virginia.edu (includes guidelines, contact information, archives). Established 1980. **Coordinating Editor:** Kimberley Roberts. **Poetry Editor:** Nura Yingling.

Magazine Needs: *Iris* is a semiannual magazine appearing in April and November that "focuses on issues concerning women worldwide. It features quality poetry, prose and artwork—mainly by women, but will also accept work by men if it illuminates some aspect of a woman's reality. It also publishes translations. Form and length are unspecified. The poetry staff consists of experienced poets with a diversity of tastes who are looking for new and original language in well-crafted poems." Poets who have appeared in *Iris* include Sharon Olds, Mary Oliver, Charlotte Matthews, Rebecca B. Rank, Lisa Russ Spaar, and Gregory Orr. As a sample the editor selected these lines from "The Lost Daughter" by Susan Imhof:

> Seven years dead and still she grows,/copper hair a strange fin/rippling through the furnace of desert
> noon,/your dream of oil spills:/birds descending/on the airstream, wings/tucked, legs unfolded to meet/
> their reflections before/the black gold swallows them,/wing tips rising a brief moment toward heaven/
> through the shimmering heat, a slow/explosion of blue flame. . . .

Iris is 78 pages, magazine-sized, professionally printed on heavy, glossy stock, saddle-stapled with a full-color glossy card cover, using graphics and photos. Press run is over 2,000 for about 40 library subscriptions, 1,000 shelf sales. Single copy: $5; subscription: $9/year; $17/2 years. Sample: $6.50.

How to Submit: Submit up to 5 poems at a time. Simultaneous submissions are discouraged. Name, address, phone number should be listed on every poem. Cover letter should include list of poems submitted and a brief bio. Publishes theme issues. Upcoming themes available for SASE and in publication. Guidelines available for SASE and on website. Responds in 6 months. Pays 1 copy and subscription. Acquires first rights.

Also Offers: Website includes info on latest issue, back issues, submission guidelines and contacts.

Advice: "Because *Iris* is a feminist magazine, it receives a lot of poetry focusing on the political experience of coming to consciousness. Interested in *all* aspects of the reality of women's lives and, because many poems are on similar topics, freshness of imagery and style are even more important."

⃠ ◎ **ISLES OF MIST REVIEW; ISLES OF MIST PRESS (Specialized: membership/subscription)**, 425 N. Barbara St., Azusa CA 91702. (661)969-2668. Established 1999. **Editor:** Jessica Lee.

Magazine Needs: *Isles of Mist Review* appears quarterly. Wants "all types of poetry." As a sample the editor selected the following lines:

> Stars burn, then fall, from the sky./Hopeless realm of night./Falling, falling to the realm of green,/Into
> our fading sight . . .

Isles of Mist Review is 24 pages, digest-sized, side-stapled, card stock cover, includes ads. Publishes 24 poems/issue. Press run is 100. Single copy: $7; subscription: $160. Sample: $7. Make checks payable to *Isles of Mist Review*.

How to Submit: Submit 3 poems at a time. Accepts previously published poems and simultaneous submissions. Accepts e-mail and disk submissions. Cover letter is preferred. "Please enclose a SASE." Reads submissions September 1 through June 30. Time between acceptance and publication is 6 weeks. Seldom comments on rejections. Occasionally publishes theme issues. Upcoming themes and guidelines available for SASE. Responds in 6 weeks. Always sends prepublication galleys. Pays 1 contributor's copy. Acquires first North American serial rights. Reviews books and chapbooks of poetry and other magazines. Poets may send books for review consideration to the editor.

Book/Chapbook Needs & How to Submit: Isles of Mist Press publishes novels, poetry, and short stories. **"A special series of chapbooks is intended as a resource for our subscribers."** Publishes 2 paperback and 8 chapbooks/year. Books/chapbooks are usually 20-30 pages, 5×8, comb, side-stapled, or book binding, paperback cover with art/graphics. "We welcome both samples and complete manuscripts." Responds to queries in 6 weeks. Pays 1 author's copy (out of a press run of 100). Order sample books/chapbooks by sending $21.

Also Offers: "We give the Isles of Mist Award each year for high achievement in literature."

N ◎ **ITALIAN AMERICANA; JOHN CIARDI AWARD (Specialized: ethnic, Italian)**, URI/CCE, 80 Washington St., Providence RI 02903-1803. (401)277-5306. Fax: (401)277-5100. E-mail: bonomo al@ital.uri.edu. Website: www.uri.edu/prov/italian/italian.html. Established 1974. **Editor:** Carol Bonomo Albright. **Poetry Editor:** Dana Gioia.

Magazine Needs: *Italian Americana* appears twice/year using 16-20 poems of "no more than three pages. No trite nostalgia; no poems about grandparents." Has published poetry by Mary Jo Salter and Joy Parini. It is 150-200 pages, 7×9, professionally printed and flat-spined with glossy card cover. Press run is 1,000 for 900 subscribers of which 175 are libraries, 175 shelf sales. Singly copy: $10; subscription: $20/year, $35/2 years. Sample: $6.

How to Submit: Submit 3 poems at a time. No previously published poems or simultaneous submissions. Cover letter not required "but helpful." Name on first page of ms only. Do not submit poetry in July,

August or September. Occasionally comments on rejected poems. Responds in 6 weeks. Acquires first rights. Reviews books of poetry in 600 words, multi-book format. Poets may send books for review consideration to Prof. John Paul Russo, English Dept., University of Miami, Coral Gables FL 33124.

Also Offers: Along with the National Italian American Foundation, *Italian Americana* co-sponsors the annual $1,000 John Ciardi Award for Lifetime Contribution to Poetry. *Italian Americana* also presents $500 fiction or memoir award annually; and $1,000 in history prizes. Website includes writer's guidelines, names of editors, poetry, historical articles and fiction.

Advice: "Single copies of poems for submissions are sufficient."

$ ☺ ITALICA PRESS (Specialized: bilingual/foreign language, translations), 595 Main St., #605, New York NY 10044-0047. (212)935-4230. Fax: (212)838-7812. E-mail: inquiries@italicapress.com. Website: www.italicapress.com (includes contact information, guidelines, bios, and editorial policy). Established 1985. **Publishers:** Eileen Gardiner and Ronald G. Musto.

Book/Chapbook Needs: Italica is a small press publisher of English translations of Italian works in paperbacks, averaging 175 pages. Has published *Contemporary Italian Women Poets*, a dual-language (English/Italian) anthology edited and translated by Anzia Sartini Blum and Lara Trulowitz, and *Women Poets of the Italian Renaissance*, a dual-language anthology, edited by Laura Anna Stortoni, translated by Laura Anna Stortoni and Mary Prentice Lillie.

How to Submit: Query with 10 sample translations of medieval and Renaissance Italian poets. Include cover letter, bio, and list of publications. Accepts simultaneous submissions, but translation should not be "totally" previously published. Accepts e-mail submissions (in text box and as attachment); no fax submissions. Responds to queries in 3 weeks, to mss in 3 months. Always sends prepublication galleys. Pays 7-15% royalties plus 10 author's copies. Acquires English language rights. Sometimes comments on rejected poems.

N ☻ JACK MACKEREL MAGAZINE; ROWHOUSE PRESS, P.O. Box 23134, Seattle WA 98102-0434. Established 1992. **Editor:** Greg Bachar.

Magazine Needs: *Jack Mackerel*, published quarterly, features poetry, fiction, and art. Has published poetry by Bell Knott, John Rose, and William D. Waltz. *Jack Mackerel* is 40-60 pages, 5½×8½, printed on bond paper, with glossy card cover stock, b&w illustrations and photos. Press run is 1,000. Subscription: $12. Sample: $5. Make checks payable to Greg Bachar.

How to Submit: No previously published poems or simultaneous submissions. Cover letter preferred. Poems are circulated to an editorial board. Seldom comments on rejected poems. Responds in 1 month. Pays with copies. Send books for review consideration.

N ☒ ☉ JADE, FREEDOM FLIGHT: THE VOICE OF ARTISTIC EXPRESSION; LUNAR ANNUAL POETRY CONTEST, 649 Bedford Park Ave., North York, Ontario M5M 1K4 Canada. Established 2002. **Publisher/Editor:** Linda Woolven.

Magazine Needs: *Jade, Freedom Flight: The Voice of Artistic Expression* appears 2 times/year as a journal of poetry, short fiction, occasional photographs, and excerpts from travel journals. Wants all kinds of poetry of good quality. "Don't really like rhyming poetry." As a sample the editor selected these lines from her poem, "Empty copper promise":

> His tin cup/clanked/empty/with a copper/promise

Jade, Freedom Flight is 10-12 pages, digest-sized, photocopied, stapled, soft cover. Publishes about 8-10 poems/ issue. Single copy: $12.95; subscription: $25. Sample: $10. Make checks payable to Linda Woolven.

How to Submit: Submit 5 poems at a time. Line length for poetry is 30 maximum. Accepts simultaneous submissions; no previously published poems. No fax, e-mail, or disk submissions. Cover letter is preferred. Reads submissions throughout the year. Submit seasonal poems 1 year in advance. Time between acceptance and publication is 1 year. "I read all material and publish what I like and what seems to have merit. If I like a piece, I will hold it for a while and see if I still like it. If I do, I will publish it." Seldom comments on rejected poems. "I'd like poets who want to submit to purchase a copy or subscription, but it's not required." Writer's guidelines are not available. "Just send your best work." Responds in up to 4 months. Pays 1 contributor's copy. Acquires one-time rights.

Advice: "If the poem poured out, that's good: now polish it. Keep writing. Write what you love, not what you think will sell."

☉ ALICE JAMES BOOKS; NEW ENGLAND/NEW YORK AWARD, BEATRICE HAWLEY AWARD, University of Maine at Farmington, 238 Main St., Farmington ME 04938. Phone/fax: (207)778-

7071. E-mail: ajb@umf.maine.edu. Website: www.umf.maine.edu/~ajb (includes information on press, guidelines, complete catalog, bios, contest info, and archives). Established 1973. **Contest Coordinator:** Alice James Books.

Book/Chapbook Needs: "The mission of Alice James Books, a cooperative poetry press, is to seek out and publish the best contemporary poetry by both established and beginning poets, with particular emphasis on involving poets in the publishing process." Has published poetry by Jane Kenyon, Jean Valentine, and B.H. Fairchild. Publishes flat-spined paperbacks of high quality, both in production and contents, no children's poetry or light verse. Publishes 4-5 books, 80 pages, each year in editions of 1,500, paperbacks—no hardbacks.

How to Submit: Query with SASE, but no need for samples: simply ask for submission guidelines. No phone queries. Send 2 copies of the ms, SASE for notification, and submission fee. Accepts simultaneous submissions, but "we would like to know when a manuscript is accepted elsewhere." Responds in 4 months.

Also Offers: Beatrice Hawley Award for poets living anywhere in the US. Also, winners of the New England/New York Competition become members of the collective with a three-year commitment to editorial board as well as a 1-month residency at the Vermont Studio Center. Each winner in both competitions receives a cash award of $2,000. Competition deadlines are in early fall and winter. Send SASE for guidelines.

$ ⊚ JAPANOPHILE (Specialized: form, ethnic/nationality), P.O. Box 7977, Ann Arbor MI 48107. (734)930-1553. E-mail: japanophile@aol.com. Website: www.japanophile.com (includes guidelines, sample material, information on the magazine and brief blurbs on the editors). Established 1974. **Editor:** Susan Aitken. **Assistant Editor:** Madeleine Vala.

Magazine Needs: *Japanophile* is a literary biannual, appearing in summer and winter, about Japanese culture (not just in Japan). Issues include articles, photos, art, a short story, and poetry. Wants haiku or other Japanese forms ("they need not be about Japanese culture") or any form if the subject is about Japan, Japanese culture, or American-Japanese relations. (Note: Karate and ikebana in the US are examples of Japanese culture.) Has published poetry by Renee Leopold, Nancy Corson Carter, Jean Jorgensen, Mimi Walter Hinman, and reprints of Bashō. As a sample the editor selected this haiku (poet unidentified):
> *first snowstorm/our old cat rediscovers/the warm airduct*

There are 10-15 pages of poetry in each issue (digest-sized, about 58 pages, saddle-stapled). Press run is 800 with 200 subscriptions of which 30 are libraries. Receives about 500 submissions/year, accepts about 70, has a 2-month backlog. Sample: $7.

How to Submit: Summer is the best time to submit. Accepts e-mail and fax submissions. Cover letter required; include brief bio and credits if any. Guidelines and upcoming themes are available for SASE or by e-mail. Responds in 2 months. Pays $3 for haiku and up to $15 for longer poems. Poets may send books for review consideration.

Book/Chapbook Needs & How to Submit: Also publishes books under the Japanophile imprint, but so far only one has been of poetry. Query with samples and cover letter (about 1 page) giving publishing credits, bio.

⊘ JEOPARDY MAGAZINE, 132 College Hall, Bellingham WA 98225. (360)650-3118. E-mail: jeopardy@cc.wwu.edu. Website: http://jeopardy.wwu.edu (includes current issue, contests, guidelines, all info about magazine). Established 1965. **Editor-in-Chief:** David McIvor.

Magazine Needs: *Jeopardy Magazine* appears annually in June or July. Wants originality, command of vocabulary, interesting perspectives, creativity. Recently published poetry by Galway Kinnell, James Bertolino, David Wagoner, Knute Skinner, and Omar S. Castañeda. *Jeopardy Magazine* is 80-150 pages, digest-sized, press-printed, book binding, color, hard stock cover, with photo, drawings, paintings, prints. Receives about 200 poems/year, accepts about 10%. Press run is 1,500 for 50 subscribers of which 30 are libraries; distributed free to students and community. Sample: $5. Make checks payable to *Jeopardy*.

How to Submit: Submit 6 poems at a time. Line length for poetry is 10 pages maximum. Accepts simultaneous submissions; no previously published poems. No disk or e-mail submissions. Cover letter is required. Include SASE. Reads submissions January 1-April 10. Time between acceptance and publication is 3 months. Poems are circulated to an editorial board. "Assistant editors read, the head editors make decision." Never comments on rejected poems. Occasionally publishes theme issues. Upcoming themes available by e-mail. Guidelines are available for SASE and on website. Responds in 3 months. Pays 2 contributor's copies. Acquires one-time rights.

⊘ ⊚ JEWISH CURRENTS (Specialized: themes, religious; ethnic/nationality), 22 E. 17th St., Suite 601, New York NY 10003-1919. (212)924-5740. Fax: (212)414-2227. Established 1946.

Magazine Needs: *Jewish Currents* is a magazine appearing 6 times/year that publishes articles, reviews, fiction, and poetry pertaining to Jewish subjects or presenting a Jewish point of view on an issue of interest, including translations from the Yiddish and Hebrew (original texts should be submitted with translations). Accepts poetry written by children. *Jewish Currents* is 40 pages, 8½ × 11, offset, saddle-stapled. Press run is 2,500 for 2,100 subscribers of which about 10% are libraries. Subscription: $30/year. Sample: $5.

How to Submit: Submit 1 poem at a time, typed, double-spaced, with SASE. Include brief bio. No previously published poems or simultaneous submissions. Accepts fax submissions. Cover letter required. Publishes theme issues. Upcoming themes include November: Jewish Book Month; December: Hanuka; February: Black History Month; March: Jewish Music Season, Purim, International Women's Day; April: Holocaust Resistance, Passover; May: Israel; July/August: Soviet Jewish History. Deadlines for themes are 6 months in advance. Time between acceptance and publication is 2 years. Seldom comments on rejected poems. Responds in up to 1 year. Always sends prepublication galleys. Pays 6 copies plus 1-year subscription. Reviews books of poetry.

$ 🖉 ◎ JEWISH WOMEN'S LITERARY ANNUAL; JEWISH WOMEN'S RESOURCE CENTER (Specialized: ethnic, women), 820 Second Ave., New York NY 10017. (212)751-9223. Fax: (212)935-3523. Established 1994. **Editor:** Dr. Henny Wenkart.

Magazine Needs: *Jewish Women's Literary Annual* appears annually in April and publishes poetry and fiction by Jewish women. Wants "poems by Jewish women on any topic, but of the highest literary quality." Has published poetry by Alicia Ostriker, Savina Teubal, Grace Herman, Enid Dame, Marge Piercy, and Lesléa Newman. As a sample the editor selected these lines from "On Schedule" by Rhina Espaillat:

> *Minutes before takeoff, did he stand/before the mirror on the men's room wall/and sicken slightly,*
> *waver at the thought/of that brown paper parcel he had brought/did his hand quiver/to hear some*
> *stranger's little son/told flight would feel like magic . . .*

Jewish Women's Literary Annual is 160 pages, 6 × 9, perfect-bound with a laminated card cover, b&w art and photos inside. Receives about 500 poems/year, accepts about 15%. Press run is 1,500 for 480 subscribers. Subscription: $18/3 issues. Sample: $7.50.

How to Submit: No previously published poems. No fax submissions. Poems are circulated to an editorial board. Often comments on rejected poems. Responds in up to 5 months. Pays 3 copies plus a small honorarium. Rights remain with the poet.

Book/Chapbook Needs & How to Submit: The Jewish Women's Resource Center holds a monthly workshop, sponsors occasional readings, and also publishes a few books of poetry. "We select only 1 or 2 manuscripts/year out of about 20 submitted. But although authors then receive editing help and publicity, they bear the cost of production. Members of the workshop we conduct and poets published in our annual receive first attention."

Advice: "It would be helpful, but not essential, if poets would send for a sample copy of our annual before submitting."

Ⓝ ◐ ◎ JOEL'S HOUSE PUBLICATIONS; NEW BEGINNING MINISTRY, INC. POETRY CONTEST (Specialized: religious/Christian; spirituality; recovery), P.O. Box 328, Beach Lake PA 18405-0328. (570)729-8709. Fax: (570)729-7246. E-mail: newbeginmin@ezaccess.net. Website: http://newbeginningmin.org (includes excerpts from Joel's House Publications). Established 1997. **Editor:** Kevin T. Coughlin.

Magazine Needs: *Joel's Hosue Publications* appears quarterly in October. Produced by New Beginning Ministry, Inc., a nonprofit corporation, *Joel's House Publications* is a newsletter featuring poetry, articles, and original art. Wants poetry that is related to recovery, spirituality; also Christian poetry. Will consider any length, positive topic, and structure. No poetry which is inappropriately sexually graphic or discriminatory in nature. Recently published poetry by Becky Welsch, Billy Burns, K.F. Homer, and K.T. Coughlin. As a sample the editor selected these lines from his poem, "Tumbleweed":

> *A beautiful snowcap/Trickling down/From the heavens/Quenching broken hearts./His mountain*
> *mastered/Our world forever changed.*

Joel's House Publications is 10-20 pages, digest-sized, offset-printed, saddle-stapled, card stock cover, with original and clip art. Receives about 100 poems/year, accepts about 50%. Publishes about 25-50 poems/issue. Press run is 500 for 100 subscribers; 300 distributed free to mailing list. Single copy: $3; subscription: $12/1 year, 1 issue. Sample: $1 plus p&h. Make checks payable to New Beginning Ministry, Inc.

How to Submit: Submit 3-5 poems at a time. No previously published poems or simultaneous submissions. No fax, e-mail, or disk submissions. Cover letter is preferred. "Always send a SASE, typed manuscript with name and address on each poem." Reads submissions all year. Time between acceptance and publication is up to 1 year. Seldom comments on rejected poems. Guidelines available for SASE. Responds in up to 6 weeks. Always sends prepublication galleys. Pays 2 contributor's copies. Acquires first rights.

Also Offers: Poetry contest (send SASE for details) and writing retreats (check website for details).

Advice: "Keep writing—revise, revise, revise! If you write poetry, you are a poet. Be true to your craft."

N ☑ **THE JOHNS HOPKINS UNIVERSITY PRESS**, 2715 N. Charles St., Baltimore MD 21218. Website: www.press.jhu.edu. Established 1878. "One of the largest American university presses, Johns Hopkins is a publisher mainly of scholarly books and journals. We do, however, publish short fiction and poetry in the series Johns Hopkins: Poetry and Fiction, edited by John Irwin. Unsolicited submissions are not considered."

⬇ ☑ JONES AV.; OEL PRESS, 88 Dagmar Ave., Toronto, Ontario M4M 1W1 Canada. (416)461-8739. E-mail: oel@interlog.com. Website: www.interlog.com/~oel (includes guidelines, contact information, subscription information, and samples). Established 1994. **Editor/Publisher:** Paul Schwartz.
Magazine Needs: *Jones Av.* is published quarterly and contains "poems from the lyric to the ash can; starting poets and award winners." Wants poems "up to 30 lines mostly, concise in thought and image. Prose poems sometimes. Rhymed poetry is very difficult to do well these days, it better be good." Has published poetry by Matt Santateresa, Elana Wolff, Duane Locke, and Ryan G. Van Cleave. As a sample the editor selected this poem, "the red apple" by Claudia K. Grinnell:

> the red apple/sliced in/two redeems/spilling flesh/surrenders/to fingertips/inviting deep/ascension
> when/halves meet

Jones Av. is 24 pages, 5½×8½, photocopied and saddle-stapled with card cover, uses b&w graphics. Receives about 300 poems/year, accepts 30-40%. Press run is 100 for 40 subscribers. Subscription: $8. Sample: $2. Make checks payable to Paul Schwartz
How to Submit: Submit 5-8 poems at a time. No previously published poems or simultaneous submissions. Cover letter required. Accepts submissions on disk and by e-mail (attachment or in text box). Include e-mail submissions in body of message. Time between acceptance and publication is up to 12 months. Often comments on rejected poems. Publishes theme issues occasionally. Guidelines available for SASE or on website. "Remember, US stamps cannot be used in Canada." Responds in 3 months. Pays 1 copy. Acquires first rights. Staff reviews books and chapbooks of poetry and other magazines in 50-75 words, multi-book format. Poets may send books for review consideration.

$ ☑ THE JOURNAL, Dept. of English, Ohio State University, 164 W. 17th Ave., Columbus OH 43210. (614)292-4076. Fax: (614)292-7816. E-mail: thejournal05@postbox.acs.ohio-state.edu. Website: www.cohums.ohio-state.edu/english/journals/the_journal/. Established 1972. **Co-Editors:** Kathy Fagan and Michelle Herman.
Magazine Needs: *The Journal* appears twice yearly with reviews, essays, quality fiction, and poetry. "We're open to all forms; we tend to favor work that gives evidence of a mature and sophisticated sense of the language." Has published poetry by Beckian Fritz Goldberg, Terrance Hayes, Bob Hicok, and Carol Potter. *The Journal* is 6×9, professionally printed on heavy stock, 128-144 pages, of which about 60 in each issue are devoted to poetry. Receives about 4,000 submissions/year, accepts about 200, and have a 3- to 6-month backlog. Press run is 1,900. Subscription: $12. Sample: $7.
How to Submit: No submissions via fax. On occasion editor comments on rejected poems. Occasionally publishes theme issues. "Autumn/Winter 2002 issue will be an all-Ohio issue; Writers from Ohio, or who have lived in Ohio for more than 3 years, may submit poems." Pays 2 copies and an honorarium of $25-50 when funds are available. Acquires all rights. Returns rights on publication. Reviews books of poetry.
Advice: "However else poets train or educate themselves, they must do what they can to know our language. Too much of the writing we see indicates poets do not in many cases develop a feel for the possibilities of language, and do not pay attention to craft. Poets should not be in a rush to publish—until they are ready."

🌐 ☑ THE JOURNAL; ORIGINAL PLUS PRESS, (formerly *Journal of Contemporary Anglo-Scandinavian Poetry*), Flat 3, Oxford Grove, Ilfracombe EX34 9HQ United Kingdom. E-mail: smithsssj@aol.com. Website: http://members.aol.com/smithsssj/index.html (includes guidelines, contact and subscription information, bios, links, and "What's On"). Established 1994. **Contact:** Sam Smith.
Magazine Needs: *The Journal* features English poetry or English translations, reviews, and articles. Wants "new poetry howsoever it comes, translations and original English language poems." Does not want "staid, generalized, all form no content." Accepts poetry written by children. Has published poetry by David H. Grubb, Gary Allen, and Ozdemir Asaf. As a sample the editor selected these lines from a poem by Lordon Hardman:

> On campaign//met the Bear again//on the fringe of the forest/as I grieved my dead//eat your cubs he
> said

The Journal is 40 pages, A4, offset printed, stapled. Receives about 1,000 poems/year, accepts approximately 5%. Press run is 100-150 for 80 subscribers of which 12 are libraries. Single copy: £2.50. For three issues: £7. Sample: £2 or £3 (sterling). Make checks payable to Sam Smith.

How to Submit: Submit up to 6 poems. Accepts previously published poems and simultaneous submissions. Accepts e-mail submissions but only from outside UK. Cover letter preferred. "Please send hard copy submissions with 2 IRCs." Time between acceptance and publication is 8 months. Often comments on rejected poems. Guidelines available for SASE (or SAE and IRC). Responds in 1 month. Always sends prepublication galleys. Pays 1 contributor's copy.
Also Offers: In 1997, Original Plus began publishing collections of poetry. Has published books by Richard Wonnacott, James Turner, Don Ammons, Idris Caffrey, and RG Bishop. Send SASE (or SAE and IRC) for details.
Advice: "I prefer poetry that has been given thought—both to what has been said and how it has been said."

JOURNAL OF AFRICAN TRAVEL-WRITING (Specialized), P.O. Box 346, Chapel Hill NC 27514. Website: www.unc.edu/~ottotwo (includes guidelines, poetry, reviews, articles, and interviews). Established 1996. **Contact:** poetry editor.
Magazine Needs: *Journal of African Travel-Writing*, published annually, "presents and explores past and contemporary accounts of African travel." Wants "poetry touching on any aspect of African travel. Translations are also welcome." Published poets include José Craveirinha, Theresa Sengova, Charles Hood, and Sandra Meek. As a sample the editor selected the poem "Traveling" by James R. Lee:
> Thought I caught a comet's tail/The end of a poem/with tom tom beat/Langston Hughes thought about/
> In one of his dreamy moments/It flashed through the skies/Of North America/Like searching phrases/
> Speaking of ancient rivers/Lifted me to the Rift Valley

Journal of African Travel-Writing is 192 pages, 7 × 10, professionally printed, perfect-bound, coated stock cover with cover and illustrative art, ads. Press run is 600. Subscription: $10. Sample: $6.
How to Submit: Submit up to 6 poems at a time. Include SASE. Accepts simultaneous submissions; no previously published poems. Cover letter preferred. Time between acceptance and publication is up to 1 year. "The poetry editor usually makes these selections." Sometimes comments on rejected poems. Guidelines available for SASE or on website. Publishes theme issues. Responds in up to 6 weeks. Always sends prepublication galleys. Pays 5 copies. Acquires first international publication rights. Reviews books, chapbooks or magazines of poetry. Poets may send books for review consideration.

JOURNAL OF NEW JERSEY POETS (Specialized: regional, New Jersey), English Dept., County College of Morris, 214 Center Grove Rd., Randolph NJ 07869-2086. (973)328-5471. Fax: (973)328-5425. E-mail: szulauf@ccm.edu. Established 1976. **Editor:** Sander Zulauf.
Magazine Needs: This periodical is "not necessarily about New Jersey—but of, by, and for poets from New Jersey." Wants "serious work that is regional in origin but universal in scope." Read the magazine before submitting. Has published poetry by Amiri Baraka, X.J. Kennedy, Brigit Pegeen Kelly, Gerald Stern, Renée and Ted Weiss, and Rachel Hadas. As a sample the editor selected these lines from "Clove" by Betty Lies:
> I never mastered any of the knots/my father tried to teach me,//those tricky tugs of love, the splice,/the
> half hitch, cat's paw, anchor bend.//A simple clove hitch draws your boat/hard to its mooring but is
> easy to undo,//he said. Ah but you clove my heart in two,/for all the times I clove to you . . .

Journal of New Jersey Poets is digest-sized, offset-printed, with an average of 64 pages. Press run is 900. Subscription: $10/2 issues, $16/4 issues; institutions: $12/2 issues, $20/4 issues; students/senior citizens: $10/4 issues. Sample: $5.
How to Submit: Send up to 3 poems; SASE with sufficient postage for return of mss required. Accepts e-mail and fax submissions. Electronic submissions will not be returned nor acknowledged. Responds in up to 1 year. Time between acceptance and publication is within 1 year. Pays 5 copies and 1-year subscription. Acquires first North American serial rights. Only using solicited reviews. Send books for review consideration.
Advice: "Read the *Journal* before submitting. Send us your best poems. Realize we vote on everything submitted, and rejection is more an indication of the quantity of submissions received and the enormous number of poets submitting quality work."

JOURNAL OF THE AMERICAN MEDICAL ASSOCIATION (JAMA) (Specialized: health concerns, themes), 515 N. State, Chicago IL 60610. Fax: (312)464-5824. E-mail: charlene_breed love@ama-assn.org. Website: www.jama.com. Established 1883. **Associate Editor:** Charlene Breedlove.
Magazine Needs: *JAMA*, a weekly journal, has a poetry and medicine column and publishes poetry "in some way related to a medical experience, whether from the point-of-view of a health care worker or patient, or simply an observer. No unskilled poetry." Has published poetry by Aimée Grunberger, Floyd Skloot, and Walt McDonald. As a sample the editor selected these lines from "In Remission" by Floyd Skloot:
> This is a spring he never thought to see./Lean dusky Alaskan geese nibbling grass/seed in his field,
> early daffodils, three/fawns moving across his lawn in the last/of a afternoon light, everything he had/
> let go with small ceremonies on dark/September nights has suddenly come back.

JAMA is magazine-sized, flat-spined, with glossy paper cover. Accepts about 7% of 750 poems received/year. Has 360,000 subscribers of which 369 are libraries. Subscription: $66. Sample: free. "No SASE needed."

How to Submit: Accepts simultaneous submissions, if identified; no previously published poems. "I always appreciate inclusion of a brief cover letter with, at minimum, the author's name and address clearly printed. Mention of other publications and special biographical notes are always of interest." Accepts fax submissions (include in body of message with postal address). "Poems sent via fax will be responded to by postal service." Accepts e-mail submissions; include in body of message. Publishes theme issues. Theme issues include AIDS, violence/human rights, tobacco, medical education, access to care, and end-of-life care. "However, we would rather that poems relate obliquely to the theme." A list of upcoming themes is available on website. Pays 1 contributor's copy, more by request. "We ask for a signed copyright release, but publication elsewhere is always granted free of charge."

N $ ☺ THE JOYFUL WOMAN; JOYFUL CHRISTIAN MINISTRIES, P.O. Box 90028, Chattanooga TN 37412. (423)892-6753. Fax: (423)892-4902. E-mail: info@joyfulwoman.org. Website: www.joyfulwoman.org. Established 1978. **Editor:** Carol Parks.

Magazine Needs: *Joyful Woman* appears bimonthly "for and about Bible-believing women who want God's best." Wants poetry "to encourage Christian women." Has published poetry by Jessie Sandberg. *The Joyful Woman* is 32 pages, magazine-sized, professionally printed on glossy paper and saddle-stapled, 4-color glossy paper cover, includes b&w and color photos. Receives about 10-20 poems/year, accepts small percentage. Press run is 6,000 for 4,300 subscribers. Single copy: $4; subscription: $19.95. Sample: $3.50 plus postage.

How to Submit: Accepts previously published poems and simultaneous submissions. Accepts submissions by e-mail (as attachment or in text box) and by fax. Cover letter preferred. Time between acceptance and publication is 6-12 months. Seldom comments on rejected poems. Publishes theme issues. Guidelines available for SASE. Responds in 6 weeks. Pays $15-20 plus 5 copies. Acquires one-time rights.

☿ ☺ JUBILAT, Dept. of English, Bartlett Hall, University of Massachusetts, Amherst MA 01003-0515. (413)577-1064. E-mail: jubilat@english.umass.edu. Website: www. jubilat.org (includes excerpts from current and past issues, links, archives, editorial policy, guidelines, subscription and contact information). Established 2000. **Editors:** Robert Casper, Christian Hawkey, Kelly LeFave, Michael Teig. **Managing Editor:** Lisa Olstein.

• Poetry published in *Jubilat* has been included in the 2001 *Best American Poetry*.

Magazine Needs: *Jubilat* appears biannually as "international poetry journal that bases itself on the notion that, to poetry, everything is relevant. To this end we publish an arresting mix of poetry, prose, art, and interviews." Wants "high quality submissions of poetry, as well as poetic prose that may or may not have anything to do with poetry per se but captures a quality of poetic thought. We publish quality work by established and emerging writers regardless of school, region, or reputation." Recently published poetry by John Ashbery, Jane Miller, Vasko Popa, Anne Carson, Reginald Shepard, and Dean Young. *Jubilat* is 150 pages, digest-sized, offset-printed, perfect-bound, 4-color glossy cover, with fine art features. Receives about 3,000 submissions/year, accepts about 2%. Publishes about 20-30 poems/issue. Press run is 2,000 for 1,000 subscribers of which 100 are libraries, 1,000 shelf sales. Single copy: $8; subscription: $14/1 year, $26/2 years, $38/3 years. Sample: $8. Make checks payable to University of Massachusetts/*Jubilat*.

How to Submit: Submit 3-5 poems at a time. Accepts simultaneous submissions if noted in cover letter and informed of acceptance elsewhere; no previously published poems. No fax, e-mail, or disk submissions. Brief cover letter preferred. "We strongly encourage poets to read an issue and look at our website before submitting." Reads submissions year round. Time between acceptance and publication varies. Poems are circulated to an editorial board. "*Jubilat* is collectively edited. All submissions are reviewed by at least one, often four editors." Seldom comments on rejected poems. Guidelines available for SASE and on website. Responds in up to 4 months. Always sends prepublication galleys. Acquires first North American serial rights; rights revert to author.

☺ JUNCTION PRESS, P.O. Box 40537, San Diego CA 92164. Established 1991. **Publisher:** Mark Weiss.

Book/Chapbook Needs: Junction Press aims to publish "overlooked non-mainstream poetry." The press publishes 2 paperback books of poetry/year. Wants "modern or postmodern formally innovative work, any form or length. No academic, Iowa school, or formal poetry." Has published poetry by Armand Schwerner, Susie Mee, Richard Elman, José Kozer, and Mervyn Taylor. Books are typically 72-96 pages, 5½×8½, offset-printed and perfect-bound with coated covers with graphics.

How to Submit: Query first with 10-15 pages of poetry and a cover letter (bio unnecessary). Accepts previously published poems; no simultaneous submissions. Often comments on rejected poems. Replies to queries in 6 months, to mss (if invited) "immediately." Pays 100 copies (out of a press run of 1,000).
Advice: "While I don't dismiss the possibility of finding a second Rimbaud, please note that all of my authors have been in their 50s and have written and published for many years."

🌐 🗋 ▢ ◪ **K.T. PUBLICATIONS; THE THIRD HALF; KITE BOOKS; KITE MODERN PO-ETS; KITE MODERN WRITERS**, 16 Fane Close, Stamford, Lincolnshire PE9 1HG England. Established 1989. **Editor:** Kevin Troop.
Magazine Needs: *The Third Half* is a literary magazine published regularly. It contains "free-flowing and free-thinking material on most subjects." Accepts poetry written by children. "Open to all ideas and suggestions. No badly written or obscene scribbling." Recently published Hannah Welfare, Michael Newman, Jack Rickand, Helen Heslop, and Margaret Pelling. As a sample we selected this poem, "Without Words," by Isabel Cortan:

> a savage sound,/sharp crack of a man's hand/across a woman's chin//a ritual sound,/her weeping in
> the dark/burying her love

The Third Half is neatly printed and perfect-bound with glossy cover, includes line drawings. Press run is 100-500. Single copy: £5.50 in UK. Sample: £10 overseas. Make checks payable to K.T. Publications.
How to Submit: Submit 6 poems at a time. No previously published poems. Cover letter preferred. Time between acceptance and publication "depends on the work and circumstances." Seldom comments on rejected poems. Occasionally publishes theme issues. Responds in 2 days. Always sends prepublication galleys. Pays 1-6 contributor's copies. "Copyright belongs to the poets/authors throughout."
Book/Chapbook Needs & How to Submit: Under K.T. Publications and Kite Books, they publish "as much as possible each year" of poetry, short stories, and books for children—"at as high a standard as humanly possible." Books are usually 50-60 pages, A5, perfect-bound with glossy cover, and art ("always looking for more.") Query first, with up to 6 sample poems and a cover letter with brief bio and publication credits. "Also include suitable SAE—so that I do not end up paying return postage every time."
Also Offers: Offers a "reading and friendly help service to writers. Costs are reasonable." Write for details. *The Third Half* showcases 2 poets per issue. "Each poet has 24 pages with illustrations."
Advice: "*Please* let your work make *sense*."

ℕ ◍ **KAEDEN BOOKS**, P.O. Box 16190, Rocky River OH 44116. (440)356-0030. Fax: (440)356-5081. Website: http://kaeden.com (includes guidelines, contact information, and catalog). Established 1990. **Vice President:** Karen Evans. **Editor:** Craig Urmston. Member: American Association of Publishers.
Book/Chapbook Needs: "*Kaeden Books* is a publisher of supplementary reading and educational materials designed for early, emergent, and fluent readers, ages 5-9. It is our goal to produce materials that have high story/character interest for the student, as well as structure suitable for instruction. Our books are 12-24 pages in length. Remember, our readers are beginners or early readers in pre-kindergarten through third grade, so vocabulary and sentence structure must be appropriate for the early reading levels. Kaeden Books are used in many reading programs such as Reading Recovery (R), English as a Second Language (ESL), and many Title I programs. Familiarity with these programs and methodologies will help you understand what we need from our authors." Publishes 3 poetry titles per year. Books are usually 12-24 pages, offset-printed and saddle-stapled, includes illustrations. Press run is usually 3,000-5,000.
How to Submit: Submit 5-6 sample poems. Accepts previously published poems and simultaneous submissions. Cover letter preferred. "Submissions should be typed and accompanied with a brief bio." No e-mail submissions. Reads submissions July, August, and December only. Time between acceptance and publication is up to 1 year. Poems are circulated to an editorial board. "Submissions are first reviewed for appropriateness to published line, then reviewed by editorial board." Guidelines available on website. Responds "if interested." Pay is negotiable. Acquires all rights.
Advice: "We do not return submissions. We retain them and could (and do) 'rediscover' new authors many years later. We do not review e-mail submissions."

$ ◎ **KALEIDOSCOPE: EXPLORING THE EXPERIENCE OF DISABILITY THROUGH LITERATURE AND FINE ARTS (Specialized: disability themes)**, 701 S. Main St., Akron OH 44311-1019. (330)762-9755. Fax: (330)762-0912. E-mail: mshiplett@udsakron.org. Website: www.udsakron.org (includes guidelines, contact and subscription information, and themes as well as information about the United Disability Services). Established 1979. **Senior Editor:** Gail Willmott. **Editor-in-Chief:** Dr. Darshan C. Perusek.
Magazine Needs: *Kaleidoscope* is based at United Disability Services, a nonprofit agency. Poetry should deal with the experience of disability but not limited to that when the writer has a disability. "*Kaleidoscope*

is interested in high-quality poetry with vivid, believable images, and evocative language. Works should not use stereotyping, patronizing, or offending language about disability." Has published poetry by Sandra J. Lindow, Gerald R. Wheeler, Desire Vail, and Sheryl L. Nelms. As a sample the editors selected these lines from "Quiet Night" by Sheryl L. Nelms:

> I see shadows/of hackberry trees/curled spinach leaves/and winter/onions/leaning Sioux-like/ear/to the ground.

Kaleidoscope is 64 pages, 8½ × 11, professionally printed and saddle-stapled with 4-color semigloss card cover, b&w art inside. Press run is 1,500, including libraries, social service agencies, health-care professionals, universities, and individual subscribers. Single copy: $6; subscription: $10 individual, $15 agency. Sample: $5.
How to Submit: Submit up to 5 poems at a time. Send photocopies with SASE for return of work. Accepts previously published poems and simultaneous submissions, "as long as we are notified in both instances." Accepts fax and e-mail submissions. Cover letter required. All submissions must be accompanied by an autobiographical sketch. Deadlines: March and August 1. Publishes theme issues. A list of upcoming themes is available for SASE, by e-mail, or on website. Themes for 2003 include "Disability and the Road Less Traveled" and "Multicultural Perspectives on Disability." Upcoming themes and guidelines available for SASE, by fax, and by e-mail. Responds in 3 weeks; acceptance or rejection may take 6 months. Pays $10-25 plus 2 copies. Rights return to author upon publication. Staff reviews books of poetry. Send books for review consideration to Gail Willmott, senior editor.

◐ THE KALEIDOSCOPE REVIEW, P. O. Box 16242, Pittsburgh PA 15242-0242. Established 2000. **Editor:** Rebecca Chembars.
Magazine Needs: *The Kaleidoscope Review* appears bimonthly as a forum for fresh, creative poetry. "We tend to prefer shorter poetry. Two pages are dedicated to haiku. One (the last) page is dedicated to witty and/or humorous submissions. Writing must be effective and interesting. No preferred style, form, or school." Does not want graphic violence or pornography. As a sample the editor selected these lines from "Olé":

> ravens swoop in greeting/as you pass through faceless crowds/papier maché hearts, pierced/cry rose petals at your crossing/I fall through, blindly/mad fiesta in my mind

The Kaleidoscope Review is 20 pages, digest-sized, laser-printed, saddle-stapled, card stock cover. Receives about 600 poems/year, accepts about 30%. Publishes about 30 poems/issue. Press run is 100 for 20 subscribers; 70 are distributed free to "friends and local business for distribution to the public." Single copy: $2; subscription: $12. Sample: $2 plus SASE. Make checks payable to *The Kaleidoscope Review.*
How To Submit: Submit 3 poems at a time, 5 if all haiku or very short poems. Line length is 35 maximum. Accepts previously published poems and simultaneous submissions. No fax, e-mail, or disk submissions. "Name and address on each sheet. Include SASE. Short cover letter highly preferred." Submit seasonal poems 3 months in advance. Time between acceptance and publication is 2-4 months. Often comments on rejected poems. "Submissions not returned to author unless SASE included." Occasionally publishes theme issues. Upcoming themes and guidelines available for SASE and in publication. Responds in up to 6 weeks. Pays 1 contributor's copy; 2 subscriber/contributor's copies. Acquires one-time rights.
Advice: "Life *is* poetry in motion. Refocus!"

⚑ $◐ ◎ KALLIOPE, A JOURNAL OF WOMEN'S LITERATURE & ART (Specialized: women, translations, themes); SUE SANIEL ELKIND POETRY CONTEST, 3939 Roosevelt Blvd., Jacksonville FL 32205. (904)381-3511. Website: www.fccj.org/kalliope (includes guidelines, contact and subscription information, archives, editorial policy, upcoming themes, contest information, table of contents of recent issues, "Lollipops, Lizards and Literature," special events). Established 1978. **Editor:** Mary Sue Koeppel.
● A poem by Denise Levertov, originally published in *Kalliope*, was selected for *Best American Poetry 1999.*
Magazine Needs: Appearing in fall and spring, *Kalliope* is a literary/visual arts journal published by Florida Community College at Jacksonville; the emphasis is on women writers and artists. "We like the idea of poetry as a sort of artesian well—there's one meaning that's clear on the surface and another deeper meaning that comes welling up from underneath. We'd like to see more poetry from Black, Hispanic and Native American women. Nothing sexist, racist, conventionally sentimental. Write for specific guidelines." Poets published include Denise Levertov, Marge Piercy, Martha M. Vertreace, Karen Subach, Maxine Kumin, and Tess Gallagher. As a sample the editor selected the following lines by Melanie Richards:

> With dried orange rind,/fragrant sage, and a blue//branch of coral, I seal/this package full of artifacts// in case the wild horses/all vanish from the earth,//or the red throat of the hummingbird/lies to us about summer;

Kalliope calls itself "a journal of women's literature and art" and publishes fiction, interviews, drama, and visual art in addition to poetry. Appearing 2 times/year, *Kalliope* is 7¼ × 8¼, flat-spined, handsomely printed on white stock, glossy card cover and b&w photographs of works of art. Average number of pages is 120. Press run is 1,600 for 400-500 subscribers of which 100 are libraries, 800 shelf sales. Subscription: $16/year or $27/2 years. Sample: $7.

How to Submit: Submit poems in batches of 3-5 with brief bio note, phone number, and address. No previously published poems. No fax or e-mail submissions. Reads submissions September through April only. SASE required. Because all submissions are read by several members of the editing staff, response time is usually up to 4 months. Publication will be within 6 months after acceptance. Criticism is provided "when time permits and the author has requested it." Guidelines and upcoming themes available on website or for SASE. Usually pays $10 or subscription. Acquires first publication rights. Reviews books of poetry, "but we prefer groups of books in one review." Poets may send books for review consideration.

Also Offers: Sponsors the Sue Saniel Elkind Poetry Contest. 1st Prize: $1,000; runners up published in *Kalliope*. Deadline: November 1. Details available for SASE.

Advice: "*Kalliope* is a carefully stitched patchwork of how women feel, what they experience, and what they have come to know and understand about their lives . . . a collection of visions from or about women all over the world. Send for a sample copy, to see what appeals to us, or better yet, subscribe!"

KARAMU, Dept. of English, Eastern Illinois University, Charleston IL 61920. Established 1966. **Editor:** Olga Abella.

• *Karamu* has received grants from the Illinois Arts Council and has won recognition and money awards in the IAC Literary Awards competition.

Magazine Needs: *Karamu* is an annual, usually published by May, whose "goal is to provide a forum for the best contemporary poetry and fiction that comes our way. We especially like to print the works of new writers. We like to see poetry that shows a good sense of what's being done with poetry currently. We like poetry that builds around real experiences, real images, and real characters and that avoids abstraction, overt philosophizing, and fuzzy pontifications. In terms of form, we prefer well-structured free verse, poetry with an inner, sub-surface structure as opposed to, let's say, the surface structure of rhymed quatrains. We have definite preferences in terms of style and form, but no such preferences in terms of length or subject matter. Purpose, however, is another thing. We don't have much interest in the openly didactic poem. If the poet wants to preach against or for some political or religious viewpoint, the preaching shouldn't be so strident that it overwhelms the poem. The poem should first be a poem." Has published poetry by Allison Joseph, Katharine Howd Machan, and Joanne Mokosh Riley. As a sample the editor selected these lines from "Anam Chara—Soul Friend" by Maureen Tolman Flannery (winner of the 2001 IAC Award for Poetry):

> Her life was marginal./She works on the edge of the solid,/like dusting fuzz from corner,/always on the
> verge of something./Her singing frames a life, drapes a valance at the rim of windows.

The format is 120 pages, 5×8, matte cover, handsomely printed (narrow margins), attractive b&w art. Receives submissions from about 500 poets each year, accepts 40-50 poems. Sometimes about a year—between acceptance and publication. Press run is 350 for 300 subscribers of which 15 are libraries. Sample: $7.50.

How to Submit: Poems—in batches of no more than 5—may be submitted to Olga Abella. "We don't much care for simultaneous submissions. We read September 1 through March 1 only, for fastest decision submit January through March. Poets should not bother to query. We critique a few of the better poems. We want the poet to consider our comments and then submit new work." Publishes occasional theme issues. Upcoming themes available for SASE. Pays 1 copy. Acquires first serial rights.

Advice: "Follow the standard advice: Know your market. Read contemporary poetry and the magazines you want to be published in. Be patient."

KARAWANE: OR, THE TEMPORARY DEATH OF THE BRUITIST (Specialized: open mic/spoken word performers), 402 S. Cedar Lake Rd., Minneapolis MN 55405. E-mail: karawane@pr odigy.net. Website: www.karawane.org (includes magazine samples, featured poets, online submissions, and open mic information). Established 1997 as *Voices From the Well*. **Editor/Publisher:** Laura Winton.

Magazine Needs: *Karawane* appears 2 times/year and "features poets, playwrights, fiction, and nonfiction writers who perform their work in public. We want innovative, thoughtful, well-crafted poetry. Poetry that needs to be poetry, rather than short stories and essays with line breaks. We are spoken word, but more in the manner of Cabaret Voltaire than a poetry slam. No poems that tell stories; no doggerel. I don't mind formal poetry, but do it well." Has published poetry by Terrence J. Folz, Ahimsa Timoteo Bodhran, Leonora Smith, and Richard Kostelanetz. As a sample the editor selected these lines from "Blue Highways" by William Sovern:

> Jimmy the guitar man made noise/the French surrealists made noise/the grand buddha poet will make
> noise/the mennonite woman walking alone/in her garden wants to make noise/i will perform a quiet/
> beat rhapsody.

Karawane is 16-28 pages, 8½×11, printed on newsprint, some inside art, ads. Receives about 300 poems/year, accepts 10-20%. Press run is 500 for 10 subscribers, 30 shelf sales; the remainder distributed free to festivals, open mics, inquiries, reviewers. Single copy: $5; subscription: $12/4 issues. Sample: $5, "donations of more appreciated." Make checks payable to Laura Winton. "To be considered, poets *must* perform their work publicly. I prefer people be an ongoing part of their spoken word scene."

How to Submit: Submit 3-6 poems at a time. Accepts previously published poems and simultaneous submissions. Accepts e-mail submissions. Cover letter preferred; "Please indicate that you perform your work publicly and tell me a little about what you do, where you perform, etc. I prefer that to knowing who has published you before. SASEs essential! I *encourage* simultaneous submissions and previously published poems if you retained subsequent rights. E-mail gets a faster response from me—try any format as long as it's PC compatible." Time between acceptance and publication is up to 6 months. Seldom comments on rejected poems. Responds in 6 months. Pays in contributor's copies. Acquires one-time rights.

Also Offers: "Our website gets better all the time, but remains unique and separate from the magazine. The website is a good first stop before you submit your work."

Advice: "Make your own scene! Don't wait for someone else to 'find' you. You can be a 'working poet,' with a little ingenuity and ambition. Poets should use every avenue available—lit mags, readings, self-publishing, cable access, leaving pamphlets on the bus, etc., to make themselves visible."

KATYDID BOOKS, 1 Balsa Rd., Santa Fe NM 87505. Established 1973. **Editors/Publishers:** Karen Hargreaves-Fitzsimmons and Thomas Fitzsimmons.

Book/Chapbook Needs & How to Submit: Katydid Books publishes 2 paperbacks and 2 hardbacks/ year. "We publish two series of poetry: Asian Poetry in Translation (distributed by University of Hawaii Press) and American Poets." Currently not accepting submissions.

KAVYA BHARATI; STUDY CENTRE FOR INDIAN LITERATURE IN ENGLISH AND TRANSLATION (SCILET) (Specialized: poetry from India or on Indian themes), Scilet, American College, Post Box 63, Madurai 625002 India. Phone: (091)0452-533609. Fax: (091)0452-531056. E-mail: scilet@md2.vsnl.net.in. Website: www.scilet.org (includes guidelines, contact and subscription information, and catalog). Established 1988. **Director:** Paul L. Love. **Editor:** R.P. Nair.

Magazine Needs: *Kavya Bharati* annually publishes "Indian poetry originally written in English and English translations from regional languages of India. We want to see poetry that makes you see life with a new pair of eyes and affirms values." As a sample they selected this poem, "Memory" by Jayanta Mahapatra:

> Out there, a line of gray windows./black spaces in them./Something is supposed to be hidden there,/
> but it just won't fit./It's like the clock—/No one disturbs it.//Does every man have to bear his./for him
> to go on?/At times it's a scar from another's,/staring moodily at the twilight body./Sometimes a wisp
> of high cirrus/that can't see its way in impossible skies.//This evening, maybe/it will stand by my bed
> again,/a hollow word, an old harlot./There was never any choice,/proof perhaps of some human grace/
> before we escape its curses.

Kavya Bharati is 5½×8½, photo typeset and hard-bound with cardboard cover. Receives about 90 poems/year, accepts approximately 20%. Publish 30 poems/issue. Press run is 1,000 for 200 subscribers of which 60 are libraries. Sample (including guidelines): $12. Make checks payable to Study Centre, *Kavya Bharati*.

How to Submit: Submit 6 poems at a time. No previously published poems. Accepts e-mail submissions (as attachment). Cover letter required. Reads submissions January through June only. Submit seasonal poems 6 months in advance. Time between acceptance and publication is 6 months. Poems are circulated to an editorial board. "A three member advisory board selects all poems." Often comments on rejected poems. Publishes theme issues occasionally. Guidelines available for SASE (or SAE and IRC), by e-mail, on website, and in publication. Responds in 6 months. Pays 2 copies. Acquires first rights. Reviews books of poetry. Poets may send books for review consideration.

Also Offers: Conducts an annual creative writing workshop. Write for details.

Advice: "Keep writing."

KELSEY REVIEW (Specialized: regional, Mercer County), Mercer County Community College, P.O. Box B, Trenton NJ 08690. (609)586-4800, ext. 3326. Fax: (609)586-2318. E-mail: kelsey.review@mccc.edu. Website: www.mccc.edu (includes address, deadlines encouragement, and announced publication). Established 1988. **Editor-in-Chief:** Robin Schore.

Magazine Needs: *Kelsey Review* is an annual published in September by Mercer County Community College. It serves as "an outlet for literary talent of people living and working in Mercer County, New Jersey only." Has no specifications as to form, length, subject matter or style, but does not want to see poetry about "kittens and puppies." Accepts poetry written by children. Has published poetry by Pat Hardigree, Bill Waters, Betty Lies, Helen Gorenstein, Ron McCall, and Shirley Wright. As a sample the editor selected these lines from "I Was Twelve" by Patricia Hardigree:

I was twelve that summer we lived in a bungalow on Coney Island/with our mother's new husband
she tried to make us call him/father but his name was Jimmy and that's how we called him/not liking
him or the strange red foods and the salty meats/and soups but we loved the company of his relations
and their/loud happy voices mocking and praising with the same words.

Kelsey Review is about 80 glossy pages, 7×11, with paper cover and line drawings; no ads. Receives about 60 submissions/year, accepts 6-10. Press run is 2,000. All distributed free to contributors, area libraries, bookstores, and schools.

How to Submit: Submit up to 6 poems at a time, typed. No previously published poems or simultaneous submissions. No fax or e-mail submissions. Deadline: May 1. Always comments on rejected poems. Information available for e-mail. Responds in June of each year. Pays 5 copies. All rights revert to authors.

$ ☑ **THE KENYON REVIEW; THE WRITERS WORKSHOP**, Kenyon College, Gambier OH 43022. (740)427-5208. Fax: (740)427-5417. E-mail: kenyonreview@kenyon.edu. Website: www.KenyonR eview.org (includes editorial policy, guidelines, contact and subscription information, excerpts from recent issues, interviews, "weekly feature," and soon *Kenyon Review* archives). Established 1939. **Editor:** David Lynn.

• Poetry published in *The Kenyon Review* is frequently selected for inclusion in *The Best American Poetry* and has won several Pushcart Prizes in each of the three considered genres: poetry, fiction, and nonfiction.

Magazine Needs: *Kenyon Review* is a triquarterly review containing poetry, fiction, essays, criticism, reviews, and memoirs. It features all styles and forms, lengths and subject matters. But this market is more closed than others because of the volume of submissions typically received during each reading cycle. Issues contain work by such poets as John Ashbery, Robert Bly, Laura Kasischke, Janet McAdams, Linda Gregerson, and Khaled Mattawa. The elegantly printed, flat-spined, 7×10, 180-page review has a press run of approximately 5,000, including individual subscribers institutions, and newsstand sales. Receives about 4,000 submissions/year, accepts 50 pages of poetry in each issue, has a 1-year backlog. The editor urges poets to read a few copies before submitting to find out what they are publishing. Sample: $10 includes postage.

How to Submit: Unsolicited submissions are typically read from September 1 through March 31. Writers may contact by phone, fax, or e-mail, but may submit mss by mail only. Responds in 3 months. Pays $15/ page for poetry, $10/page for prose and 2 copies. Acquires first North American serial rights. Reviews books of poetry in 2,500-7,000 words, single or multi-book format. "Reviews are primarily solicited— potential reviewers should inquire first."

Also Offers: Also sponsors The Writers Workshop, an annual 8-day event. 2002 dates: June 22-30. Location: the campus of Kenyon College. Average attendance is 12 per class. Open to writers of fiction, nonfiction and poetry. Conference is designed to provide intensive conversation, exercises and detailed readings of participants' work. Past speakers have included Erin Belieu, Allison Joseph, P.F. Kluge, Wendy MacLeod, Pamela Painter, Nancy Zafris, David Baker, and Reginald McKnight. Other special features include a limited-edition anthology produced by workshop writers and *The Kenyon Review* that includes the best writing of the session. College and non-degree graduate credit is offered. Cost for summer 2002 conference is $1,650, including meals, a room and tuition. Application available for SASE and on website. Early application is encouraged as the workshops are limited.

Advice: "Editor recommends reading recent issues to get familiar with the type and quality of writing being published before submitting your work."

N ◑ **KESTREL: A JOURNAL OF LITERATURE AND ART**, 1201 Locust Ave., Fairmount WV 26554-2451. (304)367-4815. Fax: (304)367-4896. E-mail: kestrel@mail.fscwv.edu. Website: www.fscwv. edu/pubs/pubs_hp.html. Established 1993. **Editor:** Mary Dillow Stewart.

Magazine Needs: *Kestrel* appears 2 times/year and publishes "living literature and art . . . a larger selection of a writer's work (typically a minimum of three poems) with an author's preface. Normally, each poem is given its own page." *Kestrel* contains poetry, fiction, creative nonfiction, translations, and artwork. Has published poetry by Michael Harper, Seamus Heaney, Lucille Clifton, Jean Valentine, Robert Bly, and Shara McCallum. As a sample the editor selected this poem, "Dispersed Light" by Angela Ball:

It shoots into the bedroom/sidelong to land/on a lover's chest/a strange slip of the tongue/about two
inches square./Freshly composed,/modest and spectacular,/lively but unalive,/not one or a selection/
but all: red orange yellow green blue/indigo violet and vice versa, insisting/and diving into each other,
plus/extensions and undetectable/by the human eye. It can't be cut;/what tries to cover it/becomes its
screen. Transitory,/permanent. Not diffuse but/spectral and actual.

Kestrel is 6×9, perfect-bound with glossy cover, includes art/graphics. Accepts approximately 10% of poems received. Press run is 700 for 275 subscribers of which 75 are libraries, 300 shelf sales. Single copy: $10; subscription: $18. Sample: $10. Make checks payable to Fairmont State College.

How to Submit: Submit 6-10 poems, or 2-3 longer poems at a time. No previously published poems or simultaneous submissions. Cover letter preferred. "SASE recommended if response is desired." Time between acceptance and publication is 6-12 months. Poems are circulated to an editorial board. "Consensus on every acceptance." Often comments on rejected poems. Publishes theme issues occasionally. Guidelines available for SASE or on website. Responds in up to 6 months. Pays 3 copies. Acquires one-time rights.

KIMERA: A JOURNAL OF FINE WRITING, 1316 Hollis, Spokane WA 99201. E-mail: kimera@js.spokane.wa.us. Website: www.js.spokane.wa.us/kimera/. Established 1996. **Publisher:** Jan Strever.

Magazine Needs: *Kimera* is a biannual online journal (appears yearly in hard copy) and "attempts to address John Locke's challenge—'where is the head with no chimeras.' " Wants poetry that "attempts to 'capture the soul in motion.' No flabby poems." Has published poetry by Gayle Elen Harvey, Janet McCann, and C.E. Chaffin. Accepts about 10% of poems/year. Press run is 300 for 200 subscribers. Single copy: $7; subscription: $14. Sample: $7.

How to Submit: Submit 3-6 poems at a time. Accepts simultaneous submissions; no previously published poems. Accepts e-mail submissions in ASCII text. Cover letter required. Poems are circulated to an editorial board. Seldom comments on rejected poems. Guidelines available on website. Responds in 3 months. Pays 1 copy. Acquires first rights.

KINGS ESTATE PRESS, 870 Kings Estate Rd., St. Augustine FL 32086-5033. (800)249-7485. E-mail: kep@aug.com. Established 1993. **Publisher:** Ruth Moon Kempher.

Book/Chapbook Needs & How to Submit: "Publishes the best contemporary poetry available; all books are illustrated." Publishes about 3 paperbacks/year. "Currently overstocked, not accepting submissions until after the year 2003."

$ ◯ ◒ THE KIT-CAT REVIEW; GAVIN FLETCHER MEMORIAL PRIZE FOR POETRY, 244 Halstead Ave., Harrison NY 10528-3611. (914)835-4833. Established 1998. **Editor:** Claudia Fletcher.

Magazine Needs: *The Kit-Cat Review* appears quarterly and is "named after the 18th century Kit-Cat Club whose members included Addison, Steele, Congreve, Vanbrugh, Garth, etc. Purpose: to promote/discover excellence and originality." Wants quality work—traditional, modern, experimental. Has published poetry by Coral Hull, Mary Kennan Herbert, Romola Robb Allrud, Harriet Zinnes, Louis Phillips, Chayym Zeldis, and Romania's Nobel Prize nominee Marin Sorescu. As a sample the editor selected these lines from "The Long Night" by Margaret J. Hoehn:

> You could be in a museum or maybe a dream/From a distance, you see the brooding scene/from what
> might be an Edward Hopper painting:/a desolate street of shadows; the desperate/obsession of a seedy
> hotel; the hum of a neon/Sign that flickers its vacancy in the window.

The Kit-Cat Review is 75 pages, 5½×8½, laser printed/photocopied, saddle-stapled with colored card cover, includes b&w illustrations. Receives about 1,000 poems/year. Press run is 500 for 200 subscribers. Subscription: $25. Sample: $7. Make checks payable to Claudia Fletcher.

How to Submit: Submit any number of poems at a time. Accepts previously published poems and simultaneous submissions. "Cover letter should contain relevant bio." Time between acceptance and publication is 2 months. Responds within 2 months. Pays up to $100 a poem and 2 copies. Acquires first or one-time rights.

Also Offers: Sponsors the annual Gavin Fletcher Memorial Prize for Poetry of $1,000.

Ⓝ ◒ KITTY LITTER PRESS; JOEY AND THE BLACK BOOTS; KATNIP REVIEWS; JOEY POETRY CONTEST, P.O. Box 3189, Nederland CO 80466-3189. E-mail: cari@kittylitterpress.com. Website: www.kittylitterpress.com (includes excerpts, guidelines, index, poet information, links to other poetry sites). Established 1994. **Editor:** Cari Taplin.

Magazine Needs: *Joey and the Black Boots* is a quarterly journal of poetry, short prose, and art. Wants free verse, blank verse, "poetry that is honest." Does not want rhyming, sentimental poetry that follows a traditional format. Recently published poetry by Lyn Lifshin, Michael Estabrook, Dave Church, Daniel Crocker, Lila Goodman, and Dan Buck. As a sample we selected these lines from "Gas Station Attendant" by Don Winter:

> He sits all night/like an overturned flower pot./His breath is sour as an orchard/after the first frost./
> Bruises under his skin are like shapes/frozen in the St. Joseph River . . .

Joey and the Black Boots is 30-40 pages, digest-sized, laser-printed, saddle-stapled, 20 lb. colored paper cover, with b&w (scannable) art. Receives about 500 poems/year, accepts about 20%. Publishes about 20-30 poems/issue. Press run is 60 for 10 subscribers of which 2 are libraries, 10 online sales; 48 distributed free to contributors. Single copy: $3; subscription: $10/4 issues. Sample: $2. Make checks payable to Cari Taplin.

How to Submit: Submit 5 poems at a time. Line length for poetry is 30 maximum. Accepts previously published poems; no simultaneous submissions. Accepts e-mail submissions; no fax or disk submissions. Cover letter is preferred. "Include SASE; put name and address on each page." Reads submissions all year. Time between acceptance and publication is 3-6 months. "Editor reads submissions and chooses desired poems, usually within one week of receipt, then responds." Seldom comments on rejected poems. Guidelines available for SASE, by e-mail, or on website. Responds in 2 weeks. Pays 1 contributor's copy. Acquires one-time rights. Also publishes *Katnip Reviews* with reviews of books and chapbooks of poetry and other magazines/journals in 100-200 words, multi-book format. Poets may send books/chapbooks for review consideration to *Katnip Reviews*, Seth Taplin, editor, P.O. Box 3189, Nederland CO 80466.

Book/Chapbook Needs & How to Submit: Kitty Litter Press publishes 4 chapbooks/year "by invitation only." Chapbooks are usually 40 pages, laser-printed, saddle-stapled, colored cardstock cover, with b&w art. "I prefer poets submit work for *Joey* first. If I'm interested, I'll solicit a manuscript for a chapbook." Responds to queries in 2 weeks; to mss in 1 month. Pays 3 author's copies (out of a press run of 20). Order sample chapbooks by sending $3 to Cari Taplin.

Also Offers: The Joey Poetry Contest; 1st Prize: $20, 2nd Prize: $10, 3rd Prize: $5, plus 4-issue subscriptions for the top 3 winners. Also awards several honorable mentions. **Entry fee:** $5/5 poems, $1 each additional poem (unlimited). **Deadline:** May 31. See website for complete guidelines.

Advice: "Poetry should be honest. What my readers like is open, honest writing that makes them think or gives a new angle on an old theme."

KOJA; KOJA PRESS (Specialized: form/style, experimental), P.O. Box 140083, Brooklyn NY 11214. Website: www.kojapress.com (includes guidelines, events, contact and subscription information, archives, links, and catalog). Established 1996. **Editor:** Michael Magazinnik.

Magazine Needs: *Koja* is published annually in August or September and "interested in experimental poetry but also publishes experimental prose and b&w artwork." Wants "visual/concrete poetry, avant-garde poetry and experimental poetry. No religious or classical work." Accepts poetry written by children. Has published poetry by Eileen Myles, David Burlyuk, K.K. Kuzminsky, I. Weiss, Richard Kostelanetz, and Bruce Andrews. *Koja* is 64 pages, 8½ × 11, various printing and binding methods, glossy color cover. Receives about 300 poems/year, accepts about 10%. Press run is 300 for 30 subscribers of which 5 are libraries, 200 shelf sales; 50 distributed free to contributors/reviewers. Subscription: $14. Sample: $7. Make checks payable to Michael Magazinnik.

How to Submit: Submit up to 10 poems at a time. No previously published poems or simultaneous submissions. "All unsolicited submissions must be accompanied by money order/check in the amount of $7 for a sample copy of the latest issue." Cover letter preferred. Time between acceptance and publication is up to 8 months. Seldom comments on rejected poems. Responds in up to 2 years. Pays 1 copy. Acquires first North American serial rights.

Book/Chapbook Needs & How to Submit: Has published *5 Underground 6* by William James Austin and *American Poetry (Free and How)* by Igor Satanovsky. Catalog available on website. Contact for more information.

Advice: "Please try to send work that fits in with our request for submissions."

KONOCTI BOOKS, 23311 County Rd. 88, Winters CA 95694. (530)662-3364. E-mail: nrpeattie@e arthlink.net. Established 1973. **Editor/Publisher:** Noel Peattie. Publishes poetry by invitation only.

KRAX (Specialized: humor), 63 Dixon Lane, Leeds, Yorkshire LS12 4RR England. Established 1971. **Editor:** Andy Robson.

Magazine Needs: *Krax* appears twice yearly, and publishes contemporary poetry from Britain and America. Wants poetry which is "light-hearted and witty; original ideas. Undesired: haiku, religious, or topical politics." 2,000 words maximum. All forms and styles considered. Has published poetry by Mike Hoy, Mandy Precious, and Patric Cunnane. As a sample the editor selected these lines from "Breathing Space" by Geoff Lowe:

> *It's an easy job now,/ever since Mr. Bandaid/invented, for cut-fingered fools,/thin air and thick water.*

Krax is 6 × 8, 64 pages of which 30 are poetry, saddle-stapled, offset-printed with b&w cartoons and graphics. Receives up to 1,000 submissions/year, accepts about 6%, has a 2- to 3-year backlog. Single copy: £3.50 ($7); subscription: £10 ($20). Sample: $1 (75p).

How to Submit: "Submit maximum of six pieces. Writer's name on same sheet as poem. Sorry, we cannot accept material on disk. SASE or SAE with IRC encouraged but not vital." No previously published poems or simultaneous submissions. Brief cover letter preferred. Responds in 2 months. Pays 1 copy. Reviews books of poetry (brief, individual comments; no outside reviews). Send books for review consideration.

Advice: "Write pieces that you would want to read for yourself and not ones which you think will please your English teacher or that are parodies of classic works."

KUMQUAT MERINGUE; PENUMBRA PRESS, P.O. Box 736, Pine Island MN 55963. (507)367-4430. E-mail: moodyriver@aol.com. Website: www.kumquatcastle.com ("includes guidelines, poetry samples and all information about *Kumquat Meringue*, and our other projects."). Established 1990. **Editor:** Christian Nelson.

Magazine Needs: *Kumquat Meringue* appears on an irregular basis, using "mostly shorter poetry about the small details of life, especially the quirky side of love and sex. We want those things other magazines find just too quirky. Not interested in rhyming, meaning of life or high-flown poetry." The magazine is "dedicated to the memory of Richard Brautigan." Has published works by Gina Bergamino, T. Kilgore Splake, Antler, Monica Kershner, Lynne Douglass, and Ianthe Brautigan. As a sample the editor selected these lines from "Leaping Lizards" by Emile Luria:

> After we made love . . . Kate said,/"You're so weird, really,/Even weirder than I thought."/And I
> thought, could she taste the salt,/Feel the sea lapping on my back?/I went to sleep wondering/About
> dinosaurs and lungfish/And the deepest reaches of the sea

Kumquat Meringue is 40-48 pages, digest-sized, "professionally designed with professional typography and nicely printed." Press run is 600 for 250 subscribers. Subscription: $12/3 issues. Sample: $6.

How to Submit: "We like cover letters but prefer to read things about who you are, rather than your long list of publishing credits. Accepts previously published and simultaneous submissions are, but please let us know." Often comments on submissions. No fax or e-mail submissions. "Please don't forget your SASE or you'll never hear back from us. E-mail address is for 'hello, praise, complaints, threats, and questions' only." Guidelines available for SASE and on website. Usually responds in 3 months. Pays 1 copy. Acquires one-time rights.

Advice: "Read *Kumquat Meringue* and anything by Richard Brautigan to get a feel for what we want, but don't copy Richard Brautigan, and don't copy those who have copied him. We just want that same feel. We also have a definite weakness for poems written 'to' or 'for' Richard Brautigan. Reviewers have called our publication iconoclastic, post-hip, post-beat, post-antipostmodern; and our poetry, carefully crafted imagery. When you get discouraged, write some more. Don't give up. Eventually your poems will find a home. We're very open to unpublished writers, and a high percentage of our writers had never been published anywhere before they submitted here."

KUUMBA (Specialized: ethnic, gay/lesbian/bisexual, love/romance/erotica, social issues), Box 83912, Los Angeles CA 90083-0912. (310)410-0808. Fax: (310)410-9250. E-mail: newsroom@blk.com or reggieh@blk.com. Website: www.kuumba.net (includes guidelines and contact information). Established 1991. **Editor:** Reginald Harris.

Magazine Needs: *Kuumba* is a biannual poetry journal of the black lesbian and gay community. Wants subject matter related to black lesbian and gay concerns. "Among the experiences of interest are: coming out, interacting with family and/or community, substance abuse, political activism, oral histories, AIDS, and intimate relationships." Does not want "gay-only subjects that have no black content, or black-only subjects with no gay content." Recently published poetry by Sharon Bridgeforth, Monica Hand, John Keene, and Norman Kester. As a sample we selected these lines from "The Sweetest Taboo" (for Gene) by Richard D. Gore:

> Forbidden,/But I loved you anyway/Dark, smouldering, and sweet/Luminous Black skin and Sloe-
> eyes . . .

Kuumba is 48 pages, 8½×11, offset-printed, saddle-stapled, with b&w cover drawing and ads. Receives about 500 poems/year, accepts about 25%. Press run is 3,000 for 750 subscribers of which 25 are libraries, 2,000 shelf sales. Subscription: $7.50/year. Sample: $4.50. Make checks payable to BLK Publishing Company.

How to Submit: Submit no more than 5 poems at a time. Accepts simultaneous submissions, if notified; no previously published poems. Accepts submissions by e-mail (in text box or as attachment) or on disk. Cover letter preferred. Seldom comments on rejected poems. Guidelines available for SASE, by e-mail, or on website. Responds in 6 weeks. Pays 4 contributor's copies. Acquires first North American serial rights and right to anthologize.

Advice: "Named for one of the Nguzo Saba (Seven Principles) which are celebrated at Kwanzaa, Kuumba means creativity." Not only dedicated to the celebration of the lives and experiences of black lesbians and gay men, but it is also intended to encourage new and experienced writers to develop their poetic craft.

HAVE A COLLECTION OF POETRY you want to publish? See the Chapbook Publishers Index or Book Publishers Index in the back of this book.

✦ ◑ ◎ KWIL KIDS PUBLISHING; THE KWIL CAFÉ NEWSLETTER; THE KWIL CLUB
(Specialized: children/teen/young adult), Box 29556, Maple Ridge, British Columbia V2X 2V0 Canada. Fax: (604)465-9101. E-mail: kwil@telus.net. Website: www.members.home.com/kwilkids/ (includes guidelines, contact information, and inspirational quotations). Established 1996. **Publisher:** Kwil.
Magazine Needs: *Kwil Kids* is a quarterly newsletter "publishing stories/poems to encourage and celebrate writers in the Kwil Club." Wants poetry that is "gentle; with compassionate truth and beauty; peace; humor; for children, by children, about children. No profane, hurtful, violent, political, or satirical work. Has published poetry by Darlene Slevin (adult), Gord Brandt (adult), Wendy Matthews (adult), Torrey Janzen (age 10), Carol McNaughton (age 6), and Ben Stoltz (age 11). As a sample they selected this poem by Kwil:

> I know that I'd sigh and grimace/When you'd fight about your play/But let peace spread from the
> playground/Throughout the world one day.

Kwil Kids is 8 pages, includes b&w graphics. Receives about 400 poems/year, accepts about 80%. Publish 8 poems/issue. Press run is 200 for 150 subscribers. Subscription: $25 (cost includes membership to the Kwil Club). Sample: SASE (or SAE and IRC) and $2. Make checks payable to Kwil Kids Publishing.
How to Submit: Submit 5 poems at a time. Include SASE and parent's signature. Cover letter preferred. Accepts fax and e-mail submissions; include in body of message, no attachments. Submit seasonal poems 3 months in advance. Time between acceptance and publication is up to 6 months. Always comments on rejected poems. "Kwil always provides encouragement and personalized response with SASE (or SAE and IRC)." Publishes theme issues occasionally. Guidelines available for SASE or on website. Responds in April, August, and December. Pays 1 copy. Acquires one-time rights.
Also Offers: "Offers 5¢ royalty (rounded to nearest dollar) on poems turned into cards for 'The Kwil Collection' sold at a local cafe, at the 'Kwil Kids Publishing Centre', and by mail order." Also sponsors The Kwil Club—a club for readers, writers, and artists of all ages. Membership features include 4 quarterly issues of the Kwil Kids newsletter, 4 quarterly issues of "Letters from the Kwil Cafe" newsletter; newsletter, newspaper, and greeting card publishing opportunities; a free subscription to Kwil's e-mail poetry list; reading, writing, and publishing tips and encouragement galore. Membership fee: $25.
Advice: "Kwil's motto: Keep your pencil moving (and your keyboard tapping!) Just be who you are, and do what you do. Miracles happen . . . when *you* love *you*."

◐ LA JOLLA POET'S PRESS; NATIONAL POETRY BOOK SERIES; SAN DIEGO POET'S PRESS; AMERICAN BOOK SERIES, P.O. Box 8638, La Jolla CA 92038. **Editor/Publisher:** Kathleen Iddings.
Book Needs: La Jolla Poet's Press and San Diego Poet's Press are nonprofit presses that publish only poets who "have published widely. No beginners here." Has published 36 individual poet's books and 5 poetry anthologies featuring poetry by Allen Ginsberg, Carolyn Kizer, Galway Kinnell, Tess Gallagher, Robert Pinsky, and Carolyn Forche. As a sample the editor included these lines from "Hester's Grammer" in *Curved Space* by Susan Terris:

> He laid his boots beside my slippers and they lay there./(Past.)/He has laid his body next to mine and
> it has lain there./(Perfect.)//Lay, lies/laid, lay/laid, lain./All quite grammatically correct and, still, it
> is not/the lay or laid that bothers him but the lies.//He may love to lie with me, yet to lie about me is
> for him/a tense not coped with in any text of standard usage./(Imperfect.)

Most books are approximately 100 pages, 5½×8½, perfect-bound, with laminated covers. Sample: $10.
How to Submit: Send 6 sample poems and SASE.

◐ THE LAIRE, INC. (Specialized: socially aware), P.O. Box 5524, Ft. Oglethorpe GA 30742. E-mail: theLaire@mindspring.com. Website: http://home.mindspring.com/~windsong/index.html (includes guidelines, subscription information, and sample poetry). Established 1995. **Editor:** Kim Abston.
Magazine Needs: *the LAIRE* is a quarterly "newsletter for poets and poetry lovers, dedicated to bringing to our readers quality poetry, and related subject matter which is both creatively and/or socially aware. Open to all forms of poetry, provided it is well executed, both creatively and technically. Poetry may be of any length or subject, but we tend to prefer poems that are 40 lines or less and socially and/or politically aware." As a sample the editor selected these lines from a poem by Gregory Fiorini:

> In that line of neglect stand revolutionaries/portable to their cause/of wings sans feathers/among
> debris/and all other ways akimbo

the LAIRE is 8 pages, 8½×11, photocopied, corner-stapled with line drawings and clip art. Receives about 1,500 poems/year, accepts 9%. Press run is 1,000 for 300-400 subscribers of which 50 are libraries, 400 shelf sales; 100 distributed free to schools, prisons, etc. Subscription: $10. Sample: $2.
How to Submit: Submit up to 5 poems at a time. No previously published poems or simultaneous submissions. No e-mail submissions. Accepts disk submissions. "Author's name, address, and telephone number must appear on each page. One poem per page. We accept 1.44meg IBM formatted floppy disk submissions, provided name, address, and phone are on label. Nothing returned without SASE." Cover letter preferred. Time between accep-

tance and publication is up to 6 months. Poems are circulated to an editorial board. "Poems are reviewed by the editorial board with the editor having final approval." Seldom comments on rejected poems. Publishes theme issues occasionally. Guidelines available for SASE and on website. Responds in 6 months. Pays 1 copy. Reviews books and chapbooks of poetry and other magazines in 150-200 words, single or multi-book format. Poets may send books for review consideration.

Also Offers: Sponsors poetry contests. Details available for SASE. Also accepts article submissions on any subject related to poetry, including critiques, biographies, book reviews, and F.Y.I. pieces.

N ◑ **LAKE EFFECT**, School of Humanities & Social Sciences, Penn State Erie, Station Rd., Erie PA 16563-1501. (814)898-6281. Fax: (814)898-6032. E-mail: gol1@psu.edu. Established 1978 as *Tempus*; renamed *Lake Effect* in 2001. **Editor-in-Chief:** George Looney. Member: CLMP.

Magazine Needs: *Lake Effect* is published annually in March/April "to provide an aesthetic venue for writing that uses language precisely to forge a genuine and rewarding experience for our readers. *Lake Effect* wishes to publish writing that rewards more than one reading, and to present side-by-side the voices of established and emerging writers." Wants "poetry aware of, and wise about, issues of craft in forming language that is capable of generating a rich and rewarding reading experience." Does not want "sentimental verse reliant on clichés." Recently published poetry by Virgil Suarez, Allison Joseph, Liz Beasley, Ryan G. Van Cleave, David Starkey, and Simon Brittan. As a sample the editor selected these lines from "If History Were a Sideshow" by Todd Pierce:

> *If history were a sideshow, the first in line would be shocked/at how little they knew of the path that led them to waiting/in line. As they'd leave the tent, they'd warn the others/but they wouldn't listen because that's how people learn/best. At night, the café sits dark in the dream of the man/with nothing but the hope of discovering what he searches for*

Lake Effect is 150 pages, digest-sized, offset-printed, perfect-bound, gloss by-flat film lamination cover. Receives about 300 poems/year, accepts about 10%. Publishes about 25-30 poems/issue. Press run is 800 for 300 shelf sales; 300 distributed free to contributors and writing programs. Single copy: $6; subscription: $6. Make checks payable to *Lake Effect*.

How to Submit: Submit 3-5 poems at a time. No previously published poems; accepts simultaneous submissions. No fax, e-mail, or disk submissions. Cover letter is required. Reads submissions year round. Time between acceptance and publication is up to 4 months. Poems are circulated to an editorial board. "The poetry staff reads the poems, meets and discusses them to come to a consensus. Poetry editor, along with editor-in-chief, makes final decisions." Seldom comments on rejected poems. Guidelines available in magazine. Responds in up to 4 months. Pays 2 contributor's copies. Acquires first North American serial rights.

Advice: "*Lake Effect* strives to provide an attractive venue for the good work of both established and emerging writers. We care about the integrity of poetry, and care for the poems we accept."

N ⊕ ◑ **THE LANTERN REVIEW**, 17 Sea Rd., Galway, County Galway, Ireland. E-mail: patjourdan@eircom.net. Established 2002. **Editor:** Pat Jourdan.

Magazine Needs: *The Lantern Review* appears quarterly. Originally founded to promote the work of a Galway writers' group but welcomes submissions from others as well. Wants modern, unforced, "preferably honest and bright" poetry. Does not want rampant rhyme, cutesy nature clichés; no sexist or sentimental poetry. *The Lantern Review* is 40 pages, digest-sized, stapled, paper cover. Receives about 500 poems/year, accepts about 25%. Publishes about 30 poems/issue. Press run is 100. Single copy: € 3.50; subscription: € 10. Sample: € 3.50. Make checks payable to Pat Jourdan.

How to Submit: Submit 3 poems at a time. Line length for poetry is 30 maximum. No previously published poems or simultaneous submissions. No fax, e-mail, or disk submissions. Send poems "preferably by letterpost only, IRCs enclosed, SAEs also." Reads submissions all year. Submit seasonal poems 3 months in advance. Time between acceptance and publication is 3 months. In choosing poems, "members of the writing group have precedence; invited poets are given several pages; others then included." Never comments on rejected poems. Guidelines available in magazine. Responds in 2 months. Pays 1 contributor's copy. Acquires first rights. Reviews books of poetry and other magazines/journals in 100 words, single book format. Poets may send materials for review consideration to Pat Jourdan.

Advice: "Try to write on what you see around you—not from other people's poetry. Go out and walk around, read the dictionary now and again to improve your vocabulary. Enjoy your own writing and others will, too."

◑ ◉ **LAURELS; WEST VIRGINIA POETRY SOCIETY (Specialized: membership)**, Rt. 2, Box 13, Ripley WV 25271. E-mail: mbush814@aol.com. Established 1996. **Editor:** Jim Bush.

Magazine Needs: *Laurels* is the quarterly journal of the West Virginia Poetry Society containing 95% poetry/5% art. Only considers work from WVPS members. Wants traditional forms and good free verse.

"If it's over 100 lines it must be very, very good. No porn, foul language, shape poems; no 'broken prose.' " Also accepts poetry written by children, if members. Has published poetry by Jane Stuart, Watha Lambert, and Thomas Downing. *Laurels* is 50 pages, digest-sized, mimeographed and saddle-stapled with paper cover, some pen-and-ink art, no ads. Receives about 2,000 poems/year, accepts about 50%. Press run is 275 for 210 subscribers. Membership: $12. Sample: $4. Make checks payable to the West Virginia Poetry Society for a subscription, to Jim Bush for a sample.

How to Submit: Requires contributors be members. For membership in WVPS, send $12 to Linda Poe, Rt. 1, Box 25, Gay WV 25244. Submit 4-5 poems at a time. Accepts previously published poems and simultaneous submissions. Accepts e-mail submissions (submit in body of message). Cover letter preferred including brief bio. Time between acceptance and publication is up to 1 year. Always comments on rejected poems. Issue deadlines are March 15, May 15, August 15, and November 15. Guidelines available for SASE. Responds "next day, usually." Sometimes sends prepublication galleys. Acquires one-time rights.

Also Offers: Sponsors a 35-category annual contest for members. Entry fee: no fee to current WVPS members or K-12 students, $1/poem for nonmembers, maximum of $12 for 12 or more categories. Guidelines available for SASE.

Advice: "Our purpose is to encourage and aid amateur poets who believe that words can be used to communicate meaning and to create beauty. Read a copy first, then join WPS."

⬤ LAZY FROG PRESS; LAZY FROG PRESS CHAPBOOK COMPETITION, P.O. Box 41253, Lafayette LA 70504-1253. E-mail: bullpen@lazyfrogpress.com. Website: www.lazyfrogpress.com. Established 2000. **Contact:** Nate Pritts.

Book/Chapbook Needs & How to Submit: "The nature of the Lazy Frog Press aesthetic is to publish and distribute bold work from new and established talents that says something about the author and his/her understanding of the form he/she is working in. Lazy Frog Press recognizes that first and foremost writing is to communicate, not to sit on a shelf and gather dust. Lazy Frog sees the best writing actively engaging the reader, forcing them to take notice of both their own place in the world and why we read." Publishes 2 chapbooks/year, one chosen through competition, one solicited. "We work with poets on all design elements." Pays 20 author's copies. Order sample chapbooks by sending $6 to Lazy Frog Press.

Also Offers: The Lazy Frog Chapbook Competition awards publication and 20 copies to a poetry manuscript in even numbered years, fiction in odd. Poems can be previously published in magazines, anthologies, online, etc., but the ms as a whole must be previously unpublished. "Enclose an acknowledgements page if you want but please DO include a cover letter with your contact information, the title of the manuscript, and a list of poem titles in the proper sequence. Also, tell us something about yourself—some brief talk about your poetry or your life: whatever." Submit 2 copies of ms of 16-32 pages, along with the $5 entry fee and a SASE for notification. Winner will be announced in June. The annual competition for poetry opens January 1 and closes May 1.

Advice: "We are looking for writers and readers both, those who challenge forms and those who like to be challenged. Lazy Frog Press wants to be the stiff breeze blowing back your hair, whether you are cruising in a T-top convertible or scaling Mt. Kilimanjaro."

◯ LEAPINGS LITERARY MAGAZINE; LEAPINGS PRESS, 2455 Pinercrest Dr., Santa Rosa CA 95403. Fax: (707)568-7531. E-mail: 72144.3133@compuserve.com. Website: http://home.inreach.com/editserv/. Established 1998. **Editor:** S.A. Warner.

Magazine Needs: *Leapings* is a semiannual literary magazine that publishes essays, book reviews, b&w artwork, literary and genre fiction, and poetry. "Open to any form, but prefer shorter verse. No rhymed for rhyming sake; no pornography." Accepts poetry written by children. Has published poetry by Kit Knight, Kenneth Pobo, Anselm Brocki, John Grey, Leslie Woolf Hedley, and John Taylor. As a sample we selected these lines from "Her love in a widened margin" by G.E. Coggshall:

> She rises at five a.m. unrebuked/for her nightgown's raveled hem. Each day/wrinkles like skin. The corners of her/wallpaper curl away from the plaster.//Her hindsight is clouded from cataracts,/yet she believes in all her layered-up/experience, her brick-and-mortar regrets.

Leapings is 35-50 pages, digest-sized, laserjet printed and saddle-stapled with cardstock cover, uses b&w graphics. Receives about 1,000 poems/year, accepts about 10%. Press run is 200 for 25 subscribers of which 5 are libraries, about 50 shelf sales. Single copy: $6; subscription: $10/year. Sample: $5. Make checks payable to S.A. Warner.

How to Submit: Submit up to 6 poems at a time. No previously published poems or simultaneous submissions. Accepts e-mail (poetry, only in body of message) and fax submissions. Cover letter preferred. "Poetry manuscripts may be submitted single-spaced and e-mailed." SASE with sufficient postage required for return of ms sent via regular mail. Time between acceptance and publication is 1 year. Often comments on rejected poems. Guidelines available for SASE, by e-mail, or on website. Responds in 3 months. Pays 2 copies. Acquires first rights. Reviews books and chapbooks of poetry and other magazines in 300 words, single book format. Poets may send books for review consideration.

THE LEDGE, 78-44 80th St., Glendale NY 11385. Established 1988. **Editor-in-Chief/Publisher:** Timothy Monaghan. **Co-Editor:** George Held. **Associate Editor:** Laura M. Corrado. **Assistant Editor:** Kimberlee A. Rohleder.

Magazine Needs: "We publish the best poems we receive. We seek poems with purpose, poems we can empathize with, powerful poems. Excellence is the ultimate criterion." Contributors include Sherman Alexie, Kurt Brown, Tony Gloeggler, Sherry Fairchok, Neil Carpathios, Marilyn L. Taylor, and Brooke Wiese. As a sample the editor-in-chief selected these lines from "Crossed Lines" by Elton Glaser:

> If you were at hand, and the night warm,/And all the crossed lines clear,/Would we undo Newton and
> confuse the physical,//Proving that two bodies can enclose/The same space at the same time,/As in
> that hybrid gift, that tourist curio//Where the Midwest finds itself/Suddenly at sea: a sand dollar/Set
> in the smooth belly of a buckeye burl.

The Ledge is 128 pages, digest-sized, typeset and perfect-bound with b&w glossy cover. Accepts 3% of poetry submissions. Press run is 1,000, including 600 subscribers. Single copy: $7; subscription: $13/2 issues, $24/4 issues or $32/6 issues.

How to Submit: Submit 3-5 poems at a time. Include SASE. Accepts simultaneous submissions; no previously published work. Reads submissions September through May only. Responds in 3 months. Pays 1 copy. Acquires one-time rights.

Also Offers: *The Ledge* sponsors an annual poetry chapbook contest, as well as an annual poetry contest. Details available for SASE.

Advice: "I believe the best poems appeal to the widest audience and consider *The Ledge* a truly democratic publication in that regard."

LIBRA PUBLISHERS, INC., 3089C Clairemont Dr., PMB 383, San Diego CA 92117. Phone/fax: (858)571-1414. **Poetry Editor:** William Kroll.

Book/Chapbook Needs: Publishes two professional journals, *Adolescence* and *Family Therapy*, plus books, primarily in the behaviorial sciences but also some general nonfiction, fiction, and poetry. "At first we published books of poetry on a standard royalty basis, paying 10% of the retail price to the authors. Although at times we were successful in selling enough copies to at least break even, we found that we could no longer afford to publish poetry on this basis. Now, unless we fall madly in love with a particular collection, we offer professional services to assist the author in self-publishing." Has published books of poetry by Martin Rosner, William Blackwell, John Travers Moore, and C. Margaret Hall.

How to Submit: Prefers complete ms but accepts query with 6 sample poems, publishing credits, and bio. Responds to query in 2 days, to submissions in up to 3 weeks. Mss should be double-spaced. Sometimes sends prepublication galleys. Send 9×12 SASE for catalog. Sample books may be purchased on a returnable basis.

THE LICKING RIVER REVIEW, Dept. of Literature and Language, Northern Kentucky University, Highland Heights KY 41099. E-mail: lrr@nku.edu. Established 1991. **Faculty Advisor:** Andrew Miller. Mail submissions to poetry editor.

Magazine Needs: *The Licking River Review,* is an annual designed "to showcase the best writing by Northern Kentucky University students alongside work by new or established writers from the region or elsewhere." No specifications regarding form, subject matter, or style of poetry. "No long poems (maximum 75 lines)." Has published poetry by David Starkey, Gail J. Peck, and James Doyle. *The Licking River Review* is 96 pages, 7×10, offset-printed on recycled paper and perfect-bound with a 16-page artwork inset (all art solicited). Accepts 5% of the poetry received. Press run is 1,000 plus. Sample: $5.

How to Submit: Submit up to 5 poems at a time. No previously published poems, no multiple or simultaneous submissions. Reads submissions September through November only. Publishes in June or July. Poems are circulated to an editorial board. Responds in up to 6 months. Pays in copies. Rights revert to author. Requests acknowledgment if poem is later reprinted.

LIGHT, Box 7500, Chicago IL 60680. Website: www.lightquarterly.com. Established 1992. **Editor:** John Mella.

Magazine Needs: *Light* is a quarterly of "light and occasional verse, satire, wordplay, puzzles, cartoons, and line art." Does not want "greeting card verse, cloying or sentimental verse." *Light* is 64 pages, perfect-bound, including art and graphics. Single copy: $5; subscription: $18. Sample: $4 with an additional $2 for first-class postage.

How to Submit: Submit 1 poem on a page with name, address, poem title and page number on each page. No previously published poems or simultaneous submissions. Seldom comments on rejected poems. Guidelines available for #10 SASE. Responds in 3 months or less. Always sends prepublication galleys. Pays 2 copies to domestic contributors, 1 copy to foreign contributors. Poets may send books for review consideration.

THE LIGHTNING BELL, 3300 Dawn Ridge Court, Greensboro NC 27403. E-mail: rfoley@ligh tningbell.org or gcuppers@lightningbell.org. Website: www.lightningbell.org/. Established 2001. **Co-Editors:** Ruth Foley and George Upper.
Magazine Needs: *The Lightning Bell* appears 3-4 times/year. "We aim to publish the best poetry we can find and especially like to see well-written formal poetry, but publish free verse poems as well. Extremely long poems and concrete poetry have very little chance with us, but we will read everything with an open mind." *The Lightning Bell* is published online. Receives about 1,250 poems/year, accepts about 5%. Publishes about 20 poems/issue. Sample free to anyone with an Internet connection.
How to Submit: Submit 2-4 poems at a time. Accepts simultaneous submissions "if notified and kept informed"; no previously published poems. Accepts e-mail submissions; no fax or disk submissions. Cover letter is preferred. "No snail mail submissions—online submissions only. See website for details." Reads submissions year round. Submit seasonal poems 5 months in advance. Time between acceptance and publication is up to 4 months. "The co-editors read every poem and only accept those that appeal to both of them." Seldom comments on rejected poems. Guidelines available on website. Responds in up to 1 month. Acquires first rights.
Advice: "Please read the poems on the website to see if *TLB* is an appropriate place for your work. Poetry takes work—if your poems did not take work, please send them elsewhere."

LILLIPUT REVIEW (Specialized: form, ten lines or less), 282 Main St., Pittsburgh PA 15201-2807. Website: http://donw714.tripod.com/lillieindex.html (includes guidelines, contact and subscription information, archives, contest information, editorial policy, and catalog). Established 1989. **Editor:** Don Wentworth.
Magazine Needs: *Lilliput* is a tiny (4½ × 3.6 or 3½ × 4¼), 12- to 16-page magazine, appearing irregularly and using poems in any style or form no longer than 10 lines. Has published *No Choice* by Cid Corman and *Half Emptied Out* by Lonnie Sherman and poetry by Gary Hotham, Pamela Miller Ness, Albert Huffstickler, and Miriam Sagan. As a sample the editor selected this poem by Ed Baker:
    Within and without/Same/Red Tulip.
Lilliput Review is laser-printed on colored paper and stapled. Press run is 250. Sample: $1 or SASE. Make checks payable to Don Wentworth.
How to Submit: Submit up to 3 poems at a time. Currently, every fourth issue is a broadside featuring the work of one particular poet. Guidelines available for SASE. Responds within 3 months. Pays 2 copies/poem. Acquires first rights. Editor comments on submissions "occasionally—always try to establish human contact."
Book/Chapbook Needs & How to Submit: Started the Modest Proposal Chapbook Series in 1994, publishing 1 chapbook/year, 18-24 pages in length. Chapbook submissions are by invitation only. Query with standard SASE. Sample chapbook: $3. Chapbook publications include *The Kingdom of Loose Board & Rusted Nail* by Christien Gholson.
Advice: "A note above my desk reads 'Clarity & resonance, not necessarily in that order.' The perfect poem for *Lilliput Review* is simple in style and language and elusive/allusive in meaning and philosophy. *Lilliput Review* is open to all short poems in approach and theme, including any of the short Eastern forms, traditional or otherwise."

LIMESTONE CIRCLE, P.O. Box 453, Ashburn VA 20146-0453. E-mail: renjef@earthlink.net. Established 1998. **Editor:** Renee Carter Hall.
   • "*Limestone Circle* will cease publication with the fall 2002 issue, due out in November 2002. The deadline for submissions is October 1, 2002."
Magazine Needs: *Limestone Circle* now appears twice annually—in spring (early May) and fall (early November). "We publish artistic, accessible poetry. Free verse is preferred." As a sample the editor selected these lines from "Cover" by Kelley Jean White:
    I lift a log and shock the thigmotactic world:/sow bugs scurry and roll, worms gleam/naked, vulnerable in the sun, a slug cowers/as my hand recoils, his thick body brown as/polished wood.
Limestone Circle is approximately 40 pages, 8½ × 5½, digitally copied, saddle-stapled, with matte cardstock cover, includes b&w artwork and photos. Each issue features 25-30 poems. Press run is 100 for 40 subscribers. Single copy: $4; subscription: $8/1 year (2 issues), $12/2 years (4 issues). Sample: $2. Make checks payable to Renee Carter Hall.

How to Submit: Submit 3-6 poems at a time, typed with name and address on each page, but "poets may submit work no more than twice in each calendar month." No previously published poems or simultaneous submissions. Accepts e-mail submissions "provided they are in the body of the message, not as attached files." Cover letter with bio preferred. Time between acceptance and publication is up to 6 months. Sometimes comments on rejected poems. Full guidelines available for SASE or by e-mail. Responds within 2 months for postal submissions; within 2 weeks for e-mail submissions. Pays 1 copy; additional copies available at a discount. Acquires first rights.

Also Offers: Also accepts submissions of b&w artwork and photos; guidelines available for SASE or by e-mail.

Advice: "We're a selective market, so we recommend that potential contributors send for guidelines and a sample copy before sending their best work."

LIMITED EDITIONS PRESS; ART: MAG, P.O. Box 70896, Las Vegas NV 89170. (702)734-8121. E-mail: magman@iopener.net. Established 1982. **Editor:** Peter Magliocco.

Magazine Needs: *ART:MAG* has "become, due to economic and other factors, more limited to a select audience of poets as well as readers. We seek to expel the superficiality of our factitious culture, in all its drive-thru, junk-food-brain, commercial-ridden extravagance—and stylize a magazine of hard-line aesthetics, where truth and beauty meet on a vector not shallowly drawn. Conforming to this outlook is an operational policy of seeking poetry from solicited poets primarily, though unsolicited submissions will be read, considered and perhaps used infrequently. Sought from the chosen is a creative use of poetic styles, systems and emotional morphologies other than banally constricting." Has published poetry by Brent McKnight, Karl Koweski, Maura Gage, Kelley Jean White, Hosho McCreesh, and Sheryl L. Helms. As a sample the editor selected these lines from "The God of Lust" by Anthony Seidman:

> Fingers have shut into fists and pounded/my chest resoundingly like an empty/steel box. And I have risen as ash/up through the black throats of suicide./I leave her skirt in disarray, and smash/open the door which divides lava from ice.

ART: MAG, appearing in 1-2 large issues of 100 copies/year, is limited to a few poets. Subscription: $10. Sample: $3 or more. Make checks payable to Peter Magliocco.

How to Submit: Submit 5 poems at a time with SASE. "Submissions should be neat and use consistent style format (except experimental work). Cover letters are optional." Accepts simultaneous submissions; no previously published poems. No fax or e-mail submissions. Sometimes comments on rejected poems. Publishes theme issues. Guidelines and upcoming themes available for SASE. Responds within 3 months. Pays 1 copy. Acquires first rights. Staff occasionally reviews books of poetry. Send books for review consideration.

Book/Chapbook Needs & How to Submit: "Recently published chapbooks for '01-02 are *Arcadia Plus* by Joyce Metzger and *Iced Amaranth* by Peter Magliocco. For any other press chapbook possibilities, query the editor before submitting any manuscript."

Advice: "The mag is seeking a futuristic aestheticism where the barriers of fact and fiction meet, where inner- and outer-space converge in the realm of poetic consciousness in order to create a more productively viable relationship to the coming 'cyberology' of the 21st century."

LINKS, Bude Haven, 18 Frankfield Rise, Tunbridge Wells TN2 5LF United Kingdom. E-mail: linksmag@supanet.com. Established 1992. **Editor:** Bill Headdon.

Magazine Needs: *Links* is published biannually in April and October and contains good quality poetry and reviews. Wants "contemporary, strong poetry to 80 lines." Has published poetry by Gross, Bartlett, and Shuttle. As a sample the editor selected these lines from "Masterpiece" by Barbara Daniels:

> I am a transparent woman,/My lover looks through me,/into a collaged landscape,/where any man can see/tamed hills and perfect pastures,/ego ego running free.

Links is up to 32 pages, A5, photocopied and saddle-stapled with card cover. Receives about 2,000 poems/year, accepts 7%. Press run is 200 for 150 subscribers of which 5 are libraries, 30 shelf sales. Subscription: £4/year (overseas £6), £7.50/2 years (overseas £10). Sample (with guidelines): £2 (£3 outside UK).

How to Submit: Submit 5-6 poems at a time. No previously published poems or simultaneous submissions. No fax or e-mail submissions. Cover letter preferred. "No long bios or list of previous publications." Time between acceptance and publication is up to 6 months. Seldom comments on rejected poems. Guidelines available for SASE or by e-mail. Responds in 2 weeks. Pays 1 copy. Acquires first rights. Reviews books and chapbooks of poetry and other magazines in 200 to 400 words, single or multi-book format. Poets may send books for review consideration.

LINTEL, 24 Blake Lane, Middletown NY 10940. (845)344-1690. Established 1977. **Poetry Editor:** Walter James Miller.

Book/Chapbook Needs: "We publish poetry and innovative fiction of types ignored by commercial presses. We consider any poetry except conventional, traditional, cliché, greeting card types, i.e., we consider any artistic poetry." Has published poetry by Sue Saniel Elkind, Samuel Exler, Adrienne Wolfert,

Edmund Pennant, and Nathan Teitel. "Typical of our work" is Teitel's book, *In Time of Tide*, 64 pages, digest-sized, professionally printed in bold type, flat-spined, hard cover stamped in gold, jacket with art and author's photo on back.
How to Submit: Not currently accepting unsolicited mss.

THE LISTENING EYE, Kent State Geauga Campus, 14111 Claridon-Troy Rd., Burton OH 44021. (440)286-3840. E-mail: grace_butcher@msn.com. Website: www.geocities.com/Athens/3716. Established 1970 for student work, 1990 as national publication. **Editor:** Grace Butcher. **Assistant Editors:** Jim Wohlken and Joanne Speidel.
Magazine Needs: *The Listening Eye* is an annual publication, appearing in late summer/early fall, of poetry, short fiction, creative nonfiction, and art that welcomes both new and established poets and writers. Wants "high literary quality poetry. Prefer shorter poems (less than two pages) but will consider longer if space allows. Any subject, any style. No trite images or predictable rhyme." Accepts poetry written by children if high literary quality. Has published poetry by Alberta Turner, Virgil Suarez, Walter McDonald, and Simon Perchik. As a sample the editor selected these lines from "71" by Simon Perchik:
> You didn't hear. Or remember. But that snow/we once believed had no memory/has returned, frantic
> now, each flake/as if the sun was still in flames/will circle down, closer and closer . . .
The Listening Eye is 52-60 pages, 5½×8½, professionally printed and saddle-stapled with card stock cover with b&w art. Receives about 200 poems/year, accepts about 5%. Press run is 300. Single copy: $4. Sample: $4. Make checks payable to Kent State University.
How to Submit: Submit up to 4 poems at a time, typed, single-spaced, 1 poem/page, name, and address in upper left-hand corner of each page, with SASE for return of work. Previously published poems occasionally accepted; no simultaneous submissions. Cover letter required. No e-mail submissions. Reads submissions January 1 through April 15 only. Time between acceptance and publication is up to 6 months. Poems are circulated to the editor and 2 assistant editors who read and evaluate work separately, then meet for final decisions. Occasionally comments on rejected poems. Guidelines available for SASE and in publication. Responds in 3 months. Pays 2 copies. Acquires first or one-time rights. Also awards $30 to the best sports poem in each issue.
Advice: "I look for tight lines that don't sound like prose, unexpected images or juxtapositions; the unusual use of language, noticeable relationships of sounds; a twist in viewpoint, an ordinary idea in extraordinary language, an amazing and complex idea simply stated, play on words and with words, an obvious love of language. Poets need to read the 'Big 3'—cummings, Thomas, Hopkins—to see the limits to which language can be taken. Then read the 'Big 2'—Dickinson to see how simultaneously tight, terse, and universal a poem can be, and Whitman to see how sprawling, cosmic, and personal. Then read everything you can find that's being published in literary magazines today and see how your work compares to all of the above."

LITERAL LATTÉ; LITERAL LATTÉ POETRY AWARDS, 61 E. Eighth St., Suite 240, New York NY 10003. (212)260-5532. E-mail: litlatte@aol.com. Website: www.literal-latte.com (includes excerpts, bios, contact and subscription information, archives, guidelines, information on events and contests). Established 1994. **Editor:** Jenine Gordon Bockman. **Contact:** Dorie Davidson.
Magazine Needs: *Literal Latté* is a bimonthly tabloid of "pure prose, poetry, and art," distributed free in coffeehouses and bookstores in New York City, and by subscription. "Open to all styles of poetry—quality is the determining factor." Has published poetry by Allen Ginsberg, Carol Muske, Amy Holman, and John Updike. As a sample we selected these lines from "What The Screech Owl Knows" by John Sokol, 1st Place winner of the annual *Literal Latté* Poetry Awards:
> That, here, in the woods/of western Pennsylvania,/life burgeons by the hour/while death rides a pig;/
> that larvae open like popcorn/and everything living/feasts on last year's detritus; . . .
Literal Latté is 24-28 pages, 11×17, neatly printed on newsprint and unbound with b&w art, graphics and ads. Receives about 3,000 poems/year, accepts 1%. Press run is 25,000 for distribution in over 200 bookstores and coffeehouses in New York City and nationwide. Subscription: $11. Sample: $3.
How to Submit: Accepts simultaneous submissions; no previously published poems. Cover letter with bio and SASE required. Time between acceptance and publication is 6 months. Often comments on rejected poems. Guidelines available for SASE, by e-mail, or on website. Responds in 3 months. Pays 10 copies and 3 subscriptions (2 gift subscriptions in author's name). All rights return to author upon publication.
Also Offers: Also sponsors the *Literal Latté* Poetry Awards, an annual contest for previously unpublished work. Offers $1,500 in awards and publication. They have added a "Food Verse" award; 1st Prize $500. Entry fee: $10 for 6 poems (or $15 includes subscription and entry fee for 6 poems). A past contest was judged by Carol Muske. Current details available for SASE, by e-mail, or on website.

$ 🖋 ◎ LITERALLY HORSES (Specialized: horses, cowboy lifestyle), Equestrienne Ltd., 208 Cherry Hill St., Kalamazoo MI 49006. (616)345-5915. E-mail: literallyhorses@aol.com. Website: www.literallyhorses.com/index.html (includes samples, guidelines, and contact and subscription information). Established 1999. **Editor:** Laurie A. Cerny.

Magazine Needs: *Literally Horses* is "a biannual venue for creative poetry/fiction and essays that have a horse/western lifestyle theme. Any style is acceptable. Nothing sexually explicit; nothing offensive; no curse words or racial overtones." Accepts poetry by children but "under 18 needs signed permission by parents." Has published poetry by Mary K. Herbert, Rod Miller, Michele F. Cooper, Mary Ruthart, Thomas Michael McDade, and Tena Bastian. As a sample the editor selected these lines from Tena Bastian:

> For in the horse's eyes, she saw a reflection of her own fear/She looked into the horse's soul/And
> understood what brought her here/God had brought the two together/The only way he could/This horse
> was not a renegade/Simply misunderstood.

Literally Horses is about 36 pages, 5½×8½, desktop-published and saddle-stapled with b&w paper cover, includes simple drawings, classified ads. Receives about 200 poems/year, accepts about 75%. Press run is 1,000. Single copy: $4.25; subscription: $7.95. Sample (including guidelines): $4.25. Make checks payable to Equestrienne Ltd.

How to Submit: Submit 1-3 poems at a time. Line length for poetry is 5 minimum, 75 maximum. Accepts previously published poems and simultaneous submissions. No fax or e-mail submissions. Cover letter required. "Cover letters with bio and release/permission to use poems. Include SASE for return of poems and acceptance." Time between acceptance and publication is 3 months. Often comments on rejected poems. Responds in 3 months. Pays $3/poem and 2 copies. Acquires one-time rights. Reviews books and chapbooks of poetry in 150 words. Poets may send books for review consideration.

Also Offers: "Annual poetry contest. Submit up to 3 poems (under 50 lines each), bio, SASE, and $9.95 entry fee (the fee includes a one-year subscription). First place: $75. Numerous smaller awards; "over 25 awards were given in the 2001 contest." Deadline: July 31 of every year. Winning entries are published in winter issue."

Advice: "Know horses and their world. The cowboy poetry I see is very good . . . so if submitting cowboy poetry, know what others are writing."

LITERARY FOCUS POETRY PUBLICATIONS; ANTHOLOGY OF CONTEMPORARY POETRY; INTERNATIONAL POETRY CONTESTS: FALL CONCOURS, SPRING CONCOURS, SUMMER CONCOURS (Specialized: anthology), P.O. Box 36242, Houston TX 77236-6242. (832)328-3881 or (281)250-2480. Fax: (281)933-0042. E-mail: adavieson@aol.com. Established 1988. **Editor-in-Chief:** Adrian A. Davieson.

Magazine Needs: Purchase of anthology may be required of poets accepted for publication. Literary Focus publishes anthologies compiled in contests, 3 times/year, with prizes of $200, $100, and $50, plus "Distinguished Mention" and "Honorable Mention." "Contemporary poetry with no restriction on themes. 20-line limit. No abusive, anti-social poetry." As a sample we selected these lines from the editor's own poem "My Deep Fears":

> Out came the fears of yester-years/Eroding my very being. As I looked/The stream of tears cascaded
> my/Cheeks, reminding me the journey/Was not over.//Only yesterday I thought of my arrival/At shore,
> but now I know it was just a/Mirage, that to be thus is nothing but/To be safely thus!

The digest-sized anthologies are either flat-spined or saddle-stapled, 70 pages, typeset.

How to Submit: Submit maximum submission 15 poems, minimum three poems. Accepts previously published poems and simultaneous submissions. Accepts submissions by fax, by e-mail (in text box or as attachment), and by regular mail. "In order to evaluate serious entries, a $5 entry fee is required for the first three poems. Poems are evaluated on an individual basis by a panel of five editors chaired by editor-in-chief. Poets are notified of acceptance two weeks after deadlines." Guidelines available for SASE. Pays up to 5 copies. Reviews books of poetry.

THE LITERARY REVIEW: AN INTERNATIONAL JOURNAL OF CONTEMPORARY WRITING, Fairleigh Dickinson University, 285 Madison Ave., Madison NJ 07940. (973)443-8564. Fax: (973)443-8364. E-mail: tlr@fdu.edu. Website: www.theliteraryreview.org (includes guidelines, links, and subscription information). Established 1957. **Editor-in-Chief:** René Steinke. **Contact:** William Zander.

Magazine Needs: *The Literary Review*, a quarterly, seeks "work by new and established poets which reflects a sensitivity to literary standards and the poetic form." No specifications as to form, length, style, subject matter, or purpose. Has published poetry by David Citino, Rick Mulkey, Virgil Suarez, Gary Fincke, and Dale M. Kushner. *The Literary Review* is 200 pages, 6×9, professionally printed and flat-spined with glossy color cover, using 50-75 pages of poetry in each issue. Press run is 2,500 with 900 subscriptions of which one-third are overseas. Receives about 1,200 submissions/year, accepts 100-150, have a 12- to 16-month backlog. Sample: $5 domestic, $6 outside US, request a "general issue."

How to Submit: Submit up to 5 typed poems at a time. Accepts simultaneous submissions. No fax or e-mail submissions. Do not submit during the summer months of June, July and August. At times the editor comments on rejected poems. Publishes theme issues. Responds in 3 months. Always sends prepublication galleys. Pays 2 copies. Acquires first rights. Reviews books of poetry in 500 words, single book format. Poets may send books for review consideration.

Also Offers: Website features original work. Has published poetry by Renée Ashley and Catherine Kasper. Website contact is Louise Stahl.
Advice: "Read a general issue of the magazine carefully before submitting."

◑ **LITTLE BROWN POETRY**, P.O. Box 4533, Portsmouth NH 03802. Fax: (240)282-6418. E-mail: editor@littlebrownpoetry.com. Website: www.littlebrownpoetry.com (includes writer's guidelines, submissions page, submissions e-mail address, about the editor, subscription info, bios, upcoming themes, archives). Established 1998. **Editor:** Sam Siegel.
Magazine Needs: *Little Brown Poetry* is an online quarterly poetry journal with collected print anthology. Wants "good quality emotional poetry, any style, any form." Has published poetry by Ric Masten, David Sutherland, Jarrett Keene, Janet Buck, Walt McDonald, Simon Perchik. As a sample the editor selected these lines by Agnes Makar:

> on december barren trees/you, man of suits and cigars/disturb the peacocks/from their far off nests,/ on some transparent glow/they fluff tails/paint eyes and lips all for the/hate of tomorrow/the consistency/day in and day out/you hear them cry/among the ruins of empty cages/vacant eyes/not belonging,/peacock woman,/a wasteland of youth.

Little Brown Poetry is over 48 pages, journal-sized, perfect-bound with original cover art. Receives about 2,500 poems/year, accepts about 15%. Press run is 1,000 for 250 subscribers. Sample: $3. "Price varies for anthology; check website or e-mail."
How to Submit: Submit at least 3 poems at a time. Accepts previously published poems and simultaneous submissions. "Please let us know whom else you have submitted your work to (the same piece of work you are submitting), and whom else you have published your work with." Accepts submissions by e-mail (as attachment or in text box), by fax, and through regular mail. Cover letter preferred. Often comments on rejected poems. Publishes theme issues. Guidelines and upcoming themes available for SASE, by e-mail, or on website. Responds in up to 3 months. Pays 1 copy. Acquires one-time rights.
Advice: "Submit your best work. Spend more time on your poetry than your cover letter and read the poetry here before submitting."

◑ **LONE STARS MAGAZINE; "SONGBOOK" POETRY CONTEST**, 4219 Flinthill, San Antonio TX 78230. Established 1992. **Editor/Publisher:** Milo Rosebud.
Magazine Needs: *Lone Stars*, published 3 times/year, features "contemporary poetry." Wants poetry that holds a continuous line of thought. No profanity. Has published poetry by Sheila Roark, Tom Hendrix, and Patricia Rourke. As a sample the editor selected these lines from "Let Life Decide" by Terry Lee:

> A midnight rainbow, a tear never cried, words spoken in silence: a light that does not shine.

Lone Stars is 25 pages, 8½×11, photocopied, with some hand-written poems, saddle-stapled, bound with tape, includes clip art. Press run is 200 for 100 subscribers of which 3 are libraries. Single copy: $5; subscription: $15. Sample: $4.50.
How to Submit: Submit 3-5 poems at a time with "the form typed the way you want it in print." **Charges reading fee of $1 per poem.** Accepts previously published poems and simultaneous submissions. Cover letter preferred. Time between acceptance and publication is 2 months. Publishes theme issues. Guidelines and upcoming themes available for SASE. Responds within 3 months. Acquires one-time rights.
Also Offers: Sponsors annual "Songbook" (song-lyric poems) Poetry Contest. Details available for SASE.

◑ **LONE WILLOW PRESS**, P.O. Box 31647, Omaha NE 68131-0647. (402)551-0343. E-mail: lonewil lowpress@aol.com. Established 1993. **Editor:** Fredrick Zydek.
Book/Chapbook Needs: Publishes 2-3 chapbooks/year. "We publish chapbooks on single themes and are open to all themes. The only requirement is excellence. However, we do not want to see doggerel or greeting card verse." Has published *Cave Poems* by Marjorie Power, *Things Like This Happen All the Time* by Eric Hoffman, *Monsters We Give Our Children* by Carolyn Riehle, and *From the Dead Before* by Clif Mason. Books are 36-50 pages, digest-sized, neatly printed on fine paper and saddle-stapled with card stock cover.
How to Submit: Query first with 5 sample poems and cover letter with brief bio and publication credits. Accepts previously published poems; no simultaneous submissions. No fax or e-mail submissions. Time between acceptance and publication is 6 months. Seldom comments on rejected poems. Guidelines available for SASE. Responds to queries in 1 month, to mss (if invited) in up to 3 months. Pays 25 author's copies. "We also pay a small royalty if the book goes into a second printing." For a sample chapbook, send $7.95 in check or money order.
Advice: "If you don't know the work of Roethke, DeFrees, and Hugo, don't bother sending work our way. We work with no more than two poets at a time."

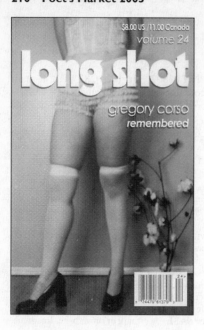

The editors of *Long Shot* selected Laurel Jensen's photograph for Volume 24's cover "because it's a striking image. Also because we thought Gregory Corso (who's honored in this edition with a special section) would approve." Cover design by Michael Fruhbeis.

LONG ISLAND QUARTERLY (Specialized: regional), P.O. Box 114, Northport NY 11768. E-mail: Liquarterly@aol.com. Website: www.poetrybay.com. Established 1990. **Editor/Publisher:** George Wallace.

Magazine Needs: *Long Island Quarterly* uses poetry (mostly lyric free verse) by people on or from Long Island. "Surprise us with fresh language. No conventional imagery, self-indulgent confessionalism, compulsive article-droppers." Has published poetry by Edmund Pennant and David Ignatow. As a sample the editor selected this poem, "The Willow," by William Heyen:

> Crazy Horse counted the leaves of willows along the river./He realized one leaf for each buffalo,/& the leaves just now appearing in the Moon of Tender Grass/were calves being born. If he could keep the trees/from the whites, the herds would seed themselves./He watched the buffalo leaves for long, & long,/how their colors wavered dark & light in the running wind./If he could keep his rootedness within this dream,/he could shade his people to the end of time.

Long Island Quarterly is 28 pages, digest-sized, professionally printed on quality stock and saddle-stapled with matte card cover. Press run is 250 for 150 subscribers of which 15 are libraries, 50-75 shelf sales. Subscription: $15. Sample: $4.

How to Submit: Submit 3 poems at a time. Name and address on each page. Accepts e-mail submissions in text box; no attachments. Cover letter including connection to Long Island region required. Submissions without SASE are not returned. Responds in 3 months. Sometimes sends prepublication galleys. Pays 1 copy.

Book/Chapbook Needs & How to Submit: Wants serious contemporary poetry of merit. Publishes up to 5 chapbooks per year. Chapbooks are usually 24-32 pages. Reviews books and chapbooks of poetry. Send books for review consideration. Terms vary.

Advice: "(1) Go beyond yourself; (2) Don't be afraid to fictionalize; (3) Don't write your autobiography—if you are worth it, maybe someone else will."

LONG SHOT, P.O. Box 6238, Hoboken NJ 07030. E-mail: dshot@mindspring.com Website: www.longshot.org. Established 1982. **Editors:** Danny Shot, Nancy Mercado, Andy Clausen, Magdalena Alagna, and Lynne Breitfeller.

Magazine Needs: Published biannually, *Long Shot* is, they say, "writing from the real world." Has published poetry by Wanda Coleman, Jayne Cortez, Amiri Baraka, Reg E. Gaines, Paul Beatty, Ishmael Reed, and Sonia Sanchez. *Long Shot* is 192 pages, professionally printed and flat-spined with glossy card cover using b&w photos, drawings and cartoons. Press run is 2,000. Subscription: $24/2 years (4 issues). Sample: $8.

How to Submit: Accepts simultaneous submissions; no previously published poems. No e-mail submissions. Responds in 2 months. Pays 2 copies.

Also Offers: Has published *Lift Off* by Herschel Silverman; *The Original Buckwheat* by Reg E. Gaines; *Sermons from the Smell of a Carcass Condemned to Begging* by Tony Medina; *Night When Moon Follows* by Cheryl Boyce Taylor; *It Concerns the Madness* by Nancy Mercado; *I Have No Clue* by Jack Wiler.
Advice: "We receive too many requests for writer's guidelines. Just send the poems."

Ⓝ Ø LONGHOUSE; SCOUT; ORIGIN PRESS, 1604 River Rd., Guilford VT 05301. E-mail: poetry@sover.net. Website: www.longhousepoetry.com (includes archives, bios, links, catalog). Established 1973. **Editor:** Bob Arnold.
Magazine Needs & How to Submit: *Longhouse* is a literary annual using poems "from the serious working poet" from any region in any style. Has published poetry by Hayden Carruth, Janine Pommy Vega, Bobby Byrd, Sharon Doubiago, John Martone, and James Koller. *Longhouse* appears as a thick packet of looseleaf 8½×14 sheets, photocopied from typescript, in a handsomely printed matte cover. Press run is 100-300. Sample: $12. Pays 2 copies. Reviews books of poetry.
Book/Chapbook Needs & How to Submit: Publishes chapbooks and books (solicited manuscripts only) under the imprints of Longhouse and Scout. Has published *Together* by Cid Corman, *Variations* by Bill Deemer, *A Cooking Book* by Lorine Niedecker as well as booklets by Michael Casey, Joanne Kyger, and Alan Chong Lau.
Also Offers: "We are also a bookshop and mail-order business for modern first editions and modern poetry and small presses. We encourage poets and readers looking for collectible modern first editions and scarce—and not so scarce—books of poetry and small press magazines to locate our website."
Advice: "Origin Press is best known as Cid Corman's press. One of the quiet giants in American poetry plus the wide scope of international work. Established in the early 1950s in Boston, it has moved around as Cid went with his life: France, Italy, Boston, for many years now in Kyoto, Japan. Cid has merged with *Longhouse* in that we now edit and publish a few items together. He continues to edit, translate, and publish from Kyoto. His own books are heavily based in our bookshop and mail-order catalog."

◐ ◎ LONZIE'S FRIED CHICKEN™ LITERARY MAGAZINE; SOUTHERN ESCARPMENT CO. (Specialized: regional, the South), P.O. Box 189, Lynn NC 28750. E-mail: lonziesfriedchic@telep lex.net. Website: www.lonziesfriedchicken.com (includes guidelines, contributors, list of bookstores, and order form). Established 1998. **Editor:** E.H. Goree.
Magazine Needs: *Lonzie's Fried Chicken*™ is "a journal of accessible southern fiction and poetry—an opportunity for writers and poets to show their stuff and satisfy readers. Our focus is well-written short fiction, self-contained novel excerpts, and poetry with a feel for the South. We welcome the best contemporary, mainstream, and historical work by published and unpublished poets and writers." Recently published poetry by Reid Bush, Gwen Hart, Wayne Hogan, Eileen Murphy, Marc Swan, and Nicole Sarrocco. *Lonzie's Fried Chicken* is about 100 pages, digest-sized, offset-printed, perfect-bound, with light card cover containing b&w photo, ads. Receives over 500 poems/year, accepts about 10%. Press run is 1,000 for about 200 subscribers, 500 shelf sales; 100 distributed free to newspapers, reviewers, and contributors. Single copy: $9.95; subscription: $16.95/year, $29.95/2 years. Sample (including guidelines): $8.95.
How to Submit: Submit up to 5 poems at a time. Accepts simultaneous submissions; no previously published poems. No fax, e-mail, or disk submissions. Cover letter preferred. Reads submissions year round. Time between acceptance and publication is up to 5 months. Poems are circulated to an editorial board. Seldom comments on rejected poems. Send SASE or postcard for return or reply. Responds in 3 months or less. Pays 3 copies. Acquires first rights and one-time anthology rights.
Advice: "We look for humor and subtlety and always reject the quaint, as well as essays, gore, violence, hate, erotica, and science fiction."

Ⓥ LOS, 150 N. Catalina St., No. 2, Los Angeles CA 90004. E-mail: lospoesy@earthlink.net. Website: http://home.earthlink.net/~lospoesy. Established 1991. **Contact:** the Editors.
Magazine Needs: *Los*, published 4 times/year, features poetry. Has published poetry by Taj Jackson, Jara Jones, Heather Lowe, Gregory Jerozal, Peter Layton, and Ed Orr. As a sample the editors selected these lines from "crossing the palm" by Christopher Mulrooney:

> Six-fourths of any chord roundabout/suggest the rest/particularity makes all the more reason/for the
> daily spotlight you give over/to a gros demesne//you make the scene

Los is 5×8½ and saddle-stapled. Press run is 100. Sample: $2. Make checks payable to Heather J. Lowe.
How to Submit: Accepts e-mail submissions (in text box). Guidelines are unavailable; "just send poems." Time between acceptance and publication is up to 6 months. Responds in 2 months. Pays 1 contributor's copy.

N ◙ ◎ **LOTUS PRESS, INC.; NAOMI LONG MADGETT POETRY AWARD (Specialized: ethnic, African-American)**, P.O. Box 21607, Detroit MI 48221. (313)861-1280. Fax: (313)861-4740. E-mail: lotuspress@aol.com. Established 1972. **Editor:** Naomi Long Madgett. **Contact:** Constance Withers.
Book/Chapbook Needs & How to Submit: "We occasionally publish sets of poster-poems on related subjects, including 'The Fullness of Earth' and 'Hymns Are My Prayers.' However, we are already committed through 2002 on publications except for award-winning manuscripts." Has published *The Force and the Reckoning* by James A. Emanuel, *Passing Over* by Houston A. Baker, Jr., *You Can See It From Here*, by Jerry Wemple, *Desdemona's Fire* by Ruth Ellen Kocher, and *Creole Journal: The Louisiana Poems* by Sybil Klein. Paperback prices vary from $5 to $15; cloth cover, $35. Pays 25 copies and 40% discount on additional copies.
Also Offers: Sponsors the Naomi Long Madgett Poetry Award. The award goes to a ms by an African-American poet. "Under the new guidelines, poets who have already had a book published by Lotus Press are ineligible. However, inclusion in a Lotus Press anthology, such as *Adam of Ifé: Black Women in Praise of Black Men*, does not disqualify them. Those who have worked over a period of years at developing their craft will have the best chance for consideration. The work of novices is not likely to be selected. Poems submitted by another person, anthologies, or collaborations by more than one poet are not eligible." Awards $500 and publication by Lotus Press, Inc. Submit 3 complete copies of approximately 60-80 pages of poetry, exclusive of a table of contents or other introductory material, with a $15 reading fee paid by money order or cashiers check. Any number of poems in the collection may be previously published individually in newspapers, magazines, journals or anthologies. Do not include author's name on any page of the ms. Include with each copy a cover sheet with the title of the collection only and no other information. Also enclose a sheet with the title of the ms, author's name, address, phone and brief statement, signed, indicating all the poems are original and uncollected and the author is an American of African descent. Mss will not be returned. Include a stamped, self-addressed postcard for acknowledgement of receipt. Submission period: April 1 through June 1. Winners will be announced no later than September 1. Send SASE or e-mail for more information.
Advice: "Read some of the books we have published, especially award winners. Read a lot of good contemporary poetry."

◙ ◎ **LOUISIANA LITERATURE; LOUISIANA LITERATURE PRIZE FOR POETRY (Specialized: regional)**, SLU-792, Southeastern Louisiana University, Hammond LA 70402. (504)549-5022. E-mail: lalit@selu.edu. Website: www.selu.edu/orgs/lalit (includes guidelines, special announcements, journal contents, and notes from the editor). **Editor:** Jack Bedell.
Magazine Needs: *Louisiana Literature* appears twice/year. "Receives mss year round although we work through submissions more slowly in summer. We consider creative work from anyone though we strive to showcase our state's talent. We appreciate poetry that shows firm control and craft, is sophisticated yet accessible to a broad readership. We don't use highly experimental work." Has published poetry by Claire Bateman, Elton Glaser, Gray Jacobik, Vivian Shipley, D.C. Berry, and Judy Longley. As a sample the editor selected these lines from "Notre Dame" by Alison T. Gray:

> Today Grandmama is as wide as Paris/and engulfs the city like smoke./She is looking for you, sister./
> You think for a moment it's raining.//but it's a trick of the dead: how/in certain light smoke can seem
> water. . . .

Louisiana Literature is 150 pages, 6¾×9¾, flat-spined, handsomely printed on heavy matte stock with matte card cover. Single copies: $8 for individuals; subscription: $12 for individuals, $12.50 for institutions.
How to Submit: Submit up to 5 poems at a time. Send cover letter, including bio to use in the event of acceptance. No simultaneous submissions. Enclose SASE "and specify whether work is to be returned or discarded." No fax or e-mail submissions. Publishes theme issues. Guidelines and upcoming themes available for SASE or on website. Sometimes sends prepublication galleys. Pays 2 copies. Send books for review consideration; include cover letter.
Also Offers: The Louisiana Literature Prize for Poetry offers a $400 award. Guidelines available for SASE. Website includes submission guidelines, special announcements, journal contents and notes from editor.
Advice: "It's important to us that the poets we publish be in control of their creations. Too much of what we see seems arbitrary."

◙ ◎ **THE LOUISIANA REVIEW (Specialized: regional, Louisiana)**, % Division of Liberal Arts, Louisiana State University at Eunice, P.O. Box 1129, Eunice LA 70535. (337)550-1328. E-mail: mgage@lsue.edu. Website: www.lsue.edu/LA-Review/ (includes table of contents, sample poems, cover of the second issue, and submission information). Established 1999. **Editor:** Dr. Maura Gage. **Associate Editor:** Dr. Susan LeJeune. **Assistant Editor:** Ms. Barbara Deger.

Magazine Needs: *The Louisiana Review* appears annually in the fall semester. "We wish to offer Louisiana poets, writers, and artists a place to showcase their most beautiful pieces. Others may submit Louisiana-related poetry, stories, interviews with Louisiana writers, and art. We want to publish the highest-quality poetry, fiction, art, and drama. For poetry we like strong imagery, metaphor, and evidence of craft, but we do not wish to have sing-song rhymes, abstract, religious or overly sentimental work." Has published poetry by Gary Snyder, Antler, David Cope, and Catfish McDaris. As a sample the editor selected these lines from "The Way We Used to Believe" by Sandra Meek:

> *if death is a shell to split open, I want to hear/ the rocking inside.*

The Louisiana Review is 100-225 pages, magazine-sized, professionally printed and perfect-bound, includes photographs/artwork. Receives about up to 2,000 poems/year, accepts 40-50 poems. Press run is 300-600. Single copy: $8.

How to Submit: Submit 5 poems at a time. Occasionally accepts previously published poems. No fax submissions, accepts e-mail submissions. Cover letter preferred. "Send typed poems with SASE, include name, and address on each poem. If including a cover letter, please tell us your association with Louisiana: live there, frequent visitor, used to live there." Reads submissions November 1 through March 31 only. Time between acceptance and publication is between 10 months and two years. Poems are circulated to an editorial board. Sometimes comments on rejected poems. Responds in up to 5 months. Sends prepublication galleys. Pays up to 2 copies "depending on the size of the issue and bulk of the print run as well as mailing expenses. Poets retain the rights to their works."

Advice: "Be true to your own voice and style."

Ø LOUISIANA STATE UNIVERSITY PRESS, P.O. Box 25053, Baton Rouge LA 70894-5053. (578)388-6294. Fax: (578)388-6461. Established 1935. **Poetry Editor:** L.E. Phillabaum. A highly respected publisher of collections by poets such as Lisel Mueller, Margaret Gibson, Fred Chappell, Marilyn Nelson, and Henry Taylor. Currently not accepting poetry submissions; "fully committed through 2003."

N Ø © THE LOUISVILLE REVIEW (Specialized: children/teen), Spalding University, 851 S. Fourth St., Louisville KY 40203. (502)585-9911, ext. 2777. E-mail: louisvillereview@spalding.edu. Website: www.louisvillereview.org (includes submission guidelines, staff, information about current and past issues). Established 1976. **Contact:** Poetry Editor.

Magazine Needs: *The Louisville Review* appears twice/year. Uses any kind of poetry except translations; has a section devoted to children's poetry (grades K-12) called The Children's Corner. Recently published poetry by Wendy Bishop, Gary Fincke, Michael Burkard, and Sandra Kohler. *The Louisville Review* is 100 pages, 6×9, flat-spined. Receives about 700 submissions/year, accepts about 10%. Single copy: $8; subscription: $14. Sample: $4.

How to Submit: Include SASE; no electronic submissions. Reads submissions year round. "We look for the striking metaphor, unusual imagery, and fresh language. Submissions are read by three readers; time to publication is two to three months after acceptance. Poetry by children must include permission of parent to publish if accepted." Guidelines available on website. Pays 2 contributor's copies.

Ø LOW-TECH PRESS, 30-73 47th St., Long Island City NY 11103. Established 1981. **Editor:** Ron Kolm. Has recently published *Bad Luck* by Mike Topp and *Goodbye Beautiful Mother* Tsaurah Litzky. "We only publish solicited mss."

Ø LSR, P.O. Box 440195, Miami FL 33144. Established 1990. **Editor/Publisher:** Nilda Cepero.

Magazine Needs: "Appearing 2 times per year, *LSR* publishes poetry, book reviews, interviews, and line artwork. Style, subject matter, and content of poetry open; we prefer contemporary with meaning and message. No surrealism, no porn, or religious poetry. Reprints are accepted." Has published poetry by Catfish McDaris, Mike Catalano, Janine Pommey-Vega, Margarita Engle, and Evangeline Blanco. As a sample the editor selected these lines by Duane Locke:

> *Death is dressed/like an old-fashioned clown/in caps and bells./Death wears silk upturned shoes./The*
> *out-of-date costume/leaves death unrecognized . . .*

LSR is 20 pages, 8½×11, offset-printed and saddle-stapled with a 60 lb. cover, includes line work, with very few ads. Receives about 300 poems/year, accepts about 30%. Publish 40-50 poems/issue. Press run is 3,000 for more than 100 subscribers of which 20 are libraries; the rest distributed free to selected bookstores in the US, Europe and Latin America. Single copy: $4; subscription: $6. Sample: $5, including postage.

How to Submit: Submit 4 poems at a time. Line length for poetry is 5 minimum, 45 maximum. Accepts previously published poems; no simultaneous submissions. Accepts disk submissions. Cover letter required. "We only accept disk submissions with print-out. Include SASE and bio." Reads submissions February 1 through October 31 only. Time between acceptance and publication is 1 year. Poems are circulated to an editorial board.

"Three rounds by different editors. Editor/Publisher acts on recommendations." Guidelines available for SASE. Responds in 9 months. Pays 2 contributor's copies. Acquires one-time rights. Reviews books. "We will not write reviews; however, will consider those written by others to 750 words."
Advice: "Read as many current poetry magazines as you can."

$◖ LUCIDITY; BEAR HOUSE PUBLISHING, 14745 Memorial Dr., #10, Houston TX 77079-5200. (281)920-1795. E-mail: tedbadger1@yahoo.com. Established 1985. **Editor:** Ted O. Badger.
Magazine Needs: *Lucidity* is a semiannual journal of poetry. **Submission fee required**—$1/poem for "juried" selection by a panel of judges or $2/poem to compete for cash awards of $15, $10, and $5. Other winners paid in both cash and in copies. Also publishes 6 pages of Succint Verse—poems of 12 lines or less—in most issues. "We expect them to be pithy and significant and there is no reading/entry fee if sent along with Cash Award or Juried poems. Just think of all poetic forms that are 12 lines or less: the cinquain, limerick, etheree, haiku, senryu, lune, etc., not to mention quatrain, triolet and couplets." In addition, the editor invites a few guest contributors to submit to each issue. Contributors are encouraged to subscribe or buy a copy of the magazine. The magazine is called *Lucidity* because, the editor says, "I have felt that too many publications of verse lean to obscurity." "Open as to form, 36-line limit due to format. We look for poetry that is life-related and has clarity and substance." Purpose: "We dedicate our journal to publishing those poets who express their thoughts, feelings and impressions about the human scene with clarity and substance." Does not want "religious, nature or vulgar poems." Published poets include Barbara Vail, Tom Padgett, John Gorman, Penny Perry, and Katherine Zauner. As a sample the editor selected these lines by Dorothy Trautfield:
> Love like fire in grate/snuffed—turns to ash then dies as/heart and hearth grow cold.
The magazine is 72 pages, digest-sized, photocopied from typescript and saddle-stapled with matte card cover. Publishes about 60 poems in each issue. Press run is 350 for 220 subscribers. Subscription: $6. Sample (including guidelines): $3.
How to Submit: Submit 3-5 poems at a time. Accepts simultaneous submissions. No e-mail submissions. Time between acceptance and publication is 4 months. Guidelines available for SASE. Responds in 4 months. Pays 1 copy plus "cash." Acquires one-time rights.
Book/Chapbook Needs & How to Submit: Bear House Press is a self-publishing arrangement by which poets can pay to have booklets published in the same format as *Lucidity*, prices beginning at 100 copies of 32 pages for $336. Publishes 8 chapbooks/year.
Also Offers: Sponsors the Lucidity Poets' Ozark Retreat, a 3-day retreat held during the month of April.
Advice: "Small press journals offer the best opportunity to most poets for publication."

◕ LULLWATER REVIEW; LULLWATER PRIZE FOR POETRY, Emory University, P.O. Box 22036, Atlanta GA 30322. (404)727-6184. Established 1990. **Poetry Editors:** Gwyneth Driskill, Janet Chan, and Laurel DeCou.
Magazine Needs: "Appearing in May and December, the *Lullwater Review* is Emory University's nationally distributed literary magazine publishing poetry, short fiction, and artwork." Seeks poetry of any genre with strong imagery, original voice, on any subject. No profanity or pornographic material. Has published poetry by Lyn Lifshin, Virgil Suarez, and Ha Jin. *Lullwater Review* is 104-120 pages, magazine-sized, full color cover, includes b&w pictures. Press run is 2,500. Subscription: $10. Sample: $5.
How to Submit: Submit 5 poems at a time. Accepts simultaneous submissions; no previously published poems. Cover letter preferred. "We must have a SASE with which to reply. Poems may not be returned." Reads submissions September 1 through May 15 only. Time between acceptance and publication is up to 6 months. Poems are circulated to an editorial board. "A poetry editor selects approximately 16 poems per week to be reviewed by editors, who then discuss and decide on the poem's status." Seldom comments on rejected poems. Guidelines and upcoming themes available for SASE. Responds in 5 months maximum. Pays 3 contributor's copies. Acquires first North American serial rights.
Also Offers: Sponsors the annual Lullwater Prize for Poetry. Award is $500 and publication. Deadline: March 15. Guidelines available for SASE. Entry fee: $8.
Advice: "Keep writing, find your voice, don't get frustrated. Please be patient with us regarding response time. We are an academic institution."

$◔ ◎ LUMMOX PRESS; LUMMOX JOURNAL; LITTLE RED BOOKS SERIES; LUMMOX SOCIETY OF WRITERS (Specialized: gay/lesbian/bisexual; writing; biography), P.O. Box 5301, San Pedro CA 90733-5301. E-mail: lumoxraindog@earthlink.net. Website: http://home.earthlink.net/~lumo xraindog/ (includes guidelines, contact information, archives, subscription information, links, and editorial policy). Established 1994 (press), 1996 (journal). **Editor/Publisher:** RD Armstrong.

Magazine Needs: *Lummox Journal* appears monthly and "explores the creative process through interviews, articles, and commentary." Wants "genuine and authentic poetry—socially conscious, heartfelt, honest, insightful, experimental. No angst-ridden confessional poetry; no pretentious, pompous, racist, and/or sexist work." Has published poetry by Diane Di Prima, A.D. Winans, John Thomas, Lindsay Wilson, and Maggie Jaffe. As a sample we selected these lines from "The False Rhapsody of Art" by Gerald Locklin:

> oppen, edward field, bukowski—/they all sought to avoid it/while keeping their ears cocked,/their
> voices clear and clean,/for the new music/of the truth/of the never old emotions.

Lummox Journal is up to 24 pages, digest-sized, photocopied and saddle-stapled with 60 lb. paper cover, includes art and ads. Receives about 1,000 poems/year, accepts about 10%. Press run is 200 for 180 subscribers. Subscription: $20/12 issues. Sample: $2. Make checks payable to *Lummox*.

How to Submit: Submit 3 poems at a time. Accepts previously published poems and simultaneous submissions. Prefers e-mail submissions (in text box); accepts submissions on disk (PC Win 98). Cover letter with bio preferred. Time between acceptance and publication is up to 6 months. Seldom comments on rejected poems. Criticism fees: $10 to critique, $25 to advise, $50 to tutor. Guidelines and upcoming themes available for SASE or by e-mail. Responds in 2 weeks. Pays 1 copy. Acquires one-time rights. Reviews books chapbooks, CDs of poetry/music, and other magazines. Poets may send books for review consideration. "Inquire first."

Book/Chapbook Needs & How to Submit: Lummox Press publishes poetry under the imprint Little Red Books. "The LRB series attempts to honor the poem as well as the poet." Publishes 12 to 15 books per year. Books are usually 48 pages, ¼ sheet-sized, photocopied/offset-printed, saddle-stapled/perfect-bound. Query first with a few sample poems and cover letter with brief bio. **Reading fee:** $5/submission ("or join LSW"). Responds to queries in up to 3 weeks; to mss in up to 2 months. Pays royalties of 10% (after second printing) plus 10% of press run. Offers subsidy arrangements (under the imprint of Plug Nickel Press) for the cost of printing and distribution plus ISBN #, $1.25 to $2.25 per book. Send check for $6 to Lummox for sample package.

Also Offers: "Lummox Society of Writers (LSW) includes a biannual newsletter listing submission guidelines and addresses for magazines and presses that the editor recommends. Future newsletters will offer helpful tips on submitting, presentation, and updates." Subscriptions is $6.

LUNA BISONTE PRODS; LOST AND FOUND TIMES (Specialized: style), 137 Leland Ave., Columbus OH 43214-7505. Established 1967. **Poetry Editor:** John M. Bennett.

Magazine Needs: John M. Bennett is a publisher (and practitioner) of experimental and avant-garde writing, sometimes sexually explicit, and art in a bewildering array of formats including the magazine, *Lost and Found Times*, postcard series, posters, chapbooks, pamphlets, labels, and audiocassette tapes. You can get a sampling of Luna Bisonte Prods for $10. Numerous reviewers have commented on the bizarre *Lost and Found Times*, "reminiscent of several West Coast dada magazines"; "This exciting magazine is recommended only for the most daring souls"; "truly demented"; "Insults . . . the past 3,000 years of literature"; "revolution where it counts, in the dangerous depths of the imagination," etc. Wants "unusual poetry, naive poetry, surrealism, experimental, visual poetry, collaborations—no poetry workshop or academic pabulum." Has published poetry by J. Leftwich, Sheila Murphy, J.S. Murnet, Peter Ganick, I. Argüelles, and A. Ackerman. As a sample the editor selected these lines from "Water" by Lewis LaCook:

> Like a capsized cloud I water the teeter/of my city below sound with clung nettle verbs./Like an absinthe
> madonna I water the babies/in the grass with a color called "bride yellow."

The digest-sized, 60-page magazine, photoreduced typescript and wild graphics, matte card cover with graphics. Press run is 350 with 75 subscribers of which 30 are libraries. Subscription: $30 for 5 numbers. Sample: $7.

How to Submit: Submit anytime—preferably camera-ready (but this is not required). Responds in 2 days. Pays 1 contributor's copy. All rights revert to authors upon publication. Staff reviews books of poetry. Send books for review consideration.

Book/Chapbook Needs & How to Submit: Luna Bisonte also will consider book submissions: query with samples and cover letter (but "keep it brief"). Chapbook publishing usually depends on grants or other subsidies and is usually by solicitation. Will also consider subsidy arrangements on negotiable terms.

Advice: "I would like to see more experimental and avant-garde material in Spanish and Portuguese, or in mixtures of languages."

LUNGFULL! MAGAZINE, 126 E. Fourth St., #2, New York NY 10003. E-mail: lungfull@rcn.com. Website: http://users.rcn.com/~lungfull. Established 1994. **Editor/Publisher:** Brendan Lorber.

WAIT! Don't mail your submission or correspondence without enclosing a SASE (self-addressed stamped envelope). If sending outside your own country, include SAE and IRCs (International Reply Coupons) instead.

• *LUNGFULL!* was the recipient of a multi-year grant from the New York State Council for the Arts.

Magazine Needs: *LUNGFULL!*, published annually, prints "the rough draft of each poem, in addition to the final so that the reader can see the creative process from start to finish." Wants "any style as long as its urgent, immediate, playful, probing, showing great thought while remaining vivid and grounded. Poems should be as interesting as conversation." Does not want "empty poetic abstractions." Has published poetry by Alice Notley, Allen Ginsberg, Lorenzo Thomas, Tracie Morris, Hal Sirowitz, Sparrow, Eileen Myles, and Bill Berkson. As a sample the editor selected this poem, "Jung and Restless: A Waitress Dreaming on Ernest Borgnines Birthday," by Julie Reid:

> Your hair is combed differently than you ever wore it and a man in gray and/green with his hands up
> inside the working of a clock flirts lightly with the woman/beside him who's applying pink lotion from
> a travel size bottle to her hands./The woman ahead of you lifts her hair off her neck so you can read
> her tattoo . . ./She says 'To the maximum 36 . . . emotions, add umbrellas, bent and broken . . ./Add
> anticipation and dread, which . . . are both forms of dread . . .

LUNGFULL! is 200 pages, 8½×7, offset-printed, perfect-bound, desktop-published, glossy 2 color cover with lots of illustrations and photos and a few small press ads. Receives about 1,000 poems/year, accepts 5%. Press run is 1,000 for 150 subscribers, 750 shelf sales; 100 distributed free to contributors. Single copy: $7.95; subscription: $31.80/4 issues, $15.90/2 issues. Sample: $9.50. Make checks payable to Brendan Lorber.

How to Submit: "We recommend you get a copy before submitting." Submit up to 6 poems at a time. Accepts previously published poems and simultaneous submissions (with notification). "However, other material will be considered first and stands a much greater chance of publication." Accepts e-mail submissions. "We prefer hard copy by USPS—but e-submissions can be made in the body of the e-mail itself or in a file saved as text." Cover letter preferred. Time between acceptance and publication is up to 8 months. "The editor looks at each piece for its own merit and for how well it'll fit into the specific issue being planned based on other accepted work." Guidelines available by e-mail. Responds in 6 months. Pays 2 copies.

Also Offers: "Each copy of *LUNGFULL! Magazine* now contains a short poem, usually from a series of six, printed on a sticker—they can be removed from the magazine and placed on any flat surface to make it a little less flat. Innovatively designed and printed in black & white, previous stickers have had work by Sparrow, Rumi, Julie Reid, Donna Cartelli, Joe Maynard, and Jeremy Sharpe, among others."

Advice: "Failure demands a certain dedication. Practice makes imperfection and imperfection makes room for the amazing. Only outside the bounds of acceptable conclusions can the astounding transpire, can writing contain anything beyond twittering snack food logic and the utilitarian pistons of mundane engineering."

THE LUTHERAN DIGEST (Specialized: humor, nature/rural/ecology, religious, inspirational), P.O. Box 4250, Hopkins MN 55343. (952)933-2820. Fax: (952)933-5708. E-mail: tldi@lutheran digest.com. Website: www.lutherandigest.com (include writers' guidelines, contact and subscription information, and select samples from current issue). Established 1953. **Editor:** David Tank.

Magazine Needs: *The Lutheran Digest* appears quarterly "to entertain and encourage believers and to subtly persuade non-believers to embrace the Christian faith. We publish short poems (24 lines or less) that will fit in a single column of the magazine. Most are inspirational, but that doesn't necessarily mean religious. No avant-garde poetry or work longer than 25 lines." Has published poetry by Kathleen A. Cain, William Beyer, Margaret Peterson, Florence Berg, and Erma Boetkher. As a sample we selected these lines from "Easter Has Arrived" by Kathleen A. Cain:

> Sun rays streak across the rugged/mountains in the east,/Sweet warblings of the finch, wren and/
> cardinal break through the morning peace./All of God's creation arrayed in its/spring beauty begins
> to unfold,/The desert is a bright splash of purple verbena and/daisies of orange and gold.

The Lutheran Digest is 64 pages, digest-sized, offset-printed and saddle-stapled with 4-color paper cover, includes b&w photos and illustrations, local ads to cover cost of distribution. Receives about 200 poems/year, accepts 20%. Press run is 110,000; 105,000 distributed free to Lutheran churches. Subscription: $14/year, $22/2 years. Sample: $3.50.

How to Submit: Submit 3 poems at a time. Line length for poetry is 30 maximum. Accepts previously published poems and simultaneous submissions. Cover letter preferred. "Include SASE if return is desired." Time between acceptance and publication is up to 9 months. Poems are circulated to an editorial board. "Selected by editor and reviewed by publication panel." Guidelines available for SASE or on website. Responds in 3 months. Pays credit and 1 copy. Acquires one-time rights.

Advice: "Poems should be short and appeal to senior citizens. We also look for poems that can be sung to traditional Lutheran hymns."

$ LYNX EYE; SCRIBBLEFEST LITERARY GROUP, 542 Mitchell Dr., Los Osos CA 93402. (805)528-8146. Fax: (805)528-7876. E-mail: pamccully@aol.com. Established 1994. **Contact:** Pam McCully.

Magazine Needs: *Lynx Eye* is the quarterly publication of the ScribbleFest Literary Group, an organization dedicated to the development and promotion of the literary arts. *Lynx Eye* is "dedicated to showcasing visionary writers and artists, particularly new voices." Each issue contains a special feature called Presenting, in which an unpublished writer of prose or poetry makes his/her print debut. No specifications regarding form, subject matter, or style of poetry. Has published poetry by Bruce Curley, Dani Montgomery, Michael Neal Morris, and Whitman McGowan. As a sample the editors selected these lines from "To Aliza . . ." by Mel C. Thompson:

> *The first man is every man/who was every woman's lover/since Brahman split in two/and became you and I.*

Lynx Eye is about 120 pages, 5½ × 8½, perfect-bound with b&w artwork. Receives about 2,000 poetry submissions/year and have space for about 75. Press run is 500 for 250 subscribers, 200 shelf sales. Subscription: $25/year. Sample: $7.95. Make checks payable to ScribbleFest Literary Group.
How to Submit: Submissions must be typed and include phone number, address, and an SASE. Accepts simultaneous submissions; no previously published poems. No fax or e-mail submissions. Name, address, and phone number on each piece. Guidelines available for SASE and by e-mail. Responds in up to 3 months. Pays $10/piece and 3 copies. Acquires first North American serial rights.

THE LYRIC, 65 VT. SR 15, Jericho VT 05465. Phone/fax: (802)899-3993. Established 1921 ("the oldest magazine in North America in continuous publication devoted to the publication of traditional poetry"). **Editor:** Jean Mellichamp Milliken.
Magazine Needs: *The Lyric* uses about 55 poems each quarterly issue. "We use rhymed verse in traditional forms, for the most part, with an occasional piece of blank or free verse. Forty lines or so is usually our limit. Our themes are varied, ranging from religious ecstasy to humor to raw grief, but we feel no compulsion to shock, embitter or confound our readers. We also avoid poems about contemporary political or social problems—grief but not grievances, as Frost put it. Frost is helpful in other ways: If yours is more than a lover's quarrel with life, we're not your best market. And most of our poems are accessible on first or second reading. Frost again: Don't hide too far away." Has published poetry by Rhina P. Espaillat, Maureen Cannon, Ruth Parks, Henry George Fisher, R.L. Cook, and R.H. Morrison. As a sample the editor selected these lines from "In Praise of Rhyme" by Barbara Loots:

> *Recurrence is the element of time/we love—the way celestial events,/the leaf, the rain, the tanager return./And so the reassertion of a rhyme/establishes both order and suspense,/like faith that builds on everything we learn.*

The Lyric is 32 pages, digest-sized, professionally printed with varied typography, matte card cover. Press run is 800 for 600 subscribers of which 40 are libraries. Receives about 3,000 submissions/year, accepts 5%. Subscription: $12 US, $14 Canada and other countries (in US funds only). Sample: $3.
How to Submit: Submit up to 6 poems at a time. Will read simultaneous submissions; no previously published poems or translations. "Cover letters often helpful, but not required." Guidelines available for SASE. Responds in 3 months (average). Pays 1 copy, and all contributors are eligible for quarterly and annual prizes totaling $750. "Subscription will not affect publication in any way."
Advice: "Our raison d'être has been the encouragement of form, music, rhyme, and accessibility in poetry. As we witness the growing dissatisfaction with the modernist movement that ignores these things, we are proud to have provided an alternative for 75 years that helps keep the roots of poetry alive."

M.I.P. COMPANY (Specialized: foreign language, erotica), P.O. Box 27484, Minneapolis MN 55427. (763)544-5915. Fax: (612)871-5733. E-mail: mp@mipco.com. Website: www.mipco.com. Established in 1984. **Contact:** Michael Peltsman.
Book/Chapbook Needs & How to Submit: M.I.P. Company publishes 3 paperbacks/year. Publishes only Russian erotic poetry and prose written in Russian. Has published poetry collections by Mikhail Armalinsky and Aleksey Shelvakh. Accepts simultaneous submissions; no previously published poems. Responds to queries in 1 month. Seldom comments on rejected poems.

THE MACGUFFIN; NATIONAL POET HUNT, Schoolcraft College, 18600 Haggerty Rd., Livonia MI 48152-2696. (734)462-4400, ext. 5327. Fax: (734)462-4679. E-mail: macguffin@schoolcrft.cc.mi. us. Website: www.macguffin.org (includes guidelines, samples from upcoming issues, special issues, and information on competitions). Established 1983. **Editor:** Arthur Lindenberg.
Magazine Needs: "*The MacGuffin* is a literary magazine which appears three times each year, in April, June, and November. We publish the best poetry, fiction, nonfiction, and artwork we find. We have no thematic or stylistic biases. We look for well-crafted poetry. Long poems should not exceed 300 lines. Avoid pornography, trite, and sloppy poetry. We do not publish haiku, concrete, or light verse." Has published poetry by Linda Nemec Foster, Virgil Suarez, and Susan Terris. *The MacGuffin* is 160 pages,

digest-sized, professionally printed on heavy buff stock, with matte card cover, flat-spined, with b&w illustrations and photos. Press run is 600 for 400 subscribers and the rest are local newsstand sales, contributor copies, and distribution to college offices. Single copy: $7; subscription: $18. Sample: $6.

How to Submit: "The editorial staff is grateful to consider unsolicited manuscripts and graphics." Submit up to 5 poems at a time of no more than 300 lines; poems should be typewritten. "We discourage simultaneous submissions." Accepts submissions by fax, on disk, by e-mail (as attachment), and through postal mail. When submitting by e-mail, "submit each work as a separate document attachment. Submissions made in the body of an e-mail will not be considered." Publishes theme issues. Upcoming themes available by fax, e-mail, and SASE. Guidelines available by fax, e-mail, SASE, and on website. Responds in 3 months; publication backlog is 6 months. Pays 2 copies, "occasional money or prizes."

Also Offers: Also sponsors the National Poet Hunt, established in 1996, offering annual awards of $500 1st Prize, $250 2nd Prize, $100 3rd Prize, 3 honorable mentions and publication. Submissions may be entered in other contests. Submit 5 typed poems on any subject in any form. Put name and address on *separate* 3×5 index card only. Upcoming themes available by fax, e-mail, SASE. Guidelines available by fax, e-mail, SASE, and on website. Entry fee: $15/5 poems. Deadline: May 31. Judge for 2001 contest was Richard Tillinghast. Winners will be announced in August, and in *Poets and Writers* in the fall.

Advice: "We will always comment on 'near misses.' Writing is a search, and it is a journey. Don't become sidetracked. Don't become discouraged. Keep looking. Keep traveling. Keep writing."

MAD POETS REVIEW; MAD POETS REVIEW POETRY COMPETITION; MAD POETS SOCIETY, P.O. Box 1248, Media PA 19063-8248. Established 1987. **Editor:** Eileen M. D'Angelo. **Associate Editor:** Camelia Nocella.

Magazine Needs: *Mad Poets Review* is published annually in October/November. "Our primary purpose is to promote thought-provoking, moving poetry, and encourage beginning poets. We don't care if you have a 'name' or a publishing history, if your poetry is well-crafted." "Anxious for work with 'joie de vivre' that startles and inspires." No restrictions on subject, form, or style. "We are not interested in porn or obscenities used for the sake of shock value." Has published poetry by Henry Braun, Leonard Gontarek, Elaine Terranova, Shulamith Caine, Daniel Moore, and Aaren Y. Perry. As a sample we selected these lines from "A Spoon of Sleep" by Lisa Barnett:

> We know the tenderness of spoons/the clean curve from bowl to stem,/as lying together at night/we curve into each other's dreams.

Mad Poets Review is about 100 pages, digest-sized, attractively printed and perfect-bound with textured card cover. Receives about 500-700 poems/year, accepts 60-70. Press run is 250. Single copy: $10. Sample: $12. Make checks payable to either Mad Poets Society or *Mad Poets Review*.

How to Submit: Submit 6 poems at a time. "Poems without an SASE with adequate postage will not be returned or acknowledged." Accepts previously published poems and simultaneous submissions. Cover letter not necessary, but "include 3-4 sentences about yourself suitable for our Bio Notes section. Mark envelope 'contest' or 'magazine.' " Reads submissions January 1 through June 1 only. Time between acceptance and publication is 8 months. Often comments on rejected poems. Responds in 3 months. Pays 1 contributor's copy. Acquires one-time rights.

Also Offers: Sponsors the annual *Mad Poets Review* Poetry Competition. "All themes and styles of poetry are welcome, no line limit, previously unpublished work only." Complete contest guidelines available for SASE. Winners published in *Mad Poets Review*. Cash prizes awarded—amount depends on number of entries. "The Mad Poets Society is an active organization in Pennsylvania. We run several poetry series; have monthly meetings for members for critique and club business; coordinate a children's contest through Del. Co. School system; run an annual poetry festival the first Sunday in October; sponsor Mad Poets Bonfires for local poets and musicians; publish an annual literary calendar and newsletters that offer the most comprehensive listing available anywhere in the tri-state area. We send quarterly newsletters to members, as well as PA Poetry Society news covering state and national events." Membership fee: $20.

Advice: "It is advised that if someone is going to submit they see what kind of poetry we publish. We sometimes receive poetry that is totally inappropriate of our mag and it is obvious the poet does not know *Mad Poets Review*."

MAD RIVER PRESS, State Road, Richmond MA 01254. (413)698-3184. Established 1986. **Editor:** Barry Sternlieb. Mad River publishes 1 broadside and 2 chapbooks/year, "all types of poetry, no bias," but none unsolicited.

MAELSTROM, P.O. Box 7, Tranquility NJ 07879. E-mail: lmaelstrom@aol.com. Website: www.geocities.com/~readmaelstrom (includes past publications, guidelines, editors' bios, and samples of some regular features). Established 1997. **Editor:** Christine L. Reed. **Art Editor:** Jennifer Fennell.

Magazine Needs: *Maelstrom*, a quarterly, "tries to be a volatile storm of talents throwing together art, poetry, short fiction, comedy and tragedy." Wants any kind of poetry, "humor appreciated. No pornography." Has published poetry by Grace Cavalieri, Mekeel McBride, Daniela Gioseffi, and B.Z. Niditch. As a sample the editor selected this poem, "Hemingway" by John Nettles:

> *Life. Too short to live/Forever in Pamplona./I'd eat my gun too.*

Maelstrom is 40-50 pages, $7 \times 8\frac{1}{2}$, saddle-stapled with color cover, includes b&w art. Receives about 600 poems/year, accepts about 20%. Press run is 500 for 100 subscribers. Single copy: $5; subscription: $20. Sample: $4.

How to Submit: Submit up to 4 poems at a time. Accepts previously published poems and simultaneous submissions. Accepts e-mail submissions "in the body of the e-mail message. Please do not send attached files." Cover letter preferred. Include name and address on every page. Send sufficient SASE for return of work. "There is no reading fee, however, submissions accompanied by a $1 donation will be answered immediately, all others will be answered in the order they are received." Time between acceptance and publication is up to 3 months. Seldom comments on rejected poems. Guidelines available by e-mail or on website. Responds in up to 3 months. Pays 1 contributor's copy. Acquires first North American serial or one-time rights. Staff reviews chapbooks of poetry and other magazines. Send books for review consideration. "Materials cannot be returned."

Also Offers: Also publishes a year anthology, *Poetography*. "Send $1 and SASE for more info."

N THE MAGAZINE OF FANTASY & SCIENCE FICTION, P.O. Box 3447, Hoboken NJ 07030. E-mail: FandSF@aol.com. Website: www.fsfmag.com (includes guidelines, nonfiction columns, scan of cover). Established 1949. **Editor:** Gordon Van Gelder.

- *The Magazine of Fantasy & Science Fiction* is a past winner of the Hugo Award and World Fantasy Award.

Magazine Needs: *The Magazine of Fantasy & Science Fiction* appears monthly, 11 times/year. "One of the longest-running magazines devoted to the literature of the fantastic." Wants only poetry that deals with the fantastic or the science-fictional. Recently published poetry by Rebecca Kavaler and Robert Frazier. As a sample the editor selected these lines from "O Pioneers" by Rebecca Kavaler:

> *Does anyone still hang around the mailbox/Expecting a reply to that picture postcard/We mailed in seventy-two?/So airily, binarily, we took a bow:/Hello, having wonderful time/Wish you were here. How/(And what) are you?*

The Magazine of Fantasy & Science Fiction is 160 pages, digest-sized, offset-printed, perfect-bound, glossy cover, has ads. Receives about 20-40 poems/year, accepts about $\frac{1}{2}$-1%. Publishes about 1-2 poems/year. Press run is 35,000 for 20,000 subscribers. Single copy: $3.50; subscription: $29.97. Sample: $5. Make checks payable to *The Magazine of Fantasy & Science Fiction.*

How to Submit: Submit 1-3 poems at a time. No previously published poems or simultaneous submissions. No fax, e-mail, or disk submissions. Time between acceptance and publication is 3-9 months. "I buy poems very infrequently—just when one hits me right." Seldom comments on rejected poems. Guidelines available for SASE or on website. Responds in up to 1 month. Always sends prepublication galleys. Pays 2 contributor's copies. Acquires first North American serial rights.

$ 🖉 ◎ THE MAGAZINE OF SPECULATIVE POETRY (Specialized: horror, science fiction, science), P.O. Box 564, Beloit WI 53512. Established 1984. **Editor:** Roger Dutcher.

Magazine Needs: *The Magazine of Speculative Poetry* is a biannual magazine that features "the best new speculative poetry. We are especially interested in narrative form, but interested in variety of styles, open to any form, length (within reason). We're looking for the best of the new poetry utilizing the ideas, imagery, and approaches developed by speculative fiction and will welcome experimental techniques as well as the fresh employment of traditional forms." Has published poetry by Terry A. Garey, Bruce Boston, and Steve Rasnic-Tem. As a sample Roger Dutcher selected these lines from "Braids of Glass" by Michael Bishop:

> *We step onto a plain of braided glass,/which rattles on its topographic loom/Like a million shattered vials of valium/Spilling everywhere the stench of emptiness.*

The Magazine of Speculative Poetry is 24-28 pages, digest-sized, offset-printed, saddle-stapled with matte card cover. Accepts less than 5% of some 500 poems received/year. Press run is 150-200, for nearly 100 subscribers. Subscription: $19/4. Sample: $5.

How to Submit: Submit 3-5 poems at a time, double-spaced with a "regular old font." "We are a small magazine, we can't print epics. Some poems run 2 or 3 pages, but rarely anything longer." No previously published poems or simultaneous submissions. "We like cover letters but they aren't necessary. We like to see where you heard of us; the names of the poems submitted; a statement if the poetry ms is disposable; a big enough SASE; and if you've been published, some recent places." Editor comments on rejected poems "on occasion." Guidelines available for SASE. Responds in up to 2 months. Pays 3¢/word, minimum $5, maximum $25, plus copy. Acquires first North American serial rights. "All rights revert to author upon publication, except for permission to reprint in any 'Best of' or compilation volume. Payment will be made for such publication." Reviews books of speculative poetry. Query on unsolicited reviews. Send speculative poetry books for review consideration.

N ◎ MAGIC CHANGES (Specialized: themes), 237 Park Trail Court, Schaumburg FL 60173. (847)517-1690. E-mail: magic-changes@attbi.com. Website: http://members.home.net/thesenate. Established 1978. **Poetry Editor:** John Sennett.

Magazine Needs: *Magic Changes* is published every 18 months, in an unusual format. Photocopied from typescript on many different weights and colors of paper, magazine-sized along the long side (you read it both vertically and horizontally), taped flat spine, full of fantasy drawings, pages packed with poems of all varieties, fiction, photos, drawings, odds and ends—including reviews of little magazines and other small press publications. It is intended to make poetry (and literature) fun and predictable. Each issue is on an announced theme. "*Magic Changes* is divided into sections such as 'The Order of the Celestial Otter,' 'State of the Arts,' 'Time,' 'Music,' and 'Skyscraper Rats.' A magical musical theme pervades." Has published poetry by Sue Standing, Caleb Bullen, Hugh Odgen, Lauren Sennett, Patricia A. Davey, and Walt Curtis. As a sample the editor selected these lines from his poem "Mourning Friend":

> Did I hear/The dying dove's song?//Today, I promise myself/To listen to pace://Footsteps/Wind in cracks/Wings.

Magic Changes has 100 pages of poetry/issue. Press run is 500 for 28 subscriptions of which 10 are libraries. Sample: $7 US, $10 foreign.

How to Submit: Submit 3-5 poems anytime. Upcoming themes available for SASE. Sometimes comments on rejected poems and offers criticism for $5/page of poetry. Responds in 4 months. Pays 1-2 copies. Acquires first North American serial rights. Reviews books of poetry in 500 words. Poets may send books for review consideration.

⊕ ◐ MAGMA POETRY MAGAZINE, 43 Keslake Rd., London NW6 6DH United Kingdom. E-mail: magmapoems@aol.com. Website: www.champignon.net/Magma (includes contact details, information about *Magma* and its policies and method of operating, as well as some examples of submissions for recent issues). Established 1994. **Editorial Secretary:** David Boll.

Magazine Needs: *Magma* appears 3 times/year and contains "modern poetry, reviews and interviews with poets." Wants poetry that is "modern in idiom and shortish (two pages maximum). Nothing sentimental or old fashioned." Has published poetry by Thom Gunn, Michael Donaghy, John Burnside, Vicki Feaurk, and Roddy Comsdrew. *Magma* is 72 pages, 8½×6, photocopied and stapled, includes b&w illustrations. Receives about 3,000 poems/year, accepts 4-5%. Press run is about 500. Single copy: £4 UK and Ireland, £5 Europe; outside Europe, £6 airmail, £5 surface mail. Subscription: £11/3 issues UK and Ireland, £14.50 Europe; outside Europe, £17.50 airmail, £14.50 surface. Make checks payable to *Magma*. For subscriptions contact Helen Nicholson, distribution secretary, 82 St. James's Dr., London SW17 7RR.

How to Submit: Submit up to 6 poems at a time. Accepts simultaneous submissions. Accepts e-mail submissions (ASCII only, no attachments). Cover letter preferred. Reads submissions September through November and February through July only. Time between acceptance and publication is maximum 3 months. Poems are circulated to an editorial board. "Each issue has an editor who submits his/her selections to a board for final approval. Editor's selection very rarely changed." Occasionally publishes theme issues. Responds in 4 months. Always sends prepublication galleys. Pays 1 contributor's copy.

Also Offers: "We hold a public reading in London three times/year, to coincide with each new issue, and poets in the issue are invited to read."

⊕ ◐ MAGPIE'S NEST, 176 Stoney Lane, Sparkhill, Birmingham B12 8AN United Kingdom. Established 1979. **Contact:** Mr. Bal Saini.

Magazine Needs: The *Magpie's Nest* appears quarterly and publishes "cutting-edge, modern poetry and fiction which deals with the human condition. No love poetry or self-obsessed work." As a sample the editor selected this poem (poet unidentified):

> There is something adhesive/about the first parent singular/Loose/images stick to her/where she lives in the shadow/of the absent father

Magpie's Nest receives about 200 poems/year, accepts about 25%. Press run is 200 for 150 subscribers, 50 shelf sales. Single copy: $2.50; subscription: $12.50. Sample: $3.

How to Submit: Submit 4 poems at a time. Line length for poetry is 10 minimum, 40 maximum. Accepts previously published poems and simultaneous submissions. Cover letter preferred. "Keep copies of poems submitted as poems which are not used are binned." Reads submissions September 1 through June 30 only. Time between acceptance and publication is 3 months. Seldom comments on rejected poems. Occasionally publishes theme issues. Responds in 3 months. Pays 1 contributor's copy. Reviews books of poetry and other magazines in 200 words, single book format. Poets may send books for review consideration.

Also Offers: "For a fee, I am willing to act as literary agent for American poets by submitting their poems to British magazines. This will save American poets postage as well as the hassle of finding out which British magazines are suitable for their poems. Please send SASE (or SAE and IRC) for further details."

Advice: "It's recommended that a sample copy be read before submission."

☑ MAIN STREET RAG, (formerly *Main Street Rag Poetry Journal*), P.O. Box 691621, Charlotte NC 28227-7028. (704)573-2516. E-mail: editor@mainstreetrag.com. Website: www.MainStreetRag.com. Established 1996. **Publisher/Editor:** M. Scott Douglass.

Magazine Needs: *Main Street Rag*, is a quarterly that publishes "poetry, short fiction, essays, interviews, reviews, photos, art, cartoons, (political, satirical), and poetry collections. . . We like publishing good material from people who are interested in more than notching another publishing credit, people who support small independent publishers like ourselves." *Main Street Rag* "will consider almost anything but prefer writing with an edge—either gritty or bitingly humorous." Has recently published work by Richard Peabody, Mark Wisniewski, Lisa Haynes, and Marie Kazalia. As a sample the editor selected these lines from "February" by Diana Pinckney:

> Crow shadows cross at dusk,//windows blink, shutters, drapes/close on grays and browns, questions/
> not yet answered, decisions/germinating, the clean slate//tarnished under a pewter moon.

Main Street Rag is approximately 80 pages, digest-sized, perfect bound with 80 lb. laminated color cover. Publishes 30-40 poems and one short story per issue out of 2,500 submissions/year. Press run is 600 for 200 subscribers of which 5 are libraries. Single copy: $7; subscription: $15. Sample: $5.

How to Submit: Submit 6 pages of poetry at a time. No previously published poems or simultaneous submissions. No e-mail submissions. Cover letter preferred with a brief bio "about the poet, not their credits." Has backlog of up to 1 year. Guidelines available for SASE. Responds within 6 weeks. Pays 1 copy and contributor's discount for the issue in which work appears. Acquires one-time rights.

Also Offers: Book-length poetry contest (64-84 pages). Deadline: January 31. 1st Prize: $500 and 100 copies. Entry fee: $20. Also offers chapbook contest. Deadline: May 31. 1st Prize: $100 and 200 copies. Entry fee: $15. Previous winners: David Chorltan, Alan Catlin, Dede Wilson.

Advice: "Small press independent exist by and for writers. Without their support (and the support of readers) we have no means or reason to publish. Sampling is always appreciated."

Ⓝ ☒ $☑ THE MALAHAT REVIEW; LONG POEM PRIZE, P.O. Box 1700, STN CSC, University of Victoria, Victoria, British Columbia V8W 2Y2 Canada. (250)721-8524. E-mail: malahat@uvic.ca. Website: http://web.uvic.ca/malahat (includes competition guidelines and current issue's contents). Established 1967. **Editor:** Marlene Cookshaw.

Magazine Needs: *The Malahat Review* is "a high quality, visually appealing literary quarterly which has earned the praise of notable literary figures throughout North America. Its purpose is to publish and promote poetry and fiction of a very high standard, both Canadian and international. We are interested in various styles, lengths and themes. The criterion is excellence." Has published poetry by Margaret Atwood and P.K. Page. As a sample the editor selected these lines from "relay" by Jan Zwicky and Don McKay:

> . . . Sleep/is a ship whose rigging keeps coming/undone in the rain,/and the self who wakes is the self
> who walks/its deck, its pockets stuffed/with all the letters you have never mailed.

Uses 50 pages of poetry in each issue, have 1,000 subscribers of which 300 are libraries. Receives about 2,000 poems/year, accepts approximately 100. Subscription: $40 Canadian (or US equivalent). Sample: $8 US.

How to Submit: Submit 5-10 poems, addressed to editor Marlene Cookshaw. Include SASE with Canadian stamps or IRC with each submission. Guidelines available for SASE (or SAE and IRC). Responds within 3 months. Pays $30/anticipated magazine page plus 2 copies and year's subscription. Acquires first world serial rights. Reviews Canadian books of poetry.

Also Offers: Sponsors the Long Poem Prize, two awards of $400 plus publication and payment at their usual rates (entry fee is a year's subscription) for a long poem or cycle 5-15 pages (flexible minimum and maximum), deadline March 1 of alternate years (1999, 2001, etc.). Entry fee: $40 Canadian or US equivalent. Include name and address on a separate page.

☑ MAMMOTH BOOKS; MAMMOTH PRESS INC., 7 South Juniata St., DuBois PA 15801. E-mail: guidelines@mammothbooks.com (for guidelines) or info@mammothbooks.com (for questions). Website: www.mammothbooks.com. Established 1997. **Publisher:** Antonio Vallone.

Book/Chapbook Needs: MAMMOTH books, an imprint of MAMMOTH press inc., publishes 2-4 paperbacks/year of creative nonfiction, fiction, and poetry through annual competitions. "We are open to all types of literary poetry." Has published *The House of Sages* by Philip Terman; *The Never Wife* by

Cynthia Hogue; *These Happy Eyes* by Liz Rosenberg; and *Subjects for Other Conversations* by John Stigall. Books are usually 5×7 or 6×9, offset-printed and perfect-bound, covers vary (1-4 color), include art.

How to Submit: Send mss to contest. Not currently reading outside of contests. For poetry mss, submit a collection of poems or a single long poem. Translations are accepted. "Manuscripts as a whole must not have been previously published. Some or all of each manuscript may have appeared in periodicals, chapbooks, anthologies, or other venues. These must be identified. Authors are responsible for securing permissions." Accepts simultaneous submissions. No e-mail submissions. Submit mss by postal mail only. Poetry mss should be single-spaced, no more than 1 poem/page. Reads submissions September 1 through February 28/29. Entry fee: $20. Make checks payable to MAMMOTH books. Time between acceptance and publication is 18 months. Poems are circulated to an editorial board. "Finalists will be chosen by the staff of MAMMOTH books and an outside editorial board and/or guest editor. Manuscripts will be selected based on merit only." Seldom comments on rejected poems. Pays royalties (10% of sales) and at least 50 free copies. Other finalist manuscripts may be selected for publication and offered a standard royalty contract and publication of at least 500 trade paperback copies. Finalists will be announced within 1 year from the end of each submission period. MAMMOTH press inc. reserves the right not to award a prize if no entries are deemed suitable. Complete rules are available for SASE or by e-mail to guidelines@mammothbooks.com. Order sample books by sending for information to their mailing address or e-mail.

Advice: "Read big. Write big. Publish small. Join the herd."

☐ MANDRAKE POETRY REVIEW; THE MANDRAKE PRESS, Box 792, Larkspur CA 94977-0792. E-mail: mandrake@polbox.com. Website: www.angelfire.com/pe/TheMandrakePress (includes magazine in its entirety). Established 1993 in New York. **Editor:** Leo Yankevich. **Editor:** David Castleman.

Magazine Needs: *Mandrake Poetry Review* appears at least twice/year. Seeks poetry in translation as well as content concerning ethnicity/nationality, politics, and social issues. Accepts poetry written by children. Has published poetry by Michael Daugherty, George Held, Hugh Fox, Errol Miller, Simon Perchik, and Joan Peternel. As a sample the editor selected these lines from "By A Philosopher's Tomb" by Cornel (Adam) Lengyel:

> How may one thank in fitting terms the maker/of new and taller windows for the soul?/I turn my
> transient eyes without and see/the world's great ghostly wheels of change reduce/our mortal home to
> essences eternal—/the terror and the grandeur, all within.

Mandrake Poetry Review is 76-150 pages, A5, offset-printed and flat-spined with glossy white card cover. Accepts about 10% of the poetry received. Press run is 500 for 100 subscribers from 3 continents. Single copy: $5 (by airmail); subscription: $20/2 years. Make checks payable to David Castleman.

How to Submit: Submit up to 7 poems at a time. "Send only copies of your poems, as we do not return poems with our reply." Accepts previously published poems and simultaneous submissions. Accepts e-mail submissions (in text box). Cover letter preferred. Guidelines available for SASE. Responds in 2 months. Pays 2 contributor's copies "sometimes more." All rights revert to author. "Poets are encouraged to send their books for review consideration to David Castleman. All editors and publishers whose books/chapbooks are selected for review will receive one copy of the issue in which the review appears. We publish 50-100 reviews yearly."

N ☐ MANGROVE, University of Miami, Dept. of English, P.O. Box 248145, Coral Gables FL 33124-4632. Website: www.as.miami.edu/english/MFA/mangrove.htm (includes contents, guidelines, staff). Established 1994. **Contact:** Poetry Editor.

Magazine Needs: *Mangrove*, published annually in the fall, is a graduate student-run magazine published by the MFA program at the University of Miami. Wants "fresh, clear poetry. Experimental encouraged." Does not want sentimental, romantic ("unless fresh and surprising"), or greeting card verse. Does not want "children's poetry." Has recently published poetry by Denise Duhamel, Lyn Lifshin, Carolyn Kizer, and Jim Murphy. *Mangrove* is digest-sized. Sample: $6. Make checks payable to *Mangrove*/Dept. of English.

How to Submit: Submit 3-5 poems at a time. Include SASE. Accepts simultaneous submissions; no previously published poems. No fax, e-mail, or disk submissions. Cover letter undesired unless "contact information and *brief* bio only. Don't try to get cute or impress us with a huge list of publications." Reads submissions postmarked from August 15 through December 15 only. Time between acceptance and publication is 6 months. Poems are circulated to an editorial board for "blind" readings. Never comments on rejected poems. Guidelines available for SASE and on website. Responds in up to 6 months. Acquires first North American serial rights.

☐ ◎ THE MANHATTAN REVIEW (Specialized: translations), 440 Riverside Dr., Apt. 38, New York NY 10027. (212)932-1854. Established 1980. **Poetry Editor:** Philip Fried.

Magazine Needs: *The Manhattan Review* "publishes American writers and foreign writers with something valuable to offer the American scene. We like to think of poetry as a powerful discipline engaged with many other fields. We want to see ambitious work. Interested in both lyric and narrative. Not interested in mawkish, sentimental poetry. We select high-quality work from a number of different countries, including the U.S." Has published poetry by Zbigniew Herbert, D. Nurkse, Baron Wormser, Penelope Shuttle, Marilyn Hacker, and Peter Redgrove. *The Manhattan Review* is now "an annual with ambitions to be semiannual." 64 pages, digest-sized, professionally printed with glossy card cover, photos and graphics. Press run is 500 for 400 subscribers of which 250 are libraries. Distributed by Bernhard DeBoer, Inc. Receives about 300 submissions/year, uses few ("but I do read everything submitted carefully and with an open mind"). "I return submissions as promptly as possible." Single copy: $5; subscription: $10. Sample: $6.35 with 6×9 envelope.

How to Submit: Submit 3-5 pages of poems at a time. No simultaneous submissions. Cover letter with short bio and publications required. Editor sometimes comments "but don't count on it." Responds in 3 months if possible. Pays contributor's copies. Staff reviews books of poetry. Send books for review consideration.

Advice: "Always read the magazine first to see if your work is appropriate."

MANY MOUNTAINS MOVING; MANY MOUNTAINS MOVING LITERARY AWARDS, 420 22nd St., Boulder CO 80302. (303)545-9942. E-mail: mmm@mmminc.org. Website: www.mmminc.org (includes guidelines, contest information, upcoming themes, excerpts, contact and subscription information, editorial policy, and general information about the magazine). Established 1994. **Editor:** Naomi Horii. **Poetry Editor:** Debra Bokur.

- Poetry published in *Many Mountains Moving* has also been included in the 1996, 1997, and 1999 volumes of *The Best American Poetry*.

Magazine Needs: Published 6 times/year, *Many Mountains Moving* is "a literary journal of diverse contemporary voices that welcomes previously unpublished fiction, poetry, nonfiction, and art from writers and artists of all walks of life. We publish the world's top writers as well as emerging talents." Open to any style of poetry, but they do not want any "Hallmark-y" poetry. Accepts poetry by children, "but quality would have to be on par with other accepted work." Has published poetry by Robert Bly, W.S. Merwin, Sherman Alexie, Lawson Fusao Inada, Allen Ginsberg, and Adrienne Rich. As a sample they selected these lines from "Bathing Susan" by Sarah Wolbach:

> *Her vertebrae are little apples softening in the heat, rocks on the river/bottom that shimmer and dissolve in the light, little tumors like the/ones within her, spreading through her lungs and glands like a flood/of mold, a village of tiny fists. Touching her body is like reading/Braille, but nothing is explained. Lifted from the water, she is wood/dripping life, she is air with light breathing through.*

Many Mountains Moving is about 88 pages, 8½×11, web offset and perfect-bound with four-color cover and b&w art and photos inside. Receives 4,000 poems/year, accepts .1%. Press run is 1,500. Single copy: $3.99; subscription: $18/year.

How to Submit: Submit 3-10 poems at a time, typed with SASE. Accepts only mailed submissions. Accepts simultaneous submissions; no previously published poems. Cover letter preferred. Poems are circulated to an editorial board. "Poems are first read by several readers. If considered seriously, they are passed to the poetry editor for final decision." Seldom comments on rejected poems. Occasionally publishes theme issues. Upcoming themes and guidelines are available for SASE or on website. Responds within 1 month, "if we are seriously considering a submission, we may take longer." Sends prepublication galleys. Pays 3 copies, additional copies available at $2/copy. Acquires first North American serial rights and "rights to publish in a future edition of the *Best of Many Mountains Moving Anthology*."

Also Offers: Sponsors the annual Many Mountains Moving Literary Awards which awards $200 plus publication in the categories of poetry, fiction, and essay. Entry fee: $15 (includes subscription). Details available for SASE.

Advice: "Although we have featured a number of established poets, we encourage new writers to submit. However, we recommend that poets read through at least one issue to familiarize themselves with the type of work we generally publish."

MANZANITA QUARTERLY, P.O. Box 1234, Ashland OR 97520. E-mail: authenticj@aol.com (for queries only; accepts only hardcopy submissions). Website: www.JesseWhiteCreations.com (includes guidelines, contact and subscription information, contest rules, editorial policy). Established 1998. **Editor:** Mariah Hegarty.

Magazine Needs: *Manzanita Quarterly* is a quarterly that publishes quality, accessible poetry. Does not want porn, rhyming poems, or Hallmark-type verse. Recently published poetry by Elizabeth Biller Chapman, Judith Barrington, Paulann Petersen, Peter Pereira, and Roger Weaver. As a sample the editor selected these lines from "Itinerary" by Paulann Peterson:

Beyond a blue city/of bees. Hives housed inside/painted boxes. This many/small squares of sky/pulled down to ground level,/snugged around the thick/thrum of wings.

Manzanita Quarterly is 75 pages, digest-sized, perfect-bound, printed card stock cover with photo. Receives about 1,000 poems/year, accepts about 25%. Publishes about 45 poems/issue. Press run is 250 for 70 subscribers of which 5 are libraries, 30 shelf sales; 10 are distributed free to libraries, reviewers. Single copy: $9 and $1 for postage; subscription: $30. Sample: $9 and $1 for postage. Make checks payable to *Manzanita Quarterly*.

How to Submit: Submit 5 poems at a time. No previously published poems or simultaneous submissions. Accepts submissions by regular mail only. Cover letter is preferred. "Send SASE, cover letter with short, serious bio, name and address on each page." Reads submissions all year. Deadlines: February 7, May 9, August 12, November 15. Submit seasonal poems 2 months in advance. Time between acceptance and publication is 2 months. Seldom comments on rejected poems. Guidelines are available in magazine, for SASE, on website, and by e-mail. Responds in 3 months from each deadline. Pays 1 contributor's copy. Acquires first North American serial rights.

Advice: "I look for vivid images, fresh language, and quality, well-crafted writing. Poetry should be accessible; I like poetry that is evocative, poignant, vital, humorous, and thoughtful. Send your best."

N ◙ **MARGIE/THE AMERICAN JOURNAL OF POETRY; THE MARJORIE J. WILSON AWARD FOR EXCELLENCE IN POETRY**, P.O. Box 250, Chesterfield MO 63006-0250. Website: www.margiereview.com (includes journal content, contest guidelines). Established 2001. **Editor:** Robert Nazarene.

Magazine Needs: *MARGIE/The American Journal of Poetry* appears annually in September. "*MARGIE* publishes superlative poetry. No limits to school, form, subject matter. Imaginative, risk-taking poetry which disturbs and/or consoles is of paramount interest. A distinctive voice is prized." Recently published poetry by Emmylou Harris, Stephen Dunn, Timothy Liu, Jane Mead, Sherod Santos, and David Wagoner. As a sample the editor selected these lines from "39 Lines on a Theme by Nicanor Parra" by Scott Coffel:

> Yet since there is also a heaven in hell,/*I feel like singing, however quietly: a few hours ago/the cello recital ended, the* Kol Nidre *delivering/its afterbirth of silence as they marched us from the auditorium,/ our wingless ankles at the mercy of flashlights.*

MARGIE is 300 pages, digest-sized, professionally-printed, perfect-bound, glossy cover with art/graphics, has ads. Receives about 4,000 poems/year, accepts about 1-2%. Publishes about 100 poems/issue. Press run is 2,000 (circulation). Single copy: $9.95; subscription: $9.95 individual; $14.95 institution and outside US (all one year/ one issue). Make checks payable to *MARGIE*.

How to Submit: Submit 3-5 poems at a time. Line length for poetry is 90 maximum. Accepts simultaneous submissions (notify in cover letter); no previously published poems. No fax, e-mail, or disk submissions. Cover letter is required. "A short bio is useful, but not required." Open reading: June 1-October 15. "Subscribers *only* may submit year round. Identify yourself as 'subscriber' on outside of submission envelope." Time between acceptance and publication is up to 1 year. Poems are circulated to an editorial board. "The editorial board meets quarterly. Recommendations are made to the editor. Editor makes final decision." *Sometimes* comments on rejected poems. Guidelines available for SASE or on website. Responds in up to 3 months. Sometimes sends prepublication galleys. Pays 2 contributor's copies. Acquires first rights. All rights revert to poet upon publication.

Also Offers: The Marjorie J. Wilson Award for Excellence in Poetry; send SASE for contest guidelines.

Advice: "Invest 90% of your literary life: reading, reading, reading; 10% of your time: writing. Be audacious, innovative, distinctive. Never, never, never give up."

◙ **THE MARLBORO REVIEW; MARLBORO PRIZE FOR POETRY**, P.O. Box 243, Marlboro VT 05344. E-mail: marlboro@marlbororeview.com. Website: www.marlbororeview.com (includes guidelines, contact and subscription information, bios, archives, contest information, and editorial policy). Established 1995. **Editor:** Ellen Dudley.

Magazine Needs: *The Marlboro Review*, published biannually, is a "literary magazine containing poetry, fiction, essays, reviews, and translations." Wants long poems. Does not want greeting card verse. Has published poetry by William Matthews, Jean Valentine, Bill Knott, and Chana Bloch. *The Marlboro Review* is 80-112 pages, 6×9, offset-printed and perfect-bound with laminated colored cover and ads. Receives about 1,000 poems/year, accepts about 7%. Press run is 1,000 for 350 subscribers of which 25 are libraries, 300 shelf sales; 50-70 distributed free to writers and institutions. Single copy: $8; subscription: $16. Sample: $8.75.

How to Submit: Submit up to 5 typed, near letter quality or better poems at a time with SASE. Accepts simultaneous submissions "if we are notified"; no previously published poems. No fax or e-mail submissions. Guidelines available for SASE and on website. Responds in up to 3 months. Sometimes sends prepublication galleys. Pays 2 copies. Acquires all rights. Returns rights on publication. Reviews books of poetry in 500-1,000 words, single book format. Poets may send books for review consideration.

Also Offers: Sponsors the Marlboro Prize for Poetry. Awards a $1,000 honorarium and publication. Submit $10 entry fee for up to 5 poems. Deadline: March 15, 2002. Include name on cover letter only, not on ms. All entrants receive the Marlboro Prize issue and are considered for publication.

MARYMARK PRESS (Specialized: form/style), 45-08 Old Millstone Dr., East Windsor NJ 08520. (609)443-0646. Website: www.experimentalpoet.com (includes samples of Mark Sonnenfeld's work, experimental writing, a spoken-word element, a listing of chapbooks with a synopsis of each, and contact information). Established 1994. **Editor/Publisher:** Mark Sonnenfeld.

Book/Chapbook Needs: Marymark Press's goal is "to feature and promote experimental poets. I will most likely be publishing only broadsides and samplers; no books at this time. I want to see experimental poetry of the outer fringe. Make up words, sounds, whatever, but say something you thought never could be explained. Disregard rules if need be." No traditional, rhyming or spiritual verse; no predictable styles. Has published poetry by Sasha Surikov, Betty Radin, Vermicious Knid, Dave Church, Barry Edgar Pilcher, Garry Freel. As a sample the editor selected these lines from a poem in *Eleven* by Mark Sonnenfeld:

> No appreciation for culture/dis married that/Fundamental/and miss/sweetheart deeply normaL/is punch drunk/Mme/interj./Having no wheels or springs/Having behaviors/Measuring its volume/they bathe me in Forget/retrieving/games

How to Submit: Submit 3 poems at a time. Accepts previously published poems and simultaneous submissions. Cover letter preferred. "Copies should be clean, crisp, and camera-ready. I do not have the means to accept electronic submissions. A SASE should accompany all submissions, and a telephone number if at all possible." Guidelines available for SASE. Time between acceptance and publication is 2 months. Seldom comments on rejected poems. Responds to queries and mss in up to 2 months. Pays at least 10 author's copies (out of a press run of 200-300). May offer subsidy arrangements. "I am new at this. And so it all depends upon my financial situation at the time. Yes, I might ask the author to subsidize the cost. It could be worth their while. I have good connections in the small press." Order sample publications by sending a 6×9 SAE. "There is no charge for samples."

Advice: "Experiment with thought, language, the printed word."

THE MASSACHUSETTS REVIEW, South College, University of Massachusetts, Amherst MA 01003. (413)545-2689. E-mail: massrev@external.umass.edu. Website: www.massreview.org (includes guidelines, contact and subscription information, bios, links, archives, and editorial policy). Established 1959. **Poetry Editors:** Paul Jenkins and Anne Halley.

● Work published in this review has been frequently included in volumes of *The Best American Poetry*.

Magazine Needs: Appearing quarterly, *The Massachusetts Review* publishes "fiction, essays, artwork, and excellent poetry of all forms and styles." Has published poetry by Marilyn Hacker, Virgil Suarez, and Miller Williams. As a sample the editors selected these lines from "Elegy" by Marianne Boruch:

> Before the basil blackened. Before plates/slept in their cupboard. Before the streets were/snow. Before the songs started in the throat or crept/sideways into the hands that hold the cello.

The Massachusetts Review is 6×9, offset-printed on bond paper, perfect-bound with color card cover with occasional art and photography sections. Receives about 2,500 poems/year, accepts about 50. Press run is 1,600 for 1,100-1,200 subscribers of which 1,000 are libraries, the rest for shelf sales. Subscription: $22/year (US), $30 outside US, $30 for libraries. Sample: $8 (US), $11 outside US.

How to Submit: No simultaneous submissions or previously published poems. Reads submissions October 1 through June 1 only. Guidelines available for SASE and on website. Responds in 6 weeks. Pays minimum of $10, or 35¢/line, plus 2 copies.

MATCHBOOK (Specialized: themes); MATCHBOOK PRESS; LCPH MEDIA SERVICES, 242 N. Broad St., Doylestown PA 18901. E-mail: matchgirl8@aol.com. Website: www.matchbook poetry.com (includes guidelines, contact information, bios, archives, upcoming themes, editorial policy, and links). Established 1994. **Editor:** Debrie Stevens.

Magazine Needs: *Matchbook* is published online and "presents intriguing poetry and reviews to readers interested in same." Wants "most any form, length, subject, style with the following restrictions, query first on long poems or translations." Does not want "rhymed verse, traditional forms, concrete poems." Has published poetry by Simon Perchik, Cid Corman, and Robert Peters. Receives about 500 poems/year, accepts about 20%. *Matchbook* is available free online.

How to Submit: Submit 5-6 poems at a time typewritten, printed out, or legible copies. Accepts simultaneous submissions OK "if noted"; previously published poems OK. Cover letter preferred. Time between acceptance and publication is 6 months. Seldom comments on rejected poems. Publishes theme issues.

Guidelines and upcoming themes available by e-mail and on website. Responds in 1 month. Staff reviews books, chapbooks, magazines, and zines in 200 words, single book format. Send books for review consideration.

MATRIARCH'S WAY, JOURNAL OF FEMALE SUPREMACY; ARTEMIS CREATIONS (Specialized: women/feminism, matriarchy), 3395-2J Nostrand Ave., Brooklyn NY 11229. (718)648-8215. E-mail: ArtemisPub@sysmatrix.net. Website: www.artemiscreations.com (includes guidelines, contact information, bios, subscription information, links). Established 1994. **Editor:** S. Oliveira.
Magazine Needs: *Matriarch's Way* is a biannual "matriarchal feminist" publication. Wants "powerful fem" poetry. *Matriarch's Way* is 125-200 pages, digest-sized, offset-printed and perfect-bound, includes art. Single copy: $10; domestic subscription: $20. Sample: $10. Make checks payable to Artemis Creations.
How to Submit: Accepts previously published poems and simultaneous submissions. Accepts e-mail submissions. Time between acceptance and publication is 1 week. Occasionally publishes theme issues. Guidelines and upcoming themes available for SASE and on website. Responds in 1 week. Sometimes sends prepublication galleys. "Book reviews needed."

$ MATURE YEARS (Specialized: senior citizen, religious), P.O. Box 801, 201 Eighth Ave. S., Nashville TN 37202. (615)749-6292. Fax: (615)749-6512. E-mail: matureyears@umpublishing.org. Established 1954. **Editor:** Marvin W. Cropsey.
Magazine Needs: *Mature Years* is a quarterly. "The magazine's purpose is to help persons understand and use the resources of Christian faith in dealing with specific opportunities and problems related to aging. Poems are usually limited to 16 lines and may, or may not, be overtly religious. Poems should not poke fun at older adults, but may take a humorous look at them. Avoid sentimentality and saccharine. If using rhymes and meter, make sure they are accurate." *Mature Years* is 112 pages, magazine-sized, perfect-bound, with full-color glossy paper cover. Press run is 70,000. Sample: $5.
How to Submit: Line length for poetry is 16 lines of up to 50 characters maximum. Accepts fax submissions; prefers e-mail submissions. Submit seasonal and nature poems for spring during December through February; for summer, March through May; for fall, June through August; and for winter, September through November. Guidelines available for SASE. Responds in 2 months; sometimes a year's delay before publication. Pays $1/line upon acceptance.

MAUSOLEUM: MORTIS ES VERITUS (Specialized: horror, dark fantasy), 6324 Locust, NE, Albuquerque NM 87113-1011. E-mail: gothia90@hotmail.com or c_ravenscar@hotmail.com. Website: www.geocities.com/crowravenscar (includes guidelines, submission info, copy prices). Established 1994. **Editor/Publisher:** Kelly Ganson (aka Crow Ravenscar).
Magazine Needs: *Mausoleum* appears annually in October, publishing fiction, poetry, and artwork. Wants "horror, Gothic horror, Wicca, dark fantasy and Renaissance horror for subject matter or genre. Free verse, rhyming verse, haiku, or humorous. Halloween themed is good. **Absolutely no** exploitation, sexual, graphic, or pornographic, cruelty to people or animals. If I see this, it'll be returned." Recently published poetry by Sean Russell Friend, John Grey, Mark Francis, and Corrine de Winter. As a sample the editor selected her poem, "Darkness":

> The Darkness/She comes on silent feet/And follows me,/Closes around me,/Swallows me,/Until I am
> no more . . .

Mausoleum is 30 pages, digest-sized, Xeroxed, saddle-stapled, b&w cardstock/colored cardstock cover, with all original artwork, some computer graphics. Receives about 20 poems/year, accepts about 8%. Publishes about 14-16 poems/issue. Press run is 40 for 8 subscribers, 20 shelf sales; 10 distributed free to contributors. Single copy: $6 US. Sample: $4.50. Make checks payable to Kelly Ganson.
How to Submit: Submit 5 poems at a time. Line length for poetry is 10 minimum, 20 maximum. Accepts previously published poems and simultaneous submissions. No fax, e-mail, or disk submissions. Cover letter is required. "Name, address, e-mail, bio, etc., in cover letter. Always include SASE or I cannot respond." Reads submissions all year. Submit seasonal poems 3 months in advance (Halloween themed especially). Time between acceptance and publication is up to 1 year (annual publication). "I read the poems; if accepted, a release form and acceptance letter are sent to contributor. If rejected, a rejection notice goes to contributor." Always comments on rejected poems. "I *do* ask that a contributor buy a sample copy of the magazine or ask for guidelines before submitting poetry, fiction, or art." Occasionally publishes theme issues. A list of upcoming themes and guidelines are available for SASE or on website. Responds in 3 weeks. Sometimes sends prepublication galleys. Pays 1 contributor's copy. Acquires one-time rights. Reviews other magazines/journals in 1-2 paragraphs. Poets may send magazines/journals for review consideration to *Mausoleam*.
Advice: "Don't be afraid to submit! And if I do reject your work, it doesn't mean you are not good enough. It just means you didn't have what I wanted. Try again and keep trying!"

⊕ ◖ **MAYPOLE EDITIONS**, 22 Mayfair Ave., Ilford, Essex IG1 3DQ England. (0181)252-0354.
Book/Chapbook Needs: Maypole Editions publishes 3 hardbacks/year of fiction and poetry, including anthologies. Wants "poems broadly covering social concerns, ethnic minorities, feminist issues, romance, lyric." Does not want "politics." Has published poetry by A. Lee Firth, Samantha Willow, Brian Jeffry, Mindy Cresswell, Denise Bell, and Paul Amphlet. As a sample we selected these lines from "Demonism Forgot" by K.M. Dersley from the anthology *Fusing Tulips: 2001-2002:*

> *Why demonise mediocrities, though?/Why do them the favor?/Do you have to attack what/is already*
> *dead?/They're decent taxpayers,/they laugh at the right places/in TV sitcoms.*

Sample: £7.95, add £2.50 US.
How to Submit: Query first with a few sample poems approximately 30 lines long and cover letter with brief bio and publication credits. Obtain samples of books by sending £1 and an A5 SAE for a catalog.

$ ◖ ◎ **MEADOWBROOK PRESS (Specialized: anthologies, children, humor)**, 5451 Smetana Dr., Minnetonka MN 55343. Website: www.meadowbrookpress.com (includes samples, guidelines, poetry contests for kids, catalog and educational info for kids and teachers). Established 1975. **Contact:** Read 'Em, Rate 'Em editor.
Book/Chapbook Needs: Meadowbrook Press "is currently seeking poems to be posted on website and to be considered for future funny poetry book anthologies for children." Wants humorous poems aimed at children ages 6-12. "Poems should be fun, light and refreshing. We're looking for new, hilarious, contemporary voices in children's poetry that kids can relate to." Accepts poetry written by children "only for website contests—not for publication in books." Has published poetry by Shel Silverstein, Jack Prelutsky, Jeff Moss, Ken Nesbitt, and Bruce Lansky. Anthologies have included *Kids Pick the Funniest Poems*; *A Bad Case of the Giggles*; and *Miles of Smiles*.
How to Submit: "Please take time to read our guidelines, and send your best work." Submit up to 10 poems; 1 poem to a page with name and address on each. Line length for poetry is 15 maximum. Include SASE with each submission. Accepts simultaneous submissions. Cover letter required "just to know where the poet found us." Time between acceptance and publication is 1-2 years. Poems are tested in front of grade school students before being published. Guidelines available for SASE and on website. Pays $50-100/poem plus 1 copy.

◖ **MEDICINAL PURPOSES LITERARY REVIEW; MARILYN K. PRESCOTT MEMORIAL POETRY CONTEST; POET TO POET, INC.**, 86-37 120th St., #2D, Richmond Hill NY 11418. (718)776-8853 or (718)847-2150. E-mail: dunnmiracle@earthlink.net. Established 1994. **Executive Editor:** Robert Dunn. **Managing Editor:** Thomas M. Catterson. **Associate Editor/Poetry Editor:** Leigh Harrison. **Prose Editor:** Anthony Scarpantonio.
Magazine Needs: *Medicinal Purposes* appears biannually and wants "virtually any sort of quality poetry (3 poems, up to 60 lines/poem). Please, no pornography, gratuitous violence, or hate mongering." Accepts poetry written by children for the young writers' column. Has published poetry by Patric Pepper, X.J. Kennedy, Rhina P. Espaillat, Paul Polansky, Charles Rammelkamp, Carol Firth, and George Dickerson. *Medicinal Purposes* is 80 pages, 8½×5½ (landscape format), professionally printed and perfect-bound with card stock cover with b&w illustration, b&w illustrations also inside. Receives 1,200 poems/year, accepts about 10%. Press run is 1,000 for 270 subscribers of which 6 are libraries, 30% shelf sales. Subscription: $16/year. Sample: $9. Make checks payable to Poet to Poet.
How to Submit: Submit 3 poems at a time, up to 60 lines per poem, typed with SASE. No previously published poems or simultaneous submissions. Accepts e-mail submissions (in text box, no attachments). Cover letter preferred. Time between acceptance and publication is up to 16 months. Often comments on rejected poems. Guidelines available for SASE or by e-mail. Responds in 3 months. Always sends prepublication galleys. Pays 2 contributor's copies. Acquires first rights.

MARKET CONDITIONS are constantly changing! If you're still using this book and it's 2004 or later, buy the newest edition of *Poet's Market* at your favorite bookstore or order directly from Writer's Digest Books (800)448-0915 or www.writersdigest.com.

Also Offers: Produces a poetry/folk music public access cable show called "Poet to Poet." Also sponsors an annual poetry contest, 1st Prize $100. Submit 3 poems of 6-16 lines each with a $5 entry fee by June 15. Winners will be published in the year's end issue. Additionally they sponsor a chapbook contest. Also administers the Marilyn K. Prescott Memorial Poetry Contest. Details available for SASE.

Advice: "Poetry cannot be created out of a vacuum. Read the work of others, listen to performances, learn the difference between the universal and the generic, and most important—Get A Life! Do Things! If you get struck by lightning, then share the light. Only then do you stand a chance of finding your own voice."

N ◯ ◎ MERIDIAN ANTHOLOGY OF CONTEMPORARY POETRY; RACHEL BENTLEY POETRY COMPETITION, P.O. Box 970309, Boca Raton FL 33497. E-mail: LetarP@aol.com. Website: www.Meridiananthology.com (includes guidelines, names of editors, excerpts). Established 2002. **Editor/ Publisher:** Phyliss L. Geller.

Magazine Needs: *Meridian Anthology of Contemporary Poetry* appears biannually and wants "poetry that is contemporary, insightful, and illuminating, that touches the nerves. It should have color, content, and be deciphering of existence." Does not want vulgarity, cliches. *Meridian Anthology* is up to 96 pages, digest-sized, offset-printed, perfect-bound, soft cover. Publishes about 75-90 poems/issue. Press run is 1,000. Single copy: $7; subscription: $12. Make checks payable to *Meridian Anthology*.

How to Submit: Submit 1-5 poems at a time. Line length for poetry is 39 maximum. Accepts simultaneous submissions; no previously published poems. No fax, e-mail, or disk submissions. Cover letter is preferred. Must include SASE. Reads submissions year round. Submit seasonal poems 6 months in advance. Time between acceptance and publication is up to 6 months. Seldom comments on rejected poems. Guidelines available for SASE or on website. Responds in "3 weeks to 3 months, depending on backlog." Pays 1 contributor's copy. Acquires one-time rights.

Also Offers: Rachel Bentley Poetry Competition awards $200 for 1st Place, plus winner will be featured with bio in an upcoming issue (3-4 line bio must be included with entry). Also awards 2nd Place: $50 and publication, 3rd Place: $25 and publication. **Entry fee:** $10 for 3 poems. **Deadline:** June 15.

Advice: "A poem must have a reason for existence, some universal tendril."

⊘ MIAMI UNIVERSITY PRESS, English Dept., Miami University, Oxford OH 45056. (513)529-5110. Website: www.muohio.edu/mupress/. Established 1992. **Editor:** James Reiss.

Book/Chapbook Needs & How to Submit: Publishes 2 books/year in paperback and cloth editions by poets who have already published at least one full-length book of poems. Recent titles include *Wind Somewhere, and Shade* by Kate Knapp Johnson, Spring 2001; and *The Printer's Error* by Aaron Fogel, Spring 2001; *Ariadne's Island* by Molly Bendall, Winter 2002; *Gender Studies* by Jeffrey Skinner, Winter 2002. Currently closed to unsolicited poetry.

Ⅶ $◎ MICHIGAN QUARTERLY REVIEW, Dept. PM, 3032 Rackham Bldg., University of Michigan, Ann Arbor MI 48109. (734)764-9265. E-mail: mqr@umich.edu. Website: www.umich.edu/~mqr (includes information about the current and forthcoming issues, special issues, subscription information, guidelines, and Lawrence Foundation Prize information). Established 1962. **Editor-in-Chief:** Laurence Goldstein.

• Poetry published in the *Michigan Quarterly Review* is frequently included in volumes of *The Best American Poetry* and has been selected for the 2002 *Pushcart Prize* anthology.

Magazine Needs: *Michigan Quarterly Review* is "an interdisciplinary, general interest academic journal that publishes mainly essays and reviews on subjects of cultural and literary interest." Uses all kinds of poetry except light verse. No specifications as to form, length, style, subject matter, or purpose. Has published poetry by Susan Hahn, Carl Phillips, Mary Oliver, and Yusef Komunyakaa. As a sample the editor selected these lines from "Spirit Cabinet" by David Wojahn:

> *House-of-Justice-One-Way-Glass: you can't see in, not to the upper floors,/where cell rows mean to prove/that here blind justice is half cured.*

Michigan Quarterly Review is 160 pages, 6×9, flat-spined, professionally printed with glossy card cover, b&w photos and art. Receives about 1,400 submissions/year, accepts about 30, has a 1-year backlog. Press run is 2,000, with 1,200 subscribers of which half are libraries. Single copy: $7; subscription: $25. Sample: $5 plus 2 first-class stamps.

How to Submit: Prefers typed mss. No previously published poems or simultaneous submissions. No fax or e-mail submissions. Cover letter preferred; "it puts a human face on the manuscript. A few sentences of biography is all I want, nothing lengthy or defensive." Publishes theme issues. Theme for autumn 2002 is "Jewish in America." Responds in 6 weeks. Always sends prepublication galleys. Pays $8-12/page. Acquires first rights only. Reviews books of poetry. "All reviews are commissioned."

Advice: "There is no substitute for omnivorous reading and careful study of poets past and present, as well as reading in new and old areas of knowledge. Attention to technique, especially to rhythm and patterns of imagery, is vital."

$□ ◎ THE MID-AMERICA PRESS, INC.; THE MID-AMERICA POETRY REVIEW; THE MID-AMERICA PRESS WRITING AWARD COMPETITION (Specialized: regional), P.O. Box 575, Warrensburg MO 64093-0575. (660)747-4602. Press established 1976. **Editor:** Robert C. Jones.

Magazine Needs: *Mid-America Poetry Review* appears 3 times/year and publishes "well-crafted poetry primarily from—but not limited to—poets living in Missouri, Illinois, Arkansas, Oklahoma, Kansas, Nebraska, and Iowa. We are open to all styles and forms; what we look for is poetry by writers who know both what they are doing and why. We have a prejudice against work with content that is primarily self-indulgent or overly private." Has published poetry by Jim Barnes, Bill Bauer, Serina Allison Hearn, Dan Jaffe, Kevin Prufer, Robert Stewart, Gloria Vando, and Jeanie Wilson. As a sample the editor selected these lines from "Why Eurydice Left" by Denise M. Rogers:

> In Hell, she'd learned, the stars/are really spiders, holding fast/to whitewashed walls./Like gods, they
> are ready to strike/when the butterflies begin to come.

The Mid-America Review is 60-70 pages, 6×9, offset-printed and perfect-bound with matte-paper cover. Receives about 700-1,000 poems/year, accepts about 20%. Press run is 750. Single copy: $6; subscription: $30/2 years. Sample: $6. Make checks payable to The Mid-America Press, Inc.

How to Submit: Submit 1-3 poems at a time. No previously published poems or simultaneous submissions. Cover letter useful. "Type submissions, single- or double-spaced, on 8½×11 white paper; name, address, telephone number, and e-mail address (if available) in top left or right corner. Keep copy of your manuscript—unused submissions will be recycled; send SASE for notification. One-page cover letter (if included) should list items to be considered; contain brief paragraphs of information about author and previous publications." Time between acceptance and publication is up to 9 months. Sometimes comments on rejected poems. Guidelines available for SASE. Responds within 2 months. Sends prepublication galleys. Pays $5/poem and 2 contributor's copies. Acquires first North American serial rights. Staff occasionally reviews books of poetry. Send books for review consideration.

Book/Chapbook Needs & How to Submit: The Mid-America Press, Inc. was established "to encourage writers and the appreciation of writing." Publishes 2-6 paperbacks per year with 1 book selected through The Mid-America Press Writing Award Competition. "At present—with the exception of entries for the competition—the Press is not reading unsolicited book-length poetry mss. The competition is limited to 48- to 148-page poetry mss (previously unpublished in book form) by poets living in Missouri, Arkansas, Oklahoma, Kansas, Nebraska, Iowa, or Illinois." Entry fee: $20. Entry guidelines and deadline date available for SASE. The winner of Writing Award 2000 was *Light and Chance* by Ardyth Bradley. Mid-America Press, Inc. award-winning publications include *Red Silk* (1999) by Maryfrances Wagner (winner of the 2000 Thorpe Menn Award for Writing Excellence) and *Living Off the Land, A Gathering of Writing from The Warrensburg Writers' Circle* (1999) edited by Robert C. Jones (First Place in The 2000 Walter William Major Work Award, from the Missouri Writers' Guild). Other publications include *Outcasts, Poems* (2000), by Brian Daldorph; *Memories & Memoirs, Essays, Poems, Stories, Letters by Contemporary Missouri Authors* (2000), edited by Sharon Kinney Hanson; and *Uncurling, Poems* (2000) by Jeanie Wilson; and *This Country or That* (2001) by Victoria Anderson. Obtain sample books by sending $13.95 per book (For *Memories & Memoirs*, send $18.95).

Ⓜ $□ ◑ ◎ MID-AMERICAN REVIEW; JAMES WRIGHT PRIZE FOR POETRY, Dept. of English, Bowling Green State University, Bowling Green OH 43403. (419)372-2725. Website: http://bgsu.edu/midamericanreview (includes sample work, guidelines, editorial policy, links, contact and subscription information, archives, contest rules, upcoming themes, and contents of previous issues). Established 1981. **Editor-in-Chief:** Michael Czyzniejewski. **Poetry Editor:** Karen Craigo.

● Poetry published in *Mid-American Review* was included in the 1999 volume of *Best American Poetry* and the 2002 *Pushcart Prize* anthology.

Magazine Needs: *Mid-American Review* appears twice/year in March and October. "Poetry should emanate from strong, evocative images; use fresh, interesting language; and have a consistent sense of voice. Each line must carry the poem, and an individual vision should be evident. We encourage new as well as established writers. There is no length limit." Has published poetry by Michelle Boisseau, Mark Cox, Denise Duhamel, Bob Hicok, Linda Pastan, and Greg Pape. The review is 192 pages, offset-printed and flat-spined with laminated card cover using full-color artwork. Receives over 2,000 mss/year, accepts 40-50 poems. Press run is 1,600. Single copy: $7; subscription: $12. Sample: $5.

How to Submit: Submit up to 6 poems at a time. Reads submissions year round; responds more slowly in summer months. Occasionally publishes theme issues. Spring 2003 edition will be an all-Ohio writers edition; deadline for submission is September 2002. Upcoming themes and guidelines available for SASE, on website, and in publication. Sends prepublication galleys. Pays $10/printed page when possible plus 2 copies. Rights revert to authors on publication. Reviews books of poetry.

Also Offers: Also publishes chapbooks in translation and award the James Wright Prize for Poetry. "To be considered for the prize, send $10 fee and three poems addressed to the James Wright Prize, or write for complete guidelines."

⌞N⌝ MIDMARCH ARTS PRESS, 300 Riverside Dr., New York NY 10025.
Book/Chapbook Needs & How to Submit: Midmarch Arts Press publishes 4-6 paperbacks/year. Query before submission. Has recently published *Split Verse* edited by Meg Campbell and William Buke; *Solo Crossing* by Meg Campbell; *Sight Lines* by Charlotte Mandel; and *Whirling Round the Sun* by Suzanne Noguerre.

$⊚ MIDSTREAM: A MONTHLY ZIONIST REVIEW (Specialized: ethnic), 633 Third Ave., 21st Floor, New York NY 10017. (212)339-6040. E-mail: info@midstream.org. Website: www.midstream.org. **Editor:** Leo Haber.
Magazine Needs: *Midstream* is an international journal appearing 8 times/year. Wants short poems with Jewish themes or atmosphere. Has published poetry by Yehuda Amichai, James Reiss, Abraham Sutzkever, Liz Rosenberg, and John Hollander. The magazine is 48 pages, about 8½ × 11, saddle-stapled with colored card cover. Each issue includes 4 to 5 poems (which tend to be short, lyric, and freestyle expressing seminal symbolism of Jewish history and Scripture). Receives about 300 submissions/year, accepts 5-10%. Press run is 10,000. Single copy: $3; subscription: $21.
How to Submit: Submit 2 poems at a time. Accepts e-mail submissions. Time between acceptance and publication is within 1 year. Publishes theme issues. Responds in 6 months. Pays $25/poem and 3 contributor's copies. Acquires first rights.

$◐ MIDWEST POETRY REVIEW, 7443 Oak Tree Lane, Springhill FL 34607-2324. (352)688-8116. E-mail: mariasingh@cs.com. Established 1980. **Editor/Publisher:** Pariksith Singh and Maria Scunziano.
Magazine Needs: *Midwest Poetry Review* is a quarterly, with no other support than subscriptions, contest entry fees, and an occasional advertisement. Looking for "quality, accessible verse. Evocative and innovative imagery with powerful adjectives and verbs. Poetry that opens the door to the author's feelings through sensory descriptions. We are attempting to encourage the cause of poetry by purchasing the best of modern poetry. Any subject is considered, if handled with skill and taste. No pornography. Nothing which arrives without SASE is read or gets reply. We are open to new poets, but they must show talent." Accepts poetry written by children. "Must be good writing." Has published poetry by Rukmini Callamchi, B.R. Culbertson, Junette Fabian, Glenna Holloway, Mikal Lofgren, and Bettie Sellers. As a sample the editor selected these lines from "Picking" by Rukmini Callamchi:

> In your yard, we are picking blackberries:/strong, blue, and full of voice./It's the thinness of this
> summer I remember,/its cliff,/its way of ending before the stains/wash off my dress//I do not want your
> mother to see this:/her hands, soft and restless/in the kitchen sink.//She is watching, waiting,/like the
> summer,/for something to snap, unravel/like the breaking of clouds before rain

Midwest Poetry Review is 56 pages, professionally printed, digest-sized, saddle-stapled with matte card cover. Subscription: $20. Sample: $7 (when available).
How to Submit: Submit up to 5 poems at a time, 1 poem/page. Line length for poetry is 100 maximum. No previously published poems or simultaneous submissions. No bios or credit lists. Accepts disk and e-mail (in text box or as attachment) submissions. Guidelines are available for SASE, by e-mail, and in publication. "We will critique up to 10 of your poems at a time." Criticism fee: $10 plus SASE. Responds in 1 month. Pays $5/poem. Acquires first rights.
Also Offers: Has varied contests in each issue, with prizes ranging from $10-250, with "unbiased, non-staff judges for all competitions." Contests have entry fees. Details available for SASE.

◐ THE MIDWEST QUARTERLY, Pittsburg State University, Pittsburg KS 66762. (316)235-4689. Fax: (316)235-4686. E-mail: smeats@pittstate.edu (queries only, no submissions). Website: www.pittstate.edu/engl/midwest.html. Established 1959. **Poetry Editor:** Stephen Meats.
Magazine Needs: *Midwest Quarterly* "publishes articles on any subject of contemporary interest, particularly literary criticism, political science, philosophy, education, biography, and sociology, and each issue contains a section of poetry usually 15 poems in length. I am interested in well-crafted, though not necessarily traditional poems that explore the inter-relationship of the human and natural worlds in bold, surrealistic

images of a writer's imaginative, mystical experience. Sixty lines or less (occasionally longer if exceptional)." Has published poetry by David Baker, Fleda Brown Jackson, Jim Daniels, Naomi Shibab Nye, Grey Kuzman, Walt McDonald, Jeanne Murray Walker, and Peter Cooley. *Midwest Quarterly* is 130 pages, digest-sized, professionally printed and flat-spined with matte cover. Press run is 650 for 600 subscribers of which 500 are libraries. Receives about 4,000 poems/year, accepts about 60. "My plan is to publish all acceptances within 1 year." Subscription: $12. Sample: $5.

How to Submit: Mss should be typed with poet's name on each page, 10 poems or fewer. Accepts simultaneous submissions; no previously published poems. No fax or e-mail submissions. Occasionally publishes theme issues. Guidelines and upcoming themes available for SASE, by fax, or by e-mail. Responds in 2 months, usually sooner. "Submissions without SASE cannot be acknowledged." Pays 3 contributor's copies. Acquires first serial rights. Editor comments on rejected poems "if the poet or poems seem particularly promising." Reviews books of poetry by *Midwest Quarterly* published poets only.

Advice: "Keep writing; read as much contemporary poetry as you can lay your hands on; don't let the discouragement of rejection keep you from sending your work out to editors."

MIDWEST VILLAGES & VOICES (Specialized: regional), P.O. Box 40214, St. Paul MN 55104. (612)822-6878. Established 1979.

Book/Chapbook Needs & How to Submit: Midwest Villages & Voices is a cultural organization and small press publisher of Midwestern poetry and prose. "We encourage and support Midwestern writers and artists. However, at this time submissions are accepted by invitation only. Unsolicited submissions are not accepted."

MIDWIFERY TODAY (Specialized: childbirth), P.O. Box 2672, Eugene OR 97402-0223. (541)344-7438. Fax: (541)344-1422. E-mail: editorial@midwiferytoday.com. Website: www.midwiferytoday.com (includes writer's guidelines, articles, and products). Established 1986. **Editor-in-Chief:** Jan Tritten. **Editor:** Bobbie Willis.

Magazine Needs: *Midwifery Today* is a quarterly that "provides a voice for midwives and childbirth educators. We are a midwifery magazine. Subject must be birth or birth profession related." Does not want poetry that is "off subject or puts down the subject." *Midwifery Today* is 75 pages, 8½ × 11, offset-printed, saddle-stapled, with glossy card cover with b&w photos and b&w artwork photos, and ads inside. Uses about 1 poem/issue. Press run is 5,000 for 3,000 subscribers, 1,000 shelf sales. Subscription: $50. Sample: $10.

How to Submit: No previously published poems. Accepts e-mail submissions (as attachment or in text box). Cover letter required. Time between acceptance and publication is 1-2 years. Seldom comments on rejected poems. Publishes theme issues. Anticipated theme issues include Winter 2002: Unity (deadline: September 1, 2002); Spring 2003: Tear Prevention (deadline: December 1, 2002); Summer 2003: The Place of Birth (deadline: March 1, 2003); Fall 2003: Fear in Midwifery and Birth (deadline: June 1, 2003). Upcoming themes available on website. Guidelines available for SASE and on website. Responds in 6 months. Pays 2 contributor's copies. Acquires first rights.

Advice: "With our publication *please* stay on the subject."

MILKWEED EDITIONS, 1011 Washington Ave. S., Suite 668, Minneapolis MN 55415-1246. (612)332-3192. Fax: (612)215-2550. E-mail: editor@milkweed.org. Website: www.milkweed.org (includes writer's guidelines, catalog, info on publishing programs and "e-verse"). Established 1979. **Contact:** Poetry Reader.

Book/Chapbook Needs: Milkweed Editions is "looking for poetry manuscripts of high quality that embody humane values and contribute to cultural understanding." Not limited in subject matter, though poetry about natural world preferred for "The World As Home: Literature About the Natural World" publishing program. Open to writers with previously published books of poetry or a minimum of 6 poems published in nationally distributed commercials or literary journals. Accepts translations and bilingual mss. Published books of poetry include *Butterfly Effect*, by Harry Humes; *Eating Bread and Honey*, by Pattiann Rogers; and *Outsiders: Poems about Rebels, Renegades and Exiles*, edited by Laure-Anne Bosselaar.

How to Submit: Submit 60 pages or more, typed on good quality white paper. Do not send originals. No submissions by fax or e-mail. Include SASE for our reply. Unsolicited mss read in January and June *only*. "Milkweed can no longer return manuscripts in stamped book mailers. In the event that manuscripts are not accepted for publication, we prefer to recycle them. If you need your work returned, *please enclose a check for $5* rather than a stamped mailer." Guidelines available for SASE. Responds in up to 6 months. Catalog available on request, with $1.50 in postage.

◯ MILKWOOD REVIEW, English Dept., Hope College, P.O. Box 9000, Holland MI 49424. (616)395-7613. E-mail: peckham@hope.edu. Website: www.milkwoodreview.50megs.com (includes all information about *Milkwood*). Established 2000. **Editors:** Joel Peckham and Susan Atefat Peckham.

Magazine Needs: *The Milkwood Review* is constantly updated and available year round in annual issues online. "*The Milkwood Review* is an interdisciplinary journal that seeks to create a web environment in which poetry, fiction, nonfiction, speculative essays, short scholarly articles, etc., are presented in a form appropriate to the material. All creative work appears with audio samples." Will consider "any kind of poetry from narrative to lyric, from traditional to experimental—no length or line-length restrictions. Because of the journal's commitment to real-audio technology, we favor work that concentrates on poetry as a musical form of literature in which sound is as important as meaning." Does not want "work that is uncrafted or facile." Recently published poetry by Minnie Bruce Pratt and Simon Perchik.

The Milkwood Review is published online with a fine art cover and art/graphics. Accepts about 10% of poems submitted. Publishes 15-30 poems/issue.

How to Submit: Submit 4-8 poems at a time. Accepts previously published poems and simultaneous submissions. Accepts e-mail and disk submissions (if Word for Windows). Cover letter is required. "Each poem printed in *Milkwood* will include an audio file. Once a poem has been accepted (not before) we will require the author to submit a recorded version of the piece." Reads submissions year-round. Submit seasonal poems anytime. Time between acceptance and publication is up to 6 months. "Poems are read by both editors and full staff. Final decisions on the publication of work in *Milkwood* rest with the founding editors." Often comments on rejections. Occasionally publishes theme issues. A list of upcoming themes is available for SASE. Guidelines are available for SASE and on website. Sometimes sends prepublication galleys. No pay; publication only. Acquires first North American serial or one-time rights, reverts to poet upon publication. Reviews books, and chapbooks of poetry and other magazines, open length, in single and multibook format. Poets may send books for review consideration to the editors.

Advice: "Read poetry—but also, *listen to it.* Pay attention not only to the precise and intentional placement of words but to the momentum they create, the surge and urge of the poem."

$◯ MILLER'S POND; LOELLA CADY LAMPHIER PRIZE FOR POETRY; H&H PRESS, RR 2, Box 241, Middlebury Center PA 16935. (570)376-3361. Fax: (570)376-2674. E-mail: cjhoughtaling @usa.net. Website: http://millerspondpoetry.com (includes guidelines, contest rules, contact and subscription information, bios, archives, links, editorial policy, and some poetry not found in print version). Established 1987. **Editor:** C.J. Houghtaling. **Web Editor:** Julie Damerell

Magazine Needs: Published in January, *miller's pond* is an annual magazine featuring contemporary poetry, interviews, reviews, and markets. "We want contemporary poetry that is fresh, accessible, energetic, vivid, and flows with language and rhythm. No religious, horror, pornographic, vulgar, rhymed, preachy, lofty, trite, or overly sentimental work." Has published poetry by Liz Rosenberg, Katharyn Howd Machan, Robert Cooperman, Ward Kelly, M.C. Leonard, and Julie Damerell. As a sample the editor selected these lines from "Bird" by James E. Cherry:

> Bird was bending notes, stretching/tones, breaking rhythms, changing times/and resetting them. And
> along with/a half pack of smokes, the bitter/lukewarm beer and all the despair that/weighed my head
> upon the table, I breathed.

miller's pond is 48 pages, 5½×8½, offset-printed and saddle-stapled with cardstock cover. Receives about 200 poems/year, accepts 20-25 poems/issue. Press run is 200. Single copy: $8. Sample (back issue) including guidelines: $6. Make checks payable to H&H Press.

How to Submit: Submit 3-5 poems at a time. Line length for poetry is 40 maximum. Accepts previously published poems and simultaneous submissions. Accepts submissions by mail only. Cover letter preferred. "No returns without SASE." Reads submissions October 1 through December 1 only. Time between acceptance and publication is up to 1 year. Seldom comments on rejected poems. Guidelines available for SASE or on website. Responds in up to 11 months; "although we try to respond sooner, we are not always able to." Sometimes sends prepublication galleys. Pays $2/poem and 1 copy for work that appears in hard copy version. Acquires one-time rights. Reviews books of poetry in up to 500 words, single book format.

Also Offers: H&H Press sponsors the Loella Lamphier Prize for Poetry. Awards $100 for 1st Place, $50 for 2nd Place and $25 3rd Place. Guidelines available on website. Send SASE. "*miller's pond* will be holding a chapbook competition. All updates will be posted on the website." Also, website features original content not found in magazine. Accepts submissions through an online submission form only. Contact web editor Julie Damerell.

Book/Chapbook Needs & How to Submit: "H&H Press is a micro-publisher of poetry chapbooks and how-to-write books, with plans to expand into nonfiction and specialty books." Publishes 1 paperback and 1 chapbook per year. Books are usually 24-36 pages, 8½×5¼, offset-printed and saddle-stapled with cardstock cover, includes some art. "By invitation only; query first for publication schedule and needs. My requirements are simple—the

insider report

Busy poet/publisher does it all

C.J. Houghtaling

When it comes to writing and publishing, C.J. Houghtaling covers all the bases. She's a former editor of Tioga County, Pennsylvania's largest weekly newspaper. Her 200 plus publishing credits include poetry, fiction, and articles in *Byline Magazine*, *Ellery Queen's Mystery Magazine*, *The Literary Journal*, *Children's Playmate*, and many others. H&H Press, which she founded in 1987, includes how-to guides for writers and poets as well as poetry chapbooks among its titles. H&H also publishes *miller's pond*, a literary journal in its fifth year with an online as well as print version. Houghtaling is also a ten-year board member of Pennwriters, Inc., a writer's organization based in Pennsylvania. Oh, and she professionally builds web pages for magazines, writers, farm equipment dealers, and other businesses, and presents web-building seminars, too.

Where does she find the time? And how does poetry fit into such a busy schedule?

"If I have just a few hours to myself within a week, and I have an idea for a poem, I'll work on that poem," says Houghtaling. "I do meet every Wednesday night with another critique partner. That kind of centers me with a goal to present her with something, a poem or a portion of a short story or novel, whatever. I'm on deadlines so much with all of the other stuff I do, it's hard for me to prioritize for myself. If I don't have a deadline, it would never get done."

For Houghtaling, the special appeal of poetry lies in "a turn of phrase, the sheer magic of the words, the way they come together on a page. It's a mini-perspective on something you may never have looked at that way otherwise."

Houghtaling and her husband sell farm machinery in Middlebury Center, Pennsylvania, and "we have all this rusty old equipment back in the hedgerows. If you've ever seen a corn picker, you know it has a very long, crooked neck. I looked at that and thought, 'Gosh, that really kind of looks like a dinosaur.' So I created a poem about this farmer trying to coax this dinosaur out of the hedgerow, to make it work one more year for him." The resulting piece appeared on an area arts calendar. "I just like to play with words, and poetry is a very easy way to put that desire to work."

Nature also is a rich source of inspiration for Houghtaling. "We live in the boondocks, with coyotes and bears in our yard, so I'm very, very close to nature. Even when I go on vacation I wind up concentrating on the nature around me and writing about that aspect of something. If I happen to see an icicle dropping off a maple leaf or something like that, a unique phrase will come to me on how to look at that, and so I write it down.

"That inspires me more than anything, just the turn of a phrase. When I read a poem that has a really unique phrase in it, I'll think, 'Oh, man, I wish I'd said that,' and I'll try to mimic that or use it in my own way."

Houghtaling decided to start her own press in response to a remark by her grandmother. "She was a really central focus in my life," Houghtaling remembers. "I just adored her. She liked my poems back when I was writing greeting card-type poems (because I didn't know anything about poetry). She said to me, 'One day you'll be famous, but I won't be around to see it.' That really bothered me, so I compiled a bunch of poems and created my own chapbook. And I thought, 'If I'm going to do this, I'm going to get the ISBN numbers and the whole nine yards.'" Houghtaling self-published the chapbook and dedicated it to her grandmother. "She thought it was just wonderful, and so did my mother," Houghtaling recalls with some amusement, "but basically it was a pretty horrible book." At that point Houghtaling had no further plans to self-publish.

Over ensuing years she founded the Northern Appalachian Writers Guild (NAWG) which later became affiliated with Pennwriters. Eventually Houghtaling volunteered to organize a writer's conference for the organization. One of the presenters, science fiction author Julia Ecklar, arrived with a hefty collection of workshop handouts. "I thought, 'This is the stuff beginning writers really need to know. This would be a great small book.'" Ecklar agreed but said she couldn't get a publisher interested. Houghtaling responded, "'I have a whole bunch of ISBNs, why don't I publish this for you?' At that point H&H Press really took off and I became a serious publishing house and published other people." The stack of handouts became *Getting There from Here: Basics for Beginning Writers*.

A similar experience lead to the publication of *Fishing Underground: A Poet's Guide to Creating, Publishing, and Beyond*, by Elaine Preston. "It's a wonderful book for a beginning poet," says Houghtaling. "It really helps unlock the chains of rhyme. The one thing I learned about beginning poets (including when I was one myself) is their main exposure to poetry has been the rhymed forms they learned in school. Curses to all English teachers who think that poetry *must* rhyme!"

Houghtaling admits she found unrhymed poetry hard to understand in the beginning, too. "Once I got used to it and started reading other poets and free verse, I started being able to recognize what was good. If beginning poets attempt to write rhyme, they're often doomed because they really don't understand. It's not just 'moon/June/spoon.'"

In 1998 Houghtaling ventured even deeper into the publishing world by starting the journal *miller's pond*. "I like to read poetry, but much of what I find in 'prestigious publications' is not what I would call 'accessible' poetry," Houghtaling explains. "Those poems have obscure elements or are so esoteric, I have a hard time understanding what the poet is trying to say. I read poetry for enjoyment, and when I come across a poem that is too 'out there,' I don't enjoy it as much. So I envisioned putting together a small poetry magazine myself where I could publish poetry I like and understand, and maybe other people would like it, too."

Houghtaling also established the Loella Cady Lamphier Prize for Poetry, named for her beloved grandmother, who died in 1999 at age 86. "She supported me so much," says Houghtaling. "She was there backing me with emotional support, and sometimes when I needed financial support, she would be there for me, too. This is a way I can hold her memory and let other people know about her. The contest focus is 'to honor a mentor or loved one.' She was both to me. She always called herself 'stupid'—no high school, a hard, typical blue collar life back in the '30s and '40s—but she was wise in so many ways."

H&H Press publishes by invitation only, and Houghtaling states this in her guidelines and market listing. Yet, she says, poets still insist on querying her about publishing their manuscripts. "If they want to see their poetry published by H&H Press, they need to *read* the books and magazines published by H&H Press," she stresses, "read the guidelines, and submit appropriate work to *miller's pond* first for consideration." Her advice applies to all magazines and publishers, and it's advice that poets everywhere should heed.

Since Houghtaling started out by self-publishing, what are her views on the subject? "I'd recommend the traditional route first, that poets actually have some of their poetry published in other magazines before they even think about putting together a chapbook of their own work," she says. "If they've never been published, submitted and only gotten rejected, that should tell them they really need to concentrate on getting their poetry critiqued and work-shopped. Never think that a poem is carved in stone. Be open to suggested changes."

Once poets have garnered 10-20 publishing credits and want to assemble those poems into a chapbook, Houghtaling says, they first should look for realistic publishing opportunities, such as chapbook competitions sponsored by "very small, obscure presses."

Houghtaling points out, though, that it definitely would be more cost effective to self-publish than go through a subsidy publisher. Even then, she says, "hire people who know what they're doing to critique your work before taking it to the printer. Even poetry can have grammatical errors; nothing is 100% poetic license just because it's a poem. If you don't know what you're doing in that respect, get someone who does. Spend your money that way instead of going through a subsidy house that's going to patronize you and tell you things for the sake of saying what they think you want to hear."

Because of her newspaper experience, Houghtaling was already familiar with the production process before she started her own publishing activities. She describes H&H Press as a "micro-press," which she defines as "a one-person operation." The work is overwhelming at times and the profit margin is small, but Houghtaling cites the satisfaction of total control and the fulfillment of helping those invited writers she publishes to realize their dreams.

"I do manage to break even with the chapbooks," she says. "I love to publish those. When a book comes out, the author is so thrilled. I love to see that. It makes me feel like Santa Claus. 'Here, here's my gift to you.' " Houghtaling chuckles ruefully. "Although it's not really a gift, because we both worked our butts off. The poet is very deserving of the book, though, and I feel really proud to be a part of that process, to make that book a reality."

—Nancy Breen

poem/poetry must speak to me on more than one level and stay with me for more than just those few brief moments I'm reading it." Responds in 4 months. Pays royalties of 7% minimum, 12% maximum and 25 author's copies (out of a press run of 200). Books are available for sale via website, phone, or fax.
Advice: "Believe in yourself. Perseverance is a writer's best 'tool.' Study the contemporary masters: Billy Collins, Maxine Kumin, Colette Inez, Hayden Carruth. Please check our website before submitting."

JOHN MILTON MAGAZINE; DISCOVERY MAGAZINE (Specialized: children/teen, religious, visual impairment), John Milton Society for the Blind, 475 Riverside Dr., Room 455, New York NY 10115. (212)870-3335. Fax: (212)870-3229. E-mail: order@jmsblind.org. Website: www.jmsblind.org (includes writer's guidelines, publications brochure, history of society, staff names, board of directors' names). Established 1928. **Executive Director:** Darcy Quigley.
Magazine Needs: *John Milton Magazine* is "a quarterly digest of more than 50 Christian periodicals, produced in large print (20 point) and sent free to visually impaired adults." The executive director says *John Milton Magazine* is 24 pages, tabloid-sized, contains clip art. Receives about 30 poems/year, accepts about 5%. Press run is 5,188 for 3,776 subscribers. Subscription is free.
Magazine Needs: *Discovery* is "a quarterly Braille magazine for blind youth (ages 8-18). Articles selected and reprinted from over 20 Christian and secular periodicals for youth." Accepts poetry written by children. The executive director says *Discovery* is 44 Braille pages. Receives about 30 poems/year, accepts 15%. Press run is 2,041 for 1,878 subscribers. Subscription is free (only available in Braille).
How to Submit: For both publications, wants "Christian themes and holidays (not exclusive), seasonal poems, subjects of interest and encouragement to blind and visually impaired persons." Submit up to 5 poems at a time. Line length for poetry is 5 minimum, 30 maximum. Accepts previously published poems and simultaneous submissions. Accepts e-mail (include in body of message) and disk submissions. Cover

letter preferred. "Please enclose a SASE with regular mail submissions." Time between acceptance and publication is up to 1 year. Seldom comments on rejected poems. Publishes theme issues. Guidelines available for SASE. Responds in 3 months. *John Milton Magazine* pays 1-3 copies. *Discovery* pays 1 Braille copy. Acquires one-time or reprint rights.
Advice: "Review list of magazines we typically reprint from (available with writer's guidelines). The bulk of our material is reprinted from other periodicals."

MIND PURGE, 6001 Skillman St., Apt. #163, Dallas TX 75231. E-mail: mind_purge@yahoo.com. Established 1994. **Editor:** Jason Hensel.
Magazine Needs: *Mind Purge* is a biannual literary and art magazine appearing in April and October that publishes poetry, short fiction, one-act plays, short screenplays, essays, book reviews, and art. Wants poetry that is "well-crafted, insightful, imagistic. No specifications as to form, length, subject matter, or style. However no greeting card verse, hackneyed themes or poetry that says nothing or goes nowhere." Has published poetry by Lyn Lifshin, Robert Cooperman, Wayne Hogan, B.Z. Niditch, and Ryan G. Van Cleave. As a sample the editors selected these lines from "The Last Days Of" by Holly Day:

> Harvest. Cultivation. The words fall alien and pleasing/from our lips, songs of summers past/of a
> people long since dead. Practice. The round gearshift cupped/smooth in your confused palm. The wide
> flat pedals creak/with rust beneath your sandaled feet. Someday/the machines will work again./
> Someday, it will rain.

Mind Purge is 36-52 pages, 5½×8½, neatly printed and saddle-stapled with matte card stock cover with b&w or color photo. Receives about 100 poems/year, accepts 10%. Press run is 100 for 10 subscribers. Subscription: $10. Sample: $4. Make checks payable to Jason Hensel.
How to Submit: Submit up to 5 poems or 10 pages at a time, name and address on each page. No previously published poems or simultaneous submissions. Accepts e-mail submissions (in body of message). Cover letter preferred. Seldom comments on rejected poems. Responds within 3 months. Pays 1 contributor's copy. Reviews books of poetry in 200 words, single book format. Poets may send books for review consideration.
Advice: "Read, read, read everything!"

THE MINNESOTA REVIEW: A JOURNAL OF COMMITTED WRITING (Specialized: political, social issues), English Dept., University of Missouri-Columbia, 110 Tate Hall, Columbia MO 65211. Fax: (573)882-5785. E-mail: WilliamsJeff@missouri.edu. Established 1960. **Editor:** Jeffrey Williams.
Magazine Needs: *The Minnesota Review* is a biannual literary magazine wanting "poetry which explores some aspect of social or political issues and/or the nature of relationships. No nature poems, and no lyric poetry without the above focus." Has published poetry by Hollander and Fuentes Lemus. *The Minnesota Review* is about 200 pages, digest-sized, flat-spined, with b&w glossy card cover and art. Press run is 1,500 for 800 subscribers. Subscription: $20 to individuals, $36 to institutions. Sample: $10.
How to Submit: Address submissions to "Poetry Editor" (not to a specific editor). No fax or e-mail submissions. Cover letter including "brief intro with address" preferred. SASE with sufficient postage required for return of mss. Publishes theme issues. Upcoming themes available for SASE. Responds in up to 4 months. Pays 2 contributor's copies. Acquires all rights. Returns rights upon request. Reviews books of poetry in single or multi-book format.

MINORITY LITERARY EXPO (Specialized: membership, minorities), 317 Third Ave. SW, Apt. 2E, Birmingham AL 35211. (205)297-9816. E-mail: kervin066@aol.com. Established 1990. **Editor/Publisher:** Kervin Fondren.
Magazine Needs & How to Submit: *Minority Literary Expo* is an annual literary professional publication featuring minority poets, novices and professionals. "Organization membership open to all minority poets nationally. I want poems from minority poets that are holistic and wholesome, less than 24 lines each, no vulgar or hate poetry accepted, any style, any form, any subject matter. Poetry that expresses holistic views and philosophies is very acceptable. Literary value is emphasized. Selected poets receive financial awards, certificates, honorable mentions, critiques and special poetic honors." Accepts poetry concerning ethnic minorities, homosexual/bisexual, students, women/feminism. No fee is charged for inclusion. Accepts poetry written by children ages 12 and up. As a sample the editor selected his poem "It's Lonely at the Top":

> No Man Can/Reach the Top of the Mountain/With Hate, Greed and Despair.//Because in Reaching the
> Top/He Soon Will Find Out that/he is the only one There.

Single copy: $21. Guidelines and upcoming themes available for SASE or by e-mail. Pays 1 contributor's copy. Accepts submissions on disk and by postal mail.

Also Offers: Also sponsors an annual poetry chapbook contest and an annual "Analyze the Poem" contest. Details available for SASE.
Advice: "We seek novices and unpublished poets to breathe the new life every poetry organization needs."

N $ ◎ THE MIRACULOUS MEDAL (Specialized: religious), 475 E. Chelten Ave., Philadelphia PA 19144-5785. (215)848-1010. Established 1928. **Editor:** Rev. William J. O'Brien, C.M.
Magazine Needs: *Miraculous Medal* is a religious quarterly. "Poetry should reflect solid Catholic doctrine and experience. Any subject matter is acceptable, provided it does not contradict the teachings of the Roman Catholic Church. Poetry must have a religious theme, preferably about the Blessed Virgin Mary." Has published poetry by Gladys McKee. *Miraculous Medal* is 32 pages, digest-sized, saddle-stapled, 2-color inside and cover, no ads. *Miraculous Medal* is used as a promotional piece and is sent to all clients of the Central Association of the Miraculous Medal. Circulation is 250,000.
How to Submit: Sample and guidelines free for postage. Line length for poetry is 20 maximum, double-spaced. No simultaneous submissions or previously published poems. Responds in up to 3 years. Pays 50¢ and up/line, on acceptance. Acquires first North American rights.

$ ◎ THE MISSING FEZ; THE RED FELT AWARD, P.O. Box 57310, Tucson AZ 85711. E-mail: missingfez@hotmail.com. Website: www.missingfez.com (includes guidelines, sample work, contest information, and a list of book and chapbook publications). Established 1999. **Poetry Editor:** Alan Brich.
Magazine Needs: Appearing in January and July, *The Missing Fez* is "a forum for the abnormal in literature. We want poems that embody some form of strangeness or oddity in either style, content, or language. Give us something different. No poems that rhyme or are about pets, or would meet parental approval." Has published poetry by Matthew Scrivner, Elise Mandernack, Ruby Jetts, Jefferson Carter, and Ian Gill. As a sample the editor selected these lines from "Mail to a Blind Man" by Michael Blackwell:
> I sit on a lamppost./Invisible tears rain down/around me and shatter like/a million broken mandalas/
> on the pavement.
The Missing Fez is 100 pages, 5½×8½, photocopied on laser quality paper and perfect-bound, includes b&w photos and illustrations. Receives about 150 poems/year, accepts 15%. Publish 3-5 poems/issue. Press run is 1,000 for 800 subscribers, 600 shelf sales; 100 distributed free to sponsored reading series. Single copy: $10; subscription: $15/year. Sample: $5. Make checks payable to Red Felt Publishing.
How to Submit: Submit 3-5 poems at a time with **$3 reading fee**. Accepts previously published poems and simultaneous submissions. No fax or e-mail submissions. Cover letter preferred. "We do require $3 reading fee and SASE since we comment on all submissions and pay on acceptance." Time between acceptance and publication is 3-6 months. Always comments on rejected poems. Occasionally publishes theme issues. Guidelines and a list of upcoming themes available for SASE or on website. Responds in 6 weeks. Pays $15 for 2-3 poems plus 2 copies. Acquires one-time rights.
Also Offers: Sponsors the annual Red Felt Award. 1st Prize winner receives $250. Complete guidelines available for SASE or on website.
Advice: "Don't write safe poetry—if you do, don't send it to us."

◎ MISSISSIPPI REVIEW, University of Southern Mississippi, Box 5144, Hattiesburg MS 39406-5144. (601)266-4321. Fax: (601)266-5757. E-mail: fb@netdoor.com. Website: www.mississippireview.com. **Editor:** Frederick Barthelme. **Managing Editor:** Rie Fortenberry.
Magazine Needs & How to Submit: Literary publication for those interested in contemporary literature. Poems differ in style, length and form, but all have craft in common (along with intriguing content). Sample: $8. Query first, via mail, e-mail, or their website. Does not read manuscripts in summer. Pays 3 contributor's copies. Sponsors contests. Guidelines available for SASE.

N $ ◎ MISSOURI REVIEW; TOM MCAFEE DISCOVERY FEATURE; LARRY LEVIS EDITORS' PRIZE IN POETRY, 1507 Hillcrest Hall, University of Missouri, Columbia MO 65211. (573)882-4474. E-mail: marta@moreview.org. Website: www.moreview.org (includes guidelines, contact and subscription information, archives, contest rules, links, editorial policy, catalog, staff photos, poetry, interviews, and discussion forum). Established 1978. **Contact:** Poetry Editor.
Magazine Needs: *Missouri Review* appears 3 times/year, publishing poetry features only—6-14 pages for each of 3 to 5 poets/issue. "By devoting more editorial space to each poet, *Missouri Review* provides a fuller look at the work of some of the best writers composing today." Has published poetry by Quan Barry, Anna Meek, Timothy Liu, Bob Hicok, George Bilgere, and Camille Dungy. As a sample the editor selected these lines from "Sheep Fair Day" by Kerry Hardie:
> I let God sip tea, boiling hot, from a cup,/and I lent God my fingers to feel how they burned/when I
> tripped on a stone and it slopped./"This is pain," I said, "there'll be more."

Subscription: $22. Sample: $8.

How to Submit: Submit 6-12 poems at a time. No previously published poems or simultaneous submissions. Include SASE. Reads submissions year round. Responds in up to 3 months. Sometimes sends prepublication galleys. Pays 3 copies and $25/page, $200 maximum. Acquires all rights. Returns rights "after publication, without charge, at the request of the authors." Staff reviews books of poetry.

Also Offers: Offers the Tom McAfee Discovery Feature at least once a year to showcase an outstanding young poet who has not yet published a book; poets are selected from regular submissions at the discretion of the editors. Also offers the Larry Levis Editors' Prize in Poetry. 1st Prize: $2,000; and publication. Three finalists receive a minimum of $100, or consideration for publication at regular rates. Enter any number of poems up to 10 pages. Guidelines available for SASE or on website. Entry fee: $15.

Advice: "We remain dedicated to publishing at least one younger or emerging poet in every issue."

◑ MÖBIUS, P.O. Box 7544, Talleyville DE 19803-0544. E-mail: mobiusmag@aol.com. Website: www.mobiuspoetry.com (includes guidelines, contact and subscription information, and links). Established 1982. **Editor:** Jean Hull Herman.

Magazine Needs: Going into its 15th consecutive year, *Möbius* is published twice/year, on Memorial Day and Thanksgiving. Looks for "the informed mind responding to the challenges of reality and the expression of the imagination in poetry that demonstrates intelligence and wit. Poets should say significant, passionate things about the larger world outside themselves, using all the resources of the English language. Preference is given to poetry that pleases the ear as well as the intellect and soul; strong preference is given to work that is fine, structured, layered, as opposed to untitled, unpunctuated jottings. General topics include usage of language and the forms of poetry; the great philosophical questions; romance; relationships; war/peace; science and technology; everyday life; and humor (the editor has a weakness for humorous lines). The magazine claims no rights to poems. Delaware's only poetry magazine, Möbius has published poetry not only from 50 states but also from all seven continents." Has published poetry by David Summers, John Horvath, Phillip Memmer, Dan Weeks, Esther Cameron, and Dessa Crawford. As a sample the editor selected these lines from "Wrong Planet" by Ward Kelly:

> *I sometimes think we're on the wrong/planet; this one doesn't appear to have/our best interests at heart.*

Möbius is 60-70 pages, magazine-sized, professionally printed and perfect-bound. Single copy: $10; subscription: $16/year (2 issues). Sample: $10.

How to Submit: Submit up to 4 poems at a time, typed with name and address on each poem, 1 submission/issue. Simultaneous submissions accepted. No electronic submissions. Submissions read year-round. Responds in 3 months. Comments on rejected poems. Pays 1 contributor's copy. Guidelines available for SASE, on website, and in publication.

Advice: "Fine poetry will be as strong on the printed page as it will if being read aloud. We want literature, good poetry, fine writing."

◪ $◯ ◎ MODERN HAIKU; FOUR HIGH SCHOOL SENIOR SCHOLARSHIPS (Specialized: translations; form, haiku/senryu/haibun), P.O. Box 1752, Madison WI 53701-1752. (608)233-2738. Established 1969. **Poetry Editor:** Robert Spiess.

• In 2000, the editor received a Masaoka Shiki International Haiku Prize in Japan for his "Outstanding Literary Endeavor and Achievement."

Magazine Needs: *Modern Haiku* appears 3 times/year in February, June, and October and "is the foremost international journal of English language haiku and criticism. We are devoted to publishing only the very best haiku being written and also publish articles on haiku and have the most complete review section of haiku books. Issues average 124 pages." Wants "contemporary haiku in English (including translations into English) that incorporate the traditional aesthetics of the haiku genre, but which may be innovative as to subject matter, mode of approach or angle of perception, and form of expression. Haiku, senryu, and haibun only. No tanka or other forms." Accepts poetry written by children. Has published haiku by Cor van den Heuvel, George Swede, and Carol Purington. As a sample the editor included this piece by Craig Barcal:

> *Winter night & the/son of man has no dogma/to fill his head*

The digest-sized magazine appears 3 times/year, printed on heavy quality stock with cover illustrations especially painted for each issue by the staff artist. Receives about 12,000-14,000 submissions/year, accepts about 800. There are over 260 poems in each issue. Press run is 775. Subscription: $20. Sample: $6.65.

How to Submit: Submit on "any size sheets, any number of haiku on a sheet; but name and address on each sheet." Include SASE. No previously published haiku or simultaneous submissions. Guidelines available for SASE. Responds in 2 weeks. Pays $1/haiku (but no contributor's copy). Acquires first North American serial rights. Staff reviews books of haiku in 350-1,000 words, single book format. Send books for review consideration.

Also Offers: Offers 4 annual scholarships for the best haiku by high school seniors. Scholarships range from $200-500 (total $1,400). Deadline is mid-March. Rules available for SASE. Also offers $200 Best of Issue Awards.

Advice: "Study what haiku really are. We do not want sentimentality, pretty-pretty, or pseudo-Japanese themes. Juxtaposition of seemingly disparate entities that nonetheless create harmony is very desirable."

⊕ $ ⌀ ◎ MODERN POETRY IN TRANSLATION (Specialized: translations), King's College London, Strand, London WC2 R2LS United Kingdom. (0)207842-2360. Fax: (0)207848-2415. Website: www.kcl.ac.uk/mpt/ (includes contents of all issues from *Modern Poetry in Translation* (1992) onwards plus subscription forms). Established 1965 (original series), 1992 (new series). **Advisory and Managing Editor:** Professor Norma Rinsler. **Editor:** Daniel Weissbort.

Magazine Needs: *Modern Poetry in Translation*, published biannually, features "translations of poems from any language into English, and essays on translation (practice rather than theory). Our aim is to further international cultural understanding and exchange and to awaken interest in poetry." Wants "only translations from any language into English—'modern' refers to translation (which should be unpublished), not to original." Does not want "self-translation by those not familiar with English; work by poets or translators who are not not familiar with a range of works in the original language rarely succeeds (unless they work with original authors)." *Modern Poetry in Translation* averages 240 pages, 5⅝ × 8½, offset-printed, perfect-bound with illustrated 2-color cover on scanchip board, matte laminated. Accept approximately 50% of the poems they receive. Press run is 500 for 350 subscribers of which 50% are libraries, 50 shelf sales. Single copy: £10 (UK/EU); £12 (foreign). Subscriptions (2 issues): £20 (UK/EU); £24 (foreign), inc. surface mail (airmail extra). Sample: £7.50. Make checks payable to King's College London (*Modern Poetry in Translation*).

How to Submit: Submit 5-6 poems at a time "unless very long, in which case 1 or 2". Disk submissions (in Word) preferred. Originals should accompany translation. No previously published poems or simultaneous submissions. Cover letter required. No fax submissions. Time between acceptance and publication is up to 9 months. The editor and managing/advisory editor discuss submissions and consult individual members of advisory board if expertise required. Often comments on rejected poems. Publishes theme issues. Upcoming themes is available for SASE (or SAE with IRC). Responds "as soon as possible—within weeks." Sometimes sends prepublication galleys. Pays £12/poem or £15/page plus 1 copy to translator, 1 for original author. "Copyright on selection as printed—general rights remain with contributors." Features reviews of poetry books often commissioned from experts in the field. Poets may send books for review consideration (translations only).

◑ MOJO RISIN'; JOSH SAMUELS BIANNUAL POETRY COMPETITION, P.O. Box 268451, Chicago IL 60626-8451. Established 1995. **Editor:** Ms. Josh Samuels.

Magazine Needs: *mojo risin'*, published quarterly, features "poetry, prose, short stories, articles, and black & white artwork in each issue." Wants "any form or style." Does not want "incest, racism, blatant sex, or anything written for shock value." Has published poetry by Daniel Crocker, Lyn Lifshin, John Grey, and Harland Ristau. As a sample we selected these lines from "The Calling" by P.F. Potvin:

> Father lowered baby to blanket and reminded/the girl to wash and pray before eating/As mother and
> father strolled through the ash/the girl bobbed her brother in the river/calling after his stillness . . .
> Galileo, Galileo, Galileo

mojo risin' is 36 pages, 8½ × 11, photocopied, saddle-stapled with colored cardstock cover and b&w artwork. Receives about 500 poems/year, accepts 30%. Press run is 300 for 200 subscribers. Subscription: $20/year; $30/ 2 years. Sample: $7.

How to Submit: Subscription not required for acceptance. Submit 3-5 poems (2 pages maximum) at a time. No previously published poems or simultaneous submissions. Cover letter preferred. Time between acceptance and publication is up to 3 months. The editor is solely responsible for all aspects of editing and publishing. Guidelines available for SASE. Responds within 10 days. Manuscripts not returned. Acquires first North American serial rights.

Also Offers: Sponsors the Josh Samuels Biannual Poetry Competition. 1st Place: $100; 2nd Place: $75; 3rd Place $50. Entry fee: $10/5 poems maximum. Any form, style or subject. No previously published poems or simultaneous submissions. Mss not returned. Deadlines: May 31 and November 30. Submissions read March through May and September through November only. Winners published and paid in February and August. Guidelines available for SASE.

⊕ ◑ MONAS HIEROGLYPHICA, 58 Seymour Rd., Hadleigh, Benfleet, Essex SS7 2HL United Kingdom. E-mail: monas_hieroglyphica@postmaster.co.uk. Website: www.geocities.com/terribleport/ (includes guidelines, contact information, archives, upcoming themes, editorial policy, and links to other sites). Established 1994. **Contact:** Mr. Jamie Spracklen.

Magazine Needs: *Monas Hieroglyphica* appears quarterly. Wants poetry concerning social issues, spirituality, the psychic/occult, and horror. No racist or sexist work. Accepts poetry written by children. Has published poetry by Sean Russell Friend and Steve Sneyd. As a sample Mr. Spracklen selected this poem, "The Passing of Life & Death," by S.R. Friend:

> Come, join the game of death;/My sweet black butterfly:/There is only cloud where/The fire should be,
> sun where/We should love the moon.

Monas Hieroglyphica is 30 pages, magazine-sized, photocopied and bound with paper cover, includes art/graphics and ads. Receives about 100 poems/year, accepts 25%. Press run is 500 for 400 subscribers. Single copy: £5; subscription: £20, English funds only please. Make checks payable to Jamie Spracklen.

How to Submit: Submit 3 poems at a time. Line length for poetry is 60 maximum. Accepts simultaneous submissions; no previously published poems. Accepts submissions by e-mail (as attachment), on disk, and by post. Cover letter required. "Poems must be typed on size A4 paper and in English." Time between acceptance and publication is 3 months. Seldom comments on rejected poems. Occasionally publishes theme issues. Upcoming themes and guidelines available on website and in publication. Responds in 2 weeks. Pays 1 copy. "Rights stay with author." Reviews books and chapbooks of poetry and other magazines in 20 words, multi-book format. Poets may send books for review consideration.

◐ **MOUNT OLIVE COLLEGE PRESS; MOUNT OLIVE REVIEW; LEE WITTE POETRY CONTEST**, 634 Henderson St., Mount Olive NC 28365. (919)658-2502. Established 1987 (*Mount Olive Review*), 1990 (Mount Olive College Press). **Editor:** Dr. Pepper Worthington.

Magazine Needs: *Mount Olive Review*, features "literary criticism, poetry, short stories, essays, and book reviews." Wants "modern poetry." *Mount Olive Review* is 7½×10. Receives about 2,000 poems/year, accepts 8%. Press run is 1,000. Single copy: $25. Make checks payable to Mount Olive College Press.

How to Submit: Submit 6 poems at a time. No previously published poems or simultaneous submissions. Cover letter preferred. Time between acceptance and publication varies. Poems are circulated to an editorial board. Seldom comments on rejected poems. Publishes theme issues. A list of upcoming themes and guidelines available for SASE. Responds in 3 months. Sometimes sends prepublication galleys. Acquires first rights. Reviews books and chapbooks of poetry and other magazines. Poets may send books for review consideration.

Book/Chapbook Needs & How to Submit: Mount Olive Press publishes 2 books/year and sponsors the Lee Witte Poetry Contest. Write to above address for guidelines. Books are usually 5½×8. Submit 12 sample poems. Responds to queries and mss in 3 months. Obtain sample books by writing to the above address.

⊘ ◎ **MOVING PARTS PRESS (Specialized: bilingual/foreign language, regional)**, 10699 Empire Grade, Santa Cruz CA 95060-9474. (831)427-2271. Fax: (831)458-2810. E-mail: frice@movingpartspr ess.com. Website: www.movingpartspress.com (includes guidelines, contact info, bios, archives, catalog, editorial policy, as well as a full history and description of Moving Parts Press). Established 1977. **Poetry Editor:** Felicia Rice. Does not accept unsolicited mss. Published *Codĕx Espangliensis: from Columbus to the Border Patrol* (1998) with performance texts by Buillermo Gómez-Peña and collage imagery by Enrique Chagoya.

▣ ◯ **MUDFISH; BOX TURTLE PRESS; MUDFISH POETRY PRIZE AWARD**, 184 Franklin St., New York NY 10013. (212)219-9278. Established 1983. **Editor:** Jill Hoffman.

Magazine Needs: *Mudfish*, published by Box Turtle Press, is an annual journal of poetry and art. Wants free verse with "energy, intensity, and originality of voice, mastery of style, the presence of passion." Has published poetry by Charles Simic, Jennifer Belle, Thomas Lux, Ronald Wardall, David Lawrence, and John Ashberry. As a sample the editor selected these lines from "Sea Cows" by Doug Dorph:

> The clogging strands of underwater flora,/great clots beneath the boat no machine can mow,/the
> wasting away of my penis each year as the thick/layers of blubber grow around my manatee waist,/
> marshmallowy, limper than simple non-tumescence,/floating like a lily bud in my underpants.

Press run is 1,200. Sample: $10 plus $2.50 shipping and handling.

How to Submit: Submit 4-6 poems at a time. No previously published poems or simultaneous submissions. Responds from "immediately to 3 months." Sends prepublication galleys. Pays 1 contributor's copy.

Also Offers: Sponsors the Mudfish Poetry Prize Award: $1,000. Submit up to 3 poems for $15, $2 for each additional poem. **Deadline:** varies. Guidelines available for SASE.

◐ **MUSE'S KISS LITERARY 'ZINE**, P.O. Box 703, Attn: L.S. Bush, Lenoir NC 28645. Fax: (208)247-4747. E-mail: museskiss@aol.com or museskiss@yahoo.com. Website: http://members.aol.com/museskiss (includes online issues, advertising information, other writing links, guidelines, and book and magazine reviews). Established 1998. **Editor:** Alex Reeves. **Publisher:** L.S. Bush. **Contact:** Anthony Scott.

Magazine Needs: *"Muse's Kiss* is a free quarterly webzine. It contains experimental and traditional poetry and short stories. We will consider general fiction, science fiction, historical fiction, and mystery for short stories and anything except erotica or haiku for poetry. Prefers free verse. Please do not send love poems or 'Hallmark' verse." Accepts poetry written by children 12 and older. Has published poetry by Duane Locke, L.B. Sedlacek, Robert Klein Engler, Julie Callinicos, Janet Buck, Taylor Graham. As a sample the editor selected these lines from "Little Britches" by Taylor Graham:

> *Whoever thought she'd go so far/on cowboy dreams from east-slope/sagebrush campsite on Independence/weekend with 4×4s all circled/and the tents and barbecues/of smoking hotdogs, Papst Blue Ribbon . . .*

Receives about 600 poems/year, accepts about 59%. Sample: $3 (by mail, online version free). Make checks payable to L.S. Bush.

How to Submit: Submit 5 poems at a time via e-mail. Line length for poetry is 8 minimum, 60 maximum. No previously published poems. Cover letter with brief bio preferred. No fax submissions. "Poems must be typed in body of e-mail—no attachments. Use plain fonts, like Arial, and single space. If you prefer, you may submit offline by sending your poems and a cover letter. If you submit offline, there is a reading fee of $1 for up to 10 poems." Time between acceptance and publication is 3 months. Guidelines available for SASE, by blank e-mail to museskiss@sendfree.com, and on website. Responds in 3 months. Acquires one-time electronic rights. Payment is publication; small honorarium "of $2 when funds are available." Staff reviews chapbooks of poetry in 100 words, multi-book format. Send books for review consideration to L.S. Bush.

Advice: "When guidelines and issues are available online for free there is no excuse for a poet who does not take the time to follow the guidelines or check out issues to see what kind of material might be appropriate for submissions. Also, just because a publication is available online does not mean it is not a quality publication or one without operating expenses—please support these publications as you would offline ones."

THE MUSING PLACE (Specialized: poets with a history of mental illness), 2700 N. Lakeview, Chicago IL 60614. (773)281-3800, ext. 2465. Fax: (773)281-8790. E-mail: sford@thresholds.org. Website: http://thresholds.org. Established 1986. **Editor:** Shannon Ford.

Magazine Needs: *The Musing Place* is an annual magazine "written and published by people with a history of mental illness. All kinds and forms of poetry are welcome." *The Musing Place* is 32 pages, 8½×11, typeset, and stapled with art also produced by people with a history of mental illness. Receives about 300 poems/year, accepts about 40. Press run is 1,000. Single copy: $3.

How to Submit: Accepts simultaneous submissions; no previously published poems. Accepts fax submissions. Cover letter required. "Poets must prove and explain their history of mental illness." Time between acceptance and publication is up to 1 year. "The board reviews submissions and chooses those that fit into each issue." Seldom comments on rejected poems. Responds within 6 months. Pays 1 copy.

MUUNA TAKEENA, Oritie 4C24, FIN-01200 Vantaa Finland. E-mail: palonen@mbnet.fi. Established 1987. **Editor:** Timo Palonen.

Magazine Needs: Appearing 2 times/year, *Muuna Takeena* publishes "reviews of underground books, zines, music, and videos. Poetry is used only to fill excess space. In every issue, I publish one or two poems that are near my hand. Also, I have now started to publish one or two poetry specials per year." Does not want to see experimental poems. As a sample we selected these lines from "From Armitage to Ovid" by Rob Morrow:

> *From Armitage to Ovid,/It's all been done before,/To go to the house/Of the one you love/And sleep at her front door.//From palace to the poorhouse,/Sometimes against the law,/From the super rich/To the common rag,/Classless while we snore.//From lunatic to lover,/For those we cannot keep,/We think about you/And dream about you/When we are lost in sleep.*

Muuna Takeena is about 30 pages, magazine-sized, photocopied and stapled, cover includes photo/drawing, also includes photos/drawings inside, some paid ads. Receives about 50 poems/year, accepts 2%. Press run is 400 for 40 subscribers. Sample: $3. "No checks."

**FOR EXPLANATIONS OF THESE SYMBOLS,
SEE THE INSIDE FRONT AND BACK COVERS OF THIS BOOK.**

How to Submit: Submit 3 poems at a time. Accepts simultaneous submissions; no previously published poems. Accepts e-mail submissions (in text box). Cover letter required. Time between acceptance and publication is 6 months. Pays 1 contributor's copy. Staff reviews books and chapbooks of poetry and other magazines in up to 100 words, single book format. Send books for review consideration.

Advice: "I read, if I like, it could be printed. If I do not like, I send forward to other zine makers."

$ □ ◎ MYSTERY TIME (Specialized: mystery, humor); RHYME TIME (Specialized: subscribers), P.O. Box 2907, Decatur IL 62524. *Mystery Time* and *Rhyme Time* established 1983. **Poetry Editor:** Linda Hutton.

Magazine Needs & How to Submit: *Mystery Time* is a semiannual containing 3-4 pages of humorous poems about mysteries and mystery writers in each issue. As a sample the editor selected the poem "The Butler of Course" by Stephen D. Rogers:

> *The butler is dead, plastic bag on his head/And a knife sticking out of his back./Two shots to the chest put digestion to rest/And the poison was easy to track./I still need to find why he felt disinclined/to believe that his life was worthwhile./I do wish he wrote a short suicide note,/So a copy could go in the file.*

Mystery Time is 44 pages, digest-sized, stapled with heavy stock cover. Receives up to 15 submissions/year, accepts 4-6. Press run is 100. Sample: $4. Submit 3 poems at a time, up to 16 lines, "typed in proper format with SASE." Accepts previously published poems. No fax or e-mail submissions. Does not read mss in December. Guidelines available for #10 SASE. Pays $5 on acceptance.

Magazine Needs & How to Submit: *Rhyme Time* is a quarterly newsletter publishing only the work of subscribers. No length limit or style restriction. Subscription: $24. Sample: $4. Cash prize of $10 awarded to the best poem in each issue. No fax or e-mail submissions.

Also Offers: Sponsors an annual poetry contest that awards a $25 cash prize for the best poem in any style or length. Submit typed poem with SASE. No entry fee; one entry/person. Deadline: November 1. (See separate listing for the Helen Vaughn Johnson Memorial Haiku Award in the Contests & Awards section.)

Advice: "Always send for guidelines before submitting."

N $ ◐ ◎ MYTHIC DELIRIUM (Specialized: science fiction, fantasy, horror, surreal, cross-genre), P.O. Box 13511, Roanoke VA 24034-3511. E-mail: mythicdelirium@dnapublications.com. Website: www.dnapublications.com/delirium/ (includes contents of current issues, contents of archives, guidelines). Established 1998. **Editor:** Mike Allen. Member: Science Fiction Poetry Association, Science Fiction & Fantasy Writers of America.

Magazine Needs: *Mythic Delirium* appears biannually as "a journal of speculative poetry for the new millennium. All forms considered. Must fit within the genres we consider, though we have published some mainstream verse." Does not want "forced rhyme, corny humor, jarringly gross sexual material, gratuitous obscenity, handwritten manuscripts." Recently published poetry by Ian Watson, Darrell Schweitzer, Laurel Winter, Amy Sterling Casil, and Wendy Rathbone. As a sample the editor selected these lines from "Reflections in a Fading *Mir*" by Ann K. Schwader:

> *Whatever we abandon gathers ghosts—/Pale dust of our ambitions, hopes & fears,/Fled out of fragile flesh to other hosts./Though doomed to suicide by thirteen years,/This worn new world will not flame out alone.*

Mythic Delirium is 32 pages, digest-sized, saddle-stapled, color cover art, with b&w interior, uses house ads. Receives about 300 poems/year, accepts about 25%. Publishes about 18 poems/issue. Press run is 150. Subscription: $9 (2 issues), $16 (4 issues). Sample: $5. Make checks payable to DNA Publications, P.O. Box 2988, Radford VA 24143-2988 (subscription address **only**).

How to Submit: No previously published poems or simultaneous submissions. No fax, e-mail, or disk submissions. Cover letter is preferred. Time between acceptance and publication is 9 months. Often comments on rejected poems. Guidelines available for SASE, by e-mail, or on website. Responds in 5 weeks. Pays $5 for poems up to 40 lines, $10 for poems over 40 lines, plus 1 contributor's copy. Acquires first North American serial rights.

Advice: "*Mythic Delirium* isn't easy to get into, but we publish newcomers in every issue. Show us how ambitious you can be, and don't give up."

N ◐ ◎ NADA PRESS; BIG SCREAM (Specialized: form/style), 2782 Dixie SW, Grandville MI 49418. (616)531-1442. E-mail: decope@yahoo.com. Established 1974. **Poetry Editor:** David Cope.

Magazine Needs: *Big Scream* appears annually in January or February and is "a brief anthology of unknown and established poets. We are promoting a continuation of objectivist tradition begun by Williams and Reznikoff. We want objectivist-based short works; some surrealism; basically short, tight work that shows clarity of perception and care in its making." Has published poetry by Antler, Richard Kostelanetz, Andy Clausen, Dianne DiPrima, Anne Waldman, and Jim Cohn. *Big Scream* is 50 pages, magazine-sized, xerograph on 60 lb. paper, side-stapled, "sent gratis to a select group of poets and editors." Receives "several hundred (not sure)" unsolicited submissions/year, use "very few." Press run is 100. Subscription to institutions: $6/year. Sample: $6.

How to Submit: Submit after March. Send 10 pages. No cover letter. "If poetry interests me, I will ask the proper questions of the poet." Accepts simultaneous submissions. Accepts submissions on disk (formatted in MS Word). Comments on rejected poems "if requested and ms warrants it." Responds in 1 month. Sometimes sends prepublication galleys. Pays 2 copies.

Advice: "Read Pound's essay, 'A Retrospect,' then Reznikoff and Williams; follow through the Beats and NY School, especially Denby & Berrigan, and you have our approach to writing well in hand. I expect to be publishing *Big Scream* regularly ten years from now, same basic format."

NANNY FANNY; FELICITY PRESS, 2524 Stockbridge Dr. #15, Indianapolis IN 46268-2670. E-mail: nightpoet@prodigy.net. Established 1998. **Editor:** Lou Hertz.

Magazine Needs: *Nanny Fanny* appears 3 times/year and "publishes accessible, high quality poetry. Some artwork wanted (b&w 5″ square for cover)." Wants "external, extroverted observations and character studies. Most poems published are free verse. Formal poetry discouraged. Prefer 30 lines or less. No internalized, self-pitying poetry. Nothing under 8 lines or over 30 unless exceptional. No pornography, extremes of violence or language. No political or overly religious poems." Accepts poetry written by children. Has published poetry by B.Z. Niditch, Diana Kwiatkowski, Rubin Lamar Thomas, and John Grey. As a sample the editor selected these lines from "At the Observatory" by Sally Molini:

> Through a window, the dome/glows in the pines like a fallen moon, this edge of the world so far from
> home/that troubles seem smaller,/as if distance were the answer.

Nanny Fanny is 36-40 pages, 5½×8½, laser-printed and side-stapled with colored 67 lb. cover, includes cover art and some b&w line drawings inside. Receives about 1,000 poems/year, accepts about 10%. Press run is 120 for 35 subscribers, 2 of which are libraries; 40 distributed free to contributors, etc. Subscription: $10/3 issues. Sample: $4. Make checks payable to Lou Hertz. "Query first about reviews."

How to Submit: Submit 3-8 poems at a time, 1 poem/page with name and address on each. Accepts previously published poems ("if writer gives credit for previous appearance"); no simultaneous submissions. No e-mail submissions. Accepts disk submissions. Cover letter with brief bio preferred. Time between acceptance and publication is up to 6 months. Usually comments on rejected poems. Guidelines available for SASE or by e-mail. Responds in up to 2 months. Sends prepublication galleys on request. Pays 1 contributor's copy. Acquires one-time rights.

Book/Chapbook Needs: Felicity Press is not currently open for submissions.

Advice: "I want good quality poetry that the average person will be able to understand and enjoy. Let's use poetic imagery to draw them in, not scare them away."

NASSAU REVIEW, English Dept., Nassau Community College, Garden City NY 11530-6793. (516)572-7792. Established 1964. **Contact:** editorial board.

Magazine Needs: *Nassau Review* is an annual "creative and research vehicle for Nassau College faculty and the faculty of other colleges." Wants "serious, intellectual poetry of any form or style. No light verse or satiric verse." Submissions from adults only. "No college students; graduate students acceptable. Want only poems of high quality." Has published poetry by Patti Tana, Dick Allen, Louis Phillips, David Heyen, Simon Perchik, and Mario Susko. *Nassau Review* is about 190 pages, digest-sized, flat-spined. Receives up to 1,700 poems/year, accepts about 20-25. Press run is 1,200 for about 1,200 subscribers of which 200 are libraries. Sample free.

How to Submit: Submit only 3 poems per yearly issue. No previously published poems or simultaneous submissions. SASE required for return of ms. Reads submissions November 1 through March 1 only. Responds in up to 4 months. Pays contributor's copies.

Also Offers: Sponsors a yearly contest with $200 poetry award. Deadline: March 31.

Advice: "Each year we are more and more overwhelmed by the number of poems submitted, but most are of an amateur quality."

$ THE NATION; "DISCOVERY"/THE NATION POETRY CONTEST, 33 Irving Place, New York NY 10003. Established 1865. **Poetry Editor:** Grace Schulman.

• Poetry published by *The Nation* has been included in the 2001 *Best American Poetry*.

Magazine Needs & How to Submit: *The Nation*'s only requirement for poetry is "excellence," which can be inferred from the list of poets they have published: Marianne Moore, Robert Lowell, W.S. Merwin, Maxine Kumin, Donald Justice, James Merrill, Richard Howard, May Swenson, Amy Clampitt, Edward Hirsch and Charles Simic. Pays $1/line, not to exceed 35 lines, plus 1 copy.

Also Offers: The magazine co-sponsors the Lenore Marshall Prize for Poetry which is an annual award of $10,000 for an outstanding book of poems published in the US in each year. For details, write to the Academy of American Poets, 584 Broadway, #1208, New York NY 10012. Also co-sponsors the "Discovery"/*The Nation* Poetry Contest ($300 each plus a reading at The Poetry Center, 1395 Lexington Ave., New York NY 10128. Deadline: mid-February. Guidelines available for SASE, on www.92ndsty.org, or by calling (212)415-5759.

☐ ◎ **NATIVE TONGUE; NATIVE TONGUE PRESS (Specialized: ethnic, African-American)**, P.O. Box 822, Eufaula AL 36072-0822. (334)616-7722. E-mail: ntp59@hotmail.com. Established 1998. **Submissions Editor:** Anthony Canada.

Magazine Needs: *Native Tongue* is published quarterly "to keep the voices and history of the black poet historic, and expand an audience for new black poets." Wants poetry "on or about the African-American experience. Open to all forms, subject matter, styles or purpose. Interested in poems which emphasize but are not limited to cultural issues, the exploration of self-esteem, and personal empowerment, and the exploration of the direction of African-American people. No submissions that do not deal with the African-American experience." As a sample the editor selected these lines from his poem "society's child":

> late nite lust on rooftops/society's child conceived/bewildered, beleagured/black bastard/preteen
> mother's screams/social service slaves/sing the welfare blues

Native Tongue is 7-10 pages, 8½×11 sheets, 3-column format, stapled. Receives about 150 poems/year, accepts about 85%. Press run is 200 for 55 subscribers, 45 shelf sales; 100 distributed free to the public, colleges, poetry groups. Subscription: $9. Sample: $2. Make checks payable to Anthony G. Canada.

How to Submit: Submit up to 5 poems at a time. Accepts previously published poems and simultaneous submissions. Accepts e-mail submissions; include text in body of message. Cover letter required. "In cover letter include basic poet information—name, address, occupation, experience, previous publishings, books, etc." SASE required for return of submitted poems. Time between acceptance and publication is 3 months. Poems are circulated to an editorial board. "Submissions reviewed by board; published pieces selected by committee." Often comments on rejected poems. Responds in 3 months. Pays 10 contributor's copies. Acquires one-time rights. Reviews books and chapbooks of poetry in 200 words, single book format. Poets may send books for review consideration.

Advice: "The aim and goal of this newsletter is to open up to a wider audience the poetic voices of our many talented brothers and sisters. The African-American community has always had a historic and rich poetic legacy. We at *Native Tongue* wish to continue and expand upon this great tradition of African-American poets. So brothers and sisters take pen to paper, and continue to make our history historic. Let your voices by heard!"

N ☐ NEBO: A LITERARY JOURNAL, English Dept., Arkansas Tech University, Russellville AR 72801-2222. (501)968-0256. Website: www.atu.edu/acad/schools/lfa/english/nebo.html. Established 1982. **Poetry Editor:** Michael Ritchie.

Magazine Needs: *Nebo* appears in May and December. Regarding poetry they say, "We accept all kinds, all styles, all subject matters and will publish a longer poem if it is outstanding. We are especially interested in formal poetry." Has published poetry by Jack Butler, Turner Cassity, Wyatt Prunty, Charles Martin, Julia Randall, and Brenda Hillman. *Nebo* is 50-70 pages, digest-sized, professionally printed on quality matte stock with matte card cover. Press run "varies." Sample: $6.

How to Submit: Submit 3-5 poems at a time. Accepts simultaneous submissions. "Please no offbeat colors." Cover letter with bio material and recent publications required. Do not submit mss between May 1 and August 15. Editor comments on rejected poems "if the work has merit but requires revision and resubmission; we do all we can to help." Responds at the end of November and February respectively. Pays 1 copy. Staff reviews books of poetry. Send books for review consideration.

N ◑ THE NEBRASKA REVIEW; THE NEBRASKA REVIEW AWARDS, Creative Writing Program, FA, University of Nebraska, Omaha NE 68182-0324. (402)554-3159. Fax: (402)554-3436. Established 1973. **Fiction and Managing Editor:** James Reed. **Poetry Editor:** Coreen Wees.

● Poetry published in *The Nebraska Review* has been included in the 2001 *Best American Poetry* and the 2002 *Pushcart Prize* anthology.

Magazine Needs: *The Nebraska Review* is a semiannual literary magazine publishing fiction and poetry with occasional essays. Wants "lyric poetry from 10-200 lines, preference being for under 100 lines. Subject matter is unimportant, as long as it has some. Poets should have mastered form, meaning poems should have form, not simply 'demonstrate' it." Doesn't want to see "concrete, inspirational, didactic, or merely political poetry." Has published poetry by Angela Ball, Virgil Suarez, James Reiss, and Katharine Whitcomb. As a sample the editors selected these lines from "Crickets" by Pamela Stewart:

In every small place the eye, toe, or caught breath turns,/crickets are singing. From that shin/just above the ground they fling an edge of sound/straight through what's left of wilderness./It swings out across the trees and yards,/up to the warm sills of September.

The Nebraska Review is 108 pages, 6×9, nicely printed and flat-spined with glossy card cover. It is a publication of the Writer's Workshop at the University of Nebraska at Omaha. Press run is 500 for 380 subscribers of which 85 are libraries. Single copy: $8; subscription: $15/year. Sample: $4.50.

How to Submit: Submit 4-6 poems at a time. "Clean typed copy strongly preferred." No fax submissions. Reads open submissions January 1 through April 30 only. Responds in 4 months. Time between acceptance and publication is up to 12 months. Pays 2 contributor's copies and 1-year subscription. Acquires first North American serial rights.

Also Offers: Submissions for The Nebraska Review Awards are read from September 1 through November 30 only. The Nebraska Review Awards of $500 each in poetry, creative nonfiction, and fiction are published in the spring issue. Entry fee: $15, includes discounted subscription. You can enter as many times as desired. Deadline: November 30.

Advice: "Your first allegiance is to the poem. Publishing will come in time, but it will always be less than you feel you deserve. Therefore, don't look to publication as a reward for writing well; it has no relationship."

Ø NEDGE, P.O. Box 2321, Providence RI 02906. Website: www.nedgemagazine.com (includes guidelines, contact info, catalog, and subscription information). Established 1994. **Editor:** Henry Gould.

Magazine Needs: *Nedge* is published by the Poetry Mission, a nonprofit arts organization. Includes poetry, fiction, reviews, and essays. Circulation is 300. Subscription: $12/2 issues. Sample: $6. Back issues available for $3.

How to Submit: Currently not accepting unsolicited submissions.

☐ Ø NERVE COWBOY; LIQUID PAPER PRESS, P.O. Box 4973, Austin TX 78765. Website: www.onr.com/user/jwhagins/nervecowboy.html. Established 1995. **Co-Editors:** Joseph Shields and Jerry Hagins.

Magazine Needs: *Nerve Cowboy* is a biannual literary journal featuring contemporary poetry, short fiction and b&w drawings. "Open to all forms, styles and subject matter preferring writing that speaks directly, and minimizes literary devices. We want to see poetry of experience and passion which can find that raw nerve and ride it." Has published poetry by Michael Estabrook, Jennifer Jackson, Wilma Elizabeth McDaniel, Dave Newman, and Mark Weber. As a sample the editors selected these lines from "Manual Transmission" by Heather Abner:

The most beautiful thing/I have seen recently/is a man driving a stick shift./Pale arm in the dark car,/blue highway of vein/running through muscle.

Nerve Cowboy is 64 pages, 7×8½, attractively printed and saddle-stapled with matte card cover with b&w cover art. Currently accepts 5-10% of the submissions received. Press run is 250 for 100 subscribers. Subscription: $16/4 issues. Sample: $5.

How to Submit: Submit 3-7 poems at a time, name on each page. Accepts previously published poems with notification; no simultaneous submissions. Informal cover letter with bio credits preferred. Seldom comments on rejected poems. Guidelines available for SASE. Responds in 2 months. Pays 1 copy. Acquires first or one-time rights.

Book/Chapbook Needs & How to Submit: Liquid Paper Press publishes 2-3 chapbooks/year but will not be accepting unsolicited chapbook mss in the foreseeable future. Only chapbook contest winners and solicited mss will be published in the next couple of years. For information on *Nerve Cowboy*'s annual chapbook contest, please send a SASE. Deadline is January 30 of each year. Entry fee: $10. Cash prizes and publication for 1st and 2nd place finishers. Chapbooks are 24-40 pages, 5½×8½, photocopied with some b&w artwork. Recent winners include Lori Jakiela, Ralph Dranow, Christopher Jones, and Belinda Subraman. Publications include *The Regulars* by Lori Jakiela; *Are You Just Getting Up?* by Joshua Bodwell; *Sunday Ritual* by Ralph Dranow; *Grappling* by Susanne R. Bowers; *The Back East Poems* by Gerald Locklin; and *Learning to Lie* by Albert Huffstickler. Send SASE for a complete list of available titles.

Ⓝ $Ø THE NEW CRITERION, The Foundation for Cultural Review, Inc., 850 Seventh Ave., New York NY 10019. **Poetry Editor:** Robert Richman.

Magazine Needs: *New Criterion* is a monthly (except July and August) review of ideas and the arts, which uses poetry of high literary quality. Has published poetry by Donald Justice, Andrew Hudgins, Elizabeth Spires, and Herbert Morris. It is 90 pages, 7×10, flat-spined. Poems here truly are open, with structured free verse and formal works. Sample: $4.75.

How to Submit: Cover letter required with submissions. Responds in 3 months. Pays $2.50/line ($75 minimum).

Advice: "To have an idea of who we are or what we stand for, poets should consult back issues."

N̂ ⦶ NEW DELTA REVIEW, English Dept., Louisiana State University, Baton Rouge LA 70803-5001. (225)578-4079. Fax: (225)578-4129. E-mail: new-delta@lsu.edu. Website: http://english.lsu.edu/journals.ndr. **Contact:** Poetry Editor.

Magazine Needs: Appearing biannually in January and May, *New Delta Review* "publishes works of quality, many of them by young writers who are building their reputations." Has published poetry by Paul Muldoon, Anne Carson, Rush Rankin, Roddy Lumsden, Stephen Dunn, and Susan Musgrove. *New Delta Review* appears twice/year, 90-120 pages, 6×9, flat-spined, typeset and printed on quality stock with matte card cover with art. Press run is 500 for 100 subscribers of which 20 are libraries; the rest are for shelf sales. Single copy: $7; subscription: $12. Back issue: $5. Make checks payable to *New Delta Review*.

How to Submit: Submit up to 5 poems "and specify on the outside of the envelope that you are submitting poetry." No previously published poems. Cover letter with author's name, address, phone number, and biographical information required. Include SASE for reply and return of work. Poetry editor sometimes comments on rejected poems, often suggesting possible revisions. Responds in 4 months. Pays 1 year subscription and discount on additional copies. Acquires first North American serial rights. Reviews books of poetry in no more than 1,000 words, single or multi-book format. Poets may also send books to poetry editor for review consideration.

Advice: "Make sure two things are present in your poems: do the heart work and attend to craft."

◼ $⦶ NEW ENGLAND REVIEW, Middlebury College, Middlebury VT 05753. (802)443-5075. Fax: (802)443-2088. E-mail: nereview@middlebury.edu. Website: www.middlebury.edu/~nereview/ (includes guidelines, editorial staff, sample poetry from current and recent issues, ordering information, and secure online ordering). Established 1978. **Editor:** Stephen Donadio.

● Work published in this review is frequently included in volumes of *The Best American Poetry.*

Magazine Needs: *New England Review* is a prestigious, nationally distributed literary quarterly, 180 pages, 7×10, flat-spined, elegant make-up and printing on heavy stock, glossy cover with art. Receives 3,000-4,000 poetry submissions/year, accepts about 70-80 poems/year; has a 3-6 month backlog between time of acceptance and publication. The editors urge poets to read a few copies of the magazine before submitting work. Has published poetry by Nick Flynn, Linda Gregerson, Marilyn Hacker, J.D. McClutchy, and Pimone Triplett. Subscription: $23. Sample: $7.

How to Submit: Submit up to 6 poems at a time. Address submissions to Poetry Editor. No previously published poems. "Brief cover letters are useful. All submissions by mail. Accepts questions by e-mail." Reads submissions September 1 through May 31 only. Response time is 12 weeks. Always sends prepublication galleys. Pays $10/page, $20 minimum, plus 2 contributor's copies. Also features essay-reviews. Send books for review consideration.

⦶ NEW ISSUES PRESS; NEW ISSUES PRESS POETRY SERIES; NEW ISSUES PRESS FIRST BOOK POETRY PRIZE; THE GREEN ROSE PRIZE IN POETRY FOR ESTABLISHED POETS, Dept. of English, Western Michigan University, Kalamazoo MI 49008-5331. (616)387-8185. Fax: (616)387-2562. E-mail: herbert.scott@wmich.edu. Website: www.wmich.edu/newissues. Established 1996. **Editor:** Herbert Scott.

Book/Chapbook Needs: New Issues Press First Book Prize publishes 3-6 first books of poetry per year, one through its annual New Issues Poetry Prize. Additional mss will be selected from those submitted to the competition for publication in the series. "A national judge selects the prize winner and recommends other manuscripts. The editors decide on the other books considering the judge's recommendation, but are not bound by it." Past judges include Chase Twichell, Philip Levine, C.D Wright, C.K. Williams, Campbell McGrath, and Marianne Boruch. Books are published on acid free paper in editions of 1,500.

How to Submit: Open to "poets writing in English who have not previously published a full-length collection of poems in an edition of 500 or more copies." Submit 48- to 72-page ms with 1-paragraph bio, publication credits (if any), and $15 entry fee. No e-mail or fax submissions. Reads submissions June 1 through November 30 only. Complete guidelines available for SASE. Winner will be notified the following April. Winner receives $1,000 plus publication of manuscript. "We offer 33⅓% discounts on our books to competition entrants."

Also Offers: New Issues Press also sponsors the Green Rose Prize in Poetry. Award is $1,000 and publication for a book of poems by an established poet who has published one or more full-length collections of poetry. Entry fee: $20/ms. Mss accepted May 1 through September 30. Winner announced in January. Winners include *Perfect Disappearance* by Martha Rhodes (2000); *When the Moon Knows You're*

Wandering by Ruth Ellen Kocher (2001); and Christopher Burskwon (2002). Other Green Rose poets include Michael Burkard, Maurice Kilwein Guevara, Mary Ann Samyn, Jim Daniels. Guidelines available for SASE or on website.

Advice: "Our belief is that there are more good poets writing than ever before. Our mission is to give some of the best of these a forum. Also, our books have been reviewed in *Publishers Weekly*, *Booklist*, and the *Library Journal* as well as being featured in the *Washington Post Book World* and the *New York Times Book Review* during 2000 and 2001. New Issues books are advertised in *Poets & Writers*, *APR*, *American Poet*, *The Bloomsbury Review*, etc. We publish 8-12 books of poems a year. New Issues Press is profiled in the May/June 2000 issue of *Poets & Writers*."

N **⬤** **◎** **THE NEW LAUREL REVIEW**, 828 Lesseps St., New Orleans LA 70117. (504)947-6001. Fax: (504)948-3834. Established 1971. **Editor:** Lee Meitzen Grue. **Poetry Editor:** Lenny Emmanuel.

Magazine Needs: *The New Laurel Review* "is an annual independent nonprofit literary magazine dedicated to fine art. Each issue contains poetry, translations, literary essays, reviews of small press books, and visual art." Wants "poetry with strong, accurate imagery. We have no particular preference in style. We try to be eclectic. We're looking for original work, without hackneyed phrases or tired thinking." Has published poetry by Jared Carter, Kalamu Ya Salaam, Melody Davis, Sue Walker, and Keith Cartwright. *The New Laurel Review* is 115 pages, 6×9, laser printed, original art on cover. Receives about 300 poems/year, accepts about 30. Circulation is 500. Single copy: $10 individuals, $12 institutions. Sample (back issue): $8.

How to Submit: Submit 3-5 poems with SASE and a short note with previous publications. No simultaneous submissions. Reads submissions September 1 through May 30 only. Time between acceptance and publication is 10 months. Guidelines available for SASE. Responds in 3 months. Pays contributor's copies. Acquires first rights. Reviews books of poetry in 1,000 words, single or multi-book format.

Advice: "Read our magazine before submitting poetry."

M **$⬤** **NEW LETTERS; NEW LETTERS LITERARY AWARD**, University of Missouri-Kansas City, Kansas City MO 64110. (816)235-1168. Fax: (816)235-2611. E-mail: newletters@umke.edu. Website: www.umkc.edu/newletters (includes guidelines, contact and subscription info, bios, and contest rules). Established 1934 as *University Review*, became *New Letters* in 1971. **Managing Editor:** Robert Stewart. **Editor:** James McKinley.

• Work published in *New Letters* appeared in the 2000 volume of *The Best American Poetry*.

Magazine Needs: *New Letters* "is dedicated to publishing the best short fiction, best contemporary poetry, literary articles, photography, and artwork by both established writers and new talents." Wants "contemporary writing of all types—free verse poetry preferred, short works are more likely to be accepted than very long ones." Has published poetry by Marilyn Hacker, Miller Williams, James Tate, Robin Becker, Amiri Baraka, and Tony Whedon. *New Letters* is 6×9, flat-spined, professionally printed quarterly, glossy 2-color cover with art, uses about 40-45 (of 120) pages of poetry in each issue. Press run is 2,500 with 1,800 subscriptions of which about 40% are libraries. Receives about 7,000 submissions/year, accepts less than 1%, has a 6-month backlog. Poems appear in a variety of styles exhibiting a high degree of craft and universality of theme (rare in many journals). Subscription: $17. Sample: $5.50.

How to Submit: Send no more than 6 poems at a time. No previously published poems or simultaneous submissions. Short cover letter preferred. "We strongly prefer original typescripts and we don't read between May 15 and October 15. No query needed." Upcoming themes and guidelines available for SASE, by e-mail, and on website. Responds in up to 10 weeks. Pays a small fee plus 2 copies. Occasionally James McKinley comments on rejected poems.

Also Offers: The New Letters Literary Award is given annually for a group of 3-6 poems. Entry guidelines available for SASE. Deadline: May 15. Also publishes occasional anthologies, selected and edited by McKinley.

Advice: "Write with originality and freshness in language, content, and style. Avoid clichés in imagery and subject."

⬤ **◎** **NEW NATIVE PRESS (Specialized: translations)**, P.O. Box 661, Cullowhee NC 28723. (828)293-9237. E-mail: newnativepress@hotmail.com. Established 1979. **Publisher:** Thomas Rain Crowe.

Book/Chapbook Needs: New Native Press has "selectively narrowed its range of contemporary 20th century literature to become an exclusive publisher of writers in marginalized and endangered languages. All books published are bilingual translations from original languages into English." Publishes on average 2 paperbacks/year. Recently published *Kenneth Patchen: Rebel Poet in America* by Larry Smith and Gaelic,

Welsh, Breton, Cornish, and Manx poets in an all-Celtic language anthology of contemporary poets from Scotland, Ireland, Wales, Brittany, Cornwall, and Isle of Man entitled *Writing The Wind: A Celtic Resurgence (The New Celtic Poetry)*. Books are sold by distributors in four foreign countries and in the US by library vendors and Small Press Distribution. Books are typically 80 pages, offset-printed and perfect-bound with glossy 120 lb. stock with professionally-designed color cover.

How to Submit: Not currently accepting submissions. For specialized translations only—authors should query first with 10 sample poems and cover letter with bio and publication credits. Accepts previously published poems and simultaneous submissions. Time between acceptance and publication is up to 12 months. Always comments on rejected poems. Responds in 2 weeks. Pays copies, "amount varies with author and title."

Advice: "We are still looking for work indicative of rare talent—unique and original voices using language experimentally and symbolically, if not subversively."

◑ ◎ NEW ORLEANS POETRY FORUM; GRIS-GRIS PRESS; DESIRE STREET (Specialized: membership), 257 Bonnabel Blvd., Metairie LA 70005-3738. Fax: (504)835-2005. E-mail: neworle anspoetryforum@yahoo.com. Poetry forum established 1971, press and magazine established 1994. **President:** Andrea S. Gereighty. **Editor:** Barbara Sahm Benjamin.

Magazine Needs: *Desire Street* is the quarterly electronic magazine of the New Orleans Poetry Forum. "The Forum, a non-profit entity, has as its chief purpose the development of poets and contemporary poetry in the New Orleans area. To this end, it conducts a weekly workshop in which original poems are presented and critiqued according to an established protocol which assures a non-judgmental and non-argumentative atmosphere. A second aim of the New Orleans Poetry Forum is to foster awareness and support for poetry in the New Orleans area through readings, publicity, and community activities. Promotion is emphasized in order to increase acceptance and support for contemporary poetry." Wants "modern poetry on any topic—1 page only. No rhyming verse; no porn, obscenity, or child molestation themes." Accepts poetry written by children over 8 years old. Has published poetry by Pinkie Gordon Lane, Ray Murphy, John Gery, Richard Katrovas, and Kalamu Ya Salaam. As a sample we selected these lines from "Bottled Mosaic" by Rebecca Morris:

> Swirls of turbulent blue/Depression spread across the canvas/Words travel around the edges/Never
> touching empty spaces//Shadows/Created by a single harsh stroke/Splashes of red/And anger enter the
> picture.//The color of whisky fills gaps/Blends the whole to a blur

Desire Street is 8-10 pages, desktop-published, downloaded photocopied and distributed, uses clip art. Receives about 550 poems/year, accepts 10%. Press run is 200 hard copies for 200 subscribers. Single copy: $3; subscription: $12/year. Sample (including guidelines): $5. Make checks payable to New Orleans Poetry Forum.

How to Submit: Submit 2 poems at a time, 10 poem limit/year. Line length for poetry is one 8½×11 page only. Accepts previously published poems; no simultaneous submissions. Accepts submissions by fax, by e-mail, and on disk (in ASCII or MS Dos text). Cover letter required. Membership in the New Orleans Poetry Forum is required before submitting work. Annual fee: $25, includes 4 issues of *Desire Street*, 52 3-hour workshops and 1 year's free critique of up to 10 poems. Time between acceptance and publication is up to 1 year. Poems are circulated to an editorial board. "First, poems are read by Andrea Gereighty. Then, poems are read by a board of five poets." Comments on rejected poems. Occasionally publishes theme issues. Upcoming themes and guidelines available for SASE, by fax, and in publication. Responds in 1 year. Pays 10 copies. Acquires one-time rights.

Also Offers: The Forum conducts weekly workshops on Wednesday nights at 257 Bonnabel Blvd. Also conducts workshops at schools and in prisons. Details available for SASE.

Advice: "Read *Desire Street* first. Take your work seriously. Send two 1-page original poems and bio. Be patient; we are all volunteers."

◙ NEW ORLEANS POETRY JOURNAL PRESS, 2131 General Pershing St., New Orleans LA 70115. (504)891-3458. Established 1956. **Publisher/Editor:** Maxine Cassin. **Co-Editor:** Charles de Gravelles.

Book/Chapbook Needs: "We prefer to publish relatively new and/or little-known poets of unusual promise or those inexplicably neglected." Does not want to see "cliché or doggerel, anything incomprehensible or too derivative, or workshop exercises. First-rate lyric poetry preferred (not necessarily in traditional forms)." Has published books by Vassar Miller, Everette Maddox, Charles Black, Malaika Favorite, Raeburn Miller, Martha McFerren, Ralph Adamo, and Charles de Gravelles.

How to Submit: This market is currently closed to all submissions.

Advice: "1) Read as much as possible! 2) Write only when you must, and 3) Don't rush into print! No poetry should be sent without querying first! Publishers are concerned about expenses unnecessarily incurred in mailing manuscripts. *Telephoning is not encouraged.*"

❧ ◢ **NEW ORPHIC REVIEW; NEW ORPHIC PUBLISHERS**, 706 Mill St., Nelson, British Columbia V1L 4S5 Canada. (250)354-0494. Fax: (250)352-0743. Established New Orphic Publishers (1995), New Orphic Review (1998). **Editor-in-Chief:** Ernest Hekkanen.

Magazine Needs: "Appearing 2 times/year, *New Orphic Review* is run by an opinionated visionary who is beholden to no one, least of all government agencies like the Canada Council or institutions of higher learning. He feels Canadian literature is stagnant, lacks daring, and is terribly incestuous." *New Orphic Review* publishes poetry, novel excerpts, mainstream and experimental short stories, and articles on a wide range of subjects. Each issue also contains a *Featured Poet* section. "*New Orphic Review* publishes authors from around the world as long as the pieces are written in English and are accompanied by an SASE with proper Canadian postage and/or US dollars to offset the cost of postage." Prefers "tight, well-wrought poetry over leggy, prosaic poetry. No 'fuck you' poetry; no rambling pseudo Beat poetry." Has published poetry by Catherine Owen, Steven Michael Berzensky (aka Mick Burrs), Robert Wayne Stedingh, John Pass, and Susan McCaslin. *New Orphic Review* is 120-140 pages, magazine-sized, laser printed and perfect-bound with color cover, includes art/graphics and ads. Receives about 400 poems/year, accepts about 10%. Press run is 500 for 250 subscribers of which 20 are libraries. Subscription: $25 (individual), $30 (institution). Sample: $15.

How to Submit: Submit 6 poems at a time. Line length for poetry is 5 minimum, 30 maximum. Accepts simultaneous submissions; no previously published poems. Cover letter preferred. "Make sure a SASE (or SAE and IRC) is included." Time between acceptance and publication is up to 8 months. Poems are circulated to an editorial board. The managing editor and associate editor refer work to the editor-in-chief. Seldom comments on rejected poems. Occasionally publishes theme issues. Guidelines available for SASE (or SAE and IRC). Responds in 2 months. Pays 1 contributor's copy. Acquires first North American serial rights.

Also Offers: New Orphic Publishers publishes 4 paperbacks/year. However, all material is solicited.

$◢ **THE NEW RENAISSANCE**, 26 Heath Rd. #11, Arlington MA 02474-3645. E-mail: wmichaud @gwi.net. Established 1968. **Editor-in-Chief:** Louise T. Reynolds. **Poetry Editor:** Frank Finale.

Magazine Needs: *the new renaissance* is "intended for the 'renaissance' person—the generalist, not the specialist. Publishes the best new writing and translations and offers a forum for articles on political, sociological topics; features established as well as emerging visual artists and writers, highlights reviews of small press, and offers essays on a variety of topics from visual arts and literature to science. Open to a variety of styles, including traditional." Has published poetry by Maria Mazziotti Gullan, Jay Griswold, Marvin Solomon, and Phillip Murray. As a sample the poetry editor selected these lines from "Works" by Stephen Todd Baker:

> To play the violin I'd have to drop this gun,/and then apply myself to it as if it had/Come upon me like
> some bejewelled aptitude/For fiddling around or from a higher, homespun/Air of cunning that deplores
> a pocket of gas,/Yet tunnels fluting to an ooze that is imbued/With traces of a baser class of dew or
> tears—

the new renaissance is 136-144 pages, 6×9, flat-spined, professionally printed on heavy stock, glossy, color cover, using 24-40 pages of poetry in each issue. Receives about 670 poetry submissions/year, accepts up to 40; has about a 1½- to 2-year backlog. Usual press run is 1,500 for 760 subscribers of which 132 are libraries. Subscriptions: $30/3 issues US, $35 Canada, $38 all others. All checks in US $. "A 3-issue subscription covers 18-22 months."

How to Submit: Submit 3-6 poems at a time, "unless a long poem—then one." Accepts simultaneous submissions, if notified; no previously published poems "unless magazine's circulation was under 250." Always include SASE or IRC. No e-mail submissions. "All poetry submissions are tied to our Awards Program for poetry published in a three-issue volume; judged by independent judges. Entry fee: $16.50 for nonsubscribers, $11.50 for subscribers, for which they choose to receive: two back issues or a recent issue or an extension of their subscription. Submissions without entry fee are *returned unread*." Guidelines available for SASE. Responds in 5 months. Pays $21-40, more for the occasional longer poem, plus 1 copy/poem. Acquires all rights but returns rights provided *the new renaissance* retains rights for any *the new renaissance* collection. Reviews books of poetry. The Awards Program gives 3 awards of $250, $125, and $60, with 3 Honorable Mentions of $25 each.

Advice: "Read, read, read! Write, write, write! Revise, revise, revise! A matter of vision is often a matter of revision. Subscribe to a variety of lit mags (or at least sample a couple of copies of each one you submit to)."

◎ **A NEW SONG; NEW SONG PRESS; NEW SONG CHAPBOOK COMPETITION (Specialized: religious, spirituality)**, P.O. Box 629, W.B.B., Dayton OH 45409-0629. E-mail: nsongpress@a ol.com. Website: www.NewSongPress.com (includes guidelines, samples, links, and subscription information). Established 1995. **Editor/Publisher:** Susan Jelus.

Magazine Needs: *A New Song* is published 2 times/year, in January and June, and "exhibits contemporary American poetry that speaks to endeavors of faith and enriches the spiritual lives of its readers. Includes poetry that takes a fresh approach and uses contemporary, natural language." Wants "free verse that addresses spiritual life through a wide range of topics and vivid imagery. No rhyming, sing-song, old-fashioned 'religious' poetry." Has published poetry by Claude Wilkinson, Janet McCann, Herbert W. Martin, and John Grey. As a sample the editor selected these lines from "Blue" by Joanna M. Weston:

> A hole in the sky/where heaven shines through/And blue. And blue./Blue the colour/of my true love's eyes,/blue the place/where my heart/is folded,/curled into safety,/seeing only the inside/of all that is:/ the wholly blue/of a prairie sky.

A New Song is 40-50 pages, 5½ × 8½, usually Docutech- or offset-printed, saddle-stapled, cardstock cover, photo or artwork on cover. Receives about 600 poems/year, accepts about 20%. Press run is 300 for 150 subscribers, 100 shelf sales; 50-75 distributed free to reviewers, bookstores, editors, professors, pastors. Single copy: $6.95; subscription: $12.95. Sample back issue: $5. Make checks payable to New Song Press.

How to Submit: Submit 3-5 poems at a time with short bio and SASE. Accepts simultaneous submissions; no previously published poems. Accepts e-mail submissions if included in body of message, "up to 3 poems only and must have a mailing address and bio." Also accepts disk submissions. Send SASE with regular mail submissions. Time between acceptance and publication is up to 18 months. Poems are circulated to an editorial board. Often comments on rejected poems. Occasionally publishes theme issues. Guidelines available for SASE, by e-mail, or on website. Responds in 3 months. Pays 1 copy. Acquires first North American serial rights. Sometimes reviews books of poetry in 750-1,000 words, single book format. Poets may send books for review consideration.

Book/Chapbook Needs & How to Submit: New Song Press's goals are "to help develop a genre of contemporary spiritual poetry." Publishes 1 chapbook per year. Has published *Remembered into Life* by Maureen Tolman Flannery. Chapbooks are usually 20-40 pages, 5½ × 8½, usually Docutech-printed, sometimes offset-printed color cover, saddle-stapled, cardstock cover, includes art/graphics. Query first, with a few sample poems and a cover letter with brief bio and publication credits. Responds to queries in 3 months; to mss in 6 months. Payment varies.

Also Offers: Sponsors chapbook contest every other year (odd-numbered years). Prize: $150 plus copies. Deadline: July 1st. Two runners-up also recognized. Entry fee for chapbook contest entries: $15, which includes a 1-year subscription to *A New Song*.

🌐 💲 📧 **THE NEW WRITER; THE NEW WRITER PROSE AND POETRY PRIZES**, P.O. Box 60, Cranbrook TN17 2ZR England. Phone: 01580 212626. Fax: 01580 212041. Website: www.thenewwriter .com. E-mail: admin@thenewwriter.com. Established 1996. **Poetry Editor:** Abi Hughes-Edwards.

Magazine Needs: Published 6 times/year, "*The New Writer* is the magazine you've been hoping to find. It's *different* and it's aimed at writers with a serious intent; who want to develop their writing to meet the high expectations of today's editors. The team at *The New Writer* are committed to working with their readers to increase the chances of publication. That's why masses of useful information and plenty of feedback is provided. More than that, we let you know about the current state of the market with the best in contemporary fiction and cutting-edge poetry backed up by searching articles and in-depth features in every issue. We are interested in short fiction, 2,000 words max.; subscribers' only; short and long unpublished poems, provided they are original and undeniably brilliant; articles that demonstrate a grasp of contemporary writing and current editorial/publishing policies; news of writers' circles, new publications, competitions, courses, workshops, etc." No "problems with length/form but anything over two pages (150 lines) needs to be brilliant. Cutting edge shouldn't mean inaccessible. No recent disasters—they date. No my baby/doggie poems; no God poems that sound like hymns, dum-dum rhymes, or comic rhymes (best left at the pub)." *New Writer* is 56 pages, A4, professionally printed and saddle-stapled with paper cover, includes clipart and b&w photos. Press run is 1,500 for 1,350 subscribers; 50 distributed free to publishers, agents. Single copy: £3.95; subscription: £33 in US. Sample: £3.95 or equivalent in IRCs. "Monthly e-mail newsletter now included free of charge in the subscription package."

How to Submit: Submit up to 6 poems at a time. Accepts previously published poems. Accepts e-mail submissions if included in body of message. Time between acceptance and publication is up to 6 months. Often comments on rejected poems. Offers criticism service: £12/6 poems. Guidelines available for SASE (or SAE with IRC) or on website. Pays £3 voucher plus 1 copy. Acquires first British serial rights. Reviews books and chapbooks of poetry and other magazines. Poets may send books for review consideration.

Also Offers: Sponsors the New Writer Prose & Poetry Prizes. An annual prize, "open to all poets writing in the English language, who are invited to submit an original, previously unpublished poem or collection of six to ten poems. Up to 25 prizes will be presented as well as publication for the prize-winning poets in an anthology plus the chance for a further 10 shortlisted poets to see their work published in *The New Writer* during the year." Write for contest rules.

$ ⊘ ⓞ NEW WRITER'S MAGAZINE (Specialized: humor, writing), P.O. Box 5976, Sarasota FL 34277-5976. (941)953-7903. E-mail: newriters@aol.com. Website: www.newriters.com. Established 1986. **Editor:** George S. Haborak.

Magazine Needs: *New Writer's Magazine* is a bimonthly magazine "for aspiring writers, and professional ones as well, to exchange ideas and working experiences." Open to free verse, light verse and traditional, 8-20 lines, reflecting upon the writing lifestyle. "Humorous slant on writing life especially welcomed." Does not want poems about "love, personal problems, abstract ideas or fantasy." *New Writer's Magazine* is 28 pages, 8½×11, offset printed, saddle-stapled, with glossy paper cover, b&w photos and ads. Receives about 300 poems/year, accepts 10%. Press run is 5,000. Subscription: $15/year, $25/2 years. Sample: $3.

How to Submit: Submit up to 3 poems at a time. No previously published poems or simultaneous submissions. No e-mail submissions. Time between acceptance and publication is up to 1 year. Guidelines available for SASE or by e-mail. Responds in 2 months. Pays $5/poem. Acquires first North American serial rights. Each issue of this magazine also includes an interview with a recognized author, articles on writing and the writing life, tips, and markets.

✪ $◖ THE NEW YORKER, 4 Times Square, New York NY 10036. E-mail: poetry@newyorker. com. Website: www.newyorker.com. Established 1925. **Contact:** Poetry Editor.

• Poems published in *The New Yorker* have been frequently included in volumes of *The Best American Poetry*.

Magazine Needs: *The New Yorker* appears weekly and publishes poetry of the highest quality (including translations). A recent edition featured poetry by Kathleen Jamie, Paul Muldoon, and Hugh Seidman. Subscription: $46/46 issues (one year), $76/92 issues (2 years).

How to Submit: Submit up to 6 poems at one time. "We prefer to receive no more than two submissions per writer per year, and generally cannot reply to more." No simultaneous submissions or previously published poems. Does not accept submissions by fax or by regular mail; send poems by e-mail only (in text box, no attachments). Mss are not read during the summer. Responds in up to 3 months. Pays top rates.

◖ NEW ZOO POETRY REVIEW; SUNKEN MEADOWS PRESS, P.O. Box 36760, Richmond VA 23235. Website: http://members.aol.com/newzoopoet. Established 1997. **Editor:** Angela Vogel.

Magazine Needs: *New Zoo Poetry Review* is published annually in January and "tends to publish free verse in well-crafted lyric and narrative forms. Our goal is to publish established poets alongside lesser-known poets of great promise. *New Zoo Poetry Review* wants serious, intellectual poetry of any form, length or style. Rhyming poetry only if exceptional. No light verse, song lyrics or greeting card copy. If you are not reading the best of contemporary poetry, then *New Zoo Poetry Review* is not for you." Has published poetry by Heather McHugh, Diane Glancy, D.C. Berry, and Martha Collins. As a sample the editor selected these lines from "Cityscape with pink rose" by Richard Bear:

> As he turns away, he sees in his mind's/eye, himself turning back to buy for her/one of her own roses,
> or bloom of her choice./Idiotic! Blooms she has, and no doubt/must throw away many; wouldn't she/
> be sick, by now, of flowers?/Trading, as she does, in these symbols/of the happiness of others, what
> would be/happiness to her, here, today?

New Zoo Poetry Review is 40 pages, digest-sized, photocopied and saddle-stapled with glossy card cover with b&w photography. Receives about 2,000 poems/year, accepts approximately 5%. Press run is 200. Subscription: $7 for 2 consecutive issues. Sample: $4.

How to Submit: Submit 3-5 poems at a time. Accepts simultaneous submissions; no previously published poems. Cover letter with brief bio required. Seldom comments on rejected poems. Responds in 2 months. Pays 1 contributor's copy. Acquires first North American serial rights. "Poets are discouraged from submitting more than once in a 12-month period. Please do not write to us for these submission guidelines."

◯ ⓞ NEWSLETTER INAGO (Specialized: free-verse), P.O. Box 26244, Tucson AZ 85726-6244. Established 1979. **Poetry Editor:** Del Reitz.

Magazine Needs: *Newsletter Inago* is a monthly newsletter-format poetry journal. "Free verse and short narrative poetry preferred. Rhymed poetry must be truly exceptional (nonforced) for consideration. Due to format, 'epic' and monothematic poetry will not be considered. Cause specific, political, or religious

---

OPENNESS TO SUBMISSIONS: ◯ beginners; ◖ beginners and experienced; ◖ mostly experienced, few beginners; ⓞ specialized; ⊘ closed to all submissions.

poetry stands little chance of consideration. A wide range of short poetry, showing the poet's preferably eclectic perspective is best for *Newsletter Inago*. No haiku, please." Has published poetry by Joshua M. Stewart, Carol Hamilton, Greg Watson, Ron Bailey, Jane Clarkson, and David Chorlton. As a sample the editor selected these lines from "Coyote Lullaby" by David Chorlton:

> *Clear the darkness from your throats/and close your eyes./Sleep in a cradle of rocks./The mountain holds you while you dream/about a country so dark/you see the universe.*

Newsletter Inago is 4-5 pages, corner-stapled. Press run is approximately 200 for subscriptions. No price is given for the newsletter, but the editor suggests a donation of $3.50 an issue or $17.50 annually ($3.50 and $21 Canada, £8 and £21 UK). Make checks payable to Del Reitz. Copyright is retained by authors.

How to Submit: Submit 10-15 poems at a time. "Poetry should be submitted in the format in which the poet wants it to appear, and cover letters are always a good idea." Accepts simultaneous submissions and previously published poems. Sometimes comments on rejected poems. Guidelines available for SASE. Responds ASAP (usually within 2 weeks). Pays in contributor copies.

N ◯ ◎ NIGHT SHADE GOTHIC POETRY (Specialized: horror; science fiction; gothic), P.O. Box 338, Slate Hill NY 10973-0338. Established 2001. **Editors:** Paul and Rhonda Jones.

Magazine Needs: *Night Shade Gothic Poetry* appears monthly to "provide a place where poets can see their work in print." Wants "gothic horror, Christian gothic, surreal, eerie science fiction. Anything strange, dark, and moody. All forms of poetry welcome." Does not want extreme violence, pornography; "no boring monologue poetry." Recently published poetry by Michael Patrick-Lanos, Jessica Henkle, Dawn Van Leuvan, Robert Holmes, and Jill Esposito. As a sample the editors selected these lines from "The Gate" by Jill Esposito:

> *Incantations fill the air/like clouds and cobwebs they appear./Specters dance like Satan's whores/while magic words will open doors./Green flies buzz on window glass/and wicked imps will echo chants.*

Night Shade Gothic Poetry is 10-20 pages, $9\frac{1}{2} \times 11$ newsletter format, computer-printed, stapled, b&w glossy cover, with b&w and some colored graphics, also ads for books, music, "anything gothic." Receives about 300 poems/year, accepts about 60%. Publishes about 35 poems/issue. Press run is 100 for 15 subscribers; 85 are distributed free to bookstores, coffee shops, and contributors. Single copy: $2; subscription: $15. Sample: $1.50. Make checks payable to Rhonda Jones.

How to Submit: Submit 5 poems at a time. Line length for poetry is 12 minimum, 15 maximum. Accepts previously published poems and simultaneous submissions. No fax, e-mail, or disk submissions. Cover letter is preferred. Include SASE. Reads submissions "yearly." Submit seasonal poems 3 months in advance. **Charges reading fee of $2 for every batch of poems.** Time between acceptance and publications is 6 months. "Editors review all submissions and choose the very best work(s) for publication. We seldom tamper with a published poet's work. We try to protect the integrity of the writer's voice and style." Seldom comments on rejected poems. Guidelines available for SASE. Responds in up to 6 months. Pays 1 contributor's copy. Acquires one-time rights.

Also Offers: Often chooses a Poet of the Month and awards a cash prize.

Advice: "We are a small but growing publication. We accept poems from beginners as well as well established writers. We try to give everyone a fair shot at publication. Know your craft and write from the heart, be yourself. Also, don't forget to use plenty of imagery when writing. Show, don't tell the reader."

▼ ⬚ NIMROD: INTERNATIONAL JOURNAL OF POETRY AND PROSE; RUTH G. HARDMAN AWARD; PABLO NERUDA PRIZE FOR POETRY, University of Tulsa, 600 S. College, Tulsa OK 74104-3189. (918)631-3080. Fax: (918)631-3033. E-mail: nimrod@utulsa.edu. Website: www.ut ulsa.edu/nimrod/ (includes guidelines, upcoming themes, contest rules, contact and subscription information, and writing samples). Established 1956. **Editor-in-Chief:** Francine Ringold. **Poetry Editor:** Manly Johnson.

● Poetry published in *Nimrod* has been included in *The Best American Poetry 1995*.

Magazine Needs: *Nimrod* "is an active 'little magazine,' part of the movement in American letters which has been essential to the development of modern literature. *Nimrod* publishes 2 issues/year, an awards issue in the fall featuring the prize winners of their national competition and a thematic issue each spring." Wants "vigorous writing that is neither wholly of the academy nor the streets, typed mss." Has published poetry by Diane Glancy, Judith Strasser, Steve Lautermilch, Reeves Kegworth, and Robin Chopman. *Nimrod* is 160 pages, 6×9, flat-spined, full-color glossy cover, professionally printed on coated stock with b&w photos and art, uses 50-90 pages of poetry in each issue. Poems in non-award issues range from formal to freestyle with several translations. Receives about 2,000 submissions/year, accepts 1%; has a 3- to 6-month backlog. Press run is 3,500 of which 200 are public and university libraries. Subscription: $17.50/year inside USA; $19 outside. Sample: $10. Specific back issues available.

How to Submit: Submit 5-10 poems at a time. No fax or e-mail submissions. Publishes theme issues. Guidelines and upcoming themes available for SASE, by e-mail, or on website. Responds in up to 12 weeks. Pays 2 contributor's copies plus reduced cost on additional copies. "Poets should be aware that during the months that the Ruth Hardman Awards Competition is being conducted, reporting time on non-contest manuscripts will be longer."

Also Offers: Send business-sized SASE for rules for the Ruth G. Hardman Award: Pablo Neruda Prize for Poetry ($2,000 and $1,000 prizes). Entries accepted January 1 through April 30 each year. The $20 entry fee includes 2 issues. Also sponsors the Nimrod/Hardman Awards Workshop, a 1-day workshop held annually in October. Cost is approximately $50. Send SASE for brochure and registration form.

N **96 INC MAGAZINE; 96 INC'S BRUCE P. ROSSLEY LITERARY AWARDS**, P.O. Box 15559, Boston MA 02215. (617)267-0543. Fax: (617)262-3568. Website: www.96inc.com (includes contact information, archives, and links). Established 1992. **Editors:** Julie Anderson, Vera Gold, and Nancy Mehegan.

Magazine Needs: *96 Inc* is an annual literary magazine appearing in July that focuses on new voices, "connecting the beginner to the established, a training center for the process of publication." Wants all forms and styles of poetry, though "shorter is better." Also accepts poetry written by teens. Has published poetry by Jennifer Barber, Peter Desmond, Dana Elder, Gary Duehr, Eugene Gloria, and Judy Katz-Levine. As a sample the editors selected this poem, "Haiku," by Peter Desmond:

> early April/buried receipts burst forth/deductions blossom

96 Inc is 38-50 pages, 8½×11, saddle-stapled with coated card cover and b&w photos and graphics. Receives around 2,000 submissions/year, accepts approximately 5%. Press run is 3,000 for 500 subscribers of which 50 are libraries, 1,500 shelf sales. Single copy: $5; subscription: $15. Sample: $7.50.

How to Submit: Accepts simultaneous submissions; no previously published poems. Time between acceptance and publication is 1 year or longer. Poems are circulated to an editorial board. Guidelines available for SASE. Responds in 6-12 months. Pays 4 copies, subscription, and modest fee (when funds are available). Copyright reverts to author 2 months after publication. Occasionally, staff reviews books of poetry. Send books for review consideration, attn: Andrew Dawson.

Also Offers: The *96 Inc's* Bruce P. Rossley Literary Awards are given to previously under-recognized writers (of poetry or fiction). Writers can be nominated by anyone familiar with their work. Send SASE for further information.

Advice: "*96 Inc* is an artists' collaborative and a local resource. It often provides venues and hosts readings in addition to publishing a magazine."

N **NITE-WRITER'S INTERNATIONAL LITERARY ARTS JOURNAL**, 137 Pointview Rd. #300, Pittsburgh PA 15227-3131. (412)885-3798. Established 1993. **Executive Editor/Publisher:** John A. Thompson Sr. **Associate Editor:** Bree Ann Orner.

Magazine Needs: A quarterly open to beginners as well as professionals, *Nite-Writer's* is " 'dedicated to the emotional intellectual' with a creative perception of life." Wants strong imagery and accept free verse, avant-garde poetry, haiku and senryu. Open to length and subject matter. No porn or violence. Has published poetry by Lyn Lifshin, Rose Marie Hunold, Peter Vetrano, Carol Frances Brown, and Richard King Perkins II. As a sample the editors selected this poem, "Love Child," by Dianne Borsenik:

> make incense from the flower/dance naked in the light/weave a blanket/fringed with stars/to cover you
> at night/breathe kisses to the morning/braid songs into your hair/blow wishes on the feathered/spores
> that surf the curls of air/and if a storm should hurt you/pour honey on the pain/chase the clouds and
> catch them/then laugh/and drink the rain

Nite-Writer is 30-50 pages, 8½×11, laser-printed, stock cover with sleeve, some graphics and artwork. Receives about 1,000 poems/year, accepts approximately 10-15%. Press run is about 100 for more than 60 subscribers of which 10 are libraries. Single copy: $6; subscription: $20. Sample (when available): $4.

How to Submit: Accepts previously published poems and simultaneous submissions. Cover letter preferred. "Give brief bio, state where you heard of us, state if material has been previously published and where. Always enclose SASE if you seek reply and return of your material." Time between acceptance and publication is within 1 year. Always comments on rejected poems. Guidelines available for SASE. Responds in 1 month.

Advice: "Don't be afraid to submit your material. Take rejection as advice—study your market. Create your own style and voice, then be heard. 'I am a creator, a name beneath words' (from my poem, 'unidentified-Identified')."

NO EXIT, P.O. Box 454, South Bend IN 46624-0454. Fax: (801)650-3743. Established 1994. **Editor:** Mike Amato.

Magazine Needs: *No Exit* is a quarterly forum "for the experimental as well as traditional excellence." Wants "poetry that takes chances in form or content. Form, length, subject matter and style are open. No poetry that's unsure of why it was written. Particularly interested in long (not long-winded) poems." Has published poetry by David Lawrence, Gregory Fiorini, and Ron Offen. *No Exit* is 32 pages, saddle-stapled, digest-sized, card cover with art. Accepts 10-15% of the submissions received. Press run is less than 500. Subscription: $12. Sample: $4.

How to Submit: Submit up to 5 poems ("send more if compelled, but I will stop reading after the fifth"). "No handwritten work, misspellings, colored paper, multiple type faces, typos, long-winded cover letters and lists of publication credits." Accepts simultaneous submissions; no previously published poems. No e-mail submissions. Time between acceptance and publication can vary from 1 month to 1 year. Sometimes comments on rejected poems, "if the poem strikes me as worth saving. No themes. But spring issues are devoted to a single poet. Interested writers should submit 24 pages of work. Don't bother unless of highest caliber. There are no other guidelines for single-author issues." Guidelines available for SASE. Responds in up to 3 months. Pays 1 contributor's copy plus 4-issue subscription. Acquires first North American serial rights plus right to reprint once in an anthology. Reviews books of poetry. "Also looking for articles, critical in nature, on poetry/poets." Poets may send books for review consideration.

Advice: "Presentation means something; namely, that you care about what you do. Don't take criticism, when offered, personally. I'll work with you if I see something solid to focus on."

NOCTURNAL LYRIC, JOURNAL OF THE BIZARRE (Specialized: horror), P.O. Box 542, Astoria OR 97103. E-mail: nocturnallyric@melodymail.com. Website: www.angelfire.com/ca/nocturnallyric (includes upcoming authors, poetry, special deals on back issues, and news about the upcoming issue). Established 1987. **Editor:** Susan Moon.

Magazine Needs: *Nocturnal Lyric* is a quarterly journal "featuring bizarre fiction and poetry, primarily by new writers." Wants "poems dealing with the bizarre: fantasy, death, morbidity, horror, gore, etc. Any length. No 'boring poetry.' " Has published poetry by Carrie L. Clark, J. Kevilus, Stan Morner, Richard Geyer, Stephen Kopel, Linda Rosenkrans. As a sample the editor selected these lines from "Visitations" by J. Kevilus:

> *Little ghosts bouncing off the walls, haunting my dreams,/my judgement, my reality. I try drowning*
> *them in the kitchen sink,/instead they dance and sing away, slipping/through my splayed fingers.*

Nocturnal Lyric is 40 pages, digest-sized, photocopied, saddle-stapled, with trade ads and staff artwork. Receives about 200 poems/year, accepts about 35%. Press run is 400 for 40 subscribers. Single copy: $3 within US, $5 for non-US addresses. Make checks payable to Susan Moon.

How to Submit: Submit up to 4 poems at a time. Accepts previously published poems and simultaneous submissions. No e-mail submissions. Seldom comments on rejected poems. Guidelines available for SASE, on website, and in publication. Responds in up to 6 months. Pays 50¢ "discount on subscription" coupons. Acquires one-time rights.

Advice: "Don't follow the trends. We admire the unique."

NOMAD'S CHOIR, % Meander, 30-15 Hobart St. F4H, Woodside NY 11377. Established 1989. **Editor:** Joshua Meander.

Magazine Needs: *Nomad's Choir* is a quarterly. "Subjects wanted: love poems, protest poems, mystical poems, nature poems, poems of humanity, poems with solutions to world problems and inner conflict. 9-30 lines, poems with hope. Simple words, careful phrasing. Free verse, rhymed poems, sonnets, half-page parables, myths and legends, song lyrics. No curse words in poems, little or no name-dropping, no naming of consumer products, no two-page poems, no humor, no bias writing, no poems untitled." Has published poetry by Steven J. Stein, Madeline Artenberg, Wayne Wilkinson, and Jill Dimaggio. *Nomad's Choir* is 10 pages, 8½×11, typeset and saddle-stapled with 3 poems/page. Receives about 150 poems/year, accepts 50. Press run is 400; all distributed free. Subscription: $5. Sample: $1.25. Make checks payable to Joshua Meander.

How to Submit: Responds in 2 months. Pays 1 contributor's copy. Publishes theme issues. Guidelines and upcoming themes available for SASE.

Advice: "Strive for timeless art—beauty and drama."

$ NORTH AMERICAN REVIEW; JAMES HEARST POETRY PRIZE, University of Northern Iowa, Cedar Falls IA 50614-0516. (319)273-6455. Fax: (319)273-4326. E-mail: nar@uni.edu. Website: http://webdelsol.com/NorthAmReview/NAR (includes history, guidelines, archive of selected work, contest information, links, and contact and subscription information). Established 1815. **Editor:** Vince Gotera.

Magazine Needs: *North American Review* is a slick magazine-sized bimonthly of general interest, 48 pages average, saddle-stapled, professionally printed with glossy full-color paper cover, publishing poetry

Gary Kelley, art director/illustrator for *North American Review*, created this painting to "reflect the issue's theme: multicultural literature and poetry. I felt the obvious ethnic portrait with the subtle surprise of the reading glasses suggested the theme, and the simplicity provides visual impact while being provocative."

of the highest quality. Has published poetry by Debra Marquart, Nick Carbó, Yusef Komunyakaa, Virgil Suárez, Nance Van Winckel, and Dara Wier. Receives about 7,000 poems/year, accepts 100. Press run is 2,500 for 1,500 subscribers of which 1,000 are libraries. Writer's subscription: $18. Sample: $5.

How to Submit: Include SASE. No simultaneous submissions or previously published poems. Accepts submissions by regular mail and by e-mail (in text box or as attachment). No fax submissions. Time between acceptance and publication is up to 1 year. Guidelines available for SASE, by e-mail, on website, and in publication. Responds in 3 months. Always sends prepublication galleys. Pays $1/line ($20 minimum) and 2 contributor's copies. Acquires first North American serial rights only. Rights revert after publication.

Also Offers: North American Review sponsors the annual James Hearst Poetry Prize. First prize $1000. Postmark deadline is October 31. Rules are available for SASE, by e-mail, by fax, or on website.

$ ◎ NORTH CAROLINA LITERARY REVIEW (Specialized: regional), English Dept., East Carolina University, Greenville NC 27858-4353. (252)328-1537. Fax: (252)328-4889. E-mail: bauerm@mail.ecu.edu. Established 1992. **Editor:** Margaret Bauer.

• *North Carolina Literary Review* was awarded best new journal in 1994 and 1999 by the CELJ.

Magazine Needs: *North Carolina Literary Review* is an annual publication appearing in October that "contains articles and other works about North Carolina topics or by North Carolina authors." Wants "poetry by writers currently living in North Carolina, those who have lived in North Carolina or those using North Carolina for subject matter." Has published poetry by Betty Adcock, James Applewhite, and A.R. Ammons. *North Carolina Literary Review* is 200 pages and magazine-sized. Receives about 250 submissions/year, accepts about 20%. Press run is 1,000 for 750 subscribers of which 100 are libraries; 100 shelf sales; 50 distributed free to contributors. Subscription: $20/2 years, $36/4 years. Sample: $10-15.

How to Submit: Submit 3-5 poems at a time. No e-mail submissions. Cover letter required. "Submit 2 copies and include SASE or e-mail address for response." Reads submissions August 1 through April 30 only. Time between acceptance and publication is up to 1 year. Often comments on rejected poems. Guidelines available for SASE, by e-mail, or on website. Responds in 2 months. Sometimes sends prepublication galleys. Pays $25-50 plus 1-2 copies. Acquires first or one-time rights. Reviews books of poetry by North Carolina poets in 2,000 words, multi-book format. Poets from North Carolina may send books for review consideration.

⛿ ◖ NORTHEAST; JUNIPER PRESS; JUNIPER BOOKS; THE WILLIAM N. JUDSON SERIES OF CONTEMPORARY AMERICAN POETRY; CHICKADEE; INLAND SEA SERIES; GIFTS OF THE PRESS, P.O. Box 8037, St. Paul MN 55108-8037. Website: www.ddgbooks.com. Established 1962. **Contact:** editors.

• "Poets we have published won the Pulitzer Prize, the Posner Poetry Prize, and the Midwest Book Award."

Magazine Needs & How to Submit: *Northeast* is an annual literary magazine appearing in January. Has published Lisel Muller, Alan Bronghton, and Bruce Cutler. *Northeast* is digest-sized and saddle-stapled. Subscription: $33/year ($38 for institutions), "which brings you one issue of the magazine and the Juniper Books, Chickadees, the William N. Judson Series of Contemporary American Poetry Books and some gifts of the press, a total of about 3-5 items. See our website or send SASE for catalog to order individual items; orders can be placed by calling the Order Dept. at (207)778-3454." Sample: $3. No submissions by fax or e-mail. Responds in up to 2 months. Pays 2 copies.

Book/Chapbook Needs & How to Submit: Juniper Press does not accept unsolicited book/chapbook mss.

Advice: "Please read us before sending mss. It will aid in your selection of materials to send. If you don't like what we do, please don't submit."

NORTHEAST ARTS MAGAZINE, P.O. Box 4363, Portland ME 04101. Established 1990. **Publisher/Editor:** Mr. Leigh Donaldson.

Magazine Needs: *Northeast Arts Magazine* is a biannual using poetry, short fiction, essays, reviews, art, and photography that is "honest, clear, with a love of expression through simple language, under 30 lines. We maintain a special interest in work that reflects cultural diversity in New England and throughout the world." Has published poetry by Steve Lutrell, Eliot Richman, Elizabeth R. Curry, Bob Begieburg, and Alisa Aran. *Northeast Arts Magazine* is 32 or more pages, digest-sized, professionally printed with 1-color coated card cover. Accepts 10-20% of submissions. Press run is 500-1,000 for 150 subscribers of which half are libraries, 50 to arts organizations. An updated arts information section and feature articles are included. Subscription: $10. Sample: $4.50.

How to Submit: Reads submissions September 1 through February 28 only. "A short bio is helpful." Guidelines available for SASE. Responds in 3 months. Pays 2 copies. Acquires first North American serial rights.

NORTHERN STARS MAGAZINE, N17285 Co. Rd. 400, Powers MI 49874. Website: http://members.aol.com/WriterNet/NorthStar.html (includes brief guidelines, poetry, and books available through North Star Publishing). Established 1997. **Editor:** Beverly Kleikamp.

Magazine Needs: *Northern Stars* is published bimonthly and "welcomes submissions of fiction, nonfiction, and poetry on any subject or style. The main requirement is good clean family reading material. Nothing you can't read to your child or your mother. No smut or filth." Accepts poetry written by children. Has published poetry by Terri Warden, Julie Sanders, Najwa Salam Brax, and Gary Elam. As a sample the editor selected these lines from "Flights of Fancy" by Gary S. Elam:

> A raven looks mysterious/With feathers black as night/An eagle perching on a cliff/Is such an awesome sight.

Northern Stars Magazine is 32 pages, $8\frac{1}{2} \times 11$, photocopied and saddle-stapled with cardstock cover, may include b&w line drawings and photographs. "Send SASE for subscription information." Single copy: $4; subscription: $19. Make checks payable to Beverly Kleikamp or *Northern Stars Magazine*.

How to Submit: Submit up to 5 poems at a time, no more than 25 lines each. Accepts previously published poems and simultaneous submissions. Cover letter preferred. "Manuscripts must be typed—please do not submit handwritten material." Often comments on rejected poems. Occasionally publishes theme issues. "No payment, but nonsubscribers are notified of publication." No fee for regular subscribers. All rights return to authors on publication.

Also Offers: Sponsors monthly alternating issues contest for poetry and fiction/nonfiction (i.e., poetry contest in March-April issue, fiction/nonfiction in May-June). Entry fee: $2.50/poem for non-subscribers, $1/poem for subscribers. Deadline: 20th of month preceding publication. Guidelines available for SASE. Publishes an annual chapbook of contest winners and honorable mentions. "I do publish many chapbooks for others now for an 'affordable' price to the writer." 100 copies or less available; sample available $5. Also has a "Somewhere In Michigan" regular column featuring people/places/events, etc., tied in with Michigan. Also includes adventures which have happened in Michigan.

Advice: "Just keep it clean and send me your best work. I do favor shorter poems over very long ones."

THE NORTHWEST FLORIDA REVIEW; OKALOOSA ISLAND PRESS; RICHARD EBERHARD AWARD IN POETRY, P.O. Box 8122, Okaloosa Island, Ft. Walton Beach FL 32548. **Poetry Editor:** Lola Haskins.

Magazine Needs: *The Northwest Florida Review* appears biannually in May and December. "A magazine of high-quality literature. We are looking for serious poetry, translations, short fiction up to 5,000 words, reviews, art and articles of literary interest." Wants the best contemporary poetry. Open to all styles and subject matter. "We want to see strong images." Does not want greeting card verse, inspirational verse, or rhymed poetry unless handled with artistic excellence. As a sample the editor selected the following lines from "Neighbors" by Susan Stewart from her book *Yellow Stars and Ice*:

> . . . *they climb, their sheets knotted/Around their waists, their clotheslines scarring the clouds, the suicides/And the maniacs, the painters and the bats,/Perch on the third story windows and slowly/Let go of the earth. A jet comes ripping/Across the ceiling, and the sky writing says,/"Jump, yes, jump"*

The Northwest Florida Review is 96 pages, digest-sized, press-printed, perfect-bound, glossy cover with art/graphics. Press run is 1,000. Single copy: $6; subscription: $10/year. Sample: $5. Make checks payable to *The Northwest Florida Review*.

How to Submit: Submit 3-6 poems at a time. Accepts simultaneous submissions; no previously published poems. No fax, e-mail, or disk submissions. Cover letter is preferred. "Include SASE. Single space for poetry, double space for fiction and nonfiction." Reads submissions year round. Poems are circulated to an editorial board. Never comments on rejected poems. Responds in up to 5 months. Pays 1 copy and $5/poem or $20/short story. Acquires first North American serial rights. Reviews books of poetry in 750 words, single book and multi-book format.

Books/Chapbooks & How to Submit: Okaloosa Island Press plans to publish 1 paperback title beginning in 2002 "by a poet who has published at least one book." Book will be at least 45-64 pages, press-printed, perfect-bound, glossy cover with art/graphics. Query first, with a few sample poems and a cover letter "but not until March 2002." Responds to queries and mss in 3 months. Pays royalties of 10-15% and 10 author's copies (out of a press run of 500).

Also Offers: The Richard Eberhart Award in Poetry. 1st Prize: $300; 2nd Prize: $50. $5 entry fee. Guidelines available for SASE.

Advice: "Read *Paris Review, Georgia Review, Poetry*, and other top 20 magazines to see what kind of poetry we want."

NORTHWEST REVIEW, 369 PLC, University of Oregon, Eugene OR 97403. (503)346-3957. Established 1957. **Poetry Editor:** John Witte.

• Poetry published by *Northwest Review* has been included in the 2001 volume of *Best American Poetry*.

Magazine Needs: "Seeking excellence in whatever form we can find it" and use "all types" of poetry. Has published poetry by Alan Dugan, Olga Broumas, and Richard Eberhart. *Northwest Review*, a 6×9, flat-spined magazine, appears 3 times/year and uses 25-40 pages of poetry in each issue. Receives about 3,500 submissions/year, accepts about 4%; has up to a 4-month backlog. Press run is 1,300 for 1,200 subscribers of which half are libraries. Sample: $4.

How to Submit: Submit 6-8 poems clearly reproduced. No simultaneous submissions. Guidelines available for SASE. Responds within 10 weeks. Pays 3 copies.

Advice: "Persist."

$ NORTHWOODS PRESS, THE POET'S PRESS; NORTHWOODS JOURNAL, A MAGAZINE FOR WRITERS; C.A.L. (CONSERVATORY OF AMERICAN LETTERS), P.O. Box 298, Thomaston ME 04861-0298. (207)354-0998. Fax: (207)354-8953. E-mail: cal@americanletters.org. Website: www.americanletters.org. Northwoods Press established 1972, *Northwoods Journal* 1993. **Editor:** Robert Olmsted.

Magazine Needs & How to Submit: *Northwoods Journal* is a quarterly literary magazine that publishes fiction, reviews, nonfiction, and poetry. "The journal is interested in all poets who feel they have something to say and who work to say it well. We have no interest in closet poets, or credit seekers. All poets seeking an audience, working to improve their craft, and determined to 'get it right' are welcome here. Accepts poetry written by children. Please request submission guidelines before submitting." *Northwoods Journal* is about 40 pages, digest-sized with full color cover. Subscription: $12.50/year. Sample: $5.50. **Reading fee:** $1/poem for nonmembers of C.A.L., 50¢/poem for members. One free read per year when joining or renewing membership in C.A.L. "Submission must accompany membership order." Guidelines are available for #10 SASE or on website; "see guidelines before submitting anything." Deadlines are the 1st of March, June, September, and December for seasonal publication. Responds within 2 weeks after deadline, sometimes sooner. Pays $4/page, average, on acceptance.

Book Needs & How to Submit: Submit book-length work to Northwoods Press Poetry Contest. Less than 10% of material may be previously published. "Submit with SASE and extra SASEs for any correspondence wanted, or clear and simple instructions to discard manuscript if not accepted." Entry fee: $10 nonmembers, $8 members. Make checks payable to CAL. Deadline: January 1. 3 prizes of $100 and offer of publication. Mss read within 72 hours of receipt. "If your manuscript is one of the best three we have, it will be retained until it is beaten." Previous winners include *Hog Killers and Other Poems* by Vernon Schmid and *Knotted Stems* by Sylvia Relation.

Advice: "Poetry must be non-trite, non-didactic. It must never bounce. Rhyme, if used at all, should be subtle. One phrase should tune the ear in preparation for the next. They should flow and create an emotional response."

◑ W.W. NORTON & COMPANY, INC., 500 Fifth Ave., New York NY 10110. E-mail: manuscripts@ wwnorton.com. Website: www.wwnorton.com/. Established 1925. **Contact:** Poetry Editor.

Book/Chapbook Needs: W.W. Norton is a well-known commercial trade publishing house that publishes only original work in both hardcover and paperback. Wants "quality literary poetry"; no "light or inspirational verse." Has published books by Rita Dove, Adrienne Rich, A.R. Ammons, Stanley Kunitz and Gerald Stein. W.W. Norton publishes approximately 10 books of poetry each year with an average page count of 64. Published in cloth and flat-spined paperbacks, attractively printed, with 2-color glossy card covers.

How to Submit: Query first with a small sampling by e-mail. Send no more than 3 pages in e-mail text box (no attachments). "Since memory space for e-mail is limited, we will not accept any complete manuscript by e-mail." No simultaneous submissions. Norton will consider only poets whose work has been published in quality literary magazines. Poems are circulated to an editorial board. Seldom comments on rejected poems. Responds to queries in 6-8 weeks.

◑ ◎ NOSTALGIA: A SENTIMENTAL STATE OF MIND (Specialized: nostalgia), P.O. Box 2224, Orangeburg SC 29116. E-mail: cnostalgia@aol.com. Website: www.nospub.com. Established 1986. **Poetry Editor:** Connie Lakey Martin.

Magazine Needs: *Nostalgia* appears quarterly with "stories of true personal experience . . . and not necessarily events that happened so long ago. 'Yesterday' can mean last week, last month. Reflective and insightful accounts of your faith, encounters, calamity, and fate. Try not to dwell solely on memories of parents, relatives, pets, holidays, etc." Wants "modern prose, but short poems, never longer than one page, no profanity, no ballads." *Nostalgia* is 24 pages, digest-sized, offset typescript, saddle-stapled, with matte card cover. Press run is 1,000. Subscription: $8. Sample: $5.

How to Submit: "If material is previously published, please advise." No e-mail submissions. Include SASE and put name and address on each poem. Guidelines available for SASE. All rights revert to author upon publication.

Advice: "I offer criticism to most rejected poems, but I suggest sampling before submitting."

◑ NOTRE DAME REVIEW, Creative Writing Program, Dept. of English, University of Notre Dame, Notre Dame IN 46556. (219)631-6952. Fax: (219)631-4268. E-mail: english.ndreview.1@nd.edu. Website: www.nd.edu/~ndr/review.htm (includes guidelines, poetry, and interviews). Established 1994. **Contact:** Poetry Editor.

Magazine Needs: Appearing biannually, *Notre Dame Review*'s "goal is to present a panoramic view of contemporary art and literature—no one style is advocated over another. We are especially interested in work that takes on big issues by making the invisible seen." Has published poetry by Ken Smith, Robert Creeley, and Denise Levertov. As a sample the editor selected these lines from "The Watchman at Mycenae" by Seamus Heaney:

> Some people wept, and not for sorrow-joy/That the king had armed and upped and sailed for Troy,/
> But inside me life struck sound in a gong/That killing-fest, the life-warm and world wrong/It brought
> to pass still argued and endured

Notre Dame Review is 170 pages, magazine-sized, perfect-bound with 4-color glossy cover, includes art/graphics and ads. Receives about 400 poems/year, accepts 10%. Press run is 2,000 for 500 subscribers of which 150 are libraries, 1,000 shelf sales; 350 distributed free to contributors, assistants, etc. Single copy: $8; subscription: $15/ year. Sample: $6. "Read magazine before submitting."

How to Submit: Submit 3-5 poems at a time. Accepts simultaneous submissions; no previously published poems. Cover letter required. Reads submissions September-November and January-April only. Time between acceptance and publication is 3 months. Seldom comments on rejected poems. Publishes theme issues. Guidelines and upcoming themes available on website. Responds in 3 months. Always sends prepublication galleys. Pays 2 copies. Acquires first rights. Staff reviews books of poetry in 500 words, single and multi-book format. Poets may send books for review consideration.

Also Offers: Sponsors the Ernest Sandeen Prize for Poetry, a book contest open to poets with at least one other book publication. Send SASE for details.

NOVA EXPRESS (Specialized: science fiction/fantasy, horror), P.O. Box 27231, Austin TX 78755. E-mail: lawrenceperson@jump.net. Website: www.novaexpress.org. Established 1987. **Editor:** Lawrence Person.

• *Nova Express* was nominated for the Hugo Award.

Magazine Needs: *Nova Express* appears "irregularly (at least once/year) with coverage of cutting edge science fiction, fantasy and horror literature, with an emphasis on post-cyperpunk and slipstream. We feature interviews, reviews, poetry, and serious (but nonacademic) critical articles on important issues and authors throughout the entire science fiction/fantasy/horror/slipstream field. *Nova Express* is no longer a market for unsolicited fiction, but we still look at poetry." Wants "poetry relating to literature of the fantastic in some way." Has published poetry by Alison Wimsatt and Mark McLaughlin. As a sample we selected these lines from "The Weatherworn Banshee Declares Her Undying Love For Some Accountant She Met At A Party" by Mark McLaughlin:

> The others threw dip and salsa at me/until you, my darling, told them to stop./These hands, callused
> and scarred/from climbing rocks and tearing apart/wild dogs, long to hold you—and these lips,/puffy
> from sucking cracked rib-bones,/burn to slather you with love.

Nova Express is 48 pages, 8½×11, stapled, desktop-published with b&w graphics and line art. Receives about 40-50 poems/year, accepts 1-2. Press run is 500 for 200 subscribers, 100 shelf sales; 100 distributed free to science fiction industry professionals. Subscription: $15. Sample: $5.

How to Submit: Submit up to 5 poems at a time. No previously published poems or simultaneous submissions. Cover letter preferred. E-mail submissions (in body of message) preferred. Time between acceptance and publication is 3 months. Often comment on rejected poems. Publishes theme issues. Upcoming themes available by e-mail. Guidelines available for SASE or by e-mail. Responds in up to 6 months. "Response will be slow until the slush pile is cleaned out." Sometimes sends prepublication galleys. Pays 2 copies plus 4-issue subscription. Acquires one-time rights.

Advice: "We are not interested in any poetry outside the science fiction/fantasy/horror genre. *Nova Express* is read widely and well regarded by genre professionals."

NUTHOUSE; TWIN RIVERS PRESS (Specialized: humor), P.O. Box 119, Ellenton FL 34222. Website: http://hometown.aol.com/Nuthouse499/index2.html. Press established 1989, magazine established 1993. **Editor:** Ludwig Von Quirk.

Magazine Needs: *Nuthouse*, "amusements by and for delightfully diseased minds," appears every 2 months using humor of all kinds, including homespun and political. Wants "humorous verse; virtually all genres considered." Has published poetry by Holly Day, Daveed Garstenstein-Ross, and Don Webb. *Nuthouse* is 12 pages, digest-sized and photocopied from desktop-published originals. Receives about 500 poems/year, accepts approximately 100. Press run is 100 for 50 subscribers. Subscription: $5/5 issues. Sample: $1.25. Make checks payable to Twin Rivers Press.

How to Submit: Accepts previously published poems and simultaneous submissions. Time between acceptance and publication is 6-12 months. Often comments on rejected poems. Responds within 1 month. Pays 1 copy/poem. Acquires one-time rights.

O!!ZONE (Specialized: visual poetry, photography, collage), 1266 Fountain View, Houston TX 77057-2204. (713)784-2802. Fax: (713)789-5119. E-mail: HarryBurrus@juno.com. Established 1993. **Editor/Publisher:** Harry Burrus.

Magazine Needs: *O!!Zone* is "an international literary-art zine featuring visual poetry, travel pieces, interviews, haiku, manifestos, and art. We are particularly intrigued by poets who also do photography (or draw or paint). We also do broadsides, publish small, modest saddle-stapled collections, and will consider book-length collections (on a collaborative basis) *as time and dinero permits.*" Wants visual poetry and collage. "I am interested in discovery and self-transcendence." No academic, traditional, or rhyming poetry. Has published poetry by Dmitry Babenko, Patricia Salas, Anthony Zoutra, Sasha Surikov, Willi Melnikov, Laura Ryder, and Joel Lipman. The editor did not offer sample lines of poetry because he says, "*O!!Zone* needs to be seen." *O!!Zone* is 80-100 pages, 8½×11, desktop-published, loaded with graphics. "Write for a catalog listing our titles. Our *O!!Zone 97, International Visual Poetry* ($25) and *O!!Zone 98* ($25) and *O!!Zone 99-00* ($25) are three anthologies that cover what's going on in international visual poetry."

How to Submit: Submit 3-6 poems at a time. No previously published poems or simultaneous submissions. No fax submissions. "Submissions of visual poetry via snail mail; textual poems may come by e-mail." Inquire before submitting via e-mail. Cover letter preferred. Has a large backlog, "but always open to surprises." Seldom comments on rejected poems. Guidelines available for SASE. Responds "soon." Pays 1-2 contributor's copies.

◯ ◎ **THE OAK; THE ACORN (Specialized: children); THE GRAY SQUIRREL (Specialized: senior citizens); THE SHEPHERD (Specialized: religious; inspirational)**, 1530 Seventh St., Rock Island IL 61201. (309)788-3980. **Poetry Editor:** Betty Mowery.

Magazine Needs & How to Submit: *The Oak*, established in 1990, is a "publication for writers with poetry and fiction." Wants poetry of "no more than 35 lines and fiction of no more than 500 words. No restrictions as to types and style, but no pornography or love poetry." *The Oak* appears quarterly. Established 1991, *The Gray Squirrel* is now included in *The Oak* and takes poetry of no more than 35 lines fiction up to 500 words from poets 60 years of age and up. Uses more than half of about 100 poems received each year. Include a SASE or mss will not be returned. Press run is 250, with 10 going to libraries. Subscription: $10. Sample: $3. Make all checks payable to *The Oak*. Submit 5 poems at a time. Accepts simultaneous submissions and previously published poems. Responds in 1 week. "*The Oak* does not pay in dollars or copies but you need not purchase to be published." Acquires first or second rights. *The Oak* holds several contests. Guidelines available for SASE.

Magazine Needs & How to Submit: *The Acorn*, established in 1988, is a "newsletter for young authors and teachers or anyone else interested in our young authors. Takes mss from kids K-12th grades. Poetry no more than 35 lines. It also takes fiction of no more than 500 words." *The Acorn* appears 4 times/year and "we take well over half of submitted mss." Press run is 100, with 6 going to libraries. Subscription: $10. Sample: $3. Make all checks payable to *The Oak*. Submit 5 poems at a time. Accepts simultaneous submissions and previously published poems. Responds in 1 week. "*The Acorn* does not pay in dollars or copies but you need not purchase to be published." Acquires first or second rights. Young authors, submitting to *The Acorn*, should put either age or grade on manuscripts. *The Shepherd*, established in 1996, is a quarterly publishing inspirational poetry from all ages. Poems may be up to 35 lines and fiction up to 500 words. "We want something with a message but not preachy." Subscription: $10 (4 issues). Sample: $3. Make checks payable to *The Oak*. Include SASE with all submissions.

Also Offers: Sponsors numerous contests. Guidelines available for SASE.

Advice: "Write what you feel. Study the markets for word limit and subject. Always include SASE or rejected manuscripts will not be returned. Please make checks for *all* publications payable to *The Oak*."

$ ◖ **OASIS**, P.O. Box 626, Largo FL 33779-0626. (727)449-2186. E-mail: oasislit@aol.com. Established 1992. **Editor:** Neal Storrs.

Magazine Needs: *Oasis* is a quarterly forum for high quality literary prose and poetry written almost exclusively by freelancers. Usually contains 6 prose pieces and the work of 4-5 poets. Wants "to see poetry of stylistic beauty. Prefer free verse with a distinct, subtle music. No superficial sentimentality, old-fashioned rhymes or rhythms." Has published poetry by Carolyn Stoloff, Fredrick Zydek, and Kim Bridgford. As a sample the editor selected these lines from "The Lightning Speech of Birds" by Corrine DeWinter:

> But now I must comply, twisting away from the clawed/lovers, shrinking from the familiar habits/of
> all three wives who have built cities and spires/under my skin/from the expectant crucifixions on the
> shoulder of the roads,/from the blessed damned on Venus' blushing sands.

Oasis is about 75 pages, 7×10, attractively printed on heavy book paper, perfect-bound with medium-weight card cover, no art. Receives about 2,000 poems/year, accepts 1%. Press run is 300 for 90 subscribers of which 5 are libraries. Subscription: $20/year. Sample: $7.50.

How to Submit: Submit any number of poems. Accepts simultaneous submissions; rarely accepts previously published poems. Accepts e-mail submissions (include in body of message). Cover letter preferred. Time between acceptance and publication is usually 4 months. Seldom comments on rejected poems. Guidelines available for SASE. Responds "the same or following day more than 99% of the time." Sometimes sends prepublication galleys. Pays $5/poem and 1 contributor's copy. Acquires first or one-time rights.

Ⓝ ⊕ ◖ **OASIS BOOKS; OASIS MAGAZINE**, 12 Stevenage Rd., London SW6 6ES England. Established 1969. **Editor/Publisher:** Ian Robinson.

Magazine Needs: *Oasis Magazine* appears 3 times/year and publishes short fiction and poetry as well as occasional reviews and other material. "No preference for style or subject matter; just quality. No long poems; *Oasis* is a very short magazine. Also, usually no rhyming poetry." Has published poetry by Andrea Moorhead, Peter Riley, and Aline Willen. *Oasis* is international A5 size, litho, folded sheets. Receives 500-600 poems/year, accepts approximately 4 or 5. Press run is 500 for 400 subscribers of which 10 are libraries. Subscription: $20/4 issues. Sample: $3.50 (US). Make checks in American funds payable to Robert Vas Dias.

How to Submit: Submit up to 6 poems at a time. Accepts previously published poems sometimes; simultaneous submissions "if work comes from outside the U.K." Include SAE and 4 IRCs for return (US postage is not valid). Seldom comments on rejected poems. Publishes theme issues occasionally. Upcoming themes available for SAE and IRC. Responds in 1 month. Pays up to 5 copies. Staff reviews books of poetry. Send books for review consideration.

Book/Chapbook Needs & How to Submit: Oasis Books publishes 2-3 paperbacks and 2-3 chapbooks/ year. Has published *Among Memory's Ruins* by Zdenek Vanicek; *From Far Away* by Harry Gilonis and Tony Baker; *Flecks* by Ralph Hawkins; *Anxious to Please* by Nicholas Moore; and *3,600 Weekends* by Ken Edwards. Responds to queries and mss in 1 month. For sample books or chapbooks, write for catalog. "No more book or chapbook publications are planned for the next two years."

Advice: "One IRC (U.S. postage is not valid) is not enough to ensure return airmail postage; three will, provided manuscript is not too thick. No return postage will ensure that the ms is junked. It's best to write first before submitting (include 2 IRCs for reply)."

$ ☑ ◎ OCEAN VIEW BOOKS (Specialized: form/style, surrealism), P.O. Box 9249, Denver CO 80209. Established 1981. **Editor:** Lee Ballentine.

Book/Chapbook Needs: Ocean View Books publishes "books of poetry by poets influenced by surrealism and science fiction." Publishes 2 paperbacks and 2 hardbacks/year. No "confessional/predictable, self-referential poems." Has published poetry by Anselm Hollo, Janet Hamill, and Tom Disch. Books are usually 100 pages, 6×9, offset-printed and perfect-bound with 4-color card cover, includes art. "Our books are distinctive in style and format. Interested poets should order a sample book for $8 (in the US) for an idea of our focus before submitting."

How to Submit: Submit a book project query including 5 poems. Accepts previously published poems and simultaneous submissions. Cover letter preferred. Time between acceptance and publication is up to 2 years. "If our editors recommend publication, we may circulate manuscripts to distinguished outside readers for an additional opinion. The volume of submissions is such that we can respond to queries only if we are interested in the project. If we're interested we will contact you within 4 months." Pays $100 honorarium and a number of author's copies (out of a press run of 500). "Terms vary per project."

Advice: "In 15 years, we have published about 40 books—most consisted of previously published poems from good journals. A poet's 'career' must be well-established before undertaking a book."

$ ◎ OF UNICORNS AND SPACE STATIONS (Specialized: science fiction/fantasy), P.O. Box 200, Bountiful UT 84011-0200. E-mail: gene@genedavis.com. Website: www.genedavis.com/magazine (includes samples from magazine and guidelines). Established 1994. **Editor:** Gene Davis.

Magazine Needs: *Of Unicorns and Space Stations*, published biannually, features science fiction/fantasy literature. "Material written in traditional fixed forms are given preference. Poetry of only a scientific slant or that only uses science fiction/fantasy imagery will be considered." *Of Unicorns and Space Stations* is currently published online only. Receives about 200 poems/year, accepts 2%. Press run is 100 for 100 subscribers; 2-3 distributed free to convention organizers and critics. Subscription: $16/4 issues. Sample: $4. Make checks payable to Gene Davis.

How to Submit: Submit 3 poems, with name and address on each page. "Manuscripts should be paper-clipped, never stapled." Accepts previously published poems; no simultaneous submissions. Accepts e-mail submissions from subscribers only. Cover letter preferred. "If sending fixed form poetry, mention what form you used in your cover letter. Editors pulling 16-hour shifts don't always spot poem types at 1 a.m." Time between acceptance and publication is up to 9 months. Poems are circulated to an editorial board of 2 editors. "Both have veto power over every piece." Seldom comments on rejected poems. Guidelines available for SASE or on website. Responds in 3 months. Pays 1 contributor's copy and "$5 flat rate for poetry." Acquires one-time rights, both electronic and hardcopy.

◐ OFFERINGS, P.O. Box 1667, Lebanon MO 65536-1667. Established 1994. **Editor:** Velvet Fackeldey.

Magazine Needs: *Offerings* is a poetry quarterly. "We accept traditional and free verse from established and new poets, as well as students. Prefer poems of less than 30 lines. No erotica." Accepts poetry written by children. Has published poetry by Charles Portolano, Diane Webster, William Davenhauer, Sheila B. Roark, William Ford Jr., and Gerald Zipper. As a sample we selected these lines from "All Things Away" by Nick R. Zemaiduk:

> *We scrubbed the room and made the bed/as if some day he may return./Kept a fire fueled, instead/of wood, with memories, to burn/away the sharper edge of pain/the mind's eye holds against all hope/of fates to which our small complaints/are no more than a way to cope.*

Offerings is 50-60 pages, digest-sized, neatly printed and saddle-stapled with paper cover. Receives about 500 poems/year, accepts about 25%. Press run is 100 for 75 subscribers, 25 shelf sales. Single copy: $5; subscription: $16. Sample: $3.

How to Submit: Submit typed poems with name and address on each page. Students should also include grade level. SASE required. No simultaneous submissions. Seldom comments on rejected poems. Guidelines available for SASE. Responds in up 1 month. All rights revert to author after publication.

Advice: "We are unable to offer payment at this time (not even copies) but hope to be able to do so in the future. We welcome beginning poets."

OFFERTA SPECIALE; BERTOLA CARLA PRESS, Corso De Nicola 20, 10-128 Torino Italy. Established 1988. **Director/Editor:** Bertola Carla. **Co-Director:** Vitacchio Alberto.

Magazine Needs: *Offerta Speciale* is a biannual international journal appearing in May and November. Has published poetry by Federica Manfredini (Italy), Bernard Heidsieck (France), Richard Kostelanetz, and E. Mycue (US). As a sample the editor selected these lines from "My Lower Back" by Sheila Murphy:

> *My lower back likes to be liquid/Dose of sugar ringside/And the thought of frost/As sacrosanct as meerschaum*

Offerta Speciale is 56 pages, digest-sized, neatly printed and saddle-stapled with glossy card cover. Receives about 300 poems/year, accepts about 40%. Press run is 500 for 60 subscribers. Single copy: $25; subscription: $100. Make checks payable to Carla Bertola.

How to Submit: Submit 3 poems at a time. No previously published poems or simultaneous submissions. Time between acceptance and publication is 1 year. Often comments on rejected poems. Guidelines available for SASE (or SAE and IRC). Pays 1 contributor's copy.

OFFICE NUMBER ONE (Specialized: form), 1708 S. Congress Ave., Austin TX 78704. Established 1988. **Editor:** Carlos B. Dingus.

Magazine Needs: Appearing 2-4 times/year, *Office Number One* is a "humorous, satirical zine of news information and events from parallel and alternate realities." In addition to stories, they want limericks, 3-5-3 or 5-7-5 haiku, and rhymed/metered quatrains. "Poems should be short (2-12 lines) and make a point. No long rambling poetry about suffering and pathos. Poetry should be technically perfect." Accepts poetry written by children, "if it stands on its own." As for a sample, the editor says, "No one poem provides a fair sample." *Office Number One* is 12 pages, 8½×11, computer set in 10 pt. type, saddle-stapled, with graphics and ads. Uses about 40 poems/year. Press run is 2,000 for 75 subscribers, 50 shelf sales; 1,600 distributed free locally. Single copy: $1.85; subscription: $8.82/6 issues. Sample: $2.

How to Submit: Submit up to 5 pages of poetry at a time. Accepts previously published poems and simultaneous submissions. Accepts e-mail submissions included in body of message. "Will comment on rejected poems if comment is requested." Publishes theme issues occasionally. Guidelines and upcoming themes available for SASE or by e-mail. Responds in 2 months. Pays "23¢" and 1 copy. Acquires "one-time use, and use in any *Officer Number One* anthology."

Advice: "Say something that a person can use to change his life."

OHIO STATE UNIVERSITY PRESS/THE JOURNAL AWARD IN POETRY, 1070 Carmack Rd., Columbus OH 43210-1002. (614)292-4856. Fax: (614)292-2065. E-mail: ohiostatepress@osu. edu. Website: www.ohiostatepress.org. **Poetry Editor:** David Citino.

Book/Chapbook Needs & How to Submit: Each year *The Journal* (see listing also in this section) selects for publication by Ohio State University Press one full-length (at least 48 pages) book ms submitted during September, typed, double-spaced, $20 handling fee (payable to OSU). Has published *Stone Sky Lifting* by Lia Purpura; *Anatomy, Errata* by Judith Hall; *Blessings the Body Gave* by Walt McDonald; and *Troubled Lovers in History* by Albert Goldbarth. Send SASE for confirmation of ms receipt. Mss will not be returned. Some or all of the poems in the collection may have appeared in periodicals, chapbooks or anthologies, but must be identified. Along with publication, *The Journal* Award in Poetry pays $1,000 cash prize. Each entrant receives a subscription (2 issues) to *The Journal*.

THE OLD RED KIMONO, Humanities Division, P.O. Box 1864, Floyd College, Rome GA 30162. E-mail: napplega@mail.fc.peachnet.edu. Website: www.fc.peachnet.edu/ork/ (includes guidelines and contact information). Established 1972. **Poetry Editors:** La Nelle Daniel, Dr. Nancy Applegate, and Erskine Thompson.

Magazine Needs: Appearing annually, *Old Red Kimono* has the "sole purpose of putting out a magazine of original, high-quality poetry and fiction. *Old Red Kimono* is looking for submissions of three to five short poems and/or one short story." Has published poetry by Walter McDonald, Peter Huggins, Midred Grear, John C. Morrison, Jack Stewart, Kirsten Fox, and Al Braselton. *Old Red Kimono* is 72 pages,

8½×11, professionally printed on heavy stock with b&w graphics, colored matte cover with art, using approximately 40 pages of poetry (usually 1 or 2 poems to the page). Receives about 1,000 submissions/year, accepts approximately 60-70. Sample: $3.

How to Submit: Submit 3-5 poems. Accepts submissions by e-mail (in text box) and by regular mail. Reads submissions September 1 through March 1 only. Guidelines available for SASE and on website. Responds in 3 months. Pays 2 copies. Acquires first publication rights.

■✿◎ $◎ ON SPEC: MORE THAN JUST SCIENCE FICTION (Specialized: regional, Canadian; science fiction/fantasy; horror), P.O. Box 4727, Edmonton, Alberta T6E 5G6 Canada. E-mail: onspec@earthling.net. Website: www.icomm.ca/onspec/ (includes guidelines, contact info, bios, past editorials, excerpts from back issues, links, and announcements). Established 1989. **Poetry Editor:** Barry Hammond.

Magazine Needs: *On Spec* is a quarterly featuring Canadian science fiction writers and artists. Wants work by Canadian poets only and only science fiction/speculative poetry; 100 lines maximum. Has published poetry by Sandra Kasturi and Alice Major. As a sample the editor selected these lines from "Wild Things" by Eileen Kernaghan:

> you can sing small songs to soothe them/make them soft and secret beds to lie in//still you will wake in winter dawns/to find them crouched upon your pillow/their sharp claws unravelling/the frayed edges of your dreams

On Spec is 112 pages, digest-sized, offset-printed on recycled paper and perfect-bound with color cover, b&w art and ads inside. Receives about 100 poems/year, accepts 5%. Press run is 1,750 for 800 subscribers of which 10 are libraries, 600 shelf sales. Single copy: $5.95; subscription: $22 (Canadian funds within Canada, US funds within US). Sample: $7.

How to Submit: Submit up to 5 poems of up to 100 lines at a time with SASE (or SAE and IRC). No previously published poems or simultaneous submissions. No submissions by fax or e-mail. Cover letter with poem titles and 2-sentence bio required. Deadlines: February 28, May 31, August 31, and November 30. Responds in 4 months maximum. Time between acceptance and publication is 6 months. Usually comments on rejected poems. Publishes theme issues. Guidelines and a list of upcoming themes are available for SASE or on website. Pays $20/poem and 1 copy, pays on acceptance. Acquires first North American serial rights.

◎ ONCE UPON A TIME (Specialized: poetry about writing or illustrating), 553 Winston Court, St. Paul MN 55118. (651)457-6223. Fax: (651)457-9151. E-mail: audreyouat@aol.com. Website: http://members.aol.com/ouatmag (includes general subscription information, sample article snippets, description of magazine, representative artwork, sample covers, comments by subscribers, guidelines, etc., plus how to get a free 4-page brochure). Established 1990. **Editor/Publisher:** Audrey B. Baird.

Magazine Needs: Published quarterly, *Once Upon A Time* is a support magazine for children's writers and illustrators. Poetry should be 20 lines maximum—writing or illustration-related. "No poems comparing writing to giving birth to a baby. Very overdone!" As a sample the editor selected this poem, "Writer at Work" by Anita Hunter:

> Spent the morning in my writing room/Sharpened pencils/Threw out stencils/Cleaned up some files/And then, all smiles/Brought my latest manuscript to bloom./By adding one small comma./After lunch, for inspiration/I read some books/Thought up new "hooks"/Made out long lists/Cleared mental mists/And with true, keen dedication/Took out the one small comma.

Once Upon A Time is 32 pages, magazine-sized, stapled with glossy cover, includes art/graphics and a few ads. Receives about 40 poems/year, accepts about 60%. Press run is 1,000 for 900 subscribers. Single copy: $6; subscription: $25. Sample: $5. Make checks payable to Audrey B. Baird.

How to Submit: Submit no more than 6 poems at a time. Accepts previously published poems and simultaneous submissions. Cover letter preferred. Accepts submissions by fax but not by e-mail. Time between acceptance and publication "can be up to 2 years. Short poems usually printed in less than 1 year." Often comments on rejected poems. Guidelines available for SASE or on website. Responds in 1 month. Pays 2 contributor's copies. Acquires one-time rights.

Advice: "Don't send your piece too quickly. Let it sit for a week or more. Then re-read it and see if you can make it better. If you're writing rhyming poetry, the rhythm has to work. Count syllables! Accents, too, have to fall in the right place! Most rhyming poetry I receive has terrible rhythm. Don't forget SASE!"

Ⓝ ◎ ONE TRICK PONY; BANSHEE PRESS, P.O. Box 11186, Philadelphia PA 19136. (215)331-7389. E-mail: lmckee4148@aol.com. Established 1997. Editor: Louis McKee.

Magazine Needs: *One Trick Pony* is published biannually and contains "poetry and poetry related reviews and essays (for reviews, essays, interviews, etc.—please query)." No limitations. Has published poetry by William Heyen, Naomi Shihab Nye, Denise Duhamel, and Michael Waters. *One Trick Pony* is 60 pages,

5½ × 8½, offset printed and saddle-stapled, glossy cover with art. Receives about 750 poems/year, accepts approximately 10%. Press run is 400 for over 150 subscribers of which 12 are libraries, 150 shelf sales. Single copy: $5; subscription: $10/3 issues. Sample: $4. Make checks payable to Louis McKee.

How to Submit: Submit 3-6 poems at a time. Accepts simultaneous submissions; no previously published poems. Responds in 1 month. Pays 2 copies. Acquires first rights. Reviews books and chapbooks of poetry. Poets may send books for review consideration.

Book/Chapbook Needs: Banshee Press publishes 1 chapbook/year. Chapbooks are *by invitation only.*

$ ☑ ◎ ONEARTH MAGAZINE (Specialized: nature/rural/ecology), (formerly *The Amicus Journal* and *e-Amicus*), 40 W. 20th St., New York NY 10011. (212)727-4412. Fax: (212)727-1773. E-mail: Onearth@nrdc.org. Website: www.nrdc.org/onearth. **Poetry Editor:** Brian Swann.

Magazine Needs: The quarterly journal of the Natural Resources Defense Council, *OnEarth* publishes about 15 poems/year and asks that submitted poetry be "rooted in nature" and no more than one ms page in length. Has published poetry by some of the best-known poets in the country, including Mary Oliver, Gary Snyder, Denise Levertov, Reg Saner, John Haines, and Wendell Berry. As a sample the editor selected these lines from "Into the Light" by Pattiann Rogers:

> There may be some places the sun/never reaches—into the stamen/of a prairie primrose bud burned/
> and withered before blooming,/or into the eyes of a fetal/lamb killed before born. I suppose . . .

OnEarth is 48 pages, about 8 × 11, finely printed, saddle-stapled, on high quality paper, with glossy cover, with art, photography, and cartoons. Circulation is 150,000. Sample: $5.

How to Submit: "All submissions must be accompanied by a cover note (with notable prior publications) and self-addressed, stamped envelope." Prefers submissions by post but accepts e-mail submissions (either in text box or as attachment). Guidelines available for SASE or by e-mail. Pays $50/poem plus 1 contributor's copy and a year's subscription.

Ⓝ ◐ ONTHEBUS; BOMBSHELTER PRESS, P.O. Box 481266, Bicentennial Station, Los Angeles CA 90048. Established 1975. **Editor:** Jack Grapes (magazine). **Poetry Editors:** Jack Grapes and Michael Andrews (press).

Magazine Needs: *ONTHEBUS*, appearing biannually, uses "contemporary mainstream poetry—no more than six (ten pages total) at a time. No rhymed, 19th Century traditional 'verse.' " Has published poetry by Charles Bukowski, Albert Goldbarth, Ai, Norman Dubie, Kate Braverman, Stephen Dobyns, Allen Ginsberg, David Mura, Richard Jones, and Ernesto Cardenal. As a sample Jack Grapes selected "Splitting Hairs" by Joyce Elaine Ross:

> After I poured my blocks onto the floor and shuffled them,/then made one last attempt to attain some
> form of poetic/fusion, like William Grant Still's Afro-American Symphony/of classical blues on jazz, I
> realized that I've never been/able to get others to understand me; that my words always/seem to turn
> into fishbones and sawdust whenever I tried/to talk about it. And if I could, I would drink my own/
> skin, erase the stain of my colors.

ONTHEBUS is 275 pages, offset printed, flat-spined, with color card cover. Press run is 3,500 for 600 subscribers of which 40 are libraries, 1,200 shelf sales ("500 sold directly at readings"). Subscription: $28/3 issues; Issue #8/9, special double issue: $15. Sample (including guidelines): $12.

How to Submit: Submit 3-6 poems at a time to the above address (send all other correspondence to: 6684 Colgate Ave., Los Angeles CA 90048). Accepts simultaneous submissions and previously published poems, "if I am informed where poem has previously appeared and/or where poem is also being submitted. I expect neatly-typed, professional-looking cover letters with list of poems included plus poet's bio. Sloppiness and unprofessional submissions do not equate with great writing." Do not submit mss between November 1 and March 1 or between June 1 and September 1. Submissions sent during those times will be returned unread. Responds in "anywhere from two weeks to two years." Pays 1 copy. Acquires one-time rights. Reviews books of poetry in 400 words (chapbooks in 200 words), single format. Poets may send books for review consideration.

Book/Chapbook Needs & How to Submit: Bombshelter Press publishes 4-6 flat-spined paperbacks and 5 chapbooks/year. Query first. Primarily interested in Los Angeles poets. "We publish very few unsolicited mss." Responds in 3 months. Pays 50 copies. Also publishes the *ONTHEBUS* Poets Anthology Series. Send SASE for details.

Advice: "My goal is to publish a democratic range of American poets and ensure they are read by striving to circulate the magazine as widely as possible. It's hard work and a financial drain. I hope the mag is healthy for poets and writers, and that they support the endeavor by subscribing as well as submitting."

Ⓝ ◙ OPEN HAND PUBLISHING INC., P.O. Box 20207, Greensboro NC 27420. (336)292-8585. Fax: (336)292-8588. E-mail: openhnd1@bellsouth.net. Website: www.openhand.com (includes catalog and contact information). Established 1981. **Publisher:** P. Anna Johnson. Open Hand is a "literary/political book publisher bringing out flat-spined paperbacks as well as cloth cover editions about African-American and multicultural issues." Has published *Where Are the Love Poems for Dictators?* by E. Ethelbert Miller, *Old Woman of Irish Blood* by Pat Andrus, and *Stone on Stone: Poetry by Women of Diverse Heritages* edited by Zoë Anglesey. Does not consider unsolicited mss.

OPEN MINDS QUARTERLY; THE WRITER'S CIRCLE ONLINE (Specialized: individuals who have experienced mental illness), The Writer's Circle, 680 Kirkwood Dr., Building 2, Sudbury, Ontario P3E 1X3 Canada. (705)675-9193, ext. 8286. Fax: (705)675-3501. E-mail: openminds@ni sa.on.ca. Website: www.nisa.on.ca/literaryprograms.htm (includes submission guidelines, mandate, contact info, *The Writer's Circle Online*). Established 1997. **Editor:** Barb Wilson, M.A.

Magazine Needs: *Open Minds Quarterly* provides a "venue for individuals who have experienced mental illness to express themselves via poetry, short fiction, essays, first-person accounts of living with mental illness, book/movie reviews." Wants unique, well-written, provocative poetry. No overly graphic or sexual violence. Recently published poetry by Derek Day, Alexander Radway, Sydney B. Smith, and Gail Kroll. As a sample the editor selected these lines from "Banff" by Derek G. Day:

> As dogs in a strange town/rush out to explore the trees and hydrants,/we come here, seek out the tavern,/and quietly get pissed.

Open Minds Quarterly is 24 pages, magazine-sized, saddle-stapled, 100 lb. stock cover with original artwork back/front, approximately 3-6 ads/issue. Receives about 125 poems/year, accepts about 65%. Publishes about 5-10 poems/issue. Press run is 1,000 for 550 subscribers of which 4-5 are libraries, 5 shelf sales; 400 distributed free to potential subscribers, published writers, advertisers. Single copy: $5 Canadian, $3.50 US; subscription: $35 Canadian, $28.25 US (special rates also available). Sample: $3.50 US, $5 Canadian. Make checks payable to NISA/Northern Initiative for Social Action.

How to Submit: Submit 1-5 poems at a time. Accepts previously published poems and simultaneous submissions. Accepts fax, e-mail, and disk submissions. Cover letter is required. "Info in cover letter: indication as to 'consumer/survivor' of the mental health system status." Reads submissions all year. Submit seasonal poems at least 8 months in advance. Time between acceptance and publication is 6-18 months. "Poems are accepted/rejected by the editor. Sometimes, submissions are passed on to a second or third party for input or a 'second opinion.' " Seldom comments on rejected poems. Guidelines available in magazine (once a year), for SASE, by fax, by e-mail, or on website. Responds in up to 4 months. Sometimes sends prepublication galleys. "All authors own their work—if another publisher seeks to reprint from our publication, we request them to cite the source."

Also Offers: "All material not accepted for our magazine/journal will be considered for *The Writer's Circle Online*, our Internet publication forum. Same guidelines apply. Same contact person."

Advice: "We are unique in that our outlets help to reduce the stigma surrounding mental illness by illustrating the creative talents of individuals suffering from mental illness."

OPEN SPACES, 6327 C SW Capitol Hwy., Suite 134, Portland OR 97201-1937. (503)227-5764. Fax: (503)227-3401. Website: www.open-spaces.com (includes guidelines, table of contents, covers, sample articles, literary essays, and overview). Established 1997. **Poetry Editor:** Susan Juve-Hu Bucharest.

Magazine Needs: "*Open Spaces* is a quarterly which gives voice to the Northwest on issues that are regional, national, and international in scope. Our readership is thoughtful, intelligent, widely read, and appreciative of ideas and writing of the highest quality. With that in mind, we seek thoughtful, well-researched articles and insightful fiction, reviews, and poetry on a variety of subjects from a number of different viewpoints. Although we take ourselves seriously, we appreciate humor as well." *Open Spaces* is 64 pages, magazine-sized, sheet-fed printed, cover art and graphics and original art throughout. "We have received many submissions and hope to use 3-4 per issue." Press run is 5,000-10,000. Subscription: $25/year. Sample: $10. Make checks payable to Open Spaces Publications, Inc.

How to Submit: Submit 3-5 poems at a time. Accepts previously published poems and simultaneous submissions. Accepts submissions by fax and by regular mail. No e-mail submissions. Cover letter required. Time between acceptance and publication is 2-3 months. Poems are circulated to an editorial board. Seldom comments on rejected poems. Guidelines available on website. Responds in up to 4 months. Payment varies. Reviews books and chapbooks of poetry."

Advice: "Poets we have published include Vern Rutsala, Pattiann Rogers, Lou Masson, and William Jolliff. Poetry is presented with care and respect."

USE THE GENERAL INDEX in the back of this book to find the page number of a specific market. Also, markets listed in the 2002 edition but not included in this edition appear in the General Index with a code explaining their absence from the listings.

OPEN UNIVERSITY OF AMERICA PRESS; OPEN UNIVERSITY OF AMERICA (Specialized: distance learning, English pedagogy), 3916 Commander Dr., Hyattsville MD 20782-1027. Phone/fax: (301)779-0220. E-mail: openuniv@aol.com. Website: www.openuniversityofamerica.com (includes catalog). Established 1965. **Co-Editors:** Mary Rodgers and Dan Rodgers.

Book/Chapbook Needs: "We buy artistic work outright before copyright or publication by the author. We include these literary pieces always with the author's name in our university publications, catalogues, lists, etc." Publishes 2 paperbacks and 2 hardbacks/year. "No restrictions on poetry. Shorter is better. One page set up for 6×9 is good. A set of poems (short chapbook) should be uniform." Interested in receiving work on the topics of "Catholic faith and culture; morality; nature; open learning and English pedagogy (teaching English) K-Ph.D. Pre-published or pre-copyrighted or book-length poems are beyond our capability." Accepts poetry written by children (negotiations only with parent, however). Has published poetry by Mark Lundberg, Mary Rodgers, Henry Tokarski, and Stavros Sitaras. As a sample we selected these lines from "Student Teaching" by Frederick Orinc in *Catholic Open University Poems, 1962-2000*:

> *I've tried to teach/this lesson/to its clean conclusion/clear objectives/but//somehow they've corrupted/*
> *in/the flesh.//Reading is easier than teaching.*

Books are usually 100-200 pages, 6×9, computer/laser printed, perfect-bound (some sewn in library binding), soft cover, includes art.

How to Submit: Submit up to 10 poems at a time. No previously published poems or simultaneous submissions. Accepts submissions by postal mail only. Cover letter preferred. "We buy poems and small sets of poems outright (price negotiable), so we need pre-copyrighted, pre-published literary work. No whole books. When we publish compilations, we always list the name of the artist/author. Literary work is accepted on its own merit and its usefulness in perpetuity to the Press and to Open University of America. Make sure you want to put your poem for final and irrevocable sale." **Reading fee:** $1/poem. Time between acceptance and publication is up to 2 years. Poems are circulated to an editorial board. "Two editors plus one consultant select work to be purchased for publication. Note that we purchase all rights for publication, total rights." Seldom comments on rejected poems. Responds to queries and mss in up to 3 weeks. Order sample books by sending $10 or order off the web.

Advice: "Today electronic publishing, overseas sales, and other mass selling mechanisms are running roughshod over the rights of writers. We buy your verbal art at a fair, negotiated price before copyright and publication. We use your poem/poems always with your name attached to enhance our literary productions. We keep it in perpetuity in our Literary Trust. This is an effective way to get publicity for your name and your work, as well as to earn income."

OPENED EYES POETRY & PROSE MAGAZINE (Specialized: membership/subscription; senior citizen; students; Afro-American, Caribbean); KENYA BLUE POETRY AWARD CONTEST, P.O. Box 21708, Brooklyn NY 11202-1708. (718)284-0569. E-mail: kenyablue@excite.com. Established 1998. **Editor-in-Chief:** Kenya Blue.

Magazine Needs: Appearing 3 times/year, *Opened Eyes* is a "venue for seniors, known poets, novice poets, and minority poets; offering a supportive environment and challenging environment." Wants "free verse, traditional forms; prose—all styles; all subject matter; short, poetic stories. No hate or sexually explicit/graphic poetry." Accepts poetry written by children. Has published poetry by Jay Chollick, Evie Ivy, and Sol Rubin. As a sample the editor selected these lines from Carol D. Meeks:

> *Among my flowers/these butterflies flaunt and flash/their stained-glass wings*

Opened Eyes is 8½×11, photocopied and either strip-bound or comb-bound with cardstock cover, includes art/ graphics and ads. Receives about 100 poems/year, accepts about 95%. Publish up to 25 poems/issue. Press run is 100 for 50 subscribers, 24 shelf sales. Subscription: $18/year. Sample: $7. Make checks payable to K. Blue.

How to Submit: Submit 1-3 poems at a time with **$3 reading fee if nonsubscriber.** Line length for poetry is 30 maximum. Accepts previously published poems and simultaneous submissions. Accepts e-mail submissions; include in body of message. "Type name, address, and e-mail in upper left hand corner. Submit typed poem in desired format for magazine and editor will try to accommodate." Time between acceptance and publication is up to 2 months. "Poems are circulated to editor and poetry consultant." Occasionally publishes theme issues; upcoming themes available for SASE. Guidelines available for SASE, by e-mail, and in publication. Responds in 3 weeks. Pays 5 copies. Acquires one-time rights.

Also Offers: "Sponsors the Kenya Blue Poetry Award contest. Winner paid in copies of magazine. Kenya Blue Award topics change yearly.

Advice: "Challenge yourself and take a first step in being creative via literature and via poetry."

OPOSSUM HOLLER TAROT, 5094 N. Co. Rd. 750 E., Orleans IN 47452. (812)865-2676. E-mail: OHT@weedmail.com. Established 1983. **Artistic Assistant:** L. Blazek.

Magazine Needs: *Opossum Holler Tarot* appears "once in awhile" as a magazine-format collage. Submit "anything you like." Does not want "hate-filled racist tripe." Recently published poetry by Geoff Sawyers, Ed Orr, Huth Argraves, Steve Sneyd, Cardinal Cox, and Giovanni Malito. As a sample the editor selected these lines from his poem "Weed" from *Transverse Nirvana*:

A sojourn flower/spreads its unlovely vagina/a lifetime passing/a painting too complete

Opossum Holler Tarot is magazine-sized, photocopied, with art/graphics. Receives about 200 poems/year, accepts about 99%. Publishes about 15 poems/issue. Press run is 5 for 1 subscriber (library); 4 distributed free to contributors. Single copy: trade or free; subscription: "send us something." Sample: "send stamps."
How to Submit: Submit 3 poems at a time. Accepts previously published poems and simultaneous submissions. Accepts e-mail submissions; no fax or disk submissions. Include SASE. Reads submissions "whenever we like." Time between acceptance and publication varies. Always comments on rejected poems. Occasionally publishes theme issues. Guidelines available for SASE or by e-mail. Responds "soon." Pays 1 contributor's copy.
Book/Chapbook Needs & How to Submit: *Opossum Holler Tarot* has discontinued its chapbook series.
Advice: "If you don't get it out there, then who's going to read it?"

$◐ ORCHISES PRESS, P.O. Box 20602, Alexandria VA 22320-1602. E-mail: lathbury@gmu.edu. Website: http://mason.gmu.edu/~rlathbur (includes submission guidelines, contact information, editorial policy, sample poems, book covers, and online catalog). Established 1983. **Poetry Editor:** Roger Lathbury.
Book/Chapbook Needs: Orchises is a small press publisher of literary and general material in flat-spined paperbacks and in hardcover. "Although we will consider mss submitted, we prefer to seek out the work of poets who interest us." Regarding poetry, Orchises has "no restrictions; it must be technically proficient and deeply felt. I find it unlikely that I would publish a ms unless a fair proportion of its contents has appeared previously in respected literary journals." Has published *Chokecherries* by Peter Klappert and *The Travelling Library* by David Kirby. Publishes about 4 flat-spined paperbacks of poetry a year, averaging 96 pages, and some casebound books. Most paperbacks are $14.95. Hardbacks are $20-21.95 each.
How to Submit: Submit 5-6 poems at a time. No e-mail submissions. Poems must be typed. When submitting, "tell where poems have previously been published." Brief cover letter preferred. Guidelines available on website. Responds in 1 month. Pays 36% of money earned once Orchises recoups its initial costs and has a "generous free copy policy."

◑ ◎ OSIRIS, AN INTERNATIONAL POETRY JOURNAL/UNE REVUE INTERNATIO-NALE (Specialized: translations, bilingual), P.O. Box 297, Deerfield MA 01342-0297. Established 1972. **Poetry Editor:** Andrea Moorhead.
Magazine Needs: *Osiris* is a semiannual that publishes contemporary poetry in English, French, and Italian without translation and in other languages with translation, including Polish, Danish, and German. Wants poetry which is "lyrical, non-narrative, multi-temporal, post-modern, well-crafted. Also looking for translations from non-IndoEuropean languages." Has published poetry by Tahar Bekri (France), Nicole Brossard (Canada), Annemette Andersen (Denmark), Athina Papadaki (Greece), and Ingrid Swanberg (US). As a sample the editor selected these lines from "Dark Summer Wind" by Ingrid Swanberg:
in your absence/the mast towers and gleams/the hiss of the moon on my shoulder
Osiris is 40-48 pages, 6×9, saddle-stapled with graphics and photos. There are 15-20 pages of poetry in English in each issue of this publication. Print run is 500 with 50 subscription copies sent to college and university libraries, including foreign libraries. Receives 200-300 submissions/year, accepts about 12. Single copy: $7.50; subscription: $15. Sample: $3.
How to Submit: Submit 4-6 poems at a time. "Poems should be sent regular mail." Include short bio and SASE with submission. "Translators should include a letter of permission from the poet or publisher as well as copies of the original text." Responds in 1 month. Sometimes sends prepublication galleys. Pays 5 contributor's copies.
Advice: "It is always best to look at a sample copy of a journal before submitting work, and when you do submit work, do it often and do not get discouraged. Try to read poetry and support other writers."

◖ OSRIC PUBLISHING; THE WHITE CROW, P.O. Box 4501, Ann Arbor MI 48106-4501. E-mail: chris@osric.com. Website: http://osric.com and http://wcrow.com (includes guidelines, contact information, reviews, and samples). Established 1993. **Editor:** Christopher™ Herdt. **Assistant Editor:** Mrrranda L. Tarrow.
Magazine Needs: *The White Crow* is a quarterly "literate, not literary journal. It contains poetry and fiction that is meaningful and that will appeal to an educated, but not necessarily high-brow audience. Something that even an electrical engineer might enjoy." Wants "nothing bigger than a breadbox. No one-pagers that use the word black more than four times and no 'throbbing, beefy torpedo' poems." Has published poetry by David Offut, Alan Catlin, Stepan Chapman, and Eileen Doherty. *The White Crow* is 32 pages, 5½×8½, sometimes photocopied, sometimes offset-printed, saddle-stapled with cardstock, black

only cover, includes art and graphics. Receives about 2,000 poems/year, accepts 5%. Press run is 400 for 50 subscribers, 200 shelf sales; 50 distributed free to reviewers and associates. Single copy: $2.50; subscription: $8. Sample (including guidelines): $2.50. Make checks payable to Osric Publishing.

How to Submit: Submit 5 poems at a time. Accepts previously published poems and simultaneous submissions. No e-mail or disk submissions. Cover letter preferred. Time between acceptance and publication is about 1 month. Poems are circulated to an editorial board. "The editors all get together and drink heavily, eat some food, and rate and berate the submissions." Guidelines are available for SASE or on website. Responds in about 6 months. Pays 1 contributor's copy. Acquires first rights. Staff reviews books and chapbooks of poetry and other magazines in 100 words, single book format. Send books for review consideration to Christopher™ Herdt.

Book/Chapbook Needs & How to Submit: Osric Publishing seeks "poetry and short fiction for the literate, not literary." Publishes 1 chapbook/year. Has published *Bench Marks* by David Offutt. Books are usually 24 pages, 8½×5½, photocopied or offset-printed and saddle-stapled with cardstock cover, uses art/graphics. Query first, with a few sample poems and a cover letter with brief bio and publication credits. Responds to queries and mss in 6 months. Pays 20 author's copies (out of a press run of 200). Order sample books by sending $2 to Osric Publishing.

Advice: "No poems about poetry, no poems about writing poetry, no stories about writing stories."

N $ M O THE OTHER SIDE MAGAZINE (Specialized: political, religious, social issues), 300 W. Apsley St., Philadelphia PA 19144. (215)849-2178. Website: www.theotherside.org. Established 1965. **Poetry Editor:** Jeanne Minahan.

Magazine Needs: "*The Other Side* is an independent ecumenical magazine that seeks to advance a broad Christian vision that's biblical and compassionate, appreciative of the creative arts, and committed to the intimate intertwining of personal spirituality and social transformation. We weave together first-person essays, insightful analyses, biblical reflection, interviews, fiction, poetry, and an inviting mix of visual art. We strive to nurture, uplift, and challenge readers with personal, provocative writing that reflects the transformative, liberating Spirit of Jesus Christ." The magazine publishes 1-2 poems/issue. "Poetry submissions should include strong imagery, fresh viewpoints, and lively language, while avoiding versifications of religious instruction or syrupy piety. Be warned that only 0.5% of the poems reviewed are accepted." Has published poetry by Kathleen Norris, Paul Ramsey, Carol Hamilton, and John Knoepfle. *The Other Side* is magazine-sized, professionally printed on quality pulp stock, 64 pages, saddle-stapled, with full-color paper cover. Circulation is 13,000 to that many subscriptions. Subscription: $24. Sample: $4.50.

How to Submit: Submit 3 poems at a time. Line length for poetry is 50 maximum. No previously published poems or simultaneous submissions. Editor "almost never" comments on rejected poems. Guidelines available for SASE. Responds in 3 months. Pays $15 plus 2 copies and 2-year subscription.

■ $ O OTHER VOICES, Garneau P.O. Box 52059, 8210-109 St., Edmonton, Alberta T6G 2T5 Canada. Established 1988. **Contact:** poetry editors.

Magazine Needs: *Other Voices* appears 2 times/year in the Spring and Fall. "We are devoted to the publication of quality literary writing—poetry, fiction, nonfiction; also reviews and artwork. We encourage submissions by new and established writers. Our only desire for poetry is that it is good! We encourage submissions by women and members of minorities, but we will consider everyone's. We never publish popular/sentimental greeting-card-type poetry or anything sexist, racist, or homophobic." Has published poetry by Bert Almon, Heidi Greco, Robin S. Chapman, Zoë Landale, and Erina Harris. As a sample the editor selected these lines from "One Breast" by Chris Smart:

> The word cancer slips/into their house/opens lace curtains, leaves/a trail of mud. A presence/breathes
> at the window/murmurs at the door.//A breast blooms/in the garden.//Once flowers bloomed/on the
> window sills/and the scent flooded/the house.

Other Voices is 100-120 pages, 21½×14cm, professionally printed and perfect-bound with color cover, includes art and ads. Receives about 800 poems/year, accepts 4%. Press run is 500 for 330 subscribers of which 7 are libraries, 60 shelf sales. Subscription: $18/year in Canada, $23 US, $28 overseas. Sample: $10.

How to Submit: Submit 2-6 poems at a time. Include SAE with IRC. "Please limit your submissions to a maximum of 6 pages of poetry and send only 1 submission every 6 months." No previously published poems or simultaneous submissions. Cover letter preferred. "Please include short bio. Phone numbers, fax numbers, and e-mail addresses are helpful." Spring submission deadline: March 15; fall deadline is September 15. "We are currently discussing moving our deadlines up to September 1 and March 1. Poets may want to submit by those dates to be on the safe side." Time between acceptance and publication is 1 month. Poems are circulated to an editorial board. "Poems are read and assessed independently by five poetry editors. After the deadline, we gather and 'haggle' over which poems to accept." Seldom comments on rejected poems. Publishes theme issues. Guidelines and upcoming themes are available for SASE (or SAE with IRC) or on website. Responds in up to

6 months. Pays small honorarium plus subscription. Acquires first North American serial rights. Reviews books of poetry in 1,000 words, single or double book format. Poets may send books for review consideration to Editorial Collective.

Also Offers: "We typically hold one contest per year, but the time, fees, and theme vary. Check our website for details."

Advice: "Please take note of our September and March deadlines. If you just miss a deadline, it could take up to six months for a reply."

OUTER DARKNESS: WHERE NIGHTMARES ROAM UNLEASHED (Specialized: horror, mystery, science fiction, dark fantasy), 1312 N. Delaware Place, Tulsa OK 74110. E-mail: odmagazine@aol.com. Established 1994. **Editor:** Dennis J. Kirk.

Magazine Needs: *Outer Darkness* is a quarterly magazine featuring short stories, poetry, and art in the genres of horror, dark fantasy, and science fiction (and also mystery with a horror/gothic slant). Wants "all styles of poetry, though traditional rhyming verse is preferred. Send verse that is dark and melancholy in nature. Nothing experimental—very little of this type of verse is published in *Outer Darkness*." Has published poetry by Carmen Willcox, Andrea Selina Thomas, and Timothy M. Walters. *Outer Darkness* is 40-60 pages, 8½ × 5½, photocopied, saddle-stapled, glossy cover, includes cover art, cartoons and illustrations and runs ads for other publications. Receives about 200 poems/year, accepts 20%. Press run is 200, 25% to subscribers, 25% to contributors, 25% sample copy sales, 25% to advertisers, free copies, etc. Single copy: $3.95; subscription: $11.95.

How to Submit: Submit up to 3 poems at a time, no longer than 60 lines each. Accepts simultaneous submissions; no previously published poems. Cover letter preferred. "Poets are encouraged to include cover letters with their submissions, with biographical information, personal interests, past publishing credits, etc. I strongly prefer hardcopy submissions rather than disks." Always comments on rejected poems. Guidelines available for SASE. Responds in up to 6 weeks. Sends prepublication galleys, when requested. Pays 2 copies. Acquires one-time rights.

Advice: "*Never* get in a hurry when composing a poem. Pay close attention to each line, each syllable, to maintain a consistent rhythm. Experiment with different forms of rhyme to avoid that sing-song feel often found in traditional verse. In short, work with each poem until you're convinced you've produced the best possible."

OUTERBRIDGE, English A324, The College of Staten Island, 2800 Victory Blvd., Staten Island NY 10314. (718)982-3651. Established 1975. **Editor:** Charlotte Alexander.

Magazine Needs: *Outerbridge* publishes "the most crafted, professional poetry and short fiction we can find (unsolicited except special features—to date rural, urban and Southern, promoted in standard newsletters such as *Poets & Writers*, *AWP*, *Small Press Review*), interested in newer voices. Anti loose, amateurish, uncrafted poems showing little awareness of the long-established fundamentals of verse; also anti blatant PRO-movement writing when it sacrifices craft for protest and message. Poems usually one to four pages in length." Has published poetry by Walter McDonald, Thomas Swiss, and Naomi Rachel. The digest-sized, flat-spined annual is 100 pages, about half poetry. Press run is 500-600 for 150 subscribers of which 28 are libraries. Receives about 500-700 submissions/year, accepts approximately 60. Sample: $6.

How to Submit: Submit 3-5 poems only, anytime except June and July. Include name and address on each page. "We dislike simultaneous submissions and if a poem accepted by us proves to have already been accepted elsewhere, a poet will be blacklisted as there are many good poets waiting in line." Cover letter with brief bio preferred. Publishes theme issues. Guidelines and upcoming themes available for SASE. Responds in 2 months. Pays 2 copies (and offers additional copies at half price). Acquires first rights.

Advice: "As a poet/editor I feel magazines like *Outerbridge* provide an invaluable publication outlet for poets (particularly since publishing a book of poetry, respectably, is extremely difficult these days). As in all of the arts, poetry—its traditions, conventions and variations, experiments—should be studied. One current 'trend' I detect is a lot of mutual backscratching which can result in loose, amateurish writing. Discipline!"

OUTRIDER PRESS, 937 Patricia Lane, Crete IL 60417-1362. (708)672-6630. Fax: (708)672-5820. E-mail: outriderpr@aol.com. Website: www.outriderpress.com (includes publication titles, prices, ordering information, general guidelines/themes, address for complete guidelines, Tallgrass Writers Guild information, and membership). Established 1988. **Senior Editor:** Whitney Scott. **President:** Phyllis Nelson.

Book/Chapbook Needs: Outrider publishes 1-3 novels/anthologies/chapbooks annually. Wants "poetry dealing with the terrain of the human heart and plotting inner journeys; growth and grace under pressure.

No bag ladies, loves-that-never-were, please." Has published poetry by Pamela Miller, David T. Lloyd, James Wheldon, Albert DeGenova, Vivian Shipley, Margo Tamez, and Cynthia Gallaher. As a sample we selected these lines from "That Year, That Icy Blackness" by Lyn Lifshin, from the anthology *A Kiss Is Still a Kiss*:

> like long hair/in tangles I/dream, if snow/melted I/could comb with/rain water

A Kiss Is Still a Kiss is 256 pages, digest-sized, attractively printed and perfect-bound with glossy card cover, $15.95.

How to Submit: Submit 3-4 poems at a time with SASE. Include name, address, phone/fax number, and e-mail address on every poem. Accepts simultaneous submissions, if specified. Guidelines and upcoming themes available for SASE, by fax, and by e-mail. Cover letter preferred. Responds to queries in 1 month, to mss in 2 months. Pays 1 copy.

Also Offers: Outrider publishes a themed anthology annually in August, with cash prizes for best poetry and short fiction. Submit up to 4 poems, no longer than 1 page in length (single spacing OK). **Reading fee:** $16, $12 for Tallgrass Writers Guild members. Guidelines available for SASE. Deadline: February 28, 2003. Published in August 2003. Our 2003 theme: Family Gatherings—weddings, wakes, holiday dinners, cookouts, and more. The press is affiliated with the Tallgrass Writers Guild, an international organization open to all who support equality of voices in writing. Annual membership fee: $35. Information available for SASE or on website.

Advice: "We look for visceral truths expressed without compromise, coyness, or cliché. Go for the center of the experience. Pull no punches."

N ⬤ OVER THE TRANSOM, P.O. Box 423528, San Francisco CA 94142-3528. (415)928-3965. E-mail: jsh619@earthlink.net. Established 1997. **Editor:** Jonathan Hayes.

Magazine Needs: *Over The Transom*, a free publication of art and literature, appears 2 times/year. Open to all styles of poetry. Recently published poetry by B.Z. Niditch, A.D. Winans, Garret Caples, Donald P. Hilla, Jr., Marie Kazalia, and Glen Chesnut. As a sample the editor selected these lines from "Because" by August Brine:

> it's the sadness of sulfur,/or the fact that suicides are just statistics,/that makes me want to love you,/while i still exist,/and fill in that empty four-letter word with all my blood and breath

Over The Transom is 32 pages, magazine-sized, saddle-stapled, cardstock cover, with b&w art. Receives about 1,000 poems/year, accepts about 20%. Publishes about 25 poems/issue. Press run is 700 for 100 subscribers; 500 distributed free to cafes, bookstores, and bars. Single copy: free. Sample: $2 to cover postage. Make checks payable to Jonathan Hayes.

How to Submit: Submit 5 poems at a time. Accepts previously published poems and simultaneous submissions. Accepts e-mail submissions; no fax or disk submissions. Cover letter is required. Must include a SASE. Reads submissions all year. Time between acceptance and publication is 2-6 months. Poems are circulated to an editorial board. "We look for the highest quality poetry that best fits the issue." Never comments on rejected poems. Occasionally publishes theme issues. Guidelines available for SASE or by e-mail. Responds in 2 months. Sometimes sends prepublication galleys. Pays 1 contributor's copy. Acquires first rights. Reviews books and chapbooks of poetry and other magazines/journals in 400 words. Poets may send books/chapbooks for review consideration to *Over The Transom*.

Advice: "All editors have differing tastes, so don't be upset by early rejection; but please ensure you always send a SASE for response, whatever it may be."

⬤ OXYGEN, 537 Jones St., PMB 999, San Francisco CA 94102. (415)776-9681. E-mail: oxygen@mind spring.com (no e-mail submissions!). Website: www.oxygeneditions.net (includes guidelines, bios, archives, contact and subscription info, etc.). Established 1991. **Editor:** Richard Hack.

Magazine Needs: *Oxygen* is published 1-2 times/year. "We are open to many forms in many categories (e.g., surrealist, expressionist, narrative, devotional, et al.). We do not like poetry that smacks too much of workshop blandness and compromise, nor do we generally like academic poetry, uninformed cafe poetry, and some others. But we are not averse to hermetic poetry, allusive poetry, or simple, clear verse. Deeper delving and passion are hoped for." Has published poetry by Victor Martinez, Sergei Yesenin, Ronald Sauer, Steve Arntson, and Maura O'Connor. *Oxygen* is 130 pages, 5½×8½, offset-printed and perfect-bound with laminated solid color cover, includes drawings and photos. Receives about 4,500 poems/year, accepts 1%. Publishes 50 poems/issue. Press run is 500. "We sell about 400 in stores and on newsstands in the Bay Area and nationally through DeBoer." Subscription: $18/4 issues. Sample: $5.

How to Submit: Submit up to 10 poems at a time. Accepts previously published poems ("as long as previous venue and its circulation are made known") and simultaneous submissions. No e-mail submissions. Always send SASE for response. Time between acceptance and publication is up to 6 months. Guidelines available for SASE. Responds in 2 months or less. Always sends prepublication galleys. Pays

2 contributor's copies. Acquires one-time rights, "plus right to use in future anthologies (spelled out in acceptance letter)." Occasionally reviews books and chapbooks of poetry and other magazines. Poets may send books for review consideration, "but no more than a notice is likely."

OYSTER BOY REVIEW; OFF THE CUFF BOOKS, P.O. Box 83, Chapel Hill NC 27514. E-mail: editors@oysterboyreview.com. Website: www.oysterboyreview.com (includes complete issues, contacts, and submission guidelines). Established 1993. **Poetry Editor:** Jeffery Beam.
Magazine Needs: *Oyster Boy Review* appears 4 times/year. "We're interested in the underrated, the ignored, the misunderstood, and the varietal. We'll make some mistakes. 'All styles are good except the boring kind'—Voltaire." Accepts poetry written by children; "We're about to publish a three year-old." Has published poetry by Jonathan Williams, Cid Corman, Lyn Lifshin, and Paul Dilsaver. As a sample the editor selected these lines from "Night" by Thomas Meyer:
> When it flowers/night fills/with a cruelty/I have done you/whose fruit is sweet

Oyster Boy Review is 60 pages, 6½×11, Docutech printed and stapled with paper cover, includes photography and ads. Receives about 1,500 poems/year, accepts 2%. Press run is 200 for 30 subscribers, 100 shelf sales; 30 distributed free to editors, authors. Subscription: $20.
How to Submit: Submit up to 5 poems at a time. No previously published poems or simultaneous submissions. Accepts e-mail submissions if poems are included in body of message. Cover letter preferred. Postal submissions require SASE. Do not submit mss in late December. "Upon acceptance, authors asked to provide electronic version of work and a biographical statement." Time between acceptance and publication is 6 months. Seldom comments on rejected poems. Guidelines are available by e-mail and on website. Responds in 3 months. Pays 2 copies. Reviews books and chapbooks of poetry in 250-500 words (1st books only), in single or multi-book format. Poets may send books for review consideration.
Book/Chapbook Needs: *Off the Cuff is not open to submissions or solicitations.* Off the Cuff Books publishes "longer works and special projects of authors published in *Oyster Boy Review.*"
Advice: *"Oyster Boy Review* responds to freshness—to the unschooled enthusiasm that leads to fresh idioms and subjects—without kowtowing to any camps, mainstream or not."

P.D.Q. (POETRY DEPTH QUARTERLY), 5836 North Haven Dr., North Highlands CA 95660. (916)331-3512. E-mail: poetdpth@aol.com Website: www.angelfire.com/biz/PoetsGuild/guide.html. Established 1995. **Publisher:** G. Elton Warrick. **Editor:** Joyce Odam.
• *"P.D.Q.* editor submits nominations for the Pushcart Prize."
Magazine Needs: *P.D.Q.* wants "original poetry that clearly demonstrates an understanding of craft. All styles accepted." Does not want "poetry which is overtly religious, erotic, inflammatory, or demeans the human spirit." Has published poetry by Jane Blue, Taylor Graham, Simon Perchik, Carol Hamilton, B.Z. Niditch, and Danyen Powell. *P.D.Q.* is 35-60 pages, digest-sized, coated and saddle-stapled with a glossy color cover and original art. Receives 1,800-2,000 poems/year, accepts about 10%. Press run is 200 of which 5 subscribers are libraries. Single: $5; subscription: $18.50 (add $10/year for foreign subscriptions). Make checks payable to G. Elton Warrick.
How to Submit: Submit 3-5 poems of any length, "typewritten and presented exactly as you would like them to appear," maximum 52 characters/line (including spaces), with name and address on every page. All submissions should include SASE (or SAE with IRC) and cover letter with short 3-10 line bio and publication credits. "Manuscripts without SASE or sufficient postage will not be read or returned." No simultaneous submissions. Accepts previously published poems "occasionally" with publication credits. Accepts e-mail submissions. Guidelines available for SASE or on website. Responds in 3 months. Pays 1 contributor's copy.

$ PACIFIC COAST JOURNAL; FRENCH BREAD AWARDS; FRENCH BREAD PUBLI-CATIONS, P.O. Box 56, Carlsbad CA 92018. E-mail: paccoastj@frenchbreadpublications.com. Website: www.frenchbreadpublications.com/pcj (includes guidelines, poetry, and contest information). Established 1992. **Editor:** Stillson Graham.
Magazine Needs: *Pacific Coast Journal* is a quarterly "unprofessional literary magazine that prints first-time authors, emerging authors, established authors, and authors who are so visible that everyone's sick of them." Wants "offbeat poetry, visual poetry, poetry that is aware of itself. We don't rule out rhyming poetry, but rarely do we accept it." Has published poetry by Nils Clausen, Joan Payne Kincaid, and Hugh Fox. As a sample the editor selected these lines by Greg Russell:
> poetry is variety, often intense,/frequently emotional, or deeply/personal. this poem isn't any of/those/things.

Pacific Coast Journal is 56 pages, 5½×8½, photocopied and saddle-stapled with a card stock cover and b&w photos and artwork. Receives 400-500 poems/year, accepts about 5-10%. Press run is 200 for 100 subscribers. Single copy: $3; subscription: $12. Sample: $2.50.

How to Submit: Submit up to 6 poems or 12 pages at a time. Accepts simultaneous submissions; no previously published poems. No e-mail submissions. Cover letter preferred. Time between acceptance and publication is up to 18 months. Seldom comments on rejected poems. Guidelines available for SASE or by e-mail. Responds in 4 months. Pays 1 contributor's copy. Acquires one-time rights. Reviews novels, short story collections, and chapbooks of poetry in 1,500 words, single format. Poets may send books for review consideration.

Book/Chapbook Needs & How to Submit: French Bread Publications also occasionally publishes chapbooks of poetry, short story collections and short novellas. Books are similar to the journal in format. Has published *Literary Junkies* by Errol Miller. Query first with 5-8 sample poems, a cover letter and a list of credits for all the poems in the ms. Responds to queries in 2 months, to mss (if invited) in 4 months. Pays royalties and 10% of press run.

Also Offers: Also sponsors the French Bread Awards for short fiction/poetry. Entry fee: $6 for a group of up to 4 poems (no longer than 8 pages total). 1st Prize: $50. 2nd Prize: $25. Deadline: August 1. Details available for SASE.

Advice: "Most poetry looks like any other poetry. We want experiments in what poetry is."

N $ PAINTED BRIDE QUARTERLY, Rutgers-Camden, English Dept. ATG Hall, 311 N. 5th St., Camden NJ 08102. E-mail: pbrideq@camden.rutgers.edu. Website: http://pbq.rutgers.edu (includes guidelines, contact and subscription information, bios, archives, contest rules, catalog, and upcoming themes). Established 1973. **Editor:** Marion Wrenn. **Contact:** Poetry Editors.

Magazine Needs: "We have no specifications or restrictions. We'll look at anything." Has published poetry by Robert Bly, Charles Bukowski, S.J. Marks, and James Hazen. "*Painted Bride Quarterly* aims to be a leader among little magazines published by and for independent poets and writers nationally." *Painted Bride Quarterly* is published quarterly online with one hardcopy anthology printed annually. Anthology: $15.

How to Submit: Submit up to 6 poems, any length, typed; only original, unpublished work. No e-mail submissions. "Submissions should include a short bio." Seldom comment on rejected poems. Occasionally publishes theme issues. September 2002 issue will be film-related essays, prose, poetry. Guidelines and themes available on website. Has a 6- to 9-month backlog. Pays 1-year subscription, 1 half-priced contributor's copy, and $5/accepted piece. Publishes reviews of poetry books. "We also occasionally publish critical essays."

Also Offers: Sponsors annual poetry contest and chapbook competition. Entry fee required for both. Send SASE for details.

PALANQUIN; PALANQUIN POETRY SERIES, Dept. of English, University of South Carolina-Aiken, 471 University Pkwy., Aiken SC 29801. E-mail: phebed@aiken.sc.edu. Established 1988. **Editor:** Phebe Davidson.

Book/Chapbook Needs: The press no longer sponsors annual contests, but continues to publish occasional chapbooks and longer books of poetry. Does not want "sentimental, religious, consciously academic" poetry. Has published poetry by Lois Marie Harrod, Robert King, and Doughtry "Doc" Long. As a sample the editor selected these lines by Robert King:

> As I drive past, a scatter of birds/startles from the field, the V's/and W's we children used in the blue//
> paint above the always green fields/or a mountain's pure purple triangle./Every tree those years . . .

Sample copy: $12 paper; $18 hardback. Make checks payable to Palanquin Press.

How to Submit: Send sample of 6-10 poems with query letter and SASE. Accepts submissions by e-mail (as attachment). Responds in 3 months.

Advice: "Read what you write; send finished work only."

PALO ALTO REVIEW (Specialized: themes), 1400 W. Villaret Blvd., San Antonio TX 78224. (210)921-5443 or 921-5017. Fax: (210)921-5008. E-mail: PALOALTOREVIEW@aol.com. Established 1992. **Editors:** Ellen Shull and Bob Richmond.

Magazine Needs: *Palo Alto Review* is a biannual publication of Palo Alto college. "We invite writing that investigates the full range of education in its myriad forms. Ideas are what we are after. *Palo Alto Review* is interested in connecting the college and the community. We would hope that those who attempt these connections will choose startling topics and find interesting angles from which to study the length and breadth of ideas and learning, a lifelong pursuit." Includes articles, essays, memoirs, interviews, book reviews, fiction, and poetry. Wants "poetry which has something to say, literary quality poems, with strong images, up to 50 lines. No inspirational verse, haiku or doggerel." Has published poetry by Walt McDonald,

Diane Glancy, Virgil Suárez, and Wendy Bishop. *Palo Alto Review* is 60 pages, 8½×11, professionally printed on recycled paper and saddle-stapled with enamel card cover with art; b&w photos, art and graphics inside. Publishes about 8 poems in each issue (16 poems/year). Press run is 600 for 400 subscribers of which 10 are libraries, 200 shelf sales. Subscription: $10. Sample: $5.

How to Submit: Submit 3-5 poems at a time. Accepts simultaneous submissions; no previously published poems. Poems are read by an advisory board and recommended to editors, who sometimes suggest revisions. Always comments on rejected poems. "Although we frequently announce a theme, the entire issue will not necessarily be dedicated to the theme." Guidelines and a list of upcoming themes available for SASE. Responds in 3 months. Pays 2 contributor's copies. Acquires first North American serial rights. "Please note poems as first published in *Palo Alto Review* in subsequent printings."

Advice: "There are no requirements for submission, though we recommend the reading (purchase) of a sample copy."

PAPER WASP: A JOURNAL OF HAIKU (Specialized: form/style, haiku/tonka/haibun); SOCIAL ALTERNATIVES (Specialized: social issues); POST PRESSED, 14 Fig Tree Pocket Rd., Chapel Hill Q 4069 Australia. E-mail: ksamuelo@bigpond.net.au. Website: http://users.bigpond.net.au/ReportWright/paperwasp/paperwasp.html (includes information about *paper wasp*, guidelines, contact information, subscription info, links, contents, and sample selections). *paper wasp* established 1972, *Social Alternatives* established 1971. **Manager:** Katherine Samuelowicz.

Magazine Needs: "*paper wasp* quarterly publishes haiku, senryu, renga, and tanka in a range of fresh tones and voices. We acknowledge a range of forms and styles from one-liners to the conventional 5-7-5 form, and variations such as development or neglect of seasonal words for regional contexts." Wants haiku, senryu, tanka, renga, linked verse, and haibun. Has published poetry by Janice Bostok, Carla Sari, Cornelis Vleeskens, Ross Clark, Tony Beyer, and Bernard Gadd. As a sample the editor selected these lines by Alan J. Summers:

   late september rain/cutting through the lane/and the mist.

paper wasp is 16 pages, digest-sized, desktop-published and saddle-stapled, cardboard cover, includes art/graphics. Receives about 2,000 submissions/year, accepts 15%. Publishes about 50 haiku/issue. Press run is 200 for 67 subscribers of which 12 are libraries. Single copy: $AUD6 within Australia, $US8 elsewhere. Subscription: $AUD20 within Australia, $US26 elsewhere. Make checks payable to *paper wasp*. "Due to very high bank charges on overseas cheques, we prefer cash or IRCs for single copies. Copies of relevant pages only are sent to published contributors who are not subscribers or who do not pay for the relevant copy."

Magazine Needs: "*Social Alternatives* is a quarterly multidisciplinary journal which seeks to analyse, critique, and review contemporary social, cultural, and economic developments and their implications at local, national, and global levels." Has published poetry by MTC Cronin, Jules Leigh Koch, ouyang yu, John O'Connor, Gina Mercer, and Michael Sariban. As a sample the editor selected these lines from "Awaiting the Barbarians (after Cavafy)" by Ron Pretty:

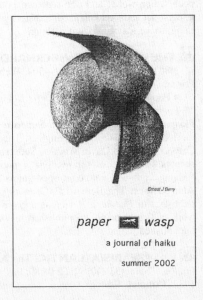

Ernest J Berry

paper ▨ *wasp*

a journal of haiku

summer 2002

The editors of *paper wasp* selected this elegant illustration by Ernest J. Berry because of its visual impact "and because it fits with the type of poetry—haiku—*paper wasp* publishes."

*It was the golden age: they were there, sure./The barbarians, but on the borders,/the northern marches,
walled out, or so/we were told, and kept in check. The city/prospered and its merchants. the constant
flow/of captives kept the mines and circuses in action*

Social Alternatives is 76 pages, magazine-sized, desktop-published, saddle-stapled with cardboard cover, includes
art/graphics, ads. Receives about approximately 1,200 submissions, accepts about 15%. Publishes about 30
poems/issue. Press run is about 800 for 587 subscribers of which 112 are libraries. Single copy: $8. Subscription:
$30, plus $40 for overseas airmail.

How to Submit: Submit up to 12 poems at a time for *paper wasp*, up to 6 poems (36 lines maximum) for
Social Alternatives. No previously published poems or simultaneous submissions. Accepts regular mail, e-mail
(in text box), and disk submissions (IBM format with Word files, plus hard copy). Cover letter required. "If mailed
within Australia, send SASE, otherwise SAE plus IRCs. Unless requested with SASE, copy is not returned." Time
between acceptance and publication is up to 6 months. Poems are circulated to an editorial board. "Read by two
editors." Sometimes comments on rejected poems. Responds within 6 months. *paper wasp* does not pay except
one copy for poets publishing with them for the first time. *Social Alternatives* pays 1 contributor's copy. Copyright
remains with authors.

**PARADOXISM; XIQUAN PUBLISHING HOUSE; THE PARADOXIST MOVEMENT AS-
SOCIATION (Specialized: form)**, University of New Mexico, Gallup NM 87301. E-mail: smarand@un
m.edu. Established 1990. **Editor:** Florentin Smarandache.

Magazine Needs: *Paradoxism*, (formerly *The Paradoxist Literary Movement Journal*), is an annual
journal of "avant-garde poetry, experiments, poems without verses, literature beyond the words, anti-
language, non-literature and its literature, as well as the sense of the non-sense; revolutionary forms of
poetry. Paradoxism is based on excessive use of antitheses, antinomies, contradictions, paradoxes in creation. It was made up in the 1980s by the editor as an anti-totalitarianism protest." Wants "avant-garde
poetry, one to two pages, any subject, any style (lyrical experiments). No classical, fixed forms." Has
published poetry by Paul Georgelin, Titu Popescu, Ion Rotaru, Michéle de LaPlante, and Claude LeRoy.
Paradoxism is 52 pages, digest-sized, offset-printed, soft cover. Press run is 500. "It is distributed to its
collaborators, U.S. and Canadian university libraries, and the Library of Congress as well as European,
Chinese, Indian, and Japanese libraries."

How to Submit: No previously published poems or simultaneous submissions. Do not submit mss in
the summer. "We do not return published or unpublished poems or notify the author of date of publication."
Responds in up to 6 months. Pays 1 contributor's copy.

Book/Chapbook Needs & How to Submit: Xiquan Publishing House also publishes 2 paperbacks
and 1-2 chapbooks/year, including translations. The poems must be unpublished and must meet the requirements of the Paradoxist Movement Association. Responds to queries in 2 months, to mss in up to 6 months.
Pays 50 author's copies. Inquire about sample books.

Advice: "We mostly receive traditional or modern verse, but not avant-garde (very different from any
previously published verse). We want anti-literature and its literature, style of the non-style, poems without
poems, non-words and non-sentence poems, very upset free verse, intelligible unintelligible language,
impersonal texts personalized, transformation of the abnormal to the normal. Make literature from everything; make literature from nothing!"

THE PARIS REVIEW; BERNARD F. CONNORS PRIZE, 541 E. 72nd St., New York NY 10021.
(212)861-0016. Fax: (212)861-4504. Website: http://parisreview.com. Established 1953. **Contact:** Poetry
Editor.
 • Poetry published in *The Paris Review* is frequently included in volumes of *The Best American
Poetry*.

Magazine Needs & How to Submit: *The Paris Review*, appearing quarterly, has published many of
the major poets writing in English. The Winter 2001 issue featured poetry by Sarah Arvic, Gabrielle
Calvocoressi, and David Wojahn. Subscription: $40/1 year, $76/2 years. No previously published poems;
accepts simultaneous submissions if notified of acceptance elsewhere. No fax or e-mail submissions.
"Manuscripts will not be returned unless accompanied by a self-addressed stampled envelope."

Also Offers: The Bernard F. Connors prize of $1,000 is awarded for the finest poem over 200 lines
published in *The Paris Review* in a given year. *The Paris Review* Discovery Prize is awarded to the best
work of fiction or poetry published in *The Paris Review* in a given year by an emerging or previously
unpublished writer.

PARIS/ATLANTIC, The American University of Paris, 31 Avenue Bosquet, Paris 75007,
France. Phone: (33 1)01 40 62 05 89. Fax: (33 1)01 45 89 13. E-mail: auplantic@hotmail.com. Established
1982. **Contact:** Editor.

Magazine Needs: *Paris/Atlantic* appears biannually and is "a forum for both new and established artists/ writers that is based in Paris and is distributed internationally. The contents vary; we publish poetry, prose, paintings, sculpture, sketches, etc." Has published poetry by Ben Wilensky, Ryan G. Van Cleave, Margo Berdeshevsky and Susan Maurer. *Paris/Atlantic* is 80-130 pages, professionally published with sewn binding and softcover, includes ads. Receives about 400-500 poems/year, accepts approximately 40%. Press run is 1,000-1,500; distributed free to bookstores, universities, literary societies, other poets, etc.

How to Submit: Submit any number of poems at a time. "There are no requirements aside from a biography and international postage so we can forward 2 free copies of *Paris/Atlantic* if your work is published." Accepts previously published poems and simultaneous submissions. Accepts e-mail (include in body of message) and disk submissions. "Please cut and paste e-mail submissions. No attachments!" Cover letter including author's name, return address with telephone number, e-mail address or fax number and a short biography required. Reads submissions September 1 through November 1 and January 1 through April 1 only. Poems are circulated to an editorial board. "The editorial board reviews work in a roundtable discussion." Send SASE (or SAE and IRC) for guidelines or request via fax or e-mail. Pays 2 copies. Acquires first rights. Rights revert to author upon publication.

Advice: "Be heard! The *Paris/Atlantic* Reading Series of Poetry and Prose takes place once a month, for which we invite two poets to perform their work in the Amex Café of The American University of Paris, followed by open mikes. Take advantage to listen and he heard in this international forum, and contact us if you would like to participate."

PARNASSUS LITERARY JOURNAL, P.O. Box 1384, Forest Park GA 30298-1384. (404)366-3177. Established 1975. **Editor:** Denver Stull.

Magazine Needs: "Our sole purpose is to promote poetry and to offer an outlet where poets may be heard. We welcome well-constructed poetry, but ask that you keep it uplifting, and free of language that might be offensive to one of our readers. We are open to all poets and all forms of poetry, including Oriental, 24-line limit, maximum 3 poems." Accepts poetry written by children. Has published poetry by Moira Bailis, T.K. Splake, Najwa S. Brax, Jean Calkins, Rod Farmer, and Matthew Louviere. As a sample the editor selected these lines from "Sizzling" by R. Riherd Green:

> *Back when I was a kid/Days were so hot/Macadam paving/Buckled and curled/like fat back strips/In*
> *a black frying pan!*

Parnassus Literary Journal, published 3 times/year, is 84 pages, photocopied from typescript, saddled-stapled, colored card cover, with an occasional drawing. Receives about 1,500 submissions/year, accepts 350. Currently have about a 1-year backlog. Press run is 300 for 200 subscribers of which 5 are libraries. Circulation includes Japan, England, Greece, India, Korea, Germany, and Netherlands. Single copy: $7 US and Canada, $9.50 overseas; subscription: $18 US and Canada, $25 overseas. Sample: $3. Offers 20% discount to schools, libraries and for orders of 5 copies or more. Make checks or money orders payable to Denver Stull.

How to Submit: Submit up to 3 poems, up to 24 lines each, with #10 SASE. Include name and address on each page of ms. "I am dismayed at the haphazard manner in which work is often submitted. I have a number of poems in my file containing no name and/or address. Simply placing your name and address on your envelope is not enough." Accepts previously published poems and simultaneous submissions. Cover letter including something about the writer preferred. "Definitely" comments on rejected poems. "We do not respond to submissions or queries not accompanied by SASE." Guidelines available for SASE and in publication. Responds within 1 week. "We regret that the ever-rising costs of publishing forces us to ask that contributors either subscribe to the magazine, or purchase a copy of the issue in which their work appears." Pays 1 copy. All rights remain with the author. Readers vote on best of each issue.

Also Offers: Conducts a contest periodically.

Advice: "Poem must make sense. Neatness *does* count."

$ PARNASSUS: POETRY IN REVIEW; POETRY IN REVIEW FOUNDATION, 205 W. 89th St., #8F, New York NY 10024-1835. (212)362-3492. Fax: (212)875-0148. Website: www.parnassuspoetry.com (includes guidelines, contact and subscription information, upcoming themes, editorial policy, links). Established 1972. **Poetry Editor:** Herbert Leibowitz.

Magazine Needs: *Parnassus* provides "comprehensive and in-depth coverage of new books of poetry, including translations from foreign poetry. We publish poems and translations on occasion, but we solicit all poetry. Poets invited to submit are given all the space they wish; the only stipulation is that the style be non-academic." Has published work by Alice Fulton, Eavan Boland, Mary Karr, Debora Greger, William Logan, Tess Gallagher, Seamus Heaney, and Rodney Jones. Subscriptions are $24/year, $46/year for libraries; has 1,250 subscribers, of which 550 are libraries.

How to Submit: Not open to unsolicited poetry. However, unsolicited essays are considered. In fact, this is an exceptionally rich market for thoughtful, insightful, non-academic essay-reviews of contemporary collections. It is strongly recommended that writers study the magazine before submitting. Multiple submissions disliked. Cover letter required. Upcoming themes available for SASE. Responds to essay submissions within 10 weeks (response takes longer during the summer). Pays $25-250 plus 2 gift subscriptions—contributors can also take one themselves. Editor comments on rejected poems—from 1 paragraph to 2 pages. Send for a sample copy (prices of individual issues can vary) to get a feel for the critical acumen needed to place here.

Advice: "Contributors are urged to subscribe to at least one literary magazine. There is a pervasive ignorance of the cost of putting out a magazine and no sense of responsibility for supporting one."

PARTING GIFTS; MARCH STREET PRESS, 3413 Wilshire, Greensboro NC 27408. E-mail: rbixby@aol.com. Website: http://members.aol.com/marchst/ (features links, guidelines, sample issues, book catalog, and news). Established 1987. **Editor:** Robert Bixby.

Magazine Needs: *Parting Gifts* is published biannually in July and November. "I want to see everything. I'm a big fan of Jim Harrison, C.K. Williams, Amy Hempel, and Janet Kauffman." Has published poetry by Eric Torgersen, Lyn Lifshin, Elizabeth Kerlikowske, and Russell Thorburn. *Parting Gifts* is 72 pages, digest-sized, photocopied, with colored matte card cover, appearing twice/year. Press run is 200. Subscription: $18. Sample: $9.

How to Submit: Submit in groups of 3-10 with SASE. Accepts simultaneous submissions; no previously published poems. "I like a cover letter because it makes the transaction more human. Best time to submit mss is early in the year." Guidelines available for SASE or on website. Responds in 2 weeks. Sometimes sends prepublication galleys. Pays 1 copy.

Book/Chapbook Needs & How to Submit: March Street Press publishes chapbooks. **Reading fee:** $20.

Advice: "Read our online archives."

PARTISAN REVIEW, Dept. PM, 236 Bay State Rd., Boston MA 02215. (617)353-4260. Fax: (617)353-7444. E-mail: partisan@bu.edu. Website: www.partisanreview.org. Established 1934. **Contact:** Brenda Pike.

• Work published in *Partisan Review* has been frequently selected for inclusion in *The Best American Poetry* (volumes 1995 and 1998).

Magazine Needs: *Partisan Review* is a distinguished quarterly literary journal using poetry of high quality. "Our poetry section is very small and highly selective. We are open to fresh, quality translations but submissions must include poem in original language as well as translation. We occasionally have special poetry sections on specified themes." Has published poetry by Charles Wright, Glyn Maxwell, Debora Greger, and Wislawa Szymborska. *Partisan Review* is 160 pages, 6×9, flat-spined. Press run is 8,200 for 6,000 subscriptions and shelf sales. Sample: $7.50.

How to Submit: Submit up to 6 poems at a time. No simultaneous submissions. No fax or e-mail submissions. Responds in 2 months. "We will only consider typed submissions. The author's name and address should appear on each page of the manuscript. Please be aware that manuscripts unaccompanied by SASE will receive no reply."

PASSAGES NORTH; ELINOR BENEDICT PRIZE, English Dept., 1401 Presque Isle Ave., Northern Michigan University, Marquette MI 49855. (906)227-1203. E-mail: passages@nmu.edu. Website: http://vm.nmu.edu/PASSAGES:HTTP/HOME.HTML. Established 1979. **Editor-in-Chief:** Kate Myers Hanson

Magazine Needs: *Passages North* is an annual magazine, appearing in spring, which contains short fiction, poetry, creative nonfiction, essays, and interviews. "The magazine publishes quality work by established and emerging writers." Has published poetry by Jim Daniels, Jack Driscoll, Bob Hicok, Gabriel Gudding, Ron Rash, Pamela McClure, and Ricardo Pau-Llosa. *Passages North* is 250 pages. Circulation is at 1,000 "and growing." Subscription: $13/year, $23/2 years. Current issue: $13; back issue: $3.

How to Submit: Prefers groups of 3-6 poems, typed single-spaced. Accepts simultaneous submissions. "Poems over 100 lines seldom published." Time between acceptance and publication is 6 months. Reads submissions September through May only. Responds in 2 months. Pays 2 contributor's copies.

Also Offers: Sponsors the Elinor Benedict Prize in poetry and the Waasmode Fiction Contest. "We have published fiction by W.P. Kinsella, Bonnie Jo Campbell, and Lisa Stolley." Details available for SASE or by e-mail.

◖ **PATERSON LITERARY REVIEW; ALLEN GINSBERG POETRY AWARDS; THE PATER-SON POETRY PRIZE; THE PATERSON PRIZE FOR BOOKS FOR YOUNG PEOPLE; PAS-SAIC COUNTY COMMUNITY COLLEGE POETRY CENTER LIBRARY**, Poetry Center, Passaic County Community College, Cultural Affairs Dept., 1 College Blvd., Paterson NJ 07505-1179. (973)684-6555. E-mail: mgellan@pccc.cc.nj.us. Website: www.pccc.cc.nj.us/poetry (includes guidelines, contact and subscription information, bios, contest rules, links, and editorial policy). Established 1979. **Editor and Director:** Maria Mazziotti Gillan.

Magazine Needs & How to Submit: A wide range of activities pertaining to poetry are conducted by the Passaic County Community College Poetry Center, including the annual *Paterson Literary Review* (formerly *Footwork: The Paterson Literary Review*) using poetry of "high quality" under 100 lines; "clear, direct, powerful work." Has published poetry by David Ray, Diane Wakoski, Sonia Sanchez, Laura Boss, and Marge Piercy. *Paterson Literary Review* is 240 pages, magazine-sized, saddle-stapled, professionally printed with glossy card 2-color cover, using b&w art and photos. Press run is 1,000 for 100 subscribers of which 50 are libraries. Sample: $10. Send up to 5 poems at a time. Accepts simultaneous submissions. Reads submissions September through January only. Responds in 1 year. Pays 1 contributor's copy. Acquires first rights.

Also Offers: The Poetry Center of the college conducts the Allen Ginsberg Poetry Awards Competition each year. Entry fee: $13. Prizes of $1,000, $200, and $100. Deadline: April 1. Rules available for SASE. Also publishes a *New Jersey Poetry Resources* book, the *Passaic County Community College Poetry Contest Anthology*, and the *New Jersey Poetry Calendar*. The Paterson Poetry Prize of $1,000 is awarded each year (split between poet and publisher) to a book of poems published in the previous year. Also sponsors the Paterson Prize for Books for Young People. Awards $500 to one book in each category (Pre-K-Grade 3, Grades 4-6, Grades 7-12). Books must be published in the previous year and be submitted by the publisher. Publishers should write with SASE for application form to be submitted by February 1 (for Poetry Prize) and March 15 (for Books for Young People Prize). Passaic County Community College Poetry Center Library has an extensive collection of contemporary poetry and seeks small press contributions to help keep it abreast. The Distinguished Poetry Series offers readings by poets of international, national, and regional reputation. Poetryworks/USA is a series of programs produced for UA Columbia-Cablevision.

◻ ◎ **PATH PRESS, INC. (Specialized: ethnic)**, P.O. Box 2925, Chicago IL 60690. (847)424-1620. Fax: (847)424-1623. E-mail: pathpressinc@aol.com. Established 1969. **President:** Bennett J. Johnson.

Book/Chapbook Needs & How to Submit: Path Press is a small publisher of books and poetry primarily "by, for, and about African-American and Third World people." The press is open to all types of poetic forms; emphasis is on high quality. Submissions should be typewritten in ms format; submissions by e-mail (as attachment) accepted. Writers should send sample poems, credits, and bio. The books are "hardback and quality paperbacks."

◖ **PAVEMENT SAW; PAVEMENT SAW PRESS; PAVEMENT SAW PRESS CHAPBOOK AWARD; TRANSCONTINENTAL POETRY AWARD**, P.O. Box 6291, Columbus OH 43206-0291. E-mail: info@pavementsaw.org. Website: www.pavementsaw.org (includes bios, subscription information, editorial policy, contest rules, and a full catalog). Established 1992. **Editor:** David Baratier.

Magazine Needs: *Pavement Saw*, which appears annually in August, wants "letters and short fiction, and poetry on any subject, especially work. Length: one or two pages. No poems that tell, no work by a deceased writer and no translations." Dedicates 10-15 pages of each issue to a featured writer. Has published poetry by Simon Perchik, Dana Curtis, Sofia Starres, Alan Catlin, Tony Gloeggler, Sean Killian, and Tracy Philpot. *Pavement Saw* is 88 pages, 6×9, perfect-bound. Receives about 14,500 poems/year, accepts less than 1%. Press run is 500 for about 250 subscribers, about 250 shelf sales. Single copy: $6; subscription: $10. Sample: $5. Make checks payable to Pavement Saw Press.

How to Submit: Submit 5 poems at a time. "No fancy typefaces." Accepts simultaneous submissions, "as long as poet has not published a book with a press run of 1,000 or more"; no previously published poems. No e-mail submissions. Cover letter required. Seldom comments on rejected poems. Guidelines available for SASE. Responds in 4 months. Sometimes sends prepublication galleys. Pays 2 copies. Acquires first rights.

Book/Chapbook Needs & How to Submit: The press also publishes books of poetry. "Most are by authors who have been published in the journal." Published "seven titles in 2000 and nine titles in 2001, eight are full-length books ranging from 72 to 612 pages."

Also Offers: Sponsors the Transcontinental Poetry Award. "Each year, Pavement Saw Press will seek to publish at least one book of poetry and/or prose poems from manuscripts received during this competition.

Competition is open to anyone who has not previously published a volume of poetry or prose. Writers who have had volumes of poetry and/or prose under 40 pages printed or printed in limited editions of no more than 500 copies are eligible. Submissions are accepted during June and July only." Entry fee: $15. Awards publication, $1,000 and a percentage of the press run. Include stamped postcard and SASE for ms receipt acknowledgement and results notification. Guidelines available for SASE. Also sponsors the Pavement Saw Press Chapbook Award. Submit up to 32 pages of poetry with a cover letter. Entry fee: $7. Awards publication, $500 and 10% of print run. "Each entrant will receive a chapbook provided a 9 × 12 SAE with 5 first-class stamps is supplied." Deadline: December 20. Guidelines available for SASE.

PEACE & FREEDOM; EASTERN RAINBOW; PEACE & FREEDOM PRESS (Specialized: subscribers), 17 Farrow Rd., Whaplode Drove, Spalding, Lincs PE12 OTS England. Established 1985. **Editor:** Paul Rance.
Magazine Needs: *Peace & Freedom* is a magazine appearing 2 times/year. "We are looking for poems up to 32 lines particularly from U.S. poets who are new to writing, especially women. The poetry we publish is pro-animal rights, anti-war, environmental; poems reflecting love; erotic, but not obscene poetry; humorous verse and spiritual, humanitarian poetry. With or without rhyme/metre." Has published poetry by Dorothy Bell-Hall, Doreen King, Bernard Shough, Mona Miller, and Andrew Savage. As a sample the editor selected these lines from "No Qualms" by Daphne Richards:

> We humans want our freedom,/and the right to choose our way,/along life's many pathways/as we tread
> them every day.//And yet we ban our animals/from all that we hold dear./We rob them of their dignity,/
> and keep them bound by fear.

Peace & Freedom has a b&w glossy cover, normally 20 A4 pages. Sample: US $4; UK £1.75. "Sample copies can only be purchased from the above address, and various mail-order distributors too numerous to mention. Advisable to buy a sample copy first. Banks charge the equivalent of $5 to cash foreign cheques in the U.K., so please only send bills, preferably by registered post." Subscription: US $16, UK £7.50/4 issues.
How to Submit: No simultaneous submissions or previously published poems. No fax or e-mail submissions. Poets are requested to send in bios. Reads submissions all through the year. Publishes theme issues. Upcoming themes available for SAE with IRC. Responds to submissions normally under a month, with IRC/SAE. "Work without correct postage will not be responded to or returned until proper postage is sent." Pays 1 copy. Reviews books of poetry.
Also Offers: Also publishes anthologies. Details on upcoming anthologies and guidelines are available for SAE with IRC. "*Peace & Freedom* now holds regular contests as does one of our other publications, *Eastern Rainbow*, which is a magazine concerning 20th century popular culture using poetry up to 32 lines. Subscription: US, $16, UK, £7.50/4 issues. Further details of competitions and publications for SAE and IRC."
Advice: "Too many writers have lost the personal touch and editors generally appreciate this. It can make a difference when selecting work of equal merit."

PEAKY HIDE (Specialized: form/style), P.O. Box 1591, Upland CA 91785. Established 1996. **Founding Editor:** Valory Banister.
Magazine Needs: *Peaky Hide* is a quarterly magazine of "almost all poetry. We use some b&w art or photos and occasionally run reviews of chapbooks." Publishes "experimental, surrealism, post-language, unconventional poetry that is as psychologically unsettling as the magazine's name. The only rule applicable is that tension is evident. We tend to favor short poems with sharp edges. We do not use poems with blatant sentimental or religious imagery. Some visual poetry is used." Has published poetry by Sheila E. Murphy, Errol Miller, Ann Erickson, Scott Keeney, John M. Bennett, and Jen Hofer. As a sample the editor selected these lines from her own poem "Tiramisu For A Monday":

> An open linoleum floor, unfettered by nothing more than/footprints lazy with haste. Semisweet chocolate
> curtains/hung only to make the sun and the cold outside disappear/do not do much against voyeurs
> or planning./What would it matter if they were purple? The injuries/are the same and a dessert for a
> Monday a decade from/now.

Peaky Hide is 26-34 pages, 8½ × 11, desktop-published and saddle-stapled with light cardstock cover, uses b&w art only. Accept approximately 40% of poems received a year. Press run is 100 for 12 subscribers; "a number of copies may be distributed to coffeehouses the editor likes." Subscription: $17 for 4 issues, $8 for 2 issues. Sample: $5. Make checks payable to Valory Banister.
How to Submit: Not accepting submissions in 2003; on hiatus.

PEARL; PEARL POETRY PRIZE; PEARL EDITIONS, 3030 E. Second St., Long Beach CA 90803-5163. (562)434-4523 or (714)968-7530. E-mail: mjohn5150@aol.com. Website: www.pearlmag. com (includes sample issues, guidelines for submission and contests, subscription information, about the editors, book catalog, and links). Established 1974. **Poetry Editors:** Joan Jobe Smith, Marilyn Johnson, and Barbara Hauk.

Magazine Needs: *Pearl* is a literary magazine appearing 2 times/year. "We are interested in accessible, humanistic poetry that communicates and is related to real life. Humor and wit are welcome, along with the ironic and serious. No taboos stylistically or subject-wise. We don't want to see sentimental, obscure, predictable, abstract, or cliché-ridden poetry. Our purpose is to provide a forum for lively, readable poetry, that reflects a wide variety of contemporary voices, viewpoints and experiences—that speaks to real people about real life in direct, living language, profane, or sublime. Our Fall/Winter issue is devoted exclusively to poetry, with a 12-15 page section featuring the work of a single poet." Has published poetry by Fred Voss, David Hernandez, Dorianne Laux, Denise Duhamel, Ed Ochester, and Nin Andrews. As a sample they selected these lines from "Amanda" by Lisa Glatt:

> *I offered up my bell and bones to you, Boy,/and you offered up your body, dropped your guard . . ./*
> *we'd have trouble here in my apartment on the sand,/a hurricane or tornado named after some good*
> *girl/on the edge of Florida*

Pearl is 96-121 pages, digest-sized, perfect-bound, offset-printed, with glossy cover. Press run is 700 for 150 subscribers of which 7 are libraries. Subscription: $18/year includes a copy of the winning book of the Pearl Poetry Prize. Sample: $7.

How to Submit: Submit 3-5 poems at a time. No previously published poems. "Simultaneous submissions must be acknowledged as such." Prefer poems no longer than 40 lines, each line no more than 10-12 words to accommodate page size and format. "Handwritten submissions and unreadable printouts are not acceptable." No e-mail submissions. "Cover letters appreciated." Reads submissions September through May only. Time between acceptance and publication is up to 1 year. Guidelines available for SASE or on website. Responds in 2 months. Sometimes sends prepublication galleys. Pays 1 contributor's copy. Acquires first serial rights.

Book/Chapbook Needs: Pearl Editions "only publishes the winner of the Pearl Poetry Prize. All other books and chapbooks are *by invitation only.*"

Also Offers: "We sponsor the Pearl Poetry Prize, an annual book-length contest, judged by one of our more well-known contributors. Winner receives publication, $1,000 and 25 copies. Entries accepted May 1 to July 15. There is a $20 entry fee, which includes a copy of the winning book." Complete rules and guidelines are available for SASE or on website. Recent books include *From Sweetness* by Debra Marquart, *A Merciful Bed* by Lisa Glatt and David Hernandez, and *Little Novels* by Denise Duhamel and Maureen Seaton.

Advice: "Advice for beginning poets? Just write from your own experience, using images that are as concrete and sensory as possible. Keep these images fresh and objective. Always listen to the music."

PECAN GROVE PRESS, Box AL 1 Camino Santa Maria, San Antonio TX 78228-8608. (210)436-3441. Fax: (210)436-3782. E-mail: hpalmer@netxpress.com. Website: http://library.stmarytx.edu/pgpress (includes submission information, chapbook contest information, catalog, and individual author pages with samples of work). Established 1988. **Editor:** H. Palmer Hall.

Book/Chapbook Needs: Pecan Grove Press is "interested in fine poetry collections that adhere. A collection should be like an art exhibit—the book is the art space, the pieces work together." Publishes 4-6 paperbacks and 2-3 chapbooks/year. Wants "poetry with something to say and that says it in fresh, original language. Will rarely publish books of more than 110 pages." Does not want "poetry that lets emotion run over control. We too often see sentiment take precedence over language." Has published *Say Hello* by Ryan G. Van Cleave, *A Small Fire* by Russell Kesler, *Live Music* by James Cervantes, *Nightwalking* by Joel Peckham, and *What the Body Knows* by Cyra Dumitru. As a sample the editor selected these lines from "Nightwalking" by Joel Peckham:

> *I'm walking out into the town/I've never visited, down a darkened street/I've traveled all my life.*
> *Where lamplights/burn out one by one, possum skitter out/on cool tar in a night become a blanket of*
> *heat/and sound—cicadas, the suffering of crickets*

Books or chapbooks are usually 50-96 pages, offset, perfect-bound, one-color plus b&w graphic design or photographic cover on index stock. Sample: $10-12.

How to Submit: Submit complete ms. Accepts previously published poems and simultaneous submissions. No fax or e-mail submissions. Cover letter required, with some indication of a poet's publication history and some ideas or suggestions for marketing the book. Time between acceptance and publication is up to 12 months. "We do circulate for outside opinion when we know the poet who has submitted a manuscript. We read closely and make decisions as quickly as possible." Seldom comments on rejected poems. "We do expect our poets to have a publication history in the little magazines with some acknowledgments." Responds to queries and mss in 3 months. After the book has paid for itself, authors receive 50% of subsequent sales and 10 author's copies (out

THE SUBJECT INDEX in the back of this book helps you identify potential markets for your work.

of a press run of 500). "We have no subsidy arrangements, but if author has subvention funds, we do welcome them. Obtain sample books by checking BIP and making purchase. We will send chapbook at random for a fee of $5; book for $10."

Advice: "We welcome submissions but feel too many inexperienced poets want to rush into book publication before they are quite ready. Many should try the little magazine route first instead of attempting to begin a new career with book publication."

N ◑ PEGASUS, P.O. Box 61324, Boulder City NV 89006. Established 1986. **Editor:** M.E. Hildebrand.

Magazine Needs: *Pegasus* is a poetry quarterly "for serious poets who have something to say and know how to say it using sensory imagery." Avoid "religious, political, pornographic themes." Has published poetry by John Grey, Elizabeth Perry, Diana K. Rubin, Lyn Lifshin, Robert K. Johnson, and Nikolas Macioci. As a sample the editor selected these closing lines from "Desert Bedlam" by Elizabeth Perry:

> The lone jacaranda tree below/droops its clusters/of purple flowers as if in shame/until the amber
> stretch of land/facing it once again assumes/the mask of silence.

Pegasus is 32 pages, digest-sized, desktop-published, saddle-stapled with colored paper cover. Publishes 10-15% of the work received. Circulation is 200. Subscription: $18. Sample: $5.

How to Submit: Submit 3-5 poems, 3-40 lines. Accepts previously published poems, provided poet retains rights; no simultaneous submissions. Guidelines available for SASE. Responds in 2 weeks. Publication is payment. Acquires first or one-time rights.

$ ◑ ◎ PELICAN PUBLISHING COMPANY (Specialized: children, regional), Box 3110, Gretna LA 70054-3110. Website: www.pelicanpub.com (includes writer's guidelines, catalog, and company history). Established 1926. **Editor-in-Chief:** Nina Kooij.

Book/Chapbook Needs: Pelican is a "moderate-sized publisher of cookbooks, travel guides, regional books, and inspirational/motivational books," which accepts poetry for "hardcover children's books only, preferably with a regional focus. However, our needs for this are very limited; we do twelve juvenile titles per year, and most of these are prose, not poetry." Accepts poetry written by children. Has published *The Teachers' Night Before Christmas* by Steven L. Layne. As a sample the editor selected these lines from *An Irish Hallowe'en* by Sarah Kirwan Blazek:

> Long ages ago/On an isle all green,/We started a feast/now called Hallowe'en

Books are 32-page, large-format (magazine-sized) with illustrations. Two of their popular series are prose books about Gaston the Green-Nosed Alligator by James Rice and Clovis Crawfish by Mary Alice Fontenot. Has a variety of books based on "The Night Before Christmas" adapted to regional settings such as Cajun, prairie, and Texas. Typically Pelican books sell for $14.95. Write for catalog to buy samples.

How to Submit: *Currently not accepting unsolicited mss.* Query first with cover letter including "work and writing backgrounds and promotional connections." No previously published poems or simultaneous submissions. Guidelines available for SASE and on website. Responds to queries in 1 month, to mss (if invited) in 3 months. Always sends prepublication galleys. Pays royalties. Acquires all rights. Returns rights upon termination of contract.

Advice: "We try to avoid rhyme altogether, especially predictable rhyme. Monotonous rhythm can also be a problem."

◑ PEMBROKE MAGAZINE, UNCP, Box 1510, Pembroke NC 28372-1510. (910)521-6358. Fax: (910)521-6688. Established 1969 by Norman Macleod. **Editor:** Shelby Stephenson. **Managing Editor:** Tina Emanuel.

Magazine Needs: *Pembroke* is a heavy (460 pages, 6×9), flat-spined, quality literary annual which has published poetry by Fred Chappell, A.R. Ammons, Barbara Guest, and Betty Adcock. Press run is 500 for 125 subscribers of which 100 are libraries. Sample: $8.

How to Submit: Sometimes comments on rejected poems. Responds within 3 months. Pays copies.

Advice: Stephenson advises, "Publication will come if you write. Writing is all."

N ⊕ ▼ $ ◑ PEN&INC; POETRY LAB; REACTIONS; PRETEXT, School of English & American Studies, University of East Anglia, Norwich, Norfolk NR4 7TJ United Kingdom. Phone: (01603)592 783. Fax: (01603)507 728. E-mail: info@penandinc.co.uk. Website: www.penandinc.co.uk (includes submission guidelines for all publications; latest news and info about Pen&inc; extracts from titles past, present, and future; contact details; book-buying facility; online writing forum). Established 1999. **Editors:** Julia Bell (*Pretext*), Esther Morgan (*Reactions*).

• *Pen&inc* was awarded a Regional Arts Lottery Board Grant; *Pretext* received a 2001-2002 award from the Arts Council of England Small Magazine Fund.

Magazine Needs: *Pretext*, appearing biannually in May and November, is "the international literary magazine from the acclaimed creative writing institution of the University of East Anglia. With over 200 pages of new poetry, prose, essays, criticism, and short fiction from new and established writers, it provides a cutting-edge platform for creative writing from Great Britain and beyond. There are no editorial restrictions on subject or style, just an insistence on quality and perspective—that the work strongly asserts where it's coming from and is well realized on the page." Recently published poetry by George Szirtes, WG Sebald, Ramona Herdman, Owen Sheers, Morgan Yasbincek, and Sibyl Ruth. As a sample the editor selected these lines from "Falldown" by Ramona Herdman:

> *Some of us are yet too scared/to take your pills like petals, wet/like the tip of a tongue on the tip/of the tongue./We watch as you dance blind/tied to the falling trapeze . . .*

Pretext is 200+ pages, book-sized magazine, litho-printed, glue-bound, full color gloss cover, with 3-5 photographs/images (b&w) within the book to illustrate text, includes ads. Receives about 500 poems/year, accepts about 25%. Publishes about 10 poems/issue. Press run is 2,000 for 100 subscribers of which 10 are libraries, 1,500 shelf sales; 200 distributed free to contributors/reviewers. Single copy: £10 (USA/ROW including postage and packing), £7 (UK including p&p), £8 (Europe including p&p); subscription: (1 year/2 issues) £14 UK including p&p, £18 USA/ROW including p&p, £16 Europe including p&p. Sample: same as single copy. Make checks payable to The University of East Anglia.

How to Submit: Submit 5 poems at a time. Accepts previously published poems and simultaneous submissions. Accepts fax, e-mail, and disk submissions. Cover letter is required. "Poems must be your own original work and must not be accepted for publication by any other magazine or anthology. Enclose a SAE. Poems submitted in electronic format should be on a floppy disk, readable by PC and Mac and be formatted in latest version on Word, or at least Word 98." Reads submissions on an ongoing basis. Time between acceptance and publication is dependent on publication date of book/magazine. "Poems are received and passed to the editorial board for relevant publication. Consultation process involving editors and contributing editors occurs. Poems are accepted or rejected, or passed back to poet for rewriting if deemed necessary." Regularly publishes theme issues ("Europe" and "Havoc/Dissent" are recent themes). Upcoming themes available on website. Guidelines available in magazine, for SASE, by e-mail, or on website. Responds in 3 months. Always sends prepublication galleys. Pays £50 UK and 1 contributor's copy. UK and international copyright remains with author at all times.

Book/Chapbook Needs & How to Submit: "Pen&inc is a small pocket of resistance and a statement of independence as part of the new wave of community-based publications which offer a fresh perspective on the writers and writing that are important at the start of the 21st century. Pen&inc aims to publish good writing, as simple as that, whether it be in poetry, short fiction, essays, criticism, or novel form." Imprints are Poetry Lab and Pen&inc Slims. Publishes 2 perfect-bound paperbacks/year selected through both open submission and competition. Books are usually 100-150 pages, glue-bound, full color or b&w gloss cover on card, with original image or photograph (color/b&w). Query first, with a few sample poems and cover letter with brief bio and publication credits. Book mss may include previously published poems. Responds to queries in 1 month; to mss in 3 months. Pays individual rates according to title and contract. Order sample books/publications by sending "cover price to Pen&inc address above. UK Sterling only accepted. Transactions by debit/credit card fine also." See website.

Also Offers: *Reactions* is "a round-up of the best new poets from around the UK and abroad. Partly selected from open submission and partly commissioned, *Reactions* features the work of poets who are at a first collection stage or working towards it and contains work by over 40 poets from both UEA and beyond. The emphasis is on emerging writers." Recently published poetry by Christopher Allan, Clare Crossman, Hannah Godfrey, Katie Landon, Nigel Lawrence, and Christine McNeill. "Submissions are invited from writers who have had a first collection or pamphlet published (but not a second) and from those who have not yet reached that stage. If you are interested in submitting work, please send to Esther Morgan. Must be accompanied by a covering letter which lists the titles of your poems, plus a short biography of no more than 70 words." See "how to submit" details above for *Pretext*.

Advice: "Write well and good and do not despair. Try and try again. If you write well, you will be recognized one day."

N 🌐 🄾 **PENNINE INK,** % Mid Pennine Arts, The Gallery, Yorke St., Burnley BB11 1HD Great Britain. Phone: (01282)703657. E-mail: sheridans@casanostra.p3online.net. Established 1983. **Editor:** Laura Sheridan. **Contact:** Joan McEvoy.

Magazine Needs: *Pennine Ink* appears annually in January using poems and short prose items. Wants "poetry up to 40 lines maximum. Consider all kinds." As a sample the editor selected the poem "Tanka" by Debra Wooland Bender:

> *My mother stands/unpinning dried laundry;/sit, be comfortable/I say, while she folds white wind/into four-cornered linens*

Pennine Ink is 48 pages, A5, with b&w illustrated cover, small local ads and 3 or 4 b&w graphics. Receives about 400 poems/year, accepts approximately 40. Press run is 500. "Contributors wishing to purchase a copy of *Pennine Ink* should enclose £3 ($6 US) per copy."

How to Submit: Submit up to 6 poems at a time. Accepts previously published poems and simultaneous submissions. Seldom comments on rejected poems. Responds in 3 months. Pays 1 copy.

Advice: "Prose and poetry should be accompanied by a suitable stamped, addressed envelope (SASE or SAE with IRCs) for return of work."

N ⊕ ♥ PENNINE PLATFORM, 7 Cockley Hill Lane, Kirkheaton, Huddersfield HD5 OHW England. Phone: (0)1484-516804. E-mail: A.E.Reiss@bradford.ac.uk. Established 1973. **Poetry Editor:** Dr. Ed Reiss.

Magazine Needs: *Pennine Platform* appears 2 times/year. Wants any kind of poetry but concrete ("lack of facilities for reproduction"). No specifications of length, but poems of less than 40 lines have a better chance. "All styles—effort is to find things good of their kind. Preference for religious or sociopolitical awareness of an acute, not conventional kind." Has published poetry by Joolz, Gaia Holmes, Milner Place, Seán Body, and Ian Parks. As a sample the editor selected these lines from "Night" by Gaia Holmes:

> The dome of the mosque glints at me/across the rooftops/like a fat mystic eye.

Pennine Platform is 48 pages, digest-sized, photocopied from typescript, saddle-stapled, with matte card cover with graphics. Circulation is 400 for 300 subscribers of which 16 are libraries. Receives about 300 submissions/year, accepts approximately 60, has about a 6-month backlog. Subscription: £10 for 2 issues (£15 abroad; £25 if not in sterling). Sample: £5.

How to Submit: Submit up to 6 poems, typed. Responds in about 3 months. No pay. Acquires first serial rights. Editor occasionally comments on rejected poems. Reviews books of poetry in 500 words, multi-book format. Poets may send books for review consideration.

◑ PENNSYLVANIA ENGLISH, Penn State DuBois, DuBois PA 15801-3199. (814)375-4814. E-mail: ajv2@psu.edu. Established 1988 (first issue in March, 1989). **Editor:** Antonio Vallone.

Magazine Needs: *Pennsylvania English*, appearing annually in winter, is "a journal sponsored by the Pennsylvania College English Association." Wants poetry of "any length, any style." Has published poetry by Liz Rosenberg, Walt MacDonald, Amy Pence, Jennifer Richter, and Jeff Schiff. *Pennsylvania English* is up to 180 pages, 5½×8½, perfect-bound with a full color cover. Press run is 500. Subscription: $10/year.

How to Submit: Submit 3 or more typed poems at a time. Include SASE. Considers simultaneous submissions but not previously published poems. Guidelines available for SASE. Responds in 6 months. Pays 3 copies.

Advice: "Poetry does not express emotions; it evokes emotions. Therefore, it should rely less on statements and more on images."

⍦ ◑ ◎ PENNY DREADFUL: TALES & POEMS OF FANTASTIC TERROR (Specialized: horror), P.O. Box 719, Radio City Station, Hell's Kitchen NY 10101-0719. E-mail: MMPendragon@aol.com. Website: www.pennydreadful.org (includes links, guidelines and subscription information). Established 1996. **Editor/Publisher:** Michael Pendragon.

● "Works appearing in *Penny Dreadful* have been reprinted in *The Year's Best Fantasy and Horror*." *Penny Dreadful* nominates best tales and poems for Pushcart Prizes.

Magazine Needs: *Penny Dreadful* is an irregular publication (Autumn, Winter, Midsummer) of goth-romantic poetry and prose. Publishes poetry, short stories, essays, letters, listings, reviews, and b&w artwork "which celebrate the darker aspects of Man, the World, and their Creator. We're looking for literary horror in the tradition of Poe, M.R. James, Shelley, M.P. Shiel, and LeFanu—dark, disquieting tales and verses designed to challenge the readers' perception of human nature, morality, and man's place within the Darkness. Stories and poems should be set prior to 1910 and/or possess a timeless quality. Avoid references to 20th and 21st century personages/events, graphic sex, strong language, excessive gore and shock elements." Has published poetry by Nancy Bennett, Michael R. Burch, Lee Clark, Louise Webster, K.S. Hardy, and Kevin N. Roberts. As a sample the editor selected these lines from "Destiny" by Tamara B. Latham:

> Sand which fills the hourglass/Scattered densely thru the sky/Blown by some eternal wind/Into some
> mere mortal's eye

Penny Dreadful is about 200 pages, 6×9, desktop-published, perfect-bound with b&w line art. Includes market listings "for, and reviews of, kindred magazines." Press run is 200 copies. Subscription: $25/year (3 issues). Sample: $10. Make checks payable to Michael Pendragon.

How to Submit: Submit 3-5 poems with name and address on opening page, and name/title/page number on all following pages. Poems should not exceed 3 pages; rhymed, metered verse preferred. Accepts previously published poems and simultaneous submissions. Prefers e-mail submissions; include in body of message with a copy attached. Include cover letter and SASE. Reads submissions all year. Time between acceptance and publica-

tion is up to 1 year. Poems reviewed and chosen by editor. Often comments on rejected poems. Guidelines available for SASE or on website. Responds in up to 1 year. Always sends prepublication galleys. Pays 1 contributor's copy. Acquires one-time rights.
Also Offers: Publishes *Songs of Innocence*/Pendragon Publications. See listing in Publishers of Poetry section.

N̄ $⊘ PENNYWHISTLE PRESS, P.O. Box 734, Tesuque NM 87574. (505)982-0066. Fax: (505)982-6858. E-mail: pennywhistlebook@aol.com. Established 1986. **Publisher:** Victor di Suvero.
Book/Chapbook Needs: Pennywhistle Press "was started as a way to present the work of notable poets to the reading public. Known for its Poetry Chapbook Series, which currently features 18 titles by some of the strongest voices of our time. The Press has branched out into the anthology market with the publication of *¡Saludos! Poemas de Nuevo Mexico*, a bilingual collection of 66 poets presenting their diverse views of this unusual tricultural state, which is also a state of being. Another bilingual anthology, *La Frontera*, is currently being completed. Edited by poet and novelist Demetria Martinez, this collection will feature important work of major poets from both sides of the U.S./Mexico border." Has published *Coming Up for Air* by Margaret Randall, *Visionary* by Douglas Kent Hall, *Harvest Time* by Victor de Suvero, *Voices from the Corner* by Mike Sutin, and *Blood Trail* by Florence McGinn. Chapbooks are usually 32 pages, 5¼×8⅜, perfect-bound; anthologies are about 200 pages, 6×9, perfect-bound.
How to Submit: Submit 10 poems at a time. Accepts previously published poems and simultaneous submissions. Poems are circulated to an editorial board. "Reviewed by editorial board and then submitted to managing editor and publisher for approval." Responds to queries in 2-4 months, to mss in 2 months. Pays honorarium; advances and royalties negotiated.
Also Offers: Publishes the "Compendium Series." "Volumes in this series include biography, memoir, poetry, photographs, and illustrations presenting a poet's entire life and work in a handy single volume." Sponsors the Pennywhistle Discovery Prize: $500 plus publication. Previously unpublished poets only.

⊘ ◎ THE PENWOOD REVIEW (Specialized: spirituality), P.O. Box 862, Los Alamitos CA 90720-0862. E-mail: penwoodreview@charter.net. Website: http://webpages.charter.net/penwoodreview/penwood.htm. Established 1997. **Editor:** Lori M. Cameron.
Magazine Needs: *The Penwood Review*, published biannually, "seeks to explore the mystery and meaning of the spiritual and sacred aspects of our existence and our relationship to God." Wants "disciplined, high-quality, well-crafted poetry on any subject. Prefer poems be less than two pages. Rhyming poetry must be written in traditional forms (sonnets, tercets, villanelles, sestinas, etc.)" Does not want "light verse, doggerel, or greeting card-style poetry. Also, nothing racist, sexist, pornographic, or blasphemous." Has published poetry by Kathleen Spivack, Nina Tassi, Rachel Srubas, and Gary Guinn. As a sample the editor selected these lines from "Mount Kenya" by Michael McManus:

> *Village elders told me,/if you love something immense/and beyond your reach, if your faith/is never*
> *diminished by famine or flood/one night the stars will turn/into white talons, and lift me to your*
> *summit./I believe them.*

The Penwood Review has about 40 pgs, 8½×11, saddle-stapled with heavy card cover. Press run is 50-100. Single copy: $6; subscription: $12.
How to Submit: Submit 3-5 poems, 1/page with the author's full name, address and phone number in the upper right hand corner. No previously published poems or simultaneous submissions. Accepts e-mail submissions in body of message. Cover letter preferred. Time between acceptance and publication is up to 12 months. "Submissions are circulated among an editorial staff for evaluations." Seldom comments on rejected poems. Responds in 2 months. Offers subscription discount of $10 to published authors and one additional free copy in which author's work appears. Acquires one-time rights.

$⊘ THE PEOPLE'S PRESS, 4810 Norwood Ave., Baltimore MD 21207-6839. Phone/fax: (410)448-0254. Press established 1997, firm established 1989. **Contact:** Submissions Editor.
Book/Chapbook Needs: "The goal of the types of material we publish is simply to move people to think and perhaps act to make the world better than when we inherited it." Wants "meaningful poetry that is mindful of human rights/dignity." Has published *Tokarski Meets Acevedo* by Henry J. Tokarski and Judith Acevedo; *The Patient Presents* Kelley Jean White, MD; and *60 Pieces of My Heart* by Jennifer Closs. Accepts poetry written by children; parental consent is mandatory for publication. As a sample they selected these lines from "Braids" by Rasheed Adero Merritt:

> *GOD fearing woman walking into building 7./"pardon me miss, did you pray for me today?/Philippians*
> *4:13 but anyway."/she grabbed me by my wife beater,/Conversation for days, butterscotch breath/and*
> *her dirty south ways.*

Books are usually 50 pages, 5½×8, photocopied, perfect-bound and saddle-stapled with soft cover, includes art/graphics.

How to Submit: Query first with 1-5 sample poems and a cover letter with brief bio and publication credits. SASE required for return of work and/or response. No submissions by fax. Time between acceptance and publication is 6-12 months. Seldom comments on rejected poems. Publishes theme issues. Guidelines available for SASE. Responds to queries in 2-6 weeks; to mss in 1-3 months. Pays royalties of 5-20% and 30 author's copies (out of a press run of 500). Order sample books by sending $8.

Also Offers: The People's Press sponsors an annual Poetry Month Contest in April. "Prizes and/or publication possibilities vary from contest to contest." Details available for SASE.

[N] [symbol] THE PERALTA PRESS, 333 E. Eighth St., Oakland CA 94606. (510)748-2340. Website: www.peraltapress.org (includes contest winners, contents, writer/contest guidelines). Established 2000. **Editor:** Jay Rubin.

Magazine Needs: *The Peralta Press* appears annually in February/March. Provides a podium for a diverse blend of both established and emerging twenty-first century voices cutting across race, gender, ethnic, age, religious, political, and sexually oriented boundaries. Wants all forms up to 30 lines (including stanza breaks); no poetry over 30 lines. Recently published poetry by Alice Jay, Vivian Shipley, Jessica Barksdale Inclan, Jessy Luanni Wolf, and Seth Kaplan. *The Peralta Press* is 144 pages, digest-sized, perfect-bound. Receives about 300 poems/year, accepts about 20%. Publishes about 50-60 poems/issue. Press run is 1,500. Single copy: $10. Sample: $12. Make checks payable to PCCD.

How to Submit: Submit 3-6 poems at a time. Line length for poetry is 30 maximum. No previously published poems or simultaneous submissions. No fax, e-mail, or disk submissions. Cover letter is required. Reads submissions August 25-September 15. Time between acceptance and publication is 5 months. Poems are circulated to an editorial board. "Editor makes first cut, teams of judges then determine contest winners." Never comments on rejected poems. "Submit through annual contests. Entry fee: $10 for 3 poems includes free copy." Guidelines available in magazine, for SASE, or on website. Responds in 1 month. Pays 1 contributor's copy, plus cash prize for winning poem. Acquires one-time print and Internet rights.

Advice: "Edit, revise, edit, revise. Preview journals before mass mailing."

[symbol] PEREGRINE; AMHERST WRITERS & ARTISTS, P.O. Box 1076, Amherst MA 01004-1076. Phone/fax: (413)253-7764. E-mail: awapress@aol.com. Website: www.amherstwriters.com (includes guidelines, masthead, contest winners, and announcements). Established 1984. **Managing Editor:** Nancy Rose.

Magazine Needs: *Peregrine*, published annually in October, features poetry and fiction. Open to all styles, forms and subjects except greeting card verse. Has published poetry by Sofía Arroyo, Charles Atkinson, Aliki Caloyeras, Allen C. Fisher, John Grey, Susan Terris, Dianalee Velie, and Jane Yolen. As a sample the editor selected these lines from "Japan Considers My Mother" by Mike Dockins:

> The shock wave/expands into its trillion/concentric circles, weakens.//At the subatomic level,/it bumps
> my pregnant/grandmother,//halfway across the planet/absently reading The Saturday Evening Post.//
> My mother shifts, gurgles/through amniotic fluid,/"What?"

Peregrine is 104 pages, digest-sized, professionally printed, perfect-bound with glossy cover. Each issue includes at least one poem in translation and reviews. Press run is 1,000. Single copy: $12; subscription: $25/3 issues; $35/5 issues; $250/lifetime. Sample: $10. Make checks payable to AWA Press.

How to Submit: Submit 3-5 poems, no more than 70 lines (and spaces) each. Accepts simultaneous submissions; no previously published work. Include cover letter with bio, 40 word maximum. No e-mail submissions. "No! No! No!" "Each ms is read by several readers. Final decisions are made by the poetry editor." Guidelines available for #10 SASE or on website. Reads submissions October through April only. Postmark deadline: April 1. Pays 2 copies. Acquires first rights.

Also Offers: The Peregrine Prize, an annual fiction and/or poetry contest. 1st Prize: $500, publication in *Peregrine*, and copies. Entry fee: $10. Submit 1-3 poems, limited to 70 lines (and spaces) per poem. *"Very specific contest guidelines!"* Guidelines available for #10 SASE or on website. After the winners of the Peregrine Prize have been chosen by an outside judge, the editorial staff will select one entry from Western Massachusetts to receive the "Best of the Nest" Award. The AWA Chapbook Series is *closed* to unsolicited submissions.

[symbol] [symbol] PERSPECTIVES (Specialized: religious), Dept. of English, Hope College, Holland MI 49422-9000. Established 1986. **Co-Editors:** Roy Anker, Leanne Van Dyk, and Dave Timmer. **Poetry Editor:** Francis Fike (send poetry submissions to Francis Fike at Dept. of English, Hope College, Holland MI 49422-9000).

Magazine Needs: *Perspectives* appears 10 times/year. The journal's purpose is "to express the Reformed faith theologically; to engage issues that Reformed Christians meet in personal, ecclesiastical, and societal life, and thus to contribute to the mission of the church of Jesus Christ." Wants "both traditional and free verse of high quality, whether explicitly 'religious' or not. Prefer traditional form. Publish one or two poems every other issue, alternating with a Poetry Page on great traditional poems from the past. No sentimental, trite, or 'inspirational' verse, please." Has published poetry by R.L. Barth, David Middleton, and Paul Willis. As a sample the editor selected these lines from "Ushering" by David Middleton:

> And when the last parishioner has gone/And all the lights are darkened we depart/A locked church—duty done—/Yet as we leave we think/On how our charge is rooted in that dawn/When God first ushered in the usher's art.

Perspectives is 24 pages, 8½×11, web offset and saddle-stapled, with paper cover containing b&w illustration. Receives about 50 poems/year, accepts 6-10. Press run is 3,300 for 3,000 subscribers of which 200 are libraries. Subscription: $24.95. Sample: $3.50.
How to Submit: No previously published poems or simultaneous submissions. No e-mail submissions. Cover letter preferred. Include SASE. Time between acceptance and publication is 12 months or less. Occasionally comments on rejected poems. Responds in up to 3 months. Pays 5 contributor's copies. Acquires first rights.

PERUGIA PRESS (Specialized: women), P.O. Box 60364, Florence MA 01062. E-mail: info@perugiapress.com. Website: www.perugiapress.com. Established 1997. **Director:** Susan Kan.
Book/Chapbook Needs: "Perugia Press publishes one collection of poetry each year, by a woman at the beginning of her publishing career. The poems that catch our attention use simple language and recognizable imagery to express complex issues, events and emotions. Our books appeal to people who have been reading poetry for decades, as well as those who might be picking up a book of poetry for the first time. Slight preference for narrative poetry." Has published *The Work of Hands* by Catherine Anderson, *Finding the Bear* by Gail Thomas, *Impulse to Fly* by Almitra David, *A Wound on Stone* by Faye Gore, and *Reach* by Janet E. Aalfs. As a sample the director selected these lines from "Ascent" by Almitra David in *Impulse to Fly*:

> Witnesses saw the children plummet,/but she watched them fly, saw each one/soar and ride the wind,/ then tucked her baby under her wings/and took off.

Books are usually 88 pages, 6×9, offset-printed and perfect-bound with 2-color card cover with photo or illustration. Print run 500-750.
How to Submit: Perugia Press is now accepting mss through annual contest only. Send 48-72 pages on white 8½×11 paper "with legible typeface, pagination, and fastened with a removable clip. Include *two* cover pages: one with title of manuscript, name, address, telephone number, and e-mail address and one with just manuscript title. Include table of contents and acknowledgments page." Cover letter and bio not required. Individual poems may be previously published. Accepts simultaneous submissions if notified of acceptance elsewhere. No translations or self-published books. Entry fee: $20/ms. Make checks payable to Perugia Press. Postmark between August 1 and November 15, 2002; "No FedEx or UPS." SASE for April 1 notification only; mss will be recycled. Judges: panel of Perugia authors, booksellers, scholars, etc. Prize: $1,000 and publication. No e-mail submissions. Order sample books by sending $14.

PHI KAPPA PHI FORUM, (formerly *National Forum*), 129 Quad Center, Mell St., Auburn University AL 36849-5306. (334)844-5200. E-mail: kaetzjp@mail.auburn.edu. Website: www.auburn.edu/natforum.html. Established 1915. **Editor:** James P. Kaetz. **Contact:** poetry editors.
Magazine Needs: *Phi Kappa Phi Forum* is the quarterly publication of Phi Kappa Phi using quality poetry. *Phi Kappa Phi Forum* is 48 pages, magazine-sized, professionally printed, saddle-stapled, with full-color paper cover and interior. Receives about 300 poems/year, accepts about 20. Press run is 115,000 for 113,000 subscribers of which 300 are libraries. Subscription: $25.
How to Submit: Submit 3-5 short (one page) poems at a time, including a biographical sketch with recent publications. Accepts e-mail submissions. Reads submissions approximately every 3 months. Responds in about 4 months. Pays 10 contributor's copies.

PHOEBE; GREG GRUMMER POETRY AWARD, MSN 206, George Mason University, 4400 University Dr., Fairfax VA 22030. (703)993-2915. E-mail: phoebe@gmu.edu. Website: www.gmu.edu/pubs/phoebe (includes guidelines for contest and submission, subscription information, etc.). Established 1970. **Editor:** Emily Tuszynska. **Poetry Editor:** Tracy Zeman.
Magazine Needs: *Phoebe* is a literary biannual, appearing September and February, "looking for imagery that will make your thumbs sweat when you touch it." Has published poetry by C.D. Wright, Russell Edson, Yusef Komunyakaa, Rosemarie Waldrop, and Leslie Scalapino. As a sample the editor selected these lines from "Why I Cannot Write At Home" by Jeffrey Schwarz:

> Does the moon yank a black comb/through the sun?/No, Mother does that.// . . .//Then where's the moon all morning?//Knocking and knocking on the outhouse door.

Press run is 3,000, with 35-40 pages of poetry in each issue. *Phoebe* receives 4,000 submissions/year. Single copy: $6; subscription: $12/year.

How to Submit: Submit up to 5 poems at a time; submission should be accompanied by SASE and a short bio. No simultaneous submissions. Does not accept e-mail submissions. Guidelines available for SASE, by e-mail, or on website. Responds in 3 months. Pays 2 copies or one year subscription.

Also Offers: Sponsors the Greg Grummer Poetry Award. Awards $1,000 and publication for winner, possible publication for finalists and a copy of awards issue to all entrants. Submit up to 4 poems, any subject, any form, with name on cover page only. No previously published submissions. Entry fee: $10/entry. Deadline: December 15. Contest receives 300-400 submissions. Back copy of awards issue: $6. Guidelines available for SASE or on website.

PHOEBE: JOURNAL OF FEMINIST SCHOLARSHIP THEORY AND AESTHETICS (Specialized: women/feminism), Women's Studies Dept., Suny-College at Oneonta, Oneonta NY 13820-4015. (607)436-2014. Fax: (607)436-2656. E-mail: omarakk@oneonta.edu. Established 1989. **Poetry Editor:** Marilyn Wesley. **Editor:** Kathleen O'Mara.

Magazine Needs: *Phoebe* is published semiannually. Wants "mostly poetry reflecting women's experiences; prefer 3 pages or less." Has published poetry by Barbara Crooker, Graham Duncan, and Patty Tana. As a sample we selected these lines from "Rosh Hodesh, In the Room of Mirrors" by Lyn Lifshin:

> *eyes over crystal/that a great aunt/might have polished/reflected in a/hall mirror,/candles float/like the moon,/a reflection of a/reflection.*

Phoebe is 120 pages, 7×9, offset-printed on coated paper and perfect-bound with glossy card cover, includes b&w art/photos and "publishing swap" ads. Receives about 500 poems/year, accepts 8%. Press run is 500 for 120 subscribers of which 52 are libraries. Single copy: $7.50; subscription: $15/year or $25/year institutional. Sample: $5.

How to Submit: No previously published poems. Accepts fax submissions. Cover letter preferred. Reads submissions October through January and May through July only. Time between acceptance and publication is 3 months. Seldom comments on rejected poems. Publishes theme issues occasionally. Guidelines available for SASE. Responds in up to 14 weeks. Sometimes sends prepublication galleys. Pays 1 contributor's copy. Staff reviews books and chapbooks of poetry in 500-1,000 words, single book format. Send books for review consideration.

PIANO PRESS; "THE ART OF MUSIC" ANNUAL WRITING CONTEST (Specialized: music-related topics), P.O. Box 85, Del Mar CA 92014-0085. (858)481-5650. Fax: (858)755-1104. E-mail: pianopress@aol.com. Website: www.pianopress.com (includes description of company, guidelines, contact and subscription information, editorial policy, catalog, contest rules). Established 1999. **Owner:** Elizabeth C. Axford, M.A. Member: The American Academy of Poets.

Book/Chapbook Needs: Piano Press regularly publishes anthologies using "poems on music-related topics to promote the art of music." Publishes 50-100 poems per year. "We are looking for poetry on music-related topics only. Poems can be of any length and in any style." Recently published *The Art of Music: A Collection of Writings Vol. I.* Includes poetry by Robert Cooperman, Gelia Dolci Mascolo, Arthur McMaster, Alana Merritt Mahattey, Bobbi Sinha-Morey, and Gerald Zipper. As a sample the editor selected these lines:

> *Friends close to home bring to mind/The times tuned to a cello or a flute/When I trace the fine vines/ And glare at the candle with the brass root/Lighting the lazy throws.*

Chapbooks are usually 64 pages, digest-sized with paper cover, includes some art/graphics.

How to Submit: Query first, with a few sample poems and cover letter with brief bio and publication credits. Accepts previously published poems and simultaneous submissions. Accepts e-mail submissions. SASE required for reply. Reads submissions September 1 through June 30 only. Submit seasonal poems 6-10 months in advance. Time between acceptance and publication is up to 18 months. Poems are circulated to an editorial board. "All submissions are reviewed by several previously published poets." Often comments on rejected poems. Responds to queries in 1 month; to mss in 3 months. Pays author's copies. Order sample chapbooks online or by sending SASE for order form.

Also Offers: Sponsors an annual writing contest for poetry, short stories, and essays on music. Open to ages 4 and up. Entry fee: $20. Entry form available online.

Advice: "Please do not send poems if they are not on music-related topics. Otherwise, all music-related poems will be considered."

$ PIG IRON; KENNETH PATCHEN COMPETITION (Specialized: themes), P.O. Box 237, Youngstown OH 44501. (330)747-6932. Fax: (330)747-0599. E-mail: pig_iron_press@cboss.com. Established 1975. **Poetry Editor:** Jim Villani.

• "Freelance manuscript moratorium resumption date to be announced."

Magazine Needs: *Pig Iron* is a literary annual devoted to special themes. Wants poetry "up to 300 lines; free verse and experimental; write for current themes." Does not want to see "traditional" poetry. Has published poetry by Frank Polite, Larry Smith, Howard McCord, Andrena Zawinski, Juan Kincaid, and Coco Gordon. As a sample the editors selected these lines from "Cat Call" by Andrenna Zawinski:

> *Curled in the corner of your couch,/like your amber eyed calico cat,/I dove when the earth quaked,*
> *fell/into the expanse of space stretched/between your arms. You caught me,/held me there,/hair on end,*
> *claws out, screeching./You held me to to your breast, your heart/beat my own rhythm; and I,/star struck*
> *and bewitched,/I purred in your ear.*

Pig Iron is 128 pages, magazine-sized, flat-spined, typeset on good stock with glossy card cover using b&w graphics and art, no ads. Press run is 1,000 for 200 subscribers of which 50 are libraries. Single copy: $12.95. Subscription: $12.95/year. Sample: $5. (Include $1.75 postage.)
How to Submit: Include SASE with submission. Accepts fax submissions. Responds in 3 months. Time between acceptance and publication is 12-18 months. Publishes theme issues. Next theme issue: "Religion in Modernity." Deadline: September 2000. Guidelines and upcoming themes available for SASE. Pays $5/poem plus 2 copies (additional copies at 50% retail). Acquires one-time rights.
Also Offers: Sponsors the annual Kenneth Patchen Competition. Details available for SASE.
Advice: "Reading the work of others positions one to be creative and organized in his/her own work."

PIKEVILLE REVIEW, Humanities Dept., Pikeville College, Pikeville KY 41501. (606)218-5002. Fax: (606)218-5225. E-mail: eward@pc.edu. Website: www.pc.edu (includes names of editors, guidelines, and most recent editions). Established 1987. **Editor:** Elgin M. Ward.
Magazine Needs: "There's no editorial bias though we recognize and appreciate style and control in each piece. No emotional gushing." *Pikeville Review* appears annually in July, accepting about 10% of poetry received. *Pikeville Review* is 94 pages, digest-sized, professionally printed and perfect-bound with glossy card cover with b&w illustration. Press run is 500. Sample: $4.
How to Submit: No simultaneous submissions or previously published poems. Editor sometimes comments on rejected poems. Guidelines available for SASE or on website. Pays 5 contributor's copies.

PINCHGUT PRESS, 6 Oaks Ave., Cremorne, Sydney, NSW 2090 Australia. Phone: (02)9908-2402. Established 1948. Publishes Australian poetry but is not currently accepting poetry submissions.

$ PINE ISLAND JOURNAL OF NEW ENGLAND POETRY (Specialized: regional, New England), P.O. Box 317, West Springfield MA 01090-0317. Established 1998. **Editor:** Linda Porter.
Magazine Needs: *Pine Island* appears 2 times/year "to encourage and support New England poets and the continued expression of New England themes." Wants poems of "up to thirty lines, haiku and other forms welcome, especially interested in New England subjects or themes. No horror, no erotica." Has published poetry by Larry Kimmel, Roy P. Fairfield, and Carol Purington. As a sample the editor selected this poem, "Trinity," by Linda Porter:

> *a trinity of apples/grace the handturned bowl/in the parlor.//just in case the pastor should call/or God*
> *himself stop by*

Pine Island is 50 pages, digest-sized, desktop-published and saddle-stapled, cardstock cover with art. Press run is 200 for 80 subscribers. Subscription: $10. Sample: $5. Make checks payable to Pine Island Journal.
How to Submit: "Writers must be currently residenced in New England." Submit 5 poems at a time. Line length for poetry is 30 maximum. No previously published poems or simultaneous submissions. Cover letter preferred. "Include SASE, prefer first time submissions to include cover letter with brief bio." Time between acceptance and publication is 6 months. Seldom comments on rejected poems. Responds in 1 month. Pays $1/poem and 1 contributor's copy. Acquires first rights.

THE PINK CHAMELEON—ONLINE. E-mail: dpfreda@juno.com. Website: www.geocities.com/thepinkchameleon/index.html (includes journal content, guidelines). Established 1985 (former print version), 1999 (online version). **Editor:** Dorothy P. Freda.
Magazine Needs: *Pink Chameleon—Online* wants "family-oriented, upbeat, any genre in good taste that gives hope for the future. For example, poems about nature, loved ones, rare moments in time. No pornography, no cursing, no swearing, nothing evoking despair." Recently published poetry by Deanne F. Purcell, James W. Collins, Craig Rondinone, Paula Freda, Kim Berger, and Robyn Sondra Wills. As a sample the editor selected these lines from "Divine Inspiration" by Deanne F. Purcell:

> *Getting up in the morning with optimism./Trying always to do the right thing,/in person, phone or*
> *writing.//Reaching out to someone, or saving another's life./Helping someone in trouble;/Being there*
> *at the right time and right place.*

The Pink Chameleon is published online with public domain illustrations and Yahoo ads. Receives about 50 poems/year, accepts about 50%. Publishes about 25 poems/issue.

How to Submit: Submit 1-4 poems at a time. Line length for poetry is 6 minimum, 24 maximum. Accepts previously published poems; no simultaneous submissions. "Only e-mail submissions considered. Please, *no attachments.* Include work in the body of the e-mail itself. Use plain text. Include a brief bio." Reads submissions all year. Time between acceptance and publication is 1 year. "As editor, I reserve the right to edit for grammar, spelling, sentence structure, flow, omit redundancy and any words or material I consider in bad taste. No pornography, no violence for the sake of violence, no curse words. Remember this is a family-oriented electronic magazine." Often comments on rejected poems. Guidelines available by e-mail or on website. Responds in 1 month. No payment. Acquires one-time, one-year publication rights. All rights revert to poet one year after publication online.

Advice: "Always keep a typed hard copy or a back-up disk of your work for your files. Mail can go astray. And I'm human, I can accidentally delete or lose the submission."

PINYON, Dept. of Languages, Literature & Communications, Mesa State College, 1100 North Ave., Grand Junction CO 81051. (970)248-1123. Established 1995. **Managing Editor:** Julia Sinclair. **Editor:** Randy Phillis.

Magazine Needs: *Pinyon* appears annually and publishes "the best available contemporary American poetry and fiction. No restrictions other than excellence. We appreciate a strong voice. No inspirational, light verse or sing-song poetry." Has published poetry by Mark Cox, Barry Spacks, Wendy Bishop, and Anne Ohman Youngs. As a sample the editor selected these lines from "The Approved Poem" by John McKernan:

> The Approved Poem sits in an oak rocker on the/front porch of a sharecropper's cabin in Logan North/
> Dakota arranging the words alphabetically in a/scrapbook.

Pinyon is about 120 pages, magazine-sized, offset-printed and perfect-bound, cover varies, includes 8-10 pages of b&w art/graphics, fiction, and poetry. Receives about 4,000 poems/year, accepts 2%. Press run is 300 for 150 subscribers of which 5 are libraries, 50 shelf sales; 100 distributed free to contributors, friends, etc. Subscription: $8/year. Sample: $4.50. Make checks payable to *Pinyon*, MSC.

How to Submit: Submit 3-5 poems at a time. No previously published poems or simultaneous submissions. Cover letter preferred. "Name, address and phone number on each page. SASE required." Time between acceptance and publication is 3-12 months. Poems are circulated to an editorial board. "Three groups of assistant editors, led by an associate editor, make recommendations to the editor." Seldom comments on rejected poems. Guidelines available for SASE. Responds in up to 3 months, "slower in summer." Pays 2 contributor's copies. Acquires one-time rights.

Advice: "Send us your best work!"

THE PIPE SMOKER'S EPHEMERIS (Specialized: pipes and pipe smoking), 20-37 120th St., College Point NY 11356-2128. Established 1964. **Editor/Publisher:** Tom Dunn.

Magazine Needs: "The *Ephemeris* is a limited edition, irregular quarterly for pipe smokers and anyone else who is interested in its varied contents. Publication costs are absorbed by the editor/publisher, assisted by any contributions—financial or otherwise—that readers might wish to make." Wants poetry with themes related to pipes and pipe smoking. Issues range from 76-116 pages, and are 8½ × 11, offset, saddle-stapled, with colored paper covers and illustrations. Has also published collections covering the first and second 15 years of the *Ephemeris* and a triennial "Collector's Dictionary."

How to Submit: Cover letter required with submissions; include any credits. Pays 1-2 contributor's copies. Staff reviews books of poetry. Send books for review consideration.

PITCHFORK; PITCHFORK PRESS, 2002 A Guadalupe St. #461, Austin TX 78705. Established 1998. **Editor:** Christopher Gibson.

Magazine Needs: *Pitchfork* is a biannual publishing "freaky goodness." Wants "erotic, psychotic and surreal poetry. No hack work." Has published poetry by Taylor Graham, Robert Cooperman, Todd Moore, and Thomas Michael McDade. As a sample the editor selected these lines from "Cupid Pro-Creator" by Robert O'Neal:

> tawdry pink hearts &/blue moons give the feathers to/foreskin, a plump-assed/cherub who splits hairs
> with his/feckless aim—love or/lust that quickens eggs into/raspberry-shellaced tadpoles?

Pitchfork is 60 pages, digest-sized, photocopied and saddle-stapled with colored paper cover. Press run varies. Single copy: $4; subscription: $6 (includes 2 issues and a chapbook of choice). Make checks payable to Christopher Gibson.

How to Submit: Submit 3-7 poems at a time. Accepts previously published poems and simultaneous submissions "but let us know." Cover letter preferred. "Include name and address on each page; always include SASE." Time between acceptance and publication is 6 months. Seldom comments on rejected poems. Response time varies. Pays 1 copy. Acquires all rights. Returns rights.

Book/Chapbook Needs & How to Submit: Pitchfork Press publishes 2 chapbooks per year. Chapbooks are usually 40-60 pages, digest-sized, photocopied and side-stapled. However, they are not accepting unsolicited mss at this time.

N ✪ PITT POETRY SERIES; UNIVERSITY OF PITTSBURGH PRESS; AGNES LYNCH STARRETT POETRY PRIZE, 3400 Forbes Ave., Pittsburgh PA 15261. (412)383-2456. Fax: (412)383-2466. Website: www.pitt.edu/~press (includes guidelines, contest rules, and catalog). Established 1968. **Poetry Editor:** Ed Ochester.
Book/Chapbook Needs: Publishes 6 books/year by established poets, and 1 by a new poet—the winner of the Starrett Poetry Prize competition. Wants "poetry of the highest quality; otherwise, no restrictions— book mss minimum of 48 pages." Poets who have previously published books should query. Accepts simultaneous submissions. Always sends prepublication galleys. Has published books of poetry by Lynn Emanuel, Larry Levis, Billy Collins and Alicia Ostriker. Their booklist also features such poets as Etheridge Knight, Sharon Olds, Ronald Wallace, David Wojahn and Toi Derricotte.
How to Submit: Unpublished poets or poets "who have published chapbooks or limited editions of less than 750 copies" must submit through the Agnes Lynch Starrett Poetry Prize (see below). For poetry series, submit "entire manuscripts only." Cover letter preferred. Reads submissions from established poets in September and October only. Seldom comments on rejected poems.
Also Offers: Sponsors the Agnes Lynch Starrett Poetry Prize. "Poets who have not previously published a book should send SASE for rules of the Starrett competition ($20 handling fee), the only vehicle through which we publish first books of poetry." The Starrett Prize consists of cash award of $5,000 and book publication. Reads in March and April only. Competition receives 1,000 entries.

✪ PLAINSONGS, Dept. of English, Hastings College, Hastings NE 68902-0269. (402)461-7352. Fax: (402)461-7480. E-mail: dm84342@alltel.net. Established 1980. **Editor:** Dwight C. Marsh.
Magazine Needs: *Plainsongs* is a poetry magazine that "accepts manuscripts from anyone, considering poems on any subject in any style but free verse predominates. Plains region poems encouraged." Has published award poems by Elizabeth Ann Bolen, James Ciletti, Michael Haskell, Scott Heflin, Brian Slusher, and Connie Wohlford. As a sample the editor selected these lines from "To Fly with the Crane" by Nancy Westerfield:

> His soul, we say to him, hopefully,/Has taken flight;/And we life our eyes/As if a contrail following its
> trajectory/Might be feathering westward towards earth's/Bounds . . .

Plainsongs is 40 pages, digest-sized, set on laser, printed on thin paper and saddle-stapled with one-color matte card cover with generic black logo. "Published by the English department of Hastings College, the magazine is partially financed by subscriptions. Although editors respond to as many submissions with personal attention as they have time for, the editor offers specific observations to all contributors who also subscribe." The name suggests not only its location on the Great Plains, but its preference for the living language, whether in free or formal verse. *Plainsongs* is committed to poems only, to make space without visual graphics, bio, or critical positions. Subscription: $10/3 issues. Sample: $4.
How to Submit: Submit up to 6 poems at a time with name and address on each page. Deadlines are August 15 for fall issue; November 15 for winter; March 15 for spring. Notification is mailed 5-6 weeks after deadlines. Pays 2 contributor's copies and 1-year subscription, with 3 award poems in each issue receiving $25. "A short essay in appreciation accompanies each award poem." Acquires first rights.
Advice: "We like to hear tension in the lines, with nothing flacid."

N ⊕ $✪ PLANET: THE WELSH INTERNATIONALIST, P.O. Box 44, Aberystwyth, Ceredigion SY23 3ZZ, Wales. Phone: 01970-611255. Fax: 01970-611197. Established 1970. **Editor:** John Barnie.
Magazine Needs: *Planet* is a bimonthly cultural magazine, "centered on Wales, but with broader interests in arts, sociology, politics, history and science." Wants "good poetry in a wide variety of styles. No limitations as to subject matter; length can be a problem." Has published poetry by Gillian Clarke and R.S. Thomas. As a sample the editor selected these lines from "On Home Beaches" by Les Murray:

> Back, in my fifties, fatter than I was then,/I step on the sand, belch down slight horror to walk/a
> wincing pit edge, waiting for the pistol shot/laughter. Long greening waves cash themselves, foam
> change/sliding into Ocean's pocket. She turns: ridicule looks down,/strappy, with faces averted, or is
> glare and families.

Planet is 128 pages, A5 size, professionally printed and perfect-bound with glossy color card cover. Receives about 500 submissions/year, accepts approximately 5%. Press run is 1,550 for 1,500 subscribers of which about 10% are libraries, 200 shelf sales. Single copy: £3.25; subscription: £15 (overseas: £16). Sample: £4.

How to Submit: No previously published poems or simultaneous submissions. SASE or SAE with IRCs essential for reply. Time between acceptance and publication is 6-10 months. Seldom comments on rejected poems. Send SASE (or SAE and IRCs if outside UK) for guidelines. Responds within a month or so. Pays £25 minimum. Acquires first serial rights only. Reviews books of poetry in 700 words, single or multi-book format.

THE PLASTIC TOWER, P.O. Box 702, Bowie MD 20718. Established 1989. **Editors:** Carol Dyer and Roger Kyle-Keith.
Magazine Needs: *The Plastic Tower* is a quarterly using "everything from iambic pentameter to silly limericks, modern free verse, haiku, rhymed couplets—we like it all! Only restriction is length—under 40 lines preferred. So send us poems that are cool or wild, funny or tragic—but especially those closest to your soul." Accepts poetry written by children. Has published poetry by "more than 400 different poets." *The Plastic Tower* is 38-54 pages, digest-sized, saddle-stapled; "variety of typefaces and b&w graphics on cheap photocopy paper. Line drawings also welcome." Press run is 200. Subscription: $8/year. Copy of current issue: $2.50. "We'll send a back issue free for a large (at least 6×9) SAE with 2 first-class stamps attached."
How to Submit: Submit up to 10 poems at a time. Accepts previously published poems and simultaneous submissions. Often comment on submissions. Guidelines available for SASE. Responds in 6 months. Pays 1 contributor's copy. Poets may send books for review consideration.
Advice: "*The Plastic Tower* is an unpretentious little rag dedicated to enjoying verse and making poetry accessible to the general public as well as fellow poets. We don't claim to be the best, but we try to be the nicest and most personal. Over the past several years, we've noticed a tremendous upswing in submissions. More people than ever are writing poetry and submitting it for publication, and that makes it tougher for individual writers to get published. But plenty of opportunities still exist (there are thousands of little and literary magazines in the U.S. alone), and the most effective tool for any writer right now is not talent or education, but persistence. So keep at it!"

THE PLAZA (Specialized: bilingual), U-Kan, Inc., Yoyogi 2-32-1, Shibuya-ku, Tokyo 151-0053, Japan. Phone: 81-3-3379-3881. Fax: 81-3-3379-3882. E-mail: plaza@u-kan.co.jp. Website: http://u-kan.co.jp. Established 1985. **Contact:** editor.
Magazine Needs: *The Plaza* is a quarterly, currently published only online (http://u-kan.co.jp), which "represents a borderless forum for contemporary writers and artists" and includes poetry, fiction, and essays published simultaneously in English and Japanese. Wants "highly artistic poetry dealing with being human and interculturally related. Nothing stressing political, national, religious, or racial differences. *The Plaza* is edited with a global view of mankind." Has published poetry by Al Beck, Antler, Charles Helzer, Richard Alan Bunch, Morgan Gibson, and Bun'ichirou Chino. As a sample the editors selected these lines from "You Who Read This Read Your Life" by Morgan Gibson:

> You who read this read your life/backwards in Alice's smeared mirror//You who see me see your face/
> before you were conceived//And who hear this hear your scream/of your own birth and dying.

The Plaza is 50 full color pages. Available free to all readers on the Internet. Receives about 2,500 poems/year, accepts 8%. Proofs of accepted poems are sent to the authors 1 month before online publication.
How to Submit: Accepts simultaneous submissions; no previously published poems. Accepts e-mail and fax submissions. "No attachments. Cover letter required. Please include telephone and fax numbers or e-mail address with submissions. As *The Plaza* is a bilingual publication in English and Japanese, it is sometimes necessary, for translation purposes, to contact authors. Japanese translations are prepared by the editorial staff." Seldom comments on rejected poems. Responds within 2 months. Reviews books of poetry, usually in less than 500 words. Poets may send books for review consideration.
Advice: "*The Plaza* focuses not on human beings but humans being human in the borderless world.

THE PLEASANT UNICORN (Specialized: humor, light verse, parody, satire). E-mail: pleasant_unicorn@yahoo.com. Website: www.tarleton.edu/students/sscarborough/pu.html (includes everything: zine, info, play toys, links). Established 2001/2002. **High Priestess of Parody and Janitor:** Stephanie Scarborough.
Magazine Needs: *The Pleasant Unicorn* appears quarterly online. "A festering pimple on the proverbial forehead of literature, we publish the best light verse, nonsense verse, parody, satire, insane musings, and other such spew. Rhyme and meter preferred, but all considered. Funny fiction, too. Must be well done, witty, strange, bewildering, random, pop-culture references good but not required. Literary humor good, too. Funny artwork, too. Nothing too cute or sentimental. Nothing serious or downtrodden or, ahem, intellectual. Nothing not well-crafted or trite. Nothing above PG-13 rating vulgarity-wise." Recently published poetry by Patricia Harrelson, Todd B. Rudy, Paul Kloppenborg, Babel, RD Larson, and Pete Geary. As a sample the editor selected these lines from "Ode to Double-Declining Depreciation" by Pete Geary:

> *Thou, who wert conceived 'neath a furrowed brow/and flew, full-formed, from some accountant's mind,/*
> *to succor those who feel the morrow's dow.//Softly, thou caress all things bottom-lined,/and offer*
> *hopeful dawns to those wary/warriors, who beg markets to be kind.*

The Pleasant Unicorn is published online only, with some funny artwork. Accepts about 25% of work submitted. Publishes about 10-15 poems/issue.

How to Submit: Submit 1-8 poems at a time. Line length for poetry is 1 minimum, 1,000 maximum. Accepts previously published poems and simultaneous submissions. Accepts e-mail submissions; no fax or disk submissions. Cover letter is preferred. "Only e-mail submissions considered, no attachments. Single-spaced. Be pleasant." Reads submissions all the time. Submit seasonal poems 2-3 months in advance. Time between acceptance and publication is 1-2 months. "I check my e-mail and read the poems. If the poem seems right for *PU* I publish it; if not, I politely reject it." Often comments on rejected poems. Occasionally publishes theme issues. A list of upcoming themes and guidelines available by e-mail or on website. Responds in 2 months. Sometimes sends prepublication galleys. No payment. Acquires one-time rights. Reviews other magazines/journals in up to 1,000 words.

Advice: "Anyone can write fragmented lines about their dysfunctional childhood, but it takes a rare breed to write light verse. There seem to be few good outlets for it. Read the poetry of Swift, Ben King, Pope and Nash, and the lyrics of Weird Al and Tom Lehrer. That's the stuff!'"

$⬭ PLEIADES; LENA-MILES WEVER TODD POETRY SERIES; PLEIADES PRESS, Dept. of English and Philosophy, Central Missouri State University, Warrensburg MO 64093. (660)543-8106. E-mail: kdp8106@cmsu2.cmsu.edu. Website: www.cmsu.edu/englphil.pleiades.edu (includes new poems and stories, guidelines, contact and subscription information, editorial policy, contest rules, contributors' notes, and contents for current issues). Established as *Spring Flight* in 1939, reestablished in its present format in 1990. **Editors:** R.M. Kinder, Susan Steinberg, and Kevin Prufer.

Magazine Needs: *Pleiades* is a semiannual journal, appearing in April and October, which publishes poetry, fiction, literary criticism, belles lettres (occasionally), and reviews. It is open to all writers. Wants "avant-garde, free verse and traditional poetry, and some quality light verse. Nothing pretentious, didactic, or overly sentimental." Has published poetry by Campbell McGrath, Brenda Hillman, Dara Wier, Rafael Campo, and David Lehman. As a sample the editor selected these lines from "How tailors are made" by Graham Foust:

> *Cipher the rate at which things are put/Together. You will discover a love for light//Sleepers who dream*
> *they are the only ones/With hands. I'll get lost on the way to your mouth.//If I could have anything I*
> *wanted, I would have/Less than I do now. Maybe your blood on a textbook,//Or your breath like some*
> *ancient hinge.*

Pleiades is 160 pages, 5½×8½, perfect-bound with a heavy coated cover and color cover art. Receives about 3,000 poems/year, accepts 1-3%. Press run is 2,500-3,000, about 200 distributed free to educational institutions and libraries across the country, several hundred shelf sales. Single copy: $6; subscription: $12. Sample: $5. Make checks payable to Pleiades Press.

How to Submit: Submit 3-5 poems at a time. Accepts simultaneous submissions with notification; no previously published poems. Cover letter with brief bio preferred. Time between acceptance and publication can be up to 1 year. Each poem published must be accepted by 2 readers and approved by the poetry editor. Seldom comments on rejected poems. Guidelines available for SASE or on website. Responds in up to 3 months. Payment varies. Acquires first and second serial rights and requests rights for *Wordbeat*, a TV/radio show featuring work published in *Pleiades*.

Also Offers: Sponsors the Lena-Miles Wever Todd Poetry Series. "We will select one book of poems in open competition and publish it in our Pleiades Press Series. Louisiana State University Press will distribute the collection." Has published *A Sacrificial Zinc* by Matthew Cooperman and *The Light in Our Houses* by Al Maginnes. Entry fee: $15. Postmark deadline: September 15 annually. Complete guidelines available for SASE.

♟ $⬭ PLOUGHSHARES, Emerson College, 120 Boylston St., Boston MA 02116. (617)824-8753. Website: www.pshares.com. Established 1971.

• Work published in *Ploughshares* is frequently selected for inclusion in volumes of *The Best American Poetry*.

Magazine Needs: *Ploughshares* is "a journal of new writing guest-edited by prominent poets and writers to reflect different and contrasting points of view." Editors have included Carolyn Forché, Gerald Stern, Rita Dove, Chase Twichell, and Marilyn Hacker. Has published poetry by Donald Hall, Li-Young Lee, Robert Pinsky, Brenda Hillman, and Thylias Moss. The triquarterly is 250 pages, 5½×8½. Press run is 6,000. Receives about 2,500 poetry submissions/year. Subscription: $22 domestic; $28 foreign. Sample: $9.95 current issue, $8.50 sample back issue.

How to Submit: "We suggest you read a few issues before submitting." Simultaneous submissions acceptable. Do not submit mss from April 1 to July 31. Responds in up to 5 months. Always sends prepublication galleys. Pays $25/printed page per poem ($50 min, $250 max), plus 2 copies and a subscription.

◩ $◻ THE PLOWMAN, Box 414, Whitby, Ontario L1N 5S4 Canada. (905)668-7803. Established 1988. **Editor:** Tony Scavetta.
Magazine Needs: *The Plowman* appears annually using "didactic, eclectic poetry; all forms. We will also take most religious poetry except satanic and evil. We are interested in work that deals with the important issues in our society. Social and environment issues are of great importance." Has published poetry by Larry Prouty, K.L. Haley, Ari Zepkin, Luther C. Hanson, and Angela Galipeau. *The Plowman* is 20 pages, 8½×11 (17×11 sheet folded), photocopied, unbound, contains clip art and market listings. Accepts 70% of the poetry received. Press run is 15,000 for 1,200 subscribers of which 500 are libraries. Single copy: $5; subscription: $10. Sample free.
How to Submit: Accepts previously published poems and simultaneous submissions. Cover letter required. No SASE necessary. Always comments on rejected poems. Guidelines available free. Responds in 1 week. Always sends prepublication galleys. Pays 1 copy. Reviews books of poetry.
Book/Chapbook Needs & How to Submit: Also publishes 125 chapbooks/year. Responds to queries and mss in 1 month. **Reading fee:** $25/book. Pays 20% royalties. Has published *A Different Kind of Quiet* by Tabitha Lady Grail; and *Words to Live By* by Geri Ahearn.
Also Offers: Offers monthly poetry contests. Entry fee: $2/poem. 1st Prize: 50% of the proceeds; 2nd: 25%; 3rd: 10%. The top poems are published. "Balance of the poems will be used for anthologies."

◪ POEM; HUNTSVILLE LITERARY ASSOCIATION, English Dept., University of Alabama at Huntsville, Huntsville AL 35899. Established 1967. **Poetry Editor:** Nancy Frey Dillard.
Magazine Needs: *Poem*, appears twice/year, consisting entirely of poetry. "We are open to traditional as well as non-traditional forms, but we favor work with the expected compression and intensity of good lyric poetry and a high degree of verbal and dramatic tension. We equally welcome submissions from established poets as well as from less-known and beginning poets." Has published poetry by Robert Cooperman, Andrew Dillon, and Scott Travis Hutchison. *Poem* is a flat-spined, 4⅜×7¼, 90-page journal that contains more than 60 poems (mostly lyric free verse under 50 lines) generally featured 1 to a page on good stock paper with a clean design and a classy matte cover. Press run is 400 (all subscriptions, including libraries). Sample: $5.
How to Submit: "We do not accept translations, previously published works, or simultaneous submissions. Best to submit December through March and June through September. We prefer to see a sample of three to five poems at a submission, with SASE. We generally respond within a month. We are a nonprofit organization and can pay only in copy to contributors." Pays 2 contributor's copies. Acquires first serial rights.

◪ POEM DU JOUR, P.O. Box 416, Somers MT 59932. Established 1999. **Editor:** Asta Bowen.
Magazine Needs: *Poem du Jour* is a "weekly one-page broadside circulated in the retail environment." Wants "accessible but not simplistic poetry; seasonal work encouraged; humorous, current events, slam favorites; topical work (rural, mountain, outdoors, environmental, Northwest). No erotica, forced rhyme, or poems of excessive length." As a sample the editor selected these lines from "Dandelions" by Lacie Jo Twiest:

> she called them flowers but I knew that they weren't/and I watched as she rubbed yellow on her cheeks
> and her lips/her entire face was the color of the sun and she beamed/and I watched her carefully craft
> the wreath that she placed atop her head/she was a princess though I knew she was too old to pretend . . .

Press run is 20-50. Sample: $2. Make checks payable to Asta Bowen—PDJ.
How to Submit: Submit up to 5 poems at a time. Line length for poetry is 50 maximum. Accepts previously published poems and simultaneous submissions. Cover letter preferred. "Prefer poems typed with name, address and phone on each page." Time between acceptance and publication varies. Seldom comments on rejected poems. Guidelines available for SASE. Responds in 2 months. Sometimes sends prepublication galleys. Pays 1 contributor's copy. Acquires one-time rights.
Advice: "New/young writers encouraged."

◪ POEMS & PLAYS; THE TENNESSEE CHAPBOOK PRIZE, English Dept., Middle Tennessee State University, Murfreesboro TN 37132. (615)898-2712. Established 1993. **Editor:** Gaylord Brewer.

Magazine Needs: *Poems & Plays* is an annual "eclectic publication for poems and short plays," published in April. No restrictions on style or content of poetry. Has published poetry by Naomi Wallace, Katia Kapovich, and Charles Harper Webb. *Poems & Plays* is 88 pages, 6×9, professionally printed and perfect-bound with coated color card cover and art. "We receive 1,500 poems per issue, typically publish 30-35." Press run is 800. Subscription: $10/2 issues. Sample: $6.

How to Submit: No previously published poems or simultaneous submissions (except for chapbook submissions). Reads submissions October 1 through December 31 only. "Work is circulated among advisory editors for comments and preferences. All accepted material is published in the following issue." Usually comments on rejected poems. Responds in 2 months. Pays 1 contributor's copy. Acquires first publication rights only.

Also Offers: "We accept chapbook manuscripts (of poems or short plays) of 20-24 pages for The Tennessee Chapbook Prize. Any combination of poems or plays, or a single play, is eligible. The winning chapbook is printed as an interior chapbook in *Poems & Plays* and the author receives 50 copies of the issue. SASE and $10 (for reading fee and one copy of the issue) required. Dates for contest entry are the same as for the magazine (October 1 through December 31). Past winners include Julie Lechevsky, David Kirby, Angela Kelly, and Rob Griffith. The chapbook competition annually receives over 100 manuscripts from the U.S. and around the world."

$□ A POET BORN PRESS, P.O. Box 24238, Knoxville TN 37933. E-mail: wm.tell.us@apoetborn.com. Website: www.apoetborn.com. Established 1998. **Contact:** Laura Skye.

Book/Chapbook Needs: A Poet Born Press publishes 6-8 paperbacks per year. Wants any style or form of poetry, 45 lines or less, including spaces. "Poems should be descriptive of the 20th Century, its people and its issues." No profanity. Has published poetry by Robin Moore, Dwhisperer, and Skye. As a sample the editor selected these lines from "One Public Servant" by J. Elsie Madding:

> *What was it like—/Going to work each morning,/Calmly ordering the affairs of state,/Striving for wisdom amidst national crises,/Seeking to achieve honorable compromise/Among arguing, bipartitie factions*

Books are usually 50-150 pages, 5½×8½, perfect-bound with 80 lb. cover stock, 1 color or full bleed color covers, includes some photographs, some drawings.

How to Submit: Query first with 1-2 sample poems and cover letter with brief bio and publication credits. Line length for poetry is 45 maximum including spaces. Accepts previously published poems and simultaneous submissions. Accepts e-mail and disk submissions. "All poetry must be accompanied by author's name and address, as well as by e-mail address and URL if applicable. Also, author must specify what submission is for: contest, certain publications or call for poems, etc." Time between acceptance and publication is up to 6 months. Poems are circulated to an editorial board. "The editorial staff reviews all submissions for publication and makes their recommendations to the Senior Editor who makes the final selections." Often comments on rejected poems. "We charge for criticism only on manuscript-length work. Price varies depending on length of manuscript. E-mail for complete details." Responds to queries in 2 months. Pays 5-35% royalties "depending on individual contract." 50% of books are author-subsidy published each year. "We have four different subsidy programs. Program is dependent upon work, audience, sales track, and author/press choice. Contracts are specifically tailored to individual authors and their work. No loyalties are paid for poems accepted for anthologies."

Also Offers: Sponsors three contests per year. 1st Place: $100 plus a brass plaque of poem; 2nd Place: brass plaque of poem; 3rd Place: A Poet Born coffee mug. "All winners receive web publication within 6 weeks of contest and print publication within one year." Entry fee: $5/poem. Website includes complete contest guidelines and submission form, Call for Poems section and permission form, Winners Circle and archive of previous winning poems, Poetry Night listings, poetry news and events, resource links and Teacher's Corner. "Teacher's Corner features lessons in poetry provided by published poets, authors, professors, editors and more. Recent appearances in the Teacher's Corner include: Robert Pinsky; Robin Moore, author of the *French Connection* and *The Green Berets*; Eugene McCarthy, statesman and published poet; and Michael Bugeja, author of *The Art and Craft of Poetry*."

◙ POET LORE, The Writer's Center, 4508 Walsh St., Bethesda MD 20815. (301)654-8664. Fax: (301)654-8667. E-mail: postmaster@writer.org. Website: www.writer.org (includes contact information, editorial policy, magazine and contest guidelines, table of contents, subscription info, current issue, and back-issue archives). Established 1889. **Editor:** Rick Canon. **Contact:** Jo-Ann Billings.

THE GEOGRAPHICAL INDEX in the back of this book helps you locate markets in your region.

Magazine Needs: *Poet Lore* is a quarterly dedicated "to the best in American and world poetry and objective and timely reviews and commentary. We look for fresh uses of traditional form and devices, but any kind of excellence is welcome. The editors encourage original translations of works by contemporary world poets." Has published poetry by Martin Galvin, Eliot Khalil Wilson, Herman Asarnow, Carmelinda Blagg, Geri Rosenzweig, and Maria Terrone. *Poet Lore* is 6×9, 120 pages, perfect-bound, professionally printed with glossy card cover. Circulation includes 600 subscriptions of which 200 are libraries. Receives about 3,000 poems/year, accepts 125. Single copy: $5.50; subscription: $18. "Add $5 postage for subscriptions outside U.S."

How to Submit: Submit typed poems, author's name and address on each page, SASE required. No simultaneous submissions. Guidelines available for SASE, by fax, by e-mail, on website. Upcoming themes available in publication. Responds in 3 months. Pays 2 contributor's copies. Reviews books of poetry. Poets may send books for review consideration.

POETCRIT (Specialized: membership), Maranda, H.P. 176 102 India. Phone: 01894-38277. Established 1988. **Editor:** Dr. D.C. Chambial.

Magazine Needs: *Poetcrit* appears each January and July "to promote poetry and international understanding through poetry. Purely critical articles on various genres of literature are also published." Wants poems of every kind. Has published poetry by Ruth Wilder Schuller (US), Danae G. Papastratau (Greece), Shiv K. Kumar (India), Joy B. Cripps (Australia), and O.P. Bhatnagar (India). As a sample the editor selected these lines from "An Existential Question" by Manas Bakashi:

> *For some days/I have lived/weaving thoughts around/All that's intractable/But poised for/An apocalypse.*

Poetcrit is 100 pages, magazine-sized, offset-printed with simple paper cover, includes ads. Receives about 1,000 poems/year, accepts 20%. Press run is 1,000 for 500 subscribers of which 100 are libraries, 200 shelf sales; 400 distributed free to new members. Single copy: $9; subscription: $15. Sample: $10. Make checks payable to Dr. D.C. Chambial. Membership required for consideration.

How to Submit: Submit 3 poems at a time. Line length for poetry is 25 maximum. Accepts simultaneous submissions; no previously published poems. Cover letter required. Reads submissions September 1 through 20 and March 1 through 20. Poems are circulated to an editorial board. "All poems reviewed by various editors and selected for publication." Occasionally publishes theme issues. Guidelines and upcoming themes are available for SASE or SAE with IRC. Responds in about 1 month. Pays 1 contributor's copy. Acquires one-time rights. Reviews books and chapbooks of poetry and other magazines in 1,000 words, single book format.

Advice: "Beginners should meditate well on their themes before writing."

POETIC HOURS, 43 Willow Rd., Carlton, Nolts NG4 3BH England. E-mail: erranpublishing@hotmail.com. Established 1993. Website: www.poetichours.homestead.com (includes magazine's history and charity work, submission guidelines, contacts, news of forthcoming issues, and *'Poetic Hours Online'*). **Editor:** Nicholas Clark.

Magazine Needs: *Poetic Hours*, published biannually, "is published to encourage and publish new poets, i.e., as a forum where good but little known poets can appear in print and to raise money for Third World charities. The magazine features articles and poetry by subscribers and others." Wants "any subject, rhyme preferred but not essential; suitable for wide ranging readership, 30 lines maximum." Does not want "gothic, horror, extremist, political, self-interested." As a sample the editor selected these lines from his poem "School Report: Human Race":

> *Does the western world now stand for judgement/Before a clock?/There's a thought!/Whole nations check two thousand years of progress/Waiting for teachers Millennium Report*

Poetic Hours is 36 pages, A4, printed, saddle-stapled and illustrated throughout with Victorian woodcuts. Receives about 500 poems/year, accepts about 40%. Press run is 400 of which 12 are for libraries, 300 shelf sales. Subscription: £7, overseas payments in sterling or US dollars ($20). For a subscription send bankers checks or cash. Sample: £3.75. Make checks payable to Erran Publishing. "Subscribe online at our site at www.firstwriter.com."

How to Submit: "Poets are encouraged to subscribe or buy a single copy, though not required." Submit up to 5 nonreturnable poems at a time. Accepts previously published poems; no simultaneous submissions. Accepts e-mail submissions in attachments; accepts disk submissions. Cover letter required. Time between acceptance and publication is 3 months. "Poems are read by editors and if found suitable, are used." Always comments on rejected poems. Publishes theme issues. Upcoming themes listed in magazine. Responds "immediately, whenever possible." Acquires one-time rights.

Also Offers: "Poetic Hours Online" features original content. "New Poets or beginners who are willing to subscribe to hard copy should submit up to 5 poems."

Advice: "We welcome newcomers and invite those just starting out to have the courage to submit work. The art of poetry has moved from the hands of book publishers down the ladder to the new magazines. This is where

rs is non-profit-making and all proceeds go to various national charities,
ational. A page of *Poetic Hours* is set aside each issue for reporting how

MAGAZINE, P.O. Box 1095, Peoria IL 61653-1095. E-mail: poeticli
w.skybusiness.com/poetic license (includes guidelines, upcoming
ast issues, editorial policy, contact and subscription information, and
. **Editor:** Denise Felt. **Children's Editor:** Nadine Shelton.
etry Magazine is a monthly publication with "the purpose of giving
o be published. It includes articles and contests that challenge poets
st free verse and rhymed poetry by adults and children. No profane,
accepted." Has published poetry by Gary Edwards, Terri Warden,
. As a sample the editor selected these lines from "Inspiration" by

the fresh print,/excitement like lightning flashing.
ages, 8½ × 11, magazine-bound with full color cover, includes graphic
/year, accepts about 95%. Press run is 80/issue. Subscription: $49/year,
s payable to *Poetic License*.
ms at a time. Accepts previously published poems and simultaneous
s in body of message. Cover letter preferred. "Send double-spaced typed
ight hand corner. Age required if poet is 18 or younger." Time between
I judge poems on a 25-point system. Adult submissions with 12 points
ons with 10 points or less are rejected." Seldom comments on rejected
s in 2 weeks. Acquires one-time rights. Guidelines and upcoming themes
bsite.
ghout the year are published in an annual poetry volume called *150 Best*
s to be found by contemporary poets." Past volumes available.
ets should concern themselves with is excellence. Whether a poem is
uldn't matter. The goal is to bring the poem to life. Then it's fit for
e people of all ages than the poets of past centuries could have dreamed.
ow and flourish through exposure to the public."

ecialized: anthology, membership), 4066 Green Park Dr., Mt
webmaster@thepoeticlink.com. Website: http://ThePoeticLink.com
ry database; submissions post immediately and receive critiques
ned 1999. **Owner:** Christopher T. Moore.
is a website devoted to poetry posted to be shared and critiqued.
n is ranked. The best-ranked poem by each poet is placed on the
r quarterly anthology. The top poems receive cash prizes." Wants
er, focus, or purpose." Does not want "poetry you have NOT given
published poetry by Charles L. East, Wayne R. Leach, CJ Heck,
ly Denise Evans. As a sample we selected these lines from "Summer

er/Amidst a drift of honeybees/Drunk on wine from flowers,//While a
me/That everything is temporary/And must be loved to last./
poems of any length at **$3/poem**. Accepts previously published poems
l submissions or disk submissions. "Submissions are ONLY accepted
fee is used to pay out the prizes each month. The critiques and advice
ll worth the small fee." Use the "submission link" on the main web
poetry is critiqued and scored on various points by website members
Guidelines available on website. Responds in 5 weeks or less. Always
thly prizes for both poetry and critiques. Acquires first rights.
y, a hardbound 8½ × 11 quarterly in which "each poet can have one
$5 shipping. Make checks payable to *The Poetic Link*.
ed poet, this is a great place to start. You will learn a great deal here
ou will teach a great deal and may earn some nice cash."

POETIC MATRIX, A PERIODIC LETTER; POETIC MA-
TRIX SLIM VOLUME SERIES, P.O. Box 1223, Madera CA 93639. (559)673-9402. E-mail: poems@poe
ticmatrix.com. Established 1997 in Yosemite. **Editor/Publisher:** John Peterson.
Magazine Needs: *Poetic Matrix, a periodic letteR* appears periodically 2-4 times/year. Wants poetry
that "creates a 'place in which we can live' rather than telling us about the place. Poetry that draws from

the imaginal mind and is rich in the poetic experience—hence the poetic matrix." Does not want poetry that talks about the experience. Recently published poetry by Jeff Mann, Grace Marie Grafton, Tony White, Kathryn Kruger, James Downs, and Brandon Cesmat. As a sample the editor selected these lines from "That Unnamed Thing" from *Where Manzanita* by James Downs:

> With shadow across his neck/Coyote pads through forest;//with fires in his eyes,/fires of worlds
> unnamed,//Coyote howls at us. Soon/his tracks fade across snow//into the dark water.

Poetic Matrix is 4-12 pages, newsletter format, photocopied, saddle-stapled, with b&w art. Publishes about 10-20 poems/issue. Press run is 500 for 250 subscribers; 150 distributed free to interested parties, etc. Subscription: $12/4 issues. Make checks payable to *Poetic Matrix*.
How to Submit: Submit through Slim Volume Series. Accepts previously published poems and simultaneous submissions. No fax, e-mail, or disk submissions. Cover letter is required. Charges reading fee for yearly Slim Volume series submissions *only*. "Poems for *letteR* are generally, but not always drawn from the call for manuscripts for the *Poetic Matrix* Slim Volume Series." Often comments on rejected poems. Guidelines available for SASE or by e-mail. Responds in 2 months. Pays 25 contributor's copies. Acquires one-time rights. Reviews books and chapbooks of poetry and other magazines/journals in 500-1,000 words, single and multi-book format. Poets may send books/chapbooks for review consideration to John Peterson, editor.
Book/Chapbook Needs & How to Submit: Poetic Matrix Press publishes books (60-90 pages), slim volumes (44-55 pages, perfect-bound), and chapbooks (20-30 pages). "Poetic Matrix Press hosts a new Slim Volume Series call for submissions of manuscripts 45-55 pages. The manuscript selected will be published with full-color cover, perfect binding, and ISBN. The selected poet will receive 50 copies of the completed book and a $200 honorarium." Full guidelines and submission dates available for SASE. For chapbook and book information, contact the publisher. Order sample copies from Poetic Matrix Press.
Advice: "If poets and lovers of poetry don't write, publish, read, purchase poetry books, etc., then we will have no say in the quality of our contemporary culture and no excuses for the abuses of language, ideas, truth, beauty, and love in our cultural life."

◻ POETIC SPACE: POETRY & FICTION, P.O. Box 11157, Eugene OR 97440. Fax: (541)683-1271. E-mail: poeticspac@aol.com. Established 1983. **Editor:** Don Hildenbrand.
Magazine Needs: *Poetic Space*, published annually in the fall, is a nonprofit literary magazine with emphasis on contemporary poetry, fiction, reviews (including film and drama), interviews, market news, and translations. Accepts poetry and fiction that is "well-crafted and takes risks. We like poetry with guts. Would like to see some poetry on social and political issues. We would also like to see gay/lesbian poetry and poetry on women's issues. Erotic and experimental OK." Prefers poems under 1,000 words. Has published poetry by Simon Perchik, Paul Weinman, Sherman Alexie, Albert Huffstickler, and Lyn Lifshin. *Poetic Space* is 30 pages, magazine-sized, saddle-stapled, offset from typescript and sometimes photoreduced. Receives about 200-300 poems/year, accepts about 25%. Press run is 800 for 50 subscribers of which 12 are libraries. Single copy: $4; subscription: $7/2 issues, $13/4 issues. Send SASE for list of available back issues ($4).
How to Submit: Ms should be typed, double-spaced, clean, name/address on each page. "Submissions without SASE will not be considered." Accepts simultaneous submissions and previously published poems. Editor provides some critical comments. Guidelines available for SASE. Responds in up to 4 months. Pays 1 contributor's copy, but more can be ordered by sending SASE and postage. Reviews books of poetry in 500-1,000 words. Poets may send books for review consideration.
Book/Chapbook Needs & How to Submit: Also publishes one chapbook each spring. First chapbook was *Truth Rides to Work and Good Girls*, poetry by Crawdad Nelson and fiction by Louise A. Blum ($5 plus $1.50 p&h).
Advice: "We like poetry that takes risks—original writing that gives us a new, different perspective."

⬛ $◻ POETRY; THE MODERN POETRY ASSOCIATION; BESS HOKIN PRIZE; LEVIN-SON PRIZE; FREDERICK BOCK PRIZE; UNION LEAGUE PRIZE; J. HOWARD AND BAR-BARA M.J. WOOD PRIZE; RUTH LILLY POETRY PRIZE; RUTH LILLY POETRY FELLOW-SHIP; JOHN FREDERICK NIMS PRIZE, 60 W. Walton St., Chicago IL 60610-3380. E-mail: poetry@p oetrymagazine.org. Website: www.poetrymagazine.org (includes contents of recent issues, featured poets, guidelines, subscription information, announcement of awards, audio clips, etc.). Established 1912. **Editor:** Joseph Parisi.
 ● Work published in *Poetry* is frequently selected for inclusion in volumes of *The Best American Poetry* and was published in the 2002 *Pushcart Prize* anthology.
Magazine Needs: *Poetry* "is the oldest and most distinguished monthly magazine devoted entirely to verse. Established in Chicago in 1912, it immediately became the international showcase that it has remained ever since, publishing in its earliest years—and often for the first time—such giants as Ezra Pound,

Juxtapositions in life and art

The world is just too vibrant and un-mellow for Wanda Coleman not to be entranced. She is on a mission to make discoveries, both at her writing desk and away from it.

Coleman is an award-winning poet, novelist, and short story and essay writer whose recent collection, *Mercurochrome: New Poems* (Black Sparrow Press), was a finalist for the 2001 National Book Award in Poetry. She absorbs her daily observations, even painful memories of growing up in the Southwest, and adamantly uses it all, in whatever form she chooses.

Coleman has published 14 books over a 30-year span and received literary fellowships from the National Endowment for the Arts and the Guggenheim Foundation. Her books, an eclectic

Wanda Coleman

Photo by Susan Carpendale

mix, often contain both poems and prose, as in *African Sleeping Sickness: Stories & Poems*, *A War of Eyes and Other Stories*, and *Heavy Daughter Blues: Poems and Stories 1968-1986*. She has published primarily with Black Sparrow Press, who helped launch her early work and to whom she's remained loyal.

Coleman writes every day and stresses that her deep-rooted values are not seduced by media, marketing, or the status quo. She's a fierce reader and observer of culture and politics who finds books a major resource as she develops her ideas on paper. Coleman says she depends a great deal on what she does *not* see on TV, in the movies, or even in the works of her contemporaries. Even when she may be "watching" TV or staring out a car window, Coleman is writing in her head, recognizing that her process of writing is continuous. Often she'll come up with lines for a poem during a commercial, put them in a notebook, and simply compile them until it's time for her to dabble more seriously.

As a high school student, Coleman's speech and debate classes instilled in her a love for the rhetorical. "It's an art unto itself, but I go for those other levels in my poems and essays," she says. She likes to play with and discover tonal variations, to get language on the page to modulate, and this harks back to the impact of those speech classes.

In her apprentice years, Coleman was a freelance journalist who wrote mainly for the "underground papers" in the 1960s and early '70s. Many of her assignments were celebrity interviews, but she also wrote short personal essays. By the late '80s she was publishing articles in more mainstream publications like *The Los Angeles Herald Examiner*, *The Los Angeles Times*, and *The Washington Post*. Many of these articles are collected in her autobiography, *Native in a Strange Land: Trials and Tremors* (Black Sparrow Press).

"I specialize in culture clashes," Coleman says, "so juxtapositions matter a lot to me. My work is experimental in that way." As a Californian, she witnesses cultural juxtapositions all the time in the Mexican influence of Los Angeles, where she resides, and that influence upon African-Americans in that area. She embraces her role as an African-American writer who can articulate this dynamic of influence, and she does all she can in her writing to exploit this relationship.

Coleman may begin a poem by "intuiting"—drawing on what she has already read over the years, or observed. Then an act of discovery will allow her poem to take a certain shape, so that constantly "playing or painting with genre has become part of what I do when examining that tension of form and content." That notion of painting is what she calls "the suppressed visual artist in me."

Coleman emphasizes the need for tension and discovery, the friction of words joining or rubbing against one another to see what evolves. This is often her way to start a piece of writing. Many times the effect is a kind of hallucinatory poetry or prose, what poet and critic Marilyn Hacker describes in Coleman's work as a "verbal mandala whose colors and textures spin off the page." The recognition several years ago that came with winning the prestigious Lenore Marshall Poetry Prize for her collection, *Bathwater Wine* (publisher), pulled Coleman's work more into the mainstream as opposed to consigning it only to the experimental.

As an artist, Coleman is never comfortable approaching a lyrical "stance" in her poems in the same way. "My sense of the rhythms of time and the universe are outside the dominant culture poets's notion of the lyrical, which is too constricting," she says. "I've groped to develop my own approach to the lyrical. I'm striving to find different ways to present what I perceive as text." For her this striving means listening only to what *she* perceives is the lyrical—a source of boundless possibility.

But how does Coleman literally try to enact these words on the page? How does she arrive at this synergy of language? Word choice is important, and Coleman's knowledge of an urban vernacular, slang, and jazz combined with her study of classic poets like Homer and Dante provide her with a diverse means to explore language. She may use a longer Whitmanian line, for example, to allow a linguistic riff to unfold.

Or, as in this passage from her poem, "Heavy Daughter Blues," Coleman's knowledge of Emily Dickinson and Langston Hughes is illustrated by her skillful emjambent of line breaks:

now that machines have finally taken over
we can get into something serious
like art

    i have my one-way ticket
    to the moon
    i am inculcated with the dangers
    of incriminating love. . . .

(reprinted with permission of the author)

It's a preoccupation, Coleman says, to play with line breaks to see how they "deepen the text while also trimming it" so that it's not just editing for editing's sake. Words that had limited meaning—like "we can get into something serious/like art"—intensify because there's a build, an emphasis on the line breaks to end with "art."

In this poem, too, there's a merging of both sophisticated and street-wise diction to drum up wordplay. "I like to tell students that I am usually the narrator in my work, when there is one," Coleman says. A reader knows that Coleman is putting a premium on language to mold her vision of an African-American culture regularly subjected to a biased European worldview. But, as this narrator sees it, she will overcome—

myth/my girlchild and me
cackle joyfully in the kitchen
as we make cookies
for the party of the world.

Much of the time, Coleman says, her poetic sensibility is driven by a force she calls "zoning," when the poem literally writes itself. This is when she is most pleased and consoled. "It's as though I'm a medium for a force," she says. While writing a poem for *Bathwater Wine*, Coleman's early drafts for the opening sequence were about a female acquaintance who had died. Months later, Coleman played with the words, the sequence, and realized the woman had served as a kind of medium for something with which Coleman was really communicating herself. That force, too, may inspire her to use a longer line and breadth of page to explore a subject. An essay or story might take shape, although her dependence on language to move even the prose comes from the poetic, as in this passage from the short story, "Gatherings":

Back in South Central, at 88th and Avalon, I'm struck by double vision.
I will always see this scrubby park through my child's eye—that Easter
way back when my brother and I discovered our brand-new Buster Browns
had been stolen while we played in the giant sandbox. I adjust my sight to
take in the five Moreno men in their 30s. They squat where the old baseball
diamond used to be. One is mid-gulp, bottoming-up the brown bag that conceals
the short dog.

As always, Coleman hopes to discover lines for poems, seeds for a story, or part of herself everywhere she looks. She never totally gives up on a piece of material. Initially she strives for the poem, her "first love," but delights in showing students how a writer can take the same material and "rework it through form and form, and how each writing form (poem, story, essay) has its own dictates, demands, and delights."

Wanda Coleman considers herself never too comfortable with a process until she's played out ideas and language on the page as much possible. She's daily awakened to some new discovery, somewhere, and she clings to it for the sake of her writing.

—Jeffrey Hillard

Robert Frost, T.S. Eliot, Marianne Moore, and Wallace Stevens. *Poetry* has continued to print the major voices of our time and to discover new talent, establishing an unprecedented record. There is virtually no important contemporary poet in our language who has not at a crucial stage in his career depended on *Poetry* to find a public for him: John Ashbery, Dylan Thomas, Edna St. Vincent Millay, James Merrill, Anne Sexton, Sylvia Plath, James Dickey, Thom Gunn, David Wagoner—only a partial list to suggest how *Poetry* has represented, without affiliation with any movements or schools, what Stephen Spender has described as 'the best, and simply the best' poetry being written." As a sample the editor selected the opening lines of "The Love Song of J. Alfred Prufrock" by T.S. Eliot, which first appeared in *Poetry* in 1915:

Let us go then, you and I,/When the evening is spread out against the sky/Like a patient etherized upon
a table;/Let us go, through certain half-deserted streets . . .

Poetry is an elegantly printed, flat-spined, 5½×9 magazine. Receives over 90,000 submissions/year, accepts about 300-350; has a backlog up to 9 months. Press run is 12,400 for 8,200 subscribers of which 33% are libraries. Single copy: $3.75; subscription: $35, $38 for institutions. Sample: $5.50.

How to Submit: Submit up to 4 poems at a time with SASE. No e-mail submissions. No simultaneous submissions. Guidelines available for SASE. Responds in 4 months—longer for mss submitted during the summer. Pays $2 a line. Acquires all rights. Returns rights "upon written request." Reviews books of poetry in multi-book formats of varying lengths. Poets may send books to Stephen Young, senior editor, for review consideration.

Also Offers: Six prizes (named in heading) ranging from $300 to $5,000 are awarded annually to poets whose work has appeared in the magazine that year. Only verse already published in *Poetry* is eligible for consideration and no formal application is necessary. *Poetry* also sponsors the Ruth Lilly Poetry Prize, an annual award of $100,000, and the Ruth Lilly Poetry Fellowship, two annual awards of $15,000 to undergraduate or graduate students to support their further studies in poetry/creative writing.

POETRY & PROSE ANNUAL, P.O. Box 1175, Seaside OR 97138. E-mail: poetry@poetryproseann ual.com. Website: www.poetryproseannual.com (includes guidelines, names of editors, poetry from previous editions, and photographs). Established 1996. **Editor:** Sandra Claire Fousheé.
Magazine Needs: *Poetry & Prose Annual*, appearing in May, "publishes work that focuses on the nature of consciousness and enlightens the human spirit. A general selection of poetry, fiction, nonfiction and photography. We are looking for excellence and undiscovered talent in poems of emotional and intellectual substance. Poems should be original with rhythmic and lyric strength. Innovation and fresh imagery encouraged. Metrical ingenuity recognized. Open to all forms." Has published poetry by Anita Endrezze, Mary Crow, Nancy McCleery, Renate Wood, Mark Christopher Eades, Donna K. Wright, and Carlos Reyes. As a sample the editor selected these lines from "All Evening" by Mary Crow:

> Beautiful to be slipping toward a greater/and greater whiteness as if moving/into invisibility or as if
> the whiteness/were a curtain that would open into/some other world, once again green, and new.

Poetry & Prose Annual is approximately 82 pages, 7×8½, offset-printed and perfect-bound with glossy card cover, cover photograph, contains line art and photos inside. Press run is about 1,000. Subscription: $15. Sample copy: $10 (includes postage).
How to Submit: A $20 entry fee is required (includes subscription and entry into the Gold Pen Award contest). "Any work submitted without submission fee or SASE will not be returned or read. " Submit no more than 200 lines of poetry at a time, typed, with line count, name, address and phone number on first page. Include SASE and brief bio. Accepts previously published poems "if author holds copyright" and simultaneous submissions. Guidelines available for SASE. Responds after deadline. Sometimes sends prepublication galleys. Pays 2 contributor's copies. Acquires one-time and reprints rights. Work may also appear in the *Poetry & Prose Annual* website.
Also Offers: The online journal contains original content not found in the print edition. "From poetry submissions we may use some original material on the website which may/may not be published in the Annual. Poetry needs are the same as for the journal. Several new writers will also be chosen from the general selection to be featured in *American Portfolio*—a special section within the journal showcasing work of several authors in a portfolio."

THE POETRY EXPLOSION NEWSLETTER (THE PEN) (Specialized: ethnic, love, subscription, nature), P.O. Box 4725, Pittsburgh PA 15206-0725. (412)886-1114. E-mail: arthurford@ hotmail.com. Established 1984. **Editor:** Arthur C. Ford Sr.
Magazine Needs: *The Pen* is a "quarterly newsletter dedicated to the preservation of poetry." Arthur Ford wants "poetry—40 lines maximum, no minimum. All forms and subject matter with the use of good imagery, symbolism and honesty. Rhyme and non-rhyme. No vulgarity." Accepts poetry written by children; "if under 18 years old, parent or guardian should submit!" Recently published poetry by Lisa Cave, Margaret A. Brennan, and Iva Fedorka. *The Pen* is 12-16 pages, saddle-stapled, mimeographed on both sides. Receives about 300 poems/year, accepts 80. Press run is 850 for 525 subscribers of which 5 are libraries. Subscription: $20. Send $4 for sample copy and more information. Make checks payable to Arthur C. Ford.
How to Submit: Submit up to 5 poems at a time (40 lines maximum) with $1 **reading fee**. Also include large SASE if you want work returned. Accepts simultaneous submissions and previously published poems. No e-mail submissions. Sometimes publishes theme issues. "We announce future dates when decided. July issue is usually full of romantic poetry." Guidelines and upcoming themes available for SASE. Responds in up to 3 weeks. Editor comments on rejected poems "sometimes, but not obligated." Pays 1 contributor's copy. Poetry critiques available for 15¢ a word. Poets may send books for review consideration.
Also Offers: Website includes writer's guidelines. Use code word 'poetry.'
Advice: "Be fresh, honest, and legible!"

POETRY FORUM; THE JOURNAL (Specialized: subscription, mystery, science fiction/fantasy, social issues); HEALTHY BODY-HEALTHY MINDS (Specialized: health concerns), 5713 Larchmont Dr., Erie PA 16509. (814)866-2543 (also fax: 8-10 a.m. or 5-8 p.m.). E-mail: 75562.670@compuserve.com Website: www.thepoetryforum.com (includes guidelines, sample poems and stories, general information, and more). **Editor:** Gunvor Skogsholm.
Magazine Needs: *Poetry Forum* appears 3 times/year. "We are open to any style and form. We believe new forms ought to develop from intuition. Length up to 50 lines accepted. Would like to encourage long

themes. No porn or blasphemy, but open to all religious persuasions." Accepts poetry written by children ages 10 and under. Has published poetry by Marshall Myers, Dana Thu, Joseph Veranneau, Ray Greenblatt, Jan Haight, and Mark Young. As a sample the editor selected these lines from his poem "Tear":

> Because the tear down the cheek of a son is the reward of a lifetime of concern, the tear down the
> cheek of a brother was what I came for

Poetry Forum is 7×8½, 38 pages, saddle-stapled with card cover, photocopied from photoreduced typescript. Sample: $3.
How to Submit: Accepts simultaneous submissions and previously published poems. Accepts electronic submissions and by fax and e-mail (include in body). Editor comments on poems "if asked, but respects the poetic freedom of the artist." Publishes theme issues. Sometimes sends prepublication galleys. Gives awards of $25, $15, $10, and 3 honorable mentions for the best poems in each issue. Acquires one-time rights. Reviews books of poetry in 250 words maximum. Poets may send books for review consideration.
Magazine Needs & How to Submit: *The Journal*, which appears twice/year, accepts experimental poetry of any length from subscribers only. Sample: $3. *Healthy Body-Healthy Minds* is a biannual publication concerned with health issues. Accepts essays, poetry, articles, and short-shorts on health, fitness, mind, and soul. Details available for SASE.
Also Offers: Offers a poetry chapbook contest. Handling fee: $12. Prize is publication and 20 copies. Send SASE for information.
Advice: "I believe today's poets should experiment more and not feel stuck in the forms that were in vogue 300 years ago. I would like to see more experimentalism—new forms will prove that poetry is alive and well in the mind and spirit of the people."

POETRY GREECE, A CYCLOPS PRODUCTION, Mitropolitou Athanasiou 10, Triti Parodos, Garitsa Corfu 49100 Greece. Phone/fax: +30(0)661 47990. E-mail: poetrygreece@hotmail.com. Website: http://users.otenet.gr/~wendyhol/poetry_greece/ (includes poetry, contents, illustrations, reviews, submission and subscription guides, competition details, and details of writing courses). Established 1999.
Director/Editor: Wendy Holborow.
Magazine Needs: *Poetry Greece* appears 3 times/year. Its purpose is "to publish good poetry in English or translated into English—to make known contemporary Greek poets to an international readership. To discuss and debate poetry and translation." Wants good, well-structured poetry with interesting themes. Does not want religious and not keen on forced rhyme. Poems do not necessarily have to be about Greece. Recently published poetry by Roger McGough, Imtiaz Dharker, Kiki Dimoula, Odysseus Elytis, and Sappho. As a sample the editor selected these lines by Adrianne Kalfopolou:

> She sits through hours/measuring cloth, her fingers/along the old lines/finding where the finer lace
> had shredded—/the white so sheer/it is the color of nightdresses.

Poetry Greece is 52 pages, magazine-sized, perfect-bound with glossy cover, includes a guest illustrator for each issue, also ads. Receives about 300 poems/year, accepts about 20%. Publishes about 40-50 poems/issue. Press run is 500 for 200 subscribers of which 50 are libraries, 250 shelf sales; 12 distributed free to Press for reviews. Single copy: $11; subscription: $33. Sample: $6. Make checks payable to Wendy Holborow.
How to Submit: Submit no more than 6 poems at a time. Accepts previously published poems and simultaneous submissions. Accepts e-mail and disk submissions. "If e-mailing, send in body of e-mail. Always include SAEs and International Reply Coupons or we can't reply." Reads submissions anytime. Time between acceptance and publication is up to 6 months. "Three to four editors all read the work and decisions are reached by majority." Seldom comments on rejected poems. Regularly publishes theme issues. Upcoming themes available for SASE. Guidelines available for SASE, by e-mail, or on website. Responds in up to 6 months. Sometimes sends prepublication galleys. Pays 1 contributor's copy. Acquires one-time rights. Reviews books and chapbooks of poetry and other magazines/journals in 1,000 words. Poets may send books for review consideration to Wendy Holborow.
Also Offers: Sponsors the annual "Keeley and Sherrard Translation Award for Poetry" (from Greek to English) with many cash prizes.

$ **POETRY HARBOR; NORTH COAST REVIEW (Specialized: regional, Upper Midwest)**, P.O. Box 103, Duluth MN 55801-0103. (218)279-3865. E-mail: poetryh@hotmail.com. Website: www.poetryharbor.com (includes current and complete info on Poetry Harbor). Established 1989. **Director:** Patrick McKinnon.
Magazine Needs: Poetry Harbor is a "nonprofit, tax-exempt organization dedicated to fostering literary creativity through public readings, publications, radio and television broadcasts, and other artistic and educational means." Its main publication, *North Coast Review*, is a regional magazine appearing 2 times/year with poetry and prose poems by and about Upper Midwest people, including those from Minnesota, Wisconsin, North Dakota, and the upper peninsula of Michigan. "No form/style/content specifications, though we are inclined toward narrative, imagist poetry. We do not want to see anything from outside our region, not because it isn't good, but because we can't publish it due to geographics." Has published poetry by Ellie Schoenfeld, Katri Sipila, and Nancy Fitzgerald. *North Coast Review* is 56 pages, 7×8½, offset

and saddle-stapled, paper cover with various b&w art, ads at back. Receives about 500 submissions/year, accepts 100-150. Press run is 1,000 for 300 subscribers of which 20 are libraries, 300 shelf sales. Subscription: $19.95/4 issues. Sample: $4.95.

How to Submit: Submit 3-5 pages of poetry, typed single-spaced, with name and address on each page. Accepts previously published poems and simultaneous submissions, if noted. Cover letter with brief bio ("writer's credits") required. "We read three times a year, but our deadlines change from time to time. Write to us for current deadlines for our various projects." Guidelines available for SASE. Responds in up to 5 months. Pays $10 plus 2-4 contributor's copies. Acquires one-time rights.

Book/Chapbook Needs & How to Submit: Poetry Harbor also publishes 1 perfect-bound paperback of poetry and 4-8 chapbooks each biennium. "Chapbooks are selected by our editorial board from the pool of poets we have published in *North Coast Review* or have worked with in our other projects. We suggest you send a submission to *North Coast Review* first. We almost always print chapbooks and anthologies by poets we've previously published or hired for readings." Anthologies include *Poets Who Haven't Moved to St. Paul* and *Days of Obsidian, Days of Grace*, selected poetry and prose by four Native American writers. Complete publications list available upon request.

Also Offers: Poetry Harbor also sponsors a monthly reading series ("poets are paid to perform"), a weekly TV program (4 different cable networks regionally), various radio programming, and other special events.

Advice: "Poetry Harbor is extremely committed to cultivating a literary community and an appreciation for our region's literature within the Upper Midwest. Poetry Harbor projects are in place to create paying, well-attended venues for our region's fine poets. Poets are now OK to people up here, and literature is thriving. The general public is proving to us that they *do* like poetry if you give them some that is both readable and rooted in the lives of the community."

⦿ POETRY INTERNATIONAL, Dept. of English, San Diego State University, San Diego CA 92182-8140. (619)594-1523. Fax: (619)594-4998. E-mail: fmoramar@mail.sdsu.edu. Website: www-rohan.sdsu.edu/dept/press/poetry.html (includes subscription information and samples from each issue). Established 1996. **Editor:** Fred Moramarco.

Magazine Needs: *Poetry International*, published annually in October, is "an eclectic poetry magazine intended to reflect a wide range of poetry being written today." Wants "a wide range of styles and subject matter. We're particularly interested in translations." Does not want "cliché-ridden, derivative, obscure poetry." Has published poetry by Adrienne Rich, Robert Bly, Hayden Carruth, Kim Addonizio, Maxine Kumin, and Gary Soto. As a sample the editor selected these lines from "My Life In Over" by Al Zolynas:

> my life, I mean that life/defined by narrow boundaries/narrow concerns, by survival/and whining and
> looking over/my shoulder, that life/of the bag of skin and bones/with the little fascist ego bitching/all
> day long/That little Mussolini is dead—or/if not dead—at least stripped of his shiny/black uniform,
> insignia cut/off pockets and collars,/epaulettes popped off shoulders./Not yet fully naked/but on the
> way, down/to T-shirts, shorts, and socks.

Poetry International is 200 pgs, perfect bound, with coated card stock cover. Press run is 1,000. Single copy: $12; subscription: $24/2 years.

How to Submit: Submit up to 5 poems at a time. Accepts simultaneous submissions "but prefer not to"; no previously published poems. No fax or e-mail submissions. Reads submissions September 1 through December 30 only. Time between acceptance and publication is 8 months. Poems are circulated to an editorial board. Seldom comments on rejected poems. Responds in 3 months. Pays 2 contributor's copies. Acquires all rights. Returns rights "50/50," meaning they split with the author any payment for reprinting the poem elsewhere. "We review anthologies regularly."

Advice: "We're interested in new work by poets who are devoted to their art. We want poems that matter—that make a difference in people's lives. We're especially seeking good translations and prose by poets about poetry."

⊕ $⦿ POETRY IRELAND REVIEW; POETRY IRELAND, Bermingham Tower, Dublin Castle, Dublin 2, Ireland. Phone: (353)(1)6714632. Fax: (353)(1)6714634. E-mail: poetry@iol.ie. Website: www.poetryireland.ie. Established 1979. **Director:** Joseph Woods.

Magazine Needs: *Poetry Ireland Review*, the magazine of Ireland's national poetry organization, "provides an outlet for Irish poets; submissions from abroad also considered. No specific style or subject matter is prescribed. We strongly dislike sexism and racism." Has published poetry by Seamus Heaney, Michael Longley, Denise Levertov, Medbh McGuckian, and Charles Wright. Occasionally publishes special issues. *Poetry Ireland Review* is 6×8 and appears quarterly. Press run is 1,200 for 800 subscriptions. Receives up to 8,000 submissions/year, accepts about 3%; has a 2-month backlog. Prints 60 pages of poetry in each issue. Single copy: IR£5.99; subscription: IR£24 Ireland and UK; IR£32 overseas (surface). Sample: $10.

How to Submit: Submit up to 6 poems at a time. Include SASE (or SAE with IRC). "Submissions not accompained by SAEs will not be returned." No previously published poems or simultaneous submissions. Accepts e-mail submissions; attach file to e-mail. Time between acceptance and publication is up to 3 months. Seldom comments on rejected poems. Send SASE (or SAE with IRCs) for guidelines. Responds in 2 months. Pays IR£25/poem or 1-year subscription. Reviews books of poetry in 500-1,000 words.
Also Offers: *Poetry Ireland Review* is published by Poetry Ireland, an organization established to "promote poets and poetry throughout Ireland." Poetry Ireland offers readings, an information service, library and administrative center, and a bimonthly newsletter giving news, details of readings, competitions, etc. for IR£6/year. Also sponsors an annual poetry competition. Details available for SASE (or SAE with IRCs).
Advice: "Keep submitting: Good work will get through."

POETRY KANTO, Kanto Gakuin University, Kamariya-cho 3-22-1, Kanazawa-Ku, Yokohama 236-8502, Japan. Established 1984. **Editor:** William I. Elliott.
Magazine Needs: *Poetry Kanto* appears annually in August and is published by the Kanto Poetry Center. The magazine publishes well-crafted original poems in English and in Japanese. Wants "anything except pornography, English haiku and tanka, and tends to publish poems under 30 lines." Has published work by A.D. Hope, Peter Robinson, Naomi Shihab Nye, Nuala Ni Dhomhnaill, and Christopher Middleton. The magazine is 60 pages, digest-sized, nicely printed (the English poems occupy the first half of the issue, the Japanese poems the second), saddle-stapled, matte card cover. Press run is 700, of which 400 are distributed free to schools, poets and presses; it is also distributed at poetry seminars. The magazine is unpriced. For sample, send SAE with IRCs.
How to Submit: Interested poets should query from October through December with SAE and IRCs before submitting. No previously published poems or simultaneous submissions. Often comments on rejected poems. Responds to mss in 2 weeks. Pays 3 contributor's copies.
Advice: "Read a lot. Get feedback from poets and/or workshops. Be neat, clean, legible, and polite in submissions. SAE with IRCs absolutely necessary when requesting sample copy."

POETRY MOTEL; POETRY MOTEL WALLPAPER BROADSIDE SERIES, P.O. Box 103, Duluth MN 55801-0103. Established 1984. **Editors:** Patrick McKinnon, Bud Backen, and Linda Erickson.
Magazine Needs: *Poetry Motel* appears "every 260 days." Poetry magazine with some fiction and memoire. Wants poetry of "any style, any length." Recently published poetry by Adrian C. Louis, Ron Androla, Todd Moore, Ellie Schoenfeld, and Serena Fusek. *Poetry Motel* is 52 pages digest-sized, offset-printed, stapled, wallpaper cover, with collages. Receives about 1,000 poems/year, accepts about 5% Publishes about 50 poems/issue. Press run is 1,000 for 400 subscribers of which 10 are libraries. Single copy: $8.95; subscription: $26/3 issues, $99/forever. Make checks payable to *Poetry Motel*.
How to Submit: Submit 3-6 pages at a time. Accepts previously published poems and simultaneous submissions. No fax, e-mail, or disk submissions. "Include SASE or brief bio." Reads submissions all year. Time between acceptance and publication varies. Never comments on rejected poems. Guidelines are available in magazine and for SASE. Responds in "1 week to never." Pays 1-5 contributor's copies. Acquires no rights. Reviews books and chapbooks of poetry and other magazines/journals in varied lengths. Poets may send books for review consideration to N. Thompson.
Advice: "All work submitted is considered for both the magazine and the broadside series."

POETRY NORTHWEST, University of Washington, P.O. Box 354330, Seattle WA 98195. (206)685-4750. Website: http://depts.washington.edu/engl/poetrynw.html (includes guidelines, subscription info, current cover image, and list of contributors). Established 1959. **Editor:** David Wagoner.
  • **Due to lack of funding, the 2002 spring issue may be the last.**.
Magazine Needs: *Poetry Northwest* is a quarterly featuring all styles and forms. For instance, lyric and narrative free verse has been included alongside a sonnet sequence, minimalist sonnets and stanza patterns—all accessible and lively. *Poetry Northwest* is 48 pages, 5½×8½, professionally printed with color card cover. Receives 10,000 poems/year, accepts approximately 160, has a 3-month backlog. Press run is 1,500. Subscription: $15. Sample: $5.
How to Submit: Submit 3-5 poems, typed and single-spaced with standard 1-inch top and bottom margins ("We need this space for copyediting marks."). No simultaneous submissions. Occasionally comments on rejected poems. Guidelines available for SASE and on website. Responds in 1 month maximum. Pays 2 contributor's copies. Awards prizes of $500, $200, and $200 yearly, judged by the editors.

N ⊕ ◯ POETRY NOTTINGHAM INTERNATIONAL; NOTTINGHAM OPEN POETRY COMPETITION; NOTTINGHAM POETRY SOCIETY, P.O. Box 6740, Nottingham NG5 1QG United Kingdom. Website: http://nottinghampoetrysociety.co.uk (includes guidelines, contact and subscription info, editorial policy, and contest rules). Established 1946. **Editor:** Julie Lumsden.

Magazine Needs: Nottingham Poetry Society meets monthly for readings, talks, etc., and publishes quarterly its magazine, *Poetry Nottingham International*, which is open to submissions from anyone. "We wish to see poetry that is intelligible to and enjoyable by the intelligent reader." Accepts poetry written by children. Has published poetry by Roberta Dewa, Anne Lewis-Smith, Michael Henry, and Alison Chisholm. As a sample the editor selected these lines from "Midas Touch" by Richard Bonfield:

> Silver Salmon/Golden trees/The alchemy/Of turning leaves//Golden water/From the well/A silver fox/
> Upon the fell//Curlew falling./Through a storm/The moonlight hedgehog/on the lawn//Jewellery from
> nature/Plucked/The Season/With the Midas Touch.

There are at least 44 pages of poetry in each issue of the 6×8 magazine, professionally printed with articles, letters, news, reviews, glossy art paper cover. Receives about 1,500 submissions/year, accepts approximately 120, usually has a 1- to 3-month backlog. Press run is 275 for 200 subscribers. Single copy: £2.75 ($9.75 US); subscriptions: £17 sterling or $34 US.

How to Submit: Submit up to 6 poems at any time, or articles up to 500 words on current issues in poetry. No previously published poems. Send SAE and 3 IRCs for stamps. No need to query but requires cover letter. Responds in 2 months. Pays 1 copy. Staff reviews books of poetry. Send books for review consideration.

Book/Chapbook Needs & How to Submit: Nottingham Poetry Society publishes collections by individual poets who are members of Nottingham Poetry Society.

Also Offers: Nottingham Open Poetry Competition offers cash prizes, annual subscriptions and publication in *Poetry Nottingham International*. Open to all. Check website for address and details. Contact for website and Nottingham Poetry Society is Jeremy Duffield, 71 Saxton Ave., Heanor, Derbyshire DE75 7PZ United Kingdom.

Advice: "We want originality, a 'surprise', apt imagery, good sense of rhythm, clear language. Poems most often rejected due to: use of tired language and imagery, use of clichés and inversions, old treatment of an old subject, sentimentality, poor rhythm and scansion, incorrect use of set forms."

◯ POETRY OF THE PEOPLE, 3341 SE 19th Ave., Gainesville FL 32641. (352)375-0244. E-mail: poetryforaquarter@yahoo.com. Website: www.angelfire.com/fl/poetryofthepeople (includes guidelines, poetry, contact info, editorial policy, and a list of back issues. Also includes original content, please contact editor). Established 1986. **Poetry Editor:** Paul Cohen.

Magazine Needs: *Poetry of the People* is a leaflet that appears monthly. "We take all forms of poetry but we like humorous poetry, love poetry, nature poetry, and fantasy. No racist or highly ethnocentric poetry will be accepted. I do not like poetry that lacks images or is too personal or contains rhyme to the point that the poem has been destroyed. All submitted poetry will be considered for posting on website which will be updated every month." Also accepts poetry written in French and Spanish. Accepts poetry written by children. Has published poetry by Max Lizard, Prof. Jerry Reminick, Ian Ayers, and Noelle Kocot. As a sample the editor selected these lines from "Lunar" by David Vetterlein:

> "I stumbled blindly/in coated forests/bound by howling wolves/I stagger/wandering endless/in that
> lunar maze/called emotion.

Poetry of the People is 32 pages, 5½×8 to 5½×4⅜, stapled, sometimes on colored paper. Issues are usually theme oriented. Samples: $4 for 11 pamphlets. "New format is being devised."

How to Submit: Submit up to 10 poems at a time. Include SASE. Accepts e-mail submissions. Cover letter with biographical information required with submissions. "I feel autobiographical information is important in understanding the poetry." Poems returned within 6 months. Editor comments on rejected poems "often." Upcoming themes available for SASE. Guidelines available by e-mail and on website. Pays 10 contributor's copies for poetry published in leaflet. Acquires first rights.

Advice: "Nature makes people happy."

N ◎ ◯ POETRY PROTOCOL; NORTH TULSA LITERARY GUILD, INC. (Specialized: members only), P.O. Box #6221, Tulsa OK 74148-0221. (918)836-5539. Fax: (918)665-4586. E-mail: amccl25089@aol.com. Website: http://hometown.aol.com/jymmeemak1/myhomepage (includes submission guidelines, contest dates and deadlines, membership info). Established 1991. **President/Co-editor:** Alton McCloud.

Magazine Needs & How to Submit: *Poetry Protocol* appears quarterly "to provide an outlet to unknown poets for international recognition." Also publishes short stories and columns. Accepts all forms; prefers free verse (20 lines or less), acrostics, haiku. Does not want very long (essay) poems. Recently published poetry by Shiela Roark, dn simmers, Sylvia Lukeman, Lisa Rye, Jean Burch, and Ashok Chakavarthy. As a sample the editor selected these lines from "Do It Now" by Vince McTigue:

Do not come and see me when I'm dead/Do not use gentle hands upon my head/Do not then touch or kiss my wrinkled brow/Do it now.

Poetry Protocol is sponsored by the North Tulsa Literary Guild, Inc., a nonprofit organization that also hosts local open mic readings and an international relationship with Poets Who Care of Liverpool, England. *Poetry Protocol* accepts submissions from members only. Contact Alton C. McCloud for information.

Also Offers: "We sponsor two contests/year that award 1st Prize: $50, 2nd Prize: $30, 3rd Prize: $20, also Honorable Mention certificates."

Advice: "*Poetry Protocol* provides an outlet for beginning poets. If your work is not accepted by us, always try again with a different form/genre of poetry. And remember that neatness and presentation count."

🌐 $⬤ POETRY REVIEW; NATIONAL POETRY COMPETITION; THE POETRY SOCIETY, 22 Betterton St., London WC2H 9BU United Kingdom. Phone: (0044)207 420 9880. Fax: (0044)207 240 4818. E-mail: poetryreview@poetrysoc.com. Website: www.poetrysoc.com. Established 1909. Editor: Peter Forbes.

Magazine Needs: *Poetry Review*, published quarterly, strives "to be the leading showcase of UK poetry and to represent poetry written in English and in translation." Wants "poems with metaphoric resonance." Does not want "inconsequential disconnected jottings." Has published poetry by John Ashbery, Miroslav Holub, Sharon Olds, and Paul Muldoon. As a sample the editor selected these lines from "*Whang* Editorial Policy" by Mark Halliday:

Do not assume that to say "Barcelona" or "heart of night"/or "blue souffle" will open every door at Whang./We look for poems that embrace God because God has failed/and not the other way around. Send only such poems/ as you would choose in lieu of a cigarette before/execution by firing squad...

Poetry Review is 96 pages, 6½×9, paperback, with b&w cartoons and photos. Receives about 30-50,000 poems/year, accepts 0.3-0.4%. Press run is 4,200 for 3,300 subscribers of which 400 are libraries, 400 shelf sales; 100 distributed free to contributors and press. Single copy: £5.95; subscription: $56. Sample: $13.

How to Submit: Submit 4 poems at a time. No previously published poems or simultaneous submissions. No fax or e-mail submissions. Time between acceptance and publication is 6 months. Poems are selected by the editor. Seldom comments on rejected poems. Publishes theme issues. Responds in up to 3 months. Sometimes sends prepublication galleys. Pays £40 plus 1 copy. Acquires UK first publication rights. Staff reviews chapbooks of poetry or other magazines in single or multi-book format.

Also Offers: Sponsors the annual National Poetry Competition run by the Poetry Society. 1st Prize: £5,000; 2nd Prize: £1,000; 3rd Prize: £500. Entry fee: £5 for first poem, £3/poem thereafter. Deadline: October 31. Guidelines available for SASE (or SAE and IRC). "The Poetry Society promotes poetry, assists poets and campaigns for poets wherever possible." Offers "Poetry Prescription" reading service: £40 for 100 lines.

🌐 ⬤ POETRY SALZBURG; POETRY SALZBURG REVIEW; UNIVERSITY OF SALZBURG PRESS, Institut für Anglistik und Amerikanistik, Universität Salzburg, Akademiestrasse 24, A-5020 Salzburg Austria. Phone: 0049662 8044 4422. Fax: 0049 662 80 44 167. E-mail: editor@poetrysalzburg.com. Website: www.poetrysalzburg.com. Established 1971. Editor: Dr. Wolfgang Görtschacher.

Magazine Needs: *Poetry Salzburg Review* appears twice/year and contains "articles on poetry, mainly contemporary, and 60 percent poetry. Also includes prose and translations. We tend to publish selections by authors who have not been taken up by the big poetry publishers. Nothing of poor quality." Has published poetry by Desmond O'Grady, James Kirkup, Robert Rehder, Raymond Federman, Rachel Hades, Alice Notley, Georgie Scott, Anne MacLeod, and Rupert Loydell. As a sample the editor selected these lines from "Starry Night" by Georgia Scott:

You sprayed your stars into my sky./Then, lying spent at my side, you wept. So,/I said "Take one back." And you did//With your lips, one was saved./With your hands, the others spread//a milky way in the night./Your glory encrusted my head.

Poetry Salzburg Review is about 170 pages, A5, professionally printed and perfect-bound with illustrated card cover, sometimes includes art. Receives about 5,000 poems/year, accepts 10%. Press run is 500 for 150 subscribers of which 30% are libraries. Single copy: about $11; subscription: $20 (cash only for those sending US funds). Make checks payable to Wolfgang Görtschacher. "No requirements, but it's a good idea to subscribe to *Poetry Salzburg Review*."

How to Submit: No previously published poems or simultaneous submissions. Accepts submissions by fax, on disk, by e-mail (as attachment), or by regular mail. Time between acceptance and publication is 6 months.

THE OPENNESS TO SUBMISSIONS INDEX in the back of this book lists markets according to the level of writing they prefer to see.

Seldom comments on rejected poems. Occasionally publishes theme issues. Responds in 2 months. Payment varies. Acquires first rights. Reviews books and chapbooks of poetry and other magazines. Poets may send books for review consideration.

Book/Chapbook Needs & How to Submit: Poetry Salzburg publishes "collections of at least 100 pages by mainly poets not taken up by big publishers." Publishes 2-30 paperbacks/year. Books are usually 100-700 pages, A5, professionally printed and perfect-bound with card cover, includes art. Query first, with a few sample poems and a cover letter with brief bio and publication credits. Suggests authors publish in *Poetry Salzburg Review* first. Responds to queries in 2 weeks; to mss in about 1 month. Pays 40 author's copies (out of a press run of 300-400).

O POETRY TODAY ONLINE; RING OF WORDS WEBRING, 5901 JFK Blvd. #5104, North Little Rock AR 72116. E-mail: editor@poetrytodayonline.com. Website: www.poetrytodayonline.com (includes how-to section by Don J. Carlson, motivations, "Poetry Request Forum" by Jim Garman, and a column by E. Clark). Established 1997. **Editor:** Margaret Perkins.

Magazine Needs: *"Poetry Today Online* has served Internet poets since 1997. Its Internet traffic is approximately 15,000 hits per month during the school year and 10,000 per month during school breaks. *Poetry Today Online* owns the Ring of Words Webring with over 5,000 membership." *Poetry Today Online* encourages all forms and styles. No "adult, erotic, or X-rated material due to the fact we are used in educational facilities. No profanity."

How to Submit: Submit 1 poem at a time. Accepts previously published poems and simultaneous submissions. Accepts e-mail submissions (in text box, no attachments); no disk submissions. "Submissions are accepted through Internet only." Time between acceptance and publication is 3 months. Seldom comments on rejected poems.

Also Offers: Additional features of *Poetry Today Online* include "a public forum, a listing of Internet poetry contests, how-to articles and more."

O POETRYBAY, P.O. Box 114, Northport NY 11768. (631)427-1950. Fax: (631)367-0038. E-mail: poetrybay@aol.com Website: www.poetrybay.com. Established 2000. **Editor:** George Wallace.

Magazine Needs: *Poetrybay* appears quarterly and "seeks to add to the body of great contemporary American poetry by presenting the work of established and emerging writers. Also, we consider essays and reviews." Recently published poetry by Robert Bly, Yevgeny Yevtushenko, Marvin Bell, Diane Wakoski, Cornelius Eady, and William Heyen. *Poetrybay* is an online publication. Publishes about 24 poems/issue.

How to Submit: Submit 5 poems at a time. Accepts simultaneous submissions; no previously published poems. Accepts e-mail submissions; no disk submissions. "We prefer e-mail with text in body. No attachments." Time between acceptance and publication is 2 months. Seldom comments on rejected poems. Occasionally publishes theme issues. Guidelines available by fax, e-mail, or on website. Sometimes sends prepublication galleys. Acquires first time electronic rights. Reviews books and chapbooks of poetry and other magazines/journals. Poets may send books/chapbooks for review consideration.

O ⊚ POETS AT WORK (Specialized: subscription), P.O. Box 232, Lyndora PA 16045. Established 1985. **Editor/Publisher:** Jessee Poet.

Magazine Needs: All contributors are expected to subscribe. "Every poet who writes within the dictates of good taste and within my 20-line limit will be published in each issue. I accept all forms and themes of poetry, including seasonal and holiday, but no porn, no profanity, horror, bilingual/foreign language, translations, feminism." Accepts poetry written by children ages 12 and up; "I have a lot of student subscribers." Has published poetry by Dr. Karen Springer, William Middleton, Ann Gasser, Warren Jones, and Ralph Hammond. As a sample he selected his poem "An Old Romance":

> I almost loved you . . . did you know?/Sometimes you still disturb my dreams./A summer romance long
> ago/I almost loved you . . . did you know?/We danced to music soft and low/Just yesterday . . . or so
> it seems/I almost loved you . . . did you know?/Sometimes you still disturb my dreams.

Poets at Work, a bimonthly, is generally 36-40 pages, magazine-sized, saddle-stapled, photocopied from typescript with colored paper cover. Subscription: $23. Sample: $3.75.

How to Submit: If a subscriber, submit 5-10 poems at a time. Line length for poetry is 20 maximum. Accepts simultaneous submissions and previously published poems. Guidelines available for SASE. Responds within 2 weeks. Pays nothing, not even a copy. "Because I publish hundreds of poets, I cannot afford to pay or give free issues. Every subscriber, of course, gets an issue."

Also Offers: Subscribers also have many opportunities to regain their subscription money in the numerous contests offered in each issue. Send SASE for flyer for separate monthly and special contests.

Advice: "These days even the best poets tell me that it is difficult to get published. I am here for the novice as well as the experienced poet. I consider *Poets at Work* to be a hotbed for poets where each one can stretch and grow at his or her own pace. Each of us learns from the other, and we do not criticize one another. The door for poets is always open, so please stop by; we probably will like each other immediately."

THE POET'S CUT, P.O. Box 937, Rio Linda CA 95673. E-mail: admin@Welkinworks.com. Website: www.poetscut.com (includes poetry, forum, guidelines, name of editor, featured poet, news, links). Established 1998. **Editor:** Leslie Laurence.
Magazine Needs: *The Poet's Cut* is a monthly online publication featuring quality, original poetry. "I am looking for poems that reflect the voice and vision of the poet, not something that reflects a current literary trend or tries to second guess what publishers want. Any form, style, or subject. Prefer works of 25 words or less." Accepts poetry written by children. Recently published poetry by Janet I. Buck, Taylor Graham, Duane Locke, Yosh, and Scott Villarosa. As a sample the editor selected these lines from "Painting Clouds" by Taylor Graham:
> In this drought, dust makes clouds./I wet it down, I spray the sky all blue/With water. In the house, Mother's/In a cloud again. Colors.

The Poet's Cut is 20 pages, published online only. Receives about 240 poems/year, accepts about 35%. Publishes about 7 poems/issue.
How to Submit: Submit up to 4 poems at a time. Line length for poetry is open. Accepts previously published poems and simultaneous submissions. Accepts e-mail submissions; no fax or disk submissions. "Submissions are accepted only as text in the body of the e-mail. Hardcopy submissions will not be read." Reads submissions year round. Submit seasonal poems 1 month in advance. Time between acceptance and publication is 3 months. Seldom comments on rejected poems. Occasionally publishes theme issues. Upcoming themes and guidelines available on website. Responds in 1 month. No payment. Acquires one-time rights.
Advice: "Read your poems aloud. You will be amazed how the weak parts stand out. Find an honest audience for your poems. Listen to what they tell you. Read the work of others. You have to know where poetry has been if you are to be a part of where it is going."

POETS ON THE LINE, P.O. Box 020292, Brooklyn NY 11202-0007. E-mail: llerner@mindspring.com. Website: www.echonyc.com/~poets. Established 1995. **Editor:** Linda Lerner. Currently not accepting unsolicited work.

POETS' PODIUM, 2-3265 Front Rd., E. Hawksbury, Ontario K6A 2R2 Canada. E-mail: kennyel@hotmail.com. Website: http://geocities.com/poetspodium/. Established 1993. **Associate Editors:** Ken Elliott, Catherine Heaney Barrowcliffe, Robert Piquette.
Magazine Needs: *Poets' Podium* is a quarterly newsletter published "to promote the reading and writing of the poetic form, especially among those being published for the first time." Poetry specifications are open. However, does not want poetry that is gothic, erotic/sexual, gory, bloody, or that depicts violence. Publish 25 poems/issue. Subscription: $10 (US). Sample: $3 (US). "Priority is given to valued subscribers. Nevertheless, when there is room in an issue we will publish nonsubscribers."
How to Submit: Submit 3 poems at a time. Line length for poetry is 4 minimum, 25 maximum. Accepts previously published poems and simultaneous submissions. Cover letter required. Include SASE (or SAE and IRC), name, address, and telephone number; e-mail address if applicable. Time between acceptance and publication varies. Guidelines available for SASE (or SAE with IRC), by fax, or by e-mail. Pays 3 copies. All rights remain with the author.
Advice: "Poetry is a wonderful literary form. Try your hand at it. Send us the fruit of your labours."

POLYGON (Specialized: bilingual/foreign language), 22 George Square, Edinburgh EH8 9LF Scotland. Phone: (0131)650 4223. Fax: (0131)662 0053. E-mail: polygon.press@eup.ed.ac.uk. Website: www.eup.ed.ac.uk/polygon/html. Established 1969. **Contact:** poetry editor.
Book/Chapbook Needs: Polygon publishes new poets, first-time collections, young voices, and Gaelic/English translations. Publishes 3 paperbacks and 1 anthology/year. Has published poetry by Ian Hamilton Finlay, Liz Lochhead, Aonghas MacNeacail, Raymond Friel, David Kinloch, and Donny O'Rourke. Books are usually 88 pages, 194×128mm, paperback. Anthologies are 350 pages, 216×138mm, paperback. Polygon is currently not accepting unsolicited manuscripts.

POLYPHONIES (Specialized: translations), 8, rue des Imbergères, 92330 Sceaux, France. Established 1985. **Editor:** Pascal Culerrier. **Editorial Committee:** Pascal Boulanger, Laurence Breysse, François Comba, Emmanuelle Dagnaud, Jean-Yves Masson, and Alexis Pelletier.

Magazine Needs: *Polyphonies* appears twice/year. "Every case is a special one. We want to discover the new important voices of the world to open French literature to the major international productions. For example, we published Brodsky in French when he was not known in our country and had not yet won the Nobel Prize. No vocal poetry, no typographic effects." Has published poetry by Mario Luzi (Italy), Jeremy Reed (Great Britain), Octavio Paz (Mexico), and Claude Michel Cluny (France). It is about 110 pages, 6½×9½, flat-spined, with glossy card cover, printed completely in French. Press run is 850 for 300 subscribers.

How to Submit: Uses translations of previously published poems. Pays 2 copies.

Advice: "Our review is still at the beginning. We are in touch with many French editors. Our purpose is to publish together, side-by-side, poets of today and of yesterday."

◐ PORCUPINE LITERARY ARTS MAGAZINE, P.O. Box 259, Cedarsburg WI 53012. E-mail: ppine259@aol.com. Website: members.aol.com/ppine259 (features writer's guidelines, cover art, table of contents, and sample poetry). Established 1996. **Managing Editor:** W.A. Reed.

Magazine Needs: *Porcupine*, published biannually, contains featured artists, poetry, short fiction, and visual art work. "There are no restrictions as to theme or style. Poetry should be accessible and highly selective. If a submission is not timely for one issue, it will be considered for another." Has published poetry by George Wallace, Robert Nazarene, Linden Ontjes, and Terri Brown-Davidson. As a sample, we selected these lines from "Deliverence" by Carol Hamilton:

> *A river song on the radio/skips after me on a dash/down the highway, slashing/my way home between*
> *fields/of feathery green tossed/by evening slant light*

Porcupine is 100-150 pages, 8½×5, offset, perfect-bound with full-color glossy cover and b&w photos and art (occasionally use color inside, depending on artwork). Receives about 500 poems/year, accepts 10%. Press run is 1,500 for 500 subscribers of which 50 are libraries, 500 shelf sales; 100 distributed free. Single copy: $8.95; subscription: $15.95. Sample: $5.

How to Submit: Submit up to 3 poems, 1/page with name and address on each. Include SASE. "The outside of the envelope should state: 'Poetry.' " No previously published poems or simultaneous submissions. Accepts e-mail submissions (include in text box). Time between acceptance and publication is 6 months. "Poems are selected by editors and then submitted to managing editor for final approval." Seldom comments on rejected poems. Guidelines available for SASE or website. Responds in 3 months. Pays 1 contributor's copy. Acquires one-time rights.

⊘ ◎ THE POST-APOLLO PRESS (Specialized: form/style, women), 35 Marie St., Sausalito CA 94965. (415)332-1458. Fax: (415)332-8045. E-mail: tpapress@dnai.com. Website: www.dnai.com/ ~tpapress. Established 1982. **Publisher:** Simone Fattal.

Book/Chapbook Needs & How to Submit: The Post-Apollo Press publishes "quality paperbacks by experimental poets/writers, mostly women, many first English translations." Publishes 2-3 paperbacks/ year. "Please note we are *not* accepting manuscripts at this time due to full publishing schedule."

Ⓝ ◯ ◎ POTATO HILL POETRY (Specialized: students, teachers), 81 Speen St., Natick MA 01760. (508)652-9908. Fax: (508)652-9858. E-mail: info@potatohill.com. Website: www.potatohill.com/ (includes poem of the week, contest and submissions guidelines, exercises, book catalog). Established 1996. **Contact:** Poetry Editor.

Magazine Needs: *Potato Hill Poetry* appears bimonthly, except in July/August, "and publishes the best student (K-12) and teacher poetry we can find and to share writing exercises." Wants poems on all topics, any length, any form. As a sample the editor selected these lines (poet unidentified):

> *I won't need to remember this/won't need to remember/the boys/the trench coats or guns/this closet or*
> *metal/shards in my arm/in my head/in my heart*

Potato Hill Poetry is 16 pages, 8½×11, saddle-stapled, 60 lb. paper stock cover, includes art/graphics and ads. Receives about 1,000 poems/year, accepts about 5%. Publishes 8-12 poems/issue. Press run is 5,000 for 2,000 subscribers of which 100 are libraries; 3,000 distributed free to schools. Subscription: $17.95. Sample: $3.

How to Submit: Submit 1-5 poems at a time with SASE. Accepts simultaneous submissions; no previously published poems. "Please include name, address, school, grade level you are in or teach, home phone number." Reads submissions September 1 through June 30 only. Time between acceptance and publication is 2 months. Poems are circulated to an editorial board. "Several editors read and make all decisions." Often comments on rejected poems. Guidelines available for SASE. Responds in 2 months. Pays 2 copies. Acquires first North American serial rights and reprint rights. Reviews books of poetry in 100-300 words, single and multi-book format. Poets may send books for review consideration.

Also Offers: Sponsors annual poetry contest.

POTLUCK CHILDREN'S LITERARY MAGAZINE (Specialized: children/teen), P.O. Box 546, Deerfield IL 60015-0546. (847)948-1139. Fax: (847)317-9492. E-mail: susan@potluckmagazine.org. Website: http://potluckmagazine.org (includes general information, "testimonials," guidelines, where to find and how to order *Potluck*, special events, and message board). Established 1997. **Editor:** Susan Napoli Picchietti.

Magazine Needs: *Potluck* is published quarterly "to provide a forum which encourages young writers to share their voice and to learn their craft. Open to all styles, forms, and subjects—we just want well crafted works that speak to the reader. No works so abstract they only have meaning to the writer. Violent, profane, or sexually explicit works will not be accepted." *Potluck* is about 40 pages, $5\frac{1}{2} \times 8\frac{1}{2}$, photocopied and saddle-stapled with 60 lb. paper cover, includes original artwork on covers. Receives about 350 poems/quarter. Publish 10-15 poems/issue. Press run is over 800 for 150 subscribers of which 5 are libraries, 625 shelf sales; back issues distributed free to hospitals/inner city schools. Single copy: $5.80; subscription: $18. Sample (including guidelines): $4.25.

How to Submit: Submit up to 3 poems at a time. Line length for poetry is 30 maximum. No previously published poems or simultaneous submissions. Accepts submissions by fax, by e-mail (in text box), and by regular mail. Cover letter preferred. "Works without a SASE or an e-mail address will not be considered." Submit seasonal poems 3 months in advance. Time between acceptance and publication is 4-6 weeks. Poems are circulated to an editorial board. "We each review each poem—make remarks on page then discuss our view of each—the best works make the issue." Always comments on rejected poems. Guidelines available for SASE, by fax, by e-mail, in publication, or on website. Responds 6 weeks after deadline. Pays 1 contributor's copy. Acquires first rights. Reviews chapbooks of poetry.

Advice: "Be present—now—write what you see, hear, taste, smell, observe and what you feel/experience. Be honest, clear, and choose your words with great care. Enjoy."

POTOMAC REVIEW: A JOURNAL OF ARTS & HUMANITIES, P.O. Box 354, Port Tobacco MD 20677. Website: www.meral.com/potomac (includes samplings of current issue, contents, guidelines, background on magazine). Established 1994. **Editor:** Eli Flam.

Magazine Needs: *Potomac Review* "prizes poetry with a vivid, individual quality that has vision to go with competence, that strives to get at 'the concealed side' of life. While regionally rooted, with a strong environmental bent, *Potomac Review* seeks poets from all quarters and focuses." Has published poetry by Judith McCombs, Virgil Suarez, and Hugh Fox. As a sample the editor selected these lines from "Open Window" by Moira Burns:

> You'd say how ocean's argument with land began:/at the exact moment a man finds himself/content,
> reclined, switching stations by remote/between the tennis match and porno flick,/and she raises her
> left hand, an empty signal,/like an isosceles flag without a country

Potomac Review is 248 pages, biannual, $5\frac{1}{2} \times 8\frac{1}{2}$, offset-printed, perfect-bound, with medium card cover, b&w graphic art, photos and ads. Receives about 1,000 poems/year, accepts 5%. Press run is 2,000 for 1,000 subscribers plus about 400 shelf sales. Subscription: $15/year (includes 2 double issues; MD residents add 5%), $25/2 years. Sample: $8.

How to Submit: Submit up to 3 poems, 5 pages at a time with SASE. Accepts simultaneous submissions; no previously published poems. Cover letter preferred with brief bio and SASE. Time between acceptance and publication is up to 1 year. Poems are read "in house," then sent to poetry editor for comments and dialogue. Often comments on rejected poems. Publishes theme issues. Fall 2002-2003 will be "On Native Grounds." Guidelines and upcoming themes available for SASE or on website. Responds in 3 months. Pays 1 contributor's copy and offers discount on additional copies. Acquires first North American serial rights. Reviews books of poetry; write first for review consideration.

Also Offers: Sponsors annual poetry contest, open January through April 15. 1st Prize: $300; winner's poem and some runners-up are published in fall/winter. To enter, send $15 (provides 1-year subscription), up to 3 poems, any subject, any form. Deadline: April 15. Competition receives about 150 entries. Guidelines available for SASE, in fall/winter issue, or on website.

POTPOURRI; DAVID RAY POETRY AWARD, P.O. Box 8278, Prairie Village KS 66208. (913)642-1503. Fax: (913)642-3128. E-mail: PotpourriEditor@aol.com. Website: www.Potpourri.org (includes general information, history, guidelines, contact and subscription information, contest rules, and archives). Established 1989. **Poetry Editor:** Terry Hoyland. **Haiku Editor:** Jeri Ragan.

Magazine Needs: *Potpourri* is a quarterly magazine "publishing works of writers, including new and unpublished writers. We want strongly voiced original poems in either free verse or traditional. Traditional work must represent the best of the craft. No religious, confessional, racial, political, erotic, abusive, or sexual preference materials. No concrete/visual poetry (because of format)." Has published poetry by Lyn Lifshin, David Ray, Richard Moore, Leslie Mcilroy, Sharon Kouros, and Carol Hamilton. As a sample the editor selected these lines from "In the Third Decade of Desire" by Leslie Mcilroy:

> There seemed to be no end to the struggle/as one by one, they began to take Prozac,/their shapeless lives taking the form of meat/grinder churning out scraps, the intestines/of childhood, the tainted liver of desperate meetings . . .

Potpourri is 80 pages, 8½ × 11, professionally printed, saddle-stapled with 2-color art on glossy cover, drawings, photos and ads inside. Press run is 1,500 for 850 subscribers. Subscription: $16. Sample: $6.95 include 9 × 12 envelope; $9.25 overseas.

How to Submit: Submit up to 3 poems at a time, one to a page, length to 75 lines (approximately 30 preferred). Address haiku and related forms to Jeri Ragan. Accepts submissions on disk, by e-mail (in text box), and by regular mail. Guidelines available for SASE, by fax, by e-mail, or on website. Responds in up to 10 weeks at most. Pays 1 contributor's copy. Acquires first North American serial rights.

Also Offers: The David Ray Poetry Award ($100 or more, depending upon grant monies) is given annually for best of volume. Another annual award is sponsored by the Council on National Literatures and offers $100 and publication in *Potpourri* for selected poem or short story; alternating years (2002 fiction). Official guidelines available for SASE. Deadline: September 1, 2002. Website includes back issues, biographies, submission guidelines, sample writings and literary links.

Advice: "Keep your new poems around long enough to become friends with them before parting. Let them ripen, and, above all, learn to be your own best editor. Read them aloud, boldly, to see how they ripple the air and echo what you mean to say. Themes of unrequited love, children, grandchildren, and favorite pets find little chance here."

$ POTTERSFIELD PORTFOLIO; POTTERSFIELD PORTFOLIO SHORT POEM COMPETITION, P.O. Box 40, Station A, Sydney, Nova Scotia B1P 6G9 Canada. Website: www.pportfoli o.com (includes guidelines, contact and subscription information, bios, contest rules, links, editorial policy, and archives). Established 1979. **Editor:** Douglas A. Brown. **Contact:** Poetry Editor.

Magazine Needs: Appearing in July and December, *Pottersfield Portfolio* is a "literary magazine publishing fiction, poetry, essays and reviews by authors from Canada. No restrictions on subject matter or style. However, we will not use religious, inspirational, or children's poetry. No doggerel or song lyrics." Has published poetry by David Zieroth, Don Domanski, Jean McNeil, and Alden Nowlan. As a sample the editor selected these lines from "The Coves" by Steve McOrmond:

> You ask the wind/hard questions. Try to see/where the horizon lies, blue seam/between ocean and air,/ between us/and the end of history.

Pottersfield is 90 pages, 8 × 11, professionally printed and perfect-bound with b&w cover, includes photos and ads. Receives about 1,000 poems/year, accepts 5%. Press run is 1,000 for 250 subscribers of which 25 are libraries, 750 shelf sales. Single copy: $9; subscription: $26. Sample: $9. "Subscribers from outside Canada please remit in U.S. dollars."

How to Submit: Submit 6 poems at a time. No previously published poems. Include SAE with IRCs. Cover letter strongly preferred. "Submissions should be on white paper of standard dimensions (8½ × 11). Only one poem per page." Time between acceptance and publication is 3 months. Guidelines available for SASE (or SAE with IRC) and on website. "Note: U.S. stamps are no good in Canada." Responds in 5 months. Pays $10/printed page to a maximum of $50 plus 1 contributor's copy. Acquires first Canadian serial rights.

Also Offers: Sponsors the *Pottersfield Portfolio* Short Poem Competition. Deadline: May 1 each year. Entry fee: $20 for 3 poems, which must be no more than 20 lines in length. Fee includes subscription. Write for details or consult website.

Advice: "Only submit your work in a form you would want to read yourself. Subscribe to some literary journals. Read lots of poetry."

$ THE PRAIRIE JOURNAL; PRAIRIE JOURNAL PRESS (Specialized: regional, prairie; themes), P.O. Box 61203, Brentwood Post Office, 217-3630 Brentwood Rd. NW, Calgary, Alberta T2L 2K6 Canada. E-mail: prairiejournal@yahoo.com. Website: www.geocities.com/prairiejournal (includes submission guidelines and poems of the month). Established 1983. **Editor:** A. Burke.

Magazine Needs: For *The Prairie Journal*, the editor wants to see poetry of "any length, free verse, contemporary themes (feminist, nature, urban, non-political), aesthetic value, a poet's poetry." Does not want to see "most rhymed verse, sentimentality, egotistical ravings. No cowboys or sage brush." Has published poetry by Liliane Welch, Cornelia Hoogland, Sheila Hyland, Zoe Lendale, and Chad Norman. *Prairie Journal* is 40-60 pages, 7 × 8½, offset, saddle-stapled with card cover, b&w drawings and ads, appearing twice/year. Receives about 1,000 poems/year, accepts 10%. Press run is 600 for 200 subscribers of which 50% are libraries, the rest are distributed on the newsstand. Subscription: $8 for individuals, $15 for libraries. Sample: $8 ("Use postal money order").

How to Submit: No simultaneous submissions or previously published poems. Does not accept e-mail submissions. Guidelines available for postage (but "no U.S. stamps, please"—get IRCs from the Post Office) or on website. "We will not be reading submissions until such time as an issue is in preparation (twice yearly), so be patient and we will acknowledge, accept for publication, or return work at that time." Sometimes sends prepublication galleys. Pays $10-50 plus 1 copy. Acquires first North American serial rights. Reviews books of poetry "but must be assigned by editor. Query first."

Book/Chapbook Needs & How to Submit: For chapbook publication, Canadian poets only (preferably from the region) should query with 5 samples, bio, publications. Responds to queries in 2 months, to mss in 6 months. Payment in modest honoraria. Has published *Voices From Earth*, selected poems by Ronald Kurt and Mark McCawley, and *In the Presence of Grace*, by McCandless Callaghan. "We also publish anthologies on themes when material is available."

Also Offers: Publishes "Poems of the Month" online. Submit up to 4 poems for $1 reading fee.

Advice: "Read recent poets! Experiment with line length, images, metaphors. Innovate."

PRAIRIE SCHOONER; STROUSSE PRIZE; LARRY LEVIS PRIZE; GLENNA LU-SCHEI AWARD; SLOTE PRIZE; FAULKNER AWARD; HUGH J. LUKE AWARD; STANLEY AWARD; JANE GESKE AWARD; READERS' CHOICE AWARDS, 201 Andrews, University of Nebraska, Lincoln NE 68588-0334. (402)472-0911. Fax: (402)472-9771. E-mail: eflanagan2@unl.edu. Website: www.unl.edu/schooner/psmain.htm (features writer's guidelines, names of editors, subscription info, history, table of contents, and excerpts from current issue). Established 1927. **Editor:** Hilda Raz.

• Poetry published in *Prairie Schooner* has also been selected for inclusion in *The Best American Poetry 1996* and the *Pushcart Prize* anthology.

Magazine Needs: *Prairie Schooner is* "one of the oldest literary quarterlies in continuous publication; publishes poetry, fiction, personal essays, interviews, and reviews." Wants "poems that fulfill the expectations they set up." No specifications as to form, length, style, subject matter, or purpose. Has published poetry by Alicia Ostriker, Marilyn Hacker, Radu Hotinceneasru, Stephen Dunn, and David Ignatow. As a sample the editor selected these lines from "How to Get in the Best Magazines" by Eleanor Wilner:

it is time to write/the acceptable poem—ice and glass, with its splinter/of bone, its pit/of an olive,/the dregs/of the cup of abundance,/useless spill of gold/from the thresher, the dust/of it filling the sunlight, the chum/broadcast on the black waters/and the fish/—the beautiful, ravenous fish—/refusing to rise.

Prairie Schooner is 200 pages, 6×9, flat-spined and uses 70-80 pages of poetry in each issue. Receives about 4,800 mss (of all types)/year, uses 300 pages of poetry. Press run is 3,100. Single copy: $9; subscription: $26. Sample: $6.

How to Submit: Submit 5-7 poems at a time. No simultaneous submissions. No fax or e-mail submissions. "Clear copy appreciated." Considers mss from September through May only. Publishes theme issues. Guidelines available for SASE. Responds in 4 months; "sooner if possible." Always sends prepublication galleys. Pays 3 contributor's copies. Acquires all rights. Returns rights upon request without fee. Reviews books of poetry. Poets may send books for review consideration. Editor Hilda Raz also promotes poets whose work has appeared in her pages by listing their continued accomplishments in a special section (even when their work does not concurrently appear in the magazine).

Also Offers: The Strousse Award for poetry ($500), the Bernice Slote Prize for beginning writers ($500), Hugh J. Luke Award ($250), the Edward Stanley Award for Poetry ($1000), the Virginia Faulkner Award for Excellence in Writing ($1,000), the Glenna Luschei Prize for Literary Distinction ($1,000), the Jane Geske Award ($200), and the Larry Levis Prize for Poetry ($1,000). Also, each year 4-8 Readers' Choice Awards ($250 each) are given for poetry, fiction, and nonfiction. All contests are open only to those writers whose work was published in the magazine the previous year. Editors serve as judges.

PRAKALPANA LITERATURE; KOBISENA (Specialized: bilingual, form), P-40 Nandana Park, Kolkata 700034, West Bengal, India. Phone: (91)(033)403-0347. E-mail: prakalpana@rediff mail.com. Website: http://prakalpana.tripod.com (includes guidelines and contact and subscription info). *Kobisena* established 1972; *Prakalpana Literature* press 1974; magazine 1977. **Editor:** Vattacharja Chandan.

Magazine Needs: "We are small magazines which publish only Prakalpana (a mixed form of prose, poetry, graphics, and art), Sarbangin (whole) poetry, experimental b&w art and photographs, essays on Prakalpana movement and Sarbangin poetry movement, letters, literary news and very few books on Prakalpana and Sarbangin literature. Purpose and form: for advancement of poetry in the super-space age, the poetry must be really experimental using mathematical signs and symbols and visualizing the pictures inherent in the alphabet (within typography) with sonorous effect accessible to people. That is Sarbangin poetry. Length: within 30 lines (up to 4 poems). Prakalpana is a mixed form of prose, poetry, essay, novel, story, play with visual effect and it is not at all short story as it is often misunderstood. Better send six

IRCs to read *Prakalpana Literature* first and then submit. Length: within 16 pages (up to 2 prakalpanas) at a time. Subject matter: society, nature, cosmos, humanity, love, peace, etc. Style: own. We do not want to see traditional, conventional, academic, religious, mainstream, and poetry of prevailing norms and forms." Has published poetry by Dilip Gupta, Bablu Roychondhuri, Nikhil Bhowmick, John M. Bennet, and Jesse Glass. *Prakalpana Literature*, an annual, is 72 pages, 7×4½, saddle-stapled, printed on thin stock, matte card cover. *Kobisena*, which also appears once/year, is 16 pages, digest-sized, newsletter format, no cover. Both use both English and Bengali. Receive about 400 poems/year, accept approximately 10%. Press run is 1,000 for each, and each has about 500 subscribers of which 50 are libraries. Samples: 10 rupees for *Prakalpana*, 4 rupees for *Kobisena*. Overseas: 6 IRCs and 3 IRCs respectively or exchange of avant-garde magazines.

How to Submit: Submit 4 poems at a time. Accepts submissions by e-mail (as attachment or in text box), on disk, or by postal mail. Cover letter with short bio and small photo/sketch of poet/writer/artist required; camera-ready copy (4×6½) preferred. Time between acceptance and publication is within a year. After being published in the magazines, poets may be included in future anthologies with translations into Bengali/English if and when necessary. "Joining with us is welcome but not a pre-condition." Editor comments on rejected poems "if wanted." Guidelines available for SAE with IRC. Pays 1 copy. Reviews books of poetry, fiction and art, "but preferably experimental books." Poets, writers, and artists may also send books for review consideration.

Advice: "We believe that only through poetry, fiction, and art, the deepest feelings of humanity as well as nature and the cosmos can be best expressed and conveyed to the peoples of the ages to come. And only poetry can fill up the gap in the peaceless hearts of dispirited peoples, resulted from the retreat of god and religion with the advancement of hi-tech. So, in an attempt, since the inception of Prakalpana Movement in 1969, to reach that goal in the experimental way we stand for Sarbangin poetry. And to poets and all concerned with poetry we wave the white handkerchief saying (in the words of Vattacharja Chandan), 'We want them who want us.' "

N ○ ◎ **PRAYERWORKS (Specialized: religious; senior citizen)**, P.O. Box 301363, Portland OR 97294-9363. (503)761-2072. E-mail: jay4prayer@aol.com. Established 1988. **Editor:** V. Ann Mandeville.

Magazine Needs: Established as a ministry to people living in retirement centers, *PrayerWorks* is a weekly newsletter encouraging "elderly people to recognize their value to God as prayer warriors." Features "prayer, ways to pray, stories of answered prayer, teaching on a Scripture portion, articles that build faith, and poems." *PrayerWorks* is 4 pages, 5½×8, photocopied, desktop-published, folded. Receives about 50 poems/year, accepts approximately 25%. Press run is 1,000 for 1,000 subscribers. Subscription: free.

How to Submit: Submit 5 poems, 1/page. Accepts previously published poems and simultaneous submissions. Accepts e-mail submissions (Wordperfect or Microsoft Word files). Cover letter preferred. Time between acceptance and publication is usually within 1 month. Seldom comments on rejected poems. Publishes theme issues relating to the holidays (submit holiday poetry 2 months in advance). Guidelines available for SASE. Responds in 3 weeks. Pays 5 or more copies.

○ **PREMIERE GENERATION INK**, P.O. Box 2056, Madison WI 53701-2056. E-mail: poetry@premie regeneration.com. Website: www.premieregeneration.com (includes guidelines, photography, video and spoken word, previews of upcoming journal, etc.). Established 1998. **Contact:** poetry editor.

Magazine Needs: *Premiere Generation Ink* appears twice yearly and publishes "high quality, honest poetry in a magazine/journal format and also in a multimedia format via website. We are also looking for art, photos, live recordings of poetry (audio or video) to be put on the Web and to be used in the journal. We also want experimental video poetry which can be mailed by VHS cassette. We would like to see poetry that is less concerned with being poetry than it is with being honest and true. We welcome any length, format, style or subject matter. We do not want to see pretentious and contrived poetry." Has published poetry by Ruth Stone, Sean Ross, Liz Rosenberg, and Virgil Suarez. As a sample the editors selected "Death Portrait of a child #10" by Adam Savage:

> I can't tell you how often I've/clipped coupons only to have them expire in my wallet./All that money
> wasted just because of a few days./I can't tell you how much a few days means to me.

Premiere Generation Ink is 30-40 pages, 8½×11, photocopied in color and saddle-stapled, cover is color or b&w "depending on issue," includes art/graphics. Single copy: $5; subscription: $16. Sample: $5.

How to Submit: Submit 5 poems at a time. Accepts previously published poems and simultaneous submissions. Accepts e-mail submissions (either in body or as attachment). Website features online submission as well. Cover letter preferred. Cover letters need not be formal, we prefer casual and personal. Time between acceptance and publication is up to 8 months. Poems are circulated to an editorial board. "Three editors review all submissions and a collective decision is reached." Often comments on rejected poems; "Always comments on first submission. Requests that author purchases sample copy before resubmitting. Comments on electronic submissions if author sends SASE." Guidelines available for SASE, by e-mail, or on website. Responds in 6 months. Pays 2-5 copies. Acquires first or reprint rights.

Also Offers: "We would like to publish books in cooperation with an author. *Premiere Generation Ink* will chiefly be a means for writers to distribute their art to a larger audience via the Web and the poetry journal. The sales proceeds will go to cover the costs associated with production. Any net profit will be divided equally between the author and the publisher. The main goal of this company is not profit, but rather to distribute quality art to a larger audience. We expect to work closely with the author on the format and layout of the book, and we hope eventually they will become just as much a part of the company as the founders." Order sample books by inquiring via regular mail, e-mail, or website. "Prior to submitting for chapbook publication, a sample copy must be purchased." *Premiere Generation Ink* is "actively seeking people to help with distribution of books journals, promotional material as well as people to help with website, multimedia, and print products."

$ THE PRESBYTERIAN RECORD (Specialized: inspirational, religious), 50 Wynford Dr., North York, Ontario M3C 1J7 Canada. (416)441-1111. Fax: (416)441-2825. E-mail: tdickey@presbyter ian.ca. Established 1876.

Magazine Needs: *The Presbyterian Record* is "the national magazine that serves the membership of The Presbyterian Church in Canada (and many who are not Canadian Presbyterians). We seek to stimulate, inform, inspire, to provide an 'apologetic' and a critique of our church and the world (not necessarily in that order!)." Wants poetry which is "inspirational, Christian, thoughtful, even satiric but not maudlin. No 'sympathy card' type verse à la Edgar Guest or Francis Gay. It would take a very exceptional poem of epic length for us to use it. Shorter poems, 10-30 lines, preferred. Blank verse OK (if it's not just rearranged prose). 'Found' poems. Subject matter should have some Christian import (however subtle)." Has published poetry by Margaret Avison, Wendy Turner Swanson, Fredrick Zydek, John Grey, T.M. Dickey, and Charles Cooper. *The Presbyterian Record* appears 11 times/year. Press run is 55,000. Subscription: $15.

How to Submit: Submit 3-6 poems at a time; seasonal work 6 weeks before month of publication. Accepts simultaneous submissions; rarely accepts previously published poems. Poems should be typed, double-spaced. Accepts fax and e-mail submissions "but will not necessarily reply to unsolicited faxes or e-mails." Pays $30-50/poem. Acquires one-time rights.

PRESENCE (Specialized: form), 12 Grovehall Ave., Leeds LS11 7EX United Kingdom. E-mail: martin.lucas@talk21.com. Website: http://members.netscapeonline.co.uk/haikupresence (includes samples of haiku, tanka, haibun, renga, articles, subscriptions, and submission information). Established 1995. **Contact:** Mr. Martin Lucas.

Magazine Needs: *Presence*, published 2-3 times/year, features haiku, senryu, renga, tanka, etc. Wants "haiku or haiku-related/haiku-influenced work. Maximum length: 16 lines (including title and spaces)." Does not want "anything longer than 16 lines (except renga)." Has published poetry by Ken Jones, Matt Morden, Patricia Prime, and Alison Williams. As a sample the editor selected this haiku by Martin Lucas:

> a night of stars/the footpath/sparkles with frost

Presence is 44-60 pages, A5, photocopied, perfect-bound, with brushdrawn art on card cover and illustrations. Receives about 2,000 poems/year, accepts about 10%. Press run is 170 for 100 subscribers of which 5 are libraries, 10 shelf sales. Subscription: £10 ($20 US) for 4 issues surface mail. £3 ($6 US) per single issue air mail. Sample: £3 ($6 US). Please pay in US bills (no checks).

How to Submit: Submit 4-12 poems at a time. "Please ensure that separate poems can be identified, and not mistaken for a sequence." No previously published poems or simultaneous submissions. Accepts e-mail submissions in body of message. Cover letter preferred. Time between acceptance and publication is 4 months. Comments on rejected poems if requested. Guidelines available for SASE (or SAE with IRC) or on website. Responds within 1 month. Pays 1 contributor's copy. Copyright remains with authors. Staff reviews books or chapbooks of poetry or other magazines in 10-500 words, single format. Poets may send books for review consideration.

Advice: "The more you read the better you'll write. Those who subscribe to read make better poets than those who are motivated solely by seeing their own name in print."

THE PRESS OF THE THIRD MIND (Specialized: form), 1301 North Dearborn #1007, Chicago IL 60610. (312)337-3122. E-mail: b_seidman@hotmail.com. Established 1985. **Poetry Editor:** Bradley Bongwater.

Book/Chapbook Needs: Press of the Third Mind is a small press publisher of artist books, poetry, and fiction. "We are especially interested in found poems, Dada, surrealism, written table-scraps left on the floors of lunatic asylums by incurable psychotics, etc." Has published poetry by Anthony Stark, Jorn Barger, Michael Kaspar, Patrick Porter, Tom Vaultonburg, and Eric Forsburg. Press run is 1,000 with books often going into a second or third printing. Sample for $1.43 postage.

How to Submit: For book publication submit up to 20 sample poems. "No anthologized mss where every poem has already appeared somewhere else." Accepts simultaneous submissions, if noted. "Cover letter is good, but we don't need to know everything you published since you were age nine in single-spaced detail." Upcoming themes available for SASE. "Authors are paid as the publication transcends the break-even benchmark." The press has released an 80-page anthology entitled *Empty Calories* and published a deconstructivist novel about the repetition compulsion called *The Squeaky Fromme Gets the Grease*.

PRINCETON UNIVERSITY PRESS; LOCKERT LIBRARY OF POETRY IN TRANSLATION (Specialized: translations, bilingual), 41 William St., Princeton NJ 08540. (609)258-2484. Fax: (609)258-6305. Website: http://pup.princeton.edu. **Associate Editor:** Fred Appel.

Book Needs: "In the Lockert Library series, we publish simultaneous cloth and paperback (flat-spine) editions for each poet. Clothbound editions are on acid-free paper, and binding materials are chosen for strength and durability. Each book is given individual design treatment rather than stamped into a series mold. We have published a wide range of poets from other cultures, including well-known writers such as Hölderlin and Cavafy, and those who have not yet had their due in English translation, such as Göran Sonnevi. Manuscripts are judged with several criteria in mind: the ability of the translation to stand on its own as poetry in English; fidelity to the tone and spirit of the original, rather than literal accuracy; and the importance of the translated poet to the literature of his or her time and country."

How to Submit: Accepts simultaneous submissions if informed. Accepts fax submissions. Cover letter required. Send mss only during respective reading periods stated in guidelines. "Manuscripts returned only with SASE." Comments on finalists only. Send SASE for guidelines to submit. Responds in 3 months.

$ PRISM INTERNATIONAL, Creative Writing Program, University of British Columbia, Vancouver, British Columbia V6T 1Z1 Canada. (604)822-2514. Fax: (604)822-3616. E-mail: prism@interc hange.ubc.ca. Website: http://prism.arts.ubc.ca (includes writer's guidelines, names of editors, samples from past issues and "virtually everything you'd want to know." Website also publishes a quarter of the poetry appearing in the print issue). Established 1959. **Contact:** Rotating Editorialship.

• *PRISM international* is known in literary circles as one of the top journals in Canada.

Magazine Needs: "*PRISM* is an international quarterly that publishes poetry, drama, short fiction, imaginative nonfiction, and translation into English in all genres. We have no thematic or stylistic allegiances:

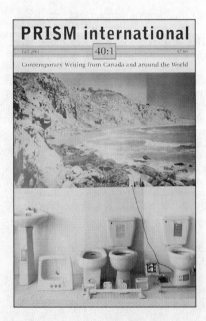

Can't stop looking, can you? Perhaps that's why Rafael Goldchain's "Appliance Store: Catemaco, Veracruz, 1986" was selected to launch *PRISM international*'s redesign. The editor adds, "It reflects our love of quirky, well-composed work."

Excellence is our main criterion for acceptance of mss. We want fresh, distinctive poetry that shows an awareness of traditions old and new. We read everything." Has published poetry by Di Brandt, Esta Spalding, Karen Connelly, Derk Wynand, and a translation by Seamus Heaney. As a sample the editors selected these lines from "The Bends" by Aurian Haller:

> *its body lost all signs of passage:/jolted out of its riverskin,/furious at the barbless hook,/red bags of reeking oil*

PRISM is 96 pages, 6×9, elegantly printed, flat-spined with original color artwork on a glossy card cover. Circulation is for 1,100 subscribers of which 200 are libraries. Receives 1,000 submissions/year, accepts about 80; has a 3 to 4 month backlog. Subscription: $18, $27/2 years. Sample: $5.

How to Submit: Submit up to 6 poems at a time, any print so long as it's typed. Include SASE (or SAE with IRCs). No previously published poems or simultaneous submissions. Accepts fax submissions. Cover letter with brief introduction and previous publications required. "Translations must be accompanied by a copy of the original." Guidelines available for SASE (or SAE with IRCs), by e-mail, or on website. Responds in up to 6 months. Pays $40/printed page plus subscription; plus an additional $10/printed page to selected authors for publication online. Editors sometimes comment on rejected poems. Acquires first North American serial rights.

Advice: "While we don't automatically discount any kind of poetry, we prefer to publish work that challenges the writer as much as it does the reader. We are particularly looking for poetry in translation."

$ ◢ PROVINCETOWN ARTS; PROVINCETOWN ARTS PRESS, 650 Commercial St., Provincetown MA 02657-1725. (508)487-3167. Fax: (508)487-4791. E-mail: cbusa@mediaone.net. Established 1985. **Editor:** Christopher Busa.

Magazine Needs: An elegant annual using quality poetry, "*Provincetown Arts* focuses broadly on the artists and writers who inhabit or visit the tip of Cape Cod and seeks to stimulate creative activity and enhance public awareness of the cultural life of the nation's oldest continuous art colony. Drawing upon a century-long tradition rich in visual art, literature, and theater, *Provincetown Arts* publishes material with a view towards demonstrating that the artists' colony, functioning outside the urban centers, is a utopian dream with an ongoing vitality." Has published poetry by Bruce Smith, Franz Wright, Sandra McPherson, and Cyrus Cassells. *Provincetown Arts* is about 170 pages, 8¾×11⅞, perfect-bound with full-color glossy cover. Press run is 10,000 for 500 subscribers of which 20 are libraries, 6,000 shelf sales. Sample: $10.

How to Submit: Submit up to 3 typed poems at a time. All queries and submissions should be via regular mail. Reads submissions October through February. Guidelines available for SASE. Responds in 3 months. Usually sends prepublication galleys. Pays $25-100/poem plus 2 contributor's copies. Acquires first rights. Reviews books of poetry in 500-3,000 words, single or multi-book format. Poets may send books for review consideration.

Book/Chapbook Needs & How to Submit: The Provincetown Arts Press has published 8 volumes of poetry. The Provincetown Poets Series includes *At the Gate* by Martha Rhodes, *Euphorbia* by Anne-Marie Levine, a finalist in the 1995 Paterson Poetry Prize, and *1990* by Michael Klein, co-winner of the 1993 Lambda Literary Award.

Ⓝ ◢ PSYCHODYSSEY; UNIQUE PORTRAYAL MAGAZINE, P.O. Box 1580, Lilburn GA 30048. E-mail: psychodyssey@yahoo.com. Website: www.uniqueportrayal.com. Established 1999. **Poetry Editor:** John V. Pepe.

Magazine Needs: *Psychodyssey* is the poetry/fiction section of *Unique Portrayal Magazine* and appears quarterly. It "exists to assist poets of all genres to showcase their creations in an arena that will facilitate capturing worldwide exposure." Wants work "in any form, embracing all subject matter, and employing any style or purpose." Does not want pornography; racist or overly violent poems; or work "laden with cliches, or poems begging to be slashed by the pernicious red pen monster." Recently published poetry by Darren Anderson, Joy Blake, Uzeyir Lokman, and John Pepe. As a sample the editor selected these lines from "Astronomer" by Joy Blake:

> *Eyes that could see into the heavens,/Words that could soothe the luminous oceans,/Resting on one false hope, he had said:/Perhaps the stars are already dead.*

Psychodyssey is published online (equivalent to 13-20 pages). Receives about 1,000 poems/year, accepts about 10%. Publishes about 20 poems/issue.

How to Submit: Submit 5 poems at a time. Accepts previously published poems and simultaneous submissions. Accepts e-mail and disk submissions; no fax submissions. "If you feel a brief cover letter will assist us in better interpreting your work, then by all means, send it along." Reads submissions year round. Submit seasonal poems 2 months in advance. Time between acceptance and publication is 3 months. "Ours is essentially a three-tier process: 1) all submissions are read several times; 2) the most potent pieces are removed for a final review; 3) only a very select few are chosen to appear on the website." Always comments on rejected poems. Occasionally publishes theme issues. List of upcoming themes and guidelines available on website. Responds in 2 months. Acquires one-time rights.

Also Offers: "There will be several scattered contests/cash awards for poetry during the course of the year, all of which are detailed in full on the website."

Advice: "Be persistent. Write relentlessly. Never offer yourself excuses. Incessantly attempt to graduate your art to the next level. Be open to honest criticism. Chuckle at rejection. And most importantly, grab life by the temples and take a giant, barbaric bite out of experience pie."

PUDDING HOUSE PUBLICATIONS; PUDDING MAGAZINE: THE INTERNATIONAL JOURNAL OF APPLIED POETRY; PUDDING HOUSE CHAPBOOK COMPETITIONS; PUDDING HOUSE BED & BREAKFAST FOR WRITERS; PUDDING HOUSE WRITERS INNOVATION CENTER (Specialized: political, social issues, popular culture), 60 N. Main St., Johnstown OH 43031. (740)967-6060. E-mail: pudding@johnstown.net. Website: www.puddinghouse. com. Established 1979. **Editor:** Jennifer Bosveld.

Magazine Needs: Pudding House Publications provides "a sociological looking glass through poems that speak to the pop culture, struggle in a consumer and guardian society and more—through 'felt experience.' Speaks for the difficulties and the solutions. Additionally a forum for poems and articles by people who take poetry arts into the schools and the human services." Publishes *Pudding* every several months, also chapbooks, anthologies, broadsides. "Wants what hasn't been said before. Speak the unspeakable. Don't want preachments or sentimentality. Don't want obvious traditional forms without fresh approach. Long poems OK as long as they aren't windy. Interested in receiving poetry on popular culture, rich brief narratives, i.e. 'virtual journalism.' (sample sheet $1 plus SASE)." Has published poetry by Knute Skinner, David Chorlton, Mary Winters, and Robert Collins. Uses up to 60 pages of poetry in each issue—$5\frac{1}{2} \times 8\frac{1}{2}$, 70 pages, offset-composed on Microsoft Word PC. Press run is 2,000 for 1,400 subscribers. Subscription: $18.95/3 issues. Sample: $7.95.

How to Submit: Submit 3-10 poems at a time with SASE. "Submissions without SASEs will be discarded." No postcards. No simultaneous submissions. Previously published submissions respected but include credits. Likes cover letters and "cultivates great relationships with writers." Sometimes publishes theme issues. Guidelines available for SASE. Responds on same day (unless traveling). Pays 1 copy; to featured poet $10 and 4 copies. Returns rights "with *Pudding* permitted to reprint." Send books for review consideration or listing as recommended. "See our website for vast calls for poems for magazine, chapbooks, and anthologies; for poetry and word games, and essays and workshop announcements."

Book/Chapbook Needs & How to Submit: Has recently published *Dancing with the Switchman* by Conrad Squires, *When I Had it Made* by Will Nixon, and *Subject Apprehended* by Hans Ostrom. Chapbooks considered outside of competitions, no query. **Reading fee:** $10. Send complete ms and cover letter with publication credits and bio. Editor sometimes comments, will critique on request for $4/page of poetry or $75 an hour in person.

Also Offers: Pudding House is the publisher of the nationwide project POETS' GREATEST HITS—an invitational. They have over 250 chapbooks and books in print. Pudding House offers 2 annual chapbook competitions—each requires a $10 reading fee with entry. Deadlines: June 30 and September 30. The competitions award $100, publication, and 20 free copies. Pudding House Bed & Breakfast for Writers offers "pretty, comfortable, clean rooms with desk and all the free paper you can use" as well as free breakfast in large comfortable home 1 block from conveniences. Location of the Pudding House Writers Innovation Center and Library on Applied Poetry. Bed & Breakfast is $85 single or double/night, discounts to writers. Reservations recommended far in advance. Details available for SASE. "Our website is one of the greatest poetry websites in the country—calls, workshops, publication list/history, online essays, games, guest pages, calendars, poem of the month, poet of the week, much more." The website also links to the site for The Unitarian Universalist Poets Cooperative and American Poets Opposed to Executions, both national organizations.

Advice: "Editors have pet peeves. I won't respond to postcards. I require SASEs. I don't like cover letters that state the obvious, poems with trite concepts, or meaning dictated by rhyme. Thoroughly review our website; it will give you a good idea about our publication history and editorial tastes."

THE PUDDIN'HEAD PRESS (Specialization: regional/Chicago), P.O. Box 477449, Chicago IL 60647. (708)656-4900. E-mail: phbooks@compuserve.com. Established 1985. **Editor-in-Chief:** David Gecic.

Book/Chapbook Needs: The Puddin'head Press is interested in "well-rounded poets who can support their work with readings and appearances. Most of our poets are drawn from the performance poetry community." Wants "quality poetry by active poets. We occasionally publish chapbook-style anthologies and let poets on our mailing lists know what type of work we're interested in for a particular project." Does not want experimental, overly political poetry, or poetry with overt sexual content; no shock or novelty poems. Recently published poetry by John Dickson, Nina Corwin, JJ Jameson, and Jeff Helgeson. As a sample the editor selected these lines from "Mythical Creatures" by John Dickson, published in *Lake Michigan Scrolls* (2002):

> *And after the last poet disappeared/it was said there had once been people/who would spend their lives stringing words together/talking their rhythms, dancing their rhymes,/making nonsense seem like reason/and logic like a drunk.*

How to Submit: Puddin'head Press publishes 1 book and 1 chapbook/year. Books/chapbooks are 30-100 pages, perfect-bound or side-stapled ("we use various formats"). Responds to queries in 1 month; to mss in 3 months. Poets must include SASE with submission. Pays various royalty rates "depending on the publication. We usually have a press run of 500 books." **About 25% of books are author-subsidy published.** Terms vary. Order sample books/chapbooks by sending $10 (price plus postage) to The Puddin'head Press (also available through Amazon).
Also Offers: "We prefer to work closely with poets in the Chicago area. There are numerous readings and events which we sponsor. We do our own distribution, primarily in the Midwest, and also do distribution for other small presses. Please send a SASE for a list of our current publications and publication/distribution guidelines."
Advice: "It is difficult to find a quality publisher. Poets must have patience and find a press that will work with them. The most important part of publication is the relationship between poet and publisher. Many good books will never be seen because the poet/publisher relationship is not healthy. If a poet is involved in the literary world, he will find a publisher, or a publisher will find him."

PUERTO DEL SOL, Box 3E, New Mexico State University, Las Cruces NM 88003-0001. E-mail: puerto@nmsu.edu. Established 1972 (in present format). **Poetry Editor:** Kathleene West. **Editor-in-Chief:** Kevin McIlvoy.
Magazine Needs: "We publish a literary magazine twice per year. Interested in poems, fiction, essays, photos, originals, and translations, usually from the Spanish. Also (generally solicited) reviews and dialogues between writers. We want top quality poetry, any style, from anywhere. We are sympathetic to Southwestern writers, but this is not a theme magazine. Excellent poetry of any kind, any form." Has published poetry by Judith Sornberger, Ana Castillo, Marilyn Hacker, Virgil Suarez, and Lois-Ann Yamanaka. As a sample the editor selected these lines from "And Seeing It" by Valerie Martínez:

> *Orange, orange. And the hand arching up/to hold it. The woman's hand, the arching./Up. And the star exploding, seeing it/where it wasn't, a telescope on the night sky./The thermonuclear flash. The explosion.*

Puerto del Sol is 6×9, flat-spined, professionally printed, matte card cover with art. Press run is 1,250 for 300 subscribers of which 25-30 are libraries. Devotes 40-50 pages to poetry in each 150-page issue. Uses about 50 of the 900 submissions (about 6,000 poems) received each year to fill up the 90 pages of poetry the 2 issues encompass. Subscription: $10/2 issues. Sample: $7.
How to Submit: Submit 3-6 poems at a time, 1 poem to a page. Accepts simultaneous submissions. No e-mail submissions. Cover letter welcome. Reads mss September 1 to March 1 only. Offers editorial comments on most mss. Responds in 6 months. Sometimes sends prepublication galleys. Pays 2 contributor's copies.
Advice: "We're looking for poems that are risk-taking and honest."

PULSAR POETRY MAGAZINE; LIGDEN PUBLISHERS, 34 Lineacre, Grange Park, Swindon, Wiltshire SN5 6DA United Kingdom. Phone: (01793)875941. E-mail: david.pike@virgin.net. Website: www.btinternet.com/~pulsarpoetry. Established 1992. **Editor:** David Pike. **Editorial Assistant:** Jill Meredith.
Magazine Needs: *Pulsar*, published quarterly, "encourages the writing of poetry from all walks of life. Contains poems, reviews and editorial comments." Wants "hard-hitting, thought-provoking work; interesting and stimulating poetry." Does not want "racist material. Not keen on religious poetry." Has published poetry by Merryn Williams, Joy Martin, Li Min Hua, Virgil Suarez, and Wincey Willis. As a sample the editor selected these lines from "The Watcher" by Lewis Hosegood:

> *Somewhere in this tall terraced house, somewhere,/somewhere lives a boy/who surely cannot see me,/ nor speak my name aloud, yet senses/my interest in origins./He will never go away though I wait here and wait. . . .*

Pulsar is 36 pages, A5, professionally printed, saddle-stapled, glossy 2-color cover with photos and ads. Press run is 300 for 100 subscribers of which 40 are libraries; several distributed free to newspapers, etc. Subscription: $30 (£12 UK). Sample: $7. Make checks payable to Ligden Publishers.
How to Submit: Submit 3 poems at a time "preferably typed." No previously published poems or simultaneous submissions. Send no more than 2 poems via e-mail; file attachments will not be read. Cover letter preferred; include SAE with IRCs. "Poems can be published in next edition if it is what we are looking for. The editor and assistant read all poems." Time between acceptance and publication is about 1 month. Seldom comments on rejected poems. Guidelines available for SASE (or SAE with IRC). Responds within 3 weeks. Pays 1 contributor's copy. "Originators retain copyright of their poems." Acquires first rights. Staff reviews poetry books and poetry audio tapes (mainstream); word count varies. Send books for review consideration.

Advice: "Give explanatory notes if poems are open to interpretation. Be patient and enjoy what you are doing. Check grammar, spelling, etc. (should be obvious). Note: we are a non-profit making society."

N ⊕ ✍ PURPLE PATCH; THE FIRING SQUAD, 25 Griffiths Rd., West Bromwich B7I 2EH England. Established 1975. **Editor:** Geoff Stevens.

Magazine Needs: *Purple Patch* a quarterly poetry and short prose magazine with reviews, comment and illustrations. "All good examples of poetry considered, but prefer 40 lines max. Do not want poor rhyming verse, non-contributory swear words or obscenities, hackneyed themes." Has published poetry by Joyce Metzger, M.T. Nowak, R.K. Avery, and Trish O'Brien. As a sample the editor selected these lines from "Echo" by M.T. Nowak:

> *I have seen your profile/in ancient Aztec carvings . . . Here you are again/ . . . cleaning tables/in an*
> *anglo chain restaurant*

Purple Patch is 24 pages, digest-sized, photocopied and side-stapled with cover on the same stock with b&w drawing. Receives about 2,500 poems/year, accepts approximately 8%. Publish 40 poems/issue. Circulation "varies." Subscription: £5 UK/3 issues; US price is $20 (submit dollars). Make checks (sterling only) payable to G. Stevens.

How to Submit: Cover letter with short self-introduction preferred with submissions. Time between acceptance and publication is 4 months. Publishes theme issues occasionally. Upcoming themes available for SASE (or SAE and IRCs) and in publication. Guidelines also in publication. Comments on rejected poems. Response time is 1 month to Great Britain, can be longer to US. Overseas contributors have to buy a copy to see their work in print. Acquires first British serial rights. Staff reviews poetry chapbooks, short stories and tapes in 30-300 words. Send books for review consideration.

Also Offers: *The Firing Squad* is a broadsheet of short poetry of a protest or complaint nature, published at irregular intervals. "All inquiries, submissions of work, etc., must include SASE or SAE and IRCs or $1 U.S./ Canadian for return postage/reply."

N $✍ QED PRESS; CYPRESS HOUSE, 155 Cypress St., Fort Bragg CA 95437. (707)964-9520. Fax: (707)964-7531. E-mail: qedpress@mcn.org. Website: www.cypresshouse.com. Established 1985. Senior Editor: John Fremont.

Book/Chapbook Needs: "QED Press has no determining philosophy. We seek clear, clean, intelligent, and moving work." Publishes 1-2 paperbacks/year. Wants "concrete, personal and spare writing. No florid rhymed verse." Has published poetry by Luke Breit, Paula Tennant (Adams), and Cynthia Frank. As a sample the editor selected this poem, "Ao Lume," by Eugenio de Andrade:

> *Nem sempre o homem é um lugar triste./Há noites em que o sorriso/dos anjos/a torna habitável e*
> *leve:/com a cabeça no teu regaço/é um cão ao lume a correr às lebres.*

Translated from Portuguese by Alexis Levitin:

> *Man is not always a place of sorrow./There are nights in which the smile/of angels/makes him habitable*
> *and light:/with his head in your lap/he's a dog by the fire chasing after hares.*

Books are usually around 100 pages, 5½×8½, offset printed, perfect-bound, full-color CS1 10 pt. cover.

How to Submit: "We prefer to see all the poems (about 100 pages worth or 75-80 poems) to be bound in a book." Accepts previously published poems and simultaneous submissions. Cover letter required. "Poets must have prior credits in recognized journals, and a minimum of 50% new material." Time between acceptance and publication is 3-6 months. Poems are circulated to an editorial board. "We publish only 1-2 poetry books each year—by consensus." Seldom comments on rejected poems. Responds to queries and mss in 3 months. Pays royalties of 7½-12% and 25 author's copies (out of a press run of 500-1,000). Order sample books by sending SASE for catalog.

Also Offers: Through the imprint Cypress House, they offer subsidy arrangements "by bid with author retaining all rights and inventory. We are not a vanity press." 50% of books are author-subsidy published each year.

⊕ $✍ QUANTUM LEAP; Q.Q. PRESS, York House, 15 Argyle Terrace, Rothesay, Isle of Bute PA20 0BD Scotland, United Kingdom. Established 1997. **Editor:** Alan Carter.

Magazine Needs: *Quantum Leap* is a quarterly poetry magazine. Wants "all kinds of poetry—free verse, rhyming, whatever—as long as it's well written and preferably well punctuated, too. We rarely use haiku." Also accepts poetry written by children. Has published poetry by Pamela Constantine, Ray Stebbing, Leigh Eduardo, Sam Smith, Sky Higgins, Norman Bissett, and Gordon Scapens. As a sample we selected these lines from "Topography of Mind" by Sky Higgins:

> *A map like none other, encompassing me: from the hard, distant stones of stars/to the blood-pulse in*
> *my eyes, and all/the time I ever savoured, stretched or lost,/where sand deserts the hourglass, is freed/*
> *into landscape whorls. . .*

Quantum Leap is 40 pages, digest-sized, desktop-published and saddle-stapled with card cover, includes clip art and ads for other magazines. Receives about 2,000 poems/year, accepts about 10%. Press run is 200 for 180 subscribers. Single copy: $10; subscription: $34. Sample: $9. Make checks payable to Alan Carter. "All things being equal in terms of a poem's quality, I will sometimes favor that of a subscriber (or someone who has at least bought an issue) over a nonsubscriber, as it is they who keep us solvent."

How to Submit: Submit 6 poems at a time. Line length for poetry is 36 ("normally"). Accepts previously published poems (indicate magazine and date of first publication) and simultaneous submissions. Cover letter required. "Within the UK, send a SASE, outside it, send IRCs to the value of what has been submitted." Time between acceptance and publication is usually 3 months "but can be longer now, due to magazine's increasing popularity." Sometimes comments on rejected poems. Guidelines available for SASE (or SAE and IRC). Responds in 3 weeks. Pays £2 sterling. Acquires first or second British serial rights.

Book/Chapbook Needs: Under the imprint "Collections," Q.Q. Press offers subsidy arrangements "to provide a cheap alternative to the 'vanity presses'—poetry only." Charges £120 sterling for 50 32-page books (A4), US $250 plus postage. Please write for details. Order sample books by sending $12 (postage included). Make checks payable to Alan Carter.

Also Offers: Sponsors open poetry competitions and competitions for subscribers only. Send SAE and IRC for details.

Advice: "Submit well-thought-out, well-presented poetry, preferably well punctuated, too. If rhyming poetry, make it flow and don't strain to rhyme. I don't bite, and I appreciate a short cover letter, but not a long, long list of where you've been published before!"

QUARTER AFTER EIGHT; PROSE WRITING CONTEST (Specialized: form/ style), Ellis Hall, Ohio University, Athens OH 45701. (740)593-2827. Fax: (740)593-2818. E-mail: quarter aftereight@hotmail.com. Website: www.quarteraftereight.com (includes guidelines, contact and subscription info, bios, editorial policy). Established 1993. **Editor-in-Chief:** Tony Viola.

● "The Art of the Snake Story" by Amy England was selected for inclusion in the 2001 volume of *Best American Poetry*.

Magazine Needs: *Quarter After Eight* is "an annual journal of prose and commentary devoted to the exploration of prose in all its permutations. We are interested in reading fiction, sudden fiction, prose poetry, creative and critical non-fiction, interviews, reviews, letters, memoirs, translations, and drama. We do not publish traditional (lineated) poetry, but we do welcome work that provocatively explores—even challenges—the prose/poetry distinction. Our primary criteria in evaluating submissions are freshness of approach and an address to the prose form." Has published poetry by Colette Inez, Maureen Seaton, Virgil Suarez, Cecilia Pinto, and Matthew Cooperman. As a sample the editors selected these lines from "Whining Prairie" by Maureen Seaton:

> I don't want to die in this wild onion smelly belly mire of the midwest stinking marsh this drenchy
> swaly swamp but I might and who would note the fragrant corruption of my poor elan this moorish
> bog this poachy few who come from sea with salt and myrrh to burn my rotting flesh?

Quarter After Eight is 286 pages, 6×9, professionally printed and perfect-bound with glossy card cover, includes b&w photos and ads. Receives about 1,000 poems/year, accepts 3%. Press run is 800 for 200 subscribers of which 50 are libraries, 300 shelf sales. Sample: $10.

How to Submit: Submit 4-6 poems at a time. Accepts simultaneous submissions; no previously published poems. Accepts disk submissions with hard copy. "Include publishing history. We encourage readers/submitters to obtain a copy of the magazine." Reads submissions September 15 through March 15 only. Poems are circulated to an editorial board. "Editorial board makes final decisions; a pool of readers handles first reads and commentary/ input on editorial decisions." Often comments on rejected poems. Guidelines available for SASE or on website. Responds in up to 4 months. Pays 2 contributor's copies. Acquires first North American serial rights. Reviews books of poetry in 800-1,200 words, single or multi-book format. Send books for review consideration to Patrick Madden, Book Review Editor.

Also Offers: Sponsors an annual Prose Writing Contest with $300 cash award. Reading fee: $15 (includes subscription). Winner is published in subsequent issue. Maximum length 10,000 words—can be a sequence of poems. Guidelines available for SASE or on website.

Advice: "*Quarter After Eight* is a somewhat specialized niche. Check out the magazine and explore the boundaries of genre."

QUARTERLY WEST, 200 S. Central Campus Dr., Room 317, University of Utah, Salt Lake City UT 84112-9109. (801)581-3938. Website: www.utah.edu/quarterlywest (includes guidelines, staff, examples of recently published poems, graphic of cover, and a list of contributors). Established 1976. **Editor:** David Hawkins. **Poetry Editors:** Julie Paegle and Nicole Walker.

MARKETS LISTED in the 2002 edition of *Poet's Market* that do not appear this year are identified in the General Index with a code explaining their absence from the listings.

• Poetry published in *Quarterly West* has appeared in *The Best American Poetry* 1997 and 2000 and has won the Pushcart Prize several times.

Magazine Needs: *Quarterly West* is a semiannual literary magazine that seeks "original and accomplished literary verse—free or formal. No greeting card or sentimental poetry." Also publishes translations. Has published poetry by Robert Pinsky, Eavan Boland, Albert Goldbarth, William Matthews, Agha Shahid Ali, and Heather McHugh. *Quarterly West* is 220 pages, 6×9, offset-printed with 4-color cover art. Receives 1,500 submissions/year, accepts less than 1%. Press run is 1,900 for 500 subscribers of which 300-400 are libraries. Subscription: $12/year, $21/2 years. Sample: $7.50.

How to Submit: Reads from September 1 to March 1. Submit 3-5 poems at a time; if translations, include original. Accepts simultaneous submissions, with notification; no previously published poems. Seldom comments on rejected poems. Guidelines available for SASE or on website. Responds in up to 6 months. Pays $15-100 plus 2 contributor's copies. Acquires all rights. Returns rights with acknowledgement and right to reprint. Reviews books of poetry in 1,000-3,000 words.

QUEEN OF ALL HEARTS (Specialized: religious), 26 S. Saxon Ave., Bay Shore NY 11706. (631)665-0726. Fax: (631)665-4349. E-mail: pretre@worldnet.att.net. Established 1950. **Poetry Editor:** Joseph Tusiani.

Magazine Needs: *Queen of All Hearts* is a magazine-sized bimonthly that uses poetry "dealing with Mary, the Mother of Jesus—inspirational poetry. Not too long." Has published poetry by Fernando Sembiante and Alberta Schumacher. *Queen of All Hearts* is professionally printed, 48 pages, heavy stock, various colors of ink and paper, liberal use of graphics and photos, has approximately 2,000 subscriptions at $22/year. Single copy: $3.50. Sample: $4. Receives 40-50 submissions/year, accepts 1-2/issue.

How to Submit: Submit double-spaced mss. Accepts fax submissions but not e-mail submissions. Responds within 1 month. Pays 6 contributor's copies (sometimes more) and complimentary subscription. Editor sometimes comments on rejected poems.

Advice: "Try and try again! Inspiration is not automatic!"

$ ELLERY QUEEN'S MYSTERY MAGAZINE (Specialized: mystery), 475 Park Ave. S, 11th Floor, New York NY 10016. E-mail: elleryqueen@dellmagazines.com. Website: www.themysteryplace. com. Established 1941. **Contact:** Janet Hutchings.

Magazine Needs: *Ellery Queen's Mystery Magazine*, appearing 11 times/year, uses primarily short stories of mystery, crime, or suspense. As a sample we selected these lines from "Lighthouse" by Katherine H. Brooks:

> *To have his shining torch usurped by tourists on vacation/would never do. He checked the view, with*
> *rising indignation./ . . ./It took a single kitchen match set it all to burning./The old man chuckled at*
> *the sight, saluted once, and turning,/Limped slowly down the spiral stairs to reach the floor below,/*
> *delighted that his beacon shone with such a lovely glow.*

Ellery Queen's Mystery Magazine is 144 pages, 5¼×8⁵⁄₁₆, professionally printed on newsprint, flat-spined with glossy paper cover. Subscription: $39.97. Sample: $3.50 (available on newsstands).

How to Submit: Accepts simultaneous submissions; no previously published poems. Include SASE with submissions. Guidelines available for SASE and on website. Responds in 3 months. Pays $15-65 plus 3 contributor's copies.

$ QUEEN'S QUARTERLY: A CANADIAN REVIEW (Specialized: regional), Queen's University, Kingston, Ontario K7L 3N6 Canada. (613)533-2667. Fax: (613)533-6822. E-mail: qquarter@post.queensu.ca. Website: www.info.queensu.ca/quarterly. Established 1893. **Editor:** Boris Castel.

Magazine Needs: *Queen's Quarterly* is "a general interest intellectual review featuring articles on science, politics, humanities, arts and letters, extensive book reviews, some poetry and fiction. We are especially interested in poetry by Canadian writers. Shorter poems preferred." Has published poetry by Evelyn Lau, Sue Nevill, and Raymond Souster. Each issue contains about 12 pages of poetry, 6×9, 224 pages. Press run is 3,500. Receives about 400 submissions of poetry/year, accepts 40. Subscription: $20 Canadian, $25 US for US and foreign subscribers. Sample: $6.50 US.

How to Submit: Submit up to 6 poems at a time. No simultaneous submissions. Submissions can be sent on hard copy with a SASE (no replies/returns for foreign submissions unless accompanied by an IRC) or by e-mail and will be responded to by same. Responds in 1 month. Pays usually $50 (Canadian)/poem, "but it varies," plus 2 copies.

N ♥ ◎ RADIX MAGAZINE (Specialized: poetry that expresses a Christian world-view), P.O. Box 4307, Berkeley CA 94704. E-mail: radixmag@aol.com. Website: www.radixmagazine.com (includes subscription and back issue information, comments from readers, a few sample articles). Established 1969. **Editor:** Sharon Gallagher. **Poetry Editor:** Luci Shaw.

Magazine Needs: *Radix* wants poems "that reflect a Christian world-view, but aren't preachy." Recently published poetry by John Leax, Walter McDonald, Evangeline Paterson, and Luci Shaw. As a sample the editor selected these lines from "Annunciation" by John Leax:

> *moving in the dawn:/the maple, stark with/all its fallen loss/is leafed with birds.*

Radix is 32 pages, magazine-sized, offset-printed, saddle-stapled, self cover 60 lb. Receives about 50 poems/year, accepts about 20%. Publishes about 2-3 poems/issue. Press run varies. Sample: $5. Make checks payable to *Radix Magazine*.

How to Submit: Submit 1-4 poems at a time. No previously published poems or simultaneous submissions. Accepts e-mail submissions; no fax or disk submissions. "Please submit poems by mail addressed to Luci Shaw and enclose SASE." Submit seasonal poems 6 months in advance. Time between acceptance and publication is 3 months-3 years. "We have a serious backlog. The poetry editor accepts or rejects poems and sends the accepted poems to the editor. The editor then publishes poems in appropriate issues. If more than one poem is accepted from any poet, there will probably be a long wait before another is published, because of our backlog of accepted poems." Seldom comments on rejected poems. "Familiarity with the magazine is helpful, but not required." Occasionally publishes theme issues. Responds in 2 months. Pays 2 contributor's copies. Acquires first rights. Returns rights upon request. Reviews books of poetry.

Advice: "*Radix* has a distinctive voice and often receives submissions that are completely inappropriate. Familiarity with the magazine is recommended before sending any submissions."

♥ ◎ THE RAINTOWN REVIEW (Specialized: form/style), P.O. Box 40851, Indianapolis IN 46240. Established 1996. **Editor:** Patrick Kanouse. **Contact:** Poetry Editor.

Magazine Needs: *The Raintown Review* is published irregularly and contains only poetry. Wants well-crafted poems—metered, syllabic, or free-verse. Has published poetry by Andrea B. Geffner, Mary Gribble, Annie Finch, Len Roberts, and Ted Simmons. As a sample the editor selected these lines from "Suicide Note" by William Baer:

> *The night that she committed suicide/her brother in New Jersey played the horses,/drinking with his buddies all night long;/her friend at Yale thumbed through a recent novel/looking in vain for meaning and for love;/her mother was asleep in New Rochelle;/her father, dead, was knocking on his box,/ hoping to distract his little girl.*

The Raintown Review is about 60 pages, chapbook-sized, desktop-published and saddle-stapled with card cover. Receives about 900 poems/year, accepts 10-15%. Press run is about 200 with most going to subscribers and contributors. Subscription: $24/year. Sample: $7.

How to Submit: Submit up to 6 poems at a time. Accepts previously published poems and simultaneous submissions. No e-mail submissions. Cover letter preferred. "We prefer contributors write for guidelines before submitting work." Guidelines available for SASE and in publication. Responds in up to 3 months. Pays 1 contributor's copy and 2 issue subscription. Acquires first or one-time rights.

◯ ◎ RALPH'S REVIEW; RC'S STAMP HOT LINE (Specialized: horror, nature/rural/ecology, psychic/occult, science fiction/fantasy), 129A Wellington Ave., Albany NY 12203. E-mail: rcpub 2000@aol.com. Established 1988. **Editor:** R. Cornell.

Magazine Needs: *Ralph's Review*, published quarterly, contains "mostly new writers, short stories and poems." Wants "horror/fantasy, environmental. No more than 30 lines." Does not want "rape, racial, political poems." Has published "Moods of Madness" by R. Cornell and poetry by Joanne Tolson, Joseph Danoski, Jim Sullivan, and Brendan J. MacDonald. As a sample the editor selected these lines from his poem "Night Beast":

> *Let the night beast,/Saunter through the streets/ . . ./The magic of life./The love of dath.*

Ralph's Review is 20-35 pages, 8½ × 11, photocopied, sometimes with soft cover, with art, cartoons and graphics. Receives about 80-100 poems/year, accepts 40%. Press run is 75-100 for 35 subscribers of which 3 are libraries; 30-40 distributed free to bookstores, toy stores, antique, and coffee shops. Single copy: $2; subscription: $15. Make checks payable to R. Cornell.

How to Submit: Submit up to 5 poems, with a **$3 reading fee** and SASE. Accepts previously published poems and simultaneous submissions. No e-mail submissions. Cover letter required. Time between acceptance and publication is 2-4 months. Seldom comments on rejected poems. Publishes theme issues. Guidelines and upcoming themes available for SASE or by e-mail. Responds in 3 weeks. Pays 1 copy. Acquires all rights. Returns rights 1 year after acceptance. Reviews books in up to 5,000 words in single-book format. Poets may send books for review consideration.

Advice: "Write good stuff, no foul language, be descriptive, colorful, short to the point, with an active ending."

◎ ☑ **RARACH PRESS** (Specialized: bilingual/foreign language, ethnic/nationality), 1005 Oakland Dr., Kalamazoo MI 49008. (616)388-5631. Established 1981. **Owner:** Ladislav Hanka. Books are handmade with original art and range in price from $100 to $3,500. Not open to unsolicited mss.

$ ☑ **RATTAPALLAX; RATTAPALLAX PRESS**, 532 La Guardia Place, Suite 353, New York NY 10012. (212)560-7459. E-mail: devineni@rattapallax.com. Website: www.rattapallax.com (includes information about the journal, submission guidelines, bios, upcoming readings, names of editors, sample poems, chat room, and links). Established 1998. **Editor-in-Chief:** Martin Mitchell.

Magazine Needs: "A biannual journal of contemporary literature, *Rattapallax* is Wallace Steven's word for the sound of thunder." Wants "extraordinary work in poetry and short fiction—words that are well-crafted and sing, words that recapture the music of the language, words that bump into each other in extraordinary ways and leave the reader touched and haunted by the experience. We do not want ordinary words about ordinary things." Has published poetry by Anthony Hecht, Kate Light, Karen Swenson, Mark Nickels, Bill Kushner, Michael T. Young, and James Rayan. As a sample the editors selected these lines from "This kindled by *Guade Virgo Salutata*, a motet by John Dunstable, c. 1400" by Mark Nickels:

> Slow-spreading English music, as though/we watched a pale drawing-off of the night/from delicate fields, and heard a haunt/of griffins in a fog close by the house./How one of the griffins, without fire, has wrought,/by a concentration of time, a face in gnarled elmwood. . . .

Rattapallax is 128 pages, magazine-sized, offset-printed, perfect-bound, with 12 pt. C1S cover, includes photos, drawings, and CD with poets. Receives about 5,000 poems/year, accepts 2%. Press run is 2,000 for 100 subscribers of which 50 are libraries, 1,200 shelf sales; 200 distributed free to contributors, reviews, and promos. Single copy: $7.95; subscription: $14/1 year. Sample (including guidelines): $7.95. Make checks payable to *Rattapallax*.

How to Submit: Submit 3-5 poems at a time. Accepts simultaneous submissions; no previously published poems. Accepts e-mail submissions from outside of the US and Canada. "SASE is required and e-mailed submissions should be sent as simple text." Cover letter preferred. Reads submissions all year; issue deadlines are June 1 and December 1. Time between acceptance and publication is 6 months. Poems are circulated to an editorial board. "The editor-in-chief, senior editor, and associate editor review all the submissions then decide on which to accept every week. Near publication time, all accepted work is narrowed and unused work is kept for the next issue." Often comments on rejected poems. Guidelines available by e-mail or on website. Responds in 2 months. Always sends prepublication galleys. Pays 2 contributor's copies. Acquires first rights.

Book/Chapbook Needs & How to Submit: Rattapallax Press publishes "contemporary poets and writers with unique powerful voices." Publishes 5 paperbacks and 3 chapbooks/year. Books are usually 64 pages, 6×9, offset-printed and perfect-bound with 12 pt. C1S cover, include drawings and photos. Query first with a few sample poems and cover letter with brief bio and publication credits and SASE. Requires authors to first be published in *Rattapallax*. Responds to queries in 1 month; to mss in 2 months. Pays royalties of 10-25%. Order sample books by sending SASE and $7.

☑ **RATTLE**, 13440 Ventura Blvd. #200, Sherman Oaks CA 91423. (818)788-3232 or (818)788-2831. Fax: (818)788-2831. E-mail: stellasuel@aol.com. Website: www.rattle.com (includes all back issues, subscription information, and shopping cart). Established 1994. **Editor:** Alan Fox. **Poetry Editor:** Stellasue Lee. Address submissions to Stellasue Lee.

Magazine Needs: *RATTLE* is a biannual poetry publication which also includes interviews with poets, essays, and reviews. Wants "high quality poetry of any form, three pages maximum. Nothing unintelligible." Accepts some poetry written by children ages 10 to 18. Has published poetry by Billy Collins, Anne Waldman, James Ragan, Philip Levine, Yusef Komunyakaa, and Simon Ortiz. As a sample the editor selected these lines from "Thinking of Li Po" by Glenn McKee:

> Island flowers blossom/unpicked by human hands./Small boats at sunset cast giant/shadows on calm waters./Adolescent Herring Gulls play the/wind's latest composition./Love searches for companionship in/a crowd of strangers./I remain stranded in time/with only words for wine.

RATTLE is 196 pages, 6×9, neatly printed and perfect-bound with 4-color coated card cover. Receives about 8,000 submissions/year, accepts 250. Press run is 4,000. Subscription: $28/2 years. Sample: $8. Make checks payable to *RATTLE*.

How to Submit: Submit up to 5 poems at a time with name, address, and phone number on each page in upper right hand corner. Include SASE. No previously published work or simultaneous submissions. Accepts e-mail ("cut and paste into text file") and fax submissions. Cover letter and e-mail address, if possible, is required as well as a bio. Reads submissions all year. Seldom comments on rejected poems unless asked by the author. Responds in up to 2 months. Pays 2 contributor's copies. Rights revert to authors upon publication. Welcomes essays up to 2,000 words on the writing process and book reviews on poetry up to 250 words. Send books for review consideration.

RAW DOG PRESS; POST POEMS, 151 S. West St., Doylestown PA 18901-4134. (215)345-6838. Website: www.freeyellow.com/members/rawdog (includes basic Raw Dog Press information, general poets' Q and A, and general writer's guidelines). Established 1977. **Poetry Editor:** R. Gerry Fabian.

Magazine Needs: "Publishes Post Poems annual—a postcard series. We want short poetry (three to seven lines) on any subject. The positive poem or the poem of understated humor always has an inside track. No taboos, however. All styles considered. Anything with rhyme had better be immortal." Has published poetry by Don Ryan, John Grey, Wes Patterson, and the editor, R. Gerry Fabian, who selected his poem, "Kiowa," as a sample:

> I placed my tired head/where the just new moon/emits your presence

How to Submit: Submit 3-5 poems at a time. Send SASE for catalog to buy samples. Always comments on rejected poems. Guidelines available on website. Pays contributor's copies. Acquires all rights. Returns rights on mention of first publication. Sometimes reviews books of poetry.

Book/Chapbook Needs & How to Submit: Raw Dog Press welcomes new poets and detests second-rate poems from 'name' poets. We exist because we are dumb like a fox, but even a fox takes care of its own."

Also Offers: Offers criticism for a fee; "if someone is desperate to publish and is willing to pay, we will use our vast knowledge to help steer the ms in the right direction. We will advise against it, but as P.T. Barnum said. . . ."

Advice: "I get poems that do not fit my needs. At least one quarter of all poets waste their postage because they do not read the requirements. Also, these are too many submissions without a SASE and they go directly into the trash!"

RB'S POETS' VIEWPOINT, Box 940, Eunice NM 88231. Established 1989. **Editor:** Robert Bennett.

Magazine Needs: *RB's Poets' Viewpoint* published bimonthly, features poetry and cartoons. Wants "general and religious poetry, sonnets, and sijo with a 21-line limit." Does not want "vulgar language." Has published poetry by Marion Ford Park, Ruth Ditmer Ream, Ruth Halbrooks, and Delphine Ledoux. As a sample the editor selected these lines from "Star Fantasy" by Mary Strand:

> On the hill where Will-O-Wisps camp/I danced to the chirpings of crickets/by the glow of the lightning-bug's lamp./When the stars in their celestial thickets/beckoned me with come-hither winks/I climbed a dangling moonbeam/& skipped on heavenly rinks.

RB's Poets' Viewpoint is 34 pages, digest-sized, photocopied, saddle-stapled with drawings and cartoons. Receives about 400 poems/year, accepts about 90%. Press run is 60. Subscription: $8. Sample: $2. Make checks payable to Robert Bennett.

How to Submit: Submit 3 poems typed single space. **Reading fee:** $1.50/poem. Accepts previously published poems and simultaneous submissions. Reads submissions February, April, June, August, October, and December only. Time between acceptance and publication is 1 month. "Poems are selected by one editor." Often comments on rejected poems. Guidelines available for SASE. Responds in 1 month. Pays 1 contributor's copy. Acquires one-time rights.

Also Offers: Sponsors contests for general poetry, religious poetry, sonnets, and sijo with 1st Prizes of $20, $6, and $5, respectively, plus publication in *RB's Poets' Viewpoint*. There is a $1.50 per poem entry fee, except the sijo category, which has a 50¢ per poem fee. Guidelines available for SASE.

RE:AL—THE JOURNAL OF LIBERAL ARTS, Dept. PM, Box 13007, Stephen F. Austin State University, Nacogdoches TX 75962. (409)468-2059. Fax: (409)468-2190. E-mail: f_real@titan.sfasu.edu. Website: www.libweb.sfasu.edu/real/default.htm (includes the entire journal). Established 1968. **Editor:** W. Dale Hearell.

Magazine Needs: *RE:AL*, printed in fall and spring, is a "Liberal Arts Forum" using short fiction, reviews, criticism, and poetry and also contains editorial notes and personalized "Contributors' Notes." Aims "to use from 90 to 110 pages of poetry per issue, typeset in editor's office. *RE:AL* welcomes all styles and forms that display craft, insight, and accessibility." Accepts poetry written by children. Receives between 60-100 poems/week. "We need a better balance between open and generic forms. We're also interested in critical writings on poems or writing poetry and translations with a bilingual format (permissions from original author)." *RE:AL* is handsomely printed, "reserved format," perfect-bound with line drawings and photos. Circulation approximately 400, "more than half of which are major college libraries." Subscriptions also in Great Britain, Ireland, Italy, Holland, the Phillipines, Puerto Rico, Brazil, Croatia, and Canada. Subscription: $40 for institutions, $30 individual. Sample: $15.

How to Submit: Submit original and copy. "Editors prefer a statement that ms is not being simultaneously submitted; however, this fact is taken for granted when we receive a ms." Writer's guidelines available for SASE. *RE:AL* acknowledges receipt of submissions and strives for a 1-month decision. Submissions during summer semesters may take longer. Pays 2 contributor's copies. Reviews are assigned, but queries about doing reviews are welcome.

N M ◎ RECYCLED QUARTERLY (Specialized: previously published work only), P.O. Box 1111, Sanford FL 32772-1111. E-mail: recycledquarterly@yahoo.com. Established 2001. **Editor:** Rob Carraway.

Magazine Needs: *Recycled Quarterly* is a literary magazine of previously published poetry, "especially if the work has changed since first publication. No specifications as to form, length, style, subject matter, or purpose. We prefer work under one page." *Recycled Quarterly* is 30-72 pages, digest-sized, laser-printed on recycled paper, saddle-stapled, glossy cover stock. Press run is 300 for 50 subscribers of which 50 are shelf sales; 200 are distributed free to general public. Single copy: $3; subscription: $10/year. Sample: $3. Make checks payable to *Recycled Quarterly*.

How to Submit: Submit 3-5 poems at a time. Accepts previously published poems. Accepts disk submissions; no fax or e-mail submissions. Cover letter is required. "We require proof of previous publication." Reads submissions all year. Time between acceptance and publication is 6-12 months. Often comments on rejected poems. Occasionally publishes theme issues. List of upcoming themes and guidelines available for SASE or by e-mail. Responds in 3 months. Sometimes sends prepublication galleys. Pays 1 contributor's copy.

◐ RED BOOTH REVIEW; RED BOOTH CHAPBOOKS, Owen House, JHU, 3400 N. Charles St., Baltimore MD 21218. (410)516-7545. E-mail: rbr@wtp62.com. Website: http://wtp62.com/rbr.htm (includes archive, current issue, guidelines). Established 1998. **Contact:** W. T. Pfefferle.

Magazine Needs: *Red Booth Review* appears 3 times/year online, 1 time/year in print. Publishes "best poetry we see, moving poems about driving, meagre love, compact and focused." Recently published poetry by John Hicks, David McNaron, and Roy Schwartzman. As a sample, the editor selected these lines by Beau Boudreaux:

> a woman approaches/who I'd shared a booth, a pitcher/in college, her touch was like an ice/cube sliding the length of your sleeve./This woman called me angel./I could not introduce her/for the life of me.

Red Booth Review is 64 pages, digest-sized, digitally-printed, perfect-bound, slick cover, with some art/graphics. Receives about 700 poems/year, accepts about 5%. Publishes about 10 poems/issue online, about 40 in print. Press run is 250 for 30 subscribers; 220 are distributed free to writers and editors. E-mail editor for sample copy prices.

How to Submit: Submit 5 poems at a time. Accepts simultaneous submissions; no previously published poems. No postal mail submissions; accepts e-mail submissions only (as attachment or in text box). Cover letter is preferred. Reads submissions all year. Time between acceptance and publication is 1 week. Usually one editor and one guest editor select poems. Often comments on rejected poems. Guidelines are available on website. Responds in 1 week. Pays 1 contributor's copy. Acquires first North American serial rights; rights revert to author upon publication.

Book/Chapbook Needs & How to Submit: Red Booth Chapbooks prefers moving and compact poetry. Publishes 1-2 chapbooks/year. Chapbooks are chosen through contest 2 times/year. First chapbook winner was Michael Cadnum with *The Woman Who Discovered Math*. Chapbooks are usually 30 pages, digitally-printed, saddle-stapled, slick cover, with art/graphics. Responds to queries in 1 month; to mss in 4 months. Pays winner $100 plus 30 copies of the finished chapbook. Order sample books/chapbooks from website.

🌐 ◐ THE RED CANDLE PRESS; CANDELABRUM POETRY MAGAZINE (Specialized: form/style, metrical and rhymed), Rose Cottage, Main Rd., Wishech PE13 2LR England. E-mail: rcp@poetry7.fsnet.co.uk. Website: www.members.tripod.com/redcandlepress (includes information about the press and its publications, a profiles link, guidelines, contact and subscription info, editorial policy, and a mini-anthology of poems). Established 1970. **Editor:** M.L. McCarthy, M.A.

Magazine Needs: Red Candle Press "is a formalist press, specially interested in metrical and rhymed poetry, though free verse is not excluded. We're more interested in poems than poets: that is, we're interested in what sort of poems an author produces, not in his or her personality." Publishes the magazine, *Candelabrum*, twice yearly (April and October). Wants "good-quality metrical verse, with rhymed verse specially wanted. Elegantly cadenced free verse is acceptable. Accepts 5-7-5 haiku. No weak stuff (moons and Junes, loves and doves, etc.) No chopped-up prose pretending to be free verse. Any length up to about 40 lines for *Candelabrum*, any subject, including eroticism (but not porn)—satire, love poems, nature lyrics, philosophical—any subject, but nothing racist, ageist, or sexist." Has published poetry by Pam Russell, Ryan Underwood, David Britton, Alice Evans, Jack Harvey, Nick Spargo. As a sample the editor selected these lines from a poem by Merryn Linford:

> On certain days there is a slant of light/that compensates for summer on the wane/And gilds the clear periphery of sight./It scintillates on hedgerows down the lane/where spiders weave geometries of silk/ And sunlight is uplifted on a skein.

Candelabrum is digest-sized, staple-spined, small type, exemplifies their intent to "pack in as much as possible, wasting no space, and try to keep a neat appearance with the minimum expense." Uses about 40 pages (some 70 poems) in each issue. Receives about 2,000 submissions/year, of which 10% is accepted, sometimes holds over poems for the next year. Press run is 900 for 700 subscribers of which 22 are libraries. Sample: $5 in bills only; non-sterling checks not accepted.

How to Submit: "Submit anytime. Enclose one IRC for reply only; three IRCs if you wish manuscript returned. If you'd prefer a reply by e-mail, without return of unwanted manuscript, please enclose one British first-class stamp, IRC, or U.S. dollar bill to pay for the call. Each poem on a separate sheet please, neat typescripts or neat legible manuscripts. Please no dark, oily photostats, no colored ink (only black or blue). Author's name and address on each sheet, please." No simultaneous submissions. No e-mail submissions. Guidelines available on website. Responds in about 2 months. Pays 1 contributor's copy.

Advice: "Traditional-type poetry is much more popular here in Britain, and we think also in the United States, now than it was in 1970, when we established *Candelabrum*. We always welcome new poets, especially traditionalists, and we like to hear from the U.S.A. as well as from here at home. General tip: Study the various outlets at the library, or buy a copy of *Candelabrum*, or borrow a copy from a subscriber, before you go to the expense of submitting your work. The Red Candle Press regrets that, because of bank charges, it is unable to accept dollar cheques. However, it is always happy to accept U.S. dollar bills."

● RED DANCEFLOOR PRESS; RED DANCEFLOOR, P.O. Box 4974, Lancaster CA 93539-4974. Fax: (661)726-0084. E-mail: dubpoet@as.net. Established 1989. **Editor:** David Goldschlag.

Magazine Needs & How to Submit: The press publishes the magazine, *Red Dancefloor*. However, the magazine has suspended publication until further notice.

Book Needs: Red Dancefloor Press also publishes full-length books and poetry audiotapes. No restrictions on form, length, or subject matter. Has published poetry by Sean T. Dougherty, Gerry Lafemina, Laurel Ann Bogen, Annie Reiner, Gary P. Walton, and Michael Stephans. As a sample the editor selected these lines from "Ladybugs" in *Estrogen Power* by Nancy Ryan Keeling:

> *Allergic to "pink,"/she camouflages/her exquisite figure/in layers of baggy clothes./She is content to live the/sexual life of a porcupine/testing and cataloging/feelings and emotions/because she knows/ nobody is ever pure twice.*

The editor suggests sampling a book, chapbook, or tape prior to submission. Send 5½ × 8½ SASE with first-class stamp for catalog. Sample: $10.

How to Submit: "We openly accept submissions for books and tapes, but *please* query first with ten samples and a cover letter explaining which area of our press you are interested in. Listing credits in a cover letter is fine, but don't go crazy." Accepts e-mail, disk, and fax submissions. "E-mail submissions may be embedded in the message itself or attached as ASCII, MS Word, or Wordperfect files." Queries and submissions via e-mail "strongly encouraged." Payment negotiable.

◪ $● RED DEER PRESS, Room 813, MacKimmie Library Tower, 2500 University Dr. NW, Calgary, Alberta T2N 1N4 Canada. (403)220-4334. Fax: (403)210-8191. E-mail: rdp@ucalgary.ca. Established 1975. **Poetry Editor:** Nicole Marcotic.

Book/Chapbook Needs & How to Submit: Red Deer Press publishes 1 poetry paperback per year under the imprint Writing West. Has published poetry by bill bissett, Susan Holbrook, Monty Reid, Stephen Scobie, Ian Samuels, and Nicole Marcotic. Books are usually 80-100 pages. Submit 8-10 poems at a time. Accepts simultaneous submissions. Cover letter required. "Must include SASE. Canadian poets only." Time between acceptance and publication is 6 months. Responds to queries in 6 months. Pays royalties.

● RED DRAGON PRESS, P.O. Box 19425, Alexandria VA 22320-0425. Website: www.reddragonpress.com (includes statement of purpose, guidelines for submissions, book list, order information, sample poems, book descriptions, and author biographical information). Established 1993. **Editor/Publisher:** Laura Qa.

Book/Chapbook Needs: Red Dragon Press publishes 3-4 chapbooks/year. Wants "innovative, progressive, and experimental poetry and prose using literary symbolism, and aspiring to the creation of meaningful new ideas, forms, and methods. We are proponents of works that represent the nature of man as androgynous, as in the fusing of male and female symbolism, and we support works that deal with psychological and parapsychological topics." Has published *Spectator Turns Witness* by George Karos and *The Crown of Affinity* by Laura Qa. As a sample the editor selected these lines from "Visitarte" by James Kerns:

> *Tonight the world is awake in the moon's embrace./I have turned everywhere but cannot outrun/the black shadow spreading from my feet./I like the brief side late light offers,/but I am unsure of what lies outside the beams/in the shade of things that have already been.*

Chapbooks are usually 64 pages, 8½ × 5⅜, offset-printed, perfect-bound on trade paper with 1-10 illustrations.

How to Submit: Submit up to 5 poems at a time with SASE. Accepts previously published poems and simultaneous submissions. Cover letter preferred with brief bio. **Reading fee:** $5 for poetry and short fiction, $10 for novels; check or money order payable to Red Dragon Press. Time between acceptance and publication is 8 months. Poems are circulated to an editorial board. "Poems are selected for consideration by the publisher, then circulated to senior editor and/or poets previously published for comment. Poems are returned to the publisher for further action; i.e., rejection or acceptance for publication in an anthology or book by a single author. Frequently submission of additional works is required before final offer is made, especially in the process for a book by a single author." Often comments on rejected poems. Charges criticism fee of $10 per page on request. Responds to queries in 10 weeks, to mss in 1 year. For sample books, purchase at book stores or mail order direct from Red Dragon Press at the above address.

$Ø RED HEN PRESS; RED HEN POETRY CONTEST, P.O. Box 3537, Granada Hills CA 91394. Fax: (818)831-6659. E-mail: editors@redhen.org. Website: www.redhen.org. Established 1993. **Publisher:** Mark E. Cull. **Editor:** Kate Gale.
Book/Chapbook Needs: Red Hen Press wants "good literary fiction and poetry" and publishes 10 paperbacks, one selected through a competition. "Translations are fine. No rhyming poetry." Has published poetry by Dr. Benjamin Saltman, Robert Peters, Eloise Klein Healy, and Terry Wolverton. Books are usually 64-96 pages, 5×7 or 6×9, professionally printed and perfect-bound with trade paper cover, includes paintings and photos.
How to Submit: Submit 5 poems at a time. Accepts previously published poems and simultaneous submissions. Cover letter preferred. Time between acceptance and publication is 1 year. Poems are circulated to an editorial board. "One main poetry editor plus three to four contributing editors review the work." Seldom comments on rejected poems. Responds to queries in 1 month. Pays 10% royalties and 50 author's copies. To obtain sample books "write to our address for a catalog."
Also Offers: Sponsors the Benjamin Saltman Poetry Contest for a full-length collection (46-68 pages). Deadline is October 31.
Advice: "Be willing to help promote your own book and be helpful to the press. Writers need to help small presses survive."

⊕ Ø RED HERRING, MidNAG, East View, Stakeford, Choppington, Northumberland NE62 5TR England. Phone: 01670 844240. Fax: 01670 844298. E-mail: n.baumfield@wansbeck.gov.uk. **Contact:** Nicholas Baumfield.
Magazine Needs: *Red Herring* appears 2-3 times/year and "welcomes new original poetry of all kinds." Accepts poetry written by children. Has published poetry by W.N. Herbert, Sean O'Brien, and Matthew Sweeney. As a sample they selected these lines from "Sometimes" by Tom Kelly:
> He's making his point,/stabbing his fingers/at the air, his kids, I presume,/stand near the mother,/as he
> seethes/intoning his hate, his troubles/to those he loves/sometimes.

Red Herring is 1 A3 sheet folded. Receives about 350 poems/year, accepts 15%. Press run is 3,000. "Most available free in Northumberland libraries." Single copy: £1. Make checks payable to MidNAG.
How to Submit: Submit up to 6 poems. Accepts simultaneous submissions; no previously published poems. Accepts submissions by fax or by e-mail (as attachment or in text box). "Copies preferred, as submissions cannot be returned." Time between acceptance and publication is 4 months. Poems are circulated to an editorial board. Seldom comments on rejected poems. Responds in 4 months. Pays 5 contributor's copies.

$♥ ◎ RED MOON PRESS; THE RED MOON ANTHOLOGY; AMERICAN HAIBUN & HAIGA (Specialized: form/style, haiku), P.O. Box 2461, Winchester VA 22604-1661. (540)722-2156. Fax: (708)810-8992. E-mail: redmoon@shentel.net. Established 1994, *American Haibun & Haiga* established 1999. **Editor/Publisher:** Jim Kacian.
Magazine Needs: *American Haibun & Haiga*, published annually in April, is the first western journal dedicated to these forms. *American Haibun & Haiga* is 128 pages, digest-sized, offset-printed on quality paper with heavy stock four-color cover. Receives several hundred submissions per year, accepts approximately 5%. Accepts poetry written by children. Expected print run is 1,000 for subscribers and commercial distribution. Subscription: $15 plus $3 shipping and handling. A brief sample of the form will be available for SASE or via return e-mail.
How to Submit: Submit up to 3 haibun or haiga at a time with SASE. No previously published work or simultaneous submissions. Accepts submissions by fax, on disk, by e-mail (as attachment or in text box), or by regular mail. Guidelines available for SASE, by e-mail, and in publication. Submissions will be read by editorial board. Time between acceptance and publication varies according to time of submission. Pays $1/page. Acquires first North American serial rights. "Only haibun and haiga will be considered. If the submitter is unfamiliar with the form, consult *Journey to the Interior*, edited by Bruce Ross, or previous issues of *American Haibun & Haiga*, for samples and some discussion."

Book/Chapbook Needs: Red Moon Press "is the largest and most prestigious publisher of English-language haiku and related work in the world." Publishes *The Red Moon Anthology,* an annual volume, the finest English-language haiku and related work published anywhere in the world in the previous 12 months. *The Red Moon Anthology* is 160 pages, digest-sized, offset-printed, perfect-bound, glossy 4-color heavy-stock cover. Inclusion is by nomination of the editorial board only. The press also publishes 6-8 volumes per year, usually 3-5 individual collections of English-language haiku, as well as 1-3 books of essays, translation, or criticism of haiku. As a sample the editor selected the following haiku from *a glimpse of red: The Red Moon Anthology of English-Language Haiku* by Joyce Austin Gilbert:

> *leftover drumsticks/ . . . first Christmas/without dad*

Under other imprints the press also publishes chapbooks of various sizes and formats.
How to Submit: Query with book theme and information, and 30-40 poems, or draft of first chapter. Responds to queries in 2 weeks, to mss (if invited) in 2-3 months. "Each contract separately negotiated."
Advice: "Haiku is a burgeoning and truly international form. It is nothing like what your fourth-grade teacher taught you years ago, and so it is best if you familiarize yourself with what is happening in the form (and its close relatives) today before submitting. We strive to give all the work we publish plenty of space in which to resonate, and to provide a forum where the best of today's practitioners can be published with dignity and prestige. All our books have either won awards or are awaiting notification."

☑ RED OWL MAGAZINE, 35 Hampshire Rd., Portsmouth NH 03801-4815. (603)431-2691. E-mail: RedOwlMag@juno.com. Established 1995. **Editor:** Edward O. Knowlton.
Magazine Needs: *Red Owl* is a biannual magazine of poetry and b&w art published in the spring and fall. "Ideally, poetry here might stress a harmony between nature and industry; add a pinch of humor for spice. Nothing introspective or downtrodden. Sometimes long poems are OK, yet poems which are 10 to 20 lines seem to fit best." Also open to poems on the subjects of animals, gay/lesbian issues, horror, psychic/occult, nature/ecology, science fiction/fantasy, and women/feminism. Has published poetry by Irene Carlson, Rod Farmer, Giovanni Malito, Robert Donald Spector, Gerald R. Wheeler, and Gerald Zipper. As a sample the editor selected these lines from "Night Eye" by Nancy McGovern:

> *colors shifting to mute tones/as though the skull of earth/held a candle within whose/wax draws sunfire to/illuminate the center/and glow in the moon.*

Red Owl is about 70 pages, 8½×11, neatly photocopied in a variety of type styles and spiral-bound with a heavy stock cover and b&w art inside. "Out of a few hundred poems received, roughly one third are considered." Single copy: $10; subscription: $20. Sample (including brief guidelines): $10 includes shipping and handling. Make checks payable to Edward O. Knowlton.
How to Submit: Submit 4 poems at a time. No previously published poems or simultaneous submissions. Accepts e-mail submissions. "Submit in the spring for the fall issue—and vice versa." Cover letter preferred. "Relay cover letter and each poem separately. I mostly use the 'Net to answer questions; this isn't the best home for 'noetics' or 'noetry.' I'd prefer to receive the submissions I get via the U.S.P.S. since I feel it's more formal—and I'm not in that big of a hurry, nor do I feel that this world has reached a conclusion. . . ." Seldom comments on rejected poems. Guidelines available in publication. Responds in up to 3 months. Pays 1 contributor's copy.
Advice: "Try and be bright; hold your head up. Yes, there are hard times in the land of plenty, yet we might try to overshadow them. . . ."

Ⓝ ☑ RED RAMPAN' PRESS; RED RAMPAN' REVIEW; RED RAMPAN' BROADSIDE SE-RIES, Bishop House, 518 East Court St., Dyersburg TN 38024-4714. Established 1981. **Poetry Editor:** Larry D. Griffin. Presently not accepting poetry.

☑ RED RIVER REVIEW, E-mail: Editor@RedRiverReview.com. Website: www.RedRiverReview.com. Established 1999. **Editor:** Bob McCranie.
Magazine Needs: "Published quarterly, *Red River Review* is a fully electronic literary journal. Our purpose is to publish quality poetry using the latest technology. *Red River* is a journal for poets who have studied the craft of writing and for readers who enjoy being stirred by language." Wants "poetry which speaks to the human experience in a unique and accessible way. No rhyming poetry or poetry that is annoyingly obscure." Has published poetry by Marin Sorescu, Padi Harman, Barbara F. Lefcowitz, Deborah DeNicola, Ed Madden, and Jeanne P. Donovan. As a sample the editor selected this poem, "This Day" by Meghan Ehrlich:

> *This is a day to wear./Grackles whistle and click in the leaves,/damp plaid flannel shirts salute, flap from balconies,/fragrant green horse-apples molder underfoot./I lay out my laundry, too, like an offering,/like a sponge. I will keep this sun in my closet/and wear it often.*

Receives about 750 poems/year, accepts about 25%.
How to Submit: Submit 4-6 poems at a time. No previously published poems or simultaneous submissions. Cover letter preferred. Electronic submissions only. Time between acceptance and publication is 3 months.

Often comments on rejected poems. Guidelines available on website. Responds in 3 months. Sometimes sends prepublication galleys. Acquires first rights and anthology rights, "if we want to do a *Red River Review Anthology*." For address and query information e-mail Editor@RedRiverReview.com.

Advice: "Write about who you are and who we are in the world. Read other writers as much as possible."

RED ROCK REVIEW; RED ROCK POETRY AWARD, English Dept. J2A, Community College of Southern Nevada, 3200 E. Cheyenne Ave., North Las Vegas NV 89030. (702)651-4094. Fax: (702)651-4639. E-mail: richard_logsdon@ccsn.nevada.edu. Website: www.ccsn.nevada.edu/english/redrockreview/index.html (includes samples from current issue, guidelines, contact and subscription information, bios, editorial policy, and contest information). Established 1994. **Editor-in-Chief:** Dr. Rich Logsdon. **Associate Editor:** Todd Moffett.

Magazine Needs: *Red Rock Review* appears biannually in May and December and publishes "the best poetry available." Also publishes fiction, creative nonfiction, and book reviews. Has published poetry by Dorianne Laux, Kim Addonizio, Ellen Bass, Cynthis Hogue, and Dianne di Prima. As a sample the editors selected these lines (poet unidentified):

> Oil paint, I've read/never completely dries./The breasts of Venus droop./Mona Lisa finally drops the smile./Glass, I've heard, is a liquid./Windows silently slide at night,/a slow motion sink, always/toward the floor, Christ ascending

Red Rock Review is about 130 pages, magazine-sized, professionally printed and perfect-bound with 10 pt. cornwall, C1S cover. Accepts about 15% of poems received/year. Press run is 1,000. Sample: $5.50.

How to Submit: Submit 2-3 poems at a time, "mailed flat, not folded, into a letter sized envelope." Line length for poetry is 80 maximum. Accepts simultaneous submissions; no previously published poems. Accepts e-mail (in body of message) and disk submissions. Cover letter with SASE required. Do not submit mss June 1 through August 31. Time between acceptance and publication is 3 months. Poems are circulated to an editorial board. "Poems go to poetry editor, who then distributes them to three readers." Seldom comments on rejected poems. Guidelines available for SASE or on website. Responds in 2 months. Pays 2 contributor's copies. Acquires first North American serial rights. Reviews books and chapbooks of poetry in 500-1,000 words, multi-book format. Poets may send books for review consideration.

Also Offers: Sponsors the annual Red Rock Poetry Award. Winner receives $500 plus publication in the *Red Rock Review*. Submit up to 3 poems of not more than 20 lines each, typed on 8½ × 11 white paper. Reading fee: $6/entry (3 poems). Deadline: October 31. Complete rules available for SASE.

RED WHEELBARROW, De Anza College, 21250 Stevens Creek Blvd., Cupertino CA 95014. (408)864-8600. E-mail: SplitterRandolph@fhda.edu. Website: www.deanza.fhda.edu/RedWheelbarrow. Established 1976. **Editor:** Randolph Splitter.

• "Note: We are not affiliated with Red Wheelbarrow Press or any similarly named publication."

Magazine Needs: This college-produced magazine appears annually in late spring/early summer. *Red Wheelbarrow* has published poetry by Steve Fellner, Nola Perez, Virgil Suarez, Al Young, and Walter Griffin. As a sample the editor selected these lines from "After Watching George Romero's *The Night of the Living Dead*" by Steve Fellner:

> Only now (as I approach sixty) do I appreciate/the zombies' slow shuffle, their refusal to hurry/someone else's death. Human flesh should be considered/a delicacy. Something to be savored. Like créme brulée/and Mel Torme albums.

Bottomfish is 100 pages, 6×9, well-printed on heavy stock with b&w graphics, perfect-bound. Press run is 500. Single copy: $5.

How to Submit: Submit 3-5 poems at a time. "Before submitting, writers are strongly urged to purchase a sample copy." Accepts e-mail submissions. Best submission times: September through December. Annual deadline: December 31. Responds in up to 6 months, depending on backlog. Include SASE for reply. "We cannot return manuscripts." Pays 2 contributor's copies.

THE REDNECK REVIEW, an online poetry journal (Specialized: regional/Southern literary tradition), PMB 167, 931 Monroe Dr. NE, Suite 102, Atlanta GA 30308-1778. E-mail: editor@redneckreview.com. Website: www.redneckreview.com (includes journal content). Established 2000. **Editor:** Penya Sandor.

Magazine Needs: *The Redneck Review* is a biannual online poetry journal "born out of the rich literary tradition of the South. We are looking for writing that is interesting, has energy, and doesn't feel like homework." Recently published poetry by Denise Duhamel, Marie Howe, Walt McDonald, Hal Sirowitz, Ben Satterfield, and Jean Trounstine. As a sample the editor selected these lines from "Differently-Abled Barbies" (reprinted from *Kinky*, Orchises Press 1997) by Denise Duhamel:

> *In Chicago, a Barbie/loses her arm. Only the boy next door knows he has taken it/to use as a toothpick.*
> *A little girl/refuses to throw that Barbie away/and knots her doll's right sleeve/that hangs limp like a*
> *sail on a breeze-less day.*

The Redneck Review is published online. Publishes about 15-20 poems/issue.

How to Submit: Submit no more than 5 poems at a time. Accepts previously published poems and simultaneous submissions. Accepts e-mail and disk submissions; no fax submissions. Cover letter is preferred. "If mailing submissions, include SASE unless you have an e-mail address. Poems won't be returned." Time between acceptance and publication "depends. *I* read the poems." Often comments on rejected poems. Guidelines available on website. Response time varies. Sometimes sends prepublication galleys. No payment. "Authors retain rights, but we ask they mention our journal if they publish the poem again." Poets may send books for review consideration to *The Redneck Review.*

Advice: "There are many respectable literary journals that publish well written but dull writing. We would prefer to read literature that is electric, not just technically well crafted."

N ◐ ◎ REFLECT (Specialized: form/style), 1317-D Eagles Trace Path, Chesapeake VA 23320. Established 1979. **Poetry Editor:** W.S. Kennedy. **Assistant Editor:** Clara Holton.

Magazine Needs: Uses "spiral poetry: featuring an inner-directed concern with sound (euphony), mystical references or overtones, and objectivity—rather than personal and emotional poems. No love poems, pornography, far left propaganda; nothing overly sentimental." Has published poetry by Marikay Brown, H.F. Noyes, Joe Malone, Ruth Wildes Schuler, and Joan Payne Kincaid. As a sample the editor selected these lines from "April Sashays in Lime Heels" by Edward C. Lynskey:

> *April sashays across ashy mews,/in lime heels and lilac breath,/swells sappy stalks, and shoos/winter*
> *north, the killing guest.//Hyacinths blush and daffodils/blink as a wisp of apple smoke/curlicues through*
> *screens until/kale yards wakes in a rainy soak.*

The quarterly is 48 pages, digest-sized, saddle-stapled, typescript. Subscription: $8. Sample: $2.

How to Submit: Submit 4 or 5 poems at a time. All submissions should be single-spaced and should fit on one typed page. No previously published poems or simultaneous submissions. Sometimes comments on rejected poems. Issue deadlines: fall—9/12 for 10/15 publication; winter—12/12 for 1/15 publication; spring—3/12 for 4/15 publication; summer—6/12 for 7/15 publication. Guidelines available for SASE. Responds within a month. Pays 1 copy to nonsubscribers, 2 copies to subscribing contributors. Acquires first rights.

N ◐ THE "REJECTION NOTICE" ZINE, 231 E. 22nd St., Paterson NJ 07514-2109. (973)279-7610. E-mail: pheekuh@aol.com. Established 1993. **Editor:** Ron Emolo.

Magazine Needs: *The "Rejection Notice" Zine* wants "any" kind of poetry. Recently published poetry by Joe Verilli, Ana Christy, Dan Buck, and Mark Sonnenfeld. As a sample the editor selected these lines from "John Kurluk Still Ever/Barks" by Dan Buck:

> *In the tallest, highest tree of a socially lonely forest, John branches out, gaining leaf by leaf, till a*
> *giving hooted owl darkly lights and clearly drops him partially limbed.*

"*Rejection Notice*" is 4-8 pages, magazine-sized, photocopied, stapled, with drawings on cover. Receives about 100 poems/year, accepts about 5%. Publishes about 5 poems/year. Press run is 80 copies distributed free to all.

How to Submit: Submit any number of poems. Accepts previously published poems and simultaneous submissions. No fax, e-mail, or disk submissions. Cover letter preferred. Include SASE. Reads submissions anytime. Time between acceptance and publication is 4-6 weeks. "I enjoy unusual poems. Anything different. I publish what moves me. Also, I'm looking for experimental poems." Never comments on rejected poems. Guidelines available for SASE. Responds in 3 weeks. "Authors responsible for copywriting their work." Poets may send books for review consideration to "*Rejection Notice*" *Zine*.

Advice: "I will work with young and new writers, if they ask."

◐ RENAISSANCE ONLINE MAGAZINE, P.O. Box 3246, Pawtucket RI 02861. E-mail: submit@renaissancemag.com. Website: www.renaissancemag.com (contains entire magazine as well as archives, guidelines, and contact information). Established 1996. **Editor:** Kevin Ridolfi. E-mail submissions only.

Magazine Needs: "Updated monthly, *Renaissance Online* strives to bring diversity and thought-provoking writing to an audience that usually settles for so much less. Poetry should reveal a strong emotion and be able to elicit a response from the reader. No nursery rhymes or profane works." Accepts poetry written by teenagers "but still must meet the same standard as adults." Has published poetry by Kevin Larimer, Josh May, and Gary Meadows. As a sample the editor selected these lines from "Dasein" by David Hunter Sutherland:

> *What can't be held send/into sleep, into turn by gentle turn/if ring worn age, covetable grace/beauty,*
> *sadness and you spread/over this air-woven awning of clouds/to defy life's strange author*

Receives about 60 poems/year, accepts about 50%.

How to Submit: Submit 3 poems at a time. Does not accept previously published poems or simultaneous submissions. Accepts only e-mail submissions (in text box). "We prefer e-mail submissions, include in body of message. Cover letter preferred. *Renaissance Online Magazine* is only published online and likes to see potential writers read previous works before submitting." Time between acceptance and publication is 3 months. Poems are circulated to an editorial board. "Poems are read by the editor, when difficult acceptance decisions need to be reached, the editorial staff is asked for comments." Often comments on rejected poems. Occasionally publishes theme issues. Guidelines available for SASE or on website. Responds in 2 months. Acquires all online publishing rights. Reviews books of poetry.

⊕ $⊚ RENDITIONS: A CHINESE-ENGLISH TRANSLATION MAGAZINE (Specialized: translations), Research Center for Translation, CUHK, Shatin, NT, Hong Kong. Phone: 852-2609-7399. Fax: 852-2603-5110. E-mail: renditions@cuhk.edu.hk. Website: www.renditions.org (includes information on *Renditions* magazine and the Research Centre for Translation, ordering information for paperbacks, books, and forthcoming issues of *Renditions*, links to related sites, authors' and translators' indexes, contact information, and sample translations). **Editor:** Dr. Eva Hung.
Magazine Needs: *Renditions* appears twice/year in May and November. "Contents exclusively translations from Chinese, ancient and modern." Also publishes a paperback series of Chinese literature in English translation. Has published translations of the poetry of Yang Lian, Gu Cheng, Shu Ting, Mang Ke, and Bei Dao. *Renditions* is about 150 pages, magazine-sized, elegantly printed, perfect-bound, all poetry with side-by-side Chinese and English texts, using some b&w and color drawings and photos, with glossy 4-color card cover. Annual subscription: $28/1 year; $45/2 years: $62/3 years. Single copy: $17.
How to Submit: Accepts e-mail and fax submissions. "Chinese originals should be sent by regular mail because of formatting problems. Include 2 copies each of the English translation and the Chinese text to facilitate referencing." Publishes theme issues. Guidelines and upcoming themes available on website. Responds in 2 months. Pays "honorarium" plus 2 contributor's copies. Use British spelling. "Will consider" book mss. Query with sample translations. Submissions should be accompanied by Chinese originals. Books pay 10% royalties plus 10 copies. Mss usually not returned. Editor sometimes comments on rejected translations.

⊘ RE:VERSE! A JOURNAL IN POETRY; RE:PRINT! PUBLISHING COMPANY, P.O. Box 8518, Erie PA 16505. E-mail: reverse@email.com. Website: www.geocities.com/reversepoetry (contains an overview of the contents, sample work from recent artists, guidelines, and a "writer's workshop" section as a poet's resource). Established 1999. **Editor:** Eric Grignol.
Magazine Needs: "*Re:Verse!* is a yearly anthology of contemporary literary poetry from American artists. We are committed to putting moving written experiences in the hands of the reading public. As the world moves into a new century, we call for a time when the American people enjoyed poetry and felt a part of the experience. We are looking for literary poetry—taut writing, which is free from affectation. Open to all forms and styles of poems; steer clear of excessively long poems. Some themes we are interested in are healing and renewal, the extraordinary in the everyday, struggles with dichotomous situations, serious explorations of social issues—but do not limit yourself to this list! No pornographic, demeaning, or vulgar poems." As a sample the editor selected "Construction Accident" by Larry Shug:

> He'd been workin'/demolition sites/since Jericho;/thought he knew/all about/tumblin' walls./But you
> know/them demo sites,/so noisy sometimes/you can't hear/a trumpet blow./

Re:Verse! is 90 pages, 5½×8½, offset-printed and perfect-bound with 2-color cardstock cover, includes line illustrations and some photos. Receives about 12,000 poems/year, accepts about 10%. Publishes 65-70 poems/issue. Press run varies according to demand. Single copy: $9.99. Sample: $6. Make checks payable to Re:Print! Publishing.
How to Submit: Submit 5 poems at a time. Accepts previously published poems and simultaneous submissions, "but both must be noted as such on cover letter." Cover letter preferred. "Due to the high volume of submissions received and our small staff, we will now only reply to accepted submissions. Do not send SASE. Enclose a manuscript that can be recycled. If we like what we see, you'll be contacted as soon as possible." Name and address atop each page, please. Has a "revolving door approach to submissions. We review them constantly up to the point when this year's issue is full. After that point, all subsequent submissions are considered for next year's volume. So your best chance of getting in is by submitting early." Time between acceptance and publication is up to 1 year. Occasionally publishes theme issues. Guidelines and upcoming themes available for SASE or on website. Responds in 5 months. Always sends prepublication galleys. Pays 1 contributor's copy. Acquires one-time rights.
Also Offers: "We are working on a companion volume to *Re:Verse!* which is intended to act as a workshop, or textbook so to speak, for poets looking to strengthen their craft by analysis of contemporary poetic works, poetry history, writing exercises and editors' comments. Contact us for details on this."
Advice: "Read constantly, explore your piece of the world, observe intently, write every day, revise your work unceasingly!"

◎ **REVISTA/REVIEW INTERAMERICANA (Specialized: ethnic, regional)**, Inter-American University of Puerto Rico, Box 5100, San Germán, Puerto Rico 00683. Phone: (787)264-1912, ext. 7229 or 7230. Fax: (787)892-6350. E-mail: reinter@sg.inter.edu. **Editor:** Anibal José Aponte.

Magazine Needs: Published online, *Revista/Review* is a bilingual scholarly journal oriented to Puerto Rican, Caribbean, and Hispanic American and inter-American subjects, poetry, short stories, and reviews.

How to Submit: Submit at least 5 poems, but no more than 7, in Spanish or English, blank verse, free verse, experimental, traditional, or avant-garde, typed exactly as you want them to appear in publication. Name should not appear on the poems, only the cover letter. No simultaneous submissions. Accepts fax and e-mail submissions. Cover letter with brief personal data required.

N ◎ RFD: A COUNTRY JOURNAL FOR GAY MEN EVERYWHERE (Specialized: gay), P.O. Box 68, Liberty TN 37095. (615)536-5176. E-mail: mail@rfdmag.org. Website: www.rfdmag.org. Established 1974. **Contact:** Poetry Editor.

Magazine Needs: *RFD* "is a quarterly for gay men with emphasis on lifestyles outside of the gay mainstream—poetry, politics, profiles, letters." Wants poetry that "illuminates the uniqueness of the gay experience. Themes that will be given special consideration are those that explore the rural gay experience, the gay perspective on social and political change, and explorations of the surprises and mysteries of relationships." Has published poetry by Antler, James Broughton, Gregory Woods and Winthrop Smith. *RFD* has a circulation of 3,000 for 700 subscribers. Single copy: $7.75; subscription: $37 first class, $25 second class. Sample: $7.75.

How to Submit: Submit up to 5 poems at a time. Accepts simultaneous submissions. Send SASE for guidelines or obtain via website. Editor sometimes comments on rejected poems. Responds in up to 9 months. Pays 1 copy. Open to unsolicited reviews.

Advice: "*RFD* looks for interesting thoughts, succinct use of language and imagery evocative of nature and gay men and love in natural settings."

⬥ ◻ **RHINO**, P.O. Box 591, Evanston IL 60204. Website: www.rhinopoetry.org (includes guidelines, ordering info, table of contents and excerpts from current issue, literary challenges and a schedule of Chicago and Illinois workshops, events, and literary links). Established 1976. **Editors:** Deborah Rosen, Alice George, Kathleen Kirk, and Helen Degen Cohen.

• "*RHINO* recently won three Illinois Arts Council Literary Awards."

Magazine Needs: *RHINO* "is an annual poetry journal, appearing in March, which also includes short-shorts and occasional essays on poetry. Translations welcome. The editors delight in work which reflects the author's passion, originality, and artistic conviction. We also welcome experiments with poetic form, sophisticated wit, and a love affair with language. Prefer poems under 100 lines." Has published poetry by Maureen Seaton, James McManus, Floyd Skoot, Lucia Getsi, and Richard Jones. *RHINO* is 100 pages, digest-sized, card cover with art, on high-quality paper. Receives 1,500 submissions/year, accepts 60-80. Press run is 1,000. Single copy: $10. Sample: $7.

How to Submit: Submit 3-5 poems with SASE. Accepts simultaneous submissions with notification; no previously published submissions. Submissions are accepted April 1 through October 1. Guidelines available for SASE or on website. Responds in up to 6 months. Pays 2 contributor's copies. Acquires first rights only.

🌐 **$ ◻ THE RIALTO**, P.O. Box 309, Alysham, Norwich, Norfolk NR11 6LN England. Website: www.therialto.co.uk (includes guidelines, contact information, subscription information, contest rules). Established 1984. **Editor:** Michael Mackmin.

Magazine Needs: *The Rialto* appears 3 times/year and "seeks to publish the best new poems by established and beginning poets. *The Rialto* seeks excellence and originality." Has published poetry by Simon Armitage, Thomas Lux, Brendan Kennelly, Selima Hill, Penelope Shuttle, George Szirtes, Philip Gross, and Ruth Padel. *The Rialto* is 56 pages, A4 with full color cover, occasionally includes art/graphics. Receives about 12,000 poems/year, accepts about 1%. Publishes 50 poems/issue. Press run is 1,500 for 1,000 subscribers of which 50 are libraries. Subscription: £16. Sample: £6. Make checks payable to *The Rialto*. "Checks in sterling only please."

How to Submit: Submit 6 poems at a time. Accepts simultaneous submissions; no previously published poems. Cover letter preferred. "SASE or SAEs with IRCs essential. U.S. readers please note that U.S. postage stamps are invalid in U.K." Time between acceptance and publication is up to 4 months. Seldom comments on rejected poems. Responds in up to 4 months. "A large number of poems arrive every week, so please note that you will have to wait at least 10 weeks for yours to be read." Pays £20/poem. Poet retains rights.

Also Offers: "*The Rialto* has recently commenced publishing first collections by poets. Andrew Waterhouse's book *In* won the 2000 Forward/Whetherstone's Best First Collection prize. Please *do not* send book length manuscripts. Write first enquiring." Sponsors an annual young poets competition as well. Details available on website and in publication.

Advice: "It is a good idea to read the magazine before submitting to check if you write our kind of poem."

RIO: A JOURNAL OF THE ARTS, P.O. Box 165, Port Jefferson NY 11777. E-mail: rioarts@angelfire.com. Website: www.engl.uic.edu/rio/rio.html and www.rioarts.com. Established 1997. **Editors:** Cynthia Davidson, Susan Pilewski, Wilbur Farley, and Gail Lukasik.

Magazine Needs: *Rio* is a biannual online journal containing "poetry, short fiction, creative nonfiction, scannable artwork/photography, and book reviews. Query for anything else." Wants poetry of any length or form. "Experiments encouraged with voice, image, or language. No greeting card verse or sentimentality." Has published poetry by Michael Anania, Liviu Ioan Stoiciu, Eleni Fourtourni, Michael Waters, Terry Wright, Ralph Mills, Jr., David Shevin, and Briar Wood. As a sample the editors selected these lines from "XI. The Sun Has Wings" by Roberta Gould:

> Each worm in the cabbage/is joyous/Each saw-toothed form/smiles freely/Even the question mark
> shimmers/flexed to new functions

Accepts about 20% of poems received/year. Back issues are available on the website.

How to Submit: Submit 5-8 poems at a time. Accepts previously published poems and simultaneous submissions "as long as you inform us of publication elsewhere." Accepts e-mail and disk submissions. "For electronic submissions, use text (ASCII) or Macintosh attachments, or e-mail submissions in body of e-mail message." Cover letter preferred. "Unaccepted entries without the SASE will be discarded." Time between acceptance and publication is 6 months. Sometimes comments on rejected poems. Guidelines available website. Responds in up to 6 months. Acquires all rights. Rights revert to authors immediately upon publication. Reviews books and chapbooks of poetry in 500-1,200 words, single book format. Send books for review consideration.

Advice: "We're looking for writers who do not fall into an easy category or niche."

RISING, 80 Cazenove Rd., Stoke Newington, London N16 6AA England. E-mail: timmywells@hotmail.com. Established 1995. **Editor:** Tim Wells.

Magazine Needs: *Rising* is a "quarterly-ish journal of poetry." Wants "short, pithy work, preferably nonrhyming; epigrams; analogies. No animals, fluffy, lazy, rhyming, anything that has 'like a . . .' in it and *no* simile!!!" Has published poetry by Salena Saliva, Francesca Beard, Cheryl B, Sean O'Brien, Gerald Locklin, and Tim Turnbull. As a sample we selected these lines from "Go Tell It to the Spartans" by Ivan Penaluna:

> It was once said by a lady friend/that I have the kind of smile that would foreshadow a nearby mailbox
> exploding/whereas the lads at the Post Office just said;//You're an anarchist aren't you?

Rising is 28 pages, A5, photocopied and saddle-stapled, colored card cover, includes b&w graphics. Receives about 300 poems/year, accepts 5%. Press run is 500 for 30 subscribers, 100 shelf sales. Sample: $3.

How to Submit: Submit 5 poems at a time. Line length for poetry is 60 maximum. Accepts previously published poems and simultaneous submissions. Accepts e-mail submissions. Cover letter required. Time between acceptance and publication is 6 months. Poems are circulated to an editorial board. "If I like it, it's in. If I'm not sure, I consult others who work on *Rising*." Seldom comments on rejected poems. Occasionally publishes theme issues. Responds in 1 month. Pays 1 contributor's copy.

Advice: "Read a copy first—don't waste our time or yours with pony poems."

$ RIVELIN GRAPHEME PRESS, Merlin House, Church St., Hungerford, Berkshire RG17 0JG England. Established 1984. **Poetry Editor:** Snowdon Barnett, D.F.A.

Book/Chapbook Needs & How to Submit: Rivelin Grapheme Press publishes only poetry. Query first with biographical information, previous publications, and a photo, if possible. If invited, send book-length manuscript, typed, double-spaced, photocopy OK. Payment is 20 copies of first printing up to 2,000, then 5% royalties on subsequent printings.

RIVER CITY (Specialized: themes), English Dept., University of Memphis, Memphis TN 38152. (901)678-4591. Fax: (901)678-2226. E-mail: rivercity@memphis.edu. Website: www.people.memphis.edu/~rivercity (includes subscription and contest info, guidelines, samples from previous issue, and contact info). Established 1980. **Editor:** Dr. Mary Leader.

Magazine Needs: *River City* appears biannually (winter and summer) and publishes fiction, poetry, interviews, and essays. Has published poetry by Marvin Bell, Maxine Kumin, Jane Hirshfield, Terrance Hayes, Paisley Rekaal, S. Beth Bishop, and Virgil Suarez. *River City* is 160 pages, 7 × 10, perfect-bound, professionally printed with 4-color glossy cover. Publishes 40-50 pages of poetry/issue. Subscription: $12. Sample: $7. Press run is 2,000.

How to Submit: Submit no more than 5 poems at a time with SASE. Accepts submissions by e-mail (as attachment). Include SASE. Does not read mss June through August. Publishes theme issues. Themes will be posted on website 6-8 months prior to deadline. Also available by e-mail and in publication. Guidelines available for SASE and by e-mail. Responds in up to 3 months. Pays 2 contributor's copies.

$⬛ RIVER CITY PUBLISHING, (formerly Black Belt Press), 1719 Mulberry St., Montgomery AL 36106. E-mail: sales@riverpublishing.com. Website: www.rivercitypublishing.com. Established 1989. **Editor:** Jim Davis. **Contact:** Staff Editor.

Book/Chapbook Needs: "We publish serious or academic poetry; no religious, romantic, or novelty material. We are not a good market for inexperienced authors." Publishes 1-3 poetry hardbacks/year. Has published *Prepositional Heaven* by Thomas Rabbitt, *White for Harvest*, by Jeanie Thompson, *The Map That Lies Between Us* by Anne George, *Blue Angels* by Peter Huggins, *Haiku: The Travelers of Eternity* by Charles Ghigna, and *Enemies of the State* by Thomas Rabbitt.

How to Submit: "Experienced poets should submit high-quality collections of at least forty poems." Most mss selected by nationally known poet, others by staff. Responds in several weeks. "E-mail submissions are permitted but not encouraged." Guidelines available for SASE, by fax, by e-mail, and on website. Pays industry-standard royalties and author's copies.

Also Offers: "We can manufacture paperback books. We accept suitable poetry projects from authors interested in partially or totally financing the project. Contact the Staff Editor for more information."

N ⬛ RIVER KING POETRY SUPPLEMENT, P.O. Box 122, Freeburg IL 62243. (618)234-5082. Fax: (618)355-9298. E-mail: riverkng@icss.net. Established 1995. **Editors:** Wayne Lanter, Donna Biffar, Phil Miller.

Magazine Needs: *River King Poetry Supplement*, published biannually in August and February, features "all poetry with commentary about poetry." Wants "serious poetry." Does not want inspirational or prose poetry and no prose cut into short lines. Has published poetry by Alan Catlin, R.G. Bishop, Phil Dacey, John Knoepfle, P.F. Allen, David Ray, and Lyn Lifshin. *River King* is 8-12 pages, tabloid-sized, press printed, folded with line art. Receives about 6,000 poems/year, accepts approximately 2%. Press run is 5,000 of which 600 are for libraries.

How to Submit: Submit 3-6 poems at a time. No simultaneous submissions or previously published poems. Accepts fax and e-mail submissions. Cover letter preferred. Time between acceptance and publication is up to 6 months. Often comments on rejected poems. Responds in 1 month. Pays 10 copies.

⬛ $⬛ RIVER STYX MAGAZINE; BIG RIVER ASSOCIATION, 634 N. Grand Ave., 12th Floor, St. Louis MO 63103. Website: www.riverstyx.org (includes guidelines, contact information, editorial policy, contest rules, subscription info, links, samples from current and recent issues, "ask the editor" section, and calendar of upcoming themes and events). Established 1975. **Editor:** Richard Newman. **Managing Editor:** Carrie Robb.

● Poetry published in *River Styx* has been selected for inclusion in past volumes of *The Best American Poetry* and *Pushcart Prize* anthologies.

Magazine Needs: *River Styx*, published 3 times/year (April, August, December), is "an international, multicultural journal publishing both award-winning and previously undiscovered writers. We feature poetry, short fiction, essays, interviews, fine art and photography." Wants "excellent poetry—original, energetic, musical and accessible. Please don't send us chopped prose or opaque poetry that isn't about anything." Has published work by Louis Simpson, Molly Peacock, David Kirby, Marilyn Hacker, Timothy Liu, and Lucia Perillo. As a sample the editor selected these lines from "The Dismal Science" by Donald Finkel:

VISIT THE WRITER'S DIGEST WEBSITE at www.writersdigest.com for books, markets, newsletter sign-up, and a special poetry page.

> *He could pick up an epic this morning/from the take-away rack at the local supermarket./All over the city young men are scribbling, scribbling,/and old women, and schoolchildren, and several chimpanzees.//The young man persists in his kitchen, parboiling a dithyramb/while the sows go farrowing on in Iowa./Welcome to the eleventh plague: plenty.*

River Styx is 100 pages, 6×9, professionally printed on coated stock, perfect-bound with color cover and b&w art, photographs, and ads. Receives about 8,000 poems/year, accepts 60-75. Press run is 2,500 for 1,000 subscribers of which 80 are libraries. Sample: $7.

How to Submit: Submit 3-5 poems at a time, "legible copies with name and address on each page." Time between acceptance and publication is within 1 year. Reads submissions May 1 through November 30 only. Publishes theme issues. Guidelines available for SASE or on website. Editor sometimes comments on rejected poems. Responds in up to 5 months. Pays 2 contributor's copies plus 1-year subscription plus $15/page if funds available. Acquires one-time rights.

Also Offers: Sponsors annual poetry contest. Past judges include Ellen Bryant Voigt, Marilyn Hacker, Philip Levine, Mark Doty, Naomi Shihab Nye, Billy Collins, and Molly Peacock. Deadline: May 31. Guidelines available for SASE.

RIVERSTONE, A PRESS FOR POETRY; RIVERSTONE POETRY CHAPBOOK AWARD, P.O. Box 1421, Carefree AZ 85377. Established 1992. **Contact:** Editor.

Book/Chapbook Needs: Riverstone publishes 1 perfect-bound chapbook/year through an annual contest. Has published chapbooks by Jefferson Carter, Marcia Hurlow, Margo Stever, Cathleen Calbert, Anita Barrows, and G. Timothy Gordan. As a sample the editor selected these lines by Martha Modena Vertreace:

> *With vertical loops/the Ferris wheel weds Navy Pier to clouds/as if the resurrection were not enough/to tether poor humans to shifting Earth./So whose permission/do I need to know your holy body?*

That's from "Creating Space with Light" in *Dragon Lady: Tsukimi*, which won the 1999 Riverstone Poetry Chapbook Award. The year 2000 winner was G. Timothy Gordon's *Everything Speaking Chinese*, which is 44 pages, digest-sized, attractively printed on 80 lb. paper and perfect-bound with spruce green endleaves and a stippled beige card stock cover.

How to Submit: To be considered for the contest, submit $8 entry fee and chapbook ms of 24-36 pages, "including poems in their proposed arrangement, title page, contents, and acknowledgments. All styles welcome." Accepts previously published poems, multiple entries, and simultaneous submissions. Include 6×9 SASE or larger for notification and copy of last year's chapbook. No further guidelines than what appears here. Contest deadline: June 30 postmark. Winner receives publication, 50 author's copies, and a cash prize of $100. Sample: $5.

RIVERWIND (Specialized: Regional), 312 Oakley Hall, Hocking College, Nelsonville OH 45764. (740)753-3591, ext. 2363. Established 1976. **Contact:** Demi Naffzigger, J.A. Fuller.

Magazine Needs: *Riverwind* is a literary annual publishing quality work by new and established writers mainly from Ohio, West Virginia, and Kentucky. Very open to various forms. Biased toward image poems and "voice" poems. No "genre poems (i.e., erotic, juvenile, etc.)." Recently published poetry by Paul Nelson, Roy Bentley, P.K. Harmon, Amy Newman, Betsy Brown. As a sample the editors selected these lines from "Mantle Dying" by Roy Bentley:

> *If I needed a hero, you'd be him/a second liver in the bloated gut,/fielding questions about the new cancer./Everyone's going where you are/and still they marvel because it's you./*

Riverwind is 112-130 pages, 7×7, offset-printed, perfect-bound, photo offset-printed cover, with art/graphics. Receives about 300 poems/year, accepts 25%. Publishes about 65 poems/issue. Press run is 400 for 300 subscribers of which 75 are libraries, 225 shelf sales; 80 are distributed free to contributors. Single copy $7.50; subscription: $7.50. Sample: $3. Make checks payable to *Riverwind*.

How to Submit: Submit 6 poems at a time. Accepts previously published poems; no simultaneous submissions. Accepts e-mail submissions; no fax or disk submissions. Cover letter is preferred. Reads submissions October 1-May 30. Time between acceptance and publication varies. Poems circulated to an editorial board. "One editor chooses what she's interested in publishing. The two editors meet to make final decision." Seldom comments on rejected poems. Occasionally publishes theme issues. Guidelines are available in magazine and for SASE. Responds in up to 3 months. Pays 2 contributor's copies. Acquires first rights. Poets may send books for review consideration to Demi Naffziger.

Advice: "Writers may want to purchase a sample copy before sending work."

ROANOKE REVIEW, English Dept., Roanoke College, 221 College Lane, Salem VA 24153. Established 1968. **Poetry Editor:** Paul Hanstedt.

Magazine Needs: *Roanoke Review* is an annual literary review which uses poetry that is "grounded in strong images and unpretentious language." Has published poetry by Peter Thomas, Norman Russell, David Citino, Susan Johnson, and Mary Balazs. *Roanoke Review* is 200 pages, 6×9, professionally printed with matte card cover with full-color art. Uses 25-30 pages of poetry in each issue. Press run is 250-300 for 150 subscribers of which 50 are libraries. Receives 400-500 submissions of poetry/year, accepts 40-60. Subscription: $10. Sample: $10.

Also Offers: Biannual Poetry Competition (2002, 2004, etc.). Send up to 5 poems. *Entry fee:* $10. Make checks payable to Roanoke College.

How to Submit: Submit original typed mss, no photocopies. Responds in 3 months. No pay.

Advice: "Be real. Know rhythm. Concentrate on strong images."

N **◐** **ROAR SHOCK**, 110 Vine St. #220, Seattle WA 98121-1442. Established 2002. **Editor:** Harvey Goldner.

Magazine Needs: *Roar Shock* appears bimonthly "to provide a print format for the best poets active in Seattle's quite lively 'open mic' scene, and to forge a link with similar genius-lunatics from sea to shining sea. At *Roar Shock*, we choose the real and the surreal, both rhymed and free, slow or rapid; we block the schlock, halt the schmaltz, and eschew the vapid, the insipid." Recently published poetry by Maged Zaher, Loraine Campbell, Vanessa Sooy, Ira Parnes, David Laterre, and John Stehman. As a sample the editor selected these lines from his poem, "State of the Art":

> *Having squandered all his inherited stash/Of medium-quality counterfeit cash,/Jack lost his place*
> *amid the gold-plated youth—/Ecstatic on Paxil, pot, gin and vermouth—/Who glittered and chattered*
> *(perhaps playing cards)/Around country club pools, or on shady yards.*

Roar Shock is 36 pages, digest-sized, photocopied, stapled, card stock cover. Receives about 1,200 poems/year, accepts about 10%. Publishes about 20-25 poems/issue. Press run is 200 for 12 subscribers, 40 shelf sales; 30 distributed free to contributors and friends. "Most copies sold at readings." Single copy: $4; subscription: $24/year. Sample: $5 p.p. Make checks payable to Harvey Goldner.

How to Submit: Submit 3-7 poems at a time. Line length for poetry is 3½ minimum, 130 maximum. Accepts previously published poems and simultaneous submissions. No fax, e-mail, or disk submissions. Cover letter is optional. Poems should be typed, single-spaced; SASE required. Reads submissions year round. Time between acceptance and publication is 6 months. Comments on rejected poems when requested. Guidelines available in magazine. Responds in 1 month. Pays 1 contributor's copy. Acquires one-time rights.

Advice: "Academic types should forget books for a while and hit the streets; street types should stay home (if they have one), read, and learn to spell. Both types should get a job and stop mooching off their mothers. And remember that, when cooking a fish, the recipe may be contemporary or ancient, but the fish must be very fresh. And you will need a fire."

◐ **THE ROCKFORD REVIEW; ROCKFORD WRITERS' GUILD**, 7721 Venus St., Loves Park IL 61111. E-mail: haikupup@aol.com. Website: www.welcome.to/rwg (includes guidelines, contact and subscription information, contest rules, and editorial policy). Established 1971. **Editor:** Cindy Guentherman.

Magazine Needs: *The Rockford Review* is a publication of the Rockford Writers' Guild which appears 3 times/year, publishing their poetry and prose, that of other writers throughout the country and contributors from other countries. *The Rockford Review* seeks experimental or traditional poetry of up to 50 lines. "We look for the magical power of the words themselves, a playfulness with language in the creation of images and fresh insights on old themes, whether it be poetry, satire, or fiction." Has published poetry by John Grey, Richard Luftig, and Laura Wilson. *The Rockford Review* is about 50 pages, digest-sized, professionally printed and saddle-stapled with card cover with b&w illustration. Press run is 350. Single copy: $6; subscription: $20 (3 issues plus the Guild's monthly newsletter, *Write Away*).

How to Submit: Submit up to 3 poems at a time with SASE. Accepts simultaneous submissions; no previously published poems. No electronic submissions. "Include a cover letter with your name, address, phone number, e-mail address (if available), a three-line bio, and an affirmation that the submission is unpublished in print or electronically." Guidelines available for SASE and on website. Responds in 2 months. Pays 1 contributor's copy and "you will receive an invitation to be a guest of honor at a Contributors' Reading & Reception in the spring." Acquires first North American serial rights.

Also Offers: Offers Editor's Choice Prizes of $25 for prose, $25 for poetry each issue. Also sponsors a Spring Stanzas Contest and a Fall Short Story Contest with cash prizes and publication in *The Rockford Review*. Accepts work by children for both contests. The Rockford Writers' Guild is a nonprofit, tax-exempt corporation established "to encourage, develop and nurture writers and good writing of all kinds and to promote the art of writing in the Rockford area." Offers lectures by Midwest authors, editors, and publishers, conducts several workshops and publishes a monthly newsletter. Membership: $30/year. Further information available for written request or on website.

$ 🖂 🔘 ROCKY MOUNTAIN RIDER MAGAZINE (Specialized: animals, regional), P.O. Box 1011, Hamilton MT 59840-1011. (406)363-4085. Fax: (406)363-1056. Website: www.rockymountainrider. com. Established 1993. **Editor:** Natalie Riehl.

Magazine Needs: *Rocky Mountain Rider Magazine* is a regional, monthly, all-breed horse magazine. Wants "cowboy poetry; western or horse-themed poetry. Please keep length to no more than 5 verses." *Rocky Mountain Rider Magazine* is 64 pages, 8½×11, web offset on newsprint and stapled. Publish 1 poem/issue.

How to Submit: Submit 1-10 poems at a time. Accepts previously published poems and simultaneous submissions. Cover letter preferred. Seldom comments on rejected poems. Occasionally publishes theme issues. Guidelines and upcoming themes available for SASE. "We'll send a free copy if requested in a letter asking for writer's guidelines." Pays $10/poem. Acquires one-time rights. Reviews books of poetry. Send books for review consideration.

🔘 ROMANTICS QUARTERLY; A.C. SWINBURNE POETRY PRIZE; ROMANTICS POETRY GROUP (Specialized: form/style, love/romance/erotica, inspirational), P.O. Box 22543, Milwaukie OR 97269. Fax: (503)296-7991. E-mail: romanticsquarter@aol.com. Website: http:// hometown.aol.com/RomanticsQuarter/index.html. Established 2000. **Editor:** Kevin N. Roberts. **Contact:** Janice, Mike, Bob.

Magazine Needs: "Our goal is to resurrect the voice of the Victorian Romantic poet and renew popular interest in traditional, rhyming, musical verse. We have no restrictions; we want to see all varieties of quality poetry. However, we are partial to traditional rhyming verse in the style of the Victorian Romantics. We do not want to see limericks, greeting card verse, political poetry, splatter-gore, children's poetry, or poems containing cliché, harsh language, or graphic violence." Has published poetry by Carmen, A.E. Stallings, Mary Rae, and Leilah Wendell. As a sample the editor selected these lines from "Ophelia" by Kevin Roberts:

> *Mad dreams drone past maiden pleasures missed,/A flood of fears and subtle, silent sighs,/Half-parted lips, as though they've just been kissed,/Half-haunted eykes grown wide and wild and wise,/Reflecting shades, like ghosted clouds of mist/But clear and calm like sultry seas and skies.*

Romantics Quarterly is 65 pages, 5½×8½, desktop-published, saddle-stapled, includes b&w line art, considers ads from gothic and poetry-related companies/publications. Receives about 1,000 poems/year, accepts about 25%. Publishes about 50 poems/issue. Press run is 500 of which 50 are libraries, 100 shelf sales; 50 distributed free to reviewers and colleagues of university. Subscription: $20. Sample: $5 (when available). Make checks payable to K. Roberts. (Cash and money orders preferred, $25 fee for returned checks.) "No requirements for contributors, but we encourage contributors to subscribe and keep in touch or become members of the Romantics Poetry Group."

How to Submit: Submit up to 5 poems at a time. Check themes on website before submitting. Accepts previously published poems and simultaneous submissions. Accepts e-mail submissions included in body of e-mail or attached in MS Word. Cover letter preferred. Include brief bio. "We prefer poems to be typed with name and address of poet on each page. Include SASE for reply. Enclose reading fee in cash, check, or money order made out to K. Roberts." **Reading fee:** $2/poem (only applies when submitting *more* than five poems). Time between acceptance and publication is up to 1 year. Poems are circulated to an editorial board. "The poetry editor reads all submissions and passes selected works on to 2-3 members of the editorial board (made up of graduate students). Editorial board makes the final decisions." Often comments on rejected poems. "If a poet wants professional criticism from graduate students/professors, please include letter stating the type of guidance you require. Include $10 per piece for thorough critique and suggestions." Upcoming themes and guidelines available for SASE, on website, or in publication. Responds in 1 month. Sometimes sends prepublication galleys. Pays 2 contributor's copies per piece accepted. Acquires one-time rights. Reviews books and chapbooks of poetry and other magazines in 35 words, multi-book format. Poets may send books for review consideration.

Also Offers: Sponsors the annual A.C. Swinburne Poetry Prize. Submit up to 5 poems with $5 entry fee. Winner will receive cash prizes, publication of poem, and 5 free copies of zine. Contest rules available for SASE.

Advice: "If you really want to impress us, study the works of Romantic poets like A.C. Swinburne, E.A. Poe, S.T. Coleridge, Lord Byron, and Shelley, and take your lead from them both in terms of music and subject matter. Make us feel it was written in the 1800s."

🔳 $ 🔘 🔘 RONSDALE PRESS (Specialized: anthology; nature/rural/ecology; social issues; regional, Canada), 3350 W. 21st Ave., Vancouver, British Columbia V6S 1G7 Canada. (604)738-4688. Fax: (604)731-4598. Website: www.ronsdalepress.com (includes catalogs, list of upcoming events, and writer's guidelines). Established 1988. **Director:** Ronald B. Hatch.

Book Needs: Publishes 3 flat-spined paperbacks of poetry/year—by Canadian poets only—classical to experimental. "Ronsdale looks for poetry manuscripts which show that the writer reads and is familiar with the work of some of the major contemporary poets. It is also essential that you have published some poems in literary magazines. We have never published a book of poetry when the author has not already published a goodly number in magazines." Has published *Taking the Breath Away* by Harold Rhenisch, *Two Shores/Deux rives* by Thuong Vuong-Riddick, *Cobalt 3* by Kevin Roberts, *Ghost Children* by Lillia Boraks-Nemetz, *Poems for a New World* by Connie Fife, *Steveston* by Daphne Marlatt, and *Cleaving* by Florence Treadwell. As a sample we selected these lines from "Flirt" in the *Green Man* by John Donlan:

> People are such flirts. Their animal spirits/rise and quit their dreary doppelgängers/as easily as you'd leave a chair./I've given up even trying to figure that out:/these tracks were laid for a lot of trains to run on—maybe escape is in our nature.

How to Submit: Query first, with sample poems and cover letter with brief bio and publication credits. Accepts previously published poems and simultaneous submissions. Often comments on rejected poems. Responds to queries in 2 weeks, to mss in 2 months. Pays 10% royalties and 10 author's copies. Write for catalog to purchase sample books.

Advice: "Ronsdale looks for poetry with echoes from previous poets. To our mind, the contemporary poet must be well-read."

N ◐ ◎ ROOK PUBLISHING (Specialized: style/rhyming poetry), 1805 Calloway Dr., Clarksville TN 37042. (931)648-6225. Fax: (931)552-3050. Established 1996. **Publisher:** Edgar A. Lawson.

Book/Chapbook Needs & How to Submit: Rook Publishing's goal is "to secure and to re-introduce meaningful sonnet/rhyming poetry in published paperback books of 100-150 pages." Wants "rhyming/sonnet poetry on any subject. We would love poems for children; 10-50 lines seem to work well, open to any style. No profanity, religion-bashing, gay/lesbian subject matter, vampires, gore, aliens, pornography, haiku, free verse, or poems in poor taste." Recently published poetry by Amanda Weaver, Sumee Sukporbee, and Lanier Devores. As a sample the editor selected these lines from his own poem "Youth":

> Here was one we all could claim/One the ancients wrote of, sang/Taken under every wing—/Ours to have for a spring/Oh the joy he cast about—/The cares he vanquished, put to rout . . .

Rook Publishing publishes 2 paperbacks/year. Books are usually 100-120 pages, 5×7, photocopied, perfect-bound, 4-color cover, with original/in-house art. "No query letter will be necessary, published poems are fine with us." Responds to queries in 10 weeks. Pays royalties of 15-25%, $100, and 3 author's copies (out of a press run of 300-500); or 5 author's copies (out of a press run of 500). Order sample books by sending $8.50 to Rook Publishing.

Advice: "We do not believe the well of great rhyming poetry has been drained. We do believe that a growing generation will be visiting it more often than ever. We seek those writers, therefore, who write and believe in this form of poetry and the challenge that it offers."

◐ ROSE ALLEY PRESS, 4203 Brooklyn Ave. NE #103A, Seattle WA 98105. (206)633-2725. E-mail: rosealleypress@juno.com. Established 1995. **Publisher/Editor:** David D. Horowitz. "We presently do not read unsolicited manuscripts."

N ◐ ROSECROFT PUBLISHING; TERRACE JOURNAL, 8517 Rosecroft Terrace, Ellicott City MD 21403. E-mail: rosecroftpub@yahoo.com. Established 2002. **Editor:** Nancy Watts.

Magazine Needs: *Terrace Journal* appears biannually in spring/fall. "I want to see all forms of well-written poetry. No foul language or sexualy explicit material. No hate poems or discriminatory poetry." As a sample we selected these lines from "Grief" by editor Nancy Watts from her chapbook, *Of My Soul*:

> And a cold numbness consumes me//So I pull it up around my chin/Waiting for the warmth of time to/ Relieve my chill and hope for the day/I can recall you without a tear

Terrace Journal is 50 pages digest-sized, side-stapled, card stock cover, with art/graphics when available. Single copy: $5; subscription: $7. Sample: $3. Make checks payable to Rosecroft Publishing.

How to Submit: Submit up to 5 poems at a time. Accepts previously published poems and simultaneous submissions. Accepts e-mail submissions. Cover letter preferred. Time between acceptance and publication is up to 6 months. Seldom comments on rejected poems. Guidelines available for SASE or by e-mail. Responds in 2 months. Pays 1 contributor's copy. Acquires one-time rights.

Book/Chapbook Needs & How to Submit: Rosecroft Publishing publishes 2-3 chapbooks/year. **Not currently receiving unsolicited material.** Chapbooks are usually 24-30 pages, side-stapled, card stock cover, with some art/graphics.

Advice: "Read other poets often and support your small presses."

◐ ROSEWATER PUBLICATIONS; THROUGH SPIDER'S EYES, 223 Chapel St., Leicester MA 01524-1115. (508)728-6564. E-mail: rosewaterbooks@yahoo.com. Established 1997. **Editor:** April M. Ardito.

Magazine Needs: *Through Spider's Eyes* appears several times/year. It's "a short zine highlighting the best of what RoseWater Publications receives. The best art is about art or has a strong message. We prefer coffeehouse and slam style poems, work that is just as powerful spoken as written. Multi-layered work always appreciated. Prefer modern and experimental work. Rhymed poetry must be exceptional; biased against 'God is great' and 'See the pretty trees and flowers' poetry." Recently published poetry by D.R. Middleton, Gwen Ellen Rider, Ed Fuqua, Jay Walker, Craig Nelson, and April M. Ardito. As a sample the editor selected these lines from "Absolutes" by Paul William Gagnon which appears in his chapbook, *The Darkness is Habitable*:

> On the way home, we talk religion. You believe in demons, hell and/original sin./You tell me Buddhists and Wiccans worship Satan./I indulge you for the sake of conversation./Outside your window, I see your devil looking in./He's big and solid as an anvil . . .

Through Spider's Eyes is 20-36 pages, digest-sized, photocopied b&w. Receives and accepts varied number of poems/year. Publishes about 10-40 poems/issue. Press run is 50. Single copy: $4.50; subscription: $20/6 issues. Sample: $4.50. Make checks payable to April M. Ardito.

How to Submit: Submit up to 5 poems at a time. Line length for poetry is 3 minimum, 250 maximum. Accepts previously published poems; no simultaneous submissions. Accepts e-mail submissions, either as attachment (.txt or .doc format) or in textbox. Cover letter is preferred. Likes "disposable manuscripts; casual, personal cover letter; SASE required." Reads submissions year round. Does not publish seasonal poems. Accepts personal checks, money orders, or PayPal for all samples and subscriptioins. Time between acceptance and publication is up to 1 year. "Editor always attempts to read all submissions personally, but has a few people who help out when submissions get overwhelming." Seldom comments on rejected poems. "Prefer that poets submit a full chapbook-length manuscript. Responds in up to 2 months. Pays 1 copy. Acquires one-time rights and reprint rights (possible inclusion in an anthology at a later date). Reviews books and chapbooks of poetry and other magazines/journals in less than 1 page, single book format. Poets may send books for review consideration to April M. Ardito.

Book/Chapbook Needs & How to Submit: RoseWater Publications "wants to create an aesthically pleasing product for poets who spend as much time on the stage as with the page." Hopes to publish full-length anthologies in the future. Publishes 5-10 chapbooks/year. Chapbooks are usually 20-64 pages, photocopied b&w, stapled, colored paper, cardstock, or business stock cover with original cover design. "Please send full manuscript (16-60 pages). We do not wish to see queries. We would prefer to see a poet's full vision." Responds to mss in up to 2 months. Pays 50% of copies (out of a press run of 50-100). **Approximately 20% of titles are author-subsidy published.** "Poet pays for layout and editing fees. RoseWater Publications would like to discontinue subsidy publishing in the next 1-2 years." Order sample books/chapbooks by sending $3.50 to April M. Ardito.

Also Offers: Also publishes poetry for vending machines. Send full ms (up to 120 lines), titled. Press run of 40, author receives 20 copies. Format is 8½×11 sheet folded in eighths.

Advice: "Spend a lot of time reading and re-reading, writing and re-writing. Always try to keep one finger on the pulse of contemporary poetry, as much to know what isn't working as what is. Stay true to yourself and your vision. Use your words to lure others into your experiences."

RUAH; POWER OF POETRY (Specialized: spirituality), Dominican School of Philosophy/Theology, 2401 Ridge Rd., Berkeley CA 94709. Fax: (510)596-1860. E-mail: cjrenzop@yahoo.com. Established 1990. **General Editor:** C.J. Renz, O.P. **Editor:** Ann Applegarth.

Magazine Needs: *Ruah*, an annual journal published in June, "provides a 'non-combative forum' for poets who have had few or no opportunities to publish their work. Theme: spiritual poetry. The journal has three sections: general poems, featured poet, and chapbook contest winners." Wants "poetry which is of a 'spiritual nature,' i.e., describes an experience of the transcendent. No religious affiliation preferences; no style/format limitations. No 'satanic verse'; no individual poems longer than four typed pages." Has published poetry by Benjamin Alire Saens, Jean Valentine, Alberto Rios, and Naomi Shihab Nye. *Ruah* is 60-80 pages, 5½×8½, photocopied and perfect-bound, glossy card stock cover, color photo, includes occasional b&w sketches of original artwork. Receives about 250 poems/year, accepts 10-20%. Press run is 250 for about 100 subscribers of which 7 are libraries, 10 shelf sales; 50 distributed free to authors, reviewers and inquiries. Subscription: $10 plus $1.50 p&h. Sample: $5 plus $1.50 postage/handling. Make checks payable to Power of Poetry/DSPT.

How to Submit: Submit 3-5 poems at a time. Accepts simultaneous submissions; no previously published poems. Accepts submissions by e-mail (MS Word 97 file attachments or in text box), by fax, on disk, by regular mail. Chapbooks, however, cannot be submitted by e-mail. "Do not mail submissions to publisher's address. Contact general editor via e-mail for current address or send written inquiries to Dominican School." Reads submissions December through March only. Time between acceptance and publication is up to 6 months. Poems are circulated to an editorial board. "Poems reviewed by writers and/or scholars in field of creative writing/literature." Guidelines available for SASE or by e-mail. Responds in up to 6 months. Pays 1 copy/poem. Acquires first rights.

Book/Chapbook Needs & How to Submit: Power of Poetry publishes 1 chapbook of spiritual poetry through their annual competition. Chapbooks are usually 24 pages, and are included as part of *Ruah*. "Poets

Jeremy Thornton designed the 2001 Winter Solstice cover of *RUNES* featuring K. Gordon's photograph, "Nepal." Explains the editor, "The theme of this issue is 'gateway.' We liked the two 'gateways,' one leading in and one leading out into another environment. This issue is filled with all kinds of gateways, traditional and unusual."

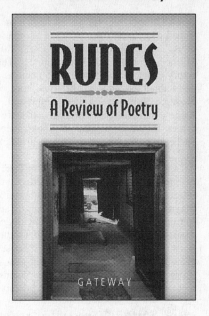

should e-mail General Editor for contest guidelines and submission address or write to Dominican School." Entry fee: $10. Deadline: December 30. Responds to queries in up to 6 weeks; to mss in up to 6 months. Winner receives publication in a volume of *Ruah* and 25 author's copies (out of a press run of 250).
Advice: "*Ruah* is a gathering place in which new poets can come to let their voice be heard alongside of and in the context of 'more established' poets. The journal hopes to provide some breakthrough experiences of the Divine at work in our world."

RUNES, A REVIEW OF POETRY, Arctos Press, P.O. Box 401, Sausalito CA 94966-0401. (415)331-2503. Fax: (415)331-3092. E-mail: RunesRev@aol.com. Website: http://members@aol.com/Runes (includes guidelines, contact and subscription info, upcoming themes, bios, contest info, archives, and interviews). Established 2000. **Editors:** Susan Terris and CB Follett. Member: SPAN, BAIPA.
Magazine Needs: *RUNES, A Review Of Poetry* appears annually. "Our taste is eclectic, but we are looking for excellence in craft." Wants "poems that have passion, originality, and conviction. We are looking for narrative and lyric poetry that is well-crafted and has something surprising to say. No greeting card verse." Recently published poetry by Jane Hirshfield, David St. John, Richard Wilbur, Ronald Wallace, Ruth Daigon, and Martha Rhodes. *RUNES* is 144 pages, digest-sized, professionally-printed, flat-spined, glossy card cover, with art/graphics. Receives about 2,000 poems/year, accepts about 100. Press run is 1,000. Single copy: $12; subscription: $12. Sample: $10. Make checks payable to Arctos Press.
How to Submit: Submit 3-5 poems at a time. Prefers poems under 100 lines. Accepts simultaneous submissions if notified; no previously published poems. No e-mail or disk submissions. SASE required. Reads submissions April 1-May 31. Time between acceptance and publication is 6 months. Seldom comments on rejections. Publishes theme issues regularly. Themes will be "Memory" in 2003, "Storm" in 2004. Guidelines and themes available for SASE, by e-mail, in publication, or on website. Responds in 4 months. Sometimes sends prepublication galleys. Pays 1 contributor's copy. Acquires first North American serial rights. Reviews books of poetry. Poets may send books for review consideration to *RUNES*.
Also Offers: Poetry competition with a judge to be announced later. Poetry competition for 2003 will have same theme as magazine—"Memory." "Three poems plus a one-year subscription for $12. For publication in *Runes*, it is *not* necessary to enter competition. All submitted poems will be read." Make checks payable to Arctos Press. (See separate listing for Arctos Press in this section.)
Advice: "No one can write in a vacuum. If you want to write good poetry, you must read good poetry—classic as well as modern work."

$ ☑ ◎ SACHEM PRESS (Specialized: translations, bilingual), P.O. Box 9, Old Chatham NY 12136-0009. Established 1980. **Editor:** Louis Hammer.

Book/Chapbook Needs: Sachem, a small press publisher of poetry and fiction, both hardcover and flat-spined paperbacks. Wants to see "strong, compelling, even visionary work, English-language or translations." Has published poetry by Cesar Vallejo, Yannis Ritsos, 24 leading poets of Spain (in an anthology), Miltos Sahtouris, and Louis Hammer. The paperbacks average 120 pages and the anthology of Spanish poetry contains 340 pages. Each poem is printed in both Spanish and English, and there are biographical notes about the authors. The small books cost $6.95 and $9.95 and the anthology $24.

How to Submit: No new submissions, only statements of projects, until January 2003. Submit mss January through April only. Royalties are 10% maximum, after expenses are recovered, plus 50 author's copies. Rights are negotiable. Book catalog is free "when available," and poets can purchase books from Sachem "by writing to us, 33⅓% discount."

N ◐ ◎ SACRED JOURNEY: THE JOURNAL OF FELLOWSHIP IN PRAYER (Specialized: religious), 291 Witherspoon St., Princeton NJ 08542. (609)924-6863. Fax: (609)924-6910. E-mail: editorial@sacredjourney.org. Website: www.sacredjourney.org. Established 1950. **Contact:** Editor.

Magazine Needs: *Sacred Journey* is an interfaith bimonthly "concerned with prayer, meditation and spiritual life" using short poetry "with deep religious (or spiritual) feeling." *Sacred Journey* is 48 pages, digest-sized, professionally printed, saddle-stapled with glossy card cover. Accepts about 10% of submissions received. Press run is 10,000. Subscription: $18. Sample free.

How to Submit: Submit 5 poems at a time, double-spaced. Accepts simultaneous submissions and "sometimes" previously published poems. Accepts submissions on disk, by e-mail (in text box), and by regular mail. Cover letter preferred. Responds in 2 months. Pays 5 copies.

◐ ◎ SAHARA (Specialized: regional/Central New England), P.O. Box 20705, Worcester MA 01602. (508)798-5672. E-mail: SaharaJournal@aol.com. Established 2000. **Managing Editor:** Lydia Mancevice.

Magazine Needs: *Sahara* appears biannually in June and December. "We are dedicated to the poetry of our region, Central New England." Wants "unaffected, clear writing in any style. Poems may exist, but they should mean something, too. No pointless obscenities." Accepts poetry written by children. Recently published poetry by Dennis Brutus, Robert Cording, Martin Espada, Carle Johnson, Laura Jehn Menides, and Francis Woodbridge. *Sahara* is 90 pages, digest-sized, offset-printed, perfect-bound, b&w printed card cover with graphics. Receives about 600 poems/year, accepts about 10%. Publishes about 30-40 poems/issues. Press run is 300 for 70 subscribers of which 5 are libraries, 100-150 shelf sales. Single copy: $10; subscription: $18. Sample: $11.50. Make checks payable to Elizabethan Press.

How to Submit: Submit 5 poems at a time. No previously published poems or simultaneous submissions. No fax, e-mail, or disk submissions. Cover letter is required. "Please state the titles of the poems and include a bio." Reads submissions continually. Submit seasonal poems 6 months in advance. Time between acceptance and publication is 6 months. "Material is circulated among several editors and must find at least one strong advocate to be considered." Seldom comments on rejected poems. "Subscribers are preferred." Responds in up to 4 months. Sometimes sends prepublication galleys. Pays 1 contributor's copy. Acquires one-time rights. Reviews books and chapbooks of poetry in 300-600 words. Poets may send books for review consideration to *Sahara*.

Advice: "Good poetry usually takes a number of drafts. If it was easy and quick, it probably is a bad poem."

$ ◐ ◎ ST. ANTHONY MESSENGER (Specialized: religious, Catholic), 28 W. Liberty St., Cincinnati OH 45210-1298. Fax: (513)241-0399. Website: www.americancatholic.org (includes guidelines, contact and subscription information, catalog, links, editorial policy, archives). **Poetry Editor:** Christopher Heffron.

Magazine Needs: *St. Anthony Messenger* is a monthly 56-page magazine, press run 340,000, for Catholic families, mostly with children in grade school, high school, or college. Some issues feature a poetry page that uses poems appropriate for their readership. Poetry submissions are always welcome despite limited need. As a sample here is "A Valentine for Darby" by Jean M. Syed:

> Why do I love you, my potbellied love?/Not for your pregnant form or shiny pate./Were these on tender
> those decades ago,/would I have been so indiscriminate/as to let you win my heart? No princess/from
> passion ever took a frog to mate.

How to Submit: "Submit seasonal poetry (Christmas/Easter/nature poems) several months in advance. Submit a few poems at a time; do not send us your entire collection of poetry. We seek to publish accessible poetry of high quality. Poems must be original, under 25 lines, spiritual/inspirational in nature a plus, but not required. We do not publish poems that have already been published—must be first run." Accepts submissions by fax or by e-mail (as attachment). Guidelines available for standard SASE, free sample for 9 × 12 SASE. Pays $2/line on acceptance and 2 copies. Acquires first worldwide serial rights. *St. Anthony Messenger* poetry occasionally receives awards from the Catholic Press Association Annual Competition.

$ ⊘ ◎ ST. JOSEPH MESSENGER AND ADVOCATE OF THE BLIND (Specialized: religious), 537 Pavonia Ave., P.O. Box 288, Jersey City NJ 07303. Established 1898. **Poetry Editor:** Sister Mary Kuiken, C.S.J.P.

Magazine Needs: *St. Joseph Messenger* is semiannual and publishes "brief but thought-filled poetry; do not want lengthy and issue-filled." Most of the poets they have used are previously unpublished. Receives 400-500 submissions/year, accepts about 50. *St. Joseph Messenger* is 16 pages, 8 × 11, and prints about 2 pages of poetry/issue. Press run 15,000. Subscription: $5.

How to Submit: Currently oversupplied; not accepting submissions. Sometimes comments on rejected poems. Publishes theme issues. Guidelines, a free sample, and upcoming themes available for SASE. Responds within 1 month. Pays $10-20/poem and 2 copies.

ℕ $ ◔ SALMON RUN PRESS; NATIONAL POETRY BOOK AWARD, Texas A&M University-Kingsville, Dept. of English, MSC 162, Kingsville TX 78363. E-mail: salmonp@aol.com. Established 1991. **Editor/Publisher:** John E. Smelcer.

Book/Chapbook Needs: Salmon Run publishes 2-3 books/year. Wants "quality poetry by established poets, any subject, any style. No poetry that is not representative of the highest achievement in the art." Has published Galway Kinnell, Ursula K. Le Guin, X.J. Kennedy, Molly Peacock, Denise Levertov, Denise Duhamel, Philip Levine, Daniel Bourne, and Luis Omar Salinas. As a sample the editor selected these lines from Philip Levine's "Peter's Gift":

> *My friend Peter found a strange newcomer/in the walnut tree. Late June,/near dusk, the soft light*
> *hanging on,/he stills us, and at first I catch nothing,/and then the soft voice, the bubbling.*

Their books are flat-spined and professionally printed on heavy, natural-colored paper with glossy color covers.

How to Submit: Query first with sample poems and cover letter with brief bio. Accepts previously published poems and simultaneous submissions. Usually comments on rejected poems. Responds to queries within 1-3 weeks, to mss in 1-2 months. Pays 10% royalties, sometimes advances and a negotiable number of author's copies.

Also Offers: Also sponsors a pamphlet series ("by invitation only") and the National Poetry Book Award for book-length mss of 60-96 pages $10 reading fee and SASE required. Entries must be postmarked by December 30 annually. The winning ms will receive $1,000 prize and national promotion.

◖ SANSKRIT, UNC Charlotte, Cone University Center, Charlotte NC 28223. (704)687-2326. Fax: (704)687-3394. E-mail: sanskrit@email.uncc.edu. Website: www.uncc.edu/life/sanskrit (features online format) or www.uncc.edu/life/smp/smp_sanskrit.html (includes guidelines and information about student media). Established 1965. **Editor-in-Chief:** Jason Keath. **Literary Editor:** Nicole Schulz.

Magazine Needs: *Sanskrit* is a literary annual appearing in April that uses poetry. "No restrictions as to form or genre, but we do look for maturity and sincerity in submissions. Nothing trite or sentimental." Has published poetry by Kimberleigh Luke-Stallings. As a sample the editor selected these lines from "The World Will Always Be With Us" by Kristina Wright:

> *The blues, the scent of lilacs on the tongue, tiny cherries/softly push from my mouth like the first buds*
> *still straining,//Though once I walked stupid-faced: shambling through dairy/products, putrid flowers,*
> *the confusion of menus, guns, women/skinny as switches on scratch and sniff pages, children with/*
> *tremulous liquid hearts like firing glass vases, . . .*

Seeks "to encourage and promote beginning and established artists and writers." *Sanskrit* is 60-65 pages, 9 × 12, flat-spined, printed on quality matte paper with heavy matte card cover. Press run is 3,500 for about 100 subscribers of which 2 are libraries. Sample: $10.

How to Submit: Submit up to 15 poems at a time. Accepts simultaneous submissions. Accepts fax and e-mail submissions (include in body of message). Cover letter with 30-70 word bio required. Submission deadline is the first Friday in November. Editor comments on submissions "infrequently." Responds in 2 months. Pays 1 contributor's copy.

$ ◖ SARABANDE BOOKS, INC.; THE KATHRYN A. MORTON PRIZE IN POETRY, 2234 Dundee Rd., Suite 200, Louisville KY 40205. (502)458-4028. Fax: (502)458-4065. E-mail: sarabandeb@aol.com. Website: www.SarabandeBooks.org (includes guidelines and application form for contest, interviews with authors, ordering information, and general information on press). Established 1994. **Editor-in-Chief:** Sarah Gorham.

Book/Chapbook Needs: Sarabande Books publishes books of poetry and short fiction. Wants "poetry of superior artistic quality. Otherwise no restraints or specifications." Has published poetry by Michael Burkard, Belle Waring, Baron Wormser, and Afaa Michael Weaver.

How to Submit: Query with 10 sample poems during the month of September only. No fax or e-mail submissions. SASE must always be enclosed. Accepts previously published poems if acknowledged as such and simultaneous submissions "if notified immediately of acceptance elsewhere." Seldom comments on rejected poems. Responds to queries in 3 months, to mss (if invited) in 6 months. Guidelines available for SASE. Pays 10% royalties and author's copies.

Also Offers: The Kathryn A. Morton Prize in Poetry is awarded to a book-length ms (at least 48 pages) submitted between January 1 and February 15. $20 handling fee and entry form required. Guidelines available in November for SASE or on website. Winner receives a $2,000 cash award, publication, and a standard royalty contract. All finalists are considered for publication. "At least half of our list is drawn from contest submissions." Entry fee: $20. Reads entries January 1 through February 15 only. Competition receives 1,200 entries. Most recent contest winner was Rick Barot for *The Darker Fall*. Judge was Stanley Plumly.

⊘ **SATURDAY PRESS, INC.**, Box 43548, Upper Montclair NJ 07043. (973)256-5053. Fax: (973)256-4987. E-mail: saturdaypr@aol.com. Established 1975. **Editor:** S. Ladov. "We do not plan to read manuscripts in the foreseeable future."

⊘ ◎ **SCORE MAGAZINE; SCORE CHAPBOOKS AND BOOKLETS (Specialized: form)**, 1111 E. Fifth, Moscow ID 83843. (208)892-8826. E-mail: orion@pullman.com. **Poetry Editor:** Crag Hill.
Magazine Needs: Score Chapbooks and Booklets is a small press publisher of visual poetry in the annual magazine *Score*, booklets, postcards, and broadsides. Wants "poetry which melds language and the visual arts such as concrete poetry; experimental use of language, words, and letters—forms. The appearance of the poem should have as much to say as the text. Poems on any subject; conceptual poetry; poems which use experimental, non-traditional methods to communicate their meanings." Doesn't want "traditional verse of any kind—be it free verse or rhymed." Has published poetry by Karl Kempton, John Vieira, Bruce Andrews, Larry Eigner, and Pete Spence. Editor says that it is impossible to quote a sample because "some of our poems consist of only a single word—or in some cases no recognizable words." *Score* is 48-72 pages, magazine-sized, offset-printed, saddle-stapled, using b&w graphics, 2-color matte card cover. Press run is 200 for 25 subscribers, of which 6 are libraries, about 50-60 shelf sales. Sample: $10.
How to Submit: We strongly advise looking at a sample copy before submitting if you are not familiar with visual poetry. Accepts previously published poems "if noted"; no simultaneous submissions. Guidelines available for SASE. Pays 2 contributor's copies. Poets may send books for review consideration.
Book/Chapbook Needs & How to Submit: For chapbook consideration send entire ms. No simultaneous submissions. Almost always comments on rejected poems. Pays 25% of the press run. Subsidy publishing available "if author requests it."

N ⊕ ⊘ ◎ **SCOTTISH CULTURAL PRESS (Specialized: nationality)**, Unit 13d, Newbattle Abbey Business Annexe, Newbattle Rd., Dalkeith EH22 3LJ Scotland United Kingdom. Phone: +44(0)131 660 6366. Fax: +44(0)131 660 6414. E-mail: info@scottishbooks.com. Website: www.scottishbooks.com. Established 1992. **Directors:** Avril Gray and Brian Pugh.
Book/Chapbook Needs: Scottish Cultural Press publishes all styles of poetry. Poet should be Scottish or have strong Scottish connections and previously published in magazines, etc. Publishes 8-12 paperbacks/year. Does not want "new poets and/or modernistic visual poetry." Has published poetry by Valerie Gillies, George Bruce, Kenneth C. Steven, Maurice Lindsay, and Alan Riach.
How to Submit: Submit 5-10 poems at a time. Accepts previously published poems and simultaneous submissions. Accepts e-mail submissions. Cover letter required and must include bio of poet and indication of whether material is available on disk. Time between acceptance and publication is "often considerable." Responds to queries in 1 month; to mss in 3 months. Pays 10% of net income royalties and 20 author's copies. "*Always* contact S.C.P. *before* sending material."

N ○ **SCRIPT MAGAZINE; BROWNISLANDPUBLISHING.COM**, 6818 N. Wayne, Chicago IL 60626. E-mail: brwneyz24@hotmail.com. Website: http://brownislandpublishing.com (includes guidelines, subscription info, *Script Magazine*). Established 2002. **Editor:** Godfrey Logan.

Magazine Needs: *Script Magazine* appears monthly. Publishes bold, honest, real-life poetry "for people who love to read as well as write poetry." Does not want racist, hateful poetry or "poetry about physically injuring a person." As a sample the editor selected these lines from "Untitled":

> *The evening envelopes us. The darkness soothing. A breeze calm and brooding./Musical in a way. Its song seems to say:/Long after the sensations have gone and there is the mutterings of the young,/there she is linked to you. Her grip unfailing to a man however in vain. This/you might heed, angels whisper.*

Script Magazine is published online and in print. Print version is desk jet-printed, stapled, newsletter format cover, with photos. Accepts about 90% of poems received. Publishes 10-20 poems/issue. No press run; is printed on demand for $3/copy.

How to Submit: Accepts print and online submissions with background information/inspiration. Reads submissions year round. "I read over poems myself with a keen open mind." Never comments on rejected poems. Occasionally publishes theme issues. Guidelines available on website. Pays for featured author ("entire issue dedicated to author") and photos ("$5 or more per print, $50 for featured artist honor"). Also pays 1 contributor's copy. Acquires one-time rights. Reviews books of poetry in single book format (**charges $5 for book reviews**). Poets may send books for review consideration to the editor.

Also Offers: Annual "end-of-year, best-of-year anthology," 30-60 pages, spiral-bound, cardstock cover with photo or artwork.

Advice: "Poetry is beauty and pain, ironies, sentiment. The single most beautiful thing in the world."

$⬭ SCROLL PUBLICATIONS INC.; SCROLL ORIGINAL ARTIST MAGAZINE, (formerly Scroll Publications), P.O. Box 562, Swink CO 81077. (917)384-8220. E-mail: goodtimes49@hotmail.com. Website: www.goodtimes.net. Established 1990. **Editor:** Cherylann Gray.

Magazine Needs: *Scroll Original Artist Magazine* contains "humor, comics, slogans, music, short stories, fiction/nonfiction, artwork, recipes, and poetry. We are strictly devoted to preserving the works and dreams of the original artist." Wants poetry of any form or style, on any subject; length, no more than 30 lines. Nothing profane or vulgar. Accepts poetry written by children. Has published poetry by Richard Perez, Harry Roman, and Natalia Radula. As a sample the editor selected these lines from "Poetry and Reason" by Robert Donald Spector:

> *Am I too prosy/In the things I write,/Striving hard to be so clear/That I lose my poetry?/How much should I sacrifice/Of those things*

Scroll is 75-80 pages, 8½ × 11½, soft paperback, includes art, ads. Receives about 1,200 poems/year, accepts about 90%. Press run is 2,300. Single copy: $6; subscription: $22.50. Sample: $4. Make checks payable to Cherylann Gray or Scroll, Inc.

How to Submit: Submit up to 5 poems at a time. **Reading fee:** $4/5 poems. Accepts previously published poems and simultaneous submissions. Cover letter preferred. Time between acceptance and publication is up to 1 month. Poems are circulated to an editorial board. Often comments on rejected poems. Occasionally publishes theme issues. Guidelines and upcoming themes available for a large SASE and also in publication. Responds in 3 weeks. Acquires first or one-time rights. Reviews chapbooks of poetry. Poets may send books for review consideration.

Book/Chapbook Needs & How to Submit: Scroll Publications publishes 3 chapbooks and 2 anthologies/year. Query first, with 3-4 sample poems and a cover letter with brief bio and publication credits. Responds to queries in 2 months; to mss in 3 months. Pays 40-60% royalties and 25 author's copies (out of a press run of 300).

Also Offers: Arrangements for co-publishing and subsidy publishing available.

Advice: "We want poetry that's strong in nature, life and real experiences, thoughts and dreams."

🌐 ⊘ SECOND AEON PUBLICATIONS, 19 Southminster Rd., Roath, Cardiff CF23 5AT Wales. Phone/fax: (02920)493093. E-mail: peter@peterfinch.co.uk. Website: www.peterfinch.co.uk. Established 1966. **Poetry Editor:** Peter Finch. Does not accept unsolicited mss.

◪⬭ SEEDS POETRY MAGAZINE; HIDDEN BROOK PRESS; SEEDS POETRY CONTEST, 412-701 King St. W., Toronto, Ontario M5V 2W7 Canada. E-mail: writers@hiddenbrookpress.com. Website: www.hiddenbrookpress.com. Established 1994. **Publisher/Editor:** Richard M. Grove.

Magazine Needs: *SEEDS* is an online publication dedicated to being an accessible venue for writers, no matter what their status is in the publishing world. "It doesn't matter whether you've ever been published or not. We publish well-crafted poetry from around the world, so send us any style of poetry you love to write. Send us your newly written or previously published work but be sure it is your absolute top shelf, best stuff. Don't save it for the bottom drawer or the future. We do not appreciate obscure, self-indulgent word games. We are not very interested in reading rhymed verse though we do on occasion publish such poetry if it suits us personally. We are not at all interested in reading about one-night stands, love-lorn angst, or the teen heart throb. Save this for your bottom drawer. Religious dogma and spiritually sappy work are usually not our cup of tea but we have published some interesting references to God, the universe, and spiritual epiphanies. Our goal is to publish well-written, memorable work whether it is humorous, traumatic, nature poems, cityscapes, or just the insight or outlook about life. Push your poetry to the edge but not too far over the edge for us. Oh, and keep the four letter words to a minimum. We have published very few of them."

How to Submit: Submit "any number of poems by e-mail or ASCII-text file on disk with hard copy." Line length for poetry is 3-200 maximum. Accepts previously published poems and simultaneous submissions. "Work, if accepted, is filed to fit with future themes, styles and formats of other works. Authors will be notified as to whether or not the editor is interested in keeping work on file." Guidelines available on website. Responds "as soon as possible."

Also Offers: Sponsors the *SEEDS* Poetry Contest, awards $100, $50, and $25 plus publication. Entry fee: $12 for 6 poems. "Send as many sets of 3 by the same author as you like on white paper, single spaced, font size 12 pt. (no fancy fonts) with your name, mailing address, phone, and e-mail address on the back of each sheet. Please no cover letter, bio, comments, or pleadings. After you have mailed your hard copy with your submission fee, then and only then, e-mail your submission in the body of the e-mail." Deadline: May 1 and October 1. Also sponsors *No Love Lost* and *The Open Window* poetry anthology contests. For *No Love Lost*, submit poems of love, hate, lust, desire, passion, jealousy and ambivalence, brotherly, sisterly, parental love, and love of country, city. Deadline: January 1. For *The Open Window*, send any style, theme, and length. Deadline: June 1. For *No Love Lost* and *The Open Window* contests, send 5 poems, previously unpublished, of any styles, any length. Submission fee: $15/£7 includes purchase of book. Authors retain copyright. 1st, 2nd, 3rd Prizes plus 10 honorable mentions will be chosen plus up to 300 poems published. Send your submissions with a SASE or SAE with IRCs to Hidden Brook Press. Electronic and hard copy submissions required. All non-Canadian destinations pay in US dollars or British sterling if from Great Britain. For overseas submissions add $1 US or £1.

Advice: "The paper-based *SEEDS* and the website *SEEDS* are two different poetry publications containing a different selection of poems and published at different times of the year."

SEEMS, P.O. Box 359, Lakeland College, Sheboygan WI 53082-0359. (920)565-1276 or (920)565-3871. Fax: (920)565-1206. E-mail: kelder@excel.net. Website: www.lakeland.edu/faculty/~elder/seemsweb.htm (currently consists of a home page with basic information, including images of the covers of two issues). Established 1971. **Editor:** Karl Elder.

Magazine Needs: *Seems* is published irregularly. This is a handsomely printed, nearly square (7×8¼) magazine, saddle-stapled, generous with white space on heavy paper. Two of the issues are considered chapbooks, and the editor suggests sampling *Seems #14, What Is The Future Of Poetry?* for $5, consisting of essays by 22 contemporary poets, and "If you don't like it, return it and we'll return your $5." *Explain That You Live: Mark Strand with Karl Elder* (#29) is available for $3. There are usually about 20 pages of poetry/issue. Has published poetry by Bruce Dethlefsen, Doug Flaherty, Janet McCann, Kevin McFadden, and Craig Paulenich. The editor said it was "impossible" to select 6 illustrative lines, but for an example of his own recent work see *The Best American Poetry 2000* or *The 2001 Pushcart Prize* anthology. Print run is 350 for 200 subscribers of which 20 are libraries. Single copy: $4; subscription: $16/4 issues.

How to Submit: There is a 1- to 2-year backlog. "People may call or fax with virtually any question, understanding that the editor may have no answer." No simultaneous submissions. No fax or e-mail submissions. Guidelines available for e-mail. Responds in up to 3 months (slower in summer). Pays 1 copy. Acquires first North American serial rights. Returns rights upon publication.

Advice: "We'd like to consider more prose poems."

SENECA REVIEW, Hobart and William Smith Colleges, Geneva NY 14456-3397. (315)781-3392. Fax: (315)781-3348. Website: www.hws.edu/~senecareview/ (includes guidelines, excerpts from current issue, profile of editors, available back issues, subscription info, info for advertisers and book stores). Established 1970. **Editor:** Deborah Tall. **Associate Editor:** John D'Agata.

• Poetry published in *Seneca Review* has also been included in the 1997, 2000, and 2001 volumes of *The Best American Poetry* and in *The 1998 Pushcart Prize* anthology.

Magazine Needs: *Seneca Review* is a biannual. Wants "serious poetry of any form, including translations. No light verse. Also essays on contemporary poetry and lyrical nonfiction." Has published poetry by Seamus Heaney, Rita Dove, Denise Levertov, Stephen Dunn, and Hayden Carruth. *Seneca Review* is 100 pages, 6×9, professionally printed on quality stock and perfect-bound with matte card cover. You'll find plenty of free verse here—some accessible and some leaning toward experimental—with the emphasis on voice, image, and diction. All in all, poems and translations complement each other and create a distinct editorial mood each issue. Receives 3,000-4,000 poems/year, accepts about 100. Press run is 1,000 for 500 subscribers of which half are libraries, about 250 shelf sales. Subscription: $11/year, $20/2 years, $28/3 years. Sample: $5.

How to Submit: Submit 3-5 poems at a time. No simultaneous submissions or previously published poems. Reads submissions September 1 through May 1 only. Responds in up to 3 months. Pays 2 contributor's copies and a 2-year subscription.

SENSATIONS MAGAZINE, 2 Radio Ave., A5, Secaucus NJ 07094. Website: www.sensationsm ag.com (includes guidelines, contact and subscription information, bios, archives, contest info, editorial policy, catalog, ordering info). Established 1987. **Publisher/Executive Editor:** David Messineo.

Magazine Needs: "*Sensations Magazine* is celebrating its 15th anniversary of independent publishing with a two issue salute to the arts. We are interested in well-crafted poetry: accent on *craft*. Beginning writers should know what a sonnet, a sestina, a pantoum, and a villanelle are (and preferably have attempted to write one of each) before submitting material to us." *Sensations Magazine* is "printed from a 600 dpi printer, hand collated and bound" with full-color photography. See website for purchasing information. Sample issue: $15.

How to Submit: "Be aware that we charge a nominal entry fee for nonsubscribers, and detailed critiques (one of our specialties) are offered only to full-year subscribers." Upcoming themes include "Art and Music" summer 2003, "Cinema" winter 2003, "Allergies" spring 2003 ("Hey, no one else thought of it . . ."). Upcoming themes and guidleines available for SASE and on website. Since 1994 has offered $3.25/line "for the top poem published every year."

Advice: "Remember to spell check your work and *always* be courteous to the publisher."

SERPENT & EAGLE PRESS, 10 Main St., Laurens NY 13796. (607)432-2990. Established 1981. **Poetry Editor:** Jo Mish. Currently not accepting poetry submissions.

$ **SETMAG—THE MAGAZINE; SETMAG.COM; TRANSCENDMAG.COM; TEEN-SFORJC.COM**, PLGK Communications, Inc., 2855 Lawrenceville-Suwane Rd., Suite 760-355, Suwanee GA 30043. Phone/fax: (770)831-8622. E-mail: uvaldes@aol.com. Website: www.setmag.com (includes includes entertainment news, school tips, tons of free stuff, published writing and art by teens). Established 2001. **Publisher:** Quentin Plair.

Magazine Needs: *Setmag* is a quarterly print magazine; *Setmag.com* appears monthly as an online publication. Both publish poetry, short stories, and essays by teen writers. As a sample we selected these lines from "Waves" by Rita Douangpannha:

> Do the pains and tears live in the waves/That sweep upon the lives of many?/Or do the waves only
> crash,/Rolling in and soon out of our lives?/Are the answers still held/Within the depths of the sea?

Setmag is 40 pages, tabloid-sized, offset-printed, saddle-stitched, glossy cover, with ads for consumer goods; *Setmag.com* is 50 pages of website content. Receives about 40 poems/year, accepts about 80%. Publishes about 4 poems/issue. Press run for *Setmag* is 50,000 for 10,000 subscribers of which 250 are libraries, 6,000 shelf sales; 4,000 distributed free to schools and others. Single copy: $3; subscription: $19. Sample: $5. Make checks payable to PLGK Communications.

How to Submit: Line length for poetry is 75 maximum. Accepts previously published poems and simultaneous submissions. Prefers disk submissions; accepts fax and e-mail submissions. Cover letter is required. Reads submissions all the time. Submit seasonal poems 3 months in advance. Time between acceptance and publication is 2 months. Regularly publishes theme issues. A list of upcoming themes and guidelines available on website. Responds in 5 weeks to submissions. Pays $20. Acquires one-time rights. Reviews books and chapbooks of poetry and other magazines/journals in 100 words. Poets may send books/chapbooks for review consideration to Quentin Plair.

Also Offers: *Transcendmag.com* (at www.transcendmag.com), an African-American teen-oriented publication offering writing by teens, entertainment news, school tips, and free stuff; and *TeensforJC.com* (at www.teensforjc.c om), a Christian teen site which offers young writers the opportunity to publish poetry, short stories, art, and opinion essays. See **How to Submit** above for details.

Advice: "We encourage teen writers to submit poetry! Short stories and essays!"

SEVEN BUFFALOES PRESS; AZOREAN EXPRESS; BLACK JACK; VALLEY GRAPE-VINE; HILL AND HOLLER ANTHOLOGY SERIES (Specialized: rural, regional, anthologies), Box 249, Big Timber MT 59011. Established 1973. **Editor:** Art Coelho.

Magazine Needs & How to Submit: "I've always thought that rural and working class writers, poets, and artists deserve the same tribute given to country singers." These publications all express that interest. Wants poetry oriented toward rural and working people, "a poem that tells a story, preferably free verse, not longer than 50-100 lines, poems with strong lyric and metaphor, not romantical, poetry of the heart as much as the head, not poems written like grocery lists or the first thing that comes from a poet's mind, no ivory tower, and half my contributors are women." Has published poetry by R.T. Smith, James Goode, Leo Connellan, and Wendell Berry. *The Azorean Express* is 35 pages, 5½×8½, side-stapled. It appears twice/year. Circulation 200. Sample: $7.75. Submit 4-8 poems at a time. No simultaneous submissions. Responds in 1 month. Pays 1 copy. *Black Jack* is an anthology series on Rural America that uses rural material from anywhere, especially the American West; *Valley Grapevine* is an anthology on central California, circulation 750, that uses rural material from central California; *Hill and Holler*, Southern Appalachian Mountain series, takes in rural mountain lifestyle and folkways. Sample of any postpaid: $7.75.

Book/Chapbook Needs & How to Submit: Seven Buffaloes Press does not accept unsolicited mss but publishes books solicited from writers who have appeared in the above magazines.

Advice: "Don't tell the editor how great you are. This one happens to be a poet and novelist who has been writing for 30 years. Your writing should not only be fused with what you know from the head, but also from what you know within your heart. Most of what we call life may be some kind of gift of an unknown river within us. The secret to be learned is to live with ease in the darkness, because there are too many things of the night in this world. But the important clue to remember is that there are many worlds within us."

$ ☑ THE SEWANEE REVIEW, University of the South, Sewanee TN 37383-1000. (931)598-1246. E-mail: rjones@sewanee.edu. Website: www.sewanee.edu/sreview/home.html (includes guidelines, contact information, subscription costs, selections from the magazine, and links to useful references, publishers, etc.). Established 1892, thus being our nation's oldest continuously published literary quarterly. **Editor:** George Core.

Magazine Needs: Fiction, criticism, and poetry are invariably of the highest establishment standards. Many of our major poets appear here from time to time. *Sewanee Review* has published poetry by Robert Bly, Neal Bowers, Catharine S. Brosman, Robert Cording, Debora Greger, John Haines, and David Middleton. Each issue is a hefty paperback of nearly 200 pages, conservatively bound in matte paper, always of the same typography. Open to all styles and forms, the issues we reviewed featured formal sequences, metered verse, structured free verse, sonnets, and lyric and narrative forms—all accessible and intelligent. Press run is 3,200. Sample: $7.25.

How to Submit: Submit up to 6 poems at a time. Line length for poetry is 40 maximum. No simultaneous submissions. No electronic submissions. "Unsolicited works should not be submitted between June 1 and August 31. A response to any submission received during that period will be greatly delayed." Guidelines available for SASE, by e-mail, and on website. Responds in 6 weeks. Pays 60¢/line, plus 2 copies (and reduced price for additional copies). Also includes brief, standard, and essay-reviews.

Also Offers: Presents the Aiken Taylor Award for Modern American Poetry to established poets. Poets *cannot* apply for this prize.

Advice: "Please keep in mind that for each poem published in *Sewanee Review*, approximately 250 poems are considered."

◐ ◎ SHEMOM (Specialized: motherhood), 2486 Montgomery Ave., Cardiff CA 92007. E-mail: peggyfrench@home.com. Established 1997. **Editor:** Peggy French.

Magazine Needs: "Appearing 2-4 times/year, *Shemom* celebrates motherhood and the joys and struggles that present themselves in that journey. It includes poetry, essays, book and CD reviews, recipes, art, and children's poetry. Open to any style, prefer free verse. We celebrate motherhood and related issues. Haiku and native writing also enjoyed. Love to hear from children." As a sample the editor selected these lines from her poem "Ode to Motherhood":

> Motherhood/that often/thankless job/yet one filled/with some of life's/greatest rewards/in the early
> years/there are diapers/sleepless nights/unread books but/priceless/infant smiles.

Shemom is a 10-20-page zine. Receives about 70 poems/year, accepts 50%. Press run is 50 for 30 subscribers. Single copy: $3; subscription: $12/4 issues. Sample: $3.50. Make checks payable to Peggy French.

How to Submit: Submit 3 poems at a time. Accepts previously published poems and simultaneous submissions included in body of message. Accepts e-mail submissions (as attachment or in text box). "Prefer e-mail submission, but not required if material is to be returned, please include a SASE." Guidelines available for SASE or by e-mail. Time between acceptance and publication is 3 months. Responds in 2 months. Pays 1 copy. Acquires one-time rights.

$ ◎ SHINEBRIGHTLY (Specialized: religious, young teens), (formerly *Touch*), P.O. Box 7259, Grand Rapids MI 49510. (616)241-5616. Established 1970. **Managing Editor:** Sara Lynne Hilton.

Magazine Needs: *SHINEbrightly* is a 24-page edition "written for girls 9-14 to show them how God is at work in their lives and in the world around them. We send out a theme update biannually to all our listed freelancers. We prefer short poems with a Christian emphasis that can show girls how God works in their lives." Has published poetry by Janet Shafer Boyanton and Iris Alderson. As a sample the editor selected this poem, "Thanks for Funny Things," by Lois Walfrid Johnson:

> *Thank You for funny things,/for the bubbling feeling of/giggles that fill my insides,/push up,/and spill*
> *over/in a shout of joy!/Thank You, Lord./Thank You!*

SHINEbrightly is published 9 times/year, magazine-sized. Receives 150-200 submissions of poetry/year, accepts 1 poem/year. Circulation is 15,500 subscribers. Subscription: $12.50 US, $15 Canada, $20 foreign. Sample and guidelines: $1 with 8×10 SASE.
How to Submit: Poems must not be longer than 20 lines—prefer much shorter. Accepts simultaneous submissions. Guidelines and upcoming themes available for SASE. Pays $10-15 and 2 contributor's copies.

N ⊘ SHIP OF FOOLS; SHIP OF FOOLS PRESS, Box 1028, University of Rio Grande, Rio Grande OH 45674-9989. (614)992-3333 or (614)245-5353. Established 1983. **Editor:** Jack Hart. **Assistant Editor:** Catherine Grosvenor. **Review Editor:** James Doubleday.
Magazine Needs: *Ship of Fools* is "more or less quarterly." Wants "coherent, well-written, traditional or modern, myth, archetype, love—most types. No concrete, incoherent or greeting card poetry." Has published poetry by Rhina Espaillat, Paula Tatarunis, Simon Perchik, and Lyn Lifshin. As a sample the editors selected these lines by Elva Lauter:

> *Sipping green tea,/I think, "Now I am there."/I will stay until stars/Streak my eyes/and the cup is*
> *empty.*

Ship of Fools as digest-sized, saddle-stapled, offset printed with cover art and graphics. Press run is 190 for 43 subscribers of which 6 are libraries. Subscription: $8/4 issues. Sample: $2.
How to Submit: No previously published poems or simultaneous submissions. Cover letter preferred. Often comments on rejected poems. Responds in 1 month. "If longer than six weeks, write and ask why." Pays 1-2 copies. Reviews books of poetry.
Book/Chapbook Needs & How to Submit: "We have no plans to publish chapbooks in the next year due to time constraints."

◎ SHIRIM, A JEWISH POETRY JOURNAL (Specialized: ethnic), 4611 Vesper Ave., Sherman Oaks CA 91403. (310)476-2861. Established 1982. **Editor:** Marc Dworkin.
Magazine Needs: *Shirim* appears biannually and publishes "poetry that reflects Jewish living without limiting to specific symbols, images, or contents." Has published poetry by Robert Mezcy, Karl Shapiro, and Grace Schulmon. *Shirim* is 40 pages, 4×5, desktop-published, saddle-stapled with card stock cover. Press run is 200. Subscription: $7. Sample: $4.
How to Submit: Submit 4 poems at a time. No previously published poems or simultaneous submissions. Cover letter preferred. Seldom comments on rejected poems. Publishes theme issues regularly. Responds in 3 months. Acquires first rights.

⊘ SIERRA NEVADA COLLEGE REVIEW, 999 Tahoe Blvd., Incline Village NV 89451. Established 1990. **Editor:** June Sylvester Saraceno.
Magazine Needs: *Sierra Nevada College Review* is an annual literary magazine published in May, featuring poetry and short fiction by new writers. "We want image-oriented poems with a distinct, genuine voice. Although we don't tend to publish 'light verse,' we do appreciate, and often publish, poems that make us laugh. We try to steer clear of sentimental, clichéd, or obscure poetry. No limit on length, style, etc." Has published poetry by Carol Frith, Simon Perchik, Taylor Graham, and Maximilian Werner. As a sample the editor selected these lines from "*Decima* to the Corn Fields in Homestead, Florida" by Virgil Suarez:

> *It was here you spent so many of cimarron sunrises,/among the green stalks, budding ears of corn,/*
> *checking for epidemias del maiz, your boots muddy,/reddened with fury of so much walking/among*
> *the tall proud stalks . . .*

Sierra Nevada College Review is about 75 pages, with cover art only. "We receive approximately 500 poems/year and accept approximately 50." Press run is 500. Subscription: $5/year. Sample: $2.50.

THE ◎ SYMBOL indicates a market with a specific or unique focus. This specialized area of interest is listed in parentheses behind the market title.

How to Submit: Submit 5 poems at a time. Accepts simultaneous submissions; no previously published poems. Reads submissions September 1 through March 1 only. Sometimes comments on rejected poems. Responds in about 3 months. Pays 2 contributor's copies.

Advice: "We're looking for poetry that shows subtlety and skill."

◐ ◎ **SILVER WINGS/MAYFLOWER PULPIT (Specialized: religious, spirituality/inspirational); POETRY ON WINGS, INC.**, P.O. Box 1000, Pearblossom CA 93553-1000. (661)264-3726. E-mail: wilcoxmyflwrplpt@aol.com. Established 1983. Published by Poetry on Wings, Inc. **Poetry Editor:** Jackson Wilcox.

Magazine Needs: "As a committed Christian service we produce and publish *Silver Wings/Mayflower Pulpit*, a bimonthly poetry magazine. We want poems with a Christian perspective, reflecting a vital personal faith and a love for God and man. Will consider poems from 3-20 lines. Short poems are preferred. Poems over 20 lines will not even be read by the editor. Quite open in regard to meter and rhyme." Has published poetry by Dave Evans, C. David Hay, and Phillip Kolin. As a sample we selected these lines from "Sonnet for the Holy Spirit" by Timothy Daniel Jones:

> The chill that bites the air this starless night/Steals the breath and settles in bone,/But now the mockingbird begins the rite./Now the first rays prepare the ancient way;/Rises the sun to take its aerial throne./Kindles my soul to feel the vital ray!

Silver Wings/Mayflower Pulpit is 16 pages, digest-sized, offset with cartoon-like art. Each issue contains a short inspirational article or sermon plus 15-20 poems. Receives about 1,500 submissions/year, accepts about 260. Press run is 300 with 250 subscribers, 50 shelf sales. Subscription: $10. Sample: $2.

How to Submit: Submit typed ms, double-spaced. Include SASE. Accepts simultaneous submissions; no previously published poems. Time between acceptance and publication can be up to 2 years. Guidelines and upcoming themes are available for SASE. Responds in 3 weeks, providing SASE is supplied. Pays 1 contributor's copy. "We occasionally offer an award to a poem we consider outstanding and most closely in the spirit of what *Silver Wings* seeks to accomplish." Acquires first rights.

Also Offers: Sponsors an annual contest. For theme and details send SASE.

Advice: "We are interested in poetry that has a spiritual content and may be easily understood by people of humble status and simple lifestyle."

$ ◐ **SILVERFISH REVIEW PRESS; GERALD CABLE BOOK AWARD**, (formerly *Silverfish Review*), P.O. Box 3541, Eugene OR 97403. (541)344-5060. E-mail: sfrpress@aol.com. Established 1979. **Editor:** Rodger Moody.

Book/Chapbook Needs & How to Submit: Silverfish Review Press sponsors the *Gerald Cable Poetry Contest*. A $1,000 cash award and publication is awarded annually to the best book-length ms *or* original poetry by an author who has not yet published a full-length collection. No restrictions on the kind of poetry or subject matter; translations not acceptable. Has published *They Grow Wings* by Nin Andrews, *Odd Botany* by Thorpe Moeckel, *Bodies that Hum* by Beth Gylys, and *Inventing Difficulty* by Jessica Greenbaum. Books are $12 and $3.50 p&h. A $20 entry fee must accompany the ms; make checks payable to Silverfish Review Press. Guidelines available for SASE or by e-mail. Pays 10% of press run (out of 1,000).

◐ **SIMPLYWORDS**, 605 Collins Ave., Centerville GA 31028. Phone/fax: (912)953-9482 (between 10 a.m. and 5 p.m. only). E-mail: simplywords@hotmail.com. Website: www.simplywords.net (includes guidelines, contact info, subscription rates). Established 1991. **Editor:** Ruth Niehaus.

Magazine Needs: *SimplyWords* is a quarterly magazine open to all types, forms, and subjects. "No foul language or overtly sexual works." Accepts poetry written by children; "there are no reading fees for children." Has published poetry by Helen McIntosh Gordon, Sarah Jensen, Barbara Cagle Ray, Betty Tuohy, Sheila B. Roark, Donald Harmande, and Daniel Green. *SimplyWords* is 20-30 pages, magazine-sized, deskjet printed and spiral-bound, photo on cover, uses clip art. Receives about 500 poems/year, accepts about 90%. Press run is 60-100 depending on subscriptions and single issue orders in house." Subscription: $18.50/year, "online version subscription $16." Sample: $5.

How to Submit: Send SASE for guidelines before submitting and write 'guidelines' in big block letters on left hand corner of envelope. No e-mail submissions. Line length for poetry is 28 maximum. "Name, address, phone number, e-mail, and line count must be on each page submitted." SASE required. Guidelines available for SASE, by fax, and on website. **Reading fee:** $1/poem. Time between acceptance and publication "depends on what issue your work was accepted for."

Advice: "It is very important that you send for guidelines before you submit to any publication. They all have rules and expect you to be professional enough to respect that. So learn the ropes—read, study, research your craft. If you want to be taken seriously prove that you are by learning your chosen craft."

SINISTER WISDOM (Specialized: lesbian, feminist), P.O. Box 3252, Berkeley CA 94703. E-mail: sw@aalexander.org. Webiste: www.sinisterwisdom.org. Established 1976. **Editor:** Alexis Alexander. **Poetry Editor:** Joan Annsfire.

Magazine Needs: *Sinister Wisdom* is a multicultural lesbian journal. "We want poetry that reflects the diversity of lesbian experience—lesbians of color, Third World, Jewish, old, young, working class, poor, disabled, fat, etc.—from a lesbian perspective. No heterosexual themes. We will not print anything that is oppressive or demeaning to women, or which perpetuates negative stereotypes." Has published work by Gloria Anzaldúa and Betsy Warland. The quarterly magazine is 128-144 pages, digest-sized, flat-spined, with photos and b&w graphics. Press run is 3,500 for 1,000 subscribers of which 100 are libraries; newsstand sales and bookstores are 1,500. Single copy: $6; subscription: $20 US, $25 foreign. Sample: $7.50.

How to Submit: No simultaneous submissions. Accepts submissions on disk, by e-mail (as attachment or in text box), and by regular mail. Time between acceptance and publication is 6 months to 1 year. Publishes theme issues. Upcoming themes available for SASE. Responds in up to 9 months. Pays 2 contributor's copies. Reviews books of poetry in 500-1,500 words, single or multi-book format.

Advice: "Send anything *other* than love poetry and want work by lesbians only."

SKALD, 2 Greenfield Terrace, Menai Bridge, Anglesey LL59 5AY Wales, United Kingdom. Phone: 1248-716343. E-mail: skald@globalnet.co.uk. Website: www.skald.co.uk. Established 1994. **Contact:** Ms. Zoë Skoulding.

Magazine Needs: *Skald* appears 2 times/year and contains "poetry and prose in Welsh or English. We focus on writers in Wales though submissions from elsewhere are welcome." Wants "interesting and varied poetry in Welsh and English. Nothing didactic, sentimental, or nostalgic." As a sample the editor selected these lines from "On the End of Pier" by Dan Wyke:

> Families stroll on what feels like terra firma/to where the wind is stronger, and candyfloss thins.//It
> blows us closer, as if it might blow us apart,/pointing at the starlings and saying to our children://
> leaves; a scarf; a cape; a genie; or nothing . . . a gull's/plaintive cry sharpens against the flinty sky.

Skald is 30-40 pages, A5, professionally printed and saddle-stapled with textured card cover, contains b&w artwork. Receives about 300 poems/year, accepts about 25%. Press run is 300 for 20 subscribers, 250 shelf sales; 20 distributed free to other magazines, art boards. Single copy: £3; subscription: £6/year (payments in sterling only).

How to Submit: Submit 2 poems at a time. No previously published poems or simultaneous submissions. Cover letter preferred. Time between acceptance and publication is 4 months. Often comments on rejected poems. Responds in 1 month. Pays 1 contributor's copy.

SKIDROW PENTHOUSE, 44 Four Corners Rd., Blairstown NJ 07825. (908)362-6808 or (212)286-2600. Established 1998. **Editor:** Rob Cook. **Editor:** Stephanie Dickinson.

Magazine Needs: *Skidrow Penthouse* is published "to give emerging and idiosyncratic writers a new forum in which to publish their work. We are looking for deeply felt authentic voices, whether surreal, confessional, New York School, formal, or free verse. Work should be well crafted: attention to line-break and diction. We want poets who sound like themselves, not workshop professionals. We don't want gutless posturing, technical precision with no subject matter, explicit sex and violence without craft, or abstract intellectualizing. We are not impressed by previous awards and publications." Has published poetry by Doug Dorph, James Grinwis, Hilary Melton, Alan Brich, David Chorlton, and Nola Perez. As a sample we selected these lines from "Nocturne for the Nocturnal" by Karl Tierney:

> the redundancies of your male side—hostile indifference—/Are doomed to glorious basking in street
> light, no other./But you need not be beautiful, only self-sustaining.

Skidrow Penthouse is 250 pages, 6×9, professionally printed and perfect-bound with 4-color cover, includes original art and photographs as well as contest announcements, magazine advertisements. Receives about 500 poems/year, accepts 3%. Publish 35-40 poems/issue. Press run is 300 for 50 subscribers; 10% distributed free to journals for review consideration. Single copy: $12.50; subscription: $20. Make checks payable to Rob Cook or Stephanie Dickinson.

How to Submit: Submit 3-5 poems at a time. Accepts previously published poems and simultaneous submissions. "Include a legal sized SASE; also name and address on every page of your submission. No handwritten submissions will be considered." Time between acceptance and publication is 1 year. Seldom comments on rejected poems. Responds in 2 months. Pays 1 contributor's copy. Acquires one-time rights. Reviews books and chapbooks of poetry and other magazines in 1,500 words, single book format. Poets may send books for review consideration.

Also Offers: "We're trying to showcase a poet in each issue by publishing up to 60 page collections within the magazine." Send SASE for details about chapbook competitions.

Advice: "We get way too many anecdotal fragments posing as poetry; too much of what we receive feels like this mornings inspiration mailed this afternoon. The majority of those who submit do not seem to have put in the sweat a good poem demands. Also, the ratio of submissions to sample copy purchases is 50:1. Just because our name is Skidrow Penthouse does not mean we are a repository for genre work or 'eat, shit, shower, and shave' poetry."

SKIPPING STONES: A MULTICULTURAL CHILDREN'S MAGAZINE; ANNUAL YOUTH HONOR AWARDS (Specialized: bilingual, children/teen, ethnic/nationality, nature/ecology, social issues), P.O. Box 3939, Eugene OR 97403. (541)342-4956. E-mail: skipping@efn.org. Website: www.efn.org/~skipping (includes guidelines, sample poetry, and details on the Youth Honor Awards). Established 1988. **Editor:** Arun Toké.

Magazine Needs: *Skipping Stones* is a "nonprofit magazine published bimonthly during the school year (5 issues) that encourages cooperation, creativity and celebration of cultural and ecological richness." Wants poetry by youth under 19; 30 lines maximum on "nature, multicultural and social issues, family, freedom . . . uplifting." No work by adults. As a sample we selected these lines from "Dry Reflections" by Amanda Marusich, age 16 from Eugene, OR:

> velvet green/carpets the wet dirt heavy with rain and a deep, rocky scent/clear, clean water/gushes
> over the riverbed with thunderous cascades/showers of mist/it is a vibrant/tangled/living web.

Skipping Stones is 8½×11, saddle-stapled, printed on recycled paper. Receives about 500-1,000 poems/year, accepts 10%. Press run is 2,500 for 1,700 subscribers. Subscription: $25. Sample: $5.

How to Submit: Submit up to 3 poems at a time. Accepts simultaneous submissions; no previously published poems. Accepts e-mail submissions included in body of message. Cover letter preferred. "Include your cultural background, experiences and what was the inspiration behind your creation." Time between acceptance and publication is up to 9 months. Poems are circulated to a 3-member editorial board. "Generally a piece is chosen for publication when all the editorial staff feel good about it." Seldom comments on rejected poems. Publishes theme issues. Guidelines and upcoming themes available for SASE. Responds in up to 4 months. Pays 1 contributor's copy, offers 25% discount for more. Acquires all rights. Returns rights after publication, but "we keep reprint rights."

Also Offers: Sponsors Annual Youth Honor Awards for 7-17 year olds. Theme for Annual Youth Honor Awards is "Multicultural and Nature Awareness." Deadline: January 20. Entry fee: $3 which includes free issue featuring winners. Details available for SASE.

SKYLINE PUBLICATIONS LITERARY MAGAZINE; SPINNINGS . . . INTENSE TALES OF LIFE QUARTERLY, P.O. Box 295, Stormville NY 12582-0295. (845)227-5171. E-mail: SkylineEditor@aol.com. Website: www.SkylinePublications.com (includes poetry, stories, and art). Established 2001. **Editor:** Victoria Valentine.

Magazine Needs: *Skyline Literary Magazine* appears monthly publishing poetry, short stories, art, and special interest columns. "Easy-read, emotional literature for all to enjoy. Collector-quality full-color magazines." Wants emotional, meaningful, understandable poetry; traditional, free verse, haiku, all styles, all genre. "We seek a smooth entertaining read for relaxation and enjoyment. Will consider experimental. No porn, religious, political, or racism." Recently published poetry by Lynn Stowe, Steven Manchester, Victoria Rose, Roger Worley, Latorial Faison, and Richard Fein. As a sample the editor selected these lines from "Where Dreams Once Flowed" by Lizette Sinclair:

> A homage to fantasy given without obligation./Pride of self, satisfaction in abundance./Kindness was
> an art; an impression of love./The days longed for the night's caress/to bring upon it, a veil of comfort./
> To dwell within the security of its motives.

Skyline is over 62 pages, tabloid-sized, laser-printed, saddle-stapled, containing 60 lb. gloss paper with color cover and interior art supplied by artists each month. Receives about 600 poems/year, accepts about 55%. Publishes about 30 poems/issue. Press run is 136 plus for store sales (orders), 60 subscribers of which 6 are libraries, 50 shelf sales; about 20 are distributed free to authors/artists. Single copy: $5.95 plus $2.50 US postage. Sample: $3.95 plus $2.50 USA postage. Make checks payable to Skyline Publications.

How to Submit: Submit 3-4 poems at a time. Line length for poetry is 35 maximum (preferred, with exceptions). Accepts previously published poems; no simultaneous submissions. Accepts e-mail and disk submissions; no fax or snail mail submissions. Short 4-5 line bio is required. Cover letter with bio is requested. Electronic submissions inside e-mail or mail CD/disk. Art attachments to e-mail or send disk. Attempts to read weekly and respond within 1 month. "I personally read, select, edit all poetry and stories." Seldom comments on rejected poems. "Must submit written Consent to Publish Agreement, prior to publication (for print only)." Occasionally publishes theme issues. List of upcoming themes available by e-mail or on website newsletter. Guidelines available on website. Responds in 1 month to submissions. Rarely sends prepublication galleys (upon request only). Pays 1 contributor's copy. Acquires one-time rights "exclusive for 30-90 days with possible reprints of back issues."

Also Offers: Cash Prize Contests. Special Edition *Tribute to America*, poetry and photo accepted. Also publishes *SpinningS. . .intense tales of life* quarterly featuring compelling short stories, provocative poetry, articles, color and art. Same quality and size as *Skyline*. "Variety of poetry and stories will be used on *Skyline* website bimonthly. Monthly print magazine publishes different original material. *SpinningS* . . . quarterly is print only with online previews and guidelines."

Advice: "Don't expect miracles overnight. Persevere! Scream loud enough and you will be heard, and always . . . reach for the sky, it's closer than you think!"

SLANT: A JOURNAL OF POETRY, Box 5063, University of Central Arkansas, 201 Donaghey Ave., Conway AR 72035-5000. (501)450-5107. Website: www.uca.edu/divisions/academic/english/Slant/HOMPAGE.html (includes guidelines, editor/board of readers, table of contents from current volume, and index 1987-1996). Established 1987. **Editor:** James Fowler.

Magazine Needs: *Slant* is an annual using *only* poetry. Uses "traditional and 'modern' poetry, even experimental, moderate length, any subject on approval of Board of Readers; purpose is to publish a journal of fine poetry from all regions of the United States and beyond. No haiku, no translations." Accepts poetry written by children ("although we're not a children's journal.") Has published poetry bySean Brendan-Brown and Susan Terris. As a sample the editor selected these lines from "I Know I Know I Know My Boundless Greed" by John McKernan:

> A thirst for color photos/of Mohican riveters/Halfway to the yellow moon/Catwalking a red & blue I-
> Beam

Slant is 125 pages, professionally printed on quality stock, flat-spined, with matte card cover. Receives about 1,500 poems/year, accepts 70-80. Press run is 200 for 70-100 subscribers. Sample: $10.

How to Submit: Submit up to 5 poems of moderate length with SASE between September and mid-November. "Put name, address (including e-mail if available) and phone on the top of each page." No simultaneous submissions or previously published poems. Editor comments on rejected poems "on occasion." Allow 3-4 months from November 15 deadline for response. Pays 1 contributor's copy.

Advice: "I would like to see more formal and narrative verse."

SLAPERING HOL PRESS, 300 Riverside Dr., Sleepy Hollow NY 10591-1414. (914)332-5953. Fax: (914)332-4825. E-mail: info@writerscenter.org. Website: www.writerscenter.org (includes listing/brief description of publications, ordering info, contest guidelines). Established 1990. **Contact:** Stephanie Strickland and Margo Stever.

Book/Chapbook Needs: "Slapering Hol Press is the small press imprint of The Hudson Valley Writers' Center, created in 1990 to provide publishing opportunities for emerging poets who have not yet published a book or chapbook, and to produce anthologies of a thematic nature. Chapbooks are selected for publication on the basis of an annual competition judged by a nationally known poet." Recently published poetry by Andrew Krivak, Rachel Loden, Ellen Goldsmith, Lynn McGee, Paul-Victor Winters, Jianqing Zheng, Sondra Upham, and Pearl Karrer. As a sample the editors selected these lines from "The Osprey" by Andrew Krivak from his chapbook *Islands*:

> When the ebb falls slack and the bay has stopped/the wind to appease the mud and stiletto reeds/
> basking in the stench of dead low tide,//the yearly visitors use their oars and ride/the current in as it
> turns. I hear them talk/of food, the smell; the flies out there are cruel.

Slapering Hol Press publishes 1 chapbook/year. Chapbooks are usually 20-24 pages, offset-printed, hand sewn, 80 lb. cover weight cover.

How to Submit: For submission guidelines, see separate listing for Slapering Hol Press Chapbook competition in the Contests & Awards section. Order sample chapbooks by sending $13.50 postage paid to Hudson Valley Writers' Center.

SLIPSTREAM, Box 2071, New Market Station, Niagara Falls NY 14301-0071. (716)282-2616 (after 5PM, EST). E-mail: editors@slipstreampress.org. Website: www.slipstreampress.org (includes guidelines, announcements, samples of poetry, annual poetry chapbook winner, chapbook competition guidelines, audio/video information, back issues, and order form). Established 1980. **Poetry Editors:** Dan Sicoli, Robert Borgatti, and Livio Farallo.

Magazine Needs: *Slipstream* is a "small press literary mag published in the spring and is about 90% poetry and 10% fiction/prose, with some artwork. Likes new work with contemporary urban flavor. Writing must have a cutting edge to get our attention. We like to keep an open forum, any length, subject, style. Best to see a sample to get a feel. Like city stuff as opposed to country. Like poetry that springs from the gut, screams from dark alleys, inspired by experience." No "pastoral, religious, traditional, rhyming" poetry. Has published poetry by M. Scott Douglass, Johnny Cordova, Douglas Goetsch, Gerald Locklin, Alison Miller, Jim Daniels, James Snodgrass, and Chrys Darkwater. As a sample the editors selected these lines from "Jack of Trades" by Martin Vest:

> one morning Jack Micheline got onto the train/and when he got off/he left his body on the seat/the
> way some people/leave a glove

The unspeakable nature of trauma

All the pundits said everything changed, changed utterly on 9/11/ 2001, but I am not so sure. As days and weeks unfolded afterward, I found myself thinking the chatter about everything changing seemed part of some after-trauma syndrome. I also thought we were all in shock, stopped in our tracks. I noted in myself a strange combination of numbed feelings and hypervigilant alertness. I began to think the ubiquitous flag-waving and nearly celebratory war-planning were masking a host of perplexities and helpless feelings.

Photo by Leslie Bowen

Fred Marchant

In Boston, where I live, there was a flurry of readings and literary benefits, and underneath them all one could hear a terrible and frightening perplexity stirring. How to talk about what had happened—and was still unfinished? How on earth could one hope to write poetry about it?

I would check in with others to see if they had been able to write at all. Some poets were generating plenty of new work; others felt they were weighed down under a pall of silence. Though I was somewhere in between, I recognized a shared feeling among my fellow poets: That words were filling the air around us but not capturing the things that most needed words. More and more had begun to feel like less and less.

The psychiatrist Judith Lewis Herman in *Trauma and Recovery* (Basic Books) helps clarify some of this moment's texture for me. She writes that to witness trauma is to be traumatized oneself (and I think we were all witnesses to trauma in the autumn of 2001). Herman also says that traumatized people often find themselves governed by a pair of contradictory desires. There is the sense that the story must be told, yet traumatic experiences by their nature are unspeakable. The traumatized person then oscillates between the desire to speak and the knowledge that no words can do the experience justice. To even speak about trauma sometimes seems the shattering of a decorous and protective silence. At the same time, one can feel something inside urgently needing words that will help bring the unspeakable back into a realm of dialogue and community.

If there is a first lesson in writing poetry at all, especially poems about traumatic material, it is that one need not try to say everything at once. One could start with the fragments or edges of the experience. In doing so, one creates a little bit of free space; that is, psychic space in which one can be freer with the material than if the intent was somehow to capture the whole experience. An "angle" of vision might yield more than the attempt at panorama. You can see this in this classic haiku by Yosa Buson (translated by Robert Hass):

I go,
    you stay;
    two autumns.

In this poem's dramatized moment of parting, it doesn't really matter whether the loved one is leaving on an ordinary journey or the parting is as final as a death. Either way, the poem is exquisite in its expression of loss. There is something more to this poem than its palpable sorrow, though. In that last line's quick, intuitive, and nonliteral connection between parting and autumn, the poet tells us that both of these people are dying just a little. Out of the friction of the two literal facts of one person going and the other staying, the third line has leapt into an expressive domain, saying something that is both "fanciful" and a measure of just how deep this parting is wounding the poet.

This haiku shows us how valuable it is to honor the fanciful, the nonliteral, the metaphorical, the nonrealistic element in the imagination. The poet has to be alert to these imaginative stirrings, even if they seem to draw us away from factual description. Just think how much would be lost from Buson's poem if he had dropped the last line saying somehow it wasn't literally true! It is in those stirrings of the nonliteral that one often finds that which is hardest to say and yet most in need of saying.

That lesson first came home to me in writing "Butterfly Chair" from my first book, *Tipping Point* (Word Works, 1994). It was just about the most difficult poem I had ever written. It concerns a scene of domestic violence, recalled from childhood.

"Butterfly Chair"

> I can see it again tonight in rough outline
> where the clear-cuts
> rise and slant up the valley:
>
> the middle room of the flat where I grew up,
> a corner space for the television,
> where I watched
>
> the quarrels spill like hot oil flowing from
> kitchen to parlor,
> my father holding my mother
>
> by the forearm to keep her steady while
> he hit her, the two of them
> silvered, and me slung
>
> in the butterfly chair, the rounded canvas
> bottom so deep, my feet
> didn't reach the floor.
>
> Transfixed, a moth awash in the light
> of what it wants so much,
> I would stare through them,
>
> into the window of the tube, and its brightness,
> holding onto a glassy wish
> that I would die.

It took me many years to write this poem, and so it is more a model of "emotion recollected in tranquility" than a model of what it means to write in the midst of difficult times. But there is some hard-earned lesson embedded in this poem. I remember the hardest thing for me was to focus the poem somehow on the little boy's helplessness. At first, I didn't consciously know that was my real topic; I thought my real concern was the horror of the violence. In taking the poem through drafts, however, I began to recognize that the helpless, almost paralyzed state was what I was really reaching for. I didn't have to explain, understand, or solve all the problems implied by this scene. What I had to do was stay with that boy's inner life and its freezing up. I had to flee with him into the snowy screen of the television. And when I did, I arrived at the comparison of the boy to a moth transfixed by a light. For me, that metaphor is the climactic moment of the poem, shifting the poem into another realm; namely, the range of feelings that include the wish he could die, happily, like a moth into a flame.

Buson's haiku and my "Butterfly Chair" are poems of more or less private trauma. But lessons similar to theirs also can be found in some very great poems about contemporary social issues. Nobel Laureate Seamus Heaney, for example, came of age as a writer in Northern Ireland during many years of sectarian violence. He could not help but feel the need to write about that suffering. His goal, he once said, was to find images and metaphors that were somehow adequate to his experience.

A breakthrough came when Heaney encountered the photographs in P.V. Glob's *The Bog People*, an archaeological book about Iron Age corpses retrieved from peat bogs in Denmark. These bodies were remarkably well preserved by the peat, and all signs indicated they had been ritual sacrifices. To Heaney's mind, these victims resonated with victims of the violence in his own time. He grasped a basic metaphorical connection between both, and this led him to write a remarkable series of poems about "bog people," presenting these bodies as appalling yet archetypal images of tribal killing, both ancient and modern, Protestant or Catholic.

The African-American poet and National Book Award winner Lucille Clifton wrote a poem in response to the dragging death of James Byrd, Jr. in Jasper, Texas, a few years ago. How to express her own horror and disgust at racist violence? She did not write directly about his violent death, but made a leap of imagination to write in this man's voice, or rather in the voice of James Byrd's ghost: "Who is the human in this place?" he asks, "the thing dragged or the draggers?" Imagining this voice, Clifton bears witness to the unspeakable nature of the trauma, and in the process finds the words to express her own disgust and despair.

The lesson I discern in these poems should not be thought of as a recipe or a road map. It is not a lesson about poetic device or strategy. It is much more a lesson in the rewards a writer gains by trusting the imagination's extensions beyond the literal facts of a trauma.

Emily Dickinson said to tell the truth, but "tell it slant." It may very well be that the most profound and heart-rending truths can enter into language only from the imaginative perimeter of consciousness. I'm reminded of what is known as "night-vision," the way the eye's iris will widen to bring in more of whatever ambient light there is, so one can really "see in the dark." This is a good analogue for what can happen when writing poetry.

—*Fred Marchant*

Slipstream appears 1-2 times/year in a 7 × 8½ format, 80-100 pages, professionally printed, perfect-bound, using b&w photos and graphics. It contains mostly free verse, some stanza patterns. Receives over 2,500 submissions of poetry/year, accepts less than 10%. Press run is 500 for 400 subscribers of which 10 are libraries. Subscription: $20/2 issues and 2 chapbooks. Sample: $7.

How to Submit: No e-mail submissions. Editor sometimes comments on rejected poems. Publishes theme issues. Guidelines and upcoming themes available for SASE and on website. "Reading for a general issue through 2002." Responds in up to 2 months, "if SASE included." Pays 1-2 copies.

Also Offers: Annual chapbook contest has December 1 deadline. Reading fee: $10. Submit up to 40 pages of poetry, any style, previously published work OK with acknowledgments. Guidelines available for SASE and on website. Winner receives $1,000 and 50 copies. All entrants receive copy of winning chapbook and an issue of the magazine. Past winners have included Sherman Alexie, Katharine Harer, Robert Cooperman, Leslie Anne Mcilroy, Serena Fusek, Rene Christopher, Gerald Locklin, Alison Pelegrin, Laurie Mezzaferro, and most recently Ronald Wardall for "The Eyes of a Vertial Cut."

Advice: "Do not waste time submitting your work 'blindly.' Sample issues from the small press first to determine which ones would be most receptive to your work."

◑ **SLOPE**, E-mail: ethan@slope.org. Website: www.slope.org. Established 1999. **Editor:** Ethan Paquin.
Magazine Needs: *Slope* "is a quarterly, online journal of poetry featuring work that is challenging, dynamic, and innovative. We encourage new writers while continuing to publish award-winning and established poets from around the world." Wants "no particular style. Interested in poetry in translation." Recently published poetry by Forrest Gander, Paul Hoover, Eleni Sikelianos, James Tate, Bruce Beasley, and Charles Bernstein.
How to Submit: Submit 3-6 poems at a time. No previously published poems; or simultaneous submissions. Accepts submissions by e-mail only (as attachments). "Submit poems via e-mail to the address at the website." Reads submissions year round. Time between acceptance and publication is 3-6 months. Seldom comments on rejections. Guidelines available by e-mail or on website. Responds in 3 months. Acquires one-time rights. Reviews books and chapbooks of poetry in 400 words, single book format. Poets may send books for review consideration; "query first."

◑ **A SMALL GARLIC PRESS (ASGP); AGNIESZKA'S DOWRY (AgD)**, 5445 Sheridan #3003, Chicago IL 60640. E-mail: asgp@enteract.com or marek@enteract.com or ketzle@ketzle.net. Website: www.enteract.com/~asgp/. Established 1995. **Co-Editors:** Marek Lugowski, katrina grace craig.
Magazine Needs: *Agnieszka's Dowry (AgD)* is "a magazine published both in print and as a permanent Internet installation of poems and graphics, letters to Agnieszka, and a navigation in an interesting space, all conducive to fast and comfortable reading. No restrictions on form or type. We use contextual and juxtapositional tie-ins with other material in making choices, so visiting the online *AgD* is assumed to be part of any submission." Single copy: $4. Make checks payable to A Small Garlic Press.
How to Submit: Submit 5-10 poems at a time. "Please inform us of the status of publishing rights." E-mail submissions only, plain text ("unless poet doesn't have the means to e-mail us—then we will accept submissions by regular mail"). Sometimes comments on rejected poems. Guidelines available on website. Responds online usually in 2 months. Pays 1 contributor's copy. Acquires one-time rights where applicable.
Book/Chapbook Needs & How to Submit: A Small Garlic Press (ASGP) publishes 2-7 chapbooks of poetry/year. Query with a full online ms, ASCII (plain text) only.
Also Offers: "See our webpage for policies and submission guidelines. The press catalog and page of links to other markets and resources for poetry and a Broadsides section are maintained online at our website."

◔ **SMALL POND MAGAZINE OF LITERATURE**, P.O. Box 664, Stratford CT 06615. (203)378-4066. Established 1964. **Editor:** Napoleon St. Cyr.
Magazine Needs: *Small Pond Magazine of Literature* is a literary triquarterly that features poetry "and anything else the editor feels is interesting, original, important." Poetry can be "any style, form, topic, except haiku, so long as it is deemed good, but limit of about 100 lines." Wants "nothing about cats, pets, flowers, butterflies, etc. Generally nothing under eight lines." Has published poetry by Marvin Solomon, Ruth Moon Kempher, Carol Hamilton, Herb Coursen, and Lynn Lifshin. *Small Pond* is 40 pages, digest-sized, offset from typescript on off-white paper, with colored matte card cover, saddle-stapled, artwork both on cover and inside. Press run is 300, of which about a third go to libraries. Subscription: $10/3 issues. Sample (including guidelines): $3 for a random selection, $4 current. "Random back issue for $2; same quality, famous editor's comments."
How to Submit: Doesn't want 60 pages of anything; "dozen pages of poems max." Name and address on each page. No previously published poems or simultaneous submissions. Brief cover letter preferred. Time between acceptance and publication is within up to 15 months. Responds in up to 30 days. Pays 2

copies. Acquires all rights. Returns rights with written request including stated use. "One-time use per request." All styles and forms are welcome here. Guidelines available for SASE and in publication. Responds quickly, often with comments to guide poets whose work interests him.

SMARTISH PACE; ERSKINE J. POETRY PRIZE, P.O. Box 22161, Baltimore MD 21203. Website: wwwsmartishpace.com (includes interviews, samples, guidelines, links, contact information, poetry submission link, advertising rates, contest information, and more). Established 1999. **Editor:** Stephen Reichert.

Magazine Needs: *Smartish Pace*, published in spring and fall, contains poetry, translations, essays on poetry, reviews, and interviews with poets. "*Smartish Pace* is an independent poetry journal and is not affiliated with any institution." No restrictions on style or content of poetry. Has published poetry by Diane Wakoski, Irving Feldman, Mark Jarman, Rachel Hadas, Sherod Santos, Allen Grossman, and X.J. Kennedy. As a sample the editor selected "World Etiquette of Cool" by Gaylord Brewer:

> *Don't try to follow the trial, child,/my woods get dark. Go to the clubhouse/and enjoy the rest of your little life./Truth's for suckers. As for cool, we have/what the gods imparted. To you, none.*

Smartish Pace is about 80 pages, 6×9, professionally printed and perfect-bound with color, heavy stock cover. Receives about 3,000 poems/year, accepts 4%; publishes 50-60 poems/issue. Press run is 500 for 300 subscribers. Subscription: $12. Sample: $6.

How to Submit: Submit no more than 6 poems at a time. Accepts simultaneous submissions; no previously published poems. "Please provide prompt notice when poems have been accepted elsewhere. Cover letter with bio and SASE is required. Electronic submissions to www.smartishpace.com are encouraged." Submit seasonal poems 8 months in advance. Time between acceptance and publication is up to 1 year. Guidelines available for SASE or on website. Responds in up to 8 months. Pays 1 copy. Acquires first rights. Encourages unsolicited reviews, essays, interviews. Poets and publishers encouraged to send review copies. All books received will also be listed in the books received sections of each issue and at the website along with ordering information and a link to the publisher's website.

Also Offers: "*Smartish Pace* hosts the annual Erskine J. Poetry Prize. Submit 3 poems with $5 entry fee in either check or money order made payable to *Smartish Pace*. Additional poems may be submitted for $1 per poem. No more than 8 poems may be submitted (8 poems = $5 + $5 = $10). Winners receive cash prizes and publication. Recent winners Mark DeFoe, Gaylord Brewer, and Susan Cavanaugh. See website for complete information."

GIBBS SMITH, PUBLISHER; PEREGRINE SMITH POETRY COMPETITION, P.O. Box 667, Layton UT 84041-0667. Website: www.gibbs-smith.com (includes guidelines, contact info, contest rules, and catalog). Established 1971. Poetry Series established 1988. **Poetry Editor:** Monica Millward Weeks.

Book/Chapbook Needs: Wants "serious, contemporary poetry of merit." Has published *You Want to Sell Me a Small Antique* by Rebecca Lilly, *Braver Deeds* by Gary Young, *The Brink* by Peter Sears, *Sister Betty Reads the Whole You* by Susan Holahan, and *How Late Desire Looks* by Katrina Roberts. Books are selected for publication through competition for the Peregrine Smith Poetry Prize of $1,000 plus publication.

How to Submit: Entries are received in April only and require a $20 reading fee and SASE. Mss should be 48-64 typewritten pages. "We publish only one unsolicited poetry ms per year—the winner of our annual Peregrine Smith Poetry Competition. For guidelines to the contest, interested poets should send a request with SASE through the mail." The winner of the 2001 contest was Rebecca Lilly's *You Want to Sell Me a Small Antique*. The judge for the series was Christopher Merrill.

SMITHS KNOLL, 49 Church Rd., Little Glemham, Woodbridge, Suffolk IP13 0BJ England. Established 1991. **Co-Editors:** Roy Blackman and Michael Laskey.

Magazine Needs: *Smiths Knoll* is a magazine appearing 3 times/year. Looks for poetry with honesty, depth of feeling, lucidity, and craft. As a sample the editors selected these lines from "Separate Paths" by Jennifer Copley:

> *She admired his jacket, loaded with studs,/which he trailed through grass/Like a thick black tongue./ He adored her creased school skirt/and her mouth that wouldn't say goodbye/as they left by separate paths.*

Smiths Knoll is 60 pages, A5, offset-litho, perfect-bound, with 2-color card cover. Receives up to 8,000 poems/year, "accepts about one in fifty." Press run is 500 for 350 subscribers. Single copy: £5; subscription: £14/3 issues (outside UK).

How to Submit: Submit up to 5 poems at a time to the co-editors. "We would consider poems previously published in magazines outside the U.K." No simultaneous submissions. Poems only. Doesn't commission work. "Cover letters should be brief: name, address, date, number of poems sent (or titles). We don't want life histories or complete publishing successes or what the poems are about. We do want sufficient IRCs for return of work. We try to offer constructive criticism of rejected poems where possible." Tries to respond within 1 month (outside UK). Pays £20 plus 1 copy/poem.

SMOKE, First Floor, Liver House, 96 Bold St., Liverpool L1 4HY England. Phone: (0151)709-3688. Established 1974. **Editor:** Dave Ward.

Magazine Needs: *Smoke* is a biannual publication of poetry and graphics. Wants "short, contemporary poetry, expressing new ideas through new forms." Has published poetry by Carol Ann Duffy, Roger McGough, Jackie Kay, and Henry Normal. *Smoke* is 24 pages, A5, offset-litho printed and stapled with paper cover, includes art. Receives about 3,000 poems/year, accepts about 40 poems. Press run is 750 for 350 subscribers of which 18 are libraries, 100 shelf sales; 100 distributed free to contributors/other mags. Subscription: $5 (cash). Sample: $1. Make checks payable to Windows Project (cash preferred/exchanges rate on cheques not viable).

How to Submit: Submit 6 poems at a time. Accepts previously published poems and simultaneous submissions. Cover letter preferred. Time between acceptance and publication is 6 months. Seldom comments on rejected poems. Responds in 2 weeks. Pays 1 copy.

$ SNOWAPPLE PRESS, P.O. Box 66024, Heritage Postal Outlet, Edmonton, Alberta T6J 6T4 Canada. Established 1991. **Editor:** Vanna Tessier.

Book/Chapbook Needs: Snowapple Press is an "independent publisher dedicated to writers who wish to contribute to literature." Publishes 4-5 paperbacks/year. Wants "contemporary, expansive, experimental and literary poetry." Has published poetry by Gilberto Finzi, Peter Prest, Vanna Tessier, Bob Stallworthy, I.B. Iskov, and Paolo Valesio. Books are usually 120-160 pages, offset-printed with #10 colored card cover with "art/graphics suitable to theme."

How to Submit: Submit 5 poems at a time, 14-70 lines each. Accepts previously published poems and simultaneous submissions. Cover letter preferred. Reads submissions September through March 31 only. Time between acceptance and publication is up to 18 months. Poems are circulated to an editorial board. Responds in 1 month. Pays 10% royalty, $100 honorarium, and 25 author's copies (out of a press run of 500).

Also Offers: Sponsors an occasional anthology contest. Send SASE (or SAE and IRC) with all correspondence. "Queries welcome for 12th anniversary 2003 Celebration Anthology to be available spring 2004."

$ SNOWY EGRET (Specialized: animals, nature), P.O. Box 9, Bowling Green IN 47833. Established 1922 by Humphrey A. Olsen. **Contact:** editors.

Magazine Needs: Appearing in spring and autumn, *Snowy Egret* specializes in work that is "nature-oriented: poetry that celebrates the abundance and beauty of nature or explores the interconnections between nature and the human psyche." As a sample the editors selected the middle and final lines of "Night Song" by Conrad Hilberry:

> All creatures/sleep,/except the fish./. . . all night long,/barracuda weave and angle/through the weeds,/
> bluefins rise, flash/in the broken moonlight,/and dive again./Sharks graze old wrecks,/and marlins/
> slice the dark.

Snowy Egret is 60-page, magazine-sized format, offset, saddle-stapled, with original graphics. Receives about 500 poems/year, accepts about 30. Press run is 800 for 500 subscribers of which 50 are libraries. Sample: $8; subscription: $12/year, $20/2 years.

How to Submit: Guidelines available for #10 SASE. Responds in 1 month. Always sends prepublication galleys. Pays $4/poem or $4/page plus 2 copies. Acquires first North American and one-time reprint rights.

Advice: "Fresh detailed observations gives poetry authenticity and immediacy."

SO TO SPEAK: A FEMINIST JOURNAL OF LANGUAGE AND ART (Specialized: women/feminism), George Mason University, 4400 University Dr., MS 2D6, Fairfax VA 22030-4444. (703)993-3625. E-mail: sts@gmu.edu. Website: www.gmu.edu/org/sts. Established 1991. **Poetry Editor:** Susan Gardner Dillon.

Magazine Needs: *So to Speak* is published 2 times/year. "We publish high-quality work about women's lives—fiction, nonfiction (including book reviews and interviews), b&w photography and artwork along with poetry. We look for poetry that deals with women's lives, but also lives up to a high standard of language, form and meaning. We are most interested in experimental, high-quality work. There are no formal specifications. We like work that takes risks successfully. No unfinished/unpolished work." Has published poetry by Marcella Durand, Jean Donnelly, Heather Fuller, Carolyn Forché, Allison Joseph, Jenn McCreary, and Elizabeth Treadwell. As a sample they selected these lines from "Sister Cell" by Allison Cobb:

> close/vanish appear/kin knees sis/my toes is/divided half whole/live split to/cry sister/the pull

So To Speak is 128 pages, digest-sized, photo-offset printed and perfect-bound, with glossy cover, includes b&w photos and art, ads. Receives about 300 poems/year, accepts 10%. Press run is 1,300 for 40 subscribers, 50 shelf sales; 500 distributed free to students/submitters. Subscription: $11. Sample: $6.

How to Submit: Submit 3-5 poems at a time. Accepts simultaneous submissions; no previously published poems. Cover letter preferred. "Please submit poems as you wish to see them in print. We do have an e-mail address but do not accept e-mail submissions. Be sure to include a cover letter with contact info, publications credits, and awards received." Reads submissions August 15 through October 15 and December 31 through March 15. Time between acceptance and publication is 6-8 months. Seldom comments on rejected poems. Occasionally publishes theme issues. Guidelines and upcoming themes available for SASE. Responds in 3 months if submissions are received during reading period. Pays 2 copies. Acquires one-time rights. Reviews books and chapbooks of poetry and other magazines in 750 words, single book format. Poets may send books for review consideration.

Also Offers: *So to Speak* runs an annual poetry contest. "Our 2001 judge was Linda McCarriston."

Advice: "We are looking for poetry that, through interesting use of language, locates experiences of women. We particularly appreciate poems that challenge tradition but remain cohesive and meaningful."

○ SO YOUNG!; ANTI-AGING PRESS, INC., P.O. Box 141489, Coral Gables FL 33114. (305)662-3928. Fax: (305)661-4123. E-mail: julia2@gate.net. Established 1992 press, 1996 newsletter. **Editor:** Julia Busch.

Magazine Needs: *So Young!* is a bimonthly newsletter publishing "anti-aging/holistic health/humorous/ philosophical topics geared to a youthful body, attitude, and spirit." Wants "short, upbeat, fresh, positive poetry. The newsletter is dedicated to a youthful body, face, mind and spirit. Work can be humorous, philosophical fillers. No off color, suggestive poems or anything relative to first night, or unrequited love affairs." *So Young!* is 12 pages, 8½×11 (11×17 sheets folded), unbound. Receives several hundred poems/ year, accepts 6-12. Press run is 700 for 500 subscribers. Subscription: $35. Sample: $6.

How to Submit: Submit up to 10 poems at a time. Accepts previously published poems and simultaneous submissions. Accepts e-mail submissions (in text box). Cover letter preferred. Time between acceptance and publication "depends on poem subject matter—usually 6-8 months." Guidelines available for SASE. Responds in 2 months. Pays 10 copies. Acquires one-time rights.

◑ ◎ THE SOCIETY OF AMERICAN POETS (SOAP); IN HIS STEPS PUBLISHING COMPANY; THE POET'S PEN; PRESIDENT'S AWARD FOR SUPERIOR CHOICE (Specialized: religious), P.O. Box 3563, Macon GA 31205-3563. (478)788-1848. Fax: (478)788-0925. E-mail: DrRev@ msn.com. Established 1984. **Editor:** Dr. Charles E. Cravey.

Magazine Needs: *The Poet's Pen* is a literary quarterly of poetry and short stories. "Open to all styles of poetry and prose—both religious and secular. No gross or 'X-rated' poetry without taste or character." Accepts poetry written by children. Has published poetry by Najwa Salam Brax, Henry Goldman, Henry W. Gurley, William Heffner, Linda Metcalf, and Charles Russ. As a sample the editor selected these lines from "Romancing the Moon" by William J. Cedar:

> A brilliant moonish glow sliding/across a starry heaven, stirring/thoughts of romance./moonbeams
> penetrating mysterious/shadows on night, softening them/into romantic tones of love

The Poet's Pen uses poetry primarily by members and subscribers, but outside submissions are also welcomed. Sample copy: $15. Membership: $25/year.

How to Submit: Submit 3 poems at a time, include name and address on each page. "Submissions or inquiries will not be responded to without a #10 business-sized SASE. We do stress originality and have each new poet and/or subscriber sign a waiver form verifying originality." Accepts simultaneous submissions and previously published poems, if permission from previous publisher is included. Publishes seasonal/theme issues. Upcoming themes and guidelines available for SASE, by fax, in publication, or by e-mail. Sometimes sends prepublication galleys. Editor "most certainly" comments on rejected poems.

Book/Chapbook Needs & How to Submit: In His Steps publishes religious and other books. Also publishes music for the commercial record market. Query for book publication.

Also Offers: Sponsors several contests each quarter which total $100-250 in cash awards. Editor's Choice Awards each quarter. President's Award for Superior Choice has a prize of $50; deadline is November 1. Also publishes a quarterly anthology that has poetry competitions in several categories with prizes of $25-100.

Advice: "Be honest with yourself above all else. Read the greats over and again and study styles, grammar, and what makes each unique. Meter, rhythm, and rhyme are still the guidelines that are most acceptable today."

N **✹** **◯** **◉** **SONGS OF INNOCENCE** (Specialized: 19th century romantic/transcenden-tal style poetry/fiction); **PENDRAGONIAN PUBLICATIONS** (Specialized: anthologies), P.O. Box 719, Radio City Station, New York NY 10101-0719. E-mail: mmpendragon@aol.com. Established 1999 (*Songs of Innocence*); 1995 (Pendragon Publications). **Editor/Publisher:** Michael Pendragon.

● Works appearing in *Songs of Innocence* have received Honorable Mention in *The Year's Best Fantasy and Horror.*

Magazine Needs: *Songs of Innocence* appears biannually publishing traditional forms of verse and fiction of a superior quality, in the romantic style. Wants "rhymed, metered, and/or employing traditional poetic elements such as alliteration, internal rhyme, metaphor, etc." Does not want "modern," free verse, quasi-diary-entry, pseudo-poetry. Recently published poetry by Louise Webster, Kevin N. Roberts, Pamela Constantine, Ann K. Schwader, and Wendy Rathbone. As a sample the editor selected these lines from "Spring Maiden" by Louise Webster:

> Upon the pastoral dawn,/a glistening, pure mist/renounces earthly desire/and glides, like a chaste/ bridal train of ethereal vapor, skyward/A winged maiden betrothed to heaven.

Songs of Innocence is 175 pages, 6×9, docutech-printed, perfect-bound, color card cover, with b&w line art. Receives about 3,000 poems/year, accepts about 5%. Publishes about 75 poems/issue. Press run is 200 for 150 subscribers of which 3 are libraries, 22 shelf sales; 25 distributed free to reviewers. Single copy: $10; subscription: $25/3 issues. Sample: $10. Make checks payable to Michael Pendragon.

How to Submit: Submit 5 poems at a time. Accepts previously published poems and simultaneous submissions. Accepts e-mail submissions; no fax or disk submissions. Cover letter is preferred. "Prefer works submitted via e-mail (in body with additional copy attached)." Time between acceptance and publication is up to 2 years. Often comments on rejected poems. Regularly publishes theme issues. "Themes are determined by content of accepted submissions." Guidelines available in magazine. Responds in 1 year. Always sends prepublication galleys. Pays 1 contributor's copy. Acquires one-time rights. Reviews books and chapbooks of poetry and other magazines/journals. Length of reviews varies. Poets may send books/chapbooks for review consideration to Michael Pendragon.

Book/Chapbook Needs & How to Submit: Pendragonian Publications publishes anthologies of poetry and fiction centered on a given theme. Publishes 1-2 paperbacks/year. Books are usually up to 250 pages, docutech-printed, perfect-bound, color card cover, with b&w line art. Pays 1 author's copy. Acquires one-time rights. "Books are multi-authored and treated as if they were magazines."

Also Offers: See separate listing for *Penny Dreadful: Tales & Poems of Fantastic Terror* in this section.

◯ **SOUL FOUNTAIN**, 90-21 Springfield Blvd., Queens Village NY 11428. Phone/fax: (718)479-2594. E-mail: davault@aol.com. Website: www.TheVault.org (includes guidelines, contact information, archives). Established 1997. **Editor:** Tone Bellizzi.

Magazine Needs: *Soul Fountain* appears 4 times/year and publishes poetry, art, photography, short fiction, and essays. "Open to all. Our motto is 'Fear no Art.' We publish all quality submitted work, and specialize in emerging voices. We are particularly interested in visionary, challenging and consciousness-expanding material. We are especially seeking poetry from North and South Dakota, Utah, Vermont, Alaska, Nevada, and Kansas for our 50 states issue. We're hungry for artwork, particularly small black on white drawings." Accepts poetry written by children, teens only. Has published poetry by Robert Dunn, Thomas Catterson, Jay Chollick, and Paula Curci. *Soul Fountain* is 28 pages, 8½×11, offset-printed and saddle-stapled. Subscription: $12. Sample: $4.50. Make checks payable to Hope for the Children Foundation.

How to Submit: Submit 2-3 "camera-ready" poems at a time. One page in length for each piece maximum. No cover letters necessary. Accepts previously published poems and simultaneous submissions. Accepts e-mail submissions (include in body of message); when e-mailing a submission, it is necessary to include your mailing address. Time between acceptance and publication is up to 2 years. Theme issues for 2003 are as follows: March, Women's Voices; September, Dangerous Visions; January, Channeling the 21st Century; June, California Dreaming. An updated list of themes is available for SASE. Pays 1 copy. "For each issue there is a release/party/performance, 'Poetry & Poultry in Motion,' attended by all poets, writers, artists, etc., appearing in the issue."

Also Offers: *Soul Fountain* is published by The Vault, "a not-for-profit arts project of the Hope for the Children Foundation; a growing, supportive community committed to empowering young and emerging artists of all disciplines at all levels to develop and share their talents through performance, collaboration, and networking."

Advice: "Fear no art—stretch."

N **INDICATES A MARKET** that did not appear in the 2002 edition.

SOUR GRAPES: ONLINE VINE FOR REJECTED WRITERS AND OTHER TOR-MENTED SOULS (Specialized), 26 Sheridan St., Woburn MA 01801-3542. E-mail: sandyberns@usa. net. Website: www.geocities.com/sourgrapesnewsletter (includes guidelines, contact info, bios, archives, market info, editorial policy, and contest info). Hardcopy established 1995, discontinued 1998, website established 1997. **Editor/Publisher:** Sandy Bernstein.

Needs: *Sour Grapes* website, published "haphazardly," is "dedicated to the discouraged, disgruntled, disillusioned, and dejected writers of the universe." Wants "insightful verse that is thought-provoking, creates an image or stirs a feeling. Poems don't have to be gripe-related, but should be of normal length— no epics, please. Almost any form style or subject is acceptable." Doesn't want " 'Experimental Poems' such as lines printed horizontally and vertically. If it looks like a crossword puzzle—don't send it here. No 'Gratuitous Profanity,' show us poetic language—not street talk."

How to Submit: Submit no more than 5 poems at one time (limit for haiku, 10; limit for very short verse, 7). Prefer e-mail submissions ("text in the body of the e-mail is preferred"). Please include cover letter with short bio and credits. Regular mail submissions should include SASE for return of mss. Often comments on rejected poems. Guidelines available for SASE or on website. Response time "may vary but will not be unreasonable." Guidelines available on the website. Pays 1 copy (include SASE).

Advice: "Only submissions that follow our guidelines will be considered."

SOUTH–A POETRY MAGAZINE FOR THE SOUTHERN COUNTIES; WANDA PUBLICATIONS, 75 High St., Wimborne, Dorset BH21 1HS England. Phone: (01202)889669. Fax: (01202)881061. E-mail: wanda@wordandaction.com. Established 1972. **Coordinating Editor:** Janet Peters.

Magazine Needs: *South* is published biannually. Has published poetry by Ian Caws, Stella Davis, Finola Holiday, Elsa Corbluth, and Brian Hinton. *South* is 68 pages, 6×9, litho-printed and saddle-stapled with gloss laminated, duotone cover, includes photographs. Receives about 1,500 poems/year, accepts about 10%. Press run is 400 for 200 subscribers of which 15 are libraries, 170 shelf sales; 15 distributed free to other magazines and reviewers. Single copy: £4.50; subscription: £8/2 issues, £15/4 issues. Make checks payable to Wanda Publications.

How to Submit: Submit 6 poems at a time. Accepts previously published poems; no simultaneous submissions. Time between acceptance and publication is up to 5 months. Responds in up to 5 months. Staff reviews books of poetry and other magazines in 400 words, multi-book format. Send books for review consideration.

$☐ THE SOUTH BOSTON LITERARY GAZETTE, P.O. Box 443, South Boston MA 02127. (617)426-0791. E-mail: johnshea@msn.com. Website: www.thesouthbostonliterarygazette.com (includes poetry and prose excerpts, guidelines, names of editors, prize descriptions, artwork). Established 1999. **Editor:** Dave Connolly.

Magazine Needs: *The South Boston Literary Gazette* appears quarterly, dedicated to promoting quality work by both new and established writers. Very open to diversity in style, content, age groups. Does not want "acid ramblings; no extreme pornography (although foul language is considered); amateurish, grammatically disordered writing." Accepts poetry written by children. Recently published poetry by Leonard Peltier, W.D. Ehrhardt, Michael Brown, Lyn Lifshin, David Connolly, and Harris Gardner. As a sample the editor selected these lines from "What Better Way to Begin" by W.D. Ehrhardt:

> You can just keep your rocket's red glare./And as for the bombs bursting in air,/with all that noise and
> fire and smoke/there has to be plenty of jagged steel/looking for someone to hit.

The South Boston Literary Gazette is 70 pages, magazine-sized, computer copied on 70 lb. higloss paper, perfect-bound, 80 lb. 4-color higloss cover. Also published in online format. Receives about 400 poems/year, accepts about 25%. Publishes about 25 poems/issue. Press run is 500 for 100 subscribers, 100 shelf sales; 50 are distributed free to contributors and donors. Single copy: $7.50; subscription: $25/year (4 issues). Sample: $8. Make checks payable to *The South Boston Literary Gazette*.

How to Submit: *The South Boston Literary Gazette* Submit up to 4 poems at a time. Maximum length for poetry is 3,000 words. Accepts previously published poems and simultaneous submissions. Accepts e-mail and disk submissions; no fax submissions. Cover letter is preferred. "Put name on each page, all pages numbered." Reads submissions at all times. Submit seasonal poems 1 month in advance. **Reading Fee: $5.** Time between acceptance and publication is 1-3 months. Poems are circulated to an editorial board, "three editors; independent reviews using a 1-3 grading system; roundtable discussions follow." Guidelines are available in magazine, for SASE, by e-mail, or on website. Responds in up to 3 months. Sometimes sends prepublication galleys. Pays 1 contributor's copy. "Author and *Gazette* share rights."

Also Offers: Each issue awards at least two $50 prizes for poetry and prose.

⬤ **SOUTH CAROLINA REVIEW**, English Dept., 801 Strode Tower, Clemson University, Box 340523, Clemson SC 29634-0523. (864)656-3151 or 656-5399. Fax: (864)656-1345. Established 1968. **Editor:** Wayne Chapman.

Magazine Needs: *South Carolina Review* is a biannual literary magazine "recognized by the *New York Quarterly* as one of the top 20 of this type." Will consider "any kind of poetry as long as it's good. No stale metaphors, uncertain rhythms, or lack of line integrity. Interested in seeing more traditional forms. Format should be according to new MLA Stylesheet." Has published poetry by Stephen Cushman, Alberto Ríos, and Claire Bateman. *South Carolina Review* is 200 pages, 6×9, professionally printed, flat-spined and uses about 25-40 pages of poetry in each issue. Reviews of recent issues back up editorial claims that all styles and forms are welcome; moreover, poems were accessible and well-executed. Press run is 600, for 400 subscribers of which 250 are libraries. Receives about 1,000 submissions of poetry/year, accepts about 60; has a 1-year backlog. Sample: $10.

How to Submit: Submit 3-10 poems at a time in an "8×10 manila envelope so poems aren't creased." No previously published poems or simultaneous submissions. "Editor prefers a chatty, personal cover letter plus a list of publishing credits." Do not submit during June, July, August, or December. Publishes theme issues. Responds in 2 months. Pays copies. Staff reviews books of poetry.

▥ ◯ **THE SOUTHEAST REVIEW; MICHAEL W. GEARHART POETRY CONTEST**, English Dept., Florida State University, 216 Williams Bldg., Tallahassee FL 32306. (850)644-2773. E-mail: southea streview@english.fsu.edu. Website: http://english.fsu.edu/southeastreview/ (includes submissions and contest guidelines, subscription info). Established 1982. **Poetry Editor:** Larry Johns.

Magazine Needs: *The Southeast Review* appears twice a year. "We look for intelligent new and established voices that speak to the contemporary aesthetic in both traditional and experimental forms." As a sample the editor selected these lines from "Face" by Emily Moore:

> *By midday the face/will be peeled from the milk/like a caul/from a newborn*

The Southeast Review is 130 pages, digest-sized. Receives about 1,300 poems/year, accepts about 10%. Publishes about 50 poems/issue. Press run is 1,200 for 800 subscribers of which 100 are libraries, 200 shelf sales; 200 are distributed free. Single copy: $10; subscription: $8/year. Sample: $2. Make checks payable to *The Southeast Review*.

How to Submit: Submit 3-5 poems at a time. Accepts simultaneous submissions; no previously published poems. No fax, e-mail, or disk submissions. Cover letter is preferred. Include SASE. Reads submissions year round. Time between acceptance and publication is 2 months. Poems are circulated to an editorial board. Seldom comments on rejected poems. Occasionally publishes theme issues. List of upcoming themes available by e-mail. Guidelines available for SASE, by e-mail, or on website. Responds in 1 month. Pays 2 contributor's copies. Acquires first North American serial rights. Reviews books and chapbooks of poetry in 250 words. Poets may send books/chapbooks to the editor, *The Southeast Review*.

Also offers: The Michael W. Gearhart Poetry Contest. Submissions must be typed, single-spaced. 1st prize: $500 and publication in the following spring issue; many finalists published as well. **Entry fee:** $10/entry (3-5 poems). **Deadline:** submit between August 1 and November 30 of each year.

◖ ◎ **THE SOUTHERN CALIFORNIA ANTHOLOGY** (Specialized: anthology); **ANN STANFORD POETRY PRIZES**, c/o Master of Professional Writing Program, WPH 404, University of Southern California, Los Angeles CA 90089-4034. (213)740-3252. Established 1983.

Magazine Needs: *The Southern California Anthology* is an "annual literary review of serious contemporary poetry and fiction. Very open to all subject matters except pornography. Any form, style OK." Has published poetry by Robert Bly, Donald Hall, Allen Ginsberg, Lisel Mueller, James Ragan, and Amiri Baraka. *The Southern California Anthology* is 144 pages, digest-sized, perfect-bound, with a semi-glossy color cover featuring one art piece. Press run is 1,500, 50% going to subscribers of which 50% are libraries, 30% are for shelf sales. Sample: $5.95.

How to Submit: Submit 3-5 poems between September 1 and January 1 only. No simultaneous submissions or previously published poems. All decisions made by mid-February. Guidelines available for SASE. Responds in 4 months. Pays 2 contributor's copies. Acquires all rights.

Also Offers: The Ann Stanford Poetry Prizes ($1,000, $200, and $100) have an April 15 deadline, $10 fee (5 poem limit), for unpublished poems. Include cover sheet with name, address, and titles as well as SASE for contest results. All entries are considered for publication, and all entrants receive a copy of *The Southern California Anthology*.

SOUTHERN HUMANITIES REVIEW; THEODORE CHRISTIAN HOEPFNER AWARD, 9088 Haley Center, Auburn University, Auburn AL 36849-5202. E-mail: shrengl@auburn.edu. Website: www.auburn.edu/english/shr/home.htm. Established 1967. **Co-Editors:** Dan Latimer and Virginia M. Kouidis.

Magazine Needs: *Southern Humanities Review* is a literary quarterly "interested in poems of any length, subject, genre. Space is limited, and brief poems are more likely to be accepted. Translations welcome, but also send written permission from the copyright holder." Has published poetry by Eamon Grennan, Donald Hall, Brendan Galvin, Susan Ludvigson, Andrew Hudgins, Bin Ramke, and Fred Chappell. *Southern Humanities Review* is 100 pages, 6×9, press run 700. Subscription: $15/year. Sample: $5.

How to Submit: "Send 3-5 poems in a business-sized envelope. Include SASE. Avoid sending faint computer printout." No previously published poems or simultaneous submissions. No e-mail submissions. Responds in 2 months, possibly longer in summer. Always sends prepublication galleys. Pays 2 copies. Copyright reverts to author upon publication. Reviews books of poetry in approximately 750-1,000 words. Send books for review consideration.

Also Offers: Sponsors the Theodore Christian Hoepfner Award, a $50 award for the best poem published in a given volume of *Southern Humanities Review*.

Advice: "For beginners we'd recommend study and wide reading in English and classical literature, and, of course, American literature—the old works, not just the new. We also recommend study of or exposure to a foreign language and a foreign culture. Poets need the reactions of others to their work: criticism, suggestions, discussion. A good creative writing teacher would be desirable here, and perhaps some course work too. And then submission of work, attendance at workshops. And again, the reading: history, biography, verse, essays—all of it. We want to see poems that have gone beyond the language of slippage and easy attitudes."

$ THE SOUTHERN REVIEW, 43 Allen Hall, Louisiana State University, Baton Rouge LA 70803-5005. (225)578-5108. Fax: (225)578-5098. E-mail: bmacon@lsu.edu. Website: www.lsu.edu/guests/wwwtsm (includes guidelines, subscription information, current table of contents, relevant addresses, names, etc.). Established 1935 (original series), 1965 (new series). **Poetry Editors:** James Olney and Dave Smith.

• Work published in this review has been frequently included in *The Best American Poetry* and appeared in *The Beacon's Best of 1999*.

Magazine Needs: *The Southern Review* "is a literary quarterly that publishes fiction, poetry, critical essays, and book reviews, with emphasis on contemporary literature in the U.S. and abroad, and with special interest in southern culture and history. Selections are made with careful attention to craftsmanship and technique and to the seriousness of the subject matter. We are interested in any variety of poetry that is well crafted, though we cannot normally accommodate excessively long poems (say 10 pages and over)." Has published poetry by Norman Dubie, Margaret Gibson, Seamus Heaney, Yusef Komunyakaa, Susan Ludvigson, and Robert Penn Warren. *The Southern Review* is 6¾×10, 240 pages, flat-spined, matte card cover. Receives about 6,000 submissions of poetry/year. All styles and forms seem welcome, although accessible lyric and narrative free verse appear most often in recent issues. Press run is 3,100 for 2,100 subscribers of which 70% are libraries. Subscription: $25. Sample: $8.

How to Submit: "We do not require a cover letter but we prefer one giving information about the author and previous publications." Prefers submissions of up to 6 pages. No fax or e-mail submissions. Guidelines available for SASE or on website. Responds in 1 month. Pays $20/printed page plus 2 contributor's copies. Acquires first North American serial rights. Staff reviews books of poetry in 3,000 words, multi-book format. Send books for review consideration.

$ SOUTHWEST REVIEW; ELIZABETH MATCHETT STOVER MEMORIAL AWARD, 307 Fondren Library West, P.O. Box 750374, Southern Methodist University, Dallas TX 75275-0374. (214)768-1037. Website: www.southwestreview.org. Established 1915. **Editor:** Willard Spiegelman.

• Poetry published in *Southwest Review* has been included in the 1995 and 1998 volumes of *The Best American Poetry* as well as the 2002 *Pushcart Prize* anthology.

Magazine Needs: *Southwest Review* is a literary quarterly that publishes fiction, essays, poetry, and interviews. "It is hard to describe our preference for poetry in a few words. We always suggest that potential contributors read several issues of the magazine to see for themselves what we like. But some things may be said: We demand very high quality in our poems; we accept both traditional and experimental writing, but avoid unnecessary obscurity and private symbolism; we place no arbitrary limits on length but find shorter poems easier to fit into our format than longer ones. We have no specific limitations as to theme."

Has published poetry by Adrienne Rich, Amy Clampitt, Albert Goldbarth, Leonard Nathan, Molly Peacock, and Charles Wright. *Southwest Review* is 6×9, 144 pages, perfect-bound, professionally printed, with matte text stock cover. Receives about 1,000 submissions of poetry/year, accepts approximately 32. Poems tend to be lyric and narrative free verse combining a strong voice with powerful topics or situations. Diction is accessible and content often conveys a strong sense of place. Circulation is 1,500 for 1,000 subscribers of which 600 are libraries. Subscription: $24. Sample: $6.

How to Submit: No simultaneous submissions or previously published work. Send SASE for guidelines. Responds within a month. Always sends prepublication galleys. Pays cash plus copies.

Also Offers: The $250 Elizabeth Matchett Stover Memorial Award is awarded annually for the best poems, chosen by editors, published in the preceding year.

THE SOW'S EAR POETRY REVIEW, 19535 Pleasant View Dr., Abingdon VA 24211-6827. (276)628-2651. E-mail: richman@preferred.com. Established 1988. **Editor:** James Owen. **Managing Editor:** Larry Richman.

Magazine Needs: *The Sow's Ear* is a quarterly. "We are open to many forms and styles, and have no limitations on length. We try to be interesting visually, and we use graphics to complement the poems. Though we publish some work from our local community of poets, we are interested in poems from all over. We publish a few by previously unpublished poets." Has recently published poetry by Andrea Carter Brown, Corrine Clegg Hales, Jerry McGuire, Virgil Suarez, Susan Terris, and Franz Wright. *The Sow's Ear Poetry Review* is 32 pages, 8½×11, saddle-stapled, with matte card cover, professionally printed. Receives about 2,000 poems/year, accepts about 100. Press run is 600 for 500 subscribers of which 15 are libraries, 20-40 shelf sales. Subscription: $10. Sample: $5.

How to Submit: Submit up to 5 poems at a time with SASE. Accepts simultaneous submissions if you tell them promptly when work is accepted elsewhere; no previously published poems. Enclose brief bio. No e-mail submissions. Guidelines available for SASE or by e-mail. Responds in up to 6 months. Pays 2 copies. Acquires first publication rights. Most prose (reviews, interviews, features) is commissioned.

Also Offers: Offers an annual contest for unpublished poems, with fee of $2/poem, prizes of $1,000, $250, and $100, and publication for 15-20 finalists. For contest, submit poems in September/October, with name and address on a separate sheet. Submissions of 5 poems/$10 receive a subscription. Include SASE for notification. 2001 Judge: Dabney Stuart. Also sponsors a chapbook contest in March/April with $10 fee, $1,000 1st Prize, publication, 25 copies and distribution to subscribers; 2nd Prize $200 and 3rd Prize $100. Send SASE or e-mail for chapbook contest guidelines.

Advice: "Four criteria help us to judge the quality of submissions: Does the poem make the strange familiar or the familiar strange or both? Is the form of the poem vital to its meaning? Do the sounds of the poem make sense in relation to the theme? Does the little story of the poem open a window on the Big Story of the human situation?"

$ ☑ ◎ SPACE AND TIME (Specialized: science fiction/fantasy, horror), 138 W. 70th St. (4B), New York NY 10023-4468. Established 1966. **Poetry Editor:** Linda Addison.

Magazine Needs: *Space and Time* is a biannual that publishes "primarily science fiction/fantasy/horror; some related poetry and articles. We do not want to see anything that doesn't fit science fiction/fantasy/weird genres." Has published poetry by Lyn Lifshin, Susan Spilecki, Mark Kreighbaum, and Cynthia Tedesco. As a sample we selected these lines from "Dark Waiting" by Catherine Mintz:

An unceasing rain/lamp light gold in the gutters./I refold bat wings.

The issue of *Space and Time* we received was about 100 pages, 5½×8½, perfect-bound. However, the magazine will be reformatted to 48 pages, 8½×11, web press printed on 50 lb. stock and saddle-stapled with glossy card cover and interior b&w illustrations. Receives about 500 poems/year, accepts 5%. Press run is 2,000 for 200 subscribers of which 10 are libraries, 1,200 shelf sales. Single copy: $5; subscription: $10. Sample: $6.25.

How to Submit: Submit up to 4 poems at a time. No previously published poems or simultaneous submissions. Time between acceptance and publication is up to 9 months. Often comments on rejected poems. Poets may send SASE for guidelines "but they won't see more than what's here." Responds in up to 6 weeks, "longer if recommended." Pays 1¢/word ($5 minimum) plus 2 copies. Acquires first North American serial rights.

☑ SPILLWAY, P.O. Box 7887, Huntington Beach CA 92615-7887. (714)968-0905. Established 1991. **Editors:** Mifanwy Kaiser and J.D. Lloyd.

Magazine Needs: *Spillway* is a biannual journal, published in March and September, "celebrating writing's diversity and power to affect our lives. Open to all voices, schools, and tendencies. We usually do not use writing which tells instead of shows, or writing which contains general, abstract lines not anchored in images. We publish poetry, translations, reviews, essays and b&w photography." Has published poetry by John Balaban, Sam Hamill, Robin Chapman, Richard Jones, and Susan Terris. *Spillway* is about 176 pages, digest-sized, attractively printed, perfect-bound, with 2-color or 4-color card cover. Press run is 2,000. Single copy: $9; subscription: $16/2 issues, $28/4 issues. Sample (including guidelines): $10. Make checks payable to *Spillway*.

How to Submit: Submit 3-6 poems at a time, 10 pages total. Accepts previously published work ("say when and where") and simultaneous submissions ("say where also submitted"). Cover letter including brief bio and SASE required. Reads submissions March through August only. "No cute bios." Responds in up to 6 months. Pays 1 copy. Acquires one-time rights. Reviews books of poetry in 500-2,500 words maximum. Poets may send books for review consideration.

Advice: "We have no problem with simultaneous or previously published submissions. Poems are murky creatures—they shift and change in time and context. It's exciting to pick up a volume, read a poem in the context of all the other pieces, and then find the same poem in another time and place. And, we don't think a poet should have to wait until death to see work in more than one volume. What joy to find out that more than one editor values one's work. Our responsibility as editors, collectively, is to promote the work of poets as much as possible—how can we do this if we say to a writer you may only have a piece published in one volume and only one time?"

SPINNING JENNY, Black Dress Press, P.O. Box 1373, New York NY 10276. Website: www.blackdr esspress.com (includes guidelines, address/contact information, subscription, links, author bios, etc.). Established 1994. **Editor:** C.E. Harrison.

Magazine Needs: *Spinning Jenny* appears once/year. Has published poetry by Denise Duhamel, Matthew Lippman, Michael Loncar, Sarah Messer, and a play by Jeff Hoffman. As a sample the editor selected these lines from "Infidelity" by Michael Morse:

> The stranger takes off his shirt,/and in your own good mind it's the kiss.//When you lean forward and
> close the eyes,/the stars and their just torments/wheel off to the somewhere-else.

Spinning Jenny is 96 pages, 5¼ × 9¼, perfect-bound with heavy card cover. "We accept less than 5% of unsolicited submissions." Press run is 1,000. Single copy: $8; subscription: $15/2 issues. Sample: $8.

How to Submit: No previously published poems; simultaneous submissions not encouraged. Accepts e-mail submissions (include in body of message). Seldom comments on rejected poems. Guidelines available for SASE or on website. Responds within 2 months. Pays contributor copies. Authors retain rights.

THE SPIRIT'S VOICE (Specialized: spiritual themes, uplifting, inspirational), 8 Rodman Rd., Ashland MA 01721. (508)875-6305. E-mail: DearAdie@aol.com. Established 1987. **Co-Editor:** Addie DiGregorio. Member: PMA, SPAN.

Magazine Needs: *The Spirit's Voice* appears quarterly to "build spiritual community in the New England region. We support people on a spiritual path, particularly *A Course in Miracles*®." Recently published poetry by Marianne Williamson, Doran Dibble, and Helen Schucman. As a sample the editor selected these lines from "Dear God" by Marianne Williamson from *Illuminated Prayers*:

> Please send to me the spirit of your peace./Then send, dear Lord, the spirit of peace from me to all
> the world./May everyone I think of and all who think of me/see only innocence and love—for that is
> what we are.

The Spirit's Voice is magazine-sized, printed in 2 colors with simple binding, paper cover, with photos, some minimal artwork. Receives about 6 poems/year, accepts about 75%. Publishes about 1-2 poems/issue. Press run is 3,000 for 3,000 subscribers; some are distributed free to spiritual teachers/leaders in the community. Single copy: annual donation/membership.

How to Submit: Submit no more than 2-3 poems at a time. Line length for poetry is no more than 1 page. Accepts previously published poems. Accepts fax and e-mail submissions. Cover letter is preferred. Submit seasonal poems 3 months in advance. Time between acceptance and publication is about 3 months. Poems are screened by co-editors and reviewed by committee. "Sorry, we don't pay."

Advice: "We are eager to hear from anyone who leads the reader to connect with God, but without linking it to a specific religion."

SPISH (Specialized: fish stories, poetry related to fishing), % Progressive, 5785 Yucca Lane North, Minneapolis MN 55446. E-mail: spishmagazine@aol.com. Website: www.spish.com (includes poetry and stories, art and photography, submission guidelines, about the editors, past issues, and links). Established 1999. **Contact:** editors.

Magazine Needs: *Spish* is an online magazine featuring fish stories, poetry, art, and photography. Appears "as we find time to produce it. We publish alternative, edgy, humorous poetry and short prose with a tie to fishing; along the lines of Brautigan, Bukowski, or Jim Harrison. We aren't likely to publish rhyming or greeting card verse. If we have to read it twice to 'get it,' it probably won't make it." Has published poetry by Charlie Bukowski, Bill Meissner, and Michael Hall. As a sample the editor selected this poem, "The Ice Fisherman" by Michael Hall:

> They sit on stools/like cats/staring into a mouse hole./Thinking perhaps,/about the unpaid loan/or the unfaithful wife,/praying/that there's something/down there/that will get them through/another winter.

How to Submit: Submit 3-5 poems at a time. Accepts previously published poems and simultaneous submissions. E-mail submissions preferred (in body of message with "Submissions" in subject line.) Include brief bio (less than 3 sentences). Time between acceptance and publication is up to 4 months. Poems are circulated to an editorial board. Often comments on rejected poems. Guidelines available on website. Responds in 1 month. Acquires one-time rights and anthology rights.
Advice: "Spend more time focusing on the story rather than the language. Write something that will be fun to read!"

SPLIZZ, 4 St. Marys Rise, Burry Port, Carms SA16 0SH Wales. E-mail: a_jmorgan@yahoo.co.uk. Website: www.stmarys4.freeserve.co.uk/Splizz.htm (includes general information about *Splizz* as well as a sample issue). Established 1993. **Editor:** Amanda Morgan.
Magazine Needs: *Splizz*, published quarterly, features poetry, prose, reviews of contemporary music and background to poets. Wants "any kind of poetry. We have no restrictions regarding style, length, subjects." However, they do not want "anything racist or homophobic." Has published Colin Cross (UK), Anders Carson (Canada), Paul Truttman (US), Jan Hansen (Portugal), and Gregory Arena (Italy). *Splizz* is 40-44 pages, A5, saddle-stapled with art and ads. Receives about 200-300 poems/year, accepts about 90%. Press run is 150 for 35 subscribers. Single copy: £1.30, 5 IRCs elsewhere; subscription: £5 UK, £10 elsewhere. Sample: £1.30 UK, 5 IRCs elsewhere. Make checks payable to Amanda Morgan (British checks only).
How to Submit: Submit 5 poems, typed submissions preferred. Include SAE with IRCs. Accepts previously published poems and simultaneous submissions. Accepts e-mail submissions in attached file. Cover letter required with short bio. Time between acceptance and publication is 4 months. Often comments on rejected poems. Charges criticism fee: "Just enclose SAE/IRC for response, and allow one to two months for delivery." Guidelines available for SASE (or SAE and IRC), by e-mail, or in publication. Responds in 2 months. Sometimes sends prepublication galleys. Reviews books or chapbooks of poetry or other magazines in 50-300 words. Poets may send books for review consideration. E-mail for further enquiries.
Advice: "Beginners seeking to have their work published, send your work to *Splizz*, as we specialize in giving new poets a chance."

THE SPOON RIVER POETRY REVIEW; EDITORS' PRIZE CONTEST, 4240/English Dept., Illinois State University, Normal IL 61790-4240. Website: www.litline.org/spoon (includes guidelines, cover art, contest guidelines, subscription information, and poems). Established 1976. **Editor:** Lucia Getsi.
Magazine Needs: *Spoon River Poetry Review* is a a biannual "poetry magazine that features newer and well-known poets from around the country and world." Also features 1 Illinois poet/issue at length for the magazine's Illinois Poet Series. "We want interesting and compelling poetry that operates beyond the ho-hum, so-what level, in any form or style about anything; language that is fresh, energetic, committed, filled with a strong voice that grabs the reader in the first line and never lets go." Also uses translations of poetry. Has published poetry by Stuart Dybek, Robin Behn, Dave Smith, Allison Joseph, Sheryl St. Germain, and Alicia Ostriker. *Spoon River Poetry Review* is 128 pages, digest-sized, laser set with card cover using photos, ads. Receives about 3,000 poems/month, accepts 1%. Press run is 1,500 for 700 subscribers, of which 100 are libraries and shelf sales. Subscription: $16. Sample (including guidelines): $10.
How to Submit: "No simultaneous submissions unless we are notified immediately if a submission is accepted elsewhere. Include name and address on every poem." Do not submit mss May 1 through September 1. Editor comments on rejected poems "many times, if a poet is promising." Responds in 2 months. Pays a year's subscription. Acquires first North American serial rights. Reviews books of poetry. Send books for review consideration.
Also Offers: Sponsors the Editor's Prize Contest for previously unpublished work. One poem will be awarded $1,000 and published in the fall issue of *Spoon River Poetry Review*, and two runners-up will receive $100 each and publication in the fall issue. Entries must be previously unpublished. **Entry fee:** $16, including 1-year subscription. **Deadline:** April 15. Write for details. Past winners were Kathleen Lynch and Aleida Rodríguez.

SPORT LITERATE (Specialized: sports/recreation), P.O. Box 577166, Chicago IL 60657-7166. Website: www.sportliterate.com. Established 1995. **Editor:** William Meiners. **Poetry Editor:** Frank Van Zant.

Magazine Needs: *Sport Literate*, published biannually, "covers leisure/sport life outside the daily grind of making a living. Stay out of your sentimental backyard where you had that eternal game of catch with dad. But don't avoid the image if it burns like a house fire. Be richly literary, but don't avoid fun. Avoid heady stuff that says nothing which matters. Send quality." Recently published poetry by Bob Harrison, Marilyn Kallet, and Ron McFarland. As a sample the editor selected these lines from "Baseball: A Short History" by Robert L. Harrison:

> The dark ages came and went,/with no night games played,/and little was known about/the bunt or hit
> and run/as the monks sold fine wine.

Sport Literate is digest-sized with glossy cover. Receives about 500 poems/year, accepts 2%. Publishes about 3-4 poems/issue. Press run is 1,500. Single copy: $7.75; subscription: $20/4 issues. Make checks payable to *Sport Literate*.

How to Submit: Submit 3 poems at a time. Accepts simultaneous submissions; no previously published poems. No e-mail or disk submissions. Reads submissions year-round. Submit seasonal poems 4 months in advance. Time between acceptance and publication is up to 6 months. Often comments on rejected poems. Occasionally publishes theme issues. Guidelines available for SASE, by e-mail, or on website. Responds in 5 weeks. Always sends prepublication galleys. Pays 3 contributor's copies. Acquires first North American serial rights.

◐ 🗹 ◎ **SPRING: THE JOURNAL OF THE E.E. CUMMINGS SOCIETY (Specialized: membership/subscription)**, 33-54 164th St., Flushing NY 11358-1442. (718)353-3631 or (718)461-9022. Fax: (718)353-4778. E-mail: EECSPRINGNF@aol.com. Website: www.gvsu.edu/english/Cummings/Index.html. **Editor:** Norman Friedman.

Magazine Needs: *Spring* is an annual publication, usually appearing in fall, designed "to maintain and broaden the audience for Cummings and to explore various facets of his life and art." Wants poems in the spirit of Cummings, primarily poems of one page or less. Nothing "amateurish." Has published poetry by John Tagliabue, Jacqueline Vaught Brogan, George Held, Richard Kostelantz, Augusto de Campos, and Gerald Locklin. *Spring* is about 180 pages, 5½×8½, offset and perfect-bound with light card stock cover. Press run is 500 for 200 subscribers of which 15 are libraries, 300 shelf sales. Subscription or sample: $17.50.

How to Submit: No previously published poems or simultaneous submissions. Accepts submissions by fax and by e-mail (as attachment). Cover letter required. Reads submissions January through March only. Seldom comments on rejected poems. Responds in 6 months. Pays 1 copy.

Advice: "Contributors are required to subscribe."

◯ ◎ **SPRING TIDES (Specialized: children)**, Savannah Country Day School, 824 Stillwood Dr., Savannah GA 31419-2643. (912)925-8800. Fax: (912)920-7800. E-mail: Houston@savcds.org. Website: www.savcds.org. Established 1989. **Contact:** Connie Houston.

Magazine Needs: Appearing in December, *Spring Tides* is an annual literary magazine by children 5-12 years of age. "Children from ages five through twelve may submit material. Please limit stories to 1,200 words and poems to 20 lines. All material must be original and created by the person submitting it. A statement signed by the child's parent or teacher attesting to the originality must accompany all work." *Spring Tides* is 28 pages, digest-sized, attractively printed and saddle-stapled with glossy card cover, includes b&w and 4-color art. Press run is 500; given to students at Savannah Country Day School and sold to others. Single copy: $5.

How to Submit: Accepts simultaneous submissions. Accepts submissions by postal mail only. SASE required. "Poems with or without illustrations may be submitted." Reads submissions January through August only. Poems are circulated to an editorial board. Always comments on rejected poems. Guidelines available for SASE and in publication. Responds in 4 months. Pays 1 copy.

$ 🗹 ◎ **SPS STUDIOS, INC., PUBLISHERS OF BLUE MOUNTAIN ARTS® (Specialized: greeting cards)**, Dept. PM, P.O. Box 1007, Boulder CO 80306-1007. Fax: (303)447-0939. E-mail: editorial@spsstudios.com. Website: www.sps.com (includes guidelines, contact information, and product information). Established 1971. **Contact:** editorial staff.

Book/Chapbook Needs: SPS Studios publishes greeting cards, books, calendars, prints, and mugs. Looking for poems, prose, and lyrics ("usually nonrhyming") appropriate for publication on greeting cards and in poetry anthologies. Also actively seeking "book-length manuscripts that would be appropriate for book and gift stores. We are also very interested in receiving book and card ideas that would be appropriate for college stores, as well as younger buyers. Poems should reflect a message, feeling, or sentiment that one person would want to share with another. We'd like to receive creative, original submissions about love relationships, family members, friendships, philosophies, and any other aspect of life. Poems and writings for specific holidays (Christmas, Valentine's Day, etc.) and special occasions, such as graduation, anniversary, and get well are also considered. Only a small portion of the material we receive is selected each year and the review process can be lengthy, but be assured every manuscript is given serious consideration."

How to Submit: Submissions must be typewritten, 1 poem/page or sent via e-mail (no attachments). Enclose SASE if you want your work returned. Simultaneous submissions "discouraged but OK with notification." Accepts submissions by e-mail (in text box), by fax, by online submission form, and by postal mail. Submit seasonal material at least 4 months in advance. Guidelines available for SASE, on website, or by e-mail. Responds in up to 6 months. Pays $200/poem all rights for each of the first 2 submissions chosen for publication (after which payment scale escalates), for the worldwide, exclusive right, $25/poem for one-time use in an anthology.

Advice: "We strongly suggest that you familiarize yourself with our products before submitting material, although we caution you not to study them too hard. We do not need more poems that sound like something we've already published. Overall, we're looking for poetry that expresses real emotions and feelings."

SPUNK, Box 55336, Hayward CA 94545. (415)974-8980. Established 1996. **Editor:** Violet Jones.
Magazine Needs: Appearing 2 times/year, *Spunk: The Journal of Unrealized Potential* contains "writings and artwork of every nature. We are an outlet for spontaneous expressions only. Save the self-satisfied, over-crafted stuff for *Paris Review*, please." Accepts poetry written by children. *Spunk* is up to 70 pages though "its size varies; silkscreened and photocopied, hand bound, no ads." Receives about 800-1,000 poems/year, accepts less than 5%. Press run is 500; all distributed free to anyone who really, really wants them. Sample: $1. No checks.
How to Submit: Submit any number of poems at a time. No previously published poems or simultaneous submissions. Cover letter preferred. "Just make us happy we opened the envelope—how you do this is up to you." Time between acceptance and publication is up to 1 year. Often comments on rejected poems. Occasionally publishes theme issues. Guidelines and upcoming themes available for SASE. Responds in up to 1 year. Pays 1 contributor's copy. Acquires first North American serial rights. Staff occasionally reviews books and chapbooks of poetry and other magazines in 100-500 words, single book format. Send books for review consideration. "Our review section has expanded, we run reviews every issue now."

SQUID INK, P.O. Box 141067, Minneapolis MN 55414-1067. Established 1999. **Editrix:** Kellie Fournier.
Magazine Needs: *Squid Ink* appears biannually. "We are here to embrace art rather than ignore it. We are especially interested in the Minneapolis scene, but all are welcome to submit." Wants "honest, feminist, beat-inspired, any form (except forced rhyme!)." Does not want anything sexist, close-minded, or Hallmark-like. Recently published poetry by Jennifer L. Moore, Scott Geisinger, and Steffanie Musich. *Squid Ink* is 24 pages, magazine-sized, photocopied, stapled. Press run is 150 which are distributed free to authors, local businesses, and colleges.
How to Submit: Submit 3-5 poems at a time. No fax, e-mail, or disk submissions. Cover letter is preferred. "Please include a SASE with submissions!" Time between acceptance and publication is up to 6 months. Seldom comments on rejected poems. Responds in 3 weeks. Pays 1 contributor's copy.
Advice: "Write what you know! Never give up on your work, you are a writer (repeat 10 times) and your work has a place somewhere."

STAPLE, Padley Rise, Nether Padley, Grindleford, Hope Valley, Derbys S32 2HE United Kingdom or 35 Carr Rd., Walkley, Sheffield S6 2WY United Kingdom. Phone: 01433-631949. Established 1982 (redesigned 2001). **Co-Editors:** Ann Atkinson and Elizabeth Barrett.
Magazine Needs: *Staple* appears 3 times/year and "accepts poetry, short fiction, and articles about the writing process." *Staple* is 100 pages, perfect-bound. Press run is 500 for 350 subscribers. Single copy: £3.50, subscription: £15/year. Sample: £3.
How to Submit: Submit 6 poems at a time. No simultaneous submissions or previously published poems. Cover letter preferred. Include 2 IRCs and SAE. Editors sometimes comment on rejected poems. Submission deadlines are end of March, July, and November. Responds in up to 3 months. Sometimes sends prepublication galleys. Pays either £5/poem (£10/story or article) or free annual subscription to *Staple*.
Also Offers: Send SASE (or SAE with IRC) for *Staple First Editions* collections (sample: £8). Published collections include *Two Plus Two* by Ruth Sharman, et al. Also produces (to order) poetry postcards of poetry published in the magazine.
Advice: "In general, we don't go for haiku, performance pieces, concrete poetry, 'found' items."

THE WALLACE STEVENS JOURNAL (Specialized: Wallace Stevens), Liberal Arts, Clarkson University, Box 5750, Potsdam NY 13699-5750. (315)268-3967. Fax: (315)268-3983. E-mail: duemer@clarkson.edu. Website: www.wallacestevens.com (includes contact and subscription information). Established 1977. **Poetry Editor:** Prof. Joseph Duemer.

Magazine Needs: *The Wallace Stevens Journal* appears biannually using "poems about or in the spirit of Wallace Stevens or having some relation to his work. No bad parodies of Stevens' anthology pieces." Has published poetry by David Athey, Jacqueline Marcus, Charles Wright, X.J. Kennedy, A.M. Juster, and Robert Creeley. As a sample the editor selected these lines from "A Holograph Draft" by Richard Epstein:

> Dear Sir:/I have received your letter of/the 26th. The offer it contains,/that in exchange for ~~mermaids~~
> a warranty deed/to 1464 we drop our claim/for 16,000 ~~blackbirds~~ dollars, will not do./Our client has
> decided to obtain/~~a pair of scarlet boots~~ a writ of execution to be served/at his discretion. I remain,
> most truly,/~~the Rajah of Molucca blithely yours~~/your obedient servant, Wallace Stevens

The Wallace Stevens Journal is 80-120 pages, 6×9, typeset, flat-spined, with cover art on glossy stock. Receives 200-300 poems/year, accepts 15-20. Press run is 900 for 600 subscribers of which 200 are libraries. Subscription: $25, includes membership in the Wallace Stevens Society. Sample: $6.

How to Submit: Submit 3-5 poems at a time. "We like to receive clean, readable copy. We generally do not publish previously published material, though we have made a few exceptions to this rule. No fax or e-mail submissions, though requests for information are fine." Responds in up to 10 weeks. Always sends prepublication galleys. Pays 2 copies. Acquires all rights. Returns rights with permission and acknowledgment. Staff reviews books of poetry. Send books for review consideration "only if there is some clear connection to Stevens." *The Wallace Stevens Journal* is published by the Wallace Stevens Society.

Advice: "Brief cover letters are fine, even encouraged. Please don't submit to *Wallace Stevens Journal* if you have not read Stevens. We like parodies, but they must add a new angle of perception. Most of the poems we publish are not parodies but meditations on themes related to Wallace Stevens and those poets he has influenced. Those wishing to contribute might wish especially to examine the Fall 1996 issue which has a large and rich selection of poetry."

STICKMAN REVIEW: AN ONLINE LITERARY JOURNAL, 2890 N. Fairview Dr., Flagstaff AZ 86004. (928)913-0869. E-mail: editors@stickmanreview.com. Website: www.stickmanreview. com. Established 2001.

Magazine Needs: *Stickman Review* is a biannual online literary journal dedicated to publishing great poetry, fiction, nonfiction, and artwork. Wants poetry "that is literary in intent, no restrictions on form, subject matter, or style. We would prefer not to see rhyming poetry." Publishes about 15 poems/issue.

How to Submit: Submit 5 poems at a time. Accepts simultaneous submissions; no previously published poems. Accepts e-mail submissions *only*; no fax or disk submissions. Cover letter is preferred. Reads submissions year round. Time between acceptance and publication is 2 months. "Currently, the editors-in-chief review all submissions." Often comments on rejected poems. Guidelines available on website. Responds in 2 months. Pays $10/poem up to $20 per author. Acquires first rights.

Advice: "Keep writing and submitting. A rejection is not necessarily a reflection upon the quality of your work. Be persistent, trust your instincts, and sooner or later, good things will come."

STONE SOUP, THE MAGAZINE BY YOUNG WRITERS AND ARTISTS; THE CHILDREN'S ART FOUNDATION (Specialized: children), P.O. Box 83, Santa Cruz CA 95063. (831)426-5557. Fax: (831)426-1161. E-mail: editor@stonesoup.com. Website: www.stonesoup.com (features writer's guidelines, sample issue, philosophy, and related materials featuring children's writing and art). Established 1973. **Editor:** Ms. Gerry Mandel.

• *Stone Soup* has received both Parents' Choice and Edpress Golden Lamp Honor Awards.

Magazine Needs: *Stone Soup* publishes writing and art by children through age 13; wants free verse poetry but no rhyming poetry, haiku, or cinquain. *Stone Soup*, published 6 times/year, is a handsome 7×10 magazine, professionally printed on heavy stock with 10-12 full-color art reproductions inside and a full-color illustration on the coated cover, saddle-stapled. A membership in the Children's Art Foundation at $33/year includes a subscription to the magazine. Receives 5,000 poetry submissions/year, accepts about 12. There are 2-4 pages of poetry in each issue. Press run is 20,000 for 14,000 subscribers, 5,000 to bookstores, 1,000 other. Sample: $5.

How to Submit: Submissions can be any number of pages, any format. Include name, age, home address and phone number. Must send SASE for response. No simultaneous submissions. No e-mail submissions. Criticism will be given when requested. Guidelines available for SASE, by e-mail, or on website. Responds in 1 month. Pays $35, a certificate, and 2 copies plus discounts. Acquires all rights. Returns rights upon request. Open to reviews by children.

◨ ◗ **STORY LINE PRESS; NICHOLAS ROERICH POETRY PRIZE**, Three Oaks Farm, P.O. Box 1240, Ashland OR 97520-0055. (541)512-8792. Fax: (541)512-8793. E-mail: mail@storylinepress. com. Website: www.storylinepress.com (includes catalog, contest guidelines, online orders, sample books, and e-mail links). Story Line Press. Established 1985. **Executive Director:** Robert McDowell.

● Books published by Story Line Press have recently received such prestigious awards as the Lenore Marshall Prize, the Whiting Award, and the Harold Morton Landon Prize.

Book/Chapbook Needs: Story Line Press publishes each year the winner of the Nicholas Roerich Poetry Prize ($1,000 plus publication and a paid reading at the Roerich Museum in New York; a runner-up receives a full Story Line Press Scholarship to the Wesleyan Writers Conference in Middletown, CT [see listing in Conferences and Workshops section]; $20 entry and handling fee). The press also publishes books about poetry and has published collections by such poets as Alfred Corn, Annie Finch, Donald Justice, Mark Jarman, and David Mason.

How to Submit: Deadline for Nicholas Roerich Poetry Prize competition is October 31st. Complete guidelines available for SASE.

Also Offers: Story Line Press annually publishes 10-15 books of poetry, literary criticism, memoir, fiction, and books in translation. Query first.

▨ ◗ ◎ **STORYBOARD; UNIVERSITY OF GUAM PRESS (Specialized: regional)**, Division of English, University of Guam, Mangilau Guam 96923. (671)735-2749. Fax: (671)734-0012. E-mail: storybd@uog9.uog.edu. Website: www.uog.edu/storyboard.html (includes guidelines, contact and subscription information, and archives). Established 1991. **General Editor:** Robert Alan Burns.

Magazine Needs: *Storyboard* appears annually and "exists primarily to encourage indigenous Pacific writers and poets to write publishable materials and to encourage writings about the Pacific region." Wants work by indigenous Pacific writers or work about the Pacific Region. Has published poetry by Mike Catalano, Kay Putney Gantt, J.Q. Zheng, Frederick Zydek, Dennis Saleh, and Canisius Filibert. As a sample the editor selected this poem (poet unidentified):

> Your face is/marble-cold/your countenances/a slab of stone./Yet your eyes are/soft fires/amd their
> glance/a feather's fall.

Storyboard is 104 pages, magazine-sized, offset printed and perfect-bound with linen cover, uses photos and b&w art. Receives about 150 poems/year, accepts approximately 10%. Press run is 500 for 100 subscribers of which 25 are libraries, 200 shelf sales; remainder distributed free to schools in the region. Subscription: $7.50. Sample: $4.

How to Submit: Submit 5 poems at a time. Line length for poetry is 8 minimum, 70 maximum. Accepts simultaneous submissions; no previously published poems. Cover letter with short bio and SASE preferred. Reads submissions September through May. Time between acceptance and publication is 6-8 months. Poems are circulated to an editorial board. "The board outright rejects poems that do not meet our criteria as to focus on Pacific region and writers. Selections made on artist aesthetic merit." Seldom comments on rejected poems. Publishes theme issues occasionally. Guidelines available for SASE, by e-mail, and in publication. Responds in 6 months "if considered for publication." Pays 2 copies. Acquires first North American serial rights.

Advice: "Write well; focus on Pacific and Asia Pacific subjects and themes."

◗ **THE STORYTELLER**, 2441 Washington Rd., Maynard AR 72444. (870)647-2137. Website: www. freewebz.com/fossilcreek. Established 1996. **Editor:** Regina Williams.

Magazine Needs: *The Storyteller*, a quarterly magazine, "is geared to, but not limited to new writers and poets." Wants "any form up to 40 lines, any matter, any style, but must have a meaning. Do not throw words together and call it a poem. Nothing in way of explicit sex, violence, horror or explicit language. I would like it to be understood that I have young readers, ages 9-18." Accepts poetry written by children of all ages. As a sample the editor selected this poem by Bryan Byrd:

> This is the land of my memories:/Where forgotten river towns leak slowly into the Mississippi;/
> Crumbling and ivy covered,/They jealously watch the trains and barges go by.

Storyteller is 64 pages, 8½×11, desktop-published with slick cover, original pen & ink drawings on cover, ads. Receives about 300 poems/year, accepts about 40%. Press run is 600 for over 500 subscribers. Subscription: $20; $24 Canada & foreign; $8 Canada & foreign. Sample: $6 (if available).

How to Submit: Submit 2 poems at a time, typed and double-spaced. Accepts previously published poems and simultaneous submissions, "but must state where and when poetry first appeared." Cover letter preferred. **Reading fee:** $1/poem. Time between acceptance and publication is 9 months. Poems are circulated to an editorial board. "Poems are read and discussed by staff." Often comments on rejected poems. Offers criticism service for $5/poem. Occasionally publishes theme issues. Upcoming themes and guidelines available for SASE. Responds in up to 5 weeks. Acquires first or one-time rights. Reviews books and chapbooks of poetry by subscribers only. Poets may send books for review consideration to associate editor Ruthan Riney.

Also Offers: Sponsors a quarterly contest. "Readers vote on their favorite poems. Winners receive copy of magazine and certificate suitable for framing. We also nominate for the Pushcart Prize."
Advice: "I want to read what comes from your heart, whether good or bad. This is probably the easiest place to get your work in print—if it is well written. Thrown together words will not find a place in *The Storyteller*."

$⬚ THE STRAIN, 11702 Webercrest, Houston TX 77048. **Poetry Editor:** Norm Stewart Jr.
Magazine Needs: *The Strain* is a monthly magazine using "experimental or traditional poetry of very high quality." Does not include sample lines of poetry here as they "prefer not to limit style of submissions."
How to Submit: Accepts simultaneous submissions and previously published poems. Guidelines issue: $5 and 8 first-class stamps. Pays "no less than $5. We would prefer you submit before obtaining the guidelines issue which mostly explains upcoming collections and collaborations." Send books for review consideration.

⬚ STRAY DOG; PRILLY & TRU PUBLICATIONS, INC., P.O. Box 713, Amawalk NY 10501. E-mail: straydog@bestweb.net. Website: www.prillyandtru.com (includes guidelines, contact information, subscription rates, editorial policy). Established 2000. **Editor/Publisher:** j.v. morrissey.
Magazine Needs: *Stray Dog* appears annually in June or July and seeks "to publish the best, most powerful work we can find," including contemporary poetry, short-shorts, and art. "We print high-quality poetry, short-shorts and b&w art in any form or style. We're looking for work that is evocative and incisive, work that will leave skid marks on the reader's emotional highway. Prior publication credits admired but not required." Does not want to see anything "preachy, whiny, obscure, pornographic, gratuitously violent, or trite." Recently published poetry by Mark Wisniewski, Linda K. Sienkiewicz, Simon Perchik, Corrine DeWinter, L.B. Sedlacek, Parker Towle, and Kelley Jean White. *Stray Dog* is 92 pages, 6¾×8⅛, Docutech printed, perfect-bound, glossy card cover with b&w art. Receives about 500 poems/year, accepts 12%. Publishes about 40-45 poems/issue. Press run is 250. Single copy: $8; subscription: $8/year, $15/2 years. Sample: $6. Make checks payable to Stray Dog.
How to Submit: Submit 3-5 poems at a time. Line length for poetry is 2 pages maximum. Accepts simultaneous submissions; no previously published poems. No e-mail or disk submissions. Cover letter is preferred. "All submissions and correspondence must be accompanied by SASE for response and return of work; name/address/phone number on each page. No handwritten work. Include 2-3 line bio." Reads submissions year round. Time between acceptance and publication is within 1 year. Sometimes comments on rejected poems. Guidelines available by fax, by e-mail, on website, for SASE. Responds in up to 5 months. Pays 1 copy; additional copies available at cost. Acquires first North American serial rights.
Book/Chapbook Needs & How to Submit: Prilly & Tru Publications, Inc. is "not publishing books or chapbooks at this time, but plans to in the future."
Advice: "Surprise me! Blow me away! Knock the neon-striped toe socks off my feet! Think 'indie' film, not network TV."

⬚ ◎ STRUGGLE: A MAGAZINE OF PROLETARIAN REVOLUTIONARY LITERATURE (Specialized: political, ethnic/nationality, gay/lesbian/bisexual, socialism, workers' social issues, women/feminism, anti-racism), P.O. Box 13261, Detroit MI 48213-0261. (313)273-9039. E-mail: timhall11@yahoo.com. Established 1985. **Editor:** Tim Hall.
Magazine Needs: *Struggle* is a "literary quarterly, content: the struggle of the working people and all oppressed against the rich. Issues such as: racism, poverty, women's rights, aggressive wars, workers' struggle for jobs and job security, the overall struggle for a non-exploitative society, a genuine socialism." The poetry and songs printed are "generally short, any style, subject matter must criticize or fight— explicitly or implicitly—against the rule of the billionaires. We welcome experimentation devoted to furthering such content. We are open to both subtlety and direct statement." Has published poetry by Kevin Knox, Kellie Jean White, Jeffrey F. Grice, Howard L. Craft, Patrick J. Melvin, and Loraine Campbell. As a sample the editor selected these lines by Matthew Eddy:

> Weep not Palestinian of the broken heart,/in apocalyptic dreams I don white gloves and swank/tuxedo
> tails carrying the torch for you . . .

Struggle is 36 pages, digest-sized, photocopied with occasional photos or artwork, short stories, and short plays as well as poetry and songs. "We need more artwork and cartoons." Subscription: $10 for 4 issues. Sample: $2.50. Make checks payable to "Tim Hall—Special Account."
How to Submit: Submit up to 8 poems at a time. Accepts e-mail submissions in body of message (no attachments). Accepted work usually appears in the next or following issue. Editor tries to provide criticism "with every submission." Tries to respond in 4 months. Pays 2 copies. "If you are unwilling to have your poetry published on our website, please in form us."
Also Offers: "Coming soon: website at STRUGGLEMAGAZINE.org."

Advice: "Show passion and fire. Humor also welcome. Prefer powerful, colloquial language over academic timidity. Look to Neruda, Lorca, Bly, Whitman, Braithwaite, Tupac Shakur, Muriel Rukeyser. Experimental, traditional forms both welcome. Especially favor: works reflecting rebellion by the working people against the rich; works against racism, sexism, militarism, imperialism; works critical of our exploitative culture; works showing a desire for—or fantasy of—a non-exploitative society; works attacking the Republican 'anti-terrorism' war frenzy and the Democrats' surrender to it."

🌐 🖋 ◎ **STUDIO, A JOURNAL OF CHRISTIANS WRITING (Specialized: religious, spirituality)**, 727 Peel St., Albury, New South Wales 2640 Australia. Phone/fax: 61 2 6021 1135. E-mail: pgrover@bigpond.com. Established 1980. **Publisher:** Paul Grover.

Magazine Needs: *Studio* is a quarterly journal publishing "poetry and prose of literary merit, offering a venue for previously published, new and aspiring writers, and seeking to create a sense of community among Christians writing." The journal also publishes occasional articles as well as news and reviews of writing, writers, and events of interest to members. In poetry, the editors want "shorter pieces but with no specification as to form or length (necessarily less than 200 lines), subject matter, style, or purpose. People who send material should be comfortable being published under this banner: *Studio, A Journal of Christians Writing*." Has published poetry by John Foulcher and other Australian poets. *Studio* is 36 pages, digest-sized, professionally printed on high-quality recycled paper, saddle-stapled, matte card cover, with graphics and line drawings. Press run is 300, all subscriptions. Subscription: $48 (Aud) for overseas members. Sample available (airmail to US) for $8 (Aud).

How to Submit: Submissions must be typed and double-spaced on one side of A4 white paper. Accepts simultaneous submissions. Name and address must appear on the reverse side of each page submitted. Cover letter required; include brief details of previous publishing history, if any. SASE (or SAE with IRC) required. Response time is 2 months and time to publication is 9 months. Pays 1 contributor's copy. Acquires first Australian rights. Reviews books of poetry in 250 words, single format. Poets may send books for review consideration.

Also Offers: The magazine conducts a biannual poetry and short story contest.

Advice: "The trend in Australia is for imagist poetry and poetry exploring the land and the self. Reading the magazine gives the best indication of style and standard, so send for a sample copy before sending your poetry. Keep writing, and we look forward to hearing from you."

🖋 **THE STYLES**, P.O. Box 7171, Madison WI 53707. E-mail: thestylesorg@yahoo.com. Website: www.t hestyles.org (includes mission statement, contributors, subscription information, submissions guidelines). Established 2000. **Poetry Editor:** Amara Verona.

Magazine Needs: *THE STYLES* appears biannually. Publishes "ambitious original and creative ideas and standards of what writing should be. *THE STYLES* encourages new ideas about how writing should be written, read, evaluated, and what it should accomplish. Experimental work." Looking for "highly experimental poetry. Most of the poetry we publish is prose poetry." Does not want "anything sentimental." Recently published poetry by Jennie Trivanovich, Sarah Lindsay, Laura Mullen, Scott Bently, Mark Terrill, and Brian Johnson. *THE STYLES* is over 100 pages, 8×8, offset-printed, perfect-bound, soft point-spot

Why did the editors of *THE STYLES* pick this intriguing visual approach for their cover? "Either we aren't telling or we don't know." They do say, however, that the cover is a collaborative effort of the editorial staff "after an anonymous source leaked us the secret of the square-themed designs."

laminated color cover. Accepts about 2% of poems submitted. Publishes 12-20 poems/issue. Press run is 1,000. Single copy: $8; subscription: $32/year (4 issues). Sample: $5. Make checks payable to *THE STYLES*.

How to Submit: Submit 3 or more poems at a time. Line length for poetry is open. Accepts simultaneous submissions; no previously published poems. No fax, e-mail, or disk submissions. Cover letter is preferred. "Always send a SASE. Cover letters and bios are appreciated, but not required." Reads submissions all year. Time between acceptance and publication is 1-9 months. Often comments on rejected poems. Guidelines are available in magazine, for SASE, or on website. Responds in 1 month. Sometimes sends prepublication galleys. Pays $3 and 2 contributor's copies. Acquires first North American serial rights. Poets may send books for review consideration. "We will make 'comments,' quotes, and advanced comments for books, chapbooks, and other magazines. We don't have a section in our publication for reviews."

Advice: "We publish very little poetry in each issue. We are looking for poets who are using language in new ways. Read our publication. Our readers enjoy work that is accessible and yet still challenging."

◎ SUB-TERRAIN; ANVIL PRESS; LAST POEMS POETRY CONTEST, P.O. Box 3008, MPO, Vancouver, British Columbia V63 3X5 Canada. (604)876-8710. Fax: (604)899-2667. E-mail: subter@porta l.ca. Website: www.anvilpress.com/subterrain (includes guidelines, contest rules, and subscription information). Established 1988. **Contact:** Poetry Editor.

Magazine Needs: Anvil Press is an "alternate small press publishing *sub-TERRAIN*—a socially conscious literary quarterly whose aim is to produce a reading source that will stand in contrast to the trite and pandered—as well as broadsheets, chapbooks and the occasional monograph." Wants "work that has a point-of-view; work that has some passion behind it and is exploring issues that are of pressing importance (particularly that with an urban slant); work that challenges conventional notions of what poetry is or should be; work with a social conscience. No bland, flowery, uninventive poetry that says nothing in style or content." As a sample the editor selected these lines from "Eidetic" by Quentin Tarantino:

> *In fluid and electrics the alligator brain holds it all/rigid, refined and encyclopedic, the chemical well/*
> *contains a green bathing suit, improbable sex acts,/inclusive results from the elector of nineteen eighty-*
> *six/a bowl of stinging Thai soup and the origin of scars/all held static and wet in the ancient clock,*
> *the first mind.*

sub-TERRAIN is 56 pages, 8½ × 11½, offset-printed, with a press run of 3,000. Subscription: $15. Sample: $5.

How to Submit: Submit 4-6 poems at a time. Accepts simultaneous submissions; no previously published poems. No fax or e-mail submissions. Responds in up to 6 months. Pays money on publication. All contest entrants receive a 3-issue subscription to *sub-TERRAIN*. Acquires one-time rights for magazine. "If chapbook contract, we retain right to publish subsequent printings unless we let a title lapse out-of-print for more than one year." Staff occasionally reviews small press poetry chapbooks.

Book/Chapbook Needs & How to Submit: For chapbook or book publication submit 4 sample poems and bio, no simultaneous submissions. No fax or e-mail submissions. "Only those manuscripts accompanied by a self-addressed stamped envelope (SASE) will be considered. But I must stress that we are a co-op, depending on support from an interested audience. New titles will be undertaken with caution. We are not subsidized at this point and do not want to give authors false hopes—but if something is important and should be in print, we will do our best. Response time can, at times, be lengthy; if you want to be assured that your manuscript has been received, include a self-addressed stamped postcard for notification." Editor provides brief comment and more extensive comments for fees.

Also Offers: Sponsors Last Poems Poetry Contest. Submit up to 4 poems. Entry fee: $15. Deadline: January 31. Winner announced March 1. Prize: $250, plus publication in Spring issue. Entrants receive a 3-issue subscription. More information is available for SASE (or SAE and IRC) and on website.

Advice: "It is important that writers intending to submit work have an idea of what work we publish. Read a sample copy before submitting."

◎ SULPHUR RIVER LITERARY REVIEW, P.O. Box 19228, Austin TX 78760-9228. (512)292-9456. Established 1978, reestablished 1987. **Editor/Publisher:** James Michael Robbins.

Magazine Needs: Appearing in March and September, *Sulphur River* is a semiannual of poetry, prose, and artwork. "No restrictions except quality." Does not want poetry that is "trite or religious or verse that does not incite thought." Has published poetry by Willie James King, Alan Britt, Nicole Melanson, Jen Besemer, Tom Chandler, and Geri Rosenzweig. *Sulphur River* is digest-sized, perfect-bound, with glossy cover. Receives about 2,000 poems/year, accepts 4%. Press run is 400 for 200 subscribers, 100 shelf sales. Subscription: $12. Sample: $7.

How to Submit: No previously published poems or simultaneous submissions. Often comments on rejected poems, although a dramatic increase in submissions has made this increasingly difficult. Responds in 1 month. Always sends prepublication galleys. Pays 2 contributor's copies.

Also Offers: "*Sulphur River* also publishes full-length volumes of poetry; latest book: *Like a Pilot: Selected Poems of Rolf Dieter Brinkman.*"

Advice: "Poetry is, for me, the essential art, the ultimate art, and there can be no compromise of quality if the poem is to be successful."

$⬤ SUMMER STREAM PRESS, P.O. Box 6056, Santa Barbara CA 93160-6056. (805)962-6540. E-mail: geehossiffer@aol.com. Established 1978. **Poetry Editor:** David D. Frost.

Book/Chapbook Needs: Publishes a series of books (Box Cars) in hardcover and softcover, each presenting 6 poets, averaging 70 text pages for each poet. "The mix of poets represents many parts of the country and many approaches to poetry. The poets previously selected have been published, but that is no requirement. We welcome traditional poets in the mix and thus offer them a chance for publication in this world of free-versers. The six poets share a 15% royalty. We require rights for our editions worldwide and share 50-50 with authors for translation rights and for republication of our editions by another publisher. Otherwise all rights remain with the authors." Accepts poetry written by children. Has published poetry by Virginia E. Smith, Sandra Russell, Jennifer MacPherson, Nancy Berg, Lois Shapley Bassen, and Nancy J. Wallace.

How to Submit: To be considered for future volumes in this series, query with about 12 sample poems, no cover letter. No e-mail submissions. Responds to query in 6 months, to submission (if invited) in 1 year. Accepts previously published poetry and simultaneous submissions. Editor usually comments on rejected poems. Always sends prepublication galleys. Pays 6 contributor's copies plus royalties.

Advice: "We welcome both traditional poetry and free verse. However, we find we must reject almost all the traditional poetry received simply because the poets exhibit little or no knowledge of the structure and rules of traditional forms. Much of it is rhymed free verse."

$⬤ THE SUN, 107 N. Roberson St., Chapel Hill NC 27516. Website: www.thesunmagazine.org. Established 1974. **Editor:** Sy Safransky.

Magazine Needs: *The Sun* is "noted for honest, personal work that's not too obscure or academic. We avoid traditional, rhyming poetry, as well as limericks, haiku, and religious poetry. We're open to almost anything else: free verse, prose poems, short and long poems." Has published poetry by William Snyder Jr., Alison Luterman, Donna Steiner, David Budbill, Susan Terris, and Michael Chitwood. As a sample the editor selected these lines from "Dog on the Floor in the Pet-Food Aisle" by Ruth L. Schwartz:

> *We watch our lives through airplane windows,/small and dim and scarred,/and even so, life noses up,/*
> *rolling before us/like a black dog,/its brown eyes steady as the sun,/its belly in the air, asking for touch.*

The Sun is 48 pages, magazine-sized, printed on 50 lb. offset, saddle-stapled, with b&w photos and graphics. Circulation is 50,000 for 48,000 subscriptions of which 500 are libraries. Receives 3,000 submissions of poetry/year, accepts about 30; has a 1- to 3-month backlog. Subscription: $34. Sample: $5.

How to Submit: Submit up to 6 poems at a time. Poems should be typed and accompanied by a cover letter. Accepts previously published poems, but simultaneous submissions are discouraged. Guidelines available for SASE. Responds within 3 months. Pays $50-200 on publication plus copies and subscription. Acquires first serial or one-time rights.

⬤ SUN POETIC TIMES, P.O. Box 790526, San Antonio TX 78279-0526. (210)349-8216. E-mail: sunpoets@hotmail.com. Website: http://clik.to/SunPoets (includes guidelines, contact information, bios, and subscription information). Established 1994. **Editor:** Rod C. Stryker.

Magazine Needs: *Sun Poetic Times, a literary & artistic magazine*, appears quarterly to "publish all types of literary and visual art from all walks of life. We take all types. Our only specification is length— 1 page in length if typed, 2 pages if handwritten (legibly)." Has published poetry by Naomi Shihab Nye, Chris Crabtree, Trinidad Sanchez, Jr., and Garland Lee Thompson, Jr. As a sample the editor selected these lines from "Omniscience" by Amanda Leigh Auchter:

> *They drank money with/each swig of amber blood,/while the mistress hung/tired linens from dirty*
> *windows,/saluting the breath of factory whispers/in midday haze, alone and silent.*

Sun Poetic Times is 24-28 pages, magazine-sized, attractively printed and saddle-stapled with glossy card stock cover, uses b&w line drawings/halftones. Receives about 200 poems/year, accepts about 30%. Press run is 300, 200 shelf sales. Subscription: $10 for 2 issues, $20/1 year (4 issues). Sample: $5 and SASE. Make checks payable to Sun Poetic Times.

NEED HELP? To better understand and use the information in these listings, see the introduction to this section.

How to Submit: Submit 3-5 poems at a time. Accepts simultaneous submissions; no previously published poems. Accepts e-mail submissions included in body of message (no attached files). Cover letter preferred. "In cover letters, we like to hear about your publishing credits, reasons you've taken up the pen and general BS like that (biographical info)." Time between acceptance and publication is up to 8 months. Seldom comments on rejected poems. Occasionally publishes theme issues. Guidelines and upcoming themes available for SASE or by e-mail. E-mail queries welcome. Responds in up to 4 months. Pays 1 contributor's copy. Rights revert back to author upon publication.

SUNSTONE (Specialized: religious, Mormon; nature/rural/ecology; social issues; spirituality/inspiration), 343 N. Third W., Salt Lake City UT 84103-1215. (801)355-5926. Established 1974. **Poetry Editor:** Dixie Partridge.

Magazine Needs: Appearing 4-6 times/year, *Sunstone* publishes "scholarly articles of interest to an open, Mormon audience; personal essays; fiction; and poetry." Wants "both lyric and narrative poetry that engages the reader with fresh, strong images, skillful use of language, and a strong sense of voice and/or place. No didactic poetry, sing-song rhymes, or in-process work." Has published poetry by Susan Howe, Anita Tanner, Robert Parham, Ryan G. Van Cleave, Robert Rees, and Virgil Suarez. As a sample the editor selected these lines from "Sonora" by Georganne O'Connor:

> . . . the wind's hot breath steals the air from your chest/and every bead of sweat from your skin./From the canyon floor, I see hills/robbed of rain, studded with giant saguaro,/the sentinels. They have seen us coming./In the accordian folds of their flesh,/elf owl rests, insulated from heat. . . .

Sunstone is 80 pages, 8½×11, professionally printed and saddle-stapled with a semi-glossy paper cover. Receives over 500 poems/year, accepts 40-50. Press run is 5,000 for 4,000 subscribers of which 300 are libraries, 700 shelf sales. Subscription: $36/6 issues. Sample: $8 postpaid.

How to Submit: Submit up to 5 poems with name and address on each poem. "We rarely use poems over 40 lines." No previously published poems or simultaneous submissions. Time between acceptance and publication is 18 months or less. Seldom comments on rejected poems. Guidelines available for SASE. Responds in 3 months. Pays 3 contributor's copies. Acquires first North American serial rights.

Advice: "Poems should not sound like a rewording of something heard before. Be original; pay attention to language, sharp imagery. Contents should deepen as the poem progresses. We've published poems rooted strongly in place, narratives seeing life from another time or culture, poems on religious belief or doubt—a wide range of subject matter."

SUPERIOR POETRY NEWS (Specialized: translations; regional, Rocky Mountain West); JOSS (Specialized: multi-cultural, philosophical); SUPERIOR POETRY PRESS, P.O. Box 424, Superior MT 59872. Established 1995. **Editors:** Ed and Guna Chaberek.

• **At press time we learned that *Superior Poetry News* has ceased publication.**

Magazine Needs: *Superior Poetry News* appears annually in January or February and "publishes the best and most interesting of new poets, as well as established poets, we can find. Also, we encourage lively translation into English from any language." Wants "general, rural, Western, or humorous poetry; translations; 40 lines or under. Nothing graphically sexual; containing profanity." Has published poetry by makyo, Roberts Mūks, Simon Perchik, Arthur Winfield Knight, and Kit Knight. *Superior Poetry News* is 12-24 pages, 8½×5, photocopied and saddle-stapled, "relevant artwork accepted, ads open to subscribers (1 free per issue)." Receives about 2,000 poems/year, accepts 10%. Press run is 75 for 50 subscribers; 3-5 distributed free to libraries. Single copy: $2; subscription: $2. Sample: $2.

How to Submit: Submit 3-5 poems at a time. No previously published poems or simultaneous submissions (unless stated). Cover letter with short bio preferred. Time between acceptance and publication is 3 months. Seldom comments on rejected poems, "but will if requested." Guidelines available for SASE. Responds in 1 week. Pays 1 copy. Acquires first rights. Staff reviews books and chapbooks of poetry and other magazines in 50-100 words, single book format. Send books for review consideration with return postage (overseas contributors please include two IRCs).

Magazine Needs & How to Submit: Superior Poetry Press also publishes *JOSS: A journal for the 21st century*. Published annually, *JOSS* features "material which serves to project and uplift the human spirit for the great adventure of the next one hundred years. Writers and poets in mainstream religious, philosophical, scientific, and social disciplines are encouraged to submit." Subscription: $2/year. Sample: $2. Submit poems of up to 40 lines in length; articles 400 words maximum. Pays 1 contributor's copy.

SUZERAIN ENTERPRISES; LOVE'S CHANCE MAGAZINE (Specialized: love/romance); FIGHTING CHANCE MAGAZINE (Specialized: horror, mystery, science fiction/fantasy), P.O. Box 60336, Worcester MA 01606. Established 1994. **Editor/Publisher:** Milton Kerr.

Magazine Needs: *Love's Chance Magazine* and *Fighting Chance Magazine* are each published 3 times/ year to "give unpublished writers a chance to be published and to be paid for their efforts." *Love's Chance* deals with romance; *Fighting Chance* deals with dark fiction, horror, and science fiction. "No porn, ageism, sexism, racism, children in sexual situations." Has published poetry by Gary McGhee, T.R. Barnes, Cecil Boyce, and Ellaraine Lockie. As a sample the editor selected these lines from "Panhandle Postcard" by Gary McGhee:

> *Amarillo Welcomes You is/in my rear view mirror and/our goodbye leaves the/taste of bile in my throat.*

Both magazines are 15-30 pages, 8½×11, photocopied and side-stapled, computer-designed paper cover. Both receive about 500 poems/year, accept about 10%. Press runs are 100 for 70-80 subscribers. Subscription: $12/ year for each. Samples: $4 each. Make checks payable to Suzerain Enterprises.

How to Submit: For both magazines, submit 3 poems at a time. Line length for poetry is 20 maximum. Accepts previously published poems and simultaneous submissions. Cover letter preferred. "Proofread for spelling errors, neatness; must be typewritten in standard manuscript form. No handwritten manuscripts." Time between acceptance and publication is 3 months. Often comments on rejected poems. Guidelines available for SASE. Responds in 6 weeks. Acquires first or one-time rights.

Advice: "Proofread and edit carefully. Read and write, then read and write some more. Don't let rejection slips get you down. Keep submitting and don't give up."

SWEET ANNIE & SWEET PEA REVIEW, 7750 Highway F-24 W, Baxter IA 50028. (515)792-3578. Fax: (515)792-1310. E-mail: anniespl@netins.net. Established 1995. **Editor/Publisher:** Beverly A. Clark.

Magazine Needs: *Sweet Annie & Sweet Pea Review*, published quarterly, features short stories and poetry. Wants "poems of outdoors, plants, land, heritage, women, relationships, olden times—simpler times." Does not want "obscene, violent, explicit sexual material, obscure, long-winded materials, no overly religious materials." Has published poetry by Anne Carol Betterton, Mary Ann Wehler, Susan Clayton-Goldner, Celeste Bowman, Dick Reynolds, and Brenda Serotte. As a sample the editor selected these lines from "Brooding the Heartlands" by M.L. Liebler:

> *There were those days/Lonesome out on/The Dakota Plains. Lonesome/In my prairie rose daydreams—/ memories brooding across the heartland.*

Sweet Annie & Sweet Pea Review is 30 pages, 5¼×8½, offset-printed, saddle-stapled, bond paper with onion skin page before title page, medium card cover, and cover art. Receives about 200 poems/year, accepts 25-33%. Press run is 40. Subscription: $24. Sample: $7. Make checks payable to Sweet Annie Press.

How to Submit: Submit 6-12 poems at a time. "Effective 2001, **reading fee** $5/author submitting. Strongly recommend ordering a sample issue prior to submitting and preference is given to poets and writers following this procedure and submitting in accordance with the layout used consistently by this Press." Accepts simultaneous submissions; no previously published poems. No e-mail submissions. Cover letter preferred with personal comments about yourself and phone number. Time between acceptance and publication is 9 months. Often comments on rejected poems. Publishes theme issues occasionally. "We select for theme first, select for content second; narrow selections through editors." Pays 1 contributor's copy. Acquires all rights. Returns rights with acknowledgment in future publications. Will review chapbooks of poetry or other magazines of short length, reviews 500 words or less. Poets may send books for review consideration.

SYCAMORE REVIEW, Dept. of English, Purdue University, West Lafayette IN 47907. (765)494-3783. Fax: (765)494-3780. E-mail: sycamore@expert.cc.purdue.edu. Website: www.sla.purdue.edu/sycamore/ (includes contact information, guidelines, archives, and subscription information). Established 1988 (first issue May, 1989). **Contact:** Poetry Editor.

- Poetry published by *Sycamore Review* was selected for inclusion in the 2002 *Pushcart Prize* anthology.

Magazine Needs: *Sycamore Review* is published biannually in January and June. "We accept personal essays, short fiction, drama, translations, and quality poetry in any form. We aim to publish many diverse styles of poetry from formalist to prose poems, narrative, and lyric." Has published poetry by Lucia Perillo, Theresa Pappas, Virgil Suarez, Dale Hushner, Christine Sneed, John O'Connor, and Kevin Prufer. *Sycamore Review* is semiannual in a digest-sized format, 160 pages, flat-spined, professionally printed, with matte, color cover. Press run is 1,000 for 500 subscribers of which 50 are libraries. Subscription: $12; $14 outside US. Sample: $7. Make checks payable to Purdue University (Indiana residents add 5% sales tax.)

How to Submit: Submit 3-6 poems at a time. Name and address on each page. Accepts simultaneous submissions, if notified immediately of acceptance elsewhere; no previously published poems except translations. No submissions accepted via fax or e-mail. Cover letters not required but invited; include phone number, short bio and previous publications, if any. "We read September 1 through March 31 only."

Guidelines available for SASE. Responds in 4 months. Pays 2 copies. Acquires first North American rights. After publication, all rights revert to author. Staff reviews books of poetry. Send books to editor-in-chief for review consideration.

Advice: "Poets who do not include SASE do not receive a response."

☐ **SYMBIOTIC PRESS, SYMBIOSIS PRESS, SLAP-DASH-UGLY CHAPBOOK SERIES**, P.O. Box 14938, Philadelphia PA 19149. Established 1997. **Editor:** Ms. Juan Xu.
   • *Symbiotic Oatmeal* is no longer being published.
Book/Chapbook Needs & How to Submit: Symbiotic Press/Symbiosis Press publishes chapbooks. Has published *River Rat Words* by Robert E. Jordon and *Childhood* by B.Z. Niditch. Query before submitting. **Reading fee:** $10 per ms. Make checks payable to Juan Xu.

$ 🖉 **SYNAESTHESIA PRESS; SYNAESTHESIA PRESS CHAPBOOK SERIES**, P.O. Box 1763, Tempe AZ 85280-1763. (602)316-1141. Fax: (480)317-9376. E-mail: jim@chapbooks.org. Website: www. chapbooks.org. Established 1995. **Editor:** Jim Camp.
Book/Chapbook Needs: Synaesthesia Press wants to publish "work seldom seen elsewhere." Under the Synaesthesia Press Chapbook Series, they publish 4 chapbooks/year. "No real specifications to form/ style; I want to read fresh poetry that stimulates the reader." He does not want to see "the same garbage most little mags publish." Has published poetry by Jack Micheline, Tszurah Litzky, Roxie Powell, and Steve Fisher. Chapbooks are usually 16 pages, digest-sized, offset/hand press printed, sewn-wrap binding, 80 lb. cardstock cover.
How to Submit: Query first with *one* sample poem. Accepts previously published poems and simultaneous submissions. Cover letter preferred. Time between acceptance and publication is 6 months. Responds to queries in 1 month. Pays honorarium of $200 and 6 author's copies (out of a press run of about 250). Order sample chapbooks by sending $15.

N 🖉 📇 **SYNERGEBOOKS**, 1235 Flat Shoals Rd., King NC 27021. (888)812-2533. E-mail: SynergE ditor@aol.com. Website: www.SynergEbooks.com (includes bookstore, featured authors and illustrators, newest releases, sales). Established 1999. **Acquisitions Editor:** Allie McCormack. Member: EPPRO, SPAN, EPC, PMA.
   • SynergEbooks won the Golden Web Award for 2001-2002.
Book/Chapbook Needs: SynergEbooks specializes in quality works by talented new writers in every available digital format, including CD-ROMs and paperback. Will accept historical, romantic, poetry from teens, etc. Does not want unedited work. Recently published poetry by Theresa Jodray, Brenda Roberts, Vanyell Delacroix, Serenity Hawk, Joel L. Young, and Minerva Bloom. As a sample the editor selected these lines from "Flies" by Rick Lawley (EPPIE award nominee, 2001) from *drowning little fireflies*:

> God, but don't you think it's odd/I get these feelings some nights like/ceramic butterflies hammer my
> brain/into dust. malignant fireflies gasp/between your talented thighs when it's/cold outside and you
> scream snowflies . . .

SynergEbooks publishes up to 40 titles/year, 2-5 of them poetry. Books are usually 45-150 pages, print-on-demand with paperback binding.
How to Submit: Query first, with a few sample poems and cover letter with brief bio and publication credits. Send by e-mail attachment whenever possible to SynergEditor@aol.com. Responds to queries in 1 month; to mss in up to 5 months. Pays royalties of 40-60%.
Advice: "We are inundated with more poetry than prose every month; but we will accept quality anthologies of any genre type that is original and high quality. New poets welcome."

🔀 ◯ ◎ **TALE SPINNERS; MIDNIGHT STAR PUBLICATIONS (Specialized: rural/pastoral)**, R.R. #1, Ponoka, Alberta T4J 1R1 Canada. (403)783-2521. Established 1996. **Editor/Publisher:** Nellie Gritchen Scott.
Magazine Needs: *Tale Spinners* is a quarterly " 'little literary magazine with a country flavour,' for writers who love country and all it stands for." Wants poetry, fiction, anecdotes, personal experiences, etc. pertaining to country life. Children's poetry welcome." No "scatological, prurient or sexually explicit or political content." Published poetry by Daniel Green, A.H. Ferguson, C. David Hay, Don Melcher, Melvin Sandberg, and Richard Arnold. As a sample the editor selected these lines from "Snow Storm" by Don Melcher:

> A wintry blast of wind and snow assail/the staunch walls of forest palisades,/Wave after wave of the
> hoary host invades/with relentless siege as deepening drifts impale

Tale Spinner is 48 pages, 5½×8, photocopied and saddle-stapled with light cardstock cover, uses clip art or freehand graphics. Receives about 100 poems/year, accepts about 80%. Press run is 75 for 50 subscribers. Subscription: $20. Sample: $5.

How to Submit: Submit up to 6 poems at a time. Accepts previously published poems. Cover letter ensures a reply. Include a SAE and IRC. "Short poems preferred, but will use narrative poems on occasion." Time between acceptance and publication is 3 months. Often comments on rejected poems. Responds in 2 weeks. Pays 1 copy.

Book/Chapbook Needs & How to Submit: "Due to health reasons, Midnight Star Publications is not accepting chapbook manuscripts at present. *Tale Spinners* will continue."

Advice: "Read the guidelines before submitting! Include return postage or I will not reply. Don't try to impress me—cuteness doesn't cut it."

TAMEME (Specialized: bilingual, regional), 199 First St., #335, Los Altos CA 94022. Website: www.tameme.org (includes overview, content, contributors notes, purchase information, and guidelines.) Established 1999. **Contact:** Poetry Editor.

• *Tameme* was awarded a grant from the Rockefeller/Bancomer Fund for US—Mexico Culture.

Magazine Needs: "*Tameme* is an annual literary magazine dedicated to publishing new writing from North America in side-by-side English-Spanish format. *Tameme*'s goals are to play an instrumental role in introducing important new writing from Canada and the United States to Mexico, and vice versa, and to provide a forum for the art of literary translation. By 'new writing' we mean the best work of serious literary value that has been written recently. By 'writing from North America' we mean writing by citizens or residents of Mexico, the United States, and Canada." Has published poetry by Alberto Blanco, Jaime Sabines, T. Lopez Mills, Marianne Toussaint, and W.D. Snodgrass. *Tameme* is 225 pages, 5½×8½. Receives about 200 poems/year, accepts 1%. Press run is 2,000. Subscription: $14.95. Sample: $14.95. Make checks payable to Tameme, Inc.

How to Submit: *Tameme* is currently closed to unsolicited mss.

$ ♡ TAMPA REVIEW, Dept. PM, University of Tampa, 401 W. Kennedy Blvd., Tampa FL 33606-1490. Website: http://tampareview.utampa.edu. Established 1964 as *UT Poetry Review,* became *Tampa Review* in 1988. **Editor:** Richard Mathews. **Poetry Editor:** Donald Morrill. Send poems to Poetry Editor, *Tampa Review*, Box 19F, The University of Tampa, Tampa FL 33606-1409.

Magazine Needs: *Tampa Review* is an elegant semiannual of fiction, nonfiction, poetry, and art (not limited to US authors) wanting "original and well-crafted poetry written with intelligence and spirit. We do accept translations, but no greeting card or inspirational verse." Has published poetry by Richard Chess, Naomi Shihab Nye, Jim Daniels, and Stephen Dunn. As a sample the editors selected these lines from "91st Birthday" by Peter Meinke:

> her brown eyes must have lit every room/she entered showing there's a brief time bright/for everyone:
> a flushed spell when our blood comes/together the music all trumpets and drums . . .

Tampa Review is 72-96 pages, 7½×10½ flat-spined, with acid free text paper and hard cover with color dust jacket. Receives about 2,000 poems/year, accepts 50-60. Press run is 1,000 for 175 subscribers of which 20 are libraries. Sample: $7.

How to Submit: Submit 3-6 poems at a time, typed, single-spaced. No previously published poems or simultaneous submissions. Unsolicited mss are read between September and December only. Guidelines available for SASE. Responds by mid-February. Sometimes sends prepublication galleys. Pays $10/printed page plus 1 contributor's copy and 40% discount on additional copies. Acquires first North American serial rights.

♡ TAPROOT LITERARY REVIEW; TAPROOT WRITER'S WORKSHOP ANNUAL WRITING CONTEST, P.O. Box 204, Ambridge PA 15003. (724)266-8476. E-mail: taproot10@aol.com. Established 1986. **Editor:** Tikvah Feinstein.

Magazine Needs: *Taproot* is an annual publication, open to beginners. "We publish some of the best poets in the U.S. *Taproot* is a very respected anthology with increasing distribution. We enjoy all types and styles of poetry from emerging writers to established writers to those who have become valuable and old friends who share their new works with us." Writers published include Hilary Koski, Lila Julius, Tammy Pegher, Charles Cingolani, B.Z. Niditch, and James Doyle. As a sample the editor selected these lines from "Autumn Croquis" by Elizabeth Howkins:

> against the sky, reaching upwards/like arms, toward something distant/our eyes, still clouded by
> summer/cannot see—a world disrobing

Taproot Literary Review is approximately 95 pages, offset-printed on white stock with one-color glossy cover, art and no ads. Circulation is 500, sold at bookstores, barnesandnoble.com, amazon.com. readings and through the mail. Single copy: $6.95; subscriptions $7.50. Sample: $5.

How to Submit: Submit up to 5 poems, "no longer than 30 lines each." Nothing previously published or pending publication will be accepted. Accepts e-mail submissions (no attached files); "we would rather have a printed copy. 'We would rather have a hard copy. Also, we cannot answer without a SASE.'' Cover letter with general information required. Submissions accepted between September 1 and December 31 only. Guidelines available for SASE. Sometimes sends prepublication galleys. Pays 2 contributor's copies. Open to receiving books for review consideration. Send query first.

Also Offers: Sponsors the annual Taproot Writer's Workshop Annual Writing Contest. 1st Prize: $25 and publication in *Taproot Literary Review*; 2nd Prize: publication; and 3rd Prize: publication. Submit 5 poems of literary quality, any form and subject except porn. Entry fee: $10/5 poems (no longer than 35 lines each), provides copy of review. Deadline: December 31. Winners announced the following March.

Advice: "We publish the best poetry we can in a variety of styles and subjects, so long as it's literary quality and speaks to us. We love poetry that stuns, surprises, amuses, and disarms."

○ TAR RIVER POETRY, English Dept., East Carolina University, Greenville NC 27858-4353. (252)328-6046 or 6467. Website: www.ecu.edu/journals (includes guidelines, masthead, sample poetry, and subscription information). Established 1960. **Editor:** Peter Makuck.

Magazine Needs: "We are not interested in sentimental, flat-statement poetry. What we would like to see is skillful use of figurative language." *Tar River* is an "all-poetry" magazine that accepts dozens of poems in each issue, providing the talented beginner and experienced writer with an excellent forum that features all styles and forms of verse. Has published poetry by Dabney Stuart, Brendan Galoin, Betty Adcock, Dannye Romine Powell, Claudia Emerson, Michael McFee. As a sample the editors selected these lines from "Chimneys" by Patrick Moran:

> If a house burns down/they have to be/the last one standing, towering over the ashes/in the charred
> cloak/of a mourner.

Tar River appears twice yearly and is 60 pages, digest-sized, professionally printed on salmon stock, some decorative line drawings, matte card cover with photo. Receives 6,000-8,000 submissions/year, accepts 150-200. Press run is 900 for 500 subscribers of which 125 are libraries. Subscription: $10. Sample: $5.50.

How to Submit: Submit 3-6 poems at a time. "We do not consider previously published poems or simultaneous submissions. Double or single-spaced OK. Name and address on each page. We do not consider mss during summer months." Reads submissions September 1 through April 15 only. Editors will comment "if slight revision will do the trick." Guidelines available for SASE or on website. Responds in 6 weeks. Pays 2 contributor's copies. Acquires first rights. Reviews books of poetry in 4,000 words maximum, single or multi-book format. Poets may send books for review consideration.

Advice: "Read, read, read. Saul Bellow says the writer is primarily a reader moved to emulation. Read the poetry column in *Writer's Digest*. Read the books recommended therein. Do your homework."

⊕ ○ TEARS IN THE FENCE, 38 Hodview, Stourpaine, Nr. Blandford Forum, Dorset DT11 8TN England. Phone: 0044 1258-456803. Fax: 0044 1258-454026. E-mail: westrow@cooperw.fsnet.co.uk. Established 1984. **General Editor:** David Caddy.

Magazine Needs: *Tears in the Fence* is a "small press magazine of poetry, fiction, interviews, articles, reviews and graphics. We are open to a wide variety of poetic styles. Work that is unusual, perceptive, risk-taking as well as imagistic, lived, and visionary will be close to our purpose. However, we like to publish a variety of work." Has published poetry by Martin Stannard, Elizabeth Cook, Joshua Bodwell, Lynne Hjelmgaard, Dave Newman, and Sheila E. Murphy. As a sample the editors selected these lines from "The Push-Up Combat Bikini" by Robert Shepard.

> Every time I open my mouth out comes a manifesto of a new literary/movement! Was that a poem,
> curling round you or its echo, nerves/ajangle on syntax's opening

Tears in the Fence appears 3 times/year, is 112 pages, A5, docutech printed on 110 gms. paper and perfect-bound with matte card cover and b&w art and graphics. Press run is 800, of which 476 go to subscribers. Subscription: $20/4 issues. Sample: $7.

How to Submit: Submit 6 typed poems with IRCs. Does not accept fax or e-mail submissions. Cover letter with brief bio required. Publishes theme issues. Upcoming themes available for SASE. Responds in 3 months. Time between acceptance and publication is 10 months "but can be much less." Pays 1 contributor's copy. Reviews books of poetry in 2,000-3,000 words, single or multi-book format. Send books for review consideration.

Also Offers: The magazine is informally connected with the East Street Poets literary promotions, workshops and events, including the annual Wessex Poetry Festival and the annual East Street Poets International Open Poetry Competition. Also publishes books. Books published include *Hanging Windchimes In A Vacuum*, by Gregory Warren Wilson, *Heart Thread* by Joan Jobe Smith, and *The Hong Kong/Macao Trip* by Gerald Locklin.

Advice: "I think it helps to subscribe to several magazines in order to study the market and develop an understanding of what type of poetry is published. Use the review sections and send off to magazines that are new to you."

♥ TEBOT BACH, P.O. Box 7887, Huntington Beach CA 92615-7887. (714)968-0905. **Editors/Publishers:** Mifanwy Kaiser

Book/Chapbook Needs & How to Submit: Tebot Bach (Welsh for "little teapot") publishes books of poetry. Titles include *48 Questions* by Richard Jones, *The Way In* by Robin Chapman, and *Written in Rain: New and Selected Poems 1985-2000* by M.L. Liebler. Query first with sample poems and cover letter with brief bio and publication credits. Include SASE. Responds to queries and mss, if invited, in 1 month. Time between acceptance and publication is up to 2 years. Write to order sample books.

⬭ ◎ **TEEN VOICES (Specialized: teen, women)**, P.O. Box 120-027, Boston MA 02112-0027. (617)426-5505. E-mail: teenvoices@teenvoices.com. Website: www.teenvoices.com (includes creative writing, horoscopes, bulletin boards, activision tips, information about the print magazine, and other topics of interest for our writers and readers). Established 1988; first published 1990. **Contact:** Submission Director.
Magazine Needs: *Teen Voices*, published quarterly, is a magazine written by, for, and about teenage girls. Regular features are family, cultural harmony, surviving sexual assault, teen motherhood, and all other topics of interest to our writers and readers. Accepts poetry written by young women ages 13-19. As a sample the editor selected these lines from "Seraph" by Rachel D.:

> Not long ago in a kingdom by the sea/winged seraphs of heaven protected me/the winds would blow
> their vow/to guide me for eternity

Teen Voices is 64 pages, with glossy cover, art and photos. "We accept 10% of the poems we receive, but can't afford to publish all of them timely." Press run is 25,000. Single copy: $3; subscription: $20. Sample: $5. Make checks payable to *Teen Voices*.
How to Submit: Submit any number of poems with name, age and address on each. Accepts simultaneous submissions; no previously published poems. Accepts submissions by fax and by e-mail (as attachment). Cover letter preferred. "Confirmation of receipt of submission sent in 6-8 weeks." Poems are circulated to a teen editorial board. Pays 5 contributor's copies. Open to unsolicited reviews.

💲◪ **TEMPORARY VANDALISM RECORDINGS; THE SILT READER**, P.O. Box 6184, Orange CA 92863-6184. E-mail: tvrec@yahoo.com. Website: http://members.aol.com/aphasiapress. Established 1991 (Temporary Vandalism Recordings), 1999 (*The Silt Reader*). **Editors:** Robert Roden and Barton M. Saunders.
Magazine Needs: *The Silt Reader*, is published biannually. "Form, length, style and subject matter can vary. It's difficult to say what will appeal to our eclectic tastes." Does not want "strictly rants, overly didactic poetry." Has published poetry by M. Jaime-Becerra, Daniel McGinn, Jerry Gordon, Margaret Garcia, and S.A. Griffin. As a sample the editor selected these lines from "The Woman Next Door" by Duane Locke:

> Under her dark hair,/a white bowl/of ashes from burnt poppies.//She is afraid/she'll hear her clothes
> drop/and become apples.//She is afraid/her hands will turn into magpies/and have shadows.//She is
> afraid her mirror might vanish./She only bares her breasts to mirrors.

The Silt Reader is 32 pages, 4¼ × 5½, saddle-stapled, photocopied with colored card cover and some ads. Accepts less than 15% of poems received. Press run is 500. Sample: $2. Make checks payable to Robert Roden.
How to Submit: Submit 5 neatly typed poems at a time. Accepts previously published poems and simultaneous submissions. Does not accept e-mail submissions. Cover letter preferred. Time between acceptance and publication is 3 months. "Two editors' votes required for inclusion." Seldom comments on rejected poems. Responds in up to 6 months. Guidelines available for SASE and on website. Pays 2 contributor's copies. Acquires one-time rights.
Book/Chapbook Needs & How to Submit: Temporary Vandalism Recordings strives "to make the world safe for poetry (just kidding)." Publishes 3 chapbooks/year. Chapbooks are usually 40 pages, photocopied, saddle-stapled, press run of 100 intially, with reprint option if needed. Submit 10 sample poems, with SASE for response. "Publication in some magazines is important, but extensive publishing is not required." Responds in 3 months. Pays 50% royalty (after costs recouped) and 5 author's copies (out of a press run of 100). For sample chapbooks send $5 to the above address.

🌐 ◪ **10TH MUSE**, 33 Hartington Rd., Southampton, Hants SO14 0EW England. Established 1990. **Editor:** Andrew Jordan.
Magazine Needs: *10th Muse* "includes poetry and reviews, as well as short prose (usually no more than 2,000 words) and graphics. I prefer poetry with a strong 'lyric' aspect. I enjoy experimental work that corresponds with aspects of the English pastoral tradition. I have a particular interest in the cultural construction of landscape." Has published poetry by Peter Riley, Andrew Duncan, Dr. Charles Mintern, Ian Robinson, John Welch, and Jeremy Hooker. As a sample the editor selected these lines from *City Walking (1)* by Jeremy Hooker:

> The brown Thames/laps against timbers.//A fragment of Roman wharf/is bound against a pillar,/ancient
> water-worn wood/against carved stone.

10th Muse is 48-72 pages, A5, photocopied, saddle-stapled, with card cover, no ads. Press run is 200. "U.S. subscribers—send $8 in bills for single copy (including postage)."

How to Submit: Submit up to 6 poems. Include SASE (or SAE with IRCs). Often comments on rejected poems. Responds in 3 months. Pays 1 contributor's copy. Staff reviews books of poetry. Send books for review consideration.

Advice: "Poets should read a copy of the magazine first."

☑ TERMINUS: A JOURNAL OF LITERATURE AND ART, (formerly *Georgia Poetry Review* and *Georgia Poetry Review* Poetry Prize), 1034 Hill St. SE, Atlanta GA 30315. E-mail: terminus@hotmail.com. Established 2001. **Editors:** Chad Prevost and Travis Denton.

Magazine Needs: Appearing in March and September, *Terminus* publishes poetry, fiction, creative nonfiction, and art. Strives "to achieve a balance between high creativity and supreme quality. We seek the best writing nationwide mostly from established writers but some from emerging writers." Wants poetry "which is quality and accessible. Innovative images. Original objects and forms welcome. Any subject, especially when handled with skill and taste." *Terminus* is 96 pages, digest-sized, perfect bound, glossy cover. Single copy: $8; subscription: $15/year. Sample: $8.

How to Submit: Submit 3-5 poems at a time. Accepts simultaneous submissions ("just please notify us as soon as you have news of publication elsewhere"); no previously published poems. No e-mail submissions "though queries and requests are welcome." Cover letter is preferred. "Manuscripts without SASE cannot be returned." Reads submissions year round. Time between acceptance and publication is 3-9 months. Usually comments on returned poems "if we'd like to see more." Responds in up to 4 months. Pays 2 contributor's copies. Acquires first rights.

Advice: "For each issue we seek to publish a journal that readers will want to come back to again and again. Please send only the work you feel most strongly about. Support us and also learn about the kind of work we accept by picking up a copy or subscribing."

☑ TERRA INCOGNITA, A BILINGUAL LITERARY REVIEW; TERRA INCOGNITA—EN-CUENTRO CULTURAL BILINGÜE (Specialized: Bilingual, Spanish/English), P.O. Box 150585, Brooklyn NY 11215-0585. (718)492-3508. E-mail: terraincognita@worldonline.es. Website: www.terrainc ognita.com (includes guidelines, archives, links, editorial policy, contact information, new content when possible, etc.). Established 1998 (first issue published in summer 2000). **US Poetry Editor:** Alexandra van de Kamp. **Spanish Poetry Editor:** Luciano Priego. Member: CLMP.

Magazine Needs: *Terra Incognita, A Bilingual Literary Review* appears annually in autumn. Goal is "to print the best work we can find from established and emerging writers in English and Spanish on both sides of the Atlantic and to act as a cultural bridge between the various Spanish and English-speaking communities. We are open to all forms and subject matter except for that of pornography and material with racist/sexist themes. We're looking for work with guts and intelligence that shows a love of the craft. We do not want to see poetry that asks only so much of itself. We want poetry that rises out of a true, sure urgency, out of a need to be written." Recently published poetry by Billy Collins, Virgil Suarez, Laurie Blauner, J'Laine Robnolt, Donna Stonecipher, and José Hierro. As a sample the editor selected these lines from "Under the Mermaid's Moon" by Laurie Blauner:

> You should see aquatic life: the twist and shouts of color,/the knots of light, the vague features of the
> drowned waving/good-bye. In our own backyard we find desire,/not the kind that endless explorers
> spread over continents,/not the gold distortion of treasure winking conspiratorially,/but the way life
> repeats itself, the retelling/of the amorous red rose.

Terra Incognita is 90 pages, magazine-sized, printed, perfectly-bound, card stock cover, with b&w photos, sketches, and selective ads for mainly independent presses and companies. Accepts about 3% of poems submitted. Publishes about 25-30 poems/issue. Press run is 1,000. Single copy $7.50; subscription: $9/year or $17/2 years (includes postage). Sample: $7 plus $2 postage. Make checks payable to Alexandra van de Kamp.

How to Submit: Submit 5 poems at a time. Line length for poetry is 100 maximum. Accepts simutaneous submissions with notification; no previously published poems. No fax, e-mail, or disk submissions. Cover letter is preferred. Note: **Submissions in Spanish should be sent to Apartado 14.401, 28080, Madrid, Spain with 2-3 IRCs.** Reads submissions all year. Time between acceptance and publication is 2-10 months. "The final decision on poetry submissions lies with the poetry editor, but other editors are consulted as well." Sometimes comments on rejected poems. Guidelines are available for SASE, by e-mail, or on website. Responds in up to 2 months. Sometimes sends prepublication galleys. Pays 2 contributor's copies. Acquires first North American serial rights. Reviews books and chapbooks of poetry in 1,000 words, single book format. Poets may send books for review consideration to Alexandra van de Kamp.

Also Offers: *Terra Incognita* is part of a larger cultural association that does bilingual readings and encourages cultural exchanges.

Advice: "We look for poetry that is not merely good or capable, but which is actually exciting and thrilling to read—something that bubbles up from deeper, more complex sources. Poetry that is not only confident but comes from a conviction of its need to be written. Beginners, ask yourself why your poem or piece *needs* to be in the world."

◎ ⊘ **TEXAS TECH UNIVERSITY PRESS (Specialized: series)**, P.O. Box 41037, Lubbock TX 79409-1037. (806)742-2982. Fax: (806)742-2979. E-mail: ttup@ttu.edu. Website: www.ttup.ttu.edu. Established 1971. **Editor:** Judith Keeling. Does not read unsolicited manuscripts.

$ ⊘ ◎ **THEMA (Specialized: themes)**, Thema Literary Society, P.O. Box 8747, Metairie LA 70011-8747. E-mail: thema@home.com. Website: http://members.home.net/thema (includes general information, guidelines and upcoming themes, archives, contact information, editorial policy, and sample writing from past issues). Established 1988. **Editor:** Virginia Howard. **Poetry Editor:** Gail Howard. Address poetry submissions to Gail Howard.

- "*THEMA* is supported in part by a grant from the Louisiana State Arts Council through the Louisiana Division of the arts as administered by the Arts Council of New Orleans."

Magazine Needs: *THEMA* is a triannual literary magazine using poetry related to specific themes. "Each issue is based on an unusual premise. Please, please send SASE for guidelines before submitting poetry to find out the upcoming themes. Upcoming themes (and submission deadlines) include: 'An Unlikely Alliance' (November 1, 2002), 'Off on a Tangent' (March 1, 2003), 'The Middle Path' (July 1, 2003). No scatologic language, alternate life-style, explicit love poetry." Poems will be judged with all others submitted. Has published poetry by John Grey, David Rachel, Constance Vogel, and L.G. Mason. As a sample the editor selected these lines from "Scrapbooks" by Kaye Bache-Snyder:

> Here are/our walking days/among the mountain peaks . . . /flattened in color photographs/fading

THEMA is 200 pages, digest-sized, professionally printed, with matte card cover. Receives about 400 poems/year, accepts about 8%. Press run is 500 for 270 subscribers of which 30 are libraries. Subscription: $16. Sample: $8.

How to Submit: Submit up to 3 poems at a time with SASE. All submissions should be typewritten and on standard 8½×11 paper. Submissions are accepted all year, but evaluated after specified deadlines. Guidelines and upcoming themes available for SASE, on website, or by e-mail. Editor comments on submissions. Pays $10/poem plus 1 contributor's copy. Acquires one-time rights.

Advice: "Do *not* submit to *THEMA* unless you have one of *THEMA*'s upcoming themes in mind. Tell us which one!"

ℕ $ ⊘ ◎ **THESE DAYS (Specialized: mainstream Christian)**, 100 Witherspoon St., Louisville KY 40202-1396. E-mail: vpatton@presbypub.com. Established 1969. **Editor:** Vince Patton.

Magazine Needs: "*These Days* is a quarterly magazine of daily devotions and devotional resources published by the Presbyterian Church (USA) in partnership with the Cumberland Presbyterian Chuch, The Presbyterian Church in Canada, The United Church of Canada, and the United Church of Christ. We publish only short religious poetry of high quality that has a contemporary but not erudite feel. We especially need church holiday and seasonal poems. We do not want to see nonreligious, nonliterary, obscure work or poetry that is outdated in form." Has published poetry by Anne Shotwell, Katherine Stewart, Sara A. DuBose, Richard Nystrom, Gordon E. Jowers and Ruth Hunt. *These Days* is 104 pages, 8½×11, offset printed and stapled with soft, glossy cover, includes full color cover art. Receives about 500 poems/year, accepts approximately 1%. Publish 1 poem/issue. Press run is 200,000 for 195,000 subscribers. Subscription: $6.95 regular print, $8.10 large print; Canada: $10.40 regular, $10.80 large print. Sample: 77¢ postage and 5×7 envelope.

How to Submit: Submit 5 poems maximum at a time. Line length for poetry is 3 minimum, 15 maximum. Accepts previously published poems. Cover letter preferred. "Please include a SASE for reply and return of submissions." Accepts submissions by e-mail (either as attachment or in text box). Submit seasonal poems 8 months in advance. Time between acceptance and publication is 1 year. Seldom comments on rejected poems. Guidelines available for SASE or by e-mail. Responds in 3 months. Pays $10 for cover poems and 5 copies. Acquires one-time rights.

Advice: "Study the publication thoroughly. If possible, subscribe and do the devotions daily."

ℕ ⊘ **THIRD COAST**, Dept. of English, Western Michigan University, Kalamazoo MI 49008-5092. (616)387-2675. Fax: (616)387-2562. Website: www.wmich.edu/thirdcoast (includes table of contents from past issues, poetry samples, names of editors, and guidelines). Established 1995. **Contact:** Poetry Editors.

Magazine Needs: *Third Coast* is a biannual national literary magazine of poetry, prose, creative nonfiction, and translation. Wants "excellence of craft and originality of thought. Nothing trite." Has published poetry by Chase Twichell, Robin Behn, Ed Ochester, Carolyn Kizer, Nance Van Winckel, Philip Levine, and Tomaž Šalamun. As a sample the editors selected these lines from "Banishing the Angels" by Dana Levin:

> *And then the cloud passed and a light came rushing down the steps/of the subway, and blazed up against the phone booth standing in the corner,/and inside it was a girl talking on the phone, all lit up amid the grime/of the subway, and when I saw her I wanted her to be/an angel, I wanted her with wings inside the station, to say/"the angel on the phone" and see it softly beating, old newspapers at its feet*

Third Coast is 140 pages, 6×9, professionally printed and perfect-bound with a 4-color cover with art. Receives about 2,000 poems/year, accepts approximately 3-5%. Press run is 1,000 for 100 subscribers of which 20 are libraries, 350 shelf sales. Single copy: $6; subscription: $11/year, $20/2 years, $29/3 years.

How to Submit: Submit up to 5 poems at a time. Poems should be typed and single-spaced, with the author's name on each page. Stanza breaks should be double-spaced. No previously published poems or simultaneous submissions. No electronic submissions. Cover letter with bio preferred. Poems are circulated to assistant poetry editors and poetry editors; poetry editors make final decisions. Seldom comments on rejected poems. Guidelines available for SASE and on website. Responds in 4 months. Pays 2 copies and 1-year subscription. Acquires first rights.

THORNY LOCUST, P.O. Box 32631, Kansas City MO 64171-5631. E-mail: editors@thornylocust. com. Website: www.thornylocust.com (includes guidelines as well as subscription and contact information). Established 1993. **Editor:** Silvia Kofler. **Managing Editor:** Celeste Kuechler.

Magazine Needs: *Thorny Locust*, published quarterly, is a "literary magazine that wants to be thought-provoking, witty, and well-written." Wants "poetry with some 'bite' e.g., satire, epigrams, black humor and bleeding-heart cynicism." Does not want "polemics, gratuitous grotesques, sombre surrealism, weeping melancholy, or hate-mongering." Has published poetry by Virgil Suarez, Patricia Cleary Miller, Michael Johnson, and Philip Miller. As a sample the editor selected these lines from "Bitter Pay Checks" by Claudine R. Moreau:

> *Bite it./taste its bitterness/ . . . Gone before it's there—/ . . . radium in your veins/poisoning the moments/ with financial responsibilities*

Thorny Locust is 28-32 pages, 7×8½, desktop-published, saddle-stapled with medium cover stock, drawings and b&w photos. Receives about 350-400 poems/year, accepts about 35%. Press run is 150-200 for 30 subscribers of which 6 are libraries; 60 distributed free to contributors and small presses. Single copy: $4; subscription: $15. Sample: $3. Make checks payable to Silvia Kofler.

How to Submit: Submit 3 poems at a time. "If you do not include a SASE with sufficient postage, your submission will be pitched!" Accepts simultaneous submissions; no previously published poems. Cover letter preferred. "Poetry and fiction must be typed, laser-printed or in a clear dot-matrix." Time between acceptance and publication is 2 months. Seldom comments on rejected poems. Guidelines available for SASE and on website. Responds in 3 months. Pays 1 contributor's copy. Acquires one-time rights.

Advice: "Never perceive a rejection as a personal rebuke, keep on trying. Take advice."

THOUGHT MAGAZINE, P.O. Box 117098, Burlingame CA 94011-7098. E-mail: thoughtmaga zine@yahoo.com. Website: www.thoughtmagazine.org (includes guidelines, contacts, recent publications). Established 2000. **Editor:** Kevin Feeney.

Magazine Needs: *Thought Magazine* is a biannual literary journal to showcase established and unpublished authors. Wants any style or form; does not want graphic sex or violence. Recently published poetry by Kim Addonizio, Gail Ylitalo, and Stacey Davis. *Thought Magazine* is 50 pages, magazine-sized, saddle-stapled, heavy stock cover, with art/graphics. Receives about 200 poems/year, accepts about 10%. Publishes about 10 poems/issue. Press run is 1,000 for 600 subscribers; 300 distributed free. Single copy: $6; subscription: $10. Sample: $6. Make checks payable to *Thought Magazine*.

How to Submit: Submit 3 poems at a time. Line length for poetry is 4 minimum, 45 maximum. Accepts previously published poems and simultaneous submissions. Accepts e-mail and disk submissions; no fax submissions. Cover letter is preferred. Reads submissions all year. Time between acceptance and publication is 3 weeks. Poems are circulated to an editorial board. Seldom comments on rejected poems. Occasionally publishes theme issues. Guidelines available in magazine, for SASE, by e-mail, or on website. Responds in up to 3 months. Pays 1 contributor's copy. Acquires one-time rights.

Also Offers: Sponsors the *Thought Magazine* Contest (see separate listing in the Contests & Awards section).

Advice: "Read a back issue."

◑ ◎ THOUGHTS FOR ALL SEASONS: THE MAGAZINE OF EPIGRAMS (Specialized: form, humor, themes), % editor Prof. Em. Michel Paul Richard, 478 NE 56th St., Miami FL 33137-2621. Established 1976. **Contact:** Editor.

Magazine Needs: *Thoughts for All Seasons* "is an irregular serial: designed to preserve the epigram as a literary form; satirical. All issues are commemorative." Rhyming poetry and nonsense verse with good imagery will be considered although most modern epigrams are prose. As a sample the editor selected this poem by Michael John Curtis:

> When a thing is ill begun/or done with ill intent/you can bet a lie will come/to cover what just went

Thoughts for All Seasons is 80 pages, offset from typescript and saddle-stapled with full-page illustrations, card cover. Accepts about 20% of material submitted. Press run is 500-1,000. There are several library subscriptions but most distribution is through direct mail or local bookstores and newsstand sales. Single copy: $6 (includes postage and handling).

How to Submit: "Submit at least one or two pages of your work, 10-12 epigrams, or two-four poems." Include SASE. Accepts simultaneous submissions, but not previously published epigrams "unless a thought is appended which alters it." Editor comments on rejected poems. Publishes theme issues. Theme for Volume 6 is "Time Travel." Guidelines available for SASE and in publication. Responds in 1 month. Pays 1 contributor's copy.

◑ THREE CANDLES, E-mail: editor@threecandles.org. Website: www.threecandles.org (includes an extensive links and resource section). Established 1999. **Editor:** Steve Mueske.

Magazine Needs: *Three Candles* is published online ("post updates when qualified poetry is available, generally once or twice a week"). "Though I am not particular about publishing specific forms of poetry, I prefer to be surprised by the content of the poems themselves. I believe that poetry should have some substance and touch, at least tangentially, on human experience." Does not want poems that are "overtly religious, sexist, racist, or unartful." Recently published poetry by Jim Moore, Deborah Keenan, Peter Kane Dufault, Jim Brock, and Jacqueline Marcus. As a sample the editor selected these lines from "Question From the Floor" by Peter Kane Dufault:

> Could you call it Dead Motion—/that of the atoms, planets,/stars, galaxies—seeing/it can no more
> cease/than dead men can collect/old bones and resume being

Three Candles is a "high-quality online journal, professionally designed and maintained." Receives about 1,000 poems/year. Publishes "approximately 4-6 poets/month, about 10 poems. Many poems I publish are solicited directly from poets." Receives 20,000 hits/month.

How to Submit: Submit 3-5 poems at a time. Accepts simultaneous submissions, if noted; no previously published poems. Accepts *only* e-mail submissions; no disk submissions. Send poems "as the body of the text or, if special formatting is used, as attachments in Word or rich text format. In the body of the e-mail, I want a short bio, a list of previous publications, and a brief note about what writing poetry means to you as an artist." Accepts submissions year round. Time between acceptance and publication is "nominal, usually less than 2 weeks." Sometimes comments on rejected poems. "Reading the journal is important to get an idea of the level of craft expected." Guidelines available on website. Responds within 2 months. Does not send prepublication galleys but "allows author to make any necessary changes before a formal announcement is e-mailed to the mailing list." No payment "at this time." Acquires first rights. Copyright reverts to author after publication.

Advice: "The online poetry community is vital and thriving. Take some time and get to know the journals that you are submitting to. Don't send work that is like what is published. Send work that is as good but different in a way that is uniquely your own."

◑ 360 DEGREES, 1229 Reece Rd., Charlotte NC 28209. E-mail: threesixtydegreesreview@yahoo.com. Established 1993. **Managing Editor:** Karen Kinnison.

Magazine Needs: *360 Degrees* is a biannual review, containing literature and artwork. "We are dedicated to keeping the art of poetic expression alive." "No real limits" on poetry, "only the limits of the submitter's imagination." However, does not want to see "greeting card verse, simplified emotions, or religious verse." Accepts poetry written by children. Has published poetry by Rochelle Holt, Anselm Brocki, Aaron Petrovich, and Christopher Brisson. As a sample the editor selected these lines from "Where Heroes Gather" by David Demarest:

> "It is the encounter of a lifetime,/the endless struggle, like Sisyphus and his rock,/where the sun
> confronts the moon's sad and silent side/and rises again the better for it,/free, perhaps, yet forever
> locked within dark gates."

360 Degrees is 40 pages, digest-sized, neatly printed and saddle-stapled. Receives about 1,000 poems/year, accepts about 80. Press run is 500 for 100 subscribers and one library. Subscription: $6. Sample: $3.

How to Submit: Submit 3-6 poems at a time. Include SASE. Accepts simultaneous submissions; no previously published poems. "Just let us know if a particular piece you have submitted to us has been accepted elsewhere." Accepts submissions by e-mail (as attachment or in text box). Cover letter preferred. Seldom comments on rejected poems. Guidelines available for SASE, by e-mail, and in publication. Responds within 3 months. Pays 1 contributor's copy.

Advice: "We are a small, but high-quality. Most of the poems we accept not only show mastery of words, but present interesting ideas. The mastery of language is something we expect from freelancers, but the content of the idea being expressed is the selling point."

☑ $ ◪ THE THREEPENNY REVIEW, P.O. Box 9131, Berkeley CA 94709. (510)849-4545. Website: www.threepennyreview.com (includes sample work, advertising and submission guidelines, internet order forms for single issues, and subscription information). Established 1980. **Poetry Editor:** Wendy Lesser.
   • Work published in this review has also been included in *The Best American Poetry* and *Pushcart Prize* anthologies.
Magazine Needs: *Threepenny Review* "is a quarterly review of literature, performing and visual arts, and social articles aimed at the intelligent, well-read, but not necessarily academic reader. Nationwide circulation. Want: formal, narrative, short poems (and others). Prefer under 100 lines. No bias against formal poetry, in fact a slight bias in favor of it." Has published poetry by Thom Gunn, Frank Bidart, Seamus Heaney, Czeslaw Milosz, and Louise Glück. Features about 10 poems in each 36-page tabloid issue. Receives about 4,500 submissions of poetry/year, accepts about 12. Press run is 10,000 for 8,000 subscribers of which 150 are libraries. Subscription: $20. Sample: $10.
How to Submit: Submit up to 5 poems at a time. Do not submit mss June through August. Guidelines available for SASE or on website. Responds in up to 2 months. Pays $100/poem plus year's subscription. Acquires first serial rights. "Send for review guidelines (SASE required)."

Ⓝ ◯ THUMBPRINTS, Thumb Area Writer's Club, P.O. Box 27, Sandusky MI 48471. Established mid-1980s. E-mail: ThPrints@yahoo.com. **Editor:** Kathleen Smith.
Magazine Needs: *Thumbprints* appears monthly "to give writers a chance to be published." Wants "any style of poetry, 40 lines maximum." No "vulgar language or sex of any kind. No satanic or witchcraft poetry." Accepts poetry written by children. Has published poetry by Janet Murphy. *Thumbprints* is 8-10 pages, 8½×11, photocopied and corner stapled with original art on cover. Receives about 300 poems/year, accepts approximately 98%. Press run is 30-60 copies depending on submissions. Subscription: $10. Sample: $1. Make checks payable to Thumb Area Writer's Club.
How to Submit: Submit up to 5 poems at a time. Include SASE with all submissions. Line length for poetry is 40 maximum. Accepts previously published poems and simultaneous submission. Accepts submissions by e-mail (in text box) and by postal mail. Cover letter preferred. Time between acceptance and publication is 1-2 months. Often comments on rejected poems. Publishes theme issues occasionally. Guidelines and upcoming themes available for SASE or by e-mail. Pays 1 copy. Author retains all rights.
Advice: "Be imaginative, descriptive. Write with deep conviction for what you are expressing."

🌐 ◪ THUMBSCREW, P.O. Box 657, Oxford OX2 6PH United Kingdom. E-mail: tim.kendall@bristol.ac.uk. Website: www.bristol.ac.uk/thumbscrew (includes an archive section for past and present issues). Established 1994. **Editor:** Tim Kendall.
Magazine Needs: "Appearing 3 times/year, *Thumbscrew* is an international poetry magazine featuring poetry and criticism from well-known and new writers." Has published poetry by Paul Muldoon, Anne Stevenson, Michael Longley, and Seamus Heaney. *Thumbscrew* is 100 pages, magazine-sized, perfect-bound with laminated board cover. Receives about 6,000 poems/year, accepts 1%. Press run is 600 for 400 subscribers of which 50 are libraries, 200 shelf sales. Subscription: $27.50. Sample: $9.50.
How to Submit: Submit 2-5 poems at a time. No previously published poems or simultaneous submissions. E-mail submissions are not accepted. Cover letter preferred. "Send clear typed copies, with each page including name and address of author." Time between acceptance and publication is 3 months. Seldom comments on rejected poems. Occasionally publishes theme issues. Responds in 3 months. Pays 1-2 contributor's copies. Acquires all rights. Copyright returned to author after publication. Reviews books and chapbooks of poetry in 1,000 words, single book format. Poets may send books for review consideration.

Ⓝ ◪ TIA CHUCHA PRESS, ℅ Guild Complex, 1212 N. Ashland Ave., Chicago IL 60622. (773)227-6117. Fax: (773)227-6159. E-mail: guildcomplex@earthlink.net. Website: www.guildcomplex.com. Established 1989. **Director:** Luis J. Rodriguez.
Book/Chapbook Needs: Publishes 2-4 paperbacks/year, "multicultural, lyrical, engaging, passionate works informed by social, racial, class experience. Evocative. Poets should be knowledgeable of contemporary and traditional poetry, even if experimenting. Ours is a culturally diverse, performance-oriented pub-

lishing house of emerging socially-engaged poetry. There are no restrictions as to style or content—poetry that 'knocks us off our feet' is what we are looking for." Has published *Talisman* by Afaa Michael Weaver and *You Come Singing* by Virgil Suarez. As a sample the editor selected these lines from "Eating in Anger" in *Fallout* by Kyoko Mori:

> *My friend lived with a man who ate/peanut butter when they fought. She/found the spoons in his pockets, sticky/inverted mirrors in which her angry/words blurred backwards. . . .*

How to Submit: Submit complete ms of 50 pages or more ("preferably 60-100 pages") with SASE. "We publish only in English, but will look at bilingual editions if they are powerful in both languages." Accepts simultaneous submissions, if notified. Only original, unpublished work in book form. "Although, we like to have poems that have been published in magazines and/or chapbooks." Deadline: June 30. Do not submit via fax. Reads submissions during the summer months. Pays 5 copies.

Advice: "We are known for publishing the best of what is usually spoken word or oral presentations of poetry. However, we like to publish poems that best work on the page. Yet, we are not limited to that. Our authors come from a diversity of ethnic, racial and gender backgrounds. Our main thrust is openness, in forms as well as content. We are cross-cultural, but we don't see this as a prison. The openness and inclusiveness is a foundation to include a broader democratic notion of what poetry should be in this country."

N ☒ $☑ TICKLED BY THUNDER, HELPING WRITERS GET PUBLISHED SINCE 1990, 14076-86A Ave., Surrey, British Columbia V3W 0V9 Canada. E-mail: thunder@istar.ca. Website: www.home.istar.ca/~thunder (includes guidelines and contact info). Established 1990. **Publisher/Editor:** Larry Lindner.

Magazine Needs: *Tickled by Thunder*, appears up to 4 times/year, using poems about "fantasy particularly, about writing or whatever. Require original images and thoughts. Keep them short (up to 40 lines)— not interested in long, long poems. Nothing pornographic, childish, unimaginative. Welcome humor and creative inspirational verse." Has published poetry by Laleh Dadpour Jackson and Helen Michiko Singh. *Tickled by Thunder* is 24 pages, digest-sized, published on Macintosh. 1,000 readers/subscribers. Subscription: $12/4 issues. Sample: $2.50.

How to Submit: Include 3-5 samples of writing with queries. No e-mail submissions. Cover letter required with submissions; include "a few facts about yourself and brief list of publishing credits." Responds in up to 6 months. Guidelines available for SASE. Pays 2¢/line to $2 maximum. Acquires first rights. Editor comments on rejected poems "80% of the time." Reviews books of poetry in up to 300 words. Open to unsolicited reviews. Poets may send books for review consideration.

Also Offers: Offers a poetry contest 4 times/year. Deadlines: the 15th of February, May, August, and October. Entry fee: $5 for 1 poem; free for subscribers. Prize: cash, publication, and subscription. Publishes author-subsidized chapbooks. "We are interested in student poetry and publish it in our center spread: *Expressions*." Send SASE (or SAE and IRC) for details.

N ☻ TIMBER CREEK REVIEW, 8969 UNCG Station, Greensboro NC 27413. (336)334-2952. E-mail: timber_creek_review@hoopsmail.com. Established 1994. **Editor:** John M. Freiermuth.

Magazine Needs: *Timber Creek Review* appears quarterly publishing short stories, literary nonfiction, and poetry. Wants all types of poetry. Does not want religious, pornography. Recently published William Miller, Bob Parham, Maura Gage, Michael McClintick, Marcia L. Herlow, and Fred Chappell. As a sample the editor selected these lines from "Dis-Ease" by Bob Parham:

> *One word may say it all/Dis-ease, for instance,/that fidgety sickness/that stirs us not to be ill,/but to agitate agitate against ourselves.*

Timber Creek Review is 80-92 pages, digest-sized, laser-printed, stapled, colored paper cover with graphics. Receives about 900 poems/year, accepts about 6-7%. Publishes about 50-60 poems/issue. Press run is 150 for 120 subscribers of which 2 are libraries, 30 shelf sales. Single copy: $4.25; subscription: $15. Sample: $4.25. Make checks payable to J.M. Freiermuth.

How to Submit: Submit 3-6 poems at a time. Line length for poetry is 3 minimum. Accepts simultaneous submissions; no previously published poems. No fax, e-mail, or disk submissions. Cover letter is required. Reads submissions year round. Submit seasonal poems 10 months in advance. Time between acceptance and publication is 3-6 months. Never comments on rejected poems. Occasionally publishes theme issues. Guidelines available for SASE or by e-mail. Responds in up to 6 months. Pays 1 contributor's copy. Acquires first North American serial rights.

$☑ TIMBERLINE PRESS, 6281 Red Bud, Fulton MO 65251. (573)642-5035. Established 1975. **Poetry Editor:** Clarence Wolfshohl.

Book/Chapbook Needs: "We do limited letterpress editions with the goal of blending strong poetry with well-crafted and designed printing. We lean toward natural history or strongly imagistic nature poetry but will look at any good work. Also, good humorous poetry." Has published *Annuli* by William Heyen,

Trance Arrows by James Bogan, *From a Collector's Garden* by Emily Borenstein, and *Harmonic Balance* by Walter Bargen. Sample copies may be obtained by sending $7.50, requesting sample copy, and noting you saw the listing in *Poet's Market*. Responds in under 1 month. Pays "50-50 split with author after Timberline Press has recovered its expenses."
How to Submit: Query before submitting full ms.

TIME OF SINGING, A MAGAZINE OF CHRISTIAN POETRY (Specialized: religious, themes), P.O. Box 149, Conneaut Lake PA 16316. E-mail: timesing@toolcity.net. Website: www.timeofsinging.bizland.com (includes themes, guidelines, sample poems, contest rules, and contact and subscription information). Established 1958-1965, revived 1980. **Editor:** Lora H. Zill.
Magazine Needs: *Time of Singing* appears 4 times/year. "We tend to be traditional. We like poems that are aware of grammar. Collections of uneven lines, series of phrases, preachy statements, unstructured 'prayers,' and trite sing-song rhymes usually get returned. We look for poems that 'show' rather than 'tell.' The viewpoint is unblushingly Christian—but in its widest and most inclusive meaning. Moreover, it is believed that the vital message of Christian poems, as well as inspiring the general reader, will give pastors, teachers, and devotional leaders rich current sources of inspiring material to aid them in their ministries. Would like to see more forms. Has published poetry by Tony Cosier, John Grey, Luci Shaw, Bob Hostetler, Evelyn Minshull, Frances P. Reid, Barbara Crooker, and Charles Waugaman. As a sample the editor selected these lines from "Stone Pillars" by Elizabeth Howard:

> Manoah brought his broken/body home. We grieved/two wheat straws leaning/into each other for succor,/but one pale day, joy/crept onto the hearth,/legs as spindly/as a grasshopper nymph's/on a frosty morning.

Time of Singing is 44 pages, digest-sized, offset from typescript with decorative line drawings scattered throughout. The bonus issues are not theme based. Receives over 800 submissions/year, accepts about 175. Press run is 300 for 150 subscribers. Single copy: $6; subscription: $15 US, $18 Canada, $27 overseas. Sample: $4.
How to Submit: Submit up to 5 poems at a time, single-spaced. "We prefer poems under 40 lines, but will publish up to 60 lines if exceptional." Accepts simultaneous submissions and previously published poems. Accepts e-mail submissions, include in body of message. Time between acceptance and publication is up to 1 year. Editor comments with suggestions for improvement if close to publication. Publishes theme issues "quite often." Guidelines and upcoming themes are available for SASE, by e-mail, and on website. Responds in 2 months. Pays 1 contributor's copy.
Also Offers: Sponsors several theme contests for specific issues. Guidelines and upcoming themes available for SASE.
Advice: "Study the craft. Be open to critique—a poet is often too close to their work and needs a critical, honest eye."

TITAN PRESS; MASTERS AWARDS, (formerly Center Press), Box 17897, Encino CA 91416. E-mail: ucla654@yahoo.com. Website: www.titanpress.info. Established 1980. **Publisher:** Stephanie Wilson.
Book/Chapbook Needs & How to Submit: Center Press is "a small press presently publishing 6-7 works per year including poetry, photojournals, calendars, novels, etc. We look for quality, freshness, and that touch of genius." In poetry, "we want to see verve, natural rhythms, discipline, impact, etc. We are flexible but verbosity, triteness, and saccharine make us cringe. *We now read and publish only mss accepted from the Masters Award.*" Has published books by Bebe Oberon, Walter Calder, Exene Vida, Carlos Castenada, and Sandra Gilbert. As a sample the editor selected these lines from "The Patriot" by Scott A. Sonders:

> Underwire bras/and other implements/of torture, are remnants of the Inquisition./It would be best to set/the breast free to hang, as a proud silk flag/on a windless day.

Their tastes are for poets such as Adrienne Rich, Li-Young Lee, Charles Bukowski, and Czeslaw Milosz. "We have strong liaisons with the entertainment industry and like to see material that is media-oriented and au courant."
Also Offers: "We sponsor the Masters Awards, established in 1981, including a $1,000 grand prize annually plus each winner (and the five runners-up in poetry) will be published on website or in a clothbound edition and distributed to selected university and public libraries, news mediums, etc. There is a one-time only $15 administration and reading fee per entrant. Submit a maximum of five poems or song lyric pages (no tapes) totaling no more than 150 lines. Any poetic style or genre is acceptable, but a clear and fresh voice, discipline, natural rhythm, and a certain individuality should be evident. Further application and details available with a #10 SASE."
Advice: "Please study what we publish before you consider submitting."

TORRE DE PAPEL (Specialized: ethnic/nationality), 111 Phillips Hall, Iowa City IA 52242-1409. (319)335-0487. E-mail: torredepapel@uiowa.edu. Website: www.uiowa.edu/~spanport. Established 1991. **Editor:** Margarita Jácome.

Magazine Needs: Appearing 3 times/year, *Torre de Papel* is a "journal devoted to the publication of critical and creative works related to Hispanic and Luso-Brazilian art, literature, and cultural production. We are looking for poetry written in Spanish, Portuguese, or languages of these cultures; translations of authors writing in these languages; or poems in English representative of some aspect of Hispanic or Luso-Brazilian culture." Does not want to see "poetry for children; no religious or esoterical work." As a sample the editor selected these lines from David William Foster and Daniel Altamiranda's translation of "Cadáveres" by Néstor Perlongher:

> Along the tracks of a train that never stops/In the wave of a sinking ship/In a small wave, vanishing/
> On the wharves the steps the trampolines the piers/There are Corpses

Torre de Papel is 110 pages, 8¾×11½. Press run is 200 for 50 subscribers of which 25 are libraries. Single copy: $7; subscription: $21. Sample: $10.

How to Submit: Submit up to 5 poems at a time. No previously published poems or simultaneous submissions. Accepts e-mail submissions, include as attached file. Cover letter with brief bio required. Include e-mail address. Submit 3 copies of each poem and a Macintosh or IBM diskette of the work. Reads submissions September through April only. Poems are circulated to an editorial board for review. "We send creative work to three readers of our advisory board for comments. However, since we publish articles and stories as well, space for poetry can be limited." Responds in 6 months. Pays 1 contributor's copy.

TOWER POETRY SOCIETY; TOWER, % McMaster University, 1200 Main St. W., Box 1021, Hamilton, Ontario L8S 1C0 Canada. (905)648-4878. Website: www.towerpoetry.icomm.ca (includes contact information, archives, links, subscription information, and essays). Established 1951. **Editor-in-Chief:** Jeff Seffinga.

Magazine Needs: "The Tower Poetry Society was started by a few members of McMaster University faculty to promote interest in poetry. We publish *Tower* twice/year. We want rhymed or free verse, traditional or modern, but not prose chopped into short lines, maximum 40 lines in length, any subject, any comprehensible style." Has published poetry by Bill Moore and Helen Fitzgerald Dougher. As a sample the editor selected these lines by Joanna Lawson:

> A poem is/a slide under a microscope/one thin slice/of then,/or now,/or what might be,/magnified for
> meaning

Tower is 40 pages, digest-sized. Press run is 250 for 60 subscribers of which 8 are libraries. Receives about 400 poems/year, accepts about 70. Subscription: $8; $9.50 abroad. Sample: $3.

How to Submit: Submit up to 4 poems at a time. Reads submissions during February or August. Responds in 2 months. Pays 1 contributor's copy.

Advice: "Read a lot of poetry before you try to write it."

TRAINED MONKEY PRESS; TRAINED MONKEY BROADSIDES, 918 York St., 1st Floor, Newport KY 41071. E-mail: trainedmonkeypress@amish2000.com. Established 2000. **Editor:** Vic Grunkenmeyer.

Magazine Needs: Trained Monkey Broadsides appear bimonthly and include poetry, album reviews, short fiction, photos. They are given away free at distribution points, and by mail for $1. Trained Monkey Broadsides are 10 pages, digest-sized, saddle-stapled, paper cover, with art/graphics and business card size and flyer size ads. Receives about 100 poems/year, accepts about 20%. Publishes about 4 poems/issue. Press run is 200 for 20 subscribers; 150 are distributed free to bars, businesses, music stores. Single copy: $1; subscription: $10/year. Sample: $1.

How to Submit: Submit 3-6 poems at a time. Line length for poetry is 1 minimum, 50 maximum. No previously published poems or simultaneous submissions. Accepts e-mail submissions; no fax or disk submissions. Cover letter is preferred. "Always use SASEs when submitting." Reads submissions year round. Time between acceptance and publication is 2 months. Submissions may be circulated within the editorial board. Seldom comments on rejected poems. Guidelines available in magazine or by e-mail. Responds in 2 weeks. Pays 1 contributor's copy. Acquires one-time rights. Reviews books and chapbooks of poetry and other magazines/journals in 200 words, single book format. Poets may send materials for review consideration to Trained Monkey Press.

Book/Chapbook Needs & How to Submit: The goal of Trained Monkey Press publications is "to get people to pick them up and read. We look for strong words; good poetry in any form that is about

---

HAVE A COLLECTION OF POETRY you want to publish? See the Chapbook Publishers Index or Book Publishers Index in the back of this book.

something. Satire is encouraged." Does not want "didactic, preachy, wishy-washy whining." Recently published poetry by Joey Shannanagins, Tom Case, David Garza, Cliff Spisak, Julie Judge, and Mr. Spoons. As a sample the editor selected these lines from "High Noon" by Robert Bartusch from his chapbook, *Bluebirds of Happiness*:

> *There's people on their lunch break/Grabbing a bite,/Gabbing with their work buddies/They hardly even notice/Him hanging out of his car/With an axe in his hand.*

Trained Monkey Press publishes 5-7 chapbooks/year. Chapbooks are usually 30 pages, saddle-stapled, with stock cover and art/graphics. Query first, with a few sample poems and a cover letter with brief bio and publication credits. Responds to queries in 2 weeks; to mss in 2 months. Pays 5 author's copies (out of a press run of 100). Order sample chapbooks by sending $5 to Trained Monkey Press.

Advice: "Get it out . . . submit to the monkey."

▢ ◎ TRANSCENDENT VISIONS (Specialized: psychiatric survivors, ex-mental patients), 251 S. Olds Blvd. 84-E, Fairless Hills PA 19030-3426. (215)547-7159. Established 1992. **Editor:** David Kime.

Magazine Needs: *Transcendent Visions* appears 1-2 times/year "to provide a creative outlet for psychiatric survivors/ex-mental patients." Wants "experimental, confessional poems; strong poems dealing with issues we face. Any length or subject matter is OK but shorter poems are more likely to be published. No rhyming poetry." Has published poetry by Bob Shelton, Gary Blankenburg, Glen Chestnut, J. Quinn Brisben, and Donna Lisle Gordon. As a sample the editor selected these lines from "Seizure City" by Beth Greenspan:

> *When the bus picks me up,/It belches "Hey baby!/Be my lover!"/Then bumpe me to sleep/And I shuffle off the bus/An hour later*

Transcendent Visions is 24 pages, 8½ × 11, photocopied and corner-stapled with paper cover, b&w line drawings. Receives about 100 poems/year, accepts 20%. Press run is 200 for 50 subscribers. Subscription: $6. Sample: $2. Make checks payable to David Kime.

How to Submit: Submit 5 poems at a time. Accepts previously published poems and simultaneous submissions. Cover letter preferred. "Please tell me something unique about you, but I do not care about all the places you have been published." Time between acceptance and publication is 6 months. Responds in 3 months. Pays 1 contributor's copy of issue in which poet was published. Acquires first or one-time rights. Staff reviews books and chapbooks of poetry and other magazines in 20 words. Send books for review consideration.

Also Offers: "I also publish a political zine called *Crazed Nation*, featuring essays concerning mental illness."

▧ ◖ ◎ TRIBUTARIES (Specialized: students of Illinois Wesleyan University only), English Dept., Illinois Wesleyan University, Bloomington IL 61702. E-mail: iwutributaries@hotmail.com. Website: www.iwu.edu/~tribut (includes content fully supplementary to the print magazine and musical and spoken-word performances). Established 2001. **Editor:** Jeff Stumpo; Jackie Waters (2002-2003).

Magazine Needs: *Tributaries* appears annually in the spring. "We are a magazine meant to showcase the diverse talents of Illinois Wesleyan University's students and add to the greater body of the fine arts. Poetry we have published ranges from the highly experimental to the highly formal. Diversity, originality, and a sense of the poet being comfortable with his or her voice are several criteria we use to distinguish the poetry we select. We do not want to see poetry with a racist or sexist agenda. Poems utilizing these themes are fine, and often riveting. However, we have no interest in propagating intolerance." Recently published poetry by Rick Boutcher, Marke Heine, Jessica Kramer, and Rachelle Street. As a sample the editor selected these lines from "Gilgamesh: Low Down and Broken Up" by Mark Heine from his collection *The Mechanism Busboys*:

> *He looked around soundly, breathing madly,/and his werewild eyes glittered and gathered the/beautiful glass and letters of rejection./He whispered suddenly in ancient Sumerian:/"You have eaten what killed Siddhartha."*

Tributaries (print version) is about 50 pages, magazine-sized, with b&w graphics. Special *Tributaries* material also appears online with color graphics. Press run is 500, distributed free to IWU students and literary magazines.

How to Submit: Accepts previously published poems and simultaneous submissions. Accepts e-mail submissions. Cover letter is required. "Include a cover letter with your name and campus phone number if you submit via campus mail. The editor will personally call you to confirm that your submission was received." Reads submissions "generally September 1-January 31." Time between acceptance and publication is about 2 months. "We have six judges on our staff who review each work. All work has the author's name removed prior to judging in order to ensure an anonymous selection process." Seldom comments on rejected poems. Guidelines available by e-mail. Responds in 1 month. Pays 3 contributor's copies.

Advice: "Poetry should be well crafted, make no mistake about that. Too many poets today, however, are either accomplished technical writers or very emotional writers. Write poetry that appeals to the emotions as well as the intellect. Always pay attention to the work of other writers and learn what you can from it."

TUCUMCARI LITERARY REVIEW (Specialized: cowboy, form/style, nature/rural/ ecology, regional, social issues, memories, nostalgia), 3108 W. Bellevue Ave., Los Angeles CA 90026. Established 1988. **Editor:** Troxey Kemper.

Magazine Needs: *Tucumcari* appears every other month. "Prefer rhyming and established forms, including sonnet, rondeau, triolet, kyrielle, villanelle, terza rima, limerick, sestina, pantoum, and others, 2-100 lines, but the primary goal is to publish good work. No talking animals. No haiku. No disjointed, fragmentary, rambling words or phrases typed in odd-shaped staggered lines trying to look like poetry. The quest here is for poetry that will be just as welcome many years later as it is now." Has published poetry byBobby S. Rivera, Helen McIntosh Gordon, Mary Gribble, Richard Moore, Virgil Suarez, and Ruth Daniels. As a sample the editor selected this quatrain by Rachel Hartnett (age 95):

> *I like the road of any kind/For they intrigue me still/I wonder what's around the bend/or just beyone*
> *the hill.*

Tucumcari Literary Review is 48 pages, digest-sized, saddle-stapled, photocopied from typescript, with card cover. Press run is 150-200. Subscription: $12, $20 for overseas. Sample: $2, $4 for overseas.

How to Submit: Submit up to 4 poems at a time. Accepts simultaneous submissions and previously published poems. Sometimes comments on rejected poems. Guidelines available for SASE and in publication. Responds within 1 month. Pays 1 contributor's copy. Acquires one-time rights.

Advice: "Many readers have commented favorably on our cover photos and the letters section, titled 'Letterrip.' Readers are encouraged to write folksy, informative scraps about what is happening in their lives."

TURKEY PRESS, 6746 Sueno Rd., Isla Vista CA 93117-4904. Established 1974. **Poetry Editors:** Harry Reese and Sandra Reese. "We do not encourage solicitations of any kind to the press. We seek out and develop projects on our own."

TURNROW, English Dept., The University of Louisiana at Monroe, Monroe LA 71209. (318)342-1510. Fax: (318)342-1491. E-mail: enryan@ulm.edu. Website: http://turnrow.ulm.edu (includes excerpts, guidelines, editors). Established 2000. **Editors:** Jack Heflin, William Ryan.

Magazine Needs: *turnrow* appears biannually and seeks submissions of nonfiction of a general interest, short fiction, poetry, translations, interviews, art, and photography. Recently published poetry by CD Wright, Mary Ruefle, Christopher Howell, Gonzalo Rojas, James Haug, and Karen Donovan. As a sample the editors selected these lines from "*Aquardiente*/Firewater" by Virgil Suárez:

> *Friends, when we speak of hands, we speak/of dead frigate birds, or ash-colored fish/poisoned on the*
> *shores of our daily labor./My father never came home in a good mood.*

"Three Orbs" by Monroe, Louisiana, artist Glenn Kennedy attracted the editors of *turnrow* for three reasons: visual impact, seasonal "feel," and Kennedy's local connection. *turnrow*'s Spring 2001 cover was designed by J. Eric McNeil.

turnrow is 130 pages, digest-sized, offset-printed, perfect-bound, full color cover, with art, graphics, photography. Receives about 5,000 poems/year, accepts about .01%. Publishes about 6-10 poems/issue. Press run is 1,000 for 100 subscribers of which 15 are libraries, 400 shelf sales. Single copy: $7; subscription: $12/1 year, $20/2 years. Sample: $7. Make checks payable to *turnrow*.

How to Submit: Submit 3 poems at a time. Line length for poetry is open. No previously published poems or simultaneous submissions. No fax, e-mail, or disk submissions. Cover letter is preferred. Reads submissions September 15 through May 15. Time between acceptance and publication is 6 months. Seldom comments on rejected poems. Occasionally publishes theme issues. A list of upcoming themes available for SASE or on website. Guidelines available for SASE. Responds in 2 months. Sometimes sends prepublication galleys. Pays $50 and 2 contributor's copies. Acquires first rights.

🖼️ ✅ $ © **TURNSTONE PRESS LIMITED (Specialized: regional)**, 607-100 Arthur St., Winnipeg, Manitoba R3B 1H3 Canada. (204)947-1555. Fax: (204)942-1555. E-mail: editor@turnstonepress.mb. ca. Website: www.TurnstonePress.com (includes writer's guidelines, list of books, and samples of writing). Established 1976. **Contact:** Acquisitions Editor-Poetry.

• Books published by Turnstone Press have won numerous awards, including the McNally Robinson Book of the Year Award, the Canadian Author's Association Literary Award for Poetry and the Lampert Memorial Awards.

Book/Chapbook Needs: "Turnstone Press publishes Canadian authors with special priority to prairie interests/themes." Publishes 2 paperbacks/year. Has published poetry by Di Brandt, Catherine Hunter, Patrick Friesen, and Dennis Cooley. Books are usually 5½×8½, offset-printed and perfect-bound with quality paperback cover.

How to Submit: Query first with 10 sample poems and cover letter with brief bio and publication credits. Accepts previously published poems and simultaneous submissions. Cover letter preferred. No e-mail submissions. "Please enclose SASE (or SAE with IRC) and if you want the submission back, make sure your envelope and postage cover it." Time between acceptance and publication is 1 year. Poems are circulated to an editorial board. "The submissions that are approved by our readers go to the editorial board for discussion." Receives more than 1,200 unsolicited mss/year, about 10% are passed to the editorial board. Responds to queries in 3 months; to mss in 4 months. Pays royalties of 10% plus advance of $200 and 10 author's copies.

Advice: "Competition is extremely fierce in poetry. Most work published is by poets working on their craft for many years."

⊘ **24.7; RE-PRESST**, 30 Forest St., Providence RI 02906. (401)521-4728. Established 1994. **Poetry Editor:** David Church. Currently not accepting submissions.

⊘ **TWILIGHT ENDING**, 21 Ludlow Dr., Milford CT 06460-6822. (203)877-3473. Established 1995. **Editor/Publisher:** Emma J. Blanch. **Co-Editor:** Martin Goorhigian.

Magazine Needs: *Twilight Ending* appears 3 times/year publishing "poetry and short fiction of the highest caliber, in English, with universal appeal." Has featured the work of poets from the US, Canada, Europe, Middle East, Japan, and New Zealand. Wants "poems with originality in thought and in style, reflecting the latest trend in writing, moving from the usual set-up to a vertical approach. We prefer unrhymed poetry, however we accept rhymed verse if rhymes are perfect. We look for the unusual approach in content and style with clarity. No haiku. No poems forming a design. No foul words. No translations. No bio. No porn." *Twilight Ending* is 5½×8½, "elegantly printed on white linen paper with one poem with title per page (12-30 lines)." Receives about 1,500 poems/year, accepts 10%. Press run is 120 for 50 subscribers of which 25 are libraries. Sample: $6 US, $6.50 Canada, $7 Europe, $8 Middle East, Japan, and New Zealand. Make checks payable to Emma J. Blanch.

How to Submit: Submit only 3-4 poems at a time, typed, single spaced. No previously published poems or simultaneous submissions nor poems submitted to contests while in consideration for *Twilight Ending*. Include white stamped business envelop for reply (overseas contributors should include 2 IRCs). No fax or e-mail submissions. "When accepted, poems and fiction will not be returned so keep copies." Submission deadlines: mid-December for Winter issue, mid-April for Spring/Summer issue, mid-September for Fall issue. No backlog, "all poems are destroyed after publication." Often comments on rejected poems. Guidelines available for SASE. Responds in 1 week. Pays nothing—not even a copy. Acquires first rights.

Advice: "If editing is needed, suggestions will be made for the writer to rework and resubmit a corrected version. The author always decides; remember that you deal with experts."

⚆ **TWO RIVERS REVIEW**, P.O. Box 158, Clinton NY 13323. E-mail: tworiversreview@juno.com (guidelines/inquiries only). Website: http://trrpoetry.tripod.com (includes guidelines, contact and subscription information, links, editorial policy, and contest rules). Established 1998. **Editor:** Philip Memmer.
Magazine Needs: *Two Rivers Review* appears biannually and "seeks to print the best of contemporary poetry. All styles of work are welcome, so long as submitted poems display excellence." Has published poetry by Billy Collins, Gary Young, Lee Upton, Baron Wormser, and Olga Broumas. *Two Rivers Review* is 44-52 pages, digest-sized, professionally printed on cream-colored paper, with card cover. Subscription: $10. Sample: $5. "Poets wishing to submit work may obtain a sample copy for the reduced price of $4."
How to Submit: Submit no more than 4 poems at a time with cover letter (optional) and SASE (required). Simultaneous submissions are considered with notification. No electronic submissions. Guidelines available for SASE, by e-mail, or on website. Responds to most submissions within 1 month. Acquires first rights.
Also Offers: Sponsors the annual *Two Rivers Review* Poetry Prize. In 2002, the *Two Rivers Review* chapbook series will also be introduced, with books chosen through a competition. Guidelines available for SASE or on website.

N ⚆ **TWO TURTLE PRESS**, P.O. Box 643, Worthington MA 01098-0643. E-mail: Rougan@rcn. com. Website: www.users.rcn.com/Rougan (includes guidelines and ordering information). Established 2001. **Publisher:** Sean Reagan.
Book/Chapbook Needs & How to Submit: Two Turtles Press publishes "anthology chapbooks, individually authored chapbooks, and broadsides." Wants "thoughtful and well-crafted poems." Publishes 1-5 chapbooks/year through open submission. Chapbooks are 16-48 pages. Printing method varies. Chapbook mss may include previously published poems. "We prefer plain text submissions via e-mail." Responds to queries in 3 weeks; to mss in 4 weeks. Pays "terms on case-by-case basis with author."
Advice: "Have fun and faith, not necessarily in that order."

$ ⚆ **U.S. CATHOLIC; CLARETIAN PUBLICATIONS**, 205 W. Monroe St., Chicago IL 60606. (312)236-7782. E-mail: aboodm@claretianpubs.org. Website: www.uscatholic.org. Established 1935. **Literary Editor:** Maureen Abood.
Magazine Needs: "Published monthly, *U.S. Catholic* engages a broad range of issues as they affect the everyday lives of Catholics." Has no specifications for poetry, but does not necessarily want poems religious in nature. No light verse. Has published poetry by Naomi Shihab Nye. *U.S. Catholic* is 51 pages, magazine-sized, printed in 4-color and stapled, includes art/graphics. Receives about 1,000 poems/year, accepts about 12 poems. Publishes 1 poem/issue. Press run is 50,000. Subscription: $22.
How to Submit: Submit 3 poems at a time. Line length for poetry is 50 maximum. Accepts simultaneous submissions; no previously published poems. Accepts e-mail submissions (include in body of message); no fax submissions. Cover letter preferred. Always include SASE. Time between acceptance and publication is 3 months. Poems are circulated to an editorial board. Seldom comments on rejected poems. Guidelines available for SASE. Responds in 3 months. Pays $75 and 5 contributor's copies. Acquires first North American serial rights.

⚆ **THE U.S. LATINO REVIEW; HISPANIC DIALOGUE PRESS**, P.O. Box 150009, Kew Gardens NY 11415. E-mail: andrescastro@aol.com or editor@uslatinoreview.org. Website: www.uslatinoreview.org (includes writer's guidelines, mission statement, poetry, interview, contact and subscription information, upcoming themes, and editorial policy). Established 1999. **Managing Editor:** Andrés Castro.
Magazine Needs: "*U.S. Latino Review* is a biannual literary review for Latinos, our friends, and critics. It is indeed a labor of love dedicated to promoting the best we as a community of creative artists have to offer. We expect truth, excellence and passion from contributors and ourselves. We include poetry, short short story, essay, sketch art and other forms considered if queried. Submissions of all content and form are considered, but writers and artists should understand that we heavily favor work that focuses concretely on the urgent social, political, economic and ecological issues of our time. We stress that *U.S. Latino Review* is not exclusionary—we are won over easily by care, craft and conscience." Has published poetry by Alma Luz Villianueva, L.S. Asekoff, Jack Agüeros, Cornelius Eady, Virgil Suarez, Kimiko Hahn, and Martín Espada. As a sample the editor selected these lines from "Black Flowers" by Ray Gonzalez:

> *Someday they will call me, diabolic antlers/erased from the unfinished drawing,/my fingers tracing letters on the paper/with charcoal, the artist standing behind me,/knife at my back, guiding my fingers/ over the ancient maps as I wonder/if my throat will burst before I trace/the first black petal.*

U.S. Latino Review is 64 pages, 5½×8½, printed on 100% recycled 24 lb. stock and flat-spined with semi-gloss card cover, includes black ink sketch art/prints. Receives about 500 poems/year, accepts 3-5%. Press run is 1,000 for 100 subscribers, 700 shelf sales. Single copy: $6 US; subscription: $12 US; $22 US/2 years. Make checks payable to *The U.S. Latino Review*.

How to Submit: Submit 3-5 poems at a time. Accepts previously published poems and simultaneous submissions. Accepts e-mail submissions in body of message (no attachments). Cover letter preferred. "SASE must accompany submissions. A short bio is requested but not necessary for contributors page." Time between acceptance and publication is up to 6 months. Poems are circulated to an editorial board. "Editor does early screening and poems forwarded to editorial board of at least three others for final selection." Guidelines available for SASE, by e-mail, on website, or in publication. Responds in up to 6 months. Sends prepublication galleys if requested. Acquires first rights.

Advice: "Please, send your best."

U.S. I WORKSHEETS; U.S. I POETS' COOPERATIVE, P.O. Box 127, Kingston NJ 08528-0127. Established 1973. **Contact:** Poetry Editors. **Managing Editor:** Winifred Hughes.

Magazine Needs: *U.S. 1 Worksheets* is a literary annual, double issue December or January, circulation 400, which uses high-quality poetry and fiction. "We use a rotating board of editors; it's wisest to query when we're next reading before submitting. A self-addressed, stamped postcard will get our next reading period dates (usually in the spring)." Has published poetry by Alicia Ostriker, James Richardson, Frederick Tibbetts, Lois Marie Harrod, James Haba, Charlotte Mandel, and David Keller. *U.S. 1 Worksheets* is 72 pages, 5½×8½, saddle-stapled, with color cover art. "We read a lot but take very few. Prefer complex, well-written work." Subscription: $7, $12/2 years.

How to Submit: Submit 5 poems at a time. Include name, address, and phone number in upper right-hand corner. No simultaneous submissions; rarely accepts previously published poems. Requests for sample copies, subscriptions, queries, back issues, and all mss should be addressed to the editor (address at beginning of listing). Guidelines available for SASE. Pays 1 contributor's copy.

[N] UMBRIATE, 710 Old Farm Rd., Point Pleasant NJ 08742-4046. (732)701-0656. E-mail: e.lovelan d@att.net. Established 2000. **Editors:** Emile Gustave and Eric Loveland.

Magazine Needs: *UMBRIATE* appears biannually. Wants "daring conceptual, concrete, or lyric poetry of which the form is driven by the content." Does not want "sloppy poetry, mawkish nonsense, bad surrealism, adolescent angst." Recently published poetry by Emile Gustave, Eric Geist, Dan Buck, and Joe Felice. As a sample the editors selected these lines from "Archimedes' Screw" by Eric Geist:

> a been of ori-/gin vised method building temp-/oral time putting

UMBRIATE is 20-25 pages, computer-generated/photocopied, saddle-stapled, with card stock cover and b&w art. Receives about 100 poems/year, accepts about 40%. Press run is 100-150; most are distributed free to poets, libraries, bookstores. Single copy: $2 or price of postage; subscription: $4 or price of postage. Sample: $1. Make checks payable to Eric Loveland.

How to Submit: Submit 3-6 poems at a time. Accepts simultaneous submissions; no previously published poems. Accepts e-mail and disk submissions. Cover letter preferred. Reads submissions all year long. Time between acceptance and publication is up to 6 months. "Poems are circulated to three members of staff and chosen by consensus." Seldom comments on rejected poems. Guidelines available in magazine. Responds in 6 weeks. Sometimes sends prepublication galleys. Pays 2 contributor's copies. Acquires one-time rights. Reviews chapbooks of poetry and other magazines/journals in 50-70 words. Poets may send materials for review consideration to Eric Loveland.

Advice: "Think, write, rewrite—then think, write, rewrite."

UNDERSTANDING MAGAZINE; DIONYSIA PRESS LTD., 20 A Montgomery St., Edinburgh, Lothian EH7 5JS Great Britain. Phone/fax: (0131)4780680. Established 1989. **Contact:** Denise Smith.

Magazine Needs: *Understanding Magazine*, published 1-2 times/year, features "poetry, short stories, parts of plays, reviews and articles." Wants "original poetry." Has published poetry by Susanna Roxman, D. Zervanou, and Ron Butlin. As a sample we selected these lines from "Private Axis" by Thom Nairn:

> The circles grow relentlessly,/His passage, inscrutably centrifugal/On this terminal cycle to silence.

Understanding is A5 and perfect-bound. Receives 2,000 poems/year. Press run is 1,000 for 500 subscribers. Single copy: £4.50; subscription: £9. Sample: £3. Make checks payable to Dionysia Press.

How to Submit: Submit 5 poems at a time. Accepts simultaneous submissions; no previously published poems. Accepts e-mail and fax submissions. Time between acceptance and publication is 6-10 months. Poems are circulated to an editorial board. Often comments on rejected poems. Responds in 6 months or more. Always sends prepublication galleys. Pays 1 contributor's copy. Acquires all rights. Returns rights after publication. Staff reviews books or chapbooks of poetry or other magazines. Send books for review consideration.

Book/Chapbook Needs & How to Submit: Dionysia Press Ltd., publishes 14 paperbacks and chapbooks of poetry/year. "Sometimes we select from submissions or competitions." Has published *Let Me Sing My Song* by Paul Hullah; *Poems* by Klitos Kyrou, translated by Thom Nairn and D. Zervnaou; *Sailing the Sands* by James Andrew; and *The Feeble Lies of Orestes Chalkiopoulos* by Andreas Mitsou. As a sample the editor selected these lines by A. Stamatis translated by T. Nairn and D. Zervanou:

> *In a dream I am shadow/in a light boat/on gleaming waters/my mouth is day/as I listen:/You know it.*
> *Why don't you look?*

Books are usually A5, perfect-bound, hard cover with art. Query first, with a few sample poems and cover letter with brief bio and publication credits. Responds to queries in 2-6 months. Pays author's copies. "We usually get arts council grants or poets get grants for themselves." For sample books or chapbooks, write to the above address.

Also Offers: Sponsors poetry competitions with cash prizes. Guidelines available for SASE.

$UNIVERSITY OF ALBERTA PRESS, Ring House 2, Edmonton, Alberta T6G 2E1 Canada. (780)492-3662. Fax: (780)492-0719. E-mail: u.a.p@ualberta.ca. Website: www.ualberta.ca/~uap (includes contact information and description of publishing program). Established 1969. **Managing Editor:** Leslie Vermeer.

Book/Chapbook Needs: "The University of Alberta Press is a scholarly press, generally publishing nonfiction plus some literary titles." Publishes 1-2 paperback poetry titles per year. Looking for "mature, thoughtful work—nothing too avant-garde. No juvenile or 'Hallmark verse.' " Has published *Bloody Jack* by Dennis Colley and *The Hornbooks of Rita K* by Robert Kroetsch.

How to Submit: Query first, with 10-12 sample poems and cover letter with brief bio and publication credits. "Do not send complete manuscript on first approach." Accepts previously published poems and simultaneous submissions. Accepts e-mail and disk submissions. Time between acceptance and publication is 6-10 months. Poems are circulated to an editorial board. "The process is: acquiring editor to editorial group meeting to two external reviewers to press committee to acceptance." Seldom comments on rejected poems. Responds to queries in 2 months. Pays royalties of 10% of net plus 10 author's copies. See website to order sample books.

UNIVERSITY OF CENTRAL FLORIDA CONTEMPORARY POETRY SERIES, % English Dept., University of Central Florida, Orlando FL 32816-1346. (407)823-2212. Established 1968. **Poetry Editor:** Judith Hemschemeyer.

Book/Chapbook Needs: Publishes two 50- to 80-page hardback or paperback collections each year. "Strong poetry on any theme in the lyric-narrative tradition." Has published poetry by Robert Cooperman, Katherine Soniat, and John Woods.

How to Submit: Submit complete paginated ms with table of contents and acknowledgement of previously published poems. Accepts simultaneous submissions. "Please send a reading fee of $7, a SASE for return of ms, and a self-addressed postcard for acknowledgment of receipt of ms." Reads submissions September through April only. Responds in 3 months. Time between acceptance and publication is 1 year.

THE UNIVERSITY OF CHICAGO PRESS; PHOENIX POETS SERIES, 1427 E. 60th St., Chicago IL 60637. (773)702-7700. Fax: (773)702-2705. Website: www.press.uchicago.edu. Established 1891. **Poetry Editor:** Randolph Petilos.

Book/Chapbook Needs: The University of Chicago Press publishes scholarly books and journals. "We may only publish four or five books in Phoenix Poets per year, and perhaps two or three books of poetry in translation per year. We occasionally publish a book of poems outside Phoenix Poets, or as a reprint from other houses." Has published poetry by Alan Shapiro, Tom Sleigh, David Ferry, Bruce Smith, and Gail Mazur.

How to Submit: By invitation only. No unsolicited mss.

UNIVERSITY OF GEORGIA PRESS; CONTEMPORARY POETRY SERIES, 330 Research Dr., Suite B100, University of Georgia, Athens GA 30602-4901. (706)369-6135. Fax: (706)369-6131. E-mail: emontjoy@ugapress.uga.edu. Website: www.uga.edu/ugapress (includes guidelines, contact and contest info, archives, and editorial policy). Press established 1938, series established 1980. **Series Editor:** Bin Ramke. **Poetry Competition Coordinator:** Emily Montjoy.

● Poetry published by University of Georgia Press has been included in the 2002 *Pushcart Prize* anthology.

Book/Chapbook Needs: Through its annual competition, the press publishes 4 collections of poetry/year, 2 of which are by poets who have not had a book published, in paperback editions. Has published poetry by Marjorie Welish, Arthur Vogelsang, C.D. Wright, Martha Ronk, and Paul Hoover.

How to Submit: "Writers should query first for guidelines and submission periods. Please enclose SASE." There are no restrictions on the type of poetry submitted, but "familiarity with our previously published books in the series may be helpful." No fax or e-mail submissions. $20 submission fee required. Make checks payable to University of Georgia Press. Manuscripts are *not* returned after the judging is completed.

UNIVERSITY OF IOWA PRESS; THE IOWA POETRY PRIZES, 119 West Park Rd., 100 Kuhl House, Iowa City IA 52242-1000. Fax: (319)335-2055. E-mail: rhonda-wetjen@uiowa.edu. Website www.uiowa.edu/~uipress (includes "all our books, some with samples").

Book/Chapbook Needs: The University of Iowa Press offers annually the Iowa Poetry Prizes for book-length mss (50-150 pages) by new or established poets. Winners will be published by the Press under a standard royalty contract. Winning entry for 2000 was *The Penultimate Suitor* by Mary Leader. (This competition is the only way in which this press accepts poetry.)

How to Submit: Mss are received annually in April only. All writers of English are eligible. Poems from previously published books may be included only in mss of selected or collected poems, submissions of which are encouraged. Accepts simultaneous submissions if press is immediately notified if the book is accepted by another publisher. $20 entry fee is charged; mss will not be returned. Include name on the title page only.

Advice: "These awards have been initiated to encourage all poets, whether new or established, to submit their very best work."

[N] THE UNIVERSITY OF MASSACHUSETTS PRESS; THE JUNIPER PRIZE, P.O. Box 429, Amherst MA 01004-0429. (413)545-2217. Fax: (413)545-1226. E-mail: info@umpress.umass.edu. Website: www.umass.edu/umpress (includes historical information about the press, guidelines, staff listing, our books-in-print and seasonal catalogs, and excerpts from recently published books). Established 1964.
Contact: Alice I. Maldonado, assistant editor.

Book/Chapbook Needs: The press offers an annual competition for the Juniper Prize, in alternate years to first and subsequent books. In even-numbered years (2000, 2002, etc.) only subsequent books will be considered: mss whose authors have had at least one full-length book or chapbook of poetry published or accepted for publication. Such chapbooks must be at least 30 pages, and self-published work is not considered to lie within this "books and chapbooks" category. In odd-numbered years (1999, 2001, etc.) only "first books" will be considered: mss by writers whose poems may have appeared in literary journals and/or anthologies but have not been published, or been accepted for publication, in book form. Has published *The Double Task* by Gray Jacobik; *Song of the Cicadas* by Mông-Lan; *Heartwall* by Richard Jackson; *At the Site of Inside Out* by Anna Rabinowitz; *Cities and Towns: Poems* by Arthur Vogelsang; and *Fugitive Red* by Karen Donovan. "Poetry books are approximately $14 for paperback editions and $24 for cloth."

How to Submit: Submissions must not exceed 70 pages in typescript. Include paginated contents page; provide the title, publisher and year of publication for previously published volumes. A list of poems published or slated for publication in literary journals and/or anthologies must also accompany the ms. Such poems may be included in the ms and must be identified. "Mss by more than one author, entries of more than one ms simultaneously or within the same year, and translations are not eligible." Entry fee: $15 plus SASE for return of ms or notification. Entries must be postmarked not later than September 30. The award is announced in April/May and publication is scheduled for the following spring. The amount of the prize is $1,000 and is in lieu of royalties on the first print run. Poet also receives 12 copies in one edition or 6 copies each if published in both hardcover and paperbound editions. Fax, call or send SASE for guidelines and/or further information to the above address. Entries are to be mailed to Juniper Prize, University of Massachusetts, Amherst MA 01003.

UNIVERSITY OF TEXAS PRESS, P.O. Box 7819, Austin TX 78713-7819. Website: www.utexas.edu/utpress. Established 1950. Not accepting unsolicited manuscripts.

UNIVERSITY OF WISCONSIN PRESS; BRITTINGHAM PRIZE IN POETRY; FELIX POLLAK PRIZE IN POETRY, Dept. of English, 600 N. Park St., University of Wisconsin, Madison WI 53706. Website: www.wisc.edu/wisconsinpress/index.html. Brittingham Prize inaugurated in 1985.
Poetry Editor: Ronald Wallace.

Book/Chapbook Needs: The University of Wisconsin Press publishes primarily scholarly works, but they offer the annual Brittingham Prize and the Felix Pollak Prize, both $1,000 plus publication. These prizes are the only way in which this press publishes poetry. Rules available for SASE or on website. Qualified readers will screen all mss. Winners will be selected by "a distinguished poet who will remain anonymous until the winners are announced in mid-February." Past judges include Henry Taylor, Carolyn Kizer, Philip Levine, Rita Dove, Donald Hall, Alicia Ostriker, Mark Doty, Ed Hirsch, and Robert Bly. Winners include Stefanie Marlis, Tony Hoagland, Stephanie Strickland, Lisa Lewis, Derick Burleson, Robin Behn, Cathy Colman, and Greg Rappleye.

How to Submit: For both prizes, submit between September 1 and October 1, unbound ms volume of 50-80 pages, with name, address, and telephone number on title page. No translations. Poems must be previously unpublished in book form. Poems published in journals, chapbooks, and anthologies may be included but must be acknowledged. There is a non-refundable $20 entry fee which must accompany the ms. (Checks to University of Wisconsin Press.) Mss will not be returned. Contest results available for SASE.

Advice: "Each submission is considered for both prizes (one entry fee only)."

◗ **THE UNKNOWN WRITER**, P.O. Box 698, Ramsey NJ 07446. E-mail: unknown_writer_2000@yahoo.com. Website: http://munno.net/unknownwriter/ (includes guidelines, subscription and contact information, editorial policy, links, samples of works from each issue, previous tables of contents). Established 1995. **Poetry Editor:** Amy Munno.

Magazine Needs: "We are a quarterly print magazine that publishes poetry and fiction by up-and-coming writers with limited publishing credits. We publish some art on covers and inner pages. We are the place for quality writers who need a start. Send us strong, rich poetry with attention to imagery, emotion, and detail. We enjoy the traditional and structured forms like sonnet and haiku as much as experimental and modern free verse. Any subject matter is acceptable as long as the poem makes a direct connection with the reader. Keep the work fresh, intelligent, and mindful." Does not want forced rhyme, limericks, or vulgar work. No profane or sexually explicit material and no graphic violence. Accepts poetry from young adults (16 or older). *The Unknown Writer* is usually 30-50 pages, digest-sized, saddle-stapled, cardstock cover and b&w line art and photos (at times). Publishes up to 6 poems/issue. Single copy: $4, subscription: $15 (4 issues).

How to Submit: Submit 3-5 poems at a time. Line length for poetry is 2 minimum, 100 maximum. Accepts simultaneous submissions; no previously published poems. Accepts e-mail (as attachment or in text box) and disk submissions. Cover letter is preferred. "Through postal mail, include a SASE, full address and e-mail address. Through e-mail, attach poems as a file or include them in the message body. With e-mail submissions, please introduce yourself in a short note; don't just send poems. Tell us if the submission is simultaneous." Reads submissions all year. Submit seasonal poems 4 months in advance. Time between acceptance and publication is 6 months. Poem may be read by some or all of editorial board members." Occasionally publishes theme issues. Guidelines available by e-mail, for SASE, or on website. Responds in 4 months. Pays 2 copies. Acquires first worldwide rights.

Advice: "We want to discover new, talented writers who need their first break or have a handful of previous acceptances, but new does not mean clichéd or careless. Proofread before submitting. Remember to keep writing regularly. Writing is a practice and a craft. If we reject your first submission but tell you to submit again, we mean it. Keep trying."

✄ ◉ **UNMUZZLED OX**, 43B Clark Lane, Staten Island NY 10304 or Box 550, Kingston, Ontario K7L 4W5 Canada. (212)226-7170. Established 1971. **Poetry Editor:** Michael Andre.

Magazine Needs & How to Submit: *Unmuzzled Ox* is a tabloid literary biannual. Each edition is built around a theme or specific project. "The chances of an unsolicited poem being accepted are slight since I always have specific ideas in mind." Has published poetry by Allen Ginsberg, Robert Creeley, and Denise Levertov. As a sample the editor selected these lines from "CL" by Daniel Berrigan:

> *Let's be grandiose, it's a game/Let's climb a balcony/Let's issue a manifesto//Why, we're turning things*
> *on their head/we're making history/we're—//Harmless.*

"Only unpublished work will be considered, but works may be in French as well as English." Subscription: $20.

🅽 ◉ **UNWOUND**, P.O. Box 835, Laramie WY 82073. (307)755-0669. E-mail: unwoundmagazine@excite.com. Website: www.FyUoCuK.com/unwound (includes poems, interview, guidelines). Established 1998. **Editor:** Lindsay Wilson.

Magazine Needs: *Unwound* appears biannually. "Looking for work that is informal and relatable that has concerns for the image. Take a risk—if not, don't send. Looking for poetry that is honest and visual.

Quality is a must. Growing more and more into the surreal image. I'm not interested in formal or Hallmark poetry. If it's strange just to be strange, or if I had to be there, don't send it." Recently published poetry by Leonard Cirino, Nathan Graziano, Daniel Crocker, Simon Perchik, Taylor Graham, and C.C. Russell. *Unwound* is 56 pages, digest-sized, copied, stapled, laser copy/silk screen cover, with b&w/silk screen art and ads. Receives about 2,500 poems/year, accepts about 2%. Publishes about 25 poems/issue. Press run is 200 for 50 subscribers of which 4 are libraries, 12 shelf sales; 50 distributed free to readings and friends, or left places. Single copy: $4; subscription: $7. Sample: $4. Make checks payable to Lindsay Wilson.
How to Submit: Submit 5 poems at a time. No previously published poems or simultaneous submissions. No fax, e-mail, or disk submissions. Cover letter is preferred. "No SASE, no chance." Does not read submissions in January or July. Time between acceptance and publication is 1-5 months. "I read all the poems and decide on my own. Seldomly I refer poems to a co-editor." Seldom comments on rejected poems. Guidelines available on website. Responds in up to 5 months. Sometimes sends prepublication galleys. Pays 1 contributor's copy. Acquires one-time rights. Reviews books and chapbooks of poetry and other magazines/journals in 1,000 words, single book format. Poets may send books/chapbooks for review consideration to Lindsay Wilson.
Advice: "At least check out the website and see if your work will fit in *Unwound*. If your gut has questions about what you're sending, listen to it and don't send. Please take a risk with your work—only send your best."

UPSOUTH (Specialized: regional, religious), 323 Bellevue Ave., Bowling Green KY 42101-5001. (502)843-8018. E-mail: galen@ky.net. Website: www.expage.com/upsouth (includes current info about the newsletter, editor's biographical information, and editor's favorite links). Established 1993. **Editor:** Galen Smith.
Magazine Needs: Appearing quarterly, *Upsouth* is an international newsletter for motivation and inspiration. "We ask for positive poems, columns, essays, etc. No works of non-motivational and non-inspirational views in nature will be accepted. Nothing negative please! But the works do not necessarily have to be motivational or inspirational in nature to be accepted. Our intention is to be a creative outlet for motivational and inspirational writers and appeal to writers and readers who desire to be motivated and inspired." Has published poetry by Rory Morse, Joyce Bradshaw, and Leah Maines. As a sample the editor selected these lines from "Dear Heavenly Father" by Raymond Flory:

> This day,/in this place/hold me once again./May I feel the touch

Upsouth is 12-16 pages, 8½×11, photocopied and corner-stapled, includes clip art. Receives about 100 poems/year, accepts about 10%. Press run is 100 for 50 subscribers of which 10 are libraries, 10 shelf sales. Subscription: $12. Sample: $4. "We are more likely to publish your poem if you subscribe."
How to Submit: Submit 3 poems at a time. Line length for poetry is 21 maximum. Include SASE. Accepts previously published poems and simultaneous submissions. No e-mail submissions. Cover letter preferred. Seldom comments on rejected poems. Occasionally publishes theme issues (related to the seasons). Guidelines available for SASE. Responds in up to 2 months. Pays 1 contributor's copy. Author retains all rights. Reviews books and chapbooks of poetry and other magazines in 250 words. Poets may send books for review consideration.
Advice: "We like for you to subscribe to *Upsouth*. We consider you as a friend and write you personal and encouraging letters. Our motto is 'your writing can change the world!' "

URTHONA MAGAZINE (Specialized: religious, Buddhism), 3 Coral Park, Henley Rd., Cambridge CB1 3EA United Kingdom. Phone: (01223) 472417. Fax: 01223 566568. E-mail: urthona.mag@virgin.net. Website: www.urthona.com. Established 1992. **Contact:** Poetry Editor.
Magazine Needs: *Urthona*, published biannually, explores the arts and western culture from a Buddhist perspective. Wants "poetry rousing the imagination." Does not want "undigested autobiography, political, or New-Agey poems." Has published poetry by Peter Abbs, Robert Bly, and Peter Redgrove. As a sample the editor selected these lines from "The Shower" by Ananda:

> And somewhere there is gold,/and a song almost getting started/in the street we're leaving by://
> something like tenderness, how/the spring light races and dies/over the washed squares

Urthona is 60 pages, A4, offset-printed, saddle-stapled with 4-color glossy cover, b&w photos, art and ads inside. Receives about 300 poems/year, accepts about 40. Press run is 900 for 50 subscribers of which 4 are libraries, 500 shelf sales; 50 distributed free to Buddhist groups. Subscription: £8.50 (surface), £11.50 (airmail)/2 issues; £15 (surface), £22 (airmail)/4 issues. Sample (including guidelines): £3.50.
How to Submit: Submit 6 poems at a time. No previously published poems or simultaneous submissions. Accepts submissions by e-mail (as attachment). Cover letter preferred. Time between acceptance and publication is 8 months. Poems are circulated to an editorial board and read and selected by poetry editor. Other editors have right of veto. Responds in 6 months. Pays 1 contributor's copy. Acquires one-time rights. Reviews books or chapbooks of poetry or other magazines in 600 words. Poets may send books for review consideration.

◓ **UTAH STATE UNIVERSITY PRESS; MAY SWENSON POETRY AWARD**, Logan UT 84322-7800. (435)797-1362. Fax: (435)797-0313. E-mail: mspooner@upress.usu.edu. Website: www.usu. edu/usupress (includes current book information, submission guidelines, May Swenson Poetry Award guidelines, and purchasing information). Established 1972. **Poetry Editor:** Michael Spooner. Publishes poetry only through the May Swenson Poetry Award competition annually. Has published *May Out West* by May Swenson; *Plato's Breath* by Randall Freisinger; *The Hammered Dulcimer* by Lisa Williams; *Necessary Light* by Patricia Fargnoli; *All That Divides Us* by Elinor Benedict; *Borgo of the Holy Ghost* by Stephen McLeod. See website for details.

◎ **VALEE PUBLICATIONS (Specialized: women from all backgrounds)**, P.O. Box 23348, Cincinnati OH 45223-0348. E-mail: hlm1961@yahoo.com. Established 2000. **Publisher:** Hilda L. McMullins.
Book/Chapbook Needs: Valee Publications wants "to publish writers who are very talented, but have not been 'discovered.' " Wants to see poetry of "any form, length, style, but no pornography or anything in bad taste." Does not want "poetry that can't be deciphered." As a sample the editor selected these lines from her own poem "Angry Eyes":

> *Teacher never taught me black was beautiful/mother never told me female was beautiful/me—tall and*
> *big boned/a female beauty from lands unknown//I have been betrayed.*

Publishes 1 chapbook/year. Books are usually 30-75 pages, stapled, glossy cover with artwork on cover. Sample: $10.
How to Submit: Send complete ms with cover letter. Accepts simultaneous submissions. No submissions by e-mail. No queries necessary, just submit complete ms. Manuscript will not be returned unless SASE enclosed. Reads submissions February through April. Guidelines available for SASE and in publication. Responds in 2 months. Pays 50 author's copies (out of a press run of 100). "Hope to give honorarium in the future."
Advice: "I seek writers who aren't in it for the money, but as an expression to share with others. Write with your heart, send out your work, have faith in God—you are a writer even if you never get published. Treasure your gift."

♞ **$◐ VALLUM MAGAZINE**, P.O. Box 48003, 5678 du Parc, Montreal, Quebec H2V 4S8 Canada. E-mail: vallummag@hotmail.com. Website: www.vallummag.com. Established 2000. **Contact:** Joshua Auerbach, Helen Zisimatos.
Magazine Needs: *Vallum Magazine* appears biannually. "We are looking for poetry that's fresh and edgy, something that reflects contemporary experience and is also well-crafted. Open to all styles. We publish new and established poets." Recently published poetry by jwcurry, David Solway, Robert Allen, Ronnie R. Brown, Blaine Marchand. *Vallum Magazine* is 60 pages, 7 × 8½, digitally-printed, perfect-bound, color images on coated stock cover, with art/graphics. Publishes about 45 poems/issue. Press run is 500. Single copy: $7; subscription: $12. Make checks payable to *Vallum Magazine*.
How to Submit: Submit 4-7 poems at a time. No previously published poems or simultaneous submissions. No fax, e-mail, or disk submissions. Cover letter is preferred. Include SASE. Time between acceptance and publication is several months. Sometimes comments on rejected poems. Guidelines are available in magazine. Responds in 3 months. Pays a "small honorarium" and 2 contributor's copies. Acquires first North American serial rights. Reviews books and chapbooks of poetry in 250-500 words. Poets may send books for review consideration to *Vallum Magazine*.
Advice: "Hone your craft, read widely, be original."

◐ **VALPARAISO POETRY REVIEW**, Dept of English, Valparaiso University, Valparaiso IN 46383-6493. (219)464-5278. Fax: (219)464-5511. E-mail: vpr@valpo.edu. Website: www.valpo.edu/english/vpr/ . Established 1999. **Editor:** Edward Byrne.
Magazine Needs: *Valparaiso Poetry Review: Contemporary Poetry and Poetics* is "a biannual online poetry journal accepting submissions of unpublished or previously published poetry, book reviews, author interviews, and essays on poetry or poetics that have not yet appeared online and for which the rights belong to the author. Query for anything else." Wants poetry of any length or style, free verse or traditional forms. Recently published poetry by Charles Wright, Jonathan Holden, Reginald Gibbons, Janet McCann, Laurence Lieberman, Beth Simon, and Margot Schilpp. As a sample the editor selected these lines from "Leaving the Scene" by Walt McDonald:

> *Sleet clicking in the trees, and finches flicking/maize and millet from the feeder. This late in spring,/*
> *and still the thin smoke whips from chimneys/a mile away. We rock and watch the dawn,/a ten-watt*
> *bulb beyond the clouds. Is all/this sideshow spring a barker's promise of warmth?*

Valparaiso Poetry Review is published online only. Receives about 500 poems/year, accepts about 7%. Publishes about 17 poems/issue.

How to Submit: Submit 3-5 poems at a time. Accepts previously published poems ("original publication must be identified to ensure proper credit") and simultaneous submissions. Accepts e-mail submissions (but prefers postal mail); no fax or disk submissions. Cover letter is preferred. Include SASE. For e-mail submissions, include text in body of message rather than as an attachment. Submit no more than 5 poems at a time. Reads submissions year round. Time between acceptance and publication is 6-12 months. Seldom comments on rejected poems. Guidelines are available on website. Responds in up to 6 weeks. Acquires one-time rights. "All rights remain with author." Reviews books of poetry in single book and multi-book format. Poets may send books for review consideration to Edward Byrne, editor.

VEGETARIAN JOURNAL; THE VEGETARIAN RESOURCE GROUP (Specialized: children/teens, vegetarianism), P.O. Box 1463, Baltimore MD 21203. Website: www.vrg.org. Established 1982.
Magazine Needs: The Vegetarian Resource Group is a publisher of nonfiction. *Vegetarian Journal* is a quarterly, 36 pages, 8½×11, saddle-stapled and professionally printed with glossy card cover. Press run is 20,000. Sample: $3.
How to Submit: "Please no submissions of poetry from adults; 18 and under only."
Also Offers: The Vegetarian Resource Group offers an annual contest for ages 18 and under, $50 savings bond in 3 age categories for the best contribution on any aspect of vegetarianism. "Most entries are essay, but we would accept poetry with enthusiasm." Postmark deadline: May 1. Details available for SASE.

VERSE, Dept. of English, University of Georgia, Athens GA 30602. Website: www.versemag.org (includes guidelines, contact information, archives, editorial policy, reviews, ordering information, and sample poems). Established 1984. **Editors:** Brian Henry and Andrew Zawacki.
   ● Poetry published in *Verse* also appeared in *The Best American Poetry* and *Pushcart Prize* anthology.
Magazine Needs: *Verse* appears 3 times/year and is "an international poetry journal which also publishes interviews with poets, essays on poetry, and book reviews." Wants "no specific kind; we look for high-quality, innovative poetry. Our focus is not only on American poetry, but on all poetry written in English, as well as translations." Has published poetry by Heather McHugh, John Ashbery, James Tate, Karen Volkman, Matthew Rohrer, and Eleni Sikelianos. *Verse* is 128-416 pages, digest-sized, professionally printed and perfect-bound with card cover. Receives about 5,000 poems/year, accepts 1%. Press run is 1,000 for 600 subscribers of which 200 are libraries, 200 shelf sales. Subscription: $18 for individuals, $36 for institutions. Current issue $9. Sample: $6.
How to Submit: Submit up to 5 poems at a time. Accepts simultaneous submissions; no previously published poems. Cover letter required. Time between acceptance and publication is up to 18 months. Guidelines available on website. Responds in 6 months. Often comments on rejected poems. "The magazine often publishes special features—recent features include younger American poets, Mexican poetry, Scottish poetry, Latino poets, prose poetry, women Irish poets, and Australian poetry—but does not publish 'theme' issues." Always sends prepublication galleys. Pays 2 contributor's copies plus a one-year subscription. Poets may send books for review consideration.

VIA DOLOROSA PRESS; ERASED, SIGH, SIGH. (Specialized: "dark" poetry and death), 701 E. Schaaf Rd., Cleveland OH 44131-1227. Phone/fax: (216)459-0896. E-mail: viadolorosapress@aol.com. Website: www.angelfire.com/oh2/dolorosa (includes VDP background/history and current catalog). Established 1994. **Editor:** Ms. Hyacinthe L. Raven.
Magazine Needs: *Erased, Sigh, Sigh.* appears biannually in January and July. Literary journal "showcasing free verse poetry/fiction with a dark tinge. Our theme is death/suicide." Prefers "free verse poetry that is very introspective and dark. We do not publish light-hearted works. No traditional or concrete poetry. Vampire poems will be thrown away." Recently published poetry by John Sweet, Karen Porter, Scott Urban, and Lara Haynes. As a sample the editor selected these lines from "that the baby will be born" by John Sweet from his chapbook, *Seasons of Rust*:
   and anything left/unsaid after the/sky bleeds away/is left unsaid for/obvious reasons
Erased, Sigh, Sigh. is about 40 pages, digest-sized, Xerox-printed, saddle-stapled/hand-bound, parchment paper cover and pages, with pen & ink drawings, print-ready ads accepted. Receives 200 poems/year, accepts about 25%. Publishes about 30 poems/issue. Press run is 500-1,000 of which 75% are shelf sales; 25% are distributed free to "other journals for review and also to charity organizations." Single copy: $3.50 and p&h, subscription rates available on request. Sample copy: $4 postage paid. Make checks payable to Hyacinthe L. Raven.
How to Submit: Submit any number of poems at a time. Line length for poetry is open. Accepts previously published poems and simultaneous submissions. No fax, e-mail, or disk submissions. Cover letter is preferred. "SASE required for response; we do not respond by e-mail." Subscription rates available on request. Reads

submissions any time. Submit seasonal poems 6 months in advance. Time between acceptance and publication is up to 1 year. "Poems are chosen by the editor. Writers will receive an acceptance/rejection letter usually within a month of receipt." Often comments on rejected poems. Publishes theme issues on "death, poets, and suicide. We publish dark poetry on these themes in every issue." Guidelines are available for 6×9 SASE with 2 first-class stamps. "Send for submission guidelines! We are strict about our theme and style. We also recommend reading a couple issue prior to considering us." Responds in 1 month. Pays 1 contributor's copy. Acquires one-time rights.

Book/Chapbook Needs & How to Submit: Via Dolorosa Press publishes "poetry, fiction, and nonfiction with an existential/humanist feel. Darker works preferred." Has published *Seasons of Rust* by John Sweet, *Ghostwhispers* by Karen Porter, and *Sestina* by Lara Haynes. Publishes 2-10 chapbooks/year. Chapbooks are usually 10-50 pages, photocopied or offset-printed, saddle-stapled or hand-bound, card stock, parchment, or other cover, with pen & ink drawings. "We ask that poets request our submission guidelines first. Then, if they think their work is fitting, we prefer to read the entire manuscript to make our decision." Responds to queries in 1 month; to mss in 2 months. Pays royalties of 25% plus 10% of press run. "See submission guidelines—our payment terms are listed in there." Send for free catalog.

Advice: "If you are repeatedly rejected because editors label your work as 'too depressing,' try us before you give up! We want work that makes us cry and that makes us think."

VIRGINIA ADVERSARIA, P.O. Box 2349, Poquoson VA 23662. E-mail: empirepub@hotmail.com. Website: www.FreshLit.com (includes guidelines, contact info, bios, contest and subscription info, archives). Established 2000. **Poetry Editor:** Nancy Powell.

Magazine Needs: Appearing biannually in May and December, *Virginia Adversaria* seeks "to further the literary arts." Wants high-quality poetry without restriction to form, style, or subject matter. Does not want greeting card-type verse. Recently published poetry by Virginia O'Keefe, Dr. Carolyn Foronda, Jack Trammell, Ann Shalaski, Ken McManus, and Doris Baker. As a sample the editor selected these lines from "Monet's Elves" by Dr. Carolyn Kreiter-Foronda:

> At first, Monet didn't see them, tricky thieves/of light, stealing forth on the backs of shadows//to deceive him. They were there in long shafts/of and humming of bees./How they carried on in the pond! Like acrobats//they swung through a willow's leafy canopy.

Virginia Adversaria is 84 pages, 7×10, digitally printed, perfect-bound, full color, 100 lb. white gloss cover, with b&w artwork/illustrations and ¼ page to full-page ads. Receives about 1,000 poems/year, accepts about 2%. Publishes about 8 poems/issue. Press run is 1,000 for 250 subscribers of which 5 are libraries, 700 shelf sales. Single copy: $6; subscription: $10. Sample: $4.50. Make checks payable to Empire Publishing.

How to Submit: Submit 3-6 poems at a time. Accepts previously published poems and simultaneous submissions. Accepts e-mail submissions (in text box). Cover letter is preferred. "Always inlcude SASE." Reads submissions all year. Submit seasonal poems 5 months in advance. Often comments on rejected poems. Guidelines are available for SASE or on website. Responds in up to 6 weeks. Pays 1¢/word and 1 contributor's copy. Acquires one-time rights.

Advice: "Read as much as possible the current poets being published today. Continue to study and work at the craft."

THE VIRGINIA QUARTERLY REVIEW; EMILY CLARK BALCH PRIZE, 1 West Range, P.O. Box 400223, Charlottesville VA 22904-4223. (434)924-3124. Fax: (434)924-1397. Website: http://virginia.edu\vgr (includes guidelines, contact and subscription information, links, editorial policy, contest information). Established 1925.

Magazine Needs: *The Virginia Quarterly Review* uses about 15 pages of poetry in each issue, no length or subject restrictions. Issues have largely included lyric and narrative free verse, most of which features a strong message or powerful voice. *The Virginia Quarterly Review* is 220 pages, digest-sized, flat-spined. Press run is 4,000.

How to Submit: Submit up to 5 poems and include SASE. "You will *not* be notified otherwise." No simultaneous submissions. Responds in 3 months or longer "due to the large number of poems we receive." Guidelines and upcoming themes available for SASE, by e-mail, and on website; do not request by fax. Pays $1/line.

Also Offers: Also sponsors the Emily Clark Balch Prize, an annual prize of $500 given to the best poem published in the review during the year.

VISTA PUBLISHING, INC. (Specialized: nursing), 422 Morris Ave., Suite 1, Long Branch NJ 07740. (732)229-6500. Fax: (732)229-9647. E-mail: info@vistapubl.com. Website: www.vistapubl.com (includes contact information and a list of all current titles with prices and ordering information). Established 1991. **Contact:** Carolyn S. Zagury, RN, PhD, CPC.

Book/Chapbook Needs: Provides "a forum for the creative and artistic side of our nursing colleagues." Publishes 10 paperback/year. Wants "poetry written by nurses, relating to nursing or healthcare." Has published *Broken Butterflies* by Jodi Lalone and *Drifting Among the Whales* by Carol Battaglia. Books are usually 100 pages, 6×9, trade paper, perfect-bound with illustrations if appropriate and 4-color cover.
How to Submit: Submit complete typed ms. "We are interested only in poetry collections with an average of 100 poems." Accepts simultaneous submissions; no previously published poems. No fax or e-mail submissions. Cover letter preferred. Has backlog to fall 2000. Time between acceptance and publication is 2 years. Often comments on rejected poems. Responds in 3 months. Pays "percentage of profits."

VOCE PIENA, 1011½ W. Micheltorena, Santa Barbara CA 93101. (805)962-7068. E-mail: dslaght@a ol.com. Established 2000. **Contact:** Deborah Slaght, editor.
Magazine Needs: *Voce Piena* appears annually in October. Publishes experimental poetry. *Voce Piena* is magazine-sized, desktop-published, white glossy 90 lb. paper cover, with abstract art. Receives varied number of poems/year. Publishes about 35-50 poems/issue. Single copy: $10; subscription: $10. Make checks payable to *Voce Piena*.
How to Submit: Submit 3-5 poems at a time. Length for poetry is 4 lines minimum, 3 pages maximum. Accepts previously published poems; no simultaneous submissions. Cover letter is required. "If there are graphics in poem, include an explanation of how the graphics should be reproduced." Reads submissions June-August. Time between acceptance and publication is up to 4 months. Never comments on rejected poems. Responds in 1 week. Pays 1 contributor's copy. Acquires first North American serial rights.
Advice: "Do not send any submissions using profanity. All experimental poetry, including experimental lyricism are read and considered thoughtfully."

VOICES ISRAEL (Specialized: anthology); REUBEN ROSE POETRY COMPETI-TION; MONTHLY POET'S VOICE (Specialized: members), P.O. Box 661, Metar Israel 85025. Phone: 972-7-6519118. Fax: 972-7-6519119. E-mail: aschatz@bgumail.bgu.ac.il. Website: members.tripod .com/~VoicesIsrael. Established 1972. **Editor-in-Chief:** Amiel Schotz; with an editorial board of 7.
Magazine Needs: "*Voices Israel* is an annual anthology of poetry in English coming from all over the world. You have to buy a copy to see your work in print. Submit all kinds of poetry (up to 4 poems), each no longer than 40 lines, in seven copies." Has published poetry by Yehuda Amichai, Hsi Muren, Alexander Volovick, Péter Kántor, and Ada Aharoni. As a sample the editor selected these lines from "Milk" by Orit Perlman:

> I want to marry a goat man/with jitter in his socks and drums in his hip/with saffron in his curls and
> sun/and blue blue wind in his eye/and crime on his teeth when he smiles.

Voices Israel is approximately 121 pages, 6½×9⅜, offset from laser output on ordinary paper, flat-spined with varying cover. Press run is 350. Subscription: $15. Sample back copy: $10. Contributor's copy: $15 airmail. "All money matters—including $35 annual membership—must be handled by the treasurer, Mel Millman, 15 Shachar St., Jerusalem, Israel 96263."
How to Submit: Accepts previously published poems, "but please include details and assurance that copyright problems do not exist." No simultaneous submissions. Accepts e-mail submissions with attachment. Cover letter with brief biographical details required with submissions. Deadline: end of November; responds as per receipt.
Also Offers: Sponsors the annual Reuben Rose Poetry Competition. Prizes: $300, $150, $100, and $50 as well as honorable mentions. Published and distributed together with the *Voices Israel* anthology as separate booklet. Send poems of up to 40 lines each, plus $5/poem to P.O. Box 236, Kiriat Ata, Israel. Poet's name and address should be on a separate sheet with titles of poems. *The Monthly Poet's Voice*, a broadside edited by Ezra Ben-Meir, is sent only to members of the Voices Group of Poets in English.
Advice: "We would like to see more humorous but well constructed poetry. We like to be surprised."

VOICINGS FROM THE HIGH COUNTRY; HIGH COUNTRY WORD CRAFTERS, 4920 South Oak St., Casper WY 82601. Established 2000. **Editor:** Ella J. Cvancara.
Magazine Needs: *Voicings from the High Country* appears annually in the spring. Accepts "poetry with substance, not just pretty words; understandable, rather than obscure; poetry that goes beyond the self. The editor is biased toward free verse that is worldly rather than introspective, tells a story, and uses many/most/all of the five senses. Also accepts haiku for a haiku page. No rhyming, pornography, violent language, 'Hallmark' verse, political poems, or overtly religious poetry. No poetry that's unsure of why it was written, is demeaning to the human spirit, or untitled." Recently published poetry by Alan M. Cvancara, Elsie Pankowski, John Parbst, and Ellen Vayo. As a sample the editor selected these lines from "High Land Grave" by Ginny Jack Palumbo:

> Summer rains sparkle/red on wildflower lips/bruised sage perfumes/still evening air as/coyotes cry a
> lullaby//Where she lies

Voicings from the High Country is 35-40 pages, digest-sized, computer-generated, stapled, 110 lb. cardstock cover, with in-house artistic photography. Receives about 50 poems/year, accepts about 50%. Publishes about 25 poems/issue. Press run is 50 of which 25 are shelf sales; 25 distributed free to contributors. Single copy: $4. Make checks payable to Ella J. Cvancara.

How to Submit: Submit 3 poems at a time. Accepts previously published poems; no simultaneous submissions. No fax, e-mail, or disk submissions. Cover letter is required with a 3-5 line biography. "Submit each poem on a separate page with name/address in upper right corner; typed or computer-generated; 35 lines or less; include a SASE for a response." Reads submissions July 1 through February 1 *only*. Submit seasonal poems 3 months in advance. Time between acceptance and publication is 3 months. "Poems are circulated to a 3-member editorial board with the names of the poets removed. They are ranked according to a ranking system." Seldom comments on rejected poems. Guidelines available for SASE. Responds in 6 months. Pays 1 contributor's copy. Acquires one-time rights.

Advice: "Beginners often write about themselves. Reach beyond yourself, avoid clichés, search for fresh language. Use metaphor and simile. Strike a spark with words. Nothing is off limits to the poet."

○ **VOIDING THE VOID**, % E.E. Lippincott, 8 Henderson Place, New York NY 10028. (718)267-6418. E-mail: eelipp@aol.com. Website: www.voidingthevoid.com (includes writer's guidelines, contact and subscription information, editorial policy, bios, archives, upcoming themes, special events, all back issues as well as the main display of the current issue of the hard copy). Established 1997. **Editor-in-Chief:** E. E. Lippincott.

Magazine Needs: *Voiding The Void* is "a monthly existential-esque reader." Their poetry needs are "very open, if author feels the work is in keeping with *Voiding The Void*'s themes of 'tangibility' and/or amusement value." Has published poetry by Bryon Howell, Sue Batterton, and Paul D. McGlynn. As a sample the editor selected these lines by Charles O'Hay:

> It is better to do one thing catastrophically/than to do a hundred acceptably./Disaster/done well/can
> set the experts chattering for decades

Voiding The Void appears both on hard copy (b&w, 8-page tabloid format) and on the web. Receives about 1,000 poetry submissions/year, accepts about 50%. First press run is about 150 for about 100 subscribers. Single copy: 1 first-class stamp; subscription: $8/year. Make checks payable to E.E. Lippincott.

How to Submit: Submit up to 5 poems at a time. Accepts simultaneous submissions. Accepts e-mail (as attachment or in text box) and disk submissions; include full name and postal address. Cover letter preferred. Time between acceptance and publication is up to 6 months. Always comments on rejected poems. Occasionally publishes theme issues. Guidelines available for SASE and on website. Responds in 2 months. Pays 4 copies. Acquires one-time rights. Reviews books of poetry. Poets may send books for review consideration.

○ **VOODOO SOULS QUARTERLY**, P.O. Box 4117, Lawrence KS 66046. E-mail: sayers@hometc. com. Established 2000. **Editor:** Meredith Sayers.

Magazine Needs: *Voodoo Souls Quarterly* is "a place where quality writing—poetry, essays, and short fiction—can find a home, regardless of the fame of its author. I've no real inclination toward a particular school of poetry. To be accepted, it will need to be precise, meaningful, and possess a sense of its own power. Innovation and clarity are appreciated." Does not want "inspirational, gratuitously violent, watered-down, imitations, or just plain poorly-written." Accepts poetry written by children. Recently published poetry by Simon Perchik, Jill Atherton, Alan Britt, Anne Gatschet, Stephen Meats, and Paul B. Roth. As a sample the editor selected these lines from "Loretta" by Anne Gatschet:

> each final dispersion where silence regains you/will wake me with night cries for nipples,/i'll call up
> your name again tiny Loretta/and the hollow compartment will shift/to the fluttering sound of your r.

Voodoo Souls Quarterly is 20-40 pages, digest-sized, high-quality photocopied, saddle-stapled, cardstock cover with b&w art/graphics. Receives about 100 poems/year, accepts about 50%. Publishes about 5-10 poems/issue. Press run is 50 for 10 subscribers of which 1 is a library, 30 shelf sales; 10 are distributed free to contributors. Single copy: $4; subscription: $12. Sample: $4. Make checks payable to Meredith Sayers.

How to Submit: Submit 3-5 poems at a time. No previously published poems or simultaneous submissions. No fax, e-mail, or disk submissions. Cover letter is preferred. "Include SASE and bio. Please tell a bit about yourself—not just your publications!" Reads submissions year round. Submit seasonal poems 6 months in advance. Time between acceptance and publication is 3-6 months. Often comments on rejected poems. Guidelines are available in magazine and for SASE. Responds in 3 months. Always sends prepublication galleys. Pays 1

WAIT! Don't mail your submission or correspondence without enclosing a SASE (self-addressed stamped envelope). If sending outside your own country, include SAE and IRCs (International Reply Coupons) instead.

contributor's copy. "Any submission without SASE will not be read or returned. Submission is considered permission to publish in *VSQ*. Rights revert to authors upon publication." Reviews books and chapbooks of poetry in single book format. Poets may send books for review consideration to Meredith Sayers.

Advice: "Put your ego on the line and send what you love. Don't bother checking popular literary mags to see if you're following the current trend. Set your own!"

N ○ ◎ VORTEX OF THE MACABRE; DARK GOTHIC (Specialized: horror, vampires, magical/occult themes), 1616 E. Barringer St., Philadelphia PA 19150-3304. E-mail: serae37378@yahoo.com. Established 1996. **Editor/Publisher:** Ms. Cinsearae S.

Magazine Needs: Publishes two biannual magazines, *Dark Gothic* and *Vortex of the Macabre*. "*Dark Gothic* is a vampire-themed zine of dark, erotic, and romantic poetry, art, and short stories. *Vortex of the Macabre* publishes weird, insane, gross poetry and art, reviews, and short-short stories. If it's twilight-zoneish, tales from the crypt-ish, insane, kooky, or just plain weird, I want it! Freestyle, prose, it doesn't matter since poetry is an art. No line limits here. No fuzzy-bunny stuff!" Has published poetry by Missy Spaulding, Mary Louise Westbrook, Rose Devi, William P. Robertson, C. David Hay, and Douglas M. Stokes. As a sample the editor selected this untitled piece by Scott Falk:

> The moon is covered in blood/And so is Mother Earth/The heavens are raining flaming/stars/That
> explode upon Mother's face/The angel of Death is/hard at work/as man's reign comes to a/violent end.

The publications are 10-20 pages (*Dark Gothic*), 20-25 pages (*Vortex of the Macabre*), 8½ × 11, photocopied and side-stapled with b&w paper cover, includes "art of an eerie or morbid tone," also ads. Receives about 80-90 poems/year, accepts approximately 95%. Press run is 100. Subscription: $14 for both, otherwise $9 for *Vortex of the Macabre*, $6 for *Dark Gothic*. Sample: $4.50 for *Vortex of the Macabre*, $3 for *Dark Gothic*. Make checks payable to Ms. Cinsearae S. "Purchase of copy is strongly encouraged. I sometimes get things too grossly obscene and almost criminal sounding! Also, contributors must send SASE with any works."

How to Submit: Submit 5 poems at a time. Accepts previously published poems and simultaneous submissions. Accepts submissions by e-mail (as attachment or in text box) or on disk. Cover letter preferred. "Poems should be single-spaced, as well as any short stories submitted to *Dark Gothic*. Send 'friendly' cover letter about you; I don't care all that much about your 'credentials.' " Time between acceptance and publication is 5 months. Often comments on rejected poems. Publishes theme issues occasionally. "Currently looking for art, poetry, and short stories of an erotic nature for special edition (fall 2003) of *Dark Gothic*." Guidelines and upcoming themes available for SASE and by e-mail. Responds in 3 months. Pays 1 copy. Acquires one-time rights. Reviews books and chapbooks of poetry and other magazines in up to 174 words. Poets may send books for review consideration to the editor, % *Vortex of the Macabre* only.

Advice: "Don't give up! If writing is your one time love, persue it! Don't give it up for anyone or anything. Believe in yourself and your work. No one has the power to make you happy but you."

◎ VQONLINE (Specialized: volcanoes and volcanology), 8009 18th Lane SE, Lacey WA 98503. (360)455-4607. E-mail: jmtanaka@webtv.net. Website: http://community.webtv.net/JMTanaka/VQ (includes contact information, bios, links, editorial policy). Established 1992. **Editor:** Janet M. Cullen Tanaka.

Magazine Needs: *VQOnline* is an "interest" publication for professional and amateur volcanologists and volcano buffs. Wants "any kind of poetry as long as it is about volcanoes and/or the people who work on them." Does not want "over-emotive, flowery stuff or anything not directly pertaining to volcanoes." Accepts poetry written by children. Has published poetry by Dane Picard and C. Martinez. As a sample the editor selected these lines from "Farewell Observatory" by C. Scarpinati, translated from Italian by Claude Grandpey:

> A coat of fire shrouded your shoulders/and your sides, as tho' you were cold./Your masks, walls of
> iron/didn't collapse.

Free on the Internet, no subscription costs.

How to Submit: Submit any number of poems. Accepts previously published poems with permission of the original copyright holder and simultaneous submissions. Accepts disk (ASCII compatible) and e-mail submissions (in body of message). Time between acceptance and publication is 6 months. Always comments on rejected poems. "I try not to outright reject, preferring to ask for a rewrite." Guidelines available for SASE, by e-mail, or on website. Responds in 1 month. Pays up to 5 copies. "Contributors may copyright in the usual fashion. But there is as yet no mechanism on the Internet to keep users honest. We also need written permission to publish on the Internet." Reviews books or chapbooks of poetry or other magazines by guest reviewers. Poets may send books for review consideration if they are about volcanoes.

Advice: "I want to concentrate on the positive aspects of volcanoes—gifts from God, 'partners' in creation, resources, beauty, awe, etc."

⊘ WAKE UP HEAVY (WUH); WAKE UP HEAVY PRESS, P.O. Box 4668, Fresno CA 93744-4668. E-mail: wuheavy@yahoo.com. Established 1998. **Editor/Publisher:** Mark Begley.

Magazine Needs: *Wake Up Heavy* is not currently publishing magazine issues, nor accepting submissions for the magazine. The first 4 issues of *Wake Up Heavy* included poetry/prose by Laura Chester, Wanda Coleman, Fielding Dawson, Edward Field, Michael Lally, and Diane Wakoski. "These out-of-print issues are available through the Web at www.abebooks.com. Many of the poems published have been reprinted in major collections by these authors, most notably three poems by Wanda Coleman that originally appeared in the premier issue of the magazine, and were later reprinted in her National Book Award nominated book *Mercurochrome* (Black Sparrow Press, 2001). Any other questions about future magazine publications should be sent to the above e-mail address."

How to Submit: *Wake Up Heavy* **is not currently accepting submissions of any kind, and the magazine has been halted indefinitely.**

Book/Chapbook Needs & How to Submit: "Chapbooks and broadsides by single authors have become our main focus. Wake Up Heavy Press has published chapbooks/pamphlets of single poems (Michael Lally's long, prose poem *¿Que Pasa Baby?*; Diane Wakoski's *Trying to Convince Robert* and *Inviting John & Barbara*), groups of poems, stories (Wanda Coleman's *Crabs for Breakfast*; Fielding Dawson's *The Dirty Blue Car* and *Backtalk*), memoirs (Wanda Coleman's Pushcart Prize-nominated *Love-ins with Nietzsche*), and chapters from novels (Laura Chester's *Kingdom Come*)." Wake Up Heavy Press publishes 2-3 chapbooks/pamphlets per year. Chapbooks/pamphlets are usually copied/offset-printed, saddle-stapled, heavy cover stock, some contain drawings or photos, and most include a signed/numbered edition. "Again, these titles are available via the Web at www.abebooks.com. Also, you can e-mail about upcoming publications/the availability of past ones. Chapbooks, pamphlets, and broadsides are *strictly from solicitations. Please do not send mss for these publications.*" Wake Up Heavy Press pays authors in copies, 50% of the press run, which is usually between 130-200 copies. Inquire about samples at the above e-mail address.

◻ **WARTHOG PRESS**, 29 South Valley Rd., West Orange NJ 07052. (973)731-9269. Established 1979. **Poetry Editor:** Patricia Fillingham.

Book/Chapbook Needs: Warthog Press publishes paperback books of poetry "that are understandable, poetic." Has published *From the Other Side of Death* by Joe Lackey; *Wishing for the Worst* by Linda Portnay; *Enemies of Time* by Donald Lev; and *Hanging On* by Joe Benevento.

How to Submit: Query with 5 samples, cover letter, and SASE. "A lot of the submissions I get seem to be for a magazine. I don't publish anything but books." Accepts simultaneous submissions. Ms should be "readable." Comments on rejected poems, "if asked for. People really don't want criticism."

Advice: "The best way to sell poetry still seems to be from poet to listener."

🌐 ◻ ◎ **WASAFIRI (Specialized: ethnic/nationality)**, Dept. of English, Queen Mary, University of London, Mile End Rd., London E1 4NS United Kingdom. Phone/fax: +44 020 7882 3120. E-mail: wasafiri@qmw.ac.uk. Website: www.english.qmw.ac.uk/wasafiri. Established 1984. **Editor:** Susheita Nasta. **Managing Editor:** Richard Dyer.

Magazine Needs: *Wasafiri*, published triannually, "promotes new writing and debate on African, Asian, Caribbean, and associated literatures." Wants "African, Asian, Caribbean, diaspora, post-colonial, innovative, high-quality poetry." Has published poetry by Vikram Seth, Fred D'Aguiar, Marlene Nourbese Philip, and Kamau Brathwaite. *Wasafiri* is 80 pages, A4, professionally-printed on coated stock, perfect-bound, with full color glossy cover, graphics, photos, and ads. Receives about 350 poems/year, accepts about 30%. Press run is 1,500 for 1,000 subscribers of which 450 are libraries, 300 shelf sales; 50 distributed free to arts council literature panel and education board. Single copy: $14; subscription: £18 individuals; £30 institutions/overseas. Sample: £5; £6 overseas.

How to Submit: Submit 3 poems at a time. No simultaneous submissions. Cover letter required. Accepts disk submissions (Word or WordPerfect). Time between acceptance and publication is 6-12 months. Poems are circulated to an editorial board. "Poems are considered by the editor and managing editor. Where guest editors are involved, poetry is considered by them also. Associate editors with expertise are asked to participate also." Often comments on rejected poems. Publishes theme issues. Guidelines and upcoming themes available for SASE, by e-mail, or on website. Themes for future issues include "Travel Writing" and "African Literature." Responds in up to 6 months. Sometimes sends prepublication galleys. Pays 1 copy. Acquires all rights. Returns rights with editor's permission. Reviews books or chapbooks of poetry or other magazines. Poets may send books for review consideration.

◖ **WASHINGTON SQUARE, A JOURNAL OF THE ARTS**, 19 University Place, Third Floor, New York University Graduate Creative Writing Program, New York NY 10003. E-mail: wsmgr@hotmail. com. Website: www.nyu.edu/gsas/program/cwp/wsr.htm. Established 1994 as *Washington Square* (originally established in 1979 as *Ark/Angel*). **Editor:** Ben Rhodes. **Contact:** Jennifer Chapis.

Magazine Needs: Published in December and May, *Washington Square* is "a non-profit literary journal publishing fiction, poetry and essays by new and established writers. It's edited and produced by the students of the NYU Creative Writing Program." Wants "all poetry of serious literary intent." Has published poetry by Rosmarie Waldrop, James Tate, Barbara Guest, Fanny Howe, Alberto Rios, and Russell Edson. *Washington Square* is 150 pages. Press run is 2,000. Subscription: $12. Sample: $6.

How to Submit: Submit up to 6 poems at a time. Accepts simultaneous submissions if noted. Time between acceptance and publication is up to 6 months. Poems are circulated to an editorial board. "The poetry editors and editorial staff read all submissions, discuss and decide which poems to include in the journal." Sometimes comments on rejected poems. Guidelines available for SASE, by e-mail, or on website. Responds in up to 6 weeks. Pays 2 copies. Acquires first North American serial rights. Sometimes reviews books and chapbooks of poetry and other magazines in 300 words. Poets may send books for review consideration.

⊘ **WATER MARK PRESS**, 138 Duane St., New York NY 10013. Established 1978. **Editor:** Coco Gordon. Currently does not accept any unsolicited poetry.

 • Note: Please do not confuse Water Mark Press with the imprint Watermark Press, used by other businesses.

N ◑ **WATERBEARER PRESS; ABOVE WATER**, 12549 Genesee St., Alden NY 14004. (716)937-7732. E-mail: waterbearerpress@hotmail.com. Website: www.waterbearerpress.com (includes Featured Artist: brief bio, photo, poem; bookstore; news/events, i.e., poetry readings). Established 2000. **Editor-in-Chief:** Tam'e Gardner.

Magazine Needs: *Above Water* is a bimonthly newsletter containing comments from the editor, upcoming events, a Featured Artist section, articles, and coffeehouse reviews. No limitations to form or content. Artists are "free to express as they see fit." Recently published poetry by Tam'e Gardner, Brian A. Menzies, and Raymond L. Waldron. *Above Water* is about 6 pages, magazine-sized, desktop-published, stapled, with photography. Publishes about 1 poem/issue. Subscription: $6.50/12 months (6 editions). First copy (sample) is complimentary. Make checks payable to Waterbearer Press.

How to Submit: Accepts previously published poems and simultaneous submissions. No fax, e-mail, or disk submissions. Cover letter is preferred. Reads submissions upon receipt. Time between acceptance and publication is within 1 year. Editor reviews all poetry and decides "if it will be published and when and where (newsletter, website)." Always comments on rejected poems. May publish theme issues. Responds in 2 weeks. "We send a proof and then the artist receives a complimentary copy of the newsletter they are published in." Acquires one-time rights.

Book/Chapbook Needs & How to Submit: Waterbearer Press mainly publishes poetry and short stories by beginning artists in all genres. "We are also interested in artwork such as painting and photography." Publishes 2 titles/year; format depends on what artist wants. "We work with the artist to determine goals and try to best reach them." Query first, with a few sample poems and cover letter with brief bio and publication credits. Responds to queries and mss in 2 weeks. Pays royalties "yet to be determined."

Advice: "Waterbearer Press is specifically designed to assist authors of poetry and short stories, as well as support artists who paint, draw, or utilize photography or other means for expression. Our goal is to work *with* the artist to accomplish *their* goals."

◐ ◎ **WATERWAYS: POETRY IN THE MAINSTREAM (Specialized: themes); TEN PENNY PLAYERS (Specialized: children/teen/young adult); BARD PRESS**, 393 St. Paul's Ave., Staten Island NY 10304-2127. (718)442-7429. E-mail: tenpennyplayers@SI.RR.com. Website: www.tenpennyplayers.org (contains "material from our publication, programs, curriculum"). Established 1977. **Poetry Editors:** Barbara Fisher and Richard Spiegel.

Magazine Needs: Ten Penny Players "publishes poetry by adult poets in a magazine [*Waterways*] that is published 11 times/year. We do theme issues and are trying to increase an audience for poetry and the printed and performed word. The project produces performance readings in public spaces and is in residence year round at the New York public library with workshops and readings. We publish the magazine *Waterways*, anthologies, and chapbooks. We are not fond of haiku or rhyming poetry; never use material of an explicit sexual nature. We are open to reading material from people we have never published, writing in traditional and experimental poetry forms. While we do 'themes,' sometimes an idea for a future magazine is inspired by a submission so we try to remain open to poets' inspirations. Poets should be guided however by the fact that we are children's and animal rights advocates and are a NYC press." Has published poetry by Ida Fasel, Albert Huffstickler, Joy Hewitt Mann, and Will Inman. *Waterways* is 40 pages, 4¼×7, photocopied from various type styles, saddle-stapled, using b&w drawings, matte card cover. Uses 60% of poems submitted. Press run is 150 for 58 subscribers of which 12 are libraries. Subscription: $25. Sample: $2.60.

How to Submit: Submit less than 10 poems for first submission. Accepts simultaneous submissions. Accepts e-mail submissions (in text box). Guidelines for approaching themes are available for SASE. "Since we've taken the time to be very specific in our response, writers should take seriously our comments and not waste their emotional energy and our time sending material that isn't within our area of interest. Sending for our theme sheet and for a sample issue and then objectively thinking about the writer's own work is practical and wise. Manuscripts that arrive without a return envelope are not sent back." Editors sometimes comment on rejected poems. Responds in less than a month. Pays 1 copy. Acquires one-time publication rights.

Book/Chapbook Needs & How to Submit: Chapbooks published by Ten Penny Players are "by children and young adults only—*not by submission*; they come through our workshops in the library and schools. Adult poets are published through our Bard Press imprint, *by invitation only.* Books evolve from the relationship we develop with writers we publish in *Waterways* and whom we would like to give more exposure."

Advice: "We suggest that poets attend book fairs and check our website. It's a fast way to find out what we are publishing. Without meaning to sound 'precious' or unfriendly, the writer should understand that small press publishers doing limited editions and all production work inhouse are working from their personal artistic vision and know exactly what notes will harmonize, effectively counterpoint and meld. Many excellent poems are sent back to the writers by *Waterways* because they don't relate to what we are trying to create in a given month."

● WAVELENGTH: A MAGAZINE OF POETRY, 1753 Fisher Ridge Rd., Horse Cave KY 42749-9706. Established 1999. **Editor/Publisher:** David P. Rogers.

Magazine Needs: *Wavelength: A Magazine of Poetry* appears 3 times/year. "We want poems approximately 30 lines or less that use lively images, intriguing metaphor, and original language. Rhyme is almost always a liability. All subjects and styles considered as long as the poem is thought-provoking or uses language in an innovative way. Prose poems are fine." Does not want "rhymed, very religious—anything that sacrifices creativity for convention." Recently published poetry by Robert Cooperman, Lyn Lifshin, Francis Blessington, Ann Taylor, Albert Haley, and Virgil Suarez. As a sample the editor selected these lines from "Dandelions Grow Behind My Tongue" by Lucille Gang Shulkapper:

> *Yellow flowers fill/my mouth and speak/to me of truth*

Wavelength is 35 pages, digest-sized, laser-printed, perfect-bound with heavy cardstock cover and cover illustration. Receives about 450 poems/year, accepts 15-20%. Publishes about 30 poems/issue. Press run is 150 for 25 subscribers, 20-25 shelf sales; 100 distributed free to the public. Single copy: $6; subscription: $15. Sample: $6. Make checks payable to Dr. David P. Rogers.

How to Submit: Submit 1-10 poems at a time. Line length for poetry is 30 maximum. No previously published poems or simultaneous submissions. No e-mail or disk submissions. Cover letter is preferred. "SASE or no response. Brief bio preferred. Poet's name and address must appear on every page. Poets who want poems returned should include sufficient postage." Submit seasonal poems 3 months in advance. Time between acceptance and publication is up to 1 year. Poems are circulated to an editorial board. "Read and write every day. We like to publish new and young poets." Seldom comments on rejected poems. Responds in 4 months. Pays 1 copy. Acquires one-time rights. Reviews books and chapbooks of poetry in 100-150 words, single book format. Poets may send books/chapbooks for review consideration to David P. Rogers.

Advice: "Read and write every day. If a poem still seems good a year after you wrote it, send it out. Be original. Say something but what will the *reader* get out of it? Send up to ten poems, SASE or no response."

□ WAY STATION MAGAZINE, 1319 South MLK, Lansing MI 48910-1340. E-mail: waystationmag @msn.com. Established 1989. **Managing Editor:** Randy Glumm. **Guest Editor:** Robin Lynch.

Magazine Needs: *Way Station*, published occasionally, strives "to provide access and encourage beginning writers, while courting the established." Wants "emerging cultures, world view, humanity direction, relationships—try all. No rhyme unless truly terrific." Does not want "religious or openly militant gay or lesbian poetry. Use common sense and discretion." Has published poetry by Charles Bukowski, Diane Wakoski, Stuart Dybek, Ethridge Knight, and Terri Jewell. *Way Station* is 7 × 8½, offset-printed, saddle-stapled, heavy card cover, with b&w art, photos, and ads. Receives about 300 poems/year, accepts 20-30%. Press run is 1,000 for 35 subscribers of which 2 are libraries, 200 shelf sales; 500 distributed free to potential advertisers, readers, libraries, and universities. Subscription: $18. Sample: $6.

How to Submit: Submit 5 poems with name and address on each page and **$5 processing fee** (returned if work is rejected). Accepts previously published poems and simultaneous submissions. Cover letter preferred. Time between acceptance and publication is 2 months, sometimes longer. "If not struck immediately, I then put it aside and re-read later 3-4 times. I might also circulate it through a panel of volunteer readers." Often comments on rejected poems. Guidelines available for SASE. Responds in 2 months. Pays 2 contributor's copies. Acquires one-time or first North American serial rights. Reviews books or chapbooks of poetry or other magazines "if I have time." Poets may send books for review consideration.

Advice: "It's best to check out your own work. Get advice from coaches, instructors prior to submitting. Also get sample copies of magazines you intend to submit to—this can only help you."

⚫ WAYNE LITERARY REVIEW, % Dept. of English, Wayne State University, Detroit MI 48202. Established 1960. **Editor:** Richard Brixton.

Magazine Needs: *Wayne Literary Review* appears biannually. "Our philosophy is to encourage a diversity of writing styles. Send your favorites. If you like them, others probably will, too." Does not want "lack of craft, gratuitous sex and violence." As a sample the editor selected these lines from "The Picture in the Shoebox" by Ray McNiece:

> I remember just where I put it, only it's gone now./Nothing there but pinches of wood-rot spaced/across
> the floor, a wad of newspaper packing,/a bit of spider chaff on the one, square window,/and a blue
> bottle fly bouncing against the pane.

Wayne Literary Review is 75 pages, digest-sized. Receives about 1,000 poems/year, accepts about 5%. Publishes about 25 poems/issue. Press run is 500 which are distributed free to the public.

How to Submit: Submit 3 poems at a time. No previously published poems or simultaneous submissions. No fax, e-mail, or disk submissions. Cover letter is preferred. "Send SASE with proper postage." Reads submissions anytime. Submit seasonal poems 6 months in advance. Time between acceptance and publication is 6 months. Poems are circulated to an editorial board. Seldom comments on rejected poems. Guidelines are available for SASE. Responds in 3 months. Pays 2 contributor's copies. Acquires first North American serial rights.

☒ $⚫ WēBER STUDIES—VOICES AND VIEWPOINTS OF THE CONTEMPORARY WEST, 1214 University Circle, Weber State University, Ogden UT 84408-1214. (801)626-6473. E-mail: weberstudies@weber.edu. Website: http://weberstudies.weber.edu (contains electronic version of the magazine). Established 1983. **Editor:** Brad L. Roghaar.

● Poetry published here has appeared in *The Best American Poetry*.

Magazine Needs: *Wēber Studies* appears 4 times/year and publishes fiction, poetry, criticism, personal essays, nonfiction, and interviews. It is an interdisciplinary journal interested in relevant works covering a wide range of topics. Wants "three or four poems; we publish multiple poems from a poet." Does not want "poems that are flippant, prurient, sing-song, or preachy." Has published poetry by William Kloefkorn, Gailmarie Pahmeier, Mark Strand, Janet Sylvester, Ingrid Wendt, and Katharine Coles. As a sample the editor selected these lines from "Rhapsody for the Good Night" by David Lee:

> nightbird/and the hum of pickup tires/on hardscrabble/I listen//behind the mockingbird behind the
> wind/behind the sound a taproot makes/working its way down to water/past that I can hear them/they
> can hear me too/if they want to

Wēber Studies is 120 pages, 7½×10, offset-printed on acid-free paper, perfect-bound, with 2-3 color cover, occasional color plates and exchange ads (with other journals). Receives about 150-200 poems/year, accepts 30-40. Press run is 1,200 for 1,000 subscribers of which 90 are libraries. Subscription: $20, $20 institutions. Sample: $7-8.

How to Submit: Submit 3-4 poems, 2 copies of each (one without name). Accepts simultaneous submissions; no previously published poems. Cover letter preferred. Time between acceptance and publication is 15 months. Poems are selected by an anonymous (blind) evaluation. Seldom comments on rejected poems. Publishes theme issues. Upcoming themes and guidelines available for SASE, by e-mail, on website, or in publication. Responds in up to 6 months. Always sends prepublication galleys. Pays 2 copies and $20-25/page; depending on fluctuating grant monies. Acquires all rights. Copyright reverts to author after first printing.

Also Offers: Cash award given every three years for poems published in *Wēber Studies*. Only poetry published in *Wēber Studies* during 3-year interval considered.

Advice: "This journal is referred by established poets—beginners not encouraged."

⊠ $⚫ ◎ WEIRD TALES (Specialized: fantasy and horror), 123 Crooked Lane, King of Prussia PA 19406-2570. (610)275-4463. E-mail: owlswick@netaxs.com. Established 1923. **Editor:** George Scithers.

Magazine Needs: *Weird Tales* appears quarterly. Publishes "fantasy and horror fiction with some poetry on those subjects." Wants poetry touching on fantasy or horror, mostly serious. Some humor accepted including limericks and double dactyls. Does not want poetry on mundane subjects. *Weird Tales* is 52

pages, magazine-sized, offset-printed, saddle-stapled, process color cover, with art/graphics and ads. Receives about 120 poems/year, accepts about 10%. Publishes about 3 poems/issue. Press run is 10,000. Single copy: $4.95; subscription: $16. Sample: $5. Make checks payable to Terminus Publishing Co.
How to Submit: Submit up to 5 poems at a time. No previously published poems or simultaneous submissions. No fax, e-mail, or disk submissions. "Double line-space poems. Include author address on every poem." Time between acceptance and publication is very irregular. Poems are circulated to an editorial board. Very seldom comments on rejected poems. Very occasionally publishes theme issues. List of upcoming themes not available. Guidelines available for SASE or by e-mail. Responds in 2 months. Always sends prepublication galleys. Pays $1 or less/line and 2 contributor's copies. Acquires first North American serial rights.
Advice: "Follow standard manuscript format."

N Ⓓ Ⓒ THE WELL TEMPERED SONNET (Specialized: form/style), 87 Petoskey St., Suite 120, New Hudson MI 48165. E-mail: jamiet@ameritech.net. Established 1998. **Publisher/Editor:** James D. Taylor II.
Magazine Needs: "Appearing biannually, *The Well Tempered Sonnet* publishes only compositions in sonnet form and caters to those who love and appreciate the form Shakespeare made famous. No erotica, blasphemy, vulgarity, or racism." *The Well Tempered Sonnet* is magazine-sized, desktop-published and spiral-bound with attractive, heavy stock cover, sometimes includes art/graphics. Subscription: $20/year. Make checks payable to James Taylor. "We encourage submissions requesting subscriptions, details included in guidelines."
How to Submit: Submit 6 poems at a time. Accepts previously published poems; no simultaneous submissions. Accepts disk submissions; no e-mail submissions. Seldom comments on rejected poems. Publishes theme issues occasionally. Guidelines available for SASE. Responds ASAP. Always sends prepublication galleys.
Also Offers: "We encourage and try to provide the means for interaction between other sonnetiers."
Advice: "A well composed sonnet is a piece of art. Understanding word usage is important in the development of the sonnet, as important as colors to a painter."

Ⓓ Ⓒ WELLSPRING: A JOURNAL OF CHRISTIAN POETRY (Specialized: religious, spirituality/inspirational). E-mail: wellspring@poetrypages.com. Website: www.angelfire.com/wa2/wellspr ing (includes complete guidelines, author biographies, the editor's statement of faith, ABC's of salvation, contact information, *Wellspring* Award of Excellence). Established 1999. **Editor:** Deborah Beachboard.
Magazine Needs: "*Wellspring* is an online journal featuring quality Christian poetry by various authors. Poems are published on an ongoing basis. I am looking for poetry that touches every aspect of Christian living—from the worship of God to the activities of daily life. No pornography, no senseless violence, nothing New Age." Has published poetry by Peter Vetrano, Robert Christopher Lutman, Kenneth Young, Frederick Lewis Allen, Jane Hutto, and Paise Gray. As a sample the editor selected these lines from "A Farmer's Prayer" by Jane F. Hutto:

> Perhaps I'll go today, dear Lord,/A tramping 'cross some fresh-tilled soil,/Then sit beside a tree-lined
> stream/To contemplate Your graciousness,/And dream . . .

Accepts about 60% of poems received/year.
How to Submit: Submit 5 poems at a time. Accepts previously published poems and simultaneous submissions. Accepts e-mail submissions included in body of message. "Currently I am accepting submissions by e-mail only. When submitting, indicate it is for *Wellspring*. Include address and name with each poem submitted." Cover letter preferred. Submit seasonal poems 1 month in advance. Time between acceptance and publication is 1 month. Seldom comments on rejected poems. Guidelines available on website. Responds in 2 weeks. Sometimes sends prepublication galleys. Acquires one-time rights.
Advice: "Heartfelt poetry is wonderful, but quality poetry will show an understanding of the craft of poetry. Learn how to incorporate poetic device into your poetry even when writing free verse!"

N $ Ⓒ WESLEYAN UNIVERSITY PRESS, 110 Mt. Vernon, Middletown CT 06459. (860)685-2420. Established 1957. **Editor-in-Chief:** Suzanna Tamminen.
Book/Chapbook Needs: Wesleyan University Press is one of the major publishers of poetry in the nation. Publishes 4-6 titles/year. Has published poetry by James Dickey, Joy Harjo, James Tate, and Yusef Komunyakaa.
How to Submit: Query first with SASE. Considers simultaneous submissions. Guidelines available for SASE. Responds to queries in 2 months; to mss in 4 months. Pays royalties plus 10 copies. Poetry publications from Wesleyan tend to get widely (and respectfully) reviewed.

◯ **WEST ANGLIA PUBLICATIONS**, P.O. Box 2683, La Jolla CA 92038. **Editor:** Wilma Lusk.
Book Needs: West Anglia Publications wants only the best poetry and short stories and publishes 1 paperback/year. Wants "contemporary poems, well wrought by poets whose work has already been accepted in various fine poetry publications. This is not a press for beginners." Has published poetry by Gary Morgan, Robert Wintringer, and John Theobald. As a sample the editor selected this poem from *Sticks, Friction & Fire, Selected and New Poems, 2001* by Kathleen Iddings:

> Obedient as dogs/we stutter to the rimless surface./No smell of parsley or almond,/no slit of starlight/
> nor sheen of whispering stream.//A stereo fugue/shrieks like a dying dream./Wardens of the wind swing
> from a gibbett./locked in a cross-grained knot.

Books are usually 75-100 pages, 5½ × 8½, perfect-bound. Sample book: $10 plus $1.50 postage and handling.
How to Submit: Query with 6 poems, cover letter, professional bio, and SASE. Pays 50 copies.

$ ◯ **WEST BRANCH**, Bucknell Hall, Bucknell University, Lewisburg PA 17837-2123. E-mail: westb ranch@bucknell.edu. Website: www.departments.bucknell.edu/stadler_center/westbranch (includes guidelines, contact information, sample issues, links). Established 1977. **Editor:** Paula Closson Buck. **Managing Editor:** Andrew Ciotola. Member: CLMP.
Magazine Needs: Appearing biannually, *West Branch* is "an aesthetic conversation between the traditional and the innovative in poetry, fiction, and nonfiction. It brings writers, both new and established, to the rooms where they will be heard, and where they will, no doubt, rearrange the furniture." Wants "well-structured verse that is both formally interesting and emotionally engaging; both short lyric and longer meditative and narrative poetry. We are especially interested in prose poetry." No confessional, genre, workshop, or slam poetry; no greeting card verse. Has published poetry by Margaret Gibson, James Harms, Jim Daniels, Denise Duhamel, Wayne Dodd, and Katherine Soniat. As a sample the editor selected these lines from "A Frantic Ode to Anticipation" by Barbara O'Dair:

> There's the moment,/and then there's what's to the side,/out of the moment, maybe even deferring it,/
> creating a sensitive circle around it, so charged/it comes to stand for it/even when it's standing on it.

West Branch is 120 pages, digest-sized, press run 1,000. Subscription: $10/year, $16/2 years. Sample: $3.
How to Submit: Submit 3-6 poems. Simultaneous submissions accepted; "ASAP notification of publication elsewhere." No disk or e-mail submissions. Reads September through May only. Time between acceptance and publication is 4-6 months. Guidelines available for SASE, on website, or in publication. Responds within 1 month. Pays 3 copies and cash (payment always subject to grant funding). Acquires first rights. Rights revert to author on publication.
Advice: *West Branch* "publishes 3% of submissions—always send your best work."

Ⓝ ◯ **WEST WIND REVIEW**, 1250 Siskiyou Blvd., Ashland OR 97520. (541)552-6518. E-mail: westwind@student.sou.edu. Website: www.sou.edu/English (includes guidelines, contact information, and content from current anthology). Established 1980. **Contact:** Poetry Editor.
Magazine Needs: *West Wind Review* publishes an annual anthology each spring in May. "Looking for sensitive but strong verse that celebrates all aspects of men's and women's experiences, both exalted and tragic. We are looking to print material that reflects ethnic and social diversity." Has published poetry by Suzanne Burns, Mark Wisniewski, Casey Kwang, Virgil Suarez, Pamela Steed Hill, and Sean Brendan Brown. As a sample the editor selected these lines from "after the burnin moon" by Clarissa Armstrong:

> given to daydreams that make her go weak in the knees; of her/limbs wrapped 'round Rooney's back
> like writhing white snakes,/of pushing a carriage full of sky-eyed babies; and her/own secret garden
> of bushes budding paper money in Spring. Of/babies bawling soft as lambs in the wake of wet-woolen
> sleep

The anthology is usually 224 pages, digest-sized, handsomely printed and perfect-bound. Receives about 1,200 submissions/year, accepts approximately 50-60 poems, 10 short stories, and 16 pages of art. Press run is 500. Single copy: $12 plus $2 s&h.
How to Submit: Submit up to 5 poems. Manuscripts should have poet's name and address on first page only. Include SASE. No simultaneous submissions or previously published poems. No e-mail submissions. Cover letter required with name, address, phone number and a brief bio. Deadline: November 15 for publication in late May. Guidelines available for SASE or on website. Responds in March. Pays 1 copy.

◯ ◎ **WESTERN ARCHIPELAGO REVIEW; WESTERN ARCHIPELAGO PRESS (Specialized: ethnic/nationality, regional)**, P.O. Box 803282, Santa Clarita CA 91380. (213)383-3447. E-mail: adorxyz@aol.com. Established 1999. **Editor:** Jovita Ador Lee.
Magazine Needs: *Western Archipelago Review* "publishes verse with a focus on the civilizations of Asia and the Pacific. All types of verse considered." As a sample the editor selected these lines (poet unidentified):

> *Angel of Death, the High Priestess dances,/Turning in her silk;/Servant of the temple, covered in black robes,/Black cloth of Bali.*

Western Archipelago Review is 12 pages, 5½ × 8½, with glossy cover. Press run is 100. Subscription: $36. Sample: $7. Make checks payable to GoodSAMARitan Press

How to Submit: Submit 3 poems at a time. Accepts previously published poems and simultaneous submissions. Accepts e-mail and disk submissions. Cover letter with SASE required. Reads submissions September to June. Time between acceptance and publication is 6 weeks. Poems are circulated to an editorial board. Guidelines available for SASE. Responds in 6 weeks. Reviews books and chapbooks of poetry and other magazines in 100 words. Poets may send books for review consideration.

Book/Chapbook Needs & How to Submit: *Western Archipelago Review* publishes chapbooks and other monographs in the Western Archipelago series. The series is a resource for subscribers.

N Y $ ○ WESTERN HUMANITIES REVIEW, University of Utah, 255 S. Central Campus Dr., Room 3500, Salt Lake City UT 84112-0494. (801)581-6070. Fax: (801)585-5167. E-mail: whr@mail.hum. utah.edu. Website: www.hum.utah.edu/whr (includes guidelines, contact information, and bios). Established 1947. **Managing Editor:** Samantha Ruckman.

● Poetry published in this review has been selected for inclusion in the 1995 and 1998 volumes of *The Best American Poetry* as well as the 2002 *Pushcart Prize* anthology.

Magazine Needs: Appearing in April and October, *Western Humanities Review* is a semiannual publication of poetry, fiction, and a small selection of nonfiction. Wants "quality poetry of any form, including translations." Has published poetry by Philip Levine, Bin Ramke, Lucie Brock-Broido, Timothy Liu, and Pattiann Rogers. *Western Humanities Review* is 96-125 pages, 6 × 9, professionally printed on quality stock and perfect-bound with coated card cover. Receives about 900 submissions/year, accepts less than 10%, publish approximately 60 poets. Press run is 1,100 for 1,000 subscribers of which 900 are libraries. Subscription: $14 to individuals in the US. Sample: $8.

How to Submit: "We do not publish writer's guidelines because we think the magazine itself conveys an accurate picture of our requirements." Accepts simultaneous submissions; no previously published poems. No fax or e-mail submissions. Reads submissions October 1 through May 31 only. Time between acceptance and publication is 1-4 issues. Managing editor makes an initial cut then the poetry editor makes the final selections. Seldom comments on rejected poems. Occasionally publishes special issues. Responds in up to 6 months. Pays $5/published page and 2 copies. Acquires first serial rights.

Also Offers: Also offers an annual spring contest for Utah poets. Prize is $250.

○ WESTVIEW: A JOURNAL OF WESTERN OKLAHOMA, 100 Campus Dr., SWOSU, Weatherford OK 73096. (580)774-3168. Established 1981. **Editor:** Fred Alsberg.

Magazine Needs: *Westview* is a semiannual publication that is "particularly interested in writers from the Southwest; however, we are open to work of quality by poets from elsewhere. We publish free verse, prose poems and formal poetry." Has published poetry by Carolynne Wright, Miller Williams, Walter McDonald, Robert Cooperman, Alicia Ostriker, and James Whitehead. *Westview* is 64 pages, magazine-sized, perfect-bound, with glossy card cover in full-color. Receives about 500 poems/year, accepts 7%. Press run is 700 for 300 subscribers of which about 25 are libraries. Subscription: $10/2 years. Sample: $5.

How to Submit: Submit 5 poems at a time. Cover letter including biographical data for contributor's note requested with submissions. "Poems on 3.5 computer disk are welcome so long as they are accompanied by the hard copy and the SASE has the appropriate postage." Editor comments on submissions "when close." Mss are circulated to an editorial board; "we usually respond within two to three months." Pays 1 copy.

○ WHISKEY ISLAND MAGAZINE, English Dept., Cleveland State University, Cleveland OH 44115. (216)687-2056. Fax: (216)687-6943. E-mail: whiskeyisland@csuohio.edu. Website: www.csuohio.edu/whi skey_island ("provides writer's guidelines, contest information, a history of the publication, and an index."). Established 1968. Student editors change yearly. **Contact:** Poetry Editor.

Magazine Needs: *Whiskey Island* appears biannually in January and July and publishes poetry, fiction, nonfiction, and art. Wants "advanced writing. We want a range of poetry from standard to experimental and concrete poetry. Thought provoking." Has published poetry by Maj Ragain, E. Maxwell, Christopher Franke, Jim Lang, Ye Qin, and Doug Manson. As a sample the editor selected these lines from "Pigeon Bones & a Pair of Pants" by Ben Gulyas:

> *he is . . . in his dreams/a man, mad with the deep blue of wooden corners/under a high eclipse where moon & sun/make dark luminous love/he is a man mad with something that breaks him open/and makes him sing—*

Whiskey Island Magazine is 86-120 pages, 6×9, professionally printed and perfect-bound with glossy stock cover and b&w art. Receives 1,000-1,500 poetry mss/year, accepts 6%. Press run is 1,200 for 200 subscribers of which 20 are libraries, about 300 shelf sales. Subscription: $12, $20 overseas. Sample: $6. Make checks payable to *Whiskey Island Magazine*.

How to Submit: Submit up to 10 pages of poetry at a time. Include SASE for reply/ms return. Include name, address, e-mail, fax, and phone number on each page. No previously published poems or simultaneous submissions. Include cover letter with brief bio. Accepts fax and e-mail submissions for mss outside of US; send as Rich Text format (.RTF) or ASCII files. Reads submissions September through April only. "Poets may fax inquiries and work that runs a few pages (longer submissions should be mailed). They may e-mail requests for submission and contest information." Poems are circulated to an editorial committee. Guidelines available for SASE, by e-mail, in publication, or on website. Responds within 4 months. Pays 2 contributor's copies, and 1 year subscription.

Also Offers: Sponsors an annual poetry contest. 1st Prize: $300; 2nd Prize: $200; 3rd Prize: $100. Entry fee: $10. Entries accepted October 1 through January 31. Query regarding contest for 2002.

Advice: "Include SASEs and your name, address, and phone for reply. List contents of submission in a cover letter."

○ WHITE EAGLE COFFEE STORE PRESS; FRESH GROUND, P.O. Box 383, Fox River Grove IL 60021-0383. E-mail: wecspress@aol.com. Website: http://members.aol.com/wecspress. Established 1992.

Magazine Needs & How to Submit: *Fresh Ground* is an annual anthology, appearing in November, that features "some of the best work of emerging poets. We're looking for edgy, crafted poetry. Poems for this annual are accepted during May and June only."

Book/Chapbook Needs: White Eagle is a small press publishing 5-6 chapbooks/year. "Alternate chapbooks are published by invitation and by competition. Author published by invitation becomes judge for next competition." "Open to any kind of poetry. No censorship at this press. Literary values are the only standard. Generally not interested in sentimental or didactic writing." Has published poetry by Timothy Russell, Connie Donovan, Scott Lumbard, Linda Lee Harper, Scott Beal, and Jill Peláez Baumgaertner. As a sample the editors included these lines from "Volunteer" in *The Wide View* by Linda Lee Harper:

> *Her Head-Start students love her bosom plush as a divan./They celebrate and grieve there, noodle/*
> *their faces deeper, deeper, dangerous comfort./But she holds their fears close as if to absorb them/into*
> *her girth like calories from so much pasta,/each little rigatoni head, a child's dread allayed.*

Sample: $5.95.

How to Submit: Submit complete chapbook ms (20-24 pages) with a brief bio, 125-word statement that introduces your writing and $10 reading fee. Accepts previously published poems and simultaneous submissions, with notice. No e-mail submissions. Deadline: September 30. Guidelines available for SASE or on website. "Each competition is judged by either the author of the most recent chapbook published by invitation or by previous competition winners." Seldom comments on rejected poems. Responds 3 months after deadline. All entrants will receive a copy of the winning chapbook. Winner receives $200 and 25 copies.

Advice: "Poetry is about a passion for language. That's what we're about. We'd like to provide an opportunity for poets of any age who are fairly early in their careers to publish something substantial. We're excited by the enthusiasm shown for this press and by the extraordinary quality of the writing we've received."

○ WHITE HERON; WHITE HERON PRESS, P.O. Box 15259, San Luis Obispo CA 93406-5259. E-mail: whiteheron@mindspring.com. Established 1997. **Editor:** Kevin Hull.

Magazine Needs: *White Heron* is a biannual magazine. "We are interested in lyric poetry, vivid imagery, open form, natural landscape, philosophical themes but not at the expense of honesty and passion; model examples: Wendell Berry, Gabriela Mistral, and Issa." Has published poetry by Penny Harter, Bill Witherup, Joseph Duemer and Michael Hannon. As a sample the editor selected the poem "Creature" by Dark Cloud:

> *Tired, so tired, it feels later than it probably is,/the wild world hushed as though obedient to poetry/*
> *or a god who wishes to be free of form and worshippers,/free, even, of consciousness, this dubious*
> *sense of self./The owl stares into its sorcery . . ./something tender and fierce disguised as a bird*

White Heron Review is 30 pages, 8½×5½, professionally printed and saddle-stapled with card stock cover, sometimes includes art. Single copy: $6; subscription: $10.

How to Submit: Submit 4 poems at a time. Accepts previously published poems "by request only" and simultaneous submissions. Accepts submissions by e-mail (as attachment or in text box) and by postal mail. Time between acceptance and publication is up to 6 months. Seldom comments on rejected poems. Responds "within a week or two." Pays 1 contributor's copy.

Book/Chapbook Needs & How to Submit: White Heron Press also considers chapbook publication. "Each manuscript considered on its own merits, regardless of name recognition. Basic production costs variable. Query or send manuscript and I'll respond."

Advice: "Do the work. Get used to solitude and rejection."

WHITE PELICAN REVIEW, P.O. Box 7833, Lakeland FL 33813. Established 1999. **Editor:** Nancy J. Wiegel.

Magazine Needs: *White Pelican Review* is a biannual literary journal dedicated to publishing poetry of the highest quality. "Although a relatively new publication, *White Pelican Review* seeks to attract writing that goes beyond competency to truly masterful acts of imagination and language. To this end, the Lake Hollingsworth prize of $100 is offered to the most distinguished poem in each issue." Has published poetry by Trend Busch, Barbara Lefcowitz, Virgil Suarez, and Peter Meinke. As a sample the editor selected these lines from "Mary in the Garden" by Jackie Bartley:

> And here is the slug, strutting its inwardness,/blank, blind, deliberate//an organ devoted to the Braille
> of a day lily stem,/ . . . She runs a finger along its swollen back,/surprised by the tear that falls onto
> her wrist.

White Pelican Review is about 48 pages, digest-sized, photocopied from typescript and saddle-stapled with matte cardstock cover. Receives about 3,000 poems/year, accepts 3%. Press run is 250 for 100 subscribers of which 10 are libraries. Subscription: $8, sample: $4.

How to Submit: Submit 3-5 poems at a time. No previously published poems or simultaneous submissions. Cover letter and SASE required. "Please include name, address, telephone number, and e-mail address when available on each page. No handwritten poems." Time between acceptance and publication is 3 months. Poems are circulated to an editorial board which reviews all submissions. Seldom comments on rejected poems. Guidelines available for SASE. Responds in 6 months. Pays 1 contributor's copy. Acquires one-time rights.

WHITE PINE PRESS; THE WHITE PINE PRESS POETRY PRIZE, P.O. Box 236, Buffalo NY 14201. E-mail: wpine@whitepine.org. Website: www.whitepine.org (includes writer's guidelines, poetry contest guidelines, list of current, and backlist titles). Established 1973. **Editor:** Dennis Maloney. **Managing Director:** Elaine LaMattina.

Book/Chapbook Needs & How to Submit: White Pine Press publishes poetry, fiction, literature in translation, essays—perfect-bound paperbacks. "We accept unsolicited work *only* for our annual competition—the White Pine Poetry Prize—and work in translation. We are always open to submissions of poetry in translation." Competition awards $1,000 plus publication to a book-length collection of poems by a US author. Entry fee: $20. Deadline: December 31. Guidelines available for SASE. No e-mail submissions. Has published *If Not for These Wrinkles of Darkness* by Stephen Frech (winner of the White Pine Poetry Prize), *Always Filling, Always Full* by Margaret Chuls, *Miracles and Mortifications* by Peter Johnson (winner of the Academy of American Poets 2001 award).

TAHANA WHITECROW FOUNDATION; CIRCLE OF REFLECTIONS (Specialized: Native American, animals, nature, spirituality/inspirational), 2350 Wallace Rd. NW, Salem OR 97304. (503)585-0564. Fax: (503)585-3302. E-mail: tahana@open.org. Website: www.open.org/tahana (includes veterans page, alcohol/drug, mental health alert). Established 1987. **Executive Director:** Melanie Smith.

Magazine Needs & How to Submit: The Whitecrow Foundation conducts one spring/summer poetry contest on Native American themes in poems up to 30 lines in length. Deadline for submissions: May 31. No haiku, Seiku, erotic or porno poems. Fees are $3 for a single poem, $10 for 4. Winners, honorable mentions and selected other entries are published in a periodic anthology, *Circle of Reflections*. Winners receive free copies and are encouraged to purchase others for $6.95 plus $2 handling in order to "help ensure the continuity of our contests." As a sample Melanie Smith selected these lines from "Colors" by Karenne Wood:

> oh, child of earth and of/a thousand generations,/our faces are/alike; our colors//they are not wrong

No fax or e-mail submissions. Guidelines available for SASE.

Advice: "We seek unpublished Native American writers. Poetic expressions of full-bloods, mixed bloods, and empathetic non-Indians need to be heard. Future goals include chapbooks. Advice to new writers: Practice, practice, practice to tap into your own rhythm and to hone and sharpen material; don't give up."

WILD VIOLET, P.O. Box 39706, Philadelphia PA 19106-9706. E-mail: wildvioletmagazine@yahoo.com. Website: www.wildviolet.net (includes current issue, back issues, message board, mailing list sign-up). Established 2001. **Editor:** Alyce Wilson.

Magazine Needs: *Wild Violet* appears quarterly. "Our goal is to democratize the arts: to make the arts more accessible and to serve as a creative forum for writers and artists." Wants "poetry that is well crafted, that engages thought, that challenges or uplifts the reader. We have published free verse, haiku, and blank verse. If the form suits the poem, we will consider any form." Does not want "abstract, self-involved poetry; poorly managed form; excessive rhyming; self-referential poems that do not show why the speaker is sad, happy, or in love." Recently published poetry by Erik Kestler, Jules St. John, Sam Vaknin, Leanne Kelly, and Rich Furman. As a sample the editor selected these lines from "Mishwa" by Erik Kestler:

> *If you, daydreaming, got off at the wrong/stop, you could discover a new country/with bare trees that*
> *bend to cartoon shapes/against a dark gray wind,/churches solar in whiteness, and weird sisters/*
> *carrying shopping bags wide as sails through the streets.*

Wild Violet is published online with photos, artwork, and graphics. Accepts about 20% of work submitted. Publishes about 10-15 poems/issue.

How to Submit: Submit 3-5 poems at a time. Accepts simultaneous submissions; no previously published poems. Accepts e-mail submissions; no fax or disk submissions. Cover letter is preferred. "Include poem(s) in body of e-mail or send as a text or Microsoft Word attachment." Reads submissions year round. Submit seasonal poems 3 months in advance. Time between acceptance and publication is 3 months. "Decisions on acceptance or rejection are made by the editor. Contests are judged by an independent panel." Seldom comments on rejected poems; comments given if requested. Occasionally publishes theme issues. A list of upcoming themes and guidelines available by e-mail. Responds in up to 6 weeks. Pays by providing a bio and link on contributor's page. All rights retained by author. Reviews books and chapbooks of poetry in 250 words, single book format. Poets may send books/chapbooks for review consideration to Alyce Wilson, editor.

Also Offers: Holds a contest with first prize being $100 and publication in *Wild Violet*. **Entry fee:** $5. E-mail wildvioletmagazine@yahoo.com for full details.

Advice: "Read voraciously; experience life and share what you've learned. Write what is hardest to say; don't take any easy outs."

THE WILLIAM AND MARY REVIEW, Campus Center, College of William and Mary, P.O. Box 8795, Williamsburg VA 23187-8795. (757)221-3290. Established 1962. **Poetry Editor:** Philip Clark.

Magazine Needs: *The William and Mary Review* is a 120-page annual, appearing in May, "dedicated to publishing new work by established poets as well as work by new and vital voices." Has published poetry by Cornelius Eady, Amy Clampitt, Edward Field, Dan Bellm, Forrest Gander, and Walter Holland. *The William and Mary Review* is about 120 pages, 6×9, professionally printed on coated paper and perfect-bound with 4-color card cover, includes 4-color artwork and photos. Receives about 5,000 poems/year, accepts 12-15. Press run is 3,500. Has 250 library subscriptions, about 500 shelf sales. Sample: $5.50.

How to Submit: Submit 1 poem/page, batches of up to 6 poems addressed to Poetry Editors. Cover letter required; include address, phone number, e-mail address (if available), past publishing history, and brief bio note. Reads submissions September 1 through February 15 *only*. Responds in approximately 4 months. Pays 5 contributor's copies.

Advice: "Write accessible but crafted poetry. Random images, navel-gazing, and intentional obscurity don't usually work."

WILLOW SPRINGS, 705 W. First Ave., MS-1, Eastern Washington University, Spokane WA 99201. (509)623-4349. Fax: (509)623-4238. Established 1977. **Editor:** Christopher Howell.

Magazine Needs: "We publish quality poetry and fiction that is imaginative, intelligent, and has a concern and care for language. We are especially interested in translations from any language or period." Has published poetry by James Grabill, Michael Heffernan, Robert Gregory, and Patricia Goedicke. *Willow Springs*, a semiannual, is one of the most visually appealing journals being published. It is 128 pages, 6×9, professionally printed, flat-spined, with glossy 4-color card cover with art. Receives about 4,000 poems/year, accepts approximately 1-2%. Editors seem to prefer free verse with varying degrees of accessibility (although an occasional formal poem does appear). Press run is 1,500 for 700 subscribers of which 30% are libraries. Subscription: $11.50/year, $20/2 years. Sample: $5.50.

How to Submit: Submit September 15 through May 15 only. "We do not read in the summer months." Include name on every page, address on first page of each poem. Brief cover letter saying how many poems on how many pages preferred. No simultaneous submissions. Guidelines available for SASE. Responds in up to 3 months. Pays 2 copies plus a copy of the succeeding issue, others at half price, and cash when funds available. Acquires all rights. Returns rights on release. Reviews books of poetry and short fiction in 200-500 words.

Also Offers: Has annual poetry and fiction awards ($200 and $250 respectively) for work published in the journal.

Advice: "We like poetry that is fresh, moving, intelligent and has no spare parts."

WIND MAGAZINE; WIND PUBLICATIONS; JOY BALE BOONE POETRY AWARD; THE QUENTIN R. HOWARD CHAPBOOK PRIZE, P.O. Box 24548, Lexington KY 40524. (859)277-6849. E-mail: wind@wind.org. Website: http://wind.wind.org (includes examples of the maga-

"We liked the combination of the comic and the outrageous," says the editor of *Willow Springs* about Abigail Rorer's "Sir Sachwerell Proboscio-Pronuncii." The drawing appeared on the June 2001 cover, designed by Scott Poole of Eastern Washington University Press.

zine and its history, submission guidelines for the magazine and contests, literary links, and essential advice to beginning writers about avoiding literary scams and selecting worthwhile literary venues). Established 1971. **Editor:** Chris Green. **Poetry Editor:** Rebecca Howell.

Magazine Needs: *Wind Magazine* appears 3 times/year. "Using poetry, fiction, and nonfiction, *Wind* operates on the metaphor of neighborly conversation between writers about the differing worlds they live in. Founded in 1971 in rural Kentucky, *Wind* looks to bring the vision and skill of writers from all concerns and walks of life into dialogue." *Wind*'s goal is "to publish a wide scope of literary work from diverse communities. Hence, we believe that each piece must be evaluated on its own terms based on its context. As not all poets and communities in America are like ourselves, and context does not travel with a poem, if you need to explain the rhetoric of your piece, please do!" Recently published poetry by Jeannette Barnes, Vivian Shipley, Richard Hagne, Kim Bridgeford, Sandra Massburn, and Glenn J. Freeman. As a sample the editor selected these lines from "The Future as an Act of the Scissor" by Mark Taksa:

> *Memory of shears weights/her head. The future is a pruning,/she tells herself. If she can cut a flower/*
> *so that it grows, she can listen*

Wind is 100 pages, digest-sized, perfect-bound, with photo portraits and line illustrations. Receives about 3,000 poems/year, accepts about 1%. Publishes 15 poems/issue. Press run is 400 for 200 subscribers of which 75 are libraries, 100 shelf sales. Single copy: $6; subscription: $15/year or $25/2 years. Sample: $4.50. Make checks payable to *Wind*.

How to Submit: Submit up to 5 poems at a time. Accepts simultaneous submissions; no previously published poems. No e-mail or disk submissions. Cover letter is preferred. Include "a brief letter of introduction letting us know a little bit about your place in life and the world." Reads submissions year round. Time between acceptance and publication is 1-2 months. "Three staff readers review each manuscript. Poetry editor makes final selection." Comments on rejections "when near misses." Guidelines available for SASE. Responds in 4 months. Pays 1 contributor's copy and discount on extras. Acquires first North American serial rights. Reviews books of poetry and other magazines in 250-500 words, single books format. Poets may send books for review consideration to Chris Green, *Wind Magazine*.

Also Offers: Joy Bale Boone Poetry Award, $500, deadline: March 1st; The Quentin R. Howard Chapbook Prize, published as summer issue of magazine; $100 and 25 copies, deadline: October 31st. Guidelines available for SASE. Each issue of *Wind* also features a portrait of a community of writers. "We highlight literary communities in the greater Ohio Valley—anywhere from Indianapolis to Knoxville, from the Mississippi to the Appalachians. Write '*Wind:* Literary Community Portraits' for guidelines."

Advice: "Be honest and relentless. There are hundreds of different poetries being written in America. As a way of selecting the appropriate place to submit work, find the community to which your voice and vision belong. Want to read every poem in whatever journal you submit to, then read them and join the conversation."

N ☐ ◎ WINDHOVER: A JOURNAL OF CHRISTIAN LITERATURE (Specialized: religious), 900 College St., Box 8008, University of Mary Hardin-Baylor, Belton TX 76513. (254)295-4564. E-mail: dwnixon@umhb.edu. Established 1996. **Editor:** Donne Walker-Nixon.
Magazine Needs: *"Windhover* annually publishes poetry and fiction by writers of faith. We're open to all types of poetry. Nothing trite or didactic." Has published poetry by Walt McDonald, Marjorie Maddox, David Brendan Hopes, and Kelly Cherry. *Windhover* is 160 pages, magazine-sized, perfect-bound. Receives about 150 poems/year, accepts approximately 10%. Press run is 500 for 50 subscribers. Subscription: $8/year. Sample: $6. Make checks payable to *Windhover.*
How to Submit: Submit 4 poems at a time. Accepts simultaneous submissions; no previously published poems. Accepts e-mail and disk submissions only. "We work best with e-mail submissions." Time between acceptance and publication is 4 months. Poems are circulated to an editorial board by e-mail. "We send poems to members of the editorial board for advisement. If poems are sent via e-mail, response time is shorter." Often comments on rejected poems. Guidelines available for SASE or by e-mail. Responds in 4 months. Sometimes sends prepublication galleys. Pays 2 copies. Acquires one-time rights. Reviews books and chapbooks of poetry in 300 words, single book format. Open to unsolicited reviews. Poets may send books for review consideration.

◎ WINGS MAGAZINE, INC., E-mail: tomjones1965@juno.com. Website: www.thepoetspress.org/wings/. Established 1991. **Publisher/Poetry Editor:** Thomas Jones. **Associate Editor:** Pamela Malone.
Magazine Needs: *Wings* is an exclusively online publication. "We want to publish the work of poets who are not as widely known as those published in larger journals but who nevertheless produce exceptional, professional material. We also publish personal essays, fiction, and plays." Wants "poetry with depth of feeling. No jingly, rhyming poetry. Rhyming poetry must show the poet knows how to use rhyme in an original way. Poetry on any theme, 80 lines or less, any style." As a sample the editor has selected these lines from "The Southern Ocean" by Robert James Berry:

> The wind blusters big waves/Glacial spring is coming/If you listen to the ocean's measured voice/In
> the wide pale eyes of Wakatipu//Sky father and earth mother/are making footsteps on the sea

Receives about 500 poems/year. "No requirements, but we encourage poets to check out our website and get an idea of the kind of material we publish."
How to Submit: Submit up to 5 poems at a time. Accepts previously published poems but no simultaneous submissions. "We take submissions through e-mail only. Send e-mail to the above juno address. Copy and paste the poem and bio into the e-mail message. The bio should be five lines or less." Always responds to submissions. Guidelines available on website. Responds in 2 months. Staff reviews books and chapbooks of poetry in single book format. Send inquiries to pamwings@juno.com.
Also Offers: "Our needs are eclectic. Content can be on any topic as long as the poet shows mastery of subject matter and craft, as well as penetration into depths." Also, published a Best of Wings CD-ROM.
Advice: "We don't want doggerel. We want sincere, well-crafted work. Poetry has been reduced to second class status by commercial publishing, and we want to restore it to the status of fiction (novels) or plays."

◎ WISCONSIN REVIEW; WISCONSIN REVIEW PRESS, 800 Algoma Blvd., University of Wisconsin-Oshkosh, Oshkosh WI 54901. (920)424-2267. E-mail: wireview@yahoo.com. Established 1966.
Contact: Martin Brick or Andrew Osborne.
Magazine Needs: *Wisconsin Review* is published 3 times/year. "We like poems with vivid images and novel subject matter. Talk about something new, or at least talk in a very new way." Has published poetry by Virgil Suarez, Baron Wormser, Doug Flaherty, Len Roberts, and B.J. Buhrow. As a sample the editor selected these lines from "Rural Madness" by B.J. Buhrow:

> I believe/in rural madness./I mean, that insanity/fluorishes in the boonies. I mean, that each/hulk
> bouncing the baby's head like a ball on the floor above the/terrified babysitter is in/a farmhouse.

Wisconsin Review is 80-100 pages, 6×9, elegantly printed on quality white stock, glossy card cover with color art, b&w art inside. Receives about 1,500 poetry submissions/year, accepts about 75; 40-50 pages of poetry in each issue. Press run is 1,600 for 40 subscribers of which 20 are libraries. Single copy: $4; subscription: $10.
How to Submit: Submit mss September 15 through May 15. Offices checked bimonthly during summer. Submit up to 4 poems at a time, one poem/page, single-spaced with name and address of writer on each page. Accepts simultaneous submissions, but previously unsubmitted works preferable. Cover letter required; include brief bio. Mss are not read during the summer months. Guidelines available for SASE. Responds in up to 9 months. Pays 2 contributor's copies.

N $ ◎ ◎ A WISE WOMAN'S GARDEN (Specialized: women, psychic, humor, nature, love/romance/erotica, fantasy, spirituality), P.O. Box 403, Racine WI 53401-0403. (262)632-2373. Established 1994. **Editor:** Katus Hortus (a.k.a. Katarzyna Rygasiewicz).

Magazine Needs: *A Wise Woman's Garden* appears 8-10 times/year "to connect readers with nature, landscape, metaphor magicks, the four elements (earth, water, air, fire) witnessed to in heart and mind." Wants "medicine-shield balanced poetry. No extensive line lengths, first drafts, typos, grammar impossibles, bleep-bleep-expletives." Has published poetry by Antler, Jane Farrell, Harvey Taylor, DyAnne Korda, Catherine Cofell, and Elaine Cavanaugh. As a sample the editor selected these lines from "Happening By" by Alice Marie Tarnowski:

> *Never pass too quickly by/overlooking what may lie/nestling, half-hidden in the dunes,/tossed up from*
> *gardens of the deep/fused and fired by the sun,/enamelled with yellow, mauve, and purple dye*

A Wise Woman's Garden is 12-16 pages, 4¼×11, photocopied on colored paper, bound by hand, "corded 2-color classic 'J' book binder stitch," occasional sketches and cartoons. Press run is 450 for 70 subscribers; most distributed free through Racine and Kenosha WI coffeehouses, stores, soirees, and art galleries. Subscription: $22 regular; $17 libraries; $11 for poets accepted for printing. Sample (including guidelines): $2 in cash. "Issues are linked to sun-sign astrological imagery at month's beginning (example: March-Pisces). Please supply birthdate for appropriate astrological linkage."

How to Submit: Submit 3-7 poems at a time. Accepts previously published poems and simultaneous submissions. Cover letter preferred, with bio or "fantastickal anecdotes." Time between acceptance and publication is up to 18 months. Often comments on rejected poems. Guidelines available in publication. Responds in up to 1 year. Sometimes sends prepublication galleys. Pays $5/poem plus 10 copies. Acquires first or one-time rights.

Advice: "Earth is capitalized (sacral respect). Poems automatically rejected for using the word 'dirt.' 'Soil' is a living organism. Find the magicks in your regional landscape and sculpt-sing them with all your knack. Wisconsin readers are ever friendly and grateful."

N ◯ ◎ THE WISHING WELL (Specialized: membership, women/feminism, lesbian/bisexual), P.O. Box 178440, San Diego CA 92177-8440. (858)270-2779. E-mail: laddiewww@aol.com. Website: www.wishingwellwomen.com (includes guidelines, contact information, links, editorial policy, subscription information, and an encouraging introductory letter to women who love women). Established 1974. **Editor/Publisher:** Laddie Hosler.

Magazine Needs: Appearing bimonthly, *The Wishing Well* is a "contact magazine for women who love women the world over; members' descriptions, photos, letters and poetry published with their permission only; resources, etc., listed. I publish writings only for and by members so membership is required." 1-2 pages in each issue are devoted to poetry, "which can be up to 8" long—depending upon acceptance by editor, 3" width column." *The Wishing Well* is 7×8½, offset printed from typescript, with soft matte card cover. Circulation is 100 members, 200 nonmembers. A sample is available for $5. Membership in *Wishing Well* is $35 for 3-5 months, $60 for 5-7 months, $90 for 7-9 months, $120 for 15 months.

How to Submit: Membership includes the right to publish poetry, a self description (exactly as you write it), to have responses forwarded to you, and other privileges. Accepts e-mail submissions (if included in body of message) for members only. Personal classifieds section, 50¢/word for members and $1/word for nonmembers.

Also Offers: Website includes membership application and introductory letter describing membership with *The Wishing Well*.

◑ ◎ WOODLEY MEMORIAL PRESS (Specialized: regional), English Dept., Washburn University, Topeka KS 66621. (785)234-1032. E-mail: zzfleury@washburn.edu. Website: www.washburn.edu/reference/woodley-press (includes contact information, editorial policy, catalog bios, and writers' guidelines). Established 1980. **Editor:** Amy Fleury. **President:** Larry McGurn. **Manuscript Editor:** Denise Low.

Book/Chapbook Needs: Woodley Memorial Press publishes 1-2 flat-spined paperbacks/year, about half being collections of poets from Kansas or with Kansas connections, "terms individually arranged with author on acceptance of ms." Has published *Horsetail* by Donald Levering, *The Gospel of Mary* by Michael Poage, *Kansas Poems of William Stafford* edited by Denise Low, *Killing Seasons* by Christopher Cokinos, and *Gathering Reunion* by David Tangeman. As a sample the editor selected these lines from "Noah's Teenage Daughters" in *Lot's Wife* by Caryn Mirriam-Goldberg:

MARKET CONDITIONS are constantly changing! If you're still using this book and it's 2004 or later, buy the newest edition of *Poet's Market* at your favorite bookstore or order directly from Writer's Digest Books (800)448-0915 or www.writersdigest.com.

> *I hate this life./They wanted to take a boy for me/but he got more interested in my best friend,/so now they're both drowned/. . . ///I think of throwing myself overboard/I think of throwing some rabbit over/ or one of the mice.*

Samples may be individually ordered from the press for $5.

How to Submit: Guidelines available on website. Accepts e-mail queries. Responds to queries in 2 weeks, to mss in 2 months. Time between acceptance and publication is 1 year.

Advice: "We look for experienced writers who are part of their writing and reading communities."

◐ ◎ WORCESTER REVIEW; WORCESTER COUNTY POETRY ASSOCIATION, INC.

(Specialized: regional), 6 Chatham St., Worcester MA 01609. (508)797-4770. Website: www.geocities. com/Paris/LeftBank/6433. Established 1973. **Managing Editor:** Rodger Martin.

Magazine Needs: *Worcester Review* appears annually "with emphasis on poetry. New England writers are encouraged to submit, though work by other poets is used also." Wants "work that is crafted, intuitively honest and empathetic, not work that shows the poet little respects his work or his readers." Has published poetry by May Swenson, Robert Pinsky, and Walter McDonald. *Worcester Review* is 160 pages, 6×9, flat-spined, professionally printed in dark type on quality stock with glossy card cover. Press run is 1,000 for 300 subscribers of which 50 are libraries, 300 shelf sales. Subscription: $20 (includes membership in WCPA). Sample: $5.

How to Submit: Submit up to 5 poems at a time. "I recommend three or less for most favorable readings." Accepts simultaneous submissions "if indicated." Previously published poems "only on special occasions." Editor comments on rejected poems "if ms warrants a response." Publishes theme issues. Guidelines and upcoming themes available for SASE. Responds in up to 9 months. Pays 2 copies. Acquires first rights.

Also Offers: Has an annual contest for poets who live, work, or in some way (past/present) have a Worcester County connection or are a WCPA member.

Advice: "Read some. Listen a lot."

◐ ◎ WORD DANCE (Specialized: children/teen), P.O. Box 10804, Wilmington DE 19850.

(302)894-1950. Fax: (302)894-1957. E-mail: playful@worddance.com. Website: www.worddance.com (includes samples of writing and art, subscription and contact information, submission guidelines, editorial policy, word games, and links for kids). Established 1989. **Director:** Stuart Ungar.

• "Listed as 'Best Bet' in *Instructor* magazine. Featured in *The New York Times*."

Magazine Needs: "Published quarterly, *Word Dance* magazine encourages the love of reading and writing in a nonthreatening, playful environment. It was created to give young people a quality vehicle for creative expression, a place where their voices can be heard. It includes short stories, poems and artwork by kids in kindergarten through Grade 8." *Word Dance* features haiku, but accepts all forms of poetry. As a sample the editors selected "7 Ways to Look at a Shell" by Matt Schwartzer:

> *Swirling ice cream cone/Phone cord spiraling down/An out of control tornado circling the air/A drill digging into the earth's molten rock/Golden jewelry/The entire ocean trapped in one little seashell*

Word Dance is 32 pages, 6×9, professionally printed and saddle-stapled, two-color card cover, includes two-color drawings. Subscription: $18/year US, $23 Canada, $28 other countries. Single copy/sample: $3.

How to Submit: Accepts poetry for four of their six sections. Field Trip accepts poems and stories about family and school trips; World Word accepts poems and short stories about the environment, war and peace, endangered species, etc.; for Haiku Corner send your Haiku poetry; Grab Bag accepts poems and short stories about any topic. "*Word Dance* receives many submissions for the Grab Bag section of the magazine, so competition is greater in this category. We recommend that students contribute to the other sections of the magazine to increase their chances of getting published." No previously published poems or simultaneous submissions. Accepts submissions by postal mail only; no fax or e-mail submissions. "Our submission form must be included with each submission." Submission form available in magazine, on website, by telephone, or by written request. Submission deadlines: February 25, May 25, August 25, November 25. Time between acceptance and publication is up to 9 months. Poems are circulated to an editorial board. Guidelines available for SASE, in publication, or on website. Copies are available at cost.

Advice: "A subscription is suggested to see examples of work. We are a nonprofit organization. Parents and teachers are encouraged to help their child/student revise and edit work."

$ ◐ WORD PRESS; WORD PRESS POETRY PRIZE, P.O. Box 541106, Cincinnati OH 45254-

1106. (513)474-3761. Fax: (513)474-9034. E-mail: connect@wordtechweb.com. Website: www.word-pres s.com (includes contact information, catalog, and guidelines). Established 2000. **Editor:** Kevin Walzer.

Book/Chapbook Needs & How to Submit: Word Press "is an independent literary press devoted to publishing and distributing the best new poetry through an annual competition and other channels." Pays winner $1,000 and 25 author's copies (out of a press run of 300-500). Runners-up receive 5 copies of their published book. Has published *No One with a Past Is Safe* by Page Dougherty Delano, *Travelers without Maps* by Lorne Mook, and *Rare Space* by Leslie Ann Mcilroy. Publishes one paperback/year chosen through the Word Press Poetry Prize. Books are 48-96 pages, offset-printed, perfect-bound, paper/laminated cover, with photos. "Submit at least 48 pages of poetry. Individual poems may be previously published, but manuscript may not." Open to both new and published poets. Guidelines available on website. Competition receives 100-200 entries/year. Judges are the Word Press staff. Annual deadline: December 1. Copies of previous winning books are available from Word Press for $15.

Advice: "We look for books that have strongly crafted individual poems and that also resonate *as books*—that have a strong thematic, narrative, or lyric depth and focus."

N ⬤ **WORD SALAD**, 3224 N. College Rd., PMB 107, Wilmington NC 28405. E-mail: whealton@wordsalad.net. Website: http://wordsalad.net. Established 1995. **Publisher:** Bruce Whealton. **Editors:** Lynn Krupey and Jean Jones.

Magazine Needs: Published quarterly online, *Word Salad* "continuously accepts original poetry. Although we do not restrict ourselves to one subject area or style, the Web allows us to receive a large number of poems and select the highest quality and we offer a world wide exposure. We are open to any form, style or subject matter; length should be no more than two typed pages. We especially like poetry dealing with oppressed/vulnerable populations, i.e., persons with mental illness, the poor/homeless. We are also planning to accept poetry in Spanish to reflect the international nature of the Internet. No greeting card verse or forced rhyme; most love poems unless you have something original to say. We invite gay/lesbian/bisexual poetry." Has published poetry by Scott Urban and Martin Kirby. As a sample we selected these lines from "Denial" by Paula Martin:

> Her every thought, word, and action/Consumed by the/Food That she will not face—/Unknowingly digesting/Her very soul/As the meal/Remains untouched/and we all stand by,/Silverware in hands,/ Ready to help her/Eat,/If only she would take/The first bite

Receives about 1,200 poems/year, accepts approximately 10%.

How to Submit: Submit 2 poems at a time. No previously published poems or simultaneous submissions. Accepts e-mail and disk submissions. Cover letter preferred. "We receive 200-300 poems per quarter and publish 20-30. Most of the submissions are received via e-mail. We ask that poets read the submission guidelines on the Web." Time between acceptance and publication is about 3 months. Seldom comments on rejected poems. Publishes theme issues occasionally. Guidelines and upcoming themes available on website. Responds in about 3 months. Sometimes sends prepublication galleys. Open to unsolicited reviews.

Also Offers: Sponsors annual poetry contest. See website for announcements. Winners are announced May 31. "*Word Salad* is linked to a directory of online resources related to writing and creativity. Additionally, we have a web-based chat program that allows live chat discussions."

⬤ **THE WORD WORKS; THE WASHINGTON PRIZE**, P.O. Box 42164, Washington DC 20015. Fax: (703)527-9384. E-mail: editor@WORDSWORKSDC.com. Website: www.WORDWORKSDC.com. Established 1974. **Editor-in-Chief:** Hilary Tham.

Book/Chapbook Needs: Word Works "is a nonprofit literary organization publishing contemporary poetry in single author editions usually in collaboration with a visual artist. We sponsor an ongoing poetry reading series, educational programs, the Capital Collection—publishing mostly metropolitan Washington, D.C. poets, and the Washington Prize—an award of $1,500 for a book-length manuscript by a living American poet." Previous winners include *Last Heat* by Peter Blair; *Following Fred Astaire* by Nathalie Anderson; *Tipping Point* by Fred Marchant; *Stalking the Florida Panther* by Enid Shomer; and *Toward Desire* by Linda Lee Harper. Submission open to any American writer except those connected with Word Works. Send SASE for rules. Entries accepted between February 1 and March 1. Postmark deadline is March 1. Winners are announced at the end of June. Publishes perfect-bound paperbacks and occasional anthologies and want "well-crafted poetry, open to most forms and styles (though not political themes particularly). Experimentation welcomed." As a sample the editors selected these lines from "Suspense" in the 2001 Washington Prize winning *One Hundred Children Waiting for a Train* by Michael Atkinson:

> Time makes me weep./Every memory I have of you now, there's rage and waiting/twisting like great arms of taffy behind your jaw

"We want more than a collection of poetry. We care about the individual poems—the craft, the emotional content and the risks taken—but we want manuscripts where one poem leads to the next. We strongly recommend you read the books that have already won the Washington Prize. Buy them, if you can, or ask for your libraries to purchase them. (Not a prerequisite.)" Most books are $10.

How to Submit: "Currently we are only reading unsolicited manuscripts for the Washington Prize." Accepts simultaneous submissions, if so stated. No fax or e-mail submissions. Always sends prepublication galleys. Payment is 15% of run (usually of 1,000). Guidelines and catalog available for SASE or on website. Occasionally comments on rejected poems.

Advice: "Get community support for your work, know your audience, and support contemporary literature by buying and reading the small press."

WORDS OF WISDOM, 8969 UNCG Station, Greensboro NC 27413. (336)334-2952. E-mail: Wowmail@hoopsmail.com. Established 1981. **Editor:** Mikhammad Abdel-Ishara.

Magazine Needs: *Words of Wisdom* appears quarterly with short stories, essays, and poetry. Wants all types of poetry. No religious, pornography. Recently published poetry by Patricia Prime, Esther Cameron, Michael Estabrook, Ulea, Millicent C. Borges, and Margene W. Hucek. *Words of Wisdom* is 76-88 pages, digest-sized, laser-printed, saddle-stapled, cover with art. Receives about 600 poems/year, accepts about 8-10%. Publishes about 10-12 poems/issue. Press run is 160 for 100 subscribers of which 2 are libraries, 50 shelf sales. Single copy: $4; subscription: $14. Sample: $4. Make checks payable to J.M. Freiermuth.

How to Submit: Submit 3-6 poems at a time. Line length for poetry is 30 maximum. Accepts simultaneous submissions; no previously published poems. No fax, e-mail, or disk submissions. Cover letter is required. Reads submissions all year. Submit seasonal poems 10 months in advance. Time between acceptance and publication is 6-9 months. Seldom comments on rejected poems. Occasionally publishes theme issues. Guidelines available for SASE or by e-mail. Responds in up to 6 months. Pays 1 contributor's copy. Acquires first North American serial rights.

Advice: "Turn off the Internet! Surf through a book of poetry."

WORDSONG; BOYDS MILLS PRESS (Specialized: children/teen/young adult), 815 Church St., Honesdale PA 18431. (800)490-5111. Website: www.boydsmillspress.com (includes info on books, book reviews, author bios, Boyds Mills Press staff, and author tours). Established 1990. **Manuscript Coordinator:** Kathryn Yerkes. **Editor-in-Chief:** Dr. Bernice E. Cullinan.

  ● Wordsong's *Been to Yesterdays* received the Christopher Award and was named a Golden Kite Honor Book.

Book/Chapbook Needs: Wordsong is the imprint under which Boyds Mills Press (a *Highlights for Children* company) publishes books of poetry for children of all ages. Wants quality poetry which reflects childhood fun, moral standards, and multiculturalism. "We are not interested in poetry for adults or that which includes violence or sexuality or promotes hatred." Has published *Storm Coming!* by Audrey Baird and *Sing of the Earth and Sky* by Aileen Fisher. As a sample the editor selected this excerpt from *Storm Coming!* by Audrey Baird:

  > *"Firebolt!"—Sparks fly/from a giant's hobnailed boots;/flinting into ebony skies./Jagged/heat/hiss-s-s-s-s-ing through space.*

How to Submit: "Wordsong prefers original work but will consider anthologies and previously published collections. We ask poets to send collections of 25-45 poems with a common theme; please send complete book manuscripts, not single poems. We publish on an advance-and-royalty basis. Wordsong guarantees a response from editors within one month of our receiving submissions or the poet may call us toll free to inquire. Please direct submissions to Kathryn Yerkes, manuscript coordinator." No fax or e-mail submissions. Always sends prepublication galleys.

Advice: "Poetry lies at the heart of the elementary school literature and reading program. In fact, poetry lies right at the heart of children's language learning. Poetry speaks to the heart of a child. We are anxious to find poetry that deals with imagination, wonder, seeing the world in a new way, family relationships, friends, school, nature, and growing up."

WORDWRIGHTS! A MAGAZINE FOR PEOPLE WHO LOVE THE WRITTEN WORD; ARGONNE HOUSE PRESS, P.O. Box 21069, Washington DC 20009. E-mail: question@wordwrights.com. Website: www.wordwrights.com. Established 1993. **Publisher/Editor-in-Chief:** R.D. Baker.

Magazine Needs: *WordWrights!* appears 4 times/year and contains "interesting and entertaining poetry and prose by both new and established writers." Wants "anything that is interesting and poetic. No bad poetry or handwritten manuscripts." Has published poetry by Henry Taylor, Grace Cavalieri, Rose Solari and David Franks. *WordWrights!* is 64 pages, 8½ × 11, offset printed and saddle-stapled with b&w author photos on cover. Receives about 1,000 poems/year, accepts approximately 10%. Press run is 5,000. Single copy: $5.95; subscription: $25/6 issues.

How to Submit: Send up to 10 poems. Accepts simultaneous submissions; no previously published poems. **Reading fee:** $5 (waived for subscribers). Time between acceptance and publication is 6 months. Seldom comments on rejected poems. Guidelines available for SASE and on website. Responds in 4 months. Always sends prepublication galleys. Pays $25/ms. Rights revert to author upon publication. Staff reviews books and chapbooks of poetry and other magazines. Send books for review consideration.

Book/Chapbook Needs & How to Submit: Argonne House Press publishes as many as 8 poetry chapbooks/year. Chapbooks are usually 40 pages, digest-sized, stapled with glossy b&w cover, includes author photos. Query first, with a few sample poems and a cover letter with brief bio and publication credits. "We only publish poets who have previously appeared in *WordWrights!*" Responds to queries in 3 months. Obtain sample chapbooks by sending $5.

Also Offers: In each issue of *WordWrights!*, three published mss are awarded "Best of Issue" awards of $100, $150, and $200.

N $ ⊘ ◎ THE WRITE CLUB (Specialized: membership), P.O. Box 1454, Conover NC 28613. (828)256-3821. E-mail: poetsnet@juno.com. Established 2001. **Club President/Editor:** Nettie C. Blackwelder.

Magazine Needs: *The Write Club* appears quarterly. "We print *one* original poem from *each* of our members in *each* quarterly club booklet. These poems are voted on by all members. We pay $1 to each member for each vote his/her poem receives. Each booklet also contains four assignments for all members who want to do them (usually poetry assignments). Our poetry specifications are open as to form, subject matter, style, or purpose. Just send your best. We don't print anything indecent or offensive." Recently published poetry by Johnnie Elma Anderson, David Bell, Lou Ellen Hoffman, Vincent J. Tomeo, Bruce Tedder, and Sallie A. Hinds. As a sample the editor selected these lines from "Mary" by Joan D. Simmons:

> A woman sits alone on a sofa/Eyes closed, as if taking a nap/Her hands rest on a big shoebox/She
> always keeps on her lap/Her blind old eyes will never again/Read the letters that it contains/Or look
> at the photos of family/Of which, she only, remains . . .

The Write Club is 24 pages, 4¼×11, computer-printed, saddle-stapled, color, light-weight, laminated cover. Receives about 200 poems/year, accepts about 90%. Publishes about 40 poems/issue. Press run is 50 for 32 subscribers; 12 distributed free to anyone who requests information. Single copy: $2; subscription: $15 (membership). Sample: $1 (or 3 first-class stamps). Make checks payable to Nettie C. Blackwelder.

How to Submit: Submit 1 poem at a time. Line length for poetry is 3 minimum, 30 maximum. Accepts previously published poems and simultaneous submissions. Accepts e-mail submissions; no fax or disk submissions. Cover letter is preferred. "Send SAE and 3 first-class stamps (or $1) for information and sample booklet before submitting poetry." Reads submissions all year. Submit seasonal poems 3 months in advance. Time between acceptance and publication is 3 months. "Poems are voted on by our members. Each vote is worth $1 to that poem's author." **Membership required** (all members receive subscription to club booklet). Guidelines available for SASE or by e-mail. Responds in 3 months. Pays $1 per vote, per poem. Acquires one-time rights.

Advice: "Rhythm is the music of the soul and sets the pace of a poem. A clever arrangement of words means very little if they have no sense of 'stop' and 'go.' If you're not sure about the rhythm of a poem, reading it aloud a few times will quickly tell you which words don't belong or should be changed. My advice is rewrite, rewrite, rewrite until you love *every* word and phrase 'as is.' "

N ◐ WRITE ON!! POETRY MAGAZETTE, P.O. Box 901, Richfield UT 84701-0901. (435)896-6669. E-mail: jimnipoetry@yahoo.com. Website: www.artistic-expressions.com/rpmagazette.html (includes guidelines). Established 1998. **Editor:** Jim Garman.

Magazine Needs: *Write On!! Poetry Magazette* appears monthly and features "poetry from poets around the world." Wants poetry of "any style, all submissions must be suitable for all ages to read. No adult or vulgar material." Recently published poetry by Diane Ashley, Kenneth Drysdale, and Lynn Lily. As a sample the editor selected these lines from "The Kiln of Naked Truth" by Diane Ashley:

> Antonement lies in the kiln fire of love/burning human straw/Exit in beauty, purified by grace/we walk
> on in peace

Write On!! is 24 pages, digest-sized, photostat-copied, saddle-stapled, with a color card cover. Receives about 500 poems/year, accepts about 50%. Publishes about 24 poems/issue. Press run is 50 for 10 subscribers of which 1 is a library, 10 shelf sales. Single copy: $4. Sample: $3. Make checks payable to Jim Garman.

How to Submit: Submit 1-6 poems at a time. Line length for poetry is 6 minimum, 24 maximum. Accepts previously published poems and simultaneous submissions. Accepts e-mail submissions; no fax or disk submissions. Reads submissions year round. Submit seasonal poems 2 months in advance. Time between acceptance and publication is 1 month. Never comments on rejected poems. Occasionally publishes theme issues. A list of upcoming themes available by e-mail. Guidelines available on website. Responds in 3 weeks. Acquires first rights.

Advice: "Send only your best material after it has been refined."

N ◐ WRITER'S BLOC, Dept. of Language & Literature, Texas A&M University-Kingsville, MSC 162, Kingsville TX 78363-8202. Established 1980.

Magazine Needs: *Writer's Bloc* is an annual journal which devotes about half of its pages to the works of Texas A&M University-Kingsville students and half to the works of writers and artists from across the nation. Wants quality poetry, fiction, and graphic art. *Writer's Bloc* is 80-96 pages, digest-sized. Press run is 300-500. Sample: $3.

How to Submit: Submit no more than 3 pages of poetry. Accepts simultaneous submissions (encouraged); no previously published poems. Submissions should be typed; SASE required for reply. Reads submissions September-January only. "Manuscripts are published upon recommendation by a staff of students and faculty." Seldom comments on rejected poems. Responds "generally in February and March." Pays in contributor's copies.

WRITERS FORUM; AND MAGAZINE (Specialized: form), 89A Petherton Rd., London N5 2QT England. Phone: 020 7226 2657. Established 1963. **Editors:** Bob Cobbing and Adrian Clarke.

Magazine Needs: Writers Forum is a small press publisher of experimental work including sound and visual poetry in cards, leaflets, chapbooks, occasional paperbacks, and a magazine. Seeks "explorations of 'the limits of poetry' including 'graphic' displays, notations for sound and performance, as well as semantic and syntactic developments, not to mention fun." Has published poetry by Bruce Andrews, Maggie O'Sullivan, Lawrence Upton, Adrian Clarke, and Karen MacCormack. *And Magazine* is published "irregularly" and uses "very little unsolicited poetry; practically none." Press run "varies."

How to Submit: Submit 6 poems at a time. "We normally don't publish previously published work." Work should generally be submitted camera-ready. Pays 2 contributor's copies, additional copies at half price.

Book/Chapbook Needs & How to Submit: Under the imprint Writers Forum they publish 12-18 books/year averaging 28 pages. Samples and listing: £3. For book publication, query with 6 samples, bio, publications. Pays 12 copies, additional copies at half price.

Advice: "We publish only that which surprises and excites us; poets who have a very individual voice and style."

WRITERS' JOURNAL, P.O. Box 394, Perham MN 56573-0394. (218)346-7921. Fax: (218)346-7924. E-mail: writersjournal@lakesplus.com. Website: www.writersjournal.com (includes guidelines, contact and subscription information, archives, catalog, contest information, and links). Established 1980. **Poetry Editor:** Esther M. Leiper.

Magazine Needs: *Writers' Journal* is a bimonthly magazine "for writers and poets that offers advice and guidance, motivation, inspiration, to the more serious and published writers and poets." Features 2 columns for poets: "Esther Comments," which specifically critiques poems sent in by readers, and "Every Day with Poetry," which discusses a wide range of poetry topics, often—but not always—including readers' work. Wants "a variety of poetry: free verse, strict forms, concrete, Oriental. But we take nothing vulgar, preachy or sloppily written. Since we appeal to those of different skill levels, some poems are more sophisticated than others, but those accepted must move, intrigue or otherwise positively capture me. 'Esther Comments' is never used as a negative force to put a poem or a poet down. Indeed, I focus on the best part of a given work and seek to suggest means of improvement on weaker aspects." Accepts poetry written by school-age children. Has published poetry by Lawrence Schug, Diana Sutliff, and Eugene E. Grollmes. *Writers' Journal* is 64 pages (including paper cover), magazine-sized, professionally printed, using 4-5 pages of poetry in each issue, including columns. Circulation is 26,000. Receives about 900 submissions/year, accepts approximately 25 (including those used in columns). Single copy: $3.99; subscription: $19.97/year (US), Canada/Mexico add $15, Europe add $30, all others $35. Sample: $5.

How to Submit: "Short is best: 25-line limit, though very occasionally we use longer. Three to four poems at a time is just right." No query. Accepts submissions by postal mail only. Responds in up to 5 months. Pays $5/poem plus 1 copy.

Also Offers: The magazine also has poetry contests for previously unpublished poetry. Submit up to 6 poems on any subject or in any form, 25 line limit. "Submit in duplicate, one with name and address, one without." Send SASE for guidelines only. Deadlines: April 30, August 30 and December 30. Reading fee for each contest: $2 first poem, $1 each poem thereafter. Competition receives 1,000 entries/year. Winners announced in *The Writers' Journal* and on website.

WRITING FOR OUR LIVES; RUNNING DEER PRESS (Specialized: women, feminism), 647 N. Santa Cruz Ave., The Annex, Los Gatos CA 95030-4350. Established 1991. **Editor/Publisher:** Janet McEwan.

Magazine Needs: Appearing annually, "*Writing For Our Lives* serves as a vessel for poems, short fiction, stories, letters, autobiographies, and journal excerpts from the life stories, experiences, and spiritual journeys of women." Wants poetry that is "personal, women's real life, life-saving, autobiographical, serious—but don't forget humorous, silence-breaking, many styles, many voices. Women writers only, please." Has published poetry by Sara V. Glover, Kennette Harrison, Sara Regina Mitcho, and Eileen Tabios. As a sample the editor selected these lines from "To the Great Blue Heron" by Joyce Greenberg Lott:

> Teach me how to swallow without chewing,/To hold a fish in my gullett until its scales become wings//
> Show me how to puff down into a secret/So only those who know me can find me/Teach me how to
> open my wings and fly,/unexpected and perfect, a crone in the sky.

Writing For Our Lives is 80-92 pages, 5¼×8¼, printed on recycled paper and perfect-bound with matte card cover. Receives about 400 poems/year, accepts 5%. Press run is 500. Subscription: $15.50/2 issues. (CA residents add 8.25% sales tax). Back issues and overseas rates available, send SASE for info. Sample: $8, $11 overseas.

How to Submit: Submit up to 5 typed poems with name and phone number on each page. Accepts previously published poems ("sometimes") and simultaneous submissions. Include 2 SASEs; "at least one of them should be sufficient to return manuscripts if you want them returned." Closing date is August 15. Usually responds in 3 days, occasionally longer. "As we are now shaping 2-4 issues in advance, we may ask to hold certain poems for later consideration over a period of 18 to 24 months." Seldom comments on rejected poems. Guidelines available for SASE. Pays 2 contributor's copies, discount on additional copies, and discount on 2-issue subscription. Acquires first world-wide English language serial (or one-time reprint) rights.

Advice: "Our contributors and circulation are international. We welcome new writers, but cannot often comment or advise. We do not pre-announce themes. Subscribe or try a sample copy—gauge the fit of your writing with *Writing For Our Lives*—support our ability to serve women's life-sustaining writing."

XAVIER REVIEW, Box 110C, Xavier University, New Orleans LA 70125. (504)483-7303. Fax: (504)485-7917. E-mail: rskinner@xula.edu. Established 1961. **Editors:** Thomas Bonner, Jr. and Richard Collins. **Managing Editor:** Robert E. Skinner.

Magazine Needs: *Xavier Review* is a biannual that publishes poetry, fiction, nonfiction, and reviews (contemporary literature) for professional writers, libraries, colleges, and universities. Wants writing dealing with African/Americans, the South, and the Gulf/Caribbean Basin. Has published *I Am New Orleans* by Marcus Christian and *Three Poets in New Orleans* by Lee Grue as well as poetry by Biljiana Obradovic and Patricia Ward. Press run is 500.

How to Submit: Submit 3-5 poems at a time with SASE. Accepts submissions by postal mail only. No e-mail or fax submissions. Pays 2 contributor's copies.

YALE UNIVERSITY PRESS; THE YALE SERIES OF YOUNGER POETS COMPETITION, P.O. Box 209040, New Haven CT 06520-9040. E-mail: yyp@yalepress3.unipress.edu. Website: http://yalebooks.com/poetry. Established 1919. **Attn:** Yale Series of Younger Poets Competition.

Book/Chapbook Needs & How to Submit: The Yale Series of Younger Poets Competition is open to poets under 40 who have not had a book previously published. Submit ms of 48-64 pages in month of January only. Entry fee: $15. Guidelines and rules are available for SASE and on website. No e-mail submissions. Poets are not disqualified by previous publication of limited editions of no more than 300 copies or previously published poems in newspapers and periodicals, which may be used in the book ms if so identified. Previous winners include Richard Kenney, Carolyn Forché, and Robert Hass.

YALOBUSHA REVIEW, University of Mississippi, Dept. of English, P.O. Box 1848, University MS 38677-1848. E-mail: yalobusha@olemiss.edu. Established 1995. **Poetry Editor:** Louis Bourgeois.

Magazine Needs: *Yalobusha Review* appears annually in April "to promote new writing and art, creative nonfiction, fiction, and poetry." Does not want anything over 10 pages. Recently published poetry by Josh Gordon, Brent S. House, Jan Wesley, Luisa Villani, Jim Natal, and David Watts. As a sample the editor selected these lines from "Panty Thief" by Juliana Gray Vice:

> The math was wrong. For one thing. Ten days' laundry/and only three pairs? All white? And nothing
> else gone?

Yalobusha Review is 126 pages, 6×9, glossy cover, with b&w photos and drawings. Receives 70-100 poems/year, accepts about 42%. Publishes about 50 poems/issue. Press run is 500; 50 are distributed free to chosen writers/artists. Single copy: $10. Sample: $8. Make check payable to *Yalobusha Review*.

How to Submit: Submit 10 poems at a time. Length for poetry is 1 page minimum, 10 pages maximum. No previously published poems. Accepts disk submissions; no fax or e-mail submissions. Cover letter is required. Include SASE. Reads submissions August 15-February 15. Submit seasonal poems 4 months in advance. Time between acceptance and publication is 4 months. Poems are circulated to an editorial board: reader to specific editor (prose/poetry) to editor-in-chief to editorial board (including advisors). Never comments on rejected poems. Occasionally publishes theme issues. Guidelines available for SASE. Responds in up to 6 months. Pays 2 contributor's copies. Acquires all rights. Returns full rights upon request.

Advice: "It seems as though poetry has become so regional, leaving us to wonder, 'Where is the universal?' "

⊘ YANKEE MAGAZINE; YANKEE ANNUAL POETRY CONTEST, P.O. Box 520, Dublin NH 03444-0520. (603)563-8111. Established 1935.

Magazine Needs & How to Submit: *Yankee Magazine* is no longer publishing poetry.

⊡ YA'SOU! A CELEBRATION OF LIFE, 2025 Taraval St., Rear, San Francisco CA 94116-2268. (415)665-0294. E-mail: poetjo@yasoumagazine.com. Website: www.joanneolivierico.com. Established 2000. **Editor:** Joanne M. Olivieri.

Magazine Needs: *Ya'sou! A celebration of life* appears quarterly. "Our purpose is to celebrate life. We like thought-provoking and uplifting material in any style and subject matter. We would like to see poetry essays, short stories, articles, and b&w artwork." Does not want "sexually explicit, violence. I'd like more poetry written by children." Recently published poetry by C. David Hay, B.Z. Niditch, Doug Lowney, Geri Ahearn, and Daphne Baumbach. As a sample the editor selected these lines from "Call of the Wild" by C. David Hay:

> The call of the wild is a restless voice/Of wind and sky and sea/Beckons all—both great and small/
> With the yearning to be free.

Ya'Sou! is 25-35 pages, magazine-sized, photocopied, side-stapled, paper cover with color photo, with art/graphics, classified ads, recipes. Receives about 200 poems/year, accepts about 75%. Publishes about 40-50 poems/issue. Press run is 50 for 25 subscribers; 10 are distributed free. Single copy: $5; subscription: $10/year. Make checks payable to Joanne Olivieri (also accepts major credit cards).

How to Submit: Submit 3 poems at a time. Line length for poetry is open. Accepts previously published poems and simultaneous submissions. Accepts e-mail submissions; no fax or disk submissions. Cover letter is preferred. "Work submitted by regular mail should be camera-ready. SASE required." Reads submissions all year. Time between acceptance and publication varies. "All work is read and chosen by the editor." Never comments on rejected poems. "Subscribers will receive preference. Subscribers only also receive special editions throughout the year." Guidelines are available in magazine, for SASE, and by e-mail. Responds in 1 week. Pays 1 contributor's copy. Acquires one-time rights.

Advice: "Let your own unique voice be heard. Remember, express your heart, live your soul, and celebrate life."

Ⓝ ⊡ YAWP MAGAZINE; YAWP'S POETRY AND SHORT STORY CONTESTS, P.O. Box 5998, Pittsburgh PA 15210. E-mail: poetrysubmissions@hotmail.com. Website: www.yawpmagazine.com (includes submission and subscription information, usually up to 7 different poets and visual artists, features, current contest information and updates, and links). Established 1999. **Poetry Contact:** Eric Bliman, editor.

Magazine Needs: *Yawp Magazine* appears biannually in winter and summer. "*Yawp* shocases the works of approximately 15-20 poets and generally a few story writers; also, *Yawp* publishes approximately 10-12 b&w reproductions of artwork, photography, and illustrations of high quality in each issue. Often, there will be a featured poet and/or artist appearing in a special section or sprinkled throughout, with a number of his or her works. *Yawp* publishes experienced and beginning poets, based solely upon the quality of the written work received." Wants "poetry that is both challenging and rewarding, stirring and intelligent, with or without a 'message'; mature voices aware of themselves and the postage stamp of earth they live on; i.e., the stuff that makes your feet tingle and your hair stand on end; joyful, desperate, confident, etc. All forms of poetry considered, only the best published. We want our readers to think and be moved; not preached or talked down to. Poems that haven't fermented for at least a month, and been revised a minimum of 10 times should not leave the house without supervision, with rare exceptions." Recently published poetry by Vivian Shipley, Andrena Zawinski, Jeff O'Brien, Jim Daniels, Allison Joseph, and John Sokol. *Yawp* is 80-130 pages, digest-sized, laser-copied, flat-spined, printed, tape-bound, heavy card stock cover with b&w illustration or photography, b&w art/graphics only. Receives about 750 poems/year, accepts about 15%. Publishes about 25-40 poems/issue. Press run is 450 for 100 subscribers of which 20 are libraries, 100 shelf sales; 100 are distributed free to contest entrants only. Single copy: $7 plus $1.50 s&h; subscription: $17/year, 2 issues. Sample: $6 includes shipping, no handling charge. Make checks payable to Yawp Magazine, Inc.

How to Submit: Submit 3-6 poems at a time. Line length for poetry is 175 maximum. Accepts previously published poems and simultaneous submissions. Accepts e-mail and disk submissions; no fax submissions. Cover letter is preferred. "Poems should be single-spaced, typed or word-processed. Brief bio of fewer than 60 words suggested but not required. Though we do accept poetry via poetrysubmissions@hotmail.com, poets should treat this medium as a convenience, not a shortcut to publication. If you use it, use it wisely and sparingly." Reads submissions March-June and September-December. Submit seasonal poems 2-4 months in advance. Time between acceptance and publication is 2-3 months. "Content of magazine is determined solely by the editors of *Yawp Magazine*; less of a process than a madness." Seldom comments on rejected poems. "No fees for noncontest submitters, but we request that our readers and contributors help keep us afloat if they like what we're doing by purchasing a subscription, as we receive no grants or university support. Also, we strongly recommend that anyone considering submitting to *Yawp* buy a subscription first, to learn what we're all about, before sending any work." Guidelines available in magazine, by e-mail, or on website. Responds in up to 4 months. Sometimes sends prepublication galleys. Pays 1 contributor's copy. Acquires first rights. Reviews books of poetry in 500 words, single book format (query first).

Also Offers: "*Yawp* holds 2 contests each year for poetry, and sometimes short stories. Grand prize: $500. Check our website periodically for all contest-related updates and guidelines."

Advice: "Read everything you can get your hands on, first; and when you do sit down to write, don't distract yourself by thinking of all the magazine editors, teachers, friends, or family members that might or might not like it. Be wary of people who give too much advice about how to write poetry. Don't rush to publish."

⬤ **YEFIEF,** P.O. Box 8505, Santa Fe NM 87504-8505. (505)753-3648. Fax: (505)753-7039. E-mail: arr@imagesformedia.com. Established 1993. **Editor:** Ann Racuya-Robbins.

Book/Chapbook Needs: *yefief* is a serial imprint of Images For Media that was originally designed "to construct a narrative of culture at the end of the century." Wants "innovative visionary work of all kinds and have a special interest in exploratory forms and language. There is no set publication schedule." Has published poetry by Michael Palmer, Simon Perchik, and Carla Harryman. *yefief* is 250 pages, printed on site and perfect-bound with color coated card cover with color and b&w photos, art and graphics inside. Initial artbook press run is 500. Single copy: $24.95. Write for information on obtaining sample copies.

How to Submit: Submit 3-6 poems at a time. Accepts previously published poems and simultaneous submissions. Responds in 2 months. Pays 2-3 contributor's copies. Poets may send books for review consideration.

🅽 ⬤ **YELLOW BAT REVIEW; RICHARD GEYER, PUBLISHER,** 1338 W. Maumee, Idlewilde Manor #129, Adrian MI 49221. E-mail: ybreview@yahoo.com. Website: www.geocities.com/rgeyer_2000/index.html (includes guidelines, names of contributors to previous issues, contact and ordering information). Established 2001. **Editor:** Craig Sernotti.

Magazine Needs: *Yellow Bat Review* appears quarterly as "a pocket-sized journal of eclectic poetry. *Yellow Bat Review* hopes to be *the* home for all types of poetry from subtle to humorous to strange and anything in between." Open to all schools and genres. No restrictions on form or content. Likes offbeat, surreal, gritty work. Nothing sentimental, no weak lines, no teenage angst. Recently published poetry by John Grey, Lyn Lifshin, and Duane Locke. *Yellow Bat Review* is 30 pages, pocket-sized ($4\frac{1}{4} \times 5\frac{1}{2}$), photocopied, saddle-stapled, glossy, b&w card stock cover. Single copy: $2.50; subscription: $8 (4 issues). Sample: $2.50. Make checks payable to Richard Geyer.

How to Submit: Submit up to 4 poems at a time. Line length for poetry is 20 maximum. Accepts previously published poems (rarely); no simultaneous submissions. Accepts e-mail submissions; no fax or disk submissions. Cover letter is preferred. Strongly prefers e-mail submissions. Poems must be given as text in the body of the message. Time between acceptance and publication is 1-6 months. Often comments on rejected poems. Occasionally publishes theme issues. Guidelines available by e-mail. Responds in up to 3 weeks. Always sends prepublication galleys. Pays 1 contributor's copy. Acquires first North American serial rights.

Book/Chapbook Needs & How to Submit: Richard Geyer, Publisher publishes pocket-sized chapbooks of dark poetry. Chapbook submissions are by invitation only. Publishes 1-2 chapbooks/year. Chapbooks are usually 10-30 pages, photocopied, saddle-stapled, glossy, b&w card stock cover. Order sample chapbooks by sending $1.50 to Richard Geyer.

Advice: "To beginners, try us, try everything. Experience only comes if you try. To everyone, we hope *Yellow Bat Review* will be a breath of fresh air in a world of dry lit mags. We don't care about being 'safe.' If the work is fresh and lively it will be published, regardless of school or style. Whether the poet is an 'unknown' or a 'well-known' is meaningless; it's the poem that counts."

⬤ **YEMASSEE; YEMASSEE AWARDS,** Dept. of English, University of South Carolina, Columbia SC 29208. (803)777-2085. E-mail: yemassee@gwm.sc.edu. Website: www.cla.sc.edu/ENGL/index.html (includes writer's guidelines, editor's names, sponsor's names, table of contents, and cover of most recent issues). Established 1993. **Editor:** Corinna McLeod.

Magazine Needs: *Yemassee* appears semiannually and "publishes primarily fiction and poetry, but we are also interested in one-act plays, brief excerpts of novels, essays, reviews, and interviews with literary figures. Our essential consideration for acceptance is the quality of the work; we are open to a variety of subjects and writing styles." Accepts 10-25 poems/issue. "No poems of such a highly personal nature that their primary relevance is to the author; bad Ginsberg." Has published poetry by Kwame Dawes, Virgil Saurez, Phoebe Davidson, Pamela McClure, Rafael Campo, David Kirby, and Susan Ludvigson. *Yemassee* is 80-100 pages perfect-bound. Receives about 400 poems/year, accepts about 10%. Press run is 750 for 63 subscribers, 10 shelf sales; 275-300 distributed free to English department heads, creative writing chairs, agents and publishers. Subscription: $6 for students, $15 regular. Sample: $5. Make checks payable to Education Foundation/English Literary Magazine Fund.

How to Submit: Submit up to 5 poems at a time. Line length for poetry is fewer than 50, "but poems of exceptional quality are considered regardless of length." No previously published poems. No fax or e-mail submissions. Cover letter required. "Each issue's contents are determined on the basis of blind selections. Therefore we ask that all works be submitted, without the author's name or address anywhere on the typescript. Include this information along with the title(s) of the work(s) in a cover letter. For longer submissions, please include an approximate word count." Reads submissions October 1 through November 15 and March 15 through April 30. Time between acceptance and publication is 4 months. "Staff reads and votes on 'blind' submissions." Seldom comments on rejected poems. Guidelines available for SASE or on website. Responds in up to 10 weeks after submission deadline. Pays 2 contributor's copies with the option to purchase additional copies at a reduced rate. Acquires first rights.

Also Offers: Sponsors the *Yemassee* Awards when funding permits. Awards $400/issue, usually $200 each for poetry and fiction.

YOMIMONO, 113-6 Ninokoshi, Kitakawamukai, Aza, Hiroshima, Matsushige-cho, Itano-gun, Tokushima-ken 771-0220 Japan. Phone/fax: (+81)886-99-7574. E-mail: kammy@mxs.mesh.ne.jp. Established 1992. Editor: Suzanne Kamata.

Magazine Needs: Published annually, *Yomimono* is "an eclectic mix of poetry, fiction, essays, interviews and artwork from around the world. We're pretty open but we tend to favor innovative and international work. We like complicated yet accessible. Be concrete. No mediocre haiku, poems about drug trips, airy philosophizing, sappy love poems, rhyming verse." Has published poetry by Virgil Suarez, Ian McBryde, Tim Wells, and Leza Lowitz. As a sample the editor selected these lines from "Life Is Difficult, Part One" by Peter Bakowski:

> The heart on my sleeve/is at the dry cleaner's/a flock of tea-bags/just circled the house/and the kettle
> won't boil/says it wants to be/a poet.

Yomimono is 66 pages, magazine-sized, desktop-published and perfect-bound, cover varies, includes b&w illustrations and photos. Receives about 100 poems/year, accepts approximately 10%. Press run is 150. Single copy: $5; subscription: $10. Sample: $4. Make checks payable to Suzanne Kamata.

How to Submit: Submit up to 5 poems at a time. Accepts previously published poems and simultaneous submissions. Accepts e-mail submissions. SASE or SAE and IRC required for reply. Time between acceptance and publication is up to 1 year. Poems are circulated to an editorial board. "Poems are discussed among three editors." Often comments on rejected poems. Responds in 6 months. Pays 3 copies. Acquires one-time rights. Reviews books and chapbooks of poetry and other magazines in 50-1,000 words, single and multi-book format. Open to unsolicited reviews. Poets may also send books for review consideration.

YORKSHIRE JOURNAL (Specialized: regional), Ilkley Rd., Otley, West Yorkshire LS2 3JP England. Phone: (01943)467958. Fax: (01943)850057. E-mail: sales@smith-settle.co.uk. Established 1992. **Editor:** Mark Whitley.

Magazine Needs: *Yorkshire Journal* is a quarterly general interest magazine about Yorkshire. Wants poetry no longer than 25 lines with some relevance to Yorkshire. Has published poetry by Vernon Scannell, Anna Adams, Ted Hughes, Andrew Motion, and Simon Armitage. As a sample the editor selected these lines from "The Herdwick Ram" by Leslie Quayle:

> As I unlatched the barn door's creaking hasp,/The grey ewes gathered, hungering, at my back,/Dawn's
> sallow glimmer pricked the tine and cusp/Of hawthorn crowns and slipped across the beck./He wasn't
> in the clamour for fresh hay,/Nor by the mistal, so I went to seek,/Hurrying through the damp grass,
> till I saw/The great, slumped shadow against the lambing creep.

Yorkshire Journal is 120 pages, highly illustrated. Receives about 200 poems/year, accepts approximately 10%. Press run is 3,000 for 700 subscribers, 2,300 shelf sales. Subscription: £12. Sample: £2.95. Make checks payable to SMITH Settle Ltd.

How to Submit: Submit up to 6 poems at a time. Accepts previously published poems and simultaneous submissions. Accepts submissions by fax and e-mail (in text box). Cover letter required including biographical information. Has a large backlog. Time between acceptance and publication varies. Sometimes comments on rejected poems. Guidelines available for SASE (or SAE and IRC). Responds within 1 month maximum. Pays 1 copy.

N ⊕ ○ ◎ YOUNG WRITER; YOUNG WRITER SUMMER ANTHOLOGY (Specialized: children/teen), Glebe House, Church Rd., Weobley, Herefordshire HR4 8SD England. Phone/fax: (01544)318901. E-mail: editor@youngwriter.org. Website: www.youngwriter.org. Established 1995. **Editor:** Kate Jones. **Editorial Assistant:** Julian Robbins.

Magazine Needs: *Young Writer* appears 3 times/year "to inspire, nurture and educate young writers of all abilities and to support teachers working with them. It contains prose and poetry, fiction and nonfiction by young people." Wants poetry by children under 18. "No poetry unsuitable to publish in magazine for readers under 18." Has published poetry by Rebecca Lawrence, Sarah Carlin, Alice Smith, Peter Ranscombe, Philip Nash, and Melanie Hobbs. As a sample the editor selected this poem, "Floppy Hat" by Claire Hughes (age 13):

> Your floppy hat lies covered in cobwebs/Untouched for years./It holds the shape of your head./It has
> been strewn carelessly into its new home,/And then forgotten./Its very presence there creates a
> spectre . . ./of our past.

Young Writer is 32 pages, 8½ × 11, 4 color printing on high quality paper, saddle-stapled with self-cover, includes art/graphics. Receives about 1,000 poems/year, accepts approximately 20%. Publish approximately 40 poems/issue. Press run is 10,000 for subscribers (individuals, schools and libraries), book club sales and shelf sales; 150 distributed free to publishers/authors. Single copy: £2.75 plus £1.24 p&h; subscription: £7.50 plus £2 p&h in Europe; £4 p&h, further afield; p&h free in UK; £4 p&h to US. Sample is free. (Send IRCs to cover postage to the US).

How to Submit: Line length for poetry is 4-5 minimum, 40 maximum. Accepts previously published poems and simultaneous submissions. Accepts e-mail and disk (Apple compatible) submissions. Cover letter preferred. Time between acceptance and publication is up to 1 year. Poems are circulated to an editorial board. "Read everything, short-list pieces that ring true, then balance the magazine." Often comments on rejected poems. Guidelines available for SASE (or SAE and IRC) or on website. Responds in 1 month. Acquires one-time rights. Reviews books and chapbooks of poetry and other magazines in up to 50 words, single and multi-book format. Open to unsolicited reviews. Poets may send books for review consideration. "Books should be suitable for readers under 18."

Also Offers: Also published an annual anthology of poetry and prose by writers 18 and under. Sponsors annual award competitions. Details on request. Website includes "a taste of the magazine plus editor's choice of children's writing, plus 'what's new?' newsboard and guidelines."

Advice: "We look for honesty and the ring of truth. We expect a level of competence in handling language. Both serious and humorous pieces considered. All material should be appropriate for our readership of children, though tough subjects may be tackled."

◗ ZILLAH: A POETRY JOURNAL, P.O. Box 202, Port Aransas TX 78373-0202. E-mail: lightningwhelk@msn.com. Established 2001. **Editor/Publisher:** Pamela M. Smith.

Magazine Needs: Appearing quarterly, *Zillah* is " 'not your mother's poetry.' Simply put, in the year 3999 an archaeologist's dig produces a copy of *Zillah* in situ and, reading it, the treasure hunter knows what it was like to live during the second and third millenia." Does not want pornography, gratuitous violence, evil or devil worship, or anything that lacks quality. *Zillah* is 40 pages, 7 × 8½, stapled, 80 lb. cover stock, with b&w original art and graphics. Single copy: $3; subscription: $12. Make checks payable to Pamela M. Smith.

How to Submit: Submit 5-6 poems at a time. Line length for poetry is 60 maximum. Accepts previously published poems and simultaneous submissions. Accepts submissions by e-mail (in text box); no fax submissions. "SASE essential, typed, double-spaced, one poem to a page." Reads submissions all year. Submit seasonal poems 6 months in advance. Time between acceptance and publication is 3 months. Never comments on rejected poems. Responds in 2 months. Pays 1 contributor's copy. Acquires first North American serial rights or second reprint rights; rights revert to author after publication.

Also Offers: The *Zillah* Poetry Contest. Winners will be published and receive 2 copies of magazine. Guidelines available for SASE.

Advice: "Everyone should write, everyone should write poetry. Take a leap of faith. Think of writing as a natural state of being. Let go from a stream of consciousness, from the heart, from depth—edit and refine later."

N ◗ ZOO PRESS, P.O. Box 22990, Lincoln NE 68542. Fax: (402)614-6302. E-mail: editors@zoopress.org. Website: www.zoopress.org. Established 2000.

Book/Chapbook Needs: "Zoo Press aims to publish the best emerging writers writing in the English language, and will endeavor to do it at the rate of at least 12 manuscripts of admirable quality a year (in print and electronic formats as they become available), providing we can find them. We're confident we can. By quality we mean originality, an awareness of tradition, formal integrity, rhetorical variety (i.e., invective, satire, argument, irony, etc.), an impressive level of difficulty, authenticity, and, above all, beauty." Wants high quality poetry mss. Does not want mss written by those who do not regularly read poetry. Recently published poetry by Priscilla Becker, Ross Martin, Siri von Reis, Kathy Fagan, Scott Cairns, and Beth Ann Fennelly. As a sample the editor selected these lines from "Because They Live on Blood Alone, Vampires" by Siri von Reis from *The Love-Suicides at Sonezaki*:

> *Because they live on blood alone, vampires//are the most specialized of the* Phyllostomidae,*/possessing a nasal thermoreceptor, anti-clotting//saliva, a tongue that transfers blood to the mouth,/and kidneys that quickly offload plasma after meals.*

Zoo Press publishes 12 paperbacks/year through open submissions and competition. Books are usually 50-100 pages, perfect-bound, 2-4 color matte covers.

How to Submit: "We only accept open submissions in January and July. Send only one copy of each manuscript, and do not send queries. Manuscripts of poetry should be between 50 and 100 pages, typed single-spaced, with no more than one poem per page. All manuscripts must be paginated and contain a table of contents. Illustrations are not accepted. Handwritten manuscripts will not be considered. A cover letter must be included with each submission. Submit a title page with each manuscript that includes the author's name, address, telephone number, e-mail if available, and the manuscript title. Each manuscript should be fastened with a single staple or binder clip. Writers who wish Zoo to acknowledge receipt of their manuscripts must enclose a self-addressed, stamped postcard. Also, a self-addressed, stamped, business-sized envelope must be enclosed in order to receive word about our decision, or an appropriately stamped envelope must be included for return of the entire manuscript, otherwise the manuscript will be discarded." Responds to mss in up to 2 months. Pays royalties of 10%, advance (varies), and 10 author's copies (out of a press run of 1,500-2,000). Order sample books by sending $10 to Zoo Press.

Also Offers: Sponsors The Paris Review Prize in Poetry and The Kenyon Review Prize in Poetry for a First Book (see separate listings in the Contest & Awards section). Also sponsors The Parnassus Prize in Poetry Criticism (contact for details).

Advice: "Please read our books or magazines published by our partners to get a feel for the quality and substance of poetry being published here."

ZUZU'S PETALS QUARTERLY ONLINE, P.O. Box 4853, Ithaca NY 14852. (607)539-1141. E-mail: info@zuzu.com. Website: www.zuzu.com. Established 1992. **Editor:** T. Dunn.

Magazine Needs: "We publish high-quality fiction, essays, poetry, and reviews on our award-winning website, which was featured in *USA Today Online*, *Entertainment Weekly*, and *Web Magazine*. Becoming an Internet publication allows us to offer thousands of helpful resources and addresses for poets, writers, editors, and researchers, as well as to greatly expand our readership. Free verse, blank verse, experimental, visually sensual poetry, etc. are especially welcome here. We're looking for a freshness of language, new ideas, and original expression. No 'June, moon, and spoon' rhymed poetry. No light verse. I'm open to considering more feminist, ethnic, alternative poetry, as well as poetry of place." Has published poetry by Ruth Daigon, Robert Sward, Laurel Bogen, W.T. Pfefferle, and Kate Gale. As a sample the editor selected these lines from "The Mind of Elizabeth Blackwell" by Jessy Randall:

> *I buy myself a daughter who will be/my only friend. I lull her to England,/then Scotland, then death. I cannot go/any further north.*

Zuzu's Petals averages 70-100 pages, using full-color artwork, and is an electronic publication available free of charge on the Internet. "Many libraries, colleges, and coffeehouses offer access to the Internet for those without home Internet accounts." Receives about 3,000 poems/year, accepts about 10%. Copies free online, printed sample: $5.

How to Submit: Submit up to 4 poems at a time. Accepts previously published poems and simultaneous submissions. Submissions via e-mail are welcome, as well as submissions in ASCII (DOS IBM) format on 3½" disks. Include e-mail submissions in the body of the message. "Cover letters are not necessary. The work should speak for itself." Seldom comments on rejected poems. Guidelines available for SASE, by e-mail, in publication, or on website. Responds in up to 2 months. Acquires one-time electronic rights. Staff reviews books of poetry in approximately 200 words. Send books, galleys, or proofs for review consideration.

Advice: "Read as much poetry as you can. Go to poetry readings, read books and collections of verse. Eat poetry for breakfast, cultivate a love of language, then write!"

Contests & Awards

This section contains a wide array of poetry competitions and literary awards. These range from state poetry society contests with a number of modest monetary prizes to prestigious honors bestowed by private foundations, elite publishers, and renowned university programs. Because there's such a variety of skill levels and degrees of competitiveness, it's important to read these listings carefully and note the requirements for each. *Never* enter a contest without consulting the guidelines and following directions to the letter (including manuscript formatting, number of lines or pages of poetry accepted, amount of entry fee, entry forms needed, and other details).

WHERE TO ENTER?

While it's perfectly okay to "think big" and aim high, being realistic may actually improve your chances of winning a prize for your poetry. Many of the listings in the Contests & Awards section begin with symbols that reflect their level of difficulty:

Contests ideal for beginners and unpublished poets are coded with the (☐) symbol. That's not to say these contests won't be highly competitive—there may be a very large number of entries. However, you may find that the work entered is more on a level with your own, increasing your chances of being "in the running" for a prize. Don't assume that these contests reward low quality, though. If you submit less than your best work, you're wasting your time and money (in postage and entry fees).

Contests for poets with more experience are coded with the (◑) symbol. Beginner/unpublished poets are usually still welcome to enter, but it's understood that the competition is keener here. Your work may be judged against that of widely published, prize-winning poets, so consider carefully whether you're ready for this level of competition. (Of course, nothing ventured, nothing gained—but those entry fees *do* add up.)

Contests for accomplished poets are coded with the (●) symbol. Note that these may have stricter entry requirements, higher entry fees, and other conditions that signal that these programs are not intended to be "wide open" to all poets.

Specialized contests are coded with the (◉) symbol. These may include regional contests; awards for poetry written in a certain form or in the style of a certain poet; contests for women, gay/lesbian, ethnic, or age-specific poets (for instance, children or older adults); contests for translated poetry only; and many others.

There are also symbols which give additional information about contests. The (N) symbol indicates that the contest is new to this edition; the (✈) symbol identifies a Canadian contest or award and the (⊕) symbol an international listing. Sometimes Canadian and international contests require that entrants live in certain countries, so pay extra close attention when you see these symbols.

ADDITIONAL CONTESTS & AWARDS

Often magazines and presses prefer to include their contests within their listings in the Publishers of Poetry section. Therefore we provide a supplement at the end of this section as a cross reference to these opportunities. For details about a contest associated with a market in this list, go to that market's page number.

WHAT ABOUT ENTRY FEES?

You'll find that most contests charge entry fees, and these are usually quite legitimate. The funds are used to cover expenses such as paying the judges, putting up prize monies, printing prize editions of magazines and journals, and promoting the contest through mailings and ads. If you're concerned about a poetry contest or other publishing opportunity, see Are You Being Taken? on page 24 for advice on some of the more questionable practices in the poetry world.

OTHER RESOURCES

Be sure to widen your search for contests beyond those listed in *Poet's Market*. Many Internet writer's sites have late-breaking announcements about competitions old and new (see Websites of Interest on page 520). Often these sites offer free electronic newsletter subscriptions, so sign up! Information will come right to you via your e-mail inbox.

The writer's magazines at your local bookstore regularly include listings for upcoming contests, as well as deadlines for artist's grants at the state and national level. (See Publications of Interest on page 514 for a few suggestions; also, State & Provincial Grants on page 461.) Associated Writing Programs (AWP) is a valuable resource, including its publication, *Writer's Chronicle*. (See Organizations, page 492.) State poetry societies are listed throughout this book; they offer many contests as well as helpful information for poets (and mutual support). To find a specific group, search the General Index for listings under your state's name or look under "society"; also consult the Geographical Index on page 538.

Finally, don't overlook your local connections. City and community newspapers, radio and TV announcements, bookstore newsletters and bulletin boards, and your public library can be terrific resources for competition news, especially regional contests.

$ THE ACORN-RUKEYSER CHAPBOOK CONTEST; THE SANDBURG-LIVESAY ANTHOLOGY CONTEST; THE HERB BARRETT AWARD (Specialized: forms/ haiku), 237 Prospect St. S., Hamilton, Ontario L8M 2Z6 Canada. (905)312-1779. E-mail: james@meklerd eahl.com. Website: www.meklerdeahl.com. **Managing Partner:** James Deahl. Offers three contests: The Acorn-Rukeyser Chapbook Contest awards $100 (US), publication, and 50 copies; runner-up receives $100 (US). Submissions may be entered in other contests. Submit a poetry ms of up to 30 pages, poems must be within the People's Poetry tradition, as exemplified by the work of Milton Acorn and Muriel Rukeyser. Guidelines available for SASE. **Entry fee:** $10 (US). All entrants receive a copy of the winning chapbook. **Postmark deadline:** September 30. Winner will be notified in the spring. The Sandburg-Livesay Anthology Contest awards 1st Prize: $250 (US) and publication; 2nd Prize: $150 (US) and anthology publication; 3rd Prize: $100 and anthology publication; and anthology publication for other prizes. Submit up to 10 poems of up to 70 lines each; poems must be within the People's Poetry tradition, as exemplified by the work of Carl Sandburg and Dorothy Livesay. **Entry fee:** $12 (US). All entrants receive a copy of the anthology ($14 value). **Postmark deadline:** October 31. Winners will be notified late summer following the contest. The Herb Barrett Award for short poetry in the haiku tradition awards publication and 1st Prize: $200 (US); 2nd Prize: $150 (US); 3rd Prize: $100 (US); and anthology publication for other prizes. Winning poems will be published in an anthology. All entrants will receive 1 copy of the anthology. "What is most important is that each haiku be a concise image of life." **Entry fee:** $10 (US). "Up to 10 poems may be submitted per entry." **Postmark deadline:** November 30. Winners will be notified the following summer. Guidelines for any of the 3 competitions are available for SASE or on website. Entry fees payable by check or bank money order to Mekler & Deahl, Publishers.

$ AKRON POETRY PRIZE, The University of Akron Press, 374B Bierce Library, Akron OH 44325-1703. (330)972-5342. Fax: (330)972-8364. E-mail: uapress@uakron.edu. Website: www.uakron. edu/uapress/(includes a list of publications, ordering information, and guidelines for poetry contest). **Award Director:** Elton Glaser. Offers annual award of $1,000 plus publication. Submissions must be unpublished and may be entered in other contests (with notification of acceptance elsewhere). Submit 60-100 pages maximum, typed, single-spaced or double-spaced, with SASE for results. Mss will not be returned. Do not send mss bound or enclosed in covers. Guidelines available for SASE or by fax or e-mail. Accepts inquiries by fax and e-mail. **Entry fee:** $25. **Deadline:** entries are accepted May 15 through June 30 only. Competition receives 450-550 entries. Most recent contest winners were John Minczeski, Dennis Hinrichsen, Beckian Fritz Goldberg, and Jeanne E. Clark. Judge for the 2002 prize was Charles Simic. Winner will be announced in September by letter (if SASE enclosed with entry) or on website. Copies of winning books are available from UAP or through your local bookstore. The University of Akron Press "is committed to publishing poetry that, as Robert Frost said, 'begins in delight and ends in wisdom.' Books accepted must exhibit three essential qualities: mastery of language, maturity of feeling, and complexity of thought."

⊘ ◎ AMERICAN ANTIQUARIAN SOCIETY VISITING FELLOWSHIPS FOR CREATIVE AND PERFORMING ARTISTS AND WRITERS (Specialized: American history and culture), Artists and Writers Fellowship, American Antiquarian Society, 185 Salisbury St., Worcester MA 01609-1634. (508)363-1131. Fax: (508)754-9069. E-mail: jmoran@mwa.org. Website: www.americanantiquarian.org/artistfellowship.htm. Established 1994. **Award Director:** James David Moran. Offers at least 3 fellowships for 4-week residencies at the Society. Awards a stipend of $1,200 plus an allowance for travel expenses. Fellowships provide recipients "with the opportunity for a period of uninterrupted research, reading, and collegial discussion at the Society in Worcester, Massachusetts." Library is devoted to pre-20th century materials. Entry form and guidelines available for SASE; additional information available on website. Accepts inquiries by fax and e-mail. **Deadline:** October 5. Winner profiles for 1995-2002 available on website. Winners will be announced in December. "Established 1812. As the country's first national historical organization, the American Antiquarian Society is both a learned society and a major independent research library. The AAS library today houses the largest and most accessible collection of books, pamphlets, broadsides, newspapers, periodicals, sheet music and graphic arts material produced through 1876 in what is now the United States, as well as manuscripts and a substantial collection of secondary works, bibliographies, and other reference works related to all aspects of American history and culture before the twentieth century." Potential candidates should "learn about the collections in the library; consult *Under Its Generous Dome, A Guide to the Collections and Programs of the American Antiquarian Society.*"

N: $◻ ◎ THE AMY AWARD (Specialized: women, form/lyric, regional/NYC or Long Island), Guild Hall of East Hampton, 158 Main St., East Hampton NY 11937. (631)329-1151. Fax: (631)329-1151*51. Website: www.guildhall.org. Established 1996. **Contact:** Paula Trachtman. Offers annual honorarium plus a reading with a well-known poet in the *Writers at Guild Hall* series. Submissions may be entered in other contests. Submit 3 lyric poems of no more than 50 lines each, with name, address, and phone on each page. Accepts entries by regular mail. Enclose SASE and bio. Entrants must be women 30 years of age or under residing on Long Island or in the New York metropolitan region. Do *not* send for guidelines; all information is contained in advertisements. **Deadline:** August. Most recent winners were Amanda Lichtenberg/Stella Padnos and Shannon Holman. Judges have included Philip Appleman, Edward Butscher, Siv Cedering, and Simon Perchik. Winners will be announced by PR mailings to all print media and by mail to winners. Guild Hall is the East End of Long Island's leading cultural center. It hosts, besides major museum, theater, and musical events, the *Writers at Guild Hall* series. Readers have included Tom Wolfe, Kurt Vonnegut, Joseph Brodsky, Maxine Kumin, Allen Ginsberg, Sharon Olds, John Ashbery, E.L. Doctorow, Eileen Myles, Linda Gregg, and Molly Peacock.

ARKANSAS POETRY DAY CONTEST; POETS' ROUNDTABLE OF ARKANSAS, 605 Higdon, Apt. 109, Hot Springs AR 71913. (501)321-4226. E-mail: vernalee@lpt.net. **Contact:** Verna Lee Hinegardner. Over 25 categories, many open to all poets. Brochure available in June; deadline in September; awards given in October. Guidelines available for SASE.

$◻ ◎ ARTIST TRUST; ARTIST TRUST GAP GRANTS; ARTIST TRUST FELLOWSHIPS (Specialized: regional/Washington state), 1835 12th Ave., Seattle WA 98122. (206)467-8734. Fax: (206)467-9633. E-mail: info@artisttrust.org. Website: www.artisttrust.org (includes applications and other grant/publication opportunities). **Program Director:** Heather Dwyer. Artist Trust is a nonprofit arts organization that provides grants to artists (including poets) who are residents of the state. Accepts inquiries by fax and e-mail. Competition receives 1,000 entries/year. Contest winners include Donna Miscolta, Thomas Gribble, and Bruce Beasley. Also publishes, three times a year, a journal of news about arts opportunities and cultural issues.

$⬚ THE BACKWATERS PRIZE, The Backwaters Press, 3502 N. 52nd St., Omaha NE 68104-3506. (402)451-4052. E-mail: gkosm62735@aol.com. Website: www.thebackwaterspress.homestead.com. Established 1998. **Contest Director:** Greg Kosmicki. Offers annual prize of $1,000 plus publication, promotion, and distribution. "Submissions may be entered in other contests and this should be noted in cover letter. Backwaters Press must be notified if manuscripts are accepted for publication at other presses." Submit up to 80 pages on any subject, any form. "Poems must be written in English. No collaborative work accepted. Parts of the manuscript may be previously published in magazines or chapbooks, but entire manuscript may not have been previously published." Manuscript should be typed (or word processed) in standard poetry format—single-spaced, one poem per page, one side only. Guidelines available for SASE, by e-mail, or on website. **Entry fee:** $25. Does not accept entry fees in foreign currencies. Send postal money order or personal check in US dollars. **Deadline:** postmarked by June 4. Competition receives 200-250 entries/year. Most recent contest winner was Susan Fiver (2001). Judges have included Carolann Russell (2001) and Hilda Raz (2002). Winner will be announced in AWP *Chronicle* ad and in *Poets & Writer's* "Recent Winners." Copies of winning books available through The Backwaters Press or Amazon. com. "The Backwaters Press is a nonprofit press dedicated to publishing the best new literature we can find. Send your best work."

$⬚ BALCONES POETRY PRIZE, Austin Community College, 1212 Rio Grande, Austin TX 78701. (512)223-3236. E-mail: dbarnett@austin.cc.tx.us. Established 1995. **Contest Director:** Dorothy Barnett. Offers annual prize of $1,000 for a book of poetry, in English, published during the award year. Submissions must be previously published in the year of the award and may be entered in other contests. Winning poet is expected to come to Austin to read from ms. Submit 42-page ms on any subject or in any form. Guidelines and information available for SASE and by e-mail. **Entry fee:** $20. **Deadline:** April 1. Competition receives approximately 80 entries. Most recent contest winner was Carol Potter. Winner will be announced in late June or early July. "The Austin Community College is a 2-year college of 26,000 students in urban Central Texas."

◎ BAY AREA BOOK REVIEWERS ASSOCIATION AWARDS (BABRA); FRED CODY AWARD (Specialized: regional/Northern California), 1450 Fourth St., #4, Berkeley CA 94710. (510)525-5476. Fax: (510)525-6752. E-mail: babra@poetryflash.org. Website: www.poetryflash.org. Established 1981. **Executive Director:** Joyce Jenkins. Offers annual awards which recognize "the best of Northern California (from Fresno north) fiction, poetry, nonfiction, and children's literature." Submissions must be books published in the calendar year. Submit 3 copies of each book entered. The authors of the submitted books must live in Northern California. Guidelines available for SASE or by fax. **Deadline:** December 1. Most recent poetry winner was Forrest Hamer. BABRA also sponsors the Fred Cody Award for lifetime achievement given to a Northern California writer who also serves the community. Also gives, on an irregular basis, awards for outstanding work in translation and publishing. The Cody Award winner for 2001 was Tillie Olsen. **Note:** *The Fred Cody Award does not accept applications.*

▦ ⬚ ◎ BBC WILDLIFE MAGAZINE POET OF THE YEAR AWARDS (Specialized: nature), *BBC Wildlife Magazine*, Broadcasting House, Whiteladies Rd., Bristol BS8 2LR United Kingdom. Phone: +44(0)117 973 8402. Fax: +44(0)117 946 7075. E-mail: wildlife.magazine@bbc.co.uk. Established 1994. **Award Director:** Nina Epton. Offers annual prize of £500, publication in *BBC Wildlife Magazine* plus the poem is read on BBC radio 4's "Poetry, Please" program. Runners-up receive cash prizes plus publication in *BBC Wildlife Magazine*. Pays winners from other countries by international money order. Submissions must be unpublished. Submit 1 poem on the natural world in any form, 50 lines maximum. Guidelines available for SASE (or SAE and IRC), by fax or e-mail. "No entry fees, but entry form appears in magazine, so you have to buy magazine to enter." Deadline varies from year to year. Competition receives 1,500-2,000 entries/year. Most recent award winner was Angela Kirby (2001). 2001 judges included Simon Rae (poet), Philip Gross (poet), Sara Davies (producer of "Poetry, Please"), Roger Deakin (poet and author), Roger McGough (poet and broadcaster), Helen Dunmore (poet and novelist), and Rosamund Kidman Cox (editor of *BBC Wildlife Magazine*). Winner announced in September *BBC Wildlife Magazine*. "Contact us for information before sending a poem in."

$ ⊘ GEORGE BENNETT FELLOWSHIP, Phillips Exeter Academy, 20 Main St., Exeter NH 03833-2460. Website: www.exeter.edu (includes information about Phillips Exeter Academy and the Fellowship with application materials). Established 1968. **Selection Committee Coordinator:** Charles Pratt. Provides a $6,000 fellowship plus residency (room and board) to a writer with a ms in progress. The Fellow's only official duties are to be in residence while the academy is in session and to be available to students interested in writing. The committee favors writers who have not yet published a book-length work with a major publisher. Application materials and guidelines available for SASE or on website. **Deadline:** December 1. Competition receives 125 entries. Recent award winners were Ilya Kaminsky (1999-2000), Laura Moriarty (2000-2001), and Anne Campisi (2001-2002).

$ ⊚ BEST OF OHIO WRITERS WRITING CONTEST (Specialized: regional/Ohio residents), P.O. Box 91801, Cleveland OH 44101. (216)421-0403. E-mail: PWLGC@msn.com. Offers annual contest for poetry, fiction, creative nonfiction, and "Writers on Writing" (any genre). 1st Prize: $150, 2nd Prize: $50, plus publication for first-place winner of each category in a special edition of *Ohio Writer*. Submit up to 3 typed poems, no more than 2 pages each, unpublished mss only. Open only to Ohio residents. "Entries will be judged anonymously, so please do not put name or other identification on manuscript. Attach entry form (or facsimile) to submission. Manuscripts will not be returned." Include SASE for list of winners. Entry form and guidelines available for SASE. **Entry fee:** $15/first entry in each category (includes 1-year subscription or renewal to *Ohio Writer*); $2 for each additional entry in same category (limit 3/category). **Deadline:** July 31. Judges have included Larry Smith, Richard Hague, Ron Antonucci, and Sheila Schwartz. Winners announced in the November/December issue of *Ohio Writer*.

$ ⊘ BLUESTEM PRESS AWARD, Emporia State University, English Dept., Box 4019, Emporia KS 66801-5087. (620)341-5216. Fax: (620)341-5547. Website: www.emporia.edu/bluestem/index.htm (includes guidelines, announcements, previous winners, and booklist). Established 1989. **Director:** Philip Heldrich. Offers annual award of $1,000 and publication for an original book-length collection of poems. Submissions must be unpublished and may be entered in other contests (with notification). Submit a typed ms of at least 48 pages on any subject in any form with a #10 SASE for notification. Guidelines and information available for SASE and by e-mail. **Entry fee:** $18. **Deadline:** March 1. Competition receives 500-700 entries/year. Recent award winner was Cheryl Lachowski. Judge was Christopher Howell. Winner will be announced in summer. Copies of winning poems or books available from the Bluestem Press at the above number. Enter early to avoid missing the deadline. Also, looking at the different winners from past years would help. Manuscripts will *not* be accepted after the deadline and will not be returned.

⊕ $ ⊚ THE BOARDMAN TASKER AWARD (Specialized: mountain literature), The Boardman Tasker Charitable Trust, 40 Wingate Rd., London W6 OUR United Kingdom. Phone/fax: 01792 386215. E-mail: margaretbody@lineone.net. Established 1983. **Contact:** Margaret Body (Pound House, Llangennith, Swansea, West Clamorgan SA3 1JQ Wales). Offers prize of £2,000 to "the author or authors of the best literary work, whether fiction, nonfiction, drama, or poetry, the central theme of which is concerned with the mountain environment. Entries for consideration may have been written by authors of any nationality but the work must be published or distributed in the United Kingdom between November 1 and October 31. (If not published in the U.K., please indicate name of distributor.) The work must be written or have been translated into the English language." Submit ms in book format. "In a collection of essays or articles by a single author, the inclusion of some material previously published but now in book form for the first time will be acceptable." *Submissions accepted from the publisher only.* Four copies of entry must be submitted with application. Accepts inquiries by e-mail; does not accept inquiries by fax. **Deadline:** August 1. Competition receives about 25 entries. Most recent winner was *The Wildest Dream*, by Peter and Leni Gillman, published by Headline.

Ⓝ $ ⊘ BOLLINGEN PRIZE, Beinecke Rare Book and Manuscript Library, Yale University, P.O. Box 208240, New Haven CT 06520-8240. A biennial prize of $50,000 to an American poet for the best poetry collection published during the previous two years, or for a body of published poetry written over several years. **By nomination only.** "All books of poetry by American poets published during the two-year period are automatically considered." Judges change biennially. Prize awarded in February of odd-numbered years.

Ⓜ $ ⊚ BP NICHOL CHAPBOOK AWARD (Specialized: regional/Canada), 316 Dupont St., Toronto, Ontario M5R 1V9 Canada. (416)964-7919. Fax: (416)964-6941. Established 1985. Offers $1,000

(Canadian) prize for the best poetry chapbook (10-48 pages) in English published in Canada in the preceding year. Submit 3 copies (not returnable) and a brief curriculum vitae of the author. Accepts inquiries by fax. **Deadline:** March 31. Competition receives between 40-60 entries on average.

🌐 $◯ **THE BRIDPORT PRIZE; INTERNATIONAL CREATIVE WRITING COMPETI-TION**, Bridport Arts Centre, South St., Bridport, Dorset DT6 3NR United Kingdom. Phone: (01308) 459444. E-mail: info@bridport-arts.com. Website: www.bridportprize.org.uk (includes entry forms, rules, info about competition, anthology order forms). Established 1980. **Contact:** Competition Secretary. Offers annual award for an original poem of not more than 42 lines and an original story of not more than 5,000 words. 1st Prize: £3,000, 2nd Prize: £1,500, and 3rd Prize: £500 in each category plus small supplementary prize. Prize-winning entries also published in anthology. Submissions must be previously unpublished. Open as to subject or form. Use online submission form to enter or submit by regular mail. Entry form and guidelines available on website. **Entry fee:** £5 sterling/entry. Accepts foreign entry fees by VISA, Mastercard. **Deadline:** June 30 of each year. Competition receives approximately 8,000 entries. 2001 poetry winner was Rowland Moloney. Recent poetry judges included Maura Dooley (2001) and Jo Shapcott (2002). Winners will be announced at the end of September. Copies of winning anthologies available by sending £11 sterling to Competition Secretary at the above address (VISA and Mastercard also accepted).

⬛ $◎ ∅ **CANADIAN AUTHORS ASSOCIATION AWARDS FOR ADULT LITERA-TURE (Specialized: regional); CANADIAN AUTHORS ASSOCIATION; AIR CANADA AWARD**, Box 419, Campbellford, Ontario K0L 1L0 Canada. (705)653-0323. Fax: (705)653-0593. E-mail: canauth@redden.on.ca. Website: www.CanAuthors.org. **Administrator:** Alec McEachern. The CAA Awards for Adult Literature offers $2,500 and a silver medal in each of 5 categories (fiction, poetry, short stories, Canadian history, Canadian biography) to Canadian writers, for a book published during the year. **Entry fee:** $20/title. **Deadline:** December 15; except for works published after December 1, in which case the postmark deadline is January 15. Competition receives 300 entries/year. Most recent award winners were Elizabeth Hay (fiction), Carmine Starnino (poetry), Lynn Coady (short stories), Will Ferguson (history), and Anna Porter (biography). The CAA Air Canada Award is an annual prize of two tickets to any Air Canada destination, awarded to a Canadian author under 30 who shows the most promise in the field of literary creation (any field or form). Most recent winner was Madeleine Thien. **Nominations are made before March 31 by CAA branches, or other writers' organizations, agents, or publishers.** All awards are given at the CAA banquet in June.

$◎ **CAVE CANEM POETRY PRIZE (Specialized: ethnic/African American); CAVE CA-NEM FOUNDATION, INC.**, 39 Jane St. GB, New York NY 10014. Fax: (434)977-8106. E-mail: cavecanempoets@aol.com. Website: www.cavecanempoets.org. Award established 1999; organization 1996. **Award Director:** Carolyn Micklem, Cave Canem director. Offers "annual first book award dedicated to presenting the work of African American poets who have not been published by a professional press. The winner will receive $500 cash, publication, and 50 copies of the book." **US poets only.** "Send two copies of manuscript of 50-75 pages. The author's name should not appear on the manuscript. Two title pages should be attached to each copy. The first must include the poet's name, address, telephone, and the title of the manuscript; the second should list the title only. Number the pages. Manuscripts will not be returned, but a SASE postcard can be included for notice of manuscript receipt. Simultaneous submissions should be noted. If the manuscript is accepted for publication elsewhere during the judging, immediate notification is requested." Guidelines available for SASE or on website. There is no entry fee. **Deadline:** May 15 of each year. Send ms to Cave Canem, P.O. Box 4286, Charlottesville, VA 22905-4286. Receives 78 entries/year (so far). Most recent award winners were Lyrae Van Clief-Stefanan (2001), Major Jackson (2000), and Natasha Trethewey (1999). Most recent judges were Kevin Young (2002) and Marilyn Nelson (2001). Winners will be announced by press release in October of year of contest. Copies of winning books are available from "any bookseller, because the publishers are Graywolf Press ('99), University of Georgia ('00), and University of Pittsburgh ('01). Cave Canem sponsors a week-long workshop/retreat each summer and regional workshops in New York City and Minnesota. It sponsors readings in cities in various parts of the country. The winner of the Prize and the judge are featured in an annual reading." Recommends "since this is a highly competitive contest, you should be at a stage in your development where some of your poems have already been published in literary journals."

$◎ **THE CENTER FOR BOOK ARTS' ANNUAL POETRY CHAPBOOK COMPETITION**, 28 W. 27th St., 3rd Floor, New York NY 10001. (212)481-0295. E-mail: info@centerforbookarts.org.

Website: www.centerforbookarts.org/ (includes guidelines, application form, center information and history, class schedule, events). Established 1995. **Executive Director:** Rory Golden. Offers $500 cash prize, a $500 reading honorarium, and publication of winning manuscript in a limited edition letterpress-printed and handbound chapbook. Pays winners from other countries in US dollars. Submissions may be previously published and entered in other contests. Submit no more than 500 lines or 24 pages on any subject, in any form. Mss must be typed on one side of 8½×11 paper. Entry form and guidelines available for SASE, by e-mail, or on website. **Entry fee:** $15/ms. Does not accept entry fees in foreign currencies; accepts US check, cash, or VISA/MasterCard number. **Postmark deadline:** December 1. Competition receives 500-1,000 entries/year. Most recent contest winner was Jack Ridl. Recent judges were Lynn Emmanuel and Billy Collins. Winner will be contacted in April by telephone. Each contestant receives a letter announcing the winner. Copies of winning chapbooks available for $25. Make checks payable to The Center for Book Arts. Reading fee credited toward the purchase of the winning chapbook. "Center for Book Arts is a nonprofit organization dedicated to the traditional crafts of bookmaking and contemporary interpretations of the book as an art object. Through the Center's Education, Exhibition, and Workspace Programs we ensure that the ancient craft of the book remains a viable and vital part of our civilization."

N $ ⬤ ◎ CHICANO/LATINO LITERARY PRIZE (Specialized: bilingual/English, Spanish), Dept. of Spanish & Portuguese, University of California at Irvine, Irvine CA 92697-5275. E-mail: cllp@uci.edu. Website: www.hnet.uci.edu/spanishandportuguese/contest/.html. Established 1974. **CLLP Director:** Prof. Juan Bruce-Novoa. Annual contest focusing on 1 of 4 genres each year: drama (2002), novel (2003), short story (2004), poetry (2005). 1st Prize: $1,000, publication of work if not under previous contract, and transportation to Irvine to receive the award; 2nd Prize: $500; 3rd Prize: $250. Work may be in English or Spanish. Only one entry/author. Open to US citizens or permanent residents of the US. Guidelines available for SASE, by e-mail, or on website. **Deadline:** June 1. Most recent contest winner for poetry was José Espinosa-Jácome. Judge was Tino Villanueva. Winners will be notified in October. Prizes will be awarded in November.

$◖ CNW/FFWA FLORIDA STATE WRITING COMPETITION, Florida Freelance Writers Association, P.O. Box A, North Stratford NH 03590-0167. (603)922-8338. E-mail: contest@writers-editors.com. Website: www.writers-editors.com (includes announcement of winners, list of previous winners, tips for poetry). Established 1978. **Award Director:** Dana K. Cassell. Offers annual awards for nonfiction, fiction, children's literature, and poetry. Awards for each category are: 1st Place: $100 plus certificate, 2nd Place: $75 plus certificate, 3rd Place: $50 plus certificate, plus Honorable Mention certificates. Submissions must be unpublished. Submit any number of poems on any subject in traditional forms, free verse, or children's. Entry form and guidelines available for SASE or on website. Accepts inquiries by e-mail. **Entry fee:** $3/poem (members), $5/poem (nonmembers). **Deadline:** March 15. Competition receives 350-400 entries/year. Competition is judged by writers, librarians, and teachers. Winners will be announced on May 31 by mail and on website.

$◎ COLORADO BOOK AWARDS (Specialized: regional), Colorado Center for the Book, 2123 Downing, Denver CO 80205. (303)839-8320. Fax: (303)839-8319. E-mail: ccftb@compuserve.com. Website: www.coloradobook.org-ccftb. **Executive Director:** Christiane Citron. Offers annual award of $350 plus promotion for books published in the year prior to the award. Submissions may be entered in other contests. Submit 6 copies of each book entered. Open to residents of Colorado. Entry form and guidelines available for SASE, by e-mail, or on website. **Entry fee:** $40. **Deadline:** January 15. Competition receives 120 entries/year. Most recent award winners were Mark Irwin and Veronica Patterson. Winner will be announced at an annual ceremony/dinner. "We are a nonprofit organization affiliated with the Library of Congress Center for the Book. We promote the love of books, reading, and literacy. We annually sponsor the Rocky Mountain Book Festival which attracts tens of thousands of people. It's free and includes hundreds of authors from throughout the country. We are located in the home of Thomas Hornsby Ferril, Colorado's late former poet laureate. This historic landmark home is used as a literary center and a tribute to Ferril's life and work."

N $◖ ◎ INA COOLBRITH CIRCLE ANNUAL POETRY CONTEST (Specialized: regional/California; members), 1415 Summit Dr., Berkeley CA 94708. (510)848-5359. E-mail: byshelrm@jps.net. **Treasurer:** Robt. Shelby. Offers annual prizes of $10-50 in each of several categories for California residents and out-of-state members only. Three poems/contestant, but no more than 1 poem in any one category. Poems submitted in 2 copies, include name, address, phone number, and member status on 1 copy only. Members of the Ina Coolbrith Circle pay no fee; others pay $2 for each poem (limit 3). Send SASE for details. **Deadline:** August.

$◎ COUNCIL FOR WISCONSIN WRITERS, INC. (Specialized: regional), Box 55322, Madison WI 53705. Offers annual awards of $500 or more for a book of poetry by a Wisconsin resident, published within the awards year (preceding the January 13 deadline). Competition receives 250 entries/ year. Entry form and entry fee ($10 for members of the Council, $25 for others) required.

⬛○◎ CRUMB ELBOW PUBLISHING POETRY CONTESTS (Specialized: themes); WIND FLOWER PRESS; HORSE LATITUDES PRESS; THE FINAL EDITION; WY'EAST HISTORICAL JOURNAL, P.O. Box 294, Rhododendron OR 97049. Established 1996. **Award Director:** Michael P. Jones. Offers annual awards of publication and tearsheets from book, "for both established poets and beginners to introduce their work to new audiences by having their work published in a collection of poetry. We are always looking for complete manuscripts. Send SASE for guidelines. Also need works for an anthology. Send at least six poems with a SASE. Would like to see b&w illustrations (pen/ink) accompany the poems." Crumb Elbow sponsors 7 contests, all having different themes. They are the Scarecrow Poetry Harvest Contest (**Deadline:** August 1), Old Traditions & New Festivities: Winter Holiday Poetry Contest (**Deadline:** October 1), Natural Enchantment: Henry David Thoreau Poetry Contest (**Deadline:** February 1), Centuries of Journeys: History & Folk Traditions Poetry Contest (**Deadline:** April 1), Onward to the New Eden! Oregon Trail Poetry Contest (**Deadline:** January 1), Westward! Historic Trails Poetry Contest (**Deadline:** November 1), and Beyond the Shadows: Social Justice Poetry Contest (**Deadline:** June 1). Submissions may be entered in other contests. Submit at least 3 poems or verses. All submissions should be typed and accompanied by SASE. Entry form and guidelines available for SASE. **Entry fees:** range from $2 for 3 poems to $15 for 22-30 poems. "Have fun with your creativity. Explore with your words and don't be afraid of themes or to try something different." Crumb Elbow also publishes *The Final Edition* and *Wy'East Historical Journal* and imprints that publish poetry like Wind Flower Press, Horse Latitudes Press, and others. Write for more information. "Please note that unless you send a SASE we will not respond due to the workload."

$◑ DANA AWARD IN POETRY, 7207 Townsend Forest Ct., Browns Summit NC 27214. (336)656-7009. E-mail: danaawards@pipeline.com (for emergency questions only). Website: http://danaawards.home .pipeline.com (includes guidelines, information on winners, judges, and the philosophy behind the awards). Established 1996. **Award Chair:** Mary Elizabeth Parker. Offers annual award of $1,000 for the best group of 5 poems. Pays winners from other countries by check in US dollars. Submissions must be unpublished "and not under promise of publication when submitted to us"; may be entered in other contests. Submit 5 poems on any subject, in any form; no light verse. Entries by regular mail only. Include SASE for winners list. No mss will be returned. Include separate cover sheet with name, address, phone, e-mail address, and titles of poems. Guidelines available for SASE, by e-mail, or on website. **Entry fee:** $10/5 poems. Does not accept entry fees in foreign currencies; accepts bank draft or check in US dollars only, drawn on US bank. No personal checks written on foreign banks. **Postmark deadline:** October 31. Competition receives 300-400 poetry entries. Recent judges were Enid Shomer and Michael White. Winner will be announced in early spring by phone, letter, and e-mail.

$○ DANCING POETRY CONTEST, Artists Embassy International, 704 Brigham Ave., Santa Rosa CA 95404-5245. (707)528-0912. E-mail: jhcheung@aol.com. Website: www.DANCINGPOETRY. com (includes description of the Dancing Poetry Festival where winners are read and performed; also description of Artist Embassy International). Established 1993. **Contest Chair:** Judy Cheung. Annual contest offers three Grand Prizes of $100, five 1st Prizes of $50, 10 2nd Prizes of $25, 20 3rd Prizes of $10. The 3 Grand Prize-winning poems will be danced, choreographed, costumed, premiered, and videotaped at the annual Dancing Poetry Festival at Palace of Legion of Honor, San Francisco. Natica Angilly's Poetic Dance Theater Company will perform the 3 Grand Prize-winning poems. Pays winners from other countries in international money orders with US value at the time of the transaction. Submissions must be unpublished or poet must own rights. Submit 2 copies of any number of poems, 40 lines maximum (each), with name, address, phone on one copy only. Foreign language poems must include English translations. Include SASE for winners list. Entry form available for SASE. No inquiries by fax or e-mail. **Entry fee:** $5/poem or $10/3 poems. Does not accept entry fees in foreign currencies; send international money order in US dollars. **Deadline:** June 15. Competition receives about 500-800 entries. Most recent contest winners include Raynette Eitel, Bonnie Nish, and Hope Vilsick-Greenwell. Judges for upcoming contest will be members of Artists Embassy International. Ticket to festival will be given to all winners. Artist Embassy International has been a nonprofit educational arts organization since 1951, "Furthering intercultural understanding and peace through the universal language of the arts."

$✐ THE DOROTHY DANIELS ANNUAL HONORARY WRITING AWARD, The National League of American Pen Women, Inc.—Simi Valley Branch, P.O. Box 1485, Simi Valley CA 93062. E-mail: cdoering@gte.net. Established 1980. **Award Director:** Carol Doering. Offers annual award of 1st Prize: $100 in each category: poetry, fiction, nonfiction. Pays winners from other countries by check in US currency. Submissions must be unpublished. Submit any number of poems, 50 lines maximum each, on any subject, free verse or traditional. Manuscript must not include name and address. Include cover letter with name, address, phone, title, category of each entry, and line count for each poem. Poem must be titled and typed on 8½ × 11 white paper, single- or double-spaced, one poem/page. Guidelines and winners list available for SASE. **Entry fee:** $5/poem. Does not accept entry fees in foreign currencies; send "checks which consider the exchange rate, or U.S. cash money." **Deadline:** July 30. Competition receives 1,500 entries/year. Recent award winner was Sandra Becker. Winners will be announced by mail in early November. "Request rules and follow them carefully—always include SASE." The National League of American Pen Women, a nonprofit organization headquartered in Washington, DC, was established in 1897 and has a membership of more than 7,000 professional writers, artists, and composers. The Simi Valley Branch, of which noted novelists Dorothy Daniels and Elizabeth Forsythe Hailey are Honorary Members, was established in 1977.

⊕ $□ DAVID ST. JOHN THOMAS CHARITABLE TRUST OPEN POETRY AWARD, David St. John Thomas Charitable Trust, P.O. Box 6055, Nairn 1V12 5YB Scotland. Phone: (01667) 453351. Fax: (01667) 452365. Established 1990. **Award Director:** David St. John Thomas. Offers annual £1,000 prize split into 2 categories plus £200 for "Winner of Winners." Cash prize paid by sterling cheque/draft only. Submissions must be unpublished. Submit any number of poems, any form. Entry form *only* available for SASE (or SAE and IRC); accepts inquiries by fax. **Entry fee:** £2.50 in sterling, IRCs to the value. Does not accept entry fees in foreign currencies ("we do accept U.S. dollars"). **Deadline:** January 31. Competition receives over 1,000 entries/year. Most recent award winner was Colin Palfrey. Judges are Alison Chisholm and Doris Corti. Winners will be announced mid-March.

Ⓝ $□ MILTON DORFMAN NATIONAL POETRY PRIZE, % Rome Art & Community Center, 308 W. Bloomfield St., Rome NY 13440. (315)336-1040. Fax: (315)336-1090. E-mail: racc@borg.com. Website: www.borg.com/~race/index.html (includes information on upcoming events at the Rome Art & Community Center, contest guidelines.) **Contact:** Deborah H. O'Shea. Annual award for unpublished poetry. Prizes: $500, $200, and $100. **Entry fee:** $5/poem (American funds only; $10 returned check penalty). Make checks payable to Rome Art & Community Center. Poets must be 18 years of age to enter. Contest opens July 1. **Deadline:** November 1. Include name, address, and phone number on each entry. Poems are printed in Center's Newsletter. Competition receives about 1,000 entries/year. Judge to be announced. Winners notified by February. Results available for SASE.

$✐ T.S. ELIOT PRIZE FOR POETRY; TRUMAN STATE UNIVERSITY PRESS, 100 E. Normal, Kirksville MO 63501-4221. (660)785-7199. Fax: (660)785-4480. E-mail: tsup@truman.edu. Website: http://tsup.truman.edu (includes T.S. Eliot Prize guidelines, past winners and judges, also books and order form). Press established 1986. **Director:** Paula Presley. Offers annual award of $2,000, publication, and 10 copies as first prize. Submit 60-100 pages, include 2 title pages, 1 with name, address, phone, and ms title; the other with only the title. Individual poems may have been previously published in periodicals or anthologies, but the collection must not have been published as a book. Include SASE if you wish acknowledgement of receipt of your ms. Mss will not be returned. Guidelines available for SASE. Accepts inquiries by fax and e-mail. **Entry fee:** $25. **Deadline:** October 31. Competition receives 500 entries/year. Recent contest winners were Christopher Bakken (2001), Harvey L. Hix (2000), and David Keplinger (1999). Truman State University Press also publishes critical books about poetry or poets, as well as hardcover and paperback originals and reprints.

⊕ $✐ T.S. ELIOT PRIZE (Specialized: regional/UK, Ireland), The Poetry Book Society, Book House, 45 East Hill, London SW18 20Z United Kingdom. Phone: (020)8874 6361. Fax: (020)8877 1615. E-mail: info@poetrybooks.co.uk. Website: www.poetrybooks.co.uk. Established 1993. **Award Director:**

Clare Brown. Offers annual award for the best poetry collection published in the UK/Republic of Ireland each year. Prize: £10,000 (donated by Mrs. Valerie Eliot) and "winning book is bound in Moroccan leather." Pays winners from other countries through publisher. Submissions must be previously published and may be entered in other contests. **Book/ms must be submitted by publisher** and have been published (or scheduled to be published) the year of the contest. Entry form and guidelines available for SASE or by fax or e-mail. Accepts inquiries by fax and e-mail. **Deadline:** early August. Competition receives 100 entries/year. Most recent contest winner was Michael Longley. Recent judges were Helen Dunmore, John Burnside, and Maurice Riordan. Winner will be announced in January.

N ⬛ ⊚ **EMERGING VOICES (Specialized: writers from minority, immigrant, and under-served communities)**, PEN USA, 672 S. Lafayette Park Place, Suite 42, Los Angeles CA 90057. (213)365-8500. Fax: (213)365-9616. E-mail: ev@penusa.org. Website: www.penusa.org (includes bro-chure, guidelines, and application form). **Literary Programs Coordinator:** Teena Apeles. Annual program offering $1,000 stipend and 8-month fellowship to writers in the early stages of their literary careers. Program includes one-on-one sessions with mentors, seminars on topics such as editing or working with agents, courses in the Writers' Program at UCLA Extension, and literary readings. Participants selected according to potential, experience, and goals. No age restrictions; selection is *not* based solely on economic need. Participants need not be published, but "the program is directed toward poets and writers of fiction and creative nonfiction with clear ideas of what they hope to accomplish through their writing. Mentors are chosen from PEN's comprehensive membership of professional writers and beyond. Participants are paired with established writers sharing similar writing interests and often with those of the same ethnic and cultural backgrounds." Program gets underway in January. **Deadline:** September 5, 2002 (for 2003 cycle). "All materials must arrive in the PEN offices by the submission deadline—no exceptions." See website for brochure and complete guidelines.

$ ⬛ **THE WILLIAM FAULKNER CREATIVE WRITING COMPETITION/POETRY CATE-GORY; THE DOUBLE DEALER REDUX**, The Pirate's Alley Faulkner Society, Inc., 632 Pirate's Alley, New Orleans LA 70116. (504)586-1612. Fax: (504)522-9725. E-mail: faulkhouse@aol.com. Web-site: www.wordsandmusic.org (includes competition guidelines, entry form, information about annual Writers' Conference, and Words & Music). Established 1992. **Award Director:** Rosemary James. Offers annual publication in *The Double Dealer Redux*, cash prize of $750, gold medal, and trip to New Orleans from any continental US city. "Foreign nationals are eligible but the society pays transportation to awards ceremony from US cities only. Winners must be present at annual meeting to receive award." Submissions must be unpublished. Submit 1 poem on any subject in any English language form. Entry form (required) and guidelines available for SASE and on website. Accepts inquiries by fax and e-mail. **Entry fee:** $25/ entry. **Deadline:** April 30. Competition receives 1,000 (for 5 categories) entries/year. Most recent contest winner was Ruth Moon Kempher (2001). Judge was Richard Katrovas. Winners will be announced on the society's website by September 1. "Competition is keen. Send your best work."

$ ⬛ ⊚ **FLORIDA INDIVIDUAL ARTIST FELLOWSHIPS (Specialized: regional)**, Florida Division of Cultural Affairs, Dept. of State, 1001 DeSoto Park Dr., Tallahassee FL 32301. (850)487-2980. Website: www.dos.state.fl.us/dca (includes general information about the Florida Department of State, Division of Cultural Affairs, and application guidelines). **Arts Administrator:** Valerie Ohlsson. Annually offers an undetermined number of fellowships in the amount of $5,000 each. "The Individual Artist Fellowship Program is designed to recognize practicing professional creative artists residing in Florida through monetary fellowship awards. The program provides support for artists of exceptional talent and demonstrated ability to improve their artistic skills and enhance their careers. Fellowships may be awarded in the following discipline categories: dance, folk arts, interdisciplinary, literature, media arts, music, theatre, and visual arts and crafts." Submissions can be previously published or unpublished. Submit 3-5 representative poems, single- or double-spaced. "Reproductions of published work may not be submitted in published format. Open to Florida residents of at least 18 years of age who are not enrolled in undergradu-ate or graduate programs. Eight copies of the work sample must be included with 8 copies of the application form. Write for entry form and guidelines." **Deadline:** January, 2003. Competitions receive 500 entries.

MARKETS LISTED in the 2002 edition of *Poet's Market* that do not appear this year are identified in the General Index with a code explaining their absence from the listings.

Most recent winner was Don Stap. Also publishes the *Dept. of State, Division of Cultural Affairs Informational Memo*, a newsletter of "information of concern to writers at state, regional, national, and international levels."

$⬛ THE ROBERT FROST FOUNDATION ANNUAL POETRY AWARD, The Robert Frost Foundation, Heritage Place, 439 S. Union St., Lawrence MA 01843. Phone/fax: (978)725-8828. E-mail: mejaneiro@aol.com. Website: www.frostfoundation.org. Established 1997. **Award Director:** Mary Ellen Janeiro. Offers annual award of $1,000. Pays winners from other countries in dollars (US). Submissions may be entered in other contests. Submit up to 3 poems of not more than 3 pages each, written in the spirit of Robert Frost. Guidelines available for SASE and on website. **Entry fee:** $10/poem. Does not accept entry fees in foreign currencies. **Deadline:** September 1st of each year. Competition receives over 200 entries/year. 2001 winner was Vivian Shipley. Winners will be announced at the annual Frost Festival and by SASE following the Festival (late October). Winning poem can be viewed on website.

N ⬛ ○ ◎ JOHN GLASSCO TRANSLATION PRIZE (Specialized: translation, regional/ Canadian), Literary Translators' Association of Canada, Université Concordia, SB 335, 1455, boul. de Maisonneuve Ouest, Montreal, Quebec H3G 1M8 Canada. (514)848-8702. Fax: (514)848-4514. E-mail: ltac@alcor.concordia.ca. Website: www.geocities.com/Athens/Oracle/9070 (includes membership form, directory of members, model contract and list of events). **Contact:** Kathleen Merken, membership secretary. $500 awarded annually for a translator's first book-length literary translation into French or English, published in Canada during the previous calendar year. The translator must be a Canadian citizen or landed immigrant. Eligible genres include fiction, creative nonfiction, poetry, published plays, and children's books. Write for application form. Accepts inquiries by e-mail. **Deadline:** June 30. Competition receives 15 entries/year. Most recent prize winner was Agnès Guitard. Winner will be announced by e-mail to members and by press release after formal presentation of award on International Translation Day (end of September).

$○ GLIMMER TRAIN'S APRIL POETRY OPEN, Glimmer Train Press, 710 SW Madison St., #504, Portland OR 97205-2900. (503)221-0836. Fax: (503)221-0837. E-mail: info@glimmertrain.com. Website: www.glimmertrain.com (includes online submission procedure, poetry presentation, top 25 winners of past contests, glimpses into issues of *Glimmer Train Stories* and *Writers Ask*). Established 1998. **Co-Editor:** Linda Swanson-Davies. Offers annual prizes. 1st Prize: $500, publication in *Glimmer Train Stories*, and 20 copies of that issue; 2nd Prize: $250; 3rd Prize: $100. Pays winners from other countries by check in US dollars. Submissions must be unpublished and may be entered in other contests. No subject or form restrictions. **Entry fee:** $6/poem. **How to submit:** Use online submission procedure at www.glimmertrain.com during the month of April. Competition receives several hundred entries/year. Most recent contest winners were Matthew Doherty and Andrea King Kelly. Judged by the editors of Glimmer Train Press. Winners will be contacted by September 1 by telephone. Glimmer Train Press publishes the quarterly *Glimmer Train Stories*, circulation 13,000, available through Amazon or most independent booksellers, and through website.

$○ GLIMMER TRAIN'S OCTOBER POETRY OPEN, Glimmer Train Press, 710 SW Madison St., #504, Portland OR 97205-2900. (503)221-0836. Fax: (503)221-0837. E-mail: info@glimmertrain.com. Website: www.glimmertrain.com (includes online submission procedure, poetry presentation, top 25 winners of past contests, glimpses into issues of *Glimmer Train Stories* and *Writers Ask*). Established 1998. **Co-Editor:** Linda Swanson-Davies. Offers annual prizes. 1st Prize: $500, publication in *Glimmer Train Stories* and 20 copies of that issue; 2nd Prize: $250; 3rd Prize: $100. Pays winners from other countries by check in US dollars. Submissions must be unpublished and may be entered in other contests. No subject or form restrictions. **Entry fee:** $6/poem. **How to submit:** Use an easy online submission procedure at www.glimmertrain.com during the month of October. Competition receives "several hundred" entries/ year. Most recent contest winners were Matthew Doherty and Andrea King Kelly. Judged by the editors of Glimmer Train Press. Winners will be contacted by March 1 by telephone. Glimmer Train Press publishes the quarterly *Glimmer Train Stories*, circulation 13,000, available through Amazon or most independent booksellers, and through website.

$⬛ GRANDMOTHER EARTH NATIONAL AWARD, Grandmother Earth Creations, P.O. Box 241986, Memphis TN 38124. (901)682-6936. Fax: (901)682-8274. E-mail: gmoearth@aol.com. Website: www.grandmotherearth.com. Established 1994. **Award Director:** Frances Cowden. Offers annual award of $1,250 with varying distributions each year. $1,250 minimum in awards for poetry and prose; $200 first, etc., plus publication in anthology; non-winning finalists considered for anthology if permission is given. Send published or unpublished work. Submissions may be entered in other contests. Submit at least 3 poems, any subject, in any form. Include SASE for winners list. Guidelines available for SASE or on website. **Entry fee:** $10/3 works, $2 each additional work. Entry fee includes a copy of the anthology. **Deadline:** July 15. Most recent award winners were Marilyn Kemph and others. Judges were Isabel Glaser and others. Winner will be announced in October at the Mid-South Poetry Festival in Memphis. Copies of winning poems or books may be obtained by writing the above address.

$☐ THE GREAT BLUE BEACON POETRY CONTEST; THE GREAT BLUE BEACON, 1425 Patriot Dr., Melbourne FL 32940. (321)253-5869. E-mail: ajircc@juno.com. Established 1997. **Award Director:** A.J. Byers. Offers prizes approximately 3 times/year, as announced, of 1st: $25; 2nd: $15; 3rd: $10. "Winning poem to be published in *The Great Blue Beacon* (amounts will be increased if sufficient entries are received.)" *The Great Blue Beacon* is a quarterly newsletter for all writers. Sample copy: $1 and 55¢ stamp (or IRC). Subscription: $10/year, students $8; outside the US $14. Submissions must be unpublished and may be entered in other contests. Submit up to 3 poems maximum on any subject in any form. "Submit three typed copies of each entry, no more than 24 lines/poem. On one copy, place your name, address, and telephone number on the upper left-hand corner of the first page. No name or address on the second copy." Guidelines available for SASE or by e-mail. Accepts inquiries by e-mail. **Entry fees:** $3/poem ($2 for subscribers to *The Great Blue Beacon*). Does not accept entry fees in foreign currencies; US dollars only. Make checks payable to Andy Byers. Competition receives 200-300 entries/year. Most recent contest winners were Denny Stein, Ren Adams, and LaVonne Schoneman. Winners will be announced approximately 2 months after deadline date. "Contestants must send SASE or e-mail address with entry to receive notification of results. Follow guidelines, particularly line limits. Submit your best work."

Ⓝ $☑ GROLIER POETRY PRIZE; ELLEN LA FORGE MEMORIAL POETRY FOUNDATION, INC., 6 Plympton St., Cambridge MA 02138. (617)253-4452. E-mail: jjhildeb@mit.edu. Website: www.GrolierPoetryBookShop.com. Established 1974. **Contact:** John Hildebide. The Grolier Poetry Prize is open to all poets who have not published either a vanity, small press, trade, or chapbook of poetry. Two poets receive an honorarium of $200 each. Pays winners from other countries by money order. Up to 4 poems by each winner and 1-2 by each of 4 runners-up are chosen for publication in the *Grolier Poetry Prize Annual*. Opens January 15 of each year; **deadline** May 1. Submissions must be unpublished and may not be simultaneously submitted. Submit up to 5 poems, not more than 10 double-spaced pages. Submit one ms in duplicate, without name of poet. On a separate sheet give name, address, phone number, and titles of poems. Only 1 submission/contestant; mss are not returned. **Entry fee:** $6, includes copy of *Annual*. Make checks payable to the Ellen La Forge Memorial Poetry Foundation, Inc. Does not accept entry fees in foreign currencies; send money order. Enclose self-addressed stamped postcard if acknowledgement of receipt is required. Winners and runners-up will be selected and informed in early June. For update of rules, send SASE to Ellen La Forge Memorial Poetry Foundation before submitting mss. Competition receives approximately 500 entries. Recent award winners include Maggie Dietz, Natasha Trethewey, and Babo Kamel. The Ellen La Forge Memorial Poetry Foundation sponsors an annual intercollegiate poetry reading and a reading series, generally 10/semester, held on the grounds of Harvard University. Poets who have new collections of poetry available are eligible. Honoraria vary. Such poets as Philip Levine, Susan Kinsolvink, Donald Hall, and Molly McQuade have given readings. Foundation depends upon private gifts and support for its activities. Copies of the *Annual* available from the Grolier Poetry Bookshop at the above address.

$☑ GUGGENHEIM FELLOWSHIPS, John Simon Guggenheim Memorial Foundation, 90 Park Ave., New York NY 10016. (212)687-4470. Fax: (212)697-3248. E-mail: fellowships@gf.org. Website: www.gf.org. Established 1925. Guggenheim fellowships are awarded each year to individuals who have already demonstrated exceptional capacity for productive scholarship or exceptional creative ability in the arts. The amounts of the grants vary. The average grant in 2001 was $36,000. Most recent award winners for poetry were Tom Andrews, Nick Flynn, Dorianne Laux, Marilyn Nelson, Wyatt Prunty, David Rivard, Charles Harper Webb, Gerardo Deniz (Juan Almela), Mercedes Roffé, and Guillermo Saavedra (2001). In 2001, 183 winners were awarded fellowships in the US out of 2,728 applications. Application deadline: October 1.

$ ● HACKNEY LITERARY AWARDS, Birmingham-Southern College, Box 549003, Birmingham AL 35254. (205)226-4921. E-mail: dcwilson@bsc.edu. Website: www.bsc.edu/events/hackneyguidelines.h tm. Sponsored by the Cecil Hackney family since 1969, offers $10,000 in prizes for novels, poetry, and short stories as part of the annual Birmingham-Southern Writing Today Conference. (See separate listing for the Writing Today Conference in the Conferences & Workshops section.) Prizes for poetry awarded at both the state and national levels. Submissions must be previously unpublished. Submit no more than 50 lines of poetry (may submit more than one poem, but total lines of all poems together must not exceed 50 lines). Guidelines available for SASE or on website. **Entry fee:** $10/50-line entry. **Postmark deadline (poems and short stories):** December 31. Most recent award winners were Susan Luther, Martin Hames, and Sue Scalf (state); Lorraine Healy, Melissa Morphew, and Lacy Schutz (national). Winners are announced at the *Writing Today* Conference.

$ ● ◎ J.C. AND RUTH HALLS AND THE CARL DJERASSI AND DIANE MIDDLE-BROOK FELLOWSHIPS IN POETRY (Specialized: MFA or equivalent degree in creative writing), Wisconsin Institute for Creative Writing, English Dept., 600 North Park St., Madison WI 53706. Website: http://creativewriting.wisc.edu. Established 1986. **Director:** Jesse Lee Kercheval. Offers annual fellowships, will pay $25,000 for one academic year. Applicants will teach one creative writing class per semester at U. of Wisconsin and give a public reading at the end of their stay. Submissions may be entered in other contests. Submit 10 poems maximum on any subject in any form. *Applicants must have a MFA or equivalent degree in creative writing.* Applicants cannot have published a book (chapbooks will not disqualify an applicant). Guidelines available for SASE or on website. **Deadline:** Applications must be received in the month of February. Competitions receive 200 entries/year. Judges are faculty of creative writing program. Results will be sent to applicants by May 1. "The fellowships are administered by the Program in Creative Writing at the University of Wisconsin-Madison. Funding is provided by the Jay C. and Ruth Halls Writing Fund and the Carl Djerassi and Diane Middlebrook Fund through the University of Wisconsin Foundation."

$ ● THE HODDER FELLOWSHIP, The Council of the Humanities, Joseph Henry House, Princeton University, Princeton NJ 08544. (609)258-4717. E-mail: humcounc@princeton.edu. Website: www.princet on.edu/~humcounc. Awarded to humanists in the early stages of their careers. Recipients have usually written one book and are working on a second. Preference is given to applicants outside academia. "The Fellowship is designed specifically to identify and nurture extraordinary potential rather than to honor distinguished achievement." **Candidates for the Ph.D. are not eligible.** Hodder Fellows spend an academic year in residence at Princeton working on independent projects in the humanities. Stipend is approximately $50,000. Most recent Hodder Fellows were Andrea Ashworth and Marlys West. Submit a résumé, sample of previous work (10 pages maximum, not returnable), a project proposal of 2-3 pages, and SASE. Guidelines available on website. Announcement of the Hodder Fellow is made in February by the President of Princeton University. **Postmark deadline:** November 1.

$ ● HENRY HOYNS POE/FAULKNER FELLOWSHIPS, Creative Writing Program, 219 Bryan Hall, P.O. Box 400121, University of Virginia, Charlottesville VA 22904-4121. (434)924-6675. Fax: (434)924-1478. E-mail: LRS9E@virginia.edu. Website: www.engl.virginia.edu/cwp (includes general information, applications, and faculty biographies). **Program Director:** Lisa Russ Spaar. Annual fellowships in poetry and fiction of varying amounts for candidates for the M.F.A. in creative writing. Sample poems/prose required with application. Accepts inquiries by fax and e-mail. **Deadline:** January 1. Competition receives 300-400 entries.

N $ ◎ INDIVIDUAL ARTIST GRANTS (Specialized: regional/Harris Co., Texas), Cultural Arts Council of Houston/Harris County, 3201 Allen Parkway, Houston TX 77019. (713)527-9330. Fax: (713)630-5210. Website: www.cachh.org. Offers awards to Houston/Harris County visual artists, writers, choreographers, and composers selected through an annual competition. Offers awards in three categories: Artist Project, General Artist Fellowship, and Emerging Artist Fellowship. Fellowship awards for writers are awarded every other year (2002), but artists are encouraged to apply for project grants in off-years. Write for deadline date, application forms, and guidelines. All information available on the website.

N ◎ THE JAPAN FOUNDATION ARTIST FELLOWSHIP PROGRAM (Specialized: US residents with Japanese affiliations), The Japan Foundation New York Office, 152 W. 57th St., 39th Floor, New York NY 10019. (212)489-0299. Fax: (212)489-0409. E-mail: katherine_wearne@jfny.org. Website:

www.jfny.org (includes program descriptions and award announcements). **Director General:** Mr. Masaya Usuda. **Program Assistant:** Katherine Wearne. Offers annual fellowships of 2-6 months in Japan (during the Japanese fiscal year of April 1 through March 31) for "accredited professional writers, musicians, painters, sculptors, stage artists, movie directors, etc." Submissions may be entered in other contests. Open to citizens or permanent residents of the US. "Affiliation with a Japanese artist or institution is required. Three letters of reference, including one from the Japanese affiliate must accompany all applications." Accepts inquiries by fax and e-mail. **Deadline:** December 1. Competition receives 20-30 entries/year.

$ ⬚ ◎ JAPANESE LITERARY TRANSLATION PRIZE (Specialized: translation/Japanese into English), Donald Keene Center of Japanese Culture, Columbia University, 507 Kent Hall, New York NY 10027. (212)854-5036. Fax: (212)854-4019. E-mail: donald-keene-center@columbia.edu. Website: www.columbia.edu/cu/ealac/dkc (includes mission and history, calendar of events, scholarly activities, translation prizes, and corporate sponsors). **Associate Director:** Becky LeGette. Established 1981. Offers annual $2,500 prize for translation of a work of Japanese classical literature into English and a $2,500 prize for translation of a work of Japanese modern literature into English. Pays winners from other countries in US dollars. "Special attention is given to new or unpublished translators, and citizens of all nationalities are eligible." Submissions may be previously published and entered in other contests. Submit 7 copies of book-length ms or published book. Entry form and guidelines available for SASE, by fax, e-mail, or on website. **Deadline:** varies. Competition receives 20-25 entries/year. Most recent award winners were James Philip Gabriel (modern Japanese literature) and Mae J. Smethurst (classical Japanese literature). Judges were Donald Keene, Hortense Calisher, Howard Hibbett, Bonnie Crown, and Robert Gottlieb. Winners will be announced through press releases and on website.

⊕ ⊘ ◎ JOHANN-HEINRICH-VOSS PRIZE FOR TRANSLATION, German Academy for Language and Literature, Alexandraweg 23, 64287 Darmstadt, Germany. Phone: (06151)40920. Fax: (06151)409299. E-mail: sekretariat@deutscheakademie.de. Website: www.deutscheakademie.de/Preise/voss.html. **President:** Prof. Dr. Christian Meier. Offers an annual award of €15,000 for outstanding lifetime achievement for translating into German, **by nomination only**.

$ ⬚ ◎ HELEN VAUGHN JOHNSON MEMORIAL HAIKU AWARD (Specialized: forms/haiku); LONG POEM CONTEST; POETRY FOR PETS (Specialized: animals), Hutton Publications, P.O. Box 2907, Decatur IL 62524. Established 2001. **Award Director:** Linda Hutton. Offers annual award for traditional haiku. 1st Prize: $25 and 1 year's subscription to *Rhyme Time*, 2nd Prize: $15, 3rd Prize: $10. Pays winners from other countries by money order. Submissions may be entered in other contests. Submit unlimited number of poems of 5 lines about nature in traditional 5-7-5 haiku format; must not refer to people; no title. Name, address, and phone number should appear in upper righthand corner of each page. Guidelines available for SASE. **Entry fee:** $1/haiku. Accepts entry fees in foreign currencies. **Deadline:** January 17 annually. Competition receives 100 entries. Judge is Linda Hutton. Winners will be announced February 20 annually. Poets may obtain copies of previous winning poems by purchasing the *Rhyme Time* winner's issue ($4). "*Rhyme Time* endeavors to encourage beginning poets. Study traditional haiku; we do not accept anything but 5-7-5." (See separate listing for *Rhyme Time* in the Publishers of Poetry section.) Also offers the Long Poem Contest. Awards 1st Prize: $25, 2nd Prize: $15, 3rd Prize: $10. Submit unlimited number of poems, no length limit, any style or theme. Include name and address on poem, mail flat with #10 SASE for contest results. No entries will be returned or published. **Entry fee:** $1/poem. **Deadline:** July 1 annually. Also offers Poetry for Pets, an annual prize of $25 each in 2 categories (rhymed and unrhymed poetry). Submissions may be previously published, must be your own work. Submit any number of poems, no more than 24 lines each (excluding title) on the subject of "pets." Entries must be typed and titled, with poet's name and address on back of page. Include #10 SASE for list of winners. **Entry fee:** $2/poem, or 3 poems for $5. **Postmark Deadline:** June 1. "Two winners will be published in a special flyer. After paying prizes and expenses of contest, the remainder of the entry fees will be donated to The Humane Society of the United States." Make all checks payable to Linda Hutton.

$ ⬚ BARBARA MANDIGO KELLY PEACE POETRY CONTEST, Nuclear Age Peace Foundation, PMB 121, 1187 Coast Village Rd., Suite 1, Santa Barbara CA 93108-2794. (805)965-3443. Fax: (805)568-0466. E-mail: wagingpeace@napf.org. Website: www.wagingpeace.org (includes posted winning poems). Established 1996. Offers an annual series of awards "to encourage poets to explore and illuminate positive visions of peace and the human spirit." Awards $1,000 to adult contestants, $200 to youth (13-18), $200 to youth (12 and under), and honorable mentions in each category. Pays winners from other countries in US currency. Submissions must be unpublished. Submit up to 3 poems on "positive visions of peace and the human spirit" in any form. Send 2 copies; maximum of 40 lines per poem. Put name, address, phone number, and age in upper right hand corner of one copy. "Poets should keep copies of all entries as we will be unable to return them." Guidelines available for SASE or on website. **Entry fee:** $5/1 poem, $10/2-3 poems. Free for youth. Does not accept entry fees in foreign currencies but will accept US money order. **Postmark deadline:** July 1. Competition receives over 500 entries. Most recent contest winner was David Ray. Judged by a committee of poets. Winners will be announced through press release and mail notification by October and on website. The Foundation reserves the right to publish the winning poems. "Nuclear Age Peace Foundation is a nonprofit peace and international security-related organization, focusing on the abolition of nuclear weapons, the strengthening of international law, the empowerment of youth, and the responsible and sustainable use of technology." Poets thinking about entering contest should "be creative and positive."

N $ KENYON REVIEW PRIZE IN POETRY FOR A FIRST BOOK, Zoo Press, P.O. Box 22990, Lincoln NE 68542. (402)770-8104. Fax: (402)614-6302. E-mail: editors@zoopress.org. Website: www.zoopress.org. Established 2000. **Contact:** Award Director. Offers annual award of $3,500 and publication. Pays winners from other countries the equivalent of $3,500 in their own currency, unless they prefer American dollars. Entrants must never have published a full-length (over 41 pages) collection of poetry. Contestants should send only 1 copy of each ms. Manuscripts must be approximately 50-100 pages in length, typed single-spaced, with no more than 1 poem/page. Manuscripts must be paginated and contain a table of contents. Illustrations are not accepted. Handwritten mss will not be accepted. Contestants who have published poems in magazines may include those in the ms submitted, along with a page of acknowledgements. Submissions may be entered in other contests. Guidelines available for SASE, by e-mail, or on website. **Entry fee:** $25/submission. Does not accept entry fees in foreign currencies; American dollars only. **Deadline:** April 15, 2003. Competition receives 500-1,000 entries/year. Beth Ann Fennelly's *Open House* won the 2001 inaugural prize. Judge for upcoming award will be David Baker. Winners will be announced in the spring of the following year. Copies of winning books are available from local bookstores, online vendors, or through www.zoopress.org. "Zoo Press is a literary publisher of poetry, fiction, drama, and essay. Please see our Paris Review Prize in Poetry [in this section] and our Parnassus Prize for a Book of Poetry Criticism." Advises, "David Baker, the prize's recurring judge, is an eclectic editor with an eye for quality. We define quality in poetry as an awareness of tradition, formal integrity, rhetorical variety (i.e., invective, satire, argument, irony, etc.), an impressive level of difficulty in the project undertaken, authenticity, and, above all, beauty. All poetry manuscripts should aspire to these ideals."

N THE STEPHEN LEACOCK MEMORIAL MEDAL FOR HUMOUR (Specialized: humor, regional/Canada); THE NEWSPACKET, Stephen Leacock Associates, P.O. Box 854, Orillia, Ontario L3V 3P4 Canada. (705)835-7061. Fax: (705)835-7062. E-mail: spruce@encode.com. Website: www.leacock.ca. **Contact:** Marilyn Rumball (corresponding secretary). **Award Chairman:** Judith Rapson. Annual prize presented for a book of humor in prose, verse, drama, or any book form—by a Canadian citizen. "Book must have been published in the current year and no part of it may have been previously published in book form." Submit 10 copies of book, 8×10 b&w photo, bio, and entry fee. **Entry fee:** $45 CAN. Prize: Silver Leacock Medal for Humour and Laurentian Bank of Canada cash award of $10,000. **Deadline:** December 31. Competition receives 40-50 entries. The 2001 winner was *The Vinyl Café Unplugged* by Stuart McLean. The committee also publishes *The Newspacket* 4 times/year, with the 4th issue being a special literary issue.

$ THE LEAGUE OF MINNESOTA POETS CONTEST, 432 Tyrol Dr., Brainerd MN 56401-2920. **Contest Chair:** Joan Wiesner. Offers 18 different contests in a variety of categories, with 3 prizes in each category ranging from $10-125 for poems up to 60 line limit. Guidelines available for SASE. **Nonmember fee:** $1/poem per category; $2/poem (limit 6) for Grand Prize category. **Members fee:** $5 for 17 categories; $1/poem (limit 6) for Grand Prize category. **Deadline:** July 31. Nationally known, non-Minnesota judges.

$ MELBOURNE POETS UNION ANNUAL NATIONAL POETRY COMPETITION (Specialized: regional/Australian poets), Melbourne Poets Union, P.O. Box 266, Flinders Lane, Victoria 8009 Australia. Established 1977. **Contact:** The Secretary. Offers annual prizes to a total of $1,000. Pays winners from other countries "with a cheque in foreign currency, after negotiation with winner." Submissions must be unpublished. Submit unlimited number of poems on any subject in any form. "Open to Australian residents living in Australia or overseas." Entry form and guidelines available for SASE (or SAE and IRC). **Entry fee:** AUS $5/poem. Accepts entry fees in foreign currencies. **Deadline:** October 31. Competition receives over 500 entries/year. Winners will be announced on the last Friday of November. "The $1,000 prize money comes directly from entry money, the rest going to paying the judge and costs of running the competition."

$⊘ MID-LIST PRESS FIRST SERIES AWARD FOR POETRY, Mid-List Press, 4324 12th Ave. S., Minneapolis MN 55407-3218. E-mail: guide@midlist.org. Website: www.midlist.org (includes information about publishing program, describes and lists titles published, and provides links to online booksellers; guidelines and entry forms are available as are special offers on most recent First Series titles). Established 1990. "The First Series Award for Poetry is an annual contest we sponsor for poets who have never published a book of poetry. The award includes publication and a $500 advance against royalties." Individual poems within the book ms may be previously published and may be entered in other contests. Submit at least 60 single-spaced pages. "Note: We do not return manuscripts. Other than length we have no restrictions, but poets are encouraged to read previous award winners we have published." Recent award winners include Margo Stever, Katherine Starke, and Adam Sol. Submissions are circulated to an editorial board. Guidelines are available for #10 SASE or on website; no inquiries by fax or e-mail. **Entry fee:** $20; must include entry form (available online). Does not accept entry fees in foreign currencies. Accepted submissions October 1 through February 1 for 2002 series. Competition receives 750 entries/year. "The First Series Award contest is highly competitive. We are looking for poets who have produced a significant body of work but have never published a book-length collection. (A chapbook is not considered a 'book' of poetry.)"

$◎ MONEY FOR WOMEN (Specialized: women/feminism); GERTRUDE STEIN AWARD; FANNIE LOU HAMER AWARD, Barbara Deming Memorial Fund, Inc., P.O. Box 630125, Bronx NY 10463. **Administrator:** Susan Pliner. Offers biannual small grants of up to $1,500 to feminists in the arts "whose work addresses women's concerns and/or speaks for peace and justice from a feminist perspective." Application form available for SASE. Applicants must be citizens of US or Canada. **Application fee:** $10. **Deadlines:** December 31 and June 30. Competition receives 400 entries/year. Most recent award winners were Kelle Groom, Danielle Montgomery, Lisa J. Parker, and Michele Thorsen. Winners will be announced in May and October. Also offers the Gertrude Stein Award for outstanding work by a lesbian, and the "Fannie Lou Hamer Award" for work which combats racism and celebrates women of color.

ℕ ◎ MONTANA ARTS; MARY BRENNEN CLAPP MEMORIAL POETRY CONTEST (Specialized: regional), P.O. Box 1872, Bozeman MT 59771. Biannual contest. Open to Montana poets or former Montana poets only, for 3 unpublished poems up to 100 lines total. Awards prizes of $100, $80, $60 and $40. Submit 3 poems and cover letter. Guidelines available for SASE. **Deadline:** September in even-numbered years.

$⊘ SAMUEL FRENCH MORSE POETRY PRIZE, English Dept., 406 Holmes, Northeastern University, Boston MA 02115. (617)373-4546. Fax: (617)373-2509. E-mail: g.rotella@neu.edu. Website: www .casdn.neu.edu/~english/pubs/morse.htm (includes info and contest rules). **Editor:** Prof. Guy Rotella. Offers book publication (ms 50-70 pages) by Northeastern University Press and an annual award of $1,000. Open to US poets who have published no more than 1 book of poetry. Entry must be unpublished in book form but may include poems published in journals and magazines. Guidelines available on website. Accepts inquiries by e-mail. **Entry fee:** $15. **Deadline:** August 1 for inquiries; September 15 for single copy of ms. Manuscripts will not be returned. Competition receives approximately 400 entries/year. Most recent award winners include Jeffrey Greene, Jennifer Atkinson, and Ted Genoways. Most recent judge was Marilyn Hacker.

$◻ NASHVILLE NEWSLETTER POETRY CONTEST, P.O. Box 60535, Nashville TN 37206-0535. Established 1977. **Editor/Publisher:** Roger Dale Miller. Offers quarterly prizes of $50, $25, and $10 plus possible publication in newsletter, and at least 50 Certificates of Merit. Pays winners from other countries with check in US funds. Submit one unpublished poem to a page, any style or subject up to 40 lines, with name and address in upper left corner. Send large #10 SASE for more information and/or extra entry forms for future contests. **Entry fee:** $5 for up to 3 poems. Must be sent all at once for each contest. Does not accept entry fees in foreign currencies but will accept check/money order in US funds. "All other nonwinning poems will be considered for possible publication in future issues." Competition receives over 700 entries/year. Most recent winners were Diane McDaniel, Cindy Mosher, Anne-Marie Legan. Recent judges were Hazel Kirby and Roger Dale Miller. *Nashville Newsletter* appears quarterly. Sample: $3. Responds in up to 10 weeks.

$⊘ NATIONAL BOOK AWARD, National Book Foundation, 95 Madison Ave., Suite 709, New York NY 10016. (212)685-0261. E-mail: natbkfdn@mindspring.com. Website: www.nationalbook.org. Offers annual grand prize of $10,000 plus 4 finalist awards of $1,000. Presents awards in fiction, nonfiction, poetry, and young people's literature. Submissions must be previously published and **must be entered by the publisher**. Entry form and guidelines available for SASE. **Entry fee:** $100/title. **Deadline:** July 8.

◯ NATIONAL WRITERS UNION ANNUAL NATIONAL POETRY COMPETITION, P.O. Box 2409, Aptos CA 95001. E-mail: lstaple@earthlink.net. Website: www.mbay.net/~NWU (includes information about local and national events and links for writers). **Chair:** Pat Hansen. **Contact:** Local 7 Coordinator. The 2002 competition is sponsored by Santa Cruz/Monterey Local 7 of the NWU. **Entry fee:** $4/poem. Prizes: $500, $300, $200, plus publication in union newsletter. Possible additional 1st place publication in *Poetry Flash*. For rules, send SASE to Local 7 Coordinator or see website. **Postmark deadline:** December 1. Competition receives about 1,000 entries/year. Past judges include Adrienne Rich and Philip Levine.

ℕ ⊘ NEUSTADT INTERNATIONAL PRIZE FOR LITERATURE; WORLD LITERATURE TODAY, University of Oklahoma, 110 Monnet Hall, Norman OK 73019-4033. (405)325-4531. Fax: (405)325-7495. Website: www.ou.edu/worldlit/ (includes general information on *World Literature Today* and the Neustadt Prize.) **Executive Director:** Robert Con Davis-Undiano. Award of $50,000 given every other year in recognition of life achievement or to a writer whose work is still in progress; **nominations from an international jury only**. Most recent award winner was David Malouf (Australia, 2000).

$◯ NEW MILLENNIUM AWARD FOR POETRY, NEW MILLENNIUM WRITINGS, P.O. Box 2463, Knoxville TN 37901. E-mail: DonWilliams7@att.net. Website: www.mach2.com (includes publication of winners, table of contents, photos of contributors, contest guidelines, cover graphics, how to order past issues, subscription information, and much more). **Editor:** Don Williams. Offers 2 annual awards of $1,000 each. Pays winners from other countries by money order. Submissions must be previously unpublished but may be entered in other contests. Submit up to 3 poems, 5 pages maximum. No restrictions on style or content. Include name, address, phone number, and a #10 SASE for notification. Printable entry form on website. Manuscripts are not returned. Guidelines available for SASE. Accepts inquiries by e-mail. **Entry fee:** $15. Make checks payable to New Millennium Writings. Does not accept entry fees in foreign currencies; send money order drawn on US bank. **Deadlines:** June 15 and November 15. Competition receives 2,000 entries/year. "Two winners and selected finalists will be published." Most recent award winners include Ken McCullough and Eduardo Corral. "Contests are not the only avenues to publication. We also accept—at no cost, no entry fee—general submissions for publication, year round. These should be addressed to Editor. There are no restrictions as to style, form, or content. Submitters should enclose SASE for correspondence purposes."

ℕ $⊘ NEW RIVER POETS QUARTERLY POETRY AWARDS, New River Poets, 5545 Meadowbrook St., Zephyrhills FL 33541-2715. Established 2000. **Awards Coordinator:** June Owens. Offers 1st Prize: $60; 2nd Prize: $40; 3rd Prize: $30 for each quarterly contest. Pays winners from other countries by international bank money order. Submissions may be previously published and may be entered in other contests. Submit 1-3 poems of up to 42 lines each on any subject, in any form. "Send 2 copies each poem on 8½×11 white paper; poet's identification on only one copy of each. If previously published, state where/when. If in a traditional form, state form. Quarter for which work is submitted must appear upper right." Guidelines available for SASE. **Entry fee:** 1-3 poems for $4; $1 each additional; no limit. Accepts entry fees in foreign currencies but prefers US funds. **Deadline:** November 15, February 15, May 15, August 15. Competition receives 510 entries/year. Most recent award winners were Norma Jagendorf,

---

VISIT THE WRITER'S DIGEST WEBSITE at www.writersdigest.com for books, markets, newsletter sign-up, and a special poetry page.

Sandra Lake Lassen, and Glenna Holloway. Most recent contest judges were Joyce Odam, Glenna Holloway, Sandra Lake Lassen, and Norma Jagendorf. (First Place winners are invited to judge a subsequent competition). Winners will be announced by mail within 45 days of deadline. "New River Poets is a chartered Chapter of Florida State Poets Association, Inc. Its purpose is to acknowledge and reward outstanding poetic efforts. Its plans include the publication of an anthology, *Watermarks*, which will not only be open to general submissions but will offer each of our 1st, 2nd, and 3rd place winners a modest honorarium for one-time use of his/her winning poem. Other plans include inviting student groups to participate and learn from specific NRP meetings. Later on, we hope to host a quarterly FSPA meeting." Advises to "send your best. Always include SASE. Our 'rules' are quite wide open, but please adhere. Remember that competition is not only good for the cause of poetry but for the poetic soul, a win-win situation."

$◑ NEWBURYPORT ART ASSOCIATION ANNUAL SPRING POETRY CONTEST, 12 Charron Dr., Newburyport MA 01950. E-mail: espmosk@juno.com. Website: www.newburyportart.org (includes contest information and guidelines). Established 1990. **Contest Coordinator:** Rhina P. Espaillat. Offers annual awards of 1st Prize: $200, 2nd Prize: $150, 3rd Prize: $100, plus 4 Honorable Mentions and certificates. "All winners, including Honorable Mention poets, are invited to read their own entries at the Awards Day Reading in May." Open to anyone over 16 years old. Pays winners from other countries with NAA check. Submissions must be previously unpublished, may be entered in other contests. Submit any number of poems, each no more than 3 pages in length. Must be typed, single- or double-spaced, on white 8½×11 paper; each poem must have a title. Send 2 copies of each poem—one without identification, one bearing your name, address, and telephone number. Include SASE for notification of contest results. Any number of poems accepted, but all must be mailed together in a single envelope with one check covering the total entry fee. Guidelines available for SASE, by e-mail, and on website. **Entry fee:** $3/poem. Does not accept entry fees in foreign currencies; send US cash, check, or money order. Make checks payable to NAA Poetry Contest (one check for all entries). **Postmark deadline:** March 15, 2003. Winners for the 2002 contest were Bill Coyle, Len Krisak, and Diana Lockward, plus 14 Honorable Mentions. Judge was Dr. Robert B. Shaw. "Please do not submit entries without first securing a copy of the guidelines, and follow them carefully."

🌐 $◎ NSW PREMIER'S LITERARY AWARD "THE KENNETH SLESSOR PRIZE" (Specialized: regional/Australia), NSW Ministry for the Arts, P.O. Box A226, Sydney South NSW 1235 Australia. E-mail: ministry@arts.nsw.gov.au. Website: www.arts.nsw.gov.au. Established 1980. Offers annual award of AUS $15,000 for a book of poetry (collection or long poem) published in the previous year. Open to Australian citizens only. Books may be nominated by poets or by their agents or publishers. Write for entry form and guidelines or check website. **Deadline:** November 30, 2002. Winners will be announced in May. "Obtain copy of guidelines before entering."

$◯ ◎ FRANK O'HARA AWARD CHAPBOOK COMPETITION; THORNGATE ROAD PRESS (Specialized: gay/lesbian/bisexual), Dept. of English and Humanities, Pratt Institute, 200 Willoughby Ave., Brooklyn NY 11205. (718)636-3790. Fax: (718)636-3573. E-mail: jelledge@pratt.edu. Established 1996. **Award Director/Publisher:** Jim Elledge. Offers annual award of $500, publication, and 25 copies. Submissions may be a combination of previously published and unpublished work and may be entered in other contests. Submit 16 pages on any topic, in any form. Another 4 pages for front matter is permitted, making the maximum total of 20 pages. Poets must be gay, lesbian, or bisexual (any race, age, background, etc.). One poem/page. Guidelines available for SASE. Accepts inquiries by fax and e-mail. **Entry fee:** $15/submission. **Deadline:** February 1. Competition receives 200-300 entries. Most recent contest winner was *Straight Boyfriend* by Peter Covino. Judge is a nationally recognized gay, lesbian, or bisexual poet. Judge remains anonymous until the winner has been announced (by April 15). Copies of winning books may be ordered by sending $6 to the above address made out to Thorngate Road Press. "Thorngate Road publishes at least two chapbooks annually, and they are selected by one of two methods. The first is through the contest. The second, the Berdache Chapbook Series, is by invitation only. We published chapbooks by Kristy Nielsen, David Trinidad, Reginald Shepherd, Karen Lee Osborne, Timothy Liu, and Maureen Seaton in the Berdache series." Although the contest is only open to gay, lesbian, bisexual, and transgendered authors, the content of submissions does not necessarily have to be gay, lesbian, bisexual, or transgendered."

N $☐ OHIO POETRY DAY CONTESTS, Ohio Poetry Day Association, 3520 St. Route 56, Mechanicsburg OH 43044. (937)834-2666. Established 1937. **Contest Chairman:** Amy Jo Zook. Offers annual slate of up to 40 contest categories. Prizes range from $75 on down; all money-award poems published in anthology (runs over 100 pages). Pays winners from other countries in cash. "The bank we use does not do *any* exchange at any price." Submissions must be unpublished. Submit 1 poem/category on topic and in form specified. Some contests open to everyone, but others open only to Ohio poets. "Each contest has its own specifications. Entry must be for a specified category, so entrants *need rules*." Entry form and guidelines available for SASE. **Entry fee:** $8 inclusive, unlimited number of categories. Does not accept entry fees in foreign currencies. **Deadline:** May 30. Competition receives up to 4,000 entries/year. Judges for most recent contest listed in winners' book. Judges are never announced in advance. Winners list available in August for SASE; prizes given in October. Copies of winning books available from Amy Jo Zook for $7 each and $1.50 postage. "Ohio Poetry Day is the umbrella. Individual contests are sponsored by poetry organizations and/or individuals across the state. OPD sponsors one, plus Poet of the Year and Student Poet of the Year; have 4 memorial funds." Advises to "revise, follow rules, look at individual categories for a good match."

$◎ OHIOANA BOOK AWARDS; OHIOANA POETRY AWARD (Helen and Laura Krout Memorial); OHIOANA QUARTERLY; OHIOANA LIBRARY ASSOCIATION (Specialized: regional), Ohioana Library Association, 274 E. First Ave., Columbus OH 43201. (614)466-3831. Fax: (614)728-6974. E-mail: ohioana@SLOMA.state.oh.us. Website: www.oplin.lib.oh.us/ohioana. **Director:** Linda Hengst. Offers annual Ohioana Book Awards. Up to 6 awards may be given for books (including books of poetry) by authors born in Ohio or who have lived in Ohio for at least 5 years. The Ohioana Poetry Award of $1,000 (with the same residence requirements), made possible by a bequest of Helen Krout, is given yearly "to an individual whose body of published work has made, and continues to make, a significant contribution to poetry, and through whose work as a writer, teacher, administrator, or in community service, interest in poetry has been developed." Nominations to be received by December 31. Competition receives several hundred entries. Most recent award winners were William Greenway (body of work) and Erin Belieu (book). *Ohioana Quarterly* regularly reviews Ohio magazines and books by Ohio authors and is available through membership in Ohioana Library Association ($25/year).

N ◎ NATALIE ORNISH POETRY AWARD (Specialized: regional/TX); SOEURETTE DIEHL FRASER TRANSLATION AWARD (Specialized: translations, regional/TX); TEXAS INSTITUTE OF LETTERS, % Paula Marks, Box 935, St. Edward's University, 3001 S. Congress, Austin TX 78704. (512)448-8702. Fax: (512)448-8767. E-mail: paulam@admin.stedwards.edu. Website: www.stedwards.edu/newc/marks/til (includes contest deadlines). **Contact:** Paula Marks. Established 1947. The Texas Institute of Letters gives annual awards for books by Texas authors in 8 categories, including the Natalie Ornish Poetry Award, a $1,000 award for best volume of poetry. Books must have been first published in the year in question, and entries may be made by authors or by their publishers. One copy of each entry must be mailed to each of 3 judges, with "information showing an author's Texas association . . . if it is not otherwise obvious." Poets must have lived in Texas for at least 2 consecutive years at some time or their work must reflect a notable concern with matters associated with the state. Soeurette Diehl Fraser Translation Award ($1,000) is given for best translation of a book into English. Same rules as those for Natalie Ornish Poetry Award. Write during the fall for complete instructions. Accepts inquiries by fax and e-mail. **Deadlines:** see website. Competitions receive 30 entries/year. Recent award winners include Isabel Nathaniel, Betty Adcock, Jack Myers, and Pattiann Rogers.

N $☐ PARIS REVIEW PRIZE IN POETRY, Zoo Press, P.O. Box 22990, Lincoln NE 68542. (402)770-8104. Fax: (402)614-6302. E-mail: editors@zoopress.org. Website: www.zoopress.org. Established 2000. **Contact:** Award Director. Offers annual award of $5,000, a reading in NYC, and publication by Zoo Press. Pays winners from other countries the equivalent of $5,000 in their own currency, unless they prefer American dollars. Contestants should send only 1 copy of each ms. Manuscripts must be approximately 50-100 pages in length, typed single-spaced, with no more than 1 poem/page. Manuscripts must be paginated and contain a table of contents. Illustrations are not accepted. Handwritten mss will not be accepted. Contestants who have published poems in magazines may include those in the ms submitted, along with a page of acknowledgements. Submissions may be entered in other contests. Guidelines available for SASE, by e-mail, or on website. **Entry fee:** $25/submission. Does not accept entry fees in foreign currencies; American dollars only. **Deadline:** October 31, 2002. Competition receives 500-1,000 entries/year. Priscilla Becker's *Internal West* won the 2000 inaugural prize. Judge for upcoming award will be

Richard Howard. Winners will be announced in the spring of the following year. Copies of winning books are available from local bookstores, online vendors, or through www.zoopress.org. "Zoo Press is a literary publisher of poetry, fiction, drama, and essay. Please see our Kenyon Review Prize in Poetry for a First Book [in this section] and our Parnassus Prize for a Book of Poetry Criticism." Advises, "Richard Howard, the prize's recurring judge, is one of the most eclectic editors of poetry in the United States, so it's difficult to qualify or quantify his aesthetic more than to say he will choose a high quality manuscript. We define quality in poetry as an awareness of tradition, formal integrity, rhetorical variety (i.e., invective, satire, argument, irony, etc.), an impressive level of difficulty in the project undertaken, authenticity, and, above all, beauty. All poetry manuscripts should aspire to these ideals."

$ ☑ PAUMANOK POETRY AWARD COMPETITION; THE VISITING WRITERS PRO-GRAM, SUNY Farmingdale, Farmingdale NY 11735. E-mail: brownml@farmingdale.edu. Website: www. farmingdale.edu/CampusPages/ArtsSciences/EnglishHumanities/paward.html (includes Paumanok Poetry Award guidelines and other links to information on the Visiting Writers Program). Established 1990. **Director:** Dr. Margery Brown. Offers a prize of $1,000 plus an all-expense-paid feature reading in their 2002-2003 series (*Please note:* travel expenses within the continental US only). Also awards two runner-up prizes of $500 plus expenses for a reading in the series. Pays winners from other countries in US dollars. Submit cover letter, 1-paragraph literary bio, up to 5 poems of up to 10 pages (published or unpublished). **Entry fee:** $25. **Postmark deadline:** by September 15. Make checks payable to SUNY Farmingdale Visiting Writers Program (VWP). Does not accept entry fees in foreign currencies. Send money order in US dollars. Send SASE for results (to be mailed by late December). Guidelines available for SASE or on website. Accepts inquiries by e-mail. Competition receives over 600 entries. Most recent contest winners include Marjorie Maddox (winner) and Elizabeth Tibbetts and Honorée Fannone Jeffers (runners-up). Poets who have read in this series include Hayden Carruth, Allen Ginsberg, Linda Pastan, Marge Piercy, Joyce Carol Oates, Louis Simpson, and David Ignatow. The series changes each year, so entries in the 2001 competition will be considered for the 2002-2003 series, and so on.

N ◎ PEN CENTER USA WEST LITERARY AWARD IN POETRY (Specialized: regional/ west of MS), PEN Center USA West, 672 S. Lafayette Park Place, #42, Los Angeles CA 90057. (213)365-8500. Fax: (213)365-9616. E-mail: awards@penusa.org. Website: www.penusa.org (includes entry forms, guidelines, press releases, membership info, and program info). **Awards Coordinator:** Christina Apeles. Offers annual $1,000 cash award to a book of poetry published during the previous calendar year. Open to writers living west of the Mississippi. Submit 4 copies of the entry. Entry form and guidelines available for SASE, by fax, e-mail, or on website. **Entry fee:** $25. **Deadline:** December 27, 2002. Recent award winner was Susan Rich. Judges were Michael C. Ford, Ruth Forman, and Peter J. Harris. Winner will be announced in a May 2003 press release and honored at a ceremony in Los Angeles.

$ ☑ ◎ PENNSYLVANIA POETRY SOCIETY ANNUAL CONTEST, 801 Spruce St., West Reading PA 19611-1448. (610)374-5848. E-mail: aubade@bluetruck.net. Website: http://home.att.net./~the paperlesspoets/index.html. **Contact:** Contest Chairman. Offers Annual Contest with grand prize awards of $100, $50, and $25; 3 poems may be entered for grand prize at $2 each for members and nonmembers alike. A total of 17 categories open to all, 4 categories for members only. **Entry fee:** varies according to category and membership. Guidelines available for SASE or on website. **Deadline:** January 15. Also sponsors the Pegasus Contest **for PA students only**, grades 5-12. For information send SASE to Carol Clark Williams, chairman, 445 North George St., York PA. **Deadline:** March 1. The Ferguson Environmental Contest is for all poets, offers prizes of $75, $25, $15, and $10. **Entry fee:** $1, 1 poem limit. **Deadline:** September 15. Kids' N Kritters contest open to all poets. Deadline: October 31. Guidelines available for SASE from Joy Campbell, chairman, 10 Polecat Rd., Landisburg PA 17040. The Wine & Roses Contest is for **PA poets only. Deadline:** October 15. Guidelines available for SASE from Ray Fulmer, chairman, 316 Park Ave., Quakertown PA 18951. The Society publishes a quarterly newsletter with member poetry

USE THE GENERAL INDEX in the back of this book to find the page number of a specific market. Also, markets listed in the 2002 edition but not included in this edition appear in the General Index with a code explaining their absence from the listings.

and challenges, plus an annual soft-cover book of prize poems from the Annual Contest. Pegasus Contest-wining poems are published in a booklet sent to schools. PPS membership dues: $15/fiscal year. Make checks payable to PPS, Inc., mail to Richard R. Gasser, treasurer, at the above address.

$◻◎ PENUMBRA POETRY & HAIKU CONTEST (Specialized: form/haiku), Tallahassee Writers' Association, P.O. Box 15995, Tallahassee FL 32317-5995. E-mail (for Carole Timin, contest director): gtimin@unr.net. Website: http://twaonline.org (includes full contest guidelines, postal address, information on Tallahassee Writers' Association membership and activities). Established 1987. Offers cash prizes plus publication in and one copy of chapbook of winners and finalists. Prizes: $200, $60, and $40 for poetry; $100, $40, and $20 for haiku. Pays winners from other countries by US check. Submission must be unpublished. No simultaneous submissions. Accepts poetry of up to 50 lines (shorter poetry is of equal value) and/or 3-line haiku. Poets may submit to both categories. Poems must be typed on 8½×11 paper; haiku on 3×5 cards. Send 2 copies of each entry. On one copy, write author's name, address, telephone, e-mail, and source of contest information, second copy should be anonymous. Include 1-paragraph bio listing publications. Guidelines available for SASE, by e-mail, or on website. **Entry fee:** $5/poem, $3/haiku. Send check or money order in US dollars only. **Deadline:** June 30. Competition receives 500-600 entries each category/year from US, Canada, Europe, and others. Most recent winners were Matt McCaw (poetry) and Tim Russell (haiku). 2001 judges were Keith Ratzlaff and Peggy Lyles. Sample copy of *Penumbra* chapbook available for $5 plus $2.50 postage from TWA Penumbra. Includes essays by judges and contributor bios.

$◎ PEW FELLOWSHIPS IN THE ARTS (Specialized: regional/PA), 230 S. Broad St., Suite 1003, Philadelphia PA 19102. (215)875-2285. Fax: (215)875-2276. Website: www.pewarts.org (includes past panelists and Pew fellows, application forms, and guidelines). Established 1991. **Award Director:** Melissa Franklin. "The Pew Fellowships in the Arts provide financial support directly to artists so they may have the opportunity to dedicate themselves wholly to the development of their artwork for up to 2 years. Up to 12 fellowships of $50,000 each (in 3 different categories) awarded each year." Must be a Pennsylvania resident of Bucks, Chester, Delaware, Montgomery, or Philadelphia county for at least 2 years; must be 25 or older. Matriculated students, full or part-time, are not eligible. Application and guidelines available mid-August for SASE. Accepts inquiries by phone, fax, and e-mail. **Deadline:** December of the preceding year. Most recently judged by a panel of artists and art professionals. Winner will be announced by letter.

$◭ THE RICHARD PHILLIPS POETRY PRIZE, The Phillips Publishing Co., 2200 E. Mountain Rd., Poetry Building: i-102, Springdale AR 72764. Established 1993. **Award Director:** Richard Phillips, Jr. Annual award of $1,000, open to all poets. Submit 48-page ms, published or unpublished poems, any subject, any form. Guidelines available for SASE. **Entry fee:** $15/ms, payable to Richard Phillips Poetry Prize. Accepts entry fees in foreign currencies. Manuscripts are not returned. **Postmark deadline:** January 31. "Winner will be announced and check for $1,000 presented by March 31." Publication is the following September. Competition receives approximately 100 entries. Most recent prize winners were: Helen Olsen (2002), Clark Doane (2001), and Patricia Lang (2000). "There are no anthologies to buy, no strings attached. The best manuscript will win the prize."

$◭ POETIC LICENSE CONTEST; MKASHEF ENTERPRISES, P.O. Box 688, Yucca Valley CA 92286-0688. E-mail: alayne@inetworld.net. Website: www.asidozines.com (includes sample poetry, editor's biography). Established 1998. **Poetry Editor:** Alayne Gelfand. Offers a biannual poetry contest. 1st Prize: $500, 2nd Prize: $100, 3rd Prize: $40, plus publication in anthology and 1 copy. Pays winners from other countries in US cash, by money order, or through PayPal. Five honorable mentions receive 1 copy; other poems of exceptional interest will also be included in the anthology. Themes and deadlines available for SASE. Submit any number of poems, any style, of up to 50 lines/poem (poems may have been previously published). Include name, address, and phone on each poem. Enclose a SASE for notification of winners. Accepts submissions by regular mail, on disk, or by e-mail (attachment or pasted within text of message). "Judges prefer original, accessible, and unforced works." Guidelines available for SASE or by e-mail. **Entry fee:** $1/poem. "We're looking for fresh word usage and surprising imagery. Each contest seeks to explode established definitions of the theme being spotlighted. Be sure to send SASE or e-mail for current theme and deadline."

N: **$** **⊘** **THE POETRY CENTER BOOK AWARD**, 1600 Holloway Ave., San Francisco CA 94132. (415)338-2227. Fax: (415)338-0966. E-mail: newlit@sfsu.edu. Website: www.sfsu.edu/~newlit/. Established 1980. **Business Manager:** Elise Ficarra. Offers award to an outstanding book of poems published by an individual author in the current year. One prize of $500 and an invitation to read at the Poetry Center. **Entry fee:** $10. Does not accept entry fees in foreign currencies; send money order in US dollars. "Please include cover sheet noting author's name, book title(s), name of person or publisher issuing check, and check number." Book must be published and copyrighted during the year of the contest and submitted by December 31. Competition receives 200-250 entries. Most recent award winner was Kevin Davies for *Comp.* (2000). Judge was Kevin Killian. Translations and anthologies are not accepted. Books should be by an individual writer and must be entirely poetry. No entry form required. Past winners include Kevin Davies, Cole Swensen, Elaine Equi, Belle·Waring, and Alicia Suskin. Winner will be announced on website and through press release. "The Poetry Center and American Poetry Archives at San Francisco State University was established in 1954. Its archives include the largest circulating tape collection of writers reading their own work in the United States."

⧗ **$⊘** **POETRY FOREVER; MILTON ACORN PRIZE FOR POETRY; ORION PRIZE FOR POETRY; TIDEPOOL PRIZE FOR POETRY**, Poetry Forever, P.O. Box 68018, Hamilton, Ontario L8M 3M7 Canada. (905)312-1779. Fax: (905)312-8285. **Administrator:** James Deahl. Poetry Forever sponsors 3 annual contests for poets everywhere—the Milton Acorn Prize, the Orion Prize, and the Tidepool Prize. Each contest awards 50% of its entry fees in 1st, 2nd, and 3rd Place prizes (amount varies, but no less than $100). The top 3 poems also receive broadsheet publication. For all 3 contests, poems may be no longer than 30 lines. "Poems should be typed or neatly printed and no longer than 30 lines. Photocopied submissions OK." Send SASE or e-mail address to receive winners' list. **Entry fee:** $3/poem. Make checks payable to Poetry Forever. **Deadlines:** May 15 (Milton Acorn), June 15 (Orion Prize), July 15 (Tidepool Prize). "The purpose of the contests is to fund the publication of full-size collections by the People's Poet, Milton Acorn (1923-1986); Ottawa poet Marty Flomen (1942-1997); and Hamilton poet Herb Barrett (1912-1995)." Recent winners include Ellen Jaffe (Orion Prize), Dorothy Stott (Milton Acorn), and Margaret Malloch Zielinski (Tidepool Prize).

$⊘ **◎** **POETS' CLUB OF CHICAGO; HELEN SCHAIBLE SHAKESPEAREAN/PETRARCHAN SONNET CONTEST (Specialized: form/sonnet)**, 1212 S. Michigan Ave., Apt. 2702, Chicago IL 60605. (312)786-1959. Fax: (312)461-0217. E-mail: toby@sxu.edu. **Chairperson:** Tom Roby. The annual Helen Schaible Shakespearean/Petrarchan Sonnet Contest is open to anyone **except** members of Poets' Club of Chicago. **For sonnets only!** Submit only 1 entry (2 copies) of either a Shakespearean or a Petrarchan sonnet, which must be original and unpublished. Entry must be typed on 8½×11 paper, double-spaced. Name and address in the upper right-hand corner on only one copy. Guidelines available for SASE or by e-mail. **No entry fee.** Prizes of $50, $35, and $15 and 3 non-cash honorable mentions. **Postmark deadline:** September 1. Competition receives 120 entries/year. Most recent contest winners were June Owens, Robert Klein Engler, Linda Bosson, and Doris Elinore Benson. Winners will be notified by mail by October 15. Include SASE with entry to receive winners' list. The Poets' Club of Chicago meets monthly at the Harold Washington Library to critique their original poetry, which the members read at various venues in the Chicago area and publish in diverse magazines and books. Members also conduct workshops at area schools and libraries by invitation.

$⊘ **◎** **POETS' DINNER CONTEST**, 2214 Derby St., Berkeley CA 94705-1018. (510)841-1217. **Contact:** Dorothy V. Benson. **Contestant must be present to win.** Submit 3 anonymous typed copies of original, unpublished poems in not more than 3 of the 8 categories [Humor, Love, Nature, Beginnings & Endings, Spaces & Places, People, Theme (changed annually), and Poet's Choice] without fee. Winning poems (Grand Prize, 1st, 2nd, 3rd) are read at an awards banquet and honorable mentions are presented. Cash prizes awarded; Honorable Mention receives books. The event is nonprofit. Since 1927 there has been an annual awards banquet sponsored by the ad hoc Poets' Dinner Committee, currently at the Holiday Inn in Emaryville. Contest guidelines available for SASE. **Deadline:** January. Competition receives about 300 entries. Recent contest winners include William Landis (Grand Prize); Sandra Bozarth, Norma King Green, Robert Eastwood, Janet Thomas, Carol Frith, and Joyce Odam (first prizes). *Remembering*, an anthology of winning poems from the Poet's Dinner over the last 25 years is available by mail for $10.33.

$⊘ **POETS OF THE VINEYARD CONTEST; VINTAGE**, 704 Brigham Ave., Santa Rosa CA 95404-5245. E-mail: jhchueng@aol.com. **President:** Judy Cheung. **Contest Chair:** Emma J. Blanch. Offers annual contest sponsored by the Sonoma County Chapter (P.O.V.) of the California Federation of Chaparral Poets. For unpublished poems in 5 categories including traditional forms, free verse poems that tell a story, short free verse, and a theme-category on grapes, vineyards, wine. Contest rules and deadline available for SASE from Contest Chair at 21 Ludlow Dr., Milford CT 06460. Prizes in each category are $50, $25, and $15, with a grand prize chosen from category winners ($75). Pays winners from other countries with international money order at US value at time of issue. **Entry fee:** nonmembers $4/poem or $10/3 poems; members $3/poem or $10/5 poems. Prize-winning poems will be published in the annual anthology, *Vintage*. Most recent contest winners were Ruth Wilder Schuler, Elizabeth Howard, and Patricia Wellingham Jones. Anthology available for $13.50 including shipping; past anthologies available for $8 including shipping.

◯ PORTLANDIA CHAPBOOK CONTEST; THE PORTLANDIA GROUP, PMB 225, 6663 SW Beaverton-Hillsdale Hwy., Portland OR 97225. E-mail: braucher@portlandia.com. Established 1999. **Award Director:** Karen Braucher. Offers annual prize of $200, publication of chapbook, and 30 free copies. Submissions may be entered in other contests. Submit 24 pages of poetry with title page, table of contents, and bio. Poems may be in free verse and/or formal verse. "See guidelines for the year you are submitting." Guidelines available for SASE and by e-mail. **Entry fee:** $12/chapbook ms (as of 2002). Does not accept entry fees in foreign currencies; accepts check on US bank or US money order. **Deadline:** check annual guidelines (was March 1 for 2002). Competition receives approximately 200 entries/year. Most recent contest winner was Elisa A. Garza for *Familia* (2001). "Panel of judges is used. Most have M.F.A. or Ph.D degrees and have published." Winner will be announced in spring of each year. Copies of winning chapbooks ($6, includes shipping) are available from The Portlandia Group. "The Portlandia Group, a fine poetry press, was founded by Karen Braucher, M.F.A., to publish the best emerging poets in the hope that they will go on to publish full-length books. This is happening. We are looking for the finest poetry being written in English. Judges are published poets who have read widely in contemporary poetry. You are unlikely to win if you have not published some poems in journals."

$◯ PULITZER PRIZE IN LETTERS, % The Pulitzer Prize Board, 709 Journalism, Columbia University, New York NY 10027. (212)854-3841. Fax: (212)854-3342. E-mail: pulitzer@www.pulitzer.org. Website: www.pulitzer.org (includes downloadable entry form and guidelines, bios and photos of winners from 1995 to present, and an archive of past winners). **Contact:** the Pulitzer Prize Board. Offers 5 prizes of $7,500 and certificate each year, including 1 in poetry, for books published in the calendar year preceding the award. Entry form and guidelines available for SASE, by fax, or on website. Accepts inquiries by fax and e-mail. Submit 4 copies of published books (or galley proofs if book is being published after November), photo, bio, entry form, and $50 entry fee. July 1 deadline for books published between January 1 and June 30; November 1 deadline for books published between July 1 and December 31. Competition receives 150 entries/year. Most recent award winner was Stephen Dunn for *Different Hours*, published by W.W. Norton & Company. Judges were Mary Karr, Anthony Hecht, and Jonathan Holden.

$◯ QUINCY WRITERS GUILD WRITING CONTEST; QUINCY WRITERS GUILD, P.O. Box 433, Quincy IL 62306. E-mail: chillebr@adams.net. Website: www.quincylibrary.org/guild.htm (includes updated guidelines). Established 1990. **Contest Coordinator:** Carol Hillebrenner. Offers annual award for original, unpublished poetry (serious poetry and light poetry), fiction, and nonfiction. Cash prizes based on dollar amount of entries; at least 70% of money returned to winners. 1st, 2nd, and 3rd Prizes awarded in all categories. Guidelines available for SASE, by e-mail, or on website. **Entry fee:** $2/poem; $4/nonfiction or fiction piece. Does not accept entry fees in foreign currencies; accepts cash in US dollars as well as Western Union and American Express checks. Entries accepted from January 1 through April 1. Competition receives 150-175 entries. Recent contest winners were Tulis McCall for "Bosses of Morning," Theodore Mangano for "Barring the Storm," and Herman Johnson for "A Soldier's Greatest Fear." Judges are QWG nonmembers. The Quincy Writers Guild meets monthly and consists of Quincy-area writers working in various genres.

◯ REDWOOD ACRES FAIR POETRY CONTEST, P.O. Box 6576, Eureka CA 95502. (707)445-3037. Fax: (707)445-1583. E-mail: ninthdaa@pacbell.net. Website: www.redwoodacres.com. **Contact:** Diane Fales. Offers an annual contest with various categories for both juniors and seniors. Prizes include Best of Show ribbon and $25; Best of Class ribbon and $5; premiums for 1st-3rd Place. Submissions must be unpublished. "For poems to be returned, entrants *must* enclose a self-addressed stamped envelope. If not picked up, entries will be destroyed." Entry form and guidelines available for SASE. **Entry fee:** 50¢/

poem for the junior contests and $1/poem for the senior contests. **Deadline:** late May. Competition receives 200 entries. Most recent winners were Ellawaine Lockie, Gene Duvall, Dan Goldstein, Angie Wolski, Kathy Keith, and Phyllis Carralho. Judge was Bill Lemley. Winners will be announced through local newspaper or by SASE.

⃞N ⃝ MARY ROBERTS RINEHART AWARDS, Mail Stop Number 3E4, English Dept., George Mason University, Fairfax: VA 22030-4444. (703)993-1180. E-mail: bgompert@gmu.edu. Website: www.gmu.edu/departments/writing. **Contact:** Barb Gomperts. Three annual grants of $2,000 each are awarded in spring for the best nominated manuscript in fiction, nonfiction, and poetry. "Grants are made only for unpublished works by writers who have not yet published a book or whose writing is not regularly appearing in nationally circulated commercial or literary magazines. Writers may see a grant in only one category in any given year; an author not granted an award one year may apply in succeeding years, but once a writer receives an award, he or she may not apply for another, even in a different genre. Grant recipients are not required to be United States citizens but only works in English will be read, and awards are made only in US dollars." **A writer's work must be nominated in writing by an established author, editor, or agent**. Nominations must be accompanied by a sample of the nominee's work (10 pages of individual or collected poems/30 pages of fiction or nonfiction). **Postmark deadline:** November 30. "Grants will be announced early in the following March on the awards web page. Candidates who wish to receive a printed announcement should submit a #10 SASE." Competition receives over 300 entries. Guidelines available for SASE, by e-mail, or on website.

⃝ ⃝ ANNA DAVIDSON ROSENBERG AWARD, FOR POEMS ON THE JEWISH EXPERIENCE (Specialized: ethnic), Judah L. Magnes Museum, 2911 Russell St., Berkeley CA 94705. E-mail: pfpr@magnesmuseum.org. Website: www.magnesmuseum.org/. Established 1987. Offers prizes of $100, $50, and $25, as well as honorable mentions, for unpublished poems (in English) on the Jewish Experience. "This award is open to all poets. You needn't be Jewish to enter."

  • There was no award given in 2001 and maybe not in 2002; poets should query regarding the status of the award for 2003 before submitting. (**Note:** the Magnes Museum and the Jewish Museum San Francisco merged as of January 1, 2002.)

⃞N ⃝ ⃝ THE CONSTANCE SALTONSTALL FOUNDATION FOR THE ARTS GRANTS (Specialized: regional), P.O. Box 6607, Ithaca NY 14851-6607. Phone/fax: (607)277-4933. E-mail: artsfound@clarityconnect.com. Website: www.saltonstall.org/. **Program Manager:** Lee-Ellen Marvin. Offers grants of $5,000 and residencies at the Saltonstall Arts Colony to visual and literary artists. Poets submit up to 15 pages. Must be 21 years or older and resident of the central and western counties of New York state. Application form available for SASE or on website. **Deadline:** January. Winners announced in April.

$ ⃝ SAN FRANCISCO FOUNDATION; JOSEPH HENRY JACKSON AWARD; JAMES D. PHELAN AWARD (Specialized: regional/CA, NV; young adult), % Intersection for the Arts, 446 Valencia St., San Francisco CA 94103. (415)626-2787. Fax: (415)626-1636. E-mail: info@theintersection.org. Website: www.theintersection.org (includes calendar of events at Intersection for the Arts and general guidelines for San Francisco Foundation awards). **Contact:** Awards Coordinator. Offers the Jackson Award ($2,000), established in 1955, to the author of an unpublished work-in-progress of fiction (novel or short stories), nonfictional prose, or poetry. Applicants must be residents of northern California or Nevada for 3 consecutive years immediately prior to the January 31 deadline and must be between the ages of 20 and 35 as of the deadline. Offers the Phelan Award ($2,000), established in 1935, to the author of an unpublished work-in-progress of fiction (novel or short stories), nonfictional prose, poetry, or drama. Applicants must be California-born (although they may now reside outside of the state), and must be between the ages of 20 and 35 as of the January 31 deadline. Manuscripts for both awards must be accompanied by an application form. The award judge will use a name-blind process. Manuscripts should be copied on the front and back of each page and must include a separate cover page that gives the work's title and the applicant's name and address. The applicant's name should only be listed on the cover page; do not list names or addresses on the pages of the ms. Applicants may, however, use the mss title and page numbers on the pages of the ms. Manuscripts with inappropriate identifying information will be deemed ineligible. Three copies of the ms should be forwarded with one properly completed current year's official application form to the address listed above. Guidelines available on website. Entries accepted November 15 through January 31. Competitions receive 150-180 entries. Recent contest writers include Richard Dry, Kristen Hanlon, and Angela Morales.

$ ☑ ◎ **SARASOTA POETRY THEATRE PRESS; EDDA POETRY CHAPBOOK COMPETITION FOR WOMEN; SARASOTA POETRY THEATRE CHAPBOOK COMPETITION; ANIMALS IN POETRY; SPRING POETRY CHAPBOOK PRIZE (Specialized: women/feminism)**, P.O. Box 48955, Sarasota FL 34230-6955. (941)366-6468. Fax: (941)954-2208. E-mail: soulspeak1 @home.com. Website: www.soulspeak.org (includes general info about Soulspeak/Sarasota Poetry Theatre, the press, competitions, and all books published, plus samples of poetry from each book). Established 1994-1998. **Award Director:** Scylla Liscombe. Offers 4 annual contests for poetry with prizes ranging from 1st Prize: $25 plus publication in an anthology to 1st Prize: $100 plus 25 published chapbooks. Honorable Mentions also awarded. Pays winners from other countries in copies. Guidelines and details about theater available for SASE or on website. Accepts queries by e-mail. **Entry fees:** range from $4/ poem to $10/ms. **Postmark deadline:** Animals in Poetry, April 30 (winners notified in July); Sarasota Poetry Theatre Chapbook Competition, August 31 (winners notified in November); Edda Poetry Chapbook Competition for women, February 28 (winners notified in May); Spring Poetry Chapbook Prize, October 31 (winners notified in January). Competitions receive an average of 1,000 entries/year. Judges for contests are the staff of the press and ranking state poets. Winners are notified by mail. "Sarasota Poetry Theatre Press is a division of Soulspeak/Sarasota Poetry Theatre, a nonprofit organization dedicated to encouraging poetry in all its forms through the Sarasota Poetry Theatre Press, Therapeutic Soulspeak for at-risk youth, and the Soulspeak Performance Center. We are looking for honest, not showy, poetry; use a good readable font. Do not send extraneous materials."

$ ☐ ◎ **CLAUDIA ANN SEAMAN POETRY AWARD (Specialized: students)**, The Community Foundation of Dutchess County, 80 Washington St., Suite 201, Poughkeepsie NY 12601. (845)452-3077. Fax: (845)452-3083. Website: http://communityfoundationdc.org. **Contact:** Karen Van Houten. Established 1983. Offers annual award of $500 (1st Prize) in national contest. Submissions must be unpublished but may be entered in other contests. Submit 1 or 2 poems on any subject, in any form. Open to students grades 9-12. "Entry must contain student and school names, addresses, and phone numbers and the name of the English or writing teacher." Entry form and guidelines available for SASE. Accepts inquiries by fax. **Deadline:** was May 1 for 2002. Recent award winner was Gemma Cooper-Novack. Judged by "a panel of judges, including Donna Seaman (Claudia's sister)." Winner announced and recognized each year at the Barnes & Noble in Manhattan (announcement date August 1 for 2002). Copies of last year's winning poem may be obtained by contacting The Community Foundation by phone or in writing. "The Community Foundation is a nonprofit organization serving Dutchess County, NY; it administers numerous grant programs, scholarship funds, and endowment funds for the benefit of the community. This is an excellent opportunity for young, previously unpublished poets to earn recognition for their work. Since there's no fee, there is little to lose; realize, however, that a national contest will have more entries than a regional competition."

$ ☐ ◎ **SENIOR POET LAUREATE POETRY COMPETITION (Specialized: senior citizen); GOLDEN WORDS**, Goodin Communications & Penny Peephole Publications, Chapbook Dept., P.O. Box 6003, Springfield MO 65801. E-mail: goldenword@aol.com. Established 1993. **Contact:** SPL Coordinator. Offers annual award to "American poets age 50 and older. Top winner will receive $75 and the Senior Poet Laureate title. Cash awards will also be given ($10 to 1st Place winners in ten poetry categories). We pay winners from other countries by money order. All winners and Honorable Mentions will be published in *Golden Words* chapbook of poems by leading older American poets." Submit any number of poems; 32 lines or less (unless specified otherwise); 1/page. Categories are haiku, short poem (12 lines or less), nostalgic, long poem (over 32 lines), sonnet, love, inspirational, light verse, western/ pioneer/patriotic poem, and Pissonnet. Poems may be previously published and entered in other contests, but poet must be able to grant rights to publish the winning poem. Entry form and guidelines available for SASE. Accepts inquiries by e-mail. **Entry fee:** $1/poem. Does not accept entry fees in foreign currencies; send money order. **Deadline:** August 1. Competition receives 1,000 entries/year. Most recent contest winner was Helen F. Blackshear (2001). Winners will be announced in October. The top winning poems from the 10 categories and the new Senior Poet Laureate's poem will also be published in *Hodgepodge* literary magazine. (See separate listing in Publishers of Poetry).

$☐ SKY BLUE WATERS POETRY CONTESTS; SKY BLUE WATERS POETRY SOCIETY, 232 SE 12th Ave., Faribault MN 55021-6406. (507)332-2803. **Contact:** Marlene Meehl. Sponsors monthly contests with prizes of $40, $30, $20, $10, plus 3 paid Honorable Mentions of $5 each. Pays winners from other countries by check. Accepts simultaneous submissions. Submit any number of poems on any subject. Guidelines available for SASE. **Entry fee:** $2 first poem, $1 each additional poem. Does not accept entry fees in foreign currencies; send check or money order. Winners will be announced by mail one month following deadline date. "The Sky Blue Waters Poetry Society is a group of Southern Minnesota poets who exist for the sheer 'love of writing.' Most members agree that writing is not just a love but a necessity. Keep writing. Keep submitting. Today's creation will be tomorrow's winner."

$⬚ SLAPERING HOL PRESS CHAPBOOK COMPETITION, The Hudson Valley Writers' Center, 300 Riverside Dr., Sleepy Hollow NY 10591. (914)332-5953. Fax: (914)332-4825. E-mail: info@writerscenter.org. Website: www.writerscenter.org (includes information about the Writers' Center and the Slapering Hol Press, including titles in print and contest guidelines). Established 1990. **Co-editor:** Margo Stever. Offers annual award of $500, publication, 10 author's copies, and a reading at the Hudson Valley Writers' Center. Pays winners from other countries with check in US currency. Submissions must be from poets who have not previously published a book or chapbook. Submit 16-20 pages of poetry with acknowledgements, any form or style, SASE, and $10 entry fee. "Manuscript should be anonymous with second title page containing name, address, and phone." Guidelines available for SASE, by fax, e-mail, or on website. **Deadline:** May 15. Competition receives 200-300 entries. Most recent contest winner was Jianquing Zheng, *The Landscape of Mind*. Copies of winning books available by requesting order form.

$☐ KAY SNOW WRITING AWARDS; WILLAMETTE WRITERS; THE WILLAMETTE WRITER, 9045 SW Barbur Blvd., Suite 5A, Portland OR 97219-4027. (503)452-1592. Fax: (503)452-0372. E-mail: wilwrite@teleport.com. Website: www.willamettewriters.com. Established 1986. **Award Director:** Elizabeth Shannon. Offers annual awards of 1st Prize: $300, 2nd Prize: $150, 3rd Prize: $50 and publication of excerpt only in December issue of *The Willamette Writer*. Pays winners from other countries by postal money order. Submissions must be unpublished. Submit up to 2 poems (one entry fee), maximum 5 pages total, on any subject in any style or form, single spaced, one side of paper only. Entry form and guidelines available for SASE or on website. Accepts inquiries by fax and e-mail. **Entry fee:** $10 for members of Willamette Writers; $15 for nonmembers. Does not accept entry fees in foreign currencies; only accepts a check drawn on a US bank. **Deadline:** May 15. Competition receives 150 entries. Most recent winners were Emily Scott, Morgan Amber Neiman, Ellavaine Lockie, Lynn Veach Sadler, Nancy Froeschle, and Tulis McCall. Winners will be announced July 31. "Write and send in your very best poem. Read it aloud. If it still sounds like the best poem you've ever heard, send it in."

Ⓝ $☐ THE SOUL OF THE POET AWARD; GRAMMAR BYTES, 3044 Shepherd of Hills, PMB 519, Branson MO 65616. E-mail: contest@grammarbytes.com. Website: www.grammarbytes.com. Established 1997. **Award Director:** Shane Jeffries. Offers annual award of 1st Prize: $250, 2nd Prize: $100, 3rd Prize: $25, plus Honorable Mention certificate. Pays winners from other countries by International Money Order. Submissions may be entered in other contests. Submit up to 30 pages of poetry on any subject in any form. "All entries must be in English. All entries may be single or double spaced but must be on standard $8\frac{1}{2} \times 11$ paper. Clean photocopies are accepted. Do not send originals." Guidelines available for SASE or on website. Accepts inquiries by e-mail. **Entry fee:** $15 for up to 30 pages. Does not accept entry fees in foreign currencies; send International Money Order. **Postmark deadlines:** May 31, 2003. Competition receives about 300 entries/year. Most recent award winner was D.P. Pool. "Previous winners select semifinalists, then a committee of 3 prominent writers will make final decision." Winners contacted by mail. "Grammar Bytes is dedicated to helping writers learn the proper usage of the English language by assisting in copyediting and proofreading. Great writing is great writing, regardless of style, technique, or subject. Submit your best work and stay positive. The Soul of the Poet Award was created to aid writers in their journey toward ultimate literary goals—whatever they might be."

$⬚ WALLACE E. STEGNER FELLOWSHIPS, Creative Writing Program, Stanford University, Stanford CA 94305-2087. (650)725-1208. Fax: (650)723-3679. E-mail: gay.pierce@forsythe.stanford.edu. Website: www.stanford.edu/dept/english/cw/. **Program Administrator:** Gay Pierce. Offers 5 fellowships in poetry of $20,000 plus tuition of over $6,000/year for promising writers who can benefit from 2 years of instruction and criticism at the Writing Center. "We do not require a degree for admission. No school of writing is favored over any other. Chronological age is not a consideration." **Postmark deadline:**

December 1. Accepts inquiries by fax and e-mail. Competition receives about 1,000 entries/year. 2002-2003 fellows in poetry include Geoffrey Brock, Robin Ekiss, Monica Ferrel, John Lundberg, and David Roderick.

N ⬛ $ ◎ STEPHAN G. STEPHANSSON AWARD FOR POETRY (Specialized: regional/ Alberta), Writers Guild of Alberta, 11759 Groat Rd., Edmonton, Alberta T5M 3K6 Canada. (780)422-8174. Fax: (780)422-2663. E-mail: mail@writersguild.ab.ca. Website: www.writersguild.ab.ca (includes awards info, job/market listing, general information on WGA, program information, and directory of writers.) **Contact:** Executive Director. Annual award in 6 categories, including poetry. Awards $1,000 and leather bound copy of book. Eligible books will have been published anywhere in the world between January 1 and December 31. Authors will have been Alberta residents for at least 12 of the 18 months prior to December 31. Contact the WGA head office for registry forms. (See separate listing for Writers Guild of Alberta in the Organizations section.) Unpublished mss not eligible, except in the drama category. Anthologies not eligible. Five copies of each book to be considered must be mailed to the WGA office no later than December 31. Submissions postmarked after this date will not be accepted. Exceptions will be made for any books published between the 15th and 31st of December, which may be submitted by January 15. Three copies will go to the 3 judges in that category; 1 will remain in the WGA library and 1 will be placed in a WGA book display around the province. Works may be submitted by authors, publishers, or any interested parties. Competition receives varied amount of entries. Most recent contest/award winner was Shane Rhodes. Additional information available by fax, e-mail, or on website.

⊕ $ ◯ THE TABLA POETRY COMPETITION; THE TABLA BOOK OF NEW VERSE, Dept. of English, University of Bristol, 3-5 Woodland Rd., Bristol BS8 1TB England. Fax: (0117)928 8860. E-mail: stephen.james@bristol.ac.uk. Website: www.bris.ac.uk/tabla. Established 1991. **Award Director:** Dr. Stephen James. Offers annual poetry competition. 1st Prize: £500, 2nd Prize: £200, 3 runners-up: £100 each plus publication. Cash prizes paid in UK sterling only. Submissions must be unpublished. Submit any number of poems on any subject in any form, any length. Poems must be typed on one side only; no names on poems to be judged. Entry form and guidelines available for SASE (or SAE and IRC) or on website. Accepts inquiries by fax and e-mail. "One free entry with purchase of *The Tabla Book of New Verse* (£6 UK); all other entries: £3 UK each. Book costs £7 (Eur), £8 (rest of world) to cover postage. Only UK standing fees and payments accepted." **Deadline:** March 1, 2003. Competition receives about 1,500 entries/year. Most recent contest winner was Siobhan Anna Toman (2001) (no competition was held in 2002). Judge was George Szirtes. Judge for upcoming contest will be Philip Gross. Winners announced by mail and on the website by June each year. "All above prices correct in 2001; subject to revision in 2002."

N $ ◯ THOUGHT MAGAZINE CONTEST, P.O. Box 117098, Burlingame CA 94011-7098. E-mail: ThoughtMagazine@yahoo.com. Website: www.ThoughtMagazine.org (includes guidelines, contacts, recent publications). Established 2000. **Award Director:** Kevin Feeney. Offers biannual award of publication and 1st Prize: $75, 2nd Prize: $50. Submissions may be entered in other contests. Submit 3 poems of 48 lines/poem. Guidelines available for SASE, by e-mail, or on website. **Entry fee:** $5 for 3 poems. Does not accept entry fees in foreign currencies. **Deadline:** April 15, 2003; August 15, 2003. Competition receives 150 entries/year. Contest judged by the editors. Winners will be announced September 1 and May 1. Copies of prizewinner issues available from *Thought Magazine*. "*Thought Magazine* is a nonprofit organization dedicated to publishing poetry and prose. Some of the proceeds are used to support community services in hospitals, shelters, and retirement homes." (See separate listing for *Thought Magazine* in the Publishers of Poetry section.)

$ ◪ ◎ TOWSON UNIVERSITY PRIZE FOR LITERATURE (Specialized: regional/Maryland), Towson University, College of Liberal Arts, Towson MD 21252. (410)704-2128. Fax: (410)830-6392. **Award Director:** Dean of the College of Liberal Arts. Offers annual prize of $2,000 "for a single book or book-length manuscript of fiction, poetry, drama, or imaginative nonfiction by a young Maryland writer. The prize is granted on the basis of literary and aesthetic excellence as determined by a panel of distinguished judges appointed by the university. The first award, made in the fall of 1980, went to novelist Anne Tyler." Work must have been published within the 3 years prior to the year of nomination or must be scheduled for publication within the year in which nominated. Submit 5 copies of work in bound form or in typewritten, double-spaced ms form. Entry form and guidelines available for SASE. Accepts inquiries by e-mail. **Deadline:** June 15. Competition receives 8-10 entries. Most recent contest co-winners were Jonathan Lowy and Dean Smith.

THE TREWITHEN POETRY PRIZE (Specialized: rural); THE TREWITHEN CHAPBOOK, Trewithen Poetry, Chy-An-Dour, Trewithen Moor, Stithians, Truro, Cornwall TR3 7DU England. Website: www.trewithenpoetry.co.uk (includes downloadable entry form and poems). Established 1995. **Award Secretary:** D. Atkinson. Offers annual award of 1st Prize: £500, 2nd Prize: £150, 3rd Prize: £75, plus 3 runner-up prizes of £25 each and publication in *The Trewithen Chapbook*. Pays winners from other countries by "sterling cheque" or draft only. Submissions may be entered in other contests "*but must not* previously have won another competition." Submit any number of poems on a rural theme in any form. Entry form available for SASE or on website. **Entry fee:** £3 for the first poem and £2 for each additional poem. Does not accept entry fees in foreign currencies; send "sterling cheque" or draft only. **Deadline:** October 31. Competition receives 1,000-1,500 entries. Recent contest winners were Lesley Quayle, Mike Sharpe, Mike Barlow, and W.R. Chadwick. Judged by a panel of 3-4 working poets who remain anonymous. Winners will be announced at the end of December by results sheet, through poetry magazines and organizations, and on website. Winning poems published biennially in March/April. Copies of *The Trewithen Chapbook* may be obtained by using order form on entry form, by writing direct to the secretary and enclosing a SAE with IRC, or on website. "We are seeking good writing with a contemporary approach, reflecting any aspect of nature or rural life in any country."

KATE TUFTS DISCOVERY AWARD; KINGSLEY TUFTS POETRY AWARD, Poetic Gallery for the Kingsley and Kate Tufts Poetry Awards, Claremont Graduate University, 160 E. 10th St., Harper East B7, Claremont CA 91711-6165. (909)621-8974. Website: www.cgu.edu/tufts/. Established 1992 (Kingsley Tufts Award) and 1993 (Kate Tufts Award). **Awards Administrator:** Betty Terrell. Kate Tufts Discovery Award offers $10,000 annually "for a first or very early work by a poet of genuine promise." Kingsley Tufts Poetry Award offers $100,000 annually "for a work by an emerging poet, one who is past the very beginning but has not yet reached the acknowledged pinnacle of his/her career." Books must be published between September 15, 2001 and September 15, 2002. Entry form and guidelines available for SASE or on website. **Deadline:** September 15. Most recent award winners were Carl Phillips (Kingsley Tufts, 2002) and Cate Marvin (Kate Tufts, 2002). Check website for updated deadlines and award information.

VER POETS OPEN COMPETITION, Ver Poets, Haycroft, 61/63 Chiswell Green Lane, St. Albans, Hertfordshire AL2 3AL United Kingdom. Phone: (01727)867005. Established 1974. **Organiser/Editor:** May Badman. Offers annual open competition with prizes totaling £1,000, plus a free copy of anthology, *Vision On* with winning and selected poems. Pays winners from other countries in sterling by cheque. Submissions must be unpublished. Submit any number of poems on any subject, "open as to style, form, contest. Poem must be no more than 30 lines excluding title, typed on white A4 sheets. Entry forms provided, pseudonyms to be used on poems." Two copies of poems required. **Entry fee:** £3/ poem. Entry form and guidelines available for SASE (or SAE and IRC). Accepts entry fees in foreign currencies. **Deadline:** April 30. Competition receives about 1,000 entries/year. Most recent contest winners were Margaret Morgan, John Godfrey, David Whitehead, and Andrew Marstand-Dauce. 2001 adjudicator was John Greening. Winners announced at an "Adjudication & Tea" event in June each year. "We have local and postal members, meet regularly in St. Albans, study poetry and the writing of it, try to guide members to reach a good standard, arrange 3 competitions per year with prizes and anthologies for members only. Plus the annual open competition. We do expect a high standard of art and skill. We make a gift to a charity each year."

WESTERN AUSTRALIAN PREMIER'S BOOK AWARDS (Specialized: regional/ Western Australia), Library & Information Service of W.A., Alexander Library Bldg., Perth Cultural Centre, Perth, Western Australia 6000 Australia. Phone: (61 8)9427 3330. Fax: (61 8)9427 3336. E-mail: jham@liswa.wa.gov.au. Website: www.liswa.wa.gov.au/pba.html. Established 1982. **Award Director:** Ms. Julie Ham. Offers annual poetry prize of AUS $5,000 for a published book of poetry. Winner also eligible for Premier's Prize of AUS $20,000. Submissions must be previously published. Open to poets born in Western Australia, current residents of Western Australia, or poets who have resided in Western Australia for at least 10 years at some stage. Entry form and guidelines available by mail or on website. Accepts inquiries by fax and e-mail. No entry fee. **Deadline:** January 4, 2003. Competition receives about 10-15 entries in poetry category/year (120 overall). Most recent winner was *Parochial* by Mark Reid. Judges were Prof. Vijay Mishra, Ms. Jill Midolo, Dr. Simon Adams, and Mr. Zolton Kovacs. Winners announced in June each year (i.e., June 2002 for 2003 awards) at a presentation dinner given by the Premier of Western Australia. "The contest is organized by the Library and Information Service of Western Australia, with money provided by the Western Australian State Government to support literature."

$⬤ STAN AND TOM WICK POETRY PRIZE, Wick Poetry Program, Dept. of English, Kent State University, P.O. Box 5190, Kent OH 44242-0001. (330)672-2067. Fax: (330)672-2567. E-mail: wickp oet@kent.edu. Website: www.kent.edu/wick (includes contest guidelines, reading series schedule). Established 1994. **Program Coordinator:** Maggie Anderson. Offers annual award of $2,000 and publication by Kent State University Press. Submissions must be unpublished as a whole and may be entered in other contests as long as the Wick program receives notice upon acceptance elsewhere. Submit 48-68 pages of poetry. Open to poets writing in English who have not yet published a full-length collection. Entries must include cover sheet with poet's name, address, telephone number, and title of ms. Guidelines available for SASE or on website. **Entry fee:** $15. Does not accept entry fees in foreign currencies; send money order or US check. **Deadline:** May 1. Competition receives 700-800 entries. 2001 contest winner was Kate Northrop. Judge for 2001 contest was Lynn Emanuel.

$◎ THE RICHARD WILBUR AWARD (Specialized: nationality), Dept. of English, University of Evansville, 1800 Lincoln Ave., Evansville IN 47722. (812)479-2963. **Series Director:** William Baca. Offers a biennial award (even-numbered years) of $1,000 and book publication to "recognize a quality book-length manuscript of poetry." Submissions must be unpublished ("although individual poems may have had previous journal publications") original poetry collections and "public domain or permission-secured translations may comprise up to one-third of the manuscript." Submit ms of 50-100 typed pages, unbound, bound, or clipped. Open to all American poets. Manuscripts should be accompanied by 2 title pages: one with collection's title, author's name, address, and phone number; one with only the title. Include SASE for contest results. Manuscripts are *not* returned. Guidelines available for SASE. **Entry fee:** $25/ms. **Next postmark deadline:** December 2, 2002. Competition receives 300-500 entries. Recent contest winner was Rhina P. Espaillat. Judge for last contest was Rachel Hadas. The winning ms is published and copyrighted by the University of Evansville Press.

$◻ WINTER WOOD POETRY AWARD, Heather's Teddy Bear Organization, Inc., 16 Oakdale Rd., Terryville CT 06786. (860)585-1735. E-mail: StarlenHTBO@aol.com. Established 1999. **Director/CEO:** Arlene M. Wood. Offers annual awards of 1st Prize: $100, 2nd Prize: $50, and 3rd Prize: $25. Pays winners from other countries with a bank check. Submissions must be unpublished and may be entered in other contests. Submit any number of poems on any subject in any style/form. Line length is 20 maximum/poem. Poems may be sent by regular mail or by e-mail (pasted within body of message). Entry form, guidelines, and winners list available for SASE. Accepts inquiries by e-mail. **Entry fee:** $5/poem. Does not accept entry fees in foreign currencies. Make checks payable to the Heather's Teddy Bear Organization, Inc., "a nonprofit organization, 501-(c)(3)." **Deadline:** for 4th annual award, submissions must be postmarked no earlier than January 1, 2002, and no later than September 30, 2002. Winners for the 3rd annual award were Ellaraine Lockie and Altaire Pare. Judges were Sue Bacon, Linda Foster, Nancy Giudice, Lisa Lavoie, Garth Pelton, and Francena Dwyer. Winners for the 3rd annual award were Ellaraine Lockie and Altaire Pare.

$⬤ ◎ WORLD ORDER OF NARRATIVE AND FORMALIST POETS (Specialized: subscription, form), P.O. Box 580174, Station A, Flushing NY 11358-0174. Established 1980. **Contest Chairman:** Dr. Alfred Dorn. Sponsors contests in a number of categories for traditional and contemporary poetic forms, including the sonnet, blank verse, ballade, villanelle, free verse, and new forms created by Alfred Dorn. Prizes total at least $5,000. Only subscribers to *The Formalist* are eligible for the competition. Complete contest guidelines available for SASE from Alfred Dorn. "We look for originality of thought, phrase and image, combined with masterful craftsmanship. Trite, trivial, or technically inept work stands

---

THE ◎ SYMBOL indicates a market with a specific or unique focus. This specialized area of interest is listed in parentheses behind the market title.

no chance." **Next deadline:** fall 2002. Competition receives about 3,000 entries. Past contest winners include Brian E. Drake, Rachel Hadas, Len Krisak, Albert Sterbak, Carolyn Raphael, and Rhina P. Espaillat. (For more information on *The Formalist*, see their listing in the Publishers of Poetry section.)

🌐 $◻ **THE WRITERS BUREAU POETRY AND SHORT STORY COMPETITION**, The Writers Bureau, Sevendale House, 7 Dale St., Manchester M1 1JB England. Phone: (0161)228 2362. Fax: (0161)228 3533. E-mail: comp@writersbureau.com. Website: www.writersbureau.com. Established 1994. **Contact:** Head of Student Services. Offers annual prizes of 1st Place: £1,000, 2nd: £400, 3rd: £200, 4th: £100, six 5th Place prizes of £50, and publication in *Freelance Market News*. Submissions must be unpublished. "Any number of entries may be sent. There is no set theme or form. Entries must be typed, and no longer than 40 lines." Accepts entries by regular mail or by fax. Entry form available for SASE or on website. Accepts inquiries by fax or e-mail. **Deadline:** late July. Contest judge was Alison Chisholm. Winner(s) will be announced in September. "The Writers Bureau is a distance learning college offering correspondence courses in Journalism, Creative Writing, and Poetry."

$◻ **THE W.B. YEATS SOCIETY ANNUAL POETRY COMPETITION; W.B. YEATS SOCIETY OF NEW YORK**, National Arts Club, 15 Gramercy Park S, New York NY 10003. (212)780-0605. Website: www.YeatsSociety.org (includes a "guestbook, where inquiries may be left; full information on our programs and links to numerous other relevant sites"). Established 1994. **President:** Andrew McGowan. Offers $250 cash prize for 1st Place, $100 cash prize for 2nd Place, and optional Honorable Mentions. Open to beginner as well as established poets. Winners are invited to read their winning entries at the Taste of the Yeats Summer School, held each April in New York; also inducted as Honorary Members of the Society (a 501(c)(3) charitable organization). Judges have included poets Eamon Grennan, L.S. Asekoff, Campbell McGrath, Billy Collins, Harvey Shapiro, and Paul Muldoon. **Annual deadline:** February 15. No entry form is required. Submit any number of unpublished poems in any style or form, up to 50 lines each, typed on letter-size paper without poet's name. Reading fee: $7 for first poem, $6 per additional poem. Attach a 3×5 card to each entry containing the poem's title along with the poet's name, address, and phone/fax/e-mail. Winners selected by March 31 and announced in April. Winning entries and judge's report are posted on the Society's website. Printed report available for SASE. Receives 200-300 entries/year. Most recent contest winners were Cameron K. Gearen, Zoe Anglesey, Elise Partridge, and John Hoppenthaler.

Additional Contests & Awards

The following listings also contain information about contests and awards. Turn to the page numbers indicated for details about their offerings.

State & Provincial Grants

Arts councils in the United States and Canada provide assistance to artists (including poets) in the form of fellowships or grants. These grants can be substantial and confer prestige upon recipients; however, **only state or province residents are eligible**. Because deadlines and available support vary annually, query first (with a SASE).

UNITED STATES ARTS AGENCIES

Alabama State Council on the Arts, *201 Monroe St., Montgomery AL 36130-1800. (334)242-4076. E-mail: staff@arts.state.al.us. Website: www.arts.state.al.us.*

Alaska State Council on the Arts, *411 W. Fourth Ave., Suite 1-E, Anchorage AK 99501-2343. (907)269-6610 or (888)278-7424. E-mail: aksca_info@eed.state.ak.us. Website: www.aksca.org.*

Arizona Commission on the Arts, *417 W. Roosevelt, Phoenix AZ 85003. (602)255-5882. E-mail: general@ArizonaArts.org. Website: www.ArizonaArts.org/.*

Arkansas Arts Council, *1500 Tower Bldg., 323 Center St., Little Rock AR 72201. (501)324-9766. E-mail: info@dah.state.ar.us. Website: www.arkansasarts.com.*

California Arts Council, *1300 I St., Suite 930, Sacramento CA 95814. (916)322-6555 or (800)201-6201. Website: www.cac.ca.gov/.*

Colorado Council on the Arts, *750 Pennsylvania St., Denver CO 80203-3699. (303)894-2617. Website: www.coloarts.state.co.us/.*

Connecticut Commission on the Arts, *755 Main St., 1 Financial Plaza, Hartford CT 06103. (860)566-4770. E-mail: artsinfo@ctarts.org. Website: www.ctarts.org.*

Delaware State Arts Council, *Carvel State Office Bldg., 820 N. French St., Wilmington DE 19801. (302)577-8278 (New Castle Co.), (302)739-5304 (Kent or Sussex Counties). E-mail: delarts@state.de.us. Website: www.artsdel.org.*

District of Columbia Commission on the Arts & Humanities, *410 Eighth St., NW, 5th Floor, Washington DC 20004. (202)724-5613. Website: http://dcarts.dc.gov.*

Florida Arts Council, *Division of Cultural Affairs, Florida Dept. of State, 1001 DeSoto Park Dr., Tallahassee FL 32301. (850)487-2980. E-mail: CulturalAffairs@mail.dos.state.fl.us. Website: www.dos.state.fl.us/dca/.*

Georgia Council for the Arts, *260 14th St., Suite 401, Atlanta GA 30318. (404)685-2787. E-mail: gaarts@gaarts.org. Website: www.gaarts.org/.*

Guam Council on the Arts & Humanities Agency, *P.O. Box 2950, Agana GU 96932. (671)646-3661. E-mail: Kahal@kuentos.guam.net. Website: www.guam.net/gov/kaha/.*

Hawaii State Foundation on Culture & the Arts, *250 S. Hotel St., 2nd Floor, Honolulu HI 96813. (808)586-0300. Website: www.state.hi.us/sfca.*

Idaho Commission on the Arts, *P.O. Box 83720, Boise ID 83720-0008. (208)334-2119 or (800)278-3863. E-mail: bgarrett@ica.state.id.us. Website: www2.state.id.us/arts.*

Illinois Arts Council, *James R. Thompson Center, 100 W. Randolph, Suite 10-500, Chicago IL 60601. (312)814-6750. E-mail: info@arts.state.il.us. Website: www.state.il.us/agency/iac.*

Indiana Arts Commission, *402 W. Washington St., Indianapolis IN 46204-2739. (317)232-1268. E-mail: arts@state.in.us. Website: www.state.in.us/iac/.*

Iowa Arts Council, *600 E. Locust, Capitol Complex, Des Moines IA 50319-0290. (515)281-6412. Website: www.culturalaffairs.org/iac/.*

Kansas Arts Commission, *700 SW Jackson, Suite 1004, Topeka KS 66603-3761. (785)296-3335.*
E-mail: KAC@arts.state.ks.us. Website: http://arts.state.ks.us/.

Kentucky Arts Council, *Old Capitol Annex, 300 W. Broadway, Frankfort KY 40601-1980. (502)564-3757.*
E-mail: kyarts@mail.state.ky.us. Website: www.kyarts.org.

Louisiana Division of the Arts, *P.O. Box 44247, Baton Rouge LA 70804-4247. (225)342-8180.*
E-mail: arts@crt.state.la.us. Website: www.crt.state.la.us/arts/.

Maine Arts Commission, *193 State St., 25 State House Station, Augusta ME 04333-0025. (207)287-2724.*
E-mail: jan.poulin@state.me.us. Website: www.mainearts.com.

Maryland State Arts Council, *175 West Ostend St., Suite E, Baltimore MD 21230. (410)767-6555.*
E-mail: tcolvin@mdbusiness.state.md.us. Website: www.msac.org/.

Massachusetts Cultural Council, *10 St. James Ave., 3rd Floor, Boston MA 02116-3803. (617)727-3668.*
E-mail: web@art.state.ma.us. Website: www.massculturalcouncil.org/.

Michigan Council for Arts & Cultural Affairs, *525 W. Ottawa, P.O. Box 30004, Lansing MI 48909.*
(513)373-1820. E-mail: artsinfo@cis.state.mi.us. Website: www.commerce.state.mi.us/arts/home.htm.

Minnesota State Arts Board, *Park Square Court, 400 Sibley St., Suite 200, St. Paul MN 55101-1928.*
(651)215-1600 or (800)8MN-ARTS. E-mail: msab@state.mn.us. Website: www.arts.state.mn.us/.

Mississippi Arts Commission, *239 N. Lamar St., Suite 207, Jackson MS 39201. (601)359-6030.*
Website: www.arts.state.ms.us/.

Missouri Arts Council, *Wainwright State Office Complex, 111 N. Seventh St., Suite 105, St. Louis MO 63101-2188.*
(314)340-6845. E-mail: moarts@mail.state.mo.us. Website: www.missouriartscouncil.org.

Montana Arts Council, *P.O. Box 202201, Helena MT 59620-2201. (406)444-6430. E-mail: mac@state.mt.us.*
Website: www.art.state.mt.us.

National Assembly of State Arts Agencies, *1029 Vermont Ave., NW, 2nd Floor, Washington DC 20005.*
(202)347-6352. E-mail: nasaa@nasaa-arts.org. Website: www.nasaa-arts/org.

Nebraska Arts Council, *Joslyn Carriage House, 3838 Davenport St., Omaha NE 68131-2329. (402)595-2122.*
E-mail: cmalloy@nebraskaartscouncil.org. Website: www.nebraskaartscouncil.org.

Nevada Arts Council, *716 N. Carson St., Suite A, Carson City NV 89701. (775)687-6680.*
Website: http://dmla.clan.lib.nv.us/docs/arts/.

New Hampshire State Council on the Arts, *40 N. Main St., Concord NH 03301-4974. (603)271-2789.*
Website: http://webster.state.nh.us/nharts.

New Jersey State Council on the Arts, *P.O. Box 306, 225 W. State St., Trenton NJ 08625. (609)292-6130.*
E-mail: njsca@arts.sos.state.nj.us. Website: www.njartscouncil.org/.

New Mexico Arts, *P.O. Box 1450, Santa Fe NM 87504-1450. (505)827-6490. Website: www.nmarts.org/.*

New York State Council on the Arts, *175 Varick St., 3rd Floor, New York NY 10014. (212)627-4455.*
Website: www.nysca.org.

North Carolina Arts Council, *Dept. of Cultural Resources, Raleigh NC 27699-4632. (919)733-2111.*
E-mail: ncarts@ncmail.net. Website: www.ncarts.org/.

North Dakota Council on the Arts, *418 E. Broadway, Suite 70, Bismarck ND 58501-4086. (701)328-3954.*
Website: www.state.nd.us/arts/.

Ohio Arts Council, *727 E. Main St., Columbus OH 43205-1796. (614)466-2613. E-mail: bob.fox@oac.state.oh.us.*
Website: www.oac.state.oh.us/.

Oklahoma Arts Council, *P.O. Box 52001-2001, Oklahoma City OK 73152-2001. (405)521-2931.*
E-mail: okarts@arts.state.ok.us. Website: www.arts.state.ok.us/.

Oregon Arts Commission, *775 Summer St. NE, Suite 200, Salem OR 97301-1284. (503)986-0082.*
E-mail: oregon.artscomm@state.or.us. Website: http://art.econ.state.or.us/.

Pennsylvania Council on the Arts, *Room 216, Finance Bldg., Harrisburg PA 17120. (717)787-6883.*
Website: www.artsnet.org/pca/.

Institute of Puerto Rican Culture, *P.O. Box 9024184, San Juan PR 00902-4184. (787)725-5137.*
Website: http://icp.prstar.net/.

Rhode Island State Council on the Arts, *83 Park St., 6th Floor, Providence RI 02903-1037. (401)222-3880.*
E-mail: info@risca.state.ri.us. Website: www.risca.state.ri.us/.

South Carolina Arts Commission, *1800 Gervais St., Columbia SC 29201. (803)734-8696.*
Website: www.state.sc.us/arts/.

South Dakota Arts Council, *Office of the Arts, 800 Governors Dr., Pierre SD 57501-2294. (605)773-3131.*
E-mail: sdac@stlib.state.sd.us. Website: www.state.sd.us/deca/sdarts/.

Tennessee Arts Commission, *Citizens Plaza, 401 Charlotte Ave., Nashville TN 37243-0780. (615)741-1701.*
E-mail: dennis.adkins@state.tn.us. Website: www.arts.state.tn.us.

Texas Commission on the Arts, *P.O. Box 13406, Capitol Station, Austin TX 78711. (512)463-5535.*
E-mail: front.desk@arts.state.tx.us. Website: www.arts.state.tx.us/.

Utah Arts Council, *617 E. South Temple St., Salt Lake City UT 84102. (801)236-7555.*
Website: www.dced.state.ut.us/arts/.

Vermont Arts Council, *136 State St., Drawer 33, Montpelier VT 05633-6001. (802)828-3291.*
E-mail: info@vermontartscouncil.org. Website: www.vermontartscouncil.org.

Virgin Islands Council on the Arts, *P.O. Box 103, St. Thomas VI 00804. (340)774-5984.*
E-mail: vicouncil@islands.vi.

Virginia Commission for the Arts, *Lewis House, 2nd Floor, 223 Governor St., Richmond VA 23219-2010.*
(804)225-3132. E-mail: vacomm@artswire.org. Website: www.arts.state.va.us/.

Washington State Arts Commission, *234 E. Eighth Ave., P.O. Box 42675, Olympia WA 98504-2675.*
(360)753-3860. Website: www.arts.wa.gov.

West Virginia Commission on the Arts, *Cultural Center, 1900 Kanawha Blvd. E., Charleston WV 25305-0300.*
(304)558-0220. Website: www.wvculture.org/arts/.

Wisconsin Arts Board, *101 E. Wilson St., 1st Floor, Madison WI 53702. (608)266-0190.*
E-mail: artsboard@arts.state.wi.us. Website: http://arts.state.wi.us.

Wyoming Arts Council, *2320 Capitol Ave., Cheyenne WY 82002. (307)777-7742. E-mail: wyoarts@artswire.org.*
Website: http://wyoarts.state.wy.us/.

CANADIAN PROVINCES ARTS AGENCIES

Alberta Foundation for the Arts, *901 Standard Life Centre, 10405 Jasper Ave., Edmonton, Alberta T5J 4R7.*
(780)427-6315. Website: www.cd.gov.ab.ca/all_about_us/commissions/arts/index.asp.

British Columbia Arts Council, *P.O. Box 9819, Stn. Prov. Govt., Victoria, British Columbia V8W 9W3.*
(250)356-1718. Website: www.bcartscouncil.gov.bc.ca.

The Canada Council, *350 Albert St., P.O. Box 1047, Ottawa, Ontario K1P 5V8. (613)566-4414.*
Website: www.canadacouncil.ca/.

Manitoba Arts Council, *525-93 Lombard Ave., Winnipeg, Manitoba R3B 3B1. (204)945-2237.*
E-mail: info@artscouncil.mb.ca. Website: www.artscouncil.mb.ca.

New Brunswick Arts Board (NBAB), *634 Queen St., Suite 300, Fredericton, New Brunswick E3B 1C2.*
E-mail: nbabcanb@nbab-canb.nb.ca. Website: www.artsnb.ca.

Newfoundland & Labrador Arts Council, *P.O. Box 98, St. John's, Newfoundland A1C 5H5. (709)726-2212.*
E-mail: nlacmail@newcomm.net. Website: www.nlac.nf.ca/.

Nova Scotia Arts Council. *New Arts and Culture Council will be established due to changes in the delivery of*
government investment. See www.novascotiaartscouncil.ns.ca/.

Ontario Arts Council, *151 Bloor St. W., 5th Floor, Toronto, Ontario M5S 1T6. (416)969-7429.*
E-mail: info@arts.on.ca. Website: www.arts.on.ca/.

Prince Edward Island Council of the Arts, *115 Richmond, Charlottetown, Prince Edward Island C1E 1H7. (902)368-6176. E-mail: artscouncil@pei.aibn.com. Website: www.gov.pe.ca.*

Quebec Council for Arts & Literature, *79 boul. René-Lévesque Est, 3e étage, Quebec, Quebec G1R 5N5. (418)643-1707. Website: www.calq.gouv.qc.ca/.*

Saskatchewan Arts Board, *2135 Broad St., Regina, Saskatchewan S4P 3V7. (306)787-4056. E-mail: sab@artsboard.sk.ca. Website: www.artsboard.sk.ca.*

Yukon Arts Branch, *Box 2703, Whitehorse, Yukon Y1A 2C6. (867)667-8589. E-mail: arts@gov.yk.ca. Website: www.artsyukon.com.*

Resources

Conferences & Workshops

As poets, we keep learning day to day. Perhaps a helpful comment on a rejection slip, feedback from a writer's group, or an enlightening essay by an admired master provides that special lesson we need to improve our writing just that much more.

However, there are times when we want to immerse ourselves in learning. Or perhaps we crave a change of scenery, the creative stimulation of being around other artists, or the uninterrupted productivity of time alone to work.

That's what this section of *Poet's Market* is all about. Not only will you find a selection of writing conferences and workshops, but also artist colonies and retreats, poetry festivals, and even a few opportunities to go travelling with your muse. These listings give the basics: contact information, a brief description of the event, lists of past presenters, and offerings that may be of special interest to poets. If an event interests you, get in touch with the director for additional information, including up-to-date costs and housing details. (Please note that most directors had not finalized their 2003 plans when we contacted them for this edition of *Poet's Market*. However, where possible, they provided us with their 2002 dates, costs, faculty names, or themes to give you a better idea of what each event has to offer.)

Before you seriously consider a conference, workshop, or other event, determine what you hope to get out of the experience. Would a general conference with one or two poetry workshops among many other types of sessions be acceptable? Or are you looking for something exclusively focused on poetry? Do you want to hear poets speak about poetry writing, or are you looking for a more participatory experience such as a one-on-one critiquing session or a group workshop? Do you mind being one of hundreds of attendees or do you prefer a more intimate setting? Are you willing to invest in the expense of travelling to a conference, or would something local better suit your budget? Keep these questions and others in mind as you read these listings, view websites, and study conference brochures.

Some listings are coded with symbols to provide certain "information at a glance." The (ℕ) symbol indicates a listing new to this edition; the (⚕) symbol denotes a Canadian listing and the (⊕) symbol an international one.

Finally, this section includes an Insider Report by poet **Jeffrey Hillard** about his experiences at the Fine Arts Work Center in Provincetown, Massachusetts. His essay (beginning on page 471) offers some general tips for potential workshop participants and examines the creation of a poem from point of inspiration to finished piece.

AMERICAN CHRISTIAN WRITERS CONFERENCES, P.O. Box 110390, Nashville TN 37222. (800)21-WRITE. E-mail: ACWriters@aol.com. Website: www.ACWriters.com. **Director:** Reg Forder. Established 1981. Annual 2-day events, 30 conferences/year held in cities including Houston, Boston, Minneapolis, Chicago, St. Louis, Detroit, Atlanta, Miami, Phoenix, and Los Angeles. Location: Usually a major hotel chain like Holiday Inn. Average attendance: 40-80.

Purpose/Features: Open to anyone. Conferences cover fiction, poetry, writing for children.

Costs/Accommodations: Cost is $99-169, participants responsible for their own meals. Accommodations include special rates at host hotel.

Additional Info: Individual poetry critiques available. Also sponsors an annual Caribbean Christian Writers Conference Cruise each November. Brochure and registration form available for SASE. Accepts inquiries by e-mail.

N̲ ⊕ ANAM CARA WRITER'S AND ARTIST'S RETREAT, Eyeries, Beara, West Cork, Ireland. Phone: 353 (0)27 74441. Fax: 353 (0)27 74448. E-mail: anamcararetreat@eircom.net. Website: www.ugr. com/anamcararetreat/ (includes information about programs, accommodations, transportation, general location). **Director:** Sue Booth-Forbes. Offers several 1-2 week workshops annually for writers and artists. Length of workshop varies with subject and leader/facilitator. 2002 programs scheduled for May through October. Location: "Beara is a rural and hauntingly beautiful part of Ireland that is kept temperate by the Gulf Stream. The retreat sits on a hill overlooking Coulagh Bay, the mountains of the Ring of Kerry, and the Slieve Miskish Mountains of Beara. The village of Eyeries is a short walk away." Average attendance: 12/workshop; 5 residents at the retreat when working individually.
Purpose/Features: "Anam Cara is a year-round retreat (except for end-of-the-year holidays) for novice as well as professional writers and artists. Applicants are asked to provide a written description on the focus of their work while on retreat. Residencies are on a first-come, first-deposit-in basis." 2002 offerings for poets included a Master Class with Billy Collins (sponsored by the Taos Institute for the Arts) and Wordpainting and Poetry with Jack McGuigan. Other workshop topics include bookmaking, printmaking, and Proprioceptive writing.
Costs/Accommodations: 2002 individual retreat costs ranged from €445-670/week depending on room and season booked. Meals and other services included except phone and Internet use. Transportation details available on website. Accommodations include full room and board, laundry, sauna, Jacuzzi, 5 acres of gardens, meadows, river banks and cascades, river island and swimming hole, and stone wall. Overflow from workshops stay in nearby B&Bs a short walk away.
Additional Info: Requests for specific information about rates and availability can be made through the website; also available for SASE or by fax or e-mail. Brochure available on website or by request.

⊕ ART WORKSHOPS IN GUATEMALA, 4758 Lyndale Ave. S., Minneapolis MN 55409-2304. (612)825-0747. Fax: (612)825-6637. E-mail: info@artguat.org. Website: www.artguat.org (includes complete information). **Director:** Liza Fourré. Established 1995. Annual 10-day creative writing courses, usually held in February or March. Location: workshops held in Antigua, the old colonial capital of Guatemala. 2003 dates to be announced. Average attendance: limit 10 students.
Purpose/Features: Art workshops in Guatemala provides the perfect getaway for creative writers of all skill levels to study with experienced instructors while being inspired by Guatemala's incredibly beautiful landscapes and warm-hearted people. Offerings for poets include "Poetry/Snapshots in Words" with Roseann Lloyd and "Voice of the Soul" with Sharon Doubiago. "This workshop is designed for those desiring to write from their true voice through aesthetic exercises, self-exploration, memory retrieval, independent writing, and lively class discussions."
Costs/Accommodations: Cost is $1,725; includes "air transportation from US, tuition, lodging in a beautiful old colonial home, a hearty breakfast, and ground transport.
Additional Info: Individual poetry critiques available. Call, write, e-mail, fax, or check website.

ASHLAND WRITERS CONFERENCE, 295 E. Main St., #5, Ashland OR 97520. (541)482-2783. Fax: (541)482-4923. E-mail: mail@ashlandwriters.com. Website: www.ashlandwriters.com. Annual five-day workshop/conference. Established in 1997. Students work with a specified instructor three hours daily for five days and in individual conferences. Usually held last week of July or first week of August. Location: Southern Oregon University. Registration limited.
  • **The conference was cancelled for 2002 but is scheduled to resume for 2003. Check website in early 2003 for latest information.**

ASPEN SUMMER WORDS WRITING RETREAT AND LITERARY FESTIVAL; ASPEN WRITERS' FOUNDATION, 110 E. Hallam St., Suite 116, Aspen CO 81611. (970)925-3122. Fax: (970)920-5700. E-mail: info@aspenwriters.org. Website: www.aspenwriters.org (includes general information about Aspen Writers' Foundation, including history; all programs; registration forms; information about past presenters; and links to visiting Aspen). **Executive Director:** Julie Comins. Established 1976. Annual 3-day writing retreat, followed by 3-day literary festival. Held the third week of June. Location: The Given Institute or other site in Aspen. Average attendance: 100-200 for the festival, 50 for the retreat.

Purpose/Features: Open to all writers and readers. Retreat includes intensive workshops in poetry, fiction, memoir, and essay. Offerings for poets include poetry workshops, craft lectures, and readings by faculty and participants. Faculty at 2002 conference included Mary Jo Salter (poetry), Pam Houston and Larry Watson (fiction), and Ted Conover (memoir and essay).
Costs/Accommodations: Cost for retreat is $375; cost for the Literary Festival is $150; cost for both is $495. Meals and other services charged separately. Information on overnight accommodations available for registrants. 2002 cost of accommodations was $60/person/day double occupancy or $120/person/day single occupancy.
Additional Info: "We accept poetry mss in advance that will be discussed during workshop." Brochure and registration form available for SASE or on website, or request by phone, fax, or e-mail. Include mailing address with all e-mail requests.

BREAD LOAF WRITERS' CONFERENCE; BAKELESS LITERARY PUBLICATION PRIZES, Middlebury College, Middlebury VT 05753. (802)443-5286. Fax: (802)443-2087. E-mail: blwc@middlebury.edu. Website: www.middlebury.edu/~blwc. **Administrative Coordinator:** Noreen Cargill. Established 1926. Annual 11-day event usually held in mid-August. Average attendance: 230.
Purpose/Features: Conference is designed to promote dialogue among writers and provide professional critiques for students. Conference usually covers fiction, nonfiction, and poetry.
Costs/Accommodations: 2002 conference cost was $1,850, including tuition, room, and board. Fellowships and scholarships for the conference available. "Candidates for fellowships must have a book published. Candidates for scholarships must have published in major literary periodicals or newspapers. A letter of recommendation, application, and supporting materials due by March 1. See website for further details. Awards are announced in June for the conference in August." Taxis to and from the airport or bus station are available.
Additional Info: Individual critiques also available. Sponsors the Bakeless Literary Publication Prizes, an annual book series competition for new authors of literary works in poetry, fiction, and creative nonfiction. Details, conference brochure, and application form are available for SASE or on website. Accepts inquiries by fax and e-mail.

BRISTOL POETRY FESTIVAL, 20-22 Hepburn Rd., Bristol BS2 8UD United Kingdom. Phone: (0044)117 9426976. Fax: (0044)117 9441478. E-mail: festival@poetrycan.demon.co.uk. Website: www.poetrycan.demon.co.uk (includes information about the festival, Poetry Can, projects, published poetry, links). **Festival Director:** Hester Cockcroft. Established 1996. Annual 10-day event held in October. Location: across the city of Bristol in a variety of venues. Average attendance: about 6,000.
Purpose/Features: Open to "everyone who is interested, from practicing poets to the general public. The festival aims to celebrate the best in local, national, and international poetry in all its manifestations, with events for everyone including performances and workshops, competitions and exhibitions, public poetry interventions, community work, cross art form, and digital projects." Offerings for poets include master classes from famous poets, workshops on poetry writing and performance, debates, and competitions.
Costs/Accommodations: Cost varies. "Discounts are available for students, elderly people, the unwaged, or the disabled."
Additional Info: Brochure available by e-mail or on website. Accepts inquiries by e-mail. "Bristol Poetry Festival is organized and funded by Bristol's Poetry Development Agency, the Poetry Can, which is based at the same address and managed by the same personnel."

CANYONLANDS WRITERS RIVER TRIP, P.O. Box 68, Moab UT 84532. (435)259-7750. Fax: (435)259-2335. E-mail: cfinfo@canyonlandsfieldinst.org. Website: www.canyonlandsfieldinst.org. **Contact:** office. Established 2000. Annual usually held for five days in July on the Colorado River. Average attendance: a maximum of 16.
Purpose/Features: Open to all. Workshop covers instruction/critique on writing about relationships to the natural world while floating down the river, Class I-III whitewater, prehistoric sites, wildlife sightings.
Costs/Accommodations: Cost: $950/person, includes instruction, outfitting, all river meals, and one night in hotel. Starts/ends in Grand Junction, Colorado.

CAPE COD WRITERS' CENTER SUMMER CONFERENCE, % Cape Cod Writers' Center, P.O. Box 186, Barnstable MA 02630. (508)375-0516. Fax: (508)362-2718. E-mail: ccwc@capecod.net. Website: www.capecodwriterscenter.com (includes event schedules, conference/workshop information, news about members). **Executive Director:** Jacqueline M. Loring. Established 1963. Annual week-long event usually held the third week of August. 2002 dates were August 19-23. Location: the Craigville Beach Conference Center in a rustic setting overlooking Nantucket Sound. Average attendance: 150.

Purpose/Features: Open to everyone. Covers poetry, fiction, mystery writing, nonfiction, children's writing, screenwriting, plus one-evening Master Class. Wednesday evening Poetry Reading by faculty and participants is open to the public. 2002 faculty included Afaa Michael Weaver (poetry) and Emily Heckman, Mcadam/Cage Publishing (Editor-in-Residence).

Costs/Accommodations: Check website for updated costs. Participants responsible for their own meals. "It is recommended that participants stay at the Craigville Beach Conference Center ((508)775-1265—early registration necessary)." Other housing information available from Bed & Breakfast Cape Cod.

Additional Info: Manuscript evaluations and personal conferences also available. For ms evaluation, submit no more than 6 pages of poetry to CCWC by July 1st. Cost is $75/ms and 30-minute conference. Cost, brochure, and registration form available for SASE or on website. Accepts inquiries by fax and e-mail. Sponsors workshops and seminars in the fall and spring.

CAVE CANEM, P. O. Box 4286, Charlottesville VA 22905-4286. E-mail: cavecanempoets@aol.com. **Contact:** Carolyn Micklem, foundation director. Established 1996. Annual week-long workshop for African-American poets. Usually held last week in June. Location: the beautiful grounds of the Cranbrook Schools in Bloomfield Hills, MI. Average attendance: 50.

Purpose/Features: Open to African-American poets. Participants selected based on a sample of 6-8 poems. Offerings include workshops by fellows and faculty, evening readings. Participants are assigned to groups of about 8 and remain together throughout session, with different faculty leading each workshop. 2002 faculty included Toi Derricotte, Cornelius Eady, Nikky Finney, Yusef Komanyakaa, Marilyn Nelson, and Al Young, with guest poets Elizabeth Alexander and Ntozake Shange.

Costs/Accommodations: 2002 cost was $495. Meals and other services included. For complete information, contact Cave Canem.

Additional Information: Poets should submit 6-8 poems with cover letter. 2002 postmark deadline was March 15, with accepted poets notified by April 30. Cave Canem Foundation also sponsors the Cave Canem Poetry Prize (see separate listing in Contest & Awards section). Brochure and registration information available for SASE and on website. Accepts inquiries by e-mail.

N CHENANGO VALLEY WRITERS' CONFERENCE, Office of Summer Programs, Colgate University, 13 Oak Dr., Hamilton NY 13346-1398. (315)228-7771. Fax: (315)228-7975. E-mail: mleone@mail. colgate.edu. Website: http://clark.colgate.edu/cvwritersconference. **Conference Director:** Matthew Leone. Established 1996. Annual week-long event usually held the last week in June, first week of July. 2002 dates were June 16-22. Location: Colgate University; has "an expansive campus, with classrooms, dormitories, libraries, and recreational facilities all in close proximity to each other." Average attendance: 75.

Purpose/Features: Open to "all serious writers or aspirants. Our purpose is to work on honing writing skills: fiction, poetry, and nonfiction prose are covered." 2002 staff included Bruce Smith, Peter Balakian, David Thoreen, Phillip Levine, and F. Bjornson Stock.

Costs/Accommodations: 2002 cost was $995 with room and board, $650 for day students; $895 and $595 before March 1; $875 and $575 for returnees. Discounts available through fellowships, typically $100-350. "Applicants for fellowships must apply before the May 1 deadline." "Will pick up airport, bus, and train station arrivals with prior notification for $30/trip." Accommodations include air-conditioned residencies (single rooms available at no extra charge), shared bathrooms; board includes breakfast, lunch, and dinner.

Additional Info: Individual poetry critiques available. Submit poems in advance to Matthew Leone. Brochures and registration forms available for SASE or on website. Accepts inquiries by fax and e-mail.

THE COLLEGE OF NEW JERSEY WRITERS CONFERENCE, College of New Jersey, Department of English, P.O. Box 7718, Ewing NJ 08628-0718. (609)771-3254. Fax: (609)637-5112. E-mail: write@tcnj .edu. **Director:** Jean Hollander. Established 1981. Annual 1-day event usually held in April at the College of New Jersey campus. Average attendance: 700-1,000.
Purpose/Features: Open to anyone. Conference covers all genres of writing. "We usually have a special presentation on breaking into print." Offers 20 separate workshops as well as readings. 2002 faculty included Margaret Atwood (featured speaker) and Jill Bialosky (poetry editor, Norton).
Costs/Accommodations: 2002 cost was $50 for 1-day session; additional cost for workshops and evening session. Participants responsible for own meals. Discounts available for students. Information on overnight accommodations available.
Additional Info: Writers of poetry, drama, journalism, literature for the young, nonfiction, and fiction may submit ms to be critiqued in writing by workshop leaders. Poetry and short story contest sponsored as part of conference. 1st Prize: $100; 2nd Prize: $50. Judges are workshop leaders and a special panel from the English Dept. Brochure and registration form available—write or call. Accepts inquiries by fax and e-mail.

COLORADO MOUNTAIN WRITERS' WORKSHOP, P.O. Box 85394, Tucson AZ 85754. (520)206-9479. E-mail: mfiles@compuserv.com. Website: www.sheilabender.com (includes information on upcoming conference, photos, and evaluations of previous conference). **Director:** Meg Files. Established 1999. Annual 5-day event. 2002 dates were June 24-28. Location: Steamboat Springs, CO, on the mountaintop campus of Colorado Mountain College. Average attendance: 50.
Purpose/Features: Open to all writers, beginning and experienced. "The workshop includes sessions on writing and publishing fiction, nonfiction, and poetry, as well as manuscript workshops and individual critiques and writing exercises." Faculty includes Sheila Bender, Jack Heffron, and Meg Files. Other special features include "a beautiful high-country site, extensive and intensive hands-on activities, individual attention, and a supportive atmosphere."
Costs/Accommodations: 2002 cost was $350 for tuition; dorm rooms and meals are available on site.
Additional Info: Individual critiques are available. Submit 5 poems in advance to Meg Files.

DESERT WRITERS WORKSHOP, P.O. Box 68, Moab UT 84532. (435)259-7750. Fax: (435)259-2335. E-mail: cfinfo@canyonlandsfieldinst.org. Website: www.canyonlandsfieldinst.org. **Contact:** office. Established 1985. Annual 5-day event usually held the first weekend in November. Location: Nature lodge accommodation. Attendance: 24.
Purpose/Features: Open to all. Workshop covers 2 categories—fiction and nonfiction (nature writing) and focuses on relationship to natural world.
Costs/Accommodations: Cost: $850, including meals, instruction, and lodging. Scholarships available.
Additional Info: Individual critiques also available. Participants will be able to mail some samples to their instructor before the workshop for critique.

[N] DJERASSI RESIDENT ARTISTS PROGRAM, Applications 2004, 2325 Bear Gulch Rd., Woodside CA 94062. (650)747-1250. Fax: (650)747-0105. E-mail: drape@djerassi.org. Website: www.djerassi. org (includes application materials). **Residency Coordinator:** Judy Freeland. Established 1979. Offers 4- to 5-week residencies, at no cost, for writers and other creative artists. Residencies available mid-March through mid-November. Location: In a spectacular rural setting in the Santa Cruz Mountains, one hour south of San Francisco.
Purpose/Features: Residencies are awarded competitively to emerging and mid-career artists as well as artists with established national or international reputations. Purpose is "to support and enhance the creativity of artists by providing uninterrupted time for work, reflection, and collegial interaction."
Costs/Accommodations: Artists selected are offered room, board, and studio space at no cost. "Three rooms in The Artists' House are set up to accommodate writers, each with a large desk, work space, and outdoor deck." Transportation to and from the airport is provided by the Program, and rides to Palo Alto for errands are generally provided by the staff once a week. There is no local public transportation for artists without cars.
Additional Info: Deadline for accepting applications is February 15 each year (i.e., 2003) for a residency in the following year (2004). Application materials available for SASE and on website.

EASTERN KENTUCKY UNIVERSITY CREATIVE WRITING CONFERENCE, Case Annex 467, Richmond KY 40475-3102. (859)622-5861. E-mail: engbrown@acs.eku.edu. Website: www.english.eku.

edu/conferences (includes the brochure which lists the visiting writers and their bios, schedule of events, registration information, cost, etc.). **Co-Directors:** Dorothy Sutton and Harry Brown. Established 1964. Annual 5-day event usually held Monday through Friday of the third week in June. Location: Eastern Kentucky University. Average attendance: 15.

Purpose/Features: Open to poetry and fiction. Provides lectures, workshops, and private conferences with visiting writers to "help writers increase their skills in writing poetry and fiction." A ms of 4-8 poems (8 pages maximum) must be submitted by May 20 and accepted before enrollment in conference is allowed. Offerings for poets include workshop discussions and individual conferences. Visiting writers have included David Citino, X. J. Kennedy, Donald Justice, Greg Orr, Maggie Anderson, and Sena Naslund.

Costs/Accommodations: Costs are $106 undergraduate and $153 graduate (in-state fees), $287 undergraduate and $418 graduate (out-of-state fees); participants responsible for their own meals, available on campus. Cost for housing in on-site facilities is $57/week single occupancy, $41/week double occupancy. "Must bring your own sheets, pillow, blanket."

Additional Info: Brochure available for SASE or request by e-mail.

FESTIVAL OF POETRY; CONFERENCE ON TEACHING AND POETRY, Robert Frost Place, Franconia NH 03580. (603)823-5510. E-mail: donald.sheehan@dartmouth.edu. Executive Director: Donald Sheehan. **Director of Admissions:** David Keller. Established 1978. Annual week-long event usually held first week of August at Robert Frost's mountain farm (house and barn), made into a center for poetry and the arts. 2002 dates were July 28-August 3. Average attendance: 50-55.

Purpose/Features: Open to poets only. 2002 guest faculty included James Tate, Paul Muldoon, David Keller, and Alicia Ostriker.

Costs/Accommodations: 2002 cost was $635 (participant), plus a $25 reading fee. Auditor fee: $585. "Room and board available locally; information sent upon acceptance to program."

Additional Info: Application should be accompanied by 3 sample pages of your work. Brochure and registration form available for SASE. Also offers the Conference on Teaching and Poetry, an annual event usually held in late June. Guest faculty for 2002 were Sydney Lea, Sue Ellen Thompson, Jeffrey Skinner, and Margaret Gibson. "The conference is intended for high school and middle school classroom teachers. Daily sessions include talks on poetry and teaching, workshops on teaching poems, workshops for teachers who write poems, and teacher sharing sessions as well as talks by working teachers on poetry in the curriculum." Fee for 4½-day program: $450 (NH teachers $350), plus $372 for 3 graduate credits from the University of New Hampshire. To apply, send letter describing current teaching situation and literary interests, along with $15 processing fee to Donald Sheehan, Teacher Conference, The Frost Place, Franconia NH 03580.

N: FINE ARTS WORK CENTER, 24 Pearl St., Provincetown MA 02657. (508)487-9960. Fax: (508)487-8873. E-mail: info@fawc.org or workshops@fawc.org. Website: www.fawc.org. Established 1968. The Fine Arts Work Center in Provincetown "is a nonprofit organization dedicated to providing emerging writers and visual artists with time and space in which to pursue independent work in a community of peers." Fellowships are awarded to poets and fiction writers in the emerging stages of their careers; professional juries make admissions decisions. See website for details and an application form.

N: FRONTIERS IN WRITING, P.O. Box 19303, Amarillo TX 79114. (806)353-3259. E-mail: kstcamp@aol.com. Website: http://users.arn.net/~ppw. **Contact:** Kim Campbell, president. Annual 2-day event usually held in mid-June. Location: Ambassador Hotel, Amarillo, TX. Average attendance: 200.

Costs/Accommodations: 2002 cost was $100 for Panhandle Professional Writers members, $135 for nonmembers. Meals and other services included. Information on separate accommodations available.

Additional Information: Individual poetry critiques available. Contest sponsored as part of workshop, guidelines available for SASE. Additional information available for SASE, by e-mail, or on website.

GIG HARBOR WRITERS' CONFERENCE, P. O. Box 826, Gig Harbor WA 98335. (253)265-1904. Fax: (253)265-8532. E-mail: ghwritersconf@aol.com. Website: www.ghkp-culturalarts.org/members/writersconf.html (includes dates, place, presenters, bios, contact info). **Director:** Kathleen O'Brien. Established 1996. Annual 3-day conference usually held the first weekend in May. 2002 dates: May 3, 4, 5. Location: Wesley Inn in Gig Harbor, "a new Best Western with conference capabilities." Average attendance: 100.

Purpose/Features: Open to all writers, with sessions offered in poetry, fiction, nonfiction, and children's writing. Offerings for poets include workshops. 2002 faculty included Heather McHugh, Linda Andrews, Linda Burmeister-Davies, Jana Harris, Kevin Miller, and Lynn Freed.

The workshop experience: Provincetown

On my first night in 4-Fish-Up, the sky was calm and there was not another writer in sight.

That would all change in the next few days. Soon the apartments near mine in Provincetown, Massachusetts, would be filled with writers and visual artists from all over the country. Like me, they'd attend workshops at The Fine Arts Work Center.

And soon my peace would be challenged by the elements. Nature would welcome me to Cape Cod in a back-handed manner—and provide inspiration for a new poem.

Jeffrey Hillard

Photo by Don Denney

4-Fish-Up, part of a duplex, was the address of my compact second story apartment at the Work Center. My writing desk, within a few feet of the stove and sink, functioned intermittently as kitchen table and bookshelf. To an artist serious about the rigors of writing, palatial conditions are a low priority. I was in a writing paradise, an amazing arts community, and I treasured my modest apartment.

The FAWC, once a busy lumberyard in the 1950s, was purchased in 1968 by a coalition of artists and writers including Stanley Kunitz, Robert Motherwell, and Alan Dugan. The area radiated potential as creative working environs, particularly for visual artists. Over the years, the Work Center would evolve into one of the premier writing and art colonies in the country, providing year-round housing, classes, lectures, readings, and exhibition space.

It loomed large as a place to live and write. I'd received a three-month writing fellowship for the summer of 2000 as part of a special program between the FAWC and the Ohio Arts Council. My objectives were to finish a new collection of poems, draft several essays, tackle several reading projects that I'd postponed, and, I hoped, draft a handful of new poems. And all in writing digs with history: The Abstract Expressionist artist Motherwell had completed many of his masterful works 30 yards across the lot.

I'd arrived early as a Work Center resident and would be alone in my stay for another week until the summer program started. I wasn't thinking about the ghosts of Motherwell or Eugene O'Neill, another FAWC alum. However, one night a clanging noise somewhere around 4-Fish-Up shifted my attention from a poem I was revising. It was past midnight. The screen windows rattled. I heard a ferocious *whoosh-whoosh* outside my window and stared at trees swaying in the cone-shaped glow of a streetlight.

As a native Ohioan, I had never travelled this far east, had never experienced what New Englanders call their "nor'easter," stormy, savage winds gusting up to 60 m.p.h. All I knew of the Cape was the big boot (the "elf shoe") I had admired on The Weather Channel.

Now Provincetown, a seaside tourist mecca in summer, twisted in the grip of a fierce nor'easter. As I anchored two windows to a latch with rubberbands and a shoestring, I imagined lines: "convulsing air," "the spill of many branches," "windows the wind keeps slamming shut," and "four rubberbands will not hold the windows closed much longer." I was thinking "poem." The lines might mimic the howling wind with jarring language—successive blends of alliteration, assonance, and consonance.

I eventually shared my rough draft of "The Nor'easter at My Window" at the FAWC. My fellowship allowed me to take three workshops at the Work Center, one of which was led by Michael Burkard, a prolific poet and teacher. We students realized we'd benefit from his expertise, so we worked with Michael to figure out a strategy for balancing critique time with his mini-lectures on poetic craft. Of our 12 workshop members, seven (including me) had brought poems from home to critique, while five anticipated simply writing poems impromptu in the workshop.

This is typical of many workshops: some students bring poems, some prefer not to. It's important to establish ground rules for both students and teacher on Day One to accommodate all students' needs. Flexibility and understanding of each other's goals are key.

I'd made it a point to bring four poems in extremely rough stages, nearly first drafts, to the Work Center. I hoped at least two would be critiqued. I was prepared with my notepad to take heavy notes, and I asked my peers to write comments on my drafts so I could further digest their feedback. Eventually we were able to critique two of the rough poems, my new nor'easter poem, and another new poem I'd written while in Provincetown. Having four poems critiqued in a five-day period gave me great satisfaction.

I recommend any poet attending a conference or workshop bring a modest number of poems to share, perhaps eight to fifteen. In such a considered time frame, neither students nor teacher have time to read a full-length manuscript. However, bringing more than a poem or two is important. When the opportunity arises (usually on the first or second day of the workshop), mention that you have a few poems. Make sure they're poems for which you really want input; you don't want to workshop poems that already have been critiqued completely.

Don't feel obligated, though, to bring poems at all. Much of a workshop experience is impromptu writing, poems created in that short, intense period. Before our week-long workshop at the FAWC ended, with Michael's guidance and prompts, each of us wrote two in-class drafts, new poems derived as total experiments. It was refreshing to read these poems aloud and see how each fared.

The reception to my nor'easter poem was mixed, as I suspected it would be. In class we'd discussed experimenting with large, imagistic contrasts in poems. "Get your contrasts to work oddly, curiously," Michael said, "and don't worry about making meaning. Just get down the incongruities and see what happens." My poem had two: "Unseen sand is certain to dance in the bedroom of a certain couple swearing off sleep," and "That certain passion that drives the sky to wrest my skimpy umbrella."

We decided these lines were decent responses to Michael's instruction. This illustrates another goal a poet can take to a workshop intensive: Do experiment and follow through with any in- or out-of-class assignments. You will make discoveries. Also, your workshop teacher is experienced, so he or she is going to offer valuable insights.

Don't wait and wait to comment and share opinions in a workshop. Students should strive for a balanced exchange, and the workshop teacher should facilitate this. There were times in Michael's workshop when a shy person made a keen comment, and the discussion followed a whole new, exciting direction.

Someone's quiet comment about my lines eventually helped me form my nor'easter poem into a litany. That inspired Michael to play, the next day, a taped reading of a litany by A.R. Ammons. It was gratifying to realize how, in just three days, our workshop group had bonded. We students fed each other new ideas, and our teacher expanded upon these, insisting we jot them down and use them in future works. Our attitude was that sharing ideas about poems is healthy, and in this way we kept energized instead of overly competitive, even if we didn't agree with every comment.

When attending a conference or workshop, especially a week-long session, it can be useful to collaborate with peers outside of the workshop environment, especially if students have brought more work they wish to trade and critique. We had productive three-hour workshops at the Work Center; however, several of us wanted to share poems we knew would not fit fairly into our limited workshop schedule.

After class one day, three of us walked to the pier on Commerical Street. A breeze from Provincetown Bay blew gently over the crowded shops and restaurants. Michael's workshop had empowered us to think of poetry in a multitude of ways; he'd energized us. We wanted to see if we could incorporate some of these ideas into our own poems, so we decided to ask our fellow students if anyone wanted to extend the workshop discussion at dinner.

The next day we sat at a large round table with blue umbrella and passed around an appetizer plate of shrimp, calamari, and chicken wings. We decided to critique one poem per person (I wanted comments on a 72-line poem I suspected we would not get to in the workshop). Four hours later, pages strewn amid cups of coffee, we finished our last poem and gathered up our notes just as the restaurant was about to close.

The energy level never seemed to wane. The day after our restaurant critique session, Michael encouraged us to visit photography and painting classes in progress below our meeting room. He'd asked the instructors if we poets could observe some of the photographs and paintings as part of a writing experiment for our class. From notes and memories of our hour-long observations, we were to write a ten-line poem based on what we perceived an image was "saying."

I was fascinated by a photograph of two greyhound dogs. Provincetown has an active Save-the-Greyhound movement, and earlier in my stay I'd noticed a curious scene on Commercial Street: A man wearing sunglasses sat glumly on a park bench, his head in his hands. A greyhound dog lay at his feet, boats were anchored behind him at the pier.

That photograph of the two greyhounds recalled the Commercial Street scene and launched me into those rough ten lines for the writing exercise. Back at my apartment I further worked out the poem, which became "Dogs in Provincetown." It had changed dramatically from those first exercise lines but continued to center on my mental image of the man on the bench:

His sad eyes. His chin stubble. His lover gone.
Dog hair his fingers sift. The paw he rubs.

This morning there was mist to fog to mist.
There was a shore bird dead, though it looked like
a clump of sand the sea could not move.

On the final day of the workshop I asked for feedback on the poem. Others, too, had finished their drafts from the photography-poem experiment. My peers persuaded me to focus on a different way to handle five very important couplets, and I had an idea for a new structure. When I left the workshop, I was fortunate to have most all I needed for the poem.

Back at 4-Fish-Up: My bedroom window was very loose and any slight breeze rattled it. I never was far removed from remembering the brunt of that first night's nor'easter, and I still had not finished my poem about it. I needed more input.

I had arranged a brief interview with Stanley Kunitz, the (then) 95-year-old former U.S.

Poet Laureate, for a magazine profile I was writing. He was gracious with his time; it helped that I was a summer-long writer-in-residence at the Work Center. I thought, "Maybe I can spring my nor'easter poem on Mr. Kunitz. When will I have the chance again to ask for an opinion from one of our greatest poets?" Not only did I get feedback, but the Poet Laureate read to me two of his own poems about winds.

My poem was not overwritten, Kunitz said. Words needed to be rearranged because lines were a bit lengthy. "The poem must retain energy with each line," Mr. Kunitz said, "and the ends of your lines in places here need to be more emphatic." I knew what he meant. Some lines dragged. He showed me a change for my "Unseen sand . . ." line:

> *A certain convulsing of air. The wider strip of shore*
> *Begets rising water. Unseen sand is certain to dance*
> *In the bedroom of a certain couple swearing off sleep.*

It was important to place "dance" and "sleep" at the end of lines because they exude an action, a physical state, and images of movement are important in the poem.

At last I knew how I needed to address my nemesis, the nor'easter. Once I finished the poem, I realized I could not have written it entirely on my own. I cherished the insights provided by my workshop peers; even more, I understood how influential a writing community can be in its diverse contributions toward enriching one's poetry.

"The Nor'easter at My Window"
a litany

> *Certain this wind will put my face in that puddle.*
> *I am certain my face will be reduced to eyelashes.*
> *Certain the four rubberbands will not hold the window*
> *closed much longer and stop the clank-clank, the audacious*
> *pounding as if a certain person is forcing a leg inside.*
> *A certain convulsing of air. The wider strip of shore*
> *begets rising water. Unseen sand is certain to dance*
> *in the bedroom of a certain couple swearing off sleep.*
> *Certain mud flats will pave a valley through clouds.*
> *Certain birds will wait for the sky to heal itself.*
> *Wind, again. Will I ever regain the certainty of walking?*
> *Is there anyone who cares that much about clarity?*
> *A certain rare moment enters a shadow and silences*
> *each cluster of poppies twisting from its roots.*
> *In that quiet moment, in calmness so certain to trick*
> *the twitching witch hazel into sleep,*
> *I know the spit curl will be jarred loose.*
> *The spill of many branches. That certain passion*
> *that drives the sky to wrest my skimpy umbrella.*
> *I'm certain my tongue will catch a falling lover.*
> *I'm certain my eyes could see fire behind*
> *every window that the wind keeps slamming shut.*
> *There must be a certain rain that weakens*

> *and falls like bits of thread in my hand.*
> *When what is certain is that the wind becomes*
> *language, is beyond language, so certain it is*
> *of the direction it pushes my legs.*
> *And the flower petal, the size of a certain wooden match,*
> *hanging onto my window sill, is not touched,*
> *and yet wants touch, as it flickers, lost in it all,*
> *flickers and spins again in place.*

It was late August—time for me to face the 22-hour drive back home to Ohio. Memories and impressions of my bountiful three-month stay at the Work Center pervaded my thoughts as I packed the car. Before I said my goodbyes, I unlatched a screen window in 4-Fish-Up and looked out. The trees were still. The streets were lined with cars. Another wicked wind would whip through here one day, but I would be far away when it happened. Yet, in my quiet writing moments, I would rely on my nor'easter poem to remind me how a poet should use any experience as subject matter—and never disregard what the world brings to his window in the most unexpected of ways.

—*Jeffrey Hillard*

Costs/Accommodations: 2002 cost was $150, including lunch. Friday full day pre-conference workshops (10 a.m.-4 p.m.): choose 1 of 3 for additional $100. Discounts for early registration. Offers special arrangements for transportation to and from the conference. Information on overnight accommodations available. Special rates available at area hotels.

Additional Information: Poetry critiques available. Contests sponsored as part of conference. Brochure and registration form available by fax, e-mail, or on website; also sent to those on mailing list. Accepts inquiries by fax and e-mail. Affiliated with AWP and WCC.

HARVARD SUMMER WRITING PROGRAM, 51 Brattle St., Dept. S810, Cambridge MA 02138. (617)495-4024. Fax: (617)495-9176. E-mail: summer@hudce.harvard.edu. Website: www.summer.harvard .edu (includes catalog, courses, program policies, and registration materials). Annual 8-week event. 2003 dates: June 23 through August 15. Location: Harvard University. Average attendance: 700.

Purpose/Features: Open to all levels, from beginner to published author. Course offerings include creative, expository, professional, and journalistic writing. Offerings for poets include beginning, intermediate, and graduate level poetry courses. Other special features include small classes, undergraduate and graduate credit, individual conferences, access to the Writing Center at Harvard, visiting writers, a reading series, and a literary magazine. Instructors are writers, editors, and faculty members from Harvard as well as other universities.

Costs/Accommodations: 2002 conference cost was $1,850/course (2 courses considered full-time), plus $3,200 for room and board (dormitory housing).

Additional Info: See website. Accepts inquiries by e-mail.

HAYSTACK WRITING PROGRAM, Summer Session, Portland State University, P.O. Box 1491, Portland OR 97207. (800)547-8887, ext. 4186 or (503)725-4186. Fax: (503)725-4840. E-mail: snydere@ses.pd x.edu. Website: www.haystack.pdx.edu. **Coordinator:** Elizabeth Snyder. Established 1969. Annual summer program. One-week and weekend courses over the 5-week program (July/August). Location: Canon Beach, OR, a small coastal community; some evening lectures and other activities. Average attendance: 10-15/ class; 400 total.

Purpose/Features: Open to all writers. One-week workshops cover fiction, poetry, mystery, screenplay, nonfiction, and more. 2002 staff included Tom Spanbauer, Ursula Le Guin, Karen Fowler, Donald Olson, and Linda Zuckerman.

Costs/Accommodations: 2002 workshop cost was $200-435; participants pay for their own lodging and meals. Wide range of options for accommodations. Listing provided upon registration.
Additional Info: Brochure and registration form available by mail. Accepts inquiries by fax and e-mail.

N HEARTLAND WRITERS CONFERENCE; HEARTLAND WRITERS GUILD, P.O. Box 652, Kennett MO 63857-0652. (618)998-8360. E-mail: hwg@heartlandwriters.org. Website: www.heartlandwriters.org (includes conference information and updates, also Heartland Writers Guild membership information). **Contact:** Coordinator. Established 1989. Biennial 3-day event. 2002 dates: June 6-8. Location: Coach House Inn, Sikeston MO. Average attendance: 150.
Purpose/Features: Open to all writers of popular fiction, nonfiction, and poetry. Offerings for poets include critique sessions. Speakers for next conference are 10 agents and editors from prominent New York-based publishing houses/agencies, as well as 12 published authors from the Midwest.
Costs/Accommodations: Most recent conference cost was $175, including meals. Information on overnight accommodations available. Accommodations include special rates at area hotels.
Additional Info: Contest sponsored as part of conference. Judges are industry professionals. Send name and address to be included on conference mailing list. Accepts inquiries by e-mail.

INDIANA UNIVERSITY WRITERS' CONFERENCE, Ballantine Hall 464, Indiana University, Bloomington IN 47405. (812)855-1877. Fax: (812)855-9535. E-mail: writecon@indiana.edu. **Director:** Amy M. Locklin. Established 1940. Annual week-long event usually held the last week in June at the university student union. Average attendance: 100.
Purpose/Features: Open to all. Conference covers fiction, creative nonfiction, and poetry. Offerings for poets include workshops and classes. 2002 faculty included Mark Doty, Andrew Hudgins, Roger Mitchell, Lucia Perillo, and Karen Volkman in poetry.
Costs/Accommodations: Most recent conference cost was $200 for conference and classes; $300 for conference, classes, and one workshop; plus $25 application fee. Information on overnight accommodations available. "Rooms available in the student union or in a dorm."
Additional Info: Individual critiques also available. Submit 10 pages of poetry in advance. "All manuscripts are considered for scholarships." Brochure and registration form available for SASE. Accepts inquiries by fax and e-mail.

IOWA SUMMER WRITING FESTIVAL, University of Iowa, 100 Oakdale Campus, W310, Iowa City IA 52242-5000. (319)335-4160. Fax: (319)335-4039. E-mail: iswfestival@uiowa.edu. Website: www.uiowa.edu/~iswfest (includes complete catalog of courses, faculty, workshop descriptions, registration forms, schedules, etc.). **Coordinator:** Amy Margolis. Established 1987. Annual event held each summer in June and July for six weeks. Includes one-week and weekend workshops at the University of Iowa campus. Average attendance: 150/week.
Purpose/Features: Open to "all adults who have a desire to write." Conference offers courses in nearly all writing forms. In 2002, offerings for poets included 17 classes for all levels. Poetry faculty included Bruce Bond, Michael Dennis Browne, Vince Gotera, Jim Heynen, Richard Jackson, and Jane Mead.
Costs/Accommodations: 2002 conference cost was $175 for a weekend course and $400-425 for a 1-week course. Participants are responsible for their own meals. Accommodations available at the Iowa House and the Sheraton. Housing in residence hall costs about $29/night.
Additional Info: Participants in week-long workshops will have private conference/critique with workshop leader. Send for brochure and registration form. Accepts inquiries by phone, fax, or e-mail.

THE IWWG SUMMER CONFERENCE, The International Women's Writing Guild, P.O. Box 810, Gracie Station, New York NY 10028. (212)737-7536. Fax: (212)737-9469. E-mail: dirhahn@aol.com. Website: www.iwwg.com. **Executive Director:** Hannelore Hahn. Established 1978. Annual week-long event usually held the second Friday in August through the following Friday. Location: Skidmore College in Saratoga Springs, NY. Average attendance: over 500.
Purpose/Features: Open to all women. Seventy workshops offered. "At least four poetry workshops offered for full week."
Costs/Accommodations: Cost is $880 for conference program and room and board.
Additional Info: "Critiquing available throughout the week." Brochure and registration form available for SASE. Accepts inquiries by e-mail (include mailing address for response). The International Women's Writing Guild's bimonthly newsletter features hundreds of outlets for poets. (See separate listing for The International Women's Writing Guild in the Organizations section.)

KALANI OCEANSIDE RETREAT, (formerly Kalani Honua Oceanside Eco Resort), RR2, Box 4500, Pahoa Beach Road HI 96778-9724. (808)965-7828 or (800)800-6886. Fax: (808)965-0527. E-mail: kalani @kalani.com. Website: www.kalani.com. Established 1980. **Director:** Richard Koob.
Purpose/Features: Offers 2-week to 2-month residencies on a year-round basis for visual, literary, folk, and performing artists. "Kalani Honua is situated near Kalapana on the big island of Hawaii on 113 acres of secluded forest and dramatic coastline, 45 minutes from the city of Hilo and 5 minutes from Hawaii Volcanoes National Park. Visitors stay in 3 two-story wooden lodges and 16 private cottage units that provide comfortable accommodations." Accommodates 100 (generally about 5 artists-in-residence) at a time in private rooms with full meal service plus optional kitchen facilities and shared or private baths; private desks and access to computer ports and reference material available. Activities include a variety of yoga, dance, drawing, fitness, and mind/body classes; also available are an olympic pool, sauna, fitness room, and nearby beach and thermal springs.
Costs/Accommodations: Residency cost ranges from $105/night to $210/night (private cottage); plus $29/day for meals. Stipends are most available in the periods of May through July and September through December. Stipends provide for 50% of lodging costs; balance is responsibility of the artist (stipends may *not* be applied toward dorm lodging or camping, or reduction in food or transportation costs).
Additional Information: Application form and guidelines available for SASE, by e-mail, or on website. When sending application, include $10 fee.

KEY WEST WRITERS' WORKSHOP, 5901 College Rd., Key West FL 33040. (305)296-9081, ext. 302 or 275. Fax: (305)292-2392. E-mail: weinman_i@firn.edu. Website: www.firn.edu/fkcc/kwww.htm (includes full details of current program/workshop leaders; all application information with form; information on travel and accommodations). **Director:** Irving Weinman. Established 1996. Five annual weekend events usually held from late January to early March. Location: "the conference room of Key West's historic Old City Hall—a modernized 1890's landmark building in the heart of the old town. Subsidiary activities (introductory get-together and optional Literary Walking Tour) also held in Old Town, Key West." Average attendance: limited to 10 for poetry weekends, 12 for fiction.
Purpose/Features: Open to all. However, "**not for beginners**." Workshop's purpose is to "bring the best writers into an intimate workshop setting with serious writers at all but beginning stages of their writing careers. Workshops are offered in poetry and fiction." Leaders for past workshops have included John Ashbery, Robert Creeley, Carolyn Forché, Sharon Olds, and Richard Wilbur.
Costs/Accommodations: 2002 conference cost was $300/weekend, tuition only. Participants responsible for their own meals. Information on overnight accommodations available.
Additional Info: Brochure and registration form available for SASE, by e-mail, or on website. Accepts inquiries by fax and e-mail. "Interested poets will be put on our brochure mailing list for the upcoming season."

LIFE PRESS CHRISTIAN WRITERS' CONFERENCE; LIFE PRESS CHRISTIAN WRITERS' ASSOCIATION, P.O. Box 241986, Memphis TN 38124. (901)682-6936. Fax: (901)682-8274. E-mail: gmoearth@aol.com. Website: www.grandmotherearth.com/ (includes contest rules, information about conference, contest, and publications). **Contact:** Frances Cowden. Established 1998. Annual 1-day event usually held the first or second Saturday in August. Location: "A church fellowship hall with nearby classroom for small critique groups." Average attendance: 45.
Purpose/Features: Open to all writers. Writing poetry or prose is the focus of the conference, with a special feature each year (for example, writing for children, humor, markets, etc.). A special humor workshop was presented in 2001. Offerings for poets include critiquing of work. 2001 speakers included Patricia Smith, Dr. Malra Treece, Mike Denington, Florence Bruce, Cherry Pryon, and Dr. Michael Ripski.
Costs/Accommodations: 2001 conference cost was $20, meals and other services included. Discounts available "upon request." Special arrangements for transportation to and from conference can be made "if prearranged and person stays in nearby hotel." Special overnight accommodations can be made.
Additional Info: Individual poetry critiques available. Poets should submit a limit of 6 works/category and $10 fee. "One payment for all entries—send with entries." Contest sponsored for "poetry and prose in general, open to all writers. Other contests require attendance. Small entry fee. Money prizes do not

THE GEOGRAPHICAL INDEX in the back of this book helps you locate markets in your region.

include publication." Special Awards for poetry (open to everyone, 50-line limit) are $50, $25, $15, $10, and $5. Conference Awards for poetry (open to those who register for the conference, 30-line limit) are $50, $15, $10. "A fee of $5 entitles you to enter one entry. $2 for each additional entry. (Three poems is an entry.) Critique from the judges is available for $10 for all entries. Write the work 'critique' on the upper right corner of each copy. (Limit 6 works in each category)." Guidelines available for SASE or on website. Winners' list available for SASE (include with entries).

MANHATTANVILLE'S WRITERS' WEEK, Manhattanville College, 2900 Purchase St., Purchase NY 10577. (914)694-3425. Fax: (914)694-3488. E-mail: dowdr@mville.edu. Website: www.manhattanville. edu. **Dean—Graduate & Professional Studies:** Ruth Dowd, RSCJ. Established 1983. Annual 5-day event usually held the last week in June at the Manhattanville College campus (June 24-28, 2002). Location: "suburban surroundings 45 minutes from downtown Manhattan." Average attendance: 100.
Purpose/Features: Open to "published writers, would-be writers, and teachers of creative writing. The conference offers workshops in five genres: short story, creative nonfiction, poetry, screenwriting, children's/young adult literature. There is also a special workshop in The Writers' Craft for beginners." Offerings for poets include a workshop conducted by Eamon Grennan. "In past years we have had such distinguished poet/workshop leaders as Mark Doty, Marie Howe, Stephanie Strickland, and Honor Moore. We generally feature a lecture by a distinguished writer."
Costs/Accommodations: 2002 conference cost was $800. Participants responsible for their own meals. Information on overnight accommodations available. "Rooms in the residence halls are available for a modest fee, or students may choose to stay at area hotels. Housing in on-site facilities costs $25-30/night."
Additional Information: Individual poetry critiques available "if students are registered for the Poetry Workshop." Additional information available on website. Accepts inquiries by fax or e-mail.

MIDLAND WRITERS CONFERENCE, Grace A. Dow Memorial Library, 1710 W. St. Andrews, Midland MI 48640. (989)837-3435. Fax: (989)837-3468. E-mail: ajarvis@midland-mi.org. Website: www. midland-mi.org/gradedowlibrary/writers.html (includes a page about the conference). **Conference Coordinator:** Ann Jarvis. Established 1979. Annual 1-day event, usually 2nd Saturday in June. 2002 date was June 8. Location: Grace A. Dow Memorial Library in Midland, MI. Average attendance: 100.
Purpose/Features: Open to any writer, published or unpublished. Conference includes sessions that vary in content. Recent keynote speaker was Arthur Golden. "We always have a well-known keynoter. In the past we have had Judith Viorst, Kurt Vonnegut, David McCullough, P.J. O'Rourke, Dave Barry, and Pat Conroy." In 2002, presenters included James W. Armstrong (poet), Ruth DuKelow (copyright), Steve Griffin (marketing), Tom Powers (self-publishing), Brenda Shannon Yee (children), and Sarah Zettle (fiction).
Costs/Accommodations: Cost for past conference $50 until 2 weeks prior to the event ($60 after that). For students, senior citizens, and handicapped participants, cost was $40 until 2 weeks prior to the event ($50 after that). Meals and other services charged separately. Information on overnight accommodations available.
Additional Info: Brochure and registration form available by mail. Accepts inquiries by fax and e-mail (include mailing address for response). Brochures mailed in late April.

MISSISSIPPI VALLEY WRITERS CONFERENCE, P.O. Box 4971, Rock Island IL 61201. (309)786-3406. E-mail: beej@qconline. Website: www.midwestwritingcenter.org (includes info for conference, poetry contest). **Conference Chair:** Bj Elsner. Established 1973. Annual 5-day event usually held the second week in June. Location: Liberal Arts College of Augustana College. Average attendance: 80-100.
 • Founder David R. Collins passed away June 17, 2001.
Purpose/Features: Open to all writers, "beginners to polished professionals." Provides a general professional focus on many genres of writing. Offers week-long workshop in poetry. Evening programs as well as daily workshops included. One-day young adult workshops in poetry, fiction, and nonfiction for writers 13-18.
Costs/Accommodations: 2002 conference cost was $25 registration, $50 one workshop, $40 each additional workshop. Meals and other services charged separately. Conferees may stay on campus or off. Board and room accommodations available at Erickson Hall on Augustana campus, 15 meals and 6 nights lodging approximately $200.
Additional Info: Individual critiques available: submit up to 10 poems. Contest sponsored as part of conference. Guidelines available for SASE, by e-mail, or on website. Awards presented by workshop leaders. Brochure and registration form available for SASE or on website. Accepts inquiries by e-mail.

MOUNT HERMON CHRISTIAN WRITERS CONFERENCE, P.O. Box 413, Mount Hermon CA 95041. (831)335-4466. Fax: (831)335-9413. E-mail: dtalbott@mhcamps.org. Website: www.mounthermon. org. **Director of Adult Ministries:** David R. Talbott. Established 1970. Annual 5-day event held Friday through Tuesday over Palm Sunday weekend. 2003 dates: April 11-15. Location: Full hotel-service-style conference center in heart of California redwoods. Average attendance: 350-450.

Purpose/Features: Open to "anyone interested in the Christian writing market." Conference is very broad based. Always covers poetry, fiction, article writing, writing for children, plus an advanced track for published authors. Offerings for poets have included several workshops, sessions on the greeting card industry, and individual 1-hour workshops. "We usually have 45-50 teaching faculty made up of publishing reps of leading Christian book and magazine publishers, plus selected freelancers." Other special features have included an advance critique service (no extra fee); residential conference, with meals taken family-style with faculty; private appointments with faculty; and an autograph party. "High spiritual impact."

Costs/Accommodations: 2002 conference cost was $915 deluxe; $760 standard; $620 economy; $545 student; including 13 meals, snacks, on-site housing, and $350 tuition fee. No-housing fee: $570. $25 airport, Greyhound, or Amtrack shuttle from San Jose, CA.

Additional Info: Brochure and registration form available on request. Accepts inquiries by fax and e-mail.

N NAPA VALLEY WRITERS' CONFERENCE, Napa Valley College, 1088 College Ave., St. Helena CA 94574. (707)967-2900. E-mail: writecon@admin.nvc.cc.ca.us. Website: www.napacommunityed.org/writersconf (includes dates for next year's conference, faculty, format and application process). **Contact:** Mark Wunderlich. **Managing Director:** Anne Evans. Established 1981. Annual week-long event usually held the last week in July or first week in August. 2002 dates were July 28-August 2. Location: Napa Valley College's new facility in the historic town of St. Helena, 30 minutes north of Napa in the heart of the valley's wine growing community. Average attendance: 48 in poetry and 48 in fiction.

Purpose/Features: "The conference has maintained its emphases on process and craft, featuring a faculty as renowned for the quality of their teaching as for their work. It has also remained small and personal, fostering an unusual rapport between faculty writers and conference participants. The poetry session provides the opportunity to work both on generating new poems and on revising previously written ones. Participants spend time with each of the staff poets in daily workshops that emphasize writing new poems— taking risks with new material and forms, pushing boundaries in the poetic process." The 2002 poetry faculty included Gillian Conoley, Forrest Gander, Brenda Hillman, and C.D. Wright. "Participants register for either the poetry or the fiction workshops, but panels and craft talks are open to all writers attending. Evenings feature readings by the faculty that are open to the public and hosted by Napa Valley wineries."

Costs/Accommodations: 2002 cost was $550, not including meals or housing. A limited number of scholarships are available. A list of valley accommodations is mailed to applicants on acceptance and includes at least one reduced-rate package. "Through the generosity of Napa residents, limited accommodations in local homes are available on a first-come, first-served basis for a fee of $30 for the week."

Additional Info: All applicants are asked to submit a qualifying ms with their registration (no more than 5 poems or 10-15 pages of fiction) as well as a brief description of their writing background. 2002 application deadline: May 23. Brochure and registration form available for SASE. Accepts inquiries by fax and e-mail.

N NORTHEAST TEXAS WRITERS' ORGANIZATION (NETWO)/NORTHEAST TEXAS COMMUNITY COLLEGE SPRING CONFERENCE, Continuing Education, Northeast Texas Community College, P.O. Box 1307, Mount Pleasant TX 75456-1307. (903)572-1911. **Conference Coordinator:** Jean Pamplin. Established 1987. Annual 1-day event held in April. Location: Northeast Texas Community College, Mt. Pleasant, Texas (90 minutes from Dallas). Average attendance: 50-60.

Purpose/Features: Open to all writers. Designed to "encourage writing by securing excellent speakers, promoting and selling our local authors' work as well as that of our speakers' work. We cover fiction and nonfiction, including poetry, plays, romance, western, mystery, short stories, childrens' stories, articles, cartoons, and young adult books." Offerings for poets "depend on our speakers. However, there are many award-winning poets in our writers' organizations with whom attendees can network." Other special features include "book tables to sell members' and speakers' books as well as magazines, articles. When we have an agent speak, he/she meets with attendees generally for 10 minutes each if they pre-register before the meeting. We usually have a reception for speakers on Friday evening before the conference on Saturday." Includes lectures, panels, and workshops.

Costs/Accommodations: 2001 cost was $50; $45 for members of the Northeast Texas Writers' Organization. Information on overnight accommodations available.
Additional Info: Brochure and registration form available for SASE. "Our conference is co-sponsored with the Northeast Texas Community College. We publish poetry in our newsletter and in regional books."

OAKLAND UNIVERSITY WRITERS' CONFERENCE, College of Arts and Sciences, 221 Varner Hall, Oakland University, Rochester MI 48309-4401. (248)370-4386. Fax: (248)370-4280. E-mail: gjboddy @oakland.edu. Website: www.oakland.edu/contin-ed/writersconf/ (includes comprehensive description of conference with photos from previous conferences; downloadable PDF copy of the conference brochure). **Director:** Gloria J. Boddy. Established 1961. Annual 2-day event. 2002 dates: October 18-19. Location: in the university student center, in meeting rooms and large dining/meeting areas, plus adjoining classroom buildings with lecture halls. Average attendance: 300.
Purpose/Features: Open to beginning through professional adult writers. "No restrictions as to geographic area." Designed to "help writers develop their skills; to provide information (and contact) for getting published; to provide a current picture of publishing markets; to furnish a venue for networking. All genres of writing are covered." Offers "critiques, both one-on-one and group, on Friday. On Saturday, 36 concurrent sessions dealing with all aspects of writing in a variety of genres are available in four time slots. A well-known professional writer is invited to be keynote speaker. A panel of the major speakers answers questions in the concluding session."
Costs/Accommodations: 2002 conference cost: $85; ms critique: $58; hands-on workshop: $48. Meals and other services charged separately. "Discounts are not offered." Information on overnight accommodations available.
Additional Info: "Submit ten pages of poetry two weeks in advance of conference. Poets will receive written feedback and have a twenty-minute one-on-one consultation with critiques on Friday." Brochure and registration form available each September 1 prior to the October conference for SASE, by fax, e-mail, or on website. Accepts inquiries by fax and e-mail. Also offers the Mary Kay Davis Scholarships for high school and college students to attend conference. Check website for details. "We will be launching one-day retreats at the 2002 conference. The retreats will be small groups lead by recognized authors. Activities and exercises will be designed to foster and nurture the creative aspects of the craft."

OZARK CREATIVE WRITERS CONFERENCE, 6817 Gingerbread Lane, Little Rock AR 72204-4738. (501)565-8889. Fax: (501)565-7220. E-mail: pvining@aristotle.net. **Conference Counselor:** Peggy Vining. Established 1968. Annual event held the second full weekend in October, Thursday through Saturday. Location: Inn of the Ozarks Convention Center in Eureka Springs, Arkansas. Average attendance: about 200.
Purpose/Features: Open to all writers.
Costs/Accommodations: Registration fee is $50 prior to September 1. "Eureka Springs is a resort town so register early for lodging (say you are with OCWI). Eighty rooms are blocked at the Inn of The Ozarks for the conference." Information on overnight accommodations available from the Chamber of Commerce of Eureka Springs.
Additional Info: Various writing contests sponsored as part of conference. Sizeable monetary awards given for all types of writing. Guidelines and brochure/registration form available for #10 SASE after April 1. Accepts inquiries by fax and e-mail. "If requesting by e-mail, please include regular mailing address."

PENNWRITERS ANNUAL CONFERENCE; PENNWRITERS, INC.; PENNWRITERS ANNUAL WRITING CONTEST; IN OTHER WORDS CONTEST; PENNWRITERS POETRY CONTEST, RR2, Box 241, Middlebury Center PA 16935. (570)376-3361(day) /2821 (evening). Fax: (570)376-2674. E-mail: cjhoughtaling@usa.net. Website: http://pennwriters.org (includes mission statement, bulletin board, events calendar and details, Board of Directors' bios, chat room, store, and membership form). **Treasurer:** C.J. Houghtaling. Established 1987. Annual 3-day event. 2002 dates were May 17-19. Location: Holiday Inn Harrisburg/Hershey; check website for 2003 location. Average attendance: 200.
Purpose/Features: Open to all writers, novice to multi-published. Covers fiction, nonfiction, and poetry. Offers workshops/seminars, appointments with agents and editors, autograph party, contests—all multi-genre oriented. Theme for 2002 conference was "Unlocking the Mysteries of Writing."
Costs/Accommodations: 2002 conference cost was $130 (members), $175 (nonmembers) for all days of conference, including some meals. Special meal events are additional. "Scholarship awards are presented

to Pennwriter members who are winners in our annual writing contests." Transportation to and from airport/ train station arranged with advance notice. Information on overnight accommodations available. Housing in on-site facilities costs $85/room single or double occupancy in 2002.

Additional Info: Pennwriters sponsors three separate contests: 1. Annual Writing Contest for novel (first chapter), article, and short story (unpublished and published). Open to members only. Complete guidelines on website. Awards scholarships to annual Pennwriters Conference. All entries receive critiques from judges. Categories receive anywhere from 5-30 submissions each. 2. In Other Words Contest, held during annual conference, open to conference attendees only. Divisions for poetry, fiction, and nonfiction (published and unpublished). Complete rules on website. Awards prizes; judged by peers. 3. Pennwriters Poetry Contest, open to all; nonmembers pay slightly higher fee. Cash prizes of $50, $25, $10. Complete guidelines on website. Brochure and registration form available for SASE or on website. Accepts inquiries by fax and e-mail. "The Pennwriters Annual Conference is sponsored by Pennwriters, Inc., a nonprofit organization with goals to help writers get published."

PIMA WRITERS' WORKSHOP, Pima College, 2202 W. Anklam Rd., Tucson AZ 85709. (520)206-6084. E-mail: mfiles@pimacc.pima.edu. **Director:** Meg Files. Established 1987. Annual 3-day event. 2002 dates were May 24-26. Location: Pima College's Center for the Arts, "includes a proscenium theater, a black box theater, a recital hall, and conference rooms, as well as a courtyard with amphitheater." Average attendance: 250.

Purpose/Features: Open to all writers, beginning and experienced. "The workshop includes sessions on all genres (nonfiction, fiction, poetry, writing for children and juveniles, screenwriting) and on editing and publishing, as well as manuscript critiques and writing exercises." Past faculty has included Robert Morgan, Sharman Apt Russell, Barbara Kingsolver, Larry McMurtry, Nancy Mairs, and others, including 2 agents. Other special features include "accessibility to writers, agents, and editors; and the workshop's atmosphere—friendly and supportive, practical and inspirational."

Costs/Accommodations: 2002 conference cost was $65. Participants responsible for their own meals. Information on overnight accommodations available.

Additional Info: Individual poetry critiques available. Submit 3 poems in advance to Meg Files. Brochure and registration form available for SASE or by fax or e-mail. Accepts inquiries by e-mail.

POETRY ALIVE! SUMMER RESIDENCY INSTITUTE FOR TEACHERS, 20 Battery Park, Suite 505, Asheville NC 28801. (800)476-8172 or (828)255-7636. Fax: (828)232-1045. E-mail: poetry@poetryalive.com. Website: www.poetryalive.com (includes photos, descriptions, dates and prices). **Contact:** Rodney Bowling. Established 1990. Annual 7-day events. 2003 dates are June 15-21, July 6-12, July 13-19. Location: University of North Carolina at Asheville. Average attendance: 20/session.

Purpose/Features: Open to anyone. Themes or panels for conference have included "creative writing (poetry), reader response techniques, poem performance techniques and teaching." Speakers at past conferences have included Allan Wolf (performance poetry, writing) and Cheryl Bromley Jones (reader response, writing). Other special features include a trip to Connemara, the Carl Sandburg Home, and dinner out in downtown Asheville.

Costs/Accommodations: 2003 conference cost is $725, including meals and housing in on-site facilities; shared dorm rooms with bed, desk, and shared bath. Private room available for additional cost. Discounts available to local commuters "who don't pay the cost of food and lodging." Transportation to and from the event not provided. "We provide transportation from the airport."

Additional Info: Brochure and registration form available by fax, e-mail, or on website. Accepts inquiries by fax and e-mail. "This workshop is designed specifically for teachers or any poet interested in working with students in the schools or as an educational consultant."

POETRY WEEKEND INTENSIVES, 40 Post Ave., Hawthorne NJ 07506. (973)423-2921. Fax: (973)523-6088. E-mail: mariagillan@msn.com. Website: www.pccc.cc.nj.us. **Executive Director:** Maria Mazziotti Gillan. Established 1997. Usually held 4 times/year in March, June, October, and December. Location: generally at St. Marguerite's Retreat House, an English manor house at the Convent of St. John the Baptist in Mendhan, NJ; also several other convents and monasteries. Average attendance: 26.

Purpose/Features: Open to all writers. "The purpose of this retreat is to give writers the space and time to focus totally on their own work in a serene and beautiful setting away from the pressures and distractions of daily life." 2001 theme was "Writing Your Way Home—Poetry of Memory and Place." "Writing weekend poets will find support and encouragement, stimulating activities leading to the creation of new work, workshop leaders who are actively engaged in the writing life, opportunities to read their work aloud to the group, a circle of writer friends, and networking opportunities." Poetry Weekend Intensives are led by Maria Mazziotti Gillan and Laura Boss. Other special features include one-on-one conferences with lead poet faculty.

Costs/Accommodations: Cost for 2002 weekends: $295, including meals. Offers a $25 early bird discount. Housing in on-site facilities included in the $295 price.

Additional Info: Individual poetry critiques available. Poets should bring poems to weekend. Registration form available for SASE or by fax or e-mail. Accepts inquiries by fax and e-mail. Maria Mazziotti Gillan is the director of the Creative Writing Program of Binghamton University—State University of New York, executive director of the Poetry Center at Passaic County Community College, and edits *Paterson Literary Review*. Laura Boss is the editor of *Lips* magazine. Fifteen professional development credits are available for each weekend.

N PORT TOWNSEND WRITERS' CONFERENCE, % Centrum, P.O. Box 1158, Port Townsend WA 98368. (360)385-3102. Fax: (360)385-2470. E-mail: carla@centrum.org. Website: www.centrum.org. **Registrar:** Carla Vander Ven. Established 1974. Annual 10-day event usually held the second week in July. Location: 400-acre state park at the entrance to Puget Sound. Average attendance: 160.

Purpose/Features: Open to "all serious writers." Conference usually covers fiction (no genre fiction), poetry, and creative nonfiction. Offerings include limited-enrollment critiqued workshops with private ms conference or open enrollment workshops. Also included are open mic readings, faculty readings, and technique classes. Faculty at the 2001 conference included Marvin Bell, Colette Inez, Greg Orr, and Rebecca Seiferle.

Costs/Accommodations: Most recent conference cost was $450 for critiqued workshop tuition, $350 for open enrollment workshop tuition (no private critique and can attend both prose and poetry); plus $285 optional for dormitory housing and 3 meals/day. Information on overnight accommodations available.

Additional Info: Members of critiqued workshops must submit no more than 10 pages of writing samples or as requested by the faculty member. Brochure and registration form available for SASE or on website.

(S.O.M.O.S.) SOCIETY OF THE MUSE OF THE SOUTHWEST; CHOKECHERRIES, P.O. Box 3225, Taos NM 87571. (505)758-0081. Fax: (505)758-4802. E-mail: somos@laplaza.com. Website: www.somostaos.org (includes calendar and descriptions of special events). **Executive Director:** Dori Vinella. Established 1983. "We offer readings, special events, and workshops at different times during the year, many during the summer." Length of workshops varies. Location: various sites in Taos. Average attendance: 10-50.

Purpose/Features: Open to anyone. "We offer workshops in various genres—fiction, poetry, nature writing, etc.," including the 2-day Annual Taos Storytelling Festival the second weekend in September. Past workshop speakers have included Denise Chavez, Alfred Depew, Marjorie Agosin, Judyth Hill, Robin Becker, and Robert Westbrook. Other special features include writing in nature/nature walks and beautiful surroundings in a historic writer's region.

Costs/Accommodations: Cost for workshops ranges from $30-175, excluding room and board. Information on overnight accommodations available.

Additional Info: Additional information available by fax, e-mail, or on website. Accepts inquiries by fax and e-mail. "Taos has a wonderful community of dedicated and talented writers who make SOMOS workshops rigorous, supportive, and exciting." Also publishes *Chokecherries*, an annual anthology.

SAGE HILL WRITING FALL POETRY COLLOQUIUM, P.O. Box 1731, Saskatoon, Saskatchewan S7K 3S1 Canada. Phone/fax: (306)652-7395. E-mail: sage.hill@saskel.net. Website: www.lights.com/sagehill/fall.html (includes program information, scholarship information, tuition, course outlines, faculty profiles, application information and down-loadable application forms). **Executive Director:** Steven Ross Smith. Established 1995. Annual event. 2002 dates: October 7-24. Location: "The peaceful milieu of St. Peter's College, adjoining St. Peter's Abbey, in Muenster, 125 kilometers east of Saskatoon."

Purpose/Features: Open to poets, 19 years of age and older, who are working in English. The colloquium offers "an intensive three-week working and critiquing retreat designed to assist poets with manuscripts-in-progress. Each writer will have established a publishing record in books or periodicals and will wish to develop his/her craft and tune a manuscript. There will be ample time for writing, one-on-one critiques, and group meetings to discuss recent thinking in poetics. Eight writers will be selected. Writers in and outside Saskatchewan are eligible." Instructor for the 2002 colloquium: Betsy Warland, with guest poet Phil Hall.

Costs/Accommodations: 2002 cost: $925, including tuition, accommodations, and meals. "A university registration fee of $25 will be added if taking this course for credit." Transportation from Saskatoon can be arranged as needed. On-site accommodations included in cost.

Additional Info: Brochure and registration form available for SASE. Most recent application deadline: July 31, 2002.

SAGE HILL WRITING SUMMER EXPERIENCE, P.O. Box 1731, Saskatoon, Saskatchewan S7K 3S1 Canada. Phone/fax: (306)652-7395. E-mail: sage.hill@sasktel.net. Website: www.lights.com/sagehill (includes program information, scholarship information, tuition, application information and down-loadable application forms). **Executive Director:** Steven Ross Smith. Established in 1990. Annual 10-day event usually held the end of July through the beginning of August. 2002 dates were July 9-August 8. Location: St. Michael's Retreat, "a tranquil facility in the beautiful Qu'Appelle Valley just outside the town of Lumsden, 25 kilometers north of Regina." Average attendance: 54, with participants broken into small groups of 5-11.

Purpose/Features: Open to writers, 19 years of age and older, who are working in English. No geographic restrictions. The retreat/workshops are designed to "offer a special working and learning opportunity to writers at different stages of development. Top quality instruction, a low instructor-writer ratio, and the rural Saskatchewan setting offers conditions ideal for the pursuit of excellence in the arts of fiction, poetry, playwriting, and creative nonfiction." Offerings for poets include a poetry workshop and poetry colloquium. 2002 faculty included Betsy Warland, Robert Kroetsch, and David Carpenter.

Costs/Accommodations: 2002 conference cost was $775, including instruction, accommodations, and meals. Limited local transportation to the conference is available. "Van transportation from Regina airport to Lumsden will be arranged for out-of-province travellers." On-site accommodations offer individual rooms with a writing desk and washroom.

Additional Info: Individual critiques offered as part of workshop and colloquium. Writing sample required with application. 2002 application deadline was April 24. Brochure and registration form available for SASE.

SAN JUAN WRITERS WORKSHOP, P.O. Box 68, Moab UT 84532. (435)259-7750. Fax: (435)259-2335. E-mail: cfinfo@canyonlandsfieldinst.org. Website: www.canyonlandsfieldinst.org. **Contact:** Registrar. Annual 4-day event usually held in March. Location: based out of the Recapture Lodge in scenic Bluff, Utah. Attendance: a maximum of 24.

• **The conference for 2002 was cancelled; contact for information regarding future conferences.**

THE SANDHILLS WRITERS CONFERENCE, Augusta State University, Augusta GA 30904. (706)737-1500. Fax: (706)667-4770. E-mail: akellman@aug.edu. Website: www.aug.edu/langlitcom/sand_hills_conference. **Conference Director:** Anthony Kellman. Established 1975. Annual 3-day event usually held the third weekend in March. 2002 dates: March 21-23. Location: campus of Augusta State University. Facilities are handicapped accessible. Average attendance: 100.

Purpose/Features: Open to all aspiring writers. Conference designed to "hone the creative writing skills of participants and provide networking opportunities. All areas are covered—fiction, poetry, children's literature, playwriting, screenwriting, and writing of song lyrics, also nonfiction." Offerings for poets include craft lectures, ms evaluations, and readings. 2002 conference speakers included poet Jayne Cortez (keynote speaker and American Book Award winner); Stephen Huff (editor, BOA Editions); Jan Dystel (literary agent); novelist Elizabeth Nunez; and music publisher Leotis Clybum (So So Def Records).

Costs/Accommodations: 2002 cost was $156 full conference registration; $110 conference-only registration (no ms critique); $76 full conference student registration. Includes lunches; participants responsible for dinners only. Information on overnight accommodations available.

Additional Info: Individual poetry critiques available. Submit 6 poems with a limit of 15 pages. Contest sponsored as part of conference. "All registrants who submit a manuscript for evaluation are eligible for the contest determined by the visiting authors in each respective genre." Brochure and registration form available for SASE or on website. Accepts inquiries by fax and e-mail.

SANTA BARBARA WRITERS' CONFERENCE, P.O. Box 304, Carpinteria CA 93014. (805)684-2250. Fax: (805)684-7003. Website: www.sbwc-online.com/. **Conference Director:** Barnaby Conrad. Established 1973. Annual event held the last week in June. 2002 dates were June 21-28. Location: Westmont College in Montecito. Average attendance: 350.

Purpose/Features: Open to everyone. Covers all genres of writing. Workshops in poetry offered. 2002 presenters included Ray Bradbury, David Lee, Gary Nale, Perie J. Longo, and Bill Wilkins.

Costs/Accommodations: 2002 conference cost including all workshops and lectures, 2 dinners, and room and board, was $1,290 single, $990 double occupancy; $400 day students. Rooms are located in the residence halls.

Additional Info: Individual poetry critiques available. Submit 1 ms of no more than 3,000 words in advance with SASE. Competitions with awards sponsored as part of conference. Brochure and registration form available for SASE or on website.

SEWANEE WRITERS' CONFERENCE, 310 St. Luke's Hall, 735 University Ave., Sewanee TN 37383-1000. (931)598-1141. E-mail: cpeters@sewanee.edu. Website: www.sewaneewriters.org (includes History, The Conference, Sewanee Writers' Series, Alumni, Contact Us, and Applications Admissions). **Creative Writing Programs Manager:** Cheri B. Peters. Established 1990. Annual 12-day event held the last 2 weeks in July. Location: the University of the South ("dormitories for housing, Women's Center for public events, classrooms for workshops, Sewanee Inn for dining, etc."). Attendance: about 105.

Purpose/Features: Open to poets, fiction writers, and playwrights who submit their work for review in a competitive admissions process. "Genre, rather than thematic, workshops are offered in each of the three areas." 2002 faculty members were Andrew Hudgins, Mark Jarman, Dave Smith, and Ellen Bryant Voigt. Charles Martin and Nigel Thompson led a 3-session translation workshop. Other speakers include editors, agents, and additional writers.

Costs/Accommodations: 2002 conference cost was $1,325, including room and board. Each year scholarships and fellowships based on merit are available on a competitive basis. "We provide free bus transportation from the Nashville airport on the opening day of the conference and back to the airport on the closing day."

Additional Info: Individual critiques available. "All writers admitted to the conference will have an individual session with a member of the faculty." A ms should be sent in advance after admission to the conference. Write for brochure and application forms; no SASE necessary. Accepts inquiries by e-mail.

SINIPEE WRITERS WORKSHOP, Continuing Education, Loras College, Dubuque IA 52004-0178. (563)588-7139. Fax: (563)588-4962. E-mail: cneuhaus@loras.edu. **Contact:** Chris Neuhaus. Established 1986. Annual 1-day event usually held the third or fourth Saturday in April. Location: the campus of Loras College. Average attendance: 50-100.

Purpose/Features: Open to anyone, "professional or neophyte," interested in writing. Conference covers fiction, poetry, and nonfiction.

Costs/Accommodations: Cost for the last workshop was $60 pre-registration, $65 at the door. Scholarships covering half of the cost are traditionally available to senior citizens and to full-time students, both college and high school. Cost includes handouts, coffee-and-donut break, lunch, snacks in afternoon, and book fair with authors in attendance available to autograph their books. Information on overnight accommodations available.

Additional Info: Annual contest for nonfiction, fiction, and poetry sponsored as part of workshop. There is a $5 reading fee for each entry (article/essay of 1,500 words, short story of 1,500 words, or poetry of 40 lines). 1st Prize in each category: $100 plus publication, 2nd Prize: $50, and 3rd Prize: $25. Competition receives 50-100 entries. Entrants in the contest may also ask for a written critique by a professional writer. The cost for critique is an additional $15/entry. Brochure and registration form available for SASE.

SOUTHAMPTON COLLEGE WRITERS CONFERENCE, 239 Montauk Hwy., Southampton NY 11968. (631)287-8175. Fax: (631)287-8253. E-mail: writers@southampton.liu.edu. Website: www.southampton.liu.edu/writing (includes information on conference, application form, and request form). **Summer Director:** Carla Caglioti. Established 1976. Annual 10-day event. 2002 dates were July 17-28. Location: Southampton College of Long Island University "in the heart of the Hamptons, one of the most beautiful and culturally rich resorts in the country." Average attendance: 12/workshop.

Purpose/Features: Open to new and established writers, graduate students, and upper-level undergraduate students. Conference covers poetry, fiction, short story, and nonfiction. Offerings for poets include a workshop. 2002 faculty included Billy Collins, Jules Feiffer, Frank McCourt, Bharati Mukkherjee, Clark Blaise, and Roger Rosenblatt.

Costs/Accommodations: 2002 conference cost was $1,950 workshop, room and board, $1,350 tuition only. Accommodations include "Writers Residence Hall, single sex suites, shared room and lavatory. Some small singles available at extra cost on first-come basis."

Additional Info: "Evening events will feature regular faculty and award-winning visiting authors. Participants will also enjoy a rich schedule of formal and informal social gatherings—author receptions, open mic nights, and special literary events. Early registration is encouraged." Brochure and registration form available for SASE, by e-mail, or on website. Accepts inquiries by fax and e-mail.

SOUTHERN CALIFORNIA WRITERS' CONFERENCE*SAN DIEGO, 4406 Park Blvd., Suite E, San Diego CA 92116. Phone/fax: (619)282-2983. E-mail: wewrite@writersconference.com. Website: www.writersconference.com. **Executive Director:** Michael Gregory. Established 1986. Annual 4-day event usually held President's Day weekend. 2003 dates: February 14-17. Location: San Diego. Average attendance: 300.

Purpose/Features: Open to all aspiring and accomplished writers of fiction, nonfiction, screen, and poetry. Conference offers 50 read-and-critique sessions as well as Q&A workshops.

Costs/Accommodations: 2002 full conference cost was $275; participants responsible for own meals (except Sunday banquet, which is included in full conference cost). Individual day rates available; see website for details. Information on overnight accommodations available. Accommodations include special rates at area hotels.

Additional Info: Individual poetry critiques available. Submit poetry in advance to Terry Hertzler at the above address. Contest sponsored as part of conference. Guidelines, brochure, and registration form available for SASE, by fax, e-mail, or on website. Competition receives 50-100 entries.

SOUTHWEST WRITERS CONTEST AND CONFERENCE, 8200 Mountain Rd. NE, Suite 106, Albuquerque NM 87110. (505)265-9485. Fax: (505)265-9483. E-mail: SWriters@aol.com. Website: www.southwestwriters.org (includes contest rules, past winners, prize information, registration forms, membership information). **Contact:** Contest Chair. Established 1982. Annual 4-day event usually held in September. 2002 dates were September 5-8. Location: "Varies—it's always a large hotel or convention center." Average attendance: 400.

Purpose/Features: Open to all writers. Workshop covers all genres, focus on getting published—over 20 editors, agents, and producers as presenters. "As part of the conference, SWW has an annual writing contest with a category for poetry. Contest judges are editors and agents." 2001 contest winners were Margaret Hoehn, Barbara Rockman, and Don Shockey. Other special features include preconference sessions; appointments with editors, agents, producers, and publicists.

Costs/Accommodations: 2002 conference cost was $180 and up (lunches included—other meals sold separately, or on one's own; accommodations not included). Early Bird discount if registered by July 15. Information on overnight accommodations available, including special rates at area hotels.

Additional Info: Individual critiques available through entry in annual contest. Submit poems with a limit of 50 lines in advance with $18 (member), $23 (nonmember) fee. Each must have separate entry form and fee. Contest receives 750 entries/year, 100 of which are poetry. **Deadline** May 1. Entry form and guidelines, brochure, and registration form available for SASE, by fax, or on website. Accepts inquiries *only* by fax and e-mail. "SWW is a year-round organization. Using outreach, education, and networking, SWW encourages, supports, and inspires all people to express themselves creatively through the written word."

SPLIT ROCK ARTS PROGRAM, University of Minnesota, 360 Coffey Hall, 1420 Eckles Ave., St. Paul MN 55108-6084. (612)625-8100. Fax: (612)624-6210. E-mail: srap@cce.umn.edu. Website: www.cce.umn.edu/splitrockarts/ (includes full catalog with program/workshop descriptions, instructor bios, registration and housing information and forms, scholarship information and application forms). **Program Associate:** Vivien Oja. Established 1983. Annual week-long workshop. 2002 dates: July 7-August 10. Location: "Workshops are held on the University's Duluth campus overlooking Lake Superior; some retreat-style workshops are held at the University of Minnesota's Cloquet Forestry Center, which offers the peaceful seclusion of the north woods." Average attendance: 550.

Purpose/Features: Open to "anyone over 18 years old who has an interest in the arts. Participants are lifelong learners from all walks of life—novices, professionals, passionate hobbyists, and advanced amateurs. Our program offers uninterrupted time and space for them to explore their art in an inviting, supportive community and an opportunity to work with renowned practising artists, writers, and craftspeople. Areas of concentration include poetry, stories, memoirs, novels, and personal essays." 2002 program instructors included Sharon Doubiago, Michael Dennis Browne, Ray Gonzalez, Kate Green, and Ruth Schwartz.

Costs/Accommodations: 2002 cost was $485/workshop noncredit; participants are responsible for their own meals. Meal tickets are available. "Limited scholarships are available based on artistic merit and financial need." Housing in on-site facilities; costs were $192-270 (shared), $540/week for private apartment.

Additional Info: Write or call for free catalog or visit website (registration forms available online beginning in March of each year). Accepts inquiries by fax and e-mail.

SQUAW VALLEY COMMUNITY OF WRITERS POETRY WORKSHOP, 10626 Banner Lava Cap, Nevada City CA 95959. (530)274-8551. E-mail: svcw@oro.net. Website: www.squawvalleywriters. org (includes "all the information contained in our brochure and more; a FAQ section which contains most information applicants will need"). **Executive Director:** Brett Hall Jones. Established 1969. Annual 7-day event usually held last full week in July. 2002 dates were July 20-27. Location: The Squaw Valley Ski Corporation's Lodge in the Sierra Nevada near Lake Tahoe. "The workshop takes place in the off-season of the ski area. Participants can find time to enjoy the Squaw Valley landscape." Average attendance: 64.

Purpose/Features: Open to talented writers of diverse ethnic backgrounds and a wide range of ages. "The Poetry Program differs in concept from other workshops in poetry. Our project's purpose is to help participants break through old habits and write something daring and difficult. Workshops are intended to provide a supportive atmosphere in which no one will be embarrassed, and at the same time to challenge the participants to go beyond what they have done before. Admissions are based on quality of the submitted manuscripts." Offerings include regular morning workshops, craft lectures, and staff readings. "Participants gather in daily workshops to discuss the work they wrote in the previous 24 hours." 2002 staff poets included Lucille Clifton, Yusef Komunyakaa, Galway Kinnell, and Sharon Olds.

Costs/Accommodations: 2002 workshop cost was $625, included regular morning workshops, craft lectures, staff readings, and dinners. Accommodations extra; information on separate accommodations available. Scholarships available. "Requests for financial aid must accompany submission/application and will be granted on the perceived quality of manuscript submitted and financial need of applicant." Transportation to workshop available. "We will pick poets up at the Reno/Lake Tahoe Airport if arranged in advance. Also, we arrange housing for participants in local houses and condominiums. Participants can choose from a single room for $400/week or a double room for $300/week within these shared houses. We do offer inexpensive bunk bed accommodations on a first come, first served basis."

Additional Info: Individual conferences available. "Only work-in-progress will be discussed." Brochure available by e-mail (include mailing address for response) or on website. Accepts inquiries by e-mail. Also publishes the annual *Squaw Valley Community of Writers Omnium Gatherum and Newsletter* containing "news and profiles on our past participants and staff, craft articles, and book advertising."

STEAMBOAT SPRINGS WRITERS CONFERENCE, P.O. Box 774284, Steamboat Springs CO 80477. (970)879-8079. E-mail: MsHFreiberger@cs.com. **Director:** Harriet Freiberger. Established 1981. Annual 1-day event usually held mid-July. 2002 conference was July 20. Location: a "renovated train station, the Depot is home of the Steamboat Springs Arts Council—friendly, relaxed atmosphere." Average attendance: 35-40 (registration limited).

Purpose/Features: Open to anyone. Conference is "designed for writers who have limited time. Instructors vary from year to year, offering maximum instruction during a weekend at a nominal cost." 2002 speaker was Stephen Topping, editor-in-chief, Johnson Books.

Costs/Accommodations: 2002 cost was $35 (early enrollment prior to May 25), including lunch. "A variety of lodgings available."

Additional Info: Brochure and registration form available for SASE or by e-mail. Optional: Friday evening dinner (cost not included in registration fee); readings by participants (no cost).

SWT SUMMER CREATIVE WRITING CAMP, Dept. of English, Southwest Texas State University, San Marcos TX 78666. (512)245-3717. Fax: (512)245-8546. E-mail: sw13@swt.edu. Website: www.Englis h.swt.edu/Camp.html (includes "an overview of our program, application details, and links to information about SWT and San Marcos"). **Director:** Steve Wilson. Established 1989. Annual week-long event usually held the last week in June. Location: "The camp is held on the campus of the 21,000-student Southwest

Texas State University, which is also home to a nationally recognized Master of Fine Arts program in creative writing. SWTSU is located in Central Texas, roughly 20 miles from Austin." Attendance: limited to 20 participants.

Purpose/Features: Open to all high school students. "Because the camp is for high school students, we ask that participants take workshops in both fiction and poetry. In addition to our standard workshops in poetry, we offer workshops in revision, and each camper takes part in one-on-one tutorials with the poetry workshop leaders. On the final day of the writing camp, campers present a public reading of their writing for friends, family, and people from the local community."

Costs/Accommodations: Cost is $250, including meals. All campers stay in SWT residence halls. Costs included in program fee.

Additional Info: Brochure and registration form available for SASE. "Our application deadline is April 15 of each year." Accepts inquiries by fax and e-mail. "Our writing camp is quite competitive, so we encourage interested poets to send their best work."

TAOS SUMMER WRITERS' CONFERENCE, (formerly Taos Summer Writers' Workshop), Dept. of English, Humanities Bldg. #255, Albuquerque NM 87131-1106. (505)277-6248. Fax: (505)277-5573. E-mail: taosconf@unm.edu. Website: www.unm.edu/~taosconf (includes e-mail link, instructor profiles, workshop descriptions, price and travel information, photos). **Director:** Sharon Oard Warner. Established 1999. Annual 7-day (weeklong) and 2-day (weekend) workshops usually held mid-July. Location: Taos, NM, at the "historic Sagebrush Inn. Beautiful views of Taos mountain. Next door sister hotel offers more modern rooms with refrigerator/microwave and computer hookups." Average attendance: 125 total; 60 places available in weekend, 120 places available in weeklong workshops. Class size limited to 12/class, usually smaller.

Purpose/Features: Open to everyone, beginners to experienced. Minimum age is 18. Friendly, relaxed atmosphere with supportive staff and instructors. Purpose is "to encourage writers in all areas. We offer both weekend and weeklong workshops in fiction, short story and novel, creative nonfiction, memoir, travel writing, magazine article writing, and poetry. We have offered classes in the past in historical fiction, screenplay writing, and children's writing." 2002 workshop presenters included Pam Houston, Carolyn Meyer, Laurie Kutchins, Elizabeth Hadas, Pat Mora, and Brent Spencer. At least one week-long workshop and one weekend devoted to poetry. Previous guest speakers have included John Nichols (*Milagro Beanfield War*) and Luci Tapahonso (*Blue Horses Rush In*). Other special features include writers craft panels and open mic sessions. "We offer free tours of the nearby D.H. Lawrence Ranch and a museum crawl—many famous artists lived and worked in Taos, including Georgia O'Keefe. All of our instructors have some connection to the Southwest."

Costs/Accommodations: 2002 conference cost was $235 for weekend, $485 for weeklong sessions, $660 combo. Breakfast and select dinners included; participants responsible for other meals. Nearest airport is Albuquerque Sunport. Shuttle bus available (a commercial service not provided by the conference) for approximately $100. Auto rental services available at the airport. Taos is about 2½ hours north of Albuquerque. Information on overnight accommodations available. Sagebrush Inn and Comfort Suites offer special rates.

Additional Info: Conference contest in both fiction and poetry. Submit 5 poems, not to exceed 10 pages/poetry entry. Prize (one for poetry, one for fiction) is a scholarship to the conference. Applicants must be registered to apply. Judges: staff from the Creative Writing Dept., University of New Mexico. Brochure and registration form available by e-mail, or on website. Accepts inquiries by fax and e-mail. Participants encouraged to submit work to the University of New Mexico's *Blue Mesa Review* (see separate listing for *Blue Mesa Review* in the Publishers of Poetry section). "Taos is a unique experience of a lifetime. The setting and scenery are spectacular; historical and natural beauty abound. Our previous attendees say they have been inspired by the place and by the friendly, personal attention of our instructors."

N **TENNESSEE MOUNTAIN WRITERS CONFERENCE**, P.O. Box 4895, Oak Ridge TN 37831-4895. Phone/fax: (865)482-6567. E-mail: tnmtnwrite@aol.com. Website: www.tmwi.org (includes complete conference info). **Executive Director:** Patricia Hope. Established 1989. Annual event usually held in April. 2003 dates: April 4-5. Location: Garden Plaza Hotel in Oak Ridge. Average attendance: 150-200.

Purpose/Features: Open to "all aspiring writers, including students." Conference covers fiction, poetry, nonfiction and writing for children, plus special classes on romance, mystery, business, etc. 2002 speakers included Kay Byer (poetry), Lou Kassem (children's), and Lee Smith (banquet speaker).

Costs/Accommodations: 2002 cost (if preregistered by April 1) was $185 for full participants, $200 after April 1. Meals and other services charged separately (except banquet, which is included). Participants make own room reservations at the Garden Plaza Hotel.

Additional Info: Individual critiques available. Submit up to 10 pages prior to conference. Consult guidelines before submitting. Also sponsors contest as part of conference; guidelines available for SASE, by e-mail, or on website. Brochure available for SASE. Registration form available on website. Accepts inquiries by e-mail.

TŶ NEWYDD WRITERS' CENTRE, Taliesin Trust, Llanystumdwy, Cricieth, Gwynedd LL52 0LW Wales, Great Britain. Phone: 0441766 522811. Fax: 0441766 523095. E-mail: tynewydd@dial.pipex.com. Website: www.tynewydd.org (includes information about courses: accommodation, tutors, travel, etc.). **Director:** Sally Baker. Established 1990. Holds 4½-day courses throughout the year, Monday evening through Saturday morning. Location: Tŷ Newydd, "a house of historical and architectural interest situated near the village of Llanystumdwy. It was the last home of Lloyd George, the former British prime minister." Average attendance: 12/course.

Purpose/Features: Open to anyone over 16 years of age. Courses are designed to "promote the writing and understanding of literature by providing creative writing courses at all levels for all ages. Courses at Tŷ Newydd provide the opportunity of working intimately and informally with two professional writers." Courses specifically for poets of all levels of experience and ability are offered throughout the year.

Costs/Accommodations: 2002 cost for a 4½-day course was £320 (inclusive), shared room; some weekend courses available, cost was £130 (inclusive). Transportation to and from Centre available if arranged at least a week in advance. Participants stay at Tŷ Newydd House in shared bedrooms or single bedrooms. "Vegetarians and people with special dietary needs are catered for but please let us know in advance. Course participants help themselves to breakfast and lunch and help to prepare one evening meal as part of a team. Participants should bring towels and their own writing materials. Some typewriters and word processors are available."

Additional Info: Brochure and registration form available for SASE. Accepts inquiries by fax and e-mail.

UND WRITERS CONFERENCE, University of North Dakota, Department of English, Grand Forks ND 58202-7209. (701)777-3321. Fax: (701)777-2373. E-mail: james_mckenzie@und.nodak.edu. Website: www.undwritersconference.org (includes biographies of visiting writers, complete conference schedule, archive listing past conferences). **Director:** James McKenzie. Established 1970. Annual 4- to 5-day event. 2002 dates were March 19-22. Location: The "UND student Memorial Union, with occasional events at other campus sites, especially the large Chester Fritz Auditorium or the North Dakota Museum of Art." Average attendance: 3,000-5,000. "Some individual events have as few as 20, some over 1,000."

Purpose/Features: All events are free and open to the public. "The conference is really more of a festival, though it has been called a conference since its inception, with a history of inviting writers from all genres. The conference's purpose is public education, as well as a kind of bonus curriculum at the University. It is the region's premier intellectual and cultural event." 2002 guests included Sharon Doubiago, Ursula Hegi, Carol Muske-Dukes, Eddy Harris, and Bill Holm. "They read, participate in panels, and otherwise make themselves available in public and academic venues." 2002 conference theme was "Explorations" to coincide with the Lewis and Clark Bicentennial. Other special features include open mic student/public readings every morning, informal meetings with writers, autograph sessions, dinners, and receptions.

Additional Info: Brochure available for SASE. Accepts inquiries by e-mail.

VICTORIA SCHOOL OF WRITING, Box 8152, Victoria, British Columbia V8W 3R8 Canada. (250)595-3000. E-mail: vicwrite@islandnet.com. Website: www.islandnet.com/vicwrite/ (includes description of school, faculty, and workshops; registration details; comments from former students and contest winners). **Director:** Ruth Slavin. Established 1996. Annual 5-day event. 2002 dates: July 14-19. Location: "Residential school in natural, park-like setting. Easy parking, access to university, downtown." Average attendance: 100.

Purpose/Features: "A three- to ten-page manuscript is required as part of the registration process, which is open to all. The general purpose of the workshop is to give hands-on assistance with better writing, working closely with established writers/instructors. We have workshops in fiction, poetry, and nonfiction; plus three other workshops which vary." Offerings for poets include 2 of the intensive 5-day workshops (16 hours of instruction and one-on-one consultation). 2002 workshop leaders included Brain Brett and Theresa Kishkan (poetry) and Audrey Thomas and Michael Winter (fiction).

Costs/Accommodations: 2002 workshop cost was $575 Canadian; included 5 lunches and 1 dinner. Other meals and accommodations available on site. "For people who register with payment in full before May 1, the cost is $525 Canadian."

Additional Info: Contest sponsored as part of conference. Most recent winners were Ariel Aue Dawn, Beth K. Ryan, and Troy Wilson. Competition receives approximately 200 entries. Brochure and registration form available for SASE. Accepts inquiries by e-mail.

WESLEYAN WRITERS CONFERENCE, Wesleyan University, Middletown CT 06457. (860)685-3604. Fax: (860)685-2441. E-mail: agreene@wesleyan.edu. Website: www.wesleyan.edu/writing/conferen. html (includes overview of conference, information on schedule and faculty, scholarship information, rates and registration form). **Director:** Anne Greene. Established 1956. Annual 5-day event usually held the last week in June. Location: the campus of Wesleyan University "in the hills overlooking the Connecticut River, a brief drive from the Connecticut shore. Wesleyan's outstanding library, poetry reading room, and other university facilities are open to participants." Average attendance: 100.

Purpose/Features: "Open to both experienced and new writers. The participants are an international group. The conference covers the novel, short story, fiction techniques, fiction-and-film, poetry, literary journalism, and memoir." Recent special sessions included "The Poetry of Engagement," "The Writer's Life," "Writing Memoirs," and "Publishing." Offerings for poets include ms consultations and daily seminars. Recent faculty include Honor Moore, C.D. Wright, Henry Taylor, Dana Gioia, Judy Jordan, and Mark Doty.

Costs/Accommodations: 2002 cost, including meals, was $725 (day rate); $850 (boarding rate). "Wesleyan has scholarships for journalists, fiction writers, nonfiction writers, and poets. Request brochure for application information." Information on overnight accommodations available. "Conference participants may stay in university dormitories or off campus in local hotels."

Additional Info: Individual poetry critiques available. Registration for critiques must be made before the conference. Accepts inquiries by fax and e-mail.

WHIDBEY ISLAND WRITERS' CONFERENCES; THE WHIDBEY ISLAND WRITERS' ASSOCIATION, P.O. Box 1289, Langley WA 98260. (360)331-6714. E-mail: writers@whidbey.com. Website: www.whidbey.com/writers (includes conference information: presenters, accommodations, links to Whidbey Island, registration forms, how to make the most of agent/editor/publisher meetings and conference opportunities). **Director:** Celeste Mergens. Established 1997. Annual event held the first weekend in March. 2002 dates: March 1-3. Location: "South Whidbey High School's state-of-the-art facility, except for Friday's Author Fireside Chats, which are held in private residences within the community." Average attendance: 250.

Purpose/Features: Open to writers of every genre and skill level. Conference covers fiction, nonfiction, poetry, children's writing, and screenwriting. Offerings for poets include workshops, panels, and readings. Past speakers have included poets Pattiann Rogers, Marvin Bell, David Lee, Peggy Schumaker, Bart Baxter, and Susan Zwinger. Other special features include "Author Fireside Chats, which are opportunities to meet and learn from the faculty in personable home settings with groups of 20 or less. Participants spend the day focusing on their chosen genre."

Costs/Accommodations: 2002 conference cost was $308, including 2 meals ($258 if registered before November 30). Volunteer discounts available. "Rideshare board available through our website." Information on overnight accommodations available. Accommodations include special rates at "local B&B's, as well as roommate share lists and dorm-style accommodations as low as $10/night.

Additional Info: Individual poetry critiques available. Submit 8 poems with a limit of 2 poems/page by February 15. "Registrants may participate in our free annual writing contest. Info on website." Offers optional 1-day writer's retreats the day prior to the conference. Brochure and registration form available for SASE, by fax, e-mail, or on website. Accepts inquiries by e-mail. Conference is sponsored by the Whidbey Island Writers' Association and is "designed to offer personable interaction and learning opportunities. We consider all presenters and participants to be part of the 'team' here. We emphasize practical application strategies for success as well as workshop opportunities. We try to invite at least one poetry publisher per year."

N **INDICATES A MARKET** that did not appear in the 2002 edition.

WINTER POETRY & PROSE GETAWAY IN CAPE MAY, 18 North Richards Ave., Ventnor NJ 08406. (609)823-5076. E-mail: wintergetaway@hotmail.com. Website: www.wintergetaway.com. **Founder/Director:** Peter E. Murphy. Established 1994. Annual 4-day event. 2003 dates: January 17-20. Location: The Grand Hotel on the Oceanfront in Historic Cape May, New Jersey. "Participants stay in comfortable rooms with an ocean view, perfect for thawing out the muse. Hotel facilities include a pool, sauna, and whirlpool, as well as a lounge and disco for late evening dancing for night people." Average attendance: 175.

Purpose/Features: Open to all writers, beginners and experienced, over the age of 18. "The poetry workshop meets for an hour or so each morning before sending you off with an assignment that will encourage and inspire you to produce exciting new work. After lunch, we gather together to read new drafts in feedback sessions led by experienced poet-teachers who help identify the poem's virtues and offer suggestions to strengthen its weaknesses. The groups are small and you receive positive attention to help your poem mature. In late afternoon, you can continue writing or schedule a personal tutorial session with one of the poets on staff." Previous staff have included Renee Ashley, Robert Carnevale, Cat Doty, Stephen Dunn, Kathleen Rockwell Lawrence, Charles Lynch, Peter Murphy, Jim Richardson, and Robbie Clipper Sethi. There are usually 10 participants in each poetry workshop and 7 in each of the prose workshops. Other special features include extra-supportive sessions for beginners.

Costs/Accommodations: 2002 conference cost was $400, including breakfast and lunch for 3 days, all sessions, as well as a double room; participants responsible for dinner only. Discounts available. "Early Bard" Discount: Deduct $25 if paid in full by November 15." Single-occupancy rooms available at additional cost.

Additional Info: Individual poetry critiques available. "Each poet may have a 20-minute tutorial with one of the poets on staff." Brochure and registration form available by mail or on website. "The Winter Getaway is known for its challenging, yet supportive atmosphere that encourages imaginative risk-taking and promotes freedom and transformation in the participants' writing."

N WRITERS@WORK, Conference Registration, P.O. Box 540370, North Salt Lake UT 84054-0370. (801)292-9285. Website: www.writersatwork.org/conference.html (includes schedule, faculty list and bios, registration form, housing info). **Contact:** Lisa Peterson. Established 1985. Annual event. 2002 dates were June 23-28. Location: the beautiful Westminster College campus in Salt Lake City. Average attendance: limited to 15/workshop.

Purpose/Features: Open to writers of all levels. Schedule includes workshops where students get feedback on mss; in-class writing sessions and craft discussions; and Blank Page workshops "where students can learn to spark their creativity when facing that blank page of paper." Offerings for poets include week-long workshop, readings by faculty and other featured poets, and daily afternoon panels providing insight to the process of writing and submitting work. 2002 faculty included Stanley Plumly, Rikki Ducornet, Ray Gonzalez, Antonya Nelson, and Robert Boswell.

Costs/Accommodations: 2002 cost was $395 for workshop, afternoon sessions (excluding "The Blank Page"), and 30-minute ms consultation. Six-hour Blank Page workshop (with John Gregory Brown in 2002) cost $175. Roundtable Box Lunch discussion also available for $15 (for full workshop participants only). Limited number of Westminster residency suites available for $150/week (must be 18 years of age). Information on other overnight accommodations available.

Additional Information: Also offers the Writers@Work Fellowship Competition for fiction, nonfiction, and poetry. See website for complete details.

WRITING TODAY, Birmingham-Southern College, Box 549003, Birmingham AL 35254. (205)226-4921. Fax: (205)226-3072. E-mail: dcwilson@bsc.edu. Website: www.bsc.edu/events/specialevents/writingtoday/. **Director of Special Events:** Anne Green. Established 1978. Annual 2-day event. "Beginning in 2003, the conference will be held the first week-end in March." 2003: March 7-8. Location: Birmingham-Southern College campus. Average attendance: over 400.

Purpose/Features: Open to "everyone interested in writing—beginners, professionals, and students. Conference topics vary year to year depending on who is part of the faculty." Past speakers/panelists have included Galway Kinnell, James Redfield, Barry Hannah, Josephine Humphries, and Grand Masters Ernest J. Gaines, Joyce Carol Oates, and Gwendolyn Brooks.

Costs/Accommodations: 2002 conference cost was $120 before deadline ($130 after deadline), including lunches. Information on overnight accommodations provided with registration confirmation. Accommodations include special rates at area hotels.

Additional Info: Individual critiques available. "Critique fees are separate and in addition to registration fees. $40/ms payable to Writing Today. Poetry—maximum of 5 pages (100-125 lines)." In addition, the Hackney Literary Awards competition is sponsored as part of the conference. Open to writers nationwide, offers $5,000 ($2,500 state level, $2,500 national level) in prizes for unpublished poetry and short stories and a $5,000 award for the novel category. (See listing for the Hackney Literary Awards in the Contests and Awards section.) Conference information and brochure available for SASE or on website.

N̳ YOSEMITE WINTER LITERARY CONFERENCE, (formerly Yosemite: Alive with Poetry), Yosemite Association, P.O. Box 230, El Portal CA 95318. (209)379-2321. Fax: (209)379-2486. E-mail: yose_yosemite_association@nps.gov. Website: www.yosemite.org (includes conference info, description of 50 other courses, a web camera broadcasting live photo of the Yosemite Valley). Coordinator: Beth Pratt. Annual 4-day event. 2002 dates were February 24-28. Location: Ahwahnee Hotel, Yosemite National Park. Average attendance: 100.

Purpose/Features: "The conference is designed for a variety of interest levels. Its goal is to attract and introduce writers and other artists to Yosemite and to engage them in literary contemplation, activity, and exchange." 2002 staff included Gary Snyder, Jane Hirshfield, and Pam Houston.

Costs/Accommodations: Cost is $535 ($510 for Yosemite Association members); participants are responsible for their own meals. Lodging is extra.

Additional Info: Call for brochures. "The Yosemite Association is a nonprofit organization dedicated to educating the public about Yosemite. We publish books, offer 68 field seminars, and give funding to the National Park Service from our book sales. We welcome new members and will honor the member fee for those individuals just joining."

Organizations

There are many organizations of value to poets. These groups may sponsor workshops and contests, stage readings, publish anthologies and chapbooks, or spread the word about publishing opportunities. A few provide economic assistance or legal advice. The best thing that organizations offer, though, is a support system where poets can turn for a pep talk, a hard-nosed (but sympathetic) critique of a manuscript, or simply the comfort of talking and sharing with others who understand the challenges (and joys) of writing poetry.

Whether national, regional, or as local as your library or community center, each organization has something special to offer. The listings in this section reflect the membership opportunities available to poets with a variety of organizations. Note, too, that many groups provide certain services to both members and nonmembers.

Certain symbols may appear at the beginning of some listings. The (N) symbol indicates an organization that is new to this edition; the (✿) symbol denotes a Canadian organization and the (⊕) symbol an international one.

Since some organizations are included in listings in the Publishers of Poetry, Contest & Awards, and Conferences & Workshops sections of this book, we've included these markets in a cross reference at the end of this section called Additional Organizations. For further details about an organization associated with a market in this list, go to that market's page number.

To find out more about groups in your area (including those that may not be listed in *Poet's Market*), contact your YMCA, community center, local colleges and universities, public library, and bookstores (and don't forget newspapers and the Internet). And if you can't find a group that suits your needs, consider starting one yourself. You might be surprised to find there are others in your locality who would welcome the encouragement, feedback, and moral support of a writer's group.

⊕ **ACADEMI–YR ACADEMI GYMREIG/THE WELSH ACADEMY; TALIESIN; NWR; A470: WHAT'S ON IN LITERARY WALES**, Mount Stuart House, 3rd Floor, Cardiff, Wales CF10 5FQ United Kingdom. Phone: 029 2047 2266. Fax: 029 2049 2930. E-mail: post@academi.org. Website: www.a cademi.org (includes contact details, list of writers, events, competitions). **Chief Executive:** Peter Finch. Established in 1959 to "promote literature in Wales and to assist in the maintaining of its standard." The Welsh National Literature Promotion Agency and Society of Writers is open to "the population of Wales and those outside Wales with an interest in Welsh writing." Currently has 2,000 total members. Levels of membership: associate, full, and fellow. Offerings include promotion of readings, events, conferences, exchanges, tours; employment of literature-development workers; publication of a bimonthly events magazine; publication of a literary magazine in Welsh (*Taliesin*) and another (*NWR*) in English. Sponsors conferences/workshops and contests/awards. Publishes *A470: What's On In Literary Wales*, a magazine appearing 5 times/year containing information on Welsh literary events. Also available to nonmembers for £15 (annual subscription). Members and nationally known writers give readings that are open to the public. Sponsors open mic readings for members and the public. Membership dues: £15/year (waged) or £7.50/year (unwaged). Additional information available for SASE (or SAE and IRC), by fax, e-mail, or on website.

THE ACADEMY OF AMERICAN POETS; FELLOWSHIP OF THE ACADEMY OF AMERICAN POETS; WALT WHITMAN AWARD; THE JAMES LAUGHLIN AWARD; HAROLD MORTON LANDON TRANSLATION AWARD; THE LENORE MARSHALL POETRY PRIZE; THE ATLAS FUND; THE RAIZISS/DE PALCHI TRANSLATION AWARD; THE WALLACE STEVENS AWARD; THE AMERICAN POET, 588 Broadway, Suite 1203, New York NY 10012-3210. (212)274-0343. Fax: (212)274-9427. E-mail: academy@poets.org. Website: www.poets.org. **Executive**

Director: Tree Swenson. Established 1934. Robert Penn Warren wrote in *Introduction to Fifty Years of American Poetry*, an anthology published in 1984 containing one poem from each of the 126 Chancellors, Fellows, and Award Winners of the Academy: "What does the Academy do? According to its certificate of incorporation, its purpose is 'To encourage, stimulate and foster the production of American poetry. . . .' The responsibility for its activities lies with the Board of Directors and the Board of Chancellors, which has included, over the years, such figures as Louise Bogan, W.H. Auden, Witter Bynner, Randall Jarrell, Robert Lowell, Robinson Jeffers, Marianne Moore, James Merrill, Robert Fitzgerald, F.O. Matthiessen and Archibald MacLeish—certainly not members of the same poetic church." The Academy Fellowship is a $35,000 award for a distinguished American poet at mid-career. **No applications are accepted.** The Walt Whitman Award pays $5,000 plus publication of a poet's first book by Louisiana State University Press. Winner also receives a 1-month residency at the Vermont Studio Center. Mss of 50-100 pages must be submitted between September 15 and November 15 with a $25 entry fee. Entry form required. Send SASE. The James Laughlin Award, for a poet's second book, is also a prize of $5,000. Submissions must be made by a publisher in ms form. The Academy distributes over 9,000 copies of the Whitman Award- and Laughlin Award-winning books to its members. Poets entering either contest must be American citizens. The Harold Morton Landon Translation Award is for translation of a book-length poem, a collection of poems, or a verse-drama translated into English from any language. One award of $1,000 is given each year to a US citizen. Write for guidelines. The Lenore Marshall Poetry Prize is a $10,000 award for the most outstanding book of poems published in the US in the preceding year. The contest is open to books by living American poets published in a standard edition (40 pages or more in length with 500 or more copies). Self-published books are not eligible. Publishers may enter as many books as they wish. Deadline: June 1. Guidelines available for SASE. The Atlas Fund assists noncommercial publishers of poetry. Guidelines available for SASE. The Raiziss/de Palchi Translation Award is for outstanding translations of modern Italian poetry into English. A $5,000 book prize and a $20,000 fellowship are given in alternate years. Submissions for the book prize are accepted in odd-numbered years from September 1 through November 1. Submissions for the fellowship are accepted in even-numbered years from September 1 through November 1. The Wallace Stevens Award of $150,000 is given annually for proven mastery in the art of poetry. **No applications are accepted.** *American Poet* is an informative periodical sent to those who contribute $25 or more/ year. Membership: $45/year. "The Academy also sponsors National Poetry Month (April), an annual celebration of the richness and vitality of American poetry; the Poetry Book Club, the only book club of its kind in the United States; the Online Poetry Classroom, an educational resource and online teaching community for high school teachers; and the Poetry Audio Archive, a collection of audio recordings of poetry readings. Additionally, the Academy maintains one of the liveliest and most comprehensive poetry sites on the Internet, at www.poets.org."

ADIRONDACK LAKES CENTER FOR THE ARTS, P.O. Box 205, Rte. 28, Blue Mountain Lake NY 12812. (518)352-7715. Fax: (518)352-7333. E-mail: alca@telenet.net. **Program Coordinator:** Darren Miller. Established in 1967 to promote "visual and performing arts through programs and services, to serve established professional and aspiring artists and the region through educational programs and activities of general interest." An independent, private, nonprofit educational organization open to everyone. Currently has 1,300 members. Levels of membership: individual, family, and business. Offerings include workshops for adults and children, reading performances, discussions, and lectures. Offers a "comfortable, cozy performance space—coffeehouse setting with tables, candles, etc." Computers available for members and artists. Publishes a triannual newsletter/schedule containing news, articles, photos, and a schedule of events. "All members are automatically sent the schedule and others may request a copy." Sponsors a few readings each year. "These are usually given by the instructor of our writing workshops. There is no set fee for membership, a gift of any size makes you a member." Members meet each July. Additional information available for SASE and by fax and e-mail.

ARIZONA AUTHORS ASSOCIATION; ARIZONA LITERARY MAGAZINE; ARIZONA AU-THORS NEWSLETTER, P.O. Box 87857, Phoenix AZ 85080-7857. (602)769-2066. Fax: (623)780-0468. E-mail: info@azauthors.com. Website: www.azauthors.com (includes information about the Arizona Authors Association, membership, meetings, and book signings as well as contest forms and guidelines, member news, and links). **Contact:** Vijaya Schartz, president. Established 1978 to provide education and referral for writers and others in publishing. State-wide organization. Currently has 150 total members. Levels of memberships: Published, Unpublished (seeking publication), Professional (printers, agents, and publishers), and Student. Sponsors conferences, workshops, contests, awards. Sponsors annual literary contest in poetry, short story, essay, unpublished novels, and published books (fiction and nonfiction). Awards publication in *Arizona Literary Magazine*, radio interview, publication of novel by 1stbooks.com in e-book and print-on-demand, and $100 1st Prize in each category. Pays winners from other countries by international money order. Does not accept entry fees in foreign currencies. Poetry submissions must be unpublished and may be entered in other contests. Submit any number of poems on any subject up to 42 lines. Entry form and guidelines available for SASE. **Entry fee:** $10/poem. **Submission period:** January 1 through July 1. Competition receives 1,000 entries/year. Most recent contest winners include Ellaraine Lockie, Cleo Lorette, Lynn Veach Sadler, Marcia Reynolds, and Gurukirn Khalsa. Judges are Arizona authors, editors, reviewers, and readers. Winners will be announced by November 15. Publishes *Arizona Literary Magazine* and *Arizona Authors Newsletter*. Membership dues: $45/year for authors, $30/year students, $60/year professionals. Members meet bimonthly. Additional information available on website.

ASSOCIATED WRITING PROGRAMS; WRITER'S CHRONICLE; THE AWP AWARD SE-RIES, MS 1E3, George Mason University, Fairfax VA 22030. (703)993-4301. Fax: (703)993-4302. E-mail: awp@gmu.edu. Website: www.awpwriter.org (includes information on AWP's core services, contest guidelines, conference information, links to other writer's organizations and creative writing programs). **Publications Manager:** Supriya Bhatnagar. Established 1967. Offers a variety of services to the writing community, including information, job placement assistance (helps writers find jobs in teaching, editing, and other related fields), writing contests, literary arts advocacy, and forums. Annual individual membership: $59; placement service extra. Publishes *The Writer's Chronicle* containing information about grants and awards, publishing opportunities, fellowships, and writing programs. Available for $20/6 issues. Also publishes a directory, *The AWP Official Guide to Writing Programs*, of over 250 college and university writing programs, available for $25.95 (includes shipping); and the *AWP Job List* magazine, approximately 20 pages, containing employment opportunity listings for writers in higher education, editing, and publishing. The AWP Award Series selects a volume of poetry (48 page minimum) each year ($10 entry fee for members; $20 for nonmembers) with an award of $2,000 and publication. Deadline: February 28. Submission guidelines available for business-sized SASE. Query after November. Competition receives approximately 1,400 entries. Recent contest winners include Joanie V. Mackowski, Alexander Parsons, Brian Lennon, and Michelle Richmond.

ASSOCIATION OF CHRISTIAN WRITERS; CANDLE AND KEYBOARD, All Saints Vicarage, 43 All Saints Close, Edmonton, London N9 9AT England. Phone/fax: 020 8884 4348. E-mail: admin@ christianwriters.org.uk. Website: www.christianwriters.org.uk. **Administrator:** Jenny Kyriacou. Established in 1971 "to inspire, train, equip, and encourage Christian writers." National charity with regional affiliations open to "anyone who affirms and practises the Christian faith and writes for pleasure or profit." Currently has 850 total members. Levels of membership: New Writers (exploring), Noncommercial Writers, Intermediate (few pieces published), and Experienced Writers (regularly published). Offerings include "market news in quarterly magazine, poetry adviser for personal manuscript critiques, postal workshops with other poets, and poetry competitions." Arranges 3 training days/year and annual contests. Publishes *Candle and Keyboard*, a quarterly magazine. Membership dues: £17 sterling/year. Additional information available for SASE and by fax and e-mail.

THE AUTHORS GUILD, INC.; THE BULLETIN, 31 E. 28th St., New York NY 10016. (212)564-5904. Fax: (212)564-8363. E-mail: staff@authorsguild.org. Website: www.authorsguild.org. **Executive Director:** Paul Aiken. Established in 1912, it "is the largest association of published writers in the United States. The Guild focuses its efforts on the legal and business concerns of published authors in the areas of publishing contract terms, copyright, taxation, and freedom of expression. The Guild provides free 75-point book and magazine contract reviews to members and makes group health insurance available to its members. The Guild also sponsors Backinprint.com, a service that allows members to republish and sell their out-of-print books. Writers must be published by a recognized book publisher or periodical of general circulation to be eligible for membership. We do not work in the area of marketing mss to publishers nor do we sponsor or participate in awards or prize selections." Also publishes *The Bulletin*, a quarterly journal for professional writers. Additional information available by mail, phone, and e-mail.

MARKET CONDITIONS are constantly changing! If you're still using this book and it's 2004 or later, buy the newest edition of *Poet's Market* at your favorite bookstore or order directly from Writer's Digest Books (800)448-0915 or www.writersdigest.com.

AUTHORS LEAGUE FUND, 31 E. 28th St., 10th Floor, New York NY 10016. **Administrator:** Sarah Heller. Makes interest-free loans to published authors and professional playwrights in need of temporary help because of illness or an emergency. No grants.

THE BEATLICKS; BEATLICK NEWS, 1016 Kipling Dr., Nashville TN 37217. (615)366-9012. Fax: (615)366-4117. E-mail: beatlick@bellsouth.net. Website: www.geocities.com/beatlick/beatlick.html (includes mission statement, poetry, pictures, calendar, and Beatlick products). **Editor:** Joe Speer. Established in 1988 to "promote literature and create a place where writers can share their work." International organization open to "anyone interested in literature." Currently has 200 members. "There is no official distinction between members, but there is a core group that does the work, writes reviews, organizes readings, etc." Offerings include publication of work (they have published poets from Australia, Egypt, India, and Holland), reviews of books and venues, readings for local and touring poets, and a poetry hotline. "We have also hosted an open mic reading in Nashville since 1988. We have read in bars, bookstores, churches, libraries, festivals, TV, and radio. We produce an hour show every Friday, Saturday, and Sunday on CATV, Channel 19. Poets submit audio and video tapes from all over. We interview poets about their work and where they are from." Publishes *Beatlick News*, a bimonthly networking tool designed to inform poets of local events and to bring awareness of the national scene. "We include poems, short fiction, art, photos, and articles about poets and venues." Submit short pieces, no vulgar language. "We try to elevate the creative spirit. We publish new voices plus well-established talents." Subscription: $12/year. Additional information available for SASE and by fax and e-mail. "We promote all the arts."

BURNABY WRITERS' SOCIETY, 6584 Deer Lake Ave., Burnaby, British Columbia V5G 3T7 Canada. E-mail: lonewolf@portal.ca. Website: www.bws.bc.ca (includes contest details, markets, resources). **Contact:** Eileen Kernaghan. Established 1967. Corresponding membership in the society, including a newsletter subscription, is open to anyone, anywhere. Currently has 150 total members. Yearly dues: $30 regular, $20 students/seniors. Sample newsletter in return for SASE with Canadian stamp. Holds monthly meetings at The Burnaby Arts Centre (located at 6450 Deer Lake Ave.), with a business meeting at 7:30 followed by a writing workshop or speaker. Members of the society stage regular public readings of their own work. Sponsors open mic readings for the public. Sponsors a poetry contest open to British Columbia residents. Competition receives about 200-400 entries/year. Past contest winners include Mildred Tremblay, Frank McCormack, and Kate Braid. Additional information available on website.

THE WITTER BYNNER FOUNDATION FOR POETRY, INC., P.O. Box 10169, Santa Fe NM 87504. (505)988-3251. Fax: (505)986-8222. E-mail: bynnerfoundation@aol.com. Website: www.bynnerfo undation.org (includes information concerning the foundation's history, mission statement, grant programs, and application process). **Executive Director:** Steven Schwartz. Awards grants, ranging from $1,000 to $15,000, exclusively to nonprofit organizations for the support of poetry-related projects in the area of: 1) support of individual poets through existing nonprofit institutions; 2) developing the poetry audience; 3) poetry translation and the process of poetry translation; and 4) uses of poetry. "May consider the support of other creative and innovative projects in poetry." Letters of intent accepted annually from August 1 through December 1; requests for application forms should be submitted to Steven Schwartz, executive director. Applications, if approved, must be returned to the Foundation postmarked by February 1. Additional information available by fax and e-mail.

THE CANADA COUNCIL FOR THE ARTS; GOVERNOR GENERAL'S LITERARY AWARDS, P.O. Box 1047, 350 Albert St., Ottawa, Ontario K1P 5V8 Canada. (613)566-4414, ext. 5576. Fax: (613)566-4410. E-mail: joanne.larocque-poirier@canadacouncil.ca. Website: www.canadacouncil.ca (includes information sheet and application forms, as well as downloadable historical listings of award nominees and winners). Established by Parliament in 1957, the Canada Council for the Arts "provides a wide range of grants and services to professional Canadian artists and art organizations in dance, media arts, music, theater, writing, publishing, and the visual arts." The Governor General's Literary Awards, valued at $15,000 (Canadian) each, are given annually for the best English-language and best French-language work in each of seven categories, including poetry. Books must be first-edition trade books written, translated, or illustrated by Canadian citizens or permanent residents of Canada and published in Canada or abroad during the previous year (September 1 through the following September 30). Collections of poetry must be at least 48 pages long and at least half the book must contain work not published previously in book form. In the case of translation, the original work must also be a Canadian-authored title. Books must be submitted by publishers with a Publisher's Submission Form, which is available from the Writing and Publishing Section. Guidelines and current deadlines available for SASE or by fax or e-mail.

CANADIAN CONFERENCE OF THE ARTS (CCA); BLIZZART, 130 Albert St., Suite 804, Ottawa, Ontario K1P 5G4 Canada. (613)238-3561. Fax: (613)238-4849. E-mail: info@ccarts.ca. Website: www.ccarts.ca (includes CCA activities and information). National, nongovernmental, not-for-profit arts service organization dedicated to the growth and vitality of the arts and cultural industries in Canada. The CCA represents all Canadian artists, cultural workers, and arts supporters. Works with all levels of government, the corporate sector, and voluntary organizations to enhance appreciation for the role of culture in Canadian life. Each year, the CCA presents awards for contribution to the arts. Regular meetings held across the country ensure members' views on urgent and ongoing issues are heard and considered in organizing advocacy efforts and forming Board policies. Members stay informed and up-to-date through *Blizzart*, a newsletter published 4 times/year, and receive discounts on conference fees and on all other publications. Membership dues: $35 (plus GST) for Canadian individual members, $40 for US members, and $45 for international members.

CANADIAN POETRY ASSOCIATION; POEMATA; THE SHAUNT BASMAJIAN CHAP-BOOK AWARD; CPA ANNUAL POETRY CONTEST, P.O. Box 22571, St. George PO, Toronto, Ontario M5S 1V8 Canada. (905)312-1779. Fax: (905)312-8285. E-mail: writers@sympatico.ca. Website: www.mirror.org/cpa. **National Coordinator:** Wayne Ray. Established 1985 "to promote all aspects of the reading, writing, publishing, purchasing, and preservation of poetry in Canada. The CPA promotes the creation of local chapters to organize readings, workshops, publishing projects, and other poetry-related events in their area." Membership is open to anyone with an interest in poetry, including publishers, schools, libraries, booksellers, and other literary organizations. Publishes a bimonthly magazine, *Poemata*, featuring news articles, chapter reports, poetry by new members, book reviews, markets information, announcements, and more. Sample: $3. Membership dues: $30/year; seniors and students: $20. Membership form available for SASE and on website. Also sponsors the following contests: The Shaunt Basmajian Chapbook Award offers $100 (Canadian) and publication, plus 50 copies. Guidelines available for SASE and on website. **Annual deadline:** April 30. The CPA Annual Poetry Contest offers prizes of $50, $40, $30, $20, $10, and $5, with up to 10 Honorable Mentions. Winning poems published in *Poemata* and on CPA website. **Postmark deadline:** June 30 annually. Guidelines available for SASE and on website.

COLUMBINE STATE POETRY SOCIETY OF COLORADO, P.O. Box 6245, Denver CO 80021. (303)431-6774. E-mail: anitajg5@aol.com. Website: http://members.aol.com/copoets. **Secretary/Treasurer:** Anita Jepson-Gilbert. Established in 1978 to promote the writing and appreciation of poetry throughout Colorado. State-wide organization open to anyone interested in poetry. Currently has 105 total members. Levels of membership: Members at Large, who do not participate in the local chapters but who belong to the National Federation of State Poetry Societies and at the state level; and Members, who belong to the national, state, and local chapter in Denver, Colorado. Offerings for the Denver Chapter include weekly workshops and monthly critiques. Sponsors contests, awards for students and adults. Sponsors the Annual Poets Fest where members and nationally known writers give readings and workshops that are open to the public. Also sponsors a chapbook contest in alternate years under Riverstone Press. Membership dues: $12 state and national; $25 local, state, and national. Members meet weekly. Additional information available for SASE, by e-mail, or on website.

COUNCIL OF LITERARY MAGAZINES AND PRESSES; DIRECTORY OF LITERARY MAGAZINES, 154 Christopher St., Suite 3C, New York NY 10014-2839. (212)741-9110. E-mail: info@clmp.org. Website: www.clmp.org (includes member directory, publishing resources, discussion boards, The Literary Landscape). **Contact:** Aimee Kelley, office manager. Currently has 350 total members. Compiles an annual directory useful to writers: the *Directory of Literary Magazines*, which has detailed descriptions of over 600 literary magazines, including type of work published, payment to contributors, and submission requirements. May be ordered by sending $17 to CLMP. Additional information available by e-mail or on website.

DALLAS POETS COMMUNITY, P.O. Box 225435, Dallas TX 75222-5435. Website: www.dallaspoets.org (includes history, mission statement, goals, guidelines for joining, and contests). **Director:** Christopher Soden. Established 1990 to provide a "safe" workshop environment for the nurturing and refining of talent, facilitate recognition for talented poets, and organize readings and events. Regional (Dallas-Ft. Worth metroplex). Organization open to poets writing at the appropriate level. Currently has 10-15 total members. "There is a 'probationary' period before a poet is allowed to join as a permanent member." Member benefits include workshops twice a month, readings throughout the year, opportunities to teach poetry in the schools and assist with the publication of *Illya's Honey*, a poetry/short fiction magazine published 4 times/year. (See separate listing for *Illya's Honey* in the Publishers of Poetry section). Sponsors conferences/workshops and contests/awards. "We have poetry workshops twice a month and an annual poetry contest to raise money for our organization." Members and nationally known writers give readings that are open to the public. Membership dues: $50/year. Members meet every two weeks (every first and third Sunday afternoon).

GEORGIA POETRY SOCIETY; BYRON HERBERT REECE CONTEST; EDWARD DAVIN VICKERS CONTEST; CHARLES B. DICKSON CHAPBOOK CONTEST; MARGERY CARLSON YOUTH AWARDS; GEORGIA POETRY SOCIETY NEWSLETTER, P.O. Box 30326, Atlanta GA 30325-0236. (404)350-0714. Website: http://pages.prodigy.net/elcampbell (includes history of GPS, membership, contests, events, publications, resources and links, outreach programs, members' news, featured poet, and acknowledgements). **President:** John K. Ottley, Jr. Established 1979 to further the purposes of the National Federation of State Poetry Societies, Inc. (NFSPS) in securing fuller public recognition of the art of poetry; to stimulate a finer and more intelligent appreciation of poetry; and to provide opportunity for study of and incentive for practice in the writing and reading of poetry. State-wide organization open to any person who is in accord with the objectives listed above. No restrictions as to age, race, religion, color, national origin, or physical or mental abilities. Currently has 251 total members. Levels of membership: Active, $20 ($35 family), fully eligible for all aspects of membership; Student, $10, does not vote or hold office, and must be full-time enrolled student through college level; Lifetime, same as Active but pays a one-time membership fee of $300, receives free anthologies each year, and pays no contest entry fees. Offerings include affiliation with NFSPS. At least one workshop is held annually, contests are throughout the year, some for members only and some for general submissions. Workshops deal with specific areas of poetry writing, publishing, etc. Contests include the Byron Herbert Reece Contest, Edward Davin Vickers Contest, Charles B. Dickson Chapbook Contest (members only), and many ongoing or one-time contests, with awards ranging from $250 downwards. Entry fees and deadlines vary. Does not accept entry fees in foreign currencies. Send US dollars or money orders. Guidelines available for SASE. Publishes *Georgia Poetry Society Newsletter*, a quarterly. Also available to nonmembers on request or on website. Readings held annually to celebrate National Poetry Day (October) and National Poetry Month (April) in public forums such as libraries; some with specified poets reading their own poetry or works of famous poets, and some open mic readings. At each quarterly meeting (open to the public) members have an opportunity to read their own poems. Members meet quarterly. "Our bylaws require rotation in office. We sponsor an active and popular Poetry in the Schools project, conducting workshops or readings in schools throughout the state by invitation. We also sponsor the annual Margery Carlson Youth Awards contest in all Georgia schools."

GREATER CINCINNATI WRITERS' LEAGUE, 2735 Rosina Ave., Covington KY 41015. (859)491-2130. E-mail: karenlgeo@aol.com. **Contact:** Karen George. Established in 1930s "to promote and support poetry and those who write poetry in the Cincinnati area and the attainment of excellence in poetry as an art and a craft. We believe in education and discipline, as well as creative freedom, as important components in the development of our own poetry and open, constructive critique as a learning tool." Regional organization open to anyone interested in and actively writing. Currently has 35 total members. Offerings include a monthly meeting/workshop or critique. Critics are published poets, usually faculty members from local universities, who critique poems submitted by members. The group also joins in the critique. Sponsors workshops, contests (none planned for 2002-2003), awards with monetary prizes, and an anthology published every few years. Members give readings that are open to the public or sponsor open mic readings at bookstores and other locations. Membership dues: $25. Members meet monthly. Additional information available for SASE.

N GUILD COMPLEX, 1212 N. Ashland, #211, Chicago IL 60622. (773)227-6117. Fax: (773)227-6159. E-mail: guildcomplex@earthlink.net. Website: www.guildcomplex.com (includes event listings, contact info, and Tia Chucha Press info). **Executive Director:** Julie Parson-Nesbitt. Established in 1989 to "serve as a forum for literary cross-cultural expression, discussion, and education, in combination with other arts. We believe that the arts are instrumental in defining and exploring human experience, while encouraging participation by artists and audience alike in changing the conditions of our society. Through its culturally inclusive, primarily literary programming, the Guild Complex provides the vital link that connects communities, artists, and ideas. Over 10,000 people attend at least one of our events each year." Offerings include "over 140 literary events each year—workshops, featured readings, open mics, youth focused events, contests, multimedia literary festivals, and a yearly writers conference. Our twice-weekly featured readings range from the solo voice to book release parties to festivals combining poetry with video or music." Events are held at The Chopin Theater in Chicago. Sponsors "a women writers conference (also open to men) each fall, and offers writing workshops with locally and nationally known writers throughout the year. We also sponsor Tia Chucha Press, the publishing wing of Guild Complex, which publishes four full-length manuscripts of poetry per year." (See separate listing in Publishers of Poetry section.) Also publishes semi-monthly calendar of events sent "to everyone on a mailing list, not just members." Locally or nationally known writers give readings that are open to the public. Sponsors open mic readings. "We present biweekly events featuring poets, writers, performance poets, and storytellers. Our Tuesday night events are youth-focused, and our Wednesday night events are for general audiences. Open mics precede most of these events." Basic membership: $20 (working artists, students, seniors), $50 (basic), $100 (patron). Additional information available for SASE, by fax, e-mail, or on website. Accepts inquiries by fax and e-mail.

THE HUDSON VALLEY WRITERS' CENTER, 300 Riverside Dr., Sleepy Hollow NY 10591-1414. (914)332-5953. Fax: (914)332-4825. E-mail: info@writerscenter.org. Website: www.writerscenter.org (includes events calendar, class schedule, publications, chapbook competition guidelines). **Executive Director:** Dare Thompson. Established 1988. "The Hudson Valley Writers' Center is a nonprofit organization devoted to furthering the literary arts in our region. Its mission is to promote the appreciation of literary excellence, to stimulate and nurture the creation of literary works in all sectors of the population, and to bring the diverse works of gifted poets and prose artists to the attention of the public." National organization open to all. Currently has 350 total members. Levels of membership: individual, family, senior, student, and donor. Offerings include public readings by established and emerging poets/writers, workshops and classes, monthly open mic nights, paid and volunteer outreach opportunities, and an annual chapbook competition. "We are housed in the former Philipse Manor Railroad Station in Sleepy Hollow, NY. The main room of the station serves as our class and performance space, with a maximum occupancy of 81 people. Our building overlooks the Hudson River. Our small press imprint, Slapering Hol Press, holds an annual chapbook competition for emerging poets who have not yet published a book or chapbook. The winner receives a cash award, publication, and a reading at the Writers' Center." (See separate listing for Slapering Hol Press in Publishers of Poetry section; see separate listing for Slapering Hol Press Chapbook Competition in the Contests & Awards section.) "We also send class and event flyers and brochures on a regular basis, averaging one per month." Available to nonmembers. Members and nationally known writers give readings that are open to the public. Sponsors open mic readings for members and the public. "Open mics are held on the third Friday of each month and are open to all writers, with a five minute limit for each reader." Membership dues: $35 individual, $45 family, and $15 senior/student. Additional information available for SASE, by fax, e-mail, or on website.

ILLINOIS STATE POETRY SOCIETY; ISPS NEWS, 1096 Onwentsia Court, Naperville IL 60563. (630)892-4862. E-mail: alharris@alharris.com. Website: www.illinoispoets.org (includes club information and member poetry). **President:** Alan Harris. Established in 1991 "to promote and enhance poetry." Statewide, affiliated with the National Federation of State Poetry Societies (NFSPS). Organization open to adult and college student members. Currently has 67 total members. Offerings include local newsletter, NFSPS newsletter (*Strophes*), meetings and workshops, annual poetry contest, and club website. Publishes *ISPS News*, a bimonthly newsletter which contains messages and news of interest to members, contest news, member poetry, and biographies of members. Not available to nonmembers. Membership dues: $15/year. Members meet bimonthly "at various libraries and other community facilities." Additional information available for SASE, by e-mail, or on website.

N INDIANA STATE FEDERATION OF POETRY CLUBS; THE POETS RENDEZVOUS CONTEST; THE POETS SUMMER STANZAS CONTEST; THE POETS WINTERS FORUM CONTEST; INDIANA POET, 808 E. 32nd St., Anderson IN 46016. (765)642-3611. E-mail: poetgglee @aol.com. **Contact:** Eleanor Cranmer, president. Established in 1941 to unite poetry clubs in the state; to educate the public concerning poetry; and to encourage poet members. State-wide organization open to anyone interested in poetry. Currently has over 150 total members. Offerings include 2 conventions each year, and membership in NFSPS. Sponsors conferences, workshops. Sponsors The Poets Rendezvous Contest. Offers more than $1,200 in prizes for poems in more than 25 categories. **Entry fee:** $5. **Deadline:** August 15. Sponsors the Poets Winters Forum and The Poets Summer Stanzas contests, with prizes of $25, $15, and $10, plus 3 honorable mentions. **Entry fee:** $1/poem. Does not accept entry fees in foreign currencies. **Deadlines:** January 15 and June 15 (respectively). Send SASE for details. Competitions receive 150-200 entries. Publishes *Indiana Poet*, a bimonthly newsletter. Members or nationally known writers give readings that are open to the public. Membership dues: $15/year (includes national membership). Members meet monthly in various local clubs. Additional information available for SASE or by e-mail.

INTERNATIONAL WOMEN'S WRITING GUILD; NETWORK, P.O. Box 810, Gracie Station, New York NY 10028. (212)737-7536. Fax: (212)737-9469. E-mail: dirhahn@aol.com. Website: www.iwwg .com (includes membership services, calendar of events, profiles of members, etc.). **Contact:** Hannelore Hahn. Established 1976 as "a network for the personal and professional empowerment of women through writing." The Guild publishes a bimonthly 32-page journal, *Network*, which includes members' needs, achievements, contests, and publishing information. A ms referral service introduces members to literary agents. Other activities and benefits are annual national and regional events, including a summer conference (see separate listing for The IWWG Summer Conference in the Conferences & Workshops section); "regional clusters" (independent regional groups); round robin ms exchanges; and group health insurance. Membership dues: $45/year (domestic and overseas). Additional information available by fax and e-mail.

N IOWA POETRY ASSOCIATION (Specialized: regional/Iowa residents), 2325 61st St., Des Moines IA 50322. (515)279-1106. **Editor:** Lucille Morgan Wilson. Established 1945 "to encourage and improve the quality of poetry written by Iowans of all ages." Statewide organization open to "anyone interested in poetry, with a residence or valid address in the state of Iowa." Currently has over 400 total members. Levels of membership: Regular and Patron ("same services, but patron members contribute to cost of running the association"). Offerings include "semiannual workshops to which a poem may be sent in advance for critique; annual contest—also open to nonmembers—with no entry fee; *IPA Newsletter*, published 5 or 6 times/year, including a quarterly national publication listing of contest opportunities; and an annual poetry anthology, *Lyrical Iowa*, containing prize-winning and high-ranking poems from contest entries, available for purchase at production cost plus postage. No requirement for purchase to ensure publication." Membership dues: $8/year (Regular); $15 or more/year (Patron). "Semiannual workshops are the only 'meetings' of the Association." Additional information (Iowa residents only) available for SASE.

N THE KENTUCKY STATE POETRY SOCIETY; PEGASUS; KSPS NEWSLETTER, 2315 S. Wilson Rd., Radcliff KY 40160. Website: http://windpub.org/ksps/index.htm (includes newsletter, contacts and membership info, contest guidelines). **Contact:** Jo Emary, president/newsletter editor. Established in 1966 to promote interest in writing poetry, improve skills in writing poetry, present poetry readings and poetry workshops, and publish poetry. Regional organization open to all. Currently has about 250 total members. Affiliated with The National Federation of State Poetry Societies. Offerings include association with other poets, information on contests and poetry happenings across the state and nation; annual state and national contests; national and state annual conventions with workshops, selected speakers and open poetry readings. Sponsors workshops, contests, awards. Membership includes the bimonthly *KSPS Newsletter*. Also includes a quarterly newsletter, *Strophes*, of the NFSPS; and the KSPS journal, *Pegasus*, published 3 times yearly: a spring/summer and fall/winter issue which solicits good poetry for publication (need not be a member to submit), and a Prize Poems issue of 1st Place contest winners in over 40 categories. Members or nationally known writers give readings that are open to the public. Membership dues: students $5; adults $20; senior adults $15. Other categories: Life; Patron; Benefactor. The 2002 Annual Awards/ Workshop is planned for October at Rough River Dam State Resort Park in Western Kentucky. Additional information available for SASE or on website.

LIVING SKIES FESTIVAL OF WORDS; THE WORD, 250 Thatcher Dr. E., Moose Jaw, Saskatchewan 56J 1L7 Canada. (306)691-0557. Fax: (306)693-2994. E-mail: word.festival@sk.sympatico.ca.

MARKETS LISTED in the 2002 edition of *Poet's Market* that do not appear this year are identified in the General Index with a code explaining their absence from the listings.

Website: www3.sk.sympatico.ca/praifes (includes excerpts from the newsletter, past presenters featured, news of upcoming events, and news of Festival). **Operations Manager:** Lori Dean. "Established in 1996, the purpose/philosophy of the organization is to celebrate the imaginative uses of languages. The Festival of Words is a registered nonprofit group of over 150 volunteers who present an enjoyable and stimulating celebration of the imaginative ways we use language. We operate year round bringing special events to Saskatchewan, holding open microphone coffeehouses for youth, and culminating in an annual summer festival in July which features activities centered around creative uses of language." National organization open to writers and readers. Currently has 285 total members. Offerings include "The Festival of Words programs with readings by poets, panel discussions, and workshops. In addition, poets attending get to share ideas, get acquainted, and conduct impromptu readings. The activities sponsored are held in the Moose Jaw Library/Art Museum complex, as well as in various venues around the city." Sponsors workshops as part of the Festival of Words. "We are also associated with *FreeLance* magazine, a publication of the Saskatchewan Writers' Guild. This publication features many useful articles dealing with poetry writing and writing in general." Also publishes *The Word*, a newsletter appearing approximately 6-7 times/year containing news of Festival events, fund-raising activities, profiles of members, reports from members. Also available to nonmembers. First issue is free. Members and nationally known writers give readings that are open to the public. Sponsors open mic readings for members and for the public. Membership dues: $5, $15/3 years. Additional information available for SASE, by fax, e-mail, or on website.

THE LOFT LITERARY CENTER (Specialized: Regional/Minnesota); A VIEW FROM THE LOFT, Suite 200, Open Book, 1011 Washington Ave. S, Minneapolis MN 55414. (612)215-2575. Fax: (612)215-2576. E-mail: loft@loft.org. Website: www.loft.org. Established 1974. "The Loft was started by a group of poets looking for a place to give readings and conduct workshops and has evolved into the most comprehensive literary center in the country, offering opportunities for Minnesota writers in all genres and at all levels of development." Managed by a 35-member board of directors and staff of 15. Currently has over 2,200 total members. In addition to membership dues, financial support comes from tuition for creative writing classes, fees from benefit performances, and contributions from individuals, corporations, and foundations. The Loft offers over 150 courses each year in addition to 80 workshops and panels. Its reading series presents established and emerging writers throughout Minnesota. Programs also bring in visiting writers from around the country to serve as mentors. The Loft publishes *A View from the Loft*, a monthly magazine on craft. Grants and fellowships are awarded only to writers who are residents of Minnesota.

MASSACHUSETTS STATE POETRY SOCIETY, INC.; BAY STATE ECHO; THE NATIONAL POETRY DAY CONTEST; THE GERTRUDE DOLE MEMORIAL CONTEST; POET'S CHOICE CONTEST; THE NAOMI CHERKOFSKY MEMORIAL CONTEST; OF THEE I SING! CONTEST; ARTHUR (SKIP) POTTER MEMORIAL CONTEST, 64 Harrison Ave., Lynn MA 01905. **President:** Jeanette C. Maes. Established 1959, dedicated to the writing and appreciation of poetry and promoting the art form. State-wide organization open to anyone with an interest in poetry. Currently has 200 total members. Offerings include critique groups. Sponsors workshops, contests including The National Poetry Day Contest, with prizes of $25, $15, and $10 (or higher) for each of 30 categories. Pays winners from other countries in US currency. **Entry fee:** $5. **Deadline:** August 1. Competition receives about 2,000 entries/year. Also sponsors these contests: The Gertrude Dole Memorial Contest, with prizes of $25, $15, and $10. **Entry fee:** $3. **Deadline:** March 1. The Poet's Choice Contest, with prizes of $50, $25, and $15. **Entry fee:** $3/poem. **Deadline:** November 1. The Naomi Cherkofsky Memorial Contest, with prizes of $50, $30, and $20. **Entry fee:** $3/poem. **Deadline:** June 30. The "Of Thee I Sing!" Contest, with prizes of $50, $25, and $15. **Deadline:** January 15. Arthur (Skip) Potter Memorial Contest with prizes of $50, $30, and $20. **Entry fee:** $3. **Deadline:** December 15 annually. Does not accept entry fees in foreign currencies. Guidelines available for SASE. Publishes a yearly anthology of poetry and a yearly publication of student poetry contest winners. Also publishes *Bay State Echo*, a newsletter, 5 times/year. Members or nationally known writers give readings that are open to the public. Sponsors open mic readings for members and the public for National Poetry Day. Membership dues: $12/year. Members meet 5 times/year. Additional information available for SASE.

MOUNTAIN WRITERS SERIES; MOUNTAIN WRITERS CENTER NEWSLETTER, Mountain Writers Center, 3624 SE Milwaukee Ave., Portland OR 97202. (503)236-4854. Fax: (503)731-9735. E-mail: pdxmws@aracnet.com. Website: www.aracnet.com/~pdxmws (includes upcoming programs, workshop registrations, and information about the MWS community). **Associate Director:** Michael Bohrer-

Clancy. Established 1973, "Mountain Writers Series is an independent nonprofit organization dedicated to supporting writers, audiences, and other sponsors by promoting literature and literacy through artistic and educational literary arts events in the Pacific Northwest." The Center is open to both members and nonmembers. Currently has about 150 total members. Levels of membership: Contributing ($100), Supporting ($500), Patron ($1,000), Basic ($50), Student/Retired ($25), and Family ($75). "Poets have access to our extensive poetry library, resource center, and space as well as discounts to most events. Members receive a seasonal newsletter as well, plus a free Lanaan video with over 60 titles to choose from. Poets may attend 1-day workshops, weekend master classes, 5-week and 10-week courses about writing." Authors who participated recently include Tony Hoagland, Robert Wrigley, Bruce Smith, Maggie Anderson, Marvin Bell, Peter Coyote, Li-Young Lee, Patricia Goedicke, Yusef Komunyakaa, and Michael Collier. "The Mountain Writers Center is a 100-year-old Victorian house with plenty of comfortable gathering space, a reading room, visiting writers room, library, resource center, garden, and Mountain Writers Series offices." Sponsors conferences/workshops. Publishes the *Mountain Writers Center Newsletter*. Also available to nonmembers for $12/year. Sponsors readings that are open to the public. Nationally and internationally known writers are sponsored by the Mountain Writers Series Northwest Regional Residencies Program (reading tours) and the campus readings program (Pulitzer Prize winners, Nobel Prize winners, MacArthur Fellows, etc.). Additional information available for SASE, by fax, e-mail, or on website.

NATIONAL FEDERATION OF STATE POETRY SOCIETIES, INC.; STEVENS MANU-SCRIPT COMPETITION; ENCORE; STROPHES; NFSPS COLLEGE/UNIVERSITY-LEVEL POETRY COMPETITION. **Publicity Chair:** Sybella Beyer-Snyder, 3444 S. Dover Terrace, Inverness FL 34452-7116. (352)344-3456. E-mail: sybella@digitalusa.net. **Membership Chairperson:** Sy Swann. 2736 Creekwood Lane, Ft. Worth TX 76123-1105. (817)292-8598 or (605)768-2127 (June and July). Fax: (817)531-6593. E-mail: JFS@flash.net. Website: www.nfsps.com (includes history, contact info, contests, publications). **Contest Chairs:** Irvin and Patricia Kimber, 1220 W. Koradine Dr., South Jordan UT 84095 (e-mail: irvkimber@lgcy.com). Established in 1959, "NFSPS is a nonprofit organization exclusively educational and literary. Its purpose is to recognize the importance of poetry with respect to national cultural heritage. It is dedicated solely to the furtherance of poetry on the national level and serves to unite poets in the bonds of fellowship and understanding." Currently has 6,000 total members. Any poetry group located in a state not already affiliated but interested in affiliating with NFSPS may contact the membership chairperson. "In a state where no valid group exists, help may also be obtained by individuals interested in organizing a poetry group for affiliation." Most reputable state poetry societies are members of the National Federation and advertise their various poetry contests through the quarterly bulletin, *Strophes*, available for SASE and $1, edited by Vera Bakker, 784 W. 1400 North, West Bountiful UT 84087 (e-mail: veraobakker@msn.com). **Beware of organizations calling themselves state poetry societies (however named) that are not members of NFSPS,** as such labels are sometimes used by vanity schemes trying to sound respectable. NFSPS holds an annual meeting in a different city each year with a large awards banquet, addressed by a renowned poet and writer. Sponsors 50 national contests in various categories each year, including the NFSPS Founders Award of $1,500 for 1st Prize; 2nd Prize: $500; 3rd Prize: $250. **Entry fees:** for members, $1/poem or $8 total for 8 or more categories, plus $5/poem for NFSPS Founders Award (limit 4 entries in this category alone); for nonmembers, $1/poem, plus $5/poem for NFSPS Founders Award (limit 4 entries in this category alone). All poems winning over $15 are published in the anthology, *ENCORE*. Rules for all contests are given in a brochure available from Vera Bakker at *Strophes* or Irvin and Patricia Kimber at the address above and on website; you can also write for the address of your state poetry society. Sponsors the annual Stevens Manuscript Competition with a 1st Prize of $1,000 and publication, 2nd Prize: $500; **deadline:** October 15. **Contact:** Doris Stengel, 1510 S. Seventh St., Brainerd MN 56401-4342 (e-mail: dpoet@brainerd.net). Information for the College/University-Level Poetry Competition available from Madelyn Eastlund, 310 S. Adams St., Beverly Hills FL 34465 (e-mail: verdure@digitalusa.net). Additional information available by fax or e-mail.

NATIONAL LEAGUE OF AMERICAN PEN WOMEN, INC.; THE PEN WOMAN, 1300 17th St. NW, Washington DC 20036-1973. Phone/fax: (978)443-2165. E-mail: nlapw1@juno.com. Website: http://members.aol.com/penwomen/pen.htm. **National Scholarship Chair:** Mary Jane Hillery (do not phone; send SASE for information). **Editor:** Anita Capps, *The Pen Woman*. Established 1897, national organization open to professional women in the creative arts. Currently has 4,000 total members. Levels of membership: "full members, those who provide proof of payment for creative work—writers, artists, composers; associate members, those in the creative arts who have not supplied proof of payment for sufficient works." Offerings include opportunities for publication and cash prizes in contests. "The National

Headquarters is in Northwest Washington DC within walking distance of the White House and many DC landmarks and memorials. It is a converted mansion in which Robert Todd Lincoln and his family lived for several months. We are near DuPont Circle with bookstores, computer center." Sponsors conferences/ workshops and contests/awards. "Anita Capps edits *The Pen Woman*, a quarterly magazine in which previously published poems are published for greater exposure." Members and nationally known writers give readings that are open to the public. Membership dues: $40 (new member); $30 (renewal). Additional information available for SASE or on website. Also sponsors a biennial $1,000 grant for which only nonmember women poets are qualified to enter; receives over 1,000 entries total. Flyer available for SASE.

NATIONAL WRITERS ASSOCIATION; AUTHORSHIP, 3140 S. Peoria, #295, Aurora CO 80014. (303)841-0246. Fax: (303)841-2607. Website: www.nationalwriters.com. **Executive Director:** Sandy Whelchel. Established 1937. National organization with regional affiliations open to writers. Currently has 3,000 total members. Levels of membership: Published Writers and Other Writers. Hosts an annual Summer Conference where workshops, panels, etc. are available to all attendees, including poets. Also offers a yearly poetry writing contest with cash awards of $100, $50, and $25. Pays winners from other countries by US check. **Entry fee:** $10/poem. Accepts entry fees in foreign currencies. **Deadline:** October 1. Send SASE for judging sheet copies. Publishes *Authorship*, an annual magazine. Sample copy available for $9×12 envelope with $1.21 postage. Also available to nonmembers for $18. Membership dues: Professional $85; others $65. Members meet monthly. Additional information available for SASE, by fax, or e-mail. Contest forms available on website.

NEVADA POETRY SOCIETY, P.O. Box 7014, Reno NV 89510. (775)322-3619. **President:** Thomas Delaplain. Established in 1976 to encourage the writing and critiquing of poetry. State-wide organization. Currently has 30 total members. Levels of membership: Active and Emeritus. Offerings include member-ship in the National Federation of State Poetry Societies (NFSPS), including their publication, *Strophes*; monthly challenges followed by critiquing of all new poems; lessons on types of poetry. Members of the society are occasionally called upon to read to organizations or in public meetings. Membership dues: $10 (this includes membership in NFSPS). Members meet monthly. Additional information available for SASE. "We advise poets to enter their poems in contests before thinking about publication."

Ⓝ THE NORTH CAROLINA POETRY SOCIETY; BROCKMAN/CAMPBELL BOOK AWARD CONTEST. (Officers change annually; please contact us through our website www.sleepycreek. net/poetry. Includes information/resources for poets; message board; poems; information on meetings, workshops, contests, etc.; poetry links). Established 1932 to "foster the writing of poetry; to bring together in meetings of mutual interest and fellowship the poets of North Carolina; to encourage the study, writing, and publication of poetry; and to develop a public taste for the reading and appreciation of poetry." State-wide and out-of-state organization open to "all interested persons." Levels of membership: Regular ($25/ year) and Student ($10/year). NCPS conducts 3 general meetings and numerous statewide workshops each year, sponsors annual poetry contests with categories for adults and students (open to anyone, with small fee for nonmembers; December/January deadline; cash prizes), publishes the contest-winning poems in the annual book *Award Winning Poems*; publishes a newsletter and supports other poetry activities. Also sponsors the annual Brockman/Campbell Book Award Contest for a book of poetry (over 20 pages) by a North Carolina poet (native-born or current resident for 3 years). Prize: $150 and a Revere-style bowl. Entry fee: $10 for nonmembers. Deadline: May 1. Competitions receive 300 entries/year. Most recent contest winners include Robert Morgan, Kathryn Byer, Mary Kratt. Additional information available on website.

OHIO POETRY ASSOCIATION; OHIO POETRY ASSOCIATION NEWSLETTER, 648 E. High St., Apt. 6, Springfield OH 45505. (937)324-3816. **President:** Renée Young. Established in 1929 as Verse Writers' Guild of Ohio to promote the art of poetry and further the support of poets and others who support poetry. "We sponsor contests, seminars, readings, and publishing opportunities for poets of all ages and abilities throughout and beyond Ohio." Statewide membership with additional members in several other states, Japan and England. Affiliated with the National Federation of State Poetry Societies (NFSPS). Organization open to "poets and writers of all ages and ability, as well as to nonwriting lovers of poetry in all its forms." Currently has over 220 total members. Levels of membership: Regular, Student, Associate, Honorary Life, Paid Life, and Honorary. Member benefits include regular contests, meeting/workshop participation, assistance with writing projects, networking; twice-yearly magazine, *Common Threads*, 4 state newsletters, 4 NFSPS newsletters, membership in NFSPS and lower entry fee for their contests.

Members are automatically on the mailing list for Ohio Poetry Day contest guidelines. "We are cosponsors of Ohio Poetry Day. Individual chapters regularly host workshops and seminars. We publish *Common Threads*, a semiannual, saddle-bound anthology of poetry (open to submission from members only)." (See separate listing for *Common Threads* in the Publishers of Poetry section; for Ohio Poetry Day in the Contests & Awards section.) Publishes the *Ohio Poetry Association Newsletter*, a quarterly which includes general news, member accomplishments, publishing opportunities, contests, editorials, items of interest to poets and writers. First issue is complementary to nonmembers. Members and nationally known writers give readings that are open to the public (at monthly meetings; public is invited). Sponsors open mic readings for members and the public. Past readers include Lisa Martinovic, David Shevin, Michael Bugeja, David Citino, and Danika Dinsmore. Membership dues: $12 senior; $15 regular; $5 associate and student. Members meet quarterly at the state level. Additional information available for SASE. "All poets need an organization to share info, critique, publish, sponsor contests, and just socialize. We do all that."

THE OREGON STATE POETRY ASSOCIATION; VERSEWEAVERS, P.O. Box 602, West Linn OR 97068. (503)655-1274. E-mail: OSPA@teleport.com. Website: www.oregonpoets.org (includes contest and organization information). **President:** David Hedges. Established 1936 for "the promotion and creation of poetry." Member of the National Federation of State Poetry Societies, Inc. (NFSPS), sponsors workshops, readings, and seminars around the state and an annual contest for students (K-12). Currently has over 400 total members. Membership dues: $18, $12 (65 and older), $5 (18 and under). Publishes a quarterly *OSPA Newsletter*, annual *Verseweavers* book, and annual *Cascadia* book of Oregon student poetry. Sponsors contests twice yearly, awards prizes in October during Fall Poetry Conference and in April during Spring Poetry Festival, with total cash prizes of $1,000 each (no entry fee to members, $3/poem for nonmembers; out-of-state entries welcome). Pays winners from other countries by International Money Order. Does not accept entry fees in foreign currencies. Send International Money Order. Themes and categories vary; special category for New Poets. Competition receives 1,400 entries/year. Most recent contest winners include Josephine Bridges, James Dott, David Lloyd, Florence Sage, Sharon Heffernan, and Marjorie Wolfson. For details send SASE to OSPA, after June 1 and December 1 each year, or check website. Members and nationally known writers give readings that are open to the public. Sponsors open mic readings for members and the public during National Poetry Month (April).

PEN AMERICAN CENTER; PEN WRITERS FUND; PEN TRANSLATION PRIZE; GRANTS AND AWARDS, 568 Broadway, New York NY 10012. (212)334-1660. Website: www.pen.org. PEN American Center "is the largest of more than 100 centers which comprise International PEN, established in London in 1921 by John Galsworthy to foster understanding among men and women of letters in all countries. Members of PEN work for freedom of expression wherever it has been endangered, and International PEN is the only worldwide organization of writers and the chief voice of the literary community." Total membership on all continents is approximately 10,000. The 2,700 members of the American Center include poets, playwrights, essayists, editors, novelists (for the original letters in the acronym PEN), as well as translators and those editors and agents who have made a substantial contribution to the literary community. Membership in American PEN includes reciprocal privileges in foreign centers for those traveling abroad. Branch offices are located in Cambridge, Chicago, Portland/Seattle, New Orleans, and San Francisco. Among PEN's various activities are public events and symposia, literary awards, assistance to writers in prison and to American writers in need (grants and loans up to $1,000 from PEN Writers Fund). Medical insurance for writers is available to members. The quarterly *PEN News* is sent to all members. The PEN Translation Prize is sponsored by the Book-of-the-Month Club, 1 prize each year of $3,000 for works published in the current calendar year. Publishes *Grants and Awards* biennially, containing guidelines, deadlines, eligibility requirements, and other information about hundreds of grants, awards, and competitions for poets and other writers: $18. Send SASE for booklet describing activities and listing publications, some of them available free.

N PEN CENTER USA WEST; ELECTRIC PEN, 672 S. Lafayette Park Place #42, Los Angeles CA 90057. (213)365-8500. Fax: (213)365-9616. E-mail: pen@penusa.org. Website: www.penusa.org (includes description of all programs, staff list, Freedom to Write alerts, awards/contest information). **Contact:** Membership Coordinator. "Established 1943, PEN Center USA West strives to protect the rights of writers around the world, to stimulate interest in the written word, and to foster a vital literary community among the diverse writers living in the western U.S. The organization, therefore, has two distinct, yet complimentary aims: one fundamentally literary and the other having a freedom of expression mandate." Regional organization open to "poets, playwrights, essayists, novelists (for the original letters in the acronym,

'PEN'), as well as television and screen writers, critics, historians, editors, journalists, and translators." Current membership: 1,000. Levels of membership: Full ("open to published or produced writers who have demonstrated work of substantial literary value and who meet the membership criteria in one or more categories"), Associate ("open to writers whose body of work only partially fulfills a criteria for full membership and to professionals, such as publishers, booksellers, literary presenters, and creative writing teachers, whose work ultimately benefits and promotes literature and writers"), and Student ("any student enrolled in a recognized writing program"). Membership dues: $65 Full, $50 Associate, $25 Student. Additional information available for SASE, by fax, e-mail, or on website.

PITTSBURGH POETRY EXCHANGE, P.O. Box 4279, Pittsburgh PA 15203. (412)481-POEM. Website: http://trfn.clpgh.org/forpoems/ (includes description of organization, activities, list of upcoming events, listing of publications by members). **Contact:** Michael Wurster. Established in 1974 as a community-based organization for local poets, it functions as a service organization and information exchange, conducting ongoing workshops, readings, forums, and other special events. No dues or fees. "Any monetary contributions are voluntary, often from outside sources. We've managed not to let our reach exceed our grasp." Reading programs are primarily committed to local and area poets, with honorariums of $25-85. Sponsors a minimum of three major events each year in addition to a monthly workshop. Some of these have been reading programs in conjunction with community arts festivals, such as the October South Side Poetry Smorgasbord—a series of readings throughout the evening at different shops (galleries, bookstores). Poets from out of town may contact the Exchange for assistance in setting up readings at bookstores to help sell their books. Additional information available for SASE or on website.

THE POETRY LIBRARY, Royal Festival Hall, London SE1 8XX United Kingdom. Phone: (0207)921 0943/0664. Fax: (0207)921 0939. E-mail: poetrylibrary@rfh.org.uk. Website: www.poetrylibrary.org.uk (includes information about library's collections and services, interactive "Lost Quotations Noticeboard"). **Poetry Librarian:** Mary Enright. Established 1953 as a "free public library of modern poetry. It contains a comprehensive collection of all British poetry published since 1912 and an international collection of poetry from all over the world, either written in or translated into English. As the United Kingdom's national library for poetry, it offers loan and information service and large collections of poetry magazines, tapes, videos, records, poem posters, and cards; also press cuttings and photographs of poets." National center with "open access for all visitors. Those wishing to borrow books and other materials must be residents of U.K." Offerings include "library and information service; access to all recently published poetry and to full range of national magazines; only source of international poetry, including magazines; and information on all aspects of poetry." Offers browsing facilities and quieter area for study; listening facilities for poetry on tape, video record, and CD. Adjacent to "Voice Box" venue for literature readings. Nationally known writers give readings that are open to the public. "Separate administration for readings in 'The Voice Box'—a year-round program of readings, talks, and literature events for all writing. Contact the literature section, Royal Festival Hall." Additional information available on website. "Our focus is more on published poets than unpublished. No unpublished poems or manuscripts kept or accepted. Donations welcome but please write or call in advance." Opened 11-8 Tuesday-Sunday; closed to visitors on Mondays, buy may be telephoned.

POETRY SOCIETY OF AMERICA; POETRY SOCIETY OF AMERICA AWARDS; CROSSROADS: A JOURNAL OF THE POETRY SOCIETY OF AMERICA, 15 Gramercy Park, New York NY 10003. (212)254-9628. Fax: (212)673-2352. E-mail: brett@poetrysociety.org. Website: www.poetrysociety.org (includes information and calendar for contests, awards, and seminars; information on journal contest winners; postcards to send; discussion groups, etc.). **Executive Director:** Alice Quinn. **Contact:** Programs Associate. Established 1910, the society is a nonprofit cultural organization in support of poetry and poets, member and nonmember, young and established. Currently has about 3,000 members. Sponsors readings, lectures, and workshops both in New York City and around the country. Peer Group Workshop is open to all members and meets on a weekly basis. Publishes *Crossroads: A Journal of the Poetry Society of America*, approximately 40 pages, letter-sized. **Poetry Society of America does not publish poems in its journal or on website.** Contest guidelines available for SASE. The following are open to members

VISIT THE WRITER'S DIGEST WEBSITE at www.writersdigest.com for books, markets, newsletter sign-up, and a special poetry page.

only: Alice Fay Di Castagnola Award ($1,000); *Writer Magazine*/Emily Dickinson Award ($250); Cecil Hemley Memorial Award ($500); Lucille Medwick Memorial Award ($500); Lyric Poetry Award ($500). Nonmembers may enter as many of the following contests as they wish, no more than 1 entry for each, for a $15 fee: Louise Louis/Emily F. Bourne Student Poetry Award, $250 for students in grades 9-12; George Bogin Memorial Award, $500 for a selection of 4-5 poems which take a stand against oppression; Robert H. Winner Memorial Award, $2,500 for a poem written by a poet over 40, still unpublished or with one book (all have a deadline of December 22; awards are made at a ceremony and banquet in late spring). The Society also has 2 contests open to works submitted by publishers only, who must obtain an entry form. There is a $20 fee for each book entered. Book awards are: Norma Farber Award, $500 for a first book; William Carlos Williams Award, a purchase prize of $500-1,000 for a book of poetry by a permanent resident of the US published by a small, nonprofit, or university press—translations not eligible. The Shelley Memorial Award of $6,000-9,000 and The Frost Medal ($2,500) are by nomination only. For necessary rules and guidelines for various contests, send an 80¢ SASE between October 1 and December 21. Additional information available for SASE or on website. Rules and awards are subject to change. Membership: $40.

N: **POETRY SOCIETY OF NEW HAMPSHIRE; THE POET'S TOUCHSTONE**, 282 Meaderboro Rd., Farmington NH 03835. (603)332-0732. E-mail: frisella@worldpath.net. **Contact:** Patricia L. Frisella, treasurer. Established in 1964 as a statewide organization for anyone interested in poetry. Member of the National Federation of State Poetry Societies (NFSPS). Currently has 155 total members. Levels of membership: $10, Junior; $20, Regular; $100, "Angel." Offerings include annual subscription to quarterly magazine, *The Poet's Touchstone*, membership in NFSPS, critiques, contests and workshops, public readings, and quarterly meetings with featured poets. *The Poet's Touchstone* available to nonmembers for $3.50 (single issue), $14 (subscription); available to nonprofit organizations for $7/year. Members and nationally known writers give readings that are open to the public. Sponsors open mic readings for members and the public. "Once a year we have a members' open mic. This year we are working with three Borders bookstores to sponsor panels of featured readers followed by open mics for National Poetry Month." Additional information available for SASE or by e-mail. "We do sponsor a national contest four times a year with $100, $50, and $25 prizes paid out in each one. People from all over the country enter and win."

POETRY SOCIETY OF TENNESSEE; TENNESSEE VOICES, P.O. Box 241986, Memphis TN 38124. (901)726-4582. E-mail: gmoearth@aol.com. Website: www.grandmotherearth.com (includes Poetry Society of Tennessee information). **President:** Frances Cowden. Established in 1953 to "promote the creative poetry of its members, poetry in the community, improving poetry writing skills, and creative poetry among young people." Statewide "but we have some associate members out of state." Affiliated with the National Federation of State Poetry Societies (NFSPS). Organization open to anyone interested in poetry. Currently has 115 total members. "We have an adult membership and a student membership." Offerings include monthly speakers, contests, and poetry readings; an annual poetry festival; and two student poetry contests each year. Sponsors conferences/workshops. "We publish a yearly anthology of poems, *Tennessee Voices*, that has won in various festival, monthly, and special contests." Also publishes a newsletter called *Tennessee Voices* 4-6 times/year as needed; contains information on meetings and speakers, contests and winners, various activities, etc. Not available to nonmembers. "We have a bimonthly reading at Deliberate Literate bookstore in Memphis. Nonmembers are invited to participate also." Membership dues: $20/year for adults, $5 for students. Additional information available for SASE, by e-mail, or on website. "Our meetings are held at 2 p.m. on the first Saturday of the month from September through May at Clough Hall at the church across from the campus of Rhodes College in Memphis." Contest brochure available after June 1 for SASE or on website.

THE POETRY SOCIETY OF TEXAS; POETRY SOCIETY OF TEXAS BULLETIN; A BOOK OF THE YEAR, 235 Shady Hill Lane, Double Oak TX 75077-8270. (817)430-1182. E-mail: jpaulholcomb @prodigy.net. Website: www.cokepoet.net/PoetrySocietyofTexas/pstindex.htm (includes history, purpose, officers, current activities, contact information, Poetry in Schools, membership application). **President:** J. Paul Holcomb. Established 1921. "The purpose of the society shall be to secure fuller public recognition of the art of poetry, to encourage the writing of poetry by Texans, and to kindle a finer and more intelligent appreciation of poetry, especially the work of living poets who interpret the spirit and heritage of Texas." PST is a member of the National Federation of State Poetry Societies (NFSPS). Has 22 chapters in cities throughout the state. Offers " 'Active' membership to native Texans, Citizens of Texas, or former Citizens of Texas who were active members; 'Associate' membership to all who desire to affiliate." Currently has 400 total members. Levels of membership: Active Membership, Associate Membership, Sustaining Membership, Benefactors, Patrons of the Poets, and Student Membership. Offerings include annual contests with prizes in excess of $5,000 as well as monthly contests (general and humorous); eight monthly meetings; annual awards banquet; annual summer conference in a different location each year; round-robin critiquing opportunities sponsored at the state level; and Poetry in Schools with contests at state and local chapter levels. "Our monthly state meetings are held at the Preston Royal Branch of the Dallas Public Library. Our annual awards banquet is held at the Harvey Hotel in Dallas. Our summer conference is held at a site chosen by the hosting chapter. Chapters determine their meeting sites." Publishes *A Book of the Year* which presents annual and monthly award-winning poems, coming contest descriptions, minutes of meetings, by-laws of the society, history, and information. Also publishes the *Poetry Society of Texas Bulletin*, a monthly newsletter that features statewide news documenting contest winners, state meeting information, chapter and individual information, news from the National Federation of State Poetry Societies (NFSPS), and announcements of coming activities and offerings for poets. "*A Book of the Year* is available to nonmembers for $8." Members and nationally known writers give readings. "All of our meetings are open to the public." Membership dues: $25 for Active and Associates Memberships, $10 for students. Members meet monthly. Additional information available for SASE, by e-mail, or on website.

POETS & WRITERS, INC.; A DIRECTORY OF AMERICAN POETS AND FICTION WRIT-ERS, 72 Spring St., New York NY 10012. (212)226-3586. Website: www.pw.org. Poets & Writers, Inc., was established in 1970 to foster the development of poets and fiction writers and to promote communication through the literary community. A nonmember organization, it offers information, support, publications, and exposure to writers at all stages in their careers. Sponsors programs such as Writers Exchange (emerging poets and fiction writers are intriduced to literary communities outside their home states), Readings/Workshops, and publication in print and online of *A Directory of American Poets & Fiction Writers*. In addition, *Poets & Writers Online* offers topical information, the Speakeasy writers' message forum, and background on all P&W programs.

N POETS' AND WRITERS' LEAGUE OF GREATER CLEVELAND; OHIO WRITER; POETRY: MIRROR OF THE ARTS; WRITERS AND THEIR FRIENDS, P.O. Box 91801, Cleveland OH 44101. (216)421-0403. Fax: (216)791-1727. E-mail: PWLGC@msn.com. **Executive Director:** Darlene Montonaro. "Established in 1974 to foster a supportive community for poets and writers and to expand the audience for creative writing among the general public." Currently has 300 total members. In 2002, PWLGC opened a Literary Center, offering classes, meeting space, and a retreat center for writers. Conducts a monthly workshop where poets can bring their work for discussion. Publishes a monthly calendar of literary events in NE Ohio; a bimonthly magazine, *Ohio Writer*, which includes articles on the writing life, news, and markets; and two chapbooks/year featuring an anthology of work by area poets. "The PWLGC also sponsors a dramatic reading series, *Poetry: Mirror of the Arts*, which unites poetry and other art forms performed in cultural settings; and *Writers & Their Friends*, a literary showcase of new writing (all genres), performed dramatically by area actors, media personalities, and performance poets." Membership dues: $25/year, includes subscription to *Ohio Writer* Magazine and discounts on services and facilities at the new Literary Center. Additional information available for SASE or by fax or e-mail.

POETS HOUSE; DIRECTORY OF AMERICAN POETRY BOOKS; THE REED FOUNDA-TION LIBRARY; THE POETS HOUSE SHOWCASE; POETRY IN THE BRANCHES; NYC POETRY TEACHER OF THE YEAR, 72 Spring St., New York NY 10012. (212)431-7920. Fax: (212)431-8131. E-mail: info@poetshouse.org. Website: www.poetshouse.org (includes Poets House news, general information about programs, comprehensive calendar of events, Directory of American Poetry Books online). **Contact:** Betsy Fagin. Established 1985, Poets House is a 40,000-volume (noncirculating) poetry library of books, tapes, and literary journals, with reading and writing space available. Comfortably furnished literary center open to the public year-round. New expanded space provides conference room, exhibition space, and a Children's Poets House. Over 50 annual public events include 1) poetic programs of cross-cultural and interdisciplinary exchange, 2) readings in which distinguished poets discuss and share the work of other poets, 3) workshops and seminars on various topics led by visiting poets, 4) an annual $1,000 award for the designated NYC Poetry Teacher of the Year, and 5) the People's Poetry Gathering. In addition, Poets House continues its collaboration with public library systems, Poetry in The Branches, aimed at bringing poetry into NYC neighborhoods through collection building, public programs, seminars for librarians, and poetry workshops for young adults (information available upon request). Finally, in April Poets House hosts the Poets House Showcase, a comprehensive exhibit of the year's new poetry releases from commercial, university, and independent presses across the country. Related Showcase events include receptions, panel discussions, and seminars which are open to the public and of special interest to poets, publishers, booksellers, distributers, and reviewers. (**Note: Poets House is not a publisher.**) Following each Showcase, copies of new titles become part of the library collection and comprehensive listings for each of the books are added to the online version of the *Directory of American Poetry Books*, accessible on www.poetshouse.org. "Poets House depends, in part, on tax-deductible contributions of its nationwide members." Membership levels begin at $40/year, and along with other graduated benefits each new or renewing member receives free admission to all regularly scheduled programs. Additional information available by fax or e-mail.

POETS THEATRE, RR2, Box 155, Cohocton NY 14826. E-mail: bobrien4@juno.com. Website: http://poetstheater.tripod.com (includes information on upcoming readings, workshops, contests). **Contact:** Beatrice O'Brien. Established 1981, sponsors monthly poetry readings and performances with limited funding from Poets & Writers, Inc. and the Hornell Arts Council. For a mostly conservative, rural audience. A featured poet, followed by open reading. Meets usually on the second Thursday of each month at the Senior Citizens Center in Hornell, NY. Additional information available by e-mail or on website.

SCOTTISH POETRY LIBRARY; SCHOOL OF POETS; CRITICAL SERVICE; SCOTTISH POETRY INDEX, 5 Crichton's Close, Edinburgh EH8 8DT Scotland. Phone: (0131)557-2876. Fax: (0131)557-8393. E-mail: inquiries@spl.org.uk. Website: www.spl.org.uk (includes About the Library; members; catalogue; publications; outreach works; SPL projects; events and diary; links). **Director:** Robyn Marsack. **Librarian:** Iain Young. A reference information source and free lending library, also lends by post and has a travelling van service lending at schools, prisons, and community centres. The library has a web-based catalogue at www.slainte.org.uk allowing searches of all the library's resources, including books, magazines, and audio material, over 20,000 items of Scottish and international poetry. Need not be a member to borrow material; memberships available strictly to support the library's work. Levels of membership: £20 individual, £10 concessionary, £30 organizational. Benefits include biannual newsletter, annual report, new publications listing, and use of members' room at the library. The School of Poets is open to anyone; "at meetings members divide into small groups in which each participant reads a poem which is then analyzed and discussed." Meetings normally take place at 7:30 p.m. on the second Tuesday of each month at the library. Also offers a Critical Service in which groups of up to 6 poems, not exceeding 200 lines in all, are given critical comment by members of the School: £15 for each critique (with SAE). Publishes the *Scottish Poetry Index*, a multi-volume indexing series, photocopied, spiral-bound, that indexes poetry and poetry-related material in selected Scottish literary magazines from 1952 to present, and an audio CD of contemporary Scottish poems, *The Jewel Box* (January 2000). Members and nationally known writers give readings that are open to the public. Additional information available by e-mail or on website.

N: SMALL PRESS CENTER/THE CENTER FOR INDEPENDENT PUBLISHING, Society of Mechanics & Tradesmen, 20 W. 44th, New York NY 10036. (212)764-7021. Fax: (212)354-5365. E-mail: smallpress@aol.com. Website: www.smallpress.org (includes general information on the center and information on events). **Executive Director:** Karin Taylor. Established in 1984, "the Small Press Center is a nonprofit reference center devoted to publishing and membership organization of small press independent publishers, writers and independent press enthusiasts." National organization open to "any person, company or organization that supports the small press." Currently has 1,400 total members—400 Friends, 1,000 Publisher Members. Offerings include workshops, readings, publishing reference center, and "support of the organization." Offers "a place in which the public may examine and order the books of independent publishers, free from commercial pressures. The Center is open five days a week." Sponsors conferences/workshops and awards. Publishes a quarterly newsletter. Members give readings that are open to the public. Publisher Membership dues: $75. Writer Membership dues start at $50. Additional information available for SASE or by fax or e-mail.

N: SOUTH CAROLINA WRITERS WORKSHOP; THE QUILL, P.O. Box 7104, Columbia SC 29202. Website: www.4bnc.com/scww. Established 1990 "to offer writers a wide range of opportunities to improve their writing, network with others, and gain practical 'how to' information about getting published." Statewide organization open to all writers. Currently has 277 total members. Offerings include "chapter meetings where members give readings and receive critiques; *The Quill*, SCWW's bimonthly newsletter which features writing competitions and publishing opportunities; an annual conference with registration discount for members; two free seminars each year; and an annual anthology featuring members' work." Chapters meet in libraries, bookstores, and public buildings. Sponsors 3-day annual conference at Myrtle Beach and literary competitions in poetry, fiction, and nonfiction. Membership dues: $50/year Individual; $75/year Family. Chapters meet bimonthly or monthly.

SOUTH DAKOTA STATE POETRY SOCIETY; PASQUE PETALS, Box 398, Lennox SD 57039. (605)647-2447. **Membership Chair/Editor:** Verlyss V. Jacobson. Established 1926 to provide a place for members to publish their poetry. Regional organization open to anyone. Currently has 200-225 total members. Levels of membership: Regular, Patron, Foreign, Student. Sponsors conferences, workshops, and 2 annual contests, one for adults and one for students, with 12 categories. **Deadlines:** August 15 for adults, February 1 for students. Competition receives 300-500 entries/year for both contests. Publishes the magazine *Pasque Petals* 4 times/year. Membership dues: $20 regular, $30 patron, $5 students. Members meet biannually. Additional information available for SASE.

N THURBER HOUSE; JAMES THURBER WRITER-IN-RESIDENCE, 77 Jefferson Ave., Columbus OH 43215. (614)464-1032. Fax: (614)280-3645. E-mail: thurberhouse@thurberhouse.org. Website: www.thurberhouse.org. **Residencies Director:** Trish Houston. Officially opened 1984. Listed on the National Register of Historic Places, Thurber House is a literary center, bookstore, and museum of Thurber materials. Programs include writing classes for children, author readings, Thurber celebrations, and an art gallery. Thurber House sponsors a writer-in-residence program that brings 2 journalists, a playwright, a poet or a fiction writer to spend a season living and writing in Thurber House while teaching a course at Ohio State University. Each writer will receive a stipend and housing in the third-floor apartment of Thurber's boyhood home. Please send a letter of interest and a curriculum vitae to Trish Houston before December 15. Please note that Thurber House is *not* a publishing house and does not accept unsolicited material. Additional information available for SASE, by fax, e-mail, or on website.

UNIVERSITY OF ARIZONA POETRY CENTER, 1216 N. Cherry Ave., Tucson AZ 85721-0410. (520)626-3765. Fax: (520)621-5566. E-mail: poetry@u.arizona.edu. Website: www.coh.arizona.edu/poet ry/ (includes info about programs and events, newsletter, and guidelines). **Director:** Alison Deming. Established in 1960 "to maintain and cherish the spirit of poetry." Open to the public. The Center is located in 3 historic adobe houses near the main campus and contains a nationally acclaimed poetry collection that includes over 40,000 items. Programs and services include a library with a noncirculating poetry collection and space for small classes; poetry-related meetings and activities; facilities, research support, and referral information about poetry and poets for local and national communities; the Free Public Reading Series of 12-18 readings each year featuring poets, fiction writers, and writers of literary nonfiction; a guest house for residencies of visiting writers and for use by other University departments and community literary activities; a 1-month summer residency at the Center's guest house offered each year to an emerging writer selected by jury; and poetry awards, readings, and special events for undergraduate and graduate students. Publishes a biannual newsletter. Additional information available for SASE, by fax, e-mail, or on website. "We do not have members, though one can become a 'Friend' through a contribution to our Friends of the Poetry Center account."

THE UNTERBERG POETRY CENTER OF THE 92ND STREET Y; "DISCOVERY"/THE NATION POETRY CONTEST, 1395 Lexington Ave., New York NY 10128. (212)415-5759. Website: www.92ndsty.org (includes guidelines). Offers annual series of readings by major literary figures (weekly readings October through May), writing workshops, master classes in fiction and poetry, and lectures and literary seminars. Also co-sponsors the "Discovery"/*The Nation* Poetry Contest. **Deadline:** January. Competition receives approximately 1,000 entries/year. Additional information available for SASE or on website. No queries by phone, fax, or e-mail.

VIRGINIA WRITERS CLUB; THE VIRGINIA WRITER, P.O. Box 300, Richmond VA 23218. Phone/fax: (804)648-0357. E-mail: charfinley@mindspring.com. Website: www.virginiawritersclub.org. **Editor/Executive Director:** Charlie Finley. Established in 1918 "to promote the art and craft of writing; to serve writers and writing in Virginia." State-wide organization with 7 local chapters open to "any and all writers." Currently has 350 total members. Offerings include networking with other poets and writers, discussions on getting published, workshops, and a newsletter, *The Virginia Writer*, published 5 times/year. Nationally known writers give readings that are open to the public. Membership dues: $25/year. Members meet 5 times/year as well as at workshops and monthly chapter meetings. Additional information available for SASE, by fax, e-mail, or on website.

Get America's #1 Poetry Resource Delivered to Your Door—and Save!

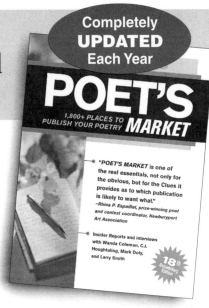

Completely UPDATED Each Year

POET'S MARKET

1,800+ PLACES TO PUBLISH YOUR POETRY

"POET'S MARKET is one of the real essentials, not only for the obvious, but for the Clues it provides as to which publication is likely to want what."
~Rhina P. Espaillat, prize-winning poet and contest coordinator, Newburyport Art Association

Insider Reports and interviews with Wanda Coleman, C.J. Houghtaling, Mark Doty, and Larry Smith

Finding the right outlets for your poetry is crucial to publishing success. With constant changes in the industry, it's not always easy to stay informed. That's why every year poets trust the newest edition of *Poet's Market* for the most up-to-date information on the people and places that will get their poetry published (more than 1,800 editors and publishers are included). This definitive resource also features insider tips from successful poets and editors that will further increase publishing opportunities.

2004 Poet's Market will be published and ready for shipment in August 2003.

Through this special offer, you can reserve your 2004 *Poet's Market* at the 2003 price—just $24.99. Order today and save!

Turn over for more books to help you write great poems and get them published!

Yes! I want the most current edition of *Poet's Market*. Please send me the *2004* edition at the 2003 price—just $24.99. (#10849-K)

# 10849-K	$ 24.99

(NOTE: *2004 Poet's Market* will be shipped in August 2003.)

I also want these books listed on back:

Book		Price
#	-K	$
#	-K	$
#	-K	$
#	-K	$
Subtotal		$
Postage & Handling		$

In the U.S., please add $3.95 s&h for the first book, $1.95 for each additional book. In OH, NY, CO and MI add applicable sales tax. In Canada, add US$5.00 for the first book, US$3.00 for each additional book, and 7% GST. Payment in U.S. funds must accompany order.

Total	$

Credit card orders call
TOLL FREE 1-800-448-0915
or visit
www.writersdigest.com/catalog

☐ Payment enclosed $ _____ (or)
Charge my: ☐ VISA ☐ MC ☐ AmEx Exp. _____

Account # _____

Signature _____

Name _____

Address _____

City _____

State/Prov. _____ ZIP/PC _____

☐ Check here if you do not want your name added to our mailing list.

30-Day Money Back Guarantee on every book you buy!

ZAH02B5

Mail to: Writer's Digest Books • PO Box 9274 • Central Islip, NY 11722-9274

More Great Books to Help You Write and Publish Your Poetry!

Pencil Dancing
New ways to free your creative spirit
by Mari Messer
Learn to dance between your right and left brain as you move between creator and critic, and creativity and logic. You'll develop creative confidence and discover how to overcome writer's block as you explore these fun and effective methods to tap into your imagination.
#10733-K/$15.99/240 p/pb

Roget's Thesaurus of Phrases
by Barbara Ann Kipfer, Ph.D.
Sure, you go to the thesaurus when you need a synonym for a word, but now you can do the same for a phrase! Need to know a different way to say "crowning achievement" or "budget deficit?" Look no further that Kipfer's indispensible reference. You'll make your writing precise and colorful, with more than 10,000 multiword entries and example lists!
#10734-K/$22.99/432 p/hc

Word Painting
A guide to writing more descriptively
by Rebecca McClanahan
Explore and improve your descriptive writing techniques through 75+ creativity exercises. You'll learn by example from Toni Morrison, Truman Capote, Gustave Flaubert, and others! If you want to elevate your writing to new levels of richness and clarity, this book is for you!
#10709-K/$14.99/256 p/pb

The Art & Craft of Poetry
by Michael J. Bugeja
Nurture your poetry-writing skills with inspiration and insight from the masters of the past and present, including Louise Glück, Dana Gioia, Walt Whitman, and Robert Frost. From idea generation to methods of expression, you'll find everything you need to create well-crafted poetry!
#10781-K/$15.99/352 p/pb

Write Your Heart Out
by Rebecca McClanahan
Discover how to turn personal experiences, ideas, and emotions into stories, essays, poems, and memoirs. McClanahan will help you learn to write deeply, honestly, and imaginatively about the most important people, events, and emotions in your life, leading you on a path to both catharsis and self-discovery.
#10735-K/$17.99/224 p/pb

**WISCONSIN FELLOWSHIP OF POETS; MUSELETTER; WISCONSIN POETS' CALEN-
DAR**, 736 W. Prospect Ave., Appleton WI 54914. E-mail: 2mutsch@vbe.com. Website: www.wfop.org.
Vice President: Cathryn Cofell. **President:** Peter Sherrill. Established in 1950 to secure fuller recognition
of poetry as one of the important forces making for a higher civilization and to create a finer appreciation
of poetry by the public at large. State-wide organization open to current and past residents of Wisconsin
who write poetry acceptable to the Credentials Chairperson. Currently has 450 total members. Levels of
membership: Associate, Active, Student. Sponsors biannual conferences, workshops, contests and awards.
Publishes *Wisconsin Poets' Calendar*, poems of Wisconsin (resident) poets. Also publishes *Museletter*, a
quarterly newsletter. Members or nationally known writers give readings that are open to the public.
Sponsors open mic readings. Membership dues: Active $25, Associate $20, Student $12.50. Members meet
biannually. Additional information available for SASE to WFOP Vice President Cathryn Cofell at the
above address. Also available by e-mail or on website; no inquiries by fax.

THE WORDSMITHS (CHRISTIAN POETRY GROUP); WORDSMITHS NEWSLETTER,
493 Elgar Rd., Box Hill North, Victoria 3129 Australia. Phone/fax: (03) 9890 5885. **Leader:** Jean Sietzema-
Dickson. Established 1987 to provide a meeting place where poets could share their work for critique and
encouragement. "We have met monthly (except in January) since 1987 and began publishing in 1990. Our
concern, as a group, has been to encourage the development of excellence in our writing and to speak out
with a distinctive voice. **We do not accept unsolicited manuscripts for publication. Our brief is to
publish *Australian* Christian poetry.**" Currently has 35 members, mostly from the greater Melbourne
area. Offerings include monthly workshops, plus "we subscribe to several magazines, have occasional
guest poets and a Quiet Day once a year when we meet from 10 a.m.-4 p.m. to spend some time together
in directed silence and writing." Holds occasional public readings. Through publishing arm, Poetica Christi
Press, has published 4 group anthologies of the writing of the Wordsmiths and the works of 5 individual
poets. Also sends out the *Wordsmiths Newsletter*, appearing "roughly" bimonthly, available to members
for AUS $20/year as part of membership. Additional information and catalogues available on request by
fax or e-mail (to Janette Fernando at fernando@mt-evelyn.net).

**WORLD-WIDE WRITERS SERVICE, INC. (3WS); WRITERS INK; WRITERS INK PRESS;
WRITERS UNLIMITED AGENCY, INC.**, 233 Mooney Pond Rd., P.O. Box 2344, Selden NY 11784.
(631)451-0478. Fax: (631)451-0477. E-mail: axelrodthepoet@poetrydoctor.com. Website: www.poetrydoct
or.com or www.worldwidewriters.com (includes editorial services; in-residence programs; college credit,
State University of New York certified and non-credit courses; publishing opportunities; and information
on conferences and workshops). **Director:** Dr. David B. Axelrod. Established 1976; Writers Ink Press
established 1978. "World-Wide Writers Service is a literary and speakers' booking agency. With its not-
for-profit affiliate, Writers Unlimited Agency, Inc., it presents literary workshops and performances, conferences, and other literary services, and publishes through Writers Ink Press chapbooks and small flat-spined
books as well as arts editions. **We publish only by our specific invitation at this time.**" *Writers Ink* is
"a sometimes newsletter of events on Long Island, now including programs of our conferences. We offer
3 conferences a year: Healing Power of Writing, Long Island Literature Conference, Florida Writing
Workshop and Poetry Conference. We welcome news of other presses and poets' activities. Review books
of poetry. We fund raise for nonprofit projects and are associates of Long Island Writers Festival and
Jeanne Voege Poetry Awards as well as the Key West Poetry Writing January Workshops, and Writing
Therapy Trainings throughout the year in various locations. Arts Editions are profit productions employing
hand-made papers, bindings, etc. We have editorial services available at small fees. Also inquire if appropriate." Also sponsors contest.

THE WRITER'S CENTER; WRITER'S CAROUSEL, 4508 Walsh St., Bethesda MD 20815.
(301)654-8664. Fax: (301)654-8667. E-mail: postmaster@writer.org. Website: www.writer.org (includes
news and information about the Washington metropolitan literary community as well as market basket for
tapes, books, membership; writers/editors registry; special "members only" page). **Founder and Artistic
Director:** Allan Lefcowitz. **Executive Director:** Jane Fox. Established 1976. An outstanding resource for
writers not only in Washington DC but in the wider area ranging from southern Pennsylvania to North
Carolina and West Virginia. Offers 260 multi-meeting workshops each year in writing, word processing,
and graphic arts. Open 7 days/week, 10 hours/day. Some 2,800 members support the center with annual
donations, which allows for 7 paid staff members. Includes a book gallery in which publications of small
presses are displayed and sold. Publishes *Writer's Carousel*, a 24-page magazine that comes out 6 times/
year. Also sponsors 80 annual performance events, which include presentations of poetry (such as open

mic Sundays), fiction, theater, and film. Also publishes *Poet Lore*—110 years old in 1999 (see separate listing for *Poet Lore* in the Publishers of Poetry section). Membership dues: $40/year individual, $25/year student, $50/year family. Additional information available by fax.

WRITERS' FEDERATION OF NOVA SCOTIA; ATLANTIC POETRY PRIZE; ATLANTIC WRITING COMPETITION; EASTWORD, 1113 Marginal Rd., Halifax, Nova Scotia B3H 4P7 Canada. (902)423-8116. Fax: (902)422-0881. E-mail: talk@writers.ns.ca. Website: www.writers.ns.ca. **Executive Director:** Jane Buss. Established in 1975 "to foster creative writing and the profession of writing in Nova Scotia; to provide advice and assistance to writers at all stages of their careers; and to encourage greater public recognition of Nova Scotian writers and their achievements." Regional organization open to anybody who writes. Currently has 650 total members. Offerings include resource library with over 2,500 titles, promotional services, workshop series, annual festivals, manuscript reading service, and contract advice. Sponsors the Atlantic Writing Competition for unpublished works by beginning writers, and the annual Atlantic Poetry Prize for the best book of poetry by an Atlantic Canadian. Publishes *Eastword*, a bimonthly newsletter containing "a plethora of information on who's doing what, markets and contests, and current writing events and issues." Members and nationally known writers give readings that are open to the public. Membership dues: $35 annually ($15 students). Additional information available on website.

WRITERS GUILD OF ALBERTA; WESTWORD, 11759 Groat Rd., Edmonton, Alberta T5M 3K6 Canada. (780)422-8174. Fax: (780)422-2663. E-mail: wga@oanet.com. Website: www.writersguild.ab .ca (includes directory of writers, job and market listings, workshop/conference information). Executive Director: Norma Lock. **Program Coordinator:** Heather Marshall. Office Administrator: Lorraine Carson. Established in 1980 "to provide a community of writers which exists to support, encourage, and promote writers and writing; to safeguard the freedom to write and read; and to advocate for the well-being of writers." Provincial organization open to emerging and professional writers. Currently has 750 total members. Offerings include workshops/conferences, bimonthly newsletter with market section, and the Stephan G. Stephansson Award for Poetry (Alberta residents only). (See separate listing for the Stephan G. Stephansson Award for Poetry in the Contests & Awards section.) Also publishes *WestWord*, a bimonthly magazine that includes articles on writing, poems, and a market section. Available to nonmembers for $60 Canadian/year. Members and nationally known writers give readings that are open to the public. Sponsors open mic readings for members. Additional information available by fax, e-mail, or on website.

WRITERS INFORMATION NETWORK, The Professional Association for Christian Writers, P.O. Box 11337, Bainbridge Island WA 98110. (206)842-9103. Fax: (206)842-0536. E-mail: WritersInfoNetwor k@juno.com. Website: www.bluejaypub.com/win. **Director:** Elaine Wright Colvin. Established in 1983 "to provide a much needed link between writers and editors/publishers of the religious publishing industry, to further professional development in writing and marketing skills of Christian writers, and to provide a meeting ground of encouragement and fellowship for persons engaged in writing and speaking." International organization open to anyone. Currently has 1,000 members. Offerings include market news, networking, editorial referrals, critiquing, and marketing/publishing assistance. Sponsors conferences and workshops around the country. Publishes a 32- to 36-page bimonthly magazine, *The Win-Informer* containing industry news and trends, writing advice, announcements, and book reviews. The magazine will also consider "writing-related poetry, up to 24 lines, with inspirational/Christian thought or encouragement. We accept first rights only." Sample copy: $5. Membership dues: $35 US/1 year, $65/2 years; $40/year in US equivalent funds for Canada and foreign, $75/2 years. Additional information available for SASE.

THE WRITERS' UNION OF CANADA; THE WRITERS' UNION OF CANADA NEWSLETTER, 40 Wellington St. E, 3rd Floor, Toronto, Ontario M5E 1C7 Canada. (416)703-8982. Fax: (416)504-7656. E-mail: twuc@the-wire.com. Website: www.writersunion.ca (includes general information about publishing, members web pages, competition information). Established 1973. Dedicated to advancing the status of Canadian writers by protecting the rights of published authors, defending the freedom to write and publish, and serving its members. National organization open to poets who have had a trade book published by a commercial or university press; must be a Canadian citizen or landed immigrant. Currently has over 1,370 total members. Offerings include contact with peers, contract advice/negotiation, grievance support, and electronic communication. Sponsors conferences/workshops. Sponsors Annual General Meeting, usually held in May, where members debate and determine Union policy, elect representatives, attend workshops, socialize, and renew friendships with their colleagues from across the country. Publishes *The Writers' Union of Canada Newsletter* 7 times/year. Membership dues: $180/year. Regional reps meet with members when possible. For writers not eligible for membership, the Union offers, for a fee, publications on publishing, contracts, and more; a Manuscript Evaluation Service for any level writer; Contract Services, including a Self-Help Package, a Contract Evaluation Service, and a Contract Negotiation Service; and three annual writing competitions for developing writers. Additional information available for SASE (or SAE and IRC), by fax, e-mail, or on website.

W.B. YEATS SOCIETY OF NEW YORK, National Arts Club, 15 Gramercy Park S, New York NY 10003. Website: www.YeatsSociety.org (includes a "guestbook, where inquiries may be left; full information on our programs; links to numerous other relevant sites"). **President:** Andrew McGowan. Established in 1990 "to promote the legacy of Irish poet and Nobel laureate William Butler Yeats through an annual program of lectures, readings, poetry competition and special events." National organization open to anyone. Currently has 450 total members. Offerings include an annual poetry competition and *Poet Pass By!*, an annual "slam" of readings, songs, and music by poets, writers, entertainers. Also sponsors conferences/ workshops. Nationally known writers give readings that are open to the public. Membership dues: $25/ year; $15/year students. Members meet monthly, September to June. Additional information available for SASE or on website; no inquiries by fax or e-mail.

(See page 512 for Additional Organizations.)

Additional Organizations

The following listings also contain information about organizations. Turn to the page numbers indicated for details about their offerings.

Publications of Interest

This section lists publications of special interest to poets, with a focus on information about writing and publishing poetry. While there are few actual markets for your work, some of these publications do identify promising leads for your submission efforts. You'll also find a wealth of advice on craft, poet interviews, reviews of books and chapbooks, events calendars, and other valuable information in these publications. While each listing includes contact information, you may also find these publications in your library or bookstore; or you may be able to order them through your favorite online bookseller.

Certain symbols may appear at the beginning of some listings. The (**N**) symbol indicates a publication new to this edition; the (◆) symbol denotes a Canadian publication and the (🌐) symbol an international one.

Some listings in the Publishers of Poetry, Contests & Awards, and Conferences & Workshops sections include informative publications (such as handbooks and newsletters). We've included these markets in a cross reference at the end of this section called Additional Publications of Interest. To find out more about a publication of interest associated with one of these markets, go to that market's page number.

🌐 **THE BBR DIRECTORY**, P.O. Box 625, Sheffield S1 3GY United Kingdom. E-mail: directory@bbr-online.com. Website: www.bbr-online.com/directory (includes "a fully searchable archive of every issue of the *BBR Directory*, plus a free Message Board facility where readers can post their publishing news for immediate viewing by other visitors to the website, network with other writers, or discuss issues relevant to small press and independent publishing.") **Editor/Publisher:** Chris Reed. Established 1996. *The BBR Directory* "is a monthly e-mail newssheet for everyone involved with or interested in the small press. Providing accurate and up-to-date information about what's happening in independent publishing all over the world, *The BBR Directory* is the ideal starting point for exploring the small press and for keeping tabs on who exactly is publishing what, and when." To subscribe, send a blank e-mail to directory-subs-on@bbr-online.com or sign up through website. Accepts inquiries by e-mail. *The BBR Directory* also has a special website of resources for writers at www.bbr-online.com/writers.

N **BOOK MAGAZINE**, 252 W. 37th St., 5th Floor, New York NY 10018. (212)659-7070. Fax: (212)736-4455. **For subscription:** P.O. Box 37601, Boone IA 50037-0601; (800)317-BOOK (or order online). E-mail: feedback@bookmagazine.com. Website: www.bookmagazine.com (includes letters, features, reviews, exclusive web content, contact info). **Contact:** Managing Editor. Established 1998. "*BOOK* is committed to being the best information source for book readers, in any medium. The print edition is published bimonthly. *BOOK* goes beyond book reviews to cover the whole world of books, from all angles . . . you'll read about authors at home and at work; publishing news, trends, and issues; great bookstores; exciting literary locations; and technological developments affecting books. You'll find excerpts, essays, and fiction by leading writers and new voices. And you'll get plenty of book reviews, too: more than 50 in every issue!" Single copy: $4.95; subscription: $20/year.

◆ **CANADIAN POETRY**, Dept. of English, University of Western Ontario, London, Ontario N6A 3K7 Canada. E-mail: shroyer@uwo.ca. Website: www.arts.uwo.ca/canpoetry. **General Editor:** Prof. D.M.R. Bentley. **Associate Editor:** R.J. Shroyer. Established 1977. A biannual journal of critical articles, reviews, and historical documents (such as interviews). Subscription: $15 CAN. **Publishes no poetry except as quotations in articles.** Also offers Canadian Poetry Press Scholarly Editions. Details available for SASE or on website.

DUSTBOOKS; INTERNATIONAL DIRECTORY OF LITTLE MAGAZINES AND SMALL PRESSES; DIRECTORY OF POETRY PUBLISHERS; SMALL PRESS REVIEW; SMALL MAGAZINE REVIEW, P.O. Box 100, Paradise CA 95967. (530)877-6110. Fax: (530)877-0222. E-mail: dustbo oks@dcsi.net. Website www.dustbooks.com. Dustbooks publishes a number of books useful to writers. Send SASE for catalog. Regular publications include *The International Directory of Little Magazines & Small Presses*, published annually with almost 6,000 entries. In addition to a wide range of magazine and book publisher listings (with full editorial information), *The International Directory* offers 1,000 pages of indexes plus sources of unique subject material for readers and researchers. *Directory of Poetry Publishers* has similar information for over 2,000 poetry markets. *Small Press Review* is a bimonthly newsprint magazine carrying updates of listings in *The International Directory*, small press needs, news, announcements, and reviews—a valuable way to stay abreast of the literary marketplace. It also incorporates *Small Magazine Review*. Additional information available by fax, e-mail, or on website.

FIRST DRAFT: THE JOURNAL OF THE ALABAMA WRITERS' FORUM; THE ALABAMA WRITERS' FORUM, Alabama State Council on the Arts, 201 Monroe St., Montgomery AL 36130-1800. (334)242-4076 ext. 233, Fax: (334)240-3269. E-mail: awf1@arts.state.al.us. Website: www.writersforum.org (includes complete coverage of forum programs and services; back issues of the quarterly journal *First Draft* are posted in PDF format). **Editor:** Jay Lamar. Established 1992. Appears 4 times/year with news, features, book reviews, and interviews relating to Alabama writers. "We do not publish original poetry or fiction." *First Draft* is 32 pages, 8½×11, professionally printed on coated paper and saddle-stapled with b&w photos inside and a full color cover. Lists markets for poetry, contests/awards, and workshops. Sponsored by the Alabama Writers' Forum, "the official literary arts advocacy organization for the state of Alabama and a partnership program of the Alabama State Council on the Arts." Reviews books of poetry, fiction, and nonfiction by "Alabama writers or from Alabama presses." Subscription: $35/year plus membership. Sample: $3.

FREELANCE MARKET NEWS, Sevendale House, 7 Dale St., Manchester M1 1JB England. Phone: (+44) 161 228 2362. Fax: (+44) 161 228 3533. E-mail: fmn@writersbureau.com. Website: http://writersbureau.com. **Editor:** Angela Cox. Established 1968. A monthly newsletter providing market information for writers and poets, *Freelance Market News* is 16 pages, A4-sized. Lists markets for poetry, contests/awards, conferences/workshops, and features how-to articles. Associated with the Writers College which offers correspondence courses in poetry. Occasionally reviews books or chapbooks of poetry. Subscription: £29. Sample: £2.50. Accepts inquiries by fax and e-mail.

THE GREAT BLUE BEACON, 1425 Patriot Dr., Melbourne FL 32940. (321)253-5869. E-mail: ajircc@juno.com. **Editor/Publisher:** Andy J. Byers. Established 1996. A quarterly newsletter for writers of all genres and skill levels. Contains writing tips, book reviews, humor, quotations, and contest/publisher information. Occasionally publishes poetry, but only through periodic contests. *The Great Blue Beacon* is 8-12 pages, magazine-sized, desktop-published, and unbound. Poets may send books for review consideration. Single copy: $4; subscription: $10, $8 for students, $14 outside US. Sample: $1 plus 2 first-class stamps or IRC. Accepts inquiries by e-mail.

HANDSHAKE; THE EIGHT HAND GANG, 5 Cross Farm Station Rd., Padgate, Warrington, Cheshire WA2 0QG England. **Contact:** John Francis Haines. Established 1992. Published irregularly to "encourage the writing of genre poetry, to provide a source of news and information about genre poetry, to encourage the reading of poetry of all types, including genre, and to provide an outlet for a little genre poetry." *Handshake* is 1 A4-sized page, printed on front and back. Lists markets for poetry and contests/awards. Single copy available for SAE and IRC.

INDEPENDENT PUBLISHER ONLINE; INDEPENDENT PUBLISHER BOOK AWARDS, Jenkins Group Inc., 400 W. Front St., Suite 4A, Traverse City MI 49684. (800)706-4636 or (231)933-0445 (main). Fax: (231)933-0448. E-mail: jimb@bookpublishing.com. Website: www.independentpublisher.com. **Managing Editor:** Jim Barnes. For 20 years the mission at *Independent Publisher* has been to recognize and encourage the work of publishers who exhibit the courage and creativity necessary to take chances, break new ground, and bring about change in the world of publishing. The annual Independent Publisher Book Awards, conducted each year to honor the year's best independently published titles (including poetry), accept entries from independent publishers throughout North America, ranging from self-publishers to major university presses. The Awards were launched in 1996 to bring increased recognition to unsung titles published by independent authors and publishers. $5,000 in prize money is divided equally among the Ten Outstanding Books of the Year, and winners and finalists in 49 categories receive plaques, certificates, and gold seals. Winner and finalists appear for an entire year in the *Independent Publisher Online* webzine, which goes out monthly to over 40,000 subscribers worldwide, many of whom are agents, buyers, and librarians.

LAUGHING BEAR NEWSLETTER; LAUGHING BEAR PRESS, P.O. Box 613322, Dallas TX 75261-3322. (817)858-9515. E-mail: editor@laughingbear.com. Website: www.LaughingBear.com. **Editor:** Tom Person. Established 1976. *Laughing Bear Newsletter* is a monthly publication of small press news, information, and inspiration for writers and publishers containing articles, news, and reviews. Subscription: $15/year. Sample copy available for SASE or by e-mail. *Laughing Bear Newsletter* uses short (200- to 300-word) articles on self-publishing and small press. Pays copies.

🌐 **LIGHT'S LIST**, 37 The Meadows, Berwick-Upon-Tweed, Northumberland TD15 1NY England. Phone: (01289)306523. E-mail: photon.press@virgin.net. **Editor:** John Light. Established 1986. *Light's List* is an annual publication "listing some 1,450 small press magazines publishing poetry, prose, market information, articles, and artwork with address and brief note of interests. All magazines publish work in English. Listings are from the United Kingdom, Europe, United States, Canada, Australia, New Zealand, South Africa, and Asia." *Light's List* is 66 pages, A5-sized, photocopied, saddle-stapled, card cover. Single copy: $6 (air $7). Accepts inquiries by e-mail.

N 🌐 **MERSEYSIDE ARTS MAGAZINE**, P.O. Box 21, Liverpool L19 3RX England. E-mail: ms.arts. mag@cableinet.co.uk. **Editor:** Bernard F. Spencer. Established 1995. A bimonthly "local news and information magazine that caters to writers/poets, theatre arts, fine arts, photography, music and dance, film, video, and digital media." Devotes roughly 15% to poetry and regularly features reviews, events, diary dates, and competitions. *Merseyside* is 44-52 pages, A4, lithographed, saddle-stapled. Lists markets for poetry, contests/awards, conferences/workshops, and readings. Associated with the Northwest Arts Board. Reviews books and chapbooks of poetry and other magazines. Poets may send books for review consideration. Single copy: £2 plus £2.17 postage. Accepts inquiries by e-mail.

OHIO WRITER. (See listing for Poets' and Writers' League of Greater Cleveland in the Organizations section.)

PARA PUBLISHING, Box 8206-880, Santa Barbara CA 93118-8206. (805)968-7277, orders (800)727-2782. Fax: (805)968-1379. E-mail: danpoynter@parapublishing.com. Website: www.parapublishing.com (over 500 pages of valuable book writing, publishing, and promoting information). Author/publisher Dan Poynter offers how-to books on book publishing and self-publishing. *Writing Nonfiction: Turning Thoughts Into Books* shows how to get your book out. *The Self-Publishing Manual, How to Write, Print and Sell Your Own Book* is all about book promotion. Also available are *Publishing Contracts on Disk, Book Fairs*, and 45 Special Reports on various aspects of book production, promotion, marketing, and distribution. Free book publishing information kit. Accepts inquiries by e-mail only.

PERSONAL POEMS, % Jean Hesse, 56 Arapaho Dr., Pensacola FL 32507. (850)492-9828. F. Jean Hesse started a business in 1980 writing poems for individuals for a fee (for greetings, special occasions, etc.). Others started similar businesses after she began instructing them in the process, especially through a cassette tape training program and other materials. Send SASE for free brochure or $20 plus $4.50 p&h for training manual, *How to Make Your Poems Pay*. Make checks payable to F. Jean Hesse.

🌐 **POETRY BOOK SOCIETY; PBS BULLETIN**, Book House, 45 East Hill, London SW18 2QZ England. Phone: +44 (0)20 8870 8403. Fax: +44 (0)20 8877 1615. E-mail: info@poetrybooks.co.uk. Website: www.poetrybooks.co.uk. Established 1953 "to promote the best newly published contemporary poetry to as wide an audience as possible." A book club with an annual subscription rate of £42, which covers 4 books of new poetry, the *PBS Bulletin*, and a premium offer (for new members). The selectors also recommend other books of special merit, which are obtainable at a discount of 25%. The Poetry Book Society is subsidized by the Arts Council of England. Please write (Attn: Clare Brown), fax, or e-mail for details.

THE POETRY CONNECTION, 13455 SW 16 Court #F-405-PM, Pembroke Pines FL 33027. (954)431-3016. Fax: (509)351-7401. E-mail: poetryconnect@webtv.net (for news) or MagicCircle@webtv.net (for poetry). Website: www.ThePoetryConnection.com (includes information on The Magic Circle). **Editor/**

Publisher: Sylvia Shichman. *The Poetry Connection*, a monthly newsletter in flyer format, provides poets, writers, and performing artists with information on how to sell their poetry/books; poetry and performing artists publications and contests; and how to obtain assistance in getting poetry published. Also info on "how to win cash for your talent." *The Poetry Connection* has information on "writing for greeting cards" directories, and a directory listing poetry contests with cash awards. Subscription: $20. Sample (including guidelines): $7. Make checks payable to Sylvia Shichman. Also sponsors The Magic Circle, a poetry publicity distribution network service. "Join the Magic Circle and have your bio and one poem sent directly to editors and publishers. Fifty copies for $60 or 100 copies for $110. The Magic Circle will distribute your flyers in a reciprocal exchange. For information, please enclose a large SASE and write to Sylvia Shichman." The Magic Circle also is a PR flyer distribution service for poets, events, and books.

POETRY FLASH; BAY AREA BOOK REVIEWERS ASSOCIATION, 1450 Fourth St. #4, Berkeley CA 94710. (510)525-5476. Fax: (510)525-6752. E-mail: editor@poetryflash.org (NOTE: **does not respond by e-mail to poetry submissions**) or BABRA@poetryflashorg. Website: www.poetryflash.org (includes editorial archives, subscription info, guidelines, and buttons for BABRA, California Poetry Series, and Watershed Poetry Festival). **Editor:** Joyce Jenkins. Established 1972. Appears 6 times/year. "*Poetry Flash*, a Poetry Review & Literary Calendar for the West, publishes reviews, interviews, essays, and information for writers. Poems, as well as announcements about submitting to other publications, appear in each issue." *Poetry Flash* focuses on poetry, but its literary calendar also includes events celebrating all forms of creative writing in areas across the nation. Lists markets for poetry, contests/awards, and workshops. *Poetry Flash* also sponsors a weekly poetry reading series at Cody's Books in Berkeley and sponsors the Bay Area Book Reviewers Association Awards. (See separate listing in Contests & Awards section.) Reviews books and chapbooks of poetry. Subscription $16/year. Sample available by submitting an online request form.

PUSHCART PRESS. Website: www.wwnorton.com/trade/affiliates.htm. **Editor:** Bill Henderson. The Pushcart Press, an affiliate publisher of W.W. Norton & Co., publishes the acclaimed annual *Pushcart Prize* anthology, Pushcart Editor's Book Award, and other quality literature, both fiction and nonfiction. "The most-honored literary series in America, *The Pushcart Prize* has been named a notable book of the year by the *New York Times* and hailed with Pushcart Press as 'among the most influential in the development of the American book business' over the past century. Recently its editor was named small press 'person of the year' by the Small Press Association." Also publishes *The Publish-It-Yourself Handbook*. Catalog available for SASE or on website.

RAIN TAXI REVIEW OF BOOKS, P.O. Box 3840, Minneapolis MN 55403. E-mail: editor@raintaxi. com or info@raintaxi.com. Website: www.raintaxi.com (includes a selection of the contents of each issue, full table of contents for current and back issues, and information about the organization). **Editor:** Eric Lorberer. Established 1996. "*Rain Taxi Review of Books* is a quarterly publication available by subscription and free in bookstores nationwide. Our circulation is 20,000 copies. We publish reviews of books that are overlooked by mainstream media, and each issue includes several pages of poetry reviews, as well as author interviews and original essays." Devotes 20% of publication to poetry. "We review poetry books in every issue and often feature interviews with poets." *Rain Taxi* is 56 pages, magazine-sized, web offset-printed on newsprint, saddle-stapled. Poets may send books for review consideration. Subscription: $12. Sample: $3. Accepts inquiries by e-mail. "We DO NOT publish original poetry. Please don't send poems."

SHAW GUIDES, INC., 10 W. 66 St., #30H, New York NY 10023. (212)799-6464. Fax: (212)724-9287. E-mail: info@shawguides.com. Website: www.shawguides.com (includes *Guide to Writers Conferences* with detailed descriptions of over 500 conferences and workshops worldwide). Established 1988 "to publish true stories of educational travel and creative career programs worldwide." **President:** Dorlene Kaplan. Publishes material on an ongoing basis on website. Accepts inquiries by fax and e-mail.

MARKET CONDITIONS are constantly changing! If you're still using this book and it's 2004 or later, buy the newest edition of *Poet's Market* at your favorite bookstore or order directly from Writer's Digest Books (800)448-0915 or www.writersdigest.com.

N ☑ WORDWRIGHTS CANADA, P.O. Box 456 Station O, Toronto, Ontario M4A 2P1 Canada. Fax: (416)752-0689. E-mail: susanio@sympatico.ca. Website: www3.sympatico.ca/susanio (includes links to Canadian writer's sites and organizations and student and chapbook writing competitions). **Director:** Susan Ioannou. Publishes "books on poetics in layman's, not academic terms, such as *A Magical Clockwork: The Art of Writing the Poem* (160 pages, perfect-bound, $16.95) and *The Workshop Guide: Poetry Writing Exercises and Resources*." Considers mss of such books for publication, paying $50 advance, 10% royalties, and 5% of press run. Also conducts editing services.

🌐 WRITERS' BULLETIN, Cherrybite Publications, Linden Cottage, 45 Burton Rd., Little Neston, Cheshire CH64 4AE United Kingdom. E-mail: helicon@globalnet.co.uk. Website: www.cherrybite.co.uk. **Editor:** Shelagh Nugent. Established 1997. "Published quarterly, *Writers' Bulletin* aims to give writers the most reliable and up-to-date information on markets for fiction, nonfiction, poetry, photographs, artwork, cartoons; information on resources, courses, and conferences; book reviews (books about writing); editors' moves, publishing news, address changes; advice and tips on writing. All markets are verified with the editor—no guesswork or second-hand information." *Writer's Bulletin* is about 28 pages, saddle-stapled, colored paper cover. Single copy: £2.40 Europe, £3 USA sterling only, £2 UK. Will accept the equivalent in US dollars (cash). Sample issue also available for 2 International Reply Coupons. Accepts inquiries by e-mail. "Because we are adding news right up to publication day, *Writers' Bulletin* has the most up-to-date information available in print."

WRITER'S DIGEST BOOKS, 4700 E. Galbraith Rd., Cincinnati OH 45236. (800)448-0915. Website www.writersdigest.com. Writer's Digest Books publishes a remarkable array of books useful to all types of writers. In addition to *Poet's Market*, books for poets include *Writing Personal Poetry* by Sheila Bender, *You Can Write Poetry* by Jeff Mock, *The Poet's Handbook* by Judson Jerome, *Creating Poetry* by John Drury, and *The Art and Craft of Poetry* by Michael J. Bugeja. Call or write for a complete catalog. Newly redesigned and expanded website includes individual web pages for fiction, nonfiction, children's, poetry, personal writing, and scriptwriting, plus markets, tips, and special content. **PLEASE NOTE:** *Writer's Digest Books publishes* only *books about the craft of writing poetry—is not a poetry publisher.*

🌐 WRITERS' NEWS; DAVID ST. JOHN THOMAS CHARITABLE TRUST, P.O. Box 168, Wellington St., Leeds LS1 1RF United Kingdom. Phone: +44(0113)2388333. Fax: +44(0113)2388330. E-mail: JanetEvans@ypn.co.uk. **Editor:** Derek Hudson. Established 1989. A monthly magazine containing news and advice for writers. Devotes up to 10% to poetry and regularly features a poetry workshop, critiques, "method and type explained," and annual and monthly competitions. *Writer's News* is 32-64 pages, A4-sized, saddle-stapled. Lists markets for poetry, contests/awards, conferences/workshops, and readings. Associated with the David St. John Thomas Charitable Trust (P.O. Box 6055, Nairn 1V12 54B) which sponsors poetry competitions. Occasionally reviews books and chapbooks of poetry and other magazines. Poets may send books for review consideration. Subscription: £49.90 overseas. Sample: £4.50. Accepts inquiries by fax and e-mail.

Additional Publications of Interest

The following listings also contain information about instructive publications for poets. Turn to the page numbers indicated for details about their offerings.

Websites of Interest

The resources for poetry on the Internet are growing daily, and there are far too many to list here. However, below you'll find those key sites every poet should bookmark. Content ranges from postal and copyright information to links, forums, articles, and reviews. (Although we confirmed every address at press time, connections can become outdated; if a site comes up "not found," enter the name of the site in a search engine to check for a new address.)

SEARCH ENGINES:

Best of the Web: www.bestoftheweb.com
Dogpile: www.dogpile.com
Google: www.google.com

RESOURCES:

Canadian Postal Service: www.canadapost.ca
IRS: www.irs.ustreas.gov/
US Copyright Office: www.loc.gov/copyright
US Postal Service: www.usps.gov

ESPECIALLY FOR POETS:

The Academy of American Poets: www.poets.org/
Alien Flower: www.sonic.net/web/alienflower
Electronic Poetry Center: http://epc.buffalo.edu
National Federation of State Poetry Societies (NFSPS): www.nfsps.com
Poetic Voices: http://poeticvoices.com/
Poetry Society of America: www.poetrysociety.org
Poetry Today Online: www.poetrytodayonline.com
Poets & Writers: www.pw.org
Rhyming Dictionary: www.rhymezone.com
Slam News Service: www.slamnews.com

OTHER GREAT SITES FOR WRITERS:

Associated Writing Programs: www.awpwriter.org
The Word Wizard: http://wordwizard.com/
Writer Beware: www.sfwa.org/beware/
The Writer's Center: www.writer.org/
Writer's Digest: www.writersdigest.com (includes special poetry pages)
Writers Write™—The Write Resource™: www.writerswrite.com
Zuzu's Petals: www.zuzu.com

Poets in Education

Whether known as PITS (Poets in the Schools), WITS (Writers in the Schools), or similar names, programs exist nationwide that coordinate residencies, classroom visits, and other opportunities for experienced poets to teach students poetry writing. Many state arts agencies include such "arts in education" programs in their activities (see State & Provincial Grants on page 461 for contact information). Another good source is the National Assembly of State Arts Agencies (see below), which includes a directory of contact names and addresses for arts education programs state-by-state. Listed below is a mere sampling of programs and organizations that link poets with schools. Contact them for information about their requirements (some may insist poets have a strong publication history, others may prefer classroom experience) or check their websites where available.

The Academy of American Poets, *588 Broadway, Suite 1203, New York NY 10012. E-mail: academy@poets.org. Website: www.poets.org (includes links to state arts in education programs).*

Arkansas Writers in the Schools. *E-mail: wits@cavern.uark.edu. Website: www.uark.edu/~wits/.*

California Poets in the Schools, *870 Market St., Suite 1148, San Francisco CA 94102. (415)399-1565. E-mail: info@cpits.org. Website: www.cpits.org.*

e-poets.network, *a collective online cultural center that promotes education through videoconferencing (i.e., "distance learning"); also includes the* Voces y Lugares *project. Website: http://learning.e-poets.net/ (includes online contact form).*

Idaho Writers in the Schools, *Log Cabin Literary Center, 801 S. Capitol Blvd., Suite 100, Boise ID 83702. (208)331-8000. Website: www.logcablit.org/wits.html.*

Indiana Writers in the Schools, *University of Evansville, Dept. of English, 1800 Lincoln Ave., Evansville IN 47722. Website: http://english.evansville.edu/english/.*

Michigan Creative Writers in the Schools, *ArtServe Michigan, 17515 W. Nine Mile Rd., Suite 1025, Southfield MI 48075. E-mail: education@artservemichigan.org. Website: www.artservemichigan.org.*

National Assembly of State Arts Agencies, *1029 Vermont Ave., NW, 2nd Floor, Washington DC 20005. (202)347-6352. E-mail: nasaa@nasaa-arts.org. Website: www.nasaa-arts.org.*

"Pick-a-Poet," *The Humanities Project, Arlington Public Schools, 1426 N. Quincy St., Arlington VA 22207. Website: www.humanitiesproject.org/.*

Potato Hill Poetry, *81 Speen St., Natick MA 01760. Website: www.potatohill.com (includes online contact form).*

Teachers & Writers Collaborative, Inc., *5 Union Square W., New York NY 10003-3306. (212)691-6590. E-mail: info@twc.org. Website: www.twc.org.*

Texas Writers in the Schools, *1523 W. Main, Houston TX 77006. (713)523-3877. E-mail: mail@writersintheschools. org. Website: www.writersintheschools.org.*

Writers & Artists in the Schools, *COMPAS, Landmark Center, 75 W. Fifth St., Suite 304, St. Paul MN 55102. (651)292-3249. E-mail: dei@compas.org. Website: www.compas.org.*

Glossary of Poetry Terms

This glossary is provided as a quick-reference only, briefly covering poetic styles and terms that may turn up in articles and listings in *Poet's Market*. For a full understanding of the terms, forms, and styles listed here, consult a solid textbook or handbook (ask your librarian or bookseller for recommendations).

Abstract poem: conveys emotion through sound, textures, and rhythm and rhyme rather than through the meanings of words.

Acrostic: poem in which initial letters of each line, read downward, form a word, phrase, or sentence.

Alphabet poem: arranges lines according to the alphabet, with first line devoted to "A" and so on.

Anapest: foot consisting of 2 unstressed syllables followed by a stress (- - ').

Avant-garde: work at the forefront of current literary practice—cutting edge, unconventional, risk-taking, revolutionary.

Ballad: narrative poem often in ballad stanza (4-line stanza with 4 stresses in lines 1 and 3, 3 stresses in lines 2 and 4, which also rhyme).

Ballade: consists of 3 stanzas rhymed *ababbcbC* (with the *C* indicating a refrain) and an envoi rhymed *bcbC*.

Beat poetry: anti-academic school of poetry born in '50s San Francisco; fast-paced free verse resembling jazz.

Blank verse: unrhymed iambic pentameter.

Chant: poem in which one or more lines are repeated over and over.

Cinquain: stanza of 5 lines, also called a "quintain."

Concrete poetry: see "emblematic poem."

Confessional poetry: work that uses personal and private details from the poet's own life.

Couplet: stanza of 2 lines; pair of rhymed lines.

Dactyl: foot consisting of a stress followed by 2 unstressed syllables (' - -).

Didactic poetry: poetry written with the intention to instruct.

Eclectic: open to a variety of poetic styles (as in "eclectic taste").

Ekphrastic poem: focuses on a piece of visual art of any genre, verbally representing something originally represented visually, though more than mere description.

Elegy: lament in verse for someone who has died, or a reflection on the tragic nature of life.

Emblematic poem: consists of words or letters arranged to imitate a shape, often the subject of the poem itself.

Enjambment: continuation of sense and rhythmic movement from one line to the next; also called a "run-on" line.

Envoi: a brief ending, usually to a ballade or sestina, and no more than 4 lines long; summarizes the subject or argument of the poem.

Epic poetry: long narrative poem telling a story central to a society, culture, or nation.

Epigram: short, witty, satirical poem or saying written to be remembered easily, like a punch-line.

Experimental poetry: work that challenges conventional ideas of poetry by exploring new techniques, form, language, and visual presentation.

Foot: unit of measure in a metrical line of poetry.

Found poem: text lifted from a nonpoetic source (such as advertisements or newspaper copy) and presented out of context as a poem.

Free verse: unmetrical verse; i.e., poetry with unmeasured lines (not counted for accents, syllables, etc.).

Ghazal: Persian poetic form of 5-15 unconnected, independent couplets; associative jumps may be made from couplet to couplet.

Greeting card poetry: poetry that resembles verses found in greeting cards, often with sing-song meter and rhyme.

Haibun: Japanese form in which prose and verse (specifically haiku) are interspersed, often in the form of a diary or travel journal.

Haiku: Japanese form of 3 lines containing 17 syllables, often arranged 5-7-5; essential elements include brevity, immediacy, spontaneity, imagery, nature, a season, and illumination.

Iamb: foot consisting of an unstressed syllable followed by a stress (- ').

Iambic pentameter: consists of 5 iambic feet per line.

Imagist poetry: consists of short, free verse lines that present images without comment or explanation; strongly influenced by haiku and other Oriental forms.

Kyrielle: French form, consists of a 4-line stanza; each line contains 8 syllables, with the final line a refrain.

Language poetry: attempts to detach words from their traditional meanings to produce something new and unprecedented.

Limerick: light verse form consisting of a 5-line stanza rhyming *aabba*; the pattern of stresses per line is traditionally 3-3-2-2-3; often bawdy or scatalogical.

Line: the basic compositional unit of a poem; measured in feet if metrical.

Long poem: exceeds the length and scope of the short lyric or narrative poem; length is defined arbitrarily, often as more than 2 pages or 100 lines.

Lyric poetry: expresses personal emotion; music predominates over narrative or drama.

Metaphor: a comparison in which 2 different things are likened by identifying one as the other (A=B).

Meter: the rhythmic measure of a line.

Modernist poetry: work of the early 20th century literary movement that sought to break with the past, rejecting outmoded literary traditions, diction, and form while encouraging innovation and reinvention.

Narrative poetry: poem that tells a story.

New Formalism: contemporary literary movement to revive formal verse.

Nonsense verse: playful, with language and/or logic that defies ordinary understanding.

Octave: stanza of 8 lines.

Ode: a songlike, or lyric, poem; can be passionate, rhapsodic, and mystical, or a formal address to a person on a public or state occasion.

Pantoum: Malayan poetic form consisting of 4-line stanzas, with lines 2 and 4 of one quatrain repeated as lines 1 and 3 of the next; final stanza reverses lines 1 and 3 of the previous quatrain and uses them as lines 2 and 4; traditionally each stanza rhymes *abab*; poem can be of any length.

Petrarchan sonnet: octave rhymes *abbaabba*; sestet may rhyme *cdcdcd, cdedce, ccdccd, cddcdd, edecde,* or *cddcee.*

Prose poem: a brief prose work that can be read as a poem because of intensity and condensed language, the use of poetic devices, and other similarities to poetry.

Quatrain: stanza of 4 lines.

Refrain: a repeated line within a poem, similar to the chorus of a song.

Regional poetry: work set in a particular locale and heavily imbued with the look, feel, and culture of that place.

Renga: Japanese collaborative form derived from the tanka; a dialogue or communal exercise in which 2 or more poets alternate writing 3 lines (haiku), then 2 lines (7 syllables each).

Rhyme: words that sound alike, especially words that end in the same sound.

Rhythm: the beat and movement of language (rise and fall, repetition and variation, change of pitch, mix of syllables, melody of words).

Rondeau: French form of 15 lines (sometimes less) in 3 parts, rhyming *aabba aabR aabbaR* (with *R* indicating a refrain that repeats the first word or phrase of the opening line).

Senryu: short, humorous stanzas in haiku form, but more direct and to the point, aiming directly at human nature.

Sequence: a group or progression of poems, often numbered as a series.

Sestet: stanza of 6 lines.

Sestina: fixed form of 39 lines—6 unrhymed stanzas of 6 lines each, then an ending 3-line stanza; each stanza uses the same 6 nonrhyming end-words, repeating them in a different order each time; all 6 end-words appear in the final 3-line stanza.

Shakespearean sonnet: rhymes *abab cdcd efef gg.*

Simile: comparison that uses a linking word (*like, as, such as, how*) to clarify the similarities.

Sonnet: poem of 14 lines (traditionally an octave and sestet), rhymed in iambic pentameter; often presents an argument but may also present a description, story, or meditation.

Spondee: foot consisting of 2 stressed syllables (' ').

Surrealistic poetry: reflects the literary/artistic movement stressing the importance of dreams and the subconscious, nonrational thought, free associations, and startling imagery and juxtapositions.

Stanza: group of lines making up a single unit; like a paragraph in prose.

Strophe: often used to mean "stanza"; also a stanza of irregular line lengths.

Tanka: Japanese form of 5 lines containing 31 syllables (arranged 5-7-5-7-7); less concentrated and mysterious, more emotional and conversational than haiku.

Tercet: stanza or poem of 3 lines.

Terza rima: a series of 3-line stanzas with an interwoven rhyme scheme (such as *aba, bcb, cdc* . . .).

Trochee: foot consisting of a stress followed by an unstressed syllable (' -).

Villanelle: French form adapted from Italian folk songs, consisting of 19 lines (5 tercets and a quatrain); line 1 serves as one refrain (repeated in lines 6, 12, 18), line 3 as a second refrain (repeated in lines 9, 15, 19); traditionally, refrains rhyme with each other and with the opening line of each stanza.

Visual poem: see "emblematic poem."

Indexes

Chapbook Publishers

A poetry chapbook is a slim volume of 24-50 pages (although chapbook lengths can vary; some are even published as inserts in magazines). Many publishers and journals solicit chapbook manuscripts through competitions. Read listings carefully, check websites where available, and request guidelines before submitting. See Frequently Asked Questions on page 7 for further information about chapbooks and submission formats.

Book Publishers Index

The following are magazines and publishers that consider full-length book manuscripts (over 50 pages, often much longer). See Frequently Asked Questions on page 7 for further information about book manuscript submission.

Openness to Submissions Index

In this section, all magazines, publishers, and contests/awards with primary listings in *Poet's Market* are categorized according to their openness to submissions (as indicated by the symbols that appear at the beginning of each listing). Note that some markets are listed in more than one category.

☐ WELCOMES SUBMISSIONS FROM BEGINNING POETS

◑ PREFERS SUBMISSIONS FROM EXPERIENCED POETS, WILL CONSIDER WORK FROM BEGINNING POETS

⊙ PREFERS SUBMISSIONS FROM SKILLED, EXPERIENCED POETS, FEW BEGINNERS

◎ MARKET WITH A SPECIALIZED FOCUS

Geographical Index

This section offers a breakdown of U.S. publishers and conferences/workshops arranged alphabetically by state or territory, followed by listings for Canada, Australia, France, Japan, the United Kingdom, and other countries—a real help when trying to locate publishers in your region as well as conferences and workshops convenient to your area.

DISCOVER A WORLD OF WRITING SUCCESS

Are you ready to be praised, published, and paid for your writing? It's time to invest in your future with *Writer's Digest*! Beginners and experienced writers alike have been enjoying *Writer's Digest*, the world's leading magazine for writers, for more than 80 years — and it keeps getting better! Each issue is brimming with:

- Inspiration from writers who have been in your shoes
- Detailed info on the latest contests, conferences, markets, and opportunities in every genre
- Tools of the trade, including reviews of the latest writing software and hardware
- Writing prompts and exercises to overcome writer's block and rekindle your creative spark
- Expert tips, techniques, and advice to help you get published
- And so much more!

That's a lot to look forward to every month. Let *Writer's Digest* put you on the road to writing success!

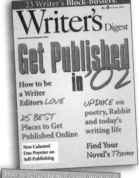

Get 2 FREE TRIAL ISSUES of Writer's® Digest

Packed with creative inspiration, advice, and tips to guide you on the road to success, *Writer's Digest* will offer you everything you need to take your writing to the next level! You'll discover how to:

- Create dynamic characters and page-turning plots
- Submit query letters that publishers won't be able to refuse
- Find the right agent or editor for you
- Make it out of the slush-pile and into the hands of the right publisher
- Write award-winning contest entries
- And more!

See for yourself by ordering your 2 FREE trial issues today!

Subject Index

This index focuses on markets indicating a specialized area of interest, whether regional, poetic style, or specific topic (these markets show a 🎯 symbol at the beginning of their listings). It also includes markets we felt offered special opportunities in certain subject areas. Subject categories are listed alphabetically, with additional subcategories indicated under the "Specialized" heading (in parentheses behind the market's name). Please note that this index only partially reflects the total markets in this book; many do not identify themselves as having specialized interests and so are not included here. Also, many specialized markets have more than one area of interest and will be found under multiple categories. Note, too, that when a market appears under a heading in this index, it does not necessarily mean it considers *only* poetry associated with that subject, poetry *only* from that region, etc. It's still best to read all listings carefully as part of a thorough marketing plan.

Poetry for Children

General Index

Markets that appeared in the *2002 Poet's Market* but are not included in this edition are identified by two-letter codes explaining their absence. These codes are: **(ED) editorial decision; (NP) no longer publishing poetry; (NR) no (or late) response to requested verification of information; (OB) out of business** (or, in the case of contests or conferences, cancelled); **(RR) removed by request of the market** (no reason given); **(UF) uncertain future; (UC) unable to contact;** and **(RP) restructuring/purchased.**

Markets that appeared in the 2002 edition but do not appear in this book are listed in the General Index with the following codes: **(ED)** editorial decision, **(NP)** no longer publishing poetry, **(NR)** no (or late) response to verification request, **(OB)** out of business, **(RR)** removed by market's request, **(UF)** uncertain future, **(UC)** unable to contact, **(RP)** restructuring/purchased.

Markets that appeared in the 2002 edition but do not appear in this book are listed in the General Index with the following codes: (ED) editorial decision, (NP) no longer publishing poetry, (NR) no (or late) response to verification request, (OB) out of business, (RR) removed by market's request, (UF) uncertain future, (UC) unable to contact, (RP) restructuring/purchased.

Markets that appeared in the 2002 edition but do not appear in this book are listed in the General Index with the following codes: (ED) editorial decision, (NP) no longer publishing poetry, (NR) no (or late) response to verification request, (OB) out of business, (RR) removed by market's request, (UF) uncertain future, (UC) unable to contact, (RP) restructuring/purchased.

Markets that appeared in the 2002 edition but do not appear in this book are listed in the General Index with the following codes: (ED) editorial decision, (NP) no longer publishing poetry, (NR) no (or late) response to verification request, (OB) out of business, (RR) removed by market's request, (UF) uncertain future, (UC) unable to contact, (RP) restructuring/purchased.